This volume of *The New Cambridge Medieval History* covers most of the period of Frankish and Carolingian dominance in western Europe, a time of remarkable political and cultural coherence, combined with crucial, very diverse and formative developments in every sphere of life. Adopting an interdisciplinary approach, the authors consider developments in Europe as a whole, from Ireland to the Bosphorus and Iceland to Gibraltar. The chapters offer an examination of the interaction between rulers and ruled, of how power and authority actually worked, and of the impact of these on the society and culture of Europe as a whole.

The volume is divided into four parts. Part I encompasses the events and political developments in the whole of the British Isles, the West and East Frankish kingdoms, Scandinavia, the Slavic and Balkan regions, Spain and Italy, and those aspects of Byzantine and Muslim history which impinged on the west between *c.* 700 and *c.* 900. Parts II, III and IV cover common themes and topics within the general categories of government and institutions, the church and society, and cultural and intellectual development.

The New Cambridge Medieval History

Volume II *c.* 700–*c.* 900

The throne of Charles the Bald (*Cathedra Petri*), Vatican, Basilica of St Peter

THE NEW
CAMBRIDGE
MEDIEVAL HISTORY

Volume II *c.700–c.900*

EDITED BY

ROSAMOND McKITTERICK

*Reader in Early Medieval European History
in the University of Cambridge
and Fellow of Newnham College*

CAMBRIDGE
UNIVERSITY PRESS

CAMBRIDGE
UNIVERSITY PRESS

University Printing House, Cambridge CB2 8BS, United Kingdom

Cambridge University Press is part of the University of Cambridge.

It furthers the University's mission by disseminating knowledge in the pursuit of education, learning and research at the highest international levels of excellence.

www.cambridge.org
Information on this title: www.cambridge.org/9781107460416

© Cambridge University Press 1995

First published 1995
Eighth printing 2013
First paperback edition 2015

A catalogue record for this publication is available from the British Library

ISBN 978-0-521-36292-4 Hardback
ISBN 978-1-107-46041-6 Paperback

CONTENTS

MAPS

FIGURE

TABLES

xi

PLATES

---

xii

CONTRIBUTORS

STUART AIRLIE: Lecturer in History, University of Glasgow

MICHEL BANNIARD: Professor of Latin, Université de Toulouse-Mirail

MARK BLACKBURN: Keeper of Coins and Medals, The Fitzwilliam Museum, Cambridge

THOMAS S. BROWN: Lecturer in History, University of Edinburgh

ROGER COLLINS: Edinburgh

JOHN J. CONTRENI: Professor of History, Purdue University, West Lafayette, Indiana

SIMON C. COUPLAND: Bath

MAYKE DE JONG: Professor of Medieval History, University of Utrecht.

PAOLO DELOGU: Professor of Medieval History, 'La Sapienza', University of Rome

PAUL FOURACRE: Lecturer in History, Goldsmiths College, University of London

JOHANNES FRIED: Professor of History, University of Frankfurt -am-Main

DAVID GANZ: Associate Professor, University of North Carolina at Chapel Hill

HANS-WERNER GOETZ: Professor of History, University of Hamburg

HUGH KENNEDY: Lecturer in History, University of St Andrews

SIMON KEYNES: Reader in Anglo-Saxon History, University of Cambridge, and Fellow of Trinity College

NIELS LUND: Lecturer in History, University of Copenhagen

MICHAEL MCCORMICK: Professor of History, Harvard University

ROSAMOND MCKITTERICK: Reader in Early Medieval European History, University of Cambridge, and Fellow of Newnham College

LAWRENCE NEES: Professor of Art History, University of Delaware

JANET L. NELSON: Professor of History, King's College, University of London

THOMAS F.X. NOBLE: Professor of History, University of Virginia

DONNCHADH Ó CORRÁIN: Professor of History, University College, Cork, National University of Ireland

ROGER REYNOLDS: Professor of History, Pontifical Institute of Medieval Studies, Toronto

JONATHAN SHEPARD: Lecturer in History, University of Cambridge, and Fellow of Peterhouse

JULIA M.H. SMITH: Associate Professor of History, Trinity College, Hartford, Connecticut

ADRIAAN VERHULST: Professor of History, University of Ghent

CHRIS WICKHAM: Professor of History, University of Birmingham

PREFACE

This volume covers most of the period of Frankish and Carolingian dominance in western Europe, a time of relative political and cultural coherence, combined with crucial, and, as the various chapters make clear, very diverse and formative developments in every sphere of life. A volume devoted to the history of western Europe between *c.* 700 and *c.* 900 in all its richness and diversity inevitably suggests a number of possible methods of organisation. The related volumes of the old *Cambridge Medieval History*, on 'The foundation of the western empire' (from *c.* 500–*c.* 814) and on 'Germany and the western empire' (from *c.* 814–*c.* 1000), were published in 1913 and 1922 respectively, and contained only a few chapters each on the period covered in the present volume. They were conceived when little was available in English on the early middle ages and there were few specialists in the English-speaking world able to write the chapters; volume III in particular was blighted by the Great War. No such impediment has presented itself for this volume. We have endeavoured to expunge the unhappy legacy of the old volume III when the principles of scholarship were sullied with political enmities and many scholars excluded as authors because of their nationality. The new series, and especially this volume, reflects the extraordinary community of interest among medievalists of all disciplines and all nationalities as well as a far greater knowledge and appreciation of medieval Europe as a whole in the academic world, among students, and in the general public. There is a far stronger acceptance of the importance of an interdisciplinary approach. There is a much greater awareness of the irrelevance of modern, or ancient, national boundaries and the need to consider developments in Europe as a whole, from Ireland to the Bosphorus, rather than focusing mainly on Anglo-Saxon England or the empires of Charlemagne and the Saxon rulers of Germany. Given the increasing economic and political integration of the European states, moreover, their common cultural inheritance adds an essential dimension to

xvii

their history. It is this that must be properly understood and which this new history is designed to serve.

Three volumes of this new series are planned, covering the centuries encompassed in the old volumes II and III. The twelve chapters devoted to the period 700–900 in the old *Cambridge Medieval History*, divided between volumes II and III, omitted many topics and regions, or at best subsumed, as short sections within narrative chapters, areas and themes which are now accorded full chapters in the *New Cambridge Medieval History*. Some of these, indeed, were rarely the subject of scholarly study at that stage. The emphasis of the old history was on the creation and maintenance of imperial domination. In place of the preoccupation with empire and the simple, blow-by-blow account of conquests and coronations, this volume offers an examination of the interaction between rulers and ruled, of how power and authority actually worked, and of the impact of these on the society and culture of Europe as a whole. There are, therefore, chapters on the 'Celtic', Slavic, Balkan and marcher regions, the aristocracy, kingship and government, Byzantium's relations with the west, Arab activities in the Mediterranean, ecclesiastical organisation, monasticism, money, the economy, rural society and social organisation, and the many different aspects of intellectual and cultural life. This greater concentration on themes reflects the current preoccupations of historical scholarship with many different facets of social and cultural history.

Thus part I of this, the second volume in the planned *New Cambridge Medieval History* but the first to be published, encompasses the events and political developments in the whole of the British Isles, the West and East Frankish kingdoms, Scandinavia, the Slavic and Balkan regions, Spain and Italy, and those events and individual actions in Byzantium and parts of the Islamic world which impinge on the west between *c.* 700 and *c.* 900. The factual and narrative portions of these chapters are blended with analysis and new interpretations of key issues. These chapters underpin those in parts II, III and IV, which cover common themes and topics within the general categories of government and institutions, the church and society, and cultural and intellectual development. In these thematic chapters all regions of Europe are considered wherever possible on a comparative basis in cases of great contrasts and in a more unified way where there is great similarity. Footnotes have been kept within strict limits, but comprehensive bibliographies for each topic will be found at the end of the volume.

Association with volume III (*c.* 900–*c.* 1030) of this new series, moreover, has been close. It is particularly to be noted in the division of chapters on the Russian lands, Celtic regions and the Scandinavian lands covering the period from *c.* 700–*c.* 1030 between the two volumes. Thus the discussion of the Russian lands for the entire period is to be found in volume III while the chapters on Scotland, Wales and Ireland and on Scandinavia are in this volume. The original intention for volume II was to devote an entire chapter to law and legal practice. Because this chapter did not arrive in time to be included, however, discussions of law and legal practice are integrated at appropriate points among a number of chapters, while a Bibliography for these topics has been added to that for the Introduction.

Josef Semmler was initially asked to provide the chapter on monasticism. Owing to ill health at a crucial stage he was obliged to withdraw, but I am immensely indebted to Mayke de Jong for filling the breach at very short notice. I am particularly grateful to my contributors, colleagues and friends from all over the world, who have joined in this enterprise, written their chapters, sometimes in very difficult circumstances, and put up with a great deal of editorial interference and cajoling from me with admirable good nature. I have incurred other debts, notably to William Davies of Cambridge University Press, for his constant support and encouragement, and to the staff at Cambridge University Press responsible for seeing the volume through the press, to the Editorial Board of the *New Cambridge Medieval History* for their preliminary advice and suggestions, to Timothy Reuter, Jonathan Shepard, Chris Wickham and John Contreni for cheering me on and offering excellent advice through all the years this volume, in its various guises, has been on my desk, to Chris Wickham, Roger Wright, Christoph Heyl, and the authors themselves, for their invaluable help with the translation of chapters 12, 27 and 5, from Italian, French and German respectively; to Vanessa Stefanak who helped with the organisation of the mountains of typescript and an intermediate version of chapter 22, to Sheila Willson of the History Faculty in the University of Cambridge, who cheerfully typed the intermediate and final versions of chapters 12 and 18, to Yitzhak Hen who compiled the composite list of primary sources, to Mary Rycroft who helped with the proofs, to Meg Davies who compiled the indexes and to Frances Brown for her meticulous copy-editing and unfailing patience. Finally, no one will be more pleased to see the volume finished, bound and quietly on the shelf than my husband David and daughter Lucy. To them both, for never-failing support, suggestions and practical assistance, I offer my heartfelt thanks, as always.

ROSAMOND MCKITTERICK

ACKNOWLEDGEMENTS

For permission to reproduce artefacts or manuscripts in their possession, the Editor is grateful to the following institutions:

Bibliothèque Municipale, Amiens; Bibliothèque Nationale, Paris; Bodleian Library, Oxford; CNMHS, France; The Royal Commission on the Ancient and Historical Monuments of Scotland, Edinburgh; National Museum of Antiquities, Scotland; The British Museum, London; Schatzkammer der Residenz, Munich and the Bayerische Verwaltung der staatliche Schlösser, Garten und Seen; Pierpont Morgan Library, New York; Stiftsarchiv, Sankt Gallen; Stiftsbibliothek, Sankt Gallen; Domschatz, Trier; Biblioteca Apostolica Vaticana; Reverenda fabbrica di S. Pietro, the Vatican; Westfälisches Amt für Denkmalpflege; ICCD, Rome; Bunge Museum; Essen, Münsterschatz.

ABBREVIATIONS

Full references for the primary sources are to be found in the Primary Source Bilbiography, pp. 867–885

AA	*Acta Archaeologica* (Copenhagen)
AASS	*Acta Sanctorum quotquot toto orbe coluntur*, ed. J. Bollandus *et al.* (Antwerp and Brussels, 1634–)
AASS OSB	*Acta Sanctorum Ordinis Sancti Benedicti*, ed. J. Mabillon, 9 vols. (Paris, 1668–1701)
AB (1)	*Annales Bertiniani*, ed. Waitz
AB (2)	*Annales Bertiniani*, ed. Rau
AB (3)	*Annales Bertiniani*, trans. Nelson
Adam of Bremen (1)	*Gesta Hammaburgensis*, ed. Trillmich and Buchner
Adam of Bremen (2)	*Gesta Hammaburgensis*, trans. Tschan
AE	*L'Anné Epigraphique*
AF (1)	*Annales Fuldenses*, ed. Kurze
AF (2)	*Annales Fuldenses*, ed. Rau
AF (3)	*Annales Fuldenses*, trans. Reuter
AfD	*Archiv für Diplomatik*
AHE	*Auctarii Havniensis Extrema*, ed. T. Mommsen, *MGH AA* ix (Berlin, 1892), pp. 337–9
AHP	*Archivum Historiae Pontificae*
AHR	*American Historical Review*
AL	*Annales Laureshamenses*
An. Boll.	*Analecta Bollandiana*
Annales ESC	*Annales: Economies, Sociétés, Civilisations*
ANOH	*Aarbøger for nordisk Oldkyndighed og Historie*
ANS	*American Numismatic Society*
API	*Archivio Paleografico Italiano*

AQ	*Ausgewählte Quellen zur deutschen Geschichte des Mittelalters*, Darmstadt
ARF (1)	*Annales Regni Francorum*, ed. Kurze
ARF (2)	*Annales Regni Francorum*, trans. Scholz
ASC	*Anglo-Saxon Chronicle*
ASE	*Anglo-Saxon England*
AV	*Annales Vedastini*
AX	*Annales Xantenses*
BAC	*Bulletino di Archeologia Cristiana*
BAR	British Archaeological Reports
BBA	Berliner Byzantinische Arbeiten, Berlin
BBCS	*Bulletin of the Board of Celtic Studies*
BBTT	*Belfast Byzantine Texts and Translations*
BCL	M. Lapidge and R. Sharpe, *A Bibliography of Celtic-Latin Literature 400–1200*, Dublin (1985)
BEC	*Bibliothèque de l'Ecole des Chartes*
Bede, *HE*	*Historia Ecclesiastica Gentis Anglorum*
Besevliev, *Inschriften*	V. Besevliev, *Die protobulgarischen Inschriften*, Berlin (1963) or Bulgarian 2nd edn, *P'rvob'lgarski nadpisi*, Sofia (1979)
BHG	*Bibliotheca Hagiographica Graeca*, ed. F. Halkin, 3rd edn (Subsidia hagiographica 8a), Brussels (1957) and *Novum Auctarium Bibliotheca Hagiographicae Graeca* (Subsidia hagiographica 65) Brussels (1984)
BHL	*Bibliotheca Hagiographica Latina* (Subsidia hagiographica 6), Brussels (1898–1901), *Supplementum* (Subsidia hagiographica 12), Brussels (1911); *Novum Supplementum* (Subsidia hagiographica 70), Brussels (1986)
BHR	*Bulgarian Historical Review*
Bib. Mun.	Bibliothèque Municipale
Bischoff, *MS* I, II, III	Bernhard Bischoff, *Mittelalterliche Studien*, Stuttgart (1966, 1967 and 1981)
Bischoff, *Schreibschulen*	Bernhard Bischoff, *Die Südostdeutschen Schreibschulen und Bibliotheken in der Karolingerzeit* I: *Die Bayerischen Diözesen*, 3rd edn, Wiesbaden (1974); II: *Die Vorwiegend Österreichischen Diözesen*, Wiesbaden (1980)
BL MS	London, British Library manuscript
BM	J.F. Böhmer and E. Mühlbacher, *Regesta*

	Imperii: Die Regesten des Kaiserreichs unter den Karolingern, 751–918, Berlin (1908; rep. Hildesheim, 1966)
BMGS	*Byzantine and Modern Greek Studies*
Bond, *Facsimiles*	E.A. Bond, *Facsimiles of Ancient Charters in the British Museum*, 4 vols., London (1873–8)
BNJ	*Byzantinische-neugriechische Jahrbücher*
BN lat.; n.a. lat.	Paris, Bibliothèque Nationale, manuscrit latin; nouvelles acquisitions latines
Brackmann, *GP*	A. Brackmann, H. Büttner, H. Jakob, W. Seegrün and T. Schieffer, *Regesta Pontificum Romanorum, Germania Pontifica*, 5 vols., Berlin and Göttingen (1910–81)
BS/EB	*Byzantine Studies/Etudes Byzantines*
BSl	*Byzantinoslavica*
BSOAS	*Bulletin of the School of Oriental and African Studies*
Byz	*Byzantion*
Byzbulg	*Byzantinobulgarica*
BZ	*Byzantinische Zeitschrift*
CA	*Chronicon Altinate*, ed. R. Cessi, *Origo Civitatum Italiae seu Venetiarum* (*FSI* 72), Rome (1933)
CAS	*Christianity among the Slavs: The Heritage of Saints Cyril and Methodius*, ed. E.G. Farrugia, R.F. Taft and G.K. Piovesana (*OCA* 231), Rome (1992)
CB	*Breviarum Ecclesiae Ravennatis (Codex Bravo)*
CC	*Codex Carolinus*
CCCC	Cambridge, Corpus Christi College MS
CCCM	*Corpus Christianorum, Continuatio Mediavalis*, Turnhout (1966–)
CCM	*Corpus Consuetudinum Monasticarum*, ed. K. Hallinger, Siegburg (1963)
CCSL	*Corpus Christianorum, Series Latina*, Turnhout (1952–)
CDF	*Codex Diplomaticus Fuldensis*, ed. E.F.J. Dronke, Kassel (1850)
CDI	*Codice Diplomatico Istriano*, ed. P. Kandler, Trieste
CDL	*Codice Diplomatico Longobardo*
CDP	*Codice Diplomatico Padovano dal secolo sesto a tutto*

	l'undecimo, ed. A. Gloria, Venice (1877)
CFHB	*Corpus Fontium Historiae Byzantinae*
ChLA	*Chartae Latinae Antiquiores*, ed. Albert Bruckner, facsimile edition of the Latin charters prior to the ninth century 1–, Olten and Lausanne (1954–)
CIG	*Corpus Inscriptionum Graecarum* iv, ed. A. Boeckh, Berlin, (1877)
CIL	*Corpus Inscriptionum Latinarum*
CL	*Codex Laureshamensis*
CLA	E.A. Lowe, *Codices Latini Antiquiores: A Palaeographical Guide to Latin Manuscripts Prior to the Ninth Century* 1–xi plus Supplement, Oxford (1935–71)
Clm	Munich, Bayerische Staatsbibliothek, Codex Latinus Monacensis
CMCS	*Cambridge Mediaeval Celtic Studies*
CNS 1	*Corpus Nummorum Saeculorum ix–xi qui in Suevia reperti sunt*, ed. B. Malmer *et al.* 1: *Gotland*, Stockholm (1975–7)
CR	*Cartulaire de l'Abbaye de Redon en Bretagne*, ed. A. de Courson, *Documents inédits sur l'histoire de France*, Paris (1863) (charters cited by editor's numbering)
CSEL	*Corpus Scriptorum Ecclesiasticorum Latinorum*, Vienna (1866–)
CSHB	*Corpus Scriptorum Historiae Byzantinae*, 50 vols., Berlin (1828–91)
CUL	Cambridge, University Library
CV	John the Deacon, *Cronaca Veneziana*
DA	*Deutsches Archiv für Erforschung des Mittelalters*
DACL	*Dictionnaire d'archéologie chrétienne et de liturgie*, ed. F. Cabrol and H. Leclercq, Paris (1924–)
DAI	Constantine VII Porphyrogenitus, *De Administrando Imperio*
DBI	*Dizionario biografico degli Italiani*, Rome (1960–)
DHGE	*Dictionnaire d'histoire et de géographie ecclésiastiques*
DÖAW	*Denkschriften der Österreichischen Akademie der Wissenschaften*
DOC	*Catalogue of the Byzantine Coins in the Dumbarton Oaks Collection and in the Whittemore Collection*

	I, ed. A.R. Bellinger, Washington, DC (1966); II, ed. P. Grierson, Washington, DC (1968); III, ed. P. Grierson, Washington, DC (1973)
DOP	*Dumbarton Oaks Papers*
DOS	*Dumbarton Oaks Studies*
DOT	*Dumbarton Oaks Texts*
DRIA	Royal Irish Academy, *Dictionary of the Irish Language*, ed. E.G. Quin, Dublin (1913–76)
EB	*Etudes Balkaniques*
EC	*Etudes Celtiques*
EHD	see D. Whitelock, *English Historical Documents* I
EHR	*English Historical Review*
ELC	*Epistolae Langobardicae Collectae*, ed. W. Gundlach, *MGH Epp.* III, Berlin (1892), pp. 691–715
EME	*Early Medieval Europe*
ESSH	A.O. Anderson, *Early Sources of Scottish History*, 2 vols., Edinburgh (1922)
fol.	folio
Fordun, *Chronica*	Johannis de Fordun *Chronica Gentis Scotorum*, ed. W.F. Skene, Edinburgh (1871)
FrSt	*Frühmittelalterliche Studien*
FSI	*Fonti per la storia d'Italia* (Instituto storico per il medio evo) (1887–)
Gä	*Gästriklands Runinskrifter*, ed. S.B.F. Jansson, *Sveriges Runinskrifter* XV, Stockholm (1981)
GEN	*Gesta Episcoporum Neapolitanorum*, ed. G. Waitz, *MGH SRL* I, Hanover (1878), pp. 398–436
GIBI	*Gr'tski Izvori za B'lgarskata Istoriia*, I–IX, Sofia (1954–74)
GMC	Georgius Monachus Continuatus, in Theoph. Cont.
GRBS	*Greek, Roman and Byzantine Studies*
Grumel	V. Grumel, *Les Regestes des actes du patriarcat de Constantinople*, I:2: *Les Regestes de 715 à 1043*, Chalcedon (1936)
GSR	*The Monks of Redon: Gesta Sanctorum Rotonensium and Vita Convoionis*, ed. C. Brett (Studies in Celtic History 10), Woodbridge (1989)

HBS	Henry Bradshaw Society
HGL	C. Devic and J. Vaissete (eds.), *Histoire générale de Languedoc*, 2 vols., Toulouse (1875)
HJb	*Historisches Jahrbuch*
HZ	*Historische Zeitschrift*
IB	*Istoriia na B'lgariia* II, Sofia (1981)
IC	*Islamic Culture*
IHS	*Irish Historical Studies*
IJMES	*International Journal of Middle Eastern Studies*
IQ	*Islamic Quarterly*
IRMA	*Ius Romanum Medii Aevi*, Milan (1961–)
ISN	*Istorija Srpskog Naroda* I, Belgrade (1981)
Jaffé, *Regesta*	P. Jaffé, S. Loewenfeld, F. Kaltenbrunner and P. Ewald, *Regesta Pontificum Romanorum*, Leipzig (1885–8)
JAOS	*Journal of the American Oriental Society*
JESHO	*Journal of the Economic and Social History of the Orient*
JMH	*Journal of Medieval History*
JNES	*Journal of Near Eastern Studies*
JÖB	*Jahrbuch der Österreichischen Byzantinistik*
JÖBG	*Jahrbuch der Österreichischen Byzantinschen Gesellschaft* (1951–68)
JRAS	*Journal of the Royal Asiatic Society*
JSS	*Journal of Semitic Studies*
JTS	*Journal of Theological Studies*
Karl der Grosse	*Karl der Grosse: Lebenswerk und Nachleben*, ed. W. Braunfels, 5 vols., Düsseldorf (1965 and 1968)
Kehr, *Regesta*	P.F. Kehr, W. Holtzmann and D. Girgensohn, *Regesta Pontificum Romanorum, Italia Pontifica*, 10 vols., Berlin and Zurich (1906–75)
Kenney, *Sources*	James F. Kenney, *The Sources for the Early History of Ireland: Ecclesiastical. An Introduction and Guide*, rev. edn Ludwig Bieler, New York (1966)
KHL	*Kulturhistorisk Lexikon for nordisk middelalder*, 22 vols. Copenhagen (1956–78)
Konst. Porph.	Konstantin Bagryanorodnij, *Ob upravlenii imperiej*, ed., Russian trans. and commentary by G.G. Litavrin, A.P. Novoselcev *et al.*, Moscow (1989)

La Neustrie	*La Neustrie: les pays au nord de la Loire de 650 à 850*, ed. H. Atsma (*Beihefte der Francia* 16), Sigmaringen (1989)
LD	*Liber Diurnus Romanorum Pontificum*, ed. Hans Foerster, Berne (1958)
LP (1)	*Liber Pontificalis*, ed. Duchesne
LP (2)	*Liber Pontificalis*, trans. Davis
Leo VI, *Takt.*	Leo VI, *Takita*, PG 107
LSCM	*The Legacy of Saints Cyril and Methodius to Kiev and Moscow. Proceedings of the International Congress on the Millennium of the Conversion of the Rus' to Christianity*, ed. A.-E.N. Tachios, Thessalonica (1992)
MA	*Le Moyen Age*
Manaresi	C. Manaresi (ed.), *I placiti del 'Regnum Italiae'*, 3 vols. (*Fonti per la storia d'Italia* 92, 96, 97), Rome (1955–60)
Mansi	J.D. Mansi, *Sacrorum Conciliorum Nova et Amplissima Collectio*, Florence and Venice (1757–98)
MBS	I. Dujčev, *Medioevo Byzantino Slavo* I–III (Storia e letteratura raccolta di Studi e Testi 102, 113, 119), Rome (1965–71)
MEC	Philip Grierson and Mark Blackburn, *Medieval European Coinage, with a Catalogue of the Coins in the Fitzwilliam Museum, Cambridge* I: *The Early Middle Ages (5th–10th centuries)*, Cambridge (1986)
MGH	*Monumenta Germaniae Historica*
AA	*Auctores Antiquissimi*, 15 vols., Berlin (1877–1919)
Cap.	*Capitularia, Legum Sectio* II, *Capitularia Regum Francorum*, ed. A. Boretius and V. Krause, 2 vols., Hanover (1883–97)
Cap. episc.	*Capitula Episcoporum*, ed. P. Brommer, Hanover (1984)
Conc.	*Concilia. Legum Sectio* III, *Concilia* II, ed. A. Werminghoff, Hanover (1906–8); III, ed. W. Hartmann, Hanover (1984)
Dip. Germ.	*Die Urkunden der Deutschen Karolinger* I, ed. P. Kehr, Berlin (1932–4); II, ed. P. Kehr, Berlin (1936–7); III, ed. P. Kehr, Berlin (1956); IV, ed. T. Schieffer, Berlin (1960)

Dip. Kar.	*Diplomata Karolinorum* I and III, ed. E. Mühlbacher and T. Schieffer, Hanover (1893–1908)
Epp.	*Epistolae* III–VIII (= *Epistolae Merovingici et Karolini Aevi*, Hanover (1892–1939)
Epp. Sel.	*Epistolae Selectae in usum scholarum*, 5 vols., Hanover (1887–91)
Fontes	*Fontes Iuris Germanici Antiqui in usum scholarum ex Monumentis Germaniae Historicis separatim editi*, 13 vols., Hanover (1909–86)
Form.	*Formulae Merowingici et Karolini Aevi*, ed. K. Zeumer, *Legum Sectio* V, Hanover (1886)
Leges nat. germ.	*Leges Nationum Germanicarum*, ed. K. Zeumer (*Lex Visigothorum*); L.R. de Salis (*Leges Burgundionum*); F. Beyerle and R. Buchner (*Lex Ribuaria*); K.A. Eckhardt (*Pactus Legis Salicae* and *Lex Salica*); E. von Schwind (*Lex Baiuariorum*), 6 vols. in 11 parts, Hanover (1892–1969)
Lib. Mem.	*Libri Memoriales*, and *Libri Memoriales et Necrologia Nova* series, Hanover (1979–)
Nec. germ.	*Necrologia Germaniae*, 5 vols + Suppl., Hanover (1886–1920)
Poet.	*Poetae Latini Aevi Carolini*, ed. E. Dummler, L. Traube, P. von Winterfeld and K. Strecker, 4 vols., Hanover (1881–99)
SS	*Scriptores* in folio, 30 vols., Hanover (1824–1924)
SRG	*Scriptores Rerum Germanicarum in usum scholarum separatim editi*, 63 vols., Hanover (1871–1987)
SRL	*Scriptores Rerum Langobardicarum et Italicarum saec. VI–IX*, ed. G. Waitz, Hanover (1878)
SRM	*Scriptores Rerum Merovingicarum*, ed. B. Krusche and W. Levison, 7 vols., Hanover (1885–1920)
MIÖG	*Mitteilungen des Instituts für Österreichische Geschichtsforschung*
Morice, *Preuves*	H. Morice, *Mémoires pour servir de preuves à l'histoire ecclésiastique et civile de Bretagne*, 3 vols., Paris (1742–6)
MLUHM	*Meddelanden från Lunds Universitets Historiska Museum*

MezhS	*Mezhdunaroden Simpozium: 1100 godini ot blazhenata konchina na sv. Metodii* I–II, ed. N. Shivarov, Sofia (1989)
MMFH	*Magnae Moraviae Fontes Historici* I–IV, Brno (1986–77)
MMS	Münstersche Mittelalterschriften
MS	Manuscript
MSHAB	*Mémoires de la Société d'Histoire et d'Archéologie de Bretagne*
N	*Nessèbre*, ed. T. Ivanov, Sofia (1969)
NAR	*Norwegian Archaeological Review*
nd	no date
NF	Neue Folge
Niceph.	Nicephorus, Patriarch of Constantinople, *Short History*, ed. and trans. C. Mango, *CFHB* XIII; *DOT* 10, Washington, DC (1990)
NIYR	*Norges innskrifter med de yngre runer*, ed. M. Olsen, 5 vols., Oslo (1941–50)
OCA	*Orientalia Christiana Analecta*
ODB	*Oxford Dictionary of Byzantium*, Oxford (1991)
Pal.	*Palaeobulgarica*, Sofia
PG	*Patrologiae Cursus Completus, Series Graeca*, ed. J.-P. Migne, 161 vols., Paris (1857–66)
PL	*Patrologiae Cursus Completus, Series Latina*, ed. J.-P. Migne, 221 vols., Paris (1841–64)
PMLA	*Publications of the Modern Language Association of America*
Porro	*Codex Diplomaticus Longobardiae*, ed. G. Porro-Lambertenghi, Turin (1873)
PP	*Pliska Preslav* I–IV, Sofia (1979–85)
PRIA	*Proceedings of the Royal Irish Academy*
QFIAB	*Quellen und Forschungen aus italienischen Archiven und Bibliotheken*
QK	*Quellen zur Karolingischen Reichsgeschichte*, ed. R. Rau, 3 vols. (= *AQ* 5–7), Darmstadt (1955–60)
RB	*Revue Bénédictine*
RE	*Paulys Realencyclopädie der classischen Altertumswissenschaft*
REI	*Revue d'Etudes Islamiques*
REB	*Revue des Etudes Byzantines*

REG	*Revue des Etudes Grecques*
RESEE	*Revue des Etudes Sud-Est Européennes*
RHEF	*Revue d'Histoire de l'Eglise de France*
RhVjb	*Rheinische Vierteljahrsblätter*
RIS	*Rerum Italicarum Scriptores*, ed. L.A. Muratori, 25 vols., Milan (1723–51); new edn G. Carducci and V. Fiorini, Città di Castello and Bologna (1900)
RN	*Revue Numismatique*
RSM	*Rivista degli Studi Medievali*
s.	*saeculum*
s.a.	*sub anno*
Sawyer	Peter H. Sawyer, *Anglo-Saxon Charters*
SBC	*Srednovekovnata B'lgariia i Chernomorieto (Sbornik dokladi ot nauchnata konferentsiia)*, ed. A. Kuzev, Varna (1982)
SBVS	*Saga-Book of the Viking Society*
Settimane	*Settimane di Studio del Centro italiano di studi sull'alto medioevo*, Spoleto (1954–)
SI	*Studia Islamica*
SM	*Studi Medievali*
SSS	*Slownik Starozytnosci Slowianskich* I–VIII, Wrocław, Warsaw and Cracow (1961–91)
StMBO	Studien und Mitteilungen zur Geschichte des Benediktiner-Ordens und seiner Zweige
SymM	*Symposium Methodianum. Beiträge der Internationalen Tagung in Regensburg (17. bis 24. April 1985) zum Gedenken an den 1100. Todestag der hl. Method*, ed. K. Trost, E. Völkl and E. Wedel (Selecta Slavica 13), Neuried (1987)
Theoph. Chron.	Theophanes, *Chronographia*, ed. C. de Boor, I, Leipzig (1883); English trans. H. Turtledove, *The Chronicle of Theophanes*, Philadelphia (1982)
Theoph. Cont.	Theophanes Continuatus, *Chronographia*, ed. I. Bekker, Bonn (1838)
TIB	Tabula Imperii Byzantini
TKAS	*Trudy Mezhdunarodnogo Kongressa Arkheologov-Slatislov, Kiev 18–25 Sentiabria 1985 g*, I–IV, Moscow and Kiev (1987–8)
TM	*Travaux et Mémoires*, Paris (1965–)

Treadgold	W. Treadgold, *The Byzantine Revival 780–842*, Stanford (1988)
TRHS	*Transactions of the Royal Historical Society*
UF	*Urkundenbuch des Klosters Fulda* I, ed. E. Stengel, Marburg (1958)
Vat. (lat.; pal. lat.; reg. lat.)	Bibliotheca Apostolica Vaticana, MS (latinus; palatinus latinus; reginensis latinus)
VA	*Vita Anskarii*, ed. Trillmich and Buchner (as under Adam of Bremen)
VC	*Vita Constantini*
VuF	Vorträge und Forschungen, herausgegeben vom Konstanzer Arbeitskreis für mittelalterliche Geschichte
VIINJ	*Vizantiski Izvvori za Istoriju Naroda Jugoslavije*
VM	*Vita Methodii*
VSWG	*Vierteljahrschrift für Sozial- und Wirtschaftsgeschichte*
VV	*Vizantijsskij Vremennik*
Whitelock, *EHD*	Dorothy Whitelock, *English Historical Documents* I, *c.* 500–1042, 2nd edn, London (1979)
ZfcP	*Zeitschrift für celtische Philologie*
ZRG	*Zeitschrift der Savigny Stiftung für Rechtsgeschichte*
GA	*Germanistische Abteilung*
KA	*Kanonistische Abteilung*
ZRVI	Zbornik Radova Vizantolosskog Instituta

PART I

POLITICAL DEVELOPMENT

CHAPTER I

INTRODUCTION: SOURCES AND INTERPRETATION

Rosamond McKitterick

THE Frankish dominance of the period covered by this volume poses special problems for the historian, not least because of the apparent concentration of a great diversity of sources from the Frankish heartlands and the relative paucity of material from everywhere else. Indeed, if our understanding of the years between 700 and 900 depended on the historical narratives produced in this period alone, we would be obliged to accept a largely Frankish proclamation of self-confidence and greatness on the part of the ruling elites of Carolingian society, and the Carolingians' distinctive celebration of the intellectual and cultural vigour of their scholarship and art, as the central points of interest for the eighth and ninth centuries.

Fortunately, however, an enormous range of other categories of evidence, drawn on in all the chapters below – charters, secular and ecclesiastical legislation, law-codes, saints' Lives, estate surveys, treatises on a wide variety of subjects, liturgical, school and library books, script, letters, tax-lists, poems, relics and relic labels, inventories, penitentials, seals, coins, library catalogues, inscriptions, confraternity books and artefacts of all kinds, ranging from pictures in manuscripts to weapons, jewellery, sculpture and buildings – redress the balance. The archaeological evidence has played a crucial role in adjusting and augmenting our understanding of many developments in this period, most notably in the economic and ecclesiastical spheres, as is clear from the chapters by Blackburn, Verhulst and de Jong.[1] The palace complexes unearthed at Aachen, Ingelheim or Pliska,[2] the fortunes of the trading emporia at Dorestad, Hamwic, Hedeby and Quentovic, the astounding range of monastic buildings at San Vincenzo al Volturno,[3] the exercise of patronage and display of wealth evident in the abundance of jewellery, metalwork and sculpture adorning churches and

---

[1] See chapters 18, 20 and 23 below; Hodges (1991) provides a useful brief survey.
[2] Randsborg (1991), pp. 65–6, and see Shepard below, p. 244.
[3] Hodges and Mitchell (1985); Hodges 1993.

filling treasuries charted by Nees,[4] add a distinctive and essential dimension also in the spheres of politics, power and social status.

Nevertheless, the principal evidence remains written material of one kind or another. Although there are many instances of texts in Irish, Old English, Old High German, Arabic, Old Slavonic and Greek, the vast bulk of our sources are in Latin. In the past, this has raised acute problems for the historian of the early middle ages, in that these Latin sources appeared to imply a major divorce between a tiny educated and clerical elite and a huge illiterate non-Latinate lay population. It has now been recognised, as Banniard explains,[5] that such problems and misconceptions arose from mistaken assumptions about the development of the Latin language in relation to the emergent Romance languages of western Europe. There was, in addition, a lack of appreciation, despite numerous modern parallels, of the degree to which a conquered people could acquire the language of their masters as a second language, especially when it was used as the language of law, religion and education.

Such was the case with Latin, adopted throughout western Europe as the language of the church, government and learning. Only in the British Isles and Scandinavia, as Keynes, Ó Corráin and Lund make clear, were the non-Latin vernaculars more widely used in law and administration.[6] Although the role of the Christian church in introducing literate modes of communication to post-Roman western Europe is undoubted, we have to reckon with continuities in the use of the written word within the areas formerly part of the Roman empire. Even in areas outside the old Roman empire, Latin was acquired, along with Christianity, and was soon exploited. This Latin, however, was subject to many local and regional variations, and differs greatly in its level of formality according to the genre for which it is used. It is certainly different from classical Latin, and different again from what is commonly understood to be 'medieval Latin', that is, a Latin understood to be conceptually distinct from the contemporary Romance vernaculars which developed out of Latin in due course. What are we to call the Latin in use in the eighth and ninth centuries? A terminological solution has been proposed by Roger Wright.[7] He argues that we have essentially complex monolingualism in the Frankish, Spanish and Italian regions once within the Roman empire. Some in the past have chosen to differentiate the elements in this monolingualism into Latin and Romance but they are more appropriately to be understood as many different spoken and written levels or registers of the same language, whether one chooses to call it 'Romance' or 'Latin'. Wright prefers 'Romance' as being less anachronistic and a way of

[4] Chapter 30 below. [5] Chapter 26 below. [6] Chapters 2a, 2b and 8 below.
[7] Wright (1993; 1994).

acknowledging undoubted differences from both classical Latin and medieval Latin.[8] Banniard below adopts an alternative position. Whatever the difference of opinion on the appropriateness of the terms, or the degree of contemporary recognition of the conceptual difference between 'Romance' and 'Latin', the upshot for the historian of the eighth and ninth centuries is that the surviving texts are in practice vernacular texts. Literacy, hitherto thought to be confined to a clerical elite, and literate skills, from the king issuing legislation and admonition and the landowner granting property to the church to the unfreed slave clinging to his new social status by means of a charter, were in fact widely dispersed throughout the society of the eighth and ninth centuries. Indeed, all the evidence available suggests that literacy and the written word were central elements of early medieval society, especially in the Frankish world. Written texts could also be made accessible to the unlettered by reading them aloud.[9] No group could remain unaffected by the activities of those able to make the most of the opportunities afforded them by their possession of literate skills.

Even with this recognition of the role of writing and uses of literacy in Europe in the eighth and ninth centuries, it is essential that oral procedures and the uses of orality be taken into account. Many of our written texts give clear indications of an oral dimension to their production or reception. Thus in legal business an essential role was played by the oral transaction in the social context of the law court, attended by the sort of people Airlie, Goetz and Wickham discuss in their chapters, where decisions were reached in public and subsequently recorded in a charter or *notitia*.[10] In the famous dispute between the monastery of Tours and Atpert, his sister Agintrude and her husband Amalgar,[11] Saraman the provost ordered that those persons who were in possession of that property should show their title deeds, *auctoritates*, at the appointed assembly in his presence. These title deeds were then brought before Saraman and other noblemen at Tours. But they could not settle the issue because of the absence of the neighbours to whom the case was known; their presence was necessary. Written charters also played a part and one of them was judged a forgery, on the grounds that the correct procedure for its redaction had not been followed, thereby fatally undermining Atpert's case. The oral witnesses, recorded in this *notitia*, told against Atpert, and we are bound to accept this formalisation of what was originally a dispute fraught with tension and grievance, with individuals of relatively modest social status attempting to uphold what they understood to be their rights in the face of a powerful institution. Even in such

---

[8] See Wright (1982; 1991); McKitterick (1989); Banniard chapter 26 below for details.
[9] McKitterick (1989; 1990).   [10] Chapters 16, 17 and 19 below.
[11] Discussed fully in Nelson (1986b).

ostensibly objective documents as the Tours case, or those charting the aspirations, claims and disputes of both urban and rural communities, therefore, we have to attempt to distinguish the rhetoric from the reality as much as we do in historical narratives.[12]

The Tours case highlights the interdependence and interweaving of oral and written procedures and discourse that is apparent in every aspect of life in the early middle ages. Often oral discourse and written documents are explicitly placed in sequence in the conduct of business. The Annals of St Bertin, for example, recount how Louis the Pious dispatched messengers to every part of his realm to bring the people the news of his own liberation, to remind them to fulfil the obligations of loyalty which they had promised him and to reassure them that he had forgiven them. Thus written messages, or messages committed to memory, were recited aloud to the people. Further, an assembly in 835, convened to discuss the problem of Ebbo of Rheims and discussed by Nelson below,[13] again demonstrates the interdependence of oral and written modes of communication and discourse. This is what happened according to the Frankish annalist:

Each one present at the assembly drew up with his own hand a full account of its findings and of their own confirmation thereof, and authenticated it with his own signature. The outcome of the whole affair, how it had been dealt with, discussed, settled and finally confirmed in suitable fashion by the signatures of everyone present: all this was put together, set out in full detail in one collection, bound as a small volume, and agreed by all to be an accurate account. They then wasted no time in making it as widely known as possible, bringing it to everyone's attention with most devoted and heartfelt and kind concern, and with an authority most worthy of so many reverend fathers. For they gathered at Metz in the church of the blessed protomartyr Stephen, completed the celebration of Mass and read out the account of the whole affair publicly to all who were present.[14]

In this inevitable stress on written materials and the contribution of oral procedures, therefore, the interplay of oral tradition is clear even if it is extraordinarily difficult to determine precisely in the light of the fact that we can only work from written testimonies. But the questions of reception, transmission and audience, and the role of listening, speaking and ritual gesture, are nevertheless crucial. Who wrote the texts we can still read, and for whom? Who then could understand and use these texts, and for what purposes? Would the texts be read privately, be read out aloud to an audience or their contents communicated in some other kind of way, in an oral paraphase, in poetic forms, or by gesture? What can be determined about rituals associated with written documents, such as liturgical *ordines*,

[12] Davies and Fouracre (1986); Balzaretti (1994).   [13] Below, p. 116.
[14] *AB s.a.* 835.

oaths, celebratory recitations, or those that have no written expression, as in gift-giving, banquets, dances or mime where in some cases written descriptions are provided of actions accompanied by formulaic spoken language? The literate modes we are able to examine in our sources may or may not have oral associations or an oral counterpart.

Occasionally we can observe the efforts of scribes to present texts in such a way as to suggest that they were designing the text for public reading out loud. Early medieval manuscripts from Britain, Frankish Gaul, Spain and Italy contain various innovations analysed by Ganz below.[15] One of these took the form of punctuation marks to indicate the structure of sentences and new layouts in order to elucidate the text transmitted to the scribe, or corrector, according to the needs of his own audience. These include the use of display scripts for titles and headings. *Diminuendo*, in which the first word of a section begins with a large letter or *littera notabilior* and the following letters gradually decrease in size, first appears in sixth- and seventh-century books and was a favoured technique with insular scribes. A hierarchy of scripts, descending from the capitals of the Roman script system, through uncials and half-uncials to minuscule scripts, flourished triumphantly in Carolingian manuscripts of the ninth century, though is to be observed in English and Frankish manuscripts of the eighth century as well.[16] In the Carolingian period the repertory of signs was increased: *litterae notabiliores* and individual letters modelled on ancient capitals were introduced at the beginnings of sentences; the question mark and various forms of *punctus* or points above or on the line were introduced to indicate minor or major medial pauses and the ends of sense units or sentences.

These signs thus have much to reveal about how such texts may have been read and understood. They establish that writing had its own autonomous conventions and structures quite distinct from those of the spoken word, and this is nowhere more apparent than in such non-literary material as the legal documents of the early middle ages and the texts of various genres designed for record-keeping alluded to above. Written language is fundamentally the textual counterpart of the spoken language, rather than writing being dependent on the spoken word. As Nees demonstrates, illustrations in manuscripts and sculpture often enjoy a close relationship with writing as well. Book illustrations enhance the meaning and associations of a text, are dependent on the text for their meaning, and are often visual translations of the written words. Other forms of art may be wordless but express no less eloquently the thought and aspirations of those who produced them.[17]

It may be that the language itself can tell us something about the intended

[15] Chapter 29 below.   [16] Parkes (1993); see also Ganz, chapter 28 below.
[17] Nees, chapter 30 below.

audience and the reception of a particular text. Just as there are several linguistic and stylistic levels in the Merovingian saints' *Vitae*, for example, so there are in Carolingian hagiography and miracle collections. Thus Alcuin in his *Vita Richarii* mentions in his prologue that the monks of St Riquier still used the Merovingian text of the *miracula* to edify the common people, while they wanted a new and more polished text for internal use. There were, in this instance therefore, two written levels, each with its own public. Hincmar of Rheims also distinguished two kinds of public for his *Vita Remigii*: the *legentes* on the one hand and the *audientia populi* on the other. Hincmar explained that he had marked the parts suitable for reading to an audience and those for study by the *illuminati*. But the difference between them is one of content rather than of syntax or style. The Carolingian hagiographers were not writing a simpler, more rustic Latin for the populace.[18] Thus the nature of the language itself does not assist us greatly in determining the audience envisaged for it so much as its message and accompanying rituals. When these can be seen to change, then ritual and language together reveal something of the society that produced them as well as a little of what religion may have meant to the laity, a subject tackled below by Smith.[19]

Fundamental changes in the rites associated with an individual's last illness and death, for example, culminated in the creation of a common and coherent, if complex, death ritual throughout the Frankish realm.[20] This ritual, and particular attitudes towards dying, death and the after-life it articulates, became the norm in Europe thereafter. Strong links between the living and the dead were created in the Carolingian period, not least by means of organised commemorative prayer on a remarkably large scale and manifest in the monastic sources de Jong confronts in her chapter.[21] The death rites and prayers were included in the Sacramentaries or Mass Books produced in large numbers in the eighth and ninth centuries for local use, described by Reynolds below.[22] Many of the later ninth-century Sacramentaries were produced at St Amand under the auspices of Abbots Adalhard and Gauzlin (also bishop of Paris) who may be credited with the elaboration of the rituals of death. With such evidence, royal involvement is nevertheless not to be discounted. It may be possible to associate the production of the eighth-century Mass Books with the Seine-basin convents and the bishops of Meaux and Paris, bearing in mind the undoubted royal connections of Chelles, chief among these convents in the time of Pippin III and Charlemagne.[23] The stories Einhard and Notker tell us about Charle-

[18] Heene (1991).   [19] Chapter 24 below.   [20] Paxton (1990).
[21] De Jong, chapter 23 below; Oexle and Schmid (1974).   [22] Chapter 22 below.
[23] See McKitterick, chapter 25 below.

magne's keen interest in liturgical chant,[24] the evidence of liturgical innovation in the royal chapel under Louis the Pious,[25] the link between St Amand and its royal patron Charles the Bald,[26] and the significance of the Mass Book, now Padua Bibloteca Capitolare D47, a member of the group of manuscripts associated with the Emperor Lothar's court school at Aachen, together suggest an abiding and active interest in liturgical matters on the part of the rulers that was closely in touch with developments within the church at large.[27] The writing down of oral literature in the early middle ages may resemble the recording of legal transactions and the transcription of music. The ecclesiastical chant tradition was one of oral performance practice, but this oral tradition was first transcribed into writing in the form of neumes in the ninth century. This is as true of the older chant traditions as of new compositions, the tropes and sequences of the later ninth century. To presuppose written composition is to envisage a very different set of mental and physical processes.[28]

A more conventional source of links between literacy and orality is literature. Poetry in particular has to be considered in relation to theories of oral recitation and composition. Was the original composition in writing or oral? If the former, to what degree do the contemporary literary genres and forms, detailed by Contreni below,[29] influence or even distort the forms of what we receive, to the extent of making it impossible really to recapture more than a faint shadow of the oral world to which they may once have belonged? Presentation in a particular form is, after all, in itself a sign language; punctuation in a written text and use of particular vocabulary, conventional metaphor and allusion can indicate appropriate rhythm stresses and patterns of phrasing. Presentation can act as a symbol of a particular cultural tradition and indicates as well as stimulates particular expectations about it. Transformations may well have been effected in an oral text when it was written down and the audience for the spoken and the written versions may well have been different. It is conceivable that the epics *Beowulf* and *Waltharius* and the victory song *Ludwigslied* were first recited at feasts in a lord's hall, composed and memorised for the purpose, but were later transcribed to accord with the needs of those accustomed to writing, or in a deliberate attempt to preserve and record them.[30] It is these written versions which survive. Analysis of the written survivor therefore has to take account of the oral conventions (no longer retrievable) which may have

---

[24] Rankin (1993).   [25] Bullough and Harting-Correâ (1989).
[26] Deshusses (1977); McKitterick (1980).   [27] See also Reynolds, chapter 22 below.
[28] Rankin (1993); Treitler (1974; 1981; 1982; 1984; 1988); Levy (1984; 1987; 1990) and Contreni, chapter 27 below.   [29] Chapter 27 below.
[30] Dronke (1977); O'Brien O'Keefe (1990).

determined the written forms we now see, as well as the literary and generic conventions which may themselves have influenced the original compositions. Words attempted to encompass and express experiences and images in the mind; in any text there is an elaborate cross-referencing system between verbal and visual signs and aesthetic responses in reading and understanding a text. Historical narrative in the eighth and ninth centuries was thus a recreation of the past in words and in a particular form, a form which was itself linked to other, possibly older literary forms. Thus the historical imagination that recorded the events regarded as central to Anglo-Saxon history in the *Anglo-Saxon Chronicle*, or the imaginations of the Frankish annalists, may have been fired as much by past imaginings and word pictures as by their response to contemporary events and wish to provide an interpretation of them for posterity.

Certainly the later eighth and the ninth centuries witnessed major developments in the secular Frankish historiographical tradition, with new forms of historical writing, such as annals,[31] biography and epic poems. These offer essentially contemporary commentary on the events of their own day and are the staple fare for the analyses presented by Fouracre, Nelson, Fried, Brown, Smith and Coupland.[32] All Carolingian historiography maintains, in one literary genre or another, a delicate balance between a profoundly and explicitly Christian and teleological sense of the past and an understanding of contemporary history which necessitated a temporary suspension of judgement in order to allow critical and constructive comment on policies or to explain setbacks. What was combined was an older Christian historiographical tradition, with its general explanation of historical change, and an annalistic and classicising approach to contemporary history. Although within this, narrative was the essential principle of organisation, subtle analysis was possible through the use of anecdote, moral fable, symbolism and parallelism in the plot. It is in this structural context that the presentations in our texts need to be understood, for, to a considerable degree, the historiography of the eighth and ninth centuries was a taught mode of organising and preserving memory.[33] The Franks had an especially keen sense both of the past and of the importance of providing a record and interpretation of contemporary events for posterity.[34] Yet in such works as the Lives of Charlemagne and Louis the Pious by Einhard, Thegan and the Astronomer, the account of the quarrels between the sons of Louis the Pious by Nithard[35] or the portions of the Annals of St Bertin written by Prudentius of Troyes and Hincmar of Rheims,[36] there is also to be

---

[31] McCormick (1975).   [32] Chapters 3–7, 9, 12 and 13 below.

[33] Compare Carruthers (1990); Morrison (1990); Morse (1991); Coleman (1992).

[34] Innes and McKitterick (1994).   [35] Nelson (1986a).   [36] Nelson (1990a).

seen an urgent political purpose in the interpretation of political events. These historians wanted us to believe the image they had created of their society and what they understood to be important in the process of events and the actions of individuals in their own day. Their motives, as well as the forms in which they chose to tell their story, need to be considered in the case of every imaginative reconstruction we encounter, in the light of the complicated relationship between the claim to be telling the truth about the past and the conventional representation in which such truths were expressed. If we consider early medieval historical narratives, we are looking at the world of authors who could manipulate conventions of writing – by omission, reducing events to narrative patterns, invention, and insistence that agents did or said things which accorded with the author's ideas about their status and character.[37]

The account Nithard gives us of the famous Strasbourg oaths of 842 is a case in point. Nithard had to present the alliance in 842 between the West and East Frankish rulers, Charles the Bald and Louis the German, positively.[38] He therefore made striking use of language differences – exchanged by the brothers but maintained by their troops – to enhance both the political difference he wished to stress and the necessity and essential logic of their reconciliation. Nithard had to continue to address fellow supporters of Charles the Bald and could do so by letting them all be united symbolically and speak with one voice, that is, in the same language, which differed from his own formal written language, just as followers of Louis the German spoke one language. By giving each army a distinctive tongue, Nithard was able to stress their unity and coherence. But in putting the language of the other army in the mouths of their leaders he could at the same time underplay the differences between them. Nithard effected this through the medium of the oath; it is repeated three times, in the two languages of the Franks, the two current spoken languages 'Early Romance' and 'Old High German' and the formal written version of Romance/Latin. The collective nature of the commitments and loyalties is heightened by this clever and essentially literary use of language. It is a rhetorical device in the traditions of the great classical history writers. It certainly cannot be understood as an accurate reflection of the linguistic affiliations or capacities of either the nobles or the rank and file of the army, as distinct from the possible range of languages and loyalties within the two armies as a whole. In any case it is unlikely that Nithard is faithfully recording the actual words spoken. What he is doing is giving literary and formulaic oral structure to what was an extempore oral promise. He wished thereby to create an

[37] Morse (1991).
[38] For historical background see Nelson and Fried, chapters 4 and 5 below.

evocative impression of what he saw as a crucial moment in the relations between the two brothers in which political and cultural loyalties on the part of the different groups serving the Frankish rulers were expressed. Yet it is important to remember that Nithard, as Nelson makes clear, intended his history to be read aloud to his military colleagues and the followers of Charles the Bald, whether literate or illiterate.[39] The oaths as written in Nithard's history are thus arguably provided by the scribe with a letter-for-sound correspondence so as to make them, when read out, intelligible and the rhetoric still more effective. That texts could be and were read aloud widens their audience dramatically, for oral communication to the illiterate made many texts accessible and helped to bridge any notional divide between clerical and non-clerical culture. Such bridges are most likely to have been needed more across social classes than across institutional groups such as the clergy and laity.[40]

Potent and persuasive image-making such as that of Nithard was also a written mode of memory keeping. Many historians, both Franks and others, were also conscientious and perceptive collectors and compilers of earlier sources, documents and traditions. Some – Bede, Paul the Deacon, Nithard or Notker – wove a story of compelling interest from the fragments they had gathered; others, such as Agnellus of Ravenna, Hincmar of Rheims, Alphonso III of the kingdom of the Asturias, or monastic annalists and episcopal chroniclers, rendered the information as they understood it in a less literary and apparently more straightforward manner. Yet it is no less subject to their own prejudices, presuppositions and aims and is no less concerned with the historical process and human chronology. Histories, biographies, annals, chronicles and saints' *Vitae* are valuable, therefore, as much for their guide to contemporary *mentalités* as for the details of events and individuals that they yield. Saints' Lives are particularly fruitful in this respect. A hagiographer to some degree was not only providing an edifying account of the deeds of a holy man or woman; he or she was also expressing the identity of a community and identifying that community's fortunes with those of the saint. The virtues of the saint were regarded as exemplary and suitable as an inducement for those reading or hearing about them to embrace the religious life as completely as possible. Accordingly a *Vita* can also be an essential key to understanding religious expectations and moral aspirations. Thus the nuns of Remiremont wrote the *Vitae* of Amatus, Romaric and Adelphius in the early ninth century to proclaim the historical identity of Remiremont as well as to promote the cult of Remiremont's patrons.[41] New communities in particular resorted to such written means of

---

[39] Nelson (1985), and see also Nelson, chapter 4 below.
[40] See the useful comments by Smith (1990).   [41] McKitterick (1991).

expressing an identity that had formed largely as a result of emotional expression and spiritual conviction. The cults or memories of founders or associated patrons were promoted. A saint's *Vita*, whether written in Spain, Ireland, Anglo-Saxon England, Francia or Italy, could represent a carefully nuanced exploitation of literate modes to further certain worldly and political ends but at the same time establish a saint within the customary oral and physical forms of religious devotion, even if the forms that devotion could take, as Smith makes plain, were often markedly dissimilar.[42] Such devotion bore fruit in orally transmitted stories on which writers of the *Vitae* could draw. The second part of Adrevald's *Miracula Sancti Benedicti*, for example, concerns miracles performed within the memory of people still living in the community. Other hagiographers, such as Berthold of Micy, are able to distinguish between what the collective memory could provide, oral tradition and what was obtainable through written sources, and how the 'monuments of letters which are set down on pages fully inundate the senses of readers and listeners', complementing the veneration and pious embellishment accorded the shrines of the saints, the churches built in their memory and the physical blessings ensuing from prayers at their tombs.[43]

Individuals ostensibly speak with their own voices in the many letters that survive from this period. They are an especially informative category of evidence in tracing the history of relations between the papacy and diverse Christian or quasi-Christian peoples,[44] from the Franks and the colonists in the Exarchate of Ravenna to the English, the new Christian communities in Hesse and Thuringia, the Bulgars and the Moravians. They provide us with many insights into the conduct of secular administration, of business within the church, and of exchanges between scholars in the Carolingian 'republic of letters'.[45] As the views of individuals, however, they speak with a distinctive voice that should not be confused with a general trend. Boniface's harsh condemnation of his Frankish episcopal colleagues, for instance, is not necessarily a fair representation of their activities.[46]

On a practical level, letters also witness to the extensive network of communications that bound Europe together, however tenuously, in the early middle ages. Willibald's pilgrimage to the Holy Places,[47] the exchange of letters across the English Channel and throughout the Frankish empire, and the messengers, embassies, merchants, pirates and pilgrims who traversed the Mediterranean, not least the Byzantines and the Arabs

---

[42] Smith, chapter 24 below. Brown (1981); Heinzelmann and Paulin (1986); Herbert (1988); Wolf (1988); Rollason (1989); Fouracre (1990); Ganz (1990); Sharpe (1991); Heinzelmann (1992).

[43] Trans. Head (1990), p. 15. See also Smith (1990; 1992).   [44] Noble, chapter 21 below.

[45] See Contreni and Ganz, chapters 27–9 below.   [46] McKitterick, p. 71 below.

[47] McKitterick, p. 78 below.

investigated by McCormick and Kennedy,[48] illustrate the practical possibilities for communications and their political and economic framework. We have to reckon with a continued use of parts at least of the Roman road network and of the Alpine passes (mostly Mont Cenis and the Great St Bernard Pass in the early middle ages). There was a system for carrying letters, even if it was more informal than the old Roman *cursus publicus*. *Xenodochia* and hospices catered to the needs of travellers. Extant documents affording safe conduct and providing introductions to potential hosts on the way indicate how common it was to travel. Surviving manuscripts, moreover, provide us with the consequences and outward and visible signs of the exchange and communication of ideas.

So far a number of primarily literary categories of sources have been considered in which a common concern has been to read not only what the text says but what it implies, the assumptions upon which it rests, and what its very existence may signify. These texts were not necessarily intended to reflect reality precisely or faithfully. To appreciate as well as to assess the accuracy of the early medieval historiographers' interpretation of their own past, we must bring in other categories of source material, as well as non-Frankish perspectives on the progress of events to balance the predominance of the Frankish versions.[49]

There were, of course, other written modes of recording memory produced with different objectives, such as all the legal records designed to establish irrefutable proof of possession which play such an important role in many of the chapters in this book. It might be thought, moreover, that it is precisely the strength of the legal sources to provide some kind of authentic and reliable voice, were it not for the fact that the legislation which comprises a major proportion of this legal material is normative and may be outlining an ideal rather than reflecting what actually went on within any one region of Europe. Legislation may well have confirmed reality, as it appears to do in many clauses in the supplementary laws of the Lombard ruler Liutprand, but in other legislation, such as some of the major capitularies of the Carolingian rulers whose implications are addressed by Nelson below, the laws are prescriptive rather than descriptive.[50] They establish and define aspirations and norms of right conduct and say what ought to be done, not what was being, nor what had been, done. When older

---

[48] Kennedy, chapter 10, and McCormick, chapter 14 below.

[49] The many surveys and bibliographical guides, such as Wattenbach, Levison and Lowe (1953–), Genicot (1972–) or van Caenegem (1978), to the wealth and diversity of the source material for this period, as well as the discussions of genre, are listed in the Bibliography to this chapter.

[50] Chapter 15 below.

secular and ecclesiastical legislation is drawn on by secular rulers and the clergy,[51] it may not always be in order to proclaim a specific ruling so much as to establish a principle or associate themselves with the wisdom of earlier law-givers.[52] Even functional documents such as law-codes are inconsistent in their terminology and an unreliable indication of reality. Yet there seems little doubt that the functioning of the law in practice was a major concern of early medieval rulers. For some the law-books produced may well have been intended as a set of guidelines and accumulated wisdom.[53] For others they were more obviously of direct social relevance and served to define group self-consciousness in a practical way.

A wide variety of early medieval texts expresses group consciousness and a sense of community in one way or another, whether or not this can be linked to nationality or ethnicity.[54] The law-codes or so-called Germanic *leges* in particular, that is the *leges* of the Salic and Ripuarian Franks, and the Bavarian, Visigothic, Lombard, Burgundian, Alemannic and Saxon laws, have been thought to express a very narrow self-consciousness linked to nationality. They may witness rather to the bestowal of political allegiance and the acknowledgement that one codification of legal customs will be the set of guiding principles in social and legal relations rather than another on the part of a number of groups. These groups might, on grounds of language or family origin, appear to be very different from one another and may have had little else in common other than the authority they recognised or had been forced to acknowledge.[55] Group identities of some kind may well therefore be reflected in a *professio iuris*, such as was required of anyone in the court, just as a judge was expected to judge according to his own law when presiding in court. Yet what established this group identity may have been allegiances subjectively determined with little reference to race, culture, religion or language, and where freedom, or lack of freedom, a distinction stressed by Goetz and Wickham below, may have been the most important social determinants of status and action.[56]

Certainly the Carolingians established the principle of the personality of the law in the early ninth century. That is, they confirmed the legal principle that different legal systems applied to different groups within the same society according to ancestry or place of origin. The Carolingian rulers legislated in their capitularies for radically new social and political situa-

---

[51] Nelson (1990b); Collins (1990).
[52] See Nelson, chapter 15, and Reynolds, chapter 22 below.
[53] See Ó Corráin, p. 50 below, on the *Senchas Mar*.   [54] Amory (1993).
[55] For political aspects of this see Fouracre, Nelson, Fried and Delogu, chapters 3, 4, 5 and 12 below.
[56] See Goetz and Wickham, chapters 17 and 19 below.

tions; as their conquests spread, so their legislation became applicable to the
new territories which came under their rule.[57] Yet they apparently endeavoured at the same time to cater to local and habitual modes of settling
business and dealing with injury and misdemeanour by allocating to certain
groups their 'own' law.[58] To this end they encouraged the production of
revised versions of the *leges* and did much to promote their dissemination. It
is certainly the case that the Carolingian rulers took a very close interest in
assembling the laws of the peoples within their realm and for ensuring that
correct texts were available to the judges in the court for use. It is even
possible to associate the production of correct texts of the Salic law and
Ripuarian laws, often accompanied by the standard early medieval digest of
Roman law, the Breviary of Alaric, with the royal writing office and notaries
of the Emperor Louis the Pious.[59] But the link between the production of
these legal codes and rulers may not always have been as direct as this. In
terms of surviving manuscripts, for example, we are often confronted with
collections that are linked with the individual enterprise of particular
bishops known to have acted as counsellors to the king, such as Hincmar,
archbishop of Rheims.[60] The thoughtfulness in providing a people with its
own written law may not always have been appreciated by the recipients. In
841, for example, the Saxons refused to follow written law and wished to
retain their own customs, regarded by the annalist as pagan and evil usage.[61]
This may be as much Saxon rejection of Frankish legislation as a specific
objection to written law as such; nevertheless, the Saxons' apparent
suspicion of what was written and preference for their own custom, held
within their collective memory, act as a warning not to overestimate the
success of the Franks in superimposing their own cultural presuppositions
and methods on another people.

While the legislation of the Carolingians, its production and distribution
have received full discussion in recent years, the role of the king in the
production of copies of the so-called customary laws of the people,
embodied in such collections as the Salic and Ripuarian laws, the Alemannic, Bavarian, Lombard and Burgundian collections, as well as the actual
dissemination, reception, function and use of these collections by the
peoples for whom they were ostensibly destined, remain a matter for
debate.[62] Although it is acknowledged that the link between literacy and the
law is an essential one to have established, the effect writing had on the law
and the degree to which it may have altered its function or affected its

[57] McKitterick (1989); Nelson (1990b).   [58] *Annales Regni Francorum s.a.* 802, ed. Rau (1974).
[59] McKitterick (1993).   [60] McKitterick (1989); Nelson (1983).
[61] See Schott (1979); Mordek (1986); Kottje (1986; 1987); McKitterick (1989); Sellert (1992b).
[62] Sellert (1992a).

practical applicability and adaptability within early medieval society still remains to be fully explored.[63] Clearer distinctions need to be maintained between the legislation of rulers, notably that of the Carolingians in capitularies, and the laws embodied in the so-called Germanic *leges*.

If laws are an ambiguous, if crucial, category of evidence, the formularies for charters and the extant charters themselves provide an indication of the special importance attached to the written word and its correct application, quite apart from what they reveal about the structure and affiliations of many early medieval communities. For the day-to-day recourse to legal procedures and documentary methods of proof, particularly in relation to land ownership, many charters survive, both in originals produced in relation to the actual transactions, and in later copies made of such originals. Notable charter collections include those of Weissenburg, Fulda and St Gall, Lucca, Farfa and Milan. But societies which displayed the greatest interest in the production of formal records, such as that of the Franks, were also those most suspicious of and best able to take steps to counter the existence of forged documents. Indeed, three of the most audacious forgeries, the Donation of Constantine, the Le Mans forgeries and the Pseudo-Isidorean decretals were produced in this period. The greater the emphasis on written records, the more determined could be the efforts to circumvent or manipulate them.[64] Charters recording the settlement of disputes, moreover, are hardly objective in their presentation of the evidence and the establishment of claims to property, in that for the most part what survives is the process of judgement as recorded by the winning party.

In all the great diversity of evidence weighed by the authors of the following chapters, it must be acknowledged that they also have had to contend with silence and a total absence of any information at all. In the light of both of these lacunae, and of the ambiguities of the evidence we do have which I have outlined in this chapter, the interpretation of the extraordinary history of the eighth and ninth centuries is one more than usually fraught with difficulties and controversy. Yet it will be seen from the rest of this volume how much can, nevertheless, be said.

---

[63] Wickham, chapter 19 below.   [64] Fuhrmann (1986).

ENGLAND, 700–900

Simon Keynes

IN his *Historia Ecclesiastica Gentis Anglorum*, written *c.* 730, Bede expounded a vision of English history which was intended to instruct his contemporaries 'in their various kingdoms', and which has always exerted a powerful influence on those who would follow in his path.[1] The 'race of the Angles or Saxons' had sprung from different Germanic tribes in northern Europe, but they shared a common language and had come to be united in their adherence to the Christian faith; so that while Bede recognised a distinction between the people of Kent, the East Saxons, the South Saxons, the West Saxons, the East Angles, the Middle Angles, the Mercians and the Northumbrians (*HE* I. 15), he also perceived them collectively as the 'English people', and his history as that 'of our nation' (*HE*, Preface). Bede's conception of the collective identity of the English people is a good example of the way in which he could distance himself, for his particular didactic purposes, from the real world of personal ambition, political aspiration, social pressure and material greed: it was a convenient and effective way of presenting his message to a wide audience but, in any political sense, it was a long way ahead of its time. One need not suppose, however, that Bede was an early advocate of the unification of 'England', as if unification on such terms was something already considered to be desirable for its own sake, and as if Bede had been concerned to set a programme for succeeding generations. The conception of unity which came most naturally to Bede was that of the island of 'Britain', implicit in his account of its Roman past (*HE* I. 1–14) and in his summary of its present state (*HE* v. 23). Bede may have felt that the 'English' were destined to prevail over the other inhabitants of the island, but he would not have presumed to deny the Picts, the *Scotti* and the *Brettones* their place.

---

[1] See Bede, *HE*, ed. Plummer (text and commentary); Bede, *HE*, ed. Colgrave and Mynors (text and trans.); and Wallace-Hadrill (1988) (commentary). See also Campbell (1986); Wormald (1983); Goffart (1988).

The general pattern of political development during the eighth and ninth centuries could be reduced to a struggle for supremacy in which success was dependent on the ability of one king or another to harness the resources at his disposal in pursuit of a preconceived political end. Such a view would depend, however, on the tacit espousal of certain concepts which have long been central to the study of Anglo-Saxon history, but which may distort the perceptions of political power current in the period itself. One is the concept of the Anglo-Saxon 'Heptarchy', which proceeds from an observed distinction between the three 'Anglian' kingdoms of Northumbria, Mercia and East Anglia, the three 'Saxon' kingdoms of Wessex, Sussex and Essex, and the 'Jutish' kingdom of Kent, and which appears to provide the framework within which political development took place. It invites the supposition that each of the kingdoms should be understood in similar terms, and it creates the impression that the kingdoms were the constituent parts of an identifiable whole; yet the concept of the 'Heptarchy' is, of course, no more than a sixteenth-century refinement of a twelfth-century rationalisation of Bede's incidental remarks on the political complexion of England in his own day. A second pervasive concept is that of the 'Bretwalda', or overlord of the southern English kingdoms. It springs from Bede's famous list of seven kings who had ruled 'all the southern kingdoms' (*HE* ii. 5), as extended by a late ninth-century chronicler who added an extra name to the list, stating that he was the 'eighth king who was *Bretwalda*'. The implication is that there was a particular form of overlordship designated by a specific title (which would appear to mean 'ruler of Britain'), and that it was the struggle for this distinction which provided the organising principle of interaction between kings in the eighth and ninth centuries. The concepts of the 'Heptarchy' and of the 'Bretwalda' are so deeply engrained in the historiography of early Anglo-Saxon England that they could never be removed from any discussion of the subject; but it is questionable whether either concept would have had much meaning in the eighth or the ninth century, and it must be said that there are other ways of approaching the complexities of political history in this period, which proceed from different assumptions and which promise to explain developments in somewhat different terms.

The nature of the available evidence creates immediate and unavoidable difficulties. We are largely dependent for our understanding of the general course of events on the annals in the *Anglo-Saxon Chronicle*, which present a view of the past as seen from the West Saxon court towards the end of the ninth century;[2] a rather different perspective is provided by a set of annals which covers events in Northumbria,[3] and one can only regret the lack of

[2] Trans. Whitelock, *EHD*, no. 1   [3] Trans. *EHD*, no. 3.

comparable material for other parts of the country. Information on aspects of the relationship which developed between the powers of church and state can be derived from the corpus of charters, which at this period were generally drawn up by churchmen acting on their own behalf as the beneficiaries of royal grants of land or privileges, or on behalf of the lay beneficiaries of royal largesse; but the various circumstances affecting the production and subsequent preservation of charters did not apply equally from one region to another, with the result that the coverage provided by this type of evidence is far from even. Further information on the development of royal power is available in the form of the law-codes issued in the names of Kentish and West Saxon kings; and analysis of the coinage reveals much about the nature of economic activity, suggesting where activity was concentrated and how kings brought it under control.[4] It is inevitably the case that the sources for one kingdom are rarely on a par with the sources for another, and of course it is true to say that fortuitous disparities of evidence should not be confused with actual disparities of substance. For example, the fact that we do not have charters or law-codes from Northumbria or East Anglia impedes the historian in any attempt to maintain a balanced view; but while it would be presumptuous to imagine that the 'quality' of government necessarily depended on the use of the written word, it would be mistaken to suppose that such records were not produced outside those areas in which they have chanced to survive. At the same time, however, the failure of evidence should not become a pretext for reducing each of the Anglo-Saxon kingdoms to a hypothetical norm. There is no reason why we should expect uniformity of structure among the kingdoms, or consistency of practice among the kings. It might be possible to observe in one kingdom a process of territorial consolidation, comple- mented by the development of certain administrative procedures, by the effective exploitation of natural resources, and by the emergence of a hierarchical and well-regulated society; but it would be a mistake to assume that one pattern of development would necessarily have been repeated elsewhere. Some 'kingdoms' may have existed only as a particular configu- ration of peoples united in their recognition of a common ruler, and might have dissolved at the time of his death, to be superseded (if at all) by alliances of a different kind; some local peoples may have retained a sense of their own identity for longer than others, and might have proved the more resistant to the imposition of the will of a distant king; and indeed, in some parts of the country the people may not have known much of the rule of any king, and might have placed their trust in a local church, or in the agents of a quite

4 See Blackburn, in Grierson and Blackburn (1986), pp. 155–89 and 267–325.

different power. It is arguable, moreover, that the sources which do survive are capable of obscuring the real differences which might have existed between the kingdoms, and which might help to account for their respective fortunes in the eighth and ninth centuries. Bede himself was not concerned to dwell on the finer points of secular affairs, and doubtless conceals a rich variety of royal and social behaviour beneath his chosen examples; similarly, the various ecclesiastics who drafted charters in different parts of the country were liable to cast the actions of kings in deceptively uniform ways, just as moneyers would strike the same types of coin in the names of kings who were themselves quite different from each other. In short, it may be that received conceptions of political development are too simplistic, or anachronistic, and that any explanation of events in this period should proceed from an assessment of the situation which is more sympathetic to the variety of conditions which might have prevailed in each of the kingdoms principally involved.

The most instructive point of departure for a review of political developments in the eighth and ninth centuries is the document known to modern scholarship as the 'Tribal Hidage'.[5] It is a short text of uncertain origin, compiled at an unknown date for a purpose which remains obscure; but it has assumed such great importance in so many respects that it cannot be ignored. The Tribal Hidage is a survey of all the land south of the river Humber, presented in the form of a list of thirty-four 'tribal' territories. Each item in the list relates to a particular group of people, giving the assessment of their land in numbers of hides. The survey begins with the land 'first called that of the Mercians', assessed at 30,000 hides; the reference is presumably to the Mercian heartland in the middle Trent valley, extending to the north and south of the river itself and including such places as Tamworth and Lichfield in Staffordshire, and Repton in Derbyshire (Map 1). From this starting-point the survey proceeds to cover the territories of the various peoples living to the west, north, east and south of the Mercian heartland, most of whom were subjected at one time or another to the authority of the Mercian kings; few of the peoples in question can be located with any degree of precision, and many cannot be identified at all. Four of the twenty-eight entries in this part of the survey relate to the substantial territories of the *W[r]ocen sætna* (in the Wrekin, Shropshire), the *Westerna* (the 'Westerners', probably in the vicinity of Hereford), the *Lindesfarona* (in Lindsey, with Hatfield Chase), and the '*Hwinca*' (presumably the Hwicce, in the Severn valley), assessed at 7000 hides apiece. Eight entries relate to

5 For the text, see Dumville (1989b). For discussion, see Stenton (1971), pp. 295–7; Russell (1947); Hart (1971); Davies and Vierck (1974); Sawyer (1978), pp. 110–13; Campbell (1982), pp. 59–61; Loyn (1984), pp. 34–9; Brooks (1989), pp. 159–61.

Map 1 Anglo-Saxon England, 700–900

territories with assessments in the range of 900 to 5000 hides, including the lands of the *Pec sætna* (1200 hides, in the Peak District of Derbyshire) and the *Ciltern sætna* (4000 hides, in the Chilterns); the lands of the *Wigesta* (900 hides), the *Herefinna* (1200 hides), the *Noxgaga* (5000 hides), the *Ohtgaga* (2000 hides), the *Hendrica* (3500 hides) and the *Unecungga* (1200 hides) cannot be so easily identified. The remaining sixteen entries in this part of the survey relate to relatively small territories assessed at 300 or 600 hides apiece, comprising the lands of the *Elmed sætna* ('Elmet-dwellers', to the east of Leeds), the *Suth Gyrwa* and the *North Gyrwa* (in the fenland around Peterborough), the *East Wixna* and the *West Wixna*, the *Spalda* (around Spalding in Lincolnshire), the *Sweord ora* (around 'Sword Point' in Whittlesea Mere, Cambridgeshire), the *Gifla* (of the Ivel valley, Bedfordshire), the *Hicca* (around Hitchen in Hertfordshire), the *Wiht gara*, the *Arosætna* (by the river Arrow, Warwickshire), the *Færpinga* (in the land of the Middle Angles), the *Bilmiga*, the *Widerigga* (around Wittering in Northamptonshire), and the *East Willa* and the *West Willa*; needless to say, the identification of many of these mysterious peoples can be no more than a matter of informed speculation, or wishful thought. The last five entries in the survey sweep rapidly through the lands of the East Angles (30,000 hides), the East Saxons (7000 hides), the people of Kent (15,000 hides), the South Saxons (7000 hides) and the West Saxons (100,000 hides). It is possible that the compiler of the Tribal Hidage was ignorant of the subdivisions which must have existed among these other peoples, or that it was not his business to provide a more detailed account; alternatively, one might draw the analogy between these peoples and those of the Mercian heartland, with the implication that the peoples who gave their names to kingdoms were considered for the compiler's purposes to have been identifiable blocs, leaving the various inhabitants of the midlands in a form of political limbo. The survey ends with a grand total, given as 242,700 hides; in fact the correct sum of the figures as transmitted is 244,100.

The significance of the Tribal Hidage depends on our judgement of its origin, date and intended purpose. The text is transmitted in one manuscript of the eleventh century, and in a post-Conquest Latin translation; but since the document itself evidently dates from a period before the Scandinavian settlements in the late ninth century, the evidence of its transmission cannot be brought to bear usefully on the circumstances of its composition. The matter must turn, therefore, on the internal evidence of the text (always assuming that the received text is a faithful copy of the lost original). It seems clear that the Tribal Hidage is in some sense a 'Mercian' document, if only because the survey proceeds from Mercia itself. It is also clear that the Tribal Hidage dates from a period when 'the land of the Mercians' would

have been understood to apply to a territory more extensive than the
original Mercian heartland, and in that sense it must represent a situation
achieved after a process of Mercian expansion, or during a period of wider
Mercian 'supremacy'. On this argument, the Tribal Hidage might be
assigned to almost any point in the period from the mid-seventh century to
the mid-ninth century. Further refinement of its date depends on one's
willingness to make certain assumptions about its purpose. The hide was the
normal unit of assessment for services due to a king, so it might be supposed
that the Tribal Hidage is a form of Mercian 'tribute-list', drawn up for the
use of royal officials responsible for ensuring that the king received what
was due to him from the various peoples under his sway; and it would follow
that the document reflects the scope of the overlordship of the king during
whose reign it was compiled. The inclusion of the 'Elmet-dwellers' would
suggest that the Tribal Hidage was compiled in the early 670s, during the
reign of King Wulfhere, since Elmet seems to have reverted thereafter to
Northumbrian control. One might, on the other hand, prefer to allow the
possibility that control of Elmet was still contested between the Mercians
and the Northumbrians in the eighth century, and to take the view that the
Tribal Hidage might thus represent a situation during the reign of King
Æthelbald (716–57) or during the reign of King Offa (757–96). Whatever
the case, the supposed significance of the Tribal Hidage would not be
affected: it would show that, at some stage, the overlordship of a Mercian
king had extended throughout England south of the river Humber,
embracing not only the numerous peoples of the midlands, but also the East
Angles, the East Saxons, the men of Kent, the South Saxons and the West
Saxons.

There can be no doubt that some Mercian rulers were powerful
overlords, that overlords took tribute from the peoples over whom they
were set, and that Mercian overlords must have taken tribute from many of
the peoples listed in the Tribal Hidage. But it is quite another matter to
regard the Tribal Hidage as an administrative document of the Mercian
regime, and as a reflection, therefore, of the scope of Mercian overlordship.
Bede himself was perfectly familiar with assessments in hides (one hide
being the amount of land capable of supporting one 'family', or household),[6] using them to convey a sense of the size of the various islands which
he had occasion to mention (Thanet, Anglesey, Man, Iona, Wight and Ely),[7]
and also to indicate the size of certain kingdoms: he remarks at one point
that the kingdom of the southern Mercians was said to contain 5000 hides
and that the land of the northern Mercians contained 7000 hides (HE III. 24),

[6] See Wallace-Hadrill (1988), p. 33; see also Verhulst, below, p. 499.
[7] HE I. 25, II. 9, III. 4, IV. 16 and IV. 19.

and elsewhere he states that the kingdom of the South Saxons contained 7000 hides (*HE* IV. 23). Information of this kind was of general interest, and probably a matter of common report. It is by no means unlikely, therefore, that at some time or another an unknown Mercian scholar was moved to compile a list of the constituent territories of 'Southumbrian' England. He may have done so merely for the sake of the exercise, or for some other reason best known to himself; and not unnaturally he chose to specify the size of each of the territories, producing a grand total at the end. It would remain uncertain when the document was compiled, though a date in the later eighth century might help to account for the discrepancy between Bede's figure for the two parts of Mercia on either side of the river Trent ($5000 + 7000 = 12,000$ hides) and the Tribal Hidage's figure for the Mercian heartland (30,000 hides). If the Tribal Hidage is interpreted in this way, it could no longer be regarded as a reflection of the scope of the overlordship of a Mercian king; but it would retain its distinction as a document of the utmost significance. Above all, the Tribal Hidage serves as an antidote to the received view of the Anglo-Saxon 'Heptarchy'. The document conveys an extraordinary impression of the number of different peoples who, at the time of its compilation, could still be distinguished from each other among the inhabitants of central England; and at the same time it suggests that the social composition of the political organism which historians recognise as the 'kingdom of Mercia' might have been quite distinctive. We cannot hope to understand in detail how the distinctions between these peoples arose, or what they might have entailed in terms of differing social customs and political organisation; but it would be dangerous to underestimate their tenacity, and it is an interesting fact that the terminology of the Tribal Hidage was still employed for at least some of the territories in the later Anglo-Saxon period. We may choose to wonder whether some of these peoples played a more significant role in the unfolding of events than their obscurity would suggest; but it is enough for the moment to recognise their existence.

Against this background, we may turn to consider more tangible evidence for political development in the eighth and ninth centuries. It emerges from the *Anglo-Saxon Chronicle* that Cædwalla of Wessex, and his brother Mul, had ravaged Kent and the Isle of Wight in 686, and Kent again in 687; but in 694 the people of Kent 'made terms' with Ine, Cædwalla's successor, involving the payment of compensation for the death of Mul, and opening the way, perhaps, for a more lasting settlement. Bede himself says little of Wihtred, king of Kent from the early 690s, beyond remarking that he came to the throne after a period of turmoil, 'and freed his people from external invasion as much by religious devotion as by hard work' (*HE* IV.

26); he has little more to say of Ine, king of Wessex from 688, beyond alluding to his subjection of the South Saxons (*HE* IV. 15), and to his departure for Rome after ruling the West Saxons for thirty-seven years (*HE* v. 7). There can be no doubt, however, that Wihtred and Ine established conditions in their respective kingdoms which lent great stability to England south of the river Thames in the first quarter of the eighth century, and indeed, it would appear that they entered into some kind of alliance which allowed the kingdoms to prosper independently of each other. The law-code promulgated by Wihtred in 695 bears comparison in certain respects with the law-code promulgated at about the same time in the name of King Ine; for example, it is evidently no coincidence that both codes contain a clause stipulating that 'a man from a distance or a foreigner' was to advertise his presence by blowing a horn, should he wander from the beaten path.[8] Yet the law-codes of Wihtred and Ine also suggest how the two kingdoms might have differed from each other in more fundamental respects. Wihtred's code projects an image of a kingdom in which ecclesiastics 'spoke in unanimity with the loyal people'. The first clause announced that the church was to be free from taxation, and that churchmen were to pray for the king and to honour him without compulsion. The rest of the code laid down, in effect, how laymen were to conduct their lives in accordance with the rules of a Christian society, and how ecclesiastics were to be accommodated in the new order. Wihtred subsequently reinforced his legislation by issuing a general charter of privileges for the Kentish minsters;[9] and given the extraordinary importance of these minsters to the religious, social and economic welfare of the kingdom,[10] it is easy to see why any ruler of Kent would have been eager to secure their support and goodwill. The law-code of King Ine, on the other hand, presents a rather different kind of picture. The code is preserved only in the form transmitted as an appendix to the law-code of King Alfred the Great, and it is a matter of some interest in itself that Alfred should have considered it worthwhile to re-issue a much earlier code in this way. The first clause enjoins 'that the servants of God rightly observe their proper rule', and other clauses serve to ensure that all men regulate their lives in the approved Christian manner. Yet the most striking feature of Ine's code is its confident assertion of royal authority. The great bulk of the code consists of provisions which seem to have been calculated to bring order to an unruly society, in ways which had not been attempted before, and to leave no one in any doubt that deviant

---

[8] Law-code of Wihtred (text, Liebermann (1903–16) I, pp. 12–14; trans. *EHD*, no. 31), ch. 28; law-code of Ine (text, Liebermann (1903–16) I, pp. 88–123; trans. *EHD*, no. 32), ch. 20.

[9] Sawyer 20. See Brooks (1984), pp. 183–4 and 195.

[10] See Brooks (1984), pp. 183–4 and 206, and Everitt (1986), pp. 187–96.

behaviour would be punished by the king or by his agents in the localities. Ine was not, however, interested in social order alone. Several of the clauses in his law-code reflect concern for the productivity of land, or for the appropriate value of livestock, and suggest that he and his councillors were well aware of the benefits which would accrue in the longer term from a well-regulated economy. There is nothing remarkable about this in itself; but it accords well with the supposition that it was Ine who promoted the development of *Hamwic* (Southampton) as a major centre of trade between Wessex and the Continent,[11] and one can sense that the West Saxons might have found themselves in a good position at a later date to turn prosperity to their political advantage.

It is more difficult to characterise the kingdom of Mercia in the early eighth century. One might suppose that royal power in Mercia had developed along the lines attested in Wessex or Kent, and that it is merely the lack of a Mercian law-code to set beside the law-codes of Ine and Wihtred that prevents us from appreciating the analogy. Yet the very absence of such evidence also permits a different train of thought. We know from Bede that the Mercian heartland lay in the middle Trent valley; and the Tribal Hidage brings home the truth that the 'kingdom of Mercia' was not so much a monolithic structure as a loose confederacy of many different peoples. Indeed, the supremacy enjoyed by a sucession of Mercian kings from Penda in the seventh century to Cenwulf in the ninth appears to have depended on the ability of these kings to exploit the resources of manpower in their natural constituency among the various peoples of midland England, thereby to bring other peoples under some form of subjection and so to gain access to the sources of wealth needed to sustain their own position. In other words, the Mercian kings derived their strength from the extension of their control over the peoples around them, and may not in this process have displayed as much concern as others to consolidate the territorial basis of their power. It is arguable, therefore, that the conditions which prevailed in the 'kingdom of Mercia' were not conducive to the emergence of a collective sense of identity which might find expression in loyalty to a particular line of kings, and indeed, that the conditions impeded the development of the institutions of government which might help to ensure continuity from one reign to the next. That is not to demean the importance of any one person styled 'king of the Mercians'. It is merely to suggest that the Mercian rulers moved in a world which suited their predatory instincts, and which brought them success for a while; but they never managed to change their world, and this proved their undoing in the end.

[11] See Hodges (1989), pp. 83–92.

In the last quarter of the seventh century the balance of power among the rulers of the English kingdoms had settled in a way that is best described as stalemate; and it was this state of affairs which persisted into the first quarter of the eighth century. Bede himself appears to have sensed that the kingdom of Northumbria was in a state of decline (*HE* IV. 26 and V. 23), and that a new order was emerging among the kingdoms in the south. In effect, the centre of gravity had moved from the river Humber to the river Thames: the Northumbrians and the East Angles were marginalised, and attention focused on control of the land stretching from the upper Thames valley downriver to the emporium of London, and thence further south into Surrey, Sussex and Kent. The rulers of Mercia were already developing their interest in the southeastern provinces, but the internal stability of Wessex and Kent seems to have presented a solid front which prevented them from breaking through. In the 720s, however, the position was suddenly transformed. Wihtred of Kent died on 23 April 725, leaving his three sons as heirs to the kingdom (*HE* V. 23); and in the following year Ine of Wessex departed as a pilgrim to Rome, leaving his kingdom in the hands of 'younger men' (*HE* V. 7). The almost simultaneous removal of these two kings, both of whom had held power since *c.* 690, must have broken the deadlock south of the Thames; and it was presumably at this point that Æthelbald, king of Mercia since 716, began to move to the fore. In the eyes of Bede, surveying the 'state of the whole of Britain' from his Northumbrian vantage point in 731, the situation which prevailed south of the Humber could be expressed in quite straightforward terms: all of the southern kingdoms, together with their various kings, were subject to Æthelbald, king of the Mercians (*HE* V. 23). Bede's seemingly incontrovertible statement represents the beginning of a period of Mercian supremacy which lasted for a hundred years, from *c.* 725 to *c.* 825, and which has long been held to mark a crucial stage in the political unification of England. We may choose to wonder whether the statement can be taken at face value; but Bede was certainly not alone in being mightily impressed by the extent of King Æthelbald's rule. The famous charter by which Æthelbald granted land at Ismere in Worcestershire to Ealdorman Cyneberht, in 736, shows how the king was perceived by a churchman in the diocese of Worcester.[12] At the beginning of the text, Æthelbald is styled 'by the gift of God king not only of the Mercians but also of all the provinces which are called by the general name "South English"'; and in an endorsement added to the charter by a different hand, he is styled 'king of the South English'. It is normally and not unnaturally assumed that the term 'South English' (*Sutangli*) was here intended to express Æthelbald's

---

[12] Sawyer 89 (trans. *EHD*, no. 67).

supremacy over all of the Southumbrian kingdoms, and that the charter thus
corroborates the word of Bede. It must be admitted, however, that the
formulation 'not only of the Mercians, but also ... of the South English' is
entirely appropriate to the conception of a Mercian king suggested by the
Tribal Hidage, as one whose royal power originated in the Mercian
heartland but had come to be extended over the 'Anglian' peoples of the
midlands ('South English', as opposed to the 'north' English of Northumbria and the 'east' English of East Anglia); and it might be safer, therefore,
to interpret the style in this more restricted sense. The feature of the Ismere
charter which remains truly remarkable is the description of Æthelbald, in
the witness-list, as 'king of Britain'. The term may reflect the grandiose
notions of Æthelbald's own entourage, or it may have come into the
draftsman's mind as an extension of his reading of Bede; whatever the case,
it certainly indicates that Æthelbald was regarded as the master of all he
surveyed. In the 740s, Boniface addressed Æthelbald as 'wielding the
glorious sceptre of imperial rule over the English';[13] and at about the same
time Felix, author of a *Life of St Guthlac*, felt it appropriate to write of
Æthelbald as one who enjoyed ever increasing prosperity from one day to
the next.[14] King Offa made no less of a mark. In some charters he is styled
'king of the Mercians and also of the other nations around', which harks
back to Æthelbald's style in the Ismere charter; in others, he is styled 'king of
the English', or even 'king of the whole country of the English', though
since none of the charters in question is preserved in its original form, it is
difficult to be sure that they represent genuine contemporary usage. Alcuin,
the scholar who had removed himself from Northumbria to the court of
Charlemagne but who retained a sensitive and abiding interest in English
affairs, heaped praise on Offa as 'the glory of Britain, the trumpet of
proclamation, the sword against foes, the shield against enemies';[15] and in
much the same vein Offa is described in a Kentish charter of the late eighth
century as 'king and glory of Britain'.[16] It is all too easy to get carried away
by the hyperbole: to forget that grandiose styles and naturally exaggerated
forms of expression are not always reliable indicators of historical truth, and
so to imagine that the Mercian overlords were intent upon breaking down
political frontiers in order to realise their own vision of a unified kingdom of
England. It is also difficult to resist the notion that the Mercian rulers would
appear in all the finery which befitted their elevated status if only we were
not otherwise so dependent on evidence supplied by those who came into

[13] Boniface, ed. Tangl (1916), no. 73 (trans. *EHD*, no. 177). For Boniface himself, see McKitterick,
below, pp. 72–8.   [14] Colgrave (1956), p. 166; see also *EHD*, no. 156 (p. 775).
[15] *MGH Epp.* IV, no. 64, p. 107; trans. *EHD*, no. 195.
[16] Sawyer 155 (trans. *EHD*, no. 80).

conflict with them;[17] or, put another way, that it is only the lack of sources emanating from the Mercian court which prevents us from seeing Offa in particular as a king on a par with Alfred the Great. Nothing could diminish our estimation of the extraordinary achievements of the Mercian overlords; the question is whether we should believe their interested admirers, or their disaffected victims.

It is essential to base our understanding of the Mercian supremacy on examination of the evidence which bears directly on the nature and extent of Mercian rule. In the case of Æthelbald, it can be shown that he held power over the rulers of the Hwicce, and since he was certainly in a position to exercise some form of control over commercial activity in London it seems likely that he brought the rulers of the East Saxons under his sway. Æthelbald's concern to foster his interests in Kent is also well attested, though it is significant that the charters issued by Kentish kings in the first half of the eighth century do not contain any obvious indication that the kings in question were operating under direct Mercian control. It is otherwise apparent that Æthelbald seized territory from the kingdom of the West Saxons, that he attacked the Welsh on several occasions, and that he even ventured on one occasion into Northumbria. The circumstances of Æthelbald's death ('treacherously killed at night by his bodyguard in shocking fashion'), and the circumstances of Offa's accession (by putting Beornred to flight, and conquering the Mercian kingdom 'with sword and bloodshed'), render it unlikely that there could have been much continuity from the one reign to the next. Charters preserved in the archives of Worcester cathedral afford evidence of Offa's control of the Hwicce, and charters preserved in the archives of Canterbury, Rochester and Selsey afford evidence of his intervention in Kent and Sussex. It emerges that Offa had to build up his power from scratch, and that his overlordship took different forms in each of the areas which came under his sway. Offa soon established his authority over the rulers of the Hwicce, though it was not until the 780s, or thereabouts, that he removed them altogether and took direct control of their realm. In the 760s Offa extended his authority into the kingdom of Kent, initially allowing the local rulers to retain their status as kings; but Kent broke free from Mercian overlordship in 776, and it was only when Offa recovered control of the kingdom, c. 785, that he suppressed the local kings, exercising direct rule in Kent for the rest of his reign. In the early 770s Offa brought the kingdom of Sussex under his sway, and in this case it would appear that those who had formerly been kings of the South Saxons were forced from the outset to abandon their royal status, though

----

[17] See Wormald, in Campbell (1982), pp. 110–11.

they were allowed to retain at least some of their power as 'ealdormen'. The South Saxons may have recovered their independence at the same time as the people of Kent; but if so, they fell back under Offa's control thereafter. Elsewhere, it seems that Offa enjoyed some form of recognition in the kingdom of East Anglia, to judge from the fact that East Anglian moneyers struck coins in his name; but the evidence is too imprecise to show whether local kings were allowed to retain their position during periods of Mercian control, or whether they only emerged in periods when the East Anglians managed to assert their independence. Little is known of the rulers of Essex in the late eighth century; but of the last two kings named in the East Saxon royal genealogy, Sigeric seems to have managed to retain his status (if not necessarily his independence) throughout Offa's reign, leaving his son Sigered to suffer the loss of his kingship under the regime of King Cenwulf. The construction of Offa's Dyke suggests that the Mercians had decided to lay down the course of their frontier with the Welsh, to defend themselves against raids from the west; but elsewhere, as it were, the options remained wide open.

The nature of the relationship between the kingdom of Mercia and the kingdom of the West Saxons requires more detailed discussion. It has been said that for most of the period from 726 to 802, 'Wessex was little more than a large, outlying province of the Mercian kingdom';[18] and if true, the fact would have a significant bearing on our general understanding of political development in the eighth and ninth centuries. Much depends in this connection on the credibility of Bede's description of Æthelbald's power in 731, on the significance to be attached to the more grandiose styles in charters, and on one's willingness to believe that the ability of Mercian rulers to take tribute from the West Saxons is attested by the Tribal Hidage. Much also depends on an observed contrast between the apparent stability of the Mercian regime, under Æthelbald and Offa, and the apparent dynastic confusion which prevailed at the same time in the kingdom of Wessex. The *Anglo-Saxon Chronicle* records a sequence of five kings between 726 and 802; yet no details are given of the parentage of any one of them, as if the main dynastic lines had failed, and as if the West Saxons were finding their kings from other branches of the extended family which they considered to be royal. It is certainly true that the West Saxon kings moved in a world of internal dissension, and were regularly confronted with (presumed) challenges to their rule: King Æthelheard fought the ætheling Oswald in 726; a certain Cynric, styled 'ætheling of the West Saxons', was slain in 748; King Sigeberht was deprived of his kingdom in 757, 'because of his unjust acts';

18 Stenton (1971), p. 204.

King Cynewulf attempted to drive out the ætheling Cyneheard, brother of
Sigeberht, in 786, leading to the death of them both; and King Brihtric was
instrumental in the expulsion of Egbert in 789. It must be emphasised,
however, that there is no particular reason to regard Wessex as a kingdom in
a state of debilitating disorder throughout these years. The brief reign of
Sigeberht (756–7) stands apart in a period otherwise marked by the longer
reigns of Æthelheard (726–40), Cuthred (740–56), Cynewulf (757–86) and
Brihtric (786–802); and while it may be difficult to gain much sense of West
Saxon affairs from the small number of surviving charters of the period,
there is enough evidence to suggest that the ability of these kings to hold
their own against their more powerful Mercian counterparts should not be
underestimated.

King Æthelheard is associated with King Æthelbald in a charter which
purports to record Æthelbald's grant of land in Berkshire to Abingdon
abbey, and which purports further to have been issued at Benson, in
Oxfordshire, at the outset (it seems) of a joint expedition to attack the British
beyond the river Severn;[19] it is difficult to judge whether any of this
information is genuine, though it is not inappropriate for the apparent date
(c. 730). If Bede can be trusted on such matters, Æthelheard was among
those kings who recognised the overlordship of King Æthelbald in 731.
According to the *Chronicle*, King Æthelbald took control of Somerton in
733, presumably as the outcome of a Mercian attack from across the river
Avon, and perhaps with the implication that the Mercian king exercised
power over much of Somerset thereafter. Cuthred of Wessex may initially
have had little option but to acknowledge Æthelbald's control of Somerset:
Æthelbald is known to have held the abbey of Bath,[20] and there is reason to
believe that his interests extended to the abbey of Glastonbury in the 740s.[21]
The *Chronicle* records that 'Æthelbald and Cuthred fought against the
Britons' in 743, which implies a joint expedition curiously reminiscent of the
one which had involved Æthelbald and Æthelheard. It was apparently in
the 750s that Cuthred earned his reputation as one who (in the chronicler's
words) 'fought stoutly against Æthelbald'. According to the annal for 750,
Cuthred 'fought against the arrogant ealdorman Æthelhun'. It would be
natural to assume that the Æthelhun in question was a West Saxon official
who had in some way given cause for offence, and so to regard this statement
as further evidence of internal dissension in Wessex. It is tempting,
however, to connect the chronicler's statement with the entry for the same
year in the set of annals preserved as a 'Continuation' of Bede, to the effect
that Cuthred rose against King Æthelbald,[22] and so to regard Æthelhun as a

---

[19] Sawyer 93.   [20] Sawyer 1257 (trans. *EHD*, no. 77).
[21] Sawyer 238, 257, 1410 and 1679.
[22] Bede, *HE*, ed. Colgrave and Mynors, p. 574; see also *EHD*, no. 5 (p. 285).

representative of the Mercian regime in some part of Wessex, whose overbearing behaviour had precipitated revolt. In 752 Cuthred is said to have fought against King Æthelbald at *Beorhford* (unidentified), apparently putting him to flight. It may be that Cuthred had resolved in the early 750s to remove the Mercians from Somerset, and elsewhere to drive them from disputed territory along the Thames valley. The West Saxons seem at about this time to have recovered their territory south of the Avon,[23] and to have resumed possession of disputed land in the middle Thames valley;[24] but one cannot tell whether this was achieved by Cuthred himself, or by one of his immediate successors.

Relations between the West Saxons and the Mercians were no less complex during the reign of King Cynewulf (757–86), and again they seem to have turned on control of various parts of the borderland between the two kingdoms. In 757 King Æthelbald (styled 'king not only of the Mercians but also of the peoples around') granted land apparently at Tockenham, in Wiltshire, to a certain abbot Eanberht, possibly of Malmesbury.[25] The charter recording the grant was attested by both Æthelbald and Cynewulf, each accompanied by his own entourage. This may indicate a certain ambiguity about the political affiliation of land in northern Wiltshire, or it may be that Cynewulf was at a disadvantage in the first year of his reign and had been obliged, in effect, to acknowledge Æthelbald's superior power in the area. But Æthelbald's death in the same year must have given Cynewulf the opportunity to recover lost ground. In 758 Cynewulf was himself in a position to grant land in northern Wiltshire to Malmesbury abbey.[26] At a council of the Southumbrian church convened at about the same time, Cynewulf granted an estate at North Stoke, on the river Avon, to the abbey of Bath;[27] the charter recording the grant was confirmed by King Offa, but the confirmation may well be an addition made on a subsequent occasion. Cynewulf is known to have exercised control over land south of the Avon, at a time when the abbey of Bath was in the hands of the bishop of Worcester;[28] but the situation seems to have changed thereafter, perhaps following the transfer of Bath into Offa's hands, since Offa was in a position, towards the end of his reign, to make at least one grant of land in Somerset.[29] It is particularly interesting to find that Cynewulf attested a charter by which King Offa granted land at Bexhill in Sussex to the bishop of Selsey, in 772.[30] In this case there is no obvious connection between Cynewulf's appearance and the nature of the grant itself; rather, it seems that Cynewulf had attended the meeting at which the grant happens to have been made, though one

[23] Sawyer 1680 and 1257.   [24] Sawyer 1258.   [25] Sawyer 96.
[26] Sawyer 260; see also Sawyer 264.   [27] Sawyer 265.
[28] Sawyer 1257 (trans. *EHD*, no. 77); see also Sawyer 261 (trans. *EHD*, no. 71) and 262 (trans. *EHD*, no. 70).   [29] Sawyer 1692.   [30] Sawyer 108.

cannot tell whether his presence signified his acknowledgement of Offa's overlordship, or whether it was simply a reflection of normal relations between the two kings. The land in the Thames valley remained the principal bone of contention. The chronicler reports that in 779 Cynewulf and Offa 'fought around Bensington [Benson, Oxfordshire], and Offa captured the town', and it emerges from another source that Offa seized the monastery at Cookham, 'and many other towns', from King Cynewulf, 'and brought them under Mercian rule'.[31] Cynewulf's eventual loss of some territory at Offa's hands does not, however, represent the subjection of his whole kingdom to Mercian rule; and although it is clear that Cynewulf must have been overshadowed by his powerful neighbour in the last years of his reign, the legates who reported to the pope on their visit to England in 786 seem to have regarded the two kings as independent rulers.[32]

Following his recovery of control of Kent, in the mid-780s, Offa was at the height of his power; and we might expect, therefore, to find more compelling signs of his 'supremacy' over Wessex. King Cynewulf was succeeded in 786 by Brihtric; and in 789 Brihtric married Eadburh, daughter of Offa. This marriage is, in fact, the only evidence for relations between the kingdoms in the last decade of Offa's reign, and it is accordingly a matter of some importance to judge it correctly. The marriage could be interpreted in political terms as an acknowledgement on Brihtric's part of Offa's overlordship, from which he might have gained some guarantee of protection against his rivals and some assurance of peace from Offa himself; alternatively, it could be interpreted as marking the establishment of a bond between the two kingdoms, which symbolised their mutual respect. The choice depends on our interpretation of a remark in the annal for 839 in the *Anglo-Saxon Chronicle*, made in connection with a record of the death of Brihtric's successor, Egbert: 'Earlier, before he became king, Offa, king of the Mercians, and Brihtric, king of the West Saxons, had driven him from England to France for three years. Brihtric had helped Offa because he had married his daughter.' As a member of the West Saxon royal dynasty, Egbert was evidently a potential threat to Brihtric; and his expulsion from England has been regarded as a case of the all-powerful Offa helping a threatened Brihtric to secure his own position in Wessex, with the implication that Brihtric ruled thereafter as Offa's 'protected dependant'.[33] Yet one should not forget that Egbert was the son of Ealhmund, who had been recognised as a king of Kent towards the end of the period of Kentish independence from Mercia (776–*c*. 785). Egbert might thus have been

---

[31] Sawyer 1258 (trans. *EHD*, no. 79).   [32] *MGH Epp.* IV, no. 3 (trans. *EHD*, no. 191).
[33] Stenton (1971), pp. 209–10; see also p. 225.

perceived as a potential threat to Offa's position in the southeast, and Brihtric would have been in the best position to secure his removal from England. Of course a West Saxon chronicler might be expected to put the best construction on the events; but his statement that it was Brihtric who helped Offa (and not *vice versa*) might reasonably be construed as an indication that, in this instance, the king of the West Saxons was performing a favour for his father-in-law, without any implication of political subordination thereafter.

The evidence bearing on relations between Wessex and Mercia in the eighth century thus falls a long way short of showing that the one was an 'outlying province' of the other for any part of the period from 726 to 802; and it is important to emphasise that the successive kings of the West Saxons appear, on the evidence of their charters, to have enjoyed a freedom of action which was denied to their counterparts elsewhere. It would be rash, therefore, to assume that the Mercian overlords entertained any serious pretensions to supremacy throughout southern England. Both Æthelbald and Offa managed to build up unprecedented power from their Mercian base, and both must have dominated their respective political scenes; yet both always remained kings 'of the Mercians'. One has to stress, in this connection, that Mercian overlordship was fundamentally a matter of degree. It meant different things to different people, from one part of the country to another and from one period to another; and it could find expression in a number of different ways. The Mercians might have maintained good relations with a kingdom, and respected its independence; they might have appropriated territory in which they had an interest, and otherwise left the local ruler to his own devices; or they might have demanded payments of tribute in return for peace. In some cases they took matters further, with more direct intervention in the internal affairs of a kingdom. They might have allowed the local ruler to retain his function as king, requiring him to acknowledge Mercian overlordship in other ways; they might have denied royal status to the local ruler, but allowed him to continue to exercise his functions as before, in a more lowly capacity; or they might have suppressed the local ruler altogether, taking direct control of the kingdom but respecting its separate identity. Needless to say, the different forms of Mercian overlordship would have left different marks, some of which are easier to detect than others; but the point remains that however extensive the 'Mercian supremacy' may have been, it should never be visualised as a uniform political system. The heart of Mercian power remained where it always had been, in the middle Trent valley, and it derived its strength from mastery of the numerous peoples of midland England; but although its separate limbs stretched out in different directions over various other parts of the country, the firmness of its grip was uneven, and there was no attempt to bring all things in reach within a single embrace.

The 'Mercian supremacy' was not, therefore, the realisation of a grand design for the unification of southern England, sustained by the emergence of a sense of collective political identity among the English people; it was simply the product of the extension of Mercian power into areas which could least resist, and so far as one can tell it was sustained essentially by a threat or display of force. Perhaps one should not attach much significance in this connection to Boniface's complaint that Æthelbald's ealdormen and companions offered 'greater violence and oppression to monks and priests than other Christian kings have done before',[34] or to Offa's overbearing behaviour in denying the right of a Kentish king to issue charters without his permission;[35] for such clashes of interest were commonplace, and could be matched in kind at any other period. Offa himself went to considerable lengths in the late 780s to secure the consecration of his son Ecgfrith as king, and even Alcuin was prepared to indulge Offa in what seems to have been his attempt in this way to put the Mercian regime on a new and more acceptable footing.[36] Yet the truth remained that Offa's position depended on the forcible suppression of his political opponents. In 789 Egbert of Wessex was driven into exile in Francia, precipitating (or perhaps compounding) a dispute between Offa and Charlemagne;[37] in 794 Æthelberht, king of the East Angles, was beheaded on Offa's orders; at about the same time Charlemagne had occasion to ask Archbishop Æthelheard to intercede with Offa on behalf of some 'miserable exiles' who had left their country with their lord Hringstan, hoping that they would now be allowed 'to return to their native land in peace and without unjust oppression of any kind';[38] and in 796, Charlemagne wrote to Offa of the exiles 'who in fear of death have taken refuge under the wings of our protection'.[39] These are the victims of Offa's regime whose own stories one should like so much to have. It must suffice, however, to reflect on the testimony of one interested observer, as he came to terms with the brutal realities of Mercian power following the deaths of both Offa and Ecgfrith in 796. Alcuin wrote to a Mercian ealdorman that Ecgfrith 'has not died for his own sins, but the vengeance for the blood shed by the father has reached the son. For you know very well how much blood his father shed to secure the kingdom on his son. This was

---

[34] Boniface, ed. Tangl (1916), no. 73 (trans. *EHD*, no. 177).
[35] Sawyer 155 (trans. *EHD*, no. 80), 1259 and 1264.   [36] Keynes (1990).
[37] *MGH Epp.* IV, no. 7 (trans. *EHD*, no. 192); see also *EHD*, no. 20.
[38] *MGH Epp.* IV, no. 85 (trans. *EHD*, no. 196).
[39] *MGH Epp.* IV, no. 100 (trans. *EHD*, no. 197)

not a strengthening of his kingdom, but its ruin.'[40] He wrote in similar terms to a Mercian bishop: 'You know very well how the illustrious king prepared for his son to inherit his kingdom, as he thought, but as events showed, he took it from him. Hence you can judge worldly wisdom, and how truly the psalmist said: "Unless the Lord builds the house, they labour in vain who guard it." Man proposes, but God disposes.'[41]

If one accepts the conception of Mercian power outlined above, there ceases to be any reason to suppose that the supremacy of the Mercian kings ended with the death of Offa in 796. Indeed, the reign of Cenwulf (796–821) seems in many respects to epitomise the Mercian regime, and to bring its most distinctive features into their sharpest focus. The extent of Cenwulf's rule was much the same as Offa's had been, and is attested in the same variety of ways; he made terms with the Northumbrians in the early years of his reign, and seems latterly to have adopted a belligerent attitude towards the Welsh; he pursued his ends with all the determination of his predecessors, meeting opposition with repression, and generating much resentment in the process; and like Offa, he may have found that he had sowed the seeds of his own destruction. It is inevitable, given the nature of the surviving sources, that we know most about Cenwulf's rule in Kent. The rebellion of Eadberht Præn had shown yet again how fragile was the power of the Mercian king outside his own kingdom, especially at the beginning of a new reign; and it is typical of the means by which supremacy was enforced that Cenwulf ravaged Kent in 798, seized Eadberht, and 'brought him in fetters into Mercia'. The nature of Mercian interests in Kent is then underlined by Cenwulf's famous dispute with Wulfred, archbishop of Canterbury, about control of the wealthy Kentish minsters;[42] yet it is striking that the Mercian king seems always to have conducted his dealings with Kent from a distance, and that he made little attempt to cultivate support among members of the local nobility. The death of Cenwulf in 821 appears to have precipitated considerable upheaval,[43] of the kind associated with the sudden release of feelings which had been suppressed during the lifetime of a potent king; and there are indications that for the rest of the 820s Mercia fell into a state of internal discord which spelt its end as a great Southumbrian power. In 823 Ceolwulf 'was deprived of his kingdom'; in 824, 'two ealdormen, Burghelm and Muca, were killed'; in 825 the Mercians suffered the military defeat which led to the loss of their control of the southeastern provinces; in 827, 'Ludeca, king of the Mercians, was killed, and his five ealdormen with

[40] *MGH Epp.* IV, no. 122 (trans. *EHD*, no. 202).
[41] *MGH Epp.* IV, no. 124 (trans. Allott (1974), no. 160); see also Bullough (1993).
[42] See Brooks (1984), pp. 175–206.   [43] Sawyer 1435.

him'; and in 829 the kingdom was 'conquered' (in whatever sense the term may imply) by Egbert of Wessex. There is no particular reason to believe that the discord persisted into the 'second reign' of Wiglaf (830–40), or into the reigns of Berhtwulf (840–52) and Burgred (852–74); but a reading of Mercian charters creates an interesting (if necessarily subjective) impression of a kingdom past its glory and now reverting to its former condition. It would appear that the 'kingdom of Mercia' remained an agglomeration of different peoples, each with its own leader, or 'ealdorman'; that the kingship of the Mercians depended on the ability of the leader of one people to gain recognition from the leaders of others; and that while particular kings may (or may not) have tried to establish dynastic rule, none succeeded in doing so. Moreover, if it was true that the Mercians lacked adequate resources of their own, and had once looked elsewhere to satisfy their needs, it may also have been true that their kings, perhaps of their nature, did not have access to land in the quantity required for the support of their men. After 825, the Mercians were obliged to turn in on themselves. The kings seem to have resorted (more so than before) to the seizure of land from some churches, and to the selling of privileges to others;[44] at the same time they would have had little option but to resign themselves to the further developments south of the Thames.

The course of events in the ninth century could be understood in its simplest terms as a story of the 'rise of Wessex' from foundations laid by King Egbert in the first quarter of the century to the achievements of King Alfred the Great in its closing decades. The outlines of the story are told in the *Anglo-Saxon Chronicle*, though the modern reader has to make all due allowance for the fact that the annals represent a West Saxon point of view and were cast in their received form by a chronicler who well knew what the outcome would be. On the day of Egbert's succession to the kingdom of Wessex, in 802, a Mercian ealdorman from the province of the Hwicce had crossed the border at Kempsford (on the Thames), presumably with the intention of mounting a raid into northern Wiltshire; the Mercian force was met by the local ealdorman, 'and the people of Wiltshire had the victory'. There is some evidence that a treaty was sworn between the Mercians and the West Saxons at about this time, in a meeting at *Colleshyl* (? Coleshill in Berkshire, not far from Kempsford);[45] and this may have inaugurated a period of peace which lasted for the next twenty years. The chronicler attached particular significance to the achievements of King Egbert in the 820s. In 825 Egbert defeated Beornwulf, king of the Mercians, at the battle

---

[44] See, e.g., Sawyer 190 (trans. *EHD*, no. 85), 192 (trans. *EHD*, no. 86), 206 (trans. *EHD*, no. 90) and 207 (trans. *EHD*, no. 91); see also Wormald, in Campbell (1982), pp. 138–9.
[45] Sawyer 154.

of *Ellendun*, precipitating the submission to the West Saxons of 'the people of Kent and of Surrey and the South Saxons and the East Saxons', and also precipitating an appeal by the East Angles to the West Saxons 'for peace and protection, because of their fear of the Mercians'. *Ellendun* (now called Wroughton) is located in that part of northern Wiltshire apparently disputed between Wessex and Mercia in the eighth century; and it is significant that Mercian supremacy in the southeast was undone in this way by a military defeat so much further to the west. In 829 Egbert went on, in the chronicler's words, to conquer 'the kingdom of the Mercians and everything south of the Humber'. It was at this point that the chronicler chose to attach Egbert's name to Bede's list of seven Southumbrian overlords (*HE* II. 5), adding that 'he was the eighth king who was *Bretwalda*'. One could argue at length about the significance of this term, and whether the 'omission' of Æthelbald and Offa from the chronicler's extended list should be construed as a sign of 'anti-Mercian bias', or as a sign of his awareness that the rule of the Mercian kings had not actually extended over the whole of Southumbria; and since the Mercians appear to have recovered their independence in 830, one might also suppose that Egbert's glory was in fact short lived. Whatever the case, Egbert is seen on this model to have been the one who began to restore West Saxon strength after the political misfortune of the period from 726 to 802, and whose victory over the Mercians at the battle of *Ellendun* in 825 enabled him and his successors to stake their own claim to the overlordship of the Southumbrian kingdoms; in short, it was essentially by virtue of Egbert's success that Alfred was able to 'inherit' what Offa had built.[46]

It is arguable, however, that the unfolding pattern of events should be understood in a rather different way. If Bede's concept of the Southumbrian overlord, and the chronicler's concept of the 'Bretwalda', are to be regarded as artificial constructs, which have no validity outside the context of the literary works in which they appear, we are released from the assumptions about political development which they seem to involve. Thus, while the chronicler in the late ninth century might have considered it appropriate to cast Egbert in the role which had been created in the first instance by Bede, we might ask whether kings in the eighth and ninth centuries were quite so obsessed with the establishment of a pan-Southumbrian state. Other issues were perhaps of more pressing concern. What mattered most to the Mercian kings was the security of their interests along the course of the river Thames, access to the emporium of London, and control of the southeast; and for much of the period from *c*. 725 to *c*. 825 they certainly had the upper hand. It

---

[46] Wormald, in Campbell (1982), p. 106.

seems, however, that Ine's successors in Wessex had managed to maintain
their independence, and that the internal affairs of the kingdom developed
without much interference from outside; but eventually Egbert broke the
Mercian hold on the southeast, and the West Saxons were able thereafter to
pursue their own objectives in their own way. It is arguable, on this basis,
that the 'rise of Wessex' should be regarded as a longer and more continuous
process: Alfred owed much to Egbert, but he owed still more to Ine, and
acknowledged the fact by re-issuing Ine's law-code as an appendix to his
own. It is also arguable, on the same basis, that to regard the West Saxon
kings of the ninth century as in any sense the 'heirs' to the supremacy
established by the Mercian kings in the eighth century, or indeed to the
supremacies established by other kings in the seventh, is to miss a more
fundamental truth. Each supremacy was a thing of its own; and Egbert, far
from following a well-trodden path towards a long-established objective,
was taking a different path towards something new.

King Egbert was essentially intent upon the creation of conditions which
would ensure the security and prosperity of England south of the Thames;
and if he had any model in mind, it was perhaps a return to the position
which had obtained in the late seventh and early eighth centuries, during the
reigns of Ine in Wessex and Wihtred in Kent. The West Saxons were no less
eager than the Mercians had been to bring Kent within their sphere of
control, but analysis of charters suggests that they set about the task in a
significantly different way.[47] The Mercians appear to have maintained their
control from a distance, and succeeded only in antagonising the Kentish
people. Egbert, on the other hand, could represent himself as one who had
some dynastic interest in Kent (through his father Ealhmund), and as one
who had delivered the southeastern provinces from Mercian oppression.
But the crucial difference was that Egbert and his successors appear to have
been careful to cultivate support in the locality: they visited Kent on what
may have been a regular basis; they came to an agreement with the
archbishop of Canterbury; and they placed responsibility for local administration in the hands of the local nobility, extending to Kent what may have
become a distinctively 'West Saxon' conception of an ealdorman as an
official appointed by the king over a designated division of land. It is
interesting, however, that both Egbert and his son Æthelwulf appear to
have respected the separate identity of Kent and its associated provinces, as
if there had been no plan at this stage to absorb the southeast into an
enlarged kingdom stretching across the whole of southern England. Nor
does it seem to have been the intention of Egbert and his successors to

---

[47] See Keynes (1993).

maintain supremacy of any kind over the kingdom of Mercia. Following his 'conquest' of Mercia in 829, Egbert had ruled the kingdom for one year; but in 830, according to the chronicler, 'Wiglaf again obtained the kingdom of the Mercians'. It is quite possible that Egbert had relinquished Mercia of his own volition; and there is no suggestion that any residual antagonism affected relations between the rulers of Wessex and Mercia thereafter. Wessex was clearly in the stronger position from a military point of view, and there is some indication that allegiances in London were already beginning to shift towards the West Saxon kings; but the general impression is one of alliance, symbolised by the two recorded instances of military co-operation and inter-dynastic marriage, in 853 and 868.

It follows from this broad view of political development in the eighth and ninth centuries that the positions established by the Mercian overlords, and the supposed 'bretwaldaship' of Egbert, had little to do with each other, and even less to do with the circumstances in which the unification of England was eventually achieved. What truly counted in the ninth century was Egbert's foundation of a 'bipartite' kingdom which stretched across southern England, and the formation of a working alliance between the West Saxon dynasty and the rulers of the Mercians.[48] In 860 the eastern and western parts of the southern kingdom were united by agreement between the surviving sons of Æthelwulf, though the union was not maintained without some opposition from within the dynasty; and in the late 870s King Alfred gained the submission of the Mercians under their ruler Æthelred, who in other circumstances might have been styled a king, but who under the Alfredian regime was regarded as the 'ealdorman' of his people. By this stage the Vikings were assuming ever increasing importance as catalysts of social and political change.[49] They constituted the common enemy, making the English the more conscious of a national identity which overrode deeper distinctions; they could be perceived as an instrument of divine punishment for the people's sins, raising awareness of a collective Christian identity; and by 'conquering' the kingdoms of the East Angles, the Northumbrians and the Mercians they created a vacuum in the leadership of the English people which was waiting to be filled. In the 870s King Alfred had been preoccupied with his own struggle for survival in the face of repeated Viking invasions of Wessex; but following his victory over Guthrum at the battle of Edington in 878 he was in a position to implement the programme of reform which he saw as the way to victory in the present and security for the future. There could be no doubt that Alfred's success depended in large measure on his adoption of practices as uncompromising as any seen in the

[48] See Keynes (1995).   [49] See Coupland, below, chapter 7.

days of the Mercian overlords. Pope John VIII had occasion to write to the archbishop of Canterbury in 877–8, encouraging him to resist demands made by the king;[50] and if there were some who actually defected to the Danes,[51] there must have been many others who took some persuading that royal policies were in a good cause. Not even Asser made much of an attempt to disguise the fact:

For by gently instructing, cajoling, urging, commanding, and (in the end, when his patience was exhausted) by sharply chastising those who were disobedient and by despising popular stupidity and stubbornness in every way, he carefully and cleverly exploited and converted his bishops and ealdormen and nobles, and his thegns most dear to him, and reeves as well (in all of whom, after the Lord and the king, the authority of the entire kingdom is seen to be invested, as is appropriate), to his own will and to the general advantage of the whole realm.[52]

Yet Alfred's true distinction lies in his determination to rise above his origins as king of the West Saxons, and to present himself as the leader of a new political order. In 886 he occupied London, 'and all the English people that were not under subjection to the Danes submitted to him'. The occupation of London marked Alfred's recognition of the city's crucial importance to the security and to the prosperity of his realm; and the fact that he promptly entrusted it to the control of Ealdorman Æthelred reflects his own faith in the Mercian alliance. Still more important, however, was the submission of the English people. It may well have involved recognition in some sense of the elevated status to which Alfred aspired, and which found more particular expression in his designation (by Asser) as 'king of the Anglo-Saxons'.[53] The title symbolised an awareness in high circles of the common interests which were beginning to bind peoples together, though there was still a long way to go: the 'king of the Anglo-Saxons' was the product of the ninth century, but the 'king of the English' would have to wait for the tenth.

[50] The letter is translated in *EHD*, no. 222.   [51] See Sawyer 362 (trans. *EHD*, no. 100).
[52] Asser, ch. 91; trans. Keynes and Lapidge (1983), pp. 101–2.
[53] See Keynes and Lapidge (1983), pp. 227–8.

IRELAND, SCOTLAND AND WALES, *c.* 700 TO THE EARLY ELEVENTH CENTURY

Donnchadh Ó Corráin

IRELAND, Scotland and Wales were all Celtic countries, but their respective medieval populations did not know this and their Celticity (however one may define it) is not the reason for grouping them together (Map 2). They did share certain terms, including elements of a legal vocabulary, that point to common institutions in earlier times but one cannot posit a genetic relationship in any real sense.[1] They were different societies, in close geographical contact, that had experiences in common, but reacted diversely. The first of these experiences was the Roman presence: Wales and part of Scotland were within the empire, Ireland and northern Scotland without, but profoundly influenced by it. The insular lands beyond the *limes* were heavily Romanised in material culture and their politico-military organisation was a reaction to Rome, in splendour and decline. Latin Christianity bound them together and set up close cultural contact between them. Their second shared experience lay in a twofold interaction with the expansionist Germanic world: first the Vikings, second the Anglo-Saxons. What began as Viking raiding opened the way to trade, settlement and urbanisation in varying degrees, tilted centres of power and influence towards the Irish Sea, and shaped the political development of all three. Finally, all experienced English aggression as a decisive force in their history – Wales, Scotland and Ireland in that order – throughout the middle ages.[2]

IRELAND

The law tracts of the eighth and ninth centuries describe a hierarchy of kings: *rí túaithe*, the king of the *túath* 'petty kingdom'; *ruiri*, the king of petty kings; and *rí ruirech* or 'king of overkings', also called *rí cóicid* 'king of a province'.[3] Muirchú in the last quarter of the seventh century lists the

---

[1] Thurneysen (1973); Ó Corráin (1986a).　　[2] Davies, R.R. (1990).
[3] Binchy (1970); Wormald (1986).

Map 2 Ireland, Wales and Scotland, 700–*c.* 1000

hierarchy as: *reges, satrapae, duces, principes, optimates populi.*[4] This structure was more complex and less static than the analysis of the lawyers (early or late) might suggest, and was the product of the power politics of competing dynasties. Notions of tribalism, much discussed in the past, are not helpful here.[5] In the eighth century and before, the petty kingdoms were going under: over-kings were conquering them and creating new principalities. Often, they took over the name, patron saints and churches of the defeated. Ireland was a land of dynastic kingship where the major dynasties competed for power and resources – and this state of affairs long ante-dated the Viking wars.[6] Political power (royal and lordly) was held by an aggressive upper class with a developed ideology of kingship and an historical awareness, both sharpened by the teachings of the clergy. It was distributed territorially but articulated hierarchically, and a learned historical myth, based on Isidore and the Bible, derived rulers and peoples from a single source.

There was no monarchy, but the clerical servitors of the paramount dynasty, Uí Néill, refer to their king as 'ruler of the whole of Ireland, ordained by God' and to Tara, their historic seat, as *caput Scottorum.* The annalists call two of them *rex Hiberniae* (642, 703). The king of Tara or *ardrí* 'high king' is the highest grade of king, the equal of the *tríath*: 'he goes through the kingdoms of Ireland from wave to wave ... The five provinces of Ireland, he goes through all their submissions as has been sung of Conchobar.'[7] The church rowed in behind rising kingly power. Adomnán talks of royal ordination. The term occurs in the book on kingship ('De regno') in the *Hibernensis* (compiled *c.* 700–50), where the canon lawyers take their text from 1 Samuel 10: 'Samuel took a flask of oil and poured it over Saul's head and kissed him and said: "Behold, the Lord has anointed you prince over your inheritance."' The annals report instances of royal ordination – 793 (king of Munster), *c.* 804 (Aed Oirnide, king of the Uí Néill), 993 (when the king of the Northern Uí Néill was given 'the order of king' by the abbot of Armagh). The lawyers favoured strong government and emphasised the king's coercive powers: 'The word of a king is a sword for beheading, a rope for hanging, it casts into prison, it condemns to exile.' Those who disobeyed the king were to be punished by death, exile, confiscation of property or imprisonment. Citing gospel authority, the lawyers demanded that royal taxes be paid and urged capital punishment for grave offences. This heady mixture of exhortation to rule firmly, to be supreme judge, to extend royal power and income, and the constant harping on the potent model of Old Testament kingship will have had a strong

---

[4] Bieler (1979), p. 84.   [5] Binchy (1954); Byrne (1971); Ó Corráin (1978).
[6] Ó Corráin (1972a), pp. 28–32.
[7] L. Breatnach (1986a); Byrne (1970; 1973), pp. 1–27, 40–69.

---

impact on the power-hungry kings of the eighth, ninth and tenth centuries who were then building up the provincial kingship that dominated Irish politics until the twelfth century.[8]

Native and Christian elements mingled in the concept of kingship – too evident to modern scholars, transparent to contemporaries. The metaphor of the sacred marriage of king and goddess and the notion of the king's righteousness that made the world fruitful were elaborately articulated in the vernacular literature[9] and skilfully integrated with Christian concepts of kingship by a learned clergy. The king ensured the good government and defence of his people (as leader, not warrior). He made peace and war, alliances and treaties, and entered into relationships (superior or subordinate) with others. His was the final court of appeal. He presided over the yearly assembly of his notables. He was a great landowner, not the allodial owner of his kingdom, but this changed as *imperium* and *dominium* merged and feudalistic institutions developed in the eleventh and twelfth centuries. Dynasties were great patrilineages articulated as competing segments. The dynasty was the royal heir: succession was determined by the power play of its segments, and consequently dynasties were often racked by segmentary struggles and weakened by secession. Successful dynasties tended to narrow the succession, and this trend becomes more common in the eleventh and twelfth centuries.[10]

Uí Néill were the leading dynasty: they had a historical mythography to prove it and a royal model in Cormac mac Airt, the Solomon of Irish kingship. There were two branches: Southern Uí Néill in Meath and the midlands, Northern Uí Néill in Ulster. Síl nAeda Sláine built Southern Uí Néill power in the seventh century (eight were kings of Tara) but their kinsmen-rivals, Clann Cholmáin, took the kingship of Tara in 743 and, except for Congalach (944–56), excluded them forever. Northern Uí Néill divided into two main segments, Cenél Conaill and Cenél Eogain. Cenél Conaill was dominant to the middle of the seventh century. Their last king of Tara abdicated in 734. Cenél Eogain had outpaced them by 789 and expanded southeast across Ulster in the eighth and ninth centuries, bringing the great monastic town of Armagh and the mid-Ulster kingdoms under their control – a base for future expansion. By the 740s the over-kingship of the whole dynasty, known as the kingship of Tara, alternated regularly between Cenél Eogain and Clann Cholmáin, and the king of Tara was usually the most powerful king in Ireland.[11]

[8] Wasserschleben (1885), pp. 76–82 (liber 25); Ó Corráin (1978), pp. 16–18; Ó Corráin, Breatnach and Breen (1984), pp. 390–1.   [9] R.A. Breatnach (1953); Mac Cana (1955–8); Dillon (1947).
[10] Ó Corráin (1972b), pp. 7–39; Binchy (1976), pp. 37–45.
[11] Byrne (1970); Byrne (1973), pp. 48–105, 254–74; Ó Corráin (1972a), pp. 14–23.

Leinster was ruled by Uí Dúnlainge, settled in the vale of Liffey and the north Leinster plains and linked with the great monastery of Kildare. Their competitors, Uí Chennselaig, dominated south Leinster. Excluded for centuries, they took the kingship in the early eleventh century. Uí Néill warred on Leinster. Donnchadh Midi, king of Tara, defeated the Leinster kings in 780 and sacked their lands and churches. His successor Aed Oirnide attacked Leinster in 804 and again in 805, deposed its king, and divided it. In 818 and 835 the Uí Néill appointed its kings. The Viking wars interfered with this conquest but conflict on the Uí Néill and Leinster frontier was to shape the history of Dublin.

The far-flung Eoganachta ruled Munster. Dynastic legends made them holy kings: God's angels revealed their royal site at Cashel to their founder and they looked back with pride to a forebear baptised there by St Patrick. A ninth-century text contrasts the gentle rule of the Eoganachta with the violence of the Uí Néill, who seize sovereignty by force and win land by the sword. Some were cleric-kings, others hereditary abbots, and they had close relations with the great monastery of Emly. The Eoganachta were divided into two rival groups: the western about Killarney and in south Munster, and the eastern at Cashel, Glanworth and Knockainy. Pressure from Uí Néill, Viking raids and dynastic disorder ruined the Eoganachta. Dál Cais, their supplanters, used their strategic position north and south of the lower Shannon to build up their power. After the 930s their rise was spectacular. They captured Viking Limerick and became the first urban Irish dynasty.[12]

Uí Briúin of Connacht became prominent in the seventh century and were dominant by 725. They claimed kinship with Uí Néill and with their predecessors, Uí Fiachrach – a signal that they had arrived. They sought Armagh's blessing by proclaiming its church-tax and wooed Clonmacnoise, eventually one of the dynastic churches. Uí Briúin limited the kingship to the immediate royal family. For most of the tenth and eleventh centuries they had a stable lineal succession. They had their reward: in the twelfth century they were kings of Ireland.[13]

The early church domesticated the landscape: holy mountains, holy wells, holy islands, and a mass of toponyms made of Christian elements (*cell* 'cell', *mainistir* 'monastery', *dísert* 'hermitage', *eclais* 'church') and saints' names organised the human environment. For the eighth- and ninth-century people Ireland's Christian history began in remote time and St Patrick, St Brigid, Columba and the monastic founders belonged to a distant 'age of the saints', though, as patrons, they were always close to their foundations and attentive to their successors' needs. Foundations and successors were rich

---

[12] Kelleher (1967); Ó Corráin (1973).
[13] Byrne (1973), pp. 230–53; Ó Corráin (1972a), pp. 9–14, 150–62.

and closely linked to royalty and nobility, for God was no equal-opportunity employer. Armagh (hereditarily ruled by local nobility)[14] and the Uí Néill kings were collaborating closely, if warily, in the late eighth and early ninth centuries. A royal residence and the mausoleum of the Uí Néill stood there. Already, in the seventh century, Kildare was a royal capital and keeper of the king's treasury. In the ninth century, its abbots and abbesses (it was a double monastery) were royal siblings or local nobles. Three or more abbots of Emly were kings of Munster and the Munster king-list was redacted there. High office in church was usually an inheritance and many clerical lineages were cadet branches of royal dynasties that survived as aristocrats in church, and there held on with remarkable tenacity.[15] But hereditary succession does not necessarily mean bad government or bad morals. The governors of great monasteries (Cork and Emly, for example) equalled the king of Munster in dignity and the rulers of Armagh, Kildare, Clonard and Clonmacnoise were great political figures, by law and by birth – more Medicis than abbots of monks and singers of matins.

Monasteries formed federations in the late seventh and eighth centuries. Property bulks large in the hagiography, its rights well guarded, its possession well justified. Greater houses encroached on the lesser, leading to consolidation and pluralism. Some monastic federations had dependants and estates all over Ireland (Kildare, for example, had far-flung properties in the late seventh century), and even abroad. Wealth brought violence and rivalry led to inter-monastic war (Clonmacnoise and Birr in 760, Clonmacnoise and Durrow in 764, Cork and Clonfert in 807, Kildare and Tallaght in 824) and violence against and amongst church personnel (the murders of the bishops of Seir and Lusk in 744, killings at Armagh in 759, a conflict at Clonard in 775 between the community and the king of Tara, a battle at Ferns in 783 between the abbot and the oeconomus). No attacker could ignore his enemy's monasteries and thus the churches were drawn into warfare.[16]

Lands and services, the offerings of the faithful, bequests, burial dues and relic circuits made the churches wealthy. Some were towns in the late seventh century. Cogitosus describes Kildare as 'a great metropolitan city', though he has to admit that it is not walled (*dum nullo murorum ambitu circumdatur*).[17] Here is evidence of self-conscious reflection on its urban nature. The community of Taghmon claimed that the layout of their town was inspired by heaven: angels appeared to the founder and said, "'Your city (*civitas*) will be in this place". And they marked out in his presence seven places on which afterwards, the principal buildings of the city were

---

[14] Ó Fiaich (1969).   [15] Ó Corráin (1981; 1973); Hughes (1966), pp. 157–72.
[16] Lucas (1967).   [17] Ó Corráin (1987), pp. 297–8.

constructed, and Fintanus placed crosses in these places.'[18] Here is a conscious corporate personality. This was deepened by reflection on the Old Testament cities of refuge and the measurements of the holy places in Ezekiel 45. The canon lawyers help fill in the picture:

There should be two or three enclosures around the sacred place; the first into which we allow no one to enter at all unless of the saints, because laymen do not approach it, nor women, only clerics; the second, into the courtyards of which we allow to enter crowds of rustics not much given to wickedness; the third into which we do not forbid to enter warriors, murderers, adulterers and whores by permission and custom. Hence the first is called most holy, the second more holy and the third holy.[19]

Evidently a monastic town was much used to a varied mix of humanity: clergy (perhaps a bishop, priests as well as monks), nuns, virgins, holy widows, the devout married laity, monastic tenants, artisans, soldiers, whores and the whole raggle-taggle of medieval life. Monastic towns where kings lived would have royal counsellors, military officers, aristocratic hangers-on and royal mistresses.[20]

There were worldly prince-abbots with aristocratic wives, great administrators, political clerics, houses of strict observance, rigorist anchorites and poor country parsons. Strongly episcopalian texts show that bishops – and a celibate bishop outranked all clerics – exercised spiritual jurisdiction over this variegated church life. Armagh and Kildare claimed to be seats of metropolitans, the canon lawyers refer to the office, but it is uncertain how developed it was.[21]

A cultivated clergy maintained high scholarship, and produced fine art[22] and a literature of distinction. The great monastery-towns that had deep pockets and high aspirations carried this activity. It was a culture of writing, and expressly so.[23] A remarkable achievement of the sixth and seventh centuries was the creation of a literary vernacular with a fixed orthography, not merely a language for homiletic-exegetical discourse but for creative literature in prose and verse. Vernacular treatises on grammar and metrics

---

[18] Heist (1965), p. 203 §19.
[19] Wasserschleben (1885), p. 175; 'Sinodus. Duo vel tres termini circa locum sanctum debent fieri: primus, in quem praeter sanctorum nullum introire permittimus omnino, quia in eum laici non accedunt, nec mulieres, nisi clerici; secundus, in cuius plateas plebium rusticorum catervas non multum nequitiae deditas intrare sinimus; tertius, in quem laicos homicidas adulteros metetricesque permissione et consuetudine intra ire non vetamus. Inde vocantur primus sanctissimus, secundus sanctior, tertius sanctus.'   [20] Doherty (1982; 1985); Ó Corráin (1987).
[21] O'Keeffe (1904); Binchy (1978), pp. 588–9 ('Miadshlechta'); L. Breatnach (1989); Sharpe (1984).
[22] Henry (1965–70); Henry and Marsh-Micheli (1985); Henry (1974); Ryan (1987).
[23] Holtz (1981); McCone (1990).

followed[24] and a wide-ranging and original imaginative literature.[25] They conceived of the pagan past as the Old Testament of their race and of its kings, queens and warriors as living according to nature in the Pauline sense, and thus fit subjects for Christian writers. This, together with their reading of Isidore, led to the cultivation of vernacular saga as written literature and the construction of a schema of human history linking the dynasties of the present, the heroes of the pagan past, and the revelations of scripture in a unifying perspective of providential history.[26] Writing in Latin – especially computistics, exegesis and hagiography – was carried on with vigour.[27]

Legal texts (Latin and Irish), the work of clerical lawyers devising a Christian law for a Christian community, survive from the seventh, eighth and ninth centuries. The *Hibernensis*, a compilation of Ruben (†725) of Dairinis and Cú Chuimne (†747) of Iona, is a systematic treatise on jurisdictions, church orders, legal procedures, government, property, bequests, theft, deposits, sanctuary, marriage and much else.[28] There are vernacular laws from the seventh century. The earliest firmly datable is 'Cáin Fhuithirbe' (AD 678–83), proclaimed at a mixed synod and dealing with the relationships of the church and kings.[29] The largest collection *Senchas Már*, eighth-century and from northern Ireland, possibly Armagh, some twenty-five tracts on private distraint, pledges, fosterage, kindred, clientship and relations of lord and dependant, marriage, personal injuries, theft, title to real estate, law of neighbourhood (trespass and liability), honour-price, and the contractual obligations of clergy and laity. Other tracts deal with legal and curial procedure, suretyship, contract, status, the professional classes (clerics, poets, judges and advocates), and much else.[30] These tracts offer a contemporary profile of society.

Society is seen, from an aristocratic perspective, in class terms: kings, lords and commons. The distinction between noble and commoner was not watertight: one could become noble over three generations by acquiring wealth and dependants, but pressure was usually downwards. What distinguished a lord from a commoner, apart from birth and wealth, was the possession of clients, men bound to him by contract, owing him renders and services in return for fiefs. Commoners were freemen who usually owned

[24] Ahlqvist (1982); Thurneysen (1891); Murphy (1961).

[25] Meyer, K. (1913; 1919); Thurneysen (1921); Murphy (1956; 1961); Carney (1955; 1966; 1967); Ó Corráin (1989).   [26] Thurneysen (1915); Ó Corráin (1985a; 1986b); Scowcroft (1987–8).

[27] Kenney, *Sources*; *BCL*, pp. 75–162; Walsh and Ó Cróinín (1988); Kelly (1988–90); Picard (1985); Sharpe (1991).   [28] Wasserschleben (1885); Mordek (1975), pp. 255–9; Fournier (1899).

[29] L. Breatnach (1986b).

[30] Binchy (1978); Kelly (1988); Charles-Edwards (1980); Ó Corráin Breatnach and Breen (1984); L. Breatnach (1984); Charles-Edwards (1986); L. Breatnach (1987).

land. Their classic representative was the *bóaire* 'cowman', who owed his lord a yearly render of a cow and subsidiary payments. There were others with lesser assets (*ócaire*). Below them were cottiers and landless men (*bothach, fuidir*), and serfs (*senchléithe*) bound to the soil.[31] There was slavery, probably extensive in the early period and common when Vikings traded slaves from abroad. Other unfortunates (for example, unwanted children and condemned prisoners released to the church) formed a servile population on monastic estates. The lawyers have a fine-tuned awareness of class precisely because it was the linchpin of the system: it determined one's legal powers and entitlements.

Clientship (*célsine*) bound lord and man in a mutual benefit relationship that favoured the lord. There are two kinds: free clientship (*sóerrath*) and base clientship (*gíallnae*), both contractual but differing in origin. Free clientship, like the *comitatus*, enabled lords to recruit a military following, ambitious aristocrats and freemen, for raiding and political in-fighting. Their reward: a share of the spoils. Base clientship was the economic basis of lordship. First, the lord made the client a payment equal to his honour price, making him the lord's man. Then the lord gave him a fief (usually of stock, but sometimes of land, chattels or implements) and took an annual render in produce, part delivered to the lord, part consumed when the lord and his retinue made a winter feasting circuit of his clients. The lord took labour services: spring ploughing, harvesting and building. He protected his client. When, for example, his client was wronged by a third party, he helped him pursue his legal rights, though he took part of any compensation received.[32]

The family, not the individual, was the socio-legal unit in matters of real estate, inheritance and legal liabilities. The legal family was the *derbfhine* 'certain family': the patrilineal descendants of a common great-grandfather. But people lived their lives in the *gelfhine* (descendants of one's grandfather) and, perhaps more usually, in the conjugal family.[33] Marriage was virilocal, apart from heiresses, and women had extensive rights. There were two types of marriage: a modified dowry marriage of church origin and an inherited bridewealth marriage. Divorce and remarriage were common, and polygamy (at least serial monogamy) was practised by the upper classes. It assured heirs and aristocratic manpower. This was not so much the survival of pagan custom, though there was some, but the continuation of early Christian and pre-Augustinian attitudes and practices.[34]

Viking raiders of coastal monasteries appeared abruptly in 795. They swept into the Irish Sea and south along the Atlantic seaboard: to Cork by 822, to Skellig in the remote southwest by 824. From the 830s they attacked

---

[31] Binchy (1941); Charles-Edwards (1986).   [32] Thurneysen (1923; 1925; 1926).
[33] Charles-Edwards (1971); Baumgarten (1985).   [34] Binchy (1936); Ó Corráin (1979; 1985b).

the immediate hinterland, especially in the northeast. In 832 Armagh was raided three times in a month, and many monasteries of the region were sacked. From c. 795 to c. 835, raids were hit-and-runs by small forces, perhaps two or three shiploads. They attacked coastal settlements, sometimes the surrounding territory, and disappeared promptly. There were no raids farther inland than twenty miles. Local levies hit back, sometimes effectively. The first deep territorial attack, with large-scale taking of prisoners (evident slaving), occurred in 836 in Southern Uí Néill. Vikings sacked Clonmore (in Co. Carlow) on Christmas Eve in 835/6 and took many prisoners; raiding and slaving at this time must mean they were over-wintering in Ireland, probably on off-shore islands, and had an organisation that could handle large numbers of captives.

They over-wintered on Lough Neagh in 840–1, at their base in Dublin in 841–2. Now inland raiding began in earnest. Large fleets arrived on the Liffey and the Boyne, ships were active on the Shannon and the Bann. Churchmen had to defend themselves. The kings turned on the enemy and reported a string of victories to Charles the Bald in 848.[35] By mid-century, landed Vikings were an accepted presence, their settlements part of the mosaic of petty jurisdictions, frequent Viking–Irish alliances occurred, and the Vikings feuded amongst themselves. In the second half of the century, they were independent adventurers with fixed bases – Dublin, Waterford, Wexford, St Mullins, Youghal, Cork, Limerick – but these, though formidable, were subject to successful Irish attack. Dublin was riven by dynastic feuds from the 870s and its decisive defeat came in 902: 'The pagans were driven from Ireland, i.e. from the fortress of Dublin ... and they abandoned a good number of their ships, and escaped half-dead after they had been wounded and broken.'[36]

The exiled Dublin Viking kings and aristocrats turned to the English littoral from the Dee to Solway Firth, to Galloway, the Western Isles and Man, and rapidly did there what they had failed to do in Ireland: established a powerful Scandinavian kingdom, based on York, and settled widely in the lands west of the Pennines.[37] The second Viking attack on Ireland came from here when the exiled kings, Ragnall and Sitric, arrived in Waterford in 917 to reinforce a Viking fleet active there since 915. Sitric defeated the Leinstermen, reoccupied Dublin and killed Niall Glúndub, king of Tara, in battle at Islandbridge, near Dublin. Ragnall led his fleet to north Britain, took York in 919, and as king of Northumbria submitted to King Edward of Wessex. A single dynasty now ruled Dublin and York. Sitric succeeded Ragnall in 920/1 and ruled until his death in 927. The Vikings in Ireland

---

[35] Rau (1980) II, p. 72.   [36] *Annals of Ulster s.a.* 902; *Annals of the Four Masters s.a.* 897 [= 902].
[37] Smyth (1975–9) I, pp. 27–116; II, pp. 1–30; Baldwin Whyte (1985).

engaged in an intense campaign to control (and settle) the Irish littoral from Dundalk to Antrim in the 920s and 930s, but this was foiled by Muirchertach, king of the Northern Uí Néill.

Godfrid of Dublin tried to take York in 927, but King Athelstan drove him out, and when he returned he was challenged by the independent Viking city of Limerick. His son Olaf, who succeeded on his death in 934, crushed Limerick in 937 and was the ringleader at the battle of *Brunanburh*, where the kings of Scotland and Strathclyde allied with Dublin to contain the rising power of Athelstan. They were defeated. On Athelstan's death in 939, Olaf returned to York and was recognised by King Edmund as king of York and Danish Mercia. He died in 941, and was succeeded by his first cousin, Olaf Cuarán, who lost York and returned to rule Dublin in 945. Here there were no easy pickings as in York. Congalach, king of Southern Uí Néill, and his allies had mercilessly sacked Dublin in 944: 'The destruction brought upon it was this: its houses, house-enclosures, its ships and its other structures were burnt; its women, children and common folk were enslaved; its men and warriors were killed; it was altogether destroyed, from four persons to one, by killing and drowning, burning and capture, apart from a small number that fled in a few ships.'[38] Olaf Cuarán was now a lightweight in Irish power play though he ruled again at York, *c.* 948 to 953.

Domnall ua Néill, king of Tara (956–80), attempted with great energy to build up a centralised over-kingdom in the north and the midlands. Olaf Cuarán sided with his regional enemies, and in the late 970s he felt strong enough to take on the Uí Néill. He was overwhelmed at the battle of Tara in 980 by Mael Sechnaill, king of Southern Uí Néill, who followed up his victory by besieging Dublin and forcing it to humiliating terms. Olaf retired to Iona as a penitent, leaving Dublin under the indirect rule of Mael Sechnaill.

Brian Boru, the most able ruler of his day, became king of Munster in 976. He dominated the Viking cities of Limerick and Waterford, and used their revenues, their fleets and their cavalry to make himself king of Ireland. In 997 Brian forced Mael Sechnaill to divide Ireland between them and hand over to him the hostages of Dublin. In 999 Sitric Silkenbeard, king of Dublin, joined with the Leinstermen and revolted. Brian and Mael Sechnaill defeated them at Glenn Máma and Brian followed this up by sacking Dublin and besieging its fortress. Finally, he restored Sitric as a dependent king. He now had Dublin's troops, fleets and taxes at his disposal in his final (and successful) effort to become king of Ireland. The Dubliners feared that their prosperous autonomous city-state would be absorbed: Brian was doing to Dublin what Athelstan and his successors had done to York, and they defied

---

[38] *Annals of Ulster s.a.* 944; *Annals of the Four Masters s.a.* 942 [= 944].

him. Their revolt really began in 1012 and by spring 1014 they had built up a powerful alliance: Leinster, Sigurd earl of Orkney, and fleets from the Hebrides and Man. The inevitable battle took place at Clontarf on Good Friday 1014: the alliance was heavily defeated but Brian was killed.[39]

Brian's successors dominated Dublin and, in the struggle for the kingship of Ireland, its possession became an economic and political prize. The tenth-century Dublin–York axis brought commercial urbanism to Ireland, the eleventh-century kings used its resources to fund their ambition to rule the entire island of Ireland, and this great struggle was the leitmotiv of Irish history until the Norman attack.[40]

SCOTLAND

In 700 the future kingdom of Scotland was occupied by three peoples – Dál Riata, Britons of Strathclyde and Picts – and under pressure from a fourth, the Northumbrians. Dál Riata, early invaders from northeast Ireland who brought Gaelic speech into Scotland, occupied Argyle and southeastern Inverness (Kintyre, Cowal and Lorn)[41] – still on the periphery after two or more centuries of conquest but probably infiltrating Pictland and settling to the north and to the east. Medieval demographic growth was slow and it would have taken time to build up the population needed to occupy central Pictland in the middle of the ninth century, Gaelicise much of mainland Scotland, and re-Gaelicise the Western Isles in the late Viking period. In the seventh century and earlier Dál Riata was ruled by Cenél Gabráin but became so riven with segmentary struggles between 680 and 740 that it is doubtful whether there was a recognised over-king of Dál Riata. Segmentation had gone far by 700 – at least seven competing groups – but this would not have prevented vigorous expansion by its sub-kingdoms. Its dynastic glories lay in the past, its present glory in the monastery of Columba at Iona, the greatest church centre in the north. Iona was ruled by Adomnán (679–704), the biographer of Columba and the most influential churchman in Britain and Ireland.[42] The expulsion of the Columban community by Nechtan, king of the Picts, in 717, following his acceptance of the Roman Easter and tonsure c. 710, was only a temporary rift.[43] Iona adopted the Roman Easter in 716, the coronal tonsure in 718.

British kingdoms had occupied the area between the Cheviot Hills and

[39] Ó Corráin (1972a), pp. 80–110; Ryan (1967); Ó Corráin (1986b).
[40] Ó Corráin (1972a), pp. 111–73; O'Grady (1889); Byrne (1987).
[41] Bannerman (1974); Chadwick (1949); Anderson (1973), pp. 119–201; (1982); Smyth (1984).
[42] Herbert (1988); Picard (1984); Smyth (1984), pp. 84–140.
[43] Dowden (1896); Haddan and Stubbs (1871), pp. 285–94.

the Forth/Clyde border with the Picts, but their history is obscure. The Northumbrians conquered the eastern half in the seventh century. The southwestern kingdom of Rheged had come under Northumbrian rule well before 700: the Bewcastle and Ruthwell crosses may mark stages of the conquest.[44] This broke the continuity between Strathclyde (the North British) and Wales. Strathclyde came under pressure from Dál Riata (battles in 678, 711, 717) and the Picts (battles 744, 750). Eadberht (737–58) conquered most of Ayrshire in 750 and attacked Dumbarton in 756, leaving Strathclyde the valley of the Clyde and little else.[45]

The Picts were heterogeneous in origin, Celtic and pre-Celtic, speaking at least two languages, one P-Celtic and one non-Indo-European.[46] Their distinguishing social custom was matrilineal succession to kingship – and one that may have eased the merger with Dál Riata if the Pictish dynasties were a group of patrilineages linked by the matriline.[47] They had strong kings, and effective defences (including a large navy). In the eighth century, the Pictish kingdoms were extensive and powerful. Dál Riata apart, the mainland and isles north of the Forth/Clyde were theirs. They held this border against the aggression of Northumbria from the late seventh century. Brude (697–706), who subscribed to Adomnán's 'Law of the Innocents' as *rí Cruithintúathi* 'king of Pictland',[48] probably ruled over a major kingdom in Pictland (*universae Pictorum provinciae*, as Bede puts it). Its divisions are not clear. An origin-legend credits the founder with seven sons, the eponyms of seven provinces – Fib (Fife), Fidach, Fotlaig (Atholl), Fortriu, Caitt (Caithness and Sutherland), Ce, Circinn (Angus) – but there may have been others and the text is of doubtful value.[49] Fortriu was the dominant province and the Irish annals use *rí Fortrenn* for 'king of the Picts'. The kingdom was powerful under Oengus/Onuist (?729–61). In 736 he harried Dál Riata, captured two princes and seized Dunadd. He defeated Dál Riata again in 741. He was fighting the Northumbrians in 740, Strathclyde in 744. He had made Dál Riata subject by 736 and established Pictish rule over it that lasted until the 770s or later.

The sources – late and suspect king-lists, synchronisms and difficult annals[50] – are not enough to construct a credible account of what followed. There was acculturalisation of Pictland and Dál Riata, so deep that neither history nor linguistics is enough to untangle the dynastic skein. Even the provenance of Cináed mac Ailpín or Kenneth I, progenitor of the dynasty

[44] Smyth (1984), pp. 26–7.   [45] Duncan (1975), pp. 59–66.
[46] O'Rahilly (1946), pp. 353–84; Jackson (1955).
[47] Boyle (1967); Kirby (1976); Miller (1979b; 1982); Sellar (1985).
[48] Ní Dhonnchadha (1982), pp. 181, 214.   [49] Skene (1867); Chadwick (1949), pp. 1–49.
[50] Anderson (1973); Miller (1979a); Jackson (1956; 1957); Skene (1867).

that dominates medieval Scotland, is debated. His descent from Cenél Gabráin is as plausible as the medieval historians intended.[51] After 768, the record of further Dál Riata/Pictish conflict ceases: this may point to a settlement, and subsequently to a union of the kingdoms under one king. Kenneth's segment may have used the disastrous Viking attack of 839 to thrust aside collaterals and seize the kingship. It is likely he was king in Dál Riata (841–2), and claimant to Pictland from 842. The Irish annals call him *rex Pictorum* on his death in 858. He made Dunkeld his new ecclesiastical centre in 848/9 and placed the relics of Columba in the church he had built there. His successor, Domnall I (852–62), enforced Dalriadic laws in Pictland: 'In his time, the Gaels with their king made the laws and ordinances of the kingdom of Aed mac Echach [*c.* 768–78], in Forteviot.'[52] This probably means that the laws of Dál Riata were imposed on Pictland.

Viking raids on Scotland began suddenly:[53] 'The devastation of all the islands of Britain by the pagans' in 794, Iona and Skye in 795, 'great incursions in Ireland and Scotland' in 798, Iona in 802 and 806 – and then silence about Scotland until the murder of Blathmac of Iona 'by pagans' in 825 and the journey of its abbot to Scotland and Ireland with the relics of Columba (829, 831). These Vikings came from Norway; they probably had already mounted unreported attacks on the Orkneys, Shetlands and Hebrides, and had begun using the islands as transit bases. Given the flurry of Viking activity around the Irish coastline, it is reasonable to think that the Vikings were at least as busy in Scotland. There are no data, for historical recording may have stopped at Iona after 825. In 839 the Vikings invaded Fortriu and won a battle in which very large numbers fell, including kings who may have governed much of Pictland. Insecurity on the west coast may have caused the drive eastwards into Pictland of Kenneth I and his followers.[54]

In 866 two of the Dublin Viking leaders, Olaf and Audgisl, brought a force of Irish and Scottish Vikings to Fortriu. They attacked Pictland, took its hostages and probably imposed a tribute on it. They were back in Ireland the next year and Audgisl was murdered by his kinsmen. In 870 Olaf went again to Scotland (accompanied by his fellow-king Ivarr). They besieged Dumbarton for four months, took it, plundered it and destroyed it. They returned to Dublin next year with 200 ships and 'a huge prey of English, Britons and Picts whom they brought to Ireland in captivity' for the slave

---

[51] Anderson (1982), pp. 106–32; Smyth (1984), pp. 179–92; Duncan (1975), pp. 54–7; Sellar (1985), pp. 31–4.

[52] Miller (1979b), p. 48; Skene (1867), p. 8: 'In hujus tempore, jura ac leges regni Edi filii Ecdach fecerunt Goedeli cum rege suo i Fochiurthabaicth.'   [53] I.A. Crawford (1981).

[54] B.E. Crawford (1987), pp. 38–62.

trade. This opened up the Clyde and central Scotland to Viking tribute-taking, if not rule. And that may be reflected in Ivarr's death notice in the Annals where he is called 'king of the Northmen of all Ireland and Britannia', the last term perhaps referring to his power over Strathclyde.[55] Ivarr's successors in Dublin were riven with feuds between at least three rival families and they came under too much pressure from the Irish kings to attempt anything significant in Scotland. The threat came rather from the Danes in Northumbria who inflicted a heavy slaughter on the Picts in 875.

It is likely that there was by now a settled Viking population in the Scottish islands, and the Gall-Goídil ('Foreigner-Gaels') who appear in Ireland as mercenaries in the 850s may be from there. Muirchertach mac Néill ravaged the Hebrides in 941: their Vikings must have posed a threat to him. A generation later Magnus son of Harold and his brother Godfrid were installed in the Hebrides and Man, and raided widely in Wales (971, 972, 980, 982, 987) and Ireland (974, 984). Vikings from the Hebrides fought on the side of Olaf Cuarán of Dublin at Tara in 980. Danes (possibly freebooters led by the earl of Orkney) landed on the coast of Dál Riata in 986,[56] raided Iona and the Western Isles on Christmas Eve 986, and killed the abbot and fifteen of the community. In 987 the son of Harold (probably Godfrid) and the Danes won a victory at Man where 1000 fell. Soon after, 360 of the Danes who had raided Iona were killed 'through the miracles of God and Columba'. Godfrid ended his career as king of the Hebrides by being killed in Dál Riata in 989. His son, Ragnall, also king of the Hebrides, died in 1005.

When and how the Orkneys were settled is unknown, the circumstantial narratives of the sagas notwithstanding.[57] These are good for the twelfth century or later, but poor before then, and the conquest of the Orkneys is a matter for pre-history and saga. The first firmly dated earl of Orkney is Sigurd son of Hlodver who fell fighting King Brian at Clontarf in 1014. If the 'Danair' raiding in the Hebrides in the 980s were really from the Orkneys, this may not have been Sigurd's first time in Ireland. The northern monastery of Derry was raided by Danair in 990 and there were Danair amongst the Viking and Leinster forces that ravaged the Southern Uí Néill seat at Loch Ennell in the same year. His son Einar may have been defeated in a coastal raid on Larne (Co. Antrim) *c.* 1018 by Conchobar, the petty king of Dál nAraide.[58]

Place-names studies point up regional differences in Viking Scotland.[59]

---

[55] *Annals of Ulster s.a.* 873: 'Imhar rex Nordmannorum totius Hiberniae 7 Brittanie uitam finiuit.'

[56] *Annals of Ulster* use the term *Danair* literally 'Danes', secondary meaning 'Vikings in general' (this is the first example of the term in these annals); *Annals of Inisfallen* use the generic *Gaill* 'Vikings, foreigners'.   [57] *ESSH* I, pp. 313–34, 346–63.

[58] *ESSH* I, p. 550.   [59] Fellows-Jensen (1984; 1985); Crawford (1987), pp. 92–115.

Place-names in the Northern Isles and in the farmlands of northeast Caithness are almost totally Norse, remarkably so because there had been a flourishing Pictish community in this area, and this was totally over-whelmed. In the Western Isles and the west coast the situation is made complex by later re-Gaelicisation of a layer of Norse names laid on previous layers of Gaelic and Pictish toponymy. There is a marked difference between the Northern and the Southern Hebrides, the one attracted by the northern Scandinavian world, the other influenced by Ireland and mainland Scotland. Nevertheless, the percentage of Scandinavian names here is significantly higher (20% and more) than in any part of the English Danelaw and points to conquest, occupation of the soil, subjection and perhaps to part-extirpation of the indigenes. Settlement is far less intense on the mainland littoral.

In 902, as stated above, the Irish kings captured Dublin and expelled its rulers from Ireland. This had an immediate impact on Scotland: it gave an impetus to the settlement of Vikings on the west coast of Britain from the Dee to the Solway and beyond and a leadership to exploit it. Here and in south Scotland, the exiled and aggressive Dublin leaders took control. In 904 two 'grandsons of Ivarr' killed the king of Pictland. In the same year, Ivarr grandson of Ivarr (who had been king of Dublin) was killed at Strathearn, warring on Pictland. Another dynast, Ragnall grandson of Ivarr, won a victory over the English and the Scots at Corbridge in 914, and was able to grant land to his followers.[60] In 917 Ragnall and his kinsman Sitric attacked southern Ireland: Sitric re-took Dublin and Ragnall returned to North Britain. He sacked Dunblane and defeated the English and Constantine II, king of the Scots, at Tynemouth. In 919 he took York and made his submission next year to Edward, king of Wessex.

The York–Dublin axis made the Viking rulers significant players in Northern politics. By 926 Athelstan was a threat to the independent kings on his periphery: Constantine II and Owain king of Strathclyde submitted to him. In 934 his fleet sailed as far north as Caithness, his land forces marched to Dunottar. Constantine and Owain joined in an alliance led by Olaf, king of Dublin, to contain Athelstan, but they were defeated at *Brunanburh* in 937. This was a setback but not a disaster for Scotland and in 945 King Edmund offered Constantine II's successor, Malcolm I, Strath-clyde and more, to detach him from the Dublin alliance. Soon Strathclyde had become a dynastic dependency.

From 954 to the late tenth century the kingship alternated between two segments, but this system broke down in violent feuding and dynastic

---

[60] Smyth (1975–9) I, pp. 62–3, 100–13.

killings and in 997 one of the royal segments was permanently excluded. This time of troubles did not end until the accession of Malcolm II (1005–34). Yet Scotland survived as a stable kingdom and stamped unity of a sort on its diverse peoples and landscapes.[61]

WALES

In Wales *rex* is the universal term for 'king', in literature and epigraphy. As in Ireland, there are gradations: greater (*rex magnus, rex inter omnes reges*) and lesser (*reguli*) kings and lords (*duces, seniores, optimates*), but there are no sociolegal sources that give a finer calibration. The vernacular terms, notably *brenhin* and *rhi* (cf. Irish *rí*), are difficult to date. Royal power was linked to well-delimited territorial kingdoms: in Wales, unlike Ireland, Scotland and England, populations took their name from the area they inhabited, not the area from the population, and this appears to be a sub-Roman inheritance.[62]

From the early sixth century Welsh politics centres on kings of large kingdoms; Gwynedd in the northwest, Powys in the northeast, Dyfed in the southwest, Glywysing in the southeast. Somewhat later, there is evidence for lesser kingdoms like Gwent and Gower, and later still for others (Brycheiniog and Ceredigion), but there may have been more (like Rhufoniog, first mentioned in the annals in 816). Dynastic origins are unclear: the genealogists of the ninth and tenth centuries give dark-age heroic and imperial Roman descents. Here there may be an element of inheritance from the late provincial Roman administration, but fifth- and sixth-century discontinuities make for uncertainty.

The kings of Gwynedd, with its island fortress of Anglesey, claimed precedence: that special position is expressed in the *Historia Brittonum* and in genealogies that trace them to the conquering Cunedda. The obit of King Rhodri describes him as *rex Brittonum* in 754 and the Irish annals give the same title to his son Cynan in 816. Intense conflict between the brother-kings led to a change of line when Merfyn, grandson of Cynan through his daughter Esyllt, succeeded. But Merfyn (†844), is called 'glorious king of the Britons' in the Bamberg cryptogram and the dynasty still boasted its Cuneddan descent. In the later ninth century Gwynedd tried to realise its claims by attacking the southern kingdoms, Dyfed and Brycheiniog – driving them into a protective alliance with King Alfred of Wessex. The southeast stood apart until the eleventh century. Ithel (*c.* 715–45) ruled as sole king of Glywysing but it and its sub-kingdoms were later shared as a dynastic possession.[63]

---

[61] Smyth, (1984), pp. 175–238; Duncan (1975), pp. 79–116.   [62] W. Davies (1990), pp. 9–31.
[63] W. Davies (1982), pp. 85–110.

As in Ireland, the king gave his clients 'fiefs' (stock, chattels, sometimes land and weapons); they fought for him. Such noble clients might be lords and have their own clients. The tie was breakable. Lower down in the social scale were lords' dependants who paid their dues in produce, who lacked powers of suretyship, and whose relationship was not terminable. Slavery was extensive and, as in Ireland, there was penal slavery.[64] Property-owning families, for law and inheritance, were patrilineages, usually four generations in depth.[65]

The Welsh church is Romano-British of unbroken tradition, but the evidence is thin. Thirty-five to forty pre-Conquest churches can be identified from non-charter material. These are on the coastal plain and in the fertile river valleys. Four have bishops – Llandaff, Llandeilo Fawr, St David's, Bangor – and there may have been more. Evidently, bishops lived in monasteries, had territorial jurisdiction if not well-defined dioceses, and there was no metropolitan structure. The charter evidence reveals an impressive density of church foundations, especially in the valley of the Wye and in the plains to the west, but it is unknown how general this was. Of the monasteries, little is known about the size of the sites or the communities, but they were significant concentrations of wealth: the Vikings found Tywyn, Clynnog and others worth raiding, though these were not the premier sites. Monasteries were landlords and had dependent monasteries (often a local bloc of churches and lands), to which the abbot appointed and from which he drew revenue. Gildas says the clergy were married: this is supported by epigraphic and documentary evidence, and the Welsh church was largely hereditary; evidence for this occurs in the seventh century, continues into the ninth and tenth, and the practice was a headache for the twelfth-century reformers.

The church was the maker of written record, from the impressive corpus of epigraphy to the charters,[66] including Gildas' *De Excidio Britanniae* (sixth-century)[67] and the *Historia Brittonum*, compiled in 829 and redolent of clerical learning.[68] The *Annales Cambriae* were kept at St David's from the late eighth century, filled out with Irish annals and royal genealogies of the tenth century.[69] Ecclesiastical learning has close affinities in the ninth and tenth centuries with Hiberno-Latin exegesis; Irish influence is strong, but Wales has a long tradition of highly conservative indigenous scholarship.[70] The dating, localisation and transmission of the outstanding vernacular

---

[64] W. Davies (1982), pp. 59–84; (1990), pp. 22–31.   [65] Charles-Edwards (1971; 1972).
[66] W. Davies (1979).   [67] Lapidge and Dumville (1984).   [68] Dumville (1975–6).
[69] Hughes (1974).   [70] Lapidge (1986); Breen (1992).

literature – in particular *Canu Aneirin*, *Canu Taliesin* and *Canu Llywarch Hen* – are problematic.[71]

Like Ireland, Wales was raided from the Irish Sea. There are some terse annalistic records of raids between 851 and 877.[72] Anglesey was ravaged by Vikings from Ireland in 853/4 and Rhodri, king of Gwynedd, killed Horm their leader in 856. The Irish annalist noted these events, and particularly Rhodri's flight to Ireland from the Vikings. They wintered in Dyfed in 878, often the prelude to setting up a base. It would be surprising if Wales escaped the intense coastal raiding Ireland suffered earlier and later. There may have been some settlement in Anglesey and elsewhere, as in Ireland. The attack came overland from England in the late ninth and tenth centuries. A Danish army reached Buttington in 893 but it was driven off by South Welsh and English forces. Within the year it was back in Chester and raided North Wales in 894. Haesten's army of Danes ravaged South Wales in 895 and evidently did much damage. But overland attacks were never as significant as those from the Irish Sea.

The next two known Viking actions involve their departure from, and return to, Ireland. When the Irish kings drove the Dubliners out of Ireland in 902 the immediate Welsh reflex was the arrival of Ingimund and his followers in Anglesey in 903. But they were driven from Wales and settled in Mercia.[73] In 914 a great fleet arrived at the Severn estuary from Brittany, ravaged Wales, and captured Bishop Cyfeiliog (who was ransomed). Local levies drove them off and King Edward took precautions to protect the estuary. Finally, they moved to Dyfed and sailed for Waterford in the autumn. It is uncertain whether they were originally bound for Ireland and took a side-swipe at Wales, but it seems likely.

Reported Viking raids increased in the second half of the tenth century while the dynasties of North and South Wales were busy with segmentary struggles. Very probably, the Vikings made stable kingdoms impossible: they intervened in dynastic disputes and milked the regions for resources. Dublin, ruled by Olaf Cuarán, mounted raids. In 961 his sons hit at Wales and Anglesey from Ireland's Eye, raiding Holyhead and the Lleyn peninsula. Magnus son of Harold, of the Western Isles, attacked Penmon in 971 and brought a great fleet from the Isles around the east of Ireland to the Shannon estuary in 974. In 972 his brother Godfrid captured Anglesey, in 980 he despoiled it and the Lleyn peninsula, in 982 Dyfed, and in 987 he ravaged Anglesey and took 2000 prisoners (and this will mean slaving). In

[71] Dumville (1977); Charles-Edwards (1978); Dumville (1988).   [72] Phillimore (1888).
[73] Radner (1978), pp. 168–72; Phillimore (1888), p. 167; Wainwright (1948).

989 Maredudd ab Owain, king of Dyfed, paid a poll-tax of a penny to the Vikings. Wales and Ireland, then, shared the attentions of these all-purpose Irish-Sea Vikings and suffered the same monastic plundering. This was fund-raising, and a matter of course: Holyhead (961), Tywyn (963), Penmon (971), Clynnog (978), St David's (982, 988, 999 when its bishop was killed), and Llanbadarn Fawr, Llanilltud and Llancarfan in 988.[74]

The literary record shows the breakers: the flows and surges of raiders, settlers, petty lords, merchants, traders and craftfolk must be sought elsewhere. There is enough 'high' evidence to expect the archaeological and place-name record to be significant. And so it is, especially in the foci of extensive raiding, Anglesey (with outliers in Flint) – hoards, graves and sculpted stones.[75] The onomastic evidence from South Wales is impressive. From Fishguard to Swansea there are some forty Scandinavian names – more than the whole of the Irish coastline – and long ago Bugge showed how twelfth-century settlers in Dublin from Cardiff, Swansea, Cardigan and Haverfordwest bore Scandinavian names.[76]

Broadly, the border with England stabilised in the seventh century, though Wales remained under English pressure. In the late ninth century, Welsh kings accepted the *dominium* of King Alfred, and formal submissions of the Welsh kings – Hywel Dda amongst them – continued from the 880s to the 950s. The powerful English kings used intimidation to secure the Welsh front and to compel resources (money and military levies) while Viking York was a menace. They tended to lose interest when that threat receded after mid-century.

Segmentary conflict is evident in Gwynedd in the early ninth century. It determined the political life of the tenth and the eleventh centuries, and probably earlier. The dynasty of Rhodri Mawr is a model of this process, an epitome of political history. His rise to power is obscure, and from the beginning his dynasty was under external threat. King of Gwynedd from 844 to his death in 878, he came under attack from the Vikings of the Irish Sea and from the English. It was assumed that the new Gwynedd dynasty had established itself and gained control of Powys to the east and Ceredigion to the south by the 870s, but this is uncertain and the Viking attack suggests otherwise. His son Anarawd was a power in Anglesey, the presumed dynastic centre, in the early tenth century. His grandson Hywel Dda was dominant in South Wales in the second quarter of the tenth century, but how and when that came about is not known.[77]

Within two or three generations the dynasty had spread widely in Gwynedd and Dyfed, mopping up local kingdoms and loyalties. This seems

---

[74] W. Davies (1982), pp. 116–20.   [75] W. Davies (1990), pp. 51–6.
[76] Loyn (1976), map 2; Bugge (1900).   [77] Dumville (1982).

reflected in the terminology: there are kings and dynasties, but king and kingdom are divorced in the records, and by the eleventh century there are new terms for areas of political power. The regionalism of the late seventh to the middle of the ninth century disappears. Power is mobile. As rulers and military leaders, kings range widely: from the middle of the tenth century to the early eleventh over all Wales except the southeast, later over the whole country and into the Marches. Kings compete along segmentary lines for hegemony, as Irish kings, but the rules are looser.

The segmentary struggles of the tenth and eleventh centuries show the Welsh kingdoms falling apart under the double stress of English pressure and Scandinavian attack. In a sense, there was dynastic decay, complicated by political succession in right of mother in a patrilineal society, the intrusion of dynastic outsiders, and alienation of a militarised ruling cadre from the regional communities subject to it. The higher ambitions and belligerence of the greater kings called for large resources and the means to gather them in, but English and, latterly, Scandinavian exploitation competed for these resources, and drew them off as levies and tribute, and the administrative infrastructure remained underdeveloped. In the eleventh century, Wales became an unstable land of unresolved segmentary struggles and quick-moving dynastic warfare.[78]

[78] W. Davies (1990), pp. 48–91.

ENGLAND AND THE CONTINENT

Rosamond McKitterick

THE first reliable evidence for links between Gaul and Anglo-Saxon England is the marriage of Bertha, a Frankish princess, to Æthelberht, king of Kent. The cordial reception given Augustine of Canterbury by Æthelberht, moreover, marks the beginnings of the distinctive English relationship with the church of Rome. Thus from the end of the sixth century the two main Continental associates of the Anglo-Saxons make their appearance; it is primarily within the context of relations between England, the Franks and Rome that English–Continental connections in the eighth and ninth centuries are to be observed. Both the Kentish marriage alliance and the ecclesiastical initiative from the pope and Gaul presuppose political and religious contacts before that, quite apart from the manœuvrings thereafter. The archaeological evidence, for instance, supports the assumption of the presence of some Franks, or contacts with Francia, south of the Thames in the early Anglo-Saxon period. There is much to be said, in fact, for Ian Wood's hypothesis that the Franks held some kind of hegemony over southern England in the sixth and early seventh centuries, while there are indications of sustained contact on the part of the Merovingians with the kingdom of Kent in particular.[1] Other fragments of information, such as the coin evidence, add to the sense of sustained contacts of which we now have no more than a faint echo. As is evident from the monetary system they adopted, for example, the Anglo-Saxons learnt the use of coinage from their Continental neighbours. At first foreign coins were used, apparently only as ornaments, but gradually they also began to play a limited monetary role before the Anglo-Saxons began to strike coins of their own.[2] Silver monometallism in the eighth century is apparent on both sides of the Channel. Innovations towards the end of the eighth century, such as the

---

[1] Leeds (1913; 1970); Evison (1965); Lohaus (1974); Myers (1986); Wood (1983).
[2] Grierson and Blackburn (1986).

coinage reforms of Offa, appear to have been inspired by Frankish example.[3] Although Frankish deniers are rarely found outside their country of origin, there appear to have been both a circulation of Anglo-Saxon sceattas on the Continent[4] and the penetration of both Frisian and Anglo-Saxon coins into Frankish Gaul.[5] The coin evidence backs up that from other sources. There is a suggestion, for example, of Frankish methods having some bearing on the production of early English charters; linguistic links have also been proposed.[6] Certainly the recent work on the main points of contact across the Channel and North Sea indicates extensive exchanges of some kind, mostly commercial, with a marked increase in traffic and the development of emporia on both sides of the Channel, at *Hamwic* (Southampton), Ipswich, London, Rouen, Boulogne, Dorestad and Quentovic in particular.[7] The literary evidence for such commercial contact has been thoroughly surveyed by Levison[8] but we can add to it the work of the numismatists, and archaeologists such as Richard Hodges and Stéphane Lebecq, who have been able to discern the beginnings of cross-Channel traffic and the importance of the Frisian middlemen in commerce by the eighth century.[9] Generally at first there was more movement eastwards than westwards, but ecclesiastical connections in the seventh century, epitomised by the activities of Bishop Wilfrid of Hexham in Frankish Gaul and Burgundy and of Bishop Agilbert of Paris in England, may well have been far closer than we can now determine with any certainty. Thus examination of the range of evidence for cross-Channel communication suggests a far more extensive, varied and influential network than has been suspected hitherto.

The historiography of relations between England and the Continent between 700 and 900 has been dominated by accounts of the activities of the English missionaries, Willibrord of Utrecht and Echternach, Boniface of Mainz, and their associates. In his classic and pioneering exposition of these activities, Levison proposed as his main theme the English contribution to the spiritual foundations and unity of western civilisation in the early middle ages.[10] He drew on the great mass of literary evidence, in particular that provided by the Lives of saints of the seventh and eighth centuries from the Rhine and Meuse region, many of which Levison had himself edited for the *Monumenta Germaniae Historica*. Levison's approach to the relations between England and the Continent, the topics he chose to discuss and the sources on

---

[3] Blackburn, chapter 20 below.   [4] Callmer (1984).   [5] Le Gentilhomme (1938).
[6] Bruckner (1967); Derolez (1974).   [7] Hodges and Hobley (1988).
[8] Levison (1946); see also Kelly (1992).
[9] Hodges (1989); Lebecq (1983); see also Ellmers (1990); McGrail (1990).
[10] Levison (1946), the first full treatment of the subject, though Hauck (1912), Dawson (1932), Crawford (1933) and Grierson (1941) had touched upon it.

which he placed emphasis have provided the agenda for subsequent accounts.[11] More recent archaeological, art historical, numismatic and palaeographical research, however, has substantially modified the picture Levison presented of the impact of the Anglo-Saxon missionaries. Not only has the overriding emphasis on the English contribution been lifted to make room for the Franks.[12] It is also clear that the work of the missionaries analysed by Levison has to be seen in the wider context of the political, diplomatic, religious, cultural and economic relations across the Channel throughout the eighth and ninth centuries. In particular, the missionaries' work was closely associated with the political development of the Frankish kingdoms. Their connections extended as far as Rome. It is this new understanding of England and the Continent in the eighth and ninth centuries that this chapter aims to present. Nevertheless the main focus of attention will still be, owing to the concentration of the evidence, the context for and activities of the Anglo-Saxon missionaries on the Continent, the establishment of new religious foundations in Hesse, Thuringia and Franconia, the Anglo-Saxons' contributions to the Frankish church, their interaction with Frankish rulers and bishops, and their legacy for subsequent connections across the Channel in the ninth century and afterwards.

The eighth century in both England and Francia was a period of rapid political change.[13] It saw the emergence in England of Mercia, and in Francia of the Carolingian family whose wealth and interests were focused in the Rhine, Moselle and Meuse region, that is, precisely the region where the English missionaries were initially most active. Information about the early life of the first of these missionaries, Willibrord, is meagre. He was born 667–8 in Northumbria and was offered up to the religious life at an early stage, where he came under the authority of Bishop Wilfrid. Possibly at the time of Wilfrid's removal from his see in 678, Willibrord departed for Ireland where, as Bede tells us, he spent twelve years as a member of the English community at Rath Maelsigi, presided over by the Northumbrian exile Egbert.[14] Nothing is known but much conjectured about this community. Bede records Egbert's own wish to evangelise Germany, the ways in which he was miraculously prevented from departing, how another companion did go for two years to Frisia and how, finally, Egbert sent Willibrord. In his calendar, BN lat. 10837, fol. 39v, Willibrord dates his departure from Ireland to 690. Despite this long Irish sojourn, and his departure for the Continent from Ireland, Willibrord's connections thereafter appear to have been retained with his native Northumbria, though there have been valiant, and in some respects successful, efforts to provide a

[11] Schieffer (1954); Reuter (1980b).   [12] *Saint Chrodegang* (1967); Angenendt (1972).
[13] Keynes, chapter 2a above and Fouracre, chapter 3 below.   [14] Ó Cróinín (1984).

greater Irish component in the initial stages of Willibrord's mission to the Frisians and monastic settlement at Echternach.[15] Wilfrid and Acca apparently stayed with Willibrord on their way to Rome in 703, St Oswald of Northumbria figures in Willibrord's calendar and a member of Willibrord's *familia* came to Lindisfarne and regained his health at the tomb of St Cuthbert.[16] Willibrord himself had many English helpers and followers: Suitberht, who preached in southern Westfalia and founded the monastery of Kaiserswerth, the martyrs Black Hewald and White Hewald, Adalbert, who went to Egmond in northern Holland, Werenfrid, who served Elst in Gelderland, and the great uncles of Liudger, who were the first Frisian priests.

The gift of the castle and the church of Utrecht to the bishopric of Cologne by Dagobert I, on the condition that the bishop of Cologne convert the Frisians to the Christian faith, suggests that the Franks, both Merovingian kings and Carolingian mayors, had clearly been aware of the need to preach to the pagan Frisians for some time. Their object was perhaps that of neutralising potentially hostile forces by making them observe the same religion as their own.[17] Eddius Stephanus records Wilfrid of Hexham's brief success some years before,[18] and the Frankish missionary Amandus had worked briefly in the east Scheldt river region. He was bishop of Maastricht and ventured northwards from there.[19] He had a base at Antwerp and built a church there dedicated to Saints Peter and Paul. Eligius, bishop of Noyon, also preached in Flanders, Antwerp and among the Frisians,[20] and in about 690 Wulframn of Sens, abbot of St Wandrille, went on a mission to Frisia, which appears to be linked to Pippin II's expansionist policies towards Frisia.[21] Utrecht itself appears to have had a church dedicated to St Martin, built under Clothar I or Theudebert I or II, who granted it immunity.[22] That the Frisians had long been an object of political interest on the part of the Franks is also indicated by a poem of Venantius Fortunatus which talks of Chilperic I (561–84) as not only trying to impose his authority on the Frisians but also to govern them.[23] The Carolingian mayors who encouraged Willibrord, therefore, appear to have been making the most of an opportunity unexpectedly offered by Willibrord's arrival and exploiting his own religious aspirations to serve established Frankish ends. It is possible, given the vulnerable political position of the Carolingian mayors at the end of the seventh century, that a relative outsider such as Willibrord, dependent

---

[15] Ó Cróinín (1984; 1989). [16] Bede, *Vita Cuthberti*, C. 44.
[17] Boniface, *Epp.*, Tangl no. 100, Talbot no. 47. [18] *Vita Sancti Wilfridi*, c. 26.
[19] *Vita Sancti Amandi, MGH SRM* v, pp. 428–49. [20] *Vita Sancti Eligii, MGH SRM* iv.
[21] *Vita Sancti Wulframni, MGH SRM* v, pp. 657–73; see also Gauthier (1980).
[22] *MGH Dip. Kar.* I, no. 5. [23] *Carmina*, IX.1.75, in Venantius Fortunatus, *Opera Poetica*.

on the Frankish ruler in a special way, was a much better prospect than any Frankish bishop might have been, for it enabled Pippin to establish an independent church, free from Cologne in particular, as well as being in an area he could be sure of politically. Indeed, it was on the close involvement with and support from the Carolingian family that the material success and physical safety of the missionaries depended. In return, the Christianisation of pagan regions carried out by the missionaries and their Frankish and Frisian helpers did much in some areas to prepare the way for, and in others to consolidate, Frankish political aggrandisement. Bede gives us some inkling of this in a comment made in passing on Willibrord's enterprise in Frisia; he tells us that Pippin II took Willibrord under his wing and sent him to Pope Sergius I to be consecrated. As Pippin had just driven King Radbod of the Frisians out of Frisia *citerior* (presumably southern Frisia) Pippin sent Willibrord there, gave him and his followers the support of his royal authority 'and bestowed many *beneficia* on those who were willing to receive the faith'.[24] The word *beneficia* in this context is to be understood in its technical sense of land in return for political submission rather than in the general one of 'favours'; Christianity and political conquest went hand in hand.

After his arrival in Frisia and successful expedition to Rome to seek papal blessing, where he was consecrated on 21 November 695, Willibrord established his see at Utrecht and built a church in the *castellum* there. Bede tells us that Pippin also made over certain localities in his own realm (that is, Austrasia) to Willibrord where he could uproot idolatrous practices and teach the newly converted people. This is probably an allusion to the establishment of Echternach, given not by Pippin (though he gave lands later) but by Pippin's mother-in-law Irmina of Oeren. Echternach not only provided a haven during the difficult period 715–19 after Pippin's death and before Charles Martel had secured his position, but was the main centre of Willibrord's activities in the latter part of his career. The early charters of Echternach witness to the extent of support and the provision of a material base Willibrord gained from the local Frankish and Frisian magnates, as well as providing evidence of missionary work. The lands granted extended from the mouth of the Scheldt, northern Brabant, Toxandria, the lower Rhine, Echternach and Trier regions into Thuringia and Franconia. The early grants in Thuringia, moreover, made in 704 and 714,[25] are the gifts of the independent duke of Thuringia over a period of thirteen years and suggest that this might have been an essential foundation for Boniface's later work in Thuringia. There are six charters recording gifts in Toxandria

---

[24] Bede, *HE* v. 11.   [25] Wampach (1929–30), nos. 8 and 26.

where there appears to have been a mixed population of Frisians and Franks.[26] In the area previously evangelised by Amandus, gifts from Rohingus, count under Pippin II, are recorded, which provided Willibrord with an Antwerp base, operating in the same area as his Frankish predecessor. Later charters refer to many small churches established in Frisia whose origins date from Willibrord's time. These provide some hint of the spread of Christianity in Frisia. By far the greater proportion of the grants, however, were of land in the Trier diocese and Moselle region, and these can be discussed in two main contexts, material wealth and piety. The first is indicated by Alcuin in his Life of Willibrord when he said that many began in their zeal for the faith to make over to the man of God their hereditary properties. The second is the degree to which the charters reveal personal relationships established by Willibrord and thus the inspiration he provided. To some extent he may have reinvigorated a movement towards the ascetic life on the part of many members of the aristocracy, begun in the wake of Columbanus in Gaul.[27] Werner, for example, has stressed the decisive role of the 'aristocracy', that is, the free landowners with surplus wealth, in the Christianisation of northern Gaul.[28] These prior developments in the Frankish church were what ensured the sympathetic reception of the Anglo-Saxon missionaries. Willibrord was able to harness latent religious zeal. It was a church promoted by the efforts and contributions of the lay landowners. The connection Willibrord established with Oeren, presided over by Irmina, is of particular importance, for it was a Pippinid family monastery enjoying close links with many other houses, such as Nivelles, Andenne, Prüm and Weissenburg, where Irmina was buried.[29] The foundation of Echternach was on land given by Irmina, where she already had churches dedicated to the Holy Trinity and Saints Mary, Peter and Paul, and a little monastery for *peregrini*. The gift was augmented a few years later in 706 by one from Plectrude and Pippin II. The text of this grant indicates that Willibrord had already built a monastery and church. Willibrord's church, a rectangular building 21 m long with a nave 7.6 m wide, with a square choir, was uncovered by a bomb in 1944. It is thought that the church may have had a baptistery as well, which has crucial implications for Willibrord's role *vis-à-vis* the surrounding population. Echternach is thus both a manifestation of local piety and a mark of Willibrord's success in winning the confidence and devotion of those inclined towards the religious life in northern Austrasia. The first grant

---

[26] Costambeys (1994).
[27] K.-F. Werner (1976); Wood (1981); Wallace-Hadrill (1983); Prinz (1965; 1988); Dierkens (1989).
[28] K.-F. Werner (1976).
[29] Werner, M. (1982); *Vita Sanctae Geretrudis, MGH SRM* 11, pp. 447–74 and van der Essen (1907).

from Irmina, clearly a well-organised, well-connected and wealthy woman, was the outcome of her own personal piety. After her death Plectrude took an interest in her mother's religious associations and expanded them. Because she was married to Pippin, who had already been using Willibrord to 'soften up' the Frisians for his own political purposes, Echternach came within the Pippinid sphere of influence. This was maintained in particular by Charles Martel once he had secured his position in Austrasia and in relation to the Neustrians. The abbot of Echternach, moreover, stayed loyal to the Carolingian family and the charters record many subsequent generous grants made by various members of the Carolingian family.[30] Echternach became a royal monastery in 751 on Pippin III's accession to the kingship and Carolingian interest in the house was maintained thereafter.[31] Echternach thus assumes political importance and continued lay support acquires the flavour of nobles simultaneously caring for their own souls and remaining in the good graces of the ascendant Carolingians. There does not appear to be any hint that they were rivals to the Carolingians for control of Echternach.

The manuscripts can add to our knowledge of texts available to and used by the English missionaries and their Frankish and Frisian helpers in Frisia and northern Austrasia, possible connections and contacts formed by the missionaries, the identity and nationality of Willibrord's followers, and whether or not a scriptorium can be associated with Willibrord and the level of competence it achieved. It is clear that while connections were maintained with England and to a lesser degree with Ireland, the main points of contact were with other Frankish regions, particularly the see of Cologne. Franks and Frisians appear to have joined Willibrord's original *familia*. The scriptorium of Echternach shows the work of both insular and Frankish scribes. It furnished Willibrord with the essential texts needed by a pastoral bishop concerned with ecclesiastical discipline and correct doctrine, drawing on his insular experience and contacts but with few intellectual pretensions.[32]

Although the evidence for Willibrord's career is relatively meagre, it nevertheless witnesses to a remarkable unity of purpose and similarity of method in the promotion of the Christian religion on both sides of the Channel. The same is true of the activities of Boniface and his followers, though here the evidence is far more abundant and explicit. Not only do we have Lives of Boniface, and of his followers Sturm, Lioba and Willibald; we

---

[30] Levison (1940); Heidrich (1965/6); Wampach (1929–30), nos. 2, 3, 4, 5, 7, 9, 10, 12, 14, 15, 17, 18, 19, 22.

[31] Wampach (1929–30), nos. 68, 93, 112, 138, 139. See also Bange and Weiler (1990) and Kiesel and Schroeder (1989).   [32] Ó Cróinín (1984); McKitterick (1985; 1989a); Netzer (1994).

also have the copious correspondence of Boniface himself to friends, acquaintances, pupils, opponents and patrons in England, Francia and Rome as well as many different kinds of Frankish documents to set against the account, inevitably partisan, provided by Boniface and his biographer.

Assessments of the contribution of both Willibrord and Boniface, however, have to be made within a realistic appraisal of the English church from which both they and their English followers came. Hitherto the assumption has tended to be of a strong and highly cultured and organised English church contributing in every way to a sadly decadent, down-at-heel and intellectually impoverished Frankish church. Bede's persuasive account has much to do with this, for he has seduced many generations of historians with his eloquence and circumstantial detail. Yet it is Bede himself who gives us the vital clues to the actual state of affairs in the English church in his letter to Egbert, archbishop of York, lamenting the shortage of ecclesiastical personnel, the weakness of the monasteries, the abuses already in evidence and the need for concerted effort and leadership. The letter to Egbert can be augmented by the clear indications in such texts as Æthelwold's *De Abbatibus*, the anonymous Life of St Cuthbert, the *Vita Sancti Wilfridi*, the *Vita Sancti Guthlaci*, Aldhelm's letters and poems, Pope Paul's letter to Eadberht and the records of English synods in the eighth and ninth centuries concerning the efforts to establish monasticism, the role of the secular church, and its relations with the secular world. It is essential to remember that England at the time of Boniface's departure was a country in which Christianity was only gradually gaining a hold. When Bishop Wilfrid converted Frisians in *c.*679 the English people itself was still being converted, for it was Wilfrid, no less, who preached the Gospel to the South Saxons in the 680s and the Isle of Wight was not officially Christian until 686.

Missionaries departing for the Continent, therefore, came from a church in which the organisation and institutions, rules of conduct and worship, were still being defined. English society was one in which monasticism, with its diverse forms, was by no means fully established. The differing political development and the lack of direct continuity with Rome that are such marked factors in early Anglo-Saxon history are also to be borne in mind. By contrast, the English came to regions on the Continent which were rarely wholly pagan; more commonly the field of enterprise was one in which the church had been established for some time within the context of the Gallo-Roman and Merovingian church, or in which Christianity, although present, was weak or had even lapsed somewhat. Boniface gives us far too prejudiced an account of the Frankish church, and he was in any case totally ignorant about whole regions. It is, furthermore, far from being the case that all Englishmen and Englishwomen who journeyed to the Continent in the eighth century were associated with Boniface, and thus it cannot be said that his work is to be understood as a concerted or co-ordinated effort by the English to preach the Gospel to pagans east of the Rhine. Recruitment for the missions was probably done not so much within an institutional framework as within the context of the personal connections of the individuals concerned.[33]

Boniface, born Wynfrith in c.675 near Exeter, rose to considerable prominence in the church in Wessex before deciding to act on a desire to convert pagans. After an abortive missionary expedition he made on his own to Frisia in 716 (it was bad timing on his part in light of the political situation) Wynfrith embarked for Rome and there he not only had his new name, Boniface, bestowed upon him by Pope Gregory II, but succeeded in persuading the pope to send him on a fact-finding mission to the north in Hesse and Thuringia, being charged by Gregory II to 'teach the heathen'.

Such a mission might be thought to corroborate the idea that it was virgin pagan territory that was to be conquered by Boniface, but this is very far from being the case. Why should the pope have been ready to send a completely strange Englishman to Germany?[34] What could the pope offer to anyone venturing northwards other than blessing and authorisation, for it is clear that he had no precise information? It is important in this context to note the visit to Rome in 716 by Duke Theodo of Bavaria who sought the help of Pope Gregory II to reorganise the church in Bavaria.[35] Bavaria had strong links with the rulers of the Lombard kingdom. The pope may well have been deciding how to help without compromising his political interests when Boniface arrived fortuitously, prepared to go, if not necessarily to Bavaria, then at least to Germany. We may note, moreover, that Bavaria had a church, albeit one in disarray. Further, a number of Rhineland bishops and monasteries had already been sending expeditions into the region east of the Rhine and attempting to consolidate Christianity by establishing churches with priests to serve them, and monasteries, notably in Bavaria. Duke Theodo himself worked through Rupert to promote Bavarian jurisdiction by evangelising the Slavs in Carinthia.[36] Irish missionaries had also been active in the Würzburg and Salzburg areas, and Christianising activity out from Burgundy, Metz, Worms and Mainz is attested by the end of the seventh century.[37] Similarly, in Bavaria, some revival in the seventh century is evident and the St Gall monks had begun to

---

[33] McKitterick (1991).   [34] See Noble, chapter 22 below.

[35] *LP* I. 398; Noble (1984), pp. 61–5.   [36] *Gesta Hrodperti, MGH SRM*; Wolfram (1972).

[37] *Vita Arnulfi, MGH SRM* v, pp. 426–46; Wolfram (1979); Büttner (1965); *St Kilian* (1989); Reuter (1980b); Prinz (1965; 1988); Ewig (1954; 1962); M. Werner (1982); Zwink (1983).

establish outposts at Fussen, Kempten and elsewhere in the first half of the eighth century, where clear links with northern Italy, especially Aquileia, can be discerned.[38] We have, therefore, a picture of a precariously maintained and sparsely distributed church outside the Frankish heartlands, of huge areas not served by bishops, and of some gradual expansion.

After preaching the Gospel in Thuringia and Frisia (where he rendered valuable assistance to Willibrord), Boniface made a second visit to Rome in 722 and was consecrated bishop, but without a fixed see. He returned to Thuringia to exhort the people to return to Christian ways and forsake their pagan gods. In a direct attack on paganism he felled the famous oak of Donau at Geismar. In 732 Boniface was granted the pallium as archbishop by Pope Gregory III and from then until 741 he was active in Hesse, Thuringia and, between 736 and 739, Bavaria, where he at last carried out the reorganisation requested by Duke Theodo so long before. Boniface divided Bavaria into four districts 'so that each bishop could have his own diocese'; this seems to have resulted in the appointment of bishops at least to Salzburg, Eichstätt, Regensburg and Passau, but there were changes subsequently as well as bishops at Freising and Augsburg; Boniface may only have been active in part of Bavaria rather than the whole duchy. Whatever the case, Boniface's account of his success in Bavaria seems to have been a considerable exaggeration. If we think only of the career of Virgil of Salzburg who collided with Boniface head on,[39] it is clear that Boniface's contribution might even be counted as interference rather than satisfactory reorganisation.[40]

The reorganisation of the church east of the Rhine was complete by the early 740s.[41] Many monasteries, notably Fulda, Fritzlar, Tauberbischofsheim, Ochsenfurt, Hersfeld, Karlburg and Holzkirchen, were established in these regions, staffed with Englishmen and women, who came out to assist Boniface, as well as with native Franks, Bavarians and Thuringians (Map 3). Sturm the Bavarian, for example, became the first abbot of Fulda.[42] The establishment of monasteries and bishoprics can be seen as part of Boniface's missionary strategy. The campaign against the Saxons by Charles Martel prompted the creation of the short-lived bishopric of Erfurt, and we may observe in this the necessity for political expansion to precede or accompany evangelisation, just as it did in Frisia. The vulnerability of the missionaries is implied not only by Boniface's acknowledgement of the protection the Carolingian mayors afforded him but also by the fact that all the new monastic foundations were established on the sites of old hill forts and

---

[38] Reindel (1964).   [39] H. Lowe (1951).   [40] H. Lowe (1955).
[41] Boniface, *Epp.*, ed. Tangl, nos. 48, 50, 51, 103, 113.   [42] See de Jong, chapter 23 below.

Map 3 The missionary areas on the Continent in the eighth century: Boniface, Chrodegang, Pirmin, Willibrord and their followers

elevated and fortified places, often commanding river crossings.[43] Among the Englishmen and women who contributed substantially to the Anglo-Saxon monastic endeavour in Germany was Lioba, possibly from Wessex, trained in grammar and the liberal arts, who became abbess of Tauberbischofsheim. She ruled her nuns, the daughters and widows of local noble families, with a rod of iron and practised hypnopedia in order not to waste time while asleep. Burchard, who became bishop of Würzburg, Denehard, who often acted as courier to England, and Lull, who succeeded Boniface at Mainz, came from Mercia. Lebuin, possibly from Northumbria, was trained by Bishop Gregory of Utrecht before going to preach to the Saxons. The brothers Willibald and Wynnebald with their sister Walpurga worked closely with Boniface in Hesse. Certainly the houses Boniface and his followers established, notably Fulda, became prominent religious and cultural centres in the Carolingian period. Much of their activity is manifest in the extant manuscripts.[44] It is clear, for example, that Boniface possessed books of his own which Schülung has characterised as the 'travelling reference library of a missionary'.[45] The libraries of Fulda and Würzburg in the eighth century possessed a fairly orthodox and narrow range of texts, with scripts and glosses in Old High German, Old English and Old Irish indicating the different nationalities represented in their communities as well as the fact that some books were sent out from England.[46] Canon law, books of the Bible and basic theology (by such authors as Gregory the Great, Augustine and Jerome) predominate.

In 741, however, Boniface's activities came far more closely within the orbit of the Carolingian mayors. Hitherto he had enjoyed the protection of Charles Martel, but the fact that Boniface had been accorded the title papal legate in 739 with a theoretical jurisdiction over the Rhineland bishoprics of Cologne, Trier, Mainz and Strasbourg, meant that friction with the doughty aristocratic warrior bishops of those sees, supporters of Charles Martel, was inevitable and relations with Charles Martel himself no doubt rendered fraught. Boniface found these bishops, Milo and his ilk, distinctly uncongenial, and worried about whether his contact with them would contaminate him with sin.[47] With the accession to the mayoralty of Austrasia and Neustria by Carloman and Pippin respectively, however, the situation changed dramatically. We can observe thereafter how closely the fortunes of the church in Austrasia and Neustria and the progress of Boniface's reforms were related to the power of particular groups of nobles and the integral part

---

[43] Parsons (1983).   [44] Bischoff and Hofmann (1952); Spilling (1978); McKitterick (1989b).
[45] Schülung (1961-3).
[46] Lull, *Epp.*, ed. Tangl, nos. 116, 124, 125 (Lull); Brown (1974); Whitelock (1960); McKitterick (1989a and b; 1992).
[47] Boniface, *Epp.*, ed. Tangl, no. 87; Ewig (1954); Wallace-Hadrill (1975).

played by the church in the gaining and exercise of power. Carloman was deeply committed to church reform and called on Boniface to assist him. The consequence was the famous *Concilium Germanicum*, which set out all the main aspects of the church that Boniface thought required remedial attention. Clerical celibacy, becoming conduct, dress, the need to desist from hunting and bearing arms and the proper definition and maintenance of Christian marriage were all discussed. The incidence of paganism was deplored. Monasteries and the nature of the religious life for monks and nuns were addressed. Pippin in Neustria was not slow to follow suit with his own synod at Soissons in 744, reinforcing the Austrasian council's decisions, though it would seem that Boniface had very little to do with Pippin. There is evidence indeed that Pippin was independently seeking advice from the Pope and bypassing Boniface.[48] After 750 Boniface seems to have had little access to the Frankish ruler and little influence and it is certainly very unlikely that he played any role in the consecration of Pippin III as king in 751. This may have contributed to his decision to return to the mission field. Consequently, he journeyed to northern Frisia and was murdered by brigands near Dokkum in 754. In 742 Boniface had been granted a special concession by Zacharias to designate his successor. The choice had fallen on Lull. Thus on Boniface's death it was Lull who succeeded as bishop of Mainz, though the papal legateship went to the Frank, Chrodegang, bishop of Metz, a staunch adviser of Pippin III.

At stake in the early Carolingian reforms were not only matters of internal discipline and the morality of the church but also the church's structure and organisation, the role of the monasteries *vis-à-vis* the bishops and that of the bishops *vis-à-vis* the priests. Many of the decisions made in the mid-eighth century were taken up, reiterated, developed and in large part acted upon in the course of the ninth century.[49] Synods are the outward and visible sign of the church being managed properly. Boniface, indeed, took the lack of synods in Francia for the eighty or so years before his advent as a sign of malaise. The decrees stress the principle of accountability with reports from priests to bishops and from bishops to synods. The synods were to be held regularly as a means of inspection. Canon law and its authority was insisted upon and, because of the involvement of the ruler in convening these synods, canon law was in effect endorsed by the rulers.

These mid-eighth-century Frankish synods to some degree reflect the end of the first stage of the reform of the Frankish church. Indications in the sphere of liturgy and canon law,[50] and the work of Chrodegang of Metz and

---

[48] Rau (1968), pp. 414–36.   [49] Levison (1946); McKitterick (1977).
[50] See Reynolds, chapter 22 below.

Pirmin of Murbach in separate spheres from those in which Boniface operated,[51] point to a groundswell for reform within the Frankish church from the end of the seventh century onwards. Chrodegang certainly reinforced the alignment to Rome so dear to the Anglo-Saxons, and was active in the restoration of episcopal authority, ecclesiastical discipline, the reorganisation of ecclesiastical provinces, marriage law according to the Christian church and the confraternities of prayer. It is very likely that Chrodegang (possibly supported by Pippin III and Bertrada) introduced Roman usage independently of Boniface and that it represents a general policy within the mid-eighth-century Frankish church that happened to coincide with Boniface's English predilections. Boniface, naturally, was inclined to exaggerate the degree of laxness he encountered, but it should also be remembered that reforms do not self-evidently improve what has gone before; they merely impose their own strong conception of what should be done in contrast to existing practice.

It is striking how soon the Frankish decisions were reported to the English bishops. The motive may have been to secure greater uniformity within the churches on either side of the Channel. Many of Boniface's letters to the pope seek guidance on matters of policy, action, ecclesiastical discipline and the interpretation of canon law. Roman and Frankish practice were sometimes at odds with English ways, particularly in the matter of episcopal succession and marriage. Thus Frankish decisions may well have played a major role in the English synods of *Cloveshoe* in 747 in that Cuthbert, to whom Boniface reported his work, stressing the necessity of maintaining the Catholic faith and unity and subjection to the Roman church, may have registered the relevance of Boniface's work to the situation prevailing in England. It remains a possibility, nevertheless, that Cuthbert informed Boniface of English proposals for reform and these gave Boniface ideas for dealing with the Frankish clergy.[52]

Whatever the case, an essential question is the degree to which the move to reform in Francia is a response to prevailing conditions rather than a consequence of Boniface's individual zealous sense of what was and was not acceptable in light of his understanding of canon law. Boniface's vehement criticisms of the English clergy, for example, are those of a man who had been away from his native land for almost thirty years. How well informed was he in formulating his proposals for reform for either England or Francia? His sources of information are clearly indicated in his letters. There is frequent reference to messengers and his own priests are sent to England to fetch and bring various items. Yet it may be that his information was not

---

[51] *Saint Chrodegang* (1967); Oexle and Schmid (1974); Angenendt (1972).
[52] Cubitt (1995).

only patchy but partial. Boniface heard what he wanted to hear, and told us in his letters what he wanted us to believe. If the account he provides of the abuses within the Frankish church can now be shown to be demonstrably distorted, the same may well go for the English church.[53]

It is not only in terms of missionary enterprise that the connections between England and the Continent are to be viewed. A lurid light, for example, is cast on connections with the Continent in Boniface's complaint that English female pilgrims were a cause for anxiety because of the danger of their being led astray, from poverty or innocence, and becoming prostitutes. That the pilgrim traffic was considerable, and not always as disreputable as Boniface implies, is suggested by many accounts, the most vivid of which is the *Hodoeporicon* of Willibald, written by Hugeburc the nun of Heidenheim (Map 4). Willibald, dedicated to the religious life by his parents and brought up in the monastery of Bishops Waltham, set out from *Hamwic* with his brother Wynnebald and their father, travelled across the Channel on a boat clearly accustomed to taking passengers, disembarked near Rouen and proceeded by land across France, visiting the shrines of various saints on the way. Once over the Alps, their father fell sick, died and was buried at Lucca. Thereafter Willibald 'with his relatives and company' journeyed to Rome, the usual goal of English pilgrims. Willibald, however, only spent the winter there before continuing to Jerusalem. He and two companions took ship and sailed, with many stops on the way – at Naples, Mount Etna, Syracuse, Monemvasia and Chios – to Ephesus. They visited Cyprus, and thereafter many cities in Asia Minor, were kidnapped by Saracens and, once they had escaped, made their way to Damascus and thence to the itinerary of Christ's ministry. In all these places they visited sacred sites and holy shrines and churches, and participated in the liturgical rites of the communities who supported them. On the journey home Willibald managed to smuggle balsam through the customs at Tyre by means of topping up a bamboo reed full of the precious oil with petroleum to disguise the smell. He sailed north, visited the site of the Synod of Nicaea and spent two years in Constantinople before returning on a ship with papal envoys, probably in 728. After making a detour to see again the wonders of the volcano at Mount Etna, Willibald settled for ten years at the monastery of Monte Cassino learning the observance of the Rule of Benedict. He then returned to Germany to assist Boniface, becoming in due course bishop of Eichstätt.

It was an extraordinary journey but, to a considerable extent, Willibald was following the well-worn paths of pilgrims before him. Pilgrims were

---

[53] For important new assessments see Brooks (1984); Cubitt (1995); Foot (forthcoming).

able to take advantage of normal trading activity, of entrepreneurs who seem to have made a living (arranging transport, keeping hostelries) from the pilgrim traffic and the occasional journeys of political envoys, religious legates and messengers in order to further their travels. Certainly, Carolingian links with England within the ecclesiastical sphere are the most obvious in our sources. Alcuin, for example, originally encountered Charlemagne at Pavia when he was a member of an English group of clergy visiting Italy. His subsequent career at the Carolingian court and retirement to Tours indicate how easily an Englishman, like many others whom we classify as 'foreigners', could be absorbed into and contribute to the mainstream of Frankish religious, political and cultural life.[54]

Nor is the contribution all one sided. Papal legates, for example, attended the famous synods of 786 in Northumbria and Mercia, but they were accompanied by the Frankish envoy Wigbod and appear to have played a political as well as an ecclesiastical role, while the political context of the legatine synods in England, dated according to Charlemagne's regnal year, was crucial.[55] One outcome of the synod was the creation of a new ecclesiastical province and archbishopric of Lichfield. This is usually interpreted as an instance of Offa's presumptuous aggrandisement in relation to the church, but it might be seen more plausibly in the context of ecclesiastical reform and an emulation of the reorganisation of ecclesiastical provinces carried out under Pippin and Charlemagne. The speed with which the decrees of Aachen in 816 were transmitted to Canterbury to figure in the records of the Synod of Chelsea in 816 is also impressive. Although thereafter the records are very scanty until the connections of Grimbald of St Bertin with King Alfred's Court, it seems likely that some political communications were sustained throughout the period. Pippin III, for example, sent presents to King Eadberht (737–58) of Northumbria, Alchred of Northumbria sent envoys to Charlemagne and Offa, Charlemagne exchanged letters on the matter of trading concessions and a marriage alliance between the two houses; and Charlemagne also received a number of English political exiles at Aachen or is said to have intervened in their political fortunes in England.[56] The contacts underlying the visit made by Æthelwulf of Wessex to the court of Charles the Bald, king of the West Franks, in 857 and the subsequent marriage of Æthelwulf to Charles' thirteen-year-old daughter Judith, and the whole spate of marriages between the daughters of Edward the Elder and various Continental rulers, not least Charles the Simple, king of the West Franks, and Otto I, king of the

[54] Bullough (1991). Compare the career of Theodulf of Orléans or that of Lombard Paul the Deacon: Dahlhaus-Berg (1981).   [55] Brooks (1984).   [56] *MGH EPP* iv, no. 100.

Map 4 Charlemagne's Europe and Byzantium, 814

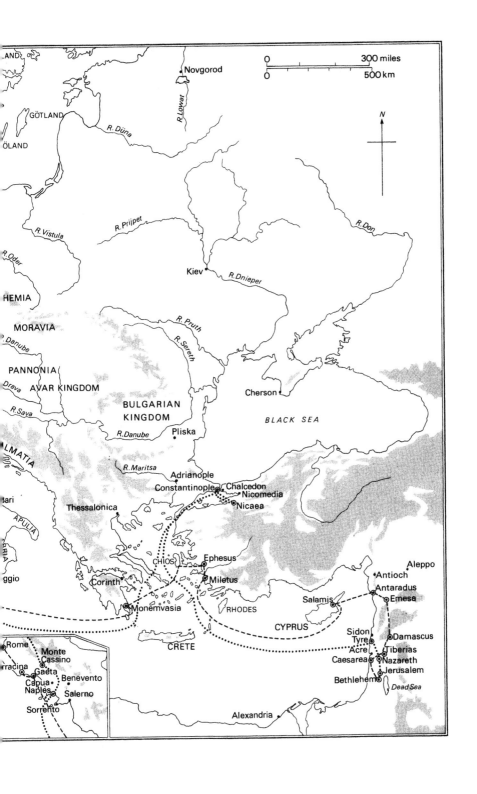

AND
Novgorod

GÖTLAND
ÖLAND

R. Düna
R. Lowat

0   300 miles
0   500 km

N

R. Prijpet

R. Vistula
R. Don

R. Oder

Kiev   *R. Dnieper*

HEMIA

MORAVIA
Danube

R. Pruth

PANNONIA
Drava

AVAR KINGDOM
R. Sava

R. Sereth

BULGARIAN
KINGDOM

Cherson

R. Danube   Pliska
BLACK SEA

LMATIA

R. Maritsa

Bari

Adrianople
Constantinople   Chalcedon
Nicomedia
Thessalonica
Nicaea

APULIA

CHIOS   Ephesus
Aleppo

ggio

Corinth   Miletus   Antioch

Antaradus

RIA

Salamis   Emesa

Monemvasia   RHODES

CYPRUS

CRETE

Sidon
Tyre   Damascus
Acre   Tiberias
Caesarea   Nazareth
Jerusalem
Bethlehem
Dead Sea

Rome
Monte
Cassino
racina
Gaëta
Capua   Benevento
Naples
Salerno
Sorrento

Alexandria

East Franks, are not to be gainsaid. Certainly the reception of Homiliary and penitential material,[57] the transmission of the Rule of Benedict and of Chrodegang's Rule in its old English version, the familiarity with Einhard's *Vita Karoli* implied by Asser, and the knowledge of early ninth-century Carolingian church reforms within the ninth-century English church, indicate a maintenance of contacts to some degree. I have argued elsewhere, moreover, that the manuscript evidence from the Anglo-Saxon missionary areas in northern Germany suggests a continued influx of English religious well into the ninth century.[58]

In the sphere of music and liturgical chant, the strongest influence on English liturgical practice until the mid-eighth century was from Rome. All information concerning English chant and its knowledge of Continental practice before the earliest extant chant books of the late tenth century that can be taken into account, however, comes from the narrative sources, such as Bede. Although the late tenth-century books reflect clear evidence of influence of both north Frankish and Lotharingian chant, we have no idea what repertory of Mass and office chants was in use in English centres between the seventh and the early tenth centuries. It is possible that the major developments of the ninth and early tenth century in Francia were known[59] but no notation survives in either English or Roman liturgical manuscripts in this period. Cantors, from both Rome and Carolingian Francia, taught music orally; chant was committed to memory. John the Cantor taught in Northumbria and Alfred brought the cantor Grimbald from St Bertin. Only in the context of the late tenth-century reforms was musical notation established in England as an indigenous practice and recognised as a means of communicating and recording the chant repertory.[60]

The manuscript evidence for links between England and the Continent in the ninth century is as ambiguous as the musical evidence. Although there are many ninth-century Carolingian manuscripts known in England before the Conquest, it is for the most part impossible to pin down the date of their arrival with any certainty.[61] It has been customary to associate their introduction with the tenth-century reform movement and the links established between such houses as Ramsey and Fleury. Yet it is a possibility that texts such as Smaragdus' *Diadema Monachorum*, copied in the late tenth century at Canterbury (CUL Ff.4.43), ninth-century copies of Martianus Capella (CCCC 153 and CCCC 330) and a volume of Boethius (CCCC 352) were available in England before that time and nearer to the date of the original compilation. Some of the texts and manuscripts can no doubt be

[57] Frantzen (1983) and Gatch (1977).   [58] McKitterick (1989b).
[59] Rankin (1994).   [60] Rankin (1985).   [61] Gneuss (1981).

accounted for by the links between Brittany and England. Julian of Toledo (CCCC 399) and other school books such as Remigius (Cambridge, Gonville and Caius College 144), Jerome *In Isaiam* (Cambridge, Pembroke College 17), Lathcen (Pembroke 88) and Hraban Maur's biblical exegesis (Pembroke 308) may have reached England in the ninth century. Future work in the spheres of liturgy and canon law in particular may well establish a tighter network than seems at present discernible. The very fact that Alfred knew whom to ask and where to go for advice is an indication that we should regard the silence of the sources with caution. Further, the texts Alfred chose to have translated, and the whole tenor of his rulership, show that he was aware, to put it no more strongly, of what was going on elsewhere.[62]

In the sphere of administration, however, there seems to be little mileage in a close investigation of the possible influence of Frankish administrative practice in England. In her classic exposition of the analogies and resemblances in methods of local government in Francia and England, Helen Cam offered many suggestions and rejected many possibilities for there being any strong influence of Frankish governmental practice on the Anglo-Saxon rulers of Wessex, even though there is sufficient fragmentary evidence of constant contact between England and Francia from the eighth to the tenth centuries, with the church acting as the main channel of communication.[63] Archaeological excavation, after all, has established the maintenance of trading links and the export of goods from and into England and the mainland. The similarities of purpose observed in the eighth-century sources are not contradicted by the little that remains for the ninth century.

How then can the contribution of the English to the Continent be defined? There are many elements common to the English and Frankish churches and to the Anglo-Saxon missionary areas on the Continent. Political and ecclesiastical expansion went hand in hand; the relationship with Rome was becoming increasingly close; there was a move towards greater coherence and uniformity in ecclesiastical organisation, monastic observance, clerical behaviour, the interpretation of canon law, liturgical practice and intellectual culture; the material base afforded the church by lay supporters was all important. Yet the distinctiveness of the Anglo-Saxon contribution at a general level remains in question, even if it can be shown on many smaller matters, such as the introduction of particular texts and methods of teaching, the conviction of the importance of papal authority, the emphasis on synodal authority, the foundation of influential monasteries and the energy devoted to establishing a coherent diocesan structure, that the English contribution was of crucial significance.

---

[62] Bullough (1972); Keynes and Lapidge (1983).   [63] Cam (1912).

The sources highlight, however, how much was due to particular individuals, how large a role chance played in the establishing of certain connections and how little modern national distinctions appear to have mattered. Further, a Frankish enterprise gathering momentum had the good fortune to coincide with the advent of some eager Anglo-Saxons on the Continent who created the necessary conditions for learning and religious culture to flourish east of the Rhine. It is impossible to define insular religious culture in terms of specific texts, customs and institutions beyond the few precarious instances cited above.[64] Apart from the visit of the legates in 786, the treaty between Charlemagne and Offa, the small indications of political intervention in English affairs, and the marriage of Charles the Bald's daughter Judith to Æthelwulf of Wessex, there appears to be no sign of institutional or official connection on matters regarded as of general policy. These exceptions may nevertheless constitute a warning not to assume that there was no such official link, at least from the 780s, even if it is clear that Boniface's mission to the Continent was in no respects promoted by the English ecclesiastical establishment. Certainly, various hints in the sources concerning Louis the Pious' policies towards his neighbours could be interpreted as part of a wider vision on the part of that ruler, but this remains to be explored. Ultimately, in the later tenth and eleventh centuries, political interests were to play a larger role, but even in the context of the late tenth-century monastic reforms we see contributions made by Franks to English monasticism very much dependent on individual initiative and invitation. Then, moreover, rather than English connections being formed with the originally Anglo-Saxon foundations on the Continent, the links were with houses of the Frankish heartlands, such as Fleury, St Bertin and Gorze. Again, as throughout the eighth- and ninth-century relations between England and the Continent, it was personal connections and local influences that were predominant.[65]

[64] See also McKitterick (1989a and b).   [65] McKitterick (1991).

CHAPTER 3

FRANKISH GAUL TO 814

Paul Fouracre

THE central theme in the history of eighth-century Francia is the rising power of its Carolingian rulers, above all of Charles Martel (715–41), Pippin III (741–68) and Charlemagne (768–814). Not only was the whole of Francia convulsed by the Carolingians' fight for domination; their success also made them the focal point of a tradition of historical writing which was king centred and increasingly court sponsored. The three principal sources for this history are the *Continuations of the Chronicle of Fredegar*, the *Prior Metz Annals* and Einhard's *Life of Charlemagne*. Given the partisan nature of these works, we must naturally guard against distortion in their view of the 'rise of the Carolingians'. It is clear, for instance, that by the early ninth century, writers of history were reordering the Merovingian past in order to date Carolingian domination back into the seventh century and so present their seizure of the throne from the Merovingians in 751 as the overdue recognition of a long-established supremacy. The clearest statement of this view is in the *Prior Metz Annals*, written *c.* 806.[1] This work took the victory of Charlemagne's great-grandfather Pippin II over the hitherto dominant Neustrians at the battle of Tertry in 687 to mark the inception of Carolingian rule, and so it has remained in many a history textbook down to this day. In reality, however, in 687 Pippin did not so much overturn the Neustrian regime of the Merovingians as join it. Although he was able to establish himself in prime position at the royal court, Pippin's power-base remained in Austrasia and his influence over the Neustrian heartlands of the Seine-Oise area was visibly limited.

By the time of Pippin II in the late seventh century, Francia, that is, the lands broadly defined as those subject to the Frankish kings since the early sixth century, comprising the regions of Neustria, Austrasia, Burgundy,

---

[1] *Annales Mettenses Priores*, p. 12. Fouracre (1984) for discussion of the Carolingian view of this period of Merovingian history.

Provence and Aquitaine, had evolved into a kingdom which was massive in size and relatively stable, despite its meagre resources and the rudimentary nature of its government. Its stability and ultimate territorial integrity were the fruits of a basically conservative political culture in which public authority lay in the hands of magnates who exercised their power more or less on behalf of the kings. What we would term the 'state' was in this period a rather loose collection of persons and institutions exercising power perceived to be derived from royal authority, an arrangement in which (at least to our eyes) the boundary between the 'public' and the 'private' uses of power was blurred. An association with royal government in turn added legitimacy to the power the magnates had over those below them. Binding people further into a single political community were shared religious beliefs and practices. Intermarriage between the most powerful families also helped break down regional differences and identities. The stability of this political entity was marked by its failure to disintegrate during the several periods of child kingship which occurred in the later seventh and early eighth centuries. On the other hand, the magnates tended to withdraw co-operation when the profits of power were perceived to be unjustly shared out, and at such times, as in the relatively well-documented 670s, the Frankish state seemed to collapse as the consensus upon which it was based disappeared and the leaders in the provinces, such as Lupus, duke of Aquitaine, ignored the government at the centre. Yet the conservative attitude of such leaders meant that they did not then go on to create new political entities and eventually they or their successors could be drawn (or forced) back into a political community focused on the palace. Pippin entered into government in the wash of this kind of political behaviour.

From 688 to his death in 714, Pippin II can be identified with the re-establishment of political consensus in Francia. Documents from the reign of Childebert III (695–711) show leaders from as far away as Provence attending the royal court in Neustria, and according to the earliest Carolingian Annals, Pippin in 709 began the slow process of bringing the 'Sueves' or Alemans back into the Frankish orbit. Though, as we shall see, the Frankish leaders fought each other again after Pippin II's death, over the next three generations the growing solidarity of the ruling elite, inspired by success in war under Carolingian leadership, raised Francia to a position of dominance in western Europe unprecedented for a single state in the post-Roman period. Of the parallels between their power and that of the Romans the Franks were well aware. Under Charlemagne's leadership there was a certain Romanisation of Frankish culture: Charlemagne even assumed the imperial title in 800 AD. Despite the novelty of their own kingship and the recent extension of Frankish power, the Carolingians themselves highlighted the ancient and customary basis of royal authority, especially at the annual assemblies of king and magnates. On these occasions not only was royal authority ritually affirmed, the basic direction of government was determined. At a local level too, in the county court or *mallus*, a recognition of custom played a large part in what was regarded as legitimate, and customary legal practice, for instance the use of amateur local worthies to decide cases, continued to operate through and in favour of a local balance of power. In most areas of government, and locally in cultural and religious life, there was therefore much continuity between Merovingian and Carolingian Francia. Nevertheless, over this period there were certainly some major changes. Above all, the German-speaking lands east of the Rhine became for the first time fully integrated into the Frankish kingdom. New impetus was given to central government, and stronger ties between king and magnates, for instance in demands for the affirmation of loyalty and for performance of military service, made it more and more difficult for regional leaders such as dukes to go their own way. All this allowed the rulers for the first time to make clear statements about the nature and purpose of public authority, beginning with calls by the sons of Charles Martel for military support, and culminating with Charlemagne's review of government following his coronation as emperor. A discussion of eighth-century history requires one first to explain how Francia became so much more powerful at this time, and secondly to consider whether the subsequent changes in political life and in its ideological reflection add up to the point at which the Carolingian state should be seen as objectively different from its Merovingian predecessor.

In 714 Francia entered into a prolonged period of political and military turmoil. In that year a crisis was provoked by the deaths of both Pippin II and his son Grimoald. Leadership of the family passed to Pippin's widow Plectrude, who had control of the family's treasure (the latter being the key to power in the short term) and ruled on behalf of Grimoald's young son Theudoald who had been designated the 'mayor of the palace' to the Merovingian king Dagobert III (711–15). This arrangement was rejected by the Neustrian Franks who drove Theudoald out, elected one Ragamfred as their own 'mayor', and then allied with the Frisians to attack the weakened Pippinid family in their Austrasian homelands. The next year King Dagobert died and was replaced by Chilperic II, a former cleric, but the only adult Merovingian available. Chilperic, Ragamfred of Neustria and Radbod, leader of the Frisians, then attacked Pippin's family again. This time the Frisian contingent was met by Charles, later to be known as Charles Martel. He was Pippin's son by a second wife from the Liège area. In 714 Charles had been imprisoned by Plectrude. He managed to escape, however, and in 715 marshalled his family's defences around the river Meuse only to suffer what was almost certainly his sole defeat in battle. The next year, 716, the Neustrian and Frisian forces penetrated to Cologne, withdrawing only after receiving treasure from Plectrude. Charles nevertheless mounted a successful ambush against the returning forces in the Ardennes. By 717 Charles had built up sufficient forces to counter-attack. He defeated the Neustrians at Vinchy near Cambrai, and then moved back to Cologne where he ousted Plectrude, secured his father's treasure and became undisputed leader of Austrasia, raising his own king, Clothar IV, to the throne of Austrasia which had been vacant for the previous forty years. Kings, it is clear, were necessary for the raising of large military forces. In 718 Charles defeated Radbod, who died the next year. He then fought again against Ragamfred and Chilperic who had allied themselves with the duke of Aquitaine, Eudo. Ragamfred fled to his base at Angers, Eudo and Chilperic retreated into Aquitaine, before Eudo came to terms with Charles, returning Chilperic to him along with the royal treasure. Charles' Austrasian king now died and from this point in 719 Charles appears as 'mayor' of a single palace claiming hegemony over all of Francia. Victory in that year brought Chilperic II and the royal treasure into Martel's hands, and the separate Austrasian kingship was allowed to lapse: Clothar IV was said to have died and he was not replaced. Charles had now created a power bloc and concentration of treasure which was stronger than any other single unit inside or on the borders of Francia, and he was able to take on the other areas of the country one by one. The next twenty years were spent enforcing his claim to hegemony.

In the early Carolingian Annals and in the *Continuations of the Chronicle of Fredegar*,[2] Charles Martel is seen to consolidate his rule in Francia through a series of military campaigns. Indeed, in contrast to the relatively peaceful seventh century, the sources for this period seem to have thought it remarkable if there was no fighting in any given year. Besides one further campaign against Ragamfred in 724, Charles fought against the Saxons in 718, in 720 and in 724. In 725 he campaigned in Alemannia and in Bavaria, again in Bavaria in 728 and in Alemannia in 730. In 731 he turned his attention to Eudo, still independent in Aquitaine. Eudo in 732 was forced to call upon the help of his erstwhile enemy Charles against Arab invaders from Spain who had raided as far north as Poitiers. Charles' response culminated in the famous battle of Poitiers (actually fought somewhere between Tours and Poitiers). Though not quite of the importance often still accorded to it, this Frankish victory did force the Arabs to retreat southwards and, partly as

---

[2] *Annales Sancti Amandi, Tiliani, Laubacenses, Petiavini, Laureshamenses s.a.* 719–41; *Continuations of the Chronicle of Fredegar*, chs. 11–21.

a result of victory at Poitiers in the following year, Charles was able to stamp his authority on south Burgundy. In 733 and again in 734 he also fought the Frisians. On Eudo's death in 735 and again in 736 he returned to Aquitaine and also brought southern Burgundy and Provence under his control. In 737 he was in Provence and Septimania fighting both against Franks who had rejected the order imposed upon them in the previous year and against the Arabs with whom they had allied. The year 738 saw Charles in Saxony again, and 739 back in Provence; 740 was without a campaign and in 741 Charles died. One can now see why he would be remembered as 'Martel', or 'the Hammer'.[3]

It is far easier to list Charles Martel's successes like this than to explain why he was so successful, or indeed to say what was really happening in Francia at this time. The key to any explanation may lie in the extent to which the Frankish political community had disintegrated after 714; the need to rally against threats from outside helped that community reintegrate around Carolingian leadership. In 714–15 the Neustrians, who had for much of the seventh century dominated Francia, recovered some of their strength thanks to Pippinid weakness, and they were plainly strong enough to oust the Pippinid family from their midst and with Frisian help to raid deep into Austrasia. Power-sharing with the Austrasians in the previous generation, however, had left them too weak to exercise much influence outside the Neustrian heartlands of the Seine-Oise area.[4] In Austrasia no other family was strong enough to replace that of Pippin as leaders, and the political crisis in Austrasia has been aptly described as a 'succession crisis' within that one family.[5] Once the succession had been resolved, Austrasia seems to have been fairly united behind Charles Martel. His emergence as leader is to be explained by the key position of his mother's family in the Liège area and hence in the front line in defence against the Frisians. Charles' successful ambush against the returning Neustro-Frisian forces in 716 brought nobles from elsewhere in Austrasia (from the Moselle, for example) into his following, and with this advantage he achieved victory against Ragamfred in 717. This in turn allowed him to get hold of his father's treasure, and he could then consolidate his position in Austrasia by raising his own king. A need for effective leadership against Saxon invaders might also have helped Charles establish his authority in Austrasia. Martel with treasure, a king and the bulk of the Austrasian forces behind him was stronger than the combined forces of Neustria and Aquitaine ranged against him in 719.

---

[3] On how Charles Martel was portrayed in the eighth and ninth centuries, see Nonn (1970), pp. 70–137, esp. pp. 124–36 for the history of his nickname 'Martel'.
[4] Gerberding (1987), pp. 92–145 is a good guide to relations between the Neustrians and Austrasians.   [5] Semmler (1977), p. 1.

Outside the Neustrian and Austrasian heartlands there was a high level of political fragmentation, except in Aquitaine where Eudo's rule was apparently generally accepted, although we can say very little about the nature of that rule.[6] Elsewhere, especially in the lands between the Seine and Loire and in mid and south Burgundy, there are gaps in the surviving lists of bishops which suggest that many sees either fell vacant or were occupied by laymen, and this has been taken to indicate a state of disorder.[7] Some notorious cases illustrate this disorder: Savaric bishop of Auxerre in Burgundy, for instance, took advantage of the fighting in the north in 714–15 to subjugate 'by military means' the surrounding towns of Orléans, Nevers, Avallon and Tonnerre, and was on the march against Lyons when he died of a stroke in 718 or 719.[8] He was followed as bishop in Auxerre by one Hainmar who was almost certainly a layman; his name appears in the list of Auxerre bishops with the qualification, 'called bishop'. Such opportunistic warlords were no match for Charles Martel when eventually he took them on with the much greater resources of Neustria and Austrasia behind him.

At the same time, it is clear that in Burgundy and Provence elements of the aristocracy were quite prepared to join forces with the northerners. As we have seen, the pressure of Arab attacks, most notably in Aquitaine, was one factor in bringing southerners into Martel's orbit. Another was the fact that the memory of a single political community was far from dead, and recent work has re-emphasised the way in which family ties between north and south remained in place.[9] Abbo, ruler of Provence, for instance, had links with other magnates in the lower Seine area and actively aided Charles Martel when he moved into Provence. For this help he was well rewarded. Finally one detail in the will which Abbo drew up leaving his property to the monastery of Novalesa suggests that political disorder and Arab invasion might have had subversive social consequences: Abbo invited Novalesa to track down and recall to subjugation those of his freedmen and servants who had dispersed during the troubles.[10] A fear that the social order was in danger may have been an added spur to the regional magnates' acceptance of a new regime.

At the level of political and military history, the growth of Carolingian power may therefore be understood in terms of an initial military success which allowed Charles Martel to take advantage of a balance of power operating progressively in his favour. Further explanations for this success

---

[6] *Vita Pardulfi* is one source which does give some idea of life in Aquitaine in the first half of the eighth century.   [7] The lists are to be found in Duchesne (1907–15).

[8] *Gesta Pontificum Autissiodorensium*, ch. 26.   [9] Geary (1985), pp. 138–43.

[10] Abbo's will is translated in Geary (1985), pp. 39–79.

have been drawn out of the reputation for despoiling the church of its lands which Charles Martel acquired in the ninth century. It was at one time suggested that he settled warriors on that land and so built up his military strength. From the small amount of evidence available to us there is no reason at all to separate Charles Martel from his peers either in the use he made of land or in the use he made of technology.[11]

The argument that Charles Martel systematically exploited church lands is not supported by eighth-century sources. This was certainly a time in which many bishoprics (such as that of Rheims) and monasteries (St Wandrille for example) lost control of a significant proportion of their very extensive estates, and, as we have seen, one in which the ecclesiastical hierarchy admitted warriors, like the notorious Savaric, into its ranks. Indeed, the Anglo-Saxon missionary Boniface complained about the falling standards of the Frankish church in terms which became famous,[12] but the loss of church lands and the increasing prominence of warrior bishops were symptoms of the general political and military turmoils of the time rather than particular causes of Martel's success. The way for this had been prepared in the seventh century which saw the growth of great ecclesiastical lordships and the entry of bishops into central politics.[13] In the eighth century, establishing control over all of Francia meant reducing the independence of such lords, driving them out where they resisted, confiscating their resources and replacing them with trusted allies. The best-documented example of this process is Martel's treatment of Eucherius bishop of Orléans who was probably a nephew of the Savaric mentioned earlier. After his victory over the Arabs in 732, when Charles consolidated his hold over Burgundy, he turned on his one-time ally Eucherius, drove him out along with his kinsmen and seized their lands to distribute to his own followers. This was not a straightforward case of 'secularisation' but rather the confiscation of the resources of a great family based on an episcopal lordship. The memory of Eucherius' treatment, preserved in the account in his Life,[14] was one of the reasons why the bishop was later venerated as a saint, and as his reputation grew, so did that of Charles Martel as a despoiler of church lands. As a result, when in the ninth century various churches drew up detailed inventories of their property, they tended to assume that what they had lost to laymen in this period had been taken away by a Charles greedy for land with which to reward his followers. It is the frequency with which this assumption was made which lends the impression

[11] See Goetz, below, pp. 473–6, and Verhulst, below, pp. 488–92.
[12] See McKitterick, pp. 75–7 above.
[13] Ewig (1953), pp. 412–30 describes the rise of episcopal power and provides the context for Boniface's strictures.   [14] *Vita Eucherii*, chs. 7–9.

that church lands were systematically turned over to lay warriors in benefice, although in fact there survives not a single contemporary document recording the granting out of land in this way. Paradoxically, it was in the next two generations that this practice really evolved, but the blame for it attached to Charles simply because, whereas his sons and grandsons were known as keen to reform the morals of the church, Charles himself was presumed to have been unconcerned about that decline in standards to which Boniface had referred. Yet it was in part precisely by voicing their concern for the church that later rulers acquired the moral authority to use its lands as their own, in order to fund a state charged with the protection of Christians. This connection was first articulated by Charles Martel's son Carloman at the council of Estinnes held at Boniface's behest in 744.[15]

As we have just seen in north Burgundy, Charles Martel consolidated his authority by installing his followers in positions of power. Another example would be Godobald who was made abbot of St Denis, the premier Neustrian monastery: Godobald was from the Liège area and closely connected with Martel's family.[16] Throughout Francia there was a sweeping change in the personnel who filled the key positions of count, bishop and abbot. At one time this was thought to have resulted in the creation of a new aristocracy made up of persons drawn, like Godobald, from the Carolingian homelands, a so-called 'imperial aristocracy' the installation of which introduced a genuinely new regime. Closer studies of individual families have now revealed greater continuities between the Merovingian and the Carolingian aristocracies.[17] Personnel change there certainly was, but also, as Abbo's behaviour demonstrates, collaboration, and intermarriage, between Martel's newcomers and families long established in each area. With the possible exception of Alemannia, this pattern would be repeated in every region into which the Carolingians expanded over the next century, for rulers naturally worked with the grain of the existing social structure. Similarly, a radical departure from traditional forms of government was inconceivable. By insisting on direct ties of loyalty between himself and the magnates in the field, Charles Martel could, in political terms, bypass the Merovingian kings to whom he was in theory subservient, but his word was not law unless it passed through a Merovingian mouthpiece.[18] Abbo's will provides an example of this: though we can be certain that it was through service to Charles that Abbo was rewarded, he still spoke of receiving that reward from

---

[15] *MGH Cap.* I, no. 11, p. 28.

[16] M. Werner (1980), pp. 126–7 for the relationship between Godobald and the family of Charles Martel.

[17] The clearest statement of this is K.-F. Werner (1965), pp. 83–142, trans. in Reuter (1978), pp. 137–202.   [18] See Nelson, below pp. 398–406.

the king, Theuderic IV (721–37), and no doubt it had been through a royal document that Abbo had received legitimate title to the land involved.[19] We should in fact take the Carolingian sources such as the *Prior Metz Annals* at their word when they suggest that eventually logic prevailed and people accepted that he who wielded the real power should become king, but, by the same token, it took the Carolingians a whole generation to prove their worth, which shows that the notion that only the descendants of Clovis could be kings of the Franks was deeply ingrained into Frankish custom.

Charles Martel and his sons proved themselves above all by success in war against other peoples and, increasingly related to the latter, by demonstrating their religious zeal. Arabs, Frisians and Saxons were all non-Christian invaders of Francia in the eighth century, and Charles Martel gained great prestige by leading forces against them. At first these wars were defensive or punitive, but they soon led to the acquisition of new territory for the Franks, in Frisia in 734–5 and in Gothia or Septimania, the formerly Visigothic province which extended from the Pyrenees east to the Rhône, in 737–8. In Frisia and east of the Rhine a rather slower process of Christianisation, largely directed by Anglo-Saxon missionaries, accompanied the establishment of Frankish control.[20] Charles Martel's father Pippin had begun the patronage of Anglo-Saxon missionaries, helping Willibrord restore the church in Utrecht, but this first effort had been bowled over in the Frisian invasions following Pippin's death in 714. In the 720s attention switched to central Germany under the leadership of Boniface. Association with this missionary in particular did a very great deal to establish the religious credentials of the Carolingians. Interestingly, the region in which Boniface worked, Hesse, had always been under Frankish control. Indeed, the Franks had since the mid-sixth century also ruled Thuringia which lay to the east of Hesse, but about the latter we know almost nothing prior to the arrival of Boniface. In fact, between the late sixth and mid-eighth centuries Hesse is mentioned only once, and this reference simply tells of an army crossing it on the way to Thuringia.[21] Such silence, and the fact that the inhabitants of the area remained largely pagan into the eighth century, reminds us that up to this point the old Rhine–Danube frontier of the Romans had remained a remarkably effective cultural and religious boundary despite the fact that Frankish power straddled it. Events east of the Rhine begin to appear more frequently in our narrative sources only after the organisation of the Christian church in the area had led to a dissemination of written culture. Equally striking is the speed at which that culture took hold. In 744 Boniface

---

[19] Geary (1985), pp. 74–5.   [20] For further details, McKitterick, pp. 68 and 73–5 above.
[21] *Chronicle of Fredegar* IV, ch. 87.

founded the monastery of Fulda in a sparsely inhabited part of Hesse. Copies of the earliest charters from Fulda show that within a decade of its foundation the local aristocracy was participating in written culture in just the same way as their counterparts who inhabited regions where habits of recording property transactions in writing had survived from Roman times.[22]

In 741, shortly before he died, Charles Martel drew up a charter which we may use briefly to indicate the position the Carolingians had reached at the end of his tumultuous career.[23] In this document Charles granted the *villa* of Clichy to the monastery of St Denis, thereby granting what had once been one of the Merovingians' favourite residences to St Denis which had once been their premier monastery. Yet though Charles Martel seemed here free to dispose of royal property as his own, and to call upon the special protection of St Denis, formerly reserved for the kings, and, as the dating clause of this charter shows, he was in the last five years of his career able to rule without a king, he nevertheless made this grant in the form of a private charter. He remained, ultimately, the most important non-royal person in the land, and, as we shall see, it was not a foregone conclusion that what he had acquired by conquest should pass to his sons. After his death there was another 'succession crisis', not as profound as the one in 714, but one which had a similar effect in drawing potential rivals into open conflict.

Before his death Charles Martel divided the Frankish territories between his sons Carloman and Pippin III, but Grifo, a third son by a later wife, contested the division and would, over the next ten years, be a focus of opposition to his half-brothers (Map 5). Another cause of conflict was that leaders who had been coerced into supporting Charles Martel renounced their allegiance on his death. In 742–3 there was a concerted effort by the dukes of Aquitaine, Alemannia and Bavaria to throw off Carolingian authority. At one moment Carloman and Pippin faced an Aleman, Bavarian, Slav and Saxon coalition to the east, whilst in the west Hunoald, son of Duke Eudo (died 735), broke out of Aquitaine and sacked the town of Chartres. At this time of crisis another Merovingian, Childeric III (743–51), was raised to the throne, presumably to disarm those who challenged the legitimacy of Carolingian authority on the basis of loyalty to the old line of kings. This Childeric, the last Merovingian king, is known only from a handful of charters, for the narrative sources are solely concerned with the seven campaigns which Pippin and Carloman mounted between the years 741–6 to break the opposition to their rule.

The narratives do not mention the church councils which were held in

---

[22] The Fulda charters are discussed in McKitterick (1989), pp. 126–9.
[23] *MGH Dip. Kar.* I, no. 14, pp. 101–2.

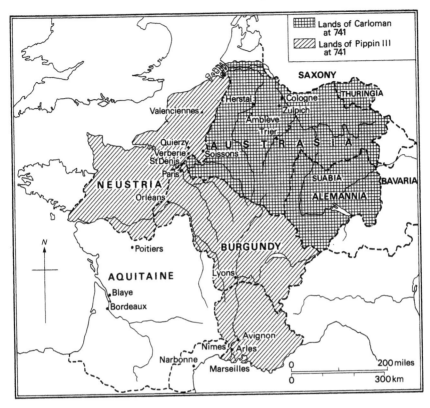

Map 5 The Frankish kingdoms, 714–40

742 or 743 and in 744, councils which addressed the lapses in clerical discipline about which Boniface had complained. These first attempts to reform the church should perhaps be seen as another aspect of the response to military pressure, to which the Council of Estinnes actually referred. Re-establishing basic order in the church was closely linked to curbing the independence of the bishops, in effect doing by the book what Charles Martel had done by force. A public commitment to reform also amounted to a call for support from church leaders. At the same time, the Carolingians reserved the right to use church lands at a time of military crisis, and the reforms did nothing to stop them taking over monasteries for their own use. Hence Pippin and Carloman could be seen as reformers whilst continuing to strip wealth from the church.[24]

---

[24] The Council of Estinnes, 3, 2 explicitly demanded the use of church property at a time of military crisis: '... propter inminentia bella et persecutiones ceterarum gentium quae in circuitu nostro sunt, ut sub precario et censu aliquam partem ecclesialis pecuniae in adiutorium exercitus nostri cum indulgentia Dei aliquanto tempore retineamus', *MGH Cap.* I, no. 11, p. 28.

Amongst the rebels east of the Rhine it was the Alemans who held out longest and were hit hardest. Carloman finally defeated them at the battle of Canstatt (near modern Stuttgart) in 746 and was said to have put several thousand to the sword afterwards. One historian, Reuter, has even argued that Canstatt was a disaster for the Alemans comparable in magnitude to that suffered at Hastings by the Anglo-Saxons, though for the former, unlike the latter, we lack the kind of evidence which could show the extent to which native landowners were dispossessed after the battle.[25] According to the *Annales Petaviani*, Carloman was so full of remorse for what he had done to the Alemans that he decided to go into a monastery.[26] Whether or not this was the real reason, Carloman did retire the next year, eventually joining the monastery of Monte Cassino in Italy. On Carloman's departure, Pippin III released his half-brother Grifo who promptly fled to the Saxons. A campaign against the Saxons was mounted, in which Pippin, as his son Charlemagne was to do several times, struck deep into eastern Saxony from Thuringia in alliance with Slav forces. Grifo then fled to Bavaria where he tried to make himself duke, but in 748 Pippin came after him again. Capturing Grifo, he gave him lands between the Seine and the Loire to rule, but from here Grifo fled to Aquitaine, where he was sheltered by the duke Waiofar until he was finally killed in 753 whilst on his way to Italy. This last phase of the struggle led to a firmer Frankish hold over Bavaria which received a new duke, Tassilo, who was both related to Pippin (his mother was Chiltrude, the latter's sister) and was under Carolingian tutelage. Another result of these events was a renewal of the tribute paid by the Saxons. They also led to a deepening of enmity between Pippin and Waiofar duke of Aquitaine. Pippin III would devote the last years of his life to destroying Aquitainian independence. First, however, he would make himself king.

Perhaps no event in early medieval history has been more comprehensively 'explained' than Pippin III's consecration in 751. We have already seen the growth of Carolingian military power which by 751 had made it impossible to resist Pippin, noting too how the Carolingians strengthened their qualifications for kingship by associating themselves with reform of the church. Yet to break with the very custom which legitimised the formal power they desired, the Carolingians had to call upon the pope to sanction their action with a divine authority which could overrule human tradition. That they should have turned to the pope in this way is put down to the influence of Boniface who in person built and cemented links between the Franks and the papacy. That the papacy responded favourably to Carol-

---

[25] Reuter (1991), p. 60.   [26] *Annales Petaviani s.a.* 747.

ingians' call for backing is explained partly by the pope's respect for Boniface and awareness that Pippin was an active reformer, but mainly by his desire for a political and military alliance with the Franks in the light of increasing Lombard pressure on Rome and the papal patrimony. Byzantium, the papacy's traditional protector, was no longer able or willing to offer much help, and the papacy had anyway long wanted to be free of interference from the east. In the main these explanations hold good, but they do require some qualification.[27] Boniface, for instance, was not quite the go-between who introduced the papacy and the Franks to each other. For there is a long history of Franco-papal relations quite separate from Boniface, whose influence anyway seems to have been much reduced after Carloman's retirement in 747. Nor are the strategic considerations of the papacy as straightforward as they first appear, for the Franks and Lombards were long-time allies with common non-Christian enemies in both Avars and Arabs. As late as 752 the papacy was still appealing for Byzantine help, and the actual agreement that the Franks should help the pope was made only in 754. In 751 itself it seems that the decision to depose Childeric III and raise Pippin to the throne was made by the Franks, carried through by the bishops who anointed him king, and endorsed, rather than enabled, by the papacy. Anointing by the bishops (Boniface may or may not have been present) was a new practice amongst the Franks. It suggested the religious function of the king, an aspect of royalty which henceforth would be progressively emphasised. Contemporary commentators such as the author of the *Prior Metz Annals*, though they did not ignore this side of things, chiefly highlighted the glaring difference in power between Merovingian king and Carolingian mayor, and their immediate concern was with the problem of the annual spring assemblies, occasions which traditionally saw a ritual expression of obedience from subjects to king and which were at the heart of Frankish custom. It was necessary to argue that people had for some time made what was only a show of obedience to the Merovingians, and that in reality they had already been obeying the Carolingians. Passages in the *Prior Metz Annals* and in Einhard's *Life of Charlemagne*, both works of the ninth century, advance this argument, but it is interesting to see it laid out in strikingly similar terms in a Byzantine source, the *Chronicle of Theophanes*.[28] This may suggest that the argument was what we might term an 'official line' formulated at the time of Pippin III's coronation and taken to Byzantium by a Frankish embassy in about 757.

---

[27] Noble (1984), pp. 62–73 is useful for the Franco-papal background to the events of 751. See also McKitterick, p. 76 above.

[28] *Annales Mettenses Priores*, p. 14; Einhard, *Vita Karoli* i, ch. 1; *Chronicle of Theophanes s.a.* 6216, trans. Turtledove (1982), pp. 94–5.

FRANKISH GAUL TO 814

After 751 Pippin III's behaviour did not change much: he continued making war each year. His enemies were the Saxons and the Aquitainians, and, after 754, the Lombards. In 753 Pope Stephen II had crossed the Alps and wintered amongst the Franks whilst lobbying them to come to the aid of the papacy against the Lombards. At their annual assembly of 754 the Franks agreed, apparently reluctantly, to campaign in Italy should the Lombard leader Aistulf refuse to withdraw from papal territory. Later that year Stephen anointed Pippin's family and stated publicly that in future the kings of the Franks should be chosen from that family alone. This gesture was not simply the *quid pro quo* for Carolingian help in Italy. It involved ties of spiritual compaternity between the 'family' of St Peter and that of Pippin, forming an alliance which was not only pragmatic but also eternal. Henceforth the Franks would (in theory) always fight to protect papal interests, and prayers for the welfare of the Carolingian family would be incorporated into the Roman liturgy. In 755 and 756 the Franks mounted what were in effect two fairly low-key campaigns against Aistulf, punishing and warning him rather than trying to conquer Lombard territory. From their very arrival in Italy in the late sixth century, the Lombards had never been able to withstand determined pressure from their much more numerous and powerful northern neighbour. Once the Franks had put their military power at the disposal of the papacy it would only be a matter of time before the Lombards would commit sufficient offence for their independence to be crushed. This eventually came about in 774.

In 753 and in 758 Pippin fought against the Saxons, continuing the 'tit-for-tat' campaigning which had been going on since the Saxons had begun encroaching upon Frankish territory around the lower Lippe and in northern Hesse at the end of the seventh century. Whilst it was possible for the Franks to raid deep in almost any part of Saxony from many points along a frontier which ran for about 400 km between the rivers Saale and Rhine, conquest was beyond them at this stage. This was partly due to the decentralised structure of Saxon society. Unlike Bavaria or Alemannia or even Frisia, in Saxony there was no paramount chief to deal with, and even the mass of warriors did not seem to be bound by any agreement made by their overlords. The difficulty also lay in terrain, for in Saxony there were no Roman roads, and communication was along river courses which were strongly defended. The Saxons were also pagans and, at least amongst the non-noble elements in society, fiercely resistant to the penetration of the Frankish religion. As we shall see, when the conquest of Saxony was eventually undertaken, it took a generation to succeed and was secured only by genocide and mass deportations. Nor could it be attempted until Aquitainian independence had been crushed.

Until the late seventh century Aquitaine had been an integral part of Frankish Gaul. Since then it had been ruled by three generations of independent dukes, but retained a political structure based on counts, counties, fiscal properties, and of course the church. Reducing Aquitainian independence meant getting the church there to accept reform and forcing the counts to pledge loyalty to Pippin rather than to the descendants of Eudo who were the dukes. Into the 760s Eudo's family still commanded enough support to marshal a formidable military force capable of raiding deep into Burgundy, and the fortifications of the towns of Aquitaine, Roman in origin, remained effective, in addition to which there were numerous 'castella' or forts at strategic points throughout the region. A further military resource was the availability of Basque troops from the lands beyond the river Garonne. Aquitaine was therefore hard to conquer: it took nearly a decade of campaigning, from 759 to 768, to subdue the duchy. The post-conquest settlement in Aquitaine meant literally going back to old ways, that is, it involved recovering royal property, securing the loyalty of counts and bishops, reinstituting ecclesiastical immunities, and installing Frankish garrisons. Pippin, however, died in 768, soon after his hard-won conquest. His two sons Charles and Carloman had already been designated kings and anointed by Pope Stephen fourteen years earlier, and Pippin was careful to secure an agreed division of the kingdom between them (Map 6). This time there would be no Carolingian succession crisis.

Under the leadership of Pippin III, the first Carolingian king, Francia was more powerful than it had ever been. Though its boundaries did not stretch much beyond those established in the sixth century, Pippin exercised far stronger control over its outlying areas than had Clovis and his descendants. In particular, Hesse, Thuringia, Alemannia and Bavaria now had a diocesan structure to match that west of the Rhine. Only Bavaria retained a native leader, and he, Tassilo, had in 757 undergone what was, according to Frankish sources, a humiliating ritual submission to Pippin. Of the German lands only Saxony remained independent, although Frisia, said to have been conquered by Charles Martel, also remained largely untouched by Frankish influence because its marshy terrain made it impenetrable. In fact it was in Frisia that Boniface was killed in 754, having returned at the end of his career to the northern part of Frisia, still largely pagan. In the south of Frankish Gaul, the old Visigothic province of Septimania had been added to Frankish territory and, as we have seen, the Franks were able to intervene in Italy at will.

The basis of Frankish power had actually changed little since the sixth

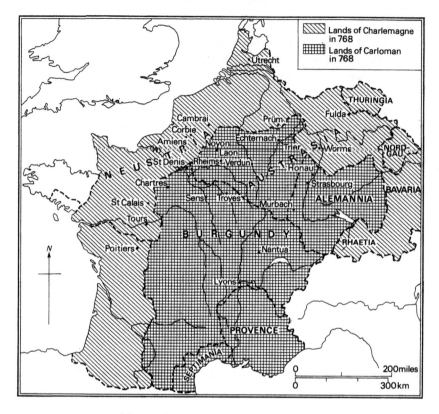

Map 6 The Frankish kingdoms, 751–68

century. That power rested ultimately on the fact that Francia was formed
out of a massive conglomeration of territories and confederation of peoples
which no other west European grouping could match. In Francia there was
never any shortage of warriors, even at times of apparent weakness. The
incessant fighting of the first half of the eighth century seems to have
strengthened the military element in society and, from the middle of the
century onwards, rulers spoke of dedicating resources to the military in a
way they had never done before. What gave Francia a cutting edge against
its unfortunate neighbours was the assertion of central control over military
organisation, for this diverted martial energies away from internal conflict
towards profitable aggression on its borders. As in the military sphere, in
other areas too the Carolingian rulers of the middle of the eighth century
rebuilt the effective power of government through the palace. It was at this
level that there had been disruption in the first half of the century, but
government had continued in traditional form at local level in the hands of

counts and bishops. Rebuilding the power of the palace meant reasserting influence over such people. Yet though it is fair to describe the structure of Carolingian government as basically unchanged, it is also true that from this time onwards there is evidence of an upsurge in activity at all levels. Quite simply, the amount of written evidence (and evidence of writing), increases rapidly from the 740s onwards. There are more charters, there are more books, there are more legislative texts, government orders and the copying of old laws.[29] In the ecclesiastical sphere too reform spread beyond the desire for clerical discipline into a review of the liturgy and into a consideration of the moral welfare of the world at large.[30] Military power, government activity and church reform all became points of marked growth in the Frankish polity once civil war died out and consensus and the co-ordination of resources returned. The leader to benefit from this development, and the one with the logistic genius to make the very most of it, was Pippin III's son Charles, or Charlemagne.

Charlemagne reigned for forty-six years, for the first three of which he ruled jointly, and unhappily it seems, with his brother Carloman until the latter's death in 771. Even a glance at the various 'annals' and 'capitularies', that is, at the narrative and normative sources for this long reign, indicates just how much it was packed with military activity and with reform of the church and of government.[31] Here there is not the space to discuss these matters in any detail; it will be possible only to make a few illustrative points. Charlemagne began his career as king by finishing off Pippin's pacification of Aquitaine. It is a measure of his success that after one season's campaigning he returned only once more to the region, in 778 when he was *en route* for Spain. Western Gaul north of the Loire, the old Merovingian stamping-ground of Neustria, also saw him rarely; he went there only once in the last thirty years of his reign. Generally his favoured residences were in the eastern part of Francia which contained the frontier zones in which there was most military activity. Roughly speaking, his itineraries were determined by military priorities. These, as Einhard stressed, lay above all in Saxony, where a campaign of pacification lasted a whole generation.[32] Richer pickings were more easily to be had in Italy, where in 774 Charlemagne responded in force to a request from Pope Hadrian I for help against the Lombards. Desiderius the Lombard king, Charlemagne's one-time ally and father-in-law, was soundly defeated and Charlemagne made

---

[29] McKitterick (1989), pp. 23–32; Nelson (1990), pp. 261–2 for recent emphasis on the increased use of writing from the mid-eighth century onwards.

[30] See Reynolds, chapter 21 below, and McKitterick (1977).

[31] See Nelson, chapter 15 and de Jong, chapter 23 below.

[32] Einhard, *Vita Karoli* II, ch. 7.

himself king of the Lombards. After a second campaign to put down a rebellion two years later, Frankish counts began to be appointed in Italy and the region became an increasingly rich source of patronage with which to reward clients of the Carolingians. Manuscripts and holy relics from Italy also began to travel northwards into Francia. The conquest moreover drew the Franks further into papal politics and brought them into direct contact, and conflict, with the Byzantine empire. Throughout this period the horizons of the Franks were being lifted, for expansion required them to seek out new allies amongst their enemies' neighbours. In this way contact was established with the ʿAbbasid caliphate in Baghdad and alliances were made with the Slavs who lived beyond the Saxons.

Conflict with the Saxons had become all-out war by 772 when Charlemagne sacked Irminsul, their most important religious centre, which probably lay near the source of the river Lippe. The Saxons took revenge by ravaging in Hesse whilst the Frankish army was away in Italy in 774. It would happen repeatedly that whilst the main Frankish force was off on campaign there would be rebellion or invasion in some other distant part of the kingdom. Each time Charlemagne would have to move very quickly over great distances to tackle the problem. In 778, for example, he had to rush back from Spain to stem a Saxon invasion of the Rhineland. This rather dramatic behaviour shows how, despite the steadily increasing range of military activity, the main force of the Frankish army retained its traditional form as the king's own following which he led in person, just as Clovis had led the forces of invading Franks nearly three centuries earlier. In this respect, the size of the empire was the measure of the king's energy. What we see in Charlemagne is a leader with phenomenal energy and with the ability to mobilise all the resources available to him in this already regicentric political culture. In contemporary terms this meant insisting on loyalty at all levels in society, for loyalty meant agreement to carry out orders without which government was inconceivable. On the one hand there was a barrage of legislation demanding loyalty and good behaviour in increasingly sophisticated ideological and theological terms; on the other hand Charlemagne inculcated loyalty amongst his magnate supporters by leading them on successful military campaigns, thereby reinforcing the group solidarity always inherent in customary aularian conviviality. Rivalry between magnates tended to be expressed through competition for royal favour and this made them eager to fight for the king. An incident in the Saxon wars, reported in the Annals, illustrates the point: in 782 there was a military disaster for the Franks in the Süntel hills as an assorted group of young nobles made an uncoordinated charge into battle against a well-organised Saxon force. Wanting too badly to claim glory for themselves, and unwilling to let a cousin of the king have the credit for victory, they raced each other towards the enemy and were cut down.[33] The sequel to this affair was that Charlemagne showed the worth of his fallen men in a terrible act of revenge, decapitating over 4000 Saxon prisoners in a single day.

Despite, or perhaps because of, this bloody episode Saxon resistance continued. Pacification was temporarily achieved with the surrender of the Saxon leader Widukind in 785. Thereafter Saxons attended the annual assemblies and fought on behalf of the Franks against other peoples, but in 792 they took advantage of a revolt by Charlemagne's son Pippin the Hunchback and of the discord within Francia which followed, and rebelled. Fear of war with the Avars fuelled political uncertainty. In 793 Frisians and Slavs joined in the revolt and the Arabs from Spain also saw an opportunity to invade. In this period of political and military crisis it is important to note the response of the regime. First Charlemagne ended the discord by putting down Pippin the Hunchback's revolt with some force, executing many of those judged to have sworn themselves into a conspiracy against him. This capital punishment reminds us that a regime based on consensus could still punish harshly, as long as the majority of the magnates could be persuaded to agree to such action. Significantly, judgement against the conspirators of 792 was made before a full assembly of magnates, and those who had stayed loyal were richly rewarded. The military response in 793 underlines both Charlemagne's genius for logistic planning, and the ability of the regime to mobilise very large amounts of labour. One instance of this is that the Franks tried to link the rivers Rednitz and Altmühl, and ultimately through them the Danube and Main, via a canal of about 3 km length. Had it succeeded, the link would have enabled the regime to deal much more easily with a war on two fronts, against both the Saxons and the Avars. In the event, the Avar threat never materialised: just as well, for the canal project failed (in fact the same project defeated Napoleon, and it is only recently, and with the aid of modern technology, that a link between the two rivers has been successfully constructed). A further response to the crisis, preceding military action against the Saxons, was the holding of a church council, the Synod of Frankfurt, at Easter 794. Here the regime reaffirmed its orthodoxy and in effect restated its commitment to Christian government.[34] Though the legislation produced from this (and other) meetings is to our eyes bafflingly jumbled and full of formulae and copying from earlier 'capitularies' (that is, royal orders and edicts organised under chapter headings – 'capitula'), it does seem to indicate the regime's sense of priorities at a time of crisis. It also shows how deeply the church had been drawn into govern-

---

33 *Revised Annals of the Kingdom of the Franks s.a.* 782, *MGH Cap.* I, no. 28, trans. King (1987), pp. 116–17.   34 *MGH Cap.* I, no. 28, trans. King (1987), pp. 224–30.

ment. Finally, after the Synod of Frankfurt, Charlemagne invaded Saxony. After campaigns in two successive years resistance amongst the South Saxons came to an end. The fighting then moved on to the lower Weser and lower Elbe regions, hitherto scarcely touched by the Franks. Eventually pacification was achieved here by mass deportations and by the use of the Saxons' enemies the Abodrite Slavs who were encouraged to occupy the lands east of the Elbe. From 803–4 onwards there was no more fighting between Franks and Saxons, and incorporation of Saxony into the Frankish political and ecclesiastical order proceeded without hindrance.

The protracted Saxon wars remind us that Frankish expansion did have its setbacks, perhaps the most famous of which was the military disaster at Roncesvalles in the Pyrenees in 778. Mostly, however, aggression towards neighbours paid off handsomely as we saw in the case of Lombard Italy. In 787 Tassilo was deprived of Bavaria in an apparently bloodless campaign, but what struck contemporaries as the greatest coup of all was the destruction and plundering of the Avar kingdom or khaganate. As the dominant force in central Europe for two hundred years, the Avars had an awesome reputation, and since the early seventh century they had posed a military threat on the eastern borders of Frankish territory. Bavaria and the Italian border region of Friuli could not be secure until that threat had been eliminated. In 791, after careful preparation, Charlemagne invaded Avar territory along the Danube with a massive army of Franks, Saxons, Frisians and Bavarians. To their surprise, the Avars offered little resistance, and the armies withdrew after reaching the confluence of the rivers Rába and Danube. The expected retaliation never came, and in fact Avar power now disintegrated, first in civil war and then through the escape of other peoples subject to them, perhaps most decisively with the departure of a large group of Bulgars who migrated to join others of their race in the Balkans.[35] In 795 and 796 Frankish forces plundered the Avar 'ring', a central complex of fortifications where a treasure of fabulous proportions was stored. According to Einhard, the influx of this treasure massively increased the wealth of the Franks.[36]

The political dividend of this success was also rich. As a letter of 796 to the Anglo-Saxon King Offa suggests, items from the Avar spoil were soon sent to impress neighbours, and they apparently did so.[37] By this time Charlemagne had already begun to take on some of the style of the Roman emperors. When he commissioned a Frankish definition of orthodoxy in relation to the vexed question of the use of images in worship, or when he presided over the condemnation of the Adoptionist heresy, moreover,

[35] See Shepard, chapter 9 below.   [36] Einhard, *Vita Karoli* ii, ch. 13.
[37] *MGH Epp.* iv, no. 100, trans. King (1987), pp. 312–14.

Charlemagne put himself forward as the leader of western Christendom. He had also had a new capital residence built, the palace complex at Aachen, with its baths and architecture Roman in inspiration.[38] It is against this background that we see Charlemagne being crowned emperor by Pope Leo III on Christmas Day in 800. In view of the history of his rule in Italy since 774, and in the context of his close relations with the papacy, any explanation of Charlemagne's acquisition of a new title to match his unprecedented stature as ruler of many peoples would seem to require little historical imagination. The Lorsch annalist even provides the further justification in that there was currently no male emperor in Byzantium. However, largely because Einhard suggested that Charlemagne did not really want to be thus crowned, and since the imperial title was not mentioned in the proposal drawn up in 806 for the division of Charlemagne's realm after his death, there has been a great deal of speculation about the sequence and the meaning of the events in 800.[39] Einhard was in fact employing the age-old literary convention of humility in the great and good, when he said that Charlemagne was reluctant to be crowned. There is no doubt that in reality the king arranged for it to be done, but what has tended to confuse historians is that he then did not seem to attach anything like as much significance to the title as later rulers and commentators would do. The great reforming capitulary issued in 802 is often said to have reflected Charlemagne's awareness of his new imperial status and responsibilities, but there is actually little in this document which cannot be found in earlier legislation.[40]

As Charlemagne grew older, he became less active and his three sons became more prominent as military leaders. Further advances were made in Spain in 801 and against the Bohemian Slavs in 805–6. The Byzantines, though ousting the Franks from Dalmatia, in 812 made peace and recognised Charlemagne as western emperor. Despite these continuing successes, legislation towards the end of the reign was increasingly concerned with getting people to perform their military service. It may be that magnates with an eye to the future were less and less willing to fight for an ageing leader far from home as the spoils of war dried up. The last campaigns, against the Danes, were hardly profitable, for the Danes could raid into Saxony and mount coastal raids into Frisia. They were in addition well protected in the Jutland peninsula, the base of which they fortified in 808 by building up an earlier earthwork. Interestingly, the apparently much more

---

[38] See Nees, p. 813 below.

[39] Einhard, *Vita Karoli* III, ch. 28; the proposed division of 806 is in *MGH Cap.* I, no. 45, trans. King (1987), pp. 251–5. For a full discussion of Charlemagne's coronation, see Folz (1974).

[40] *MGH Cap.* I, no. 33, trans. King (1987), pp. 233–42, see McKitterick (1983), pp. 93–4.

primitive Danish kingdom could mobilise labour on a scale to equal that of the Franks, as could, of course, Offa's Anglo-Saxons. By 811 Charlemagne's youngest son Louis was left as sole heir, Thus the Frankish empire was not divided as envisaged in 806. Charlemagne himself crowned Louis at Aachen in 813, a ceremony in which the pope had neither a role nor a presence, and the empire passed in its entirety to Louis when Charlemagne died in 814.[41]

As we saw earlier, the work of Charlemagne's grandfather and father in destroying rivals to their power prepared the ground for the spectacular successes of the Franks in the late eighth century. Rather as in Arabia in the seventh century, the military dynamic generated by prolonged civil war was, and had to be, directed against other peoples, for the Carolingians never quite mastered the art of living at peace. The Frankish empire created by force was held together in the first instance by Charlemagne and his army, and one cannot but be impressed by the vigour with which this was done: in just over a year in 786–7, for instance, Charlemagne travelled over 3,500 km, surely a record for any pre-modern European ruler. Over and above such prodigious feats, did the growth of territory under a single authority lead to a more systematic and cerebral approach to government? Opinion on this important question is sharply divided.

The promulgation of an increasing number of capitularies or government edicts from the time of Pippin onwards has been taken to indicate the growing importance of written government. Extrapolation from the capitulary evidence allows one to build up an impressive list of Carolingian government institutions and intentions, which, if treated as innovations, certainly suggest a thorough reform of the way Francia was ruled. Two institutions in particular are often used to illustrate this notion of progress: first the *missi dominici*, who were what we might term high-powered ombudsmen directed to check up on the work of local government, and secondly the *scabini*, experts in law directed to supplement the 'amateur' worthies in local courts and so to encourage a more 'scientific' process of judgement. In this optimistic view of Carolingian government, attention is also focused on the obligations which lords placed on their men when the latter formally swore loyalty to them. Out of these institutions and obligations, and out of the religious backing given to royal authority, it is argued, arose a political structure which went some way to reconstituting the public authority of the Roman world, the culture and titles of which it also imitated.[42] In this view, though the Carolingian state clearly did not and could not reinstitute the direct taxation upon which the later Roman state had been based, it compensated for this with its ties of loyalty and religious

[41] Classen (1972) for discussion of the succession to Charlemagne; see also Nelson, p. 110 below.   [42] For an example of this optimistic assessment, see Boussard (1968), pp. 24–42.

mandate, for bound by these its officers could be persuaded to do their public duty.

There is in contrast a more pessimistic view of Carolingian government which questions how far the good intentions expressed in the capitularies were actually put into practice.[43] There are, for instance, no case records to show that the *missi dominici* really did report on the shortcomings of local government. Where there are records, of cases heard in the courts, they do not provide evidence of a reform of the judicial process, which was, as ever, basically pragmatic in the way it operated, *scabini* or no *scabini*.[44] In this view no substantial new structure of government evolved as the Carolingian power grew.[45] What sustained that growth was instead the plunder and tribute which flowed in the wake of military success. When the empire stopped expanding the lack of structure was exposed, and the magnates who had helped build it by fighting together so profitably then began to destroy it as they fought each other in lieu of outsiders to plunder.[46] This argument has much to recommend it, in that it rests on evidence of performance rather than intention. It is, however, scarcely possible to calculate the profitability of war in the early middle ages. The bulk of fighting in Charlemagne's reign was against the relatively poor and pre-monetary Saxons, and their pacification was in the nature of a long-term investment. War, moreover, was not just the preserve of the elite, for the narrative sources also tell of armies composed of different peoples participating in very large-scale campaigns far from their homelands, requiring, in fact, the kind of logistic support which the capitularies prescribed. The canal-digging exercise in 793, for example, was rather more than an aristocratic 'work-out'.

A more equivocal approach to the development of Carolingian government allows for a more subtle treatment of sources, which are often not as straightforward as they seem. Capitularies, for instance, include a wide range of documents produced in different conditions and for different purposes.[47] Some of them expressed idealistic intentions, but others did convey real government orders, and some seem to have been drawn up in response to requests from the localities. What these documents in general reflect (and the key to their highly variegated content) is the revival of intellectual and religious activity in conjunction with the growth in power of the rulers. Revival, reform and expansion went hand in hand, promoted by an elite which benefited from them. The declared aim here was to create a justly governed society which would have the collective wisdom to live in

---

43 For the 'pessimistic' view, Reuter (1985; 1990).

44 Hübner (1891) for an inventory of records of court cases.

45 See Mordek (1986), pp. 25–50.

46 A view expressed most clearly by Reuter (1990).   47 Nelson (1990), pp. 272–96.

accordance with scriptural norms and be thus ensured of divine support. As Charlemagne's mandate, *De Litteris Colendis* (*On Cultivating Letters*), and the reforming legislation of 779, 789 and 802 made clear, the ruler was seriously interested in these ideas, even if they were not put forward very systematically, coherently or practically.[48] Though it is right to seek concrete evidence for the implementation of reform, it is also true that, in theory at least, this cleansing of the Christian community strengthened the hands of the rulers at every turn.

The reform of the church was directed at the moral welfare of the subject, with the effect of widening the brief for the state's intervention in the subject's life. The reformers did not, however, make much effort to stop the king using church property as his own, or to prevent him making gifts of monasteries to his supporters. The reform of government implied tighter control over subordinates, but the idea of just rule never remotely threatened the *status quo*, nor did judicial reform interfere with the exercise of power. Education taught the understanding of commands as well as of Scripture, and the scholars gathered at the court helped glorify the ruler as well as articulate his aims. In short, a standardisation and co-ordination of religious and cultural life worked to strengthen the hegemony of the state over these areas. In 794 the Synod of Frankfurt decreed that no new saints were to be venerated, so confining the cult of saints in effect to an officially approved list. What a contrast this is with the beginning of our period when great families, like the Carolingians themselves, sought to reinforce their identities and local independence by the establishment of new cults based on institutions under their exclusive control.

In these respects Francia in 814 seemed to have changed a great deal since the death of Charlemagne's great-grandfather a century earlier (Map 4). A single authority had replaced the disintegrating confederation of the later Merovingian period, and the strands of a common Christian culture had been gathered together in a single enterprise which was theocratic in intention. Yet the basically conservative nature of that culture, and the unmoving social order it represented, meant that on balance custom outweighed innovation when it came to putting into practice any intention to reform the kingdom. In 814 as in 714, power on the ground lay in the hands of counts and bishops who preserved the social order by protecting property. Though society could not be reformed, nor basic structures of government changed, eighth-century history demonstrates again that when the Franks pulled together they could mobilise massive power, and as long

---

[48] *MGH Cap.* I, nos. 20, 22, 33, trans. King (1987), pp. 203–5, 209–20, 233–42. See also Contreni, p. 726 below.

as Carolingian government was part of the consensus which underlay that mobilisation, it too was powerful, but not permanently so. Less spectacular, though for the future perhaps of more moment, were the changes taking place on the large estates owned by the church and by the king. The inventories of church lands, which later served as the basis for accusing Charles Martel of having plundered the church, were produced as part of a developing process of estate management which stretched back into the seventh century, but which was much stimulated by the increasing use of written records from the mid-eighth century onwards.[49] As Charlemagne's orders for his own estates demonstrate, efforts were made to maximise production to provide greater landed revenue.[50] An increase in production would slowly help to revive the depressed economy of early medieval Europe, and a greater landed revenue would help fill the gap when warfare became less profitable for the Carolingians. It would also provide local lords with more of what they needed without necessarily participating in politics at palace level. Who would benefit most from this turn in the evolution of the political economy becomes one of the most important questions of subsequent European history.

[49] See Verhulst, pp. 490–1 below.
[50] *MGH Cap.* i, no. 32, trans. Loyn and Percival (1975), pp. 65–73.

CHAPTER 4

THE FRANKISH KINGDOMS, 814–898: THE WEST

Janet L. Nelson

THE problem of the succession was always paramount and often painful for an ageing medieval ruler.[1] Charlemagne wept over the deaths of his two elder sons.[2] By 813 he had only one legitimate son left: Louis, king of Aquitaine since 781. Charlemagne summoned Louis north to a large assembly at Aachen, and 'asked everyone, from the greatest to the least, if it pleased them that he should hand over his imperial dignity to his son Louis, and they all replied enthusiastically that it was God's choice.' The following Sunday in the chapel at Aachen Charlemagne gave his son some fatherly precepts:

Love God; govern and defend God's churches from wicked men; be merciful to your sisters, and to your younger brothers, and to your nephews and nieces and all your relatives; appoint loyal and Godfearing servants who will not take bribes; do not throw anyone out of his *honor* without good grounds for the decision.[3]

Was Louis willing to follow these precepts? Yes. Then, and only then, did Charlemagne tell his son to take the crown from the altar and place it on his own head 'as a reminder of all that his father had commanded'.

Charlemagne foresaw three potential areas of conflict: churches would be assailed by wicked men; there would be dispute within the royal family; and *honores* might be wrongly given or unfairly withdrawn. Charlemagne himself had built his regime on the collaboration of churches well endowed from the forfeited resources of the Carolingians' rivals; he had given his sons sub-kingdoms to rule, and put the threads of patronage at court in the capable hands of his unmarried daughters; he had granted *honores* to a cadre of loyal servants, of whom the next best things to a list are the witnesses of his will in 811: six archbishops, including those of Cologne, Mainz, Rheims and Lyons; five bishops, including Theodulf of Orléans; the four abbots of

---

[1] Schieffer (1990).   [2] Einhard, *Vita Karoli*, c. 19.   [3] Thegan, c. 6, pp. 591–2.

St Martin, Tours, Lorsch, in the Rhineland, St Riquier near Amiens and St Germain-des-Prés, Paris; and fifteen counts, headed by Wala, Charlemagne's cousin.[4] On all three criteria he set his son – church patronage, family management and the distribution of high office – Charlemagne seemed to have excelled. But an old regime's solutions can pose problems for its successor.

In 814 Louis the Pious inherited an empire that was nominally a unit. The reality was a conglomeration of *regna* – regions, formerly independent kingdoms, and sub-kingdoms created for Charlemagne's sons (the same word served for whole and part) all of which had a great deal of autonomy. In the west, that is, the lands that lay westwards of the river Meuse and the Alpine massif, there were other *regna*:[5] Provence, Septimania and Burgundy,[6] which bordered the heartlands of Francia; Brittany; the western part of Francia – that is, the area between the Loire and the Charbonnière forest; and Aquitaine, where Louis had been born,[7] and had mostly lived since the age of three. Louis clearly planned to continue his father's system of familial devolution: immediately after his accession he sent his own second son Pippin, then aged fourteen, to rule Aquitaine and his eldest son Lothar to Bavaria.[8] Italy was not Louis' to bestow. It had been ruled since 781 by Charlemagne's son Pippin, who died in 810. In 813, just as he established Louis as his imperial successor, Charlemagne confirmed the succession to Italy of Pippin's son Bernard – despite the fact that the young man had been born to a concubine, not a wife.[9] Churchmen were now insisting on legitimacy as a qualification for kingship. This meant upsetting hitherto reasonable expectations. It was a recipe for trouble.

Louis firmly established his patriarchal position as head of the family and in the Frankish heartlands. Aachen would remain the *sedes regni*, where Louis usually wintered and often held assemblies. But Louis also looked further west – where so much of the later politics of the reign were to focus. In 816, and again in the 820s, Compiègne appeared on his itinerary as both residence and assembly site. Louis had a strong sense of continuity with the Frankish past, and with the Merovingians whose power base had lain in the Seine basin. In 816, he organised his own recoronation at Rheims as emperor, by Pope Stephen IV (816–17). At the same time his wife Irmengard was crowned empress: an echo of the papal consecration of the first Carolingian queen, Bertrada, in 754, and a declaration of intent to privilege Louis' own

---

[4] *Vita Karoli*, c. 33.   [5] See Map 4.   [6] Compare *s.a.* 778, p. 50, trans. King, p. 79.
[7] Astronomer, cc. 2 and 3, trans. King, pp. 167–8.
[8] ARF *s.a.* 814, p. 141, trans. King, p. 107.
[9] Thegan, c. 22, p. 596; Werner (1990), p. 34. For the name Bernard, apparently associated with illegitimate Carolingian birth, see p. 403 below.

descent line as against that of his deceased brother.[10] Louis had already grasped the levers of power and patronage at the court, sending his sisters to West Frankish convents, his kinsman Wala, tonsured, to Corbie, and Wala's brother Adalhard, erstwhile abbot of Corbie, into monastic exile at Noirmoutier on an island off the coast of Aquitaine. Nearly all Charlemagne's old guard were removed from positions of influence (Einhard was a rare exception[11]), and replaced with men from Louis' own entourage, a number of them from Aquitaine. When the archiepiscopal see of Rheims fell vacant, Louis appointed Ebbo, a former royal serf whose mother had been Louis' wet-nurse, and whom Charlemagne, spotting his intelligence, had freed and educated:[12] a striking (and resented) demonstration of imperial power in a society dominated by nobles.[13]

Perhaps Louis saw intimations of mortality – and divine intervention – when he was nearly killed by a collapsing beam as he processed through a wooden arcade at Aachen on Maundy Thursday 817.[14] Three months later, at the summer assembly, he announced new arrangements for the succession – which there is no reason to doubt were his own initiative.[15] The plan was not original: the idea of passing the whole of the Frankish heartlands, undivided, to his eldest son was a direct borrowing from the unimplemented *Divisio* which Charlemagne had drawn up in 806 (Maps 7 and 8).[16] Like that earlier document, this was a project to be fully implemented only on the father's death. Meanwhile, though, Pippin was confirmed as sub-king in Aquitaine; the youngest son Louis was assigned Bavaria.

As for Lothar, there was a significant difference between Charlemagne's succession plan and that of Louis: in 817 not only was the eldest son promised the whole of the Frankish heartlands in the fullness of time, but explicit provision was made for the continuance of an empire, after the father's death, as a fraternal coalition under the authority of the senior brother; furthermore, Lothar was immediately made co-emperor. Though these arrangements privileged all Irmengard's sons over other Carolingian kin, their most obvious implication was that Lothar, and a faction supporting him, had gained influence at court. His imperial title, especially after the papal involvement in the rituals of 816, suggested that Lothar was destined to rule in Italy. Certainly Louis' nephew Bernard, unmentioned in the 817 *Ordinatio*, feared total disinheritance.[17] He rebelled. And because

[10] Thegan, c. 17, p. 594.   [11] Walahfrid, preface to *Vita Karoli*.
[12] McKeon (1974). *Pace* Werner (1990), p. 55 n. 193, the story about Ebbo's mother, though recorded only in later sources, need not conflict with Charlemagne's promotion of Ebbo.
[13] Thegan, c. 44. See Martindale (1977), pp. 5–6, 16; Airlie (1990), pp. 200–2.
[14] *ARF (2) s.a.* 817, p. 146, trans. Scholz, p. 102; McKeon (1978).
[15] *Ordinatio Imperii*, MGH Cap. I, no. 136, pp. 270–3.   [16] Classen (1972).
[17] Werner (1990), pp. 40–2.

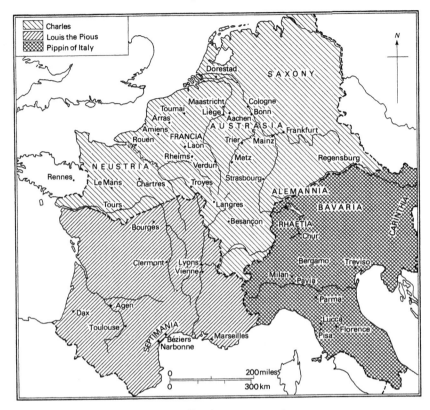

Map 7 *Divisio regnorum*, 806

aristocrats depended on kings, or would-be kings, for the securing of their interests, including *honores*, and hence conflict within the royal family always became the focus of other rivalries in the regions and at court, Bernard's rebellion, though it originated in Italy, had repercussions in Rhaetia, and – at first sight improbably – in the Loire valley.[18]

This is how it came about. Among those who had been prominent in the entourage of Charlemagne and for whom Louis' new regime had signalled an eclipse, was Bishop Theodulf of Orléans. Soon after 814, the countship of Orléans was given to Matfrid, a noble from the Rhineland and one of Louis' 'new men'. At Orléans, *ex officio*, Matfrid inevitably began to impose his *potestas* on neighbouring churches: the monasteries of St Aignan and St Benoît (Fleury), and, of course, the episcopal church of Orléans itself. Comital *potestas* meant demands for hospitality, for cash payments, for

---

[18] Noble (1974); Borgolte (1986), p. 19.

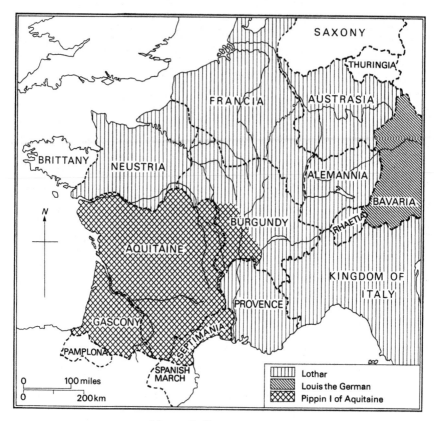

Map 8 *Ordinatio imperii*, 817

troops, for lands to distribute to the count's nominees. Theodulf of Orléans, as a courtier out of favour, and as one whose local interests were threatened by Matfrid, was accused, perhaps rightly, of supporting Bernard of Italy. He was condemned by a secular, not an ecclesiastical court, and flung into a monastic prison where he died soon after (rumour said, poisoned by those who had benefited from his absence to plunder his goods). In Theodulf's fate, we can see how Charlemagne's three strands of government – ecclesiastical patronage, royal family-management and distribution of secular offices – were enmeshed in practice.[19]

Bernard still hoped to negotiate terms with his uncle; he travelled north to meet him at Chalon. Louis had him seized, taken to Aachen, tried, condemned and blinded. Bernard died two days later. His supporters in Italy

[19] Compare Dahlhaus-Berg (1975), pp. 16–21.

and elsewhere were harshly punished – the lay leaders blinded, the clerics (like Theodulf) deposed and imprisoned. All lost their *honores* and lands.[20] To ensure there would be no more claimants to *regna* from rival descent lines of Charlemagne's offspring, Louis had his young illegitimate half-brothers Drogo and Hugh tonsured and sent to monasteries:[21] Luxeuil and Charroux – both in the western part of Louis' empire, where royal control of *honores* was firmest and where Lothar's mother Irmengard, daughter of a western Frankish magnate, probably had inherited influence.[22] Lothar and his mother, along with aristocrats in their circle, were now in the ascendant at court.

Irmengard died a few months after Bernard's execution (there were those who saw divine vengeance there[23]); and when Louis sought a new bride, he looked not west but east. Judith's family connections lay in Bavaria, Alemannia and Saxony, and Louis certainly hoped to exploit them to meet Slav attacks on the frontier, and strengthen his political hand east of the Rhine.[24] This second marriage inevitably challenged the positions of Louis' sons by his first wife, and especially Lothar, who now wanted for his own, at once, the *regnum* assigned in the past two generations to the eldest son of the ruling Carolingian: Neustria and the Loire valley, where royal estates lay thick on the ground, and the ground was fertile. Visitors admiring today the châteaux of that region glimpse something of what made it a magnet for rulers of the Franks and later the French. There were further royal assets here in the ninth century: well-endowed monasteries, and countships with *potestas*. Not least of those countships was Tours: Charlemagne had bestowed it on Hugh, a noble whose ancestors hailed from Alsace. Hugh's career prospered. When in 821, at the age of twenty-eight, Lothar sought marriage, signifying an independent household (as well as a *regnum*) of his own, the obvious choice was Hugh's daughter Ermengard.[25]

The following year, Louis organised a grand family reconciliation: there was an amnesty for the rebels of 818; Wala and Adalard were restored to favour;[26] Louis' half-brothers were soon to be given ecclesiastical *honores*. Drogo, now in his early twenties, received the bishopric of Metz and the slightly younger Hugh the abbacy of St Quentin; even Louis' half-sister Bertha reappeared at court.[27] At the summer assembly of Attigny in August 822, Louis staged a collective ritual of repentance and renewal, with himself

---

[20] Astronomer, c. 30, p. 623. Compare Werner (1990), p. 46.   [21] Nithard 1, 2.

[22] Werner (1965a), p. 119; (1990), p. 49. For queens' political influence in general, see pp. 401–2 below.

[23] Houben (1976), pp. 31–42. Irmengard's critics, significantly, were in Alemannia.

[24] Ward (1990a).   [25] Vollmer (1957), pp. 163–5.

[26] *ARF* (2) *s.a.* 822, p. 158, trans. Scholz, p. 111.   [27] Werner (1967), p. 444.

as a new Theodosius at the centre of it.[28] Immediately after Attigny, Louis 'sent Lothar to Italy' to claim it as ruler. He also arranged the marriage of Pippin of Aquitaine to the daughter of a Frankish magnate, and despatched the newly-weds back 'to the west'.[29]

It was in the west, in the largest sense, that Louis, though he resided in the 820s most frequently in the lands between Meuse and Rhine,[30] repeatedly showed his concern to remain in overall control: in western Francia, where in 829 he summoned an assembly to Paris to elaborate a great programme of reform; in Neustria, where he gave his archchancellor Theoto the abbacy of St Martin, Tours; in Brittany where he personally led a successful campaign in 824; in Aquitaine, where as former ruler he could still pull strings and still, despite his son Pippin's kingship there, intervene to banish the poet Ermold from Pippin's entourage;[31] on the Spanish March, where he had won his spurs as a youth, and which could lure him still further west. In 826 an outbreak of rebellion against the Muslim regime in Córdoba inspired Louis to write to the people of Mérida encouraging them to rebel and promising to co-ordinate with them the move westwards of a Frankish army.[32] Only hindsight persuades us to dismiss this as fantasy: in the 820s, Córdoba's star seemed to wane, while Louis' waxed. And only hindsight makes us see the Pyrenees as a barrier between discrete political units. Contemporary perceptions of real prospects for Frankish expansion, plunder and tribute here help to explain the bitterness of Louis' disappointment when in 827 a Frankish army led by Counts Hugh and Matfrid, with orders to collaborate with Pippin of Aquitaine and Count Bernard of Barcelona against the 'Saracens', arrived 'too late, owing to the negligence of its leaders'.[33] Hugh (thereafter nicknamed 'the fearful') and Matfrid lost their Neustrian *honores* because of this failure. They also lost their positions of influence at court. Their chief supplanters were Bernard, who became chamberlain (that is, in charge of the imperial treasure) in 828, and Bernard's kinsman Odo, the new count of Orléans.

Thus the roots of the crisis of Louis' reign lay in the west: where Louis himself had most to give and most to lose; where the interests of Louis and his sons most clearly collided – Lothar hankering after Neustria, Pippin resentful of his father's interference in Aquitaine; where rivalries between

---

[28] Werner (1990), p. 58. Compare de Jong (1992).

[29] *ARF (2) s.a.* 822, p. 159, trans. Scholz, p. 111.

[30] It was perhaps there, at the Aachen assembly of August 825, that Louis issued his great *Ordinatio*: Guillot (1990), p. 461; see further, p. 426 below.

[31] Ermold, *In Honorem* IV, ll. 2628–49, ed. Faral, p. 200, *Epistola* II, ll. 201–4, p. 232; see Godman (1987), pp. 106–11.   [32] *MGH Epp.* v, 1, pp. 115–16.

[33] *ARF (2) s.a.* 827, p. 173 (*ducum desidia*), trans. p. 121. Cf. Thegan, c. 28, p. 597.

Carolingians would coincide with the fissures of factional conflict between magnates; and where in 830 Hugh and Matfrid sought revenge through rebellion against Louis. Hugh and Matfrid began the revolt, and then – because only a Carolingian leader could make rebellion viable – called in Pippin, angered and shamed by his father's intervention in the government of Aquitaine.[34] Lothar's involvement was only slightly less predictable. The Empress Judith had given birth in 823 to a boy-child, Charles – the future Charles the Bald; the baby's parents had foreseen and tried to forestall trouble by enrolling Lothar as Charles' godfather and special protector.[35] In creating a *regnum* for Charles in 829, Louis had offended Lothar, granting not only Alemannia but Alsace and Chur and part of Burgundy – lands Lothar expected and which formed a strategic corridor between Francia and Italy.[36] Most of all, Lothar, who had been 'sent to Italy', resented his exclusion from Francia, and from his father's court where Judith and Bernard were in the ascendant – and their rivals responded with rumours of adultery and witchcraft.[37]

The rebels' vengeance was sharp: they blinded Bernard's brother (Bernard himself escaped), and imprisoned Judith in an Aquitainian convent, her two brothers in Aquitainian monasteries.[38] But when Louis stood firm, and when his son Louis of Bavaria stood by him, the rebels were reconciled. Bernard lost his court office, and never regained Louis' confidence. It turned out, however, that 830 had been only a dress rehearsal. Pippin's reconciliation was unreal. He insulted his father in 831 by failing to attend an assembly when summoned; at Christmas-time when he appeared at Aachen his father withheld the usual rituals of welcome, and Pippin stormed back to Aquitaine where he found a natural supporter in Bernard.[39] Louis deprived Pippin of his realm of Aquitaine and gave it instead to Charles. There, Louis hoped he could count on long-standing personal loyalties.

Unfortunately for Louis, Pippin and his brothers joined forces, and outbid him in Francia: at a place in Alsace which soon became known as the Field of Lies, Louis was deserted by enough supporters to make resistance impossible. Lothar had brought Pope Gregory IV from Italy to stiffen fainthearts.[40] He now deposed his father from his imperial office in an episcopally staged ritual (with Archbishop Ebbo of Rheims playing the leading role), and assumed sole power himself. Louis, held in rough conditions at Aachen, showed true grit, refusing to accept monastic retirement. Soon many people had second thoughts. The crucial defection from the rebel alliance was Pippin's. An Aquitainian army advanced

---

[34] *AB (3) s.a.* 830, p. 21.   [35] Nithard, I, 3; II, 1.
[36] *AX s.a.* 829, p. 7. Compare Boshof (1990), p. 183. See Map 8.   [37] Astronomer, c. 44.
[38] *AB (3) s.a.* 830, p. 22.   [39] Astronomer, c. 47.   [40] Fried (1990), pp. 266–70.

northwards to release Louis. Lothar, moving west to confront them, realised he was outmanœuvred. He left Louis to be reinstated by 'faithful' bishops at St Denis, and withdrew to the Rhône valley, where his supporters held firm. So far, inter-Carolingian conflict had consisted of ritual confrontations. It now became a war – and a war focused in the west: when Lothar took Chalon from Louis' men, he killed three counts, and had Bernard's sister drowned in the Saône as a witch. Bloodier still was the battle for control of the Loire valley, where Hugh and Matfrid clung to their *honores*: Louis' army was routed, and several counts, including Odo of Orléans and Louis' chancellor, Theoto abbot of St Martin, Tours, were all killed.[41] Nevertheless Louis recovered control in the end. This was the scene at Blois in September 834:

The emperor sat in his pavilion which was set up on a hill where the whole army could see him, and his faithful sons [Pippin and Louis] stood beside him. Lothar came and fell at his father's feet. His father-in-law Hugh the Fearful followed him, then Matfrid and the other ringleaders in crime. They all confessed their great wrongdoings.[42]

Lothar was sent back to Italy, Hugh and Matfrid along with him. Ebbo was deposed from office. In the Loire valley region, *honores* were redistributed to men handpicked by Louis. The local Franks, who apparently resented Louis' use of armies of *transrhenani* (men from across the Rhine) to defeat his opponents in this region,[43] may well have resented the appointment of the transrhenan Richwin as count of Nantes. Another 'outsider', in the traditional Carolingian mould, was Adalhard, from Middle Francia, who now became lay abbot of St Martin, Tours, and perhaps count of Tours as well.[44] But after (as before) 834 Louis also used local men as well: Rainald was count of Herbauge in northern Aquitaine, Rorigo remained a key figure in Maine, and the Breton Nominoë was formally recognised as imperial *missus* in Brittany.[45] Bishops, as ever, played a key role in stabilising political authority: Aldric of Le Mans and Jonas of Orléans were mainstays of Louis' regional control.[46]

The impulse to assert that control came from Louis' determination to settle the succession question securely, and to provide Charles with a substantial *regnum*. In 837, Louis granted him Frisia and the lands of the Meuse valley and the Seine basin, then in 838 Neustria between Seine and Loire; and when Pippin died in December 838, his sons were disinherited by their grandfather, and Aquitaine assigned to Charles. Technically, it was Louis' right to do this, but many thought it unfair and some nobles in

---

[41] *AB (3) s.a.* 834, p. 30; Nithard, I, 4.   [42] Thegan, c. 55.   [43] Adrevald, c. 27.
[44] Nelson (1990), p. 153.   [45] Smith (1992).   [46] Compare Kaiser (1981).

Aquitaine acknowledged Pippin's son and namesake as their king (there was no argument over his legitimacy). The last year or so of Louis' reign was spent trying to enforce his decision against Pippin II; and when Louis was deflected to the Rhineland to quell another rebellion by his namesake, Louis the German, Charles, helped by his mother Judith, took up the struggle on his own behalf. His forces had made a good deal of headway – though Pippin II remained at large – when on 26 June 840 came news of the emperor's death.

How far had Louis' regime, and in the longer run Frankish monarchy in general, been weakened by the events of 833? Louis' deposition was widely noticed by ecclesiastical chroniclers throughout the empire; and the absence of any capitularies for the years 834–40 has been taken to show loss of imperial authority.[47] On the other hand Louis' prestige remained high in the eyes of neighbours and foreigners (Slavs, Danes, Byzantines); and numismatic evidence shows that he recovered control of minting throughout the empire, and that coinage high in quality and quantity was produced in the latter years of the reign, as earlier.[48] If the upheavals of 833–4 had attracted the attentions of Northmen, hence the annual raids on Dorestad in 834–7, Louis met the challenge reactively, with improved defences, and proactively, by making allies among the Danes. Louis scored well on his father's three criteria. He protested vigorously against spoliations of church property in (characteristically) his sons' *regna* of Italy and in Aquitaine. He distributed *honores* skilfully, withholding from former rebels, and granting to men he could trust, often his own kinsmen. He imposed his will in the key area of family politics: disinheriting his grandsons in Charles' favour; ruthlessly suppressing Louis the German when he rebelled in response to his father's increased pressure on East Frankish resources (a shift eastwards necessitated by Charles' promotion in the West); and, most vital of all, keeping Lothar in Italy, except when summoned north in 839 to agree a prospective two-way division of the entire empire (except for Bavaria) with Charles. The West, where the conflicts of 833–4 had been fiercest fought, was where Louis intended Charles to have his inheritance: by the terms of 839 Charles was to get, on his father's death, the heartlands westwards from the Meuse valley, plus Neustria and Aquitaine (including Septimania), Burgundy and Provence.

'The best-laid schemes of mice – and men – gang aft agley.' Louis' death abruptly reopened the whole question of the empire's future. Lothar, throwing aside the 839 agreement, came north to reassert his claims to the whole of the Frankish heartlands, on the 817 model.[49] To offset the

---

[47] Forcefully restating this view: Depreux (1992). For an alternative view, see Nelson (1990).
[48] Coupland (1990).   [49] *AB (3) s.a.* 840, p. 36: Lothar breaks the *iura naturae*.

inevitable hostility of his two brothers, Louis the German and Charles, he
sought an ally: Pippin II. Thus on 25 June 841, at Fontenoy in Burgundy,
Carolingian rivals were pitted two against two. Even after Charles and
Louis won the battle, peace was a long time coming. Like all civil conflicts,
this one exposed especially clearly, and cruelly, the latent internal strains of
the society it tore apart. Contemporaries struggled to make sense of painful
experiences. It is not coincidental that the years 840–3 are the best
documented of any in the early middle ages.[50] Nithard, a participant-
observer and himself an illegitimate Carolingian, wrote the fullest record.
He had joined Charles' camp in 840 – and probably stayed there because
Lothar promptly took away his *honores*.[51] Despite this personal stake and a
personal military role, Nithard says much less about the battle than about
efforts to avert it, and about post-bellum reconciliation. Only after Charles
and Louis the German had sworn to remain united against Lothar, and their
men had sworn to hold them to it – these were the famous Strasbourg Oaths
of February 842 – did Lothar open negotiations. Nithard exposes the
mechanics of Carolingian diplomacy: the choosing of teams of noble
negotiators by each king, and the play of two intersecting factors affecting
kings and nobles alike: affinity, that is, ties and obligations of kinship and
clientship, and congruence, that is, a sense of what was fair and fitting.[52]
Nithard saw himself as a good example of the way affinity and congruence
should have worked. He had attached his fortunes to Adalhard, the dominant
figure in Charles' entourage, and at Fontenoy Nithard (as he himself
stresses) had given crucial help to Adalhard.[53] In December 842 Charles
chose as his bride Ermentrude, Adalhard's niece: Charles married her,
according to Nithard, so that Adalhard could bring over the 'majority of the
plebs'.[54] Nithard is identifying here, as in his account of the Strasbourg
Oaths, a distinct class of lesser aristocrats dependent on, but also themselves
making claims on, magnates. Nithard too, though himself of Charles' inner
circle and Charles' cousin, still depended on Adalhard, and by this time was
thoroughly disenchanted, since Adalhard, as Charles' envoy in June 842,
had negotiated away to Lothar the area west of the Meuse where, it seems,
Nithard's *honores* lay. Nithard's portrayal rings true: when kings fought, self-
interested aristocrats were seldom certain of how to pursue their interests
successfully; sometimes treacherous, they believed that noble conduct
meant loyalty unto death; violent but vulnerable, in the end they anxiously
prodded their lords towards a peace settlement. They got there after a year's
diplomacy – and many months' laborious assessing by noble *missi* of royal
resources – for it was from those (as Lothar frankly put it) that kings got 'the

---

[50] Nelson (1993).   [51] Nelson (1986), pp. 222–3.   [52] Nithard IV. 1.
[53] Nithard II. 10.   [54] Nithard IV. 6.

wherewithal to reward the men who followed them loyally'.[55] In July 843, the Treaty of Verdun was agreed between Lothar, Louis and Charles (Map 9): it was a trade-off between the competing interests of those Carolingians and also of their men.[56]

Despite the timelag, Fontenoy decisively affected Verdun: the unitary 'imperial' model of 817, which had favoured Lothar, was abandoned, and the Frankish heartlands were divided three ways with Louis and Charles getting shares alongside Lothar, and Pippin II excluded altogether. In the short run, however, Verdun itself seemed far from decisive. On the one hand, there was a continuing quest for imperial unity. Lothar tried to make good his rights as family head and as protector of an empire-wide church and, after his death in 855, first his son Louis II, then other Carolingians, aspired to maintain that imperial tradition. On the other hand, the three-way split of 843 gave way to further divisions and mergers. The Middle Kingdom was itself split three ways between Lothar's three sons, then that part of it which lay north of the Alps was redivided in 869 into two parts which were absorbed into the kingdoms of Louis and Charles respectively. These changes produced a series of ephemeral maps of the Carolingian *regna* from 843 to 879, with further redivisions down to 888 (Maps 10 and 11).

How was the frontier of the Western kingdom drawn at Verdun? The details of the boundary line between the kingdoms of Charles and Lothar, with its abrupt shifts of direction, can sometimes be attributed to particular magnates' interests: for instance it was probably personal choice and personal loyalty that kept Abbot Hugh's St Quentin and Warin's county of Chalon in Charles' kingdom rather than Lothar's.[57] The prime interest of the kings themselves was in the Frankish heartlands. Even though Lothar kept the lion's share, Charles acquired numerous royal estates there and in Burgundy, also major churches both episcopal and monastic, and important central places like markets and mints. Lothar, however, only slowly reconciled himself to their loss and continued during the later 840s to 'solicit'[58] the loyalty of aristocrats in those areas, with some success. For Charles, possibilities of plunder and tribute seemed to remain open on the Spanish March and in Brittany: the drawback was that these frontiers lay open to external aggression – as did the long coastline and river estuaries to sea-raiders. In Poitou, the silver mines at Melle had unique value; but Charles was not yet fully in control of Aquitaine.

Verdun was soon more honoured in the breach than in the observance. In Aquitaine, an unexpected defeat of Charles' troops (in his absence) in 844 gave the cause of Pippin II a new lease of life. Lothar resumed active

[55] Nithard IV. 6; cf. IV. 3.   [56] *AF (3) s.a.* 843, p. 22.   [57] Classen (1963), p. 10.
[58] Nithard's term: cf. Leyser (1994).

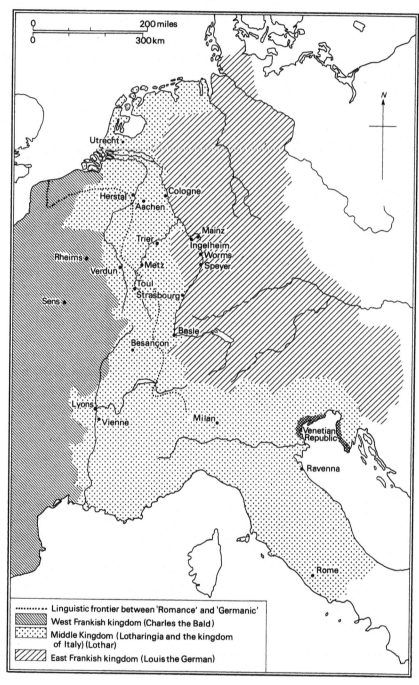

0   200 miles

0   300 km

N

Utrecht

Herstal   Cologne
Aachen

Mainz
Trier
Ingelheim
Worms
Rheims
Metz   Speyer
Verdun
Toul
Sens   Strasbourg

Basle

Besançon

Lyons
Vienne   Milan
Venetian
Republic

Ravenna

Rome

········· Linguistic frontier between 'Romance' and 'Germanic'

West Frankish kingdom (Charles the Bald)

Middle Kingdom (Lotharingia and the kingdom
of Italy) (Lothar)

East Frankish kingdom (Louis the German)

Map 9 Partition of 843 (Treaty of Verdun)

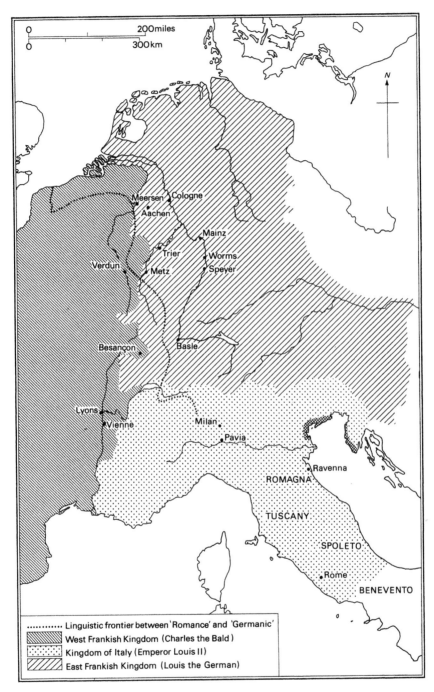

Map 10 Partition of 870 (Treaty of Meersen)

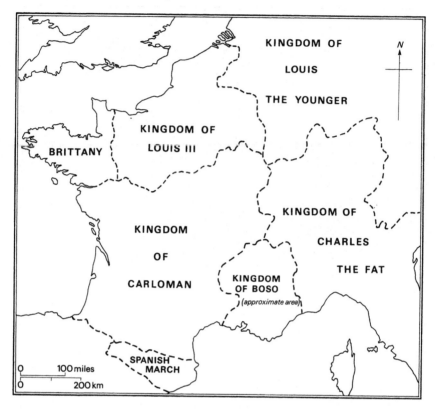

Map 11 Partition of 880

support; and so did the Bretons. Between 845 and 848 Pippin issued coins and charters in his own name as king of the Aquitainians. Charles had to work hard to eliminate him all over again – first by tonsuring,[59] then by trying to buy him off, and in the end by life-imprisonment. In the early 850s, Lothar became more conciliatory: he was anxious to arrange his own succession. Now Charles' realm was threatened from more distant Carolingian rivals; first another nephew, Louis the Younger, son of Louis the German, in 854, then Louis the German himself in 858.

Charles was already planning his own internal redivision of the realm – into *regna* for his sons: for the eldest, Louis, born 846, Neustria; for the second son, Charles, born 848/9, Aquitaine. The younger sons, significantly, Charles the Bald had tonsured, thus aiming to remove them from the pool of potential heirs. He paid them off with rich ecclesiastical *honores* –

[59] For strategies to narrow the circle of eligible candidates, see Goody (1966); and p. 402 below.

none more richly than his third son Carloman, who amassed several of the prime abbacies in Francia. New problems arose in the early 860s when the two elder sons rebelled. Each was supported by aristocrats in his own *regnum*, and the aim, apparently, was greater autonomy. Even though Charles' sons were nominally kings in their own *regna*, Charles kept them on a short rein, denying them the right to issue coins or grant charters, as the sons of Louis the Pious had done in their *regna*, and thus inhibiting their construction of aristocratic 'constituencies' of their own. Charles was in fact returning to the patriarchal style of Charlemagne. He crushed the rebellions; he humiliated his sons as Charlemagne had humiliated Pippin the Hunchback. Charles of Aquitaine died in 866. In 867 Louis, nicknamed the Stammerer,[60] was sent to Aquitaine as king with household officers chosen by Charles from his own palace.[61] By then Louis' mother had been formally consecrated queen in a ritual that explicitly requested more, and better, offspring.[62]

Now there were prospects of acquiring new *regna* through redistribution within the larger Carolingian *regnum*. Lothar's son Louis II of Italy had no son of his own. Lothar II's wife Theutberga was childless while his only son was by a woman whom many refused to acknowledge as his wife (the boy's name, Hugh, was indeed commonly chosen for Carolingian bastards). The refusers included Lothar's uncles Louis the German and Charles the Bald. Lothar used every argument to justify divorcing Theutberga and marrying Hugh's mother: in vain. He died, still undivorced, in 869, just when, coincidentally, Louis the German lay desperately ill. Charles made a grab for Lothar's kingdom: he was consecrated in September at Metz,[63] and celebrated Christmas 869 at Aachen. But Louis recovered and pressed counter-claims. In 870 Lothar's uncles divided his kingdom between them (Map 10).[64] Charles failed to hold Aachen or Metz; and even his acquisitions proved a mixed blessing, since they provoked Carloman to rebel, in pursuit of a kingdom of his own. For Charles this filial rebellion was uniquely dangerous: its location, and goal, lay in Francia, with key royal resources at stake, and the aristocrats who supported Carloman were drawn from Charles' own heartlands; further, it confirmed what Pippin II's career had already intimated, that tonsuring was not an infallible strategy for excluding surplus members of the royal family; worse still, Louis the German once more threatened to intervene. This combination of threats explains why Charles put down Carloman's rebellion with particular ferocity, and had his

---

60 Compare p. 420 below.   61 *AB (3)*, p. 138.
62 *Ordo* of 866; *MGH Cap.* ii, no. 301, pp. 453–5. *AB (3)*, pp. 133–4.
63 *AB (3)*, pp. 158–62.   64 At Meersen: *AB (3)*, pp. 168–9; *MGH Cap.* ii, no. 251, pp. 193–5.

own son blinded.[65] At the same time he retaliated by supporting Louis' sons in rebellion against their father. Carolingian family politics might have evoked from a Victorian matron the same reaction as a performance of *Antony and Cleopatra*: 'How very different from the homelife of our own dear queen!'

After 873 Charles had only one son left: Louis the Stammerer. But Charles continued to hope for more. Ermentrude had died, coincidentally, in 869, and Charles was able to choose a second bride, with what some saw as indecent haste, who could bring him the support of her kin (they included her aunt Theutberga) in Lothar's kingdom. From now on Charles hoped for further progeny – and threatened Louis the Stammerer with disinheritance. In the case of the Stammerer's own sons there was more than a threat: Charles, imitating his father's treatment of his grandsons but with a slightly different strategy, forced the Stammerer to repudiate his wife: this opened the possibility of disinheriting his sons, Charles' grandsons. At the same time Charles made his son remarry a wife of Charles' choosing – again to win the short-term political advantage of support from the bride's kin.[66] Charles was a ruthless paterfamilias. But there was no revolt from Louis, at least. Meanwhile Charles made the most of his own second wife's family as political supporters: notably his brother-in-law Boso who played a series of important roles, first in Charles' annexation of western Lotharingia in 869, when Boso used his local influence, second in Charles' acquisition of the Rhône valley and Provence in 870, where Boso was given the key position of *dux* of Vienne, and third in reconstructing the government of Aquitaine in 872, when Charles appointed Boso chamberlain to Louis the Stammerer.[67]

In 875, Louis II of Italy died. Charles had long set his sights on the imperial title, and leaving Richildis and Louis the Stammerer to guard Francia, quickly made for Italy, where he was accepted by most of the aristocracy of the Italian *regnum*, and anointed and crowned emperor at Rome by the pope on Christmas Day 875. Meanwhile Louis the German and his son Louis the Younger raided Charles' kingdom, meeting no effectual resistance. It was not really an invasion, since there was no plan to take over – only to ravage and cause maximum aristocratic dissatisfaction: but Louis' real aim was 'to make Charles leave Italy' where Louis hoped to install his own eldest son Karlmann. That hope was disappointed: Charles held on to Italy. But he did not spend long there. He arranged the marriage of Boso to Louis II's daughter, and left him as viceroy in Lombardy;[68] then he himself went back to Francia to restore his regime. In August 876 Louis the German

[65] Nelson (1988).   [66] Regino, 878, p. 114; Nelson (1992a), p. 232.
[67] See Airlie, pp. 448–9 below.
[68] Regino *s.a.* 877 (recte 876), p. 113. See *AB (3)*, pp. 189–90 nn. 3 and 5.

died, and again Charles moved fast. His aim was not to disinherit his nephews – that would have been totally unrealistic, since Louis the Younger already had solid aristocratic support in Francia and Saxony – but to acquire the lands west of the Rhine which Louis the German had acquired, against all Lothar's efforts in 843. These lands included many royal estates, the key archbishoprics of Cologne and Mainz and the sees of Worms and Speyer. Charles was thwarted: at the battle of Andernach, having failed to benefit from a planned surprise attack because the archbishop of Cologne had sent warning to Louis the Younger, Charles was heavily defeated and withdrew westwards, leaving his nephew in control of all the lands his father had held west of the Rhine before and since 870.[69] Charles lost no territory, but neither did he gain any. He lost men, and treasure and equipment; and he lost face. Aachen was beyond his reach.

Charles was nothing if not resilient. In 877 he was arranging for Compiègne to become a substitute for Aachen as his imperial palace and church.[70] He also planned a return visit to Italy to help the pope against Saracen, and Italian, enemies. At an assembly at Quierzy immediately before his departure, Charles and his faithful men agreed the conditions on which the realm would be governed in Charles' absence. Louis the Stammerer was left in charge, but he would be under the surveillance of his father's faithful men; and his rule would be temporary – terminable on Charles' return.[71] There was to be no return. In September, in Italy, when Charles waited in vain for reinforcements from Francia, he got news instead that his leading magnates – including Boso – had rebelled. It seems that their aim was to get rid of the Stammerer and to recall Charles from Italy. The rebellion, paradoxically, was for rather than against Charles' rule – but rule based firmly in Francia, not Italy. His imperial policy would have to be reconsidered. As he hastened back across the Alps he fell violently ill: he barely had time to bequeath his realm to his son, along with 'the sword known as St Peter's sword' – a clear reminder of imperial duty – before he died, on 6 October 877.[72]

SCANDINAVIANS AND OTHERS

Thus far, Carolingian family politics have predominated. They provide the context in which other themes can now be considered. The first is the impact of the Northmen.[73] Charlemagne had harboured Danish exiles, and late in

---

[69] *AB (3)*, pp. 196–7.　　[70] Tessier (1952), no. 425.
[71] *MGH Cap.* II, no. 281, pp. 355–61.　　[72] *AB (3)*, pp. 202–3.
[73] Ninth-century Frankish writers commonly use this term (never 'Vikings'). Also common is 'Danes', indicating the origin of most of the Scandinavians whom the Franks encountered.

his reign fought, and negotiated, to contain Danish expansion in the area now known as Schleswig-Holstein. In the 820s, Louis the Pious added a missionary strategy to his interventions in Danish dynastic disputes, welcoming the Danish prince Harald to Mainz and standing godfather to him at his baptism.[74] In the 830s, Louis allied with the Danish king Horik, using him to exert control over other more unruly Danes. Louis' eventual solution to the problem of defending Dorestad was to hand it over to a Danish prince named Rorik (perhaps a member of a rival branch of the Danish royal family). Meanwhile (probably in 833–4) Lothar had allied with Harald on his own account, and he exploited this alliance again in 841 against his brothers. Charles too sought a Danish ally, Ragnar, and gave him land in Flanders, which he later withdrew when Ragnar 'earned his wrath'. On one reading of the evidence, it was this Ragnar who attacked Paris in 845, and was bought off for 7000 pounds of silver, after having hanged 111 Frankish prisoners on the west bank of the Seine in a grisly display for the benefit of Charles and his men across the river.[75]

That episode is by far the nastiest reported Scandinavian atrocity on the Continent. It shows the Northmen's violent face. But the Franks needed no lessons in violence; and they understood very well what the Northmen had come for – loot and/or a warrior's wages. In the 850s Scandinavian attacks on the Loire and then the Seine became frequent: the flight of peasants soon caused disruption to normal services and local lords began to suffer. Scandinavian demands for payment were costly to both peasants and lords. Charles attempted to meet the challenge, with varied success. On the whole, the raids increased. Eventually, Charles found a twofold strategy: he targeted particular Scandinavian leaders and recruited them to his own service; and he constructed fortifications, especially on rivers.[76] By the mid-860s he had the situation on the Seine under control; and although Scandinavians remained on the Loire, they were contained in the area of Nantes. The *regnum* where their raids had been notably severe was Aquitaine; and here it was only in the 860s that Charles co-ordinated local efforts and mounted effective resistance. Churches were the main victims – as they had long been of acquisitive local aristocrats. At Bordeaux, for instance, the episcopal sequence is broken from c.860 until the late tenth century. Ecclesiastical dislocation meant that written records were no longer maintained: hence virtually nothing is known of Bordeaux after 860 until the eleventh century. It would be unsafe to infer, though, that the place was 'ruined': what can be said is that if any people prospered there, they were not

[74] Angenendt (1984), pp. 215–23; Hauck (1990), pp. 289–94.
[75] Nelson (1992a), p. 151; for Ragnar see *Vita Anskarii*, cc. 21, 36, 38, pp. 46, 71, 73. Compare Wood (1987).   [76] Coupland (1987); Gillmor (1989).

churchmen.[77] There is a little more information for Nantes, where Scandinavian raids began in earnest in 843, and where Scandinavians are more or less continuously attested throughout the ninth century. In the late 860s, the bishop sought a transfer, as the archbishop of Bordeaux had already successfully done, on the grounds that the devastation of the Northmen had made life impossible. Another Frankish prelate opposed the move however (he was, admittedly, a personal enemy of the bishop of Nantes), asserting that plenty of Christian laypeople remained at Nantes, living alongside the Northmen, and that the bishop must stay with his flock.[78] The bishop got his transfer: his move to the metropolitan see of Tours was approved by the pope, thanks to Charles' intervention.

From the king's point of view, the Scandinavians' impact was serious. It depleted the royal treasury – not least when Charles bore the brunt of Ragnar's 7000 pounds in 845 – the largest single payment of the reign. There was damage to prestige when the king seemed unable to protect his own. Charles' anguish in 845 is perfectly credible – though he redeemed, eventually, his vow to protect St Denis.[79] There were also severe problems of regional control, visible in diminishing royal interventions in Neustria (forty-six charter beneficiaries there in 840–59, only seventeen in 860–77). Yet Scandinavian activity was not unequivocally harmful to royal interests. In 859, when Danish attacks caused the peasantry between the Seine and the Loire to take up arms in self-protection, the local aristocrats (*potentiores*), fearing social disorder, slew the peasants.[80] Such attitudes tended to rally the aristocracy around the king as the unique source of legitimate force and bastion of social control. At the same time, the king wanted to harness peasant military effort in the defence against a common external enemy, and he acknowledged his own obligation to protect peasants from landlordly oppression: the Edict of Pîtres was a symptom of those converging concerns precisely in the region of the lower Seine. Then, Scandinavian demands for tribute meant that Charles was able to impose generalised taxation in town and countryside: a striking manifestation of royal authority. There was a broader impact on the economy too: it was not only cash that Northmen wanted, but Frankish food and horses and weapons, for which they were prepared to pay. The volume of transactions certainly rose in the Seine and Loire valleys especially and, as more coin was needed, debasement became widespread. In 864 Charles was able to undertake a realm-wide coinage reform, essentially a revaluation. Hoard evidence shows that it was effective, and that millions of silver coins circulated fairly rapidly within,

---

[77] For a different interpretation, see Wallace-Hadrill (1976), pp. 217–36.
[78] Hincmar, *Ep.* 31, *PL*, 126, cols. 210–30, at 221, 225, 228.   [79] Nelson (1992a), pp. 152, 219.
[80] *AB s.a.*, p. 89.

and to some extent between, regions after 864.[81] The king, of course, was by no means the only one to benefit: so did the aristocracy, but so too did peasant participants in markets.

Clearly enmeshed with Carolingian family politics is the history of the *regna* within Charles the Bald's realm. Charles' realm was just that: the *regnum Karoli*. It had no other name. It had had no existence as a political entity before 843. Modern notions of an institutionally centralised, more or less homogeneous, or ethnic, state may be misleading here. Instead, borrowing a ninth-century term, we should consider how well 'composed' was Charles' *regnum*, how firmly its parts held together, and whether they tended to grow more or less separate during Charles' reign. We also need to ask if Charles himself can be seen addressing this issue, and if so, how successfully.

Aquitaine was the largest and politically most important of the component *regna*.[82] Charles' treatment of it represented a new departure, certainly compared with his father's reign. It evolved in response to changing circumstances: in the 850s Aquitaine looked as if it might become as much of an independent *regnum* as it had been earlier in the ninth century. This had been implied when he had his son and namesake consecrated at Limoges in 855. In the 860s and 870s, after the Young Charles had rebelled, and submitted, Charles the Bald tried a different tack. Now Aquitaine was run from Francia. When the Young Charles died and Louis the Stammerer took his place, there was no consecration for him. Nominally king, Louis carried out no more of the key functions of rulership than his brother had done – in particular he issued no charters and, as Charles the Bald himself no longer visited Aquitaine, Aquitainian nobles and churchmen seeking royal favours had to journey to Francia. The result, it has been argued, was that the sinews of royal exploitation began to atrophy and the contacts between king and regional aristocracy gradually ceased to be fully operational. When the king never visited, there was no one to guard the guardians of royal estates.[83] Such problems of control were no new development, however: even when a king did reside in Aquitaine royal estates had a tendency to slip out of the king's hands; counts tended to use their comital lands (and church lands too) to reward their clients. On the other hand, the story in Charles the Bald's reign was not all one of waning royal control. Some Aquitainians still did attend Charles' assemblies in Francia; the king continued, into the 870s, to take a hand in appointments to key Aquitainian *honores*, for instance the

---

[81] Metcalf (1990). Compare Blackburn, ch. 20 below.   [82] Martindale (1990).
[83] Martindale (1985).

counties of Angoulême *c.*867 and of Bourges in 872; and Aquitainian beneficiaries figured slightly more frequently among recipients of Charles' charters in the 860s and 870s than earlier – sixteen of them between 844 and 859 but nineteen between 860 and 877. Royal government in Aquitaine never had been very intensive; it worked as before, through remote control. The coinage evidence confirms this. Aquitaine was different. Though there was overall direction, the 'new money' of 864 and after did not apply to Aquitaine.

It did apply to Brittany. Whereas earlier in his reign Charles issued no coins from Nantes and Rennes, those mints did issue his reformed coinage after 864, under Breton management but with weights and dies to the standard operating in Charles' mints elsewhere.[84] Breton distinctiveness, embedded in its Celtic history, language and institutions, became more visible in the ninth century, yet at the same time there was growing strength in the ties that bound Breton leaders to the Carolingians, and, after 840, to the realm of Charles. At first, Charles tried, as his ancestors had done, to crush the Bretons militarily, and, like his ancestors, failed. As Breton princes responded to Frankish pressure, and as the Franks adjusted, power crystallised at distinct levels. At the top one, Charles' developing imperial style of government lent credibility to his overlordship: Charles bound the Breton leaders to himself and his family by a variety of ties, notably the ritual bonds of spiritual kinship.[85] Successive Breton princes came to Francia to acknowledge Charles' authority, and so legitimise theirs. From 858 to 863, and again in 866–7, the Breton prince Salomon allied with Neustrian rebels and/or with Scandinavians to deny Charles effective control of the Loire valley, while Charles sought allies among disaffected Bretons. Thereafter, with Charles having conceded the counties, but not the bishoprics, of Avranches and Coutances, Salomon stayed loyal, co-ordinating with Charles the defence of the Loire valley against Scandinavians. During the inter-Breton conflict that followed Salomon's assassination in 874, Charles contemplated the recovery of counties transferred earlier to Breton control.[86] At levels below this, Bretons ran their own affairs.

This was equally true of the inhabitants of Gothia, which had a prehistory as Visigothic, then Frankish, Septimania, but took shape as a marcher region in the ninth century. It included the Midi from Nîmes and southwestwards to Barcelona, with, as a hinterland, the Pyrenean counties from Ampurias westwards to Ribagorza. Though the aristocrats of this region sometimes made tactical alliances with Muslim lords (frequently in rebellion against the amirs of Córdoba) across the Pyrenees, their overriding

[84] Smith (1992), pp. 142–3.   [85] See also p. 429 below.
[86] Capitulary of Quierzy (877), c. 23, *MGH Cap.* II, p. 360.

strategic concern was to defend their lands against Muslim raids. This helps explain their striking loyalty to the Carolingians.[87] Charles was appropriately depicted in a famous throne-portrait flanked by twin female personifications of Francia and Gothia.[88] Royal authority, based as it was in Francia, inevitably was exercised in more indirect and intermittent ways in Gothia; and in practice royal estates here were even likelier than in Aquitaine to fall under local control. Nevertheless one such beneficiary, Count Oliba of Carcassonne, thought it worth travelling to Francia to secure royal authorisation, and Charles' power to confiscate and reassign the lands of rebels gave him a still more effective pull on Oliba's loyalty.[89] Further, Charles kept the capacity to intervene by maintaining links with a range of local magnates, and switching between locals and outsiders in appointments to countships. Of the Frankish appointees, Hunfrid joined the rebellion of Charles of Aquitaine and was brusquely expelled from Charles the Bald's realm, while his replacement, *Marchio* Bernard, another outsider, remained loyal until 877. While in office, both Hunfrid and Bernard visited Francia from time to time, and sometimes attended Charles' assemblies.

With Burgundy Charles was in much closer and more consistent touch. Not far from Fontenoy was Auxerre, where the bishopric, and the monastery of St Germain, had both been closely linked with the Carolingian dynasty since the eighth century. Charles was able to exploit these ties to the full, and kept episcopal and abbatial appointments in his own hands throughout his reign.[90] The schools and scriptoria of Auxerre flourished under royal patronage. In the winter of 858–9 it was at Auxerre that Charles found military and spiritual reinforcement. Countships were equally crucial here: at Auxerre, Charles gave his cousin the post, while at Autun, his choice alternated between outsiders and members of magnate families with local connections. Though Eccard by the early 870s held the three countships of Autun, Chalon and Mâcon, when he died childless that bloc was dismembered to the benefit of new outsiders, one of them Charles' brother-in-law Boso. In the 870s, Boso's main interests came to lie further south in the Rhône valley (around Vienne) and Provence, regions acquired by Charles from the dismemberment of Lothar II's kingdom. When Charles moved into Italy to take up Louis II's imperial inheritance, Boso followed: marriage to Louis' daughter presaged a long-term Italian future, but Boso stayed only briefly, instead returning to consolidate his *honores* in Provence.[91]

Charles throughout his reign ruled most intensively in Francia: nearly half the beneficiaries of his charters were based in the lands between the

[87] Collins (1990b).   [88] Bible of San Paolo fuori le Mura, Rome, fol. 1r.
[89] Tessier (1952), nos. 341, 428.   [90] Sassier (1991).   [91] Airlie (1985).

Seine and the Meuse.[92] Contemporaries regarded this as 'the best part of the *regnum Francorum*'[93] – that is, fullest of royal resources. Of thirty-four men named as royal benefice-holders in Charles' charters, twenty-two were in Francia.[94] His control of episcopal appointments, and ecclesiastical benefices, is much better attested there than elsewhere. His itinerary was largely, and increasingly, based there. This is where assemblies were summoned and important decisions were made. It was the secure core-area where suspects and condemned men were held in captivity. The metropolitan sees of Rheims and Sens were central props of the regime, providing administrative skills, and the wherewithal, in the form of benefices on church lands, to maintain troops for the king's military service.[95] Francia was also the heart of the realm, containing the cult sites where the relics of saintly patrons were kept and revered and the ancestors of Frankish kings and nobles lay buried. Most important of all for Charles personally was the monastery of St Denis: the heart of the heart. Here Charles arranged for the liturgical commemoration of his parents, and of himself.[96] But he spread his favour among several churches. It was a monk of St Germain-des-Prés whom he commissioned to produce a comprehensive martyrology 'for the utility of the catholic faithful'.[97] And it was the new palatine church of St Mary that Charles chose as his Aachen-substitute in 877, with the palace of Compiègne itself designated his capital – his Carlopolis.[98]

To rule these *regna*, to collaborate with his sons, and often enough to offset their ambitions, Charles needed his aristocracy – his faithful men. In 843, immediately after Verdun, his realm riven by dissidence and factional dispute, Charles set about rebuilding consensus. At Coulaines in November, he credited his aristocracy with the initiative in forming a pact, and joined it himself. A working partnership needed a basis of mutual respect. The church, in principle all-embracing, provided a prime rallying-point: all swore to respect its *honor*. All the *fideles* then swore to observe the *honor* of the king. Last, and equally significant, Charles swore to preserve the *honor* of each *fidelis* – and in this case *honor* was spelled out as 'law and justice'. The notion of the king as guarantor of individual rights was not new but given a new precision, and set in a context of collective interests: a *societas*.[99] Constant effort was needed to maintain it. There were homoeostatic mechanisms in the Carolingian body politic: assemblies and oath-takings, processions and receptions at court. In all these, ritual was a key element.

---

[92] For the period 840–59, there were eighty-three such beneficiaries; for 860–77, there were eighty-five.   [93] Nelson (1992a), p. 95.

[94] Kienast (1990), pp. 38–85. Kienast classes all these as 'Vassallen', though very few are thus identified in the sources.   [95] Compare pp. 388–90 below.   [96] Brown (1989).

[97] Nelson (1993).   [98] Lohrmann (1976).   [99] Nelson (1992b).

Political crimes could be construed as sins, or their perpetrators accused of sexual offences: churchmen stepped in to prescribe penance or apply ordeals. While none of this was peculiar to the kingdom of Charles the Bald, nowhere was any of it more conspicuous. And the West Frankish kingdom was distinctive, largely thanks to Hincmar, in developing royal consecration rites: those for Charles, his daughter, wife and son, were to prove seminal for all future royal *ordines*. As far as ninth-century realities are concerned, Hincmar's dominance of our source materials may mislead, and so may the iconography of monarchy in West Frankish manuscripts. For Hincmar's preoccupation with anointing rites was exceptional; and few saw the manuscripts' depictions of majesty. Instead, at their assemblies and oath-swearings, the Franks saw monarchy's familiar, pragmatic face.

This did not mean the king was weak. Contemporary critics diagnosed excessive force, not weakness, as the problem about both Louis the Pious and Charles the Bald. While Charles àt Coulaines wooed aristocratic consensus, he was capable of violence and victimisation. Carolingian rivals were sometimes conciliated, but sometimes incarcerated, and in Carloman's case blinded; several aristocratic rebels were judicially (but perhaps judiciously) murdered. Charles's court remained a magnet: for every man deprived of an *honor*, there was another ready to replace him. The so-called imperial aristocracy which arguably played a key role in holding Charlemagne's empire together functioned rather differently in the mid-ninth century. Their descendants were to be found all over the Carolingian world – but they did not pull together politically.[100] The splitting of the Carolingian family (which split the empire) was paralleled in many other families. Divisions hardened as one generation succeeded another. As patrimonies passed to eldest sons, surplus siblings were shed. They had to move, and looked to kings for advancement. The mobility, spatial and political, of such ambitious individuals is a striking feature of Charles' reign. For the flow was generally from east to west, towards Charles' kingdom: witness the cases of Adalhard, already a beneficiary of Louis the Pious' largesse, then of Charles' too, in Neustria, then Francia; Robert, in Neustria, but also in Burgundy and Francia; Hugh, in Burgundy and then Neustria; Hunfrid, in Burgundy and in Gothia; Boso, in Provence and Aquitaine. Not all these men remained in the West: voluntarily or otherwise, several left for other Carolingian realms. But most stayed. Their careers suggest that the power structure in Charles' kingdom was at once more open, and more tightly controlled, than further east: that Charles had more 'wherewithal' to dispose of than had other Carolingian kings elsewhere and, as important,

---

[100] Compare Airlie, chapter 16 below.

more freedom of manœuvre in allocating power and resources at magnate level. Beneath that level (and alongside too), an indigenous aristocracy was firmly ensconced: from it the incoming magnate would recruit his clients and subordinates.

Robert, later nicknamed 'the Strong', is a well-researched case in point. Robert was an incomer to the West. Of Rhineland origin, he was granted a succession of *honores* by Charles, beginning with benefices on the lands of the church of Rheims, and proceeding to the countship of Angers in 852 where he 'inherited' some of the local network of clients assembled by the previous count, who happened to be Robert's political ally (they may have married each other's sisters).[101] Later in the 850s Robert saw his regional position threatened by the setting-up of Louis the Stammerer in Neustria with the Breton prince Erispoë, not Robert, as his father-in-law and protector. Robert rebelled, and was one of those responsible for inviting Louis the German into Charles' kingdom in 858. Only in 861 did Charles win back Robert's loyalty and the price was his restoration in the Loire valley. But his roots there were not so deep that he refused a transfer in 864, when Charles made him count of Autun. Only when he failed to establish himself there did Robert return to Angers; and he died fighting Northmen near there in 866. Robert has sometimes been cast in the role of dynast: founder of a Neustrian principality. Charles had no such intention; and was indeed able to prevent any such development occurring in his own lifetime by denying Robert's young sons succession to Robert's *honores*, and after 866 making Tours (not Angers) the focus of a reconstructed defence system in the Loire valley. Significantly, it was not in the West but in the Rhineland that Robert's death was registered as heroic.[102]

In his Western kingdom, Charles had one further special asset: churches that were not only wealthy, long established and endowed with social power, but also firmly built into the structure of the realm. In ecclesiastical personnel, the king found versatile, strenuous and generally loyal agents. Archbishops served at court as counsellors and in their provinces as *missi* and supervisors of counts. Hincmar of Rheims is the outstanding example. Bishops helped repress crime and organised the military support owed by churches to the state. Abbots in particular could be surprisingly mobile: surprisingly, that is, by the standards of monastic rules. But these abbots were not regular. Some were in minor orders, hence *clerici*, unable to marry, but otherwise living like secular lords, with their own military followings: Hugh, Charles' cousin, as abbot of St Martin served in effect as Charles' deputy in the Loire valley; and Fulk, a former palace clerk, as abbot of St

---

[101] Werner (1958).   [102] *AX s.a.* 867, p. 25.

Bertin was one of those left in charge by Charles when he departed for Italy in 877. Others were full-blown lay abbots – given lordship of the temporal goods of monasteries and responsible for granting benefices to the warriors who would serve their monastic lords and perform military service to the king. Such abbacies were luxuriant new growths of the ninth century, especially in Charles' kingdom. They were uncanonical, and in the wrong hands they could lead to depredation, but that was equally true of canonical abbacies. Even from an ecclesiastical viewpoint, lay abbots could equally bring welcome leadership and protection – as Count Vivian did to the community of St Martin, Tours, in the 840s.[103] From the king's standpoint, lay abbacies offered a ready method of granting favour without cost to royal lands. After 867, Charles himself was lay abbot of the most prestigious monastery of all: St Denis. There, appropriately, he was remembered for centuries as a major benefactor.

AFTER CHARLES THE BALD

Hindsight shows that the decade or so after Charles' death was momentous for the West. For contemporaries, change came stealthily, bit by bit. At first it seemed that there would be continuity. Charles' kingdom passed to his son Louis; and Pope John VIII wanted Louis for emperor. Louis was energetic: collaborating with Abbot Hugh against the Northmen on the Loire, acting as conciliator in aristocratic disputes, and making as much capital as possible out of the pope's visit to Francia in the summer of 878. There was nothing unusual in Louis' having begun his reign by making concessions, 'granting abbacies, countships and estates, according to what each demanded'.[104] But Hincmar when he wrote these words, perhaps as late as 882, knew what Louis could not know in 877: that Gauzlin, who received the abbacy of St Denis, and Conrad who (probably) received the countship of Paris, were to threaten the survival of Louis' realm after his death. In 877 the magnates were split into rival factions, centred on Abbots Hugh and Gauzlin, and they remained at loggerheads throughout Louis' reign.[105] It soon became clear that that reign was likely to be short: within months of his accession Louis, aged only 31, was a very sick man. Already therefore in 878 the succession problem loomed. In the summer he failed in his efforts to persuade the pope to crown his second wife Adelaide: this would have enlarged the questionmark over the legitimacy of Louis' two sons – and heirs – by his first wife Ansgard. In the autumn Louis met his cousin and namesake, Louis the Younger, at Fouron. The site was not far from Aachen; but their agreement made no mention of the imperial title except as a thing

---

[103] Kessler (1992).   [104] *AB (3) s.a.* 877, p. 203.   [105] Werner (1979).

of the past. Two separate *regna* now existed, those created by Charles the Bald and Louis the German, and they would persist into the next generation, as Louis the Younger and Louis the Stammerer mutually guaranteed to help their respective sons succeed them 'by hereditary right'.[106] On the Stammerer's side, two sons were named in the Fouron agreement: Louis [III] and Carloman. Five months later, as Louis lay dying, he bequeathed his regalia and his realm to his namesake alone.

Louis III had the support of Abbot Hugh and his allies. Gauzlin and *his* allies, Count Conrad chief among them, foresaw political extinction. At the court of Louis the Younger and his queen, Gauzlin already had contacts, made when he had been held a prisoner after Andernach in 876.[107] Now was the time to activate them by inviting the East Frankish king to intervene in the West. Perhaps Gauzlin had only wanted to encourage his opponents to divide the Western realm so that each faction had 'its' king: this indeed was the outcome. Louis III and Carloman II were both consecrated kings in September 879, and in February 880 a division of the western kingdom was agreed, Gauzlin having switched horses meanwhile: Louis got Francia and Neustria, where Gauzlin and Conrad were naturally the dominant figures, while Carloman (now supported by Hugh) got Burgundy and Aquitaine (Map 11). The new reigns started under further clouds: Louis the Younger had to be bought off with the Lotharingian lands which Charles the Bald had acquired in 870. Meanwhile, Northmen, attracted by 'news of discord', came in large numbers from England to over-winter in Francia in 879–80;[108] and Boso, perhaps after making a bid of his own for the whole Western kingdom, claiming that the Stammerer's sons were illegitimate, had himself consecrated king of Provence in October 879.[109] Louis III and Carloman faced up to these challenges: in November 879 they defeated Northmen south of the Loire and then in 880 turned on Boso and besieged him in Vienne; in August 881 Louis defeated a Scandinavian force at Saucourt in Vimeu – a victory celebrated in a vernacular German poem, the *Ludwigslied*, apparently written at St Amand where the abbacy was held (along with several others) by Gauzlin.[110] In 882 Carloman too showed that he could beat bands of Northmen plundering in the neighbourhood of Rheims. But by then Louis had died, in August 882, of injuries incurred while 'chasing a young woman on his horse for a joke (for he was a young man) while she fled into her father's house'. Scarcely two years later, Carloman too died in a hunting accident.[111] Both died without heirs. Only a tiny child remained of

---

[106] *AB (3) s.a.* 878, pp. 213–15. Louis the Stammerer reserved his claims to Italy, the imperial realm, but envisaged that it too might be divided.   [107] *AB (3) s.a.* 879, pp. 216–17.

[108] *AV s.a.* 879, p. 44.   [109] *AB (3) s.a.* 879, p. 219.

[110] Fouracre (1985); Yeandle (1989).   [111] *AV s.a.* 882, p. 52; 884, p. 56.

the descent line of Charles the Bald: Charles, later nicknamed *simplex*, the 'straightforward', or 'openhearted'. He had been born to Queen Adelaide on 17 September 879, six months after the Stammerer's death. He was passed over in 882, and in 884. In the 890s this was explained in terms of his extreme youth and the urgency of the Scandinavian threat to Francia.[112] There may have been some doubt over his paternity. But an urgent threat there certainly was. The able Louis the Younger had died leaving no son in 882. Thus the whole empire was reunited by 884 in the hands of Louis the German's youngest son Charles, known later as 'the Fat'. In the next three years the new emperor proved incapable of imposing his authority directly in the West – where he lacked roots, resources and political friends of his own. Instead he picked Odo, son of that Robert who had been killed fighting the Northmen near Angers twenty years before. The deaths of Gauzlin and Hugh within a few weeks of each other (April and May 886) left a power vacuum which Odo filled. He recovered his father's Neustrian *honores* from the emperor, and probably at the same time was made count of Paris where he now mounted a vigorous defence against Scandinavian attackers.[113]

In 887 Charles the Fat became seriously ill, and East Frankish rebels led by Arnulf, illegitimate son of Louis the German's son Karlmann, plotted his deposition. Arnulf became king of the East Franks. What would become of the West? The author of the contemporary *Annals of St Vaast* says that the 'Lower [i.e. West] Franks' (he distinguishes them from Arnulf's *australes Franci*)[114] were divided: only some favoured Odo, while others, headed by Archbishop Fulk of Rheims but including some prominent men in Burgundy, invited Duke Wido of Spoleto (a kinsman of Fulk's: his paternal ancestors were Franks) from Italy. Wido was actually consecrated at Langres by the local bishop; Odo at Compiègne by the archbishop of Sens. Wido, outplayed, returned to Italy, and his former supporters, after a brief flirtation with Arnulf who rejected their overtures, rallied to Odo. The St Vaast annalist thought that what finally turned opinion in Odo's favour was an 'unexpected victory' over the Northmen, 'through the mercy of God'. Thus, unsteadily, as it seemed unpredictably, did the kingdom of the West Franks get reconstituted in 888 – separate from other *regna*, and a single entity.

At first sight this outcome seems fortuitous. In 888 after all, several *regna* were, as Regino put it, 'detached from their structure into separate parts on the grounds that they lacked a legitimate heir, and now did not await their

---

[112] Flodoard, *Historia Remensis Ecclesiae* iv.5, p. 563. See Schneider (1973), p. 39.
[113] Celebrated in the 890s by Abbo of St Germain-des-Prés in a famous poem.
[114] *AV s.a.* p. 64.

natural lord but each *regnum* decided to create a king for itself out of its own guts' – in other words, from its indigenous nobility.[115] In Regino's view, the one 'natural lord', legitimate or no, was Arnulf, and his rejection – the rejection of a dynastic filter – opened the floodgates of conflict between more or less equally qualified Frankish magnates. Regino's diagnosis was faulty. In the minds of some contemporaries, at least, an empire survived and Arnulf held a vague hegemony over the kings. The story that Arnulf sent a crown for Odo's coronation hails from St Vaast, not Bavaria.[116] Further, the process of 'detachment' did not go far. None of the *regna* of 888 was new, for 'Burgundy' probably began as an attempt to reconstitute that Middle Kingdom[117] which since 855 had undergone so many changes and dismemberments. Italy and the East and West Frankish kingdoms had by contrast had continuous histories since 843. They did not fragment further in 888. In the West Frankish case, we can reject a Bavarian annalist's suggestion that Ramnulf, count of Poitiers, set up a separate kingdom of Aquitaine: this is belied by the evidence of Ramnulf's own charters, where no royal title is claimed, and of the annalist of St Vaast, near the heart of West Frankish affairs, that Ramnulf was acting as guardian of the eight-year-old Charles the Straightforward.[118] Ramnulf, then, acknowledged Odo belatedly because his first plan had been to promote Charles as the legitimate Carolingian heir. Neither in 888 nor in 889 did Ramnulf aim at secession.[119] His brother Ebles, abbot of St Denis since 886, already served Odo as his chancellor.

Odo's succession to the whole of what had been Charles the Bald's kingdom was therefore not really so fortuitous. What survived in the west was a *political* entity: a community neither linguistic, since the victory at Saucourt had been celebrated in German not Romance, nor ethnic, since its members were Aquitainians and Burgundians as well as Franks. This diversity in fact contributed to the realm's identity and viability in contemporary eyes. It was a kind of imperial realm: a kingdom of many kingdoms – as implied in the praise-song composed for Odo's consecration in 888:

> *Amen resultet Gallia*
> *Amen cantent Burgundia*
> *Bigorni regni spacia*
> *Wasconia et Teutonia.*[120]

---

[115] Regino, p. 129.   [116] *AV s.a.* p. 67.

[117] Hlawitschka (1968), pp. 70, 79. Compare chapter 5 below.

[118] *AV s.a.* 889, p. 67, against *AF (3) s.a.* 888, p. 116.

[119] For the myth of Ramnulf's Carolingian descent, see Martindale (1995).

[120] Schramm (1968) II, pp. 214–15. '"Amen", resounds Gaul; and Burgundy, the area of the *regnum* of Bigorre, Gascony and German-speaking lands sing "Amen"'; see further, Werner (1965).

In East Francia, the deposition of Charles the Fat resulted from uncertainties over the succession and the play of faction. In the west Charles was abandoned for other reasons. These same reasons underlay the choice of the non-Carolingian Odo. The Scandinavian threat had changed in the 880s – quantitatively but also qualitatively. Francia itself, the core of Charles the Bald's realm, was not just burdened, but menaced at its very heart. Large co-ordinated Scandinavian war-bands ravaged at will. They took Rouen (885), then penetrated the river Oise (885). Paris was besieged for eight months (885–6). Odo's success against the Scandinavians was crucial in winning the support that put him on the throne in 888.

The defence of Paris brought only temporary respite, however: Scandinavians remained on the Seine, and later in 886 their ships moved up the Yonne as far as Sens; in 888 up the Marne to Meaux; in 890 up the Oise to Noyon. No wonder the notables of these parts persuaded Odo to winter in 892–3 in Aquitaine 'so that Francia, afflicted for so many years, might recuperate a little'.[121] Odo had his own good reasons to comply. He had received recognition from a number of leading Aquitainians in 889; and in 892, when Ramnulf died, Odo assigned the countship of Poitiers to his own brother Robert, disregarding the claims of Ramnulf's young son. Ebles of St Denis promptly defected from Odo and went to Aquitaine. In pursuing him southwards, therefore, Odo was struggling to keep his position in Francia. Unfortunately for him, Archbishop Fulk of Rheims re-formed the coalition of 888. They had a rival candidate to hand: Charles the Straightforward, whom Fulk consecrated king at Rheims on 28 January 893. Although Odo had the upper hand in the ensuing struggle, he lacked a direct heir: by the peace agreement of 897, he seems to have agreed that Charles should succeed him, which he did a year later.

How far had structural change occurred in the west by 898? Odo's royal government in some ways contrasts starkly with Charles the Bald's. Odo confronted new obstacles to his authority: secular principalities well on the way to becoming hereditary and territorial,[122] gobbling up lay abbacies, for instance, as Count Baldwin of Flanders did St Vaast, and ecclesiastical principalities, equally territorial and only a little less dynastic, exploiting and sometimes flouting royal authority, as Fulk of Rheims did rather than bolstering it as his predecessor Hincmar had done.[123] Odo's power base of fisclands in Francia seems drastically diminished by comparison with Charles the Bald's. Odo is hardly ever documented as residing in a palace.[124] No capitularies of his are known. Absence of reference to royal *missi* in his reign could suggest the removal of the linchpin of Carolingian administ-

---

[121] *AV s.a.* 892, p. 72.   [122] Dhondt (1948); Dunbabin (1985).
[123] Schneider (1973).   [124] Brühl (1968), pp. 48–9.

ration. Last but not least, Odo's non-Carolingian royal person marks a break with the Carolingian past.

Some of these trends proved reversible. Full-blown ecclesiastical principalities never materialised in France: instead ecclesiastical resources remained firmly under secular control, and in the Frankish heartlands especially that control was very often royal. Hereditary secular power was conspicuous, but it was no novelty; and while principalities proved a permanent feature in general terms, particular concentrations of regional power were precarious, often ephemeral, and as subject as the kingdom itself to vagaries of dynastic accident. In the Loire valley where Odo's brother dominated the scene from his comital base of Tours, a clear distinction between comital and royal authority was not lost sight of.[125] Odo was still able to assemble magnates from the regions even if he seemed to 'ally with' them now, rather than to rule them.[126] Although royal fisclands in Francia had been alienated or damaged, Odo with his multiple lay abbacies (he had acquired those of Gauzlin after 886) vigorously exploited church resources and so was able to 'prepare himself manfully for war'.[127] After 892, the Scandinavian burden on Francia was considerably lightened. Odo's successor was able to stay frequently again in the Oise valley, and notably at Compiègne.

Odo made up for his lack of Carolingian blood by imitating the Carolingians through symbolism and rituals which, thanks to the church, remained a royal monopoly. Here Odo looked ahead to the Capetians as well as back to Charles the Bald.[128] Most important of all, Odo maintained a presence in every part of his composite realm, through visiting, in the case of Aquitaine, or through receiving leading men, in the cases of Gothia and Burgundy. Royal charters were still worth travelling for. The right to issue coinage remained, as yet, a royal one. In 893–7, the years of Odo's struggle with Charles the Straightforward, no division of the realm was mooted: the object of struggle was the realm as a whole. Charles the Bald had promoted the use of the written word, which memorialised the present (as well as the past) for the future. He had firmly locked the church into the state. He had understood the significance of rituals, and of ideology. The *res publica* he had nurtured survived the shocks of the later ninth century. The realm of 843 in the sense of a territory – 'the realm of Charles', 'the realm of the West Franks' – was preserved in the minds of men, and hence, however attenuated its institutions, in the world of politics.

---

[125] See p. 415 below.   [126] *AV s.a.* 888, 889, 892, pp. 65, 67, 72.
[127] Regino *s.a.* 893, p. 141.   [128] Schneidmüller (1979), pp. 105–21.

CHAPTER 5

THE FRANKISH KINGDOMS, 817–911:
THE EAST AND MIDDLE
KINGDOMS

Johannes Fried

LOUIS the Pious had hurt himself, but his wounds were not worth talking about.[1] Only three weeks later he was hunting again. Four months after this accident, the imperial council met. 'Suddenly, through divine inspiration', the emperor admitted, 'our faithful lieges admonished us that while we were still in good health, and God granted universal peace, we should confer on the state of the whole empire and the position of our sons, as our ancestors had done.'[2] However, the political order the emperor and 'those who know what is most salutary' came up with was revolutionary, and led to civil war. Contrary to all precedent, the empire was no longer to be divided equally among the emperor's sons (Map 8); on the contrary, the eldest son, Lothar, was to receive the imperial crown immediately and exclusively while his brothers Pippin and Louis (the German) who were both minors had to be content, the former with Aquitaine, the latter with Bavaria and its adjacent territories. All other parts of the huge Frankish realm were to fall to Lothar; his brothers were to act as viceroys 'under' him.

Lothar really received the imperial crown in 817, while his brothers were made kings. They seemed in a fair way to bring about the new order, but there was resistance from the majority of nobles. What was more, the Empress Irmengard died, and Louis took a new wife, Judith, a Welf, who feared for the inheritance of her children. She found some powerful supporters. Every time the young empress became pregnant, resistance to the new imperial order of 817 grew a little stronger; after the birth of Charles (the Bald) it came to a head. Schemes for the partition of the empire were soon put forward in rapid succession. After 829 an open struggle broke out, each son demanding his own share of Francia. Lothar was the only one to

[1] BM 643a.
[2] *MGH Cap.* I, no. 136, p. 270: 'ut nos fideles nostri ammonerent, quatenus manente nostra incolomitate et pace undique a deo concessa de statu totius regni et de filiorum nostrorum causa more parentum nostrorum tractaremus'.

cling to the settlement of 817. His brothers, Pippin and Louis, were no longer content with a subordinate role; they insisted on their full inheritance and found supporters among the nobility, as Judith did for her own son, Charles. One ominous sign was that Einhard, Charlemagne's famous counsellor, withdrew from Louis' court to retire to his estates in the Maingau region. At the assembly held at Aachen in 828, the counts Hugh of Tours and Matfrid of Orléans fell from grace after military defeats at the hands of the Saracens, to the advantage of Judith's favourite, Bernard of Septimania. Louis also deprived the margrave Baldric of Friuli of his office for military failure; after this, Baldric's fate is unknown. However, Hugh, an Etichonid, was father-in-law to the Emperor Lothar; any move against him was really aimed at his daughter's husband. Matfrid sided with the young emperor, too, whose power was to be confined to Italy alone in the following year. An opposition gathered round him against his father which was led by Wala, abbot of Corbie, Agobard, archbishop of Lyons and Ebbo of Rheims (830) and which also had the support of Pope Gregory IV. However, its only achievement was to keep the merry-go-round of partition schemes moving. For all that, in 831 all the lands east of the Rhine were for the first time assigned to the emperor's older son (who was of the same name) to form his future kingdom. When Lothar was reconciled to his father, Pippin and the younger Louis put up resistance against them; they won over their elder brother and, together with him, pitted themselves against the emperor on the 'Rotfeld' near Colmar in 833. The pope was present, too. He was among the supporters of the younger emperor, and it was thanks to him that Louis' own army defected to his sons (833). This apparent victory was regarded as the outcome of an ordeal; the abandoned emperor was relegated to a monastery, but Lothar threw away the advantage when, by virtue of the settlement of 817, he began to lord it over his brothers.

Louis the German, former king of Bavaria, had not the slightest intention of giving in, and from that time he dated his documents according to the length of his reign *in orientali Francia*. In 834 he joined with Pippin to restore their father to the throne. Louis the Pious, however, after the death of Pippin in 838, tried to confine Louis the German once again to Bavaria (839) in order to promote the interests of Charles. When Louis the Pious died in 840, the whirlwind of territorial partition had by no means been stilled. It drove the Carolingians ever deeper into war and eventually culminated in major bloodshed at Fontenoy in 841.

It is, in fact, not always easy to discern the factions of nobles backing one of the Carolingians. Among Louis the Pious' supporters in East Francia were the Poppones, the Hattones (one of whom was his biographer,

Thegan); Gebhardt, count of the Lahngau, who may have been related to
the Hattones; the Robertines, founding family of the monastery at Lorsch,
and also Archbishop Otgar of Mainz and Hraban Maur, archbishop of
Fulda. After 840, all of them were shown some (at least temporary)
disfavour by Louis the German. Without too much of an effort, his father
was able to overcome him in 832 and again in 838–40. The Alemanni also
remained largely faithful to the emperor: he was, therefore, able to earmark
this province temporarily as a sub-kingdom for the younger Charles (829).
In Saxony, the Hattone count Banzleib was loyal to Louis the Pious; the
Cobbones, from the same region, presumably also belonged to the party of
Louis and his son Charles, while the descendants of Widukind supported
Lothar.[3]

Hugh the Etichonid and his companion, Matfrid, together with those
who favoured a unified realm, declared for Lothar, as did many of the great
noble families of the West and in Italy. Our sources tell us nothing about the
force which supported Louis the German before 840: the only name known
is that of Count Ruadker of Linz and Argengau, whom Louis the Pious
demoted in favour of his wife's brother, Conrad the Welf, in 839. Only after
Louis' death did this situation change: the Eastern Franks, Alemannians,
Saxons and Thuringians now swore allegiance to the younger Louis. On the
other hand, Archbishop Otgar of Mainz and Count Adalbert of Metz
decided for Lothar and became rallying points for his supporters, albeit
briefly, for Adalbert fell in battle near the river Wornitz, in the Ries region,
in 841. It was of no avail that Lothar hatched a conspiracy in Saxony, the
'Stellinga',[4] an alliance of petty freemen and semi-freemen which eventually
drove the local nobility over to the side of Louis the German once and for
all. It was only the Bavarians whose loyalty to Louis remained unwavering.
None of the other 'Germanic' peoples had a centralised organisation of its
own; only the Bavarians were united by having an archbishopric of their
own and being led by a king. It was from Bavaria that the East Frankish
kingdom was created.

Although 'Transrhenania' was not a poor region, it was not a rich one
either; it certainly did not compare favourably with the territories west of
the Rhine. Its regions were culturally very diverse, as they comprised
territories south of the Danube, the upper Rhine and the Frankish Main
area, the woodlands of central Germany, the Harz region of Saxony and
Thuringia and the Low German heaths and marshlands. In no way could it
be considered a political or administrative unit. Except for the former
Roman provinces, towns were virtually non-existent; bishops' sees were

---

[3] Fried (1994).   [4] Compare Goetz below, p. 460.

few and far between and, with a few exceptions, comparatively poor; the most important archbishops resided west of the Rhine. Monasteries remarkable for economic strength, political importance and intellectual superiority were comparatively rare.

The royal estates were scattered unevenly throughout 'Germania', with the thickest cluster in the Franconian Rhine and Main regions, around Kassel and around Regensburg; in Saxony they were mostly ranged along the *Hellweg*, the major strategic route from Duisburg to Corvey. This had considerable influence on Carolingian politics. Charlemagne spent a good deal of time in 'Germania', but only when he had to fight or to pacify the Saxons, Bavarians and Avars. His strongholds definitely lay west of the Rhine, around Worms and Aachen; as emperor he resided almost exclusively at Aachen. Louis the Pious also lived chiefly in the capital, with regular spells at Ingelheim and Worms. He hardly ever visited his eastern lands unless the demands of war – especially the younger Louis' revolts – required it. Only in Frankfurt was the emperor seen frequently, and it was here that Charles the Bald was born in 823. Apart from Aachen, the Rhine–Main area was generally the centre of his power. Furthermore, the emperor's love of hunting often drew him to Salz on the Franconian river Saale. Nor did an imperial synod meet in any of the 'Germanic' bishoprics. The provinces east of the Rhine were peripheral to royal rule. The outcome of the battle of Fontenoy, in which Lothar was defeated by Louis and Charles, had made a division of the kingdom among the three brothers inevitable. The idea that one of the emperor's sons should rule alone, on the analogy with the monarchy of God and the unity of the indivisible church, had proved to be a failure. The independent disposition of the nobility – obscured by Charlemagne's successes, and apparently never overcome – manifested itself again with a vengeance. The political order was now determined by personal forces, ties of kinship and friendship, associations of vassals and sworn leagues and groups of nobles in support of, or in opposition to, the crown. All of these factors by means of mutual interaction eventually brought about the emergence of new unions and peoples.

The bloody battle did nothing to shift the barriers of mistrust even between the former partners. Owing to a lack of objectives, there was no such thing as a coherent concept of policy. From time to time there were ineffectual appeals to the doctrine of unity. What was most convincing as an aim was an increase of power. 'Love and peace' as it should prevail among kinsfolk could occasionally be displayed for a brief moment. By means of entering into an alliance with each other, Louis and Charles made a great display of mutual love. At Strasbourg and before their armies, they confirmed this with an oath sworn by Louis in the Romance tongue and by

Charles in *Teudisca lingua* (842).[5] The kingdoms' boundaries could now be seen as language barriers.

A committee appointed to handle a territorial partition, consisting of forty *fideles* for each king, established the boundaries in November 842. In deference to his dignity, the emperor was given first choice. The fraternal strife was ended, at least for the moment, by the Treaty of Verdun in 843. However, the form of the oath setting down the division of lands has not come down to us: only the general outcome is known[6] (Map 9). Louis received everything east of the Rhine, with the cities of Speyer, Worms and Mainz; Charles got the West, and Lothar the Middle Kingdom with Aachen and Rome. The three kings swore brotherly love, peace and friendship to one another.

The brothers wanted to tackle their great tasks together, and to this end they agreed to hold regular meetings. They made common declarations and issued statutes concerning ecclesiastical and secular government, defence against the Vikings, the persecution of criminals and the problem of how to deal with refugees. But reality lagged far behind such proclamations. Especially when it came to repelling enemies from outside such as Vikings, Saracens, Slavs and Magyars, each king was left to his own resources. The Carolingians did not stand by one another, although some of the Saxons occasionally came to Charles the Bald's aid, as in 860 and 863. For a time the meetings did at least keep up the fiction of a united Carolingian kingship. About a hundred of these meetings are known to have taken place in the period under discussion; however, the successive mutually acknowledged treaties which ensued actually accelerated the independent development of the individual kingdoms rather than restraining it. As the century drew to a close, these meetings became less frequent anyway.

Lothar never completely buried his hopes of restoring the empire to its former glory. But he could not even gain a foothold. His brother Louis did not have the slightest intention of contenting himself with what the Treaty of Verdun had dealt out to him; and Charles was soon of like mind with his brothers. Up to 840–3 the emperor dwelt mostly in Italy; after that he remained almost exclusively north of the Alps, mostly around Aachen. This was his major stronghold. His policy of gradualism aimed at letting the defeat of 841 slowly sink into oblivion did not get him far. He had one success in 844, when Pope Gregory IV made Drogo, archbishop of Metz, the papal vicar for the whole Frankish kingdom. This was an obvious attempt to weaken the Treaty of Verdun. But the measure proved ineffective, and after Drogo's death in 855 it was not repeated. Lothar strove in

---

[5] Nithard III.5 and McKitterick, above, pp. 11–12.   [6] BM 1103a.

vain to undermine the goodwill between his brothers; it did indeed turn to open enmity, with Louis waging war against Charles, but this did not in the least increase Lothar's power. Far from it! The Carolingian brothers' mutual hostility encouraged the Vikings to redouble their attacks on the Frankish kingdoms, which affected especially Lothar's territory. They repeatedly set fire to Dorestad, one of the most important ports and trading centres on the lower Rhine, in 847, and the place was permanently occupied by Rorik the Viking in 850. The emperor was no longer able to subdue the Northmen.[7]

Lothar's royal authority was also on the wane in his southern domains. Provence remained peripheral to his power. He did nothing to repel Saracen attacks. They even had the audacity to attack Rome and to loot the tombs of the apostles.[8] Then, at long last, and for the last time, Lothar hastened into Italy to set an army going against the Muslims. At Pavia he met his son Louis II (April/May 847); however, he pressed for a speedy return in February of the same year, fearing Charles' machinations in spite of the peace accord he had so recently signed with his brothers. He did at least devote some effort to a plan for a grand alliance which was to involve Pope Leo IV, the dukes of Benevento and Naples and even the Doge of Venice. In 847, the emperor summoned a synod 'in Francia' which obliged the bishops to give military support to the 'Italians', and, above all, resolved to raise a special tax throughout Lothar's kingdom to finance the construction of defences round St Peter's in Rome (also known as 'Leo's Town'). Meanwhile, all power in Italy came into the hands of Lothar's eldest son, soon to be crowned emperor by Leo IV in 850. But it was under the same pope that the papacy began to free itself from Frankish domination.

It was only the person of the king that gave some unity to the East Frankish kingdom; it did not have any tradition of its own. The army consisted of contingents from individual peoples; when the court was summoned the nobility turned up more or less in tribal groups. The areas inhabited by them and subject to their own particular laws were regularly seen as their own *patria*; the idea that the whole East Frankish kingdom should be considered as the supreme *patria* of all the peoples together remained inchoate. Neither the lay nobility nor the clergy considered themselves in any way bound by the frontiers drawn up in 842/3 nor did they (unlike the West Frankish nobility after the Treaty of Coulaines in 843) ever form a genuine union of their own. The fear was rather of renewed disintegration. The twofold process of 'internal' and 'external' consolidation was a slow one which was to be completed only in the eleventh and twelfth centuries.

---

[7] Compare Coupland, pp. 193–6.   [8] Compare Kennedy, p. 254.

Louis' reign was more or less free from major feuds among the nobility; after his death they became more frequent. Even after 843, Bavaria still remained Louis' most important power base. He repeatedly held court at Regensburg and it was from there that he addressed documents to recipients throughout his whole realm. After the Treaty of Verdun the Frankish Rhineland assumed a comparable importance; the Upper Franconia area around Forchheim was soon to play an important role for Louis while the significance of the other Frankish regions continued to decline.

What expansionism Louis indulged in was directed outwards from Bavaria. The 'true' frontier was not pushed any further eastward, but Bavarian missionaries and settlers did advance steadily down the Danube into Pannonia and pushed the 'German' frontier continually further towards the southeast. Charlemagne himself had encouraged his subjects to 'take possession of the lands in Pannonia and acquire estates there' so as to increase the property of the church; thus the province increasingly came to be part of the territory under Carolingian rule.[9]

Saxony and Alemannia were remote from the centre of royal power and Louis' appearances there were few and far between. He went only three times to Saxony, in 845, 851 and 852, and he spent only a few weeks there out of the whole of his 33-year reign after 843; each time it was in response to some threatening development.[10] Otherwise Louis left the province more and more to itself, or rather to the ecclesiastical and lay nobility. Alemannia was not nearly as marginal to the East Frankish king's itineraries as was Saxony. It formed, as it were, a convenient bridge between Bavaria and Francia, and it was actually too close to the west and the south of the kingdom to be neglected. From 850 to 860 Louis methodically consolidated his position there, particularly by means of monasteries. The convent for ladies of rank at Zurich, founded in 853, was headed by two of his daughters in turn; one was Hildegard, who died in 856, and the other was Berta, who died in 877.[11] Louis paid frequent visits to the imperial palace at Ulm. He was successful in increasing his influence in this territory; nevertheless, in about 859 he resigned his position there to his youngest son, Charles.

The clergy of the kingdom of East Francia had by now lost the dominant influence they had had under Louis the Pious. Of the twenty-five documents which the younger Louis is known to have issued before 840, however, ten were addressed to Bavarian bishops; another nine were added up till 876.[12] The rest of the episcopate received only seventeen royal missives between 840/3 and 876. The bishops' influence was obviously declining everywhere except for Bavaria. National synods which might have done something to

---

[9] *MGH Dip. Germ.* I, no. 109.   [10] BM 1386a; 1398b; 1402c–1403c.
[11] Werner (1967).   [12] Compare *MGH Dip. Germ.* I.

counter this development were very seldom convened by Louis. Only when Hraban Maur (847–56) acceded to the see of Mainz did the East Frankish synod become active, but under his successor Charles (856–63) it soon lost this impulse, and under Liutbert (863–89) it died away altogether.[13]

None of this prevented individual prelates from exerting considerable influence on the king; they did this as representatives of their own kin groups rather than of their institutions. Bishops such as Hraban Maur, Charles or Liutbert of Mainz, or Ermenrich of Passau (who died in 874) played a prominent part as counsellors or royal *fideles*. Some abbots and monasteries were more important than most of the cathedrals and bishops; however, bishops were put in charge of the major royal monasteries. Lay abbots, on the other hand, were of little importance in Louis' kingdom.

Louis was predominantly concerned with acquiring the West and the Middle Kingdom. Any sign of weakness on the part of Charles the Bald, as in 854, 858 and after 870, was an opportunity for Louis to gain a foothold in the far West.[14] Influential groups of nobles such as the Robertines and the Rorgonids sought his help and invited him to take over the throne then. First Louis sent his son Louis to Aquitaine; however, he had to withdraw without having achieved anything; in 858 Louis the German himself appeared in his brother's kingdom at the head of an army. Nevertheless, Louis was not able to do any better than his son. Hincmar of Rheims called for resistance among the West Franks, for as metropolitan archbishop he had profited most from a division which had made him the most important ecclesiastic in the kingdom.[15] In 859, Louis had to retreat precipitately. A policy of aggressive conquest beyond the old boundaries of the realm was virtually unthinkable; it was hard enough to repel enemies coming in from outside. Louis, too, pursued a generally defensive policy in the north and northeast of his kingdom, and even the active interest he took in Bavaria seemed rather less than what many of its inhabitants would have expected it to be.

When Lothar I died in 856 his Middle Kingdom was divided among his sons. Louis received Italy and the imperial crown, Lothar II the lands up to the North Sea, and Charles Burgundy and Provence. However, none of these was to be succeeded by his son, and all their reigns were constantly overshadowed by the relentless envy of their two uncles. Lothar II, whose kingdom was to bear his own name as *regnum Hlotharii* or Lotharingia, soon lost all his freedom of action. His marriage to Theutberga remained childless, and while he had a number of children by Waldrada, this liaison, blessed with offspring, bore the stigma of ecclesiastical disapproval. A king

---

[13] Hartmann (1989).   [14] Compare Nelson, pp. 124–6 above.   [15] BM 1435a; k; n.

without a son was *ipso facto* a weak ruler, and to change this situation, the
barren queen had to be removed from his side. A Lotharingian synod of the
realm was convened which granted a divorce on the grounds that Theutberga had been unfaithful.[16] The unfortunate lady and her influential family
turned to Charles the Bald (who was advised by his learned bishops) for
help; thence they appealed to the pope. In vain Lothar tried to win one or the
other uncle over to his side. In vain he lured his East Frankish relative with a
promise to cede Alsace. Both Charles and Louis immediately seized their
opportunity to attempt to get hold of Lothar's inheritance. Pope Nicholas I
went over to their side: he excommunicated Lothar's concubine for her
'obstinate determination to remain wallowing in the mire of fornication',[17]
and at a synod in Rome in 865 he deprived Bishops Gunthar of Cologne and
Thietgaud of Trier of their offices for having supported their king.
Nicholas' successor, Hadrian II, remained equally adamant. These incidents
do not only expose the personal character of political alliances; they also
point to a persistent influence on the part of the papacy during the formative
period of both Germany and France. A kingdom's chances of survival were
crucially diminished by papal interference making use of the law. Lothar II's
kingdom was further shaken by danger from outside: Viking raids were
becoming more numerous and also more efficient. The Vikings were acting,
certainly in effect if not in name, as allies of the West and East Frankish
kings.

When Lothar II died in 869, Charles II immediately invaded the Middle
Kingdom while his brother was detained at Regensburg by sickness and
warring Wends. Charles issued a stern summons to the Lotharingian nobles:
whoever did not hasten to his aid was to be stripped of all his royal fiefs and
personal estates. In 870 he had himself anointed and crowned in Metz,
ignoring Pope Hadrian's protests at this violation of the Treaty of Verdun;
his threats of excommunication (870) were also disregarded. The pope's
attempts to defend the claims of Louis II proved unavailing, for Louis –
who had no son – was another emperor without a future. As soon as Louis
recovered, Charles gave way, and 'Lotharingia' was partitioned from north
to south, a division which failed to take the linguistic boundary into
account. The Treaty of Meersen (870) confirmed the arrangement (Map 10).
Aachen became the third centre of the East Frankish kingdom, alongside
Regensburg and Frankfurt.[18] Every year Louis paid a visit to Charlemagne's
former capital, while the south of Lothar's old kingdom dwindled into a
peripheral zone of the realm.

---

[16] BM 1282a.

[17] Regino *s.a.* 866, pp. 87–8: 'nisi, obstinato animo in moechiae volutabro perenniter permanere
proposuisset'.   [18] Compare the itineraries of Louis the German and Louis the Younger.

Louis' kingdom continued to escape serious threats from without, though in 845 the Vikings attacked Hamburg, a flourishing trading centre which was about to become the metropolis of an archbishopric. Archbishop Ansgar (who died in 865) withdrew to Bremen. This was the beginning of the future archbishopric of Hamburg-Bremen eventually reorganised by Pope Nicholas I in 864.[19] It was, however, saved by a fortunate chance: in 854 an epidemic was brought in from the west and curbed the warlike spirit of the Northmen so that they took an oath to hold peace. This they really did for several decades up to 880. In return, Louis refrained from encouraging the Saxons to make small attacks against the Danes which might relieve the pressure on the Western and Middle kingdoms. Missionary endeavours in Scandinavia also came to a standstill despite a further visit by Ansgar, for the king's support for them was less than enthusiastic.

The danger from over the Elbe was also slight. Louis' 'pious' father had skilfully protected the eastern frontier by setting up a buffer zone (839).[20] The Slav peoples who had settled in the region were kept in check by occasional military campaigns. Neither in Bohemia nor in the central Elbe valley was there any outstanding sovereign ducal power. The church's missionary activity was making good progress: in 845 fourteen Bohemian *duces* were baptised in Regensburg.[21] Ten years later troops from Bavaria under Count Ernst (in 855) and the king himself (in 856) forced the Bohemians to pay tribute (Map 12).[22]

The only borderlands demanding constant attention were those close to the Moravians, Carinthians and Pannonians. Repeated expeditions under Louis, his son Carloman and the Bavarians (from 846 onwards) proved powerless to eliminate the Moravian duchy. The chief architects of Moravian power were Pribina, Mojmir and especially Rastislav (846–70) and Sventopolk (870–94).[23] They represented an ever-increasing danger to the Bavarians. Rastislav and Svatopluk even maintained contacts with a few Bavarian counts, as the former probably had a hand in the rebellion of Radbod (854), the long-serving prefect of the Bavarian frontier (he had first been appointed in 833). Rastislav even managed to win over Prince Carloman (858). But it does not appear that Louis the German ever planned to conquer Slav territories outside the established frontiers; at most he sought a kind of suzerainty over Moravia and Bohemia.

Missionary work in the southeast marches of the realm was the responsibility of the bishops of Passau, Regensburg and Salzburg. Rastislav aspired to independence from his neighbours, and therefore he made overtures to the Byzantine emperor Michael and asked him to send Greek missionaries

---

[19] Schieffer and Seegrün (1981).   [20] BM 995b.   [21] BM 1380a.
[22] BM 1411b.   [23] Compare Shepard, pp. 242–3 below.

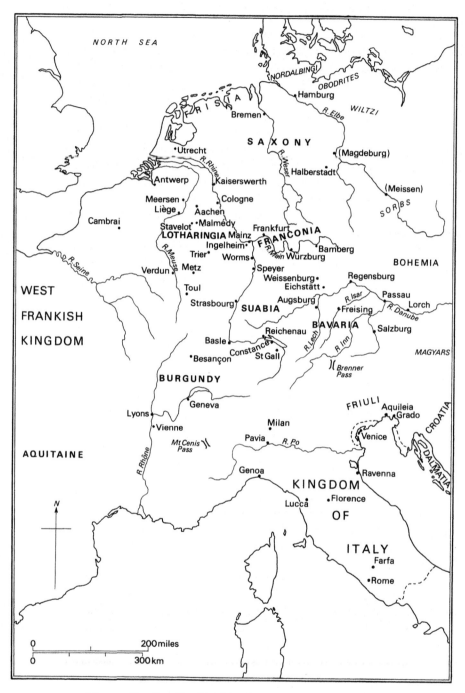

NORTH SEA

NORDALBINGI
OBODRITES
Hamburg
Bremen
R. Elbe
WILTZI

SAXONY

Utrecht
(Magdeburg)
Antwerp
Kaiserswerth
Halberstädt
(Meissen)
Meersen
Cologne
Liège
Aachen
SORBS
Stavelot
Malmedy
Cambrai
LOTHARINGIA
Mainz
Frankfurt
FRANCONIA
Ingelheim
Trier
Worms
Bamberg
Würzburg
BOHEMIA
Verdun
Metz
Speyer
Toul
Weissenburg
Regensburg
Eichstätt
Passau
WEST
Strasbourg
Augsburg
Lorch
SUABIA
Freising
R. Danube
FRANKISH
Salzburg
BAVARIA
KINGDOM
Basle
Reichenau
MAGYARS
Constance
Besançon
St Gall
Brenner
Pass
BURGUNDY

Geneva
FRIULI
Aquileia
Lyons
Grado
Vienne
Milan
Venice
Pavia
R. Po
CROATIA
AQUITAINE
Mt Cenis
Pass
Genoa
Ravenna
DALMATIA
KINGDOM
Lucca
Florence
N
OF
ITALY
Farfa
Rome

0   200 miles
0   300 km

R. Seine
R. Meuse
R. Rhine
R. Weser
R. Main
R. Isar
R. Lech
R. Inn
R. Rhône

FRISIA

Map 12 The East Frankish kingdom in the ninth century

(862). The *basileus* promptly dispatched Cyril and Methodius to the Moravians. The Bavarian bishops were furious.

At the same time, Boris, khan of the Bulgars, was aiming to build up a national church independent of Constantinople. Therefore, he sought support from the East Frankish king (866) with whom he had already established relations. A Bulgarian church established under the auspices of Bavaria would also have settled the ecclesiastical future of Moravia. Ermenrich of Passau was to lead the enterprise. In reality it was beyond the scope of the Bavarian and even the East Frankish episcopate. Even the very basics were lacking: liturgical vessels, vestments and books had to be cadged from the bishops of Charles the Bald.[24] When Ermenrich eventually arrived among the Bulgars he had come too late: missionaries from Rome were already preaching and baptising throughout the country so that the only thing left to do for the bishop of Passau was to go home again. The failure had an adverse effect on the mission to the Moravians and caused all the more ire at the Bavarian court. In 869 Louis the German sent three bodies of troops, each led by one of his sons, against the Slavs.

In 870 Rastislav finally fell victim to his treacherous nephew, Sventopolk, and was sent as a prisoner to Louis; he died in captivity. Not long afterwards, Methodius fell into the hands of the Bavarian bishops and was exiled to the innermost part of Alemannia where he spent three years before Pope John VIII intervened to free him. Meanwhile an Alemannian, Wiching by name, had become bishop of Nitra; he was later to become the most embittered enemy of Methodius.

Discontent first came to a head among the Bavarian nobility. From 854 onwards, there was increasing resistance; at that time there was an uprising after which Radbod, Prefect of the Eastern Marches, was deposed. Soon the whole eastern frontier zone boiled over. The royal house itself contributed to the turmoil. Louis, like his father, had three legitimate sons, Carloman, Louis (the Younger) and Charles (Charles III, the Fat), each of whom was to become a king in his own right. Carloman was the first to make a move. In 856 Louis put him in charge of the marches of the Bavarian east, but he put Carinthia under a count of its own. If this measure was intended to avoid the danger of revolt, it did not succeed, as Carloman married – probably without his father's permission – the daughter of Ernst, count of the Nordgau, who was the most influential of the Bavarian magnates. Immediately Carloman began to build up his own power at his father's expense. Instead of marching against the Moravians as Louis had wished, he made peace and entered into an alliance with Rastislav (858).[25] At that time Louis'

---

[24] BM 1462f.   [25] BM 1445a.

military activities detained him in the west of his kingdom. Only in 860 did he take action. Now the archbishopric of Salzburg was granted extensive royal estates in Pannonia and Carinthia: by strengthening the prelate Louis hoped to mitigate the danger from the lay nobility.[26] In the following year, Ernst was removed from office. His fall also brought down his nephews, Berengar, Udo and Abbot Waldo who belonged to the powerful Conradin family. They were exiled and lost all their possessions. Making a counter-move, Carloman subdued all Bavaria as far as the Inn. An undisguised struggle for power broke out between father and son in which Carloman eventually had to give in. In 863 he was accused of high treason and arrested. In 864 he managed to escape, but in the end he felt compelled to make peace with his father so that the latter eventually forgave him.

Louis was well aware of the threat his sons would pose to his kingdom as they grew to manhood. He tried to counter this by making preparations for the partition of his realm. As early as 859–65 he granted his sons powers less than those of a king, but greater than those of a noble, making them *principes*, 'governors' of separate tribal areas whose coherence they were bound to strengthen.[27] The king's sons thus became the predecessors and models of future dukes. In taking these measures Louis broadly followed the old tribal boundaries. Bavaria, which included Carinthia as well as (from 874) the claim to Italy and thus the imperial dignity, was to go to Carloman; Franconia and Saxony to Louis the Younger, who was also designated to receive the expected inheritance in Lotharingia and his father's hoped-for gains in West Francia. Alemannia was to go to Charles III.

Carloman, however, was the favourite of the queen, Emma. The background to this relationship is obscure, as is the exact role played by Louis' wife. Emma, who was sister to the Welf princess Judith, on whose account the imperial agreement of 817 had been abrogated, enticed her husband into machinations on her eldest son's behalf – or at least her younger offspring feared this was so. This drove the younger Louis into revolt in 865–6. Without having consulted his father, he betrothed himself to the daughter of Adalhard, whose influence in the West and Middle kingdoms was enormous, whose possessions were scattered all over the three parts of the realm and who thus represented that section of the nobility whose interests still extended over the entire Frankish realm. Together with his relatives, the Robertines, he had invited Louis the German to join his ill-fated invasion of the West kingdom in 858. Thus Louis' son was following a path which must have seemed to his father suspicious, if nothing more, while the West Frankish king could only see it as dangerous. Once again,

[26] *MGH Dip. Germ.* I, no. 102.   [27] Borgolte (1984).

Charles hastened to reconcile his brother and nephew. The younger Louis had to renounce his betrothal to Adalhard's daughter and marry the Saxon wife his father had chosen for him.

The peace remained precarious; several times Louis the Younger, deeply mistrustful of Carloman, quarrelled with his father, but each time harmony was restored. To have prevented open war among his sons was probably Louis the German's greatest achievement. He was ever willing to forgive them, and after each revolt he increased their share of power.

All in all, Louis the German's reign was a period of remarkable stability; only in the marches of eastern Bavaria was there some dangerous unrest. 'Germania' was still less developed and poorer than the West and Middle kingdoms. It was mainly for this reason, among others, that it was less troubled by over-mighty Frankish noble families who made life so difficult for Charles the Bald, and by the two Lothars. Only a handful of isolated nobles rebelled against the king; there was not a trace of any alliances (*coniurationes*) among the noble families. Louis' opponents never developed any form of organisation independent of himself or his sons; the royal court was the only place where the nobility ever appeared in a body. This made it easier for Louis to restrain the individual magnates who rebelled against him. The power of the nobles was still extensive rather than intensive. Certainly the monarchy would have needed to tighten its grip to resist the growing pressure from the nobility in the future: that Louis failed in this is revealed by the astonishing weakness of royal power after his death. Louis was in fact resting on his predecessors' laurels; he was not an innovator. His government was, as it were, backward-looking. He put most of his energy into grabbing ever larger chunks of his ancestors' original estate in which he, too, was subject to the primitive notion that it was the size of the realm which determined one's standing as a ruler.

The death of the 'great' Louis aroused the avarice of 'bald' Charles. Perhaps he had been invited in by some Lotharingians, perhaps he came of his own accord, haloed by the glory of his recent successes, for he had just taken possession of Italy (875) and of the imperial crown.[28] He had (as he claimed) entered into the Treaty of Verdun with Louis only and not with his sons; Charles' nephews were either to submit or to be blinded; their followers were to be deprived of their possessions or sent into exile unless they did him homage immediately. Near Andernach, on the Rhine, Louis the Younger inflicted a defeat on his uncle which consolidated his new kingship.

Louis the German's sons divided the realm amongst themselves in

---

[28] Compare Nelson, pp. 126–7 above.

accordance with the order of succession. They met in the Nördlinger Ries in November 876 to swear mutual loyalty. The nobility's conception of themselves must surely have been affected by this as the peoples conquered by the Franks now appeared with the same rights as their former vanquishers; the future history of East Francia was to be profoundly affected by this. The brothers came to a similar arrangement for dividing the eastern half of Lotharingia between Louis and Charles, while Carloman received Italy (877).

When Carloman surrendered his claim to Lotharingia he for the first time abandoned his policy directed towards 'Francia' and the west which his son, Arnulf, was to resume and which proved to have a future. All of his attention was focused on the east and south. The claim to Italy which Carloman had recently (874) obtained from the Emperor Louis had of course first to be asserted against Pope John VIII and Charles the Bald (875);[29] only after his uncle's death in 877 did Carloman gain a real hold on the Lombard kingdom. The pope was not amused: a king from Bavaria could more easily reach Rome than one from northern Gaul. He set out to prevent Carloman's coronation in Rome and tried to persuade Louis the Stammerer to take the imperial crown instead (878). But Louis refused. However, this did little good to Carloman the Bavarian as he was struck down by disease and died without fulfilling the hopes which had been placed in him.

Seen in the context of further developments in German history, the kingdom of Louis the Younger deserves particular attention. Louis alone still ruled as king 'in Eastern Francia' while his brothers ruled 'in Bavaria' or 'in Italy'. This was when the name formerly used for the whole realm began to be confined to the narrower ethnic territory of the German Franks. The archbishop of Mainz had his see, his diocese and most of his province within Louis' kingdom. Archbishop Liutbert was also Louis the Younger's chancellor, and Louis' marriage into the Liudolfing dynasty raised it above the generality of the Saxon nobility. Louis' realm united the peoples who, to the Ottonians, were the pillars of the kingdom, that is, the Franks and the Saxons, to which could be added the Lotharingians. He was married to Liutgard, of the Liudolfing family, kept close contacts with the Babenbergers and also received the Conradins, whom his father had stripped of power, at his court. By gathering these three noble houses around himself, Louis was conciliating not only his father's enemies, but also, more importantly, the representatives of the most respected noble families in the East who, through their West Frankish relations, had enormous influence

[29] Fried (1982).

throughout the whole realm. Thus it was at the court of the younger Louis that the configuration first arose which was to govern the fate of Eastern Francia at the beginning of the tenth century. The West of his realm, together with Lotharingia, was the object of Louis' closest attention. The Treaty of Fouron which he made with his cousin Louis the Stammerer in 878 guaranteed the integrity of both kingdoms even in the case of their sons' succession.[30] The West Frankish nobility's loyalties were divided, of course, and when Charles' son died, some great West Frankish nobles invited the East Frankish king, Louis, to come over even though their own king had left two sons. Louis the Younger paid scant regard to the treaty to which he had just sworn and accepted the invitation. Once again Hincmar of Rheims organised the resistance and compelled Louis to abandon the enterprise in return for the transfer of the Lotharingian West. For the first time the western frontier of Lotharingia appeared as the frontier of the East Frankish kingdom; the Treaty of Ribémont (880) sealed the agreement.

The inheritance of Lotharingia altered the demands on the East Frankish king, for now he had to beat back the Vikings. What is more, Hugh, the bastard son of Lothar II, was in league with them and was busy doing his foul work there. At first (873) the Vikings were driven back, but three years later the next band of pirates was bivouacking and wreaking havoc in Frisia, and from 879 onwards a 'great host' led by a number of 'kings' made an attempt to settle permanently on the lower Rhine. Louis' moves against them were unsuccessful. In 880 he had to abandon his siege of Nijmegen prematurely and let the besieged Vikings escape. In the same year the Northmen annihilated a Saxon force led by the Liudolfing Brun. Louis' West Frankish cousin and namesake had better luck: in 881 he defeated the Vikings at Saucourt. The 'great host' shifted its sphere of operations to Lotharingia and thus into the kingdom of Louis the Younger. The whole area between the Rhine and the Meuse was ravaged; the Vikings kept their horses in the lady chapel at Aachen. Cologne and Bonn were burned down; Trier lost its Roman character which it had hitherto managed to preserve (881–2).[31] After his uncle had died and his brother Carloman had fallen ill in 878, Louis was the oldest legitimate Carolingian who enjoyed full freedom of action. Opposition groups in Bavaria turned to him. In order to steal a march on his brother Charles, therefore, he accepted the succession in Bavaria and its adjoining lands while ceding his claims to Italy to Charles (879–80). This settlement did not, however, prove to be a lasting one. Louis died prematurely of disease in 882 while the Vikings were still wreaking havoc in Lotharingia.

---

[30] *MGH Cap.* II, no. 246, pp. 168–70.   [31] Anton (1987).

Louis had been a man who stood, as it were, at the intersection of two major conflicting trends causing a good deal of polarised tension. He regarded neither the East Frankish kingdom of his father nor the part of the realm he himself had inherited as a self-contained unit. However, Louis was the nucleus of a grouping of nobles who insisted on the validity of the partition of 843 and thus became instrumental in the transition from Frankish to German history.

Louis' inheritance passed to his youngest brother, Charles. He seemed to have attained what every Carolingian king aimed at: a united empire well under his control. Italy (879), the imperial crown (881) and finally the West (885) also fell to him without any effort on his part; only Burgundy and Provence, where Boso had made himself king in 879 in defiance of the Carolingians, escaped his suzerainty. Yet since 843 the nobles of the various sub-kingdoms had been going their separate ways. The sub-kingdoms did not simply disappear after the reunification, as is shown by the royal documents which continued to be dated according to Charles' reign 'in Italy' (from 882), 'in Gaul' (from 885) and 'in Francia' (in the East Frankish kingdom), indicating that the former royal chanceries still existed.[32] However, this was of little significance, as the reunification lasted for barely three years, that is until 887–8. A more successful emperor might have made a good many changes.

For a short time, there was renewed hope for a restoration of the empire's unity. However Charles achieved very little; worst of all, he could not shake off his Alemannian past; most of his counsellors were Alemannians. This was a source of discontent, and it alienated the Franks, who gathered around Liutbert of Mainz.[33] This archbishop, who could easily have become instrumental in bringing about the unity of the East Frankish kingdom, had been royal chaplain since 870. As soon as Charles had succeeded his brother in 882, he deprived Liutbert of that office and gave it to Liutward who had already been made bishop of Vercelli in 880. Bavaria also did badly out of the change of rulers, and under Charles it eventually came to share Saxony's role as a neglected territory. The Bavarian nobility were more divided among themselves than ever; Charles, indeed, had no intention of allowing the province to be ruled by one man, not even by his nephew Arnulf. Further east, the change of rulers proved equally disastrous. Under Svatopluk, Moravia's unabated rise to the status of a powerful kingdom continued. Soon there was open war between Bavarians and Moravians.

Charles proved unequal to his initial good fortune. Having just succeeded his brother, he led an attack on the Vikings. They were besieged at Asselt,

---

[32] Brühl (1990), pp. 90–4.   [33] Keller (1966).

on the Meuse, in 882, and seemed on the brink of annihilation when Charles made peace with them, accepted their king Godfrid as his vassal and marched off again. The annalist of Fulda (who was closely associated with Liutbert of Mainz) was fuming with impotent rage as he recorded the events of that year. There were also disputes over policy as Liutward thought it better to negotiate rather than fight: instead of attempting to drive out the Vikings, they should be given fiefs in the threatened regions so that they owed a duty to the king and could be burdened with the defence of the territory. However, the Alemannian was not to have his way. The Franks held open war in higher esteem, and Charles' reputation was shaken and rapidly diminished. Eventually he had to part with Liutward, who was replaced in 887 by his most inveterate enemy, Archbishop Liutbert. Although the latter hastened to change sides and became a supporter of Charles while the disgraced Liutward went over to Arnulf of Carinthia, the new archbishop of Mainz was unable to undo the harm that had already been done.

The Viking incursions were worse than ever: the 'great host' was back, and this time it meant to stay. In 884 and 885 the Northmen appeared again in Saxony, but were driven back; when they entrenched themselves at Duisburg, the most convenient of the Rhine ports, for several winters, the menace could be contained. The defence was organised by Heinrich, an early 'Babenberger', the former *princeps militiae* of Louis the Younger. But he was killed trying to relieve Paris, which was besieged by the Vikings, in 886. The gap he left was filled by his brothers-in-law, the Liudolfings, in Saxony.

Fresh dangers were also brewing in the East. A murderous struggle for power flared up in Thuringia among the leading families: the 'Babenberger Feud' was in its early stages. Unrest was growing in Bavaria, stirred up by both the native nobility and the prince of Moravia. And even in Alemannia rivalry was growing amongst factions of nobles who alternated between supporting and opposing the king; Liutward fell victim to them in 887. All in all, there was mounting discontent with the unsuccessful emperor.

Charles strove to put his house in order. Although Richardis had borne him no children, he did have a son, one Bernard, by a concubine, to whom he planned to bequeath his realm. He did his best to safeguard this arrangement, but it was all in vain. The nobility were little inclined to submit to a minor. Bernard did not succeed his father. Apparently, the long series of disasters forced Charles the Fat into the greatest concession that could be wrung from a Carolingian: he had to relinquish the restored unity and consent to a new partition of the realm. It is probable, however, that this split into a number of *regna*, some not even ruled by Carolingians, had already been planned during Charles' reign in the form which it actually took after the emperor's downfall.

Arnulf, for his part, was not going to be satisfied with a subordinate position. He had every reason to be angry with his uncle. Under Louis the Younger he had occupied a prominent position in Bavaria, but Charles had confined him to Carinthia and Pannonia and had kept him 'short of estates and within narrow bounds'.[34] This really amounted to a considerable come-down for Charles' nephew. Arnulf accordingly began to gather his uncle's enemies around himself. When power began to slip between the ailing emperor's fingers, Arnulf knew that his time had come. He came in force to an assembly near Tribur in 887, ousted his uncle and went to nearby Frankfurt to receive the homage of the nobles who were present, and who may have been in collusion with him. Soon afterwards, probably at Forchheim, he had himself formally elected as king by all the tribes and was eventually crowned at Regensburg. Charles survived this humiliation for about eight weeks before succumbing to his illness. His son Bernard was killed three years later (891) when he rebelled against the upstart Arnulf.

The new king was an usurper. After the premature death of his father he had no overriding claim to the throne, and he unscrupulously exploited his uncle's sickness to elbow him out and forestall the superior claims of other Carolingian magnates and pretenders to the throne. Nearer to the throne than he, or at least as near, were two minors, Bernard and Charles the Simple; however, Lothar II's son Hugh was ineligible as he had been blinded. There was no noble family in Eastern Francia, apart from the royal line, which had come to be prominent enough to aspire to the throne, as happened in the West and in Italy. There were not many obstacles to Arnulf's recognition. Although he did have some opponents, he did not have to fear a rival.

The West Franks did not participate in this upheaval, and neither did the 'Italians'; nevertheless the event was of considerable significance. Everywhere, new kings were appearing: January 888 saw the rise in Italy of the Unruoching Berengar of Friuli, and in Upper Burgundy of the Welf Rudolf, who had his eye on Alemannia and Lotharingia. In Gaul there was the Robertine Odo who stole a march on Wido of Spoleto; in Provence, there was Louis, the grandson of a Carolingian; and in Aquitaine, there was Ramnulf, the only one to give in prematurely (in 888). Here, decisive action was taken without questions of law having been settled in advance. Arnulf could do nothing about it because he had no better title to his kingship than the others had to theirs, although as king of the whole East Frankish realm

[34] Notker, *Gesta Karoli* II. 34.

he was powerful enough to exercise a kind of hegemony over the other 'petty kings'.[35]

In the first years after he had seized the throne, Arnulf made an appearance in all the provinces of his realm. Yet he made no attempt to fight for the whole empire even when in 890, after Odo's uprising, Fulk of Rheims offered him the crown of the West Frankish kingdom, and Pope Stephen V that of Rome. Arnulf bowed to the inevitable, recognised Odo (888–98), acknowledged Berengar as king of Italy and, for the time being, Rudolf as king of Upper Burgundy (888), while confirming Louis' claim by presenting him with a sceptre (889). Thus, Arnulf sanctioned Charles the Fat's plan for a partition of the empire – if there really had been such a plan – with only one exception: he took Bernard's place for himself. As a token of 'friendship' Arnulf sent the Robertian a crown, with which Odo did in fact have himself crowned by the metropolitan bishop of Rheims. Only Wido, whose appearance had disturbed the partition of the realm which may already have been planned under Charles III, and who even seemed to be striving for the hegemony over the whole of the Frankish realm, remained unrecognised by Arnulf.

Arnulf's defence of his kingdom was put to its most severe test by the Vikings. He gave battle to them on the Dyle near Leuven in 892: this was one of the last combats against the Vikings within what was to become the 'German' empire. For the Vikings were of course no longer entering the Frankish kingdom only to plunder it: now they wanted to stay there. They were ferociously driven back. Then, at last, the 'great host' turned back to England, overrunning the east of that country, which became the Danelaw.[36] The pressure on the Frankish kingdom was substantially reduced. The church proved to be the strongest support to the late Carolingian king: there existed a relationship characterised by mutual dependence. While sections of the lay nobility often rebelled, the bishops remained loyal. Bishops and abbots from all over the realm regularly attended the royal assemblies in large numbers. Arnulf allowed them greatly to influence his decisions. The synods, especially, gained an importance which was unprecedented in the East Frankish realm; this is all the more surprising in that in the West, after the death of the great Hincmar in 882, a contrary tendency had been perceptible. It was also on Frankish soil that the most important assembly of this era met: this was at Tribur, southwest of Frankfurt, in 895.[37] Twenty-six bishops from all the provinces of the realm assembled under the leadership of Hatto of Mainz, Heriman of Cologne and Ratbod of Trier, and

---

[35] Regino *s.a.* 888, p. 129: 'Multos enim idoneos principes ad regni gubernacula moderanda Francia genuisset'.   [36] Compare Keynes, p. 42 above.

[37] *MGH Cap.* II, no. 252, pp. 196–249.

almost sixty canons were promulgated. The reforms they agreed on formed a coherent programme. However, it was not granted to Arnulf to implement this programme. He was remarkably generous in his frequent endowments from which the bishops benefited: monasteries, forests, rights of coinage, the right to hold markets and to exact customs dues were granted to them in unprecedented measure. In return, the bishops took on increased military responsibilities and were both expected and able to create their own followings of vassals as the lay nobility had already been doing for some time.

While Arnulf favoured the bishops, this did not mean that he neglected the laity. Notable regional differences can be discerned. Alongside Franconia, Bavaria once again became the centre of royal power: most of the recipients and interveners of Arnulf's documents lived there. It was this *regnum* that was Arnulf's power base, and it was in its palaces that he preferred to reside. He seldom held assemblies there, however, and the documents he issued in Bavaria (apart from Regensburg) were normally intended for Bavarian recipients only and seldom for those who lived in other parts of the realm. The latter tended to go to Franconia, especially the Rhine–Main area, in order to meet the king there. It was there that he had won his kingdom, and it was mainly from there that he ruled it.

Bavaria was exceptionally important to Arnulf. Probably as early as 876, Carloman had entrusted the defence of his eastern frontier to his son; here he had risen to prominence; all his past bound him to the East of his realm. The duke of Carinthia had already turned his whole attention to the continuing disputes with the Slavs of Moravia. He had soon clashed with Svatopluk Moravia. In 884 and 885 Arnulf was compelled to make peace, surrendering Bohemia and maybe even parts of Pannonia to Svatopluk, but as soon as he became king he tried to wipe off this disgrace. He immediately started to build fortified refuges, thus preparing for a military confrontation. In vain did the margrave Aribo try to convince him that the Moravians desired only peace. From 892 onwards he made war on them, even calling on the Magyars for aid. After Svatopluk's death in 894 when his sons, Mojmir II and Svatopluk II, quarrelled over the succession, Arnulf began to do much better. The Bohemians at once (895) did homage to the Frankish king, but again some of the Bavarian nobles had sided with the Moravians, which made it difficult, and eventually impossible, to make radical changes here.

Arnulf's conflicts with the nobility became more and more embittered, and they were not confined to Bavaria. The 'Babenberger' Poppo, the 'duke of the Thuringians', rather surprisingly lost his fiefs and allodia in 892; at the same time, the Conradin Rudolf received the bishopric of Würzburg, whereby his family extended its influence to the East Frankish border and brought it to bear on the Babenbergers. This step had certainly been brought about by the queen, Uta, who was also a Conradin. The emperor realised his mistake, but it was too late: the 'Babenberger Feud' which turned Babenbergers and Conradins into irreconcilable enemies, and in which the Liutpoldings of Bavaria became involved as well, continued to run its course and laid an unendurable burden on the reign of his son, Louis.[38] Other nobles also felt the weight of Arnulf's anger. It seems odd, in this context, that the margrave Aribo had scarcely been demoted when he was again restored to his 'prefecture'; only his son continued to be out of favour and did not become reconciled until later, with Louis the Child.[39] Evidently Arnulf had no such thing as a clear-cut policy.

The king was especially perturbed by an alliance between Hildegard, a legitimate daughter of Louis the Younger, and Engildeo, count of the Northern Gau of Bavaria, who had clashed with Arnulf when he had merely been a duke. Arnulf deposed the count and, 'according to the counsel and judgement of the Franks, Bavarians, Saxons and Alemanni' stripped his cousin of all her possessions and banished her to a nunnery at Frauenchiem-see (895).[40] Hildegard was soon free again; however, the noble Liutpold took over the role of Engildeo. Legal proceedings in the royal court deserve particular attention. The princess was judged by a royal court of justice whose members were drawn from all the peoples who had elected Arnulf as king. This was new at the time, but it was to become ever more common. It was not the constitution of law courts that had changed, but the ideology of kingship. It now embraced more than the narrow circle around the ruler: the nobility also had a part in it. This pointed to a hitherto unknown unity between king and nobles which was henceforth to represent the realm.

In 889 the king paid another visit to Saxony in the course of an expedition against the Obodrites. He had not been there for a long time. However, all he did there was to acknowledge the status quo which had been emerging during the last thirty years. He only renewed his influence over the royal monasteries of Corvey and Herford,[41] and his relationship with the nobility was made clearer than it had been under his predecessors: he obviously made considerable efforts to win them over. The cathedrals also received rich gifts. This relationship had been inverted since the beginning of the century: then, the Saxon nobility had attained to power and influence by cultivating connections with the Frankish king, but now the Carolingian was streng-thening his support in the province through the power which the nobility had gained there. The Liudolfings kept on good terms with the royal house, as the marriage mentioned above amply demonstrates;[42] in the borderlands

---

[38] Dümmler (1887–8) III, pp. 521–45.   [39] Schwarzmeier (1972).
[40] Arnulf, *DDArn* 132.   [41] *DDArn* 28; 60; 105; 155.   [42] Compare p. 156.

of Saxony, Thuringia and Franconia they were competing more and more with the Conradins. Other families, such as the Ekbertines, were generously endowed with royal lands, perhaps in order to strengthen them against the Liudolfings. The constellation which was to dominate the early years of the next century was already in preparation: it was to be Conradins and Ekbertines versus Liudolfings and Babenbergers.

Alemannia, where the nobility had offered some opposition to the coup of 887, became a marginal zone seldom visited by the king, who nevertheless did make his influence felt by means of documents. For this region, which bordered on Burgundy and with whose king, a Welf, Arnulf had been at war shortly after he had recognised him (888), could distress him. Once again it was to the monasteries of St Gall and Reichenau that the king showed the greatest favour. His chancellor Salomo, Bishop of Constance since 890, was an Alemannian; in 891 he received the monastery of St Gall. The abbot of Reichenau, Hatto, was made archbishop of Mainz in 891. While Arnulf kept a steady interest in the East of his realm, he was content to leave the West largely to its own devices. His attention was very unevenly distributed. He focused on what had been the kingdom of Louis the German, including Italy. His attitude towards Lotharingia, and to the West in general, was somewhat ambiguous. Having subdued these regions in the campaigns of 891 and 893, he then handed them over to his incompetent and illegitimate son Zwentibold in 895.[43] The latter never managed to bridle the local nobility and frittered away his strength in useless campaigns, in the last of which (900) he was killed. The Lotharingians then sided with his brother Louis.

The Western Kingdom was even more divorced from Arnulf's immediate concerns than was Lotharingia. He was content with a suzerainty which he exercised only once, when Fulk of Rheims rescued Charles, the last remaining agnatic nephew of Arnulf, from the oblivion into which he had sunk. Fulk had never been a friend to the Robertines, having previously (888) given his support to his kinsman, Wido of Spoleto; he reluctantly did homage to Odo, but on the first opportunity (893) presented him with a rival. He anointed the young Charles the Simple,[44] who eventually, hard pressed by Odo, asked Arnulf to confirm his title to his 'paternal kingdom' (894). Arnulf accepted his newphew's title, but he did not break with Odo. Evidently he was toying with the idea of a further partition of the West Frankish kingdom, but he left the execution to the kings most directly involved (895). When, in 898, Odo died without a male heir, Charles' claim was generally accepted.

---

[43] BM 1908a.   [44] Dümmler (1887–8) III, p. 383.

Arnulf was no more willing to lose his grip on Italy than his father had been. That country came to be entirely at the mercy of the nobles: Berengar of Friuli, the Widones and Adalbert of Tuscany were competing for the Carolingian inheritance and, even during Arnulf's lifetime (in 898), Louis of Provence also reached for the imperial crown. Earlier, in 890, Pope Stephen had sought help from Arnulf, but then the latter had turned him down. Therefore Wido and his son Lambert were crowned emperors (891). Only in 896 did Arnulf come to Rome. The Romans opposed this foreign master, however, and when the Carolingian appeared, they barred their gates against him. Arnulf had to break the gates down before he could be crowned by the pope – a prophetic scene. He then compelled the Romans to swear allegiance to him, but to little effect: they swore the oath only to abjure it immediately afterwards. Moreover, Wido's son, the Emperor Lambert, was still alive (he died in 898): he was a youth of sixteen and he had no intention of resigning the crown. So when Arnulf was crowned in St Peter's, he was merely a rival emperor.

The end of Arnulf's reign was as paralysed as its beginning had been confident. Soon after he had assumed the Roman crown he had a stroke. He became a sick man, and royal power declined with him. This decline was heralded by gloomy auspices. Arnulf eventually died in 900 while a new enemy, the Magyars, laid waste Pannonia and Bavaria. Arnulf had called them in himself years before, when, in 892, he had been campaigning against the Moravians. Although the first defeats of 862 and 881, and raids on Bulgaria, Carinthia and Moravia (889), ought to have warned him, the king evidently underestimated the danger from the Magyars; at least he strengthened his eastern borders, built castles and reorganised his border defences. It was then (893) that Luitpold was made margrave of Carinthia and Upper Pannonia. Just when the danger seemed to have been averted, the Magyars suddenly appeared in northern Italy and annihilated a Lombard army on the Brenta. Very soon after Arnulf's death they were invading Bavaria (900); they advanced over the Enns, and year after year they kept coming back. The Moravian kingdom against which both Carolingians and Bavarians had struggled in vain succumbed to their attacks in 905/6, as did the Slav principality of Lower Pannonia with its centre Moosburg-Zalavar on Lake Balaton. The main field for the emergence of Slav power shifted to the Prague basin and thus to the court of the Premyslids.

The local defence contingents were too clumsy for intercepting these swift warriors of the steppes; what is more, the Magyars' weaponry and tactics were unfamiliar to mail-clad horsemen. In 907 a Bavarian force suffered a crushing defeat on the Marchfeld near Pressburg, where margrave Luitpold and many other nobles were slain. Wreaking havoc all the way, the

Magyars reached the far west. This situation called for self-help. Bishop
Thietlach of Worms (891–914), for example, issued regulations concerning
the building of town walls which had some influence on bringing the
concept of town life back into higher esteem. Elsewhere, manors and
villages were fortified as well.

People like Arnulf of Bavaria, the son of Luitpold who had fallen in 907,
who proved their worth under these circumstances thus established their
own right to exert power. Several times (in 909, 910 and 913) he triumphed
over Magyars as they hastened to get home and, subduing Bavaria, secured
for himself a ducal power verging on kingship. This involved seizures of
royal and church property. Arnulf imposed himself as *de facto* ruler, tolerated
at best by the king, but not formally recognised. Similar developments took
place elsewhere both before and after this. A notable case is Saxony where
Otto the Illustrious, father of the later King Henry, founded a Saxon duchy.
A basically similar development took place in Alemannia. In all these *regna*
the king's influence dwindled almost to nothing, except for the occasional
church which preferred the lordship of a distant king to that of a nearby
duke.

Arnulf's son, Louis the Child, ascended the throne in 900 at the age of six.
Great hopes were vested in the boy who was expected to reach out for the
imperial crown, but he died ingloriously, at just seventeen years old. The
obvious consequences were to follow. 'Few are peaceably inclined, all are
quarrelling, the bishop, the count and their retainers; fellow townsmen and
kinsmen fight among themselves; the townsfolk grumble, and unrest is rife
in the towns, too.' The poet, an Alemannian, probably Salomo of Constance,[45] was no doubt not only thinking of the notorious 'Babenberger
Feud' into which the infant king had been drawn by his mother's relations:
violence was rife everywhere. The feud just mentioned was ended when
Hatto of Mainz intervened and Adalbert of Babenberg was executed. It had
almost looked as if the whole family had been doomed to extinction. Again,
decisive steps such as the confiscation of the Babenbergers' property (903),
were approved by jurors from all the peoples of the East Frankish kingdom:
the nobility of the entire kingdom were to appear jointly responsible for the
king's actions.

Others were ready to step into the king's shoes: his godfather and tutor
Adalbero of Augsburg; Salomo III of Constance; the most important, Hatto
of Mainz, also godfather to the child; and, last but not least, the Conradins,
who had their eye on Lotharingia. The boy king was brought up mainly in

---

[45] *MGH Poet.* IV, p. 301, vv. 116–19: 'Rari sint nostrum quorum mens tendat in unum/Discordant
omnes, praesul, comes atque phalanges,/Pugnant inter se concives contribulesque,/Urbica turba
strepit, machinantur et oppida bellum.'

Franconia and also in Alemannia, that is, in Hatto's and the Conradins' sphere of influence, but less in Bavaria (especially after the battle of Pressburg); there, his family had enjoyed the strongest support from 817. Louis almost completely avoided going to the remaining regions of his kingdom. However, all the noble families were still represented at his court and mentioned in his documents, and nobody invited a foreign king to help himself to the East Frankish throne. Lotharingia, too, was seldom visited by Louis. Trusting in the boy king's authority, the Conradin Gebhard tried to seize the ducal power there; the nobility, headed by the Matfridings, resisted these attempts. When he fell in battle against the Magyars in 910, the Lotharingians abandoned the child king (910) and, immediately after his death, paid homage to the West Frankish king Charles III, the Simple.

When young Louis died, the *stirps regia*, to which the East Franks had remained more faithful than others, died with him. There, after all – in contrast to the Lotharingians – nobody seemed inclined to accept the only remaining scion of the old ruling house, the undisputed ruler of the West, Charles the Simple.[46] The later Carolingians had proved less and less able to control the nobility because they had nothing left to offer. Their resources were exhausted, but their kingly duty of generosity still remained. Charlemagne's successors had given away so much that they had eroded the substance of their power. Charles the Fat saw the results, as did his rebellious cousin Arnulf. The nobles were no longer prepared to bow to these kings; their demands increased, and more and more they came to pursue aims of their own. There was nothing 'fearful' any more about this outworn monarchy. Instead, the slow agony of the ruling house led to a kind of shadow kingship, ever more hotly contested by the leaders of the lay nobility with their pretensions to ducal status; they no longer derived their power from the king. No longer were the raising of armies, the keeping of the peace and the right of judgement over freemen royal prerogatives; the nobility even usurped the control over churches. Nevertheless the uniqueness of the name of king outlived the Carolingians themselves – more a chance than a reality, but as such it did become the basis for the re-establishment of kingship by the Ottonians. Bishops and monks, menaced by the local nobility, fell back on the king and continued, being literate men and thus guardians of the collective memory, to develop the concept of a suprapersonal kingship.

The ninth century was an extremely troubled and eventful period. Everything was changing. This does not necessarily imply that new impulses came to the fore; however, old ones grew stronger. Memories of

---

[46] Compare Nelson, pp. 138–41 above.

the old Carolingian unity grew faint; the cohesiveness of the Eastern realm, united under one king, increased; the nobility strengthened its position, and the Saxon north gained in importance. The different peoples made the East Frankish, or German, kingdom a multiracial state, a jigsaw of many *patriae* whose sole visible element of unity was the royal court. Only the basic acceptance of the king by the nobles of all the 'peoples' safeguarded the links which allowed royal power to penetrate, albeit with widely varying intensity, into every part of the realm. There still was no such thing as a sense of national identity common to all the 'peoples'. The nobles of each people established themselves in its own territory, there aspiring to earldoms and seigneurial power; there they sought consolidation of power and property, there they were busy building up a network of relationships, marriage alliances and vassals; there they put their relatives in cathedral chapters and on bishops' thrones and founded monasteries. It was mainly in the regions peripheral to royal rule that the nobility could strengthen its position, and it was in Saxony that royal power was reborn, a royal power both going back to Carolingian tradition and, at the same time, assuming a new shape.

CHAPTER 6

FINES IMPERII: THE MARCHES

Julia M.H. Smith

'Have a Frank as a friend, not as a neighbour.'
Byzantine proverb. Einhard, *Vita Karoli*, 16

A VENERABLE historiographical tradition tells the story of the Frankish kingdoms from the perspective of the royal court. Viewed from this angle, the expansion of the Carolingian realm and the establishment of its frontiers offer a straightforward narrative of military success, interspersed with the occasional setback. Celebrated by Einhard, such a view reduces the frontiers of the Carolingian empire to insignificance, of moment only when invasion or revolt drew royal attention to them.[1] This chapter offers an inverse picture of the Carolingian polity. It takes the reader from royal capitals and palaces to the cliffs of Brittany, the high plateaux of the Pyrenees, the mountains of southern Italy and of the eastern Alps, and the arterial waterways of the Danube and the Elbe (see Map 4). By concentrating on these outlying regions, it asks questions about the limits and limitations of Carolingian power. In studying the interaction of centre and periphery, it provides a cross-section of the Carolingian empire. By analysing ways of securing borders, asserting influence and manipulating neighbours, it highlights vital administrative and political skills. Since all political entities define themselves in part through the nature of their boundaries, 'peripheral vision' may assist in focusing our images of the centre.[2]

CHARLEMAGNE'S EMPIRE

Exploration of frontier regions must begin by noting where the outer limits of the Carolingian empire lay, and by ascertaining why they were located

---

[1] Compare Fouracre, Nelson and Fried, chapters 3–5 above. For complementary approaches to two of the regions to be discussed in this chapter, see Shepherd and Collins, chapters 9 and 11 below.   [2] Cf. Eadie (1977).

where they were. The crucial question underlying both points, why Frankish expansion under Charlemagne halted *where* it did, has received little attention from historians, who have preferred to contemplate why it ceased *when* it did. Rather than assuming (as so often has been done) a thwarted Carolingian urge towards constant aggrandisement, we should credit Charlemagne with a clear sense of the appropriate and attainable bounds of his power. A propagandist at work very shortly after Charlemagne's imperial coronation offers an explanation of what those bounds were. For the author of the *Annales Mettenses Priores*, Charlemagne completed the task begun by Pippin II of reconstituting under direct Carolingian rule all those territories which had once either acknowledged direct Merovingian rule or submitted to Merovingian hegemony.[3] Even including the Lombard kingdom, seized in 774 as the logical culmination of the Franco-papal entente, there was 'something profoundly conservative and definitive in early Carolingian conquests'.[4] In its essentials, the Carolingian empire renewed the Merovingian sphere of influence, but substituted direct rule for overlordship wherever possible. Certainly Theudebert I's boast to Justinian I in *c.*535 that he ruled 'from the Danube and the frontiers of Pannonia to the Ocean' is also an apt description of the extent of Carolingian rule by the end of the eighth century.[5] For the most part then, Carolingian frontiers were not established by deliberate strategic choice: they were inherited from the outlying *regna* newly subjected to Frankish rule.

Where pre-existing limits were extended, local circumstances governed their advance. In Saxony, arguably, the exigencies of security necessitated the extension of Carolingian rule to the Elbe and even the establishment of fortifications on the right bank. Charlemagne moved into Istria in the wake of the Lombard Desiderius.[6] In Bavaria, he inherited from Tassilo in 788 the Agilolfing duke's claims to hegemony over the Slavs of Carentania, where Bavarian churches were already busy colonising and converting. These activities pulled direct Frankish rule ever further eastwards; one century later, by the death of Louis the German (876), East Frankish counts were established some 200 km further east and south, in Pannonia, Carniola and Carentania.[7] By contrast, the gradual extension of new settlement down the southern flanks of the eastern Pyrenees in the course of the ninth century led to the expansion of Carolingian administrative structures but no direct extension of royal authority, for by 885, when the colonisers were incorporated into the new county of Vich, direct West Frankish intervention in the affairs of this area had already ceased.[8]

---

[3] *Annales Mettenses Priores*, pp. 12–13; Werner (1973).   [4] Noble (1990), p. 339.
[5] *Epistolae Austrasiacae* 20, *MGH Epp.* III, p. 133; Wood (1983); James (1988), pp. 91–108.
[6] Cessi (1940).   [7] Reindel (1965); Mitterauer (1963), pp. 1–7, 85–90, 160–9.
[8] D'Abadal i de Vinyals (1958), pp. 73–114; Freedman (1991), pp. 57–61.

At its fullest extent, Charlemagne's empire comprised an essentially Frankish 'heartland' in Austrasia and Neustria, surrounded by a ring of non-Frankish *regna*. Preferred royal haunts tended to be in the interior region where family ties and landholdings were concentrated. Two implications of this for an analysis of peripheral regions are immediately apparent. In the first instance, Austrasia/Neustria only abutted the outer margin of the empire in two adjacent stretches. The sea coast from the Rhine delta south to the Bay of Mont-Saint-Michel formed the only maritime frontier. Immediately south of this, a short border across the neck of the Armorican peninsula separated western Neustria from the Bretons. Everywhere else, a shield of conquered *regna* insulated the Frankish *Kerngebiet* from the ravages of raiding by *exterae gentes* and from the need for special defensive organisation. Secondly, all frontier regions lay far from the areas that enjoyed close royal government. Only in the later ninth century, when Louis the German and his successors began to spend significant amounts of time in the Bavarian palace at Regensburg, did royal government move to the frontier. This East Frankish fusion of centre with periphery became one of the crucial distinctions between the ailing Carolingian West Frankish kingdom and the nascent Ottonian *Reich* of the tenth century. But for the period under discussion here, frontier regions generally lay far from the centre, with such conquered *regna* as Aquitaine, Bavaria or Thuringia forming mediating buffers. Exploration of peripheral regions therefore inevitably becomes a study both of the ethnic pluralism of the Carolingian empire and of the means by which Carolingian government transcended huge distances in maintaining its rule.

Landward or maritime, inherited with or without adjustment, the geographical limits of Carolingian power fall into no tidy pattern. Each frontier region established a compromise with local circumstances, taking into account the particular nature of the political and social situation beyond the frontier.[9] In exercising the royal prerogative of defining and defending the frontiers of empire, Charlemagne (and his successors likewise) maintained a careful, panoramic concern with the entire periphery of the territory under his rule. A brief glance at one year towards the end of his reign highlights the need for constant alert, stresses the uniqueness of each sector of the frontier and draws attention to some common strategies.

The year in question is the twelve months from October 810. Three peaces engaged Charlemagne's attention during the autumn and winter; three campaigns marked the spring of 811. In October 810, Charlemagne reached agreements with both al-Ḥakam I, amir of Córdoba, and the Byzantine emperor, Nicephorus. Muslim support for Pippin III's Aquitainian

9 Cf. Reuter (1991), p. 78.

opponents in the 740–50s had pulled Carolingian power into Septimania; appeals from independent-minded Muslim governors of the cities of the Ebro valley had drawn Charlemagne even further south, most famously in the disastrous expedition of 778. In the depopulated eastern flanks of the Pyrenees (the area known to the Franks as *Gothia* or *Hispania*, not until the twelfth century to emerge as *Catalonia*) there rapidly emerged a pattern of shifting local alliances, cutting across the grain of the religious cleavage, and further complicated by the participation of the Basques at the western end of the Pyrenean chain. Appeals to the amir or emperor for help forced both distant rulers to pay attention to 'la pre-Catalunya'. Just such a situation had arisen in 810 when the governor of Zaragoza, ʿAmrūs b. Yūsuf, made overtures to the Franks. The affirmation of peace between Charlemagne and al-Ḥakam indicated the successful resolution of the situation, and also secured the return of a noble Frankish hostage.[10] As for the simultaneous negotiations with the Emperor Nicephorus, their substance was not dissimilar. It concerned the status of Venice. Nominally Byzantine, effectively independent and of growing economic significance, the lagoon community originated as a place of refuge during the fifth-century invasions. Although competing Roman and Greek claims to ecclesiastical jurisdiction over the lands around the head of the Adriatic remained unresolved throughout the ninth century, the efforts of the Venetian doge in 810 to play the Franks off against the Byzantines terminated when Charlemagne recognised Byzantine lordship over the city that October; in return, when a formal peace was concluded with Nicephorus' successor, Michael I, in 812, Charlemagne secured recognition of his claims to Istria and the Dalmatian hinterland.[11]

The winter of 810–11 saw Charlemagne concerned with the northern perimeter of his empire. In much the same manner as the Byzantines secured their frontiers, the Frankish emperor attempted wherever possible to establish a ring of friendly client rulers in the immediate periphery of his territory. Sound in theory, delicate to execute in practice, the strategy indicated a balancing-act between protecting Frankish interests and provoking an anti-Carolingian backlash. Along the middle and lower reaches of the Elbe, Germanic settlement shaded off into the Slavic lands of the Sorbs (beyond Thuringia), Obodrites (from Holstein east to the river Havel) and beyond them, controlling the Baltic coast and its hinterland as far east as the

---

[10] Wolff (1965), p. 281; Lévi-Provençal (1950), p. 156. Collins (1986) assesses what little we know of the Basques in the early middle ages; Nelson (1992), pp. 150–1, 161–2 demonstrates the persistence of this pattern of alliances into the later ninth century.

[11] *ARF* s.a. 812; Einhard, *Vita Karoli*, 15. Norwich (1982), pp. 15–25; Krahwinkler (1991), pp. 179–83; Classen (1981), pp. 933–5.

river Oder, the Wilzi. Further north still, and secure behind the formidable
earthwork thrown up in 737 across the neck of the Jutish peninsula, lived
the Danes.[12] Traditional patterns of relationships between Saxons, Slavs and
Danes were upset by the Frankish conquest of Saxony, concluded by
securing the northern bank of the Elbe with friendly Obodrite settlers in
804; they were further distorted by the beginning of Danish raiding
enterprises along the Baltic and North Sea coasts. Throughout the second
half of the eighth century, the Danes had helped the Saxons against the
Franks, who had relied on the support of the Obodrites to offset the Danes.
The death of the Danish king Godfrid in 810 gave Charlemagne the
opportunity to exert some influence over the Danes, which he did by
immediately recognising the succession of Godfrid's brother Hemming and
by sending twelve Frankish counts to swear a formal peace with the Danes
on their border, the river Eider. However, Hemming's death in 812
inaugurated fifteen years of rivalry for the Danish throne, in which
Charlemagne and then Louis the Pious found that to favour one claimant
was to promote aggression from another. By 817, the Obodrites had been
sucked in, and had deserted their traditional Frankish allies in favour of
Danish protection for their trading centres. Thereafter, the Franks could
never again rely upon a friendly neighbour in the trans-Elbe regions, and
not even the skilful *Ostpolitik* of Louis the German would neutralise the
persistent threat of revolt in the northeast.[13]

Having concluded three different peace negotiations in the autumn and
winter of 810, in the spring of 811 Charlemagne sent out three armies, each
to deal with an unruly tributary people: the Linones, the Avars and the
Bretons. The Linones, a Slav people on the right bank of the middle Elbe,
were caught in the tensions between the Danes and the Obodrites. The
Carolingian army contented itself with ravaging their land and rebuilding a
Frankish fortification on the right bank of the Elbe, at Höhbeck which the
Wilzi had recently razed. The second army marched down the Danube into
Pannonia, that region where, more than anywhere else, Frankish expansion
precipitated fundamental changes in the political geography of the later
eighth and ninth centuries. Avar support for opponents of the Carolingian
takeover of Bavaria and the Lombard kingdom had led to the virtual
annihilation of the powerful Avar khaghanate of the middle Danube basin
in 795–6. The remnants, established as a tributary principality under a
Christian Avar ruler, offered an easy prey to the neighbouring Slav peoples
recently released from Avar hegemony. Charlemagne's army seems to have
been sent on a peace-keeping exercise: after fighting between Slavs and

12 For the *Danevirke*, see Roesdahl (1982), pp. 141–6.
13 Kötzschke (1920); Jankuhn (1965); Ernst (1974; 1977); Friedmann (1986).

Avars had been terminated, leaders of both groups were brought back to Aachen. Although the Avar lands were not fully incorporated into the Frankish empire until 828, the power vacuum left by the collapse of the khaghanate had repercussions long after the unrest of 811. In place of the Avar empire, there emerged in the middle years of the ninth century a vigorous and expansionist Slav principality whose centre, *Velehrad*, is usually, though not indisputably, located in the valley of the northern river Morava, some distance north of Bratislava and south of Olomouc. The wide-ranging coalition of Slav peoples who fell under Moravian hegemony was to become the focus of attention throughout the long reign of Louis the German, his son Karlmann and grandson Arnulf of Carinthia.[14] As for the third army dispatched in 811, it marched against the Bretons, the Christian, Celtic inhabitants of the Armorican peninsula of westernmost Gaul whose conquest had been proclaimed twelve years earlier. Their revolt in 811 betokened the reluctance with which they had accepted the imposition of Frankish rule; by the third quarter of the ninth century the Bretons would become as formidable an opponent and as crucial an ally for Charles the Bald as the Moravians were for his brother, Louis the German.[15]

Our survey of the year concludes in October 811, at Boulogne. In response to the Viking raids which were already beginning to hit Francia, Charlemagne had in the previous summer ordered the construction of a fleet, to assist in the defence of the shoreline along the North Sea and English Channel. Whilst inspecting the new ships at Boulogne he took further measures to institute coastal watches, and also issued a detailed ordinance regulating frontier defence and military service throughout the empire.[16] The maritime frontier always posed particular problems for the Carolingians. Whether the challenge came from the increasingly persistent Viking attacks along the Atlantic seaboard or the ninth-century Saracen raids on the coasts of Provence and Italy, the Carolingians were rarely in a position to take the offensive. Details of the defensive provisions for seaward watches and the levying of ships remain generally elusive.

The events of 810–11 offer a synoptic view of the major trouble-spots along the Carolingian periphery. Two further regions also deserve mention, Frisia and southern Italy. Although tranquil throughout 810–11, they both manifested significantly different problems and opportunities from those encountered elsewhere. Frisia had been brought under Carolingian control in piecemeal fashion by Pippin II, Charles Martel and Charlemagne, but its

---

[14] Wolfram (1987), esp. pp. 259–60; Bosl (1966); Poulik (1982); Pohl (1988). For the arguments for the location of Greater Moravia in the valley of the southern, Serbian Morava, see Boba (1971) and Bowlus (1987). [15] Brunterc'h (1989); Smith (1992).
[16] *MGH Cap.* I, pp. 166–7, no. 74.

conquest was not completed until the final submission of the Saxons, the Frisians' close allies. Consisting largely of coastal islands and isolated villages rising on *terpen* above the dunes and fens of the coast between the Scheldt and the mouth of the Weser, Frisia remained largely inaccessible by land throughout the early middle ages and therefore of restricted political significance. Its importance for the Carolingians lay rather in access to the wealth generated by the immense trading network centred on Dorestad and Domburg, and in the ease with which Vikings preyed upon these trading centres. Indeed, it had been the devastating Danish raid on Frisia in 810 and the exaction of a heavy tribute which had prompted Charlemagne to take in hand the defences of the North Sea coast.[17]

As to southern Italy, Charlemagne's conquest of the Lombard kingdom in 774 had left the swathe of papal lands across the centre of Italy formally under a Frankish protectorate, but in practice a buffer zone between the northern core of the *regnum Langobardorum* and the turbulent politics of the southern half of the peninsula.[18] South of Rome, the two duchies of Spoleto and Benevento had been associated with the old Lombard kingdom. Although Spoleto did pass under direct Carolingian control, the duchy of Benevento eluded anything more stringent than nominal overlordship, only prompting brief intervention from Charlemagne in 787. Much later Louis II renewed the interest, managing in 849 to end the civil war which had rent the duchy apart, and returning rather later (865–71) as emperor to wrest Bari from the Saracens.[19] But in general, southern Italy held limited interest for the Carolingians. Neither Louis the Pious nor Lothar I could be bothered with it. After Charlemagne's treaty with Michael I in 812, the Lombards constituted no great threat, preferring to turn on each other rather than on papal lands. The distinctiveness of southern Italian politics anyway made Carolingian influence harder and harder to achieve. In the middle years of the ninth century, an inexorable process of redistribution of power began: it created such a mosaic of competing Lombard, Greek and Saracen authorities that imperial overlordship could not operate effectively in the face of the rapid privatisation and fragmentation of authority.[20] As Louis II discovered in 871 in the wake of recapturing Bari, Carolingian imperial overlordship brought no prestige, only humiliation.

This brief survey of all the frontier regions of the Carolingian empire reveals some persistent themes in Carolingian frontier policy which transcend the individuality of each peripheral region. In the first place, negotiation combined with a readiness to use force to prosecute Carolingian

---

[17] Reuter (1991), p. 69; Lebecq (1978); Blok (1979).   [18] Noble (1984), pp. 138–83.

[19] Kreutz (1991), pp. 40–6; Cilento (1966), pp. 106–9.

[20] Wickham (1981); von Falkenhausen (1983).

interests always characterised Frankish strategy. Secondly, the Carolingians participated in the common early medieval diplomatic practices of receiving, entertaining and dismissing envoys; royal gift-exchange; demanding hostages to keep at court; extracting tribute and oaths of loyalty; welcoming and sheltering political exiles from other kingdoms; concluding truces and treaties. Such strategies expressed the relative status of the parties involved. Only with the Byzantine emperor and the amir of Córdoba did negotiations proceed on equal terms: all other rulers of peripheral kingdoms, pagan or Christian, were expected to defer to Carolingian superiority and recognise Frankish overlordship. Thirdly, the Carolingian imperial rhetoric of a Christian, Latin empire broke down at the frontier. It was not simply that Beneventans, Bretons and Basques – all Christian – only reluctantly admitted Carolingian suzerainty; rather that shifting alliances of Christian with non-Christian were a normal part of frontier politics. In addition to Muslim *walis*, pagan Slav princes or Danish warlords all at one time or another served as valuable allies. Fourthly, Charlemagne, and his successors after him, saw the specific issues of security along each frontier as interlocking facets of a single puzzle of immense complexity. Because they did so, we may discern certain patterns in the administrative arrangements made for frontier zones, in the connections between the centre and the periphery of the empire, and in the implications for the surrounding peoples of having the Franks as their neighbours. These three themes occupy the remainder of this chapter.

DEFINING THE FRONTIER

What constituted the outer limits of the Carolingian empire? An older generation of constitutional historians saw in the term *marca* (a word of vernacular derivation) an institution specifically created by Charlemagne to organise Carolingian power at the periphery.[21] In practice, however, the word occurs interchangeably with the classical terms *limites, confinia, termini* and *fines.* These words do not correspond to the modern categories commonly used by geographers and anthropologists, who distinguish between a boundary (linear) and a frontier (zonal). All could refer to either a particular line or a swathe of land at the margin of the empire. In their linear sense, they might also refer to the boundary of either a piece of property, or a village, *pagus, civitas* or diocese: Carolingian Latin had no vocabulary specific to the farthest reaches of imperial power.

Behind the words lies the fact that most Carolingian frontiers were *both*

---

[21] Lipp (1892); Hofmeister (1907); Klebel (1938; 1963); Werner (1980) cf. Cessi (1940); Wolff (1965); Brunterc'h (1989); Zibermayr (1956), p. 278.

linear and zonal. In their zonal sense, Carolingian frontiers were sometimes only loosely associated with the political and administrative structures of the empire. Hence the distinction between action 'both within the kingdom and outside it in our marches' came easily to Lothar I.[22] From a local perspective, the *marca* was 'a relative idea ... the region where the danger was greater than elsewhere ... a zone of ill-defined or undefined domination'.[23] Characteristically, these zones constituted regions where defensive organisation was concentrated in the hands of a count, prefect, duke or marquis: the internal boundary of these regions was clear, even if the outer edge was sometimes indeterminate.

In the linear sense, the *marca*, *fines* or *terminus* might be either the internal boundary of the frontier region, or a clearly designated external boundary. In the former sense, Carolingian armies were expected to refrain from plundering until they reached the frontier.[24] Here too began the three-month period for which they had brought rations: for troops recruited on the right bank of the Rhine, the border was the Elbe, and for those sent from Aquitaine into Spain, the Pyrenees formed the equivalent demarcation.[25] As a precise external boundary, the same terms referred to a line which was known to parties on both sides, might be designated by mutual negotiation, or breached as an act of provocation. Such boundaries were precisely known, if often contested. In Italy, where the Roman administrative heritage remained strong, frontiers achieved a degree of specificity unprecedented elsewhere: 'Let the border between Benevento and Capua be from *Sanctus Angelus ad Cerros*, proceeding along the ridge of *Mons Virginis* to the place called *Fenestella*.'[26] Defining the frontier by means of boundary-markers – *definitio per signa* – could be an imperial responsibility.[27]

Whether designated boundaries or marginal zones of militarised living, Carolingian frontiers were varied and complex. Throughout European history, political demarcations have rarely conformed neatly to geographic features (the mis-named 'natural' frontiers), or to ethnic and linguistic distinctions. Carolingian frontiers were no exception. The political frontier along the Elbe did not follow the linguistic divide between German and Slav, any more than the boundary between Brittany and Neustria conformed to that between Breton and the emerging Romance vernacular. Istria and Dalmatia may have been a polyglot region of Latin, Greek and

---

[22] *MGH Cap.* II, p. 74, no. 205: 'et infra regnum et extra regnum per marchas nostras'.

[23] Zimmermann (1983), p. 14, note 35 quoting Pierre Bonnassie.

[24] *MGH Cap.* I, p. 305, no. 150, c. 16.   [25] *MGH Cap.* I, p. 167, no. 74, c. 8.

[26] *Divisio* between Radelgisus of Benevento and Siginulf of Salerno, *MGH Leges* IV, p. 222, c. 10: 'Inter Beneventum et Capuam sit finis ad Sanctum Angelum ad Cerros, perexiens per serram montis Virginis usque ad locum qui dicitur Fenestella.'   [27] Toubert (1973), II, pp. 942–3.

Slav.[28] Nor were Carolingian frontiers clear-cut in religious terms. The situation along the Spanish frontier may be adduced here, for the division between Christian and Muslim applied only at the level of the ruling elites: the Muslim garrisons controlled a Mozarab population which remained largely Christian until well into the tenth century.[29] As for the northern and eastern circumference, conversion to Christianity preceded extension of political control in some places, though in others conquest leapfrogged ahead of conversion.[30]

Understanding of the frontier requires instead a look at administrative and judicial procedures. At its most fundamental, crossing the frontier meant escaping beyond the reach of the Carolingian state. A Lombard opponent of Charlemagne's who sought out the Avars; a palatine cleric who converted to Judaism and fled to Zaragoza; a wife-snatcher who removed himself to Moravia; and a distressed monk who had run into theological trouble and sought refuge in Dalmatia: all had in common a search for a bolt-hole beyond the reach of reprisals.[31] Even Louis the German had to escape beyond the frontiers to avoid his father's wrath, and his brother Lothar contemplated a similar flight after his defeat at Fontenoy in 841.[32] It is not surprising, then, that extant *pacta* regulating Italian borders (notably between Naples and Benevento in 836, or between Lothar I and Venice in 840) make a prominent concern out of the fate of fugitives escaping across the border.[33] In defining a frontier, we define the state which it encompassed.

Other people crossed frontiers legitimately, however. Merchants were chief among these. Their greatest concern was the fiscal aspect of the Carolingian frontier. Legislation restricted legal tender to the coins minted at official mints: on entering Carolingian territory, a trader's first encounter with a royal agent probably came with a visit to an official money-changer. Paying a special toll on departure formed his last obligation. Traders who passed from East Francia into Moravia in the reign of Louis the Child owed

---

[28] On Germanic and Slav settlements, see Herrmann (1985); Nitz (1988). On the limits of Breton speech, Chédeville and Guillotel (1984), pp. 89–112; Smith (1992), pp. 35–6. On Istria and Dalmatia, Obolensky (1988); Vlasto (1970), pp. 187–97; Krahwinkler (1991), pp. 199–243.

[29] Bonnassie (1975–6) I, pp. 119–20.

[30] Frisia provides a case study of the complex interaction of conquest and conversion. Lebecq (1986); Wood (1993).

[31] For the Lombard Aio, see *MGH Dip. Kar.* I, p. 251, no. 187. For the Deacon Bodo, see *AB s.a.* 839. On Albgis, who had eloped with Patrichus' wife, see the Council of Mainz (852), c. 11, *MGH Conc.* III, pp. 248–9. For Gottschalk's own account of his activities among the Slavs and Bulgars, see *Œuvres théologiques et grammaticales de Godescalc d'Orbais*, pp. 163, 325, and on the chronology of his exile, the comments of L. Traube, *MGH Poet.* III, pp. 711–13.   [32] *AF s.a.* 840, 841.

[33] *MGH Leges* IV, pp. 216–21; *MGH Cap.* II, pp. 130–5, no. 233.

one *denarius* per ship at Mautern on their outward journey, though nothing on their return.[34] But fiscal regulation was concentrated in specified places which lay well within the reach of the Carolingian administration, not at its extreme limits. Of the nine trading checkpoints on the eastern periphery listed in the capitulary of Thionville (805), the southernmost one – Lorch, near the confluence of the Enns and the Danube – was the command centre of the new prefect of the Bavarian *plaga orientalis*, but it lay on the border between Bavaria and the marcher region, far up the Danube from the furthest reach of the prefect's operations.[35]

Except where precise boundaries demarcated the limits of Carolingian administrative powers, the authority of officials on the periphery probably petered out rather than terminated abruptly. Where new secular and ecclesiastical units of administration were created in the Pyrenees in the later ninth and tenth centuries, they embraced regions never totally depopulated, but only for the first time brought under comital control. In the years before Count Wifred the Hairy undertook the resettlement and organisation of the plain of Vich we must envisage small, scattered settlements where the judicial, fiscal and military control of Carolingian counts rarely, if ever, penetrated, a no-man's land equally beyond the reach of Muslim control.[36] Similar zones of uncertain allegiance doubtless marked the long eastern periphery as well, especially in such heavily forested areas as the Böhmerwald, or the forests between the Elbe and the Eider.

The zonal nature of Carolingian frontiers – especially those in Spain, Pannonia and along the Elbe – thus becomes clearer. The reach of Carolingian justice was not coterminous with the fiscal border. Neither represented the limits of military operation. With the exception of the precisely demarcated borders of Italy (perhaps too the Breton border) and the sea coasts, the Carolingian empire simply shaded off at the outer edges into ill-defined territoriality.

THE POLITICS OF THE PERIPHERY

It would be easy to write a political history of the Carolingian centuries in terms of a grim narrative of revolts and rebellions. Two strands run through this catalogue of conflict. The competing claims to power of the adult males of the Arnulfing dynasty provide one thread, present even before the acquisition of royal title in 751. The second theme consists of the frequent

---

34 *Inquisitio de Theloneis Raffelstetensis* (903 × 906), *MGH Cap.* II, pp. 250–2, no. 253, reflecting regulations in place since the reign of Louis the German; Mitterauer (1964).

35 *MGH Cap.* I, p. 123, no. 44, c. 7; Wolfram (1987), p. 263.

36 Freedman (1991), p. 59; Bonnassie (1975–6) I, pp. 120–1.

revolts around the margin of the empire, whether the unrest of Frankish magnates in border regions, or the uprisings against Carolingian overlordship of neighbouring *gentes*. Both strands, that of the dynastic centre and that of the far-flung periphery, intertwine so closely for much of the time that they are not easily separable. Tracing the recurring patterns in this braid enables us to discern the vital role which the periphery played in the politics of the centre.

Perhaps the most obvious motif is the case with which those members of the *stirps regia* who felt themselves denied access to adequate power could find support and succour in peripheral regions. Neighbouring rulers, on the watch for an opportunity to elude Carolingian overlordship, might be relied on to provide help. The earliest clear example of this is the career of Grifo, son of Charles Martel by Swanahild, his second, Bavarian wife. Half-brother of Pippin III and Carloman, Grifo had made a bid for a share of their father's power in 741, and after Carloman had withdrawn to the religious life in 747, Grifo challenged Pippin's position as sole mayor of the palace. His efforts to secure support took him to those places where Carolingian claims were least secure: Saxony then Bavaria then Gascony, whose Basque ruler took him in. For two years, Pippin gave chase; only after Grifo had been killed in 753 was his rule secured.[37]

This pattern features especially clearly in the ninth century, when Charlemagne's skilful maintenance of a harmonious family had given way to much more overt dynastic rivalries.[38] Rumours of Breton unrest at the same time as the first revolt against Louis the Pious (830) may be a case in point.[39] But it is during the reigns of Louis' sons and grandsons that this theme recurs with insistence. Charles the Bald's nephew, Pippin II of Aquitaine, sought help from the Basques in his efforts to recover his father's inheritance.[40] As for Charles the Bald's eldest son, Louis the Stammerer, his impatience for a stake in his father's kingdom led him to make common cause with the rebellious Breton ruler, Salomon, in 862.[41] Only the previous year, Charles' half-brother Louis the German had faced an identical revolt from his eldest son, in the course of which Karlmann had turned to the Moravian prince Rastislav.[42] The situation was symptomatic of royal longevity: if sons grew to adulthood and political maturity long before their father's death, challenges were almost inevitable. When, by the turn of the century, the dynastic imperative became to produce any adult, legitimate

[37] *ARF s.a.* 741 (revised entry), 747, 748, 753; *Annales Mettenses Priores s.a.* 741, 749. Reindel (1965), pp. 220–1; Mikoletsky (1952).   [38] Cf. Nelson (1991).   [39] *AB s.a.* 830.
[40] *AB s.a.* 852; Nelson (1992), p. 162.
[41] *AB s.a.* 862, pp. 89–90; Smith (1992), pp. 104–5; Nelson (1992), p. 204.
[42] *AF s.a.* 861; *AB s.a.* 861.

and competent heir, this particular threat to the peace diminished commensurately.

Alliances between restive prince and rebellious client ruler often grew out of mutual interests in a common border zone. Again dating back to the 740s, outlying regions had frequently been set aside as sub-kingdoms for young princes, especially eldest sons. Pippin III had briefly invested Grifo with the outlying western countries of Neustria which faced towards Brittany, but the most important precedent was set when Charlemagne gave the future Louis the Pious the sub-kingdom of Aquitaine in 781. The eastern periphery of Bavaria became the region where Karlmann first established his own court and government in 856 (a sub-kingdom which passed to his own son, Arnulf of Carinthia); Charles the Bald had likewise hoped to create a sub-kingdom in western Neustria for Louis the Stammerer in 856. Frontier apanages gave young heirs the opportunity to hone their military skills in a tough environment, obliged them to learn to mediate disputes involving client rulers or marcher magnates, and familiarised them with the ritual displays of power that accompanied hegemony over subordinate princes. In addition, they brought royal presence into distant regions of the kingdom, but thereby created alternative foci of patronage and loyalty. A Carolingian prince and the ruler of a neighbouring *gens* had a common cause in their remoteness from the political centre – remoteness not merely in terms of a long journey, but also in terms of the check which subordination to the king placed upon their own appetite for power.

In these circumstances, the equilibrium between royal and aristocratic interests could be at risk. Where Frankish counts had been sent from court to secure and govern border areas, their initial position owed much to royal patronage, but their continued enjoyment of it depended upon a combination of military aptitude and the ability to balance local needs with those of the palace. An effective frontier commander was one like Thaculf, who, as commander of the frontier against the Sorbs, 'had knowledge of the laws and customs of the Slavic people'.[43] An ineffective one, either, like Cadolah, prefect of the Friuli frontier, provoked accusations of 'high-handed cruelty' or, like Bernard of Septimania, simply exported palace intrigue to the frontier.[44] The introduction of a young sub-king to a peripheral region might upset frontier counts who had grown habituated to the self-reliance which distance from the centre made inevitable. Certainly the establishment of Louis the Stammerer and Karlmann as sub-kings in 856 precipitated serious aristocratic unrest both in western Neustria and on the eastern

---

[43] *AF s.a.* 849.
[44] Cadolah: *ARF s.a.* 818. Bernard: Collins (1990b); Nelson (1992), pp. 80–1, 102–3, 139–40.

periphery.[45] Local aristocratic rivalries for influence and benefices could have an equally destabilising effect, especially when neighbouring rulers were drawn in. The involvement of Svatopluk of Moravia in a feud over the countships from the Traungau to the rivers Drava and Rába culminated in 884 in horrendous devastation and cruel mutilations perpetrated on both sides of the dispute, a devastating blow to Charles the Fat.[46] Exceptional only in its ferocity, this episode serves as a sharp reminder of the fragility of Carolingian control at the periphery.

The interweaving of dynastic and peripheral politics was more intricate still. Little surprise attends the observation that frontier revolt also punctuated the line of succession to the Carolingian throne. Behind laconic references to Pippin and Carloman's campaigns in Aquitaine and Alemannia in 742 we may suspect tumult caused by the death of Charles Martel the previous year.[47] Certainly, when Pippin himself died in 768, having just celebrated in triumph the apparent completion of his conquest of Aquitaine, Charlemagne and his brother's very first task became to resubjugate the same province.[48] Charlemagne's 46-year reign kept the lid firmly on the pot: his death in January 814 gave the signal for revolts or the renegotiation of borders along virtually the entire length of the imperial periphery.[49] The pattern recurs throughout the ninth century: in 877 Louis the Younger inaugurated his reign by suppressing the efforts of the Linones and Siusli (Slavs of the middle Elbe) to overthrow Carolingian hegemony, and in 878 his cousin, Louis the Stammerer, inaugurated his by dealing with a revolt which included the Bretons.[50]

Customary though it was for each new ruler to have to reassert his own lordship at the periphery of his kingdom, the unrest of 840 deserves particular mention, because it introduces a new twist to the pattern. Peripheral *gentes* now had to choose between the claims to hegemony of competing Carolingian kings. For the sons of Louis the Pious, this meant the opportunity to stab each other in the back by fomenting unrest along the borders. Lothar I quickly adopted this tactic, which he used to considerable effect in 840–3. Exploiting his position as emperor and as ruler of the Middle Kingdom, he not only turned Danes and Slavs against Louis the German but also Bretons against Charles the Bald.[51] Others followed where Lothar had led: when relations between Charles the Bald and Louis the German reached their nadir in 853, Charles incited the Slavs and Bulgars to make

[45] Smith (1992), pp. 102–3; Wolfram (1987), pp. 283–5.
[46] *AF s.a.* 884 (Regensburg recension); Reuter (1991), pp. 116, 124; Wolfram (1987), pp. 284–92.
[47] *ARF s.a.* 742; *Continuationes Fredegarii*, 25.   [48] *ARF s.a.* 768, 769; Einhard, *Vita Karoli*, 5.
[49] Smith (1992), pp. 64–5.   [50] *AF s.a.* 877; *AB s.a.* 878.
[51] Smith (1992) pp. 94–9 for all details.

trouble for his brother, thus effectively pinning down the East Frankish army as far away as possible.[52] In the rough-and-tumble of the fraternal wrestling bouts of the 840s–50s, the deliberate creation of border unrest was an effective ploy.

The close interlocking of dynastic and peripheral politics presumes an environment where the rituals of overlordship were integral to politics. To the traditional means of asserting their superiority over neighbouring peoples, such as demanding tribute, taking hostages, requiring military service, the Carolingians added two further expressions of overlordship. One (reflecting Anglo-Saxon and Byzantine precedents) involved the sponsorship at baptism of pagan rulers, whose conversion to Christianity was itself an act of submission. First mobilised by Charlemagne when he stood godfather to the Saxon leaders Widukind and Abbi in 785, baptism created bonds of spiritual kinship (compaternity) which effectively replicated the relationship of son to father. Avars, Danes, Moravians and Bohemians all encountered Christianity in this way; Bretons and Venetians, though already Christian, were also pulled into the network of political kinship.[53] The second addition to these rituals comprised the granting of benefices on the margin of the Carolingian realm. Louis the Pious set the precedent here, when he endowed the Danish prince Harald with the Frisian county of Rüstringen (at the mouth of the Weser) at the same time as he stood godfather to him in 826. Such lands were held strictly at the king's will: Charles the Bald installed but soon dismissed another Dane, Ragnar, in Flanders in the early 840s, whilst Louis the German granted lands between the rivers Rába and Drava, centring on Lake Balaton, to the Slav prince Pribina in 838/40, converting this benefice into an allod in 847.[54] Baptism and benefices, separately or together, completed the ritual expressions of overlordship.

Here too dynastic ambitions and peripheral politics intertwined, providing the final motif in this complex embroidery. Before 840, the rituals of overlordship were a natural expression of imperial power. But after 840, hegemony over peripheral peoples became another arena for competition as brothers, sons and nephews vied with each other for status, influence, resources and, ultimately, the imperial crown. Louis the Pious' sons all played this game with vigour. Lothar lost no time in affirming that

[52] *AB s.a.* 853.

[53] For baptismal sponsorship in the context of conversion to Christianity, see Angenendt (1984). On the Bretons and Venetians, see, respectively, Smith (1992), pp. 108–15 and *La Cronaca Veneziana del diacono Giovanni*, p. 116.

[54] Ragnar: Nelson (1992), p. 151. Pribina: *Conversio Bagoariorum et Carantanorum*, 11–12; *MGH Dip. Ger.* I, pp. 62–3, no. 46; Wolfram (1987), p. 276.

overlordship over the periphery of his Middle Kingdom accompanied the
imperial title. In 841 he gave the Frisian island of Walcheren to the Danish
prince Harald as a benefice; he had already reached a *pactum* with Venice
which confirmed the city's self-government but put Lothar's name on
Venetian coins. At his installation as *rex Langobardorum* in 844, his son Louis
II received recognition from Siconulf of Benevento, and when he intervened to end civil war between Benevento and Salerno in 849, Louis was the
first Carolingian since 801 to take an interest in southern Italian affairs. By
852, the Croatian ruler Trpimir may have become a client of Lothar's too.[55]
Charles the Bald followed suit. Almost nothing is known of the Basques
during his reign – except that he was occasionally able to bring influence,
however ephemeral, to bear on their ruler. Although the Muslim frontier of
the Ebro valley was not suited to conventional expressions of overlordship,
he nevertheless exploited its local rivalries in such a way as to encourage rich
conciliatory gifts from the amir of Córdoba. But the frontier most able to
provide Charles with the trappings of overlordship was Brittany. He
installed the native Breton princes Erispoë (851–7) and Salomon (857–74) as
dependent kings holding Frankish benefices in moves which brought only
modest tribute but much prestige.[56] In this fraternal contest for overlordship Louis the German far outbid his brothers, however. To him fell
responsibility for the long, open East Frankish frontier stretching all the
way from Schleswig to Szombathely. Danes, Obodrites, Sorbs, Bohemians,
Moravians and Pannonian Slavs all had to be played off against each other,
and all admitted their dependence at some point during Louis' reign. To
achieve this, Louis adroitly manipulated the full range of hegemonic rituals:
he baptised fourteen Bohemian princes in 845; he installed Rastislav as ruler
of the Moravians in 846 (though of uncertain loyalty, both Rastislav (846–
70) and his nephew Zwentibald (= Svatopluk, Zwentopulk) (870–94)
conducted a politics predicated upon Frankish overlordship); he created a
Pannonian client principality for Pribina; he accepted the submission of the
Danish kings Sigfrid and Halfdan who placed themselves under him as sons
to a father.[57] Even as the Carolingian empire gradually lost its internal
political coherence in the third quarter of the ninth century, the external

---

[55] Frisia: *AB s.a.* 841. Venice: *Pactum Hlothari I, MGH Cap.* II, pp. 130–5, no. 233; Grierson and
  Blackburn (1986), p. 196. Louis II and Benevento: Cilento (1966), pp. 90–1; Kreutz (1991), pp.
  28–30. Croatia: Krahwinkler (1991), pp. 253–4.

[56] Basques: Collins (1986). Muslim Spain: Nelson (1993). Brittany: Smith (1992), pp. 108–115.

[57] General: Reuter (1991), pp. 77–84. Bohemia: *AF s.a.* 845; Angenendt (1984), pp. 237–8.
  Rastislav: *AF s.a.* 846; Bosl (1966); Wolfram (1987), pp. 359–69; Graus (1980), pp. 41–51.
  Pribina: as note 54 above. Danes: *AF s.a.* 873.

expression of lordship became ever more crucial in the competition for the imperial title.

THE TRANSFORMATION OF THE PERIPHERY

Carolingian hegemony over peripheral peoples entailed far more than rituals of subordination or demands for loyalty. The pressures to conform to the Carolingian will led gradually but inexorably to the creation of new political systems. If unrest and revolt induced repeated tremors and seismic shocks all around the rim of the empire, they registered a fault line whose other manifestation was the formation of new polities.

This transformation had least effect in regions characterised by ancient traditions of Christian worship combined with a sophisticated and literate territorial administration, notably southern Italy and the former Visigothic counties of Septimania together with northeastern Spain. Its scale may also have been modest in places too unstable to permit the development of hereditary, territorial lordships, such as the secluded Basque lands of the western Pyrenees or the Slav lands in the valleys of the Rába, Drava and Sava rivers, buffeted between Bulgars and Moravians. But by 900, all other peripheral *gentes* had been changed beyond recognition.

In the first instance, Carolingian policy consistently preferred dealings with a single, relatively powerful prince to a competing medley of claimants. Louis the Pious intervened repeatedly in the succession disputes of both Danes and Obodrites, clearly hoping in both cases to promote a stable, hereditary dynasty.[58] In Brittany, the princely dynasty which emerged after 831 as rulers of the entire peninsula owed everything to Carolingian initiative. Here princely hostages found their calling. In 788 Charlemagne released a Beneventan prince to return home to rule his own people.[59] There is every reason to suspect that the Breton and Moravian princes who participated so skilfully in Frankish political intrigue in the 850s–60s were exploiting lessons learned and contacts made as hostages.[60]

But Carolingian intevention to mould the political systems of client kingdoms did not stop with the choice of ruler – or even with the show trials of dissident princes staged at Aachen for public appreciation.[61] Other strategies carried Carolingian influence far afield, supreme among them being the acquisition and control of landed resources. Merovingian kings

[58] *ARF s.a.* 814, 817, 819, 821, 826.
[59] Erchempert, *Historia Langobardorum Beneventanorum*, 4, MGH *SRL*, p. 236.
[60] Cf. Bosl (1966), p. 17.
[61] *ARF s.a.* 819 describes the removal of both the Abodrite Sclaomir and the Basque Lupus Centulli.

had had the prudence to reserve for the royal fisc or for loyal monasteries lands in such strategic locations as the Alpine passes or the Breton border area. The Agilolfing dukes of Bavaria had done likewise, notably in the eastern Alps.[62] Heirs to both, the Carolingians emulated and surpassed them. Though evident everywhere, nowhere was their land hunger greater than on the eastern periphery.[63] In the wake of the annihilation of the Avar khaghanate, Charlemagne permitted Bavarian monasteries to 'seize and possess' whatever lands they could, and did not trouble himself to provide them with legal, written title.[64] Other lands, absorbed into the royal fisc, can be traced when later alienated. Even private individuals took advantage of this opportunity to grab land. Much of the property acquired in this way initially lay beyond the limits of effective Carolingian policing: on the eastern frontier, landowners were the earliest representatives of the Carolingian state.[65]

Land implies jurisdiction. In this too, Carolingian practices eroded the autonomy of peripheral communities. Cathedrals and monasteries undertook the economic and administrative regulation of their Slav properties and their native tenants, often entitled to collect from them a proportion of the tribute owed to the king.[66] Elsewhere, when conquest pulled old-established monasteries into the Carolingian sphere of influence, the judicial privilege of immunity might tie these communities closely to the royal court. Such grants followed upon Charlemagne's conquest of Brittany, his 787 expedition to pacify Benevento and his organisation of Carolingian authority in Septimania and the eastern Pyrenees.[67] Immunity created islands where (in theory, at least) all local jurisdictions were set aside in favour of the king's. On this basis, the Beneventan houses of Monte Cassino and San Vincenzo al Volturno could appeal to Louis II for help against the Saracens.[68]

In Benevento, where the Carolingians encountered an administrative and

---

[62] Störmer (1987).   [63] Dopsch (1962) I, pp. 194–5 stresses the long-term significance of this.

[64] Louis the German's diploma for Niederaltaich makes clear that Charlemagne had given the monastery verbal permission *carpere ac possidere hereditatem*: *MGH Dip. Ger.* I, pp. 156–8, no. 109. See also *MGH Dip. Ger.* I, pp. 2–4, nos. 2–3.

[65] See the convenient, though error-ridden, listing of charters in Kuhar (1962) and the texts assembled by Herrmann (1965).

[66] Examples include: Tassilo's foundation charter for Kremsmünster (reproduced in Herrmann (1965), pp. 60–1); Charlemagne's confirmation of Fulda's immunity (*MGH Dip. Kar.* I, pp. 123, no. 85); charters of Pippin III, Carloman and Louis the Pious for Würzburg, as confirmed by Arnulf of Carinthia in 889 (*MGH Dip. Ger.* III, pp. 103–4, no. 69); Louis the German's grant of 860 to Salzburg (*MGH Dip. Ger.* I, pp. 147–8, no. 102).

[67] Morice, *Preuves*, I, pp. 225–6; *MGH Dip. Kar.* I, pp. 211–17, 231–3, nos. 156–9, 173.

[68] Cilento (1966), pp. 106, 164.

legal system comparable to their own, additional judicial expressions of overlordship accompanied grants of immunity. Charlemagne stipulated that his own name must replace that of Grimoald III on Beneventan coins and charters. (At the same time, he ordered the Beneventans to abandon their Greek haircut in favour of a Frankish coiffure.) Coins bearing the name of Carolingian rulers from Benevento, and also from Rome and from Venice, survive to witness the impact of Carolingian power in these virtually autonomous places.[69] Carolingian influence in Brittany found similar conduits. Charles the Bald continued to mint in cities under Breton rule, and the local princes manifested their recognition of his overlordship by modelling their own charters on those of the West Frankish king.[70]

As Grimoald knew, injunctions to adopt Carolingian charter or coin forms were unlikely to be enforced with insistence. A quite different situation arose when Carolingian judicial officers intervened. The Frankish appointees to border countships exercised surveillance over the dependent client rulers beyond; that surveillance might extend to jurisdictional intervention. Instances could be adduced from Brittany or Moravia, but the best example of the impact of Carolingian justice upon local practices comes from Istria. In *c.* 804, local residents of Pula, Koper, Novigrad and other towns arraigned *dux Iohannes* before the representatives of Pippin, sub-king of Italy. There ensued detailed allegations that he had abused his powers, ridden rough-shod over traditional local procedures and rights, made extortionate demands and seized local properties.[71] We do not know whether *Iohannes* lived up to his undertaking to mend his ways, but the case serves as a reminder of the Carolingian readiness to intervene judicially in the affairs of neighbouring *gentes*.

Land acquisition, judicial obligations and administrative supervision all helped mould the periphery in the image of the Carolingian state. The Carolingian church offered a complementary contribution. Not merely as a landowner – in Frisia, beyond the Elbe, in the Pyrenees and Brittany as well as in the Danubian basin – but as the carrier of Carolingian cultural norms and as an organising, administering body in its own right, the church left its imprint too. We may note the extension of Benedictine monasticism, that form of monastic life promoted by Louis the Pious as the defining motif of his religious policies. From the Atlantic coast of Brittany to the high valleys of the Pyrenees, the introduction of the Benedictine Rule entailed

---

[69] Erchempert, 4; Grierson and Blackburn (1986), pp. 195–6; Martin (1980), pp. 558–9.
[70] Smith (1992), pp. 116–46.
[71] Edited by Manaresi (1955–60) I, pp. 48–56, no. 17 and commented upon by Krahwinkler (1991), pp. 199–243.

membership of the imperial church and recognition of Carolingian lordship.[72] Even more significant, however, were the activities of Carolingian missionaries. Anskar undertook his work among the Danes at Louis the Pious' behest; a generation later, German missionaries vied with the Greek brothers, Cyril and Methodius, for the souls of the Moravians.[73] Carolingian churchmen made clear that they expected Christians round the imperial periphery to be incorporated within the jurisdiction of the Frankish church. Their views sometimes clashed with the papacy, however. Nicholas I and his successors did support the West Frankish bishops in their fight to prevent the Breton bishops, led by the church of Dol, from breaking away to establish their own independent province. But at the other end of the empire, the popes were not prepared to yield their own plans for a metropolitan see for the Moravians and Pannonian Slavs to the claims of the archbishopric of Salzburg. Despite heated interchange with the papacy, the Bavarian bishops persisted in promoting their own missionary priests, and in fighting attempts to establish a liturgy in Old Church Slavonic for the fledgling Christian communities in Pribina's Pannonian principality and in Moravia.[74]

The Christian religion, Carolingian schemes of ecclesiastical administration and Benedictine monasticism all contributed to political transformation, and might be as corrosive of older ways as were the administrative and judicial agents of Carolingian kings. Whatever its particular tint, Carolingian influence almost always stained indelibly. The map of Europe in c. 1100 reveals the trace of the Carolingian periphery in a ring of polities whose origins lie in our period: Brittany, Catalonia, Carinthia, Bohemia, Denmark. Normandy deserves a place on this list, for though its formal establishment only dates from 911, it was simply the last in the long series of peripheral fiefs entrusted to Viking warlords. Moravia is absent only because effectively annihilated by 907 in the Hungarian onslaught, and by c. 1100 the Normans had mopped up all the fragments of the southern Italian landscape.

It takes but a glance at the historiography of European state formation to reveal this legacy at its most pervasive. The outer reaches of Carolingian influence extended through the territories of eleven present-day states (as of 1995): Germany, the Czech Republic, Austria, Hungary, Slovenia, Croatia, Italy, Spain, France, Belgium and the Netherlands. The development of

---

[72] Brittany: Smith (1986); Smith (1992), p. 72. Pyrenees: Wolff (1965), pp. 297–300; Collins (1983), p. 263.   [73] Anskar: *VA* 7. Cyril and Methodius: Vlasto (1970), pp. 26–85.

[74] Archbishop of Dol: Smith (1982), Smith (1992), pp. 151–61. Archbishop of Moravia: Angenendt (1984), pp. 238–47 offers the clearest account of the textual and political controversies; also Dopsch (1986), Löwe (1982).

ideas of national identity in some of these nations or their constitutent ethnic groups has been profoundly affected by the fact of Carolingian conquest. In the high and later middle ages, Catalans hailed Charlemagne as the liberator with whom their history began; Bretons identified the struggle against Carolingian overlordship as crucial in the formation of their nation. All West- and South-Slavic languages derive their word for 'king' from the name *Carolus*. The nineteenth-century efforts by the French and the Germans each to appropriate Charlemagne for themselves contributed to their respective efforts to build the historiography of the nation-state. Until recently, issues of the interaction of German and Slav along the Elbe were polarised by the existence of the Iron Curtain, in one further twist to the sensitive issues raised by the long history of German *Ostbewegung*.[75] The historiography of the Carolingian frontier is disputed territory – the inevitable legacy of early medieval imperialism.

[75] Catalonia: Freedman (1988). Brittany: Kerhervé (1980). Slav peoples: Graus (1980), pp. 17–37; Ernst (1974), pp. 20–33. French and German historiography of Charlemagne: Borst (1965).

CHAPTER 7

THE VIKINGS IN FRANCIA AND ANGLO-SAXON ENGLAND TO 911

Simon Coupland

EVEN though Scandinavian coastal raids on England and the Continent were recorded long before the eighth century, the attacks which began in the 790s were perceived by contemporaries as something new in their nature, scope and extent. Over the next 120 years these Scandinavian incursions would increase to such a pitch that they would threaten to overwhelm the Anglo-Saxon and West Frankish kingdoms, and ultimately leave an enduring mark in the form of the settlement of Normandy and the Danelaw.

The first wave of attacks offered only a hint of what was to come. From the first raids in the 790s until 840, the sources record only small Viking fleets making hit-and-run attacks along the coast. The Viking longships with their shallow draught were ideally suited to surprise raids on coastal locations, being uniquely able to land raiding parties close to poorly defended monasteries or trading centres, then to row away as swiftly as they had come. Against this new form of warfare the Franks and Anglo-Saxons had little defence.

Two areas of the Carolingian empire came under attack at this time: Frisia, where the culprits were Danes, making their way south along the Frankish coast, and Aquitaine, where the raiders were probably Norwegians coming from Ireland, which suffered a wave of Norse invasions in the early ninth century (Map 13). Information about the raids on Aquitaine is sparse, primarily because most of the longer annals were written in the north of the empire. Nonetheless, local sources reveal a continuing Scandinavian menace throughout the early years of the ninth century. The most notable is an account of the flight of the monks of the island monastery of Noirmoutier which was written soon after the event by Ermentarius, himself a member of the community. Ermentarius describes how at first the brothers spent only the summers on the mainland, returning to the monastery when the rough autumn seas ended the threat of Viking attack. In the 830s, however, the

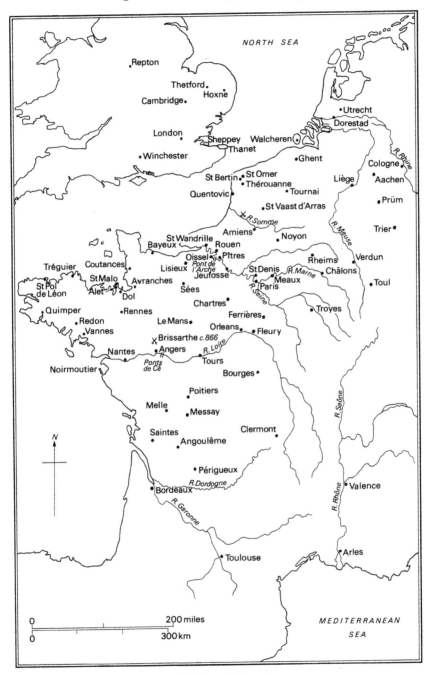

Map 13 The Vikings in Francia, 789–895

raids became so frequent that the community decided that the island was no longer safe, and abandoned it, taking the body of their patron with them.[1] Various defensive measures were undertaken in the region, including the construction of a fleet, the stationing of coast guards, and the fortification of Noirmoutier, but they appear to have been ineffectual.

In Frisia the Vikings' principal targets were trading centres, particularly the prosperous market of Dorestad, which was first sacked in 834. The Annals of St Bertin report that 'they ravaged everything, killed some of the men, carried others off as captives, and burned down part of the emporium'.[2] The port was pillaged again in each of the following three years, along with other Frisian markets, and it was apparently only a storm which saved the region from further attack in 838, wrecking a Viking fleet as it sailed south (AB s.a. 835, 836, 837, 838). Here, too, Louis the Pious made strenuous efforts to protect the coast by stationing garrisons, building a fleet, and constructing small ring fortresses, but again his endeavours were largely ineffectual, most probably because of the unwillingness of local counts to obey his orders.

The timing of this upsurge in raiding in Frisia was evidently not accidental. The year 834, when Dorestad was first pillaged, marked the failure of a revolt by Lothar I and his exile to Italy, while 839, when the attacks subsided, witnessed his return to favour. That this was not mere coincidence was suggested by several West Frankish authors, who claimed that Lothar had actively encouraged certain Danish leaders to make the raids in order to harm his father Louis the Pious, and rewarded them with grants of land on his accession in 840.[3] Unfortunately, Lothar's actions were tantamount to sowing the wind, for the return of the successful raiders, their ships laden with captives and loot, undoubtedly encouraged others to follow in their footsteps.

The wide range of Continental sources, which include annals, chronicles, letters, capitularies, charters, miracle texts, and even hymns and prayers referring to the Viking raids, is unfortunately not matched on the other side of the Channel, where the *Anglo-Saxon Chronicle* provides nearly all our information about the raids. At this early stage, they seem to have been few and sporadic, and after the initial shock caused by the sack of Lindisfarne in 793 and Monkwearmouth in 794, little Scandinavian activity was reported until the late 830s. Then Sheppey was attacked in 835, and Egbert of Wessex fought the invaders at Carhampton in 836 and Hingston Down in 838.

---

[1] *De Translationibus et Miraculis Sancti Filiberti*, Preface to Book I, in Poupardin (1905), pp. 23–5.
[2] 'Omnia diripuerunt, homines autem quosdam occiderunt, quosdam captivatos abduxerunt partemque eius igni cremaverunt.' *AB s.a.* 834, p. 14.
[3] *AB s.a.* 841, p. 39; Nithard, *Historiarum Libri IIII*, IV.2, p. 122.

Although the *Chronicle* referred to all the raiders as 'Danes', it seems that, even if this was true of those who pillaged Sheppey, those who were active in the west are more likely to have been Norwegians from Ireland.

The second phase of Scandinavian activity, from 841 to 875, was characterised by a marked increase in the number, scope and scale of the raids. At first it was a kind of *Blitzkrieg*, with the Vikings arriving unexpectedly, plundering, burning and killing or enslaving the inhabitants, then leaving as swiftly as they had come. The contemporary description of an incursion on the Seine in 841 is typical:

> The Northmen appeared on 12 May, led by Oskar. They set fire to the city of Rouen on 14 May and left on 16 May. On 24 May they burned down the monastery of Jumièges, on 25 May the abbey of St Wandrille was ransomed for 6 pounds [of silver], and on 28 May monks arrived from St Denis and redeemed sixty-eight captives for 26 pounds. On 31 May the pagans made for the sea, and although Vulfard, a royal vassal, opposed them with an army, the pagans were not at all prepared to fight.[4]

As this account suggests, one of the main reasons for the Vikings' success was the surprise and speed of their attacks. They fell upon unprepared and often defenceless settlements, plundered whatever they could find, then withdrew before the locals could muster sufficient force to resist them. Raids of this type were reported on both sides of the Channel in the early 840s, with London, Rochester, *Hamwic* (Southampton), Quentovic, Nantes, Hamburg and Paris among the many victims.

As time went by, the profitability of such raids and the lack of effective resistance led to a change in the Vikings' tactics, as they began to winter on foreign soil instead of returning to Scandinavia each autumn. The first reported instance of this was in 843, when a fleet landed on an island off southern Aquitaine, 'brought houses from the mainland, and decided to spend the winter there as if in a permanent settlement'.[5] From this date onwards Aquitaine was hardly ever free of a Viking presence, with fleets camped on the Loire almost every year, and other incursions on the Garonne and the Charente. It was likewise a fleet coming from Aquitaine

---

[4] 'Quarto Idus Maii venerunt Nortmanni, Oscheri quoque dux. Pridie Idus Maii incensa est ab eis urbs Rotomagus; 17 Kal. Iunii egressi sunt a Rothomago; 9 Kal. Iunii Gemmeticum monasterium igne cremarunt; 8 Kal. Iunii redemptum est Fontinella coenobium libris 6; 5 Kal. Iunii venerunt monachi de sancto Dyonisio, redemeruntque capita sexaginta octo libris viginti sex. Pridie Kal. Iunii pagani mare petierunt. Obviusque illis factus est Vulfardus regis homo cum populo, sed pagani minime ad pugnam se praeparaverunt.' Chronicon Fontanellense *s.a.* 841, ed. Laporte (1951), p. 75.
[5] 'Insulam quandam ingressi, convectis a continenti domibus, hiemare velut perpetuis sedibus statuerunt.' *AB s.a.* 843, p. 44.

which first wintered on the Seine, in 851, and although that particular band was persuaded to leave the river by the payment of a tribute in 853, another fleet which entered the river in 856 remained for fully six years, until 862. That the Seine was not permanently occupied, like the Loire, was due largely to Charles the Bald's determination to expel the invaders from the Frankish heartlands; distant (and unruly) Aquitaine does not seem to have concerned him as much. Thus a fleet which entered the Seine in 865 was swiftly bought off with a tribute, and departed the following year.

Meanwhile, the *Anglo-Saxon Chronicle* had reported a similar change of Viking tactics in England in 850. One version of the *Chronicle* recorded the location, Thanet, while the other noted the significance of the event, when 'The heathen for the first time remained over the winter' (*s.a.* 851). That fleet does not appear to have stayed long in England, but it started a trend which others subsequently followed. In particular, the army which arrived in 865 remained over many winters, and part of it later settled what became known as the Danelaw. This was the 'Great Army', a name by which it was described on both sides of the Channel (the term was used by the *Chronicle* in England and by Adrevald of Fleury on the Continent).

The formation of the 'Great Army' highlights another new factor in this second phase of the Scandinavian attacks, namely the increased size of the Viking war-bands. Before 840, relatively small Scandinavian fleets are recorded in contemporary sources, but thereafter the numbers increase. Thus three ships were reported *s.a.* 789 (*ASC*), nine in 835,[6] thirteen in 820 (*ARF*), and twenty-five or thirty-five in 836 (*ASC*). By contrast, the fleet which sacked Nantes in 843 numbered sixty-three ships,[7] Ragnar's fleet on the Seine in 845 contained 120 ships (*AB*), the fleet which stormed Canterbury and London in 851 reportedly numbered 350 ships (*ASC*), and 260 ships were said to make up the two fleets which occupied the Seine in 861 (*AB*). If each ship could transport some thirty to forty men, as archaeological discoveries suggest, then these Viking armies probably numbered in their thousands, but not tens of thousands. Although Sawyer has cited a text of 1142 as evidence that even the 'Great Army' consisted of no more than a thousand men,[8] he fails to take several important points into account. First, it is unclear whether the ships used by the ninth-century Viking armies were identical to those employed three centuries later. Secondly, although the presence of horses on board the Viking longships would have reduced the number of men they could carry (as would indeed the presence of captives and plunder), it must be recalled that Viking armies

---

[6] *De Miraculis Sancti Filiberti* II. 11, in Poupardin (1905), pp. 66–7.

[7] *De Miraculis Sancti Filiberti*, Preface to Book II, in Poupardin (1905), p. 59.

[8] Sawyer (1971), p. 128.

are never said to have consisted of cavalry alone: on the contrary, mounted forces are mentioned alongside footsoldiers. Thirdly, as Brooks has observed, the sizes of Viking fleets and the numbers of casualties reported in contemporary sources both suggest that the armies contained thousands, rather than hundreds, of men.[9] In this context it is significant that two raiding parties sent out by the Vikings on the Seine in 865 numbered 200 and 500 men respectively (*AB s.a.* 865), while a similar force which raided St Omer in 891 reportedly consisted of 550 men.[10] Bearing in mind that in each case a sizeable contingent must have been left to guard the fleet, the Viking armies in question probably both contained upwards of a thousand men.

Not only were the Scandinavian armies of this period larger, there were also more of them on campaign. In 845, for instance, one fleet attacked Hamburg in the East Frankish kingdom, another fought in Frisia in the Middle Kingdom, yet another sacked Paris in Charles the Bald's kingdom, while a fourth raided Saintes in Aquitaine. This was admittedly an exceptional year, but it highlights an observable trend, with more fleets attacking ever more widely. To cite another example, towards the end of 850 a large Danish fleet in Frisia divided into three, with one group occupying Dorestad, another attacking Flanders, and a third wintering on Thanet in Kent. The next year another large fleet stormed London and Canterbury, while yet another army entered the Seine, in this instance from Aquitaine.

This brings out the point that Viking armies were continually changing in their composition, leadership and location. New elements arrived as old elements left, and the theatre of operations could change from year to year. It is therefore misleading to speak of 'the Seine Vikings', 'the Loire Vikings' or even 'the Great Army', except with reference to a specific army at a particular time. Similarly, it is important to recognise that there was no plan or co-ordination behind the raids, no concerted assault on western Europe. Each war-band fought for itself, and on occasion Viking armies fought each other, as for instance on the Loire in 853, when one fleet blockaded another Viking war-band and forced it to hand over a large amount of booty.

A third development which can be discerned during this second phase of the Viking incursions was that the invading fleets travelled ever further in their search for fresh targets. The most striking examples of this are the two Scandinavian expeditions into the Mediterranean. The first took place in 844, when Frankish and Arab sources reported that a fleet which had previously sacked Nantes and Toulouse attacked Gijòn, Lisbon and Seville before being defeated by an Umayyad army, whereupon they left the Guadalquivir and returned to Aquitaine. The second expedition lasted

---

[9] Brooks (1979), pp. 4–11.   [10] *Miracula Sancti Bertini*, c. 6: *MGH SS* xv:1, p. 512.

longer and travelled considerably further. After leaving the Loire in 858, the fleet raided the coasts of Spain and North Africa before wintering in the Camargue. They subsequently sacked Nîmes and Arles, travelled up the Rhône as far as Valence, and, after suffering defeat at the hands of the count of Vienne, set sail for Italy, where they looted Pisa and other towns. Later medieval accounts of how Hasting captured the town of Luna by trickery, then put the inhabitants to the sword when he discovered that the town was not Rome as he had thought, are, sadly, unsubstantiated by contemporary sources, and almost certainly legend. The fleet finally returned to the Atlantic coast in 862, having plundered the shores of southern France and Spain en route.

As this account has indicated, the Viking armies also penetrated further upriver than before, threatening areas which had previously been unscathed. This was a gradual development, so that on the Loire, for instance, offshore islands are the only known targets before 840, Nantes was sacked in 843, Tours in 853, Orléans in 856, and Fleury in 865. Similarly, in the southeast of England only the Isle of Sheppey was raided before 840, then Romney Marsh in 841, Rochester and London in 842, and Canterbury in 851.

At the same time, the Northmen also began to leave their ships and travel across country, either on foot or on horseback. At first, the Vikings' base camps were almost always their ships, moored in the rivers, or islands in midstream. For instance, Adrevald of Fleury, writing in the 870s, described how 'The Northmen meanwhile made an anchorage for their ships and a refuge from all dangers on an island below the monastery of St Florent, putting up huts in a sort of village in which to keep their gangs of prisoners in irons, and to rest their bodies from their labours for a time, ready to serve on campaign.'[11] Because the Franks and Anglo-Saxons did not have suitable ships with which to attack these island bases, they were virtually impregnable. On the one occasion when Charles the Bald tried to assemble a river fleet to assault an island base, at Oissel, near Rouen, the campaign ended disastrously, with the entire fleet falling into enemy hands.[12] As time went by, however, the Vikings became emboldened by success and greedy for new targets, and so began to venture away from the rivers, building fortified camps or occupying existing strongholds. The 'Great Army' was the first to adopt this strategy, initially in England, and then on the Continent after its passage there in 879.

---

[11] 'Interea stationem navium suarum acsi asylum omnium periculorum in insula quadam coenobio Sancti Florentii subposita conponentes, mappalia quoque instar exaedificavere burgi, quo captivorum greges catenis asstrictos adservarent ipsique pro tempore corpora a labore reficerent, expeditioni ilico servitura.' Adrevald, *Miracula Sancti Benedicti*, c. 33: MGH SS xv:1, p. 494.

[12] *Vita Faronis*, c. 125; MGH SRM v, p. 201.

The fact that Viking armies were now remaining for ever longer periods on foreign soil meant that they posed an increased political threat to the local rulers, and this brings us to a final development which can be observed during the period in question, namely the Vikings' increasing entanglement in internal politics. One form which this took was the Vikings' exploitation of internal political disputes to their own ends, either independently or in collusion with local rebel factions. Thus in the Frankish kingdoms they capitalised on the internecine struggles between the Carolingian rulers by attacking while the royal host was elsewhere, or by joining forces with the king's enemies, whether the Bretons or the Aquitainian pretender, Pippin II. In Anglo-Saxon England the invaders' influence was considerably greater, for they were able not only to exploit the feuds between and within the various kingdoms, as on the Continent, but even to appoint puppet kings, Ceolwulf in Mercia in 873, 'a foolish king's thane' (*ASC*), and perhaps others in Northumbria in 867 and East Anglia in 870.

The other side of the coin was that the Anglo-Saxon and Frankish rulers absorbed a number of Viking leaders into the internal political scene by buying them off with cash, or lands, or both. It is true that some of these poachers-turned-gamekeepers appear to have been less than reliable, such as a certain Rodulf, who 'though he had been baptised, ended his dog's life with a fitting death' in Frisia in 873.[13] Others were successfully integrated into the local political milieu, however, including a former king of Denmark, Hemming, 'a most Christian leader', who died defending the island of Walcheren from Viking attack in 837.[14]

This offers a timely reminder that the Franks and the Anglo-Saxons alike vigorously resisted the Viking armies, albeit with limited success. Coastal defence has already been mentioned, and coast guards or coastal fleets did on occasion repel Scandinavian raiders, as for example when Frankish shore guards prevented a fleet of thirteen ships from plundering the Flemish coast and the mouth of the Seine in 820 (*ARF*), or when the men of Dorset and Somerset defeated a Viking fleet at the mouth of the Parret in 845 (*ASC*). On land, too, the Vikings suffered a number of defeats, a fact which has often been overlooked. For example, Charles the Bald captured nine longships on the Dordogne in 848, and won a resounding victory near Chartres in 856,[15] while the 'Great Army' was defeated twice in 871, at Englefield by ealdorman Æthelwulf and at Ashdown by Alfred (*ASC s.a.* 871).

Such defeats rarely seem to have deterred the Northmen, however. They simply regrouped, perhaps retreated, and turned their attentions elsewhere.

13 'Quamvis baptizatus esset, caninam vitam digna morte finivit.' *Annales Xantenses s.a.* 873, p. 33.
14 'Dux christianissimus.' Thegan, *Vita Hludowici Imperatoris*, Appendix; *MGH SS* II, p. 604.
15 *Chronicon Fontanellense s.a.* 848, 855; Laporte (1951), pp. 81, 91.

Carolingian and Anglo-Saxon rulers alike therefore frequently resorted to
the payment of tribute, a time-honoured method of buying off one's
opponent. Although this practice has been much vilified by contemporaries
and modern historians, it does appear to have been the most effective means
of removing the Vikings. Contrary to popular opinion, the Scandinavian
leaders who took tributes did normally keep their side of the agreement and
leave the kingdom which paid them, while there is no indication that such
payments encouraged others to seek similar deals. What is more, the written
and numismatic evidence suggests that the Anglo-Saxon and Frankish
kingdoms were able to afford the sums paid, even if they did sometimes
prove difficult to raise in a short time. The odium with which the practice
has been regarded can in fact largely be attributed to the barbed comments
of the ninth-century Frankish ecclesiastics who wrote virtually all of the
surviving Continental texts. They saw the defence of the realm as the
responsibility of the secular nobility, not the church, and therefore deeply
resented having to dig into their coffers to buy off the invaders. It is
instructive to compare the expression which is consistently used by the more
sympathetic writer of the *Anglo-Saxon Chronicle*: 'they made peace'. Historians have all too often accepted the highly negative reports of the Frankish
clerics without recognising the self-interest which coloured them.

The other successful tactic adopted on both sides of the Channel to
oppose the Vikings was that of fortification, including the fortification of
strategically located bridges. In 862 Charles the Bald fortuitously discovered
that closing a river by blocking the span of a bridge could prevent the
passage of Viking fleets, and even force them to leave the kingdom. He
therefore ordered the fortification of the bridge nearest the mouth of the
Seine, at Pont-de-l'Arche near Pîtres, in order to be able to close the river in
the case of future incursions. When the upper Loire was finally clear of
Vikings in 873, the king seems to have followed a similar strategy there,
fortifying the bridge at Les Ponts-de-Cé near Angers to perform the same
function.[16] It is unclear how successful these bridges were, in that there is no
record of them having actually stopped any Viking fleets, but they appear to
have been judged worthy of imitation by later monarchs, including Alfred
in England in the 880s. Charles the Bald also encouraged a limited
programme of urban fortification against the Vikings in the late 860s, when
Tours, Le Mans, Orléans, St Denis and probably also Angoulême were
fortified.

It is therefore clear that the Vikings were offered stout resistance on both
sides of the Channel during this second wave of invasions, but that their
increased numbers, increased mobility and increased political influence

[16] Coupland (1991a).

made them extremely difficult and dangerous enemies. In the third phase of the attacks, from 876 to 911, the Scandinavians capitalised on this position of strength to colonise areas of England and Francia.

In 876 the *Anglo-Saxon Chronicle* contained the significant report: 'In this year Halfdan shared out the lands of the Northumbrians, and they proceeded to plough and to support themselves.' Although Scandinavian chieftains had previously ruled fiefdoms in Frisia, with the most famous of them, Rorik, holding a large area around Dorestad for nearly all of the period between 840 and 875, there does not appear to have been any attempt by the Danes to settle the region.[17] It is precisely this aspect of Scandinavian activity on both sides of the Channel, namely the settlement of occupied territory, which distinguishes the third phase of the Viking invasions, from 876 to 911.

Before going on to examine in more detail the events of that period, it is appropriate at this point to consider the aims of the invasions. Were the Vikings seeking political conquest? Were they engaged on a pagan crusade, as some have claimed? Or were they simply after loot? We are hampered by the fact that the Vikings themselves left no contemporary record of their intentions, so that all accounts of their activities were compiled by their victims, who may have been ill informed or even malicious in their reports. Even so, there is broad agreement among commentators that the quest for loot was the principal, if not the only motivation behind the raids.

With regard to the first possibility, political conquest, there is little sign that this was ever the deliberate intent of the invaders, even if at times it seemed to their victims that they threatened to overrun the kingdom. We have already noted that Scandinavian chiefs ruled large tracts of Frisia for long periods without any apparent attempt by their followers to colonise the region, and until the mid-870s the armies which occupied Frankish or Anglo-Saxon territory over many years likewise gave no indication of wishing to take political control. Furthermore, when Viking leaders 'made peace' with Carolingian or Anglo-Saxon rulers, they consistently sought tributes rather than political power, and even after the establishment of the Danelaw and Normandy the primary concern of the settlers appears to have been colonisation, not conquest.

As for the second possibility, that the raids were motivated by militant paganism, there is equally little support for this in contemporary sources. Although the idea was revived by Wallace-Hadrill,[18] the texts which he cited are evidence not so much of any pagan zeal on the part of the Vikings, as of the militant Christianity of the ecclesiastical Carolingian writers.[19]

The thirst for loot is, by contrast, clearly attested in all contemporary

---

[17] Blok (1978), pp. 37–47.   [18] Wallace-Hadrill (1975).   [19] Coupland (1991b).

descriptions of the Scandinavian incursions. It accounts for their choice of targets, their avoidance of battle wherever possible, and their willingness, even eagerness, to accept tributes and ransoms.

This motivation is also just as evident in the third phase of the invasions, the era of settlement, as it was from the 790s to 875. The 'Great Army' went wherever it could find the richest pickings, crossing the Channel when faced with resolute opposition, as in England in 878, or with famine, as on the Continent in 892. As time went by, however, others emulated the example of Halfdan and his followers, settling in Mercia in 877, and East Anglia in 879–80 and 896. The rest of the army meanwhile continued to harry and plunder on both sides of the Channel, with new recruits evidently arriving to swell its ranks, for it clearly continued to be a formidable fighting force.

One contemporary cleric testified to the terror the 'Great Army' inspired:

The Northmen never stopped enslaving and killing the Christian people, pulling down churches, demolishing fortifications and burning towns. And on every road lay the corpses of clergy and laity, noblemen and commoners, women, youngsters and babies. Indeed there was no village or highway where the dead did not lie, and all were filled with grief and torment as they saw the Christian populace being destroyed to the point of extinction.[20]

This was, it is true, the reaction of a local man written by a monk from Arras, which lay at the heart of the area of the operations of the 'Great Army' on the Continent, between the Seine and the Rhine. It is nonetheless an eloquent testimony to the panic engendered by the Viking raids, which led to many monastic communities fleeing with the relics of their patron saints, and seeking refuge in safer regions. The monks of Noirmoutier, who had left their island monastery so many years earlier, ended up in Tournus in Burgundy, while the community of St Vaast fled Arras for less distant Beauvais. A similar reaction was also reported on the other side of the Channel, so that for instance the monks of Lindisfarne removed the relics of St Cuthbert from his tomb in 875, and wandered with the body until they found a safe resting place at Chester-le-Street in 883, apparently after making a deal with the local Danes.

Meanwhile the military response to the 'Great Army' varied markedly from one ruler to another. In England, Alfred needed several years to devise an effective strategy of resistance, but after a decisive victory at Edington in 878 offered vigorous opposition. Whereas he had previously been forced to

---

[20] 'Nortmanni vero non cessant captivari atque interfici populum Christianum atque ecclesias subrui, destructis moeniis et villis igne crematis. Per omnes enim plateas iacebant cadavera clericorum, laicorum nobilium atque aliorum, mulierum, iuvenum et lactentium. Non enim erat via vel locus, quo non iacerent mortui, et erat tribulatio omnibus et dolor, videntes populum Christianum usque ad internitionem devastari.' *Annales Vedastini s.a.* 884, pp. 54–5.

offer repeated tribute payments, after 878 he established a chain of fortresses across the south of England, reorganised the army, 'so that always half its men were at home, and half out on service, except for those men who were to garrison the burhs' (*ASC s.a.* 893), and in 896 ordered a new type of craft to be built which could oppose the Viking longships in shallow coastal waters. When the Vikings returned from the Continent in 892 they found that they could no longer roam the country at will, for wherever they went they were opposed by a local army. After four years the Scandinavians therefore separated, some to settle in Northumbria and East Anglia, the remainder to try their luck again on the Continent.

On the other side of the Channel, the memory of the presence of the 'Great Army' between 879 and 892 was still strong, and Charles the Simple was doubtless aware that his grip on the kingdom depended on the strength of his opposition to the invaders. Only nine years earlier Charles the Fat had been deposed because he had apparently let the Vikings off the hook at Elsloo in 882 and before Paris in 886, while the choice of Odo, Count of Paris, to replace him as West Frankish king had evidently been prompted by his successful defence of his besieged city in 885–6. So Charles the Simple opposed the newly arrived army with the twin approaches of tribute and attack, and although contemporary sources are frustratingly silent during the decade after 900, in 911 Charles' army won a significant victory over the Vikings at Chartres. It is likely that some of them had already started to settle around the mouth of the Seine, and in a treaty with their leader Rollo, Charles recognised his control over the area and his followers' right to colonise the region, in return for Rollo's baptism and pledge of allegiance to Charles. Many comparable agreements had previously been made, but hindsight affords this one particular significance. For it was by this treaty that the Vikings became Normans, the pagans became Christians, and thereby, in the eyes of contemporaries, the barbarians joined civilisation.

CHAPTER 8

SCANDINAVIA, *c.* 700–1066

Niels Lund

AT the beginning of the eighth century Scandinavia was politically amorphous. By the end of the three and a half centuries surveyed in this chapter three independent kingdoms and one 'republic' had formed in this part of Europe (Map 14).

The political structure of Scandinavia before the eighth century eludes us. The claims made for a dark-age kingdom of the Svear controlling all Sweden and large parts of the Baltic area are no doubt exaggerated. The Götar are not mentioned in ninth-century sources and this has led some scholars to assume that at some point between 500 and 900 they had been absorbed by the Svear. Later evidence, however, shows conclusively that the Götar were recognised as an independent people well into the twelfth century. Foreign observers often give a misleading impression because they were familiar only with the Svear. At the beginning of the eighth century Sweden was divided into several regions effectively separated from each other by natural obstacles, mainly thick and trackless forests (Map 15).

In Norway geographical conditions similarly determined the limits for any concentration of power. Most communication was by sea. Naval forces therefore were prerequisites for anyone aspiring to power over larger tracts of Norway. Distances were vast; the distance between the southern and northern limits of Scandinavia matches that from York to Gibraltar. Southeast Norway therefore came as naturally into the sphere of interest of Danish princes as into that of princes based in western or northern Norway, and there is nothing to suggest that Norway was ever united under one ruler or even regarded as a separate territorial or national entity before the Viking period. This is reflected in Norwegian graves well into the Viking period. Centres of princely or aristocratic burial are found in several parts of Norway.

In Denmark the geography is much more favourable to the exercise of power: a larger population is concentrated within a much smaller area. It is

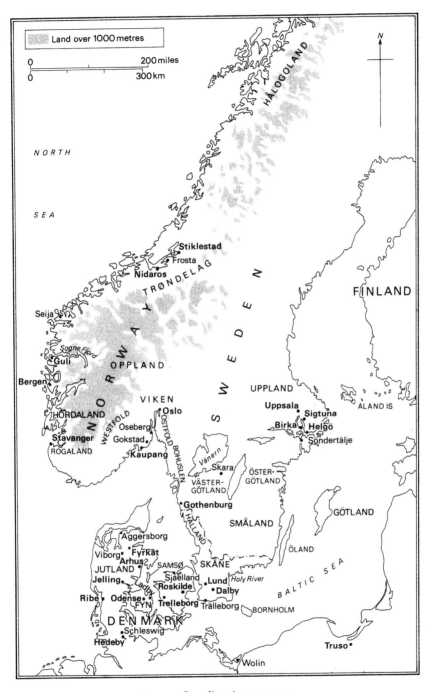

Map 14 Scandinavia, 700–1050

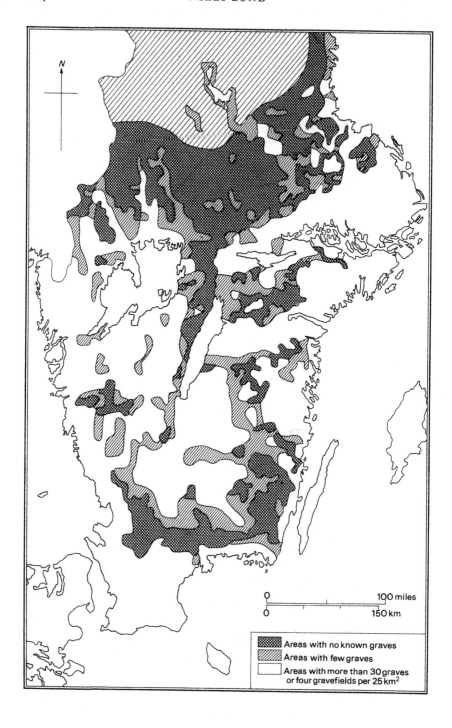

N

0   100 miles
0   150 km

    ▨ Areas with no known graves
    ▨ Areas with few graves
    ☐ Areas with more than 30 graves
        or four gravefields per 25 km^2

understandable, therefore, that the first concentration of power emerges in Denmark.

The first signs of this are manifest in the first quarter of the eighth century. Between 704 and 710 a centre for commerce was created at Ribe in southwest Jutland and there are several indications of a royal hand in this. By 720 coins may have been struck in Ribe. In 726 the Kanhave canal was dug across the island of Samsø in the Kattegat, enabling ships to be dragged from one side of the island to the other. This suggests that some king was trying to exercise control over traffic in both the Great and the Little Belt, and in 737 another earthwork which certainly presupposes a royal or other authority capable of organising great resources was put up, namely, the first Danevirke, an earthwork extending over 10 km for the protection of the southern Danish frontier.

There is no certainty that Ribe, the Kanhave canal and the oldest Danevirke were all due to the same king, or that he is identical with the only Danish king of this period known from written sources. It seems unlikely, however, that such a limited area could offer scope for more than one king able to wield the resources required for each of these ventures. Ribe's contacts were very much with Frisia and England, and before 714 Willibrord, the Anglo-Saxon missionary to the Frisians, tried to extend his mission to Scandinavia but found the Danish king Ongendus inaccessible to the truth.[1] It is this Ongendus who is the only known Danish king of the first half of the eighth century. Thus he or his dynasty is likely to be behind this first manifestation of central power in Denmark. It has been suggested that this Danish kingdom was able to take over the maritime hegemony of the North Sea exercised by the early Merovingians and maintain peaceful conditions for the trade in the region.[2]

For the best idea of what Scandinavian society was like before kingship developed one must go to Iceland. This island was populated largely from Scandinavia and therefore may be expected to differ from the rest of Scandinavia mainly in having no king. Authority in Iceland was exercised

---

[1] Alcuin, *Life of Willibrord*, ch.9.   [2] Wood (1983), p. 19.

Map 15 Sweden, distribution of prehistoric burial sites. This shows the extent to which Uppland was separated from Västergötland and, to a lesser extent, from Östergötland, and also illustrates why Skåne and Halland came naturally to belong to Denmark. From Åke Hyenstrand, *Fasta fornlämningar och arkeologiska regioner* (Riksantikvarieämbetet 1984:7) Stockholm, 1984.

by chieftains called *goðar*. Their power was personal, not territorial; their jurisdiction, called a *goðorð*, was formed by freemen who had commended themselves to a particular *goði*. Over two or three centuries the number of *goðorð* was reduced through rivalries between the *goðar*, and larger lordships called *ríkir* were formed; these were territorial.

Although the existence of slavery in the Scandinavian societies has been recognised, it has been generally believed that the majority of the population was formed by the free peasantry and that the land was owned and run by freemen and their families. These freemen were thought to have the decisive word at the popular assemblies called 'thing'. However, recent studies have shown not only that agricultural holdings were generally quite large in the Viking period, so large that they required much more than a family to run them; a great number of dependants must have been attached to these large farms. It has also been recognised that much land was owned by magnates whose land was run by tenants. By a recent estimate no more than 3 or 4% of the population were freemen with a say at the assemblies,[3] and one should not idealise procedures at these assemblies. They were dominated by the chieftains. Matters were settled by the number of their armed followers rather than by voting. It is no coincidence that decisions were taken by the brandishing of weapons, *vapnatak*.

A process similar to the one found in Iceland no doubt was at work in the rest of Scandinavia but the evidence does not permit us to follow it very closely. Apart from its use in three Danish runic inscriptions the term *goði* does not occur outside Iceland. In Norway there are suggestions of *ríkir* like Ranrike and Romerike, and in the ninth century Viking bands in western Europe could be traced back to Vestfold, the region on the western banks of Oslo Fjord,[4] and to Hordaland in southwest Norway.[5] In Denmark Bornholm is described as a separate kingdom towards the end of the ninth century.

A king who wanted to control larger parts of Scandinavia would have to secure recognition of his overlordship from the rulers of *goðorð* and *ríkir* or similar territorial units, and by the year 800 the Danish king Godfrid appears to be in control of most of the lands surrounding the Kattegat and the Skagerrak.

The conquest of Saxony made the Franks neighbours of the Danes; thus the Danes get mentioned more often in Frankish sources. In 782, for example, the Danish king, Sigfrid, sent envoys to a Frankish assembly also attended by the Saxons, except Widukind, the leader of Saxon resistance,

---

[3] Porsmose (1988), p. 259; a census taken in 1096 of the Icelandic population recorded 4560 fully free. The total population was probably about 80,000: Sawyer (1982), p. 59.

[4] *Chronicon Aquitanicum*, 843, *MGH SS* II, pp. 252-3.   [5] *ASC s.a.* 789, D, E, F.

who had fled to Denmark, and in 798 a Frankish envoy was killed by the Saxons on his way to Denmark to see Sigfrid.[6] Nothing more is known about Sigfrid, but his successor, and probably son, Godfrid plays a large role. He seems to have extended his power over most of the Skagerrak and Kattegat area; the princes and people of the Oslo Fjord region refused his successors allegiance in 813:[7] by implication they must have accepted Godfrid's overlordship and paid him tribute. In 811 one member of a Danish legation to Charlemagne was a man from Skåne;[8] while he could have been a noble in Hemming's entourage who just happened to be a native of Skåne, it seems more likely that he was there as a representative of that province.

Godfrid's imperial ambitions were not confined to Scandinavia. They extended to neighbours like the Obodrites and the Frisians as well and on both fronts his interests clashed with those of Charlemagne. Frisia, of course, was part of the Carolingian empire. When Godfrid began to levy tributes in Frisia, this, from a Frankish point of view, amounted to attempted conquest. The Obodrites had apparently acknowledged the Danes as overlords at some stage before the Frankish subjection of Saxony was complete. Godfrid had received tribute from the Obodrite port of Reric,[9] but when Saxony had been subdued but was not yet reliable, the Obodrites became valuable allies of Charlemagne. With this support the Obodrites tried to liberate themselves of the Danish yoke.

In 804, when Charlemagne deported the Saxons living north of the Elbe and gave their land to the Obodrites, Godfrid concentrated his fleet and his army at Schleswig, apparently prepared to intervene, and in 808 he invaded the Obodrites to ensure continued payments of tribute from them. He moved the merchants of Reric to Schleswig for the same reason. On this occasion Godfrid is also said to have built a wall to protect his Saxon border. This wall has not been identified with certainty.

Godfrid's ambitions even included Saxony which he is said to have regarded as his own province.[10] Einhard does not exclude the possibility that Godfrid might attack Charlemagne in Aachen itself. Charlemagne was considering an attack on Denmark when it was reported to him that a Danish fleet of 200 ships had devastated all the Frisian islands, had beaten the mainland Frisians three times and had levied a tribute of 100 pounds of silver.[11]

This crisis subsided when Godfrid was murdered in 810. It is a distinct possiblity that Charlemagne had a hand in this. Godfrid's successor, his nephew Hemming, immediately sought peace with the emperor. Danish

[6] *ARF s.a.* 782, 798.　　[7] *ARF s.a.* 813.　　[8] *ARF s.a.* 811.　　[9] *ARF s.a.* 808.
[10] Einhard, *Vita Karoli* ii. 14.　　[11] *ARF s.a.* 810.

and Frankish peace delegations met on the Eider in the spring of 811 to conclude a formal peace. Among the members on the Danish side were two of Hemming's brothers but none of Godfrid's sons.

Hemming had already died in 812 and the succession was contested between Sigfrid, another nephew of Godfrid, and Anulo, who was the nephew of a former king, Harald; they both lost their lives in the ensuing battle and two of Anulo's brothers, Harald and Reginfrid, were accepted as kings. They sent envoys to the emperor to make their own peace with him and to secure the return of their brother Hemming from Francia. Hemming is likely to have been a hostage.

Charlemagne obliged and returned Hemming but Harald and Reginfrid were not there to welcome him. They were in Vestfold, the northwestern-most part of their *regnum*, to re-establish their authority. The princes and people in these parts had apparently taken the opportunity afforded by the civil wars in Denmark to shake off their tributary obligations.[12]

These civil wars continued when the sons of Godfrid returned from their exile in Sweden together with a number of Danish magnates. They defeated Harald and Reginfrid in 814; the latter was killed and Harald sought refuge with Louis the Pious. Louis promised to help him but the army which he sent into Jutland in 815 failed to restore Harald to power.

Harald was now left in Saxony and continued to harass Godfrid's sons in Denmark, until in 819 Louis had the Obodrites escort his Danish protégé back to Denmark. This time the sons of Godfrid, four of whom were co-ruling, were forced to accept him as joint ruler. In the following years the emperor repeatedly had to sort things out between the Danish kings, very much in the manner he dealt with dissensions among the Slav princes. In 823, for example, Harald appeared before Louis complaining about God-frid's sons and Louis sent a couple of counts to Denmark to inquire into the matter. In 825 and 826 Godfrid's sons sent envoys to Louis, and in the latter year Harald appeared with numerous followers in Mainz and was baptised, hoping that would make the emperor back him more firmly. On the same occasion he was given Rüstringen in north Frisia as a fief and place of refuge and in 827 he was finally expelled from Denmark. He probably never re-entered Denmark after his baptism, and Anskar, a monk from Corbie whom Louis had sent to Denmark with Harald to evangelise, must also have failed to gain access. After 827 one of Godfrid's sons, Horik I, emerged as sole king of Denmark and ruled until his death in 854.

Harald apparently soon gave up hope that Louis' support would benefit him; the emperor probably realised that as an exile Harald was no longer

---

[12] *ARF s.a.* 813.

useful to him and began pinning his hopes for the dissemination of the Gospel on Horik.[13] After 828, when Harald impatiently ruined Louis' efforts on his behalf, Harald deserted Louis in favour of his rebellious son Lothar, and in the following years he appears to have been behind the attacks on Dorestad, some of which were timed remarkably to put a spoke in Louis' wheel when he was on his way to Italy to deal with Lothar. In 841 Harald was duly rewarded by Lothar who, once he had succeeded his father, gave Walcheren and some nearby settlements to Harald.[14]

Louis' change of attitude towards Horik soon showed. Having made an unlucky choice of partner as far as a mission in Denmark was concerned, Anskar turned his efforts to Sweden, and Horik's control of south Scandinavian waters must have been such that the mission to Birka, 829–31, would not have been possible against an unfriendly attitude on Horik's part. Anskar's later mission to Birka took place explicitly with the support of Horik.[15] Envoys from Horik repeatedly attended Louis' courts, offering peace and even obedience, and the emperor paid indemnities to Horik for the murder of some of his envoys near Cologne.[16] Louis did find, however, that Horik was overreaching himself when in 838 he demanded the lordship of Frisia as well as of the Obodrites, those very provinces that Godfrid had coveted, in return for the execution of some leaders of Vikings who had attacked the empire.[17]

EARLY ATTEMPTS TO INTRODUCE CHRISTIANITY

The first recorded attempt to evangelise in Scandinavia took place at the beginning of the eighth century when Willibrord extended his activity into Denmark.[18] His seeds fell on stony ground, however, and he does not seem to have had any royal backing. Under Charlemagne, interest in converting the Danes was renewed. Alcuin asked a Saxon abbot whether there was any hope for this goal;[19] we do not know the answer but apparently it was regarded as an unenviable task. Charlemagne once asked Paul the Deacon whether he would rather carry heavy chains, be in harsh prison, or go to Denmark to convert King Sigfrid.[20]

Not until the reign of Louis the Pious, however, was something really done. In 823 Pope Paschal II authorised Ebbo, archbishop of Rheims, to evangelise *in partibus aquilonis*, and Ebbo soon after actually visited Denmark. One result of his efforts was that Harald Klak was induced to travel to Mainz where he was baptised and paid homage to the emperor. When he

[13] Wood (1987), p. 45.   [14] Lund (1989), pp. 47–50.   [15] *VA*, 26.

[16] *AB s.a.* 831, 836.   [17] *AB s.a.* 838.   [18] See McKitterick, pp. 68–70 above.

[19] *MHG Epp.* IV, no. 6.   [20] *MGH Poet.* I, p. 51.

headed for Denmark two missionaries, Anskar and Autbert, followed him. As Harald was denied entry to Denmark, however, Anskar and Autbert were unable to intensify the work begun by Ebbo. Little more is heard about the mission in Denmark before the middle of the century.

After failing to enter Denmark, Anskar was sent to Sweden to evangelise. According to Rimbert's *Life of St Anskar* the Swedes themselves sent to Louis the Pious in 829 for missionaries to be despatched to Sweden, so a friendly reception was only to be expected. The mission was successful in the sense that in 830–1 a number of converts were won. Although the prefect of Birka built a church on his own land, no permanent community resulted. By the middle of the century, when Anskar returned to Birka, he had to start all over again.

In 831/2 Pope Gregory IV confirmed the foundation of an archdiocese at Hamburg and conferred a pallium on Anskar. The special responsibility of this see was the mission to the Swedes, the Danes and the Slavs, and while Ebbo was mentioned as co-responsible he vanished from the northern scene after 835 when he fell from favour. In 845 Anskar's metropolis was sacked by a Danish fleet and while Rimbert does not mention Horik as responsible other sources make it clear that he was. The sources do not permit us to follow the vacillations of the Dano-Frankish relationship in these years but a few years later Horik showed himself friendlily disposed towards the missionaries. Anskar was permitted to build churches in Schleswig and Ribe, the king making the land available, and Horik supported the resumption of the mission to the Swedes. There can be little doubt that at this time there were a number of people in Scandinavia interested in Christianity nor that the mission was, in fact, quite successful. Horik's successor, Horik II, even sent presents to the pope and received a letter back thanking him for these gifts and strongly urging him to give up idolatry.[21] At this time Anskar felt able to report to his fellow German bishops that the Church of Christ was firmly established among the Swedes and the Danes and that the priests could work unhindered.[22]

END OF THE FIRST DANISH EMPIRE

Another century passed, however, before Christianity took permanent root in Denmark and even longer in Sweden. The reason for this probably is that the political stability gave way to a period of insecurity. Slightly before 800 Scandinavians began to ravage western Europe with Viking raids and by the middle of the ninth century this activity had assumed large proportions. The

[21] *MGH Epp.* VI, no. 27.   [22] *MGH Epp.* VI, no. 116.

leaders were often members of royal families who had been exiled from Scandinavia,[23] and when they had enriched themselves abroad and were able to maintain powerful forces they represented a threat to the rulers back home in Scandinavia. Not rarely one or more of them would return home to assert their claims. In 850 Horik I was forced to share power with two nephews,[24] and in 854 Horik and many others lost their lives in a civil war started by another nephew whom Horik had hitherto denied a share in power, thereby forcing him to live *piratico more*.[25]

Little is known about his successor, Horik II 'the Child', except that he apparently maintained the friendly attitude towards Anskar's work that Horik I had adopted towards the end of his reign. The last of him is heard in 864 when he sent presents to the pope. After this the foreign sources that have permitted us at least to outline Danish history dry up for a century or more. In 873 the two Danish kings Halfdan and Sigfrid, apparently co-ruling, conducted negotiations with Louis the German. Halfdan has been identified with the Halfdan known from England but this is very unlikely; there is a greater possibility that Sigfrid may be identical with the Sigfrid who took part in the siege of Paris, 885–7, but as Abbo describes this Sigfrid as a king without any land he must then in the meantime have lost whatever position he had in Denmark.

The next rulers of Denmark that we learn about belong to the so-called Swedish dynasty. According to Adam of Bremen, Denmark was first ruled by one Helgi and after him by Olaf and his sons who came from Sweden. It has been generally believed that this amounted to a conquest of at least southern Denmark by a powerful Swedish dynasty wishing to unite Birka and Hedeby in a commercial empire controlling the assumed west to east trade route via the Baltic and Russia. Neither Adam nor any other source suggests that these kings ruled only part of Denmark, and among the Svear there was at this time no central authority capable of drafting, let alone pursuing, policies on this scale. By the middle of the ninth century, Birka was ruled by a king named Olof, whose power was not great enough to prevent an exiled rival, Anund, from attacking him with a mere eleven ships of his own and twenty-one collected in Denmark. Anskar's second visit to Birka also depended on Danish support. If a Swedish Baltic empire had emerged after 850, it ought to have included Bornholm. This island, however, was an independent kingdom in the last quarter of the ninth century.[26] In all probability Olaf and his dynasty were another group of exiles who took a favourable opportunity to return to Denmark.[27]

We have no clue as to why Danish power crumbled in this period. Adam

[23] Lund (1989), p. 53.   [24] *AB s.a.* 850.   [25] *AF s.a.* 854.
[26] *Old English Orosius*, p. 16.   [27] Lund (1980); against this, Moltke (1985).

blamed it on a crushing defeat suffered by a force of Vikings at the hands of
Arnulf, king of the eastern Franks, at the Dyle in 891. In reality this battle
was a relatively unimportant skirmish. Nevertheless, the very idea that the
defeat of a band of Vikings somewhere in Europe could have serious
consequences for the kingdom of Denmark does raise the question of the
connection between the rulers of the Scandinavian kingdoms and the
Viking armies abroad. If, in general, the leaders of the Viking raids were
exiles from Denmark and their possible return to Denmark presented a
danger to its rulers, then the defeat of a Viking force in Europe ought to be
welcomed by the king of Denmark. It is, however, difficult to generalise
about this and there are suggestions that the Vikings abroad were not
completely beyond the control of the king of Denmark. Horik I, in
negotiations with Louis the Pious, claimed to have punished some of those
Vikings that visited the empire. The facts that Ragnar, the leader of the
Vikings who attacked Paris in 845, was able to return to Denmark with his
booty *and* that Horik entered into negotiations with the Frankish kings and
returned some of the booty taken by Ragnar suggest that the Frankish kings
were not being entirely unfair when in 847 they sent envoys to Horik
threatening to attack him in Denmark if he did not stop his subjects from
attacking the Christians.[28]

HARALD FAIRHAIR IN NORWAY

The decline of Danish power created scope for local rulers in parts of
Scandinavia that had hitherto accepted Danish overlordship. What hap-
pened in Sweden remains obscure but in Norway the first attempt by a
Norwegian king to unite Norway was made.

Some time in the last quarter of the ninth century Ottar, a Norwegian
chieftain from Hålogaland, visited the court of King Alfred of Wessex and
gave an account of his travels in Scandinavian waters.[29] He described the
journey into the White Sea and the journey from his home in north Norway
to the ports of Sciringesheal in south Norway and Hedeby in south
Denmark, giving us information about the population of the regions and
the conditions of communications. Norway was populated by Norwegians,
who had permanent settlements mainly in the coastal regions and by
nomadic Sami who utilised the vast inland wastes. From Ottar's account and
other information in the *Old English Orosius*, Denmark emerges as split
between south Danes in Jutland and north Danes on the islands and in
Skåne, Halland and Bohuslen.[30] Virtually no political information is given

---

[28] *AB s.a.* 847.   [29] *Old English Orosius*, pp. 13–16.   [30] Lund (1991a).

in these texts, only that Bornholm formed a separate kingdom, but Ottar and his contemporaries clearly recognised three separate peoples in Scandinavia: the Norwegians, the Danes and the Swedes.

For information about the political conditions of the area we have to rely upon much later evidence. Denmark is covered to some extent by Adam of Bremen, while for Norway we have to rely on authors writing in the twelfth and thirteenth centuries. Some tenth- and eleventh-century skaldic poetry was available to these authors but neither medieval nor modern historians could mould a coherent political story on this basis. Skaldic poetry was meant to embroider fact, not record it. It has therefore been very difficult to get away from the picture of Norwegian history drawn up by Snorre in the thirteenth century in his collection of sagas of Norwegian kings known as *Heimskringla*.

According to Snorre the first successful attempt to unite Norway under a native king was made by Harald Fairhair who is said to have been the son of a petty king in Vestfold. He set out to subdue the rest of Norway, one kingdom or chieftaincy after another, crowning his efforts in the legendary battle in Hafrsfjord. Snorre's account obviously bears little relation to reality. In fact, Harald Fairhair was probably a king of Rogaland or Hordaland in western Norway, and his power in the rest of Norway never extended beyond an overlordship. Claims that he founded the unified kingdom of Norway and that afterwards the kingship was recognised as the paternal heritage of his descendants are baseless[31] and it is very doubtful that later kings like Olav Tryggvesson and Olav Haraldsson were in fact his descendants. Harald Hardrada based his claim to legitimacy on being the uterine brother of St Olav, not a descendant from Harald Fairhair. The idea that the throne of Norway was hereditary and the dynasty very old was very much in the interest of King Sverrir and his descendants in the late twelfth and early thirteenth centuries and was cultivated by historians of that period. Harald Fairhair allegedly had many wives but one of them, Ragnhild, was the daughter of a Danish king called Erik of Jutland, presumably Horik II. Ragnhild was treated with such respect that almost a dozen other wives are said to have been rejected because of her.[32] In spite of the fictitious character of much genealogy in Snorre this does suggest that Harald Fairhair began his career as a vassal of the Danish king but made himself independent when the Danes could no longer assert their authority in Norway.

The chronology of Harald's reign is very uncertain. Traditionally, the

---

[31] Krag (1989).
[32] *Saga of Harald Fairhair*, ch. 21, quoting the skald Torbjørn Hornklove; see Sturluson (1941–51).

battle of Hafrsfjord was dated 872, but Halfdan Koht put it as late as *c.* 900. He also put Harald's death *c.* 950 while tradition places it two decades earlier.

ICELAND

In very much this same period the settlement of Iceland took place. Beginning *c.* 870 it was explained as a consequence of Harald Fairhair's harsh rule in Norway but as the battle of Hafrsfjord was probably somewhat later in the century the validity of this explanation is more than doubtful. According to Are Thorgilsson's *Íslendingabók*, 'Book of the Icelanders',[33] from which it comes, the settlement was complete *c.* 930, and in this year an all-Iceland assembly, the Althing, was instituted at Thingvellir near Reykjavik.

The settlement is described in *Landnámabók*, which names over 400 original colonists. *Landnámabók* was, however, drawn up in the first half of the twelfth century to legitimise contemporary landholding and many names are demonstrably invented on the basis of place-names. It is therefore no reliable guide to the original settlement.

Most of the settlers came from western Norway but a contingent also came from the Celtic parts of the British Isles. In Ireland the Scandinavians suffered considerable setbacks in the late ninth century. Many Scandinavians with Irish wives, some of them perhaps themselves the offspring of mixed marriages, therefore left Ireland, and while some of them settled in England others found their way to Iceland. The Celtic element in Iceland is traceable in the personal names used and in the composition of blood-types found in the Icelandic population.[34]

The first settlers carved out huge lumps of land, rather like little principalities, and within these they settled their family and retainers. When the Althing was instituted thirty-six *goðar* emerged as the men in power in Iceland and as those able to control the Althing. In 965 Iceland was divided into quarters for which law assemblies were held twice a year, presided over by three *goðar*.

As the ninth century drew to a close Viking attacks on western Europe practically came to an end. England had its last serious visit 892–6 but defended itself well, and in the first decades of the tenth century Edward the Elder, king of Wessex, was able to conquer those parts of England where the Danes had settled, except for Northumbria. This did not imply any expulsion of the Danes from eastern and northern England and therefore had no traceable consequences in the Scandinavian homelands or in other

---

[33] *Íslendingabók*, ed. Anne Holtsmark.   [34] Constandse-Westermann (1972).

settlement areas, although the Danish earl Thurketil of Bedford and his followers left for Normandy.[35] In France little is heard of fresh attacks after 911 when Normandy was ceded to Rollo, who undertook to stop compatriots from entering the Seine.[36]

DANISH RECOVERY: THE JELLINGE DYNASTY

The recovery of Danish royal power began some time in the first quarter of the tenth century when, according to Adam, one Hardegon, the son of Svein, came from *Nortmannia*, which could be either Normandy or Norway, and evicted Sigtryg, the last member of the Olaf dynasty. Very little is known about his reign. When Archbishop Unni of Hamburg-Bremen visited Denmark in 936 Hardegon had been succeeded by Gorm, apparently his son. If we are to believe Widukind, very little scope is left for Hardegon. Widukind claims that in 934 Henry the Fowler defeated the Danes and their king Chnuba, who was the father of Sigtryg,[37] and forced them to pay tribute and to accept Christianity. Widukind's information should, however, probably be rejected. His source, the annals of Corvey, mentions neither the name of the Danish king nor any tribute nor baptism. Tribute and baptism are Widukind's own inferences, not necessarily wrong, from defeat.

We are better informed about Gorm's death than about his life. He was buried in 958 in the north mound at Jelling, where he had put up a runic monument in memory of his queen Thyre. Gorm himself was commemorated together with Thyre in another inscription by his son Harald Bluetooth. Later he was transferred to a Christian grave in the church at Jelling built by his son after his conversion in 965. Gorm described Thyre as *tanmarkar but*, 'the pride of Denmark', and this is probably the first instance of the name 'Denmark' in Danish. It had appeared before 900 in Old English, in Ottar's account of his voyage from Sciringesheal to Hedeby. The *Old English Orosius*, as suggested above, gives the impression that the territory inhabited by the Danes was divided between south Danes and north Danes. Apparently the name 'Denmark' covered the territory of the North Danes, that is, the Danish islands and Skåne, Halland and Bohuslen on the Scandinavian mainland. It is possible, therefore, that Gorm's marriage was an attempt to unite the Danes and that it paved the way for his son who makes the claim for himself that he won all Denmark: 'King Harald

---

[35] *ASC s.a.* 916. Lucien Musset (1959) has suggested that the English flavour of many Scandinavian place-names in Normandy may be due to immigration of Scandinavians who had spent a number of years in England. [36] See Coupland, above, p. 201.

[37] *Danmarks Runeindskrifter*, nos. 2 and 4.

had these *kumbl* [memorial complexes] made in memory of Gorm, his father, and Thyre, his mother, that Harald who won for himself all Denmark, and Norway, and Christianised the Danes.'[38]

The dynasty to which Gorm and Harald belonged is generally called the Jellinge dynasty because of its association with the monuments there. By the end of the century, however, the centre of power had moved to Roskilde and this does suggest that the achievement Harald boasted was indeed the unification of his own south Danish Jutland with the north Danish islands and parts of the Scandinavian mainland. The four or five circular fortresses found in Denmark should possibly be understood in the context of his conquest of Denmark. They were built 980–1 and may have functioned as royal strongholds in newly subdued provinces.

It has also been suggested, but this is less probable, that Harald was referring to his reconquest of parts of southern Jutland from the Germans. During most of the tenth century the Germans exerted pressure on their eastern and northern neighbours. This gave Danes and Slavs common interests. Harald indeed married an Obodrite princess, no doubt for political reasons.[39]

The second claim that Harald made for himself was that he won Norway. The presence of Hákon, earl of Lade, on Harald's side against the Germans in 974 lends substance to this claim. In spite of the decline of Danish power Danish influence in Norway does not seem to have faded completely. Harald Fairhair was married to a Danish princess, and so was his oldest son and immediate successor, Erik Bloodaxe, whose wife was a sister of Harald Bluetooth.

By 948 Erik Bloodaxe had been ousted by Hákon the Good, another son of Harald Fairhair who had been brought up in England at the court of King Athelstan.[40] His return to Norway was probably backed by the English and

---

[38] 'Haraltr kunukR baþ kaurua kubl þausi aft kurm faþur sin auk aft þaurui muþur sina sa haraltr ias saR uan tanmaurk ala auk nuruiak auk tani karþi kristna': *Danmarks Runeindskrifter*, no. 42.

[39] She had a runic inscription, now in the church of Sdr. Vissing in north Jutland, carved in memory of her mother, without naming her: *tufa let kaurua kubl mistiuis tutir uft muþur sina kuna harats hins kuþa sunar kurms*; 'Tove, daughter of Mistivoi, wife of Harald the Good Gormsson, had these kumbl made in memory of her mother': *Danmarks Runeindskrifter*, no. 55. Harald and Mistivoi attacked Germany jointly in 983, and links were maintained when a daughter of Svein Forkbeard married a grandson of Mistivoi. Their son Gotskalk spent some time with Knut the Great in England and later married a daughter of Svein Estridson. Another indication of Slav–Danish connections is the presence at Knut's court of one *Wrytsleof dux*, who signed a charter of 1026(?): Sawyer 962.

[40] Snorre Sturluson, *Saga of Harald Fairhair*, chs. 39–41; *Saga of Hákon the Good*, ch. 1. Snorre's account of how Hákon came to be brought up at the court of Athelstan is untrustworthy. Probably the arrangement was part of an alliance between Athelstan and Harald Fairhair against

Erik Bloodaxe was now welcomed as a king in York by the Northumbrians, still resisting south English attempts to incorporate them in the English kingdom.

Hákon the Good based his power, like his father, on western Norway but he secured the submission to his lordship of Sigurd, earl of Lade, and thus controlled considerable parts of Norway. He returned from England a Christian but his attempts to promote Christianity were unsuccessful.

Harald Bluetooth involved himself in Norwegian politics on the side of his nephews, the sons of Erik Bloodaxe, and supported Harald Greycloak. In about 960 they managed to kill Hákon. Harald Greycloak, however, soon developed policies more independent than Harald Bluetooth liked, trying to take over control not only of western and northern Norway but of Viken as well, and the Danish king therefore transferred his support to the new earl of Lade, Hákon, whose father, Sigurd, Harald Greycloak had killed. Hákon defeated Harald Greycloak in a naval battle in Danish waters. As Hákon afterwards acknowledged Harald Bluetooth as his overlord and was the most powerful chieftain in Norway, the Danish king was justified in claiming that he had won Norway. He had restored traditional Danish overlordship.

Harald's third claim on the Jellinge stone is that he Christianised the Danes. This was a matter of organising a church more than of converting the Danes. Indeed, Widukind claims that they were Christians of old.[41] Almost a century after Anskar was allowed to build churches in Schleswig and Ribe, however, Denmark had no organised church, and the archbishop in Hamburg had no suffragans. In 948 three bishops were appointed to sees in Denmark: Hored to Schleswig, Liafdag to Ribe and Reginbrand to Arhus.[42] These bishops probably never set foot in Denmark but their appointment was a warning to the king of Denmark that Otto intended to promote the church in Denmark much as he was promoting it among the Slavs. This implied annexation to Germany. The only way Harald could forestall a similar process in Denmark was by adopting Christianity and thereby making himself acceptable as the protector of the church within his kingdom. There are suggestions that Harald tried to evade the influence of Hamburg, which as part of the imperial German church would still be an agent of the empire. Poppo, the missionary who is reported to have convinced the Danes through ordeal of hot iron, certainly was not brought

---

the Danes and possibly against the Northumbrians. According to William of Malmesbury many foreign kings sought the friendship of Athelstan, and Harald did so by presenting him a magnificent ship (*Gesta Regum* I, 149).

[41] Widukind, *Rerum Gestarum Saxonicarum* III. 65.

[42] *MGH Leges*, sectio 4: *Constitutiones et Acta Imperatorum et Regum* I, pp. 13–14.

in from Hamburg. Harald soon established friendly relations with the archbishop, however, and was remembered as a great friend of Hamburg; there is even a hint of plans to sanctify him.[43]

Otto the Great quickly acknowledged Harald as head of the Danish church, probably because he wanted to concentrate on his Slav frontier. In 965 he issued a charter formally relinquishing all imperial rights over the church in Denmark.[44] However formal these rights may have been, and there is no evidence that Otto exercised any real power in Denmark before 965, the way the Germans saw it and the perspectives it would hold to the Danish king are probably well enough expressed by Adam of Bremen: the Danish kingdom was in Otto's power to such an extent that he even gave away the bishoprics.[45]

However much the Christianisation of the Danes may have done to alleviate German pressure on the kingdom it did not remove it. Three years later Harald fortified his German border with extensive works on the Danevirke, linking the very recent semicircular fortifications at Hedeby with the old main wall of the Danevirke from 737. In 968, indeed, the Saxons expected a war with Denmark.[46] Nothing, as far as we know, came of this but when news of the death of Otto the Great in 973 reached Denmark, Harald himself invaded the land south of the Eider. The following year, however, a German counter-attack was successful; Harald lost Hedeby and the Danevirke and possibly larger parts of south Jutland. This situation persisted until 983 when Harald as well as the Obodrite prince Mistivoi, Harald's father-in-law, took the opportunity provided by the defeat of Otto II at the hands of the Saracens at Capo Colonne to repair their losses.

Harald Bluetooth was a great builder. At Jelling he built the north mound, in which his father was first buried, the south mound, empty and completed after his adoption of Christianity, and a large wooden church to which he transferred the remains of Gorm, and he put up a runic stone there; he fortified the Danevirke, repairing old parts of it and adding new; and he built five circular fortresses, a fifth one having been discovered recently in Trelleborg in Skåne in addition to the four long-familiar ones. Bridges and roads, too, were built on a large scale. We have no direct evidence that Harald demanded bridgework, roadwork or the building of fortifications from his subjects like contemporary west European rulers, but a building activity on this scale would hardly have been possible without them. Such demands are a possible reason, therefore, for the rebellion staged by

---

[43] Adam of Bremen II, p. 28: 'at ille noster Haraldus, qui ... ille, inquam, innocens vulneratus et pro Christo expulsus martyrii palma, ut spero, non carebit'.

[44] *MGH Diplomata Regum et Imperatorum* I, no. 294.   [45] Adam of Bremen II. 3.

[46] Widukind III. 70.

Harald's son Svein in the 980s. Another possible reason is that Svein and the party supporting him disapproved of Harald's concessionary policy towards Hamburg-Bremen. There is no suggestion, however, of opposition to Christianity as such. Heathen practices disappeared quietly within a generation of the adoption of Christianity.

Harald Bluetooth died on 1 November 987 from the wounds he incurred when Svein rebelled against him. After the battle he fled to the Wends and died there but was allegedly buried in Denmark.[47] An immediate sequel to Svein's victory was the expulsion of the German bishops from Denmark; in 988 Adaldag, archbishop of Hamburg-Bremen, solicited a charter from Otto III permitting Danish ecclesiastics to acquire privileged lands within the empire.[48] This hostility of Svein's towards prelates loyal to Hamburg gave him a very bad name in the records of the church. To Adam of Bremen it amounted to apostasy and he treated Svein as a heathen until shortly before the battle of Svold in which the Lord turned out to be on Svein's side; Adam could then no longer be against him.

This attitude has led to a severely distorted account of Svein's early career in Adam's *Gesta* as well as in Thietmar who hated Svein for family reasons. According to these authors Svein spent his early years in captivity, from which he had to be ransomed more than once, and in exile, driven from his country by foreign enemies. In fact Svein turned his interests against England soon after his accession to the throne. Viking raids on England had been resumed on a modest scale in about 980 but when Svein entered the business in the 990s they increased dramatically. Svein is first mentioned by name in the *Anglo-Saxon Chronicle* under 994 but he very probably also took part in the campaign in 991 which involved the famous battle of Maldon.[49]

One of Svein's companions in the 994 campaign was Olav Tryggvesson, a Norwegian chieftain of obscure lineage. According to Snorre his father was Tryggve Olavsson, a petty king in Vestfold and a grandson of Harald Fairhair,[50] but this genealogy, as well as Snorre's account of Olav's youth, is fictitious.[51] What their partnership was like is uncertain but there is little reason to doubt that Svein regarded himself as the overlord of Norway much as his father had been. Nor can there be any doubt that a Norwegian prince would take any opportunity afforded to break loose from Danish

---

[47] According to the oldest source, the *Encomium Emmae Reginae*, Harald fled to the Wends. In later sources, like Adam of Bremen, he is made to escape to Jumne, which has been identified with Wollin on an island near the Oder estuary, and in still later sources, like the legendary *Jomsvikinga Saga*, this becomes a stronghold which Harald had founded himself. The likeliest place for Harald to seek refuge was with his father-in-law, Mistivoi, with whom he had recently campaigned against the Germans.   [48] *MGH Diplomata Regum et Imperatorum* II, no. 41.

[49] Lund (1991b), pp. 132–3.   [50] *Saga of Harald Fairhair*, ch. 42; *Saga of Olav Tryggvesson*, ch. 1.

[51] Krag (1991).

domination. Olav was given one such opportunity by Æthelred the Unready, king of England, when, after the 994 campaign, he accepted a peace offer from Æthelred. They concluded a treaty by which peace was to obtain between the parties.[52] Olav undertook never to return to England with hostile intentions, a promise that he fulfilled, the *Anglo-Saxon Chronicle* confirms. In 995 he returned to Norway, apparently, like Hákon the Good almost half a century earlier, with English financial support. Æthelred was playing off two enemies against each other, hoping to give Svein worries at home that would keep him away from England.[53]

OLAV TRYGGVESSON IN NORWAY

In Norway Olav managed to secure recognition of his rule in Trøndelag after the murder of Earl Hákon by his slave. Hákon's government appears to have grown increasingly unpopular with the Norwegians but a direct link between his murder and Olav's return from England cannot be demonstrated. Olav's rule was brief and, though he was the first king of all Norway to rule Trøndelag directly, it left no permanent traces. Some 200 years later he was depicted as a great missionary king to whose influence the adoption of Christianity also in Iceland was due, and in the nineteenth century he became the great national hero of Norway.[54] This all tells us more about those centuries than about Olav himself. In 999 or 1000 he faced a coalition of the Danish and Swedish kings, Svein Forkbeard and Olof Skötkonung, and Erik Earl Hákonsson; although the Jomsvikings are reported to have come to his assistance, Olav lost his life in the battle of Svold. There can be little doubt that a showdown with Olav must have been on Svein's agenda since 995 and this battle restored his control of Norway. He seems to have assumed direct control of Viken while the government of the remoter parts of the country was left in the hands of the sons of Earl Hákon, Erik and Svein, as it had been in those of Hákon himself.

The appearance of the Swedish king on the Danish side reflects Svein's influence in Sweden. We have no reliable information about kings of the Svear between the middle of the ninth century and the end of the tenth. Svealand did not have any central authority and such attempts as there were to establish authority over larger parts of Sweden seem to have originated in east Götaland, west Götaland being too exposed to Danish influence. About 970 Sigtuna was founded, apparently by a king connected with Götaland, conceivably Erik, known as 'the Victorious', father of Olof Skötkonung. Little else is known about this Erik except that he was married to a Polish

---

[52] II Æthelred; Whitelock, *EHD*, no. 43; Leibermann (1903) I, pp. 220–5.
[53] Andersson (1987); Sawyer (1987).   [54] Bagge (1992).

princess who after Erik's death married Svein Forkbeard and became the mother of Harald, king of Denmark 1014–18, and of Knut the Great. Svein's marriage to Erik's widow indicates a superiority over the Swedes and it made him the stepfather of Erik's successor Olof. Olof's epithet, *Skötkonung*, designates him as a tributary king, and that must have been to the Danes.

Thietmar of Merseburg depicted Svein as a king who ravaged his own country but the little that is known about the domestic side of Svein's reign suggests that Denmark was thriving. To replace the German bishops, Svein brought in ecclesiastics from England. In his lifetime churches were built in new towns like Roskilde and Lund. The latter was previously thought to have been founded by Knut the Great but its first church has now been dated *c.* 990; it was soon followed by more, and Roskilde grew to be a remarkably big place in a short time. It seems to have replaced a local centre of power at Lejre.

Svein also began, as the first king of Denmark, to strike coins with his name on them, after the English pattern. Coins had, of course, been struck in Ribe and Hedeby in the eighth and ninth centuries and Harald Bluetooth had struck an ostensibly Christian coinage after his conversion. Svein's coins are imitations of coins of Æthelred and on the surface of it his moneyer was also English. Coins with the same moneyer's name on them were also struck in Norway for Olav Tryggvesson and at Sigtuna for Olof Skötkonung at much the same time. There are such technical differences between these coins, however, that they could not have been struck by one moneyer travelling from one Scandinavian court to another; they are rather independent imitations. While Svein's coinage was emphemeral, minting went on in Sigtuna. A coinage of considerable volume, largely consisting of imitations of English coins, was minted in the reigns of Olof Skötkonung and his successor Anund Jacob (1022–50). This coinage suggests that Swedish kings were experimenting with the exercise of royal power but did not really know how to run a coinage.[55]

THE DANISH CONQUEST OF ENGLAND

In 1013 Svein embarked on the conquest of England. He had already raided England several times but does not seem to have intended any conquest before. What changed his mind may have been the achievements of Thorkell the Tall. This chieftain had set out on a raid in 1009 and had had great success. He accumulated much gold and silver, and when the fleet dispersed

---

[55] See Blackburn, p. 558 below.

in 1012, he himself with a number of ships took service with Æthelred, king of England.

Thorkell's relationship with Svein is ambiguous. According to the *Encomium Emmae Reginae* he was one of Svein's military leaders who had now deserted with part of Svein's army; Svein therefore invaded England to discipline him. Thorkell was connected with the legendary Jomsvikings based somewhere in the Baltic, and if there is any truth in the legends collected in the *Jomsvikinga Saga* this band ought to have been Svein's enemies. They were on Olav Tryggvesson's side in 1000 at Svold. It is likely, however, that after this defeat they had been forced to acknowledge Svein's overlordship. In that sense Thorkell could therefore be regarded as one of Svein's captains. From Thorkell's point of view, however, it was a question of an allegiance that he chose to break and replace with an allegiance to Æthelred. This was dangerous for Svein. Æthelred depended so much on his forces that Thorkell might very well achieve a dominant position in England. Should that happen Thorkell would become a very dangerous rival for Svein, commanding much greater resources than Svein himself.

In a swift campaign Svein managed to drive Æthelred from his country and secure recognition as king of England himself. He died soon after, however, on 3 February 1014, unmourned by the *Anglo-Saxon Chronicle*, which refers to 'the happy event of Svein's death'.

This created a very unstable situation in England and in Scandinavia. With Svein in England was his younger son Knut. When the Danish fleet elected Knut king, the English *witan* chose to recall Æthelred from his exile in Normandy and the English managed to drive out Knut's forces. In Denmark Svein had been succeeded by his elder son Harald, who had presumably been left in charge while Svein was away in England. Knut therefore had to start all over again, collecting fresh forces and launching a new attack on England.

Thorkell the Tall remained faithful to Æthelred and helped him defend England against the new Danish onslaught. With him was Olav Haraldsson, a Norwegian chieftain who had fought many of Thorkell's battles and also been away on his own campaigns on the Continent. With the riches he had collected, and apparently with more supplied by Æthelred, who once more tried to give his Danish enemies trouble in Scandinavia, he now turned towards Norway, taking the opportunity offered by Svein's death and the heavy demands on the resources of Denmark made by the campaigns in England. In Norway Olav Haraldsson came across Svein Earl Hákonsson and defeated him in the battle of Nesjar, 26 March 1016. Svein's brother Erik had joined Knut in England.

It has been suggested that there was a deal between Knut and Olav, to the effect that Olav was given Norway in return for giving up his support for

Æthelred. But Knut was in no position to give away Norway at this time, and it was hardly in the interest of his brother Harald to do so. The Danish hegemony of Scandinavia was badly shaken after the death of Svein Forkbeard. Olof Skötkonung in Sweden took advantage of the situation as well. The Danes did not reverse their policy towards Hamburg-Bremen until the mid-twenties when Knut came to terms with the German emperor, but Olof immediately sent to Hamburg for a bishop to come to Sweden.[56] He also married off one of his daughters to Olav Haraldsson. Both these acts amount to a clear defiance of his Danish overlord and an attempt to ally with the enemies of the Danes.

In spite of stiff resistance Knut succeeded in making himself lord of England.[57] In 1019, having consolidated his hold on that country, he travelled to Denmark to succeed his brother Harald. The main problem facing Knut in Denmark was apparently that his dismissal of his fleet had created a great number of redundant Vikings in Scandinavia. Although some found employment in Russia and Byzantium and on raids in the east, there was a great danger that someone might rally them for fresh attacks on England. How Knut solved this problem we cannot tell but in a letter written from Denmark to his English subjects he claims to have done so.[58]

The *Anglo-Saxon Chronicle*[59] informs us that in 1023 Knut entrusted Denmark to Thorkell whom he had outlawed two years before but with whom he was now reconciled. This is unlikely. Although Thorkell, who had only joined Knut at a late stage, had been given a very high position in England in Knut's first years, he seems to disappear from history after his outlawry. Denmark is more likely to have been entrusted to Knut's brother-in-law Ulf. Nothing is heard of his appointment but he emerges as regent of Denmark in 1026 when he joined Knut's enemies.

Little is known about the government of Denmark in Knut's time. He attempted twice to introduce a coinage modelled on the English coinage, the first time imitating English types, the second introducing a series of local types. Knut continued his father's policy against Hamburg-Bremen; he brought in bishops from England, and it is even possible that he intended to organise the Danish church as an ecclesiastical province with the metropolitan see at Roskilde, under the primacy of Canterbury. If so, his plans were thwarted when the archbishop of Hamburg intercepted Gerbrand, bishop of Roskilde, and kept him a prisoner until he promised to submit to Hamburg-Bremen.[60] These problems were probably finally settled in 1027 when Knut met Conrad II and attended his coronation.

[56] Adam of Bremen II, 58.   [57] See vol. III, chapter by S.D. Keynes.
[58] Whitelock, *EHD*, no. 48; Keynes (1986), pp. 81–99.   [59] *ASC*, MS c.
[60] Adam of Bremen II. 55.

OLAV HARALDSSON IN NORWAY

Olav Haraldsson did not bring large forces back to Norway from England so much as substantial means. He relied on these to buy the loyalty of the Norwegian chieftains. After Nesjar he co-operated with the old aristocracy in so far as they were willing, but he tried to balance their power in regions where they were dominant by placing lesser vassals among them. Rather than outright battle against the established chieftains his device was *Divide et impera*. He introduced reeves, *ármenn*, on the royal estates and used these as local representatives of royal authority. His government was, however, based on personal links and allegiances. A government apparatus independent of the person of the king only developed in Norway in the twelfth century.

Olav's attempts to introduce centralised government were unacceptable to some of the magnates, not least those in control of the trade and taxation in Finnmark and Biarmia, and by 1026 they had rebelled against Olav.

Olav has a name as a champion of Christianity in Norway. Christianity had already gained a footing in Norway, especially in the western parts, since the mid-tenth century; Olav concentrated his efforts in the Opplands and other places where the old faith was still strong and they were to some extent violent. It is difficult, however, to distinguish missionary zeal from political ambition.

Olav brought in a bishop from England, Grimkell, and, significantly, immediately had him seek recognition from Hamburg-Bremen.[61] Later sources ascribe to Olav and Grimkell the introduction of certain ecclesiastical laws but this is highly dubious. The provisions ascribed to them, particularly those regarding consanguinity, are likely to be later. There is also, therefore, no basis for regarding Olav as the organiser of the Norwegian church. His bishop was a member of his household and permanent sees were not created in Norway until *c.* 1100.

Posterity has made Olav Haraldsson the great national king of Norway, the real unifier of Norway and 'the eternal king of Norway'. However, as little of his efforts had any lasting effect, his reign was, realistically, little more than 'an episode in an era during which Danish kings were overlords over greater or lesser parts of Norway, particularly neighbouring Viken'.[62]

KNUT, KING OF NORWAY AND PART OF THE SWEDES

In 1026 Olav and the king of the Swedes, Anund, who had succeeded Olof Skötkonung *c.* 1022, attacked Denmark and this brought Knut over from

---

[61] Adam of Bremen II. 57, IV. 34.   [62] Helle (1991), p. 29.

England with an army. On his arrival he apparently found that Ulf had joined his enemies. The location as well as the outcome of the ensuing battle is very much debated. The location is given as Helgeå or 'Holy River'.[63] This was traditionally thought to be in Skåne but a persuasive case has been made for its location in Uppland.[64] According to Scandinavian sources Knut was victorious but the *Anglo-Saxon Chronicle* claims that the Swedes had control of the battlefield. This discrepancy can only be resolved by recourse to the aftermath of the battle which clearly suggests that whichever party may have been able to claim a victory was unable to exploit it. Knut, at least, suffered so little from his enemies that he was able in early 1027 to travel to Rome. In a letter to his English subjects written on his way home Knut informs the English that he is going to Denmark to conclude 'peace and a firm treaty with those nations and peoples who wished, if it had been possible for them, to deprive us of both kingdom and life, but could not'.[65] Knut apparently was in no position to dictate a settlement to his opponents.

When Olav Haraldsson had alienated the Norwegian magnates Knut stepped in and persuaded many of them to shift their allegiance to him. He styled himself 'king of Norway' already in 1027. His means of persuasion were the traditional ones, also used by Olav on his return from England in 1014: gold and silver. So many turned to Knut that Olav gave up and sought refuge in Russia in 1028. Knut appointed Hákon Earl Eriksson, son of Earl Erik of Northumbria, ruler of Norway, but when Hákon died before he had taken up office Knut made an appointment which seems to have helped change Norwegian attitudes to Danish overlordship fundamentally. On hearing about Hákon's death in 1029, Olav attempted a return but the Norwegians were still loyal to Knut and defeated and killed Olav in the battle of Stiklestad. Yet, when after this Knut sent an alien, his son Svein, backed up by his mother Ælfgifu of Northampton, he alienated the Norwegians. Svein's and Ælfgifu's rule, apparently based on English ideas of kingship, was very unpopular. On Knut's death in 1035 they were driven out and the Norwegians recalled from exile in Russia Magnus, the young son of Olav, and made him king. Olav himself began to be treated as a saint. He was recognised as one within a year of his death, largely owing to the efforts of Grimkell, and churches were dedicated to him in York and in Novgorod, among other places, remarkably soon afterwards.

In his letter of 1027, Knut also styles himself 'king of part of the Swedes'. This probably means that he had secured the allegiance of a number of Swedish chieftains and may have been on his way to do what he had done in

---

[63] *ASC* MS e: 'to þam holme æt ea þære halgan'.   [64] Gräslund (1986).
[65] Whitelock, *EHD*, no. 49; Liebermann (1903) I, 276–7.

Norway with his gold and silver. A group of runic inscriptions including the
titles 'thegn' and 'dreng' may be evidence of Knut's influence in Sweden.[66]
A number of coins with the legend CNUT REX SW struck in Sigtuna have also
been taken as corroboration of Knut's claim to Sweden but they have now
been shown to be imitations; they are all struck from one pair of dies and
form only a small part of a coinage struck around 1030 by Anund.[67]

Knut's son Svein died soon after his father. His mother's interests now lay
in England with her other son Harold. By Knut's arrangement with Emma,
their son Harthaknut was designated Knut's successor in England. But he
was held up in Denmark and before he was able to come to England,
Ælfgifu, backed by her powerful northern English family, had secured the
recognition of Harold Harefoot. Harold remained in power until his death
in 1040 and the invasion that Harthaknut was preparing to unseat him
proved unnecessary.

MAGNUS THE GOOD AND HARALD HARDRADA IN NORWAY

In Norway, Magnus took up the idea of a North Sea empire and after
Harthaknut's death secured power in Denmark. His claim was contested by
Svein Estridson, a son of Knut's sister Estrid and Ulf, the regent of
Denmark killed after the battle of the Holy River. Svein may, or may not,
have ruled Denmark on behalf of Harthaknut after 1040 and now asked for
English support against Magnus. He was a natural ally of Edward the
Confessor in so far as Magnus seems to have had aggressive intentions
against England as well, but his request was apparently turned down.
Towards the end of his reign, Magnus was forced to share power with his
nephew Harald, later known as 'Hardrada', who returned from Byzantium
and Russia, having served the Byzantine emperor for ten years. Harald
Hardrada was recognised as sole king on Magnus' death in 1047 and his
most important achievement was that he managed to complete what his
half-brother had begun, namely the establishment of direct control over all
Norway. He killed or exiled the most important members of the old
aristocracy, notably those who had wielded the greatest influence during
Magnus' minority, and subordinated the rest.

Harald carried on Magnus' foreign policy. He is reported to have sought
recognition as king of Denmark in Viborg but failed. He fought endless
wars with Svein Estridson. According to skaldic poetry he won a crushing
victory over Svein in 1062 in the battle of Niså but was unable to exploit it
because of a rebellion in a Norwegian province;[68] one may doubt the

---

[66] Löfving (1991).   [67] Sawyer (1989), p. 92.   [68] *Saga of Harald Hardrada*, chs. 61 ff.

character of his victory if it did not discourage the people of Oppland. In any case, he soon gave up his Danish plans to concentrate on the conquest of England after the death of Edward the Confessor, a venture that ended in disaster at Stamford Bridge.

SVEIN ESTRIDSON IN DENMARK

In Denmark, Svein Estridson managed to establish himself as king. Although a reconciliation was effected with Knut, for the first time since the reign of Harald Bluetooth a Danish king entered into friendly relations with Hamburg-Bremen. This friendship was severely tested when the archbishop forced Svein to repudiate his wife because of consanguinity. Nevertheless it survived this strain and in Svein's reign Denmark was properly organised into eight dioceses. In Iceland a diocese was created in 1056 at Skálholt. Towards the end of his reign Svein also negotiated with the pope for recognition of an autonomous Danish ecclesiastical province, but this was not achieved until 1103.

Sweden seems, after the death of Knut, to have enjoyed relief from external pressure. It was hardly to be counted as united under one king, however, and there seems to have been no idea as yet of Sweden as one nation or one people. Indeed, in the late eleventh century Pope Gregory VII was taught to distinguish between *rex sueonum* and the *reges wisigothorum*.[69] A peace treaty between Denmark and Sweden purporting to have been concluded in the mid-eleventh century has been regarded as evidence that Sweden had by then been united through the subjection by the Svear of the Gautar. Such serious doubts about the authenticity and date of this treaty have now been raised, however, that its validity in this context can no longer be accepted.[70] The most powerful factor in the unification of Sweden seems to have been the creation of the archdiocese of Uppsala in 1164, at a time when Frederick Barbarossa looked like increasing his influence in Denmark and the pope wanted to keep imperial influence out of as much of Scandinavia as possible.

[69] Sawyer (1988a), p. 17.   [70] Sawyer (1988b), pp. 165–70.

CHAPTER 9

SLAVS AND BULGARS

Jonathan Shepard

AT the beginning of the eighth century only three political structures of substance impinged upon the Balkans. Two of them belonged to quite recent arrivals from the Eurasian steppes, the Avars and the Bulgars, while the third comprised the remnants of the eastern Roman empire which had, until the sixth century, encompassed the entire peninsula. It must be emphasised that the empire never unreservedly gave up its claim to ultimate authority over the whole area south of the lower or middle Danube, for all the treaties which it had perforce to ratify with the more formidable of the intruders. Equally, the most numerous immigration – of the Slavs – was also, by and large, the least systematically violent, leaving intact many visible symbols of the empire, for example, governors' residences and churches. The Byzantine government's periodic assertions of its rights of proprietorship were therefore not wholly lacking in physical corroboration, while the presence of Greek-speaking and, presumably, largely Christian communities was a further reminder of a past order. Not all Greek-speakers, however, necessarily regarded themselves as owing service to the remote and apparently ineffectual emperor on the Bosphorus.

The secession of Greek Christian and other groups from the Avar khanate[1] points to the strains which a federation of steppe nomads and subject peoples was liable to undergo, as the momentum of campaigning and plundering gradually gave way to a sedentary, less martial way of life. This tendency was already pronounced by the late seventh century and continued through the eighth. The majority of the population engaged in agriculture, as the many finds of sickles in burial grounds attest, although some Avars may have maintained a degree of pastoral nomadism. The Avars' stance was essentially defensive and the strongpoints indicated by the

---

[1] See Lemerle (1979) I, pp. 222–4; Lemerle (1981) II, pp. 142–52. The descendants of the Greek-speaking captives of the Avars who appeared near Thessalonica in the 680s were, whether justly or not, viewed with some suspicion by the imperial authorities.

concentration of warrior graves in their southeastern quarter, near modern Belgrade, served primarily to block Bulgar forays up the Danube. Nonetheless, they remained, with their bows and arrows, sabres and horsemanship, a far from negligible military power and could be described by a Frankish writer in the mid-eighth century as *robusta gens Avarorum*.[2] They probably acted as a check upon the westwards adventurism of their Bulgar neighbours.

The exact ethnic origins of the Danubian Bulgars is controversial. It is in any case most probable that they had enveloped groupings of diverse origins during their migration westwards across the Eurasian steppes,[3] and they undoubtedly spoke a form of Turkic as their main language. The Bulgars long retained many of the customs, military tactics, titles and emblems of a nomadic people of the steppes. They were still carrying into battle horses' tails as banners in the 860s.[4] The Bulgars in the eighth and ninth centuries had a pressing practical reason for retaining a military organisation appropriate for the open steppes. The fertile stretch of steppe northeast from the Danube as far as the environs of the Dniester basin was still their grazing ground, and it needed guarding against other military formations from further east. The Danubian Bulgars were, in a sense, obliged to remain on a steppe-warfare footing to a much greater extent than were the Avars behind their Carpathian screen: Pliska, the Bulgars' focal point in the plain south of the Danube, formed a colossal encampment and refuge for their families and livestock soon after they crossed the Danube and appropriated the plain to its south in 680–1 (Map 16). They raised an earthen rampart some 3 m high, enclosing an area of approximately 23 sq km; in its middle was a much smaller earthwork, concentric in plan with the outer rampart, containing the khan's residence and the halls of senior nobles.[5] These structures were not, in the late seventh or eighth century, of stone but the remains of stone Byzantine churches and public buildings were still extant. One of the main attractions of the area was abundant pastureland and the newly arrived Bulgars created several similar large fortified encampments within a few kilometres of Pliska.[6] Another advantage was the protection which the Danube afforded from sudden attacks by other peoples of the steppes.

To the south lay the 'Greeks', against whose perfidy and sudden attacks strict vigilance must also be maintained. The tribute or subsidies which Bulgar khans from Asparuch onwards seem to have received from the emperor may have served as an appetiser for further treasure to be had from

---

[2] Arbeo of Freising (1920), p. 33; Deér (1977), p. 328.   [3] Dimitrov (1987), pp. 65–70.
[4] *MGH Epp.* VI, p. 580.   [5] *IB*, p. 181; *PP* IV, pp. 9–12.
[6] *PP* IV, p. 15. On the re-use of spolia in the ninth century, see p. 244 below.

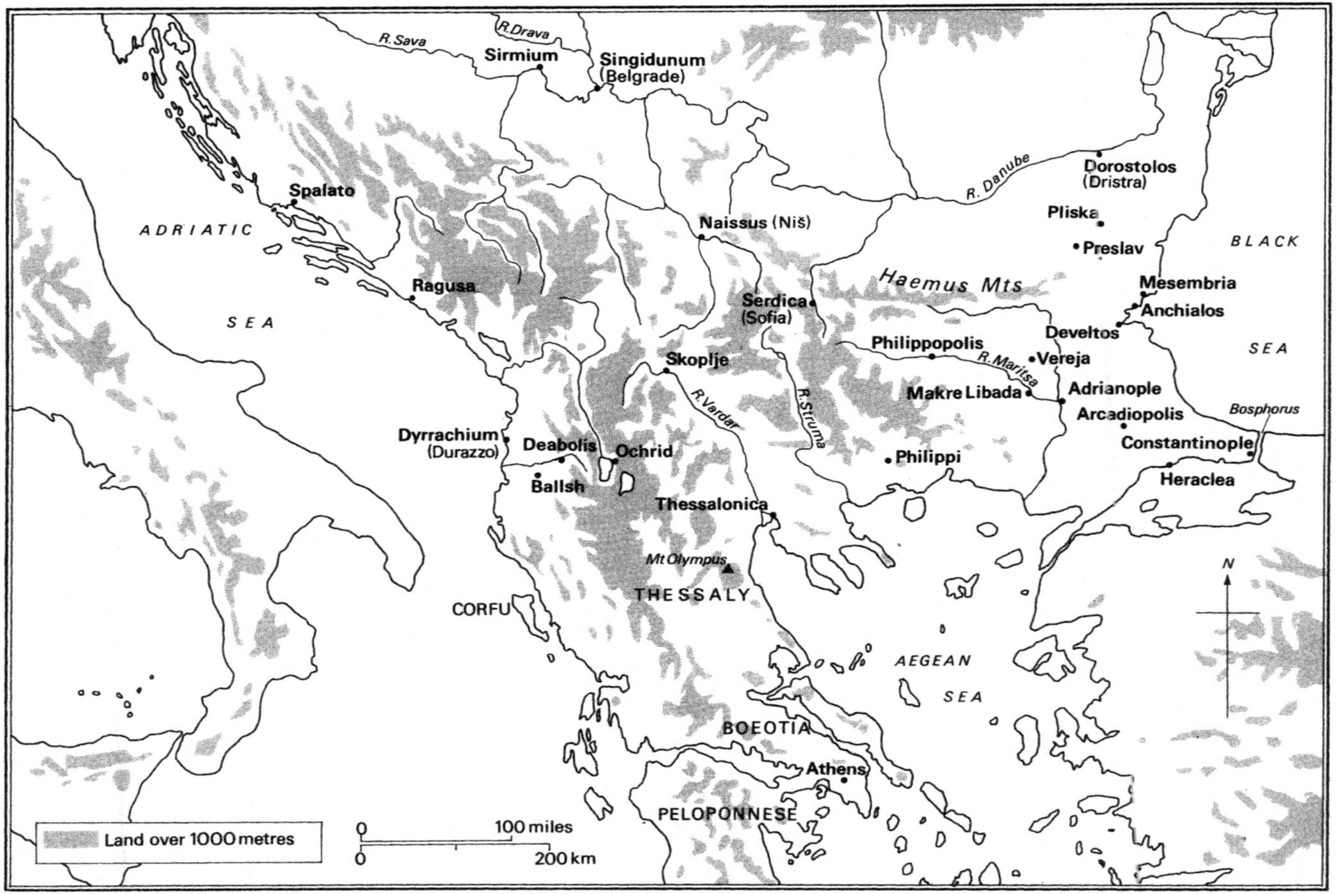

Map 16 The Balkans, 700–900

Rivers and seas:
BLACK SEA
AEGEAN SEA
ADRIATIC SEA
R. Danube
R. Drava
R. Sava
R. Maritsa
R. Struma
R. Vardar
Bosphorus

Places:
Dorostolos (Dristra)
Pliska
Preslav
Mesembria
Anchialos
Develtos
Vereja
Adrianople
Arcadiopolis
Constantinople
Heraclea
Philippopolis
Makre Libada
Philippi
Serdica (Sofia)
Naissus (Niš)
Skopje
Thessalonica
Mt Olympus
THESSALY
Singidunum (Belgrade)
Sirmium
Ragusa
Spalato
Dyrrachium (Durazzo)
Deabolis
Ballsh
Ochrid
CORFU
BOEOTIA
Athens
PELOPONNESE

Haemus Mts

N

100 miles
200 km

Land over 1000 metres

raiding, but it could also encourage acceptance of the *status quo*. It seems to have been principally the readiness of Byzantine contenders for the throne to call for Bulgar military aid that upset this equilibrium. The most notable instance was in 705–6. Justinian II, intent upon recovering power after years in exile north of the Black Sea, enlisted Khan Tervel's support with the promise of 'many gifts, and his own daughter as wife',[7] and appeared before Constantinople with Tervel and his warriors. The sight of this host failed to cow the city's defenders into surrender, but Justinian managed to slip inside the walls with a few followers and in the ensuing mêlée he regained the throne. Tervel was rewarded with the almost imperial title of Caesar and, sitting enthroned beside the emperor, he received the obeisance of the citizenry. He displayed his new trappings on a seal which was perhaps struck for him while he was still in Constantinople.[8] Tervel also commissioned a large relief carving (2.6 m high, 3.1 m wide) high up on a cliff face at Madara, some way south of Pliska. Tervel is depicted on horseback, trampling down a lion which he has speared.[9] He was, in the role of triumphant huntsman, appropriating a royal motif.

Tervel's stance of wary collusion with the emperor, suggested by a contemporary inscription,[10] was not absurd. Byzantine rulers, hard pressed to contain the Arabs' pressure which mounted in the early eighth century, and unsure of their own generals' loyalties, were inclined to treat the Bulgar occupation of the lower Danubian basin as a *fait accompli*. Probably in 716, and in any case no later than *c*.750, a treaty was concluded between a Bulgarian ruler (probably Tervel) and an emperor, providing for travel between the regions under their respective sway; traders were to be equipped with 'certificates and seals' (*sigilliōn kai sphragidōn*), and their possessions were to be inviolate; garments and red leather up to a total value of 30 or 50 pounds of gold could be bought by the Bulgars.[11] The treaty gave suppleness and credibility to the khan's military overlordship: in future, he and his agents would have the right to supervise the regular contacts of whoever lived north of the Haemus range with the imperial authorities in Constantinople or the fortified ports which studded the Black Sea coast; the port of Mesembria seems to have been the principal entrepôt.[12]

One might expect, on analogy with the Avars and other steppe federations, that the Bulgar polity would undergo stress once the momentum of

---

[7] 'pleista … dōra kai tēn heautou thygatera eis gynaika', Theoph. Chron., p. 374, trans. Turtledove, p. 71; cf. Niceph., pp. 102–3.

[8] Zacos and Veglery (1972) I.3, p. 1441; Beševliev (1979), p. 231; Jurukova (1984), pp. 224–6.

[9] Beševliev (1979), p. 89, 100–1.   [10] Beševliev (1979), p. 91.

[11] Theoph. Chron., p. 497, trans. Turtledove, p. 176; *IB*, p. 115; Oikonomides (1988), pp. 29–30.

[12] Oikonomides (1988), p. 31.

conquest and massive influxes of booty died away and non-nobles engaged to a greater or lesser extent in agriculture. The camp at Pliska contained no equivalent to the Avar Ring's treasure and, in so far as the eighth-century Byzantine economy was preponderantly agrarian, few rich pickings lay within reach in southern Thrace, even in such towns as Philippopolis. Such tribute as was exacted from the Slavs must have been in kind, and agrarian produce, wax and skins were not the aptest cogs for a durable political mechanism of rewards and patronage. Nor does the tribute rendered, at uncertain intervals, by Byzantium seem to have been really substantial.

These speculations, which must needs be highly tentative, have some bearing on the events recorded in the third quarter of the eighth century, when warfare brought the Bulgars back into the Byzantine chronicles' beam. The emperor Constantine V (741–75) was a talented military man, confident in the loyalty of his *tagmata*. Taking advantage of the turmoil in the Muslim world, he attacked well-populated regions on his eastern frontier and transferred their Syrian and Armenian Christian inhabitants to Thrace. Constantine was also concerned to tighten control over the mainly Slav occupants of the strip of land between the Rhodope range and the Aegean Sea. One expedition – probably essentially punitive and intimidatory – sent against the Bulgars *c*. 760 came to grief in a mountain pass,[13] but subsequent events seemed to vindicate Constantine's dismissive treatment of his northern neighbours. Many Slavs seized the opportunity presented by discord between their overlords to flee to the emperor, who resettled them in Bithynia.

The successive expeditions of Constantine V against the Bulgars in the later years of his reign are mostly depicted in Byzantine chronicles as fatuous and vainglorious affairs.[14] He seems, in 773, to have needed only to sail up to Varna for the Bulgars collectively to sue for peace, and when he subsequently routed a Bulgar army that had breached the newly made written agreements, he made much of victory celebrations in Constantinople, and did not pursue the foe far northwards. His expeditions by land and sea may in reality have had the limited aim of overawing the Bulgars and discouraging them from intervening in his efforts to destabilise such Slav political structures as existed to the south of the Haemus range. The empire's urgent requirement, probably aggravated by recurrent plagues, was not so much for pastureland as people, both to garrison the fortresses which Constantine built or refurbished in the borderlands, and to produce the agricultural

---

[13] Theoph. Chron., p. 431, trans. Turtledove, p. 120; for a positive version of what could be the same campaign, see Niceph. pp. 144–5, 219.

[14] Niceph., pp. 148–53, 156–7; Theoph's tone is far more negative: pp. 432–3, 436–7, 446–8, trans. Turtledove, pp. 122, 125–6, 133–5.

surpluses upon which such defences had to rest. His concern to keep up, if not expand, the size of the population in Thrace is suggested by the decisiveness of his response to the Bulgars' scheme to transplant the inhabitants of Berzetia to their own country in 774.[15]

If this interpretation of Constantine's aims is sound, it tempers the scale of the Bulgars' achievement in weathering the blows his armies dealt them. In Constantine's reign, they had their first hostile encounter with a firmly based and undistracted soldier emperor, and the effect of their repeated reverses was to exacerbate the political instability which was already astir. The numerous 'secret friends' who kept Constantine informed about Bulgar plans perhaps bear witness to the politico-cultural magnetism of the imperial court rather than simply to the efficacy of Byzantine bribery and intelligence-gathering. In 776 Khan Telerig, following in the footsteps of at least one predecessor, sought asylum in Constantinople, was baptised and wedded a cousin of the emperor's wife. But it would be wrong to infer from the volatility at the top that the entire ruling elite was demoralised or culturally bankrupt. Distrust of 'the Greeks' is a motif of the so-called 'Protobulgar' inscriptions and it may, paradoxically, have helped maintain cohesion among the warrior class, in that a high degree of military alertness was imperative. The 'council' (*kombenton*) which denounced Khan Sabinos in 763 is supposed to have declared: 'Thanks to you, the Romans will enslave Bulgaria!'[16] This utterance foreshadows other, indubitably historical, expressions of Bulgar fear and distrust of the Byzantine state.

The turn of the eighth and the ninth centuries is celebrated for a series of invasions and counter invasions on the part of Byzantines and Bulgars. Lurid as some of these clashes were, they did not, in themselves, alter the balance between the two powers. They were, however, symptoms of more fundamental developments which the virulent early ninth-century conflicts probably accelerated. First, and most dramatically, the collapse of the Avar khaganate must be noted. In 796 the khagan submitted to Charlemagne and in 803 the last significant Avar resistance gave out.[17] The Bulgars under their new khan, Krum, were quick to exploit the Avars' predicament. Around 804 they launched a devastating raid, prompting one group of Avars to request permission to migrate westwards into the territory of their Frankish overlords.[18]

A second fundamental development *c.* 800 was the tightening of the links

---

[15] Theoph. Chron., p. 447, trans. Turtledove, p. 134; Turner (1990a), p. 426; Soustal (1991), pp. 80, 336.

[16] 'dia sou hē Boulgaria mellei doulousthai tois Rōmaiois': Theoph. Chron., p. 433, trans. Turtledove, p. 122.   [17] Pohl (1989), pp. 321–2.

[18] *Suidae Lexicon* (1928, 1), pp. 483–4; Pohl (1989), p. 322.

between Byzantium and the diverse inhabitants of the Balkan hinterland, and the Bulgars' reaction to this. The imperial government in the late eighth century took spectacular steps to proclaim dominion over the Slav communities to its west and southwest. In 784 Empress Irene celebrated with a triumph in the capital the success of her chief minister, Staurakios, in allegedly 'making tribute-payers' of 'all' the Slav tribes in the regions of Thessalonica and northern Greece,[19] and subsequently she herself went on a kind of imperial progress through Thrace, accompanied by a large force and taking with her organs and other musical symbols of majesty. Irene's itinerary marked an attempt to establish enclaves centred on fortresses across a broad swathe of the debatable lands looking towards Bulgaria. Irene's journey to a point as far up the Hebros (Maritsa) as Philippopolis (Plovdiv) took her well beyond the previous limits of imperial security. Her foundation of a new theme, 'Macedonia', gave administrative form to Byzantine dominance over the coastal strip west of the Hebros and the choice of name served notice on the Bulgars of imperial claims to Macedonia proper, far to the west.

If Irene and her counsellors supposed from the instability among the Bulgar ruling elite that their reclamation work would meet with acquiescence, they were soon to be disillusioned. The Bulgar polity proved far more resilient *vis-à-vis* the Byzantines than was the Avar khaganate before the Franks. In fact, it was the Byzantine state that now experienced volatility at the top for over two decades, giving the Bulgars the chance to reverse the trend of recent years.

The Byzantine chronicles record a few colourful bouts in a largely unrecorded struggle for control not only of forts such as Markellai but also of the entire length of the main river valleys leading down to the Aegean from the Balkan interior.[20] The Bulgars may well have felt threatened by the Byzantine shows of force and acts of consolidation outlined above. But they were not devoid of some spirit of adventurism and expansionism, as their assault on the Avars *c.* 804 shows.

The khan who mounted this assault, Krum, had come to power *c.* 802 and his *démarches* have left their mark in certain inscriptions. These were set up at his instigation in the borderlands or at strategic points in order to propagate claims and publicise rights. It is noteworthy that strongholds far inland were

---

[19] *hypophorous epoïēse*: Theoph. Chron., p. 456, trans. Turtledove, p. 142; Treadgold, p. 73. Imperial authority had been established in larger towns such as Adrianople well to the west of the capital, judging by the attendance list of bishops at the Seventh Oecumenical Council at Nicaea in 787: Soustal (1991), p. 81.

[20] Theoph. Chron., pp. 463–4, 467–8, 470, trans. Turtledove, pp. 148, 150–1, 153; Treadgold, pp. 91–2, 98–100, 106; Soustal (1991), pp. 82, 348–9.

now at issue, as well as points on eastern Thrace's coastal plain. In 809 Krum gained entry to Serdica (Sofia) and massacred not only its large garrison but also the civilian population; this was, probably, mainly made up of Greek-speakers transplanted there in the recent past. Nicephorus' response was twofold. First, he stepped up the transfer of 'Christians ... from every theme' (*Christianous ... ek pantos thematos*) to preponderantly Slav-settled regions over which he claimed dominion.[21] Secondly, Nicephorus determined to inflict a humiliating blow on Khan Krum, preventing further disruption of the burgeoning pattern of strongholds. The emperor led a huge army up to Krum's seat of authority in the Danubian plain, burning his residence and setting seals and bars on his 'treasury buildings', thereby proclaiming a change of ownership.[22] Within a few days Nicephorus' grand army was withdrawing through the deep mountain passes. Even so, the Bulgars had sufficient time in which to prepare wooden barricades which they threw up at either end of a valley, trapping the Byzantines within it. The Bulgars overran the emperor's camp before dawn on Saturday, 26 July 811, killing Nicephorus; panic set in and many more soldiers perished in trying to break out over the palisades. The Byzantine losses have been described as 'immense'.[23] Krum seems to have proposed peace terms which were more or less a renewal of the treaty of almost a century earlier. A clause concerning the repatriation of runaways, including political refugees, apparently an innovation, proved to be a sticking-point.[24] Thereupon Krum took by means of bombardment the key naval base of Mesembria and harried parts of Thrace. Emperor Michael I (811–15) eventually abandoned his reluctance to do battle, but his ill-equipped and largely untrained troops were easily routed at Bersinikia on 22 June 813. Krum's forces were considerably fewer than the Byzantines' and he had hitherto shown wariness. Now he led his men up to Constantinople and demanded that his spear be affixed to the Golden Gate, evidently as a symbol of victory. He was probably merely posturing, prior to peace talks, and, at his request, a meeting between him and the newly acceded emperor, Leo V, was arranged. It may well have been exasperation after a Byzantine assassination attempt that drove Krum on a whirlwind tour of destruction. After sacking the suburbs of the capital, Krum and his warriors devastated many forts and walled towns along the northern shore of the Sea of Marmara, a prosperous, hitherto secure area.

Krum published on an inscribed stone the hierarchy of commanders of

---

[21] Theoph. Chron., p. 486, trans. Turtledove, p. 166.

[22] *tois tameiois*: Theoph. Chron., p. 490, line 24, trans. Turtledove, p. 171. It is in my view unlikely that there had already been a Byzantine expedition into the Danubian plain as far as Pliska in 809; see, however, Treadgold, p. 158. [23] Treadgold, p. 174.

[24] Theoph. Cont., pp. 12–13; p. 231 above.

his newly won border fortresses. He also had the names of more southerly fortified towns, which had been sacked but not occupied, inscribed on marble columns standing in Pliska. Twenty-one examples of these are known.[25] Krum now sought to add to the list the name of Constantinople. Weight of numbers and siege equipment were prerequisite for this task, so he set about assembling a huge army, recruiting Avars and many Slavs.[26] He prepared an arsenal of enormous catapults and other devices, which were to be drawn by 10,000 oxen. But sudden death cut short the enterprise. Krum died of a cerebral haemorrhage on 13 April 814.

Thus ended one of the more martial phases in Byzantino-Bulgarian relations. The various invasions had re-affirmed what was probably obvious already: that neither side could overwhelm the other. The speed of Nicephorus' incursion in 811 was probably dictated by fear for his lines of withdrawal: his response to the news that the passes had been blocked was, reportedly, 'Even were we to grow wings, none could hope to survive.'[27] Bulgar incursions continued after Krum's death, but the effective stalemate created by the natural barrier of the Haemus and by the walls of the City were recognised in a peace treaty (probably for thirty years) concluded between Leo V and Krum's son, Omurtag (815–31) in, most probably, 816.[28] Its contents were summarised on an inscribed column at Pliska: the border area was specified mainly in terms of various fortresses running inland from Develtos (which seems to have been returned to Byzantium).

The inscription is incomplete and very few of the place-names are free from controversy about their form or their present-day location.[29] It is on the one hand clear that Konstanteia, strategically situated on the Hebros, and Makre Libada nearby, were well to the south of the Haemus and brought the Bulgars footholds in the fertile river valley. On the other hand, the inscription's provisions also imply a return to coexistence and the removal of *casus belli*. The very fact of its erection at the khan's seat suggests as much, and it may well have been at this time that the Bulgars raised a great earthen rampart. The earthwork is still discernible for some 137 km, running from the coast near Develtos to the environs of Konstanteia and rising to a height of up to 1 m.[30] The rampart is a mark of considerable powers of organisation and, while evincing distrust of the Greeks, it also suggests an intention to stay put. The khan still accounted the steppe

---

[25] Beševliev (1979), pp. 32–3, 143–51, 173–4; cf. Soustal (1991), pp. 83–4.

[26] Dujčev, *MBS* II, p. 425; Pohl (1989), p. 327.

[27] 'k'an pterōtoi genōmetha, mēdeis elpisoi diaphygein ton olethron', Theoph. Chron., p. 490, trans. Turtledove, p. 171.   [28] Treadgold (1984), pp. 217–18.

[29] Beševliev (1979), pp. 152–63; Soustal (1986), pp. 150–4.

[30] Beševliev (1981a), pp. 476–7; Soustal (1991), pp. 261–2.

northeast of the Danube as his domain and a sizeable colony of Byzantine captives was maintained there, probably in the vicinity of the Dniester. The community was allowed its own leaders and these agriculturalists, who seem to have been armed, served as a buffer against raiders from the east. There exist 'Protobulgar' inscriptions which apparently confirm or supplement the forementioned treaty,[31] and in 822–3 Omurtag came to the assistance of Michael II against the rebellion of Thomas the Slav, perhaps in fulfilment of a treaty clause.[32]

There were, however, serious tensions engrained in the Bulgar polity's relations with the empire. That military preparedness remained a top priority of the khan is indicated in the correspondence between Khan Boris and Pope Nicholas I in 866. Before going to war, the khan sent out an inspector of keen intelligence to scrutinise 'all weapons, horses and things essential for battle ... and whoever proves to be ill-prepared is punished with death'. Death was also the lot of border-guards who let slip unauthorised freemen or slaves.[33] This grim state of constant alert suggests abiding fear of sudden strikes from the Byzantines by land or sea, while the steppes to the northeast swarmed with unpredictable marauders.[34] But the Bulgars' energies could find outlets in expansionism when the occasion arose, and the demands of their ninth-century military organisation for *matériel* as well as manpower probably encouraged them to extend the compass of their exactions from amenable populations. By the mid-820s they were seeking some sort of overlordship over the Slavs and Avars living beyond the Iron Gates to the east of the river Theiss. In 827 a Bulgar fleet sailed up the river Drava and an attempt was made to wrest control of the local Slavs from the Franks.[35] Khan Presian (836–52) waged war for three years with the Serbs and although his objectives are not clear, it is likely that, as in the clash with the Franks, rights of overlordship and, ultimately, exactions were at issue. This, in turn, would suggest that towards the middle of the century the khan's sphere of exactions reached far to the west beyond Serdica (Sofia). Where exactly the khan's sway ended and the emperor's began was probably undecided, and in any case the Bulgar rulers did not attempt fully to press home the opportunities which the fragility of Byzantine hegemony over

---

[31] Beševliev (1979), pp. 163–9.

[32] Treadgold, p. 240 and n. 332 on p. 445. On evidence suggestive of a Bulgar contingent serving with the Byzantines against the Arabs in Asia Minor in 837, see Ditten (1984), pp. 70–9.

[33] 'cuncta arma et caballos et quae necessaria pugnae existunt ... et, apud quem inutiliter praeparata inventa fuerint, capite punitur', *MGH Epp.* VI, p. 582; cf. *ibid.*, p. 579.

[34] E.g. the Magyars who harassed the above-mentioned Byzantine captives upon their flight, apparently during the 830s: GMC, pp. 818–19.

[35] Deér (1977), p. 358; Pohl (1989), p. 327.

certain of its *Slaviniai* in the 820s and 830s might seem to have offered.[36] Krum's successors seem rather to have probed into the mountainous interior of the Balkans and upstream along the Danube, beyond the striking range of the emperor's fleets or armies.

Their eyes, though, were cocked on the *basileus* and his court. This is the inescapable conclusion to be drawn from the inscriptions which the khans had cut in Greek by employees who may very often themselves have been ethnic Greeks; the inscriptions' language is spoken, not formal literary Greek. Some were essentially functional, but the majority were set up, often on marble columns, at royal residences for purposes of display. The title the 'prince-from-God' is first attested on inscriptions of Omurtag. It can hardly be a coincidence that 'emperor-from-God' (*ek theou basileus*) was a term in use on contemporary Byzantine coins and seals and, probably, in contemporary acclamations.[37]

Our sources for the reign of Boris (852–89, 893) are fuller than for the reigns of his predecessors, but they are very difficult to evaluate. Remarks about the political background to Boris' conversion and even about the course of events must therefore be highly tentative. It seems most likely that soon after Boris' accession he ratified a treaty with Byzantium, probably seeking to deal with the pattern of raids and counterraids that appear to have burgeoned in the Byzantino-Bulgar borderlands during the later 840s, after the expiry of the thirty-year treaty.[38] Certain Byzantine sources claim that Boris had been deterred from military initiatives by Empress Theodora's firm stance, but the reality may have been a strategic calculation of the khan: being aware of Byzantium's substantial reserves of wealth, military man-power and diplomatic connections, Boris may have sought stability to his south and northeast, in order to extend his overlordship westwards. In 853 he attacked the territory of Louis the German in Pannonia 'fiercely' (*acriter*), albeit unsuccessfully.[39] It may perhaps have been in the same decade that he

---

[36] On routine banditry, and an outright revolt, see Dvornik (1926b), pp. 35–6, 54, 61–2. The part played by the Bulgars in this unrest hinges mainly on the interpretation of an incomplete and much discussed inscription (Karayannopoulos (1986), pp. 14–19, 26–48). Any such involvement as the khan may have had was not sustained.

[37] Beševliev (1979), p. 70; Beševliev (1987), pp. 58–9; Zacos and Veglery (1972) I.1, p. 47; Grierson (1973) I, pp. 366–7, 376–7, 395–6, 412, 430, 432–3. Two inscriptions wish the khan long life in terms virtually identical to Byzantine acclamations while a third's allusion to the ritual trampling in imperial victory celebrations presupposes that its readers will be acquainted with this: Beševliev (1979), pp. 192–3, 200–1, 209–10; cf. McCormick (1990), pp. 57–8, 144; Schreiner (1989), pp. 53, 57–8.

[38] Leo Grammaticus (1842), p. 235; Pseudo-Symeon, p. 657; Theoph. Cont., p. 162.

[39] *AB s.a.* 853, p. 68.

attacked the Serbs and met with humiliating failure.[40] An indication of more successful Bulgar expansion westwards comes in the form of an incomplete inscription found at Ballsh, and datable to the year 1 September 865 to 31 August 866, in present-day southern Albania.[41] The wording implies that Boris reigned over the area, but it offers no clue as to when Ballsh had come under Bulgar dominion.

Probings westwards such as those outlined above made Boris a major figure, of concern to the East Frankish king as well as the *basileus*. Louis the German did not only have to reckon with the possibility of further Bulgar ventures up the middle Danube; he also had to contend with the emergence of a Slav political structure much closer to his borders, in fact within his sphere of influence, in the form of Moravia. Prince Rastislav had been imposed on the Moravians by Louis himself, but Louis' ineffectual expedition against him in 855 highlights the intractability of this Slav potentate: Louis' camp was almost overwhelmed during his withdrawal.[42] Boris and Louis had a common interest in curbing the power of Rastislav and in the early 860s they achieved some sort of *rapprochement*, eventually amounting to an alliance. There were exchanges between Boris and Louis concerning conversion to Christianity to the point where Louis felt able to profess optimism that the khan 'might be willing to be converted' (*velit converti*) in a message directed to the papacy in the first half of 864.[43] But in the event it was from Byzantium, and not Louis, that Boris received the faith. The Christian name which he assumed was that of the emperor, Michael III, who became his godfather.

The precise date of Boris' baptism, 864, 865 or even (implausibly) 863 or 866, remains contentious, as do the circumstances.[44] One group of Byzantine chronicles relates that Boris was converted under duress.[45] But one must also consider the possibility that the chronicles are relaying the imperial explanation for a decision that was essentially of Boris' making. His

---

[40] *DAI*, ch. 32, lines 42–53. The date is controversial: *VIINJ* II, p. 51, n. 163; Jenkins (1962), p. 134; Maksimović (1979), pp. 69–76; *ISN*, p. 148; *IB*, p. 236; *SSS* VII, p. 510.

[41] This mentions 'Boris whose name has been changed to Michael' and 'the people given to him by God' (*Borēs ho metonomastheis Michaēl; tō ek theou dedomenō autō ethnei*): Beševliev (1979), p. 139; Cankova-Petkova (1973), pp. 31–2. It was, most probably, cut soon after Boris's conversion.

[42] *AF s.a.* 855, p. 45. On Louis the German's problems with Moravia, see Reuter (1991), pp. 82–3.

[43] Louis, as the object of rebukes from Nicholas I at that time, had his reasons for propagating such hopes. Similar caution should be exercised with the statement in *AB* (*s.a.* 864, p. 113) that Boris 'had promised that he wished to become a Christian' (*christianum fieri velle promiserat*); this would, even if actually made, have been only the vaguest of undertakings.

[44] See, e.g., Obolensky (1971a), p. 84; Cankova-Petkova (1973), pp. 30–4; Hannick (1978), pp. 308–9; *SSS* VII, p. 510; Gjuzelev (1988), p. 133.

[45] GMC, p. 824; Leo Grammaticus (1842), p. 238.

baptism could represent a proposal which he voluntarily presented to Byzantium in exchange for territorial concessions from Byzantium in Thrace.[46] It need not have been determined solely by apprehensions of a Byzantine invasion.

If, as is likely, Boris was seriously considering baptism already before the onset of famine, apparent abandonment by the gods and strategic vulnerability, he was at least partly motivated by a desire to come to terms with a religion whose magnetic force was evident. Some of Boris' subjects were Christians, and not all of them were Greek-born. Boris' own sister is said to have been converted while living (as a hostage) in Constantinople and, supposedly, upon her return home she urged the faith upon him. In fact, nunneries, as well as monasteries, seem to have been in existence among the Bulgars for some time before Boris' conversion,[47] and Orthodox religious often made the most dedicated proselytisers. This could have a demeaning, if not downright disruptive, effect upon the rites, such as sacrifices, over which the khan presided. On the other hand, the cohesiveness, order and written learning of Christian worship, together with the energies of its practitioners, might be harnessed to Boris' rule, lending credibility to his title 'prince-from-God'. A cult which might predispose the Slavs, Vlachs and other autochthonous inhabitants of his lands to accept that they belonged to 'the people given to him from God' would be of obvious advantage to Boris.[48] It may well have been considerations such as these, and not just diplomatic manœuvring, which raised the question of Boris' conversion during his exchanges with Louis the German. Not dissimilar considerations may have underlain his acceptance of Christianity from Michael III, whether or not this was preceded by serious imperial sabre-rattling.

Imperial propaganda inclined to treat the adoption of the Orthodox creed by the Bulgar khan as a triumph for the Byzantine state: Boris and his people had now submitted to the emperor. Boris' subsequent conduct suggests that subservience to an external ruler was precisely what he was seeking to avert. Having made the decision to convert, he committed himself whole-heartedly to mastering the intricacies of the new religion's ritual and discipline, and to inculcating Christian behavioural norms in his people in a characteristically thorough way. But his stance was still exploratory, in the

[46] Theoph. Cont., p. 165; GMC, p. 824; Leo Grammaticus (1842), p. 238; Soustal (1986), pp. 149, 153–5.   [47] Florja and Litavrin (1988), pp. 187–8.

[48] On archaeological attestation of long-lasting differences in burial and cremation ritual between Bulgars and Slavs, see Georgiev et al. (1975), p. 87; V'zharova (1976), pp. 424–6, 435–6. On the non-Slav population, see Schramm (1981), pp. 134–7, 178–9, 399; Winnifrith (1987), pp. 88–100; Risos (1990), pp. 202–3.

sense that he sought information from more than one ecclesiastical authority. His strategic position soon recovered from such temporary dislocation as the famine of the early 860s may have induced, and his internal
position was greatly strengthened in 866 by his defeat in battle of a major
uprising of nobles opposed to his adoption of the new religion; they may
have regarded Boris' *démarche* with the same disfavour that their predecessors had greeted Sabinos' conciliatory policy towards Constantine V a
century earlier. 'All their leaders' (*omnes primates eorum*) are said to have been
executed by Boris.[49] Within a year or two of baptism Boris felt able to risk
Byzantine outrage by seeking clergy from Louis the German, and counsel
and a patriarch from Pope Nicholas I. The pope's answers, dated 13
November 866, match the detail of Boris' enquiries as to how to implant the
new religion into everyday life.[50] Nicholas sent a high-ranking delegation,
together with numerous junior clergy, to see through what he envisaged as
the incorporation of the barbarian occupants of the old ecclesiastical
province of Illyricum into the mother church.

Boris seems, throughout his negotiations with the papal representatives
and the papacy, to have acted on the assumption that the new cult's priests
should be answerable to him and that their hierarchy should correspond
with his own status as a wholly independent ruler: hence his desire for a
patriarch as his high priest.[51] He was most probably well aware of, and
perhaps not uninfluenced by, the efforts which the chief prince of Moravia
had been making in the early 860s to acquire a hierarchy independent of the
Frankish church hierarchy. Rastislav's aim was much more modest than
Boris', in that he seems merely to have been seeking a bishop and clergy to
form a diocese coterminous with his dominions. But his rationale was
comparable. Upon failing to procure a bishop from Nicholas I, Rastislav put
a similar request to the emperor of Byzantium, and may also have sought
general recognition of his right to rule over the Moravians.[52]

Rastislav received not a full-blown mission but two brothers, Constantine and Methodius. Both were pious and Slav-speakers, and Constantine
was a supremely gifted linguist who seems already to have experimented
with designing an alphabet for the Slavic language, perhaps even translating
some Gospel readings.[53] The Byzantine government may well have
intended the mission to be exploratory rather than permanent, and in any
case Rastislav's bid for institutionalized autonomy suffered a major setback

---

[49] *MGH Epp.* VI, p. 577; *AB s.a.* 866, p. 133.
[50] *MGH Epp.* VI, pp. 568–600; Sullivan (1966), pp. 53–139. Boris had already received a letter from
Patriarch Photius, prescribing the duties of a Christian prince: Photius (1983) I, pp. 1–39.
[51] *MGH Epp.* VI, pp. 592–3; Gjuzelev (1988), p. 147.   [52] *VC*, ch. 14; Richter (1985), p. 283.
[53] Vavřínek and Zástěrová (1982), p. 174.

in 864, soon after the arrival of Constantine and Methodius in Moravia. Surprised in his stronghold of Děvín, he was obliged to surrender to Louis the German and swore *fides* to the king; thereupon Frankish churchmen were able to resume their pastoral work. Constantine and Methodius left Rastislav's lands at the end of 866 or the beginning of 867.[54]

Nonetheless, the repercussions of the brothers' activities were wide ranging. Constantine, acting with his brother and apparently at their own initiative, translated during their stay in Moravia several lengthy texts fundamental to the liturgy. The four Gospels, the Acts of the Apostles and, apparently, the entire Book of Psalms were elegantly rendered and written down in the script that Constantine had devised, almost certainly Glagolitic.[55] The papacy, at odds with Byzantium concerning jurisdiction over the church in Bulgaria (as falling within Illyricum, to which the Constantinopolitan patriarchate, too, laid claim),[56] began to show interest in the brothers. Constantine and Methodius, who were in the summer of 867 lodged in Venice, received an invitation to Rome, where Pope Hadrian II accorded them a ceremonial welcome.[57]

Pope Hadrian's manifest sympathy and respect for the translation work of Constantine and Methodius was not, however, without high-placed critics in Rome. Nonetheless, shortly after his brother's death in 869 Methodius was able to return to the middle Danube Slavs as papal legate armed with a papal bull sanctioning the use of the new Slavonic script. Soon afterwards he was ordained in Rome as archbishop of 'the Pannonians'. The nomenclature, reviving the western part of the province of Illyricum, reflected the fact that Methodius enjoyed the active support of Kocel, prince of the Pannonian Slavs, with whom he and his brother had stayed on their way from Moravia to Venice in 867 and who now welcomed the prospect of an archbishopric, as a bar to the archbishop of Salzburg's right to intervene in Pannonian affairs. Nonetheless, Methodius continued to encounter great difficulties, including a period in detention. Upon Kocel's death *c.* 875 he moved on to Moravia and took charge of church life in the dominions of Svatopluk, the nephew and ouster of Rastislav. Methodius strenuously devoted himself to teaching and translating and, increasingly with the help of his pupils, created a very extensive repertory, including most of the Bible and also excerpts from the Church Fathers, prayers and a work of church

---

[54] *VC*, ch. 15; Wolfram (1987), p. 294.

[55] *VC*, ch. 15; *VM*, ch. 15. It seems, however, that the Gospels and the Acts were not translated in their entirety; those parts read out in church services were translated: Floria (1981), p. 128, n. 14; p. 168, n. 5.

[56] Dvornik (1948), pp. 91–4, 100–3; Hannick (1978), pp. 311–12; *IB*, pp. 224–7; Döpmann (1981), pp. 62–6; *SSS* vii, p. 510.   [57] *VC*, ch. 17.

law, the *Synagoge of 50 Titles*, adapted to conditions in Moravia. Although Svatopluk showed no enthusiasm for a Slavonic liturgy, Methodius in 880 received permission from Pope John VIII to celebrate the liturgy in Slavonic, a concession which the papacy had denied him hitherto.

Boris of Bulgaria was, in the late 860s, in a far stronger position than Rastislav, Svatopluk or Kocel, being master of his own land without serious fear of deposition. The Roman clergy had proved to be very active, but he had not reached agreement with the pope on a choice of archbishop: he had fairly rapidly abandoned his quest for a patriarch. For reasons which are not fully clear, he began to contemplate a *rapprochement* with Byzantium; the recently acceded emperor, Basil I, for his part, may well have been interested in some means of tempering the Bulgarian problem, at a time when his missionaries were making progress among the Serbs and other western neighbours of the Bulgars.[58] An occasion for both parties – Boris and Basil – to formalise an arrangement was provided by the dispute between the Roman and the Constantinopolitan churches, which Nicholas I's refusal to recognise Photius as patriarch in lieu of the deposed Ignatius had precipitated. Basil, eager for legitimisation of his recent palace coup and in particular for Rome's recognition of his patriarch (the now-restored Ignatius), convened a Council, attended by heads or representatives of all five patriarchates, from October 869 to March 870. The papacy's own condemnation of Photius was confirmed and he was excommunicated. However, Basil, acting in collusion with Boris, had some hidden agenda for the delegates, concerning Bulgaria; the papacy seems to have suspected as much in advance, but its legates were unable to halt the reconvening of the Council to consider a question posed by the khan's envoys: to which patriarchate did his land belong? The answer of the delegates – the Romans alone dissenting – can have come as no surprise to Basil or to Boris. The judgement was, according to Anastasius Bibliothecarius, that 'the country of the Bulgars which, as we have ascertained, was formerly under Greek rule and had Greek clergy, is now returned through the Christian faith to the holy church of Constantinople, from which it had been removed through paganism'.[59]

The church in Bulgaria thus gained the ambivalent status of an 'autocephalous' archbishopric: the only other such see encompassed the island of Cyprus. Although owing his status directly to an imperial decision and

---

[58] *DAI*, ch. 29/70–98; Radojičić (1952), pp. 253–6; *VIINJ* II, p. 49, n. 152; Dujčev (1961), pp. 53–5; Hannick (1978), p. 312; *ISN*, pp. 151–2.

[59] 'Quapropter Bulgarum patria ex Grecorum potestate dudum fuisse et Grecos sacerdotes habuisse comperimus, sanctae ecclesiae Constantinopolitanae a qua per paganismum recesserat, nunc per christianismum restitui iudicamus', *LP* II, p. 184.

under the moral aegis of the Constantinopolitan patriarch, who consecrated at least the first incumbent, the archbishop seems in effect to have possessed autonomy. His appointment can only have been made with the approval of the 'prince-from-God' and Basil's agreement on this point may well have been the essence of the settlement.[60] Boris could feel confident of obtaining an acceptable high priest.

He planned that the first archbishop, named variously in our sources as Stephen or Joseph, should live with him at Pliska, probably in a monastery situated in the fortified outer town; his chambers seem to have been connected by vaulted galleries to the Great Basilica which Boris had caused to be built, or rather, rebuilt. The huge structure, some 29.5 m wide by 99 m long (including its colonnaded atrium), was raised on the foundations of a ruined basilica that is probably datable to the early Byzantine period.[61] The church's size and the lavishness of its columns and other ornamentation – much of it spolia from earlier buildings[62] – served to display the prince's special relationship with God.

The sources for Boris' conduct after his final adoption of the Byzantine rite are mostly ecclesiastical in origin, and it is quite conceivable that the Christian prince engaged in aggressive warfare against the Croats, and possibly against the Serbs.[63] It was, however, peaceful promotion of the new cult that served the ruler's interests most systematically, entitling him to intervene legitimately in communities whose dealings with him and his agents had hitherto been mainly in the form of tribute payments and military service. As is apparent in Boris' questions to Nicholas I, he saw it as his duty to enforce correct observance of the cult's rites and disciplines on all his subjects: the severe demands traditionally placed on Bulgar nobles and freemen owing military service were now supplemented, if not supplanted, by the ruler's responsibility to God for their moral and spiritual welfare,[64] and his new duties did not stop with Bulgars. Boris seems to have been well aware of the opportunities which Christianity gave him to define his role as ruler and to extend it to the outer reaches of his dominions. The location of the inscription commemorating his conversion is suggestive: Ballsh was over 600 km southwest of Pliska and very few indeed of the local inhabitants can have been ethnic Bulgars. Several of the episcopal sees were also on the

---

[60] See, e.g. Svoboda (1966), pp. 73–8; Döpmann (1967), pp. 803–4; *SSS* III, p. 495; *IB*, p. 236; Darrouzès (1981), pp. 93, 153, and n. 1.

[61] Mavrodinov (1959), pp. 54ff.; *IB*, p. 427; Mango (1986), p. 173; Totev (1987), pp. 187–9.

[62] *PP* II, pp. 190–8.

[63] The attack on the Croats is related in the *DAI*, ch. 31/62–4 without clear chronological indicators. The *DAI*'s account of Boris' expedition against the Serbs is ambivalent in its clues as to the date: above, n. 40.   [64] A point put to him by Pope Nicholas, *MGH Epp.* VI, p. 582.

fringes of Boris' realm – Belgrade, for example, and the nearby town of Morav-Margus in the northwest; Ochrid and Bregalnitsa in the southwest; and, in Thrace, Philippopolis.[65] Boris is described by an eleventh-century churchman as having 'girdled' (*perizōsanta*) all Bulgaria with metropolitan churches, which he claims numbered seven in all.[66] The pattern of Bulgarian sees to some extent registers those areas where Orthodox Christianity was long established. However, Boris' interest in founding bishoprics and building churches probably also sprang from awareness of the benefits to his authority of a network of cult centres which relied upon him for patronage and resources. The southern and western sees of the new archbishopric were mostly in areas which had only come under Bulgar dominion within living memory, and which were not devoid of strategic significance.

That Slavic developed as a literary language in Bulgaria seems to have owed much, although by no means everything, to providence or chance. In 885, after Methodius' death Pope Stephen V(VI) re-imposed the ban on worship in Slavic in Moravia. Moravian priests and deacons, approximately two hundred in number, all of them celebrants of the Slavic liturgy, were imprisoned, enslaved or expelled.[67] One small group made its way to Bulgaria, where its three leaders were received by Boris. Naum apparently took up residence in Pliska, but Boris assigned Clement to the southwest extremities of his territories. Clement is depicted in his *Vita* as conducting an extraordinarily active mission, teaching and showing the same zeal for book-learning that his mentors, Constantine-Cyril and Methodius, had done; he gave up much time to the young, whom he drilled vigorously in reading, writing and comprehension.[68]

Several of the claims made for Clement by his *Vita* are borne out by independent sources, notably by a sizeable body of works attributed – with varying degrees of plausibility – to him. Panegyrics of saints and at least fifteen sermons can safely be ascribed to him.[69] And there is no doubt that his pastoral care encompassed Ochrid, where he soon founded a monastery, Deabolis (Devol), and other recesses of what is now southern Albania. There is no firm evidence that Boris was, in the late 880s, contemplating a wholesale substitution of Slavonic for Greek as the language of worship or of the Scriptures. On the other hand, he seems to have sanctioned some translation work by Bulgarians such as John the Exarch even before the arrival of Methodius' pupils.

---

[65] *SSS* III, map on p. 495; p. 497; *IB*, p. 231.
[66] Milev (1966), p. 132. The figure of seven metropolitanates for ninth-century Bulgaria may well be an anachronism on the part of the writer, Theophylact of Ochrid.
[67] Milev (1966), p. 110.   [68] Milev (1966), p. 126.
[69] Iliev (1987), pp. 72–5; Obolensky (1988b), pp. 30–1.

One must, in particular, beware of possible distortion or simplification of the original purpose of Clement's mission, let alone of the lack of clarity concerning Boris' motives, in the longer of his two *Vitae*. Its author, Theophylact of Ochrid, was writing two centuries afterwards and he had reasons of his own for aggrandising his see as having been the cradle of the young Bulgarian church.[70] At any rate, Clement was initially allotted residences and, apparently, instructed to evangelise, in largely pagan regions which had only come under Bulgar dominion quite recently and many of whose inhabitants were not Bulgars or even Slavs, but Albanians and Vlachs.[71] Clement's fluency in Slavonic would therefore have been of limited impact. It is likely that Boris regarded both individuals such as Clement and institutions – monasteries and sees – as important means of demarcating the zones of his legitimate rule. Together, they constituted a sort of dynamo of fixed bases and mobile individuals which could bring a measure of order to the disparate communities of the region, at least in the valleys.

There was, then, a profoundly political dimension to Boris' furtherance of Christianity and patronage of such cults as that of the Fifteen Martyrs of Tiberioupolis.[72] But if in earlier days his preoccupation was with a well-drilled series of rituals, new means of underpinning his rule through social control, he came to cherish the faith as the pathway to his own spiritual improvement and redemption. A German chronicler, Regino of Prüm, whose evident admiration for Boris was based on factual information, recounts that by night he would don 'sackcloth and, entering the basilica secretly, he would prostrate himself on a goat's hair covering spread directly on the church pavement, and lie there in prayer'.[73] This portrayal gains some substance from the fact that in 889 Boris abdicated, exchanging earthly power for the cloister. Several of his close relatives were already monks or nuns. Munificence towards the church, strict personal piety and thirst for learning may well have appeared ingrained in the new political culture of Bulgaria, and Boris was presumably confident, upon abdicating, that things would continue thus under his eldest son and heir Vladimir.

---

[70] Nonetheless, the detailed and at least partly verifiable information, together with occasional phraseology befitting a pupil of Clement, suggests that Theophylact was drawing on an early source, such as a *Vita*. Cf. Obolensky (1988b), p. 63.

[71] Milev (1966), p. 124. One of the properties was at Ballsh, where stood the Greek inscription commemorating the conversion of Boris and his 'people': above, n. 41. Intensive Slav settlement of this area is, however, propounded by Gjuzelev (1991), pp. 79–82.

[72] Theophylact of Ochrid, *Martyrium*, cols. 201–6; *SSS* III, p. 495; *SSS* V, p. 440; Obolensky (1988b), pp. 73–5.

[73] 'sacco vestitus latenter ecclesiam intrans super pavimentum ipsius basilicae substrato sibi tantum cilicio prostratus in oratione iaceret': Regino of Prüm (1890), p. 96.

In the event, Vladimir attempted a pagan reaction in which blood was spilt.[74] Vladimir's failure suggests that Christian statehood was a now irreversible trend in Bulgaria, as nearly everywhere else in southeastern Europe, even though Boris, at the time of his abdication, had left unresolved major questions as to the relative merits and uses of Greek and Slavonic in worship, religious instruction and secular administration. Cognate with this was the wider issue of Bulgaria's relationship with Byzantium. Notionally, in the eyes of senior Byzantine churchmen at least, the Bulgarian people were the 'spiritual children' of the Byzantines,[75] and Boris was willing to disseminate an image of piety and submission to Constantinopolitan authority on his lead seals. Some earlier khans had issued seals or medallions, notably Tervel and Omurtag; they were portrayed with vestments and regalia largely of Byzantine cut. Boris, in contrast, eschewed portrayal of himself on his seals. On their face is a bust of Christ; on their reverse is a bust of the Mother of God with her arms raised in prayer.[76]

To all appearances, then, the Byzantines and the Bulgarians were united in the body of Christ. The fact remained that the khan's dominions now included a far broader swathe of the Balkans than those of his predecessors had done. Boris' adoption of Christianity as a state religion provided him with an array of new means for the ordering of his subjects. The lower Danube area remained his base.[77] At the same time, a high proportion of Boris' bishoprics lay in the vicinity of his borders with Byzantium. Boris' main concern may have been with the inculcation of his authority among the heterogeneous inhabitants of his southern and western borderlands. It may well be that Boris was partly seeking to counter the religious, cultural and ultimately political gravitational field which centres such as Dyrrachium, Thessalonica and Constantinople itself inevitably exerted.

Such measures of Boris as this had no direct military purpose, but the imperial government cannot have failed to note the potential strategic problems which an enlarged, better-ordered Bulgaria under an interventionist Christian monarch might pose. Even during the later part of Boris' reign, when his Christian piety was manifest, the Byzantine state took

---

[74] See *New Cambridge Medieval History* III, forthcoming.   [75] Dölger (1939), p. 227, n. 17.

[76] The face and the reverse of Boris' seals respectively invoke, in a standard Byzantine formula, the aid of Christ and the Mother of God for 'Michael, prince of Bulgaria' (*Michaēl archonta Boulgarias*): Jurukova (1981), pp. 3–4, 5–6; Jurukova (1984), pp. 226–8; Jurukova (1985), p. 17. For Tervel's seal, see above, n. 8; for Omurtag's medallions, see Beševliev (1979), p. 234; Jurukova (1984), p. 226; Beševliev (1987), p. 62.

[77] Fortuitous as are the finds of such objects as seals, it is significant that at least eight examples of Boris' seals are known, whereas no lead, 'functional' seals of his ninth-century predecessors are known; equally significantly, most of Boris's seals have been found in the lower Danube area: Beševliev (1979), pp. 232–4; Jordanov (1984), pp. 89–90.

precautions in the form of the rebuilding of fortifications at their key naval base of Mesembria.[78] Photius in 886 tried to impress upon Boris the continuity of policy which Basil's sons and heirs would maintain, urging him to reciprocate their desire for concord; the word 'peace' (*eirene*) occurs four times in this relatively brief letter.[79] Photius' very preoccupation with this theme may well betray unease. The lengthy spell of peace between Byzantines and Bulgarians had owed much to the congruence of interests and policies between Boris and Basil I which had been expressed in the ecclesiastical arrangement of 870 of which, unfortunately, no textual evidence survives. The question remained open: would a new generation of Byzantine rulers willingly concede to their Bulgarian counterpart the fellowship, paternal solicitude and consideration which their rhetoric professed and which Christian teaching gave him the right to expect?

[78] Beševliev (1960), pp. 291–3; Venedikov (1969a), pp. 143–4; Venedikov (1969b), pp. 159–60; Velkov (1969), pp. 214–16; Oikonomides (1981, 1984–5), pp. 271–2; Soustal (1991), p. 356. The date of Byzantium's recovery of Mesembria is uncertain: this could have formed part of the arrangement between Basil and Boris in 870.

[79] Photius (1985) III, pp. 113–14, lines 36, 39, 43, 47.

CHAPTER 10

THE MUSLIMS IN EUROPE

Hugh Kennedy

THE MUSLIMS IN THE MEDITERRANEAN

THE confrontation and interaction between Muslin and Christian worlds spread throughout the Mediterranean from east to west. In the east, the conflict was essentially between the Islamic states, notably the Umayyads and ʿAbbasids in the eighth century and the ʿAbbasids and Tulunids in the ninth, on the one hand, and the Byzantines on the other. This conflict was played out on the long land frontier which ran roughly along the southeastern borders of the Anatolian plateau. It was also played out at sea where, by the beginning of the eighth century, the Muslims had shown themselves adept at naval warfare. The city of Constantinople was able to defend itself, but many of the coastlines and islands of the empire were subject to raids, and some islands, notably Crete, were occupied (Map 4). This struggle lies outside the scope of this volume (for further reading see the bibliography for this chapter). In the western half of the Mediterranean, however, the Muslims were able to establish sustainable states on the European shores and it is with these states that this chapter is concerned.

THE MUSLIMS IN SICILY AND SOUTHERN ITALY

Sicily, with its ancient Greek and Latin legacies, had long been a half-way house between two cultures. While in Gregory the Great's time, Latin influence, and especially ecclesiastical connections, remained strong, it seems that the seventh and eighth centuries saw the island becoming increasingly Greek in language, administration and religion. The loss of Syria and Egypt to the Muslims appears to have increased the importance of Sicily to Byzantium. In the eighth century, the island had no imperial pretensions, but it remained an integral part of the Byzantine empire, governed by the *strategos* of Syracuse.

Sicily was no more immune from Arab attacks than any other part of the Mediterranean coastline. The first raid was sent by the governor of Syria, Muʿāwiyah, later to be the first Umayyad caliph, in 642. In 667 a more extensive raid led to the capture of booty, some of which was forwarded to the caliph. In 693–4 the Muslims took Carthage and established their rule over the province they called Ifrīqiyyah (from the Latin Africa: essentially modern Tunisia) with its capital at Qayrawān. This meant that Sicily was now in the front line and the early seventh century saw numerous raids cross the straits. At first these were simply forays in search of booty but in 740 it seems that Ḥabīb b. Abī ʿUbayda was attempting an attack on Syracuse and a more permanent occupation.

The Arab assaults on Sicily were brought to a halt by the great Berber rebellion of 741. This resulted in a complete breakdown of Umayyad control in Africa and the absorption of Arab and Berber alike in internecine strife. The coming of the ʿAbbasids did not immediately put an end to this: Berbers, mostly giving their allegiance to the Kharijite sect of Islam, continued to dominate the province. In 761 a large army of mostly Khurasānī soldiers (Khurasānīs, from northeast Iran, formed the backbone of the early ʿAbbasid armies) was sent to Ifrīqiyyah under the command of Muḥammad b. al-Ashʿath al-Khuzāʿī. They eventually defeated the Berbers and re-established government in Qayrawān. Soon afterwards, however, the ʿAbbasid administration was challenged by the *jund*, the soldiers of the Khurasānī army; the governor was expelled and in 765 power was seized by the leaders of the military. Thereafter, while governors continued to be appointed from Baghdad, the *jund* exercised an effective veto over appointments since only they could protect Ifrīqiyyah from the Berber Kharijites, now usually confined to the Aurès mountains of modern Algeria and the Zāb to the south and west.

In 800 the power of the *jund* was formalised when Hārūn al-Rashīd accepted Ibrāhīm b. al-Aghlab, son of a Persian officer who had arrived in the province in 761, as governor. In practice, therefore, the caliph gave up his right to interfere in appointments. The pill was sweetened by the fact that the defence of Ifrīqiyyah had been a constant drain on central government finances, some 100,000 *dirham*s per year being forwarded from Egypt for this purpose. The governor Ibrāhīm actually agreed to send taxes east, though it is not clear that this was ever done. He attempted to consolidate his personal power by importing black slave soldiers as a private guard. This naturally alienated the *jund* who rebelled and were only pacified with difficulty. When Ibrāhīm died in 812, the Caliph al-Amīn was embroiled in a bitter civil war with his brother al-Maʾmūn. He was thus in no position to challenge the right of Ibrāhīm's son ʿAbd Allāh to succeed him. Similarly

ʿAbd Allāh's brother, Ziyādat Allāh, succeeded him in 817 without interference and the independence of the Aghlabid amirate from the ʿAbbasid caliphate was effectively established.[1] This did not, however, solve the problem of finding a role for the expensive and demanding *jund* at a time when Berber opposition was steadily declining. Sicily was rich, near and inviting.

Since the great Berber rebellion of 740, Muslim raids on Sicily had largely ceased. Ziyādat Allāh (817–38) was faced by continuous unrest among the *jund* but, according to the traditional story, it was an invitation from Sicily and the naval commander Euphemios which was the immediate cause of the first major expedition. In response Ziyādat Allāh decided to send an expedition and appointed Asad b. al-Furāt as its leader. Asad's background was similar to many members of the *jund*. He had been brought up in Tunis and had studied Islamic law in the east before being made *qāḍī*.

The history of the Muslim conquest of Sicily in the ninth century is largely based on much later Arabic chronicles, notably the compilations of Ibn al-Athīr (d. 1234) and Ibn Idhārī (fl. c. 1300). The only near-contemporary Sicilian source to have survived is the so-called Cambridge Chronicle.[2] It exists in both Arabic and Greek texts and covers the years 827 to 965. It is useful for establishing chronologies but is otherwise very brief and uninformative. Both Ibn al-Athīr and Ibn Idhārī are precise and careful about names and dates but are rather austere in their approach: there is little circumstantial detail or anecdote which we can use to reconstruct patterns of administrative or social life. Muslim Sicily, unlike Muslim Spain, never developed an intellectual milieu in which people collected and elaborated their early history. As Amari and, more recently, Ahmad[3] have found moreover, the material we have does not enable us to go much further than a bare narrative of the incidents of conquest.

In June 827 Asad led a force said to have consisted of 10,000 men of whom only 900 were horsemen. Contrary, perhaps, to the popular image, most Muslim armies before the mid-ninth century were composed largely of footsoldiers. In the first campaign, the Muslims took Mazara in the southwest. Syracuse, however, was stoutly defended by the governor. The next winter saw the Muslim army reduced by disease, and the death of Asad himself, who was replaced by one Muḥammad b. Abī'l-Jawārī. By March 829, the Muslims only held the bridgehead at Mazara and were under siege in the small fortress of Mineo in the southwest from the new Byzantine commander Theodotus.

The history of Muslim Sicily might have ended at this point but for the

---

[1] Kennedy (1981), pp. 187–95.   [2] Lagumina (1892).
[3] Amari (1933–9) I, pp. 368–677; Ahmad (1975), pp. 6–24.

arrival of reinforcements in the shape of a fleet from Spain led by a Berber chief Aṣbagh b. Wānsūs al-Hawwārī. After a year-long siege, the Muslim forces took Palermo at the beginning of September 831.

Thereafter the Muslims consolidated their power in the Val di Mazara and made a number of unsuccessful sorties against Castrogiovanni (Enna) and other Byzantine strongholds. The Aghlabid rulers of Ifrīqiyyah attempted to establish their control by appointing members of the ruling dynasty as amirs (governors). None of the family seems to have participated in the original invasion and their attempt to take over power aroused opposition which sometimes erupted in violence. Much of the hostility between *jund* and dynasty which characterised the politics of Ifrīqiyyah seems to have been transmitted to Sicily. In 832 Ziyādat Allāh appointed his cousin Muḥammad b. ʿAbd Allāh who remained governor until he was killed in a mutiny in 835. Ziyadatallāh sent al-Faḍl b. Yaʿqūb as a stop gap replacement, and in the few months he was in charge al-Faḍl led two expeditions against the Sicilian Christians. Although his power was short lived, al-Faḍl was the founder of a family which was to provide leaders of the Muslims of Sicily for the next three-quarters of a century. During most of this period, the internal politics of the Muslims of Sicily were dominated by the struggle between the Aghlabids of Qayrawān and the family of al-Faḍl b. Yaʿqūb and their Sicilian Muslim supporters to control the office of amir. This time, however, Ziyādat Allāh soon replaced al-Faḍl with the dead amir's brother Ibrāhīm who remained immovably in post in Palermo until his death sixteen years later in 851.

From 841 onwards the Muslims began to make further conquests in the Val di Noto and raided increasingly close to Syracuse and Catania. This phase culminated in the conquest of the powerful fortress at Castrogiovanni in January 859. After 842 the Muslims enjoyed the benefits of their alliance, begun in 837, with Naples which enabled them to conquer some of the northern coastal towns, including Messina. This left only the east coast and the Val Demone in Byzantine hands and even here the Muslims were able to raid the countryside almost at will. When Ibrāhīm b. ʿAbd Allāh died in 851, the Muslims of Sicily chose as his successor a soldier who had frequently led them on campaign, al-ʿAbbās b. al-Faḍl b. Yaʿqūb. This choice was then accepted by the Aghlabid Amir Muḥammad (841–56). The choice of a governor by the Muslim inhabitants of a province was rare in the Islamic world, although no doubt local opinion was sometimes taken into account. It is likely that the remote and precarious nature of these Muslim settlements encouraged the locals to take matters into their own hands. Al-ʿAbbās extended his power by constant campaigns and by appointing both his brother ʿAlī and his uncle al-Rabāḥ b. Yaʿqūb to military commands.

The fall of Castrogiovanni was by no means the end of Byzantine resistance. In response to the fall of the city, the Emperor Michael III (842–67) sent a fleet of 300 ships to encourage resistance. Although they were defeated by the Muslims, the period from 859 onwards saw bitter fighting in the east of the island. Final Muslim victory was also postponed by almost continuous conflict within the Muslim camp between the Aghlabids and local leaders from the family of al-Faḍl b. Yaʿqūb. In 878 Syracuse finally fell to the Muslims, half a century after they had first attacked it. Alone of all the military campaigns of the time, we have a contemporary description of this from the surviving letter of the monk Theodosius,[4] written while he was a captive in Palermo. He makes it clear that this was a very hard-fought siege, that the Arabs were skilful in the use of siege engines and that the defenders endured terrible hardships and maintained a stout defence.

Despite this success, civil strife among the Muslims continued. Aghlabid governors were constantly opposed by the *jund* and other Sicilian Muslims who were quite prepared to make alliances with local Christian leaders; local autonomy was a more pressing preoccupation than Holy War. In these circumstances little progress was made in the conquests and it was not until 902 that Taormina and the rest of the Val Demone were taken. In that year the Aghlabid Amir Ibrāhīm b. Aḥmad (875–902) resigned and, leaving his throne to his son, decided to devote himself to the Holy War. He thereupon succeeded in destroying the city and the last vestiges of Christian rule in the island.

The conquest took more than three-quarters of a century. During that time most of western Sicily was comparatively peaceful under Muslim rule. We must assume that some rudimentary administration was set up: certainly coins were minted and we hear of a *qāḍī*; a mosque is said to have been built in Castrogiovanni and we must suppose that there was one in Palermo. Our sources, however, give us very little indication of the extent of Muslim settlement or the development of governmental and fiscal structures and it would be rash to project later developments back to the ninth century. It is more likely that the Muslims remained a permanent raiding band based in Palermo, living off booty as much as from the collection of taxes or the cultivation of fields. Only in the next century did this predatory society begin to change and the beginnings of state organisation emerge.

The main arena for Arab raids was mainland southern Italy. Here the incessant rivalries between the Byzantine authorities in Apulia and Calabria, Lombard princes in Benevento and cities such as Naples meant that there were many opportunities for raiding. As in Sicily and Spain, the first Muslim

[4] See Lavagnini (1959–60), pp. 267–79.

intervention is said to have occurred when they acted as allies of one party in inter-Christian disputes. In this case they assisted Naples in 837 to preserve its independence from the advancing Lombard Prince Sicard of Benevento. Neither the Byzantines nor the Venetians could match them at sea. In 840 the Muslims established a permanent presence for the first time at Taranto and the next year they took Bari and Brindisi as allies of one Lombard prince against another, building up their power in a way curiously similar to that used by the Normans two centuries later.

Thereafter emphasis shifted from the Adriatic to the more accessible west coast. The most spectacular result of this was the attack on Rome in 846 when the Vatican was pillaged, though the city itself was saved. Both east and west coasts were subject to continuing attack and only the repeated efforts of the Emperor Louis II (d. 875), sometimes in alliance with the Byzantines, prevented the Muslims from occupying the whole of southern Italy. His efforts were partially successful when he reconquered Bari in 871 with naval support from the Byzantines. From the 870s the Byzantines began to dominate Apulia, the Adriatic was secured and the Muslims were eventually defeated at sea at Milazzo and driven out of Taranto in 880. The Byzantines meanwhile moved on to take most of Calabria over the next decade. On the west coast, however, the Muslims established a permanent raiding camp on the Garigliano river in the late 870s which they continued to use as a base until they were finally expelled in 915. Ironically the year of victory at Taormina in 902 also saw their final defeat in mainland Italy. From the end of the ninth century until the mid-eleventh Calabria and Apulia were under Byzantine hegemony and Sicily was under Muslim rule. The Muslims did occupy some Italian towns for considerable periods – Bari from 841 to 871 and Taranto from 840 to 880 – but they founded no sort of state. Like the early conquerors of Sicily and Spain, they sought to live off booty and when this dried up or became too dangerous, their raids ceased. It is not clear how closely they were connected with the Muslims of Sicily and it is likely that many of those who invaded the Adriatic coast were from Crete and other areas of the eastern Mediterranean. One Mufarraj b. Sallām, of unknown origin, proclaimed his independence at Bari. The west-coast Arabs were probably Sicilian. In 871 the Aghlabids seem to have tried to seize the initiative by appointing ʿAbd Allāh b. Yaʿqūb of the well-known Sicilian military family as governor of southern Italy. He was sent to Taranto but died soon after his arrival and there is no evidence that he was replaced. Despite the impermanence of their presence, there can be no doubt that the half-century of their raids had a major effect on the society of central and southern Italy, destroying Carolingian patterns and the wealth and independence of the papacy and forcing people to retreat to mountain strongholds: *incastallamento* (the concentration of the population in fortified hill-top sites) had begun.

THE MUSLIM WEST: THE CONQUEST AND ESTABLISHMENT OF AL-ANDALUS (711–912)

The earliest phases of Arabic historical literature from Muslim Spain, known as al-Andalus in the Arabic sources, are represented by *akhbār*, or individual anecdotes. These often seem to have been preserved orally to keep fresh the memory of great men and deeds. These *akhbār* offer detailed circumstantial accounts of particular instances but the collections usually lack any overall chronological or thematic structure. *Akhbār* literature is most clearly represented by two surviving texts. The anonymous early eleventh-century *Akhbār al-Majmūʿah* (Collected Anecdotes)[5] is arranged roughly chronologically with the latest, rather thin, material dating from the early tenth century. The second *akhbār* text is the *Taʾrīkh Iftitāḥ al-Andalus* (History of the Conquest of Spain)[6] which again takes the story down to the early tenth century. This vivid and gossipy collection is attributed to Ibn al-Qūṭiyyah (839–926). Originally from Seville he claimed descent from the Visigothic royal family (his name means 'son of the Gothic woman') but the work was compiled at the court of the Amir ʿAbd al-Raḥmān III (912–61) in Córdoba. Again there is a roughly chronological framework and Ibn al-Qūṭiyyah is especially interesting on the politics of the court under the early Umayyad amirs.

The arranging of this material more strictly into chronological order as *Taʾrīkh* or history was the achievement of the Rāzī family, Aḥmad b. Muḥammad (d. 955) and his son ʿIsa (d. 989) from Iran via North Africa. They brought with them an understanding of the historical techniques developed in the east by such writers as al-Madaʾini (d. 839). Their work does not survive in its original form but it is the basis for the surviving portions of the great history of Ibn Hayyan (d. 1076); all later compilers like Ibn Idhārī (*fl. c.* 1300) and al-Makkari (d. 1632) were ultimately dependent on it.

The reliability of this material is variable. There can be little doubt that the basic chronology developed by the Rāzīs was more or less correct. On the other hand some at least of the *akhbār* have been shown to be eastern Islamic stories attached to figures in Andalusi history. The material is not 'biased' in a pro-Muslim anti-Christian sense except that the unbelievers are treated to conventional curses and Muslim victories stressed; in general it is

---

[5] Anonymous (1867).   [6] Ibn al-Qūṭiyyah (1926).

not concerned with Muslim–Christian relations. The writings do, however, suffer from the fact that they represent a limited, Córdoban viewpoint of a restricted social group. Ibn al-Qūṭiyyah and Aḥmad al-Rāzī were both members of the court circle in the early days of ʿAbd al-Raḥmān III and they reflected the opinions and interests of the Umayyad house and the courtiers. Even when dealing with much earlier history, they tend to concentrate on the doings of the amirs and ancestors of their friends and colleagues.[7] With the exception of the historical geography of Aḥmad b. ʿUmar al-ʿUdhrī (d. 1085) of Almeria,[8] which deals with the Levante and the Ebro valley in some detail, no source gives a non-Córdoban perspective. This is especially misleading when trying to assess the effectiveness of the Umayyad amirs who are always treated as if they held sway over all of al-Andalus when in fact their power was confined to the capital and the south. Despite these limitations, however, the Arabic sources for the early history of al-Andalus are relatively full and reliable.

The Muslim conquest of the Iberian peninsula from 711 to 716 was a logical extension of the conquest of North Africa. Muslim troops had reached Tangier in 703 and it was natural that their leaders should look beyond the narrow straits of Gibraltar to the richer and more fertile lands of southern Spain. The conquest of North Africa had been a rolling process: as the Muslim armies moved west, they recruited Berbers to swell their numbers and these new converts were anxious to enjoy the material, as well as the spiritual, advantages of belonging to a conquering army. A continuous supply of booty was required to satisfy the troops and prevent its disintegration into warring factions.

The Iberian peninsula had been ruled from Toledo by Visigothic kings. In the early eighth century there was a succession crisis, as was all too common in Visigothic politics. When Witiza died in 710, Roderick, a member of the nobility, was elected to succeed him. His accession aroused widespread opposition. Arabic sources suggest that some important members of the nobility, including the sons of Witiza, actively encouraged the Muslims to invade, intending, no doubt, that the Muslims should defeat the new monarch and then return, or be sent back, across the straits. Thus in 711 Ṭāriq b. Ziyād, a Berber chief who had been made governor of Tangier, led the first Muslim invasion. The numbers involved are very difficult to estimate but Ṭāriq's army was probably no more than 7000, of whom the largest part were Berbers. They crossed the straits at Gibraltar and moved north, presumably heading for Seville. Roderick had been leading the Visigothic army against the Basques in the north of the country but, hearing

[7] See Manzano Moreno (1991), pp. 11–218.   [8] Ed. Al-Ahwani, (1965).

of the invasion, he hurried south to face it. Towards the end of July 711, a battle was fought in the extreme south of Spain near Medina Sidonia. Roderick's army was decisively defeated, the king himself being killed in the battle or shortly after. Ṭāriq followed up his victory with rapid conquests; Córdoba was taken after some resistance but his men encountered little opposition elsewhere in the south. He then pushed on to Toledo, which he found largely deserted. He was able to spend the winter of 711–12 in the old capital.

Ṭāriq's superior, Mūsā b. Nuṣayr, governor of Qayrawān, set out the next year with an army of perhaps 18,000, including a large number of Arabs, to ensure that he and his men received a share of the profits of conquest. He did not join Ṭāriq immediately but went first to Seville and then to Mérida, which fell after a brief siege in July 713. Only then did the two leaders meet and in spring 714 they launched an extensive campaign in the north, taking Zaragoza and the upper Ebro, León and Astorga. If they had hopes of permanent power in the land they had conquered, these were shattered when in September 714 they were both summoned by the Caliph al-Walīd (705–15) to Damascus and left, never to return.

Mūsā left his son ʿAbd al-ʿAzīz in charge. He continued the conquests. In his period of office (714–16), Santarem and Coimbra in the west, Pamplona in the north, Barcelona, Girona and Narbonne in the northeast all fell to Muslim commanders. ʿAbd al-ʿAzīz himself led an expedition to the Murcia area where he concluded an agreement with the local Visigothic commander, Theodemir, which allowed the Christians to retain their possessions and their religion in exchange for a modest tribute. By 716 virtually all the peninsula had been conquered by, or at least received an unopposed visit from, the Muslim troops. Leading men of the Visigothic state actively and rapidly sought incorporation into the new elite. The sons of Witiza retained a vast amount of their personal wealth and are found advising the Muslim governors. According to later tradition, the Banū Qāsī of the upper Ebro valley sprang from one Fortun, a Visigothic noble who embraced Islam in 714 when the Muslim armies first appeared. Only in the Asturias, where Pelayo led an embryo resistance movement, among the Basques who had never really accepted Visigothic control, and in the isolated valleys on the southern flanks of the Pyrenees, was there real opposition.

Muslim settlement was widely dispersed throughout the peninsula with the exception of the northern mountains. In general the centres of Arab settlement were the fertile river valleys of the Guadalquivir and the Ebro and cities like Córdoba, Seville and Zaragoza. Most of the Arabs who settled in Spain at this time came originally not from Bedouin backgrounds but

from the Yemen where their ancestors had always been farmers; they seem
to have adapted easily to the agricultural life. The Berbers, many of whom
were pastoralists and who may have crossed the straits with their flocks,
occupied the southern uplands and the central plateau of the Meseta (later,
of course, the centre of the great Castilian sheep-rearing economy). No
attempt seems to have been made to establish garrison cities like Kūfah and
Baṣra in Iraq or Fusṭāṭ in Egypt and the settlers mingled with the local
people without arousing great opposition. The settlement was largely
unplanned. That the settlers lived so close to the land from which they made
their living may have contributed to the fact that, in contrast to the Muslim
east, no elaborate bureaucratic structure emerged to collect taxes from the
conquered people and redistribute them as salaries.

The period from 714 to 741 saw a succession of governors ruling al-
Andalus from Córdoba, which became the capital from early on. They were
usually appointed by the governor of Qayrawān or by his superior, the
governor of Egypt; with few exceptions, they did not have local roots and
their spell of office was too short for them to build up any local power base.
Links with the Umayyad government in Damascus must always have been
tenuous and it is not clear that any revenue was exported from the new
province to the capital after the first wave of conquests. Conquest and
expansion remained very important. The governors led frequent raids, not
on the hard and poverty-stricken mountains of northern Spain but into
southern France. Their route was either up the Rhône valley reaching as far
as Langres and Sens in 725, or through Pamplona and Bordeaux. This last
was the route taken by ʿAbd al-Raḥmān al-Ghāfiqī in 732 when he led the ill-
fated expedition defeated by Charles Martel at the battle of Poitiers.[9]
Thereafter, large-scale raids were suspended.

Conquest and booty had been a major, possibly the major, source of
revenue for the government and an outlet for the energies of ambitious or
dissatisfied Muslims. When the chance of easy pickings dried up, competition for resources within al-Andalus and North Africa intensified and gave
rise to open civil war. The most dangerous of these was the great Berber
rebellion of 741 which spread throughout North Africa and Spain. The
Caliph Hishām sent a large army, mostly recruited in Syria and al-Jazīrah to
deal with it. They were defeated and a large body of them, perhaps 10,000,
led by Balj b. Bishr al-Qushayrī, was cut off by the Berbers in the western
Maghreb. Meanwhile the Arabs of al-Andalus were also faced by a Muslim
uprising in the central plateau which they were unable to put down.

---

[9] See Collins (1989), pp. 90–1 for further discussion of the date.

Desperate for help, they invited Balj's ragged and starving army across the straits to help them.

With these reinforcements, the Berbers were soon defeated but the problems for the Arab settlers were only beginning. Seeing the prosperity of the country and the wealth of the Arabs established there, the newly arrived Syrians, despite their original agreement, refused to leave; civil war developed again. For the next fifteen years there were continuous struggles between the original settlers (the *Baladiyūn*) and the Syrians (*Shāmiyūn*) and their Berber allies for control of the governorate. Soon after they had arrived, in an effort at compromise, the Syrians had been systematically settled in Andalucia. Each of the *ajnād* (sing: *jund*; essentially regiments recruited from the same district of Syria) were settled in different areas from Elvira (Granada) in the east to Sidonia in the west. In exchange for land they were obliged to perform military service when the amir requested. The establishment of these *ajnād* gave an important impetus to the Arabisation of southern Spain.

In the short term, civil strife remained acute and it was exacerbated by the hostility between the Qays-Mudar and Yemen parties. This conflict originated in Syria and Iraq where it had polarised the Arab tribes. By the time it reached Spain, its origins were as obscure and irrelevant as those of the Welf–Ghibelline dispute in late medieval Italy. The early Arab settlers mostly came from the Yemeni tribal bloc, from both Yemen and Syria, and there was no friction between them and the comparatively small number of Qaysis. Most of the Syrians, by contrast, came from the Qays group and brought with them memories of the bitter disputes then raging in their homelands. Both sides attempted to use tribal solidarity to win recruits in the other party. This led to confusions of alliance and rapidly shifting balances of power, compounded by events in the east where, between 747 and 750, the Umayyad caliphate was overthrown by the ʿAbbasids. There was now no outside authority to appoint governors. Nevertheless, it had become clear that control of Córdoba and the title of amir were the major prizes and the only possible means of political control. Secondly, no group was powerful enough to seize and retain this power on a stable basis.

It was into this scorpions' nest that the emissaries of ʿAbd al-Raḥmān b. Muʿāwiyah the Umayyad first arrived. By 756 the governor in Córdoba was Yūsuf b. ʿAbd al-Raḥmān al-Fihrī, a direct descendant of the famous ʿUqbah b. Nāfiʿ, hero of the Muslim conquest of North Africa. He was, despite his illustrious ancestor, aged and ineffective and the real power behind him was al-Ṣumayl b. Hātim al-Kilābī, a Syrian Qaysi of modest origins but of great determination and ruthlessness. Predictably there was widespread opposition from early settlers and Yemenis. ʿAbd al-Raḥmān b. Muʿāwiyah was the grandson of the last great Umayyad Caliph Hishām (724–43). He had escaped the massacre of most of his family by the ʿAbbasids, and by a series of hair-breadth escapes, graphically recounted in the Arab sources,[10] had made his way to North Africa where he took refuge with his mother's Berber relations. From this sanctuary he sent his trusted envoy Badr to al-Andalus to see if there were any political opportunities. Receiving favourable reports he arrived in person at Almuñecar on the south coast in August 755. From there he began to tour the southern uplands, recruiting supporters, mostly among the Yemenis and the Berbers, until he was strong enough to challenge the governor. In May 756 his forces defeated Yūsuf and al-Ṣumayl just outside Córdoba; he took the city and the palace and was proclaimed amir. His descendants were to rule there until 1031.

The fugitive scion of a dispossessed dynasty, ʿAbd al-Raḥmān had few obvious advantages. He was only twenty-six years old, had no experience of government and no significant financial resources, and neither he nor any member of his family had ever visited al-Andalus before. Apart from his own ability and longevity, however, ʿAbd al-Raḥmān did have a number of crucial political assets. His ancestors had been caliphs of the entire Muslim world; he himself came from the prestigious Prophet's tribe of Quraysh, and Qurashis were felt to be above and somewhat separate from the Qays/Yemen dispute, able to attract support from both sides. There was also the Syrian connection: the Umayyads had ruled the Islamic world from Syria with Syrian support and a large number of the Arabs in al-Andalus boasted Syrian origins. Many of these people had a tradition of loyalty to the Umayyad house and would have vigorously rejected the claims of the rival ʿAbbasid dynasty. ʿAbd al-Raḥmān, therefore, was the only leader who could appeal across and above tribal loyalties to a wide cross-section of Arab society in Spain.

Perhaps the most important asset he had, however, was a group of Umayyad *mawālī* on whose absolute loyalty he could count. The *mawālī* (sing. *mawlā*) were clients of Arab families. When members of conquered populations, whether Syrian, Aramaean, Greek, Persian or Berber, wished to convert to Islam and share the privileges of the ruling group, they attached themselves to an individual or family who became, so to speak, their godfather. Many of these were ex-prisoners of war or ex-slaves and, while they were now freemen, they had no tribal connections and owed their loyalty to their sponsors. Ṭāriq b. Ziyād, governor of Tangier and first

10 Anonymous (1867), pp. 46–56.

Muslim invader of Spain, and probably an important Berber chief in his own right, was one such *mawlā*. No family had more *mawālī* than the ruling Umayyads and many of them came from Syria with the Syrian troops of Balj or fled there after the ʿAbbasid revolution. They had little status or power in the tribal elites which fought for control in pre-Umayyad al-Andalus and were happy to offer their support to ʿAbd al-Raḥmān's messenger, himself a *mawlā*. After ʿAbd al-Raḥmān took power, more Umayyad *mawālī* continued to arrive from the east. Thus, alone of all the contenders for power, ʿAbd al-Raḥmān could count on the devotion of a coherent group of supporters whose loyalty extended beyond the bounds of tribal solidarity. These *mawālī* and their descendants, families like the Banū Shuhayd and the Banū Abī ʿAbda, were the backbone of the Umayyad state and provided generals and bureaucrats for the Umayyads for the next three centuries, as well as both authors and patrons for the golden age of Andalusi literature in the tenth and eleventh centuries.

ʿAbd al-Raḥmān b. Muʿāwiyah ruled as amir from 756 to 788. We have little beyond brief annals of his reign but it is clear that he faced a number of rivals for power, such as the Fihrīs, finally defeated in 785, and the ʿAbbasids. Soon after his accession, ʿAbd al-Raḥmān dropped the name of the ʿAbbasid caliph from the *khuṭbah* (the sermon in the mosque on Friday) and the last formal ties with the eastern caliphate were broken. The determined ʿAbbasid Caliph al-Manṣūr (754–75) tried to foment an insurrection in al-Andalus by subsidising an Arab chief from Beja, al-ʿAla b. Mughīth al-Yaḥṣubī, to raise a revolt in 763. The ʿAbbasids sent money and moral support but no troops and the attempt was defeated. The ʿAbbasids could not count on any significant body of support in al-Andalus, and after this setback they confined themselves to sending abusive letters.

By his death in October 788, ʿAbd al-Raḥmān had firmly established his status as amir and his control over much of Córdoba and the south. He had built a palace near the city and begun the first stage of the great mosque, parts of which can still be seen today. He had established a rudimentary administration which differed somewhat from eastern models: rather than the *wazīr* (vizier) being the main official, this role was filled in al-Andalus by the *ḥājib* (chamberlain) who was both a civil and military commander, assisted by about half a dozen *wazīr*s. As far as we can tell, almost all his *wazīr*s and military commanders were members of the Umayyad family or *mawālī*: Arab chiefs were almost entirely excluded from positions of power.

ʿAbd al-Raḥmān was far from being an absolute ruler of al-Andalus. The amir's authority did not extend to Mérida, Toledo or Zaragoza and the Ebro valley, where occasional punitive raids were the only sign of Umayyad authority. The Berber tribes of the Meseta were kept in check in the same way. He also had to contend with Christian pressures on the frontier (see below).

ʿAbd al-Raḥmān died without naming a successor. The Umayyad family had a strong hereditary tradition and there could be no doubt that one of his sons should succeed him, but in a political culture which did not believe in primogeniture, it was difficult to know which one it was to be. The dispute soon developed into open warfare between the eldest son Sulaymān and his younger brother Hishām. Sulaymān seems to have appealed to the Berber and Arab tribal constituencies who had supported the Fihrīs. Hishām had the backing of the *mawālī* and probably the other members of the Umayyad family. Sulaymān was defeated near Jaen and retreated to Toledo whence he was forced to leave for North Africa, albeit with a large pension.

The chronicle tradition[11] gives the next two amirs, Hishām I (788–96) and al-Ḥakam I (796–822) distinctive characters, Hishām modest and pious, al-Ḥakam, choleric and violent, fond of poetry and wine. The evidence for their reigns amounts to little more than brief annals interspersed with anecdotes more picturesque than reliable. It does seem, however, that Hishām's reign saw the arrival in al-Andalus of the Mālikī school of Islamic law. Mālik b. Anas himself died in Madīnah in 795 and his writings bequeathed to the Islamic world a system of law based on the practice of Madīnah, clear and concise but somewhat rigid and restricting. As a result there was little academic debate of legal issues but it did mean that al-Andalus was spared the often violent disputes which disturbed the eastern Islamic world in the ninth and tenth centuries. It also gave great status and prestige to the *qāḍī*s who interpreted and taught the law. Almost all *qāḍī*s claimed Arab descent, were practically an hereditary profession, and were recruited from different groups than were the bureaucrats or military men. Throughout the Umayyad period, the Amīrs seem to have retained the right to appoint *qāḍī*s in the whole of al-Andalus, even in towns like Zaragoza and Toledo where amirs seldom enjoyed any other political powers. Many of these *qāḍī*s were educated in Córdoba. This system may well have encouraged a sense of religious and cultural unity which would otherwise have been lacking.

Before he died in 796, Hishām was careful to designate his son al-Ḥakam as his heir. Nevertheless al-Ḥakam's rights were challenged by his uncle Sulaymān, who was not finally captured and executed until 800. Sulaymān's younger brother ʿAbd Allāh went to Aachen with the intention of seeking Carolingian support against his nephew but returned empty handed. In the

---

[11] Ibn Idhari (1948–51) II, pp. 65–6, 78–80.

end ʿAbd Allāh established himself in the Valencia region where he was given what amounted to an independent appanage. His arrival here inaugurated a new wave of Muslim naval activity in the western Mediterranean. In 798 ʿAbd Allāh's Berber followers launched a major raid on the Balearic Islands and this was followed by a series of raids between 805 and 813 on Corsica and Sardinia. Carolingian sources also mention attacks on Nice and Civitavecchia. The marked lull after 813 coincides with the appearance of the Andalusian pirates who took over Alexandria in 815–16.

Al-Ḥakam's reign was marked by two major insurrections in Córdoba itself. These revolts were supported both by members of the elite and by ordinary Muslims. The underlying motive was, apparently, resentment at al-Ḥakam's employment of professional soldiers. Rather than rely on the *ajnād*, he built up a guard of slave-soldiers, *ʿabīd*, commanded by a Christian officer, al-Rabīʿ. It is likely that, instead of being asked to do military service, the members of the *ajnād* were required to pay taxes to support this new army. No doubt al-Ḥakam saw this development as an essential stage in the construction of a stable regime but inevitably it aroused fear and hostility among many Arabs who felt that they were being excluded from power and saw the amir's actions as heavy handed and dictatorial.

The first outbreak came in 805 and in 818 there was a mass uprising in Secunda, the suburb of Córdoba which lay to the south of the river. The rebels attempted to cross and take the town but were defeated by loyal troops led by the *ḥājib*, ʿAbd Allāh b. al-Mughīth and members of the Umayyad family. The amir's vengeance was terrible. He ordered mass executions, and that the suburb be razed to the ground and any surviving inhabitants sent into exile.

After this there was no more open opposition to the Umayyads in the city. Indeed, the loyalty of Córdoba to the dynasty was a striking feature of the Umayyad state right down to the abolition of the caliphate in 1031. The amir, moreover, now had the power to push ahead with building a standing army and a bureaucratic apparatus, not to speak of a large and luxurious court, without effective opposition from the Muslim Arab leaders, many of whose families had been in al-Andalus much longer than the Umayyads. Many of the exiles went to Morocco where they settled near the newly established colony of people from Qayrawān (Qarawiyīn) at Fes. Here, on the opposite side of the river, they established their own quarter of the Andalusiyīn. Some went further afield and sailed to the east, where they occupied first Alexandria, and then Crete which they won from the Byzantines in 826. Crete remained a Muslim possession until 961.

The development of an apparatus of government begun under al-Ḥakam was extended by his son ʿAbd al-Raḥmān II (822–52). His accession was itself an indication of the enhanced status of the amirate. During his father's last illness, the leading members of the court swore the oath of allegiance (*bayʿah*) to him. When al-Ḥakam died, ʿAbd al-Raḥmān sent his brother al-Mughīrah to receive in public in the mosque in Córdoba the oaths of the leading Cordobans. This formal installation ceremony was based on the one used by ʿAbbasid caliphs in Baghdad. It is evidence both of the aspirations of the new amir and of his reliance on eastern models.

The new amir began to recruit supporters from many quarters. The old *mawālī* families continued to be important, ʿIsā b. Shuhayd, for example, was made a *wazīr* and then *ḥājib*, but there were new sources of recruits as well. ʿAbd al-Raḥmān rejected his father's policy of employing Christian guards. Two of his first acts were to execute al-Rabīʿ, head of the guard, and to close down the wine market in Córdoba. Instead of turning to local Arabs to replace the Christian guards, ʿAbd al-Raḥman engaged two Berber princes from the ruling dynasty of Tahert in North Africa, ʿAbd al-Raḥmān and Muḥammad b. Rustam, as military commanders presumably with their followers. Towards the end of the reign, ʿAbd al-Raḥmān increasingly relied on Naṣr, a eunuch of unknown origin; the growing importance of eunuchs was another sign of the increasing eastern Islamic influence at the Umayyad court. Both Berber princes and eunuchs, often of northern European origin, had the advantages of being without local contacts and were completely reliant on the ruler.

The recruitment of this new military, not to speak of an increasingly elaborate and luxurious court, complete with *ḥarīm* and poets recruited from the Islamic east, necessitated a fiscal system to support it. We have virtually no information about taxation from the time of the early amirs and it seems likely that, with the Muslims dispersed and living off the land, only the most rudimentary fiscal structures were required. Poll-tax (*jizyah*) paid by Christians and Jews probably formed an important part of the amir's income. From the time of al-Ḥakam we have details of a more developed system. It appears that a major source of income was payment, presumably by the *jund*, to be excused military service, a sort of scutage, as well as general, unspecified taxes and dues for the right to fly falcons; none of these taxes has parallels in eastern Islamic fiscal practice. There is mention of substantial quantities of goods in kind, wheat and barley, but the bulk of the income was raised in, or at least accounted in, gold *dīnār*s. In one recorded assessment, Córdoba provided 142,000, Seville 35,000. Sidonia, 50,600, Moron, 21,000 and Niebla in the far west, 15,600 *dīnār*s. Córdoba and its district thus provided more than all the other areas put together and only the southern areas where the Syrian *ajnād* were settled made contributions. It may be that the fragmentary record leaves out important areas but it is more likely that this reflects the heavy reliance of the Umayyads on the Guadalquivir valley and areas to the west and south for their income. The gross income of the amirate is said to have increased from 600,000 *dīnār*s under al-Ḥakam to 1,000,000 under ʿAbd al-Raḥmān II. It was the latter who appointed treasurers (*khuzzān*) as specifically financial officials.

With new military and fiscal resources to support him, ʿAbd al-Raḥmān II made a determined effort to assert Umayyad rule over the whole of Muslim Spain. While the authority of Córdoba may have been more or less effective in the south, it did not extend to the three areas known as the Marches (*thughūr*), namely the Lower March in the west based on Mérida, the Middle March based on Toledo in the centre and the Upper March based on Zaragoza and the Ebro valley in the north and northeast. Each of these had different characteristics.

Apart from the old Roman centre at Mérida itself, the Lower March was largely pastoral country, with villages and castles few and far between. Not many Arabs had settled in these harsh, wide-open landscapes, and the Muslim population were largely Berbers or *muwallad*s, that is, native Spanish converts. The Berbers lived a pastoral life and tribal structures and tribal leaders remained powerful among them throughout the early middle ages. The *muwallad*s, on the other hand, were probably the inhabitants of the villages and river valley settlements. It was very difficult country to control and the early amirs could do little more than make alliances with the most powerful chiefs in the area. Only after 828 did ʿAbd al-Raḥmān II assert the power of Córdoba by sending a governor and a garrison to Mérida and building a citadel, dated by inscription to 835,[12] whose walls still survive above the Guadiana river. Despite this show of strength, it is doubtful that Umayyad authority extended much beyond the city itself.

The situation in the Middle March was very similar. Toledo itself, more than any other city in al-Andalus, was dominated by *muwallad*s who formed the elite of the city and frequently asserted their independence. To the east and south lay the upland plains of the central Meseta rising in the east to the desolate slopes of the Montes Universales and the Sierra de Cuenca. These were Berber lands where direct rule from Córdoba was virtually impossible and where a fragile peace depended on diplomacy and punitive raids. Toledo itself had a vigorous tradition of political independence but the sources are too fragmentary for us to know how the government of the city was organised. There is some indication that al-Ḥakam attempted to use a *muwallad* ally of his, ʿAmrūs b. Yūsuf, to govern the city. It was not until the 830s that real control was established and then only as a response to the

---

12 Lévi-Provençal (1932), nos. 39, 40, pp. 50–1; Creswell (1940), pp. 197–205.

aggression of the Toledans. In 836–7 the city was finally occupied by Umayyad troops and, as at Mérida, a governor was installed and a citadel was constructed on the site of the present, much rebuilt, Alcazar.

Although the Murcia area was not technically part of the Marches, it too was outside the scope of Umayyad power. The agreement with Theodemir seems to have broken down by the early ninth century, if not before, and many Arabs settled in the district. At the beginning of ʿAbd al-Raḥmān's reign, this was the scene of the last major outbreak of Qays–Yemen conflict in al-Andalus. Typically, ʿAbd al-Raḥmān combined diplomacy with force to bring this bloody civil war to an end in 828–9. After the Umayyad forces were victorious, the dominant Yemeni leader, Abū'l-Shammākh Muḥammad b. Ibrāhīm, was given a military command in the amir's forces (one of the few Arabs to be so honoured). Further, a new fortress and administrative centre was founded in 831 at Murcia; it became the seat of government and the most important city in the area.

The history of the Upper March in the Ebro valley is complex. The city of Zaragoza itself was dominated by Arabs, mostly of Yemeni origin, but the other cities and much of the country were ruled by powerful *muwallad* families, the Banū Qāsī of Tudela and the upper Ebro area and ʿAmrūs b. Yūsuf and his family in Huesca. Al-Ḥakam had used his alliance with ʿAmrūs to try to exert some influence in the region but after his death in 812 the Banū Qāsī under Mūsā b. Mūsā became the dominant force. Not only were they powerful in their own lands around Tudela but they also had close relations with the Basque kings of Pamplona into whose family they had married. In addition, it is possible that they recruited Basque soldiers for their forces. Mūsā b. Mūsā generally remained on good terms with ʿAbd al-Raḥmān II and in 844 Mūsā gave ʿAbd al-Raḥmān valuable military support against the Vikings who had attacked Seville. Nevertheless he continued to act as an independent power and called himself the 'third king of Spain'.[13] The city of Zaragoza itself was conquered by the amir in 844 and entrusted to his son Muḥammad. By the end of ʿAbd al-Raḥmān's reign, Murcia, Zaragoza, Toledo and Mérida all had Umayyad governors, usually members of *mawālī* families and garrisons. Events after ʿAbd al-Raḥmān's death in 852 were to show how precarious this assertion of central control was.

Beyond the Marches lay the Christian lands (below, pp. 272–89). The frontier fell into two distinct sectors, west and east. In the west, roughly from the headwaters of the Duero to the Atlantic, the Muslims had briefly occupied outposts as far north as Galicia and Oviedo. The occupation must have been very transitory and the Berber revolt in 741 (most of the Muslims

---

[13] *Chronicle of Alfonso III*, cap. 25.

in this area were Berbers) and the famines of the 750s, when many Berbers returned to North Africa, led to the abandonment of this area. From this point the northern boundary of Muslim settlement was marked by the Cordillera Central, and Coimbra, Coria, Talavera, Toledo and Madinaceli were the frontier towns. North of the mountains lay the plains of the Duero, a vast no-man's land with little if any permanent settlement, which only ended at the southern Christian outposts like León and Astorga. The western sector of the frontier region changed little between 750 and 912, the only difference being the slow advance of Christian settlement into the no-man's land.

The frontier in the Ebro valley was a very different matter. Here there were no empty spaces and Christians and Muslims fought to control the towns and fertile plains. The rise of Carolingian power led to a gradual but sustained Christian advance, aided by the willingness of dissident Muslims in the provinces to appeal for Christian help against their Muslim neighbours. In 798 Pamplona fell and the nucleus of the Basque Kingdom of Navarre was established. Girona was taken in 785 and Barcelona in 801; both were later incorporated into the Spanish March of the Carolingian empire. The plains of the Ebro valley remained in Muslim hands and attempts to take Zaragoza (by Charlemagne in 778) and Tortosa (by Louis the Pious between 804 and 809) were unsuccessful.

The Muslims regularly took the offensive against the Christians in raids known as *ṣawā'if* (sing. *ṣā'ifah*). They were directed at all points of the Christian-held lands. Galicia, the Asturias and Pamplona were regularly attacked, but the lands of the Alava and Old Castile were the most common objectives. These raids do not seem to have been an attempt to conquer Christian territory. When the Muslims did capture a city, such as León in 846, they simply made breaches in the walls and abandoned it. It is a significant contrast with Christian advances; when the Christians took a town like Girona or Barcelona they installed a garrison and fortified it and the Muslims never regained it. León, in contrast, was resettled by the Christians as soon as the Muslim armies were out of sight.

The purpose of these raids was to assert the power and status of the amir and his family by demonstrating that they were leaders of the Muslims against the infidel. They had the added advantages of bringing in booty, though this was unlikely to have been vast, and enabling the amir to make contact with magnates of the outlying parts of al-Andalus. Yet the raids never threatened the existence of the Christian states.

The Christian community in Al-Andalus was not, so far as we can tell, actively persecuted by the Umayyad authorities. Christians had to pay the *jizyah*, there were restrictions on processions and the use of church bells, and they played a much smaller part in administration than their co-religionists in, say, Fatimid Egypt. Nonetheless, an ecclesiastical hierarchy of sorts seems to have been maintained and some monasteries existed. The bulk of the Christian population began to take on the language and dress of their Muslim masters, being referred to as Mozarabs (from an Arabic word meaning 'one who seeks to become an Arab'). It was possibly in protest against this easy acceptance that a group of Christians, led by the priest Elogius and centred on the small monastery of Tabanos outside Córdoba, began to seek a confrontation with the Muslim state. They did this by publicly insulting the Prophet and encouraging converts to Islam to apostasise: both crimes, as they knew well, were punishable by death under Islamic law. After all attempts to make them recant had failed, thirteen were executed before Elogius left for the Christian north. In 853 he returned and the martyrdoms resumed and there were fourteen more executions until in 859 Elogius himself, now bishop of Córdoba, was executed and the movement came to an end. Attempts to portray this as a proto-nationalist movement have not been convincing. It seems more probable that this self-sacrifice was a product of the intense devotion and cult of martyrdom in the small group which gathered round the charismatic figure of Elogius.[14]

ʿAbd al-Raḥmān II died in 852 and was succeeded by his son Muḥammad, who seems to have been a capable if unexceptional ruler. He continued at first in the tradition of his father, but power gradually slipped out of his hands. Personal failings aside, the major underlying problem came, ironically, from the very success of Islam. The circumstantial evidence suggests that the second half of the ninth century was a period of very rapid conversion to Islam,[15] with large numbers, rather than a few elite individuals like the Banū Qāsī of earlier generations, converting. The likelihood is that this happened most rapidly in the areas where Muslim settlement had been densest, that is, in the area of the Guadalquivir valley and the southern mountains. The new converts sought to participate in the political life of the Muslim community they had just joined and they supported leaders like Ibn Marwān al-Jillīqī and Ibn Ḥafṣūn who attempted to secure places in the military elite for themselves and their followers. This in turn aroused the resentment of the older established military elements, the mawālī, Arabs and Berbers, who found a leader in Hāshim b. ʿAbd al-ʿAzīz, and led to both Ibn Marwān and Ibn Ḥafṣūn being obliged to leave Córdoba for their homelands whence they defied the government.

This change also undermined the fiscal basis of the government. The jizyah (poll-tax) was an important source of revenue and clearly the more

---

[14] For the best recent discussion see Wolf (1988).   [15] Bulliet (1979), pp. 114–27.

people who converted to Islam and were consequently exempt from the *jizyah*, the less money was collected. The new converts, moreover, now enjoyed a more favourable tax position than members of the *jund* who were obliged to pay the *ḥashd* as a substitute for military service. It was probably pressure from them which persuaded Muḥammad to abolish their obligation to military service, thus freeing them from this tax burden. In times of famine in 865–8 and 873–4 further fiscal problems arose when the collection of the *ʿushūr* (the tithes all Muslims are required to pay) had to be abandoned.

The Umayyad government in consequence became increasingly weak and impoverished. It was not long before the separatist tendencies, superficially restrained in the final years of ʿAbd al-Raḥmān II's reign, manifested themselves once more. In Mérida and the Lower March the initiative was taken by ʿAbd al-Raḥmān b. Marwān al-Jillīqī, son of the *muwallad* leader who had dominated the area in the early years of the ninth century. He was persuaded to come to Córdoba and given an honoured position at court. In 875, however, he was driven out by the hostility of Hāshim b. ʿAbd al-ʿAzīz. He returned to the Lower March. Here from his newly developed centre at Badajoz ʿAbd al-Raḥmān b. Marwān al-Jillīqī and his family ruled what was essentially an independent state. The Toledans were actively aggressive and the amir was again obliged to fortify Calatrava to block their access to the south. In 854 the amir won a notable victory over them and their Asturian allies but the city was not really brought back under Umayyad control. The eventual agreement in 873 allowed a large measure of autonomy to the city including the right of the people to choose their own governor. Muḥammad's only effective response was to seek an alliance with the Berber chiefs of the areas east and south of the city who were as hostile to the *muwallad* Toledans as he was. It was in this way that Muḥammad first built up the power of the Banū Zannūn (Arabised to Banū' l-Dhū' l-Nūn) who were to dominate the area in the tenth century and took over Toledo itself in the eleventh. Zaragoza and the Upper March escaped Córdoban control as early as 856 when Mūsā b. Mūsā b. Qāsī asserted his independence again. With one brief interval, the Banū Qāsī asserted their independent control over the city and the Ebro area and were effectively independent monarchs until driven out of the city by the rival Arab Tujībī family in 890. After this, the power of the Banū Qāsī was confined to the Tudela region whence they had sprung and was finally eclipsed in the first decade of the tenth century by the Tujībīs and other local dynasts.

The loss of power in the Marches was a blow to prestige but it did not challenge Umayyad power in the southern heartlands. The rebellion of Ibn Ḥafṣūn was much more dangerous in this respect. Ibn Ḥafṣūn was a *muwallad* landowner of some means with estates in the mountains to the east of Ronda, who gradually acquired a considerable following among *muwallad*s and Mozarabs alike, and a permanent base at the mountain stronghold of Bobastro. In 883 Hāshim b. ʿAbd al-ʿAzīz led a military expedition against Ibn Ḥafṣūn and he agreed to come to Córdoba where he was given a military command and joined the *ṣāʾifah* against Alava. Despite this demonstration of loyalty, Ibn Ḥafṣūn was not accepted by the Cordoban elite. After a quarrel with the governor of the city, he retreated to his mountain fastness and began a revolt which soon spread throughout the southern mountains. Not only was this area now outside Umayyad control but the power of this *muwallad* had the effect or rousing Arab notables, especially in the Elvira (Granada) area, to protect themselves against him by building castles and raising their own war-bands.

By Muḥammad's death in 886 the disintegration of the amirate was far advanced. It was only in the Guadalquivir valley and the area immediately around the city itself that the Umayyad amir had any real power but he lacked the resources to expand it significantly. Elsewhere local political forces had taken over.

Muḥammad was succeeded for two years by his able son al-Mundhir, who, although he made a determined effort to reduce Bobastro and put an end to the power of Ibn Ḥafṣūn, died in mysterious circumstances while on campaign. In 888 he was succeeded by his brother ʿAbd Allāh, whose reign marks the nadir of Cordoban power. The new amir seems to have been indolent, possibly clinically depressed, and capable of taking little initiative apart from occasional bursts of murderous cruelty against members of his family, including his own sons. He seldom left Córdoba, except to go on hunting expeditions in the immediate vicinity, and made little effort to restore the fortunes of the amirate.

In addition, areas which had not hitherto shown signs of separatist tendencies began to go their own way. The province of Elvira (Granada) was torn apart by fierce hostility between Arabs and *muwallad*s and the latter, having appealed in vain to the amir for protection, threw in their lot with Ibn Ḥafṣūn. In the city of Seville, probably the largest in al-Andalus after Córdoba itself, there was a vicious feud between Arab patrician families (the Banū Ḥajjāj and the Banū Khaldūn) and those of *muwallad* origin (Banū Angelino and Banū Savarico) which finally left Ibrāhīm b. al-Ḥajjāj as ruler of an independent city-state.

ʿAbd Allāh remained as amir until his death in 912. The Umayyad amirate survived less because of his abilities than because of the divisions amongst its enemies, more intent on fighting each other than attacking Córdoba. No rival magnate attempted to take the title of amir or to capture the capital city and many, like the *muwallad*s in both Elvira and Seville, looked to the Umayyads for support against their local rivals. The conflicts were the expression of widespread social and ethnic tensions rather than a determination to end Umayyad rule. The amir was still able to count on the loyalty of the people of Córdoba and despite his poverty he never seems to have increased the taxes on them. He could rely also on the support of the *mawālī* families who had always been the mainstay of the dynasty; both the Banū Shuhayd and the Banū Abī ʿAbda figured prominently in his rudimentary administration. He maintained an army of sorts. In the absence of tax revenues, this army existed mostly by plundering neighbouring areas which had rejected the amir's authority, setting out at harvest time and returning with supplies or with cash given to them to induce them to go away. It was left to ʿAbd Allāh's grandson, who became amir as ʿAbd al-Raḥmān III on ʿAbd Allāh's death in 912, to create on this modest foundation what was to be the most powerful state in tenth-century western Europe.

SPAIN: THE NORTHERN KINGDOMS AND THE BASQUES, 711–910

Roger Collins

THE KINGDOM OF THE ASTURIAS, 718–910

THE disintegration of the unitary Visigothic kingdom in the Iberian peninsula in the years 710–12, as a consequence of civil war and military defeat at the hands of the invading Arab armies, was both sudden and unforeseen. The actual course of events cannot easily be recovered, owing to the limitations of the extant sources. Arab texts, upon which historians have placed the greatest reliance, are in no case datable to any period earlier than the late tenth century, and even ones that may have originated then are only transmitted in fragmentary form in later works, or show serious indications of interpolation. This and similar evidential problems, together with the inevitable growth of ideologically slanted interpretations of the key episodes, makes it very difficult to assess the immediate consequences of the collapse of the Visigothic kingdom, not least the emergence *c.* 720 in the north of the peninsula of a minute but independent Christian kingdom in the Asturias (Map 17). That this was the product of the northwards flight of refugees from the other regions of the former Visigothic realm is highly unlikely, as the Arab conquerors made treaties with the regional authorities, the Visigothic counts in most cases, that guaranteed local autonomy in matters of law, administration and religion in return for the payment of fixed capitation and other taxes. For the first half-century or so of Arab domination in Spain local conditions were probably very little affected by changes in central authority. One effect of this was to limit the perspectives of the Latin historiography of this period. Thus the author of the only substantial contemporary Latin chronicle written in the peninsula, probably in Toledo *c.* 754, records nothing of the events that led to the creation of the Asturian monarchy. For that, reliance has to be placed exclusively on the indigenous historiographical tradition of the kingdom, and this presents its own particular problems.[1]

[1] Collins (1989b), pp. 23–36.

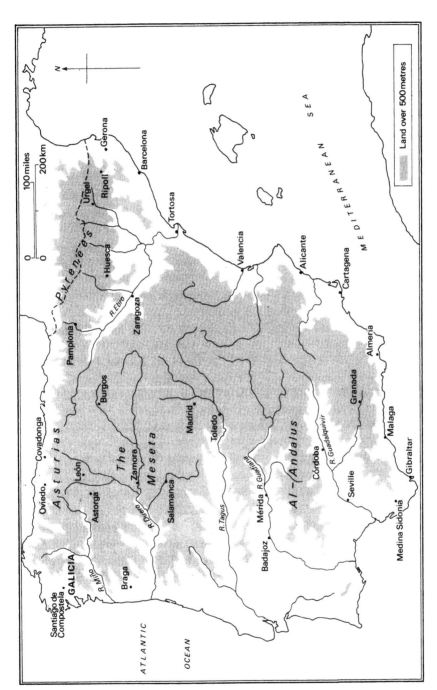

Map 17 The Iberian peninsula, 700–900

Any political narrative derives from the two brief chronicles initially written in the 880s. The first of these, the *Chronicle of Albelda*, was composed in 883/4, and received a brief continuation in the Riojan monastery of Albelda around the year 976. The second Asturian chronicle, known from the presumed author of its original version as the *Chronicle of Alfonso III*, was probably composed at the Asturian court, but now survives only in two slightly later recensions, completed in the reigns of Alfonso's sons García (910–913/14) and Ordoño II (913/14–924), the first kings of León. Considerable uncertainty exists as to how much, if any, of the original text may be the work of Alfonso III (866–910), and as to the identity of the compilers of the two extant recensions. It has been suggested that the original core text may be no more than the section concerning the reign of Alfonso's father Ordoño I (850–66).[2] In all respects, though, it is clear that the only available historiographical perspective on the 200-year history of the Asturian kingdom is one that comes from a very late period in its existence and is strongly influenced by the ideological perspectives and political conditions of that time. Attempts to argue that the initial sections of the chronicles depend on a lost earlier text, perhaps dating to the reign of Alfonso II (791–842), have not attracted much support.[3]

The outline narrative that may be derived from the Asturian chronicles can be supplemented on occasion by the works of Arab historians. These refer primarily to military and diplomatic encounters, and can make entirely contradictory statements as to their outcome in comparison with those of the Asturian chronicles. By and large, however, such Arab sources are of relatively late date, the earliest extant being fragments of a compilation made in the last quarter of the eleventh century. Although they give greater grounds for confidence in the validity of their information bearing on the ninth century, especially the later part, their veracity can be seriously impugned in respect of the eighth. More exactly contemporary information can be expected from the small corpus of charters that survives from the Asturian kingdom.[4] The earliest of these documents dates to 775, but it is one of the few of the eighth-century texts that has not been suspected of being forged or severely interpolated. The problems of authenticity improve as far as the charters of the second half of the ninth century are concerned, but their testimony is still very restricted in what it can offer. Largely, such texts record the making of sales and exchanges of land, or the foundations of monasteries. Very few of them are royal documents, and little evidence survives for the practical functioning of the administration of the Asturian kings.

---

[2] Gil, Moralejo and Ruiz de la Peña (1985), pp. 88–105.
[3] Sánchez-Albornoz (1967), pp. 111–60. [4] Floriano (1949/51).

Problems of evidence and its interpretation are probably most concentrated in the materials relating to the foundation of the kingdom and the reign of its first monarch, Pelagius (718/22–737). His successful revolt against the authority of the recently installed Arab governors of Spain marked both the creation of the independent kingdom and the establishment of its ruling dynasty. Hence, it is not surprising to find considerable contradiction in the sources, and that their narratives of the events are quite disproportionate to the scale of the treatment afforded other, subsequent episodes in Asturian history. Pelagius' origins and the reasons for his taking refuge in the Asturias are differently explained in each of the chronicles. By the time of the revisions of the Alfonsine chronicle the royal court had moved south to León, and there was less reason to make the dynastic founder a primarily Asturian leader. Similarly, the second version of that of Alfonso III, which is known either from the dedicatory letter at the head of it as the *Ad Sebastianum* (Bishop Sebastian of Orense), or from its more literary character as the 'erudite' recension, claims that Pelagius was a member of an unspecified Visigothic royal family. This is typical of the way that the Asturian and Leonese kings from the ninth century onwards tried to present themselves as the natural heirs to the Visigothic kingdom that had embraced the whole Iberian peninsula.

Pelagius' revolt, which is normally dated on the basis of ninth-century king-lists to 718, is variously presented as being motivated by the desire to restore liberty to the Christians living in the Asturias or the need to defend the honour of his sister from the advances of the Arab governor of León or Gijón. Although this Arab governor features as the leader of the Arab forces in all of the chronicles, a role of greater infamy is ascribed to a Bishop Oppa, who is erroneously presented as being a son of the former Visigothic king Witiza, and whose see is said to be Toledo and Seville by the *Rotensis* and 'erudite' versions respectively.[5] In both texts of the *Chronicle of Alfonso III* this Oppa, who has accompanied the Arab army sent to crush Pelagius, engages in a lengthy dialogue with the rebel leader prior to the battle on 'Mount Auseva', later known as Covadonga, in which the Asturian forces would emerge triumphant. It has been suggested that this, clearly fictional, exchange has been taken from an otherwise lost oral epic.[6] Other legendary accretions relating to the battle of Covadonga include the miraculous swallowing up by the mountain of 63,000 of the Arab and Berber troops.

Despite the obviously tendentious and contradictory nature of the accounts of the revolt and of the defeat of an Arab punitive expedition, it is

---

[5] Collins (1989), pp. 145–9 shows the impossibility of this claim.
[6] Sánchez-Albornoz (1967), pp. 161–202.

clear that the rising led by Pelagius in the eastern Asturias did lead to the establishment of a tiny independent kingdom in that region. Further Arab and Berber attempts to suppress it were not forthcoming, largely because the governors of al-Andalus had little interest in maintaining their authority in the remote northern mountain regions of the peninsula.[7] This was accentuated by the period of Berber revolts and conflicts between Arab factions that affected all of southern Spain and North Africa in the 730s and 740s.[8] The seizure of power in Córdoba by the Umayyad ʿAbd al-Raḥmān I (756–88) in 756 further protected the nascent Christian kingdom, in that it took him over twenty years to impose his authority effectively over the southern and central regions of the peninsula and over the Ebro valley. Thus, it was not until the last decade of the eighth century that serious military conflict ensued between the Asturian kingdom and the Umayyad amirate of Córdoba.

The intervening years had been spent very effectively by the Asturian kings in enlarging their realm, largely at the expense of their fellow Christian inhabitants of the northern mountains and the Meseta. Inevitably, in the ideologically charged perspective of the late ninth- and early tenth-century chronicles the process of aggressive conquest and assimilation is obscured. Wars of conquest were thus presented as the repression of rebellions on the part of the inhabitants of Galicia in the west and by the Basques in the east, over both of whom the Asturian kings had no prior title to authority. The process of expansion was initiated in the reign of the third of these monarchs, Alfonso I (739–57). Of the founder of the kingdom, Pelagius, little is recorded after his success over the Arabs in 718 (or 722 as has been argued).[9] His only son Fafila (737–9) was killed by a bear, but is otherwise known to have founded a church dedicated to the Holy Cross at Cangas de Onis, which appears to have been the centre of the kingdom at this time.[10] He was succeeded by his brother-in-law, Alfonso, the son of a Duke Peter of Cantabria. The latter may have exercised authority in the period following the Arab invasion over a region to the east of the Asturias, and the merging of the two dynasties through the marriage of Alfonso to Pelagius' daughter Ermosinda represents the first territorial expansion of the kingdom.

Under Alfonso I, later known as 'the Catholic', and his son Fruela I the Cruel (757–68), the authority of the Asturian monarchy was extended westwards into Galicia as far as the valley of the Miño. In the same period, a series of raids were conducted into the lower valley of the Duero and across the Meseta, leading to the capture of a number of the major towns in these

[7] See above, Kennedy, p. 257.
[8] Collins (1989b), pp. 141–51.   [9] Sánchez-Albornoz (1972–5) II, pp. 97–135.
[10] For the now lost inscription: Vigil (1887) I, pp. 304–5; II, plate IV.

regions. These settlements were said by the late ninth-century chroniclers to include Braga, Oporto, Astorga, León, Zamora, Simancas, Osma, Avila and Segovia, amongst others. The Christian sources attribute primary responsibility to Alfonso: the Arab ones to Fruela. These expeditions across the Meseta and south of the Miño were not, however, intended to promote a further territorial extension of the Asturian kingdom in these directions, as the Christian inhabitants of these settlements are reported to have been carried off northwards by their captors.

The process thus laconically described in the chronicles has generated much controversy, though few of the questions that need to be posed can be answered. Were these mid-eighth-century Asturian kings seeking to depopulate a broad swathe of territory running from the Atlantic to the upper Duero and from the Sierra de Guadarrama to the Asturian and Cantabrian mountains, and if so how effectively could they have achieved it?[11] Equally uncertain are both the size and nature of the captured settlements, and what if any was the need for a resettling of population in the northern mountains and Galicia, areas not known otherwise to have been deprived of inhabitants. No mention is made of these processes of depopulation and transportation in the Arab sources, and there exists a real danger that the Asturian chronicles were validating the subsequent imposition of royal authority over most of the Meseta and southern Galicia in the ninth century. In other words, the imposition of lordship and regalian rights in the later period was being justified by a supposed prior period of Asturian rule over these areas.

The murder of Fruela I in 768, possibly in a vendetta initiated by his own killing of his brother Vimara, marked the end of this period of raiding the Arab-ruled towns of the Meseta. Fruela's infant son Alfonso was passed over in favour of a cousin of the late king called Aurelius (768–74). Unlike the preceding Visigothic kingdom, the Asturian monarchy was able to maintain dynastic continuity, largely by adopting a flexible approach to the rules of succession and avoiding strict adherence to primogeniture. Thus, when Aurelius died the palace nobility, who seem normally to have been the determining force in the selecting of a new king, chose Silo (774–83), the husband of Alfonso I's daughter Adosinda. On his death his widow, required by canonical regulations of the Visigothic period to enter a convent, tried to secure the succession for her nephew Alfonso.[12] Here, however, the palace nobility were thwarted by a coup led by Mauregatus (783–8), an illegitimate son of Alfonso I. He in turn was succeeded by

---

[11] Sánchez-Albornoz (1966).

[12] For the survival of Visigothic rules relating to royal widows see Orlandis (1962), pp. 117–23.

Vermudo I (788–91), the brother of the former King Aurelius. Only a crushing defeat of the new king at the hands of an Arab army led to the long-postponed succession of Fruela I's son Alfonso II (791–842): whether voluntarily or otherwise, the military disaster led Vermudo to retire into a monastery.[13]

The seizure of the kingdom by Mauregatus in 783 represents the first manifestation of a phenomenon that would increasingly dominate the political life of the Asturian monarchy and also of its Leonese successor (910–1037). This was the power of the frontier nobility to defy or on occasion to overturn the central authority of the kings. The conquests of Galicia and of territory of the later Basque provinces of Alava and Vizcaya had depended on and were reinforced by the establishment of territorial lordships, both lay and ecclesiastical, in these regions. Although the lack of survival of charters makes it impossible to document individual cases before the later ninth century, it is possible to detect the building up of substantial marcher lordships in the eighth.[14] By the end of this century, what had been an Asturian domination of peripheral territories to the east and to the west of its heartlands had been transformed into an almost equal partnership of the three principal components of the kingdom: the Asturian palatine nobility and the marcher lords of Galicia and of the western Basque regions.

Individual monarchs depended for the maintenance of their practical authority, or in cases of disputed successions for their claim to the throne, on securing the backing of at least one or more of these groups. Thus, Mauregatus and also Vermudo I depended primarily on the support of the Galicians, and were able to expel and keep in exile the young Alfonso. The latter, on the other hand, because of his father's marriage to the Basque Muña, was able to call upon elements of his mother's people. He took refuge amongst them in 788. He himself never married, and apparently earned his later sobriquet of 'the Chaste'. This created a disputed succession on his death. After Alfonso's long reign his designated heir and nephew, Nepotian (842), was rapidly overthrown by the Galician-backed Ramiro I (842–50), the son of Vermudo I. His grandson, Alfonso III (866–910), was himself briefly expelled in 867 by a Galician coup, and in due course was to be deposed by his own sons with the support of the Leonese frontier aristocracy. In the later ninth century the southward expansion of the frontiers of the Asturian kingdom created new marcher regions in the north of what would eventually become the kingdom of Portugal and in Castile. The leading landowners and office holders of these regions became in their

---

[13] Collins (1989b), pp. 160–7.   [14] Baliñas (1989); Barreiro Somoza (1987), pp. 61–70.

turn in the tenth century the principal arbiters of the political stability of the kingdom, replacing their predecessors in Galicia and Alava.

Other social groups in the Asturian kingdom are much harder to delineate, again largely thanks to the limited nature of the evidence. In the reign of Aurelius (768–74) a servile revolt broke out. The chronicles make the briefest of mention of this, stating only that 'When he was reigning the slaves (*servi*) who were in revolt against their lords were captured by his zeal and returned to their previous servitude.'[15] The nature of the revolt and of the *servi* themselves is not easily defined. It has usually been assumed that they were slaves, entirely lacking in any form of personal liberty.[16] However, documents from the ninth century indicate that such men could own property, which might be transmitted to their sons with their lords' consent. Unfortunately, such texts give no further information as to the other ties of dependency between the lords and *servi*. The revolt under Aurelius is the only instance of such an uprising in the Asturian period, and the chronicles fail to give it any precise geographical location.

Under the relatively short-reigned kings from Aurelius to Vermudo I the southern frontiers of the kingdom were generally tranquil. However, the establishment in power of the second Umayyad amir, Hishām I (788–96) led, not least for reasons concerned with the internal stability of the Arab state in al-Andalus, to the launch of almost biannual campaigns against the Christian populations of northern Spain. The defeat of Vermudo I at the battle of Burbia in 791 was one consequence of this, and his successor, Alfonso II, routed an Arab army at Lutos in 794. The latter was presented as a victory by the Arab chronicles, but the Asturian accounts are probably more credible.[17] Less intensive campaigning followed the accession of al-Ḥakam I (796–822), and in general no serious effort was ever made by the Arab rulers to destroy the Asturian kingdom.

One consequence of the fighting in the 790s was the establishment of diplomatic contacts between Alfonso II and Charlemagne. In 797 the Asturian king, taking advantage of the disorder in the south following the premature death of Hishām I, launched a raid on Lisbon, that was probably intended to co-ordinate with a Frankish offensive in the Ebro valley. The latter failed to materialise, owing to difficulties with the Saxons, but some of the loot from Alfonso's raid was sent to Charlemagne.[18] However, no such Asturian co-operation is recorded when the Franks finally did capture Barcelona in 801. This may well have been a product of the brief overthrow

---

[15] *Chronica Albeldensia* xv 5: 'Eo regnante serbi dominis suis contradicentes eius industria capti in pristina sunt serbitute redacti.'   [16] Sánchez-Albornoz (1972–5) II, pp. 209–10.
[17] Sánchez-Albornoz (1972–5) II, pp. 483–90.   [18] *ARF* s.a. 798.

of Alfonso II in that year and his imprisonment in the monastery of Ablaña. The name of his supplanter is not recorded, and he was restored in a countercoup led by a certain Teuda.[19]

Most of the latter part of the reign of Alfonso II appears to have been peaceful, and from 812 onwards he is recorded in the chronicles as having devoted himself to the construction of a series of churches in Oviedo, which he had made his capital. By the time of Silo (774–83) the principal royal residence had moved from Cangas de Onis to Pravía, and early in his reign Alfonso established himself at Oviedo, which had also once been patronised by his father Fruela. None of these places had been towns in the Roman period, and it would be misleading to think of them as such at this time either. They were little more than ceremonial centres, housing a royal palace and one or more churches, together with small populations serving the court. The kings themselves may be assumed to have been largely peripatetic for much of the year, but Alfonso II seems deliberately to have built up Oviedo to mimic the role of Toledo in the Visigothic kingdom.[20] Several of the extant buildings of ninth-century date in Oviedo have been dated to the reign of Alfonso II on the basis of attributions in the chronicles. However, a number of significant discrepancies can be detected within the literary texts and also between them and the existing structures. Greater caution is probably needed in stating that any of the latter actually date from this reign. Furthermore, the frequently made claim that Alfonso's principal architect can be named as a certain Tioda is entirely without foundation, in that it depends upon a spurious interpolation in a late copy of a charter. It is likely that the name derives from a confusion, deliberate or otherwise, with the Teuda who rescued Alfonso from captivity in 801/2.[21]

The same kinds of problems are to be encountered in the study of the buildings attributed to Alfonso's successor, Ramiro I (842–50), who is recorded in the chronicles as having built a palace, a bath house and a church on Monte Naranco, immediately to the north of Oviedo. The buildings now to be found on this site are so fundamentally different in both their architecture and their decoration from other churches of the Asturian period that a distinctive artistic style has been ascribed to the period of the reigns of Ramiro I and his son, Ordoño I (850–66), known as the 'estilo ramirense'. Once again, however, the evidence of the literary texts can be found not to tally with the material remains. An inscription in the church of Sta María de Naranco, for example, indicates that Ramiro restored rather than founded the building, and the commonly held view that this was originally created by the king as the audience hall of his palace has no

---

[19] *Chronica Albeldensia* xv 9.   [20] Sánchez-Albornoz (1972–5) II, pp. 623–39.
[21] Collins (1989a), pp. 3–12.

foundation.[22] Only with the churches of the reign of his grandson, Alfonso III the Great (866–910), can anything like certainty be achieved, largely because these can be dated exclusively on the basis of inscriptions, and do not feature in chronicle texts.

Although a more stable *modus vivendi* was reached with the Umayyad amirate in the second part of the reign of Alfonso II, the growing weakness of the central authority of that state in the course of the ninth century led to the development of more localised conflicts and problems for the Asturian kingdom. Thus for example, in 833, under the Amir ʿAbd al-Raḥmān II (822–52), Maḥmūd ibn ʿAbd al-Djabbar, an Arab leader who had failed in a bid to establish an independent realm for himself in the city of Mérida, fled north and sought the protection of Alfonso II. The latter established him and his followers on the Galician frontier. But within seven years he was treating the Asturian king in the same way as he had the amir, by trying to carve an independent regional base for himself out of his overlord's territories. In 840 Alfonso attacked him with the royal army and destroyed him.[23]

Under Ramiro I, although a Cordoban army sacked León in 846, the most dramatic military threat to the Asturian kingdom came in the form of the first Viking attack on Spain. The Danish fleet that had previously based itself in the Garonne came along the Bay of Biscay in the summer of 844 and descended on the Galician coast.[24] The Vikings were successfully driven off by Ramiro, and continued south to sack both Lisbon and Seville. As well as having to face these periodic external difficulties, the brief reign of Ramiro was more seriously beset by internal disorders. Although the chronicles written in the time of his grandson present him as having the natural right to the throne, he had in fact deposed, following a successful invasion of the Asturias, the designated heir of Alfonso II the Chaste. This short-lived ruler, Nepotian, is treated as a legitimate king in some Asturian regnal lists, although mendaciously portrayed as a usurper by the chroniclers.[25] After his overthrow he was blinded and confined to a monastery. Such a seizure of the throne led to a period of internal instability, and Ramiro is recorded as having to face the revolts of two of the Asturian palatine nobility. One of these, Piniolus, held the rank of Count of the Palace, the principal officer of the royal court. Overall, the reign of Ramiro was marked by a defensive stance, imposed by such combinations of external and internal threats. In general, the territorial expansion of the kingdom, that had been such a

[22] Collins (1989a), pp. 12—18.
[23] *Adefonsi Tertii Chronica, Rotensis* and *Ad Sebastianum* versions, 22; Ibn al-Athir *s.a.* 213–25.
[24] *AB* trans. Nelson, p. 60; ed. Rau, p. 64 and see Coupland, above, pp. 195–6.
[25] Casariego (1969).

marked feature of its history in the mid-eighth century, does not seem to have been renewed before the 850s.

For Ramiro I's son Ordoño I (850–66), on the other hand, greater opportunities existed in the increasingly disturbed state of the Umayyad amirate. The rebellion of Toledo against the new ruler of Córdoba, Muḥammad I (852–86), led to its inhabitants appealing to Ordoño for aid, and this enabled him to launch the first Asturian expedition south of the Sierra de Guadarrama in 854. In the ensuing battle the Toledans and their Asturian allies were defeated by the amir's army, though probably not as seriously as the Arab sources imply.[26] The city remained in revolt until 859, and the whole episode initiated a new and dynamic period of expansion on the part of the northern kingdom. In 859 Ordoño launched an attack on Mūsā ibn Mūsā (d. 862), the patriarch of the Banū Qāsī, a *muwallad* dynasty of ultimately Visigothic origin, who had built up a dominant position for themselves in the upper Ebro valley, and had recently gained control of Tudela and Zaragoza.[27] Ordoño destroyed the fortress that Mūsā had been building at Albelda, and routed his army in a battle fought on Mount Laturce. Although Mūsā, who had been in almost continuous revolt against Córdoba since 840, had achieved such a regional dominance as to be known as 'the third king of Spain', this disaster broke his power, and even his son Lubb (Lope), who had recently been installed as governor of Toledo, temporarily submitted to the authority of Ordoño.[28]

Although this Asturian ascendancy over the former Visigothic capital was short lived, once the Amir Muḥammad I (852–86) was able to reassert himself, the reign of Ordoño's son Alfonso the Great (866–910) marked the re-establishment of Christian control over most of the Meseta and the valley of the Duero. Regrettably, the chronicle that bears the king's name ends with his accession, but the *Chronicle of Albelda* becomes uncharacteristically detailed for the period 866–83. This was a time marked by expectations of the collapse of Arab power in Spain, as indicated by the so-called *Prophetic Chronicle*, a text that became attached to the Albeldan chronicle collection, and which calculated on the basis of pseudo-biblical prophecies that Islamic domination in the peninsula would come to an end in 884. Heartened by such hopes or by the more positive military achievements of the previous reign, a more aggressive stance on the part of the Asturian kingdom was linked to an intensive repopulation and development of the southern frontier districts.

Most notable here was the expansion of settlements in Castile and in the north of what was to become Portugal.[29] The latter included Braga, Oporto,

[26] Porres Martín-Cleto (1985), pp. 31–4.   [27] Cañada Juste (1980).
[28] Sánchez-Albornoz (1969).   [29] Merea (1949).

Viseo and Lamego, which were given new Christian populations, as was the newly created town of Zamora, which was said to have been occupied by refugees from Toledo. At the same time raids were directed into Muslim territory, reaching as far to the south as Mérida in 881. In Castile, where the process of repopulation was under way by the 860s, an entirely new settlement was founded at Burgos in 883 by Count Diego (873–90), to provide the administrative centre of the recently created county. These processes were facilitated by the increasing fragmentation of the Umayyad state in the last years of Muḥammad. Cordoban expeditions launched against the Asturian kingdom achieved little, and in 882 the amir negotiated a truce with Alfonso III, part of the consequences of which were the translation to Oviedo of the relics of the Cordoban martyr Eulogius (executed 859) and with them a corpus of literary and poetic texts.[30]

The origins of the Asturian kingdom, in the northern mountains and far removed from the cultural centres of the previous Visigothic period, together with its subsequent essentially military character, made it a less than flourishing abode of learning. Few monasteries existed in the kingdom prior to the ninth century, and there are no traces of anything that could be called a 'court school' to be found in it. No extant manuscripts can be ascribed to Asturian scriptoria. Even so, some traces of the intellectual culture of the Asturian period can be detected in the few new works that were produced at this time. Of the latter the *Commentary on the Apocalypse*, probably though not certainly written by the monk Beatus in 786, is by far the most substantial, and, although offering nothing original in itself, is testimony to the existence of a rich collection of exegetical texts in late eighth-century Asturias. Beatus quoted from, amongst others, the works of Apringius, the Donatist Tyconius, Augustine, Gregory the Great and Isidore. A different kind of erudition was displayed by the late ninth-century anonymous author who put together the collection of chronological texts that accompanied the *Chronicle of Albelda*. This included regnal lists, not only of the Roman emperors and the Austurian and Visigothic kings, but also of the governors and amirs of al-Andalus.

Although a small number of monastic communities is recorded as having come into existence, especially in Galicia, in the Asturian period none of them achieved any great size or significance at this time. On the other hand, it did see the discovery of the supposed body of the Apostle St James, and the subsequent rapid development of a cult based on the relic and its place of burial.[31] The discovery was made in a late Roman cemetery at Compostela during the episcopate of Bishop Theodemir of Iria Flavia (*c.* 818–47), who

---

[30] Collins (1983b).   [31] Barreiro Somoza (1987), pp. 59–78.

erected the first church on the site. This was replaced by a more substantial
basilica in 899, built by Alfonso III and Bishop Sisnando of Iria (*c.* 880–
c. 920). Little evidence exists for royal interest in the cult before this reign,
but Alfonso made substantial donations of land and treasure to the church,
as well as adopting St James as one of his patron saints. It is possible that
pilgrimage to the shrine of Santiago from outside the Asturian kingdom was
already under way by the end of the ninth century.[32]

The ending of the chronicle itself in 883 has meant that the second half of
the reign of Alfonso III is much less well recorded than the first. However,
the Arab sources confirm that this was a relatively peaceful period for the
Asturian kingdom, not least owing to the problems that the Amir ʿAbd
Allāh (888–912) had to face in the south, notably the escalating revolt of
Umar ibn Ḥafṣūn. For Alfonso III the main concern may have been
maintaining royal authority over expanding and increasingly independent
frontiers. In 910 he was deposed in a conspiracy led by his eldest son García,
who had the backing of the Leonese frontier nobility, and he seems to have
died soon afterwards. The claim that he retired to the monastery of San
Salvador de Valedíos, that he himself had founded in 892, is based only on
late medieval chronicle accounts. The deposition of Alfonso was followed
by the moving of the capital of the kingdom from Oviedo to León, south of
the Cantabrian mountains: a change that was symbolic of the greater
security that was then felt and of the enhanced importance of the southern
frontier regions, now firmly established along the line of the Duero.
Although this process may not have been completed until the reign of
Alfonso's second son, Ordoño II (913/14–24), 910 is always taken as
marking the transition between the Asturian and Leonese kingdoms.

THE KINGDOM OF PAMPLONA, 799–905

While the mountainous southern fringes of the Bay of Biscay, Cantabria, the
Asturias and Galicia broke free of the domination of the Arab and Berber
conquerors by the middle of the eighth century, the western Pyrenees
remained longer under their rule. However, many of the problems of
maintaining order in this region that had faced the Visigothic kings from the
late sixth century onwards remained for the successors. Raids into the upper
Ebro valley by the Basques posed a substantial military threat, and Yūsuf
ibn ʿAbd al-Raḥmān, the last of the governors or, arguably, the first of the
independent Arab rulers of al-Andalus, lost a detachment of his army to the

---

[32] Fletcher (1984), pp. 53–77.

Basques in 756.[33] His overthrow in the same year at the hands of the Umayyad ʿAbd al-Raḥmān was blamed on the loss of these forces in one Arab account. It took the new ruler of Córdoba over twenty years to impose his authority on the Ebro valley and, in the meantime, power passed into the hands of a series of local potentates, of mixed Arab and *muwallad* origin. Their reluctance to accept the authority of ʿAbd al-Raḥmān led to an appeal for help from Charlemagne, and the latter's fruitless intervention in the Ebro valley in 778.[34] One consequence of this had been the Frankish conquest of Pamplona, but the city, whose walls were then destroyed, had to be given up in the course of the subsequent retreat across the Pyrenees. By 799 Pamplona was in the hands of Mutarrif ibn Mūsā, a member of the Banū Qāsī, who was murdered by the citizens in that year. A restoration of Frankish rule over Pamplona and the western Pyrenees took place in 806, matching the recent establishment of Frankish control over Barcelona and the formation of a march that was centred on it. However, the western Pyrenean region was less enthusiastic for Frankish rule than the eastern, and in 812 and 819 revolts occurred that had to be suppressed by King Louis of Aquitaine and his son Pippin I. In 824, in the course of a further revolt, a Frankish army led by two counts was ambushed and routed by the Basques in the second battle of Roncesvalles. As a probable result of this, a small kingdom came into being in Pamplona, and Frankish control over the area was never restored.

The history of the kingdom of Pamplona has to be reconstructed on a far smaller evidential basis than that of the neighbouring Asturian realm. No chronicles at all were produced, and few genuine charters originating in the kingdom can be found dating from earlier than the late tenth century. The principal indigenous historical text is a collection of royal and comital genealogies, which were probably compiled in Nájera, then a royal centre, in the later tenth century.[35] Otherwise, recourse has to be made to the occasional notices afforded the kingdom in Asturian and Arab historiography. This makes the history of the Pamplonan monarchy, especially in the ninth century, both very obscure and highly controversial.[36] Much scholarly argument has been devoted to problems of the geographical extent of the kingdom, its regnal dating, and the identification of individuals briefly mentioned in the genealogical and other sources.

It is accepted on the basis of the king-list, and confirmed by Arab narratives, that the first king of Pamplona was a certain Iñigo Arista. It may be assumed, though it is not provable, that he came to power in the

[33] Collins (1989b), pp. 119–26.   [34] Collins (1989b), pp. 168–82.   [35] Lacarra (1945).
[36] Lévi-Provençal (1953); Pérez de Urbel (1954); Sánchez-Albornoz (1957); Collins (1986), pp. 123–63.

aftermath of the second battle of Roncesvalles in 824. His death in 851 is
recorded in a fragment of the Arab historian Ibn Ḥayyān. Few other
chronological statements concerning his dynasty can be made with anything
like such assurance. His son García Iníguez seems to have succeeded him
without interruption, but his date of death is not known. It has been
suggested that, as his eldest son Fortún Garcés was still possibly a captive in
Córdoba following an earlier military defeat, a regency occurred on the
death of King García. This may have been exercised by one of his other
sons.[37] Fortún Garcés probably began his own personal reign in the early
880s, and is thought to have died in 905. Although the genealogies record
him as having sons, he proved to be the last member of the founding line of
the kings of Pamplona, as he was succeeded by Sancho Garcés I (905–25),
the son of a certain García Jiménez and thus the representative of a different
dynasty.[38]

One of the distinguishing features of the early history of the kingdom of
Pamplona is the close relationship that existed between its ruling dynasty
and the *muwallad* Banū Qāsī. The mother of Mūsā ibn Mūsā (d. 862), the
most powerful of the latter, was the sister of Iñigo Arista. The tiny Basque
kingdom was faced by predatory enemies in several directions. Although
never realised, the threat of Frankish attempts to regain control over the
western Pyrenees was a real one. In practice even more menacing was the
gradual eastwards expansion of the Asturian kingdom; while in the south
lay the amirate of Córdoba, ever anxious to impose its authority over the
frontier regions, not least the Upper March, which embraced the Ebro
valley. For such reasons the alliance of Pamplona and the Muslim Banū Qāsī
offered significant mutual benefits, if also shared dangers. Thus, Mūsā and
Iñigo joined forces to ambush and capture one of ʿAbd al-Raḥmān II's
commanders in 843, but the consequence was a massive military response
from Córdoba, led by the amir in person, which led to the defeat of the allies
and much destruction and the taking of slaves in the vicinity of Pamplona. A
second retaliatory expedition in 844 inflicted a further defeat, in which one
of King Iñigo's brothers was killed. Even so, the Pamplonans are found
acting together with the Banū Qāsī in defiance of Córdoba again in 847 and
in 850. The defeat of Mūsā ibn Mūsā by Ordoño I in 859, however, left the
kingdom of Pamplona peculiarly exposed to threats from the south. In 860
an expedition led by the Amir Muḥammad I entered the kingdom and
captured Fortún Garcés, the heir to the throne, who was taken to Córdoba
and kept there as a hostage, probably for the next twenty years.[39]

[37] Sánchez-Albornoz (1971).
[38] Ubieto Arteta (1960); Sánchez-Albornoz (1961).
[39] See Kennedy above, pp. 268–9; Al-Makkarī, vi.4.

Although the events of 859–60 left both the Banū Qāsī and the rulers of Pamplona weakened during the course of the ensuing decade, their alliance was resumed in the early 870s. In 872 the four sons of Mūsā ibn Mūsā succeeded in seizing power in all of the major towns of the Upper March: Zaragoza, Tarazona, Huesca, Lérida and Tudela. Although Huesca was regained for the amir in 873, the Banū Qāsī could not be dislodged from their hold over the rest of the region. In consequence almost annual expeditions were launched into the Ebro valley from Córdoba, and these normally included the ravaging of the districts around Pamplona in their programme. However, neither the Christian city nor any of the strongholds of the Banū Qāsī fell to the amir's forces. Close relations, based on mutual reaction to a common threat, were also established with the kingdom of the Asturias, whose king Alfonso III married a Pamplonan wife called Jimena; one of his sons, the future Ordoño II, was sent to be brought up in one of the courts of the Banū Qāsī, probably that of Muḥammad b. Lubb ibn Mūsā, who became the dominant member of that dynasty in the mid-870s.[40]

This long-established pattern of relationships was broken in the 880s. Muḥammad ibn Lubb found it expedient to renew his allegiance to the amir, and return Zaragoza to Umayyad control, while being recognised as the Umayyad ruler's governor of Tudela and Tarazona. The emergence of another rival local dynasty, the Tujibids, to whom the Umayyads then entrusted Zaragoza and Calatayud, led to a fragmentation of Banū Qāsī power in the Ebro valley and increasing conflict with all of their neighbours. This could include raids on both Pamplonan and Asturian lands. Muḥammad ibn Lubb was killed in 898 in the course of a protracted siege of Zaragoza, and the Christian monarchs, whose ties to the Banū Qāsī had been broken in the course of the previous decade, attempted unsuccessfully to annexe his territories. Alfonso III, possibly acting in concert with Fortún Garcés of Pamplona, was defeated in the vicinity of Tarazona in 899 by Muḥammad's son Lubb. Another Asturian invasion of the upper Ebro valley was driven back in 904, but Lubb ibn Muḥammad's raid on Pamplona in 907 proved fatal to his brief restoration of Banū Qāsī dominance in the Ebro. He fell into an ambush prepared by Sancho Garcés I, the first king of the second Pamplonan dynasty, and was killed.

The events surrounding the replacement of the line of Iñigo Arista as kings of Pamplona are peculiarly impenetrable, because of the lack of narrative sources. The story that King Fortún Garcés abdicated *c.* 905 to become a monk seems to be a later rationalisation of what may have been a disputed succession or even a *coup d'état*. The last of the Arista kings was

[40] Cañada Juste (1980), p. 57.

buried, as possibly had been his predecessors, in the monastery of Leyre. This was one of a small number of monastic houses known to have existed in Pamplona in the ninth century. It is probable that some may have owed their foundation to Frankish influence and patronage in the period 806–24.[41] By 848, when the Cordoban priest Eulogius visited the kingdom of Pamplona, a number of these monasteries, notably Leyre and the Aragonese house of Siresa, were flourishing. In another of them called St Zacharias, the precise location of which is now unknown, Eulogius found a corpus of poetic and other texts, including the *De Civitate Dei* of Augustine, which were then unavailable in Córdoba. From the copies that he took back with him sprang a brief renaissance of Latin metrical composition in al-Andalus.[42]

The lack of documentary evidence makes it impossible to determine how far in the ninth century the authority of the kings of Pamplona extended northwards into such regions as the later Basque provinces of Vizcaya and Guipúzcoa. Across the Pyrenees, the Basque-settled areas south of the Garonne were controlled by a line of dukes, theoretically subject to the West Frankish kings, but from the 830s onwards in practice independent rulers of the region. Not before the eleventh century would the authority of the kings of Pamplona extend northwards across the mountains. Similarly, to the south of Pamplona the power of the Banū Qāsī and other local dynasts in the upper Ebro valley, together with the military threats from Córdoba, made territorial expansion of the realm in this direction almost impossible at this time. No southern conquests were to be achieved before the reign of Sancho Garcés I. To the west the Asturian monarchy had pre-empted its smaller Pamplonan counterpart in establishing its authority over the primarily Basque-speaking inhabitants of Alava. However, possibilities existed for the aggrandisement of the kingdom in an eastwards direction, along the line of the Pyrenees.

Here the neighbour of the Pamplonan monarchy was the county established by the Franks in the valley of the river Aragón. As with other central Pyrenean counties, formal loyalty to the Frankish crown was preserved in Aragón after the second battle of Roncesvalles. One of the two Frankish commanders taken prisoner by the Basques in that victory was probably Count Aznar of Aragón, who was released because he was of the same race as his captors. At some point probably soon after, if the brief statements in the Genealogies of Roda be followed, this Aznar was overthrown by his son-in-law, García the Bad, who transferred his allegiance from the Frankish ruler to King Iñigo of Pamplona. Even after Aznar's son Galindo regained the county some time after 842/3, he too

[41] Collins (1990).   [42] Collins (1983b).

found it expedient to maintain this new relationship, and he married his son Aznar Galíndez to a daughter of García Iníguez of Pamplona. A line of counts of this dynasty continued to rule the upper valley of the Aragón until the late tenth century, but under the suzerainty of the kings of Pamplona. The other Pyrenean counties, such as Pallars and Ribagorza to the west of Aragón, remained throughout this period under at least formal Frankish rule.

By the later ninth century some of the distinctive ideology of the later 'Reconquista' had come into being. Christian writers, such as the anonymous author of the so-called 'Prophetic Chronicle' of 883/4, could look forward to the expulsion of the Arabs from Spain, and a sense of both an ethnic and a religious-cultural divide between the inhabitants of the small northern kingdoms and the dominant elite in the south was marked in the writings of both sides. On the other hand, it is unwise to be too linear in the approach to the origins of the 'Reconquista', as tended to be the way with Spanish historiography in the earlier part of the twentieth century. Periods of peaceful co-existence or of limited and localised frontier disturbances were more frequent than ones of all-out military conflict between al-Andalus and the Christian kingdoms. As has been mentioned, the former never made any serious effort to eliminate the latter. Moreover, as in the case of relations between the Arista dynasty in Pamplona and the Banū Qāsī, mutual interest could be a stronger bond than ideological divisions based on antagonistic creeds. These tendencies were, if anything, to be reinforced in the tenth century.

CHAPTER 12

LOMBARD AND CAROLINGIAN ITALY

Paolo Delogu

THE LOMBARD STATE

THE laws which were promulgated by the Lombard king Liutprand (712–744) depict the model of an ideal state, based on elevated political ideas, peculiar to that prince and his age.

One basic principle was the solidarity of the king with the freemen who constituted the political body of the kingdom. This was in part a heritage of the ancient Germanic idea of the people participating in national sovereignty. This concept had not weakened after the Lombards established themselves in Italy. Under Liutprand it could be found in the recognition, implicit in his legislation, that it was the body of the free Lombards that ensured the two basic expressions of national sovereignty: military activity, and the ability to provide themselves with legal regulations. Thus the laws of Liutprand were promulgated in assemblies consisting of judges and royal *fideles* from all the *partes* of the kingdom, representing the entire Lombard people, who could no longer physically gather together. As for military activity, it should be noted that in Liutprand's laws the free Lombard is usually identified with the *exercitalis* – the man who performs military service for the public authority. The traditional nature of this concept was stressed through the use of the ancient Lombard term *arimannus* as a synonym for *exercitalis*.

Taking an active part in public military service was considered as the most complete and honourable form of freedom, whereby the free-born cooperated in maintaining both order and justice within the kingdom, and its independence or superiority with respect to other peoples. It was also an indication of economic independence, since military service was performed at the private expense of the *exercitalis*. As a recognition of all this, the king declared his concern for the free, and safeguarded their needs and interests (*Liutprandi Leges*, cc. 1–4). The solidarity of the king with the freemen seems to have been reinforced at the time by a personal oath of fidelity sworn by all the *arimanni* (*Notitia de Actoribus Regis*, c. 5).

On the other hand, the kingdom was described in Liutprand's laws as an orderly structure made out of judicial districts – the *iudiciariae* – with a hierarchy of powers which ensured the administration of justice at increasing levels of authority. Within each *iudiciaria*, corresponding as a rule to the territory of a city, every settlement was supervised in its legal affairs by a public official, called a *decanus* or a *saltarius*. The *decani* and *saltarii* depended on a *sculdhais*, who was the lowest official permitted to administer justice to the free. The jurisdiction of the *sculdhais* was, however, limited. If the case rose above a certain level of importance, the *sculdhais* was supposed to pass it on to a superior authority, the *iudex* of the *iudiciaria*. Whenever the case could not be settled by the *iudex*, he was to pass the matter on to the highest level of jurisdiction, the royal court in the city of Pavia, then the capital of the kingdom. The king, too, received appeals against allegedly unjust sentences. The administration of justice was the primary aim of public authority and was subordinated to, and made dependent on, the king, who presented himself as the supreme judge and the surety for justice for all Lombards (*Liutprandi Leges*, cc. 25–27, 44, 85).

Power within the kingdom was thus thought of as jurisdiction, and made dependent on the king's authority. It was given the legal nature of a public function exerted in the interests of the community. Roman and Christian influences are apparent in this complex idea of the state which manifests how refined the political culture was at the Lombard court in the first decades of the eighth century.

Nonetheless, King Liutprand's concepts were more aims to attain through royal government, than objective reflections of the institutional machinery for the time being. In reality, political and jurisdictional powers were not as evenly ordered as the *iudiciaria* system might suggest. Not all of the Lombard territories, for instance, were equally subject to royal authority. This extended over the greater part of northern Italy, comprising the Po valley, Trentino and Friuli; in that part of Italy only the provinces of the Byzantine empire – Venetiae, the Exarchate and the Pentapolis – escaped royal control. South of the Apennines, Tuscia, approximately corresponding to modern Tuscany, was also subject to the king, perhaps in a looser form. Further east and south, the duchies of Spoleto and Benevento, two vast regions named after the seats of the Lombard dukes who presided over them, did not fully recognise the authority of the king, even though they shared the laws and customs of the kingdom.

This was possible because of the complex nature of the Lombard state. All over Lombard Italy, the dukes were the titular holders of local power, but their ties with the kings had different degrees of intensity and subordination. Only in northern Italy were the dukes really bound to the kingdom and the kings. This was the result of bitter struggles that had been fought out after the Lombard conquest of Italy, during the last decades of the sixth century. The kings had then managed to impose themselves over the dukes, who had led the conquest with them and had settled in the cities. Nonetheless, the Lombard dukes had not simply been transformed into royal officials. They usually belonged to families of ancient origin which formed a sort of national nobility, or else were war-leaders renowned for their deeds. Their authority derived from their family or their prestige, as well as from royal consent; they were not totally dependent on the kings, although they certainly co-operated with them. Kings for instance could appoint dukes in vacant duchies, but found it very difficult to remove them; this happened only in extreme cases and usually by force. Indeed, the kings themselves originated from ducal families, because among the Lombards, unlike among the Franks or the Anglo-Saxons, there was no *stirps regia*, though family links between successive kings and the handing down of royal power from father to son were frequent.

Still in the eighth century, kings could overcome individual dukes because the kings had a wider political consensus behind them, and had access to administrative, fiscal and military resources which were greater than those of each duke; but the constitutional ties between kings and dukes were more like an alliance than a relationship of service. The bigger and the further away a duchy was, the weaker the duke's subordination to the kings. This explains not only the autonomy of Spoleto and Benevento, but also the special status of border dukes even in northern Italy, such as the dukes of Friuli and Trento.

The political and administrative organisation of the Lombard kingdom at the beginning of the eighth century did not, however, consist exclusively of a complex of duchies of various sizes variously related to the authority of the king. Alongside this, there was a network of public officials, the *gastaldii*, who were the administrators of the fiscal property distributed throughout the kingdom, which constituted the economic basis for the monarchy. The *gastaldii* also collected the proceeds of justice reserved for the kings, and held military commands similar to those of the dukes; they even governed a number of cities which had no dukes. Unlike the dukes, the *gastaldii* were strictly dependent on the royal authority. They usually belonged to the upper social stratum of the area in which they were to govern, but not to the national aristocracy. The kings could remove them from their office without the military actions which were often necessary to get rid of a duke. The office of the *gastaldius* was not necessarily antagonistic to the authority of the duke, but it was an important administrative tool by which the royal authority could make itself effective throughout the whole kingdom, without depending on the intermediation of the dukes; for this reason, royal *gastaldii* did not exist in the autonomous duchies of Spoleto and Benevento. It now becomes evident that the *iudices* of Liutprand's laws represent both a unification of the offices of duke and *gastaldius* and the idealisation of their subjection to royal authority. The king traced a new model of the state, simple and rational, which he endeavoured to make effective throughout his reign.

In fact, other forces were also active within the kingdom and had a growing political importance, even though they were not recognised as having an official role in the state's organisation. In the Po valley and in Tuscia, the cities, by the end of the seventh century, had once again become central settlement places, which dominated the countryside around them because they were the residences of the public authorities and of many landowners. Commerce and crafts were also carried on in them. Commerce in this case meant the exchange not only of goods produced within the city and its territory, but also of food and other commodities brought from further away. Salt, for example, was imported all over the Po valley from the lagoons of Comacchio, together with less indispensable seasonings, such as pepper and *garum*; silver came from as far afield as England and Frisia; and silk cloth probably came from southern Italy, as well as, sometimes, from the eastern Mediterranean (*CDL* I, no. 50). The inhabitants of the towns constituted active political bodies which could collectively guard and protect their own interests, take part in the internal political events of the kingdom, or raise an army. They could even oppose the local holders of public authority, the *iudices* of the royal administration.

The Liutprandine model of the state also did not take into account the clienteles gathered around powerful personages, whether or not they exercised public functions. The clientele was an early Germanic tradition, originally linked to the military activity of the migrant peoples; King Rothari had made reference to it in his Edict of 643. At the beginning of the eighth century such clienteles had lost their primary military functions, but still constituted political and social groupings, held together by bonds of interest, collaboration and honour. Although they were different from the ties of vassalage which were at that time spreading through the kingdom of the Franks, they had a similar influence on the social structure of the Lombard people. The kings also had their own followings of *fideles*, known as their *gasindii*, distributed throughout the whole kingdom. They helped to support the king's authority in political ways, though they had no institutional role.

Finally, ecclesiastical institutions, too, were gaining greater importance in the organisation of society. The conversion of the Lombards to Christianity having been completed, the territorial organisation of the church gained a secular role as well. Both the *plebes*, the rural churches where baptism and other religious services were performed for the local population, and the cathedrals, which carried out the same functions for the people of the cities and which exercised control over the *plebes* of their dioceses, became centres of social cohesion for the inhabitants of the kingdom. In addition, the churches as landowners exercised influence, patronage and authority over local society and thus also acquired influence in political and administrative affairs. The bishops were not granted a definite function within the Lombard state. They did, however, enjoy a *de facto* influence, which consolidated itself in the course of the eighth century, when they sometimes supported the public *iudices* in the administration of justice, and were also obliged to provide military service on the basis of their landed property.

THE KINGS AND ITALY

After the conquests of Byzantine territory by King Rothari in the 640s, the Lombard kings for a long time limited their military activity to internal affairs and to occasional defence against invasions, by the Franks to the west and the Avars to the east. In *c.* 680 a peace treaty with the Byzantine empire made the political borders within Italy definitive, thus removing the justification for further military undertakings. Only the dukes of Benevento still launched a few expeditions against the Byzantine lands, annexing some small territories as a result.

This static situation suddenly came to an end during the reign of Liutprand. The external cause for this was the crisis of Byzantine imperial authority in Italy. From the first years of the eighth century, the Byzantine provinces openly showed their discontent with and intolerance of the imperial administration. A series of rebellions culminated in 727 in the assassination of the imperial governor, the exarch Paul. It was in this context that Lombard expansion into Byzantine territory began again: in that year Sutri in the Roman duchy was conquered directly; and the cities of Bologna, Imola and Osimo, as well as the inhabitants of some rural districts in Emilia, the Frignano and Persiceta, offered their submission, apparently spontaneously, to Liutprand (Map 18).

These events, although mostly not provoked by the king, may also have suggested to him the possibility that he might profit from the disturbances of the political order in Italy, so as to affirm royal authority over the duchies

Map 18 (a) Italy, 700–900; (b) territories under Byzantine rule

of Spoleto and Benevento. This programme was not in itself aimed against
the Byzantine empire; indeed, in order to carry it out, Liutprand originally
came to an agreement with the new exarch, Eutychius, in exchange for a
promise of aid to bring back order to the imperial provinces. The plan is
likely to have depended on Liutprand's strong idea of royal authority, which
had already caused him to reaffirm hegemony over the duke of Friuli.
Liutprand probably intended to impose a systematic institutional hierarchy
throughout the Lombard world, along the lines of the model expressed in
his law-code. Given that every political institution in the Lombard world
was supposed to be placed inside a hierarchy dependent on the king, it
would have been right and proper that the dukes of Spoleto and Benevento,
too, should be fully subject to him. This certainly fits with a law of 727, in
which Spoleto and Benevento were mentioned for the first time, alongside
the other parts of the kingdom, as areas where the royal law applied
(*Liutprandi Leges*, c. 88). The achievement of this plan proved difficult,
however, because it conflicted with the interests of the other powers in Italy.
The dukes and the leading political groups of the two southern duchies
transformed their *de facto* autonomy into a programme of resistance to the
king. This was particularly true in the duchy of Spoleto, where Duke
Trasamund II not only opposed the Lombard king, but also aimed at
playing a part in the crisis which the imperial authority was experiencing in
Italy. He endeavoured to form an alliance with the papacy and the Exarchate
in order to create a Romano-Lombard political area in central Italy, which
could protect itself both from abuses of power on the part of the empire and
from extensions of Lombard royal authority. As a result, the Spoleto area
began to gravitate towards Rome from the 730s onwards. This was to
remain a constant feature of Italian political geography for at least the next
two centuries.

The political situation in Benevento was less clear-cut. It would seem,
however, that the local aristocracy was divided into two parties, of which
one, opposed to royal authority, was keen to maintain the autonomy of the
duchy, whilst the other was perhaps more prepared to reach an understanding with the king.

Notwithstanding local resistance, Liutprand achieved considerable successes in his policy towards the peripheral duchies. In 729 he entered the
duchy of Spoleto and forced Duke Trasamund and the duke of Benevento,
Romuald II, to swear fealty to him. A few years later, in 732, he went again
with the royal army to Benevento, where he prevented Romuald II's son
from succeeding to the duchy on the grounds of his still being a minor; he
entrusted the duchy for the time being to his own nephew Gregory, duke of
Chiusi.

Outside the Lombard world, Liutprand now had to face the opposition of the exarch Eutychius and of Pope Gregory II (731–41). These two had formed an alliance aimed at re-establishing order in the Byzantine provinces by means of a curious form of joint control, in which the pope extended his jurisdiction over the Roman duchy (the area depending on the city of Rome), while the exarch restricted himself to the Exarchate and the Pentapolis. The exarch also renounced the imposition of iconoclasm – the imperial law forbidding the veneration of holy images, which had given rise to opposition from the Italian subjects of the empire and condemnation from the popes – in return for the moral and political protection of the papacy. An additional aim of this arrangement was to prevent the expansion of the Lombard king, by supporting the resistance of the southern Lombard duchies and by direct military action on the part of the exarch. As a result, Liutprand's policies became increasingly hostile to the Exarchate and eventually led to repeated invasions of imperial territory, including attacks on the exarchal capital at Ravenna.

In these wars with the Byzantines, it is possible to pick out a guiding thread: Liutprand's aim was not the conquest of the Exarchate, but the control of a strategic route between the Po region and the duchy of Spoleto, which was essential for the exercise of royal authority over the southern duchies. (Once having arrived in the district of Spoleto, it was possible for the king to reach Benevento without having to cross any further Byzantine territory.) Liutprand's conquests in imperial territory were in fact limited to the cities of Faenza, Cesena, Ancona and Numana along the way to Spoleto; other castles which were temporarily occupied by the king in the duchy of Rome, such as Amelia, Orte and Bomarzo, also controlled access from Lombard Tuscia to the duchy of Spoleto. The attacks on Ravenna itself, which occurred twice under Liutprand, were only undertaken in response to the hostile activities of the exarch. It seems, furthermore, that Liutprand recognised the special administrative powers assumed by the popes in the Roman duchy, which were confirmed in his eyes by the religious authority of the head of all the Catholic churches. So it was that after the death of Gregory III, a Syrian who seems to have nourished a violent hatred for the Lombards, Liutprand agreed to give back to his successor Zacharias (741–52) the castles in the duchy of Rome and even, at the request of the pope, to return Cesena to the exarch.

Notwithstanding this dual opposition, Liutprand's policies with regard to the outlying Lombard duchies produced lasting successes. In 742, the duchy of Spoleto was once and for all made subject to the kingdom, with the deposition of Duke Trasamund II and the nomination in his place of a nephew of the king, Agiprand. In the course of the same military campaign,

Liutprand reached Benevento, where he forced the new Duke Godeschalk, who was a supporter of local autonomy, to flee, and restored the ducal power to Romuald II's son Gisulf (another nephew of the king, through his mother), whom Liutprand had previously removed from the duchy and had brought up in Pavia.

Once established, the subjection of the southern dukes was kept up under Liutprand's successors, Ratchis, Aistulf and Desiderius, who were the last independent Lombard kings. Spoleto was fully united to the kingdom: the kings continued to impose men from among their own followers as dukes and indeed on occasion ruled the duchy directly. In the duchy of Benevento, which was larger and further away, royal hegemony showed itself principally in the protection given to the ducal family of Gisulf II, who, thanks to renewed intervention by the kings, retained power after Gisulf's death, in spite of his son being again a minor. Nevertheless, aspirations to self-government continued to be felt by the aristocracy and the inhabitants of the duchies, and reappeared when royal power weakened.

Liutprand's successors also inherited from him the difficult relationship with the complex system of powers which ruled and protected the imperial provinces. Ratchis (744–9), who succeeded after the very brief reign of Liutprand's nephew, Hildeprand, tried to follow the direction of Liutprand's policies; he made a peace with the pope which would have left him free to confront the exarch militarily. But when in 749 he invaded the Pentapolis and besieged Perugia – another key to overland communications between Tuscia and Spoleto, as well as between the Exarchate and Rome – he was forced to realise that the pope in fact considered even the lands subject to the exarch untouchable. Indeed, Zacharias used all his religious authority to force the king to abandon his undertaking, as he had already done in the past with Liutprand. It was by now clear that it was not possible to separate the cause of the pope from that of the exarch.

The reasons, however, which led Ratchis to wage war must have been very pressing; for, after his capitulation before the pope, the king was forced to abdicate and royal power passed to his brother Aistulf (749–56), a man already known for his aggressiveness and daring. Aistulf immediately resumed hostilities against the Exarchate and in 750, in the course of a lucky expedition, conquered Ravenna and all the provinces subject to the Exarchate, proclaiming himself king of the 'Romans' – in other words the subjects of the empire in Italy – 'by the grace of God'. Having thus taken over the imperial power, he apparently next intended to impose his authority over the Roman populace and the duchy of Rome as well; in fact, he demanded that every inhabitant should pay him a golden *solidus* as tribute. He offered the pope, Stephen II, who succeeded Zacharias in 752, peace and recognition of his religious authority, and probably also a limited independence for the Roman duchy, under the hegemony of the Lombard kingdom.

Aistulf probably thought that he had finally found a permanent solution to the problems of the security of the kingdom and the territorial connection with the outlying duchies – indeed, after the conquest of Ravenna, he placed Spoleto under direct royal control without nominating a duke. In fact, however, this radical and revolutionary undertaking had the consequence – which was also revolutionary – of extending the pope's politico-religious protection, which he already exercised over the Roman duchy, to include the populations of the Exarchate and the Pentapolis as well, thus making the pope both the victim and the opponent of every action undertaken by the king to confirm his dominion over the lands which had previously belonged to the empire. The authority of the pope to act against Lombard rule was officially confirmed by the Emperor Constantine V (741–75), who, considering the pope to be the only surviving representative of imperial authority in Italy, charged him with obtaining the restitution of the Exarchate and the Pentapolis.

Since Aistulf considered that the supremacy of the empire in Italy was henceforth extinct, Stephen II was not able to exercise over him the same pastoral diplomacy that Zacharias had successfully put into operation with Liutprand and Ratchis. On the contrary, Aistulf increased both his threats and his military pressure, so as to force the Romans to submit. Realising that he could not count on any military aid from the empire, the pope appealed to the new king of the Franks, Pippin, who had only recently (751), with the moral support of the papacy, deposed the last king of the Merovingian dynasty, thus completing the political ascent of the Carolingians. The pope's appeal to the Franks had probably been agreed in advance with the Byzantine emperor. The aim was to force Aistulf to return his conquests 'to those who had a right to them' (*LP*, 246; I, p. 449). But Stephen II must have made it quite clear to the Franks that it was the Roman church that exercised a religious, moral and political authority over all the lands which had previously belonged to the empire. This enabled the pope to act in their defence, but also established his right to receive them back from the Franks. Furthermore, the pope honoured Pippin and his sons with the title 'Patricians of the Romans'; this was a term with no precise institutional meaning, but was sufficient to make Pippin antagonistic to Aistulf's claims to sovereignty over the Romans.

Pippin's military campaign in Italy in the summer of 754 fulfilled papal expectations. Aistulf, defeated in a battle on the borders of the kingdom, was forced to promise Pippin that he would return Ravenna and the other cities which he had conquered. The restitutions were probably to be received by the pope, who to some extent still acted as the representative of constitutional legitimacy within the imperial territories.

What remained uncertain and ambiguous in this situation was largely resolved by the events of this same year and the following one. Once the Frankish army had withdrawn, Aistulf refused to hand over the stipulated territory; moreover, considering the pope to be his declared enemy, he tried to take possession of Rome itself in order to complete his plans and put an end to papal political activities. Meanwhile, Stephen II's attitude to the empire changed after the end of 754. In that year, Emperor Constantine V summoned a council at Constantinople which greatly intensified the iconoclastic movement, declaring the worship of images heretical. In 756, at the anxious request of the pope, Pippin returned to Italy with the Frankish army, again defeated the Lombards on the border of the kingdom, besieged Aistulf at Pavia and forced him to surrender. This time, the terms were stiffer: envoys from the king of the Franks would directly supervise the return of the lands in question. The beneficiary was now explicitly the Church of Rome, represented by the pope; indeed, when approached by the Byzantine ambassador, Pippin refused to recognise any imperial claim to the liberated provinces (*LP*, 251; I, p. 453). Thus the royal plan to substitute Lombard for Byzantine domination in Italy suffered a final blow; and so did all hope of unifying all the Lombard territories, since the demand for self-government soon regained strength in the outlying duchies. Furthermore, the Lombard kingdom was henceforth bound to pay an annual tribute to the Franks; this meant virtual political subjection.

The order thus achieved still rested on a fragile basis. The Lombard kingdom was not completely subjugated, and the political and military alliance between the Franks and the papacy was not solid enough to allow the latter to act very effectively against the Lombards. Desiderius, who succeeded Aistulf in 756, was able to re-establish royal control over the duchies of Spoleto and Benevento, and to maintain strategic strongholds in Emilia and the Pentapolis. He managed to put off or to avoid part of the land restitutions, and cleverly took advantage of the difficulty encountered by the papacy in having its authority recognised by the populace and the local authorities of the Exarchate, now grouped around the archbishop of Ravenna. The popes who succeeded Stephen II could no longer count on the Byzantine empire for support, whilst Pippin was reluctant to undertake further military operation in Italy. They were further weakened by the struggles for political and economic control of Rome between various factions within the city.

On the death of Pippin in 768, the Frankish kingdom was divided between the king's two sons, who were in conflict with each other. For some years Desiderius succeeded in presenting himself as an important point of reference on the international scene, and even as a protector for Pope Stephen III and Pippin's widow Bertrada. The latter in 770 came to Pavia to arrange for the marriage of her son Charles (the future Charlemagne) to one of the daughters of the Lombard king. Desiderius took advantage of this to reconquer lands in the former Byzantine provinces, although he now aimed only to seize strategic points along the borders. One has, however, the impression that Desiderius' successes depended more on the temporary weakening of the opponents of the Lombards than on any real strength on his own part. When, between the end of 771 and the beginning of 772, Charlemagne became the sole king of the Franks, and the new pope, Hadrian I, succeeded in restoring peace among the various factions in Rome, Desiderius was immediately driven into a critical position. Charlemagne broke off the marriage alliance by repudiating his Lombard wife; Hadrian, for his part, demanded the return of conquests old and new. Desiderius' attempts to exercise military pressure on the pope, and to raise up a Frankish faction against Charlemagne in support of the hereditary rights of the latter's nephews, only resulted in a revival of Frankish hostility to the Lombards, and hastened a new agreement between the pope and the king of the Franks.

In the spring of 773, Charlemagne, now defending his own interests, appeared on the borders of Italy, routed the Lombard army without difficulty and besieged Desiderius at Pavia, forcing him to yield in 774. Charlemagne's attitude after the victory was very different from that of his father. He wanted to eliminate the roots of what he felt to be a permanent threat to the new political order that he was planning, based on the hegemony of the Frankish kingdom over the Christian society of western Europe. For this reason, he exiled Desiderius to Francia, took the title of king of the Lombards for himself, and forced the Lombards to swear an oath of fealty.

The failure of the Lombard kingdom against the Franks raises many questions. Above all, the fact throws doubt on the political cohesion and moral determination of the Lombards at a moment at which they should have been defending their own survival as a sovereign people. A number of hypotheses have been brought forward to explain this. In general, they focus on the social complexity and the loose political organisation of Lombard society, a complexity that the kings never fully managed to dominate. The existence of an aristocratic opposition to King Desiderius has been pointed out: Lombard nobles had indeed fled to Francia, seeking hospitality from Charlemagne. Other explanations have stressed the symptoms of a moral unease, revealed for instance by the longing for monastic life which spread throughout Lombard society at the time of the clashes with Pippin.[1] A sort of renunciation of Lombard national identity which reached an extreme of treachery occurred when the people of Spoleto, in an attempt to obtain papal protection when Charlemagne was besieging Pavia, actually submitted themselves to the pope's authority, asking to have their hair cut after the Roman fashion (*LP*, 311; 1, p. 495). It has also been argued that, two hundred years after their settlement in Italy, the Lombards had lost their taste for war, in favour of the civilised values of urban life.

Although all these circumstances undoubtedly characterise the cultural development of the eighth century, none of them seems to have gone so far as to make the collapse of the kingdom inevitable. Feeling for the national tradition remained alive among the Lombard nobility, and there were still moments of rebellion against Frankish dominion after 774. Lombard national consciousness was also expressed very clearly in the 'History' which the Friulan Paul the Deacon composéd, some ten years after the end of the Lombard kingdom, in praise of his people. In it, the dignity and power of the Lombards were expressed through their warlike deeds and military virtues thus showing that these values were still held in honour by the Lombards up to 774 and after. Christianity did not militate against them; rather it was integrated into them, much as in the case of the Franks, given that faith was perceived as a confirmation and support for the excellence of the race. Certainly, Christianity raised the question of the legality of war, which should only be waged against the enemies of the faith. The Lombard attacks on the papacy may well for this reason have raised doubts and unease at the time. But it should be observed that the kings avoided, as far as possible, direct action against Rome. They generally recognised the inviolability of the papacy and its territory. As for the opposition of the nobility to the king at the time of Desiderius, this was probably motivated by personal rivalries, perhaps depending on the social origins of the king; it is very doubtful that Desiderius' opponents meant to favour the establishment of Frankish sovereignty in Italy.

Supplementary explanations for the failure of the Lombard kingdom can be found in the new political determination of the Franks under Charlemagne, and in the frailty of the Lombard military apparatus. This last deserves a few comments.

The Lombard national army was quite possibly unsuited for the mounting of a major co-ordinated effort. It would seem that the Lombard *exercitales*, although they were defined in institutional terms as warriors, practised only a very limited military activity in normal circumstances. This consisted above all in the *caballicatio* in the retinue of the local judge for

---

[1] See Schmid (1972).

police operations, and in the safeguard of their local territories (Ratchis, *Leges*, c. 4). Occasionally, disputes between neighbouring communities could result in violence as well. These activities could be carried out with very limited military training, and without the fighters concerned being fully armed. Furthermore, the *exercitalis* was normally a small- or medium-scale landowner, directly involved in the running of country estates with the help of serfs and other dependants. Hence, there was a tendency for them to obtain exemption from military duties. This could fit with the interest that *iudices* had in profiting by illicit favouritism, given that they relied mostly on their personal adherents in the exercise of their authority. The normal military activities of the *exercitales* took place, therefore, within a local framework and were of limited commitment and duration, so as not to interfere seriously with the management of their economic interests.

The royal wars, by contrast, were waged on the frontiers of the kingdom; good equipment and training were required, and the risks were greater. The kings imposed by law the minimum equipment of weapons that each economic level had to possess, but they could not affect the military training of the freemen. Furthermore, it seems that the recruitment and the military service of the *arimanni* were organised on a local basis. The contingent from each city went to war together and took joint decisions on how they were to act. Loyalty towards the king and national solidarity were balanced against local political and economic interests. There are in fact examples of whole groups from one city or region taking the decision to defect in the course of individual wars (Paul the Deacon, *Historia Langobardorum* v, cc. 39, 41). It is probable that the kings and the most powerful aristocrats had groups of trained warriors who made up their entourage and were rewarded by gifts and favours; these were not sufficient, however, to fight full-scale battles, and had to be supplemented by the local contingents, so as to form what the sources call the *exercitum generale* (LP 303; I, p. 491). An army composed of independent groups and largely made up of untrained soldiers could be held together when the tasks were easy and the hope for booty high, as was the case under Liutprand and Aistulf. But in the pitched battles against the expert military organisation of the Franks, the general army of the Lombards found itself at a disadvantage. After a defeat in the field, each component group among the Lombards retreated whence it came, looking only to its own safety.

THE DOMINATION OF THE FRANKS

After the Frankish conquest, the Lombard kingdom survived as a distinct state, but at the price of losing its national foundation. Despite Pope

Hadrian's attempt to dismember the kingdom and place a major portion of it under his own authority (*LP* 319; 1, p. 498), Charlemagne did not carry out the pope's request, and indeed in 781 he had the pope anoint his son Pippin as king of the Lombards, although the child was then only four years old. Since Charlemagne kept the Lombard royal title for himself as well, his son was a sub-king: at first, a simple figurehead for the Frankish administration in Italy. Later, however, as an adult, Pippin was an alert and energetic executor of instructions which came nevertheless from his father. The subordination of the Lombard kingdom to the convenience of Frankish politics and strategic considerations was so firmly entrenched that in the *Divisio regnorum* of 806 Charlemagne decreed that, should Pippin die, the kingdom was to be divided between his two other sons (*MGH Cap.* 1, no. 45, c. 4).

In fact, the kingdom was not divided up. By 813 only one of Charlemagne's sons, Louis, was still alive, and in that year his father shared the imperial title with him, in preparation for his own succession. At the same time, however, Charlemagne conferred the royal title for Italy on Pippin's son Bernard. The separate identity of the former Lombard kingdom was thus confirmed, although it took some decades for it to recover autonomous government. After his succession in 814, Louis the Pious allowed Bernard to keep the title of king, but proclaimed the kingdom dependent on the imperial authority. A rebellion from Bernard in 817 was soon repressed, and Louis entrusted the control of the kingdom to his elder son Lothar, whom he had already associated with himself in the rule of the empire.

Lothar exercised his authority over Italy for more than ten years without living there, and without even adopting the title of king, purely on the strength of his imperial dignity.[2] Paradoxically enough, however, it was his political career which afterwards led to the confirmation of the independent existence of the kingdom of Italy. Having come into conflict with his father over the unity of the empire and the hereditary rights of his brothers, Lothar was forced to live in Italy more or less permanently for ten years, from 829 onwards. Although he did not, even then, identify himself with the royal Lombard tradition, nevertheless the continuous presence of a sovereign whose sphere of activity was *de facto* limited to the kingdom gave back to it a life of its own. The resolution, in 839, of Lothar's quarrel with his father marked a new confirmation of Italian autonomy, for, probably as part of the settlement, Lothar's first-born son, Louis II, was appointed king for Italy. In 844 Louis was sent to Rome to be anointed, and to receive the crown of

---

[2] *Contra* Jarnut (1991), p. 354; but the reference in *ARF* to a *corona regni* conferred by the pope on Lothar is generic, and does not indicate with any certainty the crown of the Lombards.

the Lombards from the pope. Although Lothar maintained control of Italy through his imperial authority, the existence of the kingdom as a separate entity was never again called into question. The events of the reign of Louis II definitively confirmed this.

Many aspects of the Carolingian government of Italy up to Lothar depended on the role the kingdom played within the empire. On several fronts the boundaries of the kingdom coincided with those of the empire. The ancient enmity between the Lombards and their eastern neighbours, the Avars, was inherited by the Carolingians, who had a common border with the Avars, in Bavaria as well. In southern Italy, the duke of Benevento, Arichis, the son-in-law of King Desiderius, having escaped the Frankish invasion thanks to the sheer distance of the duchy from the theatre of military operations, assumed the rank of an independent prince in 774 and severed the old links between the duchy and the kingdom. Charlemagne succeeded in making Arichis recognise his hegemony, but was not able to exercise any effective authority over the principality. Soon, the Beneventans sought the support of the Byzantine empire and fought the Franks along the border (Erchempert, *Historia Langobardorum Beneventanorum*, cc. 2, 3; Leo Ostiensis, *Chronica Monasterii Casinensis* I, c. 9). The Tyrrhenian coast also gradually acquired the characteristics of a frontier, because of the attacks carried out by the Saracens from the beginning of the ninth century, first against Sicily, Sardinia and Corsica (this latter a dependency of Tuscia), and afterwards against the Italian mainland as well.

The defence of the borders of the kingdom was thus essential not only for the maintenance of control in Italy, but also to confront forces which were essentially hostile to the empire. The Carolingians therefore preserved the regional structure of the Lombard duchies of Friuli and Spoleto, and they increased the authority and lands of the duke of Lucca, so as to create a substantial duchy in Tuscia too. These border districts took on the nature and functions of the marches of the Frankish political system. The Carolingian emperors chose their dukes from among the nobles they trusted most, and kept them under direct control, regardless of the presence of a sub-king in Italy. Inefficient dukes were replaced by other nominees; and efforts were made to provide them with adequate troops for campaigns beyond the border (*MGH Cap.* I, no. 99). A king was not therefore strictly necessary in Italy, as the country's strategic position could be secured by the keepers of the marches. The duke of Spoleto was also made a permanent representative of the emperors for the protection of the popes in Rome. When kings were appointed for Italy, therefore, as under Charlemagne, this happened more for dynastic than for strategic reasons, even though local kings helped to control the activity of the public officials and to gain consensus from the local populace, as a Carolingian king was ideologically bound to keep justice and to protect the feeble in his kingdom. As regards military activity, Pippin's role basically consisted in supporting the frontier wars of the dukes in the marches. Louis II at first performed the same duty under Lothar.

One problem for the Carolingians was the role that the Lombards themselves would have in the kingdom. It would not have been possible for the Franks to obliterate the identity of the Lombards, who, after all, were the majority of the population in the country. As king of the Lombards, Charlemagne to some extent took on the duty of acting as their protector; indeed he allowed them, for instance, to preserve their national law. But the Lombard ruling class was gradually removed from public positions; their places were taken by members of the Frankish, Alemannic and Burgundian aristocracy who had come in with the Carolingian conquest. These were appointed to the judicial districts of the kingdom, with the titles of counts, dukes and *marchiones* (marquises). Others were settled as royal vassals to control strategic points in the kingdom and to provide the counts with armed support. The replacement of Lombard officials was almost complete by 800, but the influx of Frankish vassals, officials and ecclesiastics continued after Charlemagne's death in 814. The last substantial wave occurred in 834, when many Frankish nobles, supporters of Lothar, followed him into exile and were rewarded by him with possessions and positions in Italy.

The imposition of the Franks as the governing class went with the elimination of Lombard tradition as the political ideology of the kingdom. Although Pippin and Louis II bore the official title of 'kings of the Lombards', in fact the Frankish sources normally refer to them as 'kings of Italy'. Even in a capitulary promulgated by Charlemagne in 801, reference was made to the 'provinces of Italy' (*MGH Cap.* 1, no. 98). This usage derived from the Carolingian custom of indicating the various parts of the empire by geographical rather than ethnic names, but it effectively served the purpose of stressing the newness of the regime in Italy and of masking the Lombard roots of the kingdom. It is significant that, from the reign of Lothar onwards, it also became customary for notaries to date documents according to the regnal years of the sovereigns 'in Italy'.

The prominence of Lombard law was also reduced. The Carolingian rulers promulgated special laws for the kingdom of Italy, sometimes presenting them as the continuation and completion of the Lombard legislation. But, in general, these laws were intended to regulate a new situation, in which people of different origins lived together in Italy and all had the right to call upon their own national law. Such legislation was still aimed at the free, but these were no longer qualified as Lombards or *arimanni*: under Lothar they were described as 'the whole populace living in the kingdom of Italy' (*MGH Cap.* 1, no. 201). Even the basis of legislative authority was new. Only in the earliest capitulary of Pippin is there any trace of the Lombard custom of promulgation in front of an assembly, in which Franks already took part (*MGH Cap.* 1, no. 91). After this, the Italian capitularies were prepared on the basis of written instructions which arrived from across the Alps or else were simply extensions to Italy of decisions already taken in Francia (*MGH Cap.* 1, no. 94). On one occasion, Charlemagne imposed Frankish customs to supplement the Lombard law (*MGH Cap.* 1, no. 98). Carolingian legislation was royal, supranational; the use of the Lombard law was allowed in so far as it did not conflict with the perspectives of the new sovereignty.[3]

The institutional organisation of the kingdom was altered as well. The Frankish government aimed at unifying and rationalising the Lombard administrative system through the office of the count. The counts, who took over the functions and frequently the districts of the Lombard dukes, formed an aristocracy of officials who derived their position from royal appointment, and had no organic ties with the society they governed. Thus the complexity of the duke-*gastaldius* structure was reduced. The *gastaldii* retained their original function as administrators of royal fiscal estates (*MGH Cap.* 1, no. 159, c. 4), but they no longer formed an alternative system of representatives of royal authority inside the kingdom. Towards the middle of the ninth century, many *gastaldii* were assimilated to Frankish viscounts, and were quite simply subordinated to the counts. All other local officials with jurisdictional powers were considered from the very beginning of the Frankish domination as *ministri* of the counts (*MGH Cap.* 1, nos. 98, 102).

This administrative reorganisation was not, however, so coherent as to eliminate all conflict. The Carolingians brought the church into the running of the state, making churchmen into supporters and advisers of the kings, and collaborators with and controllers of the counts. The relationship with the church was essential for the Carolingians, whose policy was supposed to have religious ends. In addition, the church in Italy already exercised influence over lay society, both in political and in economic terms. With its bishoprics and *plebes* it also offered a complete and systematic network of territorial districts, which could be useful in establishing control over the lay population. Thus the bishops were quickly absorbed into the governing

---

[3] Compare also *MGH Cap.* 1, no. 158, cc. 13, 14 (of Lothar), which validated Lombard legal customs by imperial authority.

class of the kingdom, and received jurisdictional powers similar in nature to those of the counts with whom they were urged to collaborate. Many bishops were sent to the Italian dioceses from Francia, but in general the foreign presence was less notable in ecclesiastical positions than in lay ones: ecclesiastical careers were generally the product of local recruitment. On the other hand, the religious and moral ideology of the Carolingian state implied the consent and collaboration of the church. Hence, the clergy, even those of Lombard origin, did not become spokesmen for a specifically Lombard politics. If they held to their own indigenous traditions, this basically occurred in the ecclesiastical field and at a local level. Within the structure of the kingdom as a whole, the bishops came increasingly to form a political body, loyal to the kings and endowed with remarkable influence over them. As far as their relationship with the counts was concerned, collaboration on the local level could easily evolve into competition.

Quite apart from these legal and institutional changes, Frankish domination was accompanied by a radical transformation of the social organisation of Italy, caused by the imposition – often by force – of seigneurial powers over the ranks of the free, which considerably weakened the common liberties of the Lombard tradition. The representatives of the new order, above all the counts themselves, used their powers of coercion to acquire for themselves huge landed estates. They exploited the subject population in every possible way with no regard for the rights of the free. Immediately after the conquest, a serious famine – and, probably, the uncertainty of the political situation – compelled many people to sell their estates for less than their worth, or make them over to powerful lords and to ecclesiastical institutions. Some of the free even sold themselves into servitude together with their families, in exchange for money or security (*MGH Cap.* 1, no. 88). Subsequently, Charlemagne and Pippin more than once complained that the counts, supported by armed bands in their service, were forcing freemen to work on their lands, make over part of the harvest, construct buildings, and give them hospitality at their own expense. Justice itself in the hands of the counts was frequently neglected, bent to suit personal interests, or else used as a means of blackmailing or coercing the free-born. Even the movement of people and goods was affected by the imposition of arbitrary tolls. The counts also oppressed the churches on their landed property as they unlawfully burdened the farmers, free or servile, who worked on it with both private and public services (*MGH Cap.* 1, nos. 90, c. 8; 91, cc. 7, 10; 93, cc. 5, 6; 102, c. 12; 103).

The most immediate result was the impoverishment of the weakest and, in extreme cases, the flight of the peasants from the land (*MGH Cap.* 1, no. 93, c. 6). In the longer term, the state too was damaged. Since the free owed public service in so far as they possessed landed properties, many freemen gave up their lands and even their freedom, agreeing to be the dependants of richer landowners in legally binding contracts, and then leasing back the same lands, which were now encumbered with rents and services; in this way, thanks to the spread of immunities from public obligations on the lands of the powerful, they at least escaped from the control of the counts, and in particular from the three services imposed on the free, which by now they often considered oppressive: the army, attendance at courts of justice, and the maintenance of public buildings, bridges and roads. The class of freemen was thus consistently diminished, while the rural seigneurie took on an increasing importance as a means of social organisation. Not even the ecclesiastical world escaped this process. Bishops began to change their long-established right of disposal over dependent churches into landlordship. They treated the *plebes* as estates from which they took rents and tolls over and above the canonical norms, and they appointed rectors to these churches on the basis of friendship and private interest (*MGH Cap.* I, nos. 92, 157).

The kings' attempts to change this situation were ineffectual, whether because they were only occasional, or because they went against the interests of the kings' own supporters. Charlemagne and Pippin probably succeeded in exercising a certain degree of control, but later the situation degenerated further. The abuses inflicted on the weak by the administrators of the kingdom gave rise to scandal even in Francia (Paschasius Radbertus, *Vita Walae* I, c. 26). Nonetheless, the laws by Lothar in the first years of his reign were concerned neither with administrative fairness nor with the protection of his subjects, but only with the prerogatives of the state. All that Lothar did was ordain that whosoever made over a landed estate to another while preserving the use of it was still bound to public service; to this effect he simply cancelled the immunity. Thus the powerful continued to act as they wished. At the beginning of his reign, Louis II had an enquiry made into the activities of the counts and their subordinates, which still listed the well-known abuses: arbitrary exercise of justice, violence, the misappropriation of landed estates and the oppression of the weak (*MGH Cap.* II, nos. 209, 210, 212). This predatory and oppressive aspect of the public authorities led not only to the weakening and shrinking of the social stratum of freemen, but also to a widespread sense of alienation from the state, which appeared as a structure offering advantages only to those who held power.

The cities provide a partial exception to this. During the Carolingian period, city-dwellers no longer had the political importance they had enjoyed under the Lombards. They did, however, preserve a certain capacity to act as organised bodies, which they exercised in the defence of their common economic interests, in the fulfilment of their obligations to maintain and restore public buildings, and in the administration of their collectively owned property. Besides the solidarity produced by these common interests, other elements gave rise to conditions favourable for preserving the freedom, both legal and economic, of the citizens. Individuals and groups in urban society had privileged relations with the holders of power, who often had their residence in the city, and, through them, they could protect their positions. Judges and notaries, the urban elite, collaborated in the administration of justice; merchants and artisans provided essential services; their own family members filled the various ecclesiastical offices within the cities. Even the landowners, who probably made up the largest sector of city-dwellers, were more protected from the oppressions which burdened the rural population through the mere fact of living in a city. The ties of vassalage which also existed among them did not involve a decline in freedom.

The peculiar character of the cities was probably recognised and sanctioned by the state through the practice of appointing *gastaldii* to administer the cities under the supervision of the counts. But the citizens felt that their individuality and their aspirations to local self-government were better represented by the bishop. Not only was the bishop separate from the authority of the count and able to act as a counterweight to the latter's oppressive tendencies, but he was also bound to the local traditions of the city, which to a large extent were expressed in ecclesiastical ritual. Foreign origins were less common among the bishops than among the counts. The episcopal church was also an economic focus for the city, in that it bought goods and services and leased out lands. It also offered career possibilities. Relations between bishops and city-dwellers were not always harmonious – there is evidence of conflicts in which bishops pursued the advantage of their churches without any regard for their city. Nevertheless, in the course of the ninth century there was an increasing convergence of interest between the economic expansion of the cities and the ambition of the bishops to play an ever more important political role. This process, on the other hand, did nothing to consolidate the body of the state, or to provide it with widely based consensus. The cities were concerned with their own independence, and saw the bishop above all as a local power capable of understanding their own needs, and of representing them before the king.

THE AUTONOMOUS KINGDOM

The political configuration of the kingdom of Italy took on a new character during the reign of Louis II (850–75). Following the division between

Lothar's sons, Louis II, although inheriting the imperial title, exercised real power only over the kingdom of Italy. As a result, the kingdom ceased to be an appendix to the empire, and became the privileged and indeed the sole sphere of imperial activity. This resulted in a weakening of the imperial dignity, but was a favourable opportunity for the kingdom itself.

Louis II asserted the kingdom's hegemony over the whole of Italy, in a way reminiscent of Lombard royal policy during the eighth century. The relationship with the papacy took on a particular importance. In 824 Louis' father, Lothar, had intervened authoritatively in Rome to put an end to the violent internal conflicts which were involving the papacy. He had compelled Pope Eugenius IV (824–7) to sign an agreement whereby both the election of the popes and their political and administrative activities were placed under imperial control, which was to be exercised by a permanent representative, living in Rome. Lothar also imposed on the pope and on the Romans the swearing of an oath of loyalty to the emperor (*MGH Cap.* I, no. 161).

Louis II clung to these prerogatives. He intervened, sometimes with force, in all the papal elections that occurred during his reign, to ensure that his preferred candidate won. Through his authority as emperor, he exercised strong control over the internal politics of Rome, favouring those groups of powerful people, whether lay or clerical, who supported the amalgamation of the Roman state within the body of the empire. He also made imperial prerogatives felt in the Exarchate, overriding the papal jurisdiction which had been instituted there by Pippin. He installed imperial vassals in the Pentapolis. Furthermore, he upheld the claims to autonomy of Archbishop John of Ravenna against Pope Nicholas I (858–67), although he was aware that the archbishop, with the help of his brother, planned to establish temporal domination over the whole ecclesiastical province of Ravenna.

Louis II also re-established a more effective royal control over the duchy of Spoleto. Lothar had preserved the duchy's function as a frontier region, establishing there in 842 Guy, son of his supporter Lambert, formerly count of Nantes, who had followed him into exile in Italy. As was the custom, Lothar committed to Guy the defence of Rome and responsibility for frontier relations with the Lombard principality of Benevento. Guy interpreted his function in very much his own way. He intervened in the struggles of the Lombard aristocracy after the murder of Prince Sicard in 839. In about 843 Guy married the late prince's sister and supported her brother Siconulf as a contestant for the princely power against Sicard's successor in Benevento. He thus opened the way for a political event of great consequence: the division of the state of Benevento into two independent principalities, one with its capital at Benevento and the other at Salerno. This was sanctioned in 849 by the young Louis II, on the orders of Lothar. Among other troubles, the fighting among the factions of the Beneventan aristocracy had favoured the spread of the Muslims in the south; they had begun the conquest of Sicily in 827, and now appeared in the Lombard lands, offering themselves as mercenaries to the various warring parties. The Carolingian government could no longer remain indifferent. Nowhere was royal intervention sufficient to stabilise the political situation in southern Italy. So in 858, Guy of Spoleto took further advantage of the lasting troubles of the Lombard principalities, and annexed a large complex of border lands to his duchy (Erchempert, *Historia*, c. 25). Although his activities increased the influence of the Frankish empire in southern Italy, they also reinforced the duke's personal power: Guy could now call on a network of alliances outside the Frankish world, and could turn himself into a prince capable of independent policy-making in the heart of central Italy. This represented a risk for royal authority. In 860, Guy's son Lambert, who had succeeded to Spoleto, rebelled against Louis II and, when faced with the latter's prompt military reaction, fled to Benevento, where he received hospitality from Prince Adelchis. A typical situation of the Lombard period, the alliance of the duchy of Spoleto with that of Benevento, was now recurring, and threatened Carolingian authority in central Italy.

Louis II was, however, able to cope with this situation. He entered Spoleto with his army in that same year, 860, and went as far as the northern territories of the principality of Benevento, conquering a number of cities. Prince Adelchis came to terms with him, and succeeded in having Lambert taken back into favour and re-installed in his position as duke. From that time on, however, Louis limited the duke (or, by now, usually marquis) of Spoleto's mandate with respect to the Lombard south. Instead, he made the assertion of his own direct hegemony over these far territories a major aim of his policy. Through it, Louis' imperial role regained its identity. A new understanding was reached with the papacy, which redefined the origin, nature and function of Carolingian imperial power. The Beneventan division of 849 had not solved the problem of the Muslim presence in the south of Italy. On the contrary, the Muslims had settled in various cities, in particular Bari, escaping the control of the Lombard princes, and waging war and practising piracy on their own account. The religious establishments of the south, including the monasteries of Monte Cassino and San Vincenzo al Volturno, together with the papacy, urged Louis to fulfil the imperial mission, which to them consisted of the defence of Christianity and of the church. War against the Muslims, which was to confirm his imperial role and demonstrate his power, and, if possible, widen his dominions, became his dominant preoccupation.

In 865, Louis II proclaimed a levy of all the freemen of the kingdom, according to Lombard tradition, and in May 866 he entered southern Italy. There he stayed for the next five years, hunting down the Muslims, settling his supporters in cities and castles, and imposing his sovereignty on the local potentates. The great southern expedition marked the summit, but also the limits, of Louis II's imperial policies. In fact, the general army was only mustered for a year, and was later reduced to vassal forces alone. In spite of Louis' numerous successes, including the taking of Bari, a lasting Lombard resentment against the Franks prompted the rebellion of the Beneventan prince Adelchis. He took the emperor captive and refused to free him until he had sworn neither to revenge himself nor to re-enter the principality. Thus, once again, the Beneventan region confirmed its autonomy versus the kingdom of the north.

This defeat did not mark the end of Louis' career. On his return to the kingdom, he prepared for a new expedition to the south, again at the request of the pope and the southern clergy, but his death in 875 prevented any further developments. A new sort of problem then emerged. For the first time since the Carolingian conquest, an emperor had left no male heirs. Under these circumstances, the far-reaching consequences of Louis II's reign became apparent. Throughout the period, the Franco-Italian ruling class, composed of the counts, the bishops and the royal vassals, had changed in both role and prospects. They were no longer put in charge of a subject province by an external ruler, but had become collaborators and participators in a local political system, which not only bestowed advantages and honours on those who ran it, but also in some sense involved them in the exercise of sovereignty, through their military and decision-making functions. Moreover, the survival of the autonomous kingdom was essential for them to maintain their power and prestige. During the second half of the ninth century, it had become difficult for members of the aristocracy to hold lands and wield political influence in widely separated regions of the empire. The kingdoms which emerged from the divisions among Louis the Pious' descendants of the empire were based on pacts between the bearers of the royal title and the aristocracy of a limited area. Whoever did not take part in these pacts was deprived of any real political participation. In Italy, likewise, the descendants of the immigrants from across the Alps had by this time taken root, and their chances of political action and influence lay within the kingdom. Thus, at the death of Louis II, the holders of public positions, both lay and ecclesiastical, acted as the collective upholders of Italian sovereignty. They gathered in an assembly to elect a ruler who would be able to ensure the continuance of the kingdom and to guarantee their new political role.

The reign of Louis II left one more legacy, however: the close relationship between the kingdom of Italy, the imperial title and the papacy. To some extent this conflicted with the desire of the nobility for self-rule. The kings of the Lombards had never been chosen by the papacy, even if their Carolingian successors had been anointed by the popes in Rome. Nonetheless, Pope John VIII (872–82) drew the final conclusion from the association of the Italian kingdom with the imperial dignity. He maintained that since the essential purpose of the emperor was the military defence of the papacy, the pope had the right not only to choose the emperor from among the various candidates, but also to impose him as king of Italy given that the experience of Louis II had shown that the emperor could only effectively defend Rome against pagans and wicked Christians when he had Italy as his base.

In choosing its new king, the Italian aristocracy was also limited by the prerogative of the Carolingian family, who were still recognised to have the right to take for themselves any royal post within the empire's boundaries. As a consequence, for the twelve years between the death of Louis II and the deposition of Charles the Fat, with whom the Carolingian domination came to an end, the Italian aristocracy was obliged to confer the royal title upon sovereigns who were not of local origin, and who had no intention of moving permanently to Italy. These were Charles the Bald, king of the West Franks (875–7) and two Carolingians of the German branch; Carloman (877–80) and Charles the Fat (880–7). Nonetheless, the influence of the aristocracy in the kingdom continued to rise. Not only was the choice formally expressed by their assembly recognised as the way royal power was constituted; but the foreign kings also needed support, collaboration and representation in Italy, and were willing to remunerate the help received from Italian aristocrats by conferring upon them titles and powers. To some extent all this modified the administrative organisation of the kingdom.

There were no institutional reforms in this period, but only individual concessions, depending on particular circumstances and personal relationships, which bound only the sovereign who conferred them. Charles the Bald gave the bishops of the kingdom the function of imperial *missi* within their bishoprics, and tried to create a new duchy in the Po region of Italy to control the kingdom in his absence. Carloman granted the bishop of Parma the *districtus*, that is, the public right of command and constraint, over his own city, as well as other fiscal advantages. Charles the Fat was lavish in granting the bishops exemptions from the jurisdictional powers of the counts, and extended these exemptions to all free inhabitants of church lands. Some among the lay lords were able to establish special relationships with the king, expressed in the title *consiliarius*, and were on occasion endowed with special powers, delegated directly by the king.

All this strengthened the tendency of the aristocracy to extend its authority, and to take advantage of the administration of the state. It explains the ever more frequent succession of son to father in the offices of count and marquis. The illegal practice of acquiring lands and services at the expense of ecclesiastical bodies and of the weak also revived again. Even the public services of the surviving *arimanni* were exploited for private ends.

The longing for increased power on the part of the aristocracy did not take place regardless of any interest in the preservation of the kingdom or in plans for its government. Underneath the fluid shifts of alignments and interests among the ruling classes, two distinct and stable positions may be distinguished with regard to the choice of the sovereign. All of northeastern Italy, including Friuli, the Veneto and the county of Verona, as well as almost all the bishops of the province of Aquileia, tended to support the position consistently and tenaciously held by the duke-marquis of Friuli, Berengar. This meant that they supported the candidature of the German Carolingians as heirs to the kingdom and as continuators of the policies of Louis II, who in fact had designated a German Carolingian his successor. The ideological background for this choice appears to have been a preference for a strong royal power and for the prospect of making the kingdom of Italy part of the constellation of states that the German kings were then creating north of the Alps and in Lotharingia.

A different orientation was pursued in northwestern Italy: its most conscious exponents were the bishops of the province of Milan, co-ordinated and led by their archbishop, Anspert, who had taken for himself the role of keeper of the royal tradition in Italy, by burying Louis II beside Kings Pippin and Bernard in the church of Sant'Ambrogio in Milan. These bishops seem to have been concerned as much with the independence of the kingdom as with the assertion of ecclesiastical control over the kings, much as Archbishop Hincmar of Rheims acted in the same period in the kingdom of the western Franks. The Milanese faction supported Charles the Bald for king in Italy, and remained thereafter hostile to Berengar, who tended to loose royal authority from ecclesiastical conditioning. Lay aristocrats who did not favour an authoritarian king grouped themselves around these bishops.

Weakened royal power also favoured the tendency towards self-government in the marches of Tuscia and Spoleto. This was particularly evident when, at the beginning of the 880s, new marquises succeeded those who had ruled under Louis II. In Spoleto, Guy II carried on the traditional family policies towards southern Italy and the papacy, with such unscrupulousness that he seemed to disdain royal and imperial authority, and was declared a traitor by Charles the Fat.

These divisions of groups, geo-political regions and programmes survived and were accentuated after the deposition of Charles the Fat in 887, which gave the Italian aristocracy complete freedom to choose a king, who after a long interval could again originate from and reside in Italy. In fact, this time there was no deliberative assembly, such as had gathered on the occasion of previous successions. Instead, the two most powerful marquises of the time, Berengar of Friuli and Guy of Spoleto, put themselves forward as candidates: the choice between them was from the first dependent on the outcome of armed conflict. Possibly these two represented opposing views of royal authority. Berengar based himself on Carolingian legitimism, since he was the grandson of Louis the Pious through his mother. He probably still aimed at a strong royal power, based on the military resources of the northeastern regions which he ruled as marquis, as well as at freeing the kingdom from its complex connection with the papacy. Certainly Berengar was the first king of Italy after the Carolingian conquest not to be consecrated by the pope.

Guy of Spoleto at first made an unsuccessful attempt at having himself made king outside Italy (*Annales Vedastini s.a.* 888; Liutprand, *Antapodosis* 1, c. 16). This may confirm either the lack of interest in the kingdom which he showed as marquis, or the originality and high level of his political aspirations. Whatever the case, he subsequently transferred his royal plans to Italy. There Guy sought and found supporters in the group of bishops of the province of Milan and in the lay nobility of the same region. Adalbert, marquis of Tuscia, a kinsman of Guy, also supported him.

Although not a Carolingian, Guy offered his supporters, and in particular the bishops, the restoration of Carolingian principles of government, accepting the concept that the royal office could be conditioned by the other political forces of the kingdom. He restarted the legislative activities interrupted at the death of Louis II, so as to revive the essential principles of good government. As a king he aimed to protect what survived of the free inhabitants of Italy, and to promote the collaboration between bishops and counts in local administration (*MGH Cap.* II, nos. 222–4). Guy also took on the defence of the church of Rome as the prime duty connected with his power. This enabled him to have himself anointed emperor in 891 by Pope Stephen V.

It is worth noting that neither of the two contestants for the kingdom of Italy referred back to Lombard tradition to give the kingdom an independent ideological basis. Memories of the Lombard kingdom survived in some sectors of Italian society, thanks to the historical information handed down by Paul the Deacon and to the continued observance of Lombard law. But, judging from the most relevant surviving evidence, the historical summary compiled at the end of the 870s by Andrea, a priest from Bergamo (*MGH SRL*, pp. 221ff.), these memories were incoherent and had no political implications. Furthermore, the social groups which did cultivate them did not include either the aristocracy, which preserved a very precise memory of its Frankish origins, or the upper clergy, which was linked to the Carolingian tradition of government. For this ruling elite, the autonomy of the kingdom merely implied a new balance of power between the aristocracy and the king within an essentially Carolingian ideological and constitutional framework. The aristocracy quickly took to behaving as if their powers were independent of royal appointment, even though these remained consistent with the institutional structure of the kingdom. As they were now accustomed to consider themselves the co-holders of sovereignty with the kings, they did not intend to admit that their governmental powers were dependent on the authority of one of themselves, even if he now held the royal title. The main exponent of this attitude was Adalbert of Tuscia, who boasted both a dynastic tradition and family connections equal to those of either of the aspirants to the crown. As he controlled enough economic and military resources to allow either faction to prevail, Adalbert throughout his political career used these resources to prevent any strong royal power from asserting itself, by giving and withdrawing his support to and from the conflicting kings, none of whom was ever able to trouble him in his own domains. Nevertheless, he continued formally to recognise the royal authority.

Other lay lords adopted similar attitudes, including those who through the fighting between Guy and Berengar had gained dominant positions within the aristocracy. At that time, a new march was created in north-western Piedmont, with its centre at Ivrea; the counts of Milan and Verona also adopted the title of marquis, and their power grew. Around them gathered less influential counts and vassals. The simultaneous operation of conflicting ambitions and attitudes was responsible for the many uncertainties revealed by the institutional organisation and the political activity of the kingdom during the first decades of re-acquired independence after 887. In spite of a general agreement to maintain the institutional structure of the kingdom, royal power was divided, for neither Guy nor Berengar was able to prevail over the other. Both of them kept the royal title, and exercised their power simultaneously; Berengar in northeastern Italy, Guy in the rest of the kingdom. After Guy's death in 894, an agreement between Lambert, his son and successor, and Berengar seemed to ratify this situation. Shortly after the death of Lambert, who had no heirs, in 898, Berengar was able to extend his rule over the whole kingdom, but the opposing aristocrats soon reinstated the system of two kings, by summoning Louis, king of Provence, to Italy in 901; Louis was related to the marquis of Tuscia and descended on his mother's side from the king and emperor Louis II. By this initiative, the aristocracy seems again to have put into question not only the unity of the kingdom, but also its independence. It is true that when in 894–5 the king of Germany, Arnulf, the bastard son of Carloman, had made an attempt to subjugate the kingdom of Italy, he failed more through the resistance of the aristocracy than because of the actions of the titular kings of Italy. Nonetheless, this summoning of a king from Provence makes it clear that, for a solid section of the aristocracy, independence did not necessarily imply an indigenous king, but simply one who would sanction aristocratic independence, formally unifying them by his legal authority. Resistance to Arnulf seems in fact to have been more a matter of that king's aggressiveness and intransigence than of his foreign origins.

The institution of the empire offered a partial corrective to these contradictions. There has always been some uncertainty about what the real value of the imperial title was, when it was held by sovereigns whose power was limited to the kingdom of Italy, or indeed only to parts of it. Since the time of Louis II, however, the universal nature of the imperial title depended on the special relationship between the emperor and the pope, rather than on the extent of his political control. In this sense the Italian kings could feel themselves to be true emperors, and were considered as such by the popes, as long as they carried on the essential duty of defending the papacy. Furthermore, again following the tradition of Louis II, the imperial authority in Italy had a wider and deeper role than the regal one. It was recognised not only in Rome, but also in the lands which had made up the Exarchate and the Pentapolis. The emperor could claim papal support and a privileged relationship with the church, even in territories over which he did not exercise authority as king. Within the kingdom, the imperial title at least in theory could resolve paradoxical coexistence of two rulers, by making whichever one was also emperor superior. The aristocracy, too, was prepared to grant greater prerogatives to the emperor than to the king. Hence Guy, Lambert and later Berengar himself did their best to have the popes consecrate them emperors. Hence, also, the aristocracy which was hostile to Berengar hastened to have Louis of Provence anointed emperor. Even after the dramatic failure of this attempt in 905, they went to great lengths to prevent Berengar receiving the title.

Thanks to this web of symbols and aspirations, the kingdom of Italy continued to exist, in the form that it had acquired during the Carolingian period. Royal power, however, while maintaining its ideal and legal position and much of its traditional economic resources, nevertheless lost its dominance as an institution. It had now to be exercised in a series of political confrontations between the kings on the one hand and, on the other, the holders of public authority, as well as the new forces which arose in northern Italy at the beginning of the tenth century: the expanding cities, and an emerging lower aristocracy, which tended to develop a jurisdictional competence quite alien to the order of the Carolingian state.

CHAPTER 13

BYZANTINE ITALY, *c. 680–c. 876*

T.S. Brown

BYZANTINE ITALY IN 680

BY the last quarter of the seventh century the Byzantine areas of Italy had experienced over a century of upheaval. Within decades of their first invasion of Italy in 568 the Lombards had established a powerful kingdom consisting of the territories north of the river Po, Tuscany and the two outlying duchies of Spoleto and Benevento. The empire was confined to the areas of Rome and its duchy, Ravenna and the neighbouring areas of the Exarchate and Pentapolis, approximating to the present-day Romagna and Marche, and a few coastal areas elsewhere. The Byzantines had only been able to hold on to their possessions by initiating a thorough-going militarisation of society, which involved the concentration of land in military hands and the concentration of authority in the hands of the commander-in-chief in Ravenna (the exarch) and his subordinates (*duces* and *magistri militum* at a provincial level and *tribuni* in the localities). In many areas, such as the Roman Campagna, this process was accompanied by a steady shift of population, as settlement became concentrated on military strongholds and refuges, usually located on promontory sites. Although the pressure eased somewhat in the seventh century, Liguria and most of the remaining settlements on the Venetian mainland were lost to the Lombards in the reign of King Rothari (636–52), and the duchy of Benevento made continual encroachments in the south, which accelerated after the unsuccessful expedition of Constans II to southern Italy (663–8). Internal tensions were reflected in a series of revolts, the determined opposition led by the papacy to the Emperor Constans II's monothelite doctrines (which culminated in the exile and death of Pope Martin I in the Crimea in 653) and a bitter conflict between the sees of Rome and Ravenna over the same emperor's grant of ecclesiastical autonomy (*autocephalia*) to the latter in 666.[1]

---

[1] On Lombard–Byzantine relations Delogu, Guillou and Ortalli (1980). On the Byzantine territories Guillou (1969), Brown (1984) and Ferluga (1991). On the movement of settlement to defensive *castra* Brown and Christie (1989).

In two letters addressed to his successor, Pope Agatho (678–81) bemoaned the dislocation caused by the 'gentiles' and complained that lack of food forced the clergy to work the land.[2]

By 680, however, the outlook appeared more hopeful. In that year, or shortly before, the empire had concluded a treaty with the Lombards which seems to have incorporated formal recognition of their kingdom.[3] Constantine IV (668–85) pursued a policy of reconciliation with the papacy which was reflected in his abandonment of support for Rome's ecclesiastical rival, the archbishopric of Ravenna, reduced taxation of papal patrimonies and a renunciation of monotheletism in favour of Chalcedonian orthodoxy at the Sixth Ecumenical Council, held in Constantinople in 680/1.[4] The process of absorbing the Lombards into the Roman and Christian mainstream was facilitated when the Arian beliefs which had long served as an anti-Roman rallying point for many Lombard kings and their followers were finally repudiated by King Perctarit (672–88). Complete unity within the catholic ranks was at last achieved when the damaging schism over the 'Three Chapters' was resolved by the Synod of Pavia (698). Byzantine influence was considerable in many respects, as can be seen through the strong presence of eastern clerics and artists not only in imperial territories such as Rome, but also in the kingdom of Italy, and in the Greek, Syrian or Sicilian origin of eight of the nine pontiffs who sat on the throne of St Peter between 676 and 715.

Any euphoria was short lived because the situation within the remaining Byzantine enclaves was inherently unstable. Successful resistance to the Lombards had been achieved through the concentration of power in the hands of elites formed locally from the local garrison units (*numeri*) of the imperial army. Bureaucrats and soldiers of eastern origin had married into native families, accumulated property locally and assumed a dominant hereditary position within their communities. This group, which probably included some more adaptable elements from among the middle-ranking civilian landowners surviving from the late Roman period, came to identify strongly with local interests and traditions, and was in a position to flex its muscles whenever it saw its position threatened by an imperial government which it regarded as remote and alternately impotent or oppressive. As a result of this process, and the empire's preoccupation with more immediate threats from the Arabs, Bulgars and Slavs and its consequent shortage of resources, the position of the exarch and other officials sent out from the east became increasingly marginal. Exarchal power was further limited in the early 690s by the elevation of Sicily into a theme, whose governor (*strategos*)

---

[2] *PL* 87, cols. 1164, 1219, 1220. [3] Dölger (1924), no. 240. The precise date is uncertain.
[4] Dölger (1924), no. 238 and references; Dölger (1924), no. 250; Mansi XI.

was also granted authority over Naples and the other imperial territories in the southern mainland.[5] In this context the transformation of the Lombards from barbarian bogeymen to Romanised catholics served to weaken allegiance to the empire further.

THE LAST DECADES OF BYZANTINE RULE

The delicate equilibrium was soon destabilised by the autocracy and impetuosity which the youthful Emperor Justinian II displayed in his first reign (685–95). After a brief honeymoon period with the papacy[6] the emperor in 691–2 convoked a council in Constantinople, the Quinisextum, or Council in Trullo, which promulgated a number of canons in conflict with the customs of the Roman church. Faced with resistance from Pope Sergius I, Justinian resorted to the same strong-arm tactics which his grandfather had attempted against Martin I. On this occasion, however, military contingents from Ravenna and the Pentapolis intervened to prevent Sergius' arrest by the *protospatharius* Zacharias.[7] The antagonism of Ravenna to Justinian found expression in 695, when a number of its citizens resident in Constantinople joined in the emperor's deposition and muti-lation.[8] Italian hostility to the empire was visible again in 701, when 'the army of all Italy' moved to protect Pope John VI against the newly appointed exarch Theophylact, who had presumably been sent to Rome by Tiberius III to pressurise the pontiff into accepting the Quinisextum decrees.[9]

The situation deteriorated further when Justinian recovered his throne with Bulgar help in 705. The chronology and motives of imperial policy are far from clear. However it is likely that while he harboured plans for revenge against Ravenna his approach to Rome was more accommodating. Papal support was seen as crucial to the emperor's desire for political and religious unity and the see of Rome appears to have enjoyed enhanced power as the representative of imperial authority in Rome.[10] John VII (705–7), the son of

---

[5] Oikonomidès (1964), pp. 121–30.

[6] A continuation of his father's pro-papal policy is demonstrated by a letter of 687 asserting his adherence to Chalcedonian orthodoxy (Dölger (1924), no. 254) and by a reduction of taxation on papal patrimonies in Sicily and southern Italy (Dölger (1924), nos. 255, 256).

[7] *LP* I, pp. 373–4.

[8] Agnellus, c. 137, p. 367. Although Agnellus' account has many legendary elements, support for this episode is offered by the known presence of Italian troops in Constantinople (Mansi XI, col. 737).   [9] *LP* I, p. 383.

[10] Llewellyn (1986). Noble (1984) approaches the question from a different perspective (of increasing tension and papal independence), but his interpretation is broadly compatible for the position between *c.* 680 and the outbreak of iconoclasm.

a Greek official, was offered a compromise over the Quinisextum decrees, which he refused. The pope then proceeded to establish a papal palace on the previously imperial preserve of the Palatine hill, and carried out a lavish programme of artistic production, best reflected in the superb frescoes of the church of Sta Maria Antiqua.[11] The strongly 'Byzantine' character of John's programme lends support to the notion of a positive element to relations between Justinian and the pope. For example, the emperor appears to have sided with Rome in a renewed conflict with its fractious suffragan, Ravenna. At his ordination in 709 the city's archbishop, Felix, refused to offer the traditional pledges of loyalty to the pope, and with the support of the (by now independent-minded) Ravenna officials (*iudices*) submitted his own version. The emperor's despatch of a punitive expedition led by the patrician Theodore, *strategos* of Sicily, can best be seen as retribution for this snub to papal authority on the part of the new exarch, rather than vengeance for Ravennate opposition to the emperor in 693 or 695.[12] By a ruse Theodore succeeded in arresting Felix and the leading citizens of Ravenna, who were taken to Constantinople and tortured.[13] In fear of further moves by Justinian the remaining citizens organised an elaborate local defence force under an elected duke named George.[14] It is probable that this new force caused the 'revolting death' suffered by the new exarch John Rizokopos when he sought to take up his post in Ravenna in late 710.[15] The whole episode led to a turning point in Ravenna's relations with the empire: the general allegiance associated with benign imperial *laissez-faire* in the late seventh century turned to marked antipathy and an even more marginal role for the exarchs in the eighth. It is hardly surprising that there was rejoicing in Ravenna when the emperor was deposed and his severed head was transported to Italy.[16]

Meanwhile a *rapprochement* between Rome and the empire had finally been

---

[11] Nordhagen (1988), pp. 600–10.

[12] My interpretation of this episode differs radically from that of Guillou (1969), pp. 211–18, who argues that the Ravenna *iudices* forced Felix to climb down and places Theodore's expedition after the murder of John Rizokopos. The latter chronology runs counter to the contemporary account in the *LP* (I, pp. 389–90) and my interpretation of the phrase *sed per potentiam iudicum [Felix] exposuit ut maluit* is supported by the translation of Davis (1989), p. 89.

[13] The outlines of the dramatic account in Agnellus, cc. 137–8, pp. 367–9, can probably be accepted because (a) the episode clearly loomed large in Ravenna folk memory and the traditions of Agnellus' family and (b) it is broadly confirmed by the *LP* account.

[14] Agnellus, c. 140, pp. 369–70. George was the son of Iohannicius, a learned secretary at the exarch's court who had served for a time in the capital before becoming one of the unfortunates arrested by Theodore.

[15] The account in *LP* I, p. 390 is vague; *suis nefandissimis factis iudicio Dei illic (sc. Ravennae) turpissima morte occubuit*.

[16] Agnellus, c. 142, p. 371, and cf. Niceph., p. 47, and Theoph. Chron. *s.a.* 6203, p. 381.

achieved in early 711, when Pope Constantine I (708–15) visited Constanti-nople, was honourably received by Justinian II and accorded privileges. However Justinian appears to have been playing a double game, since in the pope's absence the newly appointed exarch John Rizokopos executed four prominent papal officials, presumably to punish advisers considered anti-imperial and to intimidate the pope.[17]

Justinian was assassinated in December 711 and relations between Rome and Constantinople deteriorated during the short reign of his successor, Philippikos Bardanes (711–13), who was refused recognition in Rome on the grounds of his monophysite sympathies. As the *de facto* authority in the city Constantine had to make peace between the warring factions.[18] An improvement in relations followed Bardanes' deposition in 713, but once again events made this short lived. After years of instability the Lombard kingdom became a potent force under Liutprand (712–44), who adopted a policy of unifying the peninsula under Lombard rule. Meanwhile the empire came under renewed pressure from the Arabs which culminated in a year-long seige of Constantinople. In Sicily the *strategos* Sergios, in apparent despair of the empire's survival, rebelled and proclaimed a certain Basil emperor. Leo responded by sending an expedition under a replacement *strategos*, Paul, and Sergios was forced to seek refuge among the Lombards of southern Italy.

More serious was the Lombards' exploitation of the empire's difficulties. In 717 the duke of Benevento seized Cumae, the duke of Spoleto occupied Narni and the king himself invaded the Exarchate and occupied Classe. Although the loss of Narni proved permanent, Liutprand promptly withdrew from Classe and the Roman pontiff Gregory II (715–31) was able to recover Cumae. Once his position in the east was secure Leo III attempted to reassert the empire's authority in Italy. In 724 or 725 the emperor imposed an increase in taxation which hit the papal patrimonies, hitherto exempted from fiscal burdens by a privilege of Constantine IV, particularly hard.[19] In the light of Gregory's opposition a plot to kill the pontiff was hatched by imperial *duces* in collaboration with papal officials. When this failed the exarch Paul sent forces in support of another plot on the pope's life. However the Romans, together with the Lombards of Spoleto and Benevento, rallied to the pope's defence and forced the exarch's troops to withdraw.

Stronger resistance arose to Leo III's publication of decrees prohibiting the veneration of icons in 727. Gregory II's vehement reaction is reflected in the words of both the Roman *Liber pontificalis* ('he took up arms against the

[17] *LP* I, p. 390.   [18] *LP* I, p. 392.
[19] *LP* I, p. 402; on the circumstances see Marazzi (1991), pp. 231–46.

emperor as if against an enemy'[20]) and the Byzantine chronicler Theophanes ('he removed Rome and all Italy from his [Leo III's] rule'[21]). In areas such as Venetia and the Pentapolis this dispute reinforced existing discontent and prompted local army units to revolt and elect their own dukes. When the notion was mooted of electing a rival emperor and setting him up in Constantinople, however, Gregory refused his support in the hope that Leo could still be won back to orthodoxy, and urged the empire's subjects 'not to renounce their love and loyalty to the Roman empire'.[22] Serious divisions soon appeared within the Byzantine provinces. While in Rome the population killed one pro-imperial duke and blinded another, in the duchy of Naples iconoclasm appears to have attracted widespread support;[23] in the Exarchate there was serious conflict between pro- and anti-Byzantine factions, in which the exarch Paul lost his life.[24] Gregory's position reflects not only the durability of the imperial ideal in the absence of any ideological alternative, but also his need to retain a protector against the Lombards, still regarded as barbarians intent on exploiting the situation to dominate the peninsula. In fact, while the dukes of Spoleto and Benevento showed solidarity with the pontiff, King Liutprand seized western portions of the Exarchate.

Later in the same year (727) a new exarch, Eutychius, disembarked in Naples but was unable to enter Rome or to enforce his authority there.[25] When Liutprand moved south to establish control over Spoleto and Benevento, however, he and Eutychius found it expedient to make a surprising alliance against the pope. However Gregory was able to play upon the king's catholic piety to induce him to leave for the north, and a revolt in Roman Etruria in 728 gave Gregory an opportunity to demonstrate his continuing loyalty to the imperial ideal. The pope encouraged the exarch to defeat and capture the usurper, Tiberius Petasius, and Eutychius then also headed north in order to reimpose imperial control over Ravenna.

The empire's position was soon undermined by Leo III's promulgation of stronger decrees against icons in 730. After diplomatic remonstrations failed, the new pope, Gregory III (731–41), summoned a council in Rome in December 731 which resolutely upheld the iconodule position. Leo III responded by transferring the papal provinces of southern Italy, Sicily and

---

[20] *LP* I, p. 404: *contra imperatorem quasi contra hostem se armavit.*
[21] Theoph. Chron. *s.a.* 6221, p. 409.   [22] *LP* I, p. 407.   [23] P. Bertolini (1974).
[24] *LP* I, 405. the view of Guillou (1969), p. 220, that Leo responded by sending a punitive expedition, is based on a misunderstanding of Agnellus, c. 153, p. 377. The expedition referred to was probably intended to recover the city after its capture by the Lombards (cf. Bertolini, O. (1986b)), but Agnellus may also have confused it with the attack of the *strategos* Theodore in 710.
[25] *LP* I, p. 406.

Illyricum to the jurisdiction of the patriarch of Constantinople. However the attitude of the pope and the imperial authorities in Italy was surprisingly conciliatory. While Gregory took a principled stand in opposing iconoclasm and imperial persecution in the east, in practice he co-operated with Eutychius in defending the Italian provinces against the Lombards. In turn the exarch appears to have made no attempt to impose the iconoclast decrees in Italy and even sent the pope a gift of onyx columns for St Peter's. Eutychius' alliance with Liutprand had proved short lived, and imperial forces even attempted to recover some of the Lombard conquests. Lombard forces occupied Ravenna at an uncertain date in the middle or late 730s, forcing Eutychius to flee to Venice. Possibly after the failure of an imperial expedition to recover the city, Pope Gregory III wrote to the duke of Venetia and the Patriarch of Grado requesting their help in restoring Ravenna 'to the holy republic and the imperial service of our sons Leo [III] and Constantine [V]'.[26] A Venetian fleet dúly recovered the city.

In 739 Duke Trasamund II of Spoleto captured the stronghold of Gallese from the duchy of Rome. Gregory III resorted to negotiation to recover it for 'the holy republic and the Christ-loved Roman army'. The duke then rebelled against King Liutprand and, when ejected from his duchy by royal troops, sought refuge in Rome. In his fury the Lombard king then devastated the area around Rome and seized four strategic strongholds on the Via Flaminia, prompting Gregory to appeal to the Frankish mayor of the palace, Charles Martel. When the king returned northwards Trasamund was able to recover his duchy with Roman support.

Gregory's successor, the Greek Zacharias (741–52), had to face another period of uncertainty when the more militantly iconoclast Constantine V succeeded his father in 741 and was faced with a revolt by his brother-in-law Artavasdos. Liutprand appeared characteristically opportunistic in applying renewed pressure against both Spoleto and Rome. Zacharias resumed negotiations, obtained the four disputed *castra*, together with lost papal patrimonies in the Pentapolis and the duchy of Spoleto, and concluded a treaty of twenty years' peace with the Lombard kingdom (742). In the following year Liutprand prepared to attack Ravenna again, and in alarm the exarch and the city's archbishop appealed to the pope to intervene. Zacharias set off for Ravenna, where he was received with great honour by the exarch and population, and then on to Pavia, where he persuaded the exarch to return most of the territories seized from the Exarchate (summer 743). The pope acted independently of the empire, and appears for the first time to have staked the kind of proprietorial claims to the Exarchate which

---

[26] *ELC* 11, *MGH Epp.* III, p. 702 (= Jaffé and Ewald (1885), no. 2177).

he had to the duchy of Rome. Soon after, in 743, Constantine V granted the pope two estates south of Rome, probably in order to restore the pope's allegiance to his rule (Zacharias had recognised for a time the usurper Artavasdos) and to offer compensation for the loss of papal jurisdiction and property in 732/3.

751 AND ITS CONSEQUENCES

In early 744 Liutprand died, and Zacharias was able to confirm the twenty-year treaty with his successor-but-one, Ratchis. For obscure reasons Ratchis abandoned his pro-Roman policy in 749 and launched a campaign against the Pentapolis. Zacharias met the king and prevailed upon him to renounce his conquests, but within a short time Ratchis became a monk and was succeeded by his brother Aistulf (749–56). Aistulf adopted a more aggressive policy, including attacks on Istria, Ferrara, Comacchio and Ravenna itself, which was in his hands by 4 July 751. The ease with which the capital was finally taken may be explained by Eutychius' realism in surrounding the city in the face of considerable odds and by a pro-Lombard party among the Ravennati hostile to the only viable alternative, papal overlordship. This group may have included the city's archbishop, Sergius, who, according to Agnellus, had aspirations to rule the area 'just like an exarch'.[27] Certainly Aistulf showed himself aware of Ravennate sensibilities by observing the forms and titles of Roman rulership, patronising the city's churches and showing deference to its patron, St Apollinaris. Nor did he attempt a military occupation of the Exarchate, relying on control exercised on its border through the foundation of the royal monastery of Nonantola and the foundation of the duchy of Persiceto under a loyal Friulian noble.

The long-term consequences of the fall of Ravenna in 751 proved dramatic for the papacy and the Lombard and Frankish kingdoms, especially since the same *annus mirabilis* saw the deposition of the last Merovingian king with the sanction of Pope Zacharias, and the anointing of Pippin III as king of Franks by the Frankish bishops. Ironically the fall of the capital with more of a whimper than a bang had little direct effect on the remaining territories of Byzantine Italy (Map 18). The process of decentralisation had been under way for decades, with effective power in the hands of local elites led by *duces*. Nevertheless the history of the surviving provinces is best studied by examining them in three separate blocks, since in each the relatively uniform social structure of the imperial period was gradually transformed by particular local factors. In the north Venetia and Istria

---

[27] Agnellus, c. 159, p. 380.

retained their imperial allegiance, in the south Sicily and the duchies of Calabria, Otranto and Naples continued to come under the authority of the *strategos* of the Sicilian theme, and in central Italy the Exarchate, Pentapolis and duchies of Perugia and Rome were the subject of a tug of war between the Lombards, the papacy and entrenched local elites.

ROME AND ITS DUCHY

Zacharias' successor, Pope Stephen II (752–7), was alarmed when Aistulf followed up his conquests by demanding a tribute from the duchy of Rome, and sought help from Constantine V. At the emperor's behest, he entered into frantic negotiations with Pavia, but all to no avail. As Lombard pressure on Rome increased in 753, the pope made overtures to Pippin III, paid a fruitless visit to Pavia on imperial orders, and then proceeded over the Alps to meet Pippin at Ponthion (January 754). The upshot was that Stephen granted Pippin the title *patricius Romanorum* (with its echoes of the rank held by the Byzantine exarch), a Frankish army was sent to beseige Pavia and Aistulf was compelled to hand over to Stephen II territories formerly belonging to the Exarchate. When these promises were broken, the Frankish king returned to Italy in 756 and conceded all the territories of the Exarchate to the pope by the 'Donation' of Pippin. Although this represented a serious snub to imperial claims, a complete break between the papacy and the empire cannot be postulated before at least the 770s, when the pontiff's name replaced that of the emperor on Roman coins and documents. In practice, however, ties became increasingly close between the papacy and the Franks, and it was also to this period (*c.* 752–71) that most recent scholars would date the forging of the 'Donation of Constantine' (*Constitutum Constantini*) by a Roman cleric working in the Lateran chancery. Although it is nevertheless doubtful that this document can be seen as an official production intended to legitimise papal claims to Byzantine territory, it appears to reflect the predominant ideology of clerical milieux in Rome who were working towards a wholly independent status for the 'patrimony of St Peter'.

The following years were ones of uncertainty. Widespread fears of Byzantine attempts to recover their territory failed to materialise, while the new Lombard king Desiderius (757–74) showed himself at first conciliatory, but later hostile, to papal claims. Although after Stephen II's death in March 757 Desiderius failed to deliver all the areas he had promised and Pippin was too preoccupied with other concerns to intervene, an uneasy *modus vivendi* was achieved between the Lombard king and Pope Paul I (757–67). Following Paul's death, however, the duchy of Rome sank into bitter internal conflicts, whose key element appears to have been a struggle between an elite of military officials with their power base in the country and the clerical bureaucrats of the Lateran palace in the city. One such official, Duke Toto of Nepi, succeeded in having his brother, Constantine, 'elected' as anti-pope in June 767. Soon the clerical party regained power with Lombard help and had their candidate elected as Pope Stephen III in August 768, but serious difficulties continued, including anti-papal activity in the Exarchate and dissension among the papacy's Frankish allies. A coup staged in 771/2 against the clerical regime of Christopher and his son Sergius led to the rise to power of the pro-Lombard papal chamberlain Paul Afiarta. However, after the death of the vacillating Stephen III, a new pope from a leading Roman family was elected in 772 as Hadrian I, who proved no mere tool in Paul's hands. He had Paul arrested in Ravenna and resisted Desiderius' attempts to enter Rome and to have his protégés, the sons of the Frankish king Carloman, anointed there. When Desiderius proceeded to occupy strategic towns in the Exarchate, Hadrian prevailed upon the new Frankish king Charles to order their return. When Desiderius refused to comply, Charles led an army into Italy, besieged Desiderius in Pavia and took over the Lombard kingdom.

In Hadrian's pontificate (772–95) the papacy's alliance with its Frankish protectors grew increasingly close and cordial, especially after Charles conquered the Lombard kingdom in 774 and renewed the grants made by his father. Hadrian went to the length of addressing Charles as a new Constantine in 778.[28] Ties with the eastern empire were not formally broken (in 772 criminals were sent to Constantinople for punishment) but in practice turned to hostility. The pope's implicit claim to independence is evident in a letter addressed to Constantine VI in which he wrote of how Charles had 'restored by force to the apostle of God the provinces, cities, strongholds, territories and patrimonies which were held by the perfidious race of the Lombards'.[29] Hadrian's letters reflect his constant fear of a *reconquista* led by the Greeks in alliance with Duke Arichis of Benevento and Desiderius' exiled son Adelchis. The pope was unable to prevail upon Charles to intervene militarily against Benevento. In Rome and his hinterland the pope established new levels of prosperity and stability, largely as a result of his personal position as a powerful family magnate with influential relatives and allies among both the Lateran bureaucracy and the secular

---

28 *CC*, no. 60, *MGH, Epp.*, iii, p. 587. The passage appears to be based on the *Actus Sylvestri*, the main source of the forged Donation of Constantine.

29 'Tam provincias, quam civitates, seu castra et cetera territoria, imo et patrimonia quae a perfida Longobardorum gente detinebantur, brachio forte eidem Dei apostolo restituit': Mansi xii, cols. 1075–6 (= Jaffé and Ewald (1885), no. 2442).

aristocracy. The pope also succeeded in strengthening papal authority in the countryside round Rome by setting up six papal estate complexes known as *domuscultae* such as Sta Cornelia 25 km north of Rome. Here he was continuing a policy initiated by Zacharias, who had set up five such complexes, and more estates were set up by his successor, Leo III. These had a number of purposes, including the more efficient management of land and the securing of food supplies for the city at a time when it had lost its traditional sources of provisions in Sicily and southern Italy. However their primary role was to strengthen papal control in the face of the endemic disorder of the countryside, and to serve as papal strongholds against local warlords such as Duke Toto. The peasant workforce was organised into a loyal *familia S. Petri*, and furnished militia contingents which were used to suppress a *coup d'état* in 824 and to fortify the area around St Peter's in 846.[30]

Hadrian, however, experienced continuing difficulties in enforcing his authority over the wider complex of cities, villages and patrimonies often anachronistically termed 'the papal state'. These were particularly acute in areas where the papal claim to be heirs of the Roman state was somewhat dubious, such as the Sabine territories around the monastery of Farfa, which had been held by Lombard settlers for generations. Even in the Exarchate and Pentapolis, although opposition to papal rule subsided somewhat with the death of Archbishop Leo of Ravenna in 778, Hadrian complained in 783 that lay officials (*iudices*) from Ravenna had appealed directly to Charles and in 790/1 elements in the city were denying the pope's legal authority (*dicio*). The pope did however receive additional territories on the occasion of Charles' visit to Italy in 787 when the king made over a grant of part of Lombard Tuscany stretching from Città di Castello in the north to Viterbo and Orte in the south and a number of towns in the duchy of Benevento (although some, including Capua, remained in practice in Lombard hands). The pope also had problems in establishing his rights to various papal patrimonies in the duchy of Naples, and it was probably to apply pressure for their return as well as to secure the southern flank of the duchy of Rome that papal troops seized Terracina from the Neapolitan duchy in 788.[31]

Hadrian's successor, Leo III (795–816), was a less powerful character from a non-aristocratic background. As a result his position was much weaker, and his dependence on the Franks for protection even greater. His first action was to treat Charles in the manner that preceding popes had adopted towards their Byzantine sovereigns by sending him the protocol of his election, together with a pledge of loyalty and the keys and banner of the city of Rome. Matters were brought to a head by a coup in 799, when

[30] Christie (1991), pp. 6–8.   [31] *CC*, nos. 61, 64, *MGH Epp.*, III, pp. 588, 591–2.

aristocratic elements associated with Hadrian I accused Leo of various offences and sought to arrest and mutilate him. Leo first fled to Spoleto and then over the Alps where he met Charles at Paderborn. He then returned in the autumn with an investigating commission of bishops and officials in order to restore his position in Rome. In the following November Charles visited Rome and was crowned emperor in St Peter's on Christmas Day 800. The intentions of the parties involved in this event are the subject of considerable debate, but here it need only be pointed out that the papacy's action represents the culmination of a long process of distancing from the Byzantine empire and that one possible motive for Charles may have been to win support in the 'Roman areas' of Italy such as the Exarchate and Rome by exploiting vestigial nostalgia for the Roman imperial title.[32]

As a result of the events of 800, Rome burnt its boats with the Byzantine empire on a political level. An alternative ideological model was instituted, clerical control of the government was enhanced, and Frankish influence became more marked. The pope adopted a strongly pro-Frankish policy as long as the Carolingian empire lasted (until 888), and the chronicler Theophanes wrote, 'now Rome is in the hands of the Franks'.[33] Thus in 817 Louis the Pious issued the privilege known as the *Ludovicianum* in which the grants of his father and grandfather were made more tidy and precise on terms favourable to the papacy.[34] In 824, however, a less generous line was taken by the *Constitutio Romana*, which weakened the papacy's independence by setting up two *missi*, one papal and one imperial in Rome and in demanding from the Romans an oath of loyalty to the empire.[35] Byzantium remained a factor, but only of limited importance, in the first half of the ninth century. Fears were expressed of plans for a Byzantine *reconquista*, and there may well may have been links between the eastern empire and elements of the secular aristocracy nostalgic for the Byzantine period and eager for an end to the influence of the 'barbarian' Franks. Certainly in 853 a *magister militum*, Gratian, was accused of accepting Byzantine bribes. The situation changed, however, as a result of the growing threat of Muslim naval power to the coasts of Italy, especially after the sack of St Peter's in 846 and the

---

[32] Classen (1951). Such a policy certainly appears to have had the desired effect in Ravenna since the normally xenophobic local writer Agnellus accepted the legitimacy of Charles' imperial title: Agnellus, c. 94, p. 338: cf. Brown (1986), pp. 109–10.

[33] Theoph. Chron. *s.a.* 6289, p. 472.

[34] Ed. Sickel (1883). Louis promised not to interfere in papal jurisduction or to intervene in papal elections.

[35] *MGH Cap.* I, no. 161, pp. 322–4. Noble (1984), p. 308, argues that the traditional contrast between the two documents is exaggerated and that the *Constitutio* was a logical extension of the *Ludovicianum*. Useful as this corrective view is, it has to be remembered that from 822 Italy was under the rule of Lothar who in general took a firmer line with the papacy than his father.

occupation of Bari in the same year. Although the papacy looked primarily to Louis II to deal with the Saracen danger, it supported his attempts to secure Byzantine naval co-operation, and when his efforts in southern Italy proved a failure, John VIII (872–82) resorted increasingly to diplomatic overtures to Byzantium aimed at involving the empire in a Christian 'crusade' against the infidel. These papal efforts were not crowned with success, however, until the successful storming of the Arab base on the river Garigliano by a league of Christian forces assembled by John X in 915.[36]

On an ecclesiastical level relations with Byzantium were strained by the second wave of iconoclasm in the east (815–43) and even after the restoration of icons contentious issues remained. The transfer of jurisdiction and patrimonies in southern Italy and Illyricum to the patriarchate of Constantinople and the closely associated problem of authority over missions to the Balkans proved sources of conflict, especially during the pontificate of Nicholas I (858–67). Nevertheless the papacy retained its claims to primacy over the eastern as well as the western churches, and Rome remained a magnet for eastern pilgrims and exiles. In many respects Rome remained within the Byzantine cultural orbit. Eastern artistic influence on the city remained strong, expressed through a flow of liturgical objects and in all probability also an influx of artists. A number of Greek monasteries continued to flourish in the city, and Rome became a major centre of translation activity, best exemplified by the Latin versions of Greek historical and hagiographical texts produced by the papal librarian Anastasius.

On an institutional level the extent and durability of the Romano-Byzantine inheritance has been a subject of controversy, mainly because of the paucity of evidence for the ninth century. Certain titles from the imperial period continue, such as *consul, dux* and *magister militum*, while others, such as *tribunus*, disappear. There is similar uncertainty over whether the apparently lay judges known as *iudices dativi* constitute a survival from the Roman period. It is clear that any notion of a strong centralised secular authority on the traditional Byzantine model has to be rejected. This had already broken down in the last decades of the imperial rule, to be replaced by a decentralised power system in the hands of local warlords. On the other hand it is likely that most of the families to which the latter belonged established their position in the Byzantine period, and they remained deeply attached to the old imperial titles, even though these were used in an increasingly vague and debased way. In the city of Rome certain institutions persist which can be traced to the imperial past, such as the local militia units

---

[36] Brown (1988b), p. 38.

(*scholae*) and the strong sense of public rights and property, but these were taken over and transformed under papal control. The papal bureaucracy itself modelled its workings and titles on that of the empire. In certain respects the popes themselves can be seen behaving in self-conscious imitation of emperors, as with Gregory's naming of the refortified Ostia as Gregoriopolis and Leo IV's short-lived foundation of Leopolis following the Arab attack on nearby Civitavecchia. In general there appears to have been a striking nostalgia for all those things Byzantine, especially in the sphere of titles, names and dress, and this became if anything stronger as the century progressed as a result of the growing disenchantment with Frankish barbarism and impotence. Northern writers pointed to the resemblance between the Romans and the Greeks, especially in the pejorative sense of their effeminacy and cowardliness.[37] The impact of *le snobisme byzantinisant*[38] proved more than a passing fashion, since it helped build support for renewed political relations between the Roman elite and Byzantium in the tenth century.

THE EXARCHATE AND THE PENTAPOLIS[39]

The other major areas within the central bloc of formerly Byzantine territories, the Exarchate and the Pentapolis, was also claimed by the popes after 751 but their authority was always much less effective. The two closely related areas had developed such strong local institutions in the last decades of imperial rule that the area's takeover by Aistulf had little effect. The short-lived Lombard overlordship appears to have been benign, and the king was compelled to hand over both areas to papal authority in 755, in accordance with a peace agreement made at Pavia[40]. This settlement aroused bitter opposition in Ravenna and, when Pope Stephen II decided to visit Ravenna in that year in order to make the necessary administrative arrangements, he was refused admission into the city by the local lay and clerical aristocracy, with the apparent connivance of Archbishop Sergius (744–69). A second Frankish expedition proved necessary to make Aistulf fulfil his promises, and a commission of Frankish officials was sent to the Exarchate led by Abbot Fulrad. Stephen II sent two influential Romans, the priest Philip and Duke Eustachius to assume authority in his name and they succeeded in

---

[37] For references see Toubert (1973) II, p. 1007.
[38] The phrase is that of Toubert (1973) II, p. 966.
[39] The valuable studies in Carile (1991, 1992) deal at length with these areas before and after 751.
[40] The tangled history of the early years of papal rule over the Exarchate has been convincingly clarified by Bertolini, O. (1950) and a number of articles published in the collection of Bertolini, O. (1968a).

sending the leaders of the local opposition to Rome, where they were imprisoned. Papal administrators such as a *vestararius* were then sent to the area, but it is unclear how much practical power they were able to exercise. Certainly they faced widespread obstruction and hostility from the local population, and considerable *de facto* power remained in the hands of the archbishop, whom the local writer Agnellus describes as ruling the areas 'just like an exarch' and 'arranging everything as the Romans were accustomed to doing'.[41] When Archbishop Sergius entered into negotiations with Aistulf to re-establish Lombard rule, he too was arrested and sent to Rome for trial by a tribunal of judges. At that moment Stephen II died, and his successor as pope, his brother Paul I, considered it expedient to reach a compromise, possibly out of fear of a Byzantine attempt to reconquer the Exarchate. Sergius was therefore sent back to his city with the right to conduct the day-to-day administration while the pope's overall authority was upheld. This arrangement seems to have worked relatively well until Sergius' death. The Lombard king Desiderius then joined forces with local military elements led by Duke Maurice of Rimini to impose a strongly anti-Roman cleric named Michael as archbishop, but he was deposed after a year as a result of popular outrage at his avarice and the arrival of Frankish *missi*. However the next, legitimately elected, archbishop, Leo (771–8), was equally hostile to papal claims and proceeded to send an embassy to Charles, much to the anger of Pope Hadrian I. The pope complained to Charles that Leo had taken over the cities of Faenza, Forlì, Cesena, Sarsina, Comacchio and Ferrara and expelled papal officials in them and in Ravenna itself. Charles took no immediate steps against the Ravenna prelate, who went on a personal visit to Francia to defend his position in the spring of 775. Charles' reactions are unclear, but Leo certainly behaved as if he had independent control of the Exarchate. He claimed that the king had granted him Bologna and Imola, prevented papal representatives from obtaining oaths of loyalty to St Peter, expelled papal officials and imprisoned a certain Dominicus, appointed count of Gavello by the pope.[42]

After the bitter resistance to the papacy led by the archbishops Sergius and Leo, the situation appears to have become more settled for the greater part of Charlemagne's reign, probably as a result of a compromise agreement.[43] The popes retained overall political authority, together with extensive but imprecisely known rights and lands. At the same time practical power was largely in the hands of the archbishop by virtue of his vast

---

[41] Agnellus c.159, p. 380. 'Iudicavit iste ...totum Pentapolim veluti exarchus... sic omnia dispondebat, ut soliti sunt modo Romani facere.' In general see Fasoli (1979).

[42] *CC*, no. 54.

[43] Noble (1984), pp. 172, 251, terms this arrangement a 'double dyarchy'.

patrimonies, his close political and economic ties with the local aristocracy, and his traditional role as focus for the Exarchate's traditions and aspirations. The details of these rights and powers cannot be reconstructed from the very patchy sources, and even the lively and contemporary local writer Agnellus (*fl. c.* 840) is of little help, since the biographies of most of the bishops of this period are missing in the one surviving manuscript of his work. In addition the presence of the Frankish rulers as kings of Italy complicated matters; even though most of them respected papal claims, they were susceptible to the imperial associations of Ravenna and aware of the strategic importance of the area with its seaports on the Adriatic and its proximity to the Byzantine possessions in Venetia. Frankish *missi* were also active in the area; Pope Leo III (795–816) had been receptive to scandalous utterances made by Archbishop Valerius (806–10) and others had seized material from the palace of Ravenna.[44] This interest was exploited with some success by the archbishops of Ravenna in order to obtain privileges.[45]

The rule of Pope Leo III (795–816) appears to have been particularly unpopular in Ravenna and encouraged the archbishops to solicit Frankish support. Charles seems to have turned a deaf ear to such requests, but the strongly anti-Roman Martin (810–17) apparently had success in winning Frankish support against papal claims through a mixture of sycophancy and bribes. The line taken by his successor, Petronax (817–34) was arguably more pro-papal, to judge from critical allusions in Agnellus' work and the privilege which he received from Pope Paschal I in 819. When Louis the Pious' son Lothar took *de facto* control over Italy in 822 he seems to have built up strong links with major sees such as Ravenna. The next archbishop, George (834–46), attempted to exploit Lothar's poor relations with Rome to undermine the papal position, and his policy may have been to seek a return to the autocephalous status granted by Constans II rather than the more limited autonomy sought by Sergius and Leo.[46] Certainly the gradual penetration of Frankish authority continued within the Exarchate, as is demonstrated by a legal case brought about by the *advocatus* of the archbishop and decided by imperial *missi* at Rovigo in 838.[47] However, he incurred the opposition of his clergy through his personal greed and his costly recourse to bribery of his royal benefactors.[48] Even more bitter hostility to papal overlordship broke out under archbishops Deusdedit

---

[44] *Leonis III Epistolae*, nos. 2 and 9, in *MGH Epp.* v, pp. 91, 101 (the expression used in the former is *turpitudo*).

[45] For details of what follows see Brown (1990).

[46] The suggestion is that of Fasoli (1979), p. 102.   [47] Manaresi, no. 43, pp. 139–44.

[48] George's personal visit to Lothar in 841 ended in fiasco when his imperial patron was defeated at the battle of Fontenoy and the see's treasures were plundered: Agnellus, c. 174, p. 389.

(846–50) and John VIII (850–78). The latter dominated the Exarchate in conjunction with his brother Duke Gregory and displayed his independence at the time of his consecration by altering the pledges of loyalty to the papacy and empire which new prelates were expected to sign. He co-operated closely with Louis II, who may have been attempting to incorporate the Exarchate within the kingdom of Italy. Unfortunately, like other ambitious Ravenna prelates, he appears to have feathered his own nest and alienated local interests in his opposition to Rome. In February 861 Pope Nicholas I responded to complaints against John by summoning a council in Rome. There the archbishop was excommunicated for heresy, violation of the rights of his clergy, especially his suffragan bishops, and interference with Roman rights in the Exarchate. John's appeals to Louis for help proved fruitless and in a second synod of November 861 John acknowledged his guilt and suffered the humiliation of receiving back his see from the pope on strict conditions. Nevertheless he continued to make trouble for the succeeding popes, Hadrian II and John VIII, and was roundly denounced in the latter's letters for usurpation of papal property.[49] The crisis over the succession to the empire which followed the death of Louis II in 875 gave John new opportunities. He sided with the Roman faction of Formosus, bishop of Porto, which supported Louis the German and Charles the Bald, and in 876 armed pro-Formosan elements sacked the property of papal followers, seized the keys of Ravenna from the papal *vestararius* and handed them over to the archbishop.[50]

Despite their difficulties the popes had some success in countering this separatist feeling through the backing of their officials and pro-Roman elements in the Exarchate and by holding regular synods in Ravenna, as in 874, 877 and 898. Thus Archbishop Romanus (878–88), was excommunicated for his anti-Roman policy in 881 and failed in his attempt to appoint his successor. However an important change in the balance of forces occurred towards the close of the ninth century. The rule of the Carolingian emperors was replaced by that of local Italian monarchs, who visited the Exarchate more frequently and held assemblies representing their whole kingdom in Ravenna. As a result the Exarchate and Pentapolis became more integrated into the kingdom of Italy, as is reflected in the dating system of the Ravenna documents from *c.* 898. Since royal authority was weak, the main beneficiaries were the archbishops who retained their metropolitan status and great prestige, wealth and patronage networks.[51] By the end of the ninth century,

---

[49] Belletskie (1980).

[50] *Fragmenta Registri Iohannis VIII Papae*, no. 62, in *MGH Epp.* VII, p. 55.

however, the area had lost much of its traditional Romano-Byzantine character since a centralised administration system had been replaced by family and patrimonial ties between the Ravenna elite and local elements, and dynastic links were beginning to be forged with neighbouring Germanic families from Tuscany and the Po valley.[52]

The nature of the Byzantine legacy in the Exarchate is difficult to assess despite the comparative wealth of evidence, furnished especially by the local writer Agnellus and the papyrus and parchment documents preserved by the church of Ravenna.[53] The evidence of the documents reveals remarkable continuity in the Greek and Roman names employed, in the use of Romano-Byzantine titles such as *magister militum, dux, tribunus* and *consul*, in the division and management of land, and, most significantly, in the close relations of the lay military elite with the see of Ravenna. This nexus was cemented through the leasing out of church land on generous terms and had its origins in an officially encouraged policy of the imperial period.[54] Paradoxically clear Greek cultural elements were limited in Ravenna, the residence of the emperor's representative. Although there is some evidence for the continued existence of Greek monasteries after 751, it is very limited compared with Rome and the liturgical or other influence from the east on the see was slight. Nor was there any trace of the translation activity or literary composition in Greek so evident in Rome.[55] Although the work of the local writer Agnellus includes a sizeable number of Greek terms, his attitude to the Byzantines is one of contempt, and this view appears to have been shared by most of his compatriots.[56] A letter which the patriarch Photius addressed to the archbishop of Ravenna is likely to have been less a reflection of the traditional links between Rome and the east than a desire to cause difficulties for the pope with a prelate known to be independent minded.[57] Even so there may have been a vestigial attachment to the eastern

---

[51] Fasoli (1979), pp. 106–9. The exact date and significance of the Exarchate's incorporation within the kingdom of Italy is the subject of debate. Some ties with Rome remained, as is shown by Archbishop John IX's election as Pope John X in 914.

[52] Fasoli (1979), pp. 110–11; Curradi (1977), pp. 17–64.

[53] Agnellus, in *MGH SRL*, pp. 273–391. Tjäder (1954–82) includes documents up to 700. The collection is known as the Codex Bavarus (Munich, Bayerische Staatsbibliothek, col. 44; *CB*, ed. Rabotti, *Breviarium*) records transactions as early as the seventh century. Most of the parchment documents (rare for the eighth century and before, more numerous for the ninth century) are still only available in Fantuzzi (1801–4).   [54] Brown (1979).

[55] Brown (1988a), pp. 148–9; Sansterre (1983), *passim*. Translation activity, especially of medical works, had of course been common earlier, in the sixth century.

[56] E.g. c. 140, *MGH SRL*, p. 369.

[57] Photius, *Epistulae et Amphilochia* II, no. 267, pp. 217–18.

empire in certain outlying areas of the Exarchate, especially those close to the Byzantine province of Venetia; thus a document from Rovigo near Padua was dated by the regnal years of the Byzantine emperors as late as 826.[58]

VENICE AND ISTRIA

In the early stages of imperial rule in Italy *Venetia et Istria* constituted a single province but at some stage in the seventh century it was divided into two. Istria embraced most of the peninsula, but its northern limits are uncertain, since it came under continual pressure from the Lombards, Avars and especially the Slavs. Extremely little is known of it during the imperial period, and it fell into Lombard hands for brief periods in or soon after 751 and again between 768 and 772. By 774 it was again in the emperor's possession, but at some stage in the late eighth century it was conquered by the Franks, possibly at the time of Charlemagne's victory over the Byzantines in southern Italy in 788.[59] It is all the more ironic that the most informative document on the society of Byzantine Italy survives from this obscure region and from the period immediately after imperial rule. In 804 three Frankish *missi* met at Rizana with the patriarch of Grado, the duke of Istria, the local bishops and 172 representatives of the local towns to examine the rights and exactions customary in the times of the Greeks. The resulting report, known as the Plea of Rizana or Risano, reveals the considerable local power exercised by the landowners and their leaders (*primates*), their attachment to their military offices (such as tribune) and to the titles obtained from the empire (*hypatos* or consul) and the relatively local level of taxes paid to the empire.[60]

Istria's neighbour to the west, Venetia, remained under Byzantine authority and experienced the most dramatic development in our period. The area also presents serious problems because the evidence is scanty and often late and unreliable. The islands of the lagoon from Chioggia in the southwest to Grado in the northeast had received an influx of refugees at the time of the Lombard invasion of 568 and became the predominant element of the Byzantine province of Venetia when the mainland city of Oderzo fell to the Lombards and the residence of the *magister militum* or governor was transferred to Eraclea (also known as Cittanova). The area followed the

---

[58] The document is referred to in a Frankish *placitum* of 838: Manaresi, I, no. 43.

[59] Ferluga (1988), pp. 174–5.

[60] Edited Manaresi, I, no. 17, pp. 50–6 and Guillou (1969), pp. 294–307. The tax paid by nine towns amounted to 344 *solidi mancosi* in addition to levies in kind and labour exacted by the duke and various obligations to the church, over which there was an argument.

general pattern of Byzantine Italy, with political and economic power concentrated in the hands of a local elite drawn from the ranks of the imperial garrison but increasingly identified with local interests. Within the islands, however, economic activity must have been based on fishing and local trade as much as agriculture. It was probably as a result of its growing trading role that the duchy was able to make an agreement with the Lombard king Liutprand which defined its boundaries on the mainland.[61] The area's distinctiveness was fostered by the existence of its ecclesiastical structures separate from the mainland under the authority of the patriarch of Grado. According to later tradition a period of a century and a half of rule by the indigenous nobility of *tribuni* was followed by the election of the first local doge or duke supposedly in either 697 or *c.* 715.[62] In fact this event occurred only in 727, with the election of the Eraclean leader Ursus, and was part of a more general process. As we have seen, many provinces elected their own *duces* that year as a result of the general discontent with the policies of Leo III. Also the step turned out not to denote any decisive break with the empire, since Ursus was soon recognised by the Byzantines as an autonomous *dux* with the title of *hypatos* and the area's continued loyalty to the empire was demonstrated by the help given to the exarch Eutychius in recovering Ravenna in the 730s. As elsewhere, the decline of imperial authority and the growing pressure from the Lombards led to an increase in conflict between local factions. The details of these are obscure, but they appear to have stemmed from rivalries between different families and islands, as in 742 when Malamocco revolted against the capital, Eraclea, and elected as duke Deusdedit, the son of Ursus. These internal pressures were exacerbated by the powerful presence of the Franks in the region from the 770s on. Venetia and Istria were not included in the papal claims to former imperial territories expressed in the 'Donations' of Quierzy and Pavia (754 and 756), but they did figure among the lands promised to Pope Hadrian I by Charlemagne in 774. Loyalty to Byzantium nevertheless remained paramount, and was reflected in the use of imperial titles and customs. For example the family of Maurizio Galbaio was probably following imperial practice when the founder's son and later his grandson were co-opted as dukes. Meanwhile Frankish power in the region was further enhanced by Charles' takeover of Friuli and Istria and defeat of the Avars, and certain factions found it expedient to side with the new western empire. Such a pro-Frankish group seized power in the person of Obelerius in 802. When Charlemagne recognised Venice as a Frankish fief under his son, Pippin, king of Italy, the emperor Nicephorus I retaliated by sending a fleet under

---

[61] Referred to in *Pactum Lotharii*, c. 26.   [62] Andrea Dandolo, p. 105; John the Deacon, p. 91.

the command of the patrician Nicetas. A compromise was reached whereby Obelerius' position as doge was confirmed with his accepting the title of *spatharios* as an imperial official. A truce between the two empires was signed in 807. However hostilities broke out again when Obelerius showed renewed signs of disloyalty to the empire and a second Byzantine fleet came into conflict with the Franks. Pippin intervened and sacked several of the settlements of Venice shortly before his death in July 810.

In the face of this crisis the Venetians sank their differences and established a new centre of settlement and administration at the Rialto under a new doge, Agnello Partecipazio (or Particiaco). Local opinion had shifted decisively in favour of attachment to Byzantium[63], and Venetia was recognised as Byzantine territory by the terms of the treaty which was agreed between the Frankish and eastern empires in 812. Venice benefited from its new-found stability to develop into an important emporium, trading in the luxury items of the east, exporting western timber, slaves, salt and fish, and serving as the empire's listening post in the west. The growth and sophistication of Venice's commercial role is reflected in the will of Doge Giustiniano Partecipazio, who died in 829: in addition to extensive property-holdings it lists investments in long-distance trading ventures.[64] Venice's relations with Byzantium remained cordial, with widespread use of Byzantine titles and fashions, but in practice the province was increasingly independent.

The doges also wished Venice to enjoy ecclesiastical independence, especially after the suffragan sees of the patriarchate of Grado were placed under the patriarch of Aquileia by the Synod of Mantua of 827. In the following year the body of St Mark was seized in Alexandria by Venetian seamen and deposited in a new basilica adjoining the ducal basilica in Rialto. The city's new patron rapidly became a symbol of Byzantine pride and independence.

The middle years of the ninth century were a period of both danger and opportunity for Venice. The Byzantine and western missions to the Slavs helped open up new areas to Venetian enterprise, but also led to new tensions which complicated Venice's position as a 'middle-man'. Even more serious was the wave of naval raids launched by the Arabs of North Africa. Venice's growing naval strength was called upon by the Byzantines to help combat these attacks on Sicily in 827 and in the Adriatic in the 830s and 840s. In 840 a treaty was signed with the Emperor Lothar which guaranteed Venice's neutrality, boundaries and right to trade freely. The Frankish

---

[63] Constantine Porphyrogenitus, *De administrando imperio*, c. 38, states that the Venetians told Pippin that they preferred to be subjects of the emperor of the Romans.

[64] 'De laboratoriis solidis, si salva de navigatione reversa fuerint'; ed. Cessi, *Documenti*, I, pp. 93–9.

recognition of Venice's power and independence was reflected in confirmations of the agreement in 856 and 880 and by a state visit by Louis II to the city in the former year. At the same time Venice faced new dangers from Slav disorder and piracy within its Istrian and Dalmatian spheres of influence and from the reassertion of Byzantine power in the western Adriatic following the reconquest of Dalmatia in 868 and of southern Italy from 876 onwards. Despite this powerful new presence, Byzantium continued to recognise the need for Venetian naval assistance, especially when a planned alliance with the Franks against the Arabs fell through, and in 879 an imperial embassy travelled to Venice to confer upon Doge Ursus I Partecipazio gifts and the title of *protospatharios*. Ursus' dogeship also saw the creation of *iudices* as magistrates and advisers to curb the doge's authority and the establishment of new bishoprics, including Torcello. From the late ninth century, therefore, many of the characteristic features of medieval Venice were in place, including some distinctive constitutional arrangements, a marked independence in outlook and government and wide-ranging naval and commercial activities, but the city retained its powerful but ambiguous links with the east.

THE DUCHY OF NAPLES

The duchy of Naples included the coast and islands of the Bay of Naples, the Terra di Lavoro inland and the outlying towns of Sorrento, Amalfi and Gaeta. Little is known of its history in the seventh century, and the traditional view that its first local *dux* was Basilius, confirmed by Constans II around 661, is now rejected. Its institutions followed the usual Italian model, with a concentration of power and property in the military elite of the *exercitus*, but its loyalty to the empire was consistently greater than the territories to the north, probably because of its maritime links with the east and the need for imperial protection against the constant threat posed by Lombard Benevento. Thus the Neapolitans allowed the exarch Eutychius to disembark in their city in 727, when most of Byzantine Italy was in revolt. The duchy was also sympathetic to the Isaurian policy on images, to the extent that the episcopal see was held by an outright iconoclast, Calvus, between 750 and 762. The duchy was unaffected by the fall of Ravenna in 751, having come under the nominal authority of the *strategos* of the theme of Sicily for several decades.

Nevertheless Naples experienced the same trend towards increased autonomy as other areas, and by 755 it had its first locally elected *dux*, Stephen. After his election as bishop in 767 Stephen was able to pass on the ducal office to his two sons, Gregory and Caesarius, in succession, and then to his son-in-law Theophylact. As in Venice, relations with the empire oscillated considerably, probably as a reflection of the ascendancy of rival factions. While the duchy supported the *strategos* of Sicily in opposing papal claims to Campania in 779/80, in 812 Duke Anthimus refused to send his fleet to help his nominal superior fend off an Arab raid on Ischia. In 818 the citizens petitioned the *strategos* to appoint a *dux* to govern them, but in 821 one such imperial appointee was deposed in favour of a candidate from the family of Stephen. The decisive stage in the detachment of Naples from the empire came, however, with the Arab invasion of Sicily in 827, when the *strategos* was too preoccupied to intervene in the duchy and Naples was left to its own devices to resist the growing pressure from the Arabs by sea and the Lombards on land. As an example of the delicate balancing act required, Duke Andrew employed Muslin mercenaries in 835 against Prince Sicard of Benevento and then gave his allies help in conquering Messina from the empire (842/3). Although Naples attracted considerable criticism for these opportunistic alliances with the infidel, the strengthened position thus attained enabled Andrew to conclude a favourable treaty with the Lombards in 836 (the *pactum Sicardi*), and in 839 Lombard pressure was for a time alleviated by the civil war which split the Lombard principality into two parts, Benevento and Salerno. Later, in the 840s, Duke Sergius, together with his son, the consul Caesarius, turned against the Arabs and won a series of victories culminating in the battle of Ostia (849). Later, however, the Neapolitans established friendly relations with the Saracens, perhaps in order to prevent raids form the Muslims' strongholds of Benevento and Taranto. Such a policy, while necessary to safeguard the duchy's political survival and commercial interests, drew bitter denunciations from the papacy. Once again outside intervention served to foment internal factional strife. Duke Sergius II was deposed and replaced by his brother, Bishop Athanasius II in 877. *Realpolitik* however compelled the new duke to make a new deal with the Arabs, thus earning excommunication by his former patron, Pope John VIII.

Already in the ninth century Naples began to assume an important role as a centre of translation activity from Greek, although this reached its height in the tenth century. Other evidence also demonstrates that the cultural and economic influence of Byzantium was pervasive. Imports of pottery from the east were numerous, signatures to documents in Greek characters were common and a penchant for Byzantine titles such as consul remained strong.[65]

To the north Gaeta had become increasingly important as a centre of

---

[65] Luzzati Laganà (1980); Brown (1988b), p. 34.

communications after Formia was destroyed by the Arabs and its bishopric transferred to the nearby port in the eighth century. It remained nominally part of the Neapolitan duchy until 839, although in practice it often had to align itself with the papacy, whose territories surrounded it. On occasion it acted independently of Naples, as when it responded to a request from a *strategos* of Sicily for help against Muslim raiding parties.[66] From around 839 its greater measure of independence is reflected in the title of *hypatos* held by city leaders such as Docibilis. Although its continuing ties with the Byzantine empire were reflected in the dating of documents by the regnal years of emperors and by the elite's custom of signing their names in Greek characters, the town was forced to adopt policies favourable to the Muslims. In the 880s Aghlabid raiders were allowed to set up a pirate nest near the mouth of the nearby Garigliano river – a move which provoked bitter denunciation on the part of Pope John VIII.[67]

To the south was the non-Roman settlement of Amalfi, first recorded in 596 as a *castrum* populated by refugees from the Lombards. By the eighth century it was recorded as a naval base used in conflicts with the Lombards, Franks and Arabs and assumed increasing importance as a trading centre, while remaining part of the duchy of Naples, perhaps because of the continual pressure it faced from the Lombards. Although its population was temporarily transferred to Salerno following its sacking by Prince Sicard of Benevento in 839, it soon after achieved independence from Naples under its own leaders (*comites* and later *praefecturii*). By the late ninth century its tiny territory consisted of a small coastal strip, the Monti Lattari in the hinterland and the island of Capri, and a dynasty was established by the *praefecturius* Manso which lasted for seventy years. Although the Greek element was never as strong as in Naples and its foreign policy became steadily more independent of the empire, its trading links with the east became increasingly important.[68]

THE DUCHIES OF CALABRIA AND OTRANTO

The term Calabria was originally applied to a late Roman civilian province corresponding to the Terra d'Otranto. In the mid-seventh century the imperial possessions underwent a severe crisis with their final breakdown of civilian administration and the capture of large areas by the Lombard dukes of Benevento. It is likely that, as a result of an administrative reorganisation in the late seventh century, the name was applied to a duchy ruled from

---

[66] Leo III, *Ep.* 6, *MGH Epp.* v, p. 96.
[67] Merores (1911), especially p. 15, but cf. the comments of von Falkenhausen (1980), p. 348 and Skinner (1992), pp. 353–8.   [68] Schwarz (1978), especially pp. 16–17.

Reggio and covering both the areas remaining under Byzantine rule, the Terra d'Otranto and southern Calabria (i.e. the areas south of a line running from the Crati to the south of Cosenza to Amentea on the Tyrrhenian coast).[69] This period marked an important stage in the hellenisation of both areas, probably largely as a result of immigration from Greece and Sicily rather than settlements of refugees from the Muslim invasions further east or official transfer of soldiers or peasants. In the early eighth century Otranto was lost to the Lombards and the term was confined to the old civilian province of Bruttium in the southwest toe of Italy, which came under the authority of the *strategos* of Sicily. The duchy is mentioned in a Byzantine rank-list of 842/3 but does not appear in another of 899, presumably because it became the main power base of the *strategos* of Sicily, when most of the latter island had fallen to the Arabs.[70] Disappointingly little is known of the duchy in this period from written sources, but archaeological research has pointed to a move away from settlements on the plains and coast towards hill-top sites and to fairly widespread circulation of eastern goods such as pottery.[71] Only after 885–6, when Lombard Calabria was conquered by Basil I's general Nikephoros Phokas, does the position become clearer.

Even less is known of Calabria's imperial neighbour on the heel of Italy, the duchy of Otranto. Otranto and Gallipoli remained Byzantine at the time of the Lombard advances of the late seventh century, but some time after 710 Otranto was lost. It was restored to the empire in 758 by King Desiderius in return for Byzantine help against a rebel duke of Benevento. The case for the area's status as a separate duchy depends on a seal of uncertain date, and the 'duchy's' non-appearance in a rank-list of 842/3 suggests that at some stage it was reincorporated in the duchy of Calabria.[72] The boundaries of imperial rule are uncertain: the duchy may have been confined to the dioceses which clearly came under the jurisdiction of Constantinople, Gallipoli and Otranto, or it may have included all the Terra d'Otranto including Oria. Excavations have suggested that Otranto was a rich centre, probably as a result of its strategic importance as the main point of entry for imperial troops and officials sent to the west.[73] However, following the swift *reconquista* of Lombard Apulia from 876 the capital became Benevento and later Bari.

---

[69] Von Falkenhausen (1978), p. 7; the boundary with the Lombards can be reconstructed from the *divisio* of the principality of Benevento: *MGH Leges nat. germ.* IV, p. 222.

[70] Oikonomidès (1972), p. 57, and cf. pp. 351 and 356. The lists in question are the *Taktikon Uspenskij* and the *Kleterologion* of Philotheos. Von Falkenhausen (1978), p. 7, suggests that after 843 Calabria became a *tourma* within the theme of Sicily.   [71] Noyé (1988).

[72] Cf. von Falkenhausen (1978), p. 9.   [73] Brown (1992), pp. 27–30.

SICILY

In radical contrast to the separatism evident in most of the Byzantine territories in the Italian peninsula, Sicily assumed a more central place within the imperial orbit from the seventh century. In the first half of the century it appears to have been a prosperous backwater secure from the Lombard assaults which devastated much of the mainland and retaining civil government under a *praetor* and resilient elements of civilian society. Following the first major raid by the Arabs in 652, repulsed by an expedition led by the exarch Olympius, it assumed a more central role on the political stage. After Constans II's decision to abandon Constantinople in 661 and his unsuccessful campaigns against the Lombards of southern Italy, the imperial court moved to Syracuse in 663. Although the emperor was murdered in 668, the island gained new importance as a naval base used to oppose Muslim advances in North Africa, and Justinian II elevated it into a theme in the early 690s. Its governor (*strategos*) came to assume authority over imperial territory in southern Italy and after the fall of the exarchal government in 751 also came to play a leading role in diplomatic negotiations with the Franks, Lombards and papacy.

The effects of these changes were mixed. The influx of officials and soldiers from the east accelerated a wide-scale process of hellenisation. The origins of this are uncertain, but there is evidence that a dual Greek and Latin culture existed in the Roman period and that the Greek substrata were reinforced by immigration, most notably from Greece and the Balkans, by the early seventh century. The church remained under the jurisdiction of the see of Rome, but the hellenisation, reflected in the Greek monks encountered by eastern visitors such as Maximus the Confessor and by the Greeks from Sicily who ascended the papal throne, is in sharp contrast to the impression of Latin predominance given in the letters of Gregory the Great. On the other hand the militarisation and decentralisation involved in theme organisation must have served to strengthen local elements. One reflection of this was the revolt of the *strategos* Sergios in 717–18, who responded to the Arab seige of Constantinople by crowning one of his subordinates, Basil Onomagoulós, as emperor. However after his defeat of the Arabs, Leo III had no difficulty in quelling the rebellion, executing Basil and forcing Sergios to seek refuge with the Lombards across the Straits of Messina.

The new emperor was prompt to recognise the economic as well as political and military value of the island. He ordered that the vast revenues previously paid to the Roman church should be transferred to the imperial fisc, and Sicily was one of the areas transferred from papal jurisdiction to that of the patriarch of Constantinople by his edict of *c.* 733. Partly as a result of these moves, the Latin element virtually disappeared and the process of hellenisation continued apace, as is demonstrated by a number of important saints' Lives and the importance of Greek scholars and ecclesiastics from Sicily in the eighth and ninth centuries such as Gregory Asbestas, Joseph the Hymnographer, Constantine the Sicilian and the Patriarch Methodios, whose reign saw the restoration of icons in 843. The dominant Greek culture, with its strong cosmopolitan links with the capital, appears to have been largely confined to elite groups and was limited in its local impact and character. Although several iconodules were sent into exile to Sicily and its neighbouring islands, there appears to have been large-scale migration as a result of iconoclast persecution. In general the iconoclast crisis seems to have had little impact on the island, apart from the execution of the *strategos* Antiochos together with eighteen other iconodule officials in Constantinople in 766, and the appointment of the strongly iconoclastic Theodore Krithinos as archbishop of Syracuse during the second wave of the movement.[74] Rather, the island's attachment to icons and to Greek saints helped to bind it more closely to the empire.

Nevertheless, unrest was clearly growing by the eighth century, although the pattern of this was different from the mainland. One likely factor here was economic decline. Although a full picture is only gradually emerging from archaeological surveys[75], the island's prosperity was probably adversely affected by the increasing frequency of Arab raids and by a severe plague in 745–6.

The island's ties with the centre were so strong that revolts seem to have reflected personal ambition or the political and religious conflicts of the capital rather than purely local separatism. A case in point is the crisis of 781, when the *strategos* Elpidios was accused by the Empress Irene of conspiring with her brother-in-law and the Sicilian *exercitus* prevented his arrest. Irene responded by sending an expedition, which defeated Elpidios' forces and compelled him to seek refuge in Africa, where he had himself crowned as emperor with Arab support.[76] Unlike the mainland provinces of Italy, Sicily lacked one dominant political and cultural centre analogous to Ravenna, Rome or Naples, or an independent-minded military elite with a strong sense of local collective identity and a tradition of autonomy. As a result the population's reaction to a crisis such as that of the 820s was divided and in some respects passive.

Discontent broke out early in the decade, possibly sparked off by the revolt of Thomas the Slav in the east (821–3). An attempt by Michael II to raise taxation from the island led to a rising by an anti-imperial faction. By

---

[74] Gouillard (1961), pp. 386–401.   [75] For a useful survey see Johns (1993).
[76] For details see Treadgold, pp. 66–7.

826 this faction was led by the ambitious commander of the Sicilian fleet, the turmarch Euphemios, who had led successful raids against North Africa.[77] When the *strategos* Constantine moved to arrest him, probably for his disloyalty rather than as result of the romantic excesses ascribed to him by later legend,[78] Euphemios responded by seizing Syracuse, proclaiming himself emperor and then defeating and killing his superior in Catania. However, some of his supporters then switched their loyalty to the imperial government and Euphemios was forced to flee to Africa, where the Aghlabid amir Ziyadāt Allāh I recognised his title and granted him a fleet to attack the island. In June 827 the predominantly Arab force landed at the western port of Mazara and soon after defeated the Byzantine *strategos* Plato. Despite fierce resistance and some Byzantine successes the Arabs gradually extended their hold over the island, conquering Palermo in 831, Cefalù in 857 and Enna (Castrogiovanni) in 859. A decisive blow was struck when the capital, Syracuse, fell after a nine-month siege in 878 and its population was massacred[79], although a few outposts survived into the tenth century.

SARDINIA

The worst-documented Byzantine province in the Italian theatre is Sardinia. In the seventh century it had close administrative ties with the Exarchate of Africa, although ecclesiastically it came under the authority of the see of Rome. It suffered from Lombard naval attacks, but these appear to have been successfully repulsed, to judge from an inscription attributing victories to the emperor (either Constans II or Constantine IV).[80] After the fall of the Exarchate of Carthage in 698 imperial rule over the island became increasingly nominal. However, Byzantine-style institutions and Greek titles apparently survived in the eighth and ninth centuries. By the latter century numerous attacks from the Arabs further weakened links with Constantinople and power became concentrated in the hands of locally appointed officials (*iudices*).

CONCLUSION

Over the two centuries Byzantium's position in Italy had turned virtually full circle from the outwardly hopeful but in practice precarious position of

---

[77] Alexander (1973), pp. 9–14.

[78] Later accounts claim that Euphemios had abducted his niece from a nunnery and forced her into marriage.

[79] For the contemporary but melancholy and impersonal account of Theodosios Monachos see Zuretti (1910).　　[80] Mazzarino (1940), pp. 292–313.

680 to the verge of a new period of power and influence in the late ninth century. Despite, and in some measure because of, the short-lived political and ecclesiastical peace which prevailed at the beginning, discontent and separatist feeling had grown rapidly. As a result of the election of local military leaders as *duces* the power of the emperor and his representative, the exarch, had become marginal from the late 720s. The fall of Ravenna in 751 was only one stage in the fragmentation of the Byzantine territories, but it did promote distinct development in each area. Only in the theme of Sicily and the associated duchies of Calabria and Otranto was traditional imperial control effective, assisted by a steady process of hellenisation. In Venetia and the various component parts of the duchy of Naples nominal loyalty to the empire survived side by side with growing economic sophistication and political independence under locally chosen leaders from the traditional military elite. Elsewhere, as in the Exarchate, Pentapolis and duchy of Rome, the predominant power came into the hands of high ecclesiastics, but these had to work out a *modus vivendi* with lay aristocratic families, and with the Frankish rulers of the kingdom of Italy after 774. In each area, however, developments were conditioned by the decentralisation which had got under way as early as the seventh century, and distinctive traditions and institutions, more often Roman than strictly Byzantine, remained powerful, as can be seen in the persistence of titles, names and legal institutions.

If Byzantium's power and influence were in decline for most of the period, it still remained a force to be reckoned with, as can be seen in its successful defence of its interests in Venetia, and the preoccupation of both the Franks and the popes with their relations with the empire. In the economic, artistic and literary spheres Byzantium's impact was as considerable as ever, and was channelled through Rome as much as through the nominally Byzantine centres. Byzantine naval power was always a powerful factor, and it is this which especially enabled the empire to come into its own again as a player on the Italian scene in the second half of the ninth century. Byzantium's position was reinforced by the devastation of the Arab raids, by disenchantment with Frankish political and military weakness and by the aggressive yet pragmatic policy pursued by Michael III and Basil I. The conquest of much of the Lombard territories in Apulia, Calabria and Lucania, including Bari and Taranto (conquered in 876 and 880 respectively) ushered in a new era of nearly two centuries of Byzantine domination in southern Italy.

CHAPTER 14

BYZANTIUM AND THE WEST, 700–900

Michael McCormick

THE early medieval societies of Byzantium and western Europe that emerged from the late Roman world shared more than a few institutions, traditions and religious experiences. They sometimes rubbed shoulders in ways we overlook. Rome's clerical elite was so hellenised that the pope who reigned at Charlemagne's birth spoke Greek as his mother tongue. Under Charlemagne's grandsons, the entourage of St Methodius, who was born in Thessalonica, was once an imperial official in Macedonia and was later a monk in Bithynia, used Greek majuscules in the memorial book of a German monastery to record their stay. Conversely, Franks served in the Byzantine emperor's military household and figured at palace banquets.[1]

Facts like these raise the broader question of how the two main entities of Christendom interacted over the six or seven generations from *c.* 700 to *c.* 900. The historical problem is not without snares. 'Influence' can be misleading: interaction between cultures rarely has one society passively undergoing the active influence of another. Once something is available, the borrowing civilisation must take the initiative in appropriating it from the other culture. So when, where and how Byzantium and the west came into direct or indirect contact needs clarifying. Moreover, though these early medieval societies evolved away from their late antique roots, those common roots are everywhere discernible, and it is easy to mistake residual for recent borrowing.[2] Even over seven generations, patterns of interaction changed. And Byzantium took as well as gave.

Around 700, a kind of community of imagination preserved lingering mental links where real ones had lapsed. In England, Bede still synchronised his universal chronicle with contemporary Byzantine regnal years.[3] And

---

[1] *Verbrüderungsbuch Reichenau*, 53D4–5; compare Zettler (1983); Philotheus, *Kleterologion*, p. 177.

[2] McCormick (1987).

[3] Bede, *De Temporum Ratione*, 591. Compare *De Temporibus*, 22; Bede gives mainly the eastern, not the western Roman imperial succession.

Frankish celebrants, eager to use authoritative new Mass texts imported from the Byzantine duchy of Rome, sometimes seem scarcely to have noticed that they were still praying for the Roman emperor.[4] Anglo-Saxon missionaries, heirs of a Byzantine missionary who had come to them from Tarsus via Rome, encouraged obedience to St Peter and a fascination with Italy that fostered face-to-face meetings with Byzantine provincial civilisation.

Paradoxically, by 900 actual contacts had increased and the old imaginary links were gone. In Byzantine eyes western Europeans' Christianity still created the basis for special relations with the empire. Traditional barbarian stereotypes still prevailed at Constantinople: the Franks were brave but stupid fighters, emotional and undisciplined, and recent experience confirmed their avid corruptibility.[5] If eighth-century Byzantines imagined Rome as a typical Byzantine town and the popes as obedient functionaries reverently storing imperial communiqués near the tomb of Peter or routinely transmitting them to western barbarians, ninth-century strains induced an angry emperor to brand the pope and his Latin language as 'barbarian'.[6] 'Byzantines', of course, never existed as such: the empire of Constantinople was known to inhabitants and enemies alike as Roman, a usage into which even a hostile Einhard slips.[7] Its subjects might simply identify themselves as 'Christians'.[8] Westerners might lump the empire's inhabitants together under the simplistic linguistic heading *Graeci*, particularly when they wished to ignore the uncomfortable political implications of eastern imperial continuity. Beneath the uniformity of its Greek public language and tax payments to the emperor in Constantinople, the empire was multi-ethnic: Armenians, Syrians, Slavs, Italians, Istrians all swore allegiance to the Roman emperor, and as cultivated a man as Einhard casually identifies a eunuch with a Slavic name as a 'Greek'.[9] But the ancient empire had changed since the days of Justinian's reconquests.

EARLY MEDIEVAL BYZANTIUM

The upheavals of the seventh century had transformed Byzantium. The old urban fabric of the Roman empire largely gave way. Though the precise causes and chronology remain controversial, archaeological evidence shows that, in the long run, the cities of Asia Minor and the Balkan peninsula fared

---

[4] Tellenbach (1934/5), pp. 19–21.

[5] Leo VI, *Taktika, 18*, 77; *18*, 85–9; cf. Dagron (1987), pp. 217–18.

[6] Pseudo-Gregory II, *Ep.* 1; recent arguments assigning these texts to Rome have left me unconvinced. For Michael III on Latin, Nicholas I, *Ep.* 88.   [7] *Vita Karoli*, 28.

[8] Mango (1980), p. 31.   [9] *Translatio Marcellini et Petri*, 4, 1.

little better than those of western Europe. Starting in 542 and recurring cyclically until 767, the great Justinianic plague and connected infections presided over sharp demographic contraction.[10] The provincial towns that limped on served mainly as seats of ecclesiastical and political administration. Despite streams of refugees, even the capital of Constantinople shrank dramatically in population.[11]

The rise of Islam had violently reduced the empire's geographic scale and institutional structures. Heraclius' (610–41) bitter war to free the wealthy eastern provinces from Persian occupation was wasted by cataclysmic Islamic victories from the Golan Heights (636) to Carthage (698). In 674–8 and 717–18, the Arabs besieged the capital itself. The old Danube frontier and much of the Balkans were overrun by Slavs, Avars and Bulgars, though the imperial government still clung to coastal strongholds like Thessalonica or Monemvasia. Rome and Ravenna hung by a thread as the Lombards expanded their power down Italy's mountainous spine. Emperor Constans II's (641–68) bold attempt to defend the empire's southern flank by transferring imperial headquarters back to Italy (663–8) collapsed with his murder.[12]

For a government whose professional bureaucracy and military forces were sustained largely by a land tax levied on the provinces, the fiscal implications of such territorial losses were devastating, amounting to as much as three-quarters of revenues.[13] Defeat and the fiscal crunch forced radical administrative and military reconfigurations in the empire's besieged remnants. And conjugated disaster opened more than a political crisis in a society which lived and breathed its religious sentiment: the challenge of Islam was ideological no less than political and military. Was the sect in whose sign the Roman empire had conquered since Constantine's conversion no longer stamped with God's seal of success?

Life-style and mental attitudes underwent a sea change as the amenities of late Roman daily life became a thing of the past outside the court's island of archaism.[14] By the seventh century, Greek had supplanted Latin as the characteristic language of the central administration. Outside the Latin-speaking outposts of Dalmatia and Italy, only the Latin lettering of coins and imperial documents, a few fossilised acclamations and the massive presence of Latin loan words in the technical jargon of the state offered a faint linguistic echo of the old Roman past.

Byzantine culture no longer coincided with the Byzantine polity. For a few generations, Constantinople ceded Hellenic cultural leadership to the

---

[10] Biraben and Le Goff (1969); Dols (1974); Allen (1979).
[11] Haldon (1990), pp. 92–124; Mango (1985), pp. 51–62.
[12] Corsi (1983).   [13] Hendy (1985), p. 620.   [14] Mango (1981).

empire's geographic edges. John of Damascus (d. 753/4?), the greatest Byzantine thinker of his time, wrote his Greek theological treatises under the Arab caliphs; the best Byzantine art adorned the shrines and pleasure palaces of the new Islamic empire, while remarkable Byzantine hagiography of the eighth century was produced in Italy or Palestine.

Small wonder that one of the few pieces of contemporary Byzantine literature translated into Latin around 700 is an apocalyptic vision of the Arab conquest, the last Byzantine emperor's return to Jerusalem and the impending end of the world![15] But events would follow an unforeseeable path. Transformed and reorganised, Byzantium was about to begin a remarkable resurgence. Bede, who had earlier succumbed to optimistic reports of the Roman reconquest of Africa, accurately reported the successful defence of Constantinople from the final Arab siege of 717–18.[16] That victory inaugurated an era whose scarce sources cannot obscure the renewal of Byzantine civilisation which, by 900, stood on the threshold of its great medieval expansion.

The changes that produced this revamped empire are much debated. The Byzantines themselves located the defining moments of their history in dynasties and doctrines, a vision which says as much about emperor and faith in Byzantine mentality as about historical trends. By these lights, confusion and usurpation followed the toppling and execution of Heraclius' last descendant, Justinian II (d. 711), until the usurper general Leo III (717–41) defended the capital from the Arabs and launched the 'Isaurian' or Syrian dynasty. The victorious Leo promoted a new cult practice whose affinity with Islam many observers feel is undeniable: he proscribed most religious images and their veneration as a form of idolatry. His dynasty championed iconoclasm almost to the end, uncovering powerful stresses within the Byzantine ruling class which succeeding generations memorialised as religious persecution.

Three generations later, the regent Empress Irene (780–90; 797–802) recruited Pope Hadrian I's support to overturn the imperial doctrine at the Second Ecumenical Council of Nicaea in 787. Charlemagne's ambassadors witnessed the palace coup that ended Irene's independent rule and the Isaurian dynasty in 802. Another period of short reigns, including too a toned-down iconoclasm, led to a coup by Michael II (820–9) who established the Amorian dynasty, named after his home town in Asia Minor. Another regent, Empress Theodora (842–56), finally abolished iconoclasm in 843. Her son Michael III (842–67) and the Amorian house were overturned by a palace parvenu, Basil I (867–86), who founded the

---

[15] Latin Pseudo-Methodius; cf. Prinz (1985).

[16] *De Temporibus*, 22; *De Temporum Ratione*, 592.

Macedonian dynasty, destined to reign if not always to rule for the next two centuries. Down to Michael III's time, soldier emperors predominated: Leo III and his son Constantine V (741–75) were particularly successful commanders.

Reorganisation and re-establishment of control characterise this era, whether we look at theology, the classical cultural inheritance or the hierarchy of church and state. Survival required first and foremost the military stabilisation of the eastern front, where Arab incursions into the empire's new agrarian heartland of western Asia minor were increasingly checked thanks to new provincial defence systems, known as themes. These *themata* spread sporadically as events dictated. The word's derivation is contested but it refers simultaneously to autonomous military units and to the large territorial districts in which they were permanently stationed and of which the empire was composed. They may have been inspired at least in part by the western Exarchates, earlier administrative and military structures elaborated in reconquered Italy and Africa. By the time of Charlemagne, themes and the generals or military governors (*strategoi*) who headed them had everywhere ended the late Roman tradition that strictly separated civil and military administration, and government had shifted to a permanent war footing.[17]

The mighty themes of Asia Minor helped slow the Arab advance. The European themes straddled the capital's western approaches and defended Constantinople from the rising power of the Bulgarians. But the very concentration of power that facilitated the generals' defensive tasks complicated the political structure of the empire, since *strategoi* like the future Leo III often challenged the emperor resident in Constantinople. The last great revolt of the themes in particular had serious consequences. The civil war between Michael II in Constantinople and Thomas the Slav (821–3) and the ensuing disarray contributed to the empire's greatest territorial losses in our period: the Arab conquest of Crete (*c.* 824–8) and the beginning in 826 of the fall of Sicily.

To counter their own provincial armies, the Isaurian emperors created a new, imperial army of cavalry and infantry, known simply as 'the regiments' (*ta tagmata*) and headquartered in the capital. The *tagmata* spearheaded offensive operations and played a key role in the Isaurians' notable successes in the Balkans and Asia Minor. At sea, the seventh-century Karabisianoi (from *karabos* 'ship') fleet, essentially conceived to defend the central coastal areas and sea approaches to Constantinople, was superseded by provincial fleets organised as maritime themes in the course of the eighth and ninth

[17] Lilie (1984).

centuries. An imperial fleet equipped with Greek fire was stationed at Constantinople and chiefly destined for long-range intervention, flanked by elements of the thematic fleets.[18]

Despite occasional setbacks, the new military apparatus proved effective in preserving the empire. Conciliar subscriptions between 680/1 and 879 document the progressive recovery of bishoprics whose territories had slipped out of Byzantine control in the 600s, as the empire expanded its reach westward across the Balkans and back into Greece, and eastward across Asia Minor. The government organised large-scale population transfers aimed at repeopling first the environs of the capital and then other critical regions of Asia and Europe. As surviving inscriptions attest, the emperors began refurbishing critical infrastructures. The return of imperial administration always meant the return of tax collectors, so that the tightening of central control was a mixed blessing for any provincial landowners who might have survived the century of storms. But whatever the local discomfort, the dynamic was probably powerful: imperial armies brought coinage, administrators and bishops, who sent back to Constantinople the newly restored tax revenues, which in turn reinforced the imperial treasury which financed the bureaucracy and military apparatus and enabled the empire to extend its reach even further.[19]

In the capital, the few great late Roman ministers like the Praetorian Prefects or Masters of the Offices, into whose offices various vertical chains of administrative institutions formerly converged, had disappeared. They were replaced by the omnipresent 'accountants' or logothetes ever vigilant for income and expenditure of a state straining against the abyss. These new sub-ministers reported directly to the emperor and so brought more direct lines of authority into his hands. Administrative structures were far more institutionalised than in the west, as professional bureaucracies looked after imperial finances and justice. The loss of Egypt and North Africa combined with Arab raids in Asia Minor to diminish the relative importance of great estates in the countryside, and enhance that of peasant villages as the predominant unit of rural organisation.[20] Whatever survived or now emerged as a ruling class owed much to government service as the source and sign of its wealth and power. The stresses of a ruling class in the making mark the top echelon of society: frequent *coups d'état*, political shake-ups and church schisms start to stabilise only in the tenth century. From *c.* 800, Byzantine and Frankish sources yield the earliest glimpses of family names

[18] Ahrweiler (1966), pp. 7–107.
[19] Recovery: Hendy (1985), pp. 77–85; 90–1; population transfers: Lilie (1976), pp. 227–54; inscriptions: e.g. Mango and Ševčenko (1972), pp. 384–93.
[20] Harvey (1989), pp. 14–22.

and clans like the Phocades or the Argyroi who would dominate the social scene at Byzantium's apogee and who seem to ride a rising tide of economic and demographic recovery.[21] A state hierarchy structured this emerging power elite, as imperial promotion granted life-long, non-hereditary state dignities like patrician or *protospatharios* ('first sword-bearer') and salaries to leading officials who trumpeted their titles on numerous surviving lead seals. Each official's place in the hierarchy was communicated by his position in imperial ceremonies and delineated in official lists of precedence, the earliest surviving example of which dates from 843.[22] For all its factions, the power of this senatorial order was such that a prudent pope might demand that it confirm by oath guarantees issued to his legates by a shaky regency, and it is this social group that supplied most of the challenges to imperial authority, whether they came in the form of conspiracies, usurpations or doctrinal dissidence.[23]

Iconoclasm, the most lasting and disruptive doctrinal quarrel of the era, had many consequences. Resistance to the imperial heresy challenged the emperor's power in matters of doctrine and, implicitly, in other matters as well. The considerable efforts subsequently devoted to restoring the emperor's prestige and redefining relations with the ruling class are most visible in the refurbishing of imperial ceremonial. Iconoclasm affected the institutional history of the church even more deeply. The patriarchs resided only a stone's throw from the imperial palace and were often under the emperor's thumb. The secular church's relative tractability with respect to imperial doctrinal shifts fostered internal conflict. Churchmen, who sought to resolve conflict without throwing the ecclesiastical hierarchy into chaos, clashed with zealots. A monastic party centring on the great cenobitic reformer Theodore of Stoudios (759–826) burned to root out any who had temporised with what had been the empire's official doctrine over nine of the last twelve decades, factionalising the church in ways which paralleled and were perhaps connected with fissures in the lay aristocracy. In any case conflict spilled over into other issues and spawned a series of bitter schisms from the Moechian controversy – a dispute centring on Emperor Constantine VI's decision to divorce and remarry in 795 – to the 'Tetragamy' in which the Italian patriarch and former imperial adviser, Nicholas I Mysticus (901–7; 912–25) bitterly opposed emperor Leo VI's (886–912) fourth marriage. Since partisans of each faction challenged their opponents'

21 On elite factionalism: Winkelmann (1987), pp. 75–7; families: Kazhdan (1974), pp. 124–5.

22 For seals, an essential source for prosopography and institutional history, see Nesbitt and Oikonomidès (1991); for the precedence lists: Oikonomidès (1972).

23 Mansi XII, col. 1073B.

ecclesiastical appointments, Byzantine bishops' careers seemed noticeably unsettled in this era.

Factionalism in the upper echelons of church and state provoked sudden political shifts which affected relations with the west. Since the days of Pope Leo I, whose memory the iconophile hero Theodore Graptus (d. 841/4) still celebrated, the Roman see and its doctrinal rectitude had enjoyed great prestige in the Constantinopolitan church. This prestige was only enhanced by Rome's role in the earlier monothelite controversies and Pope Martin I's (649–53) resistance, arrest and death in imperial custody which led the Byzantine church to venerate him as a martyr: a Greek account of his suffering was composed in eighth-century Rome. Rome had become the authority to which Byzantine religious thinkers under pressure appealed for support. That the duchy of Rome was slipping out from under the emperor's effective administrative reach only increased its attraction, hence efforts to persuade western authorities to curtail the activities of eastern *émigrés* at Rome.[24]

Culturally, four generations of theological debate for and against icons spurred renewed examination of the Hellenic theological and cultural heritage. The hunting out and recopying of old books to uncover or rebut authorities on icons mark the earliest stages in the birth of Byzantine humanism, the encyclopaedic movement. The political and economic recovery of a society based in large part on written administration equally invigorated literary culture. Imperial bureaucrats like the future patriarch Nicephorus I figure prominently in the early phases of the revival.[25] They were reinforced by intellectuals and others like Michael Syncellus or Patriarch Methodius who immigrated back to a recovering imperial centre from Arab-controlled Palestine or the Italian borderlands. As in the west (see Ganz below, chapter 29) so in Byzantium a new minuscule book script was the tool and hallmark of the new culture. So too the new Greek writing required and conditioned the phenomenon of transliteration. Ancient exemplars in the old script were sought out, compared and copied in the new script which has preserved in such Byzantine 'editions' most of what has survived of classical Greek and patristic literature.

In the capital, the receding danger of Arab siege was replaced by the imminent menace of Bulgar attack. Repairs were made to the city walls.[26] Behind their protective bulk, renewal stirred in a city where nature had reconquered much of the urban fabric. Though on a much smaller scale and with a more religious focus than the colossal monuments of the old Roman

---

[24] *Vita Martini I, BHG* 2259; cf. Mango (1973), pp. 703–4; Michael II and Theophilus, *Ep.*; Photius, *Ep.* 290.   [25] Mango (1975).

[26] Müller-Wiener (1977), pp. 288, 293, 303, 308; cf. p. 313.

state, construction and redecorating were nonetheless significant by recent standards and invite comparison with contemporary western efforts. In 768, Constantine V restored the aqueduct of Valens, which had been interrupted since 626 and was essential to the water-starved site of Constantinople. Numerous churches were remodelled in the ninth century. Theophilus (829–42) built a new suburban palace, 'Bryas', modelled, significantly, on the Arab caliphs', the new standard-bearers of luxury. Basil I constructed a splendid new chapel, the Nea, for the Great Palace, and the ebb and flow of icon veneration required redecoration of religious shrines according to the dictates of the moment.[27]

It was then a changing Byzantium which bordered on western Christendom. As the threat of political extinction receded, the reorganised empire reasserted control. The progress of imperial administration allied with an improving general situation and sporadic disarray amongst the empire's most lethal enemies to allow renewed, if staccato, campaigns of intervention at the empire's extremities, which despite all setbacks and reversals steadily continued to extend outwards from Constantinople.

BYZANTINE–WESTERN TRADE?

Broader economic structures had once spanned the Mediterranean and fostered Byzantine commercial interaction with the west. The sweeping changes of the seventh century naturally affected communications between the two former *partes imperii*. The occasional western shipwreck confirms that dwindling economic links to the eastern Mediterranean persisted into the 630s, perhaps reinforced by supply efforts to the last garrisons perched along the Ligurian coastline.[28] But even the trickle of sea communications between Constantinople and the west seems almost to dry up between *c.* 650 and 700.[29]

The reason remains controversial; certainly there were multiple causes. Trading networks of easterners residing in the west may have withered under the cyclical plagues, whose contagion contemporaries linked with shipping. Declining economic fortunes presumably shrank western purchasing power even before the Islamic conquests redistributed eastern wealth and reorganised macro-economic structures, fanning demand in the east. To grant Pirenne his due, warfare around the Mediterranean rim probably played a role. Greek and Coptic papyrus archives of 698–711 from

---

[27] See in general Mango (1985).
[28] For a ship from Constantinople that sank off Narbonne *c.* 630–1, see Solier *et al.* (1981), pp. 26–52; for Italy: Christie (1989).
[29] Claude (1985), pp. 303–9; cf. Christie (1989), pp. 259–63 and Panella (1989), pp. 138–41.

the inland town of Aphrodito (Kom Ishgau) on the Nile paint an astonishing picture of how the new rulers mobilised local wealth and conscripts for sea raids (*koursa*) launched from Africa, Egypt and the east.[30] Land travel too was disrupted: Byzantine loss of control in the Balkans blocked the old Roman overland routes to the west. Finally, Byzantium's own long-distance trade in the eighth century seems to have been reorientated along a new axis linking the Aegean and the Black Sea.[31]

Direct documentary evidence of trade between Byzantium and the west is slim, and complicated by the ambiguity of the notions of trade and 'Byzantine'. Should Venetian merchants, who recognised Byzantine sovereignty and sailed between Italy and Africa, Egypt and Palestine, be classified as Byzantine middlemen? In any event, over the next two centuries the old infrastructures of travel gradually recovered or were replaced. A gradual increase in exchanges seems to follow the nadir of *c.* 700, particularly in Italy. For instance a growing volume of goods shipped on the Po probably lies behind the appearance of new shippers.[32]

Practically in the shadow of the Alps, the more or less autonomous Byzantine outpost of Venice rose out of the Adriatic mists from insignificance to embody this change. The ancient trunk route linking the Tyrrhenian coast with the Middle East via the straits of Messina, around southern Greece and across the Aegean had never ceased completely to function and indeed, in 746–7, transmitted eastward the last major seaborne outbreak of the bubonic plague until 1347.[33] But over the next century, branch routes show increasing liveliness on the Adriatic or through the gulf of Corinth, feeding piracy along the coast. Even the old Balkan overland route returns to life.[34] However, the rare data on Venetian shipping between *c.* 750 and 850 point mostly to trade between Italy and the Islamic world. A slave trade appears to have run along the west coast of Italy and involved Rome and the shipment to Africa of enslaved Europeans by Venetian and Greek merchants *c.* 750–75, and emperor Leo V (813–20) was eager to block Venetian commerce with the caliphate.[35] It may be more than coincidence that all three of the 'early medieval' shipwrecks recently discovered off the French Riviera were apparently carrying goods from the Islamic world.[36] Similarly, not Byzantine but Arabic 'mancus' (Ar. *manqush*) coins served as an

---

[30] Bell (1910), pp. xxxii–xxxv; cf. e.g. no. 1350 (AD 710).   [31] Lilie (1976), pp. 276–9.

[32] On the competition of new ninth-century shippers, Hartmann (1904), pp. 80–2.

[33] Pryor (1988), pp. 93–111 and 137–49; Biraben and Le Goff (1969), p. 1497.

[34] The changing infrastructure of travel will be treated in detail in my forthcoming monograph. On Balkan travel, see in the meantime Obolensky (1988).

[35] *CC* 59, from 776; *LP* 1, p. 433; Dölger (1924), no. 400.

[36] Pomey, Long *et al.* (1987–8), pp. 19, 39, 49–50.

international medium of exchange along the edges of Byzantine Italy. Contemporary Latin references document the influx of Arab coinage – and, one would think, intensifying economic links – in eighth-century Italy.[37]

Merchants make only rare appearances in Carolingian sources, and 'Greeks' are rarest among them. Traders who do show up tend to be Frisians, Anglo-Saxons, Jews or Italians. The last two may have included subjects of the Byzantine emperor; in any event commercial contacts with Byzantium seem often to have been realised through non-Greek intermediaries.[38] Nonetheless, a few 'Greek' merchants crop up in the eighth-century Tyrrhenian sea. Towards the tenth century, some Italo-Byzantines imitated their neighbours in Amalfi, Naples and Gaeta, like the slave trader from Armo near Reggio di Calabria who would not sacrifice his trade's superior profits for less reprehensible commercial ventures. A near contemporary life of a Sicilian saint compared his crossing from Africa back to Sicily *c*. 880 to 'some huge ship filled with all kinds of merchandise'. Such hints perhaps explain the concession of a landing for Greek merchants to the church of Arles by one of the last Carolingians, Louis the Blind who, as we shall see, had other connections with Constantinople.[39] The North African connection underscores that Greek merchants, like their Venetian peers, might have found more profit linking western Europe with the huge Islamic economy than with Constantinople. In other words, western contacts with Byzantine merchants may have been an indirect result of commercial relations with the Islamic world. But this does not diminish the significance either of the intermediaries or of the overall growth in infrastructures which permitted and channelled relations between Byzantium and the west.

POLITICAL AND DIPLOMATIC RELATIONS

Constantinople took the diplomatic initiative in order to defend its own vital interests on its western flanks, especially in Italy. Over time both Franks and Byzantines expanded their imperial reach and their concerns converged or collided in other regions as well. Thus Charlemagne's destruction of the Avars in central Europe opened a power vacuum into which the dynamic Bulgarian kingdom expanded from its headquarters some 300 km north of Constantinople. Bulgaria's Greek inscriptions or inhabitants make its Byzantine cultural cachet unmistakable, and it may have acted occasionally as an intermediary.[40] Ninth-century Franks and

[37] Brühl and Violante (1983), pp. 48–9.   [38] Compare Pryor (1988), pp. 136–9.
[39] Eighth-century 'Greek' merchants: *CC* 59; slave trader: *Vita Eliae Speliotis*, 18; crossing from Africa: *Vita Eliae Iunioris*, 25; Louis III: Poupardin (1920), no. 59, p. 108.
[40] Venedikov (1962), pp. 273–7 and see Shepard above, p. 238.

Byzantines shared powerful and dangerous neighbours in the Bulgars. The new Slavic society of the Moravians which sprang up between the destruction of the Avars and the arrival of the Magyars would greatly concern the eastern Franks and allow Byzantium to cultivate yet another power situated to Bulgaria's rear. Finally, tenth-century links between Byzantium and northern Europe were foreshadowed by the Scandinavians' appearance on the Black Sea, a fact perhaps not unconnected with the new northeastern axis of Byzantine shipping. In 839 Emperor Theophilus sent some mysterious newcomers called 'Rhos' with his ambassadors to Louis the Pious. Louis knew a Viking spy when he saw one and so informed his Byzantine colleague.[41] A couple of years later, the Byzantine ambassador to the Franks and Venice apparently entered into contact with the Baltic trading emporium of Haithabu.[42]

Ideas as well as realities conditioned Byzantium's approach to the west. Byzantines viewed Constantinople as the capital of the Roman empire, a unique historical entity established by God to foster the spread of Christianity. Various barbarians had occupied parts of the whole but the empire retained theoretical claim to territories which were, for the time being, not effectively administered. This attitude affected imperial ideas about Italy, for example in Constantine V's pressure on Pippin III to restore the Exarchate of Ravenna to Byzantine control.

A second idea conditioned Byzantine policy and was linked with the first: just as the Roman empire was a unique historical entity, so its ruler, the *basileus* – the Greek word had come gradually to occupy the semantic zone of the Latin word *imperator*, triumphing officially by 629 – was God's lieutenant on earth and incomparably superior to other terrestrial rulers (*archontes*) or kings (*reges*). A family hierarchy of powers projected onto foreign relations the conceptions that structured domestic society. The Roman emperor reigned supreme as the father of all other rulers, although the exception once made for the Persian shah was now extended to the caliph, who was reckoned worthy of fraternal status. This would give a particular edge to the Frankish imperial usurpation, as it was viewed in Constantinople.[43]

The means by which Constantinople sought to effect its aims ranged from carefully calibrated gifts to armed intervention. They included religious co-operation or conversion, subsidising potential rivals and cultivating satellite powers as buffers as well as dangling prospects of marriage with the imperial family. A favourite tactic was to encourage hostile action by the enemies of

---

[41] *AB*, pp. 30–1; compare Ahrweiler (1971), pp. 46–9.   [42] Laurent (1978).
[43] See Ahrweiler (1975), esp. pp. 129–47; *ODB* I, p. 264 and III, p. 1945; Grierson (1981), pp. 890–914.

Byzantium's enemies.[44] All these approaches featured in the diplomatic dialogue with the west.

Geographically and historically, a fragmented Italy and its complicated local politics held the key to Byzantine dealings in the west. The Lombard principalities of the Po basin, Spoleto and Benevento pressed against the increasingly autonomous Byzantine coastal areas stretching from Ravenna to Naples via Rome. At the extreme south of the Italian boot, first Sicily and later Calabria and Apulia anchored Constantinople's power in Italy. The loss of Rome to the barbarians – for this is how Constantinople viewed the papal alliance with the Franks – and Carolingian ascendancy in Italy inevitably intensified Byzantine interest in the new transalpine power.[45]

Three successive trends characterise the political situation. As elsewhere in its former dominions, Constantinople sought in the early eighth century to reintegrate Italy into the imperial structure, and so to restore late antique patterns of political domination. But local and distant forces conspired to loosen Constantinople's grasp on the Italo-Byzantine societies. From the north, expanding Lombard power absorbed Ravenna in 751 and menaced Rome. The Franks would soon swallow the Po kingdom and extend the Lombard pattern into an attempt to restore a Roman empire in the west. They forcibly removed northern Italy from the Byzantine sphere and so strengthened its transalpine political, cultural and economic links that it looked much like the southernmost extension of northern Europe. The even greater vitality of the Islamic world capitalised on the complexities of southern Italy to drive Byzantium from Sicily and establish toeholds on the Italian mainland. Finally, the collapse of the Frankish empire combined with the resurgence of Byzantine power to shift the dynamics in a new direction so that, as far north as Rome, the peninsula again appeared as the northwestern edge of a southeastern Mediterranean world.

If Italy was the key to Byzantine and western interaction, Rome was the key to Italy. The city's cultural and religious significance outweighed its economic or strategic importance, although the wealth of its churches would tempt Arab and Frankish looters alike, and great prestige accrued to its master. It was uniquely suited to intensive cross-cultural contacts. Politically it lay on the fluctuating frontier of Byzantine and northern power zones. Culturally, it attracted pilgrims from all parts of the Christian world: Irish, Anglo-Saxons, Franks, Lombards, Byzantines, even Arabs made their way to its fabled shrines.[46] From 700 to 900, its elite culture changed. Around 725, the church of Rome was nearing the last generation of its

---

[44] Obolensky (1963).   [45] Von Falkenhausen (1978–9), p. 152.
[46] Byzantine pilgrims: von Falkenhausen (1988), pp. 644–6; cf. the semi-fabulous description associated with Harun ibn Yahyah: ibn Rusteh (1955), pp. 144–6.

'Byzantine period'. The papal bureaucracy, the lay elite and monasteries all
show signs of Greek predominance, as some befuddled Anglo-Saxons
learned in 704 when the papal advisers they were meeting began joking and
discussing the matter among themselves in Greek.[47] The city produced Greek
literature, including the Life of Martin I and Miracles of St Anastasius, while
surviving fragments suggest that Greek inscriptions were not uncommon.[48]
The public face of the papal court owed much to Byzantine provincial
officialdom, naturally enough given the prominence of descendants of
refugees from the eastern upheavals. Although the process is difficult to track,
such families must increasingly have assimilated the local language, even as
innovations rooted in the immigration flourished, whether we look to the
name stock of the Roman elite, saints' cults or new liturgical feasts like the
Assumption, all imported from the east.[49] From about the middle of the
eighth century Latin prevails, but a Greek heritage perdured: the person who
forged the Donation of Constantine wrote a Greek-accented Latin, the
Lateran Palace probably had a library of Greek manuscripts and Pope Paul I
supplied Pippin III with Greek books.[50] Two or three generations later, the
Greek presence at Rome appears to have been concentrated in the monasteries, which had received fresh reinforcements fleeing the upheavals in the
Byzantine church. Papal distributions to the monastic establishments of the
eternal city reveal that in 807, six of the most important monasteries and one
convent were Greek.[51] A fragment from their liturgical services shows that
one community used the Greek liturgy associated with Jerusalem when
praying for Pope Hadrian.[52] In the later ninth century, some Roman
aristocrats may still have felt nostalgia for Byzantine rule, Anastasius
Bibliothecarius may have been able to compare different manuscripts of
Pseudo-Dionysius in Rome, and the occasional Greek monk might work
purple cloth or copy texts there. But the instruction and use of Greek was
becoming rarer and more private.[53] As Roman ambassadors insisted in
Constantinople in 870, some churches under Roman jurisdiction were Greek
in language, and clergy appointed to them were chosen for their linguistic
qualifications.[54] But Anastasius stands head and shoulders above his

---

[47] Eddius Stephanus, *Vita Wilfridi*, 53.

[48] In general: Sansterre (1982); cf. 1.138–9 on the *Vita Martini* (BHG 2259); *Miracula Anastasii*
(BHG 89); inscriptions: Cavallo (1988), pp. 484–92.

[49] Provincial ceremonial: McCormick (1990), pp. 252–9; names: Llewellyn (1981), pp. 360–1;
saints: Sansterre (1982, 1), pp. 147–9 and Detorakès (1987), pp. 94–6.

[50] Donation: Loenertz (1974); library: Riedinger (1989), pp. 13–15 on BN grec. 1115; *CC* 24.

[51] *LP* 405; II, pp. 22–5; Sansterre (1982) I, pp. 32–4 and 90–1.   [52] Sansterre (1984).

[53] Nostalgia: Brown (1988a), pp. 39–44; Anastasius' MSS: Chiesa (1989), p. 198; cloth and
calligraphy: *Vita Blasii*, 14; changing character of Greek learning: Cavallo (1988), pp. 490–2.

[54] *LP* 634–6; II, p. 183.

contemporaries. By 900 immigration from the east had shrunk to undetectable levels and the old Greek monasticism of Rome was entering its final decline even as Byzantine power was resurgent in the south.[55]

In some ways, the very recovery of the imperial centre distanced the two societies: a reorganising empire sought to tighten slackened links with provincial society by restoring old standards of political, fiscal and religious integration and subordination long in abeyance and now newly resented. A carrot and stick approach seems unmistakable: *c*. 710 Justinian II violently repressed a rebellion in Ravenna and blinded and exiled its archbishop Felix; later the same prelate was restored and enriched. Pope Constantine and his entourage were summoned to Constantinople for a year-long consultation and celebration of unity, during which the future Pope Gregory II's theological expertise impressed the emperor, who confirmed earlier privileges of the Roman church, while imperial envoys arrested and executed the papal officials who had stayed behind in Rome.[56]

Some time between *c*. 724 and 755, a series of distinct developments coalesced to undermine the old assumptions which governed the church of Rome's thinking about the empire. The precise chronology and relative weight of each development is disputed, but the overall result is clear. As Constantinople reorganised, it increased the tax burden on the lands of the Roman church. The papal establishment resisted paying. Despite imperial efforts to stabilise the Arab threat from the south, expanding Lombard power menaced Rome and Ravenna ever more acutely, even as pressing military threats closer to home kept Constantinople from shoring up Italy's defences. Leo III's new doctrine of iconoclasm met papal opposition. The imperial government responded to papal tax delinquency by confiscating the papal properties in Sicily and Calabria; then or somewhat later, the emperor transferred ecclesiastical jurisdiction over southern Italy and Illyricum from Rome to the patriarch of Constantinople.[57]

According to their loyal biographers, the popes vociferously protested at doctrinal and administrative measures of which they disapproved even as they dutifully represented imperial power in security matters. Thus in 713 Constantine I intervened to quell a murderous riot against an official who had accepted an appointment in the name of Emperor Philippicus (711–13), whose orthodoxy the pope himself had challenged.[58] Gregory II is supposed to have quashed an Italian plan to elect a rival emperor to oppose Leo III's

---

[55] Sansterre (1988), pp. 709–10.   [56] Agnellus, 137; 143–4; *LP* 170–4, 177; I, pp. 389–91, 396.

[57] Arab threat: 728: Pope Leo III, *Ep. X*, 7; cf. Amari (1933), pp. 350–1; taxes: *LP* 183; I, p. 403, ll.22–4; Theoph. A.M. 6217 and 6224; cf. Sansterre (1982) II, p. 165, nn. 176–7; on the date of the transfer: von Falkenhausen (1978–9), pp. 151–5; cf. Schreiner (1988), pp. 369–79.

[58] *LP* 176; I, p. 392.

iconoclasm and attack Constantinople, despite purported Byzantine plots on his life.[59] Pope Zacharias intervened twice with the Lombard kings to protect Ravenna. Despite recognition of the usurper Artarasdos (741–3), he even obtained the imperial estates of Ninfa and Norma in Campania from Constantine V.[60]

To judge from the imperial largesse, papal opposition sounded louder locally and beyond Byzantine borders than inside the Great Palace in Constantinople. Nonetheless, the pope had held a local synod in 731 to clarify his position against iconoclasm. Roman links with the Greek milieux of Jerusalem which were ardently defending icons from the safety of the caliphate, and with monks fleeing from Constantinople, perhaps stiffened papal attitudes. The measures concerning the papal patrimonies and jurisdiction were certainly not tailored to soften Roman doctrine.

Doctrinal and administrative differences might have remained just that, as they had in far more dramatic circumstances a hundred years earlier, were it not for the inexorable Lombard threat. This pressure produced a triangular relationship among Constantinople, Rome and whoever controlled the Po valley, in which every *rapprochement* between two partners might threaten the third partner. When Rome urged Constantinople to check the Lombard threat, it nonetheless dreaded that Constantinople might sacrifice Rome to accommodate the Lombards. So, too, when the popes entered their alliance with the Franks, Constantinople attempted to bind the Carolingian kings to itself to the popes' detriment. Paradoxically, when Rome seemed strictly subordinated, relations between the Franks and Byzantines were on the best footing, for instance immediately after Pope Leo III's restoration by Frankish arms.

In its last century of existence, the Lombard kingdom of Pavia must have had fairly intensive contacts with Byzantium, not least because of its ongoing absorption of the Exarchate of Ravenna. But records are rare. Diplomatic exchanges for instance are known only in so far as the papacy was involved. The extent of contacts is suggested by a few hints: a Byzantine jester named Gregory entertained King Liutprand's court; Lombard royal charters emulated Byzantine models; and in 750, King Aistulf forbade business with the Byzantines during periods of conflict.[61]

The same pope who convened the synod condemning iconoclasm in 731 had secretly invited the Franks to attack the Lombards in what was, after all, only a classic manœuvre of Byzantine diplomacy. In 732, a Roman synod

[59] *LP* 183–5; I, pp. 403–6.

[60] Bertolini (1968) II, pp. 695–701; compare the different interpretation of Speck (1981), pp. 114–22.

[61] Lounghis (1980), pp. 133–4; *MGH Dip. Kar.* I, no. 183; Brühl (1977), pp. 9–10; Aistulf, *Leges*, 4.

very publicly ignored imperial sovereignty. A decade or two after the fact, a member of the Carolingian family remembered that the pope had promised *to defect from Byzantium* if Charles Martel helped him. True or not, it shows that under Pippin III the Carolingian clan fully grasped the Byzantine implications of intervening in Italy.[62]

Theological tension perhaps converged with Lombard military pressure to drive the papacy into the arms of the Franks: Pope Stephen II's trip across the Alps to seek Frankish intervention effectively put him and his chief advisers out of Byzantine reach for the iconoclast council scheduled in Constantinople for February 754. In any event, King Pippin's twin invasions of Italy in 754 and 756 signalled to Constantine V that his power counted in the ancient territories over which Constantinople was reasserting control. That Byzantium viewed the Franks in the light of Italy emerges from every aspect of the diplomatic opening: it followed Pippin's first intervention there; John *silentiarios*, one of the ambassadors, had headed previous negotiations with the Lombards; he stopped at Rome to co-ordinate with the pope before heading to Pippin's court.[63] Papal assertions to the contrary notwithstanding, Constantine V's efforts to woo the Franks for his version of an anti-Lombard alliance clearly tempted the Franks and frightened the Romans. In May 757, Byzantine ambassadors pressed their case and presents, including an organ, on Pippin's court at a general assembly at Compiègne. More than simply symbolising superior technology, a Byzantine organ was a strictly secular instrument used chiefly in ceremonies glorifying the emperor. Its ostentatious presentation to the usurper king at the assembly of his unruly magnates suggests that Byzantium curried royal favour by supplying the means to magnify a nascent monarchy.[64]

In the last twelve years of his reign, Pippin's frequent diplomatic contacts with Constantinople provoked papal anxiety and efforts to examine Frankish correspondence with Byzantium and to stress the heretical character of imperial theology. This explains for instance the staging of a theological debate between imperial and papal representatives at Gentilly in 767. The popes supplied Pippin's court with specialists who could advise him on the Byzantines. To the pope's horror, Pippin solidified his Byzantine relations by betrothing his daughter Gisela to Constantine V's son Leo IV.[65] But the fragile Frankish political consensus which had allowed intervention in Italy disintegrated with the king's death. The Frankish aristocracy turned inward

---

[62] Mordek (1988); Fredegarius Continuatus 22; compare Classen (1983), pp. 102–3.
[63] *LP* 232, 237–41, 250–53; I, pp. 442, 444–6, 452–3.   [64] *ARF s.a.* 757.
[65] Papal anxiety: e.g. *CC* 11, 30; Gentilly: *ARF s.a.* 767; specialists: McCormick (1994a); Gisela: *CC* 45.

to his sons' succession, as Italy and Byzantium receded to the far periphery of Carolingian politics.

Yet this very issue triggered decisive Frankish intervention in Italy. Among the reasons which spurred Charlemagne to invade the Lombard kingdom in 773, the escape of his brother's wife and sons to her father's capital of Pavia when Charles pounced on his dead brother's kingdom, was critical. There his kin constituted a permanent threat. The papacy's position appears ambivalent. It had worked hard to foster warm relations with the Carolingians and benefited from the virtual Frankish protectorate in N. Italy. But despite its differences with the emperors, Rome continued formally to recognise imperial sovereignty.[66] In fact, the year before Charlemagne's invasion, Hadrian I was comfortable enough with the iconoclast regime to send his political enemies to Constantinople for safekeeping.[67] In any event, Charlemagne's conquest of Pavia brought renewed relations with Constantinople. A marriage alliance was resurrected and formally concluded in Rome in 781; the eunuch official Elissaeus was dispatched to Charles' court to prepare his daughter Rotrud for her new life as a Byzantine empress.[68] Rome again faced the disturbing prospect of its two major partners making arrangements over its head, when Pope Hadrian responded cautiously but positively to Empress Irene's overtures in 784 and 785 about restoring icons and doctrinal – and therefore political? – unity.[69]

The second Frankish–Byzantine entente was short lived. Why it collapsed is unclear. Einhard claims Charlemagne simply could not bear to lose his daughter and torpedoed the alliance. It is no less likely that the Franks had inherited Pavia's conflicts with Constantinople, notably in the Adriatic, where Venice already presented an inviting target and the Lombard assimilation of Byzantine Istria was pursued.[70] To the south, the allegiance of the powerful duchy of Benevento oscillated. Charlemagne's efforts to impose his overlordship met with patchy success and the policies of the dukes there and in Bavaria – both of whom had married sisters of Adelchis, the Lombard co-king who had escaped to Constantinople – were unpredictable. Hadrian's growing disillusionment with Frankish domination can be read in his constant, vain entreaties to Charlemagne to fulfil his part of the bargain struck by his father.[71]

The break came early in 787, when Charlemagne met with Byzantine ambassadors at Capua, even as he reasserted his authority over the Beneventans. Hadrian frantically relayed reports of Beneventan collusion

---

[66] Deér (1972).   [67] LP 299–300; I, p. 490.

[68] Annales Mosellani s.a. 781; Theoph. Chron. s.a. 6274.

[69] Dölger (1924), no. 341 (= Mansi XII, cols. 986B–C); Grumel no. 352.

[70] Bullough (1955), pp. 161–6.   [71] CC 49, 53–6.

with an impending Byzantine invasion which would restore Adelchis. The invasion occurred early in 788; it coincided – perhaps not coincidentally – with attacks by the Bavarians and Avars. The Byzantine expeditionary force expected aid from Benevento. But the new duke sided with the Franks and the imperial troops were crushed in Calabria. Alcuin boasted that 4000 Byzantines were killed and another 1000 captured. Among the latter was Sisinnius, Patriarch Tarasius' brother, who would spend the next decade in western captivity. The Byzantine defeat secured the Frankish position in Italy and left relations with Constantinople at a standstill.[72]

There was a complication. Even as Byzantine forces and the Lombard king were disembarking to drive the Franks from Italy, Hadrian's ambassadors were *en route* or just back home from Constantinople with their copy of the acts of the second Nicene council. The Greek text of the proceedings proclaimed the perfect unity of the Byzantine rulers and the pope on icon veneration, punctuated by the usual acclamations of imperial power, the whole, of course, signed and approved by papal legates. To make matters worse, the Greek text had silently excised references to Charlemagne from its quotations of Hadrian's correspondence with the emperors.[73] Exactly when Charles and his advisors learned about all this is unclear. Their reaction is not: it can be read in the enraged pages of the *Libri Carolini*, whose context was clearly more than purely theological.

Hadrian's relations with Charlemagne survived this crisis, but the Frankish court persisted in a modified version of its iconoclast views as the synod of Frankfurt shows, and the next pope's court made its differing opinion known to the Roman public and visitors by raising huge icons in the city's main pilgrim shrines. In the south, Byzantium recouped its position somewhat by marrying the emperor's sister-in-law Evanthia to the duke of Benevento.[74] Starting again in 797, Byzantium attempted to normalise relations with the increasingly powerful Charlemagne, whose contacts with the caliphate and Byzantine milieux in Palestine could scarcely have escaped Constantinople.[75] Two more legations had arrived at the Frankish court by late 798. But the crisis in Rome pre-empted whatever was cooking between the two courts, and Charlemagne's actions in subsequent months appeared hostile. The Frankish crack-down which restored Leo III was soon followed by the famous visit to Rome at Christmas 800.

In Constantinople, Charlemagne's coronation as emperor naturally appeared as the latest in a long series of Italian usurpations, the most recent

---

[72] *ARF* and *Annales Einhardi s.a.* 786 and 798; Theoph. Chron. *s.a.* 6281; *CC* 80, 82–4 and App. 1–2; Alcuin, *Ep.* 7; Classen (1985), pp. 28–34.   [73] Mansi XII, cols. 1075C–6A.

[74] Frankfurt: Hartmann (1989), pp. 108–10; icons: *LP* II.1; Evanthia: Classen (1985), p. 33.

[75] Borgolte (1976), pp. 46–58; *DAI* 26.

of which had occurred only nineteen years before, and it was believed an
invasion of Sicily would soon follow.[76] When that did not materialise, Irene
continued her contacts and two of Charlemagne's right-hand men travelled
to Constantinople, according to a Byzantine witness, in order to discuss a
marriage between Charlemagne and the increasingly beleaguered empress.[77]
Irene was toppled, however, and subsequent contacts led nowhere, as
Charlemagne's imperial pretensions poisoned an atmosphere of increasing
hostility. Again Italy supplied the kindling, as an internal power struggle in
Venice spilled over into Frankish politics: the new Venetian leaders and two
key officials of Byzantine Dalmatia shifted their allegiance to Charles in 805.
The result was Charles' second war with Byzantium, which ended only
when the Franks, whose Adriatic successes were mitigated by naval defeat
and the death of Charlemagne's son, renounced their claim to Venice. In
return Byzantine ambassadors acclaimed Charlemagne as *basileus* – without
specifying of what or whom – in the new chapel of Aachen. Byzantine silver
coins henceforth entitled their rulers *basileis Rhomaion*: 'emperors of the
Romans'.[78] This compromise would govern the two powers' basic *modus
vivendi* for over a quarter of a century.

The compromise facilitated some military co-ordination in Italy. Arab
raids increasingly menaced the peninsula's western coast, and the pope was
able to act as intermediary between the Byzantine governor of Sicily and
Charlemagne. Border disputes along the western Balkans were the subject
of two Byzantine missions in 817. But the crisis of the Carolingian political
structure that overtook Louis the Pious' court interrupted the progress
realised by missions of 824 and 827, aimed at a deepened diplomatic and
theological union. Further embassies in 833 and 839 found the Franks
enmeshed in civil war and a looming succession crisis, which dashed
Theophilus' hopes of Frankish military support.[79]

By the middle of the ninth century, the context had changed dramatically.
The Frankish empire had fragmented even as Mediterranean infrastructures seemed to recover. The duchy of Rome was regaining autonomy,
Venice grew in wealth and power, while Arab attacks on the coasts
intensified and Sicily slowly slid under Arab control. Yet Byzantine power
was on the upsurge at home and abroad. Between the Frankish kingdoms
and Constantinople, new centres of power were emerging among the

---

[76] Classen (1983), pp. 34, 40–1.
[77] Grierson (1981), pp. 906–8; however, compare Classen (1985), pp. 83–6.
[78] Classen (1985), pp. 91–7; Grierson (1981), pp. 910–11.
[79] Papal go-between: Leo III, *Ep.*x, 7–8; compare 1 and 6; 817: Böhmer-Mühlbacher nos. 642b and
655a; 824: *ibid.* nos. 793a and 842b; 833 and 839: *ibid.* nos. 926a and 993b; 'Genesius' *Reges*, 3, 16
and 18; Theoph. Cont. 3, 37; compare Dölger (1953), pp. 330–1.

Moravians and the Bulgarians. These changes combined with the recent past to shape the final phase of Byzantine–Carolingian interaction. Frankish imperial ambitions continued to irritate the Roman emperors of Constantinople. And the old papal claims to jurisdiction in the Balkans lost none of their relevance as that area figured anew on the historical stage.

The installation of Arabs on the Italian mainland from 838 combined with the sack of St Peter's (846) to dramatise the need for co-operation. Louis II's residence in Italy deepened his involvement in the complex politics of Rome and southern Italy, and·consequently with Constantinople. At least two more marriage alliances were contracted between Lothar I's family and its Constantinopolitan counterpart, although again the marriages never took place.[80] Co-operation focused on the key strongholds of Apulia, where the complementarity of Frankish land forces and the Byzantine navy was obvious. Bari had been an Arab stronghold since 841; its coastal site counselled a land and sea operation. Joint Byzantino-Frankish operations were foreseen in 869 and 870 but co-ordination broke down. In 871 Louis II finally captured Bari in an operation in which the Byzantine sources claim they participated. He then failed to take Taranto.[81] It was in this context that Louis II sent his famous letter to Basil I, composed probably by Anastasius Bibliothecarius, newly returned from a Frankish mission to Constantinople. The letter responded vigorously to Basil's criticism of the Carolingian imperial title, even as Louis requested more naval support and suggested that he and Basil had agreed to liberate Sicily once Calabria was cleared of Arabs.[82]

The ambivalent tone of Louis' letter foreshadowed how interests which had converged at Bari now collided. Both powers aimed to control southern Italy and both focused on Benevento in this respect. Louis II had turned Bari over to the duke of Benevento rather than the Byzantine admiral. But the duke soon turned on him, capturing and humiliating the Frankish ruler. Louis' further efforts to subdue the duke were frustrated in part because of the duke's new alliance with Constantinople.[83] Louis' subsequent death without an heir precipitated a struggle over northern Italy which Charles the Bald's short-lived success failed to resolve, even as the pace of Byzantine intervention accelerated in the south. Already in 872 the Byzantine fleet had scored one success off the Campanian coast to the relief of Pope John VIII.[84]

---

[80] Dölger (1953), pp. 334–7.

[81] Theoph. Cont. v, 55; *DAI* 29; Constantine VII, *De Thematibus* II, II; cf. Dölger (1953), pp. 337–8.

[82] Amari (1933, 1), pp. 518–23; Böhmer-Mühlbacher, nos. 1242a, 1246abc, 1246ef, 1247; Gay (1917), pp. 84–96; Louis II, *Epistola ad Basilium* I.   [83] Böhmer-Mühlbacher, no. 1261a.

[84] *Fragmenta Registri*, 5.

When Rome itself was occupied by the duke of Spoleto early in 878, John VIII felt himself driven into the arms of Constantinople. As his letter to Basil I shows, the Roman see was now led to look with a different eye on the latest in the Byzantine church's continuing upheavals and to seek resolution of its own bitter conflicts with recent patriarchs.[85]

These conflicts had arisen despite the final restoration of icons and the appointment as patriarch of Methodius (843–7), a Sicilian who had been ordained during the few years he had lived in Rome. In fact, however, Roman resentment over its jurisdictional losses had not disappeared. It was exacerbated by the expansion of Bulgarian power in the Balkans, that is Illyricum. Papal suspicion of the patriarchate was plain to see right from 787, when Hadrian had couched his co-operation in long-standing papal objections against the patriarchal title *oikoumenikos* or 'universalis', as well as against Tarasius' elevation from lay official to patriarch.[86] Two generations later new developments were to mix different sources of contention in explosive fashion: Roman primacy, lost jurisdiction over southern Italy and Illyricum, growing awareness of disciplinary divergences and the factionalisation of the Byzantine elite.

Monastic pressure on Methodius to purge all bishops compromised under second iconoclasm was given new life by his rigorist succesor, the monk Ignatius (847–58; 867–77), a castrated son of Emperor Michael I. For reasons that are unclear, Ignatius deposed one of Methodius' close associates, Gregory Asbestas, archbishop of Syracuse, who appealed to Rome. While this was pending, Ignatius himself was swept away by a political crisis and replaced by the head of the imperial chancery, the great lay intellectual Photius, who was consecrated by none other than Gregory Asbestas. In spring 859, the deposed Ignatius' supporters met in Constantinople and claimed to depose Photius; Photius retorted with a synod which attacked Ignatius.

At this point, the opposing factions seemed to stall in stalemate. Photius and Michael III sent an embassy to the new pope, Nicholas I, seeking his support for a council which would deal finally with iconoclasm and the current schism within the Byzantine church.[87] Bishops Radoald of Porto and Zacharias of Anagni, the papal legates, apparently exceeded their mandate at the ensuing synod held at Constantinople in April 861, by approving the deposition of Ignatius; but they failed to recover Illyricum.[88] The remaining Greek monastic communities in Rome again added an

---

[85] *Ep.* 72, 69.   [86] Mansi XII, cols. 1074A–5B.

[87] Nicholas I, *Ep.* 82; compare Dölger (1924), no. 457; Grumel, no. 464.

[88] Deusdedit, *Collectio Canonum* IV, 428–31; compare e.g. Beck, in Kempf, Beck *et al.* (1969), p. 178; see Shepard, p. 243 above.

internal dimension to papal relations with Constantinople. Ignatius clearly had vociferous supporters there, particularly the monk Theognostus. Nicholas convened a synod which repudiated his legates' actions and declared Photius and Asbestas deposed, eliciting from Michael III the famous and contemptuous letter about the barbarity of Latin Rome.[89]

On an already complex situation, further complications now obtruded, as the Bulgar ruler was having second thoughts over his contacts with Constantinople and approached Louis the German about converting to Frankish rather than Byzantine Christianity. At about the same time Constantinople dispatched two veteran diplomats and missionaries to the edges of East Francia, in response to the Moravians' expression of interest in conversion. It is a sign of the rapid development of both Bulgar and Moravian societies that they now looked to conversion and therefore cultural integration with the dominant neighbouring cultures. It is a measure of their political astuteness that each explored the advantages of converting to the church most removed from their respective borders. The Bulgar initiative, which was soon notified to the pope, opened up the unexpected prospect of recovering jurisdiction over Illyricum regardless of the Byzantine emperor's attitude. In 866, the Bulgar ruler expressed dissatisfaction with the Greek missionaries working in his kingdom by approaching Nicholas I, who answered with legates and a remarkable document responding to the khan's queries about Byzantine criticism of Bulgar customs. The pope expressed a fairly enlightened attitude towards Bulgar practices even as he slammed the customs of rival Constantinople. Photius retorted by enumerating western doctrinal and disciplinary deviations in an eastern encyclical. He convoked a synod which deposed Nicholas I and dispatched emissaries to Louis II to solicit his help in toppling the pope, even as Nicholas sought theological support from the dynamic cultural centres of the Frankish kingdoms.[90]

At that very moment, the power constellation with which Photius was identified crumbled when Basil I had Michael III assassinated. The new emperor soon restored Ignatius and requested papal support, offering to have the rival patriarchal parties submit to the pope for judgement. Only Ignatius' legation made it to Rome intact, and Nicholas I's successor, Hadrian II, unsurprisingly found for Ignatius. Papal legates then travelled to Constantinople for a council convened over the winter of 869–70 to sort

---

[89] Dölger (1924), no. 464; Nicholas I, *Ep.* 88; *ODB* III, p. 2055; for the intricacies of the Photian schism, see Hergenröther (1867–9) I, pp. 357–9 and Dvornik (1948) which must be used with caution. Compare Beck, in Kempf, Beck *et al.* (1969), pp. 174–93.

[90] Nicholas I, *Ep.* 99, on which compare *ODB* III, p. 1785; and *Epp.* 100–2; Photius, *Ep.* 2; compare p. 374 below.

out the implications of the recent upheavals. At the same time, Louis II's ambassadors – including Anastasius Bibliothecarius – were busy in Constantinople discussing a marriage alliance and the military co-operation we have already noted. The intractable papal legates imposed their own views on the council. But afterwards, they were confronted and confounded by Bulgarian ambassadors and a Byzantine hierarchy led by Ignatius, backed by Basil and supported by the eastern patriarchates, which forcefully denied Roman claims in Bulgaria. The resulting strain would endure until events in Italy drove John VIII in 878 to seek political *rapprochement* with Byzantium.[91]

Ignatius had died in 877 and Photius resumed the patriarchal office. The pope allowed his legation to participate in another winter council in 879–80. The text of the Roman documents presented there appears to have been toned down; Photius emphasised that he had never opposed Roman jurisdiction over Bulgaria: he had only bowed to the imperial will in the matter. Concord of a sort was re-established. Although Roman jurisdiction over Bulgaria was never to become a reality, old and new Rome were again in communion and the way was open for military co-operation.[92]

The need was great: the Byzantine stronghold of Syracuse had fallen to the Arabs a few weeks after John VIII wrote to Basil seeking his support, and Constantinople reacted strongly. In 879, the Byzantine navy attacked the Arabs off Naples, and the pope complained that the detachment had not continued up the coast to receive his blessing and defend Rome. After the latest council in Constantinople the pope received the seeming good news about Bulgaria, the loan of several warships and the restoration of Roman rights over the elegant Justinianic church of Saints Sergius and Bacchus next door to the Great Palace.[93] A powerful military force from the western themes reconquered Taranto, even as a Byzantine fleet won an important victory off the northern coast of Sicily. Basil I's hold on Calabria expanded considerably, as the Byzantines occupied some strongholds while others recognised eastern overlordship.[94] Charles the Fat, who now claimed his family's inheritance in Italy, rightly feared that Rome and even the Frankish family who ran the duchy of Spoleto were turning away from the Carolingians to Constantinople. Duke Wido had in fact sent his own embassy to Constantinople.[95]

As post-Carolingian chaos descended on the north of Italy, the Byzantines briefly occupied Benevento (891–5), organised the new theme of

---

[91] Mansi XVI, cols. 1–208; *LP* II.180–5; cf. Stiernon (1967); John VIII, *Epp.* 69, 72.
[92] Mansi XVII, cols. 373–526; Dvornik (1948), pp. 159–201.
[93] John VIII, *Epp.* 245, 259.   [94] Von Falkenhausen (1967), pp. 19–20.
[95] Rome: Böhmer-Mühlbacher, no. 1604d; Wido: Hiestand (1964), pp. 27–9.

Langobardia and seemed more significant to Italy's fate than ever. That significance expressed itself in the dating formulae of local charters or the dispatch of Venetian bells to adorn Basil I's splendid new palace chapel of the Nea. Monasteries scurried to obtain Byzantine confirmations of their privileges, local Italian elites flaunted Greek court titles. Reinforced by population transfers from the east, the Byzantine south became increasingly active in the renewed writing and copying of Greek texts.[96] Italians made pilgrimages to St Demetrius' shrine in Thessalonica and Leo VI invited to his court holy men from Italy, even as Eugenius Vulgarius sent him fawning panegyrical poems in Latin.[97]

Presumably in anticipation of the impending Carolingian succession in Italy, in 872 and 873 Basil I had reopened diplomatic contacts with a northern Frankish court by concluding an alliance (*amicitia*) with Louis the German.[98] Italy motivated, at least in part, the Byzantine envoy who travelled to Regensburg in 894 for an audience with King Arnulf after his Italian expedition. So too another embassy in 896 followed Arnulf's imperial coronation.[99] Pope John IX's ambassadors to Constantinople in 899 consecrated the renewed harmony between Rome and the east and may have played a hand in arranging the marriage of Louis III, king of Provence – whose mother Ermengard had once been promised to the Byzantine emperor – to Anna, daughter of Leo VI. Louis III 'the Blind', who sporadically controlled areas of northern Italy between 900 and 905, fathered the only Carolingian also descended from the Byzantine Macedonian house, Charles-Constantine, count of Vienne. The union perhaps clarifies the mention of Greek merchants in Louis' privilege of 921.[100] In any event, Rome's relations with Constantinople and renewed Byzantine power in Italy would soon be symbolised by the victorious joint operation against the Arab colony on the Garigliano river in 915.[101]

CULTURAL INTERACTION BETWEEN BYZANTIUM AND THE WEST

Diplomatic interaction fostered cultural ramifications. The several dozen embassies which travelled between Constantinople and western courts

[96] Dating, confirmations, titles, transfers: von Falkenhausen (1967), pp. 10–12, 21–4, 31–7; bells: *CV*, p. 126; MSS: Irigoin (1969).

[97] *Miracula Sancti Demetrii* (*BHG* 529), pp. 222–6; *Vita Eliae Iunioris* 66; compare *Vita Blasii*, 19; Eugenius: *ODB* ii, p. 744.

[98] Böhmer-Mühlbacher, no. 1490b, with Dümmler (1887–8) ii, pp. 336–7; Dölger (1924), nos. 489 and 491.

[99] Dölger (1924), nos. 525 and 533; Böhmer-Mühlbacher, no. 1922a; Hiestand (1964), pp. 70 and 75–6.   [100] Compare p. 359 above; Hiestand (1964), pp. 90–107.

[101] Gay (1917), pp. 147–54.

constituted privileged intermediaries and much cultural exchange bears their stamp. Men of great influence led them: for instance Charlemagne's ambassador Count Hugh became father-in-law of Lothar I. Some, like Amalarius of Metz or Anastasius Bibliothecarius were distinguished intellectuals. Amalarius, for example, used his experience of the Greek liturgy in his own commentaries and wrote a poem about his trip to Constantinople.[102] The numbers involved are surprising: at least fifty-five diplomats travelled between the Frankish court and Constantinople between 756 and 840. What is more, the structure and size of the parties they led means that the heads of embassies – whose names alone the sources usually supply – were only the tip of the iceberg: thus these ambassadors were probably accompanied by a very large number of attendants of varying status.[103]

Byzantine gifts were carefully chosen for their impact, as the ceremonial organ mentioned earlier suggests. The manuscript of Pseudo-Dionysius the Areopagite (BN grec. 257) presented to Louis the Pious' court in 827 was tailored to the pretensions of Louis' adviser, Hilduin, abbot of St Denis, who identified the Areopagite with his abbey's patron saint. Diplomatic contacts required translators: we have already noted how the Roman church supplied Pippin III with Byzantine experts. One relic of such contacts survives in the Latin translation of Michael II and Theophilus' letter to Louis the Pious.[104] The embassies help explain why transalpine interest in Byzantine culture clustered around the Frankish courts.

Because of its diplomatic implications, the Frankish court mediated western discussion about religious images, which was launched by the debate on iconoclasm between representatives of Constantine V and the Roman church at Gentilly and echoed through the court-produced *Libri Carolini* and the synods of Frankfurt (794) and Paris (825). Frankish theologians joined the Photian fray when, at Pope Nicholas I's request, Hincmar of Rheims raised the matter before Charles the Bald's court over Christmas 867. The result was that at Paris and Corbie, Bishop Aeneas and the monk Ratramn refuted Byzantine objections against the *filioque*, papal primacy and various disciplinary issues. The East Frankish bishops offered their own response in a synod held at Worms in 868.[105]

So too the Byzantine practice of inviting foreign ambassadors to witness important state rituals explains western court familiarity with some Byzantine ceremonies: Count Hugh and Bishop Haito's embassy of 811 accounts for Charlemagne's crowning his son Louis the Pious in 813 in a manner resembling that of Theophylact by Emperor Michael I in 811. Notker claims

---

[102] *ODB* I, pp. 72–3.   [103] McCormick (1994a).   [104] *MGH Conc.* II: 2, pp. 475–80.
[105] Iconoclasm: *CC* 36; Haendler (1958) and McCormick (1994b); Hincmar: Devisse (1976) II, pp. 628–31; Aeneas and Ratramn: Bouhot (1976), pp. 60–7; Worms: Hartmann (1989), pp. 301–9.

that a Byzantine delegation's sweet chanting prompted Charlemagne to obtain an isosyllabic translation, the antiphon *O veterem hominem*, so that it could be sung in his chapel, and independent Byzantine evidence appears to bear him out.[106] Hilduin of St Denis' and John Scottus' translations of Pseudo-Dionysius both show court connections and used the manuscript conveyed in 827. Conversely, the eastern missions to the court of Louis the Pious resulted in Byzantine translations of Latin hagiography. Hilduin's fantastic passion of St Denis was rendered into Greek soon thereafter, while the Latin passion of St Anastasia was translated during the Roman leg of the embassy of 824.[107] Outside the royal courts, sustained Byzantine cultural contacts north of the Alps were rarer. Two exceptions were Reichenau and, especially, St Gall, religious houses which, probably not coincidentally, lay where a great complex of Alpine passes met the Rhine, Francia's main north–south axis.[108]

Even left to their own devices, Carolingian scholars needed to understand the Greek expressions which littered St Jerome's letters or even Priscian: hence the collection of lists of Greek terms organised by the Latin authors where they occur.[109] The drive to understand the Bible deepened interest in Greek. Bilingual Psalters like those connected with Sedulius Scottus' circle did double duty. The prophetic character Christian exegesis recognised in the Septuagint gave the Greek text great prestige, while the fact that the Psalms were often known by heart allowed them to serve as a crude dictionary in which Greek equivalents for Latin phrases might be hunted down. Although not every Carolingian crumb of Greek need reflect a personal contact with Byzantines, such contacts may have played a larger role than usually suspected. So Thegan claims that Charlemagne consulted Greeks and Syrians about the text of the Gospels.[110] Northern scribes who delighted in spelling their names with Greek letters may strike us as superficial pedants, but they were perhaps inspired by Italians from Byzantine borderlands who had been using Greek letters for Latin subscriptions since the days of Justinian.[111] The lists of Greek numbers frequently found in Carolingian manuscripts give the modern rather than the classical names, and so derive from contemporary Greek speakers.[112] Linguistic contacts left tangible traces in Lupus of Ferrières' comment on the accent of a Greek loan word or in bilingual phrase collections for travellers. The St

---

[106] Theophylact: Wendling (1985), pp. 207–23; Notker, *Gesta Karoli* II, 7; compare Strunk (1964).

[107] Loenertz (1950; 1951); *Passio Anastasiae* (*BHG* 81–81a), Epilogue.

[108] Kaczynski (1988); compare the Rhenish connections of the Hiberno-Greek data in Bischoff (1977), pp. 51–3.   [109] Dionisotti (1988), pp. 13, 49–50.   [110] *Vita Hludowici*, 7.

[111] von Falkenhausen (1968/9), pp. 177–80; compare the somewhat different interpretation of Luzzatti Laganà (1982), pp. 740–7.   [112] Bischoff, *MS* II, p. 264.

Gall-Angers list has useful Greek expressions like 'do me a favour'; one at Monza in early Italian and Greek may have been connected with an early tenth-century travelling doctor.[113]

Outside Europe, the Greek-speaking church of Jerusalem offered a privileged place for cross-cultural encounter. Royal involvement with Christians there is documented by an extraordinary Frankish fiscal roll indicating revenues, personnel and languages of prayer of the churches of Palestine. Alcuin sought a prayer association with the Greek patriarch of Jerusalem and, by Charlemagne's last years, seventeen nuns and many monks from the Frankish empire had established communities in the Holy City, one of which survived at least for another half-century, when its members were still displaying the splendid Bible, presumably from Charlemagne's court-school, sent to them by the emperor. They formed a natural focus for contacts among western pilgrims, Italian merchants and the Greek clergy, which explains why the *filioque* controversy over the wording of the Creed arose there, when Greek monks heard Latins chanting the offending passage.[114]

But like political ones, cultural contacts between Byzantium and the west pivoted on Italy. As far back as the Lombard court's Greek jester, the Po basin had channelled western encounters with Byzantine civilisation. Although Ravenna's gateway role in our period has perhaps been overrated, Agnellus' historical memory and Charlemagne's exportation of Ravennate artwork testify to its enduring Byzantine after life. If it is genuine, Charles the Bald's mention of the Greek liturgy to the clergy of Ravenna need not reflect its performance there. Already in 826, a Venetian came to Louis the Pious' court, promising to construct a Byzantine organ. Across the Adriatic, *missi dominici* grappled with the intricacies of Byzantine provincial administration during an inquest into the Frankish absorption of Istria.[115] Some slight evidence for translations in the Po basin anticipates the Monza glossary, and Anastasius Bibliothecarius found a Greek manuscript of the Translation of St Stephen in Mantua.[116] The controversial Gottschalk of Orbais drew on his experience in Byzantine Dalmatia and Venice when delineating the semantic fields of key words in his defence of predestination.[117]

---

[113] Lupus, *Ep.* 8 (Levillain); St Gall: Kaczynski (1988), pp. 70–1; Monza: Aerts (1972); compare Bischoff (1984), p. 255.

[114] Fiscal roll, nuns, etc.: *Breve commemoratorii*, esp. p. 302; cf. Borgolte (1976), pp. 45–107; Alcuin, *Ep.* 210; Bible: *Itinerarium Bernardi*, 10; merchants: *Miracula Sancti Genesii*, 2; *filioque*: Peri (1971).

[115] Ravenna overrated as a conduit for Hellenic 'influence': Brown (1988b), pp. 131–41; *ODB* 1, p. 37; *CC* 81; Charles the Bald: Jacob (1972); organ: *ARF s.a.* 826; inquest: Margetić (1988).

[116] Chiesa (1989), pp. 173–5.   [117] *De Praedestinatione* 9, 6.

Rome was a propitious place for translations. Hadrian I ordered a Latin translation of the Greek acts of II Nicaea brought back by his legates.[118] The Roman translator Anastasius Bibliothecarius was Carolingian Europe's pre-eminent Byzantine specialist. He translated the usual fare of hagiography and councils, but Anastasius' interest in 'modern' Byzantine literature is even more noteworthy, since he rendered into Latin the work of the most outstanding historian of the period, a sermon by Theodore Studite and a work by his contemporary Constantine-Cyril.[119] A fellow papal emissary, Bishop John of Arezzo – precisely one of the legates who presided over Charles the Bald's experiment in Byzantine ceremonial at Ponthion in July 876 – may have translated a Byzantine text on the Assumption.[120] Rome is virtually unique in so far as it was also a centre for translation from Latin into Greek. Thus Pope Zacharias' rendering of Gregory the Great's Dialogues was perhaps intended for circulation at home as well as abroad: a manuscript (Vat. grec. 1666) probably copied at Rome survives from 800; the Greek translation of the passion of St Anastasia mentioned above used a Latin manuscript at the saint's Roman shrine.

Latin-speakers rubbed shoulders with hellenophones in the south. Late ninth-century Taranto for instance had Latin bishops but counted many Greeks among its elite.[121] The renewal of Byzantine power and culture helps explain the sudden bloom of Latin translations along the Campanian frontier. The church of Naples fostered rather superior translations. For instance, the deacon Paul sought to capitalise on Charles the Bald's enthusiasm for things Greek by dedicating to the Frankish ruler his translations of the Life of St Mary the Egyptian and the Faustian Penance of Theophilus. Both works enjoyed enormous success north of the Alps and fuelled the veneration of Mary as an intercessor for sinners.[122] Deacon John who continued his see's episcopal *Gesta c.* 900 and enjoyed the patronage of the bishop and the abbot of St Severinus also collaborated with a Greek-speaker to produce Latin adaptations of hagiographical classics like Cyril of Scythopolis' sixth-century Life of Euthymius as well as patriarch Methodius' Life of Nicholas.[123]

Not a few instances of apparent western appropriation of Byzantine iconography and style have been challenged. Even when derivation from 'Byzantine' style or iconography is uncontested, it is often unclear whether we have a direct appropriation from a contemporary Byzantine exemplar, or a residual rather than recent borrowing from Byzantium. The art historical

---

[118] *LP* 353 1, p. 512; compare Freeman (1985), pp. 75–81.   [119] *ODB* 1, pp. 88–9.

[120] Philippart (1974); Schieffer (1935) pp. 16–25.   [121] Von Falkenhausen (1968), p. 149.

[122] Kunze (1969), p. 40; Meersseman (1963).

[123] Dolbeau (1982); Corsi (1979); Chiesa (1989), pp. 183–5.

problem is only complicated by the scarcity of securely dated and localised surviving eastern comparanda.

Some Byzantine models were nonetheless certainly available for imitation in the west: *c.* 850 a party of Irish pilgrims to Italy jotted down a description of a Greek Gospel cycle and left the codex at St Gall. Even its sophisticated Islamic neighbours appreciated ninth-century Byzantium's outstanding metalwork and locks. Diplomacy documents the dispatch of Byzantine luxury products like the bejewelled Gospel Book and chalice conveyed to Pope Leo IV. Nor were such gifts destined only for royal treasure hoards: Constantinople had a shrewd grasp of the power structure at a western court and, as the lists of presents intended for King Hugh of Provence and his court in 935 reveals, imperial diplomacy distributed its gifts accordingly, placing Byzantine prestige items in the hands of key royal associates who were no less active than the kings as patrons of art. A prominent early ninth-century traveller and diplomat proudly bequeathed to the churches of Grado expensive reliquaries purchased in Constantinople. Nor was the traffic exclusively one way: we have already noted Basil's bells from Venice, while the technique of making cloisonné enamel may have travelled from the west to Byzantium around the same time, and a high Byzantine official acquired religious art at Rome late in the eighth century.[124]

Linguistic evidence yields some tentative insights into technology transfers and material culture, since words could be borrowed with the thing they designated. Of course the problem of residual borrowings is compounded by that of the potential lag between the borrowing and a word's earliest attestation in the rare written records. Still, Byzantium's apparent linguistic impact in this period does not contradict the picture derived from the other evidence. Most securely identified Byzantine loanwords relate to expensive items associated with the lay or clerical elite; virtually all seem to enter usage through Italy, whether via the Po basin or Rome. Byzantium's impact on religious life and art is suggested by the Italian Latin loanword *icona* (Gr. *eikon*; acc. *eikona*) or, late in the tenth century, the word *olibanum* for incense (< [*t*]*o libanon*). At Rome Byzantium appears as the west's intermediary with the Islamic world with *magarita* and *magarizare* ('apostate', 'to convert to Islam') from Arabic *muhadzhir* ('Muslim Arab settler in newly conquered territory') via Greek *moagarites* or *magarites*. On the other hand, *cendatum*, a word from the good life ('fine silk cloth', 'brocade'), probably derives from Persian *sundus* via Byzantine Greek

[124] Gospel cycle: Mütherich (1987); metalwork: Pellat (1954), p. 159; compare on the date Lewis (1977), p. 13; Leo IV: *LP* 574; II, pp. 147–8; Hugh of Provence: Constantine VII, *De ceremoniis* 2, 44; Fortunatus of Grado's will: Cessi (1942) I, pp. 76–7; enamel: Buckton (1988); Roman religious art: *Vita Nicetae Patricii* (*BHG* 1342e), 3.

sendes and shows up almost simultaneously in milieux connected with the Carolingian court and northern Italy. Military contacts such as we have seen in southern Italy can be traced in words for 'catapult' which seem to have been borrowed at this time, and the Byzantine word *chelandion*, perhaps derived from 'eel', designated Constantinople's sleek warships in Latin. Technology is probably represented by the ancestors of the modern English words 'bronze' and 'varnish'.[125] Transfers in the other direction seem rarer, but so are the sources. One very likely candidate for our period is *kortes* (Lat. *cortis*) apparently in the sense of 'royal tent'.[126]

CONCLUSIONS

Despite the renewed dynamism of the Byzantine south, Italy from Rome northwards was now fastened to transalpine Europe to an extent and in ways no one could have imagined in 700. Venice was well on its way to becoming a distinctively Italo-Byzantine amalgam and a gateway city to the populations of the Po basin and across the Alps. The issue of the imperial legacy and legitimacy was posed and would rarely leave the forefront of diplomatic relations. Rome's paper victory in defending its ecclesiastical claims to Illyricum would be swept aside by the Bulgar–Byzantine confrontation and the Magyar attacks. While Greek monasticism in the environs of Rome would not cease altogether, the dynamic provincial society of Byzantine Calabria probably provided a more characteristic note than Constantinople.

Byzantium's interaction with the west appears chiefly political and cultural. Economic links to the imperial metropolis seem distinctly secondary. But whatever the kind of interaction, Italy was pivotal, simultaneously a privileged locus of encounter and the stakes of competition. Three essential zones appeared there: the Po-Adriatic basin; Rome and vicinity; and the Byzantine south. Other secondary, eccentric zones of encounter followed the itinerant human networks that were the Frankish courts; farther afield, significant contacts certainly occurred between westerners and Byzantines in Jerusalem.

Generally speaking, the extent to which transalpine Europe controlled parts of Italy was the chief factor affecting the intensity of political and direct cultural interaction north of the Alps. Such contacts first peaked between 756 and 768. They intensified again in the 780s and once more in the first three decades of the ninth century. After that, the possibility for

---

[125] Kahane and Kahane (1970–6), pp. 368–71, 380, 412, 385 respectively.
[126] For example, Theoph. Chron. *s.a.* 6284.

Constantinople to deal directly with a Carolingian ruler in Italy made this kind of contact more sporadic.

The sociology of interaction suggests mostly an affair of elites. But this social slant may be in part the product of our aristocratically minded source material. The content of exchanges is pretty clear. Elite life-style concerns played an important role: westerners imported eastern political rituals and symbols, liturgical pieces, theological treatises, and political and military support where Byzantium's capacities complemented but did not threaten their own. Constantinople was interested in obtaining political support on its own terms, as well as western warriors. The religious traditions of Rome provided useful sanctions to competing factions of the Constantinopolitan elite, while the inability of Constantinople to project its power there made it a safe haven for dissidents. Both societies avidly discovered each other's saints and the texts describing their wonders. The Greek church of Jerusalem sought Frankish wealth for its own local purposes, even as the semi-autonomous Byzantine outposts of Italy provided inoffensive go-betweens among the huge economy of the house of Islam, a resurgent Byzantium and a recovering west.

In this crucial period of some seven generations, Byzantium and the west began again to know one another. In so doing, each began to discover with amazement how different the sibling had become. Like the Creed, once-identical shared traditions had begun to show slight variations which were all the more disturbing for the substantial sameness of their backgrounds. The Photian schism had been overcome, but these centuries' interaction left scars: the issues of papal primacy, the *filioque* and disciplinary divergences between Rome and Constantinople were so many ticking time-bombs, awaiting future moments of tension. And the Carolingian claim to have restored the Roman empire, despite brief periods of mutual acceptance, constituted a permanent challenge to all that was essential to the Byzantine identity. The stage was set for the co-operation and competition that would mark the future of Byzantium's interaction with the west.

PART II

GOVERNMENT AND INSTITUTIONS

CHAPTER 15

KINGSHIP AND ROYAL
GOVERNMENT

Janet L. Nelson

INTRODUCTION

WITH the demise of a political economy based around the Mediterranean, the early eighth century signalled a new beginning in the history of Europe. Henri Pirenne, writing in the early decades of the twentieth century, was the first historian to underline the significance of the break: but his monochrome picture of regression, and 'an economy of no markets', is no longer acceptable; nor is his explanation in terms of an external factor, the rise of Islam.[1] Instead, the new economy can be credited with its own dynamic, and the collapse of a system driven by the Roman state seen not as putting an end to exchanges but diversifying them. The new economy had a dual base, in the agrarian wealth of the western European land mass from the Pyrenees to central Germany, and in an exchange system orientated towards the northern seas into which the great rivers of the land mass drained.[2] The vast wealth on which Roman emperors had gorged was a thing of the past: eighth- and ninth-century kings had to make do with smaller slices of diminished cakes. Yet a revised, revived, version of the past seemed still within reach. The resources available to kings, in moveables as well as land, were increasing, and competition, inside and outside realms, produced a new momentum. The reorientation of the west brought into view societies around the northern periphery of the Roman empire which, though remote from its centre, had felt the impact of the empire's existence: Scandinavians, Irish and Anglo-Saxons would all respond to the creation of a new concentration of power in the west.

In Constantinople, emperors saw themselves as Rome's direct heirs. Severe economic and military problems (in the east, Arab expansion meant

---

[1] Pirenne (1938); Hodges and Whitehouse (1983).
[2] Devroey (1993); Hodges and Hobley (1988); Verhulst (1989); Fried (1991), pp. 37–42. See also Verhulst, below, ch. 18.

substantial territorial losses) helped concentrate minds, and resources. The institutions and the ideology of the late Roman state survived in attenuated form. In the west, the two successor states which at first seemed to have inherited the largest concentrations of Roman state power had undergone profound change by the early eighth century. The Ostrogothic kingdom had been only partly replaced by that of the Lombards. Much of eastern and southern Italy remained in Byzantine hands. For all its Roman-legal veneer, the Lombard kingdom depended on a warrior aristocracy. Visigothic Spain fell to North African Muslims in 711 and its own tiny successor kingdom in the Asturias was fragile (and exiguously documented) until the mid-ninth century.[3] Further north, the kingdom of the Franks, less obviously Roman in origin, now appropriated what remained of Rome's political and cultural inheritance and came to dominate the west. Pirenne's Francocentric focus, which obscured important aspects of the sixth and seventh centuries, took him to the heart of the eighth and ninth.

In the eighth century, the Frankish empire, under Carolingian leadership, expanded to absorb neighbouring peoples. In the ninth century, as Frankish expansion halted, the surrounding world of *exterae gentes* was ravaged, plundered, exploited when possible; otherwise converted, traded and treated with, recruited and borrowed from. Charlemagne had made substantial acquisitions in northeastern Spain, and his successors were tantalised by the possibilities of further intervention: in 826 the Frankish emperor wrote to the men of Mérida urging revolt against the amir in Córdoba,[4] and in the 850s Frankish monks with a safe conduct from the Muslim governor of Zaragoza fetched relics of Christians recently martyred by Muslim authorities in Córdoba.[5] But ninth-century Frankish rulers gained no territory in Spain or Italy, and could not prevent damaging Saracen raids on Mediterranean coasts. Charlemagne's elephant, sent from Baghdad by the caliph, died in 810 in Westfalia preparing to campaign on the Danish frontier,[6] as symbolically apt a termination of diplomatic relations in one direction as it was a portent of new concerns in another. In 805, Charlemagne listed eight frontier-posts on a north–south line from Saxony to Austria: only by way of these, and with royal licence, were merchants to export Frankish swords and byrnies eastwards to the Slav peoples.[7]

Even before 800, when the papacy legitimised a new empire in the west, Latin Christendom had asserted its identity and autonomy by rejecting the 'errors' of the Greeks.[8] In the ninth century, the rulers of east and west

---

[3] See above, Collins, chapter 11.   [4] *MGH Epp.* v: 1, pp. 115–16.   [5] Nelson (1993b).
[6] *ARF s.a.* 810, p. 131, trans. King, p. 102.
[7] *MGH Cap.* I, no. 44, c. 7, p. 123; Siems (1992), p. 487.
[8] *Libri Carolini, MGH Conc. Supp.*, p. 5.

competed in sending missions to convert the Slavs in central Europe. Byzantium had become an alien power. Yet its monarchic style, and symbols, continued to fascinate powerful kings. More inspiration came from the past. Latin legal texts that preserved, in the west, not just the style but something of the substance of Roman government began to be reread and reused by royal counsellors, rekindling ideas of restoration and renewal.[9]

THE BASES OF POWER

In modern times, capitalism and transport technology have partly dissociated geography from political history. The kingdoms of the eighth and ninth centuries depended on the location, and quality, of the lands and central places controlled by the king. The heart of the Lombard kingdom remained centred in the cities of the Po valley, which had passed directly from imperial control in the later sixth century.[10] West Saxon kings controlled estates in Somerset which their predecessors had gained from the Britons in the fifth and sixth centuries: this region was *principalior*, 'more royal', than the more recently acquired Kent, Surrey and Sussex.[11] The kings of the Asturias ruled, in the eighth and ninth centuries, a kingdom not much larger than Wessex, its heartlands around Oviedo.[12] In the Frankish realm, royal lands, often called by the old Roman term fisc, derived in part from the fifth-century take-over of Roman *civitates* and imperial estates. When the Carolingian dynasty replaced the Merovingians in 751, they took over old fisclands and added their own family lands, augmented through astute marriages, in the valleys of the Meuse and Moselle, and in the Rhineland.[13] Though modern historians have only partly uncovered the origins of the royal demesne, in every kingdom a core of royal lands apparently remained intact over long periods. This was sometimes the outcome of kings' successful efforts to secure the succession of a single heir, but equally often of the failure of such efforts reflected in assassinations and usurpations. Dynastic discontinuity could favour the continuity of an undivided royal demesne. Thus in the Seine basin Merovingian palaces disappeared from the record in the early eighth century to reappear after 751 in Carolingian hands. Compiègne, for instance, used as a residence by late Merovingian kings, then by Pippin in the 750s, became in the ninth century the favourite palace of Charles the Bald, who also hunted in the same royal forests as Dagobert.[14] When, as sometimes occurred in the eighth and ninth

---

[9] Wood and Harries (1993); Nelson (1989b).   [10] Delogu (1980).
[11] Sawyer (1982); Asser, c. 15.   [12] Sanchez-Albornoz (1972)
[13] Ewig (1965), map at p. 176.   [14] Lohrmann (1976).

centuries, a kingdom was divided between heirs, there could be a partition
of these corelands – as between Charlemagne and his brother in 768, or the
three sons of Louis the Pious in 843:[15] such divisions were made after
exhaustive surveys of royal resources.

The estates' careful management[16] was geared to the perpetuation of royal
power: to maintaining the stock of horses for the war-band, and to
providing the wherewithal to equip men. It was geared, still more
fundamentally, to the sustenance of the royal household – for kings
regularly stayed throughout winter (and often much of the summer too,
when not campaigning on or beyond the borders) in the heartlands of the
realm. The notion of royal itinerancy, helpful as it is, can be overplayed.
Kings made prolonged stays at a few places. Sometimes a single central place
emerged. In the eighth century, Pavia was the effective capital of the
Lombard kings. By the early ninth century, King Alfonso II of the Asturias
had established his main residence at Oviedo. Even in the case of rulers who
spent more time in the saddle, there is no evidence of regular journeyings
around their kingdoms. Most of Charlemagne's empire was never visited by
its ruler at all: royal travelling was essentially for campaigning purposes.
From 794, Aachen became Charlemagne's *sedes regni*, the seat of his realm.[17]
The largest constellations of royal lands were organised around such
residences, or palaces. Kings jealously guarded their forest rights to ensure
meat supplies for winter. Though no written constitution declared the
demesne inalienable, it was the prerequisite for the kingdom's survival. This
is quite clear in ninth-century Wessex, thanks to information derivable from
royal wills, but is evident in other kingdoms too. Members of the royal
family might have a life-interest in particular estates: queens, for instance,
might be given particular estates as dowerlands[18] which reverted to the fisc
at the holder's death.

The fisc was not a fixed quantum. The king received lands by gift or
inheritance or acquisition. Treason, and disloyal service, were punished by
the con*fisc*ation of estates. The royal lands also supplied (as a ninth-century
king put it) 'the wherewithal to reward followers':[19] estates confiscated from
the faithless could be regranted to the faithful. Grants were quite often made
in areas outside the heartlands where they were, in any case, difficult to
manage.[20] Conquest could mean the acquisition of a defeated dynasty's fisc,

---

[15] See Map 9, p. 122.

[16] *Capitulare de Villis, MGH Cap.* I, no. 32, pp. 82–91, trans. Loyn and Percival (1975), pp. 65–73;
Quierzy letter, *MGH Conc.* III, no. 41, c. 12, pp. 420–2.

[17] Brühl (1968), pp. 9–115; Reuter (1991), p. 24.

[18] Capitulary of Quierzy *s.a.* 877, *MGH Cap.* II, no. 281, c. 5, p. 357; Alfred's Will, trans. Keynes
and Lapidge (1983), p. 177. See Stafford (1983), pp. 101–4.   [19] Nithard IV. 3.

[20] Compare Martindale (1985).

for instance when the Carolingians acquired Lombardy, or Bavaria – regions excentric *vis-à-vis* former heartlands. These brought new resource bases for ruling an extended realm. The empire of Charlemagne was 'amplified' (Einhard's word[21]) to some 1,200,000 sq km in extent. Distance increased the difficulties of control. Though rivers provided access routes to areas far inland and Roman roads and even staging posts survived in some regions,[22] the preservation of fisc lands in outlying parts of the realm was always problematic, and unless military concerns were likely to bring the king back (as Charles the Bald kept returning to western Anjou, or Louis the German to eastern Bavaria) could be a thankless task. As power radiated out from palaces and heartlands, it inevitably became less regular, and less intensive, nearer the periphery.

But power less direct was nonetheless real. The paradox of early medieval states was that their stability depended on chronic instability, as kings made constant efforts to expand their territory and the range of their raiding and tribute-taking, inevitably at their neighbours' expense. 'If a Frank is your friend, he's certainly not your neighbour', was a saying quoted by Einhard as 'a Greek proverb', implying a reference to Frankish pressure on Byzantine southern Italy.[23] Expansion provided kings with the wherewithal to maintain the loyalty of aristocrats and of potential competitors within the royal family. The kingdom of the Asturias was vulnerable to Muslim raids, but eighth-century kings could sometimes lead their little armies southwards to plunder the towns of the Duero valley, and eventually extended their control over Galicia. More powerful Anglo-Saxon kings gained territory at the expense of lesser ones and granted lands to their own faithful men in what had formerly been independent kingdoms.[24] Few neighbours were less friendly than Offa of Mercia. The ninth-century Welsh remembered that 'tyrant', but suffered now from the 'tyranny' of his successor Æthelred.[25] Your likeliest friend was your neighbour's neighbour on the other side: so for the Welsh, Alfred of Wessex, or, for those threatened by the Franks, fellow-victims on other Frankish frontiers – Danes and Wilzes, for example. Other neighbours were no more friendly, only less strikingly successful expanders, than the Franks.

The subduing of neighbours, and the acquisition of *regna*, set Frankish rulers new lessons in resource management. The kingdom of Aquitaine created for the three-year-old Louis the Pious in 781 covered (including Gascony and Septimania) some 120,000 sq km.[26] It could be more or less

---

[21] *Vita Karoli*, c. 15.
[22] Astronomer, c. 55, p. 641; *AB(3) s.a.* 868, 874, pp. 150, 186; *AF(3) s.a.* 852, p. 34.
[23] *Vita Karoli*, c. 16.   [24] Sanchez-Albornoz (1972), pp. 185–221; Kirby (1991), pp. 163–9.
[25] Asser, c. 81; see Davies (1982), pp. 112–16.   [26] Martindale (1985; 1990).

self-contained; but before long Charlemagne had to intervene to prevent the misappropriation of royal estates by local magnates. He reorganised the Aquitainian fisc to provide for four major rural palaces where Louis could over-winter: Chasseneuil and Doué in Poitou; Angeac in the Saintonge; Ebreuil in southern Berry.[27] There were also residences at places that in the ninth century can be called urban, *civitates* like Limoges, Clermont, Toulouse, Bourges, and from the 830s onwards kings of Aquitaine preferred these – a pattern that can be observed in other ninth-century kingdoms too. After being ruled from 781 to 838 as a separate kingdom, Aquitaine became just a part of Charles the Bald's larger realm. Though Charles later recreated the sub-kingdom, he denied his sons the power to alienate lands by charter: Charles managed Aquitaine from a distance, never even visiting there after the 850s, but continuing to welcome Aquitainians to his palaces in Francia and occasionally to make grants in Aquitaine. While the Gascons remained beyond Frankish control (as they always had), Septimanians, threatened by their Spanish-Muslim neighbours, cherished the Frankish connection and were prepared to travel 500 km to Francia to get confirmation of the king's protection.[28] A succession of royal residents (however young or frail) maintained a royal presence in Aquitaine itself.[29] Late in the ninth century, King Odo was able to spend long spells of time in Aquitaine, which implies that royal control of some fisclands had been retained and/or that alternative accommodation was available in *civitates*. That accommodation, and the support system sustaining it, was very often ecclesiastical. The same was true of Alemannia, another of the Carolingians' acquired *regna*. Its place within a larger structure changed similarly, with changes in the configuration of the Carolingian family and in the shape of the ninth-century East Frankish kingdom. When in 839 strategic needs made Alemannia a key area, Louis the Pious was apparently able to take up the threads of royal control. The palace of Bodman on the Bodensee became his base for several weeks. Here again, royal estates were not the only royal assets: it was the proximity of the great royal abbey of Reichenau that helped Louis make the most of his stay at Bodman.[30]

   In Gaul, thanks to generations of pious royal and aristocratic benefaction, the secularisation, that is, lay reappropriation, of church lands was well under way in the eighth century. The very establishment of Carolingian power used to be credited to a 'feudal revolution' whereby church lands were seized by Charles Martel to be granted to his vassal-cavalrymen. It is

---

[27] Astronomer, c. 7, p. 610, trans. King, p. 171.

[28] Tessier (1952), nos. 244, 245, 289, 290, 320, 321, 322, 340, 341, 360, 415.

[29] For differing interpretations of these changes, compare Martindale (1990) and Nelson (1992a), pp. 210–12.   [30] Zotz (1990).

now clear that Martel did nothing new in appropriating church lands, nor did he exploit the church particularly vigorously. (Disgruntled ecclesiastics projected their grievances back into the past: in the ninth century, it was safer to portray Charles Martel burning in hell than Charles the Bald.[31]) What Martel did was to 'crush the tyrants',[32] that is, the bishops who had been building up ecclesiastical principalities at Auxerre and Orléans, for instance. Martel was driven less by reforming zeal (since he himself gave the two key sees of Rheims and Trier to a notoriously unreformed character, but trusty supporter, Milo) than by the need to remove political rivals in strategically key areas and to put ecclesiastical resources at the disposal of men who would fight for him. Martel set his heirs on the way to a royal destiny.[33] His son Pippin, king from 751, picked up threads left by powerful Merovingians. He continued Martel's strategy of controlling key churches, expropriating most of the lands of the see of Auxerre, for instance, and installing noble supporters thereon. He also extended that strategy, in a complex *quid pro quo* of patronage and exploitation, into a truly realm-wide *Einstaatung* – incorporation into the state – of the Frankish church.[34] Pippin, after all, had been consecrated king by the bishops of Gaul. He personally appointed bishops and abbots to major establishments (a century later, this was rightly claimed as Frankish royal custom[35]); summoned their attendance at councils and assemblies, which reinforced their corporate involvement in royal designs; required the military service of the men, often kin and/or clients of bishops and abbots, endowed with grants of ecclesiastical lands; and obtained the prayers of senior churchmen for himself, his family, his regime. The map of Carolingian resources thus needs to include major churches along with palaces and royal estates. The lands of the bishopric of Auxerre enabled Pippin to secure control of Burgundy in the 750s, thus opening the way to Aquitaine. The Frankish takeover of Alemannia was followed up by extensive grants of former ducal fisclands to Abbot Fulrad of St Denis, the monastery Pippin had designated his burial-place. Once Charlemagne had annexed the Lombard kingdom, endowments to St Denis and St Martin, Tours, in the Val d'Aosta secured the route to Italy.[36] Royal grants of jurisdictional immunities to monasteries need to be understood in this context. Since such churches were firmly under royal protection, and hence still open to royal influence and intervention, this was a form of devolution, not disengagement (any more than similar arrangements had been in the Merovingian period). Thus, while the Carolingians' relations

---

31 Nonn (1970). 32 *Vita Karoli*, c. 2.
33 Wallace-Hadrill (1983), pp. 134–8; Wood (1993b), pp. 273–87.
34 Prinz (1971), pp. 70–3, 91. 35 Lupus, *Ep.*, 26 (842).
36 Wickham (1981), p. 48; compare Geary (1985), pp. 123–5.

with favoured churches had a strong flavour of private interest, their church policy, overall and in detail, deployed and built public authority.

In theory church lands were the property of saints 'forever', but in practice this did not exclude their continuing availability to meet royal demands. These demands grew heavier as needs increased and alternative sources of reward diminished. Louis the Pious listed monasteries owing gifts, military service and prayers – in some cases all three.[37] Sometimes a king's exploitation was barefaced, as when Charles the Bald, having granted the see of Laon over 2000 manses so that military service could be performed for him, that is, by benefice-holders chosen by himself, was irate when the bishop proved less than compliant.[38] Royal generosity could be explicitly conditional: Charles the Fat granted lands to St Gall on condition that they were used to commemorate his father: 'but if not, they are to be made public lands again [and returned] to the fisc'.[39] Royal access to church resources was fully institutionalised. Peasants on the estates of the royal monastery of St Germain-des-Prés owed renders earmarked for provisioning troops (*hostilicium*).[40] The armies of ninth-century Carolingians included large contingents of troops, holders of benefices on ecclesiastical lands, who were organised for campaign by bishops, abbots and abbesses. The loyalty, perhaps too the efficiency, of those ecclesiastical dignitaries was generally more reliable than that of secular office-holders.

This system clearly played an important part in the expansion of the Carolingian empire. In nearly every *regnum* absorbed by the Franks (Saxony was the exception), well-endowed churches were of much more recent date than those of Gaul; and there is no evidence that anything like the Carolingian system was in place. The well-documented military arrangements of the Lombard kingdom include no ecclesiastical contributions to royal armies. A letter of complaint by the patriarch of Aquileia to Charlemagne in 789/90 seems to imply that the imposition of such service on Lombard churches was new: the patriarch asked to be permitted 'to serve only in the camps of the Lord', and reminded Charlemagne that 'no man can serve two masters'.[41] Dual service, to God and to the king, was precisely what Frankish bishops had learned to perform well, and the Carolingians made Lombard bishops follow suit.[42]

In Ireland, where no overkingship emerged sufficiently powerful to buttress a realm-wide institutional church, links between local churches and little kingdoms became so close, with kings who were also abbots and even

---

[37] *CCM* I, pp. 493–9.   [38] Nelson (1991b), p. 26.
[39] Wartmann III, p. 688: an interesting use of the verb *publicare*.
[40] Durliat (1984)   [41] *MGH Epp.* IV, p. 525.
[42] *MGH Cap.* II, no. 218, c. 4, p. 96.

bishops, that ecclesiastical resources became scarcely distinguishable from royal ones. Ecclesiastical wealth was despoiled by Irishmen before as well as during the ninth-century Scandinavian raids, and it was not restored.[43] In England an accident of historical geography, the location of the primatial see in Kent, meant that after the Mercians' suppression of the Kentish kingdom in the eighth century, the archbishops of Canterbury became representatives of Kentish autonomy. They continued to mint their own coins, and from time to time used their exceptionally close contacts with the papacy to gain leverage against the demands of Mercian and then West Saxon kings and so resist incorporation in anything like a Carolingian system.[44] Later in the ninth century, Viking raids on archiepiscopal lands weakened Canterbury's capacity to withstand West Saxon pressure: Alfred and his successors could be more successful imitators of the Carolingians. The see of York underwent rather different trials: recurrent disputes over the Northumbrian throne spelled danger for archbishops' security (one archbishop's brother, Alcuin, preferred exile) and removed the bulwark against aristocratic domination of church resources. Bede denounced bogus monasteries set up to evade, rather than fulfil, obligations of military service.[45] Nevertheless powerful ecclesiastical institutions survived, and although most lost their endowments when the kingdom succumbed to Scandinavian conquest in 866, a few found forms of accommodation with the new powers that were. By the 880s, the community of St Cuthbert was helping install one Scandinavian king, while the archbishop of York was making space available in the cathedral graveyard for the burial of another.[46] But neither in Ireland nor England did the church contribute institutionally to the state as it did in the Carolingians' kingdoms.

The Frankish system could work well only as long as, and where, powerful monarchs bolstered the church's institutional integrity and helped it keep and protect its own. Charlemagne's heirs gladly made this investment. Dependent as they were on the church's military service, they sincerely believed themselves yet more dependent on the church's prayers. After 774, monasteries in the conquered Lombard kingdom were expected to pray for their conqueror, and such prayer could become a litmus-test of loyalty: the abbot of San Vincenzo was lucky to keep his job when Charlemagne heard allegations of his reluctance to join in the intercessory liturgy.[47] Entry in the book of life at Reichenau, or the endowment of feasts at St Denis where the community, through a 'pious gastric alchemy'[48] which was itself a form of prayer, ate their way to the welfare of their patron and his

[43] Hughes (1966), pp. 197–214; Davies (1993).   [44] Brooks (1984), pp. 111–206.
[45] *EHD*, no. 170.   [46] *EHD*, no. 6, p. 287; Loyn (1977), p. 61.
[47] McCormick (1984), pp. 3–4   [48] Rouche (1984), p. 276.

family, gave kings that most precious of all resources: confidence in success. In West Francia, the clearest evidence for some slippage of royal power in the late ninth century is the passing of key royal monasteries into local aristocratic hands: St Vaast to the counts of Flanders; St Denis to Odo son of Robert; St Martin to Odo's brother Robert.[49] Episcopal 'tyranny' of the sort overcome by Martel returned in Fulk of Rheims' bid for regional dominance based on the systematic building of *castella* in his diocese.[50] Royal failure to hold distant churches was one thing: to lose control of Rheims, in the very centre of the West Frankish royal heartlands was another. The East Frankish kings were more successful, and in their kingdom the Carolingian church system, after a temporary blip, became the Ottonian one.[51]

This hugely significant ecclesiastical contribution to the Carolingian state tells against the gloomy analysis of the ninth-century political economy offered by the Belgian scholar Jan Dhondt. Dhondt argued (with the west mainly in mind) that the squandering of the Carolingian fisc by Charlemagne's successors fatally undermined Carolingian power, and that the empire thus collapsed from within through lack of resources. There are methodological problems here: reign cannot be compared with reign, for the eighth century is poorly documented compared with the ninth; and grants of benefices, which depleted the fisc's recurrent *income* as much as did outright grants, were seldom recorded in writing even in the ninth century.[52] In any event, patronage in the form of land-grants was a positive instrument of royal government: political crisis can be documented by a fall in numbers of grants, the defusing of crisis by a marked rise as the ruler rewarded supporters.[53] Moreover, a managerial rationale is sometimes suggested by the nature and location of lands conceded: those furthest from the heartlands were hardest to run; and relatively recent acquisitions (for instance, through confiscation) made prudent concessions to the rivals of the disgraced.[54] But the critical point against Dhondt is simply this: that the political geography of the Carolingian empire must include the ecclesiastical alongside the secular. The great majority of extant Carolingian charters are grants to churches, and so, given the system just described, can hardly be categorised as losses to the state.

Kings depended not only on their lands, but on moveable wealth. In 793 Charlemagne rewarded non-defectors after a serious rebellion by giving out 'gold and silver and precious cloths'.[55] How had Charlemagne acquired

---

[49] See ch 23. Also p. 415 below.   [50] Schneider (1973); Kaiser (1981).
[51] Even allowing for reservations of Reuter (1982); see Schieffer (1990).
[52] Martindale (1985).   [53] Depreux (1992); Nelson (1992a), p. 191.
[54] Tessier (1952), no. 428 is a good example.
[55] *Annales Laureshamenses*, p. 35, trans. King, p. 140.

these items? In his reign, plunder and tribute were major forms of royal income and royal reward/inducement. Einhard described the profits of empire: cartloads of Avar treasure that accrued from the victories of the 790s and made the Franks so wealthy that 'it seemed as if they had been almost paupers before'.[56] Charlemagne distributed Avar loot to favoured churches; and to foreign potentates: Offa of Mercia received a sword. The Beneventans were not conquered, but made to pay a hefty tribute.[57] Charlemagne's huge treasure-hoard was at once a proof of his authority and a means of wielding it. Einhard describes some of it near the end of Charlemagne's life: the three great silver tables; the hangings, carpets, silks, gold and silver vessels, vestments, bullion and cash, books, especially liturgical ones.[58] Such exceptionally precious and exotic possessions – and there were also the organ, the clock, and (briefly) the elephant – marked out their owner as uniquely prestigious.[59] Most precious of all were the relics encased in splendid reliquaries of gold and silver encrusted with gems. The *Domschatz* at Aachen to this day gives a faint impression of what the ninth-century original must have been: a spiritual powerhouse indeed, of incalculable psychological value in terms of morale and prestige; but of economic value too, as the potential stuff of gift or exchange. The well-protected Jewish traders at the courts of Charlemagne's successors purveyed the wherewithal for conspicuous consumption.[60]

Plunder and tribute are fragile bases for such consumption. Treasure need not indicate sustainable economic activity. A hoard can be very easily dispersed. Apparently strong kingdoms could fade into impotence. Denmark posed a serious threat to Charlemagne, but King Godfrid was assassinated in 809 and a long-running succession dispute cut the royal share of the realm's moveable wealth. In 845 King Horik, and a Carolingian king's envoy at his court, looked on as the Danish warlord Ragnar showed off the loot he had brought back from his attack on Paris.[61] Frankish wealth was passing into Danish hands but they were not royal hands. A further succession dispute brought the deaths of 'King Horik and other kings and almost the entire nobility' in 854.[62] Despite the efforts of Frankish missionaries Horik had remained pagan: no ecclesiastical resources cushioned the Danish kingdom from near-collapse. At this very time, on the Carolingians' 'Wild East frontier',[63] the Moravian kingdom was becoming an empire. It

---

[56] *Vita Karoli*, c. 13.
[57] *MGH Epp.* IV, nos. 96, 100, pp. 140, 146; *ARF (1) s.a.* 787, trans. King, p. 84.
[58] *Vita Karoli*, c. 33.
[59] *ARF s.a.* 757, p. 14 (and cf. 826, p. 170), 801–2, pp. 116–17 (trans. King, p. 94–5); 807, p. 124 (trans. p. 98). [60] *MGH Form.*, nos. 30–2, pp. 309–11. [61] Nelson (1992a), p. 152.
[62] *AB(3) s.a.* p. 80. [63] Reuter (1991), p. 81.

did so, like the Carolingian empire itself, by growing: kings based in passable imitations of *sedes regni* amplified the lands under their direct control, then made neighbours into clients and tributaries. They had the luck of continuity: just as two exceptionally long-lived kings made Mercian hegemony in eighth-century England (716–96), so three kings as long-lived held Moravian hegemony in ninth-century eastern Europe (*c.* 830–94). 'Greater Moravia' apparently covered a large area including modern Czechia and Slovakia and extending far south of the Danube.[64] But amplification was not sustainable indefinitely in time or space. The Moravian empire succumbed to the familiar problem of dynastic disputes which were exploited by an external enemy, the Hungarians. The collapse was total: the bases of Moravian power have had to be reconstructed by archaeologists.

Charlemagne's empire was differently built. It had reached its utmost ('natural'?) limits by about 806 and ceased to expand.[65] Charlemagne's treasure-hoard was dispersed at his death in 814. There were to be serious dynastic disputes in the ninth century. Yet the Carolingian state did not implode. Partly through (not despite) divisions, its rulers found homoeostatic mechanisms of their own. External attack came: the successor states of the ninth century did not succumb. The first part of the explanation lies in readjustment of the bases of power. Internal redistribution of wealth was an alternative to external expansion. The preservation of a single Carolingian *regnum* after 840, with brothers, uncles and nephews all retaining stakes in their patrimony, in spite of division and (in 855) further division, allowed expansion as between Carolingian kingdoms through the working of inheritance: Louis the German and Charles the Bald significantly extended their realms by exploiting the infertility of one nephew's queen and the sonlessness of another. The Carolingian empire's *Auflösungsprozess* – process of dissolution[66] – was also one of resolution and reformation. Kings could put increasing pressure on ecclesiastical resources, granting abbacies, that is, the temporal lordship that went with them, to laymen, using church lands to grant benefices to their men, and dipping into church treasuries. Further, income from fisclands could be increased through more vigorous management, that is, extracting from peasants heavier labour services, and increased dues in kind and especially in cash. Hincmar of Rheims advised Louis the German and Charles the Bald not to let their estate-managers oppress the peasantry in this way: chests heavy with silver and gold meant souls weighed down with sin. Hincmar insisted that if the managers did their job properly,

---

[64] Following Reuter (1991), but partly accepting Bowlus (1987).   [65] Reuter (1990).
[66] Schlesinger (1965).

the king could support his household quite satisfactorily from the fisc, without imposing demands for hospitality on 'bishops, abbots, abbesses and counts', thus pushing *them* to increase their demands on the local tenantry.[67] The shift from an economy of plunder to an economy of profiteering[68] was already under way.

The aristocracy too grew richer in the eighth and ninth centuries by participation in the spoils of war, and also by more aggressive landlordship (*Grundherrschaft*) which imposed just the sort of heavier burdens on the peasantry that Hincmar warned against. Did growing aristocratic wealth necessarily mean diminishing royal resources? True, the elites of the Carolingian world took a very much bigger slice of the available cake than their predecessors in the Roman empire had of theirs, because the Carolingian state did not tax its elites as the Roman state had done. (The cake as a whole was very much smaller than the Roman one: what matters here are the relative sizes of slices as between state and elites.) Carolingian rulers did however impose a regular levy on aristocratic wealth through institutionalised 'annual gifts'. Horses as well as gold and silver were always welcome to kings.[69] There were other less regular levies too: rulers since the sixth century had assigned a high office for a price. In the case of ecclesiastical offices this was called simony. Complaints in the reign of Charles the Bald suggest that his prices were high.[70] Powerful Carolingians may also have been able to limit the size of the cut taken by an office-holder from the fines and gifts (*munera*) which together constituted the profits of justice. This was a form of power-sharing in which the king could contrive to retain the lion's share. But it was possible for *both* the aristocracy's *and* the king's shares to grow, if the total cake was expanding, that is, if there were increased proceeds from expanding economic activity and, at the same time, from increasingly active royal government.

Unlike Roman coinage, which functioned almost exclusively to meet the needs of the state, early medieval currency operated in an economy driven by the interests, and the quest for profit, of private individuals as well as rulers.[71] That was one reason why as early as *c.* 700 Frisian merchants had begun to try their hands at issuing coin.[72] Yet kings were quick to follow and to reimpose a royal monopoly. Hence the coinage reforms of Pippin and Charlemagne on the one hand, Offa on the other, are among the surest signs both of newly active internal and external markets offering kings, and

[67] *MGH Conc.* III, no. 41, c. 14, pp. 422–3.

[68] Davies (1987), p. 157 (in the context of twelfth-century Wales).

[69] Reuter (1985), Compare *De Ordine Palatii*, c. 29, trans. Herlihy, p. 222.

[70] Nelson (1992a), p. 240.   [71] Hendy (1988), and see Blackburn, below, chapter 20.

[72] Wood (1993), pp. 39–40.

others, possibilities for profit, and of revived royal authority in Francia and
England. Kings were able to maintain, or restore, the quality of the coinage
against debasement because this served the interests of other coin-users. If
the volume of currency in circulation in the Frankish lands west of the
Rhine, and also in England, amounted to millions of coins in the earlier
eighth century, and again in the earlier ninth century, as some numismatists
think,[73] there were potential large benefits to all involved including kings.
Coinage oiled the wheels of trade; and tolls contributed substantially to
royal income. Eighth-century Mercian kings were well aware of this, and so
were the Carolingians.[74] So too was the Danish king Godfrid: in 808 he
'destroyed the *emporium* on the Baltic sea-coast at *Reric* [?Old Lübeck, or
Wolin] whence he used to extract a large benefit from tolls, and putting the
traders on board ship, he made for the *portus* of Schleswig [Hedeby, in
eastern Denmark], which he then decided to protect with a rampart'.[75] The
portus was evidently easier than the *emporium* for the king to protect, and
exploit. Archaeologists have been able to show at Hedeby and on many
other sites the material evidence of the revival of an economy of
exchanges.[76] Written sources record more merchants, and more markets.[77]
Kings played some part in stimulating these changes, as protectors of
merchants and patrons of *emporia*.[78] More significant still, kings benefited
from them, in terms of consumption and exaction.

Charlemagne's prohibition of Sunday markets[79] suggests the stimulus
given to more local commercial transactions involving peasants. Charles the
Bald's 864 legislation envisages peasants as among regular coin-users; and
anecdotal evidence in hagiography confirms that peasants got their coins
through selling in local markets.[80] There were potential benefits for kings
here too, as landlords, and as controllers of markets within their realms. The
interest of kings in coinage and commerce was fiscal rather than economic:
witness Godfrid transferring the traders from whose tolls he profited to his
portus of Hedeby; witness the wealth of Charles the Bald and Alfred, diligent
creamers-off, both, of other people's surpluses. Charles' critics in 858 alleged
that he finished off the 'plundering' of his own people that the Northmen
had begun![81] In 860 he raised the money to pay a Scandinavian war-band he
hoped to recruit (to turn against other Scandinavians) by taxing not only
landowners but traders, 'even very small-scale ones'.[82] The *renovatio monetae*

---

[73] Metcalf (1967; 1990); Coupland (1990), against Hendy (1988), pp. 39–40.
[74] Sawyer (1977); Kelly (1992); Siems (1992), pp. 448–52.   [75] *ARF(3)*, p. 100.
[76] Randsborg (1980), pp. 85–92; Verhulst (1989).   [77] Johanek (1988).
[78] Sawyer (1982); Hodges (1990).
[79] *MGH Cap.* I, no. 61 (809), c. 8, p. 149. Siems (1992), pp. 491–2.
[80] Nelson (1992a), pp. 24–5.   [81] *AF(3)*, pp. 49–50, trans., p. 42.   [82] *AB(3)*, p. 92.

of 864 in the West Frankish kingdom entailed the calling-in of all coins, many of them very debased, their demonetisation (the old coins would no longer be accepted as currency) and their replacement by a distinctive new issue of purer coin – a substantial revaluation in fact. Those who brought in old pennies to mints would receive many fewer new pennies. The charge thus imposed on coin-users (later known as seigneurage) seems to have amounted in the Carolingian period to some 10%, shared between the king and those who managed each mint, namely the moneyers and the local count or viscount. *Renovatio* meant taxation on all who held and used money: profits flowed from every mint to the royal treasury. The purity of the reformed coins, their standardised dies, the hoard evidence for the disappearance from currency of the old money, all prove Charles' success in carrying out this ambitious plan.[83] In 866, he was able to impose realm-wide direct taxation, calculated on land-units, to pay off tributes owed to Scandinavian war-bands.[84] Alfred organised a monetary reform in Wessex for similar purposes in the 870s, and again the hoard evidence proves his success.[85] He, like the Mercian king in the 860s, paid Vikings tributes that were apparently raised realm-wide. [86] Charles the Bald was also able (in 864) to attempt to prohibit unlicensed markets, and so if not to limit, at least to check, and insist on payment from, other beneficiaries of market activity.[87] In the more monetised parts of western Europe, that is, west of the Rhine and in England, kings had problems less because they were poor (if they were poor compared with Roman emperors, they were not so poor compared with seventh- or tenth-century kings), than because they had to share so much social power with other *potentes*, inside as well as outside the royal family. When Charles the Bald tried to increase the aristocracy's contribution to taxation in 877, he was confronted by rebellion. His 864 legislation implies that local aristocrats, counts no doubt in the lead, were already vigorously exploiting market control. The firmly king-centred sources for Wessex make Alfred seem more dominant than his Continental counterparts; but Alfred too had to cajole the great men of his kingdom – and it was a small kingdom. In the East Midlands and East Anglia, Scandinavian warlords called themselves kings and imitated Alfred's coinage on their own account. Alfred had to be as firm (if not so ruthless) as Charles the Bald in excluding his kinsmen, and his own sons too, from more than nominal shares in his regime. If silver stocks dwindled later in the ninth century,[88] kings would have needed to drive harder to maintain their shares.

---

[83] Compare Spufford (1988), pp. 44–73; Metcalf and Northover (1989); Metcalf (1990); Coupland (1991).   [84] *AB(3)*, p. 130.   [85] Maddicott (1992); Blackburn (1993).
[86] Sawyer 354. For Mercian tributes, Sawyer 1278.
[87] Edict of Pîtres, c. 19, *MGH Cap.* II, no. 273, pp. 317–18.   [88] Blackburn (1993).

Alfred's successors re-engaged in 'imperial' expansion; Charles the Bald's were unable to increase internal or external income. Thus the fiscality of royal government, as of landlordship, in this period was precarious as well as limited.[89] Though Roman ways were alluring, practical politics drew kings in other directions.

THE SOCIOLOGY OF POWER

Sketches of official hierarchies or feudal pyramids can bear about as much relationship to reality as the paper constitutions of many twentieth-century states. Like colonial District Officers-turned-anthropologists, historians of early medieval government have increasingly interested themselves in the social relations within and through which government worked. Yet, something of the social scientist's analytical clarity has to be sacrificed when the focus is on change and variety. The obligations of kinship played through institutions, dynastic power through structures of office-holding, in complex and contradictory ways.[90] Kinship was crucial to the political workings of all kingdoms, whatever the level of economic activity, whatever the administrative arrangements. While an elective element in royal succession was common, inheritance within a more or less restricted family or kindred was the norm. Changes of dynasty were masked by the construction of fictive genealogical ties.[91] In Francia, the frequent creation of child-rulers in this period implies both the overriding importance of dynasticism, and (paradoxically) a firmly institutionalised regnal authority able to weather periods of temporary royal incapacity, because aristocrats could so actively participate in royal government.[92] Kinship itself, imposing the most fundamental of social obligations, and acting as the template for a variety of political relationships, contained another paradox. Fictive, spiritual, kinship could strengthen political ties, as when successive popes became co-fathers of the Carolingian kings whose offspring they baptised, or when the Moravian ruler Svatopluk (Zwentibold) signalled his entry into the Carolingian orbit by standing godfather, and passing his exotic name, to the illegitimate son of the East Frankish king Arnulf.[93] But when godparenthood was used to reinforce relationships *within* a royal family, as when a Carolingian uncle became his nephew's godfather, it plainly hinted at mistrust between close kinsmen. The closest nexus of loving relationships, maintained by the most sacred of social duties, was also the site of tension and

---

[89] For a different view, see Durliat (1990).   [90] Althoff (1990). Compare Wickham (1991).
[91] Dumville (1977); Hlawitschka (1989).
[92] Compare Reynolds (1984), p. 254: 'regnal' government would be a better term.
[93] Angenendt (1984); Lynch (1986); Althoff (1990), pp. 77–84; Smith (1992), pp. 111–13.

often ferocious conflict. Charlemagne forbade his sons 'to kill, blind, mutilate their nephews, or force them to be tonsured against their will'.[94]

Women are good guides to the sociology of power, for men relate to each other and gain power from each other through women, and powerful men legitimise their status and their authority by protecting and exploiting women. In the early medieval period, such social realities, barely surmisable, are obscured by the tendency of texts produced in a more or less misogynistic clerical culture to ignore or devalue women. Key pieces in genealogical jigsaw-puzzles are often missing, therefore.[95] In the modern historiography of medieval politics and government, a long-standing neglect of women is now being rectified. Women's importance as conduits of property and power, as peace-weavers, as the foci of interest-groups at court, is becoming increasingly clear. 'It frequently happens that women are sought as marriage-partners between regions and realms': Charlemagne's *Divisio*-project of 806, in explicitly acknowledging the role of such marriages in binding *regna* together, also signalled a problem. What would happen when the empire was divided? Women moving from one realm to another, said Charlemagne, were to keep their lands in the realm whence they came.[96] One suspects (but cannot quite prove) that powerful rulers in the eighth and ninth centuries, as later, had a voice in the marriages of magnates' daughters.[97] Certainly, rulers were well aware that an aristocratic marriage-alliance, proposed or effected, bonded not just the couple but their wider families, and that the breaking-off of a betrothal, the repudiation of a wife, could provoke realm-wide 'scandals and seditions'. Hence Charles the Bald's concern to smooth over one such row involving Aquitainian *viri potentes* on whose co-operation he relied. Hence too the delicate situation which arose when the lady Northild, unable any longer to bear her husband's perverse sexual practices, appealed to Louis the Pious: he referred the case to bishops, who, pleading ignorance of such matters, passed it on to a court of laymen – who declared that the lady must remain with her husband.[98] Just as aristocrats would 'marry into' wealth and probably (given a pattern of hereditary office-holding,[99] and the demographic probability of heiresses rather than heirs within three generations) into high office too,[100] so kings pursued marriage strategies of their own. They chose partners for themselves and their offspring from the aristocracy of their own or neighbouring realms, or, more rarely, intermarried with foreign royalty. Royal marriages were critical events in the political process. They figure frequently in court-directed historical writing. Kin by marriage (affines)

---

[94] *Divisio* of 806, *MGH Cap.* I, no. 45, c. 18, pp. 129–30.   [95] Bouchard (1988).
[96] *MGH Cap.* I, no. 45, c. 12, p. 129.   [97] Compare Hodgson (1993), pp. 245–6.
[98] *PL* 125, col. 655.   [99] Below, pp. 412–13.   [100] Bouchard (1986).

could offer political support. Both maternal and paternal kin could transmit claims on wealth and prestige to the next generation.

In ruling families, women occupied centrally important positions: as individuals they could strengthen, yet also imperil, dynastic security, could be powerful, yet vulnerable in a patriarchal world. Useful as a marriage-partner for her father's ally, the bride could find herself alone in a foreign court when an alliance cooled. In the early eighth century, the heiress Plectrude consolidated the power of her husband the mayor of the palace, Pippin, by bringing him lands between the rivers Meuse and Moselle. After Pippin's death, Plectrude's stepson Charles Martel defeated her and her grandsons by exploiting the support of his own mother's kinsmen in the region of Liège.[101] He entered into Pippin's inheritance, and bettered it, becoming the *princeps* of the Franks. Martel's own son Pippin dared to assume the title of king, deriving his prestige in part from the high, possibly Merovingian, birth and rich inheritance of his wife Bertrada.[102] Pippin's sister Chiltrude had flouted the authority of her male relatives by marrying the Bavarian duke without their consent in one of the great scandals of the age:[103] her son Tassilo was to be the most dangerous rival of Pippin's son Charlemagne.

In the complex 'international relations' of Charlemagne's early years, Lombard royal women, seldom included in textbook genealogies, actually played key roles. King Desiderius, demonstrating the aspirations of a new Theodoric, married off three daughters to the Lombard Duke Arichis of Benevento, to Tassilo of Bavaria and to Charlemagne, while a fourth daughter became abbess of the convent of San Salvatore which Desiderius and his wife founded at his home-city of Brescia. Charlemagne's repudiation of his Lombard bride earned him the hatred of her sisters. When Arichis died, his widow continued successful Lombard resistance to a Frankish takeover.[104] In 788 when Charlemagne finally ousted Tassilo he not only tonsured him and his son but carried off his wife and daughters into captivity.[105] Authority in Bavaria was now given to Gerold, brother of the woman whom Charlemagne had married after rejecting the Lombard bride. Though Gerold's sister Queen Hildegard had died in 783, Gerold was the maternal uncle of her and Charlemagne's son Pippin, destined, had he lived, to inherit Bavaria. Thus dead as well as living, a royal woman acted as a focus for the loyalties of a subset of Carolingian kin and enabled one group to define itself against others. But a woman could act too as a focus for a people's identity and such an identity mattered especially in the *regna* east of

---

[101] Gerberding (1987), chapter 6.   [102] Hlawitschka (1965); Nelson (1991).
[103] Astronomer, c. 21, p. 618; Jarnut (1977).   [104] Goffart (1988), pp. 332, 336–49.
[105] Stoclet (1986).

the Rhine: Charlemagne had picked Hildegard in the first place because she was descended, through her mother, from the Alemannic ducal line:[106] the marriage assuaged Alemans' resentment at the ousting of their dynasty and legitimised Carolingian rule in Alemannia. Hildegard bore eleven children in as many years of marriage (771–83). Her successors, Charlemagne's queens Fastrada (d. 794) and Liutgard (d. 800), *ex officio* took some part in managing the royal estates to provision the royal household; and since that household included ambitious young warriors, were responsible for 'nurturing' them through disbursing annual gifts. Fastrada's 'cruelty' was the alleged cause of the two serious rebellions (786, 792) of Charlemagne's reign. With unique access to her husband, the queen could be a significant channel of patronage, benefiting her own kinsmen.[107] A widower-king's remarriage could pit one royal descent line, one kin-cluster, against another: after Louis the Pious married for a second time, and seemed to favour the son of his new wife Judith over his sons by his first wife, family discord eventually erupted into civil war. When Judith was suspected of adultery, her brothers as well as she were banished to monastic imprisonment.[108] In Wessex twenty years later, when King Æthelwulf married that Judith's granddaughter (and daughter of Charles the Bald), his adult son rebelled. When Æthelwulf died soon after, the son married his stepmother, presumably thereby gaining political advantages that outweighed the denunciations of clerical contemporaries.[109]

Carolingians, unlike some Merovingians, took their wives from the aristocracy; and royal fathers normally selected, and sometimes dowered, their sons' wives. Marriage with a local heiress could give a king's son a grip on his sub-kingdom. Louis the German arranged the marriages of his three sons in the 860s to noble heiresses in Bavaria, Saxony and Alemannia respectively, while Charles the Bald's two elder sons, when scarcely adult, jumped the gun (and infuriated their father) by choosing their own brides in Neustria and Aquitaine.[110] The activities of queens were more than a matter of personal or familial influence, however: they reflected the centrality of the court in the political system and the institutionalised powers of kingship, hence the extent to which the Carolingian realm functioned as a state. In order to do his job, a king needed a queen. She played a key role in running his household, dispensing annual payments to the *milites*; and she could have a household, and household officers, of her own.[111] This was why the affair of Lothar II's divorce was not just scandalous but a political disaster.[112] Queenship began to take its place alongside kingship as the subject of

---

[106] Thegan, c.2, pp. 590–1.   [107] Compare, Notker 1, 4. See further Nelson (1993a).
[108] Ward (1990b).   [109] Asser, c. 17; see Stafford (1990), p. 151.   [110] See Table 9.
[111] *De Ordine Palatii*, c. 22, trans. Herlihy, p. 219; *MGH Form.*, p. 368.   [112] See above, p. 150.

political thought.[113] At the same time, the queen's role reflected the special loyalty expected of close kin. A king shared his parent's kin with his brothers: a king's wife's kin were his own. When kinsmen on mother's or father's side threatened rivalry or defection, in-laws promised an individual king firmer support, as did the young Emperor Lothar's father-in-law Hugh, and Charles the Bald's brother-in-law Boso in the 870s. The marriages of daughters, on the other hand, threatened to bring too many in-laws with claims on shares of the patrimony. Charlemagne kept his daughters unmarried: their influence at court during his last years became a scandal that was never permitted to recur. Nearly all the daughters of the ninth-century Carolingians were placed in convents. It was a safer way to narrow the circle of in-laws claiming familial resources and influence at court. But a royal descent line could become too narrow: in the later ninth century the Carolingians themselves were faced with no threat more severe than 'the sterility of their wives'.[114] It may be true that the Carolingians overrated the binding-power of marriage-alliances:[115] it is hard to think, though, of any better strategy available to them. Who could predict a woman's infertility, or her arousing of *inrevocabile odium* in the heart of her royal husband?[116]

Kingship was an exceptionally scarce resource, and sub-kingdoms were limited. Kings' sons 'surplus to requirement' had therefore to be shed. After Charlemagne and his younger brother Carloman had partitioned Pippin's kingdom in 768, relations deteriorated so badly that they were, according to Einhard, on the point of open war when Carloman died. The flight of Carloman's widow and her two young sons to Pavia (Einhard affects surprise) was a major reason for Charlemagne's conquest of the Lombard kingdom.[117] No more is known of Charlemagne's nephews, but they may have been in his mind when he told his sons what *not* to do to *their* nephews. Louis the Pious' nephew Bernard, excluded from the Carolingian inheritance in favour of Louis' sons, rebelled: he died after being blinded on his uncle's orders. This was not only a family tragedy. Bernard had many sympathisers and his revolt had threatened the stability of Louis' regime. Louis' spectacular performance of public penance in 822 was a well-judged gesture to restore harmony and re-establish his authority.[118] Few kings escaped the problem of rebellion by a close kinsman. One of the most dangerous rebels was Charles the Bald's son Carloman: only after the young

---

[113] Sedulius Scottus, *De Rectoribus Christianis*, c. 5, trans. Doyle, pp. 56–61. Compare Stafford (1983), pp. 27–8, 100; Nelson (1993a).   [114] Regino *s.a.* 880, p. 117.

[115] Althoff, (1990), p. 48.

[116] *AB(3) s.a.* 860, p. 92, on Lothar II's feeling about his wife Theutberga.

[117] *Vita Karoli*, c. 3.   [118] Werner (1990), pp. 57–69; de Jong (1992).

man's capture and, after a show-trial, blinding on his father's orders, did his aristocratic supporters abandon him.[119]

Conflict between dynastic branches, or rival dynasties, could leave a kingdom vulnerable to rivals and external aggressors. Northumbria and Mercia fell victim to such troubles. So did Denmark and the Moravian empire. The nascent Breton kingdom of Salomon was aborted by a succession dispute, and Salomon's successors were counts, not kings. Careful management rather than luck enabled West Saxon kings to avoid disaster, by fraternal pacts, publicly attested pre-mortem arrangements, and downgrading of the kings' wives who reproduced rival descent lines.[120] Naming was a means of staking, and denying, claims to power. The names of two of Charlemagne's sons, Clovis and Clothar, linked the new dynasty with the traditions of the old more securely than blood.[121] Through another set of names, other Carolingians were identified as illegitimate offspring. Pippin I's illegitimate half-brother Bernard remained in secular life, but was denied any share in the patrimony of Charles Martel.[122] Bernard, Louis the Pious' nephew, may have been so named to indicate illegitimacy; but if so, his grandfather Charlemagne had second thoughts, for Bernard's kingship of Italy was recognised in 813. Charlemagne gave his eldest son the 'right' name, Pippin, but belatedly excluded him from the succession in *c* 790 to make way for half-brothers: after his revolt in 792 had been crushed, Pippin was tonsured. In the ninth century, Carolingians used tonsuring to exclude princes from the ranks of potential kings. The bastard sons Hugh and Drogo who were the product of Charlemagne's liaisons during his latter years were tonsured by their half-brother Louis the Pious 'lest they should solicit the people' and rebel in their turn.[123] Charles the Bald, king of a much smaller realm than his father and grandfather, tried to exclude *legitimate* younger sons by tonsuring them as children, and tonsured his adult nephews too. Neither illegimitacy nor canonical disqualification proved definitive bars to royal succession. In 887, when the Carolingian line in East Francia was endangered, Arnulf was acknowledged king despite being illegitimate; and in 870, Charles the Bald's long-since tonsured son Carloman found substantial support for his bid for a kingdom.

At the palace, kinship with the king defined a group of men with presumptive claims to political influence. An aspiring youth was encouraged by his mother to cultivate 'the king's *parentes* and *propinqui*, both by paternal descent and by marriage'.[124] Stray hints in the sources suggest there were many of them. Some were more equal than others. Nithard, though

---

[1)] *AB(3) s.a.* 870–1, 873, pp. 167, 171–5, 180–1.   [120] Stafford (1981); Nelson (1991a), p. 55.
[121] Jarnut (1985).   [122] Nelson (1991c), p. 196.   [123] Nithard I. 2.
[124] Dhuoda, p. 166.

Charlemagne's grandson, was a Carolingian only through his mother. When conflicts between his maternal kinsmen resulted in Nithard's being deprived of lands, he fell back on paternal resources.[125] A much more powerful figure than Nithard in Charles' entourage in the early 840s was Adalhard, whose niece Charles married, Nithard says, 'because he thought Adalhard could bring the support of most of the *plebs*'.[126] Adalhard was distantly related to the king, but his power in 842 derived from years of influence at Louis the Pious' court when he had been able to direct patronage towards his own clients. Adalhard had become a *potens* ('powerful one'), through closeness to the ruler. Modern German historians have coined the apt term *Königsnähe* for this valuable quality. The presence of *potentes* at the king's side, as one *potens* put it, 'enabled men from the regions to come to the palace *familiarius*, 'more familiarly', that is, with more confidence of finding a patron.[127] For if *potentes* owed much to royal favour, they ploughed its benefits back into the roots of their social power, acknowledging their obligations to allies, dependants, neighbours: chosen by rival Carolingians to help divide the empire, they could be relied on (as Nithard recorded with some pride) to take precisely these considerations of 'affinity and congruence' into account. Their participation, in other words, gave settlements a chance of success. It was the king's business to ensure such persons did not form a focus of faction at court, nor of rebellion in the regions: or if they did, to restore consensus. A kingdom would hold together when aristocrats functioned, and saw themselves, as the king's *consiliarii*, 'the givers of counsel'.[128] When, as often happened in the eighth and ninth centuries, *potentes* moved from one kingdom to another, they retained old links as well as forging new ones. Adalhard, for instance, finding his position at Charles' court a less than commanding one (and his niece seems to have had a mind of her own, for her marriage to Charles was rapidly followed by the eclipse of Charles' mother), soon moved back east to his inherited lands and power in the neighbourhood of Trier. He had already taken the precaution of assuring Lothar I's wife the Empress Ermengard of his reliability.[129] In 865 Adalhard tried to reconstruct *Königsnähe* with one of the next Carolingian generation by betrothing his daughter to the son of Louis the German, but Louis made his son break off the engagement.[130] On the whole Adalhard's Carolingian patrons kept the whip hand: in the long run, he needed them more than they him.

A king's court teemed with the sons of the nobility sent there by their parents to learn social, political and military skills, to shine among their

---

[125] Nelson (1986a), p. 233.   [126] Nithard IV. 6.

[127] Hincmar, *De Ordine Palatii*, c. 18, trans. p. 217.   [128] See pp. 419–20 below.

[129] *MGH Epistolae Karolini Aevi* v, Epp. Variorum no. 27, pp. 343–5.   [130] *AB(3)*, p. 128.

commilitones, to grow up with the benefit of *Königsnähe*. The idea of selecting even non-noble boys to join the court may have appealed to kings as a way of keeping nobles on their toes: Notker has a story about Charlemagne as a kind of school-inspector, shaming lazy young nobles by praising the zeal of their non-noble fellows.[131] From this material a young king could shape his own entourage, or a mature king the next generation of *fideles*. The queen too played an important part, as pay-mistress, as well as surrogate mother, to the youths of the household. Gift-giving cemented the king's authority: Louis the Pious apparently gave the members of his retinue a new suit of clothes each year, Alfred gave his men money.[132] In due course, the hoped-for gifts might include an heiress, land, a countship, a lay abbacy. Alongside the young laymen were young clerics, equally ambitious. Later in life, they would recall fondly the companionship of the years at court.[133] Most bishops came from this milieu. Just occasionally, a ruler promoted a cleric of relatively humble birth: Ebbo of Rheims and Liutward of Vercelli used their episcopal positions to advance their low-born kin in secular life too, by arranging prestigious marriages and land-grants.[134]

Kings thus had access to social levels below the great aristocracy. Alfred's Laws protected the legal status, and the right to a defended residence, of free ceorls; and even slaves, thanks to Alfred, had the right to holidays when they could trade their surplus goods.[135] In the Frankish realm, the difference between free and slave[136] was important in differentiating those who could be called on for military service from those who could not. Among the free, kings could use *utilitas* where they found it. Whatever his birth, a man with a mission from the king, and armed with royal protection, had authority vested in him. The gulf between *potentes* and *pauperes* was wide, but nowhere was there simply a two-class society. There were squirearchies, and there were prosperous free peasants. Kings and magnates alike depended on the deference and political support of their social inferiors, and so shared a vested interest in maintaining a hierarchical order. Elites in Francia feared *coniurationes*, sworn associations formed by lesser folk to provide a kind of social security, for instance against fire or shipwreck. Such horizontal groupings could seem to the powerful like threats to social control.[137] Hierarchy mattered more than ethnicity. When Saxon peasants rebelled in 841, 'resisting their lawful lords', Frankish and Saxon elites rallied behind King Louis the German who crushed the rebels 'nobly, yet with lawful

---

[131] Notker I. 3; compare Asser, c. 75.
[132] Notker II. 21; Alfred's Will, trans. Keynes and Lapidge (1983), p. 177.
[133] Airlie (1990), p. 196.   [134] Thegan, c. 44, p. 599; *AF(3) s.a.* 887, pp. 101–2.
[135] Laws, c. 43, trans. Keynes and Lapidge (1983), p. 170.
[136] *MGH Cap.* I, no. 58, p. 145. See Reuter (1991), p. 31.   [137] Althoff (1990), pp. 119–21.

slaughter'.[138] A generation later, Scandinavian attacks on Saxony evoked a similar rallying in response.[139] Elsewhere the Scandinavians exploited fissures in the local societies and kingdoms they attacked. The peasants (*vulgus*) of the region between Seine and Loire who attempted resistance on their own account were ruthlessly slaughtered by the local Frankish nobility. Nobles, Breton and Flemish, Aquitainian and Frankish, as individuals and as groups, threatened to, and sometimes actually did, ally with Scandinavians to put pressure on Carolingian kings. Rival Carolingians themselves recruited Scandinavian war-bands, and allied with Danish princes.[140] In Ireland, kings made alliances with Norsemen against each other.[141] In Northumbria, Mercia and East Anglia, Scandinavian warlords extinguished existing kingdoms and set themselves up as kings partly by winning the support of indigenous collaborators. Alfred was able to keep and expand his kingdom in part by outbidding Scandinavian competitors: while he recruited individual Danes into his own war-band, he managed to persuade his own aristocracy that they had more to gain than to lose by supporting his kingship.[142] For any king, the worst danger was noble *coniuratio*, conspiracy against himself. Protecting *pauperes* was good, but promoting lordship was better. That was the basis of a king's entente with the aristocracy. Alfred's Laws, which he 'showed to all my councillors (*witan*) and they then said that it pleased them all to observe them', had the same ends in view: oaths must be kept, unless a man 'promised treachery to his lord', in which case 'it is better to leave the promise unfulfilled than to perform it'.[143] Obligations to lords overrode even the bonds of kinship: 'a man may fight on behalf of his born kinsman ... unless it is against his lord; that we do not allow'.[144] Most significant of all, Alfred coupled his treason-law, 'if anyone plots against the king's life ... he is to be liable for his life', with a further decree: 'thus also do we determine concerning all ranks, both *ceorl* and noble: he who plots against his lord's life is to be liable for his life'.[145] Kingship and lordship went together, and reinforced each other.

THE LOGISTICS OF POWER

Size was a fundamental constraint. An Irish king in his tiny kingdom some 50 km from end to end, would know everyone who mattered, be able to visit

---

[138] *AF(3) s.a.* 842, p. 21; Nithard IV. 4.   [139] *AF(3) s.a.* 880, p. 88.

[140] Nelson (1992a), pp. 77–8, 151, 170, 183, 187–8, 193, 204–6; Smith (1992), p. 105.

[141] Smyth (1977), pp. 122–42.   [142] Nelson (1986a).

[143] Laws Int. 49.10, Laws 1, 1.1, trans. Keynes and Lapidge (1983), p. 164.

[144] Laws 4, 2.6, trans. Keynes and Lapidge (1983), p. 169.

[145] Laws 4, 4.2, trans. Keynes and Lapidge (1983), p. 165.

every settlement, settle disputes personally.[146] In an empire the size of Charlemagne's, the ruler could govern only a relatively small part directly. Most of it he would never visit. The empire was a conglomerate of previously separate *regna*, each with its own hereditary nobility. In the *regna* of the East Frankish kingdom, and in Lombardy, the aristocracy had a strong sense of collective identity, and Charlemagne had to reckon with this. Existing regional (as well as local) power had to be accommodated. If Charlemagne summoned, say, Bavarians to his host, they fought together, as Bavarians. The establishment of a king's son in a sub-kingdom was an acknowledgement of regional power, and only to a lesser extent a limitation on it – an intrusion from the centre. Some aristocrats would retain and enhance their positions by collaborating with the new regime, seeking *Königsnähe*. More tensions arose from the relationship of son to father than from regional, or regnal, resistance to central directives, which anyway were few. The sons of Charlemagne and, still more, those of Louis the Pious, though given effective powers to make grants of lands and privilege in their own names, and even to issue coinage, resented their fathers' occasional interventions such as Charlemagne's reorganisation of Louis' Aquitainian fisc, or, still more contentious, Louis' redrawing of the boundaries of his sons' sub-kingdoms. Louis the German, in the next generation, explicitly distinguished levels of power when in 865 he delegated to his sons certain fisclands and responsibility for 'lesser judicial cases', while himself retaining control of bishoprics, countships, the bulk of the fisc and 'more important cases'.[147] Building up powerful military retinues and support within their own lands, yet unable to issue charters or coins, the sons oscillated between loyalty and restiveness as long as their father lived. Charles the Bald, by appointing men from his own entourage as court officials for his son Louis in Aquitaine, ensured loyalty of a kind.[148]

The heart of the political system within each kingdom, large or small, was a royal household. Size and scale made a difference to its operations. In an Irish kingdom, it was small, and specialisation of function minimal. In any Christian court specialist staff were required to perform religious services, and an Irish king might call on a neighbouring monastery for those. In larger and more complex kingdoms, specialised personnel were in more or less permanent attendance on the king. There are hints of palatine staff serving, and sometimes conspiring against, the ninth-century kings of the Asturias. In Wessex, the Welsh priest Asser had special permission to reside at Alfred's court only half the year, and the rest with his home community of

---

[146] Davies (1993).   [147] *AF(3)* s.a. 866, p. 54 n. 1.
[148] *AB(3)* s.a. 867, 872, pp. 138, 177.

St David's in South Wales. Quite where Alfred usually resided is unknown: Winchester may have become a favoured residence later in his reign, and that is where he was buried. In Francia, the court clergy were organised as a cadre of chaplains (*capellani*), custodians of the royal relic-collection whose centre-piece was the half-cloak (*cappa*, *capella*) of St Martin.[149] The chamber, literally the royal bed-chamber, was traditionally where the treasure was stored. According to Hincmar's treatise, *The Government of the Palace*, the chamberlain, along with the queen, looked after the treasure-hoard, dispensing annual gifts to the warriors of the household. Scarcely less important were the butler and seneschal, who saw to the provisioning of the king's table and the feeding of the court, including all those who visited it as guests or envoys. The constable, in charge of the king's horses, seems also to have co-ordinated the military activities when the king's retinue, on campaign, operated as a war-band.[150] Royal foresters, falconers and hunts-men played a key part in the hunting that fed the court and, in semi-ritualised fashion, bonded the king with the young aristocrats who rode with him. Ushers, literally doorkeepers, controlled admittance and so access to the king. In all these 'departments', the chief post would be given by the king to a favoured aristocrat, who presumably placed clients in junior posts. All senior household positions involved a political dimension. Though the numbers involved may have been fewer, a royal household's structure and functioning were not essentially different from what we know of the better-documented twelfth-century or fifteenth-century *domus regis*.

In much of western Europe in this period, the functions of royal households were governmental, that is, routinely involved in centralised administration by agents of public authority. Nearly everywhere, some traditions of late Roman imperial government survived, or were revived. Ireland was an exception, not only because Roman traditions were lacking, but because kingdoms were so small: an Irish king scarcely needed agents to act on his behalf at court or away from it because he could act in person, through face to face meetings and confrontations; and legal business was dealt with in part by members of the indigenous learned class, the brehons.[151] In Francia, the expansion of empire, and the sheer volume of business coming to the king's court, generated new requirements for delegation and co-ordination, for the multiplying of royal agents, and for forms of communication, therefore, between those agents and the king.[152] Charlemagne and his successors west of the Rhine and in Italy were heirs to

---

[149] Fleckenstein (1966) I, pp. 11–16. The story of St Martin's dividing his cloak with a beggar was one of the best known in medieval hagiography. Notker I. 4, says the Franks always carried the *cappa* into battle.   [150] *De Ordine Palatii*, cc. 22–5, trans. pp. 219–20.

[151] Ó Córráin above, p. 50. Wormald (1986), pp. 154–6; Davies (1993).   [152] Werner (1980).

Frankish and Lombard kingdoms in which forms and traditions of late Roman government had been preserved. These included the use of the written word. Royal charters, that is, records of grants and confirmations of predecessors' grants of land and/or privileges, survive in their hundreds for the reigns of ninth-century Carolingians, including those east of the Rhine. These documents, which had standardised forms and could be subjected to stringent tests of authenticity, were treated as firm proof of legal tenure.[153] A charter, with seal attached bearing the imprint of the king's seal-ring, was a precious item in the archive of a lay aristocrat or of a church, to be produced in court if a dispute arose over the property or rights in question. Individuals, and representatives of ecclesiastical institutions, travelled great distances, and laid out substantial sums, to get charters issued or confirmed. Even though charter-writing was very far from a full-time occupation, and the team of notaries at a Carolingian's court at any one time consisted of no more than three or four men, their work met the needs of the governed. Royal notaries had plenty of opportunity to amass wealth through gifts; and the chancellor, the man in charge of their output and of the king's seal, was invariably a leading ecclesiastic who enjoyed special *Königsnähe*. The fact that the number of Carolingian royal judgements surviving is extremely small compared with those of the Merovingian period suggests that still more importance now attached to charters as expressions of the royal will and vehicles of royal command.[154]

Kings had a unique capacity to confer and legitimise property rights and to confirm ecclesiastical privileges. Similarly, Carolingian royal authority lent unique and realm-wide force to legal and administrative measures embodied in capitularies. Not a single capitulary survives as an original 'official' text, and it may well be that few were produced, or kept, centrally. Instead, the manuscript evidence suggests that drafts were made by interested parties with influence at court. These drafts formed the basis for legislation. Once that had been enacted, those same interested parties might make their own copies of it, as *aides-mémoire*.[155] There is even one piece of evidence showing the swift translation into local judicial practice of capitulary instructions on legal procedure.[156] There are hints, too, that some royal agents, mainly west and south of the Rhine, had copies made of capitularies, as they were supposed to do.[157] Bits of Carolingian legislation, in short, were 'received' both because they had royal authority and because

---

153 For this and for what follows, McKitterick (1989).

154 Goffart (1990), pp. 920–3.

155 Mordek (1986a), pp. 462–9, and (1986b), pp. 32–5.

156 Ganshof (1971), pp. 585–603; compare Nelson (1986b), pp. 47, 63.

157 McKitterick (1980); compare Nelson (1990b), p. 283.

they served the purposes of those who had applied them. In the latter part of Charlemagne's reign when Aachen was his *de facto* capital, and in the reigns of Louis the Pious and Charles the Bald, despite their more mobile residence pattern, there clearly was a royal archive, in which master-copies of at least some capitularies were kept, presumably made by royal notaries, and into which royal agents sent or placed the written reports and lists required of them. Ninth-century chancery output was significant not only in the Carolingian kingdoms, but also in Wessex where King Æthelwulf had a Frankish chief notary, and in the kingdom of the Asturias, where the trickle of surviving royal charters became a stream.[158] As significant is the fugitive evidence of royal mandates conveying instructions to agents, of letters and seals which kept the king in touch with other potentates in and beyond their realms, and in which, as Alfred put it, 'you can know your lord's intention'.[159] Written messages did not displace oral ones. The couriers (*veredarii*) and envoys on whose comings and goings the annalists of the court depended for their information and royal agents for their instructions must have dealt far more often in the spoken word than in the written word.[160]

Keeping control of their agents was a constant problem for kings in this period. Alfred in his small kingdom needed to chastise as well as cajole his ealdormen, thegns and managers of royal estates. Charlemagne recommended that *maiores* (village-headmen) be recruited 'not from among the *potentiores*, but from the middling ranks, who are faithful' (*mediocres qui fideles sunt*).[161] Estate-managers were required to report to the monarch thrice annually, and to present accounts: if not numerate themselves, they would need to find help. Some *actores* worked efficiently, at least in the sense that they reacted vigorously against theft of royal property. There are also complaints of corruption. Not surprisingly, some *actores* seem to have been the kinsmen of magnates, whose interests would have been hard to ignore.[162] Moneyers may have found themselves in a similar position. Counts should appoint their subordinates rightly, thought Hincmar: such men would imitate the counts, 'their *seniores*', in being well-disposed to the locals (*pagenses*).[163]

Counts (*comites*, literally 'companions'), then, were the essential middle-men between ruler and people in the kingdoms of the Carolingians.

---

[158] Wessex, Stafford (1990), pp. 142–2; Asturias, Floriano (1949) I and II; compare the fifteen eighth-century charters, with 36 for the period 800–50, and 112 for the period 850–900.

[159] Keynes and Lapidge (1983), p. 141; compare Nelson (1990b), pp. 293–4.

[160] Nelson (1990b), pp. 275–6.   [161] *Capitulare de Villis*, c. 60, MGH Cap. II, no. 32, p. 88.

[162] Airlie (1990), pp. 197–9.

[163] Quierzy letter, c. 12, MGH Conc. III, no. 41, p. 420.

Originally troubleshooters of later Roman emperors, counts had become all-purpose agents of government in the post-Roman west.[164] Carolingian capitularies show rulers instructing counts to act in three main government capacities: first, to keep social order in their localities, presiding over local courts to 'do justice' between local landowners, and repressing crime; second, to look after royal estates in their localities; third, to summon men to the host when the king campaigned. Ealdormen in Anglo-Saxon kingdoms apparently performed similar functions. In Lombardy, dukes (*duces*) had originally been military appointees of kings, and in the eighth century were still pre-eminently war-leaders, while gastalds looked after royal estates. When the ninth-century kings of the Asturias extended their realms southwards, they claimed overlordship of the counts of Castile, but there is no clear evidence that this meant the imposition of official duties. Some of the earliest Castilian charters, from the later ninth century, refer in the same breath to 'the king ruling in Oviedo' and 'the count ruling in Castile'.[165] Prescriptive texts sometimes show what counts and dukes were supposed to do. Evidence of them at work is scrappy. In Alemannia, a small-scale landowner would have the record of his grant to St Gall formally noted 'done under count so-and-so'; but this may be no more than a formula, for there is no sign that the count was present, or had approved the transaction. Sometimes counts certainly did what they were *not* supposed to do: in Alsace, Count Erkanger, having received one estate from the fisc of Lothar I, 'abstracted' another.[166] Counts themselves complained in 811 that men were refusing to obey their summons to military service, and alleging instead a duty to their own lords.[167]

Neat lists of functions can mislead. Early medieval reality was untidy. Counts, for instance, were far from homogeneous. East of the Rhine where no structure of Roman *civitates* had existed, the countships created by the Carolingians were not always discrete territorial units, but were interspersed with areas of others' jurisdiction. In the empire at large there were 'greater' and 'lesser' counts:[168] some were great magnates, since some counties were much larger and wealthier than others; others were of merely local importance. Counties were sometimes (perhaps increasingly through the ninth century) held in plurality; but on the empire's periphery, several counts could be jointly responsible for a single frontier area (march, mark) and were called *marchiones*. The system evolved over time, local concentrations of power were formed, and discrepancies grew. Titles acquired new

---

[164] Barnwell (1992).   [165] Collins (1983), p. 234.   [166] Borgolte (1983), pp. 25–35.
[167] *MGH Cap.* I, no. 70, cc. 6, 8, p. 165.   [168] *MGH Cap.* I, no. 21, p. 52 (*fortiores; mediocres*).

meanings – *marchio* for instance, came to denote a powerful count.[169] *Vassus*, meaning 'boy' (cf. French *garçon*), was applied, originally half-humorously perhaps, to the man vested with the authority of a royal agent.

Countships tended, like kingships, to be, or become, hereditary. Counts were nobles, who seem generally to have operated in areas where they possessed lands: hence the 'official' lands associated with the countship – the count's 'salary' – would tend to be assimilated to his own estates, privatising the public. Counts seem to have chosen their own subordinates (viscounts)[170]; *vicarii; centenarii; notarii*), and used their lands to build up what would later be called affinities of men (often kinsmen) holding land from them and dependent on their patronage. Counts, and *missi* too, were aristocrats first, royal agents second. 'Officials' is a misleading term for such men, whatever notions of office some kings tried to instill.

Frankish aristocratic collaborators made possible the initial expansion of Carolingian power. They were also prime beneficiaries, rewarded with *honores* in the acquired *regna*. Charlemagne's conquest of Aquitaine was sealed by his appointment of nine Frankish *fideles* to key countships.[171] So many Franks were 'exported' to posts in the Italian *regnum* 'to enforce the authority of laws and cause the custom of the Franks to be observed' that it was said – and this was a Francocentric view – that '[Charlemagne's] palace was emptied of the leading men of the people'.[172] Charles the Bald was able to destroy his rival, and nephew, Pippin II, by convincing a majority of Aquitaine nobles that he himself would be a better lord. In his legislation, he safeguarded certain legal arrangements of the *Romani*, that is, Aquitainians who used Roman law.[173] What enabled Charlemagne to acquire Bavaria was the abandonment of Tassilo by key members of the Bavarian aristocracy.[174] Despite occasional Frankish outbursts of imperialist rhetoric, the Bavarian and Alemannic and Lombard aristocracies kept their own laws – which meant much in terms of collective self-consciousness and autonomy. Hence the embodiment of those laws in written codes, along with a more protracted process of the incorporation of custom into written tradition, eased the Bavarians' accommodation to Frankish overlordship.[175] In practice law was mostly territorial, not personal, in the ninth century. But it was the possession of the people (*gens*) whose social leaders were the resident nobility.

---

[169] Werner (1980), pp. 210–11.

[170] Perhaps a new invention of Louis the Pious, Werner (1990), p. 76, n. 273.

[171] Astronomer, c. 3, p. 607, trans. King, p. 168.

[172] Adrevald, *Miracula Sancti Benedicti*, c. 18, *MGH SS* xv: 1, p. 486.

[173] Notably in the Edict of Pîtres (864), *MGH Cap.* ii, no. 272, cc. 13, 16, 20, 23, 28, 31, 34, pp. 315–27.   [174] Faussner (1988), pp. 76–83.   [175] Compare Hammer (1989).

In attempting to ensure the loyal co-operation of counts, kings worked with the grain of their society. It would never have occurred to them to challenge heritability. If there were no adult male heir to a countship, there might be a choice between kinsmen as potential successor.[176] If there were no suitable kinsmen, the king might appoint another local man, or more rarely an outsider (this was hardly possible east of the Rhine, however). The ebb and flow of familial conflict, royal and aristocratic, ensured a supply of rebels and traitors whose *honores* the king could take and redistribute to faithful men. Thus kings exploited 'natural' opportunities to check the entrenchment of comital dynastic power. The Carolingians used artifice as well, in the form of alternative agents of two types. First, *missi dominici* were appointed to inspect and report back on counts. *Missi* were not bureaucrats: often chosen from among the greater counts of the region in which they operated, they were already *potentes* in their own right. That was why they could pack a considerable punch in their localities – why, for instance, Charlemagne could realistically tell his *missi* to supervise the selection of the local panels of knowledgeable men (*boni homines*) to serve in comital courts, or to hear and remedy complaints of lesser folk against counts. But *missi* were also empowered by royal authority. Local *potentes* who failed to attend the assemblies summoned by *missi* were, Charlemagne ordered, to be listed and the black-lists brought to him. *Missi* could hold local *inquisitiones*, and require locals to give sworn testimony on particular cases, as Charlemagne's *missus* Vernarius did at Marseilles (his report back to Charlemagne survives).[177] An Alemannian count, who had confiscated someone's property on the grounds of incest, was overridden by royal *missi*.[178] The answer to the question, 'who will guard those guards?' was: the ruler himself.

Secondly, the Carolingians used *vassi*, men with personal obligations to themselves, and sometimes endowed with lands (benefices) by them. At the palace vassals might help the king in making judgement, or be sent on diplomatic missions. Six vassals (along with six counts) swore on Lothar II's behalf that he would treat his wife 'as a king should a queen'.[179] Writing with a Welsh accent but borrowing Frankish terminology, Asser says that Alfred's *faselli* were the men who stood by him in 878.[180] Vassals could function as agents of royal authority in centre and province.[181] In 869

---

[176] *MGH Cap.* II, no. 281, c. 9, p. 358.   [177] Nelson (1990b), p. 285.

[178] *MGH Form.*, p. 357.

[179] *AB(3) s.a.* 865, p. 124; compare Tessier (1952), nos. 228, 259 (where counts and vassals are clearly distinguished), 314.   [180] Asser, cc. 53, 55.

[181] Kienast (1990), pp. 113–39 offers a helpful guide to secondary literature on vassals, but uses the term unhelpfully to translate a range of Latin words (*fideles, homines, milites*). Compare Odegaard (1945), maintaining the distinction between *vassi* and *fideles*; and, definitively, Reynolds (1994).

Charles asked his vassals in each county to make check-lists of benefices held
by counts (counts were to do the same for their own vassals) in order to
assess contributions to royally ordered fortifications on the Seine.[182] Thus,
though vassals were vulnerable to the pressure of *potentes*, the king could
keep direct access to their loyalty and services. In all the above contexts,
vassals were clearly distinguished from counts; and the absence of any case
of career-progression from vassal to count suggests that ninth-century
vassals were recruited, sometimes at least, from the ranks of the *mediocres*.[183]

Most *missi* were already *potentes*, but kings could choose high ecclesiastics
to serve alongside laymen. As *missi*, bishops might organise oath-takings,
supervise mints. Abbots held immunities, that is, rights of jurisdiction over
persons on the lands of their church, thus presided over courts where
disputes were settled and criminals punished. Carolingians, especially in the
ninth century, could compensate for lack of fisclands in certain regions by
the granting of ecclesiastical *honores* to favoured clerics. Clerical abbots, that
is, secular clergy, often in minor orders, endowed with lordship of abbeys
whose lands they then controlled, were as significant as lay abbots here.[184]
The king urged co-operation between bishops and counts, or might simply
deploy episcopal authority or episcopal military retinues as substitutes for
comital equivalents. The military contribution, euphemistically known as
the 'solace', *solatium*, organised by senior ecclesiastics (and here abbesses
were drummed into service along with bishops and abbots) covered the
equipment and mustering and dispatch of troops when the king summoned
them.[185] If violence was never far below the surface of politics, kings had, in
the form of their own household troops and the men of their bishops, abbots
and court clergy, a means to keep it under control.[186] Charles the Bald may
sometimes have kept countships vacant, relying on ecclesiastical agents
instead.[187] Alternatively, archbishops, as regional magnates, were responsible for 'their counts'.[188]

What sanctions had rulers for agents' non-fulfilment of their duties?
Removal from post; deprivation of patrimonies (allods); exile. The Lombard King Liutprand threatened gastalds who took royal lands that he
would have their property confiscated (*inpublicare faciat*).[189] It is hardly
surprising that rulers rarely imposed such drastic punishments – remark-

---

[182] *AB(3)*, p. 153; compare *s.a.* 837, p. 38; and compare *MGH Cap.* I, no. 48 (807), pp. 134–5.

[183] Also implied by Notker I. 13: 'With this income or that estate... I can make as good a vassal out
of some faithful man as can any of my counts, and perhaps a better one.'

[184] Nelson (1992a), p. 62.   [185] Nelson (1986a), pp. 122–3.

[186] *MGH Cap.* II, no. 278 (dealing with witches), p. 281.   [187] Kaiser (1981).

[188] *MGH Cap.* I, no. 150, c. 26, p. 307.

[189] Liutprand, c. 59, trans. K.F. Drew, *The Lombard Laws*, Philadelphia (1973), pp. 168–9.

able, though, that they sometimes did, and that not only counts but bishops might sometimes be punished by removal from office (*dishonoratio*). The only cases to reach the historical record were reprisals for acts of treason or rebellion: Charlemagne after 792, Louis the Pious after 818 and 833, Charles the Bald after 858, Louis the German in 861, Charles the Fat in 833, and apparently Alfred after 878. The seriousness of these revolts showed the fragility of royal power. Charlemagne's sigh of relief in 792–3 is audible through the contemporary account of his largesse to the loyal.[190] His biographer was anxious to explain that rebels had been killed in 786 only when they drew their swords to resist arrest[191] and Louis the Pious granted rebels 'life and limb and their hereditary possessions', commuting death-sentences to exile.[192] Charles the Bald had traitors executed[193] and, in the case of a bishop, blinded,[194] but took care to secure condemnations for treason 'by judgement of the Franks'. Carolingians frequently reminded, and occasionally berated, counts in their capitularies. Alfred threatened his ealdormen with loss of their posts if they failed to learn to read.[195] In practice, even powerful rulers found difficulty in removing counts. Louis the Pious did manage to remove Count Matfrid of Orléans and sent *missi* to encourage the locals who had suffered Matfrid's 'misdeeds' to come forward and complain.[196] The new count would have to replace some, at least, of Matfrid's men by his own supporters. High politics were behind all this, and the revolt of 833 was part of the backlash against Louis. Some suffering locals were no doubt better off under Matfrid's successors.

A king's very existence offered hope of redress. Because King Odo happened to be at Tours in June 890, the canons of St Martin, displeased at comital failure to remedy a grievance, were able to threaten an appeal directly to the king. The case was a complicated one: certain lands of St Martin in the county of Maine hitherto held as an advocacy, that is, entrusted to a local layman who would defend the community's interests, had passed into the hands of Patrick, a vassal of Count Berengar of Le Mans (Maine). The community appealed first to Berengar, therefore, only to be told that Patrick was 'rather the vassal of Robert [count of Tours] because he held more [as a] benefice from him'. It was at this point that St Martin's men came before Robert's court at Tours and announced that they would appeal to the king (who also happened to be Robert's brother). Robert hastily replied that he would do justice; and after checking that the benefice in question yielded 'three shields', that is, the service of three armed warriors, settled the affair with a joke: 'So – am I going to harm my soul for the sake of

---

[190] See n. 54 above. [191] *Vita Karoli*, c. 20. [192] *AB(3) s.a.* 831, 834, pp. 23, 31.
[193] Nelson (1992a), pp. 139, 171, 212. [194] *AV s.a.* 878, p. 43. [195] Asser, c. 106.
[196] *MGH Cap.* II, no. 188, c. 3, p. 10.

three shields?' The canons got the outcome they sought, and so kept a record of it.[197] The count evidently had to strike a balance between the expectations of a variety of people and groups within his own patronage-network, but wanted above all not to lose face: what weighed in Robert's mind was that, to use his own words, 'I am their abbot, and who else should see that they get their *iustitia*...?' The threat of royal intervention was enough to impel the count to 'do justice' for those under his protection.

In Alfred's small kingdom of Wessex, many judicial cases were taken before the king: 'if every judgement that King Alfred gave is set aside, when will there ever be an end to disputing?'[198] In the 1,200,000 sq km of the Carolingian empire, or even the 1200 sq km of a Carolingian sub-kingdom, distance affected the accessibility of royal justice. There were parts the king could not reach. In the autumn of 852, Louis the German went from Bavaria to Mainz, where he settled disputes; returned to Bavaria; then went back north via the Rhineland to Saxony and more dispute-settlement before returning to Regensburg for Christmas.[199] This was an exceptionally busy three months in the life of a Carolingian; otherwise, Louis rarely visited Saxony. In Brittany, Carolingian rulers formally devolved jurisdiction to regional princes who functioned rather like sub-kings. Their title advanced between the 830s and the 860s from *missus* to *rex*. Here were distinct levels of power: the small world of local courts where the squirearchy (in Brittany called machtierns) dealt with peasant disputes, and above it the aristocratic world of princes and war-bands.[200] The monastery of Redon participated in both worlds: it benefited from judgement of Breton princes, and imposed its own jurisdiction on local landowners and peasants. It also received Carolingian largesse, and in 850 its abbot visited Charles the Bald's court to secure a grant of immunity.[201] Redon derived its power from its extensive lordship (as distinct from landowning) which included public rights, for instance to take tolls and to settle disputes. At the same time the regional rulers of Brittany, Nominoë and his successors, exercised public rights of their own, and over Redon too. Yet the Breton rulers acknowledged the overlordship of Charles. Government was multi-layered, but small worlds remained part of greater ones.

East of the Rhine, deeply rooted patterns of lordship over people, in the hands of local and regional aristocrats, were what new Carolingian over-lords had to come to terms with, while local and regional nobles came to terms with the Carolingians. Noble lordship, wielded now as public

---

[197] *Gallia Christiana*, ed. D. de Ste Marthe, 16 vols., Paris (1715–1865), XIV, no. xxxvii.
[198] Keynes (1992).   [199] *AF(3)*, p. 33–4.   [200] Davies (1988), pp. 201–10.
[201] Tessier (1943), no. 132 – though the Redon area was effectively beyond Charles' control at this point.

authority in the king's name, coexisted with sporadically intrusive royal power. East Francia is not the only part of the empire where it is hard to find evidence for royal appointment of men bearing the title of count. Everywhere there was exercise of public jurisdiction through local lordship: for instance when a *missus* (with the local *boni homines* firmly in tow) sat as judge in his own county in a dispute between himself as lord and a peasant who claimed to be of free, not servile, status.[202] There was little practical difference between such local government, and a seigneurie. In West Francia, one and the same clause of the Edict of Pîtres (864) shows both that immunities had been granted to lay *potentes* and that the king claimed the right to send his agents into those immunities in pursuit of criminals.[203] In the various *regna*, and in localities, details of court cases show trade-offs and reconciliations between royal and local aristocratic interests. In Carolingian government there was inevitably a good deal of subsidiarity, untidy as that always is.

There were times, nevertheless, when 'persons from the regions came to the palace'. They came to pursue their own cases, to seek redress, to lodge appeals. Pressure of daily business meant that Charlemagne buckled down to judging cases when he was scarcely out of bed.[204] Peasants might still come to the palace seeking judgement from the king and his *vassi*.[205] Those were private initiatives. But the palace – Hincmar said the word was 'nowadays in normal use to mean [what in Antiquity had been called] the *praetori[um]*'[206] – was a public place: made so by what people perceived as the king's relatively frequent, hence expected, residence in it. The palace was where you would find the king. Many routes led to the king's *tun*, as Alfred said. Once there, even if not actually beside the king, you were in his presence.[207] The palace was so much the king's place that the killing there of one of Arnulf of East Francia's leading men without express royal command was a peculiarly shocking event.[208] When Louis the Pious seemed to fail to maintain the palace's moral order, he was losing his grip on the realm.[209] Conversely, in the later ninth century, an Asturian chronicler epitomised the significance of the reign of Alfonso II as 'the re-establishment of the order of the Goths both in church and in palace'.[210]

Regnal 'order' was never clearer than when the king summoned an assembly. It was a court, an occasion and a shared experience that surely

---

[202] Nelson (1986a), p. 47.   [203] *MGH Cap.* II, no. 273, c. 18, p. 317.
[204] *Vita Karoli*, c. 24.   [205] Tessier (1952), no. 228.
[206] *De Ordine Palatii* c. 15, trans. p. 216.
[207] Alfred's version of Augustine's *Soliloquies*, trans. Keynes and Lapidge (1983), pp. 143–4. Compare modern scholars' definitions of *Pfalzlichkeit*: Brühl (1968), p. 92.
[208] *AF(3) s.a.* 893, p. 125.   [209] Ward (1990a).   [210] Collins (1983), p. 232.

reinforced participants' sense of themselves as a group. Such a perception seems to be reflected in the title given by a scribe, writing about 870, to a capitulary collection: 'Capitula of Bishops, Kings, and Especially All The Noble Franks'.[211] Judicial business was always on the assembly agenda. Legislation consisted, in part, in generalising from the particular, as Charles the Bald apparently did when he addressed the problem of luring back emigrant peasants to work on estates in the Seine valley, and as Alfred did when he settled a case arising out of an accident with a spear.[212] There was no clear-cut distinction between 'local' and 'central' issues. Judgement on all matters required similar kinds of practical wisdom. It was no coincidence that in Anglo-Saxon kingdoms the body of those assembled was called simply the *witan*: 'the wise men'. Through the regnal assembly,[213] royal government was applied to every kind of problem. The agenda of Charlemagne's great council at Frankfurt in 794 included: clearing up after the rebellion of 792, sorting the faithless from the faithful, and confirming the downfall of Tassilo of Bavaria; dealing with a serious famine, fixing prices, punishing profiteers; and (we can see, with hindsight, a premonition of empire) establishing orthodoxy for Latin Christendom.[214] In June 864, the Edict of Pîtres, the most substantial piece of administrative law produced by a Carolingian assembly, launched a counter-assault on crime; spelled out details of a *renovatio monetae*; regulated royal estate management; vigorously reformed military organisation; and last but not least made arrangements for its own diffusion to the realm at large.[215]

Obviously only a selection of persons attended the king's assembly. If the meeting was a small one, as often in wintertime, the king might summon only a few *potentes* and counsellors. Abbot Lupus of Ferrières' letters reveal the changing moods of a *potens*: anxiously awaiting the king's messenger, for the benefits of proximity to the king and his *familiares* were great, yet weighing the burdens of attendance, for the king's demands were constant, and pressing. Lupus, knowing that the king's wrath could be terrible, did not refuse an invitation. He hoped for the king's smile – even while knowing it could be a mask.[216] To participate was not always to feel home and dry. As Alfred pointed out, 'not all are similarly at ease when they get there. Some are received with greater respect and greater familiarity than others, some with less; some with virtually none, except for the one fact, that

---

[211] Nelson (1986a), p. 110.
[212] Edict of Pîtres, c. 31, *MGH Cap.* II, no. 272, p. 323; Alfred, Laws, c. 36, see Wormald (1977), p. 113.   [213] Compare above, n. 90.
[214] *MGH Cap.* I, no. 28, trans. King, pp. 224–30.   [215] *MGH Cap.* II, no. 273, pp. 310–28.
[216] Lupus, *Epp.* 17, 41, 45, 58, 67; and cf. *Ep.* 52.

he [the king] loves them all.'[217] The gathering at Savonnières in November 862 was exceptionally large for a winter meeting because three Carolingian kings were involved: a participant estimated that 'nearly 200 *consiliarii*, bishops and abbots as well as laymen, were under one roof'.[218]

Summer meetings were normally large affairs, attended not only by magnates, but by lesser men too: a potential army. *Consiliarii* would have retinues, which however were not to be multiplied beyond the king's view of necessity – and that view would depend, in turn, on a magnate's standing at court, and on the wider political scene. A bishop who turned up with 'the whole company of his men' (but he was in dispute with the king, and perhaps already suspected of plotting defection) was brusquely told by royal officers that 'ten or twelve retainers' (*casati homines*), plus clergy and servants, was a sufficient retinue; fifty (perhaps including clergy and servants?) was considered a reasonable entourage when the bishop toured his diocese.[219] A hundred Bavarian nobles happen to be named in a document produced at the great assembly of Verdun in August 843, suggesting a total attendance of well over a thousand nobles from the three kingdoms represented on this occasion; and bishops certainly were at Verdun too.[220] The scale of some ninth-century public buildings permitted large gatherings. At two places, the modern visitor gains a vivid impression of this: first, in Asturias, at the church of St Julian, Oviedo, built in Alfonso II's reign, and not far away, at the palace complex of Ramiro I; second, at Aachen, where Charlemagne's church is still standing, and can apparently accommodate (at a pinch) 7000 people, and where archaeologists have exposed the foundations of a ninth-century hall nearly 50 m long.[221] At St Julian, the style if not the content of the wall-paintings was intended to remind the viewer of the Gothic past. At Ingelheim, a little imagination re-erects on the excavated foundations of Louis the Pious' 35 m hall the lavishly painted walls which once displayed Orosian world history complemented by the series of Frankish victories won under Carolingian leadership.[222] No building, anyway, constrained the size of assemblies that flowed out into the open air.[223] Tents were a normal part of royal equipment, hence the aptness of specially fine ones as

---

217 Keynes and Lapidge (1983), pp. 143–4 (translation slightly modified). Alfred was drawing a parallel between the king's centripetal force, and that of Wisdom.

218 *MGH Cap.* II, no. 243, p. 165. Compare an attendance-list of fifty ecclesiastics at the synod of Ponthion, *MGH Cap.* II, no. 279, pp. 349–50.   219 Nelson (1986a), p. 125.

220 Bitterauf (1905), no. 661, pp. 556–8.

221 Oviedo, Schlunk (1947), pp. 398–405; Aachen, Lammers (1979), pp. 228–32, 283, and for the church's capacity, if the gallery too is packed: Schramm (1968) I, p. 209, n. 47.

222 Lammers (1979).   223 Compare *De Ordine Palatii* c. 35, trans. p. 226.

diplomatic gifts.[224] The presence of large numbers of young men, touchy, aggressive, ambitious, with their own brand of humour and a taste for horseplay, must have posed one logistical problem. Horses were another. Constables and marshals organised their grooming, their fodder (supplies became available in May/June), and the disposal of tons of dung.[225]

The somewhat idealised description of a Carolingian summer assembly in *The Government of the Palace*, shows the 'counsellors', that is, the magnates highest in royal favour, conferring in private on an agenda supplied by the king. Meanwhile lesser men conducted their own discussions. As for the king, he joined the counsellors if requested; otherwise 'he would be occupied with the rest of the assembled people, receiving gifts, greeting the more important, exchanging news with those he did not see often, expressing sympathy with the old, sharing their pleasures with the young...'[226] When the counsellors had 'found counsel', and framed this in *capitula*, 'the less important heard that counsel, sometimes deliberated on it, and confirmed it, not because they were forced to do so but from their own understanding and freely expressed opinion'.[227] Idealised this may be, but it reflects more than one man's ideal. Hearing and seeing were as vital as at a nineteenth-century election rally, for assembly proceedings were punctuated by royal speech-making: a welcoming address, a statement of intent, a pep-talk, an agreed legislative programme, an envoi. That was why it mattered if a king had a stammer, as did Charles the Bald's son Louis (his nickname was contemporary[228]) – and why Charles' own blend of irony, intimacy and panache still makes an impression even in the stilted Latin of the official record (it would have been read out in the vernacular[229]). A king won the aristocracy's confidence by confiding – demonstratively – in them. Alfred addressed his bishops 'lovingly and friendlily', in a formula which was apparently already standard in Anglo-Saxon royal letters.[230]

Assembly proceedings, and decisions, have left some residue in the written word. From Mercia and Wessex, there are the attendance-lists and decrees of ecclesiastics at royally summoned synods, and witness-lists to royal charters that probably emanated from meetings of the *witan*. Carolingian rulers wanted counts and *missi* to take copies of the *capitula* agreed at

---

[224] *ARF(3) s.a.* 807, p. 98.

[225] Marshals and fodder: *MGH Cap.* II, no. 260, c. 13, p. 274; dung, compare Bachrach (1986), pp. 11–15.   [226] *De Ordine Palatii*, c. 35, trans. p. 226 (slightly adapted).

[227] *De Ordine Palatii*, c. 29, trans. p. 222; compare also Capitulary of Quierzy (877), *MGH Cap.* II, no. 281, c. 22, p. 360: 'Let each say what he thinks is best, and when all have spoken, let them choose what seems best.'   [228] Regino *s.a.* 878, p. 114.

[229] Compare Banniard, Chapter 26 below.

[230] Alfred's version of Gregory's *Pastoral Care*, prose preface, Keynes and Lapidge (1983), p. 124; Harmer (1952; repr. 1989), p. 62.

assemblies and bring these copies back to their localities. Some *capitula* required special publicity: Count Stephen, *missus* for a group of counties centred on Paris in 802[231], brought home from an Aachen assembly a set of additions to *Lex Salica*[232]

so that he might make these manifest in the *civitas* of Paris in the public assembly, and so that he might read them out before the judgement-finders (*scabini*). And this he did. And all consented together, saying that they were willing to observe it [*sic*] at all times and forever. Further, all the *scabini*, bishops, abbots and counts confirmed these *capitula* by writing beneath in their own hands.

Those who attended regnal assemblies thus in a sense represented local communities: and their *annuntiationes* were a kind of report-back. Disputes were settled at the local assembly, in Wessex called the 'moot' (*gemot*), in Francia known as the *mallus*. Charlemagne let the conquered Saxons continue to settle cases within their *patria*, that is, within Saxony, 'through local men (*pagenses*) in local courts with neighbourhood-dwellers according to custom'. Appeals could be 'brought to the palace'.[233] In all these public courts, crime was punished as an offence against the king's authority, his *bann*, to which the Saxons were now subject along with the Franks. Heavy fines were imposed, in cash or in kind. Who enforced the settlements, extracted the fines, punished the criminals? Though there was no doubt a good deal of self-help, individual and collective, there were customary public procedures, like the Saxons' burning down of the houses of criminals, which Charlemagne decreed should continue to be carried out 'for coercion to judgement on our behalf'.[234] In West Francia, the oath of the hundredmen (*centenarii*) in 853 shows that one category of freemen, at least, the *Franci homines*, were supposed to swear that they would report and pursue criminals.[235] Criminals, after all, were faithless to the Franks as well as to their king.[236] Charlemagne, though he did not personally choose local judgement-finders wanted *missi* to provide him with lists of them.[237] Alfred declared that the careful keeping of oath and pledge by every man was 'most necessary'[238] and decreed that a man involved in a feud should 'ask justice', that is seek legal remedy, before attacking his enemy 'at home'.[239] There was much disorder; but kings took seriously their God-sent obligation to

[231] *MGH Cap.* i, no. 39, pp. 111–12.
[232] See further McKitterick (1989), pp. 40–60.
[233] *MGH Cap.* i, no. 27, c. 4, p. 71, trans. pp. 230–1.   [234] *Ibid.*, c. 8.
[235] *MGH Cap.* ii, no. 260, p. 274; for *Franci homines* as free men under special royal protection, Werner (1980), pp. 212–13 and n. 86.   [236] *MGH Cap.* i, no. 67, p. 156.
[237] *MGH Cap.* i, no. 40, c. 3, p. 115; no. 49, c. 4, p. 136.
[238] Laws 1, trans. Keynes and Lapidge (1983), p. 164.
[239] Laws 42, trans. Keynes and Lapidge (1983), pp. 168–9.

preserve peace and order in their realms, and strove to engage their people along with them.

Military obligation was fundamental, failure to perform it a most serious breach of the ruler's authority. All were involved when external enemies attacked. 'All must come to the defence of the fatherland.' In 864, Charles the Bald laid down the death penalty for those who failed to do so, and for those who supplied the enemy.[240] Alfred's Laws, imposing double compensation for attacks on the fortified residences of king and archbishop, bishops, ealdormen, nobles and ceorls 'when the army had been called out', imply a similar universal obligation, alongside royal responsibility, to defend the land.[241] In 896 at Winchester, Alfred hanged captured Danes: treating them as oath-breakers, he was imposing the death penalty prescribed in his Laws for those who committed treason.[242]

THE IDEOLOGY OF POWER

At the beginning of this chapter Pirenne's view of the economic changes of the eighth and ninth centuries was reckoned half-right. The same goes for Pirenne's view of the equally fundamental ideological changes of this period. There was, as Pirenne thought, a transformation in the representation and self-presentation of kingship. In part this resulted, as Pirenne thought, from the augmented authority of the church in the west. From the eighth century onwards, for instance, not just individual holy men but the church as a sacramental institution legislated on marital matters. It defined the prohibited degrees in marriage between kin, and required marriages to be made 'publicly', that is, openly, so that the knowledge of priest, kin and neighbours could avert any incestuous union. Such regulations affected the private as well as the public lives of the Christian laity, 'noble as much as non-noble'.[243] The publicly kept concubines, and the repudiation of successive wives, which had been such a feature of Merovingian family life, were increasingly firmly forbidden by church councils. Kings were urged to practise as well as to prescribe monogamy.[244] For royalty, the personal was political: in setting themselves new goals of conduct and self-control, kings claimed a new authority; and in imposing sexual restraint on their people by incorporating church canons into their own legislation, kings claimed new powers.[245] The confidence with which Pippin asserted his rulership over the

---

[240] *MGH Cap.* II, no. 273, cc. 25, 27.

[241] Laws 40, 40.1, trans. Keynes and Lapidge (1983), p. 168.

[242] *ASC s.a.* 896; Laws 4, trans. p. 165.

[243] *MGH Cap.* I, no. 36, c. 15, p. 36 compare no. 22, *Admonitio Generalis*, c. 68, p. 59. See Ritzer (1962), pp. 260–1.   [244] Enright (1985).   [245] Wemple (1981), pp. 76–7.

Franks, and Charlemagne his leadership over Latin Christendom, are definitive traits of the new regime. As mayor of the palace Pippin had lacked, hardly needed, special legitimation: his position rested on the social facts of ancestry and wealth.[246] The question put to the pope by Pippin's envoys in 750 was not whether he ought to have *regalis potestas*, but whether he who already had it ought now to have the title of king as well. Pippin's success and sheer good fortune in the 740s had pointed towards this destiny. But *potestas* was the hallmark of regality, not its source, and could not in itself legitimise the substitution of Pippin's own dynasty for that of the Merovingians.

In so strongly emphasising the role of ecclesiastical, and especially papal, authority in creating a new legitimacy, and in conferring divine grace through the new ritual of consecration, Pirenne overlooked three things. First, the royal ideology espoused by the Carolingians' advisers, and shared by the papacy, reflected the variousness of the traditions at work in the post-Roman world:[247] from the law-books of the Old Testament, as glossed by Irish and Anglo-Saxon churchmen, and treated as a blue-print for government, it took an overriding concern with justice and judgement, and a lively sense of the interconnectedness of royal conduct and general well-being; from late antiquity, it incorporated a kind of welfare-statism and the notion of multi-gentile empire; from the histories of 'barbarian' kingdoms, pagan as well as Christian, it drew a hard-headed appreciation of military prowess and its rewards. Many tributaries flowed into the Carolingian mainstream. Thus the expositors of political ideas included biblical commentators and liturgists, historians and lawmen, from Ireland and Spain, Northumbria and Italy, as well as from Francia. The ideology of power in this period was far more eclectic and 'international' than Pirenne allowed. Second, the transformation that so impressed Pirenne was a longer-term process than he admitted: Merovingian kings, even though they had not been clerically consecrated, attended to ecclesiastical demands, and (as did their unconsecrated contemporaries elsewhere) claimed divine approval; and like their Carolingian successors, the Merovingians were committed to dynastic survival. The third and fundamental aspect of kingship, demonstrating both continuities with the Frankish past and similarities with other early medieval realms, Christians and pagan alike, was its basis in a *gens*, a people, and hence in the bonding of ruler and ruled. Neglecting this, Pirenne seriously underestimated the role of the Frankish aristocracy in the advent of the Carolingian dynasty, and missed the involvement of a wider constituency than kings and clerics in the ideology of power.

---

[246] *Vita Karoli*, c. 2 (*claritas generis ... opes*).   [247] Compare Nelson (1988a).

The one contemporary Frankish account of Pippin's accession says that, 'with the consent of the Franks', he sent to the pope and obtained approval, then 'by the election of all the Franks to the throne of the kingdom, by the consecration of bishops and by the acknowledgement of lay magnates, with Queen Bertrada as the rules of ancient tradition require he [Pippin] was elevated into the kingdom'.[248] The wording expresses, painstakingly, the coincidence of Frankish with papal legitimation. That same pope had written three years before to Pippin and the Frankish magnates explaining how, in Francia as in Italy, 'their fighting and our praying' could work together 'to save the province'.[249] In the eyes of a monastic charter-draftsman, Pippin's consecration conveyed an infusion of divine grace, and imposed new obligations: he had become a sublime *rector*, charged by God with the task of governing and educating the needy and powerless.[250] *Legislatores* at Pippin's court, using the more public and official medium of a new longer prologue (763/4) to *Lex Salica*, sounded another note: 'the bodies of holy martyrs, which the Romans burned with fire, and mutilated by the sword, and tore apart by throwing them to wild beasts: these bodies the Franks have found, and enclosed in gold and precious stones.' The Franks' devotion to the martyrs proved the strength of their Christian faith, demonstrated and explained the divine favour they had recently gained. *Vivit qui Francos diligit Christus*: 'Christ lives who loves the Franks.' Pippin and his people had surpassed the Romans, and merited special divine approval.[251] The new sexual *mores* marked out the people as well as the king. Pippin's consecration in the manner of Old Testament kings presupposed a new Israel. In 754, Pippin, his queen and their two sons received papal anointings which established links not just between the pope and the royal family but between St Peter and the Franks. 'You, dearest ones, you, "a holy *gens*, a royal priesthood, a special people", whom the Lord God of Israel has blessed, rejoice and be glad, for the names of your kings and your names are written in heaven':[252] the pope subtly evoked the contemporary religious practice whereby individuals' names were entered in monastic Books of Life for liturgical commemoration that was believed to assure well-being in this world and the next. The Franks and their king would share the potency of omnipotent God, and gain an everlasting name. In the eighth century success in war, royal generosity to magnates, the subjection of other *gentes*

---

[248] Continuator of Fredegar, ed. Wallace-Hadrill (1960), c. 33, p. 102.
[249] *Codex Carolinus*, no. 3, p. 480.   [250] *MGH Dip. Kar.* I, no. 16, p. 22.
[251] *Lex Salica, 100-Titel Text*, pp. 6–8; cf Ewig (1956), pp. 16–17, 47–9. *Legislatores*, Nelson (1986a), p. 57, n. 41.   [252] *Codex Carolinus*, no. 39, p. 552, with citation from I Peter 2:9.

and the flourishing of churches were prayers that came true for the Franks.[253]

Once Charlemagne's realm had expanded to include many peoples, new themes, of wider reference, appeared in the regime's self-representation. The realm acquired firmer territorial identity, its boundaries clearer delineation. In practice, law became a matter of territoriality, not gentile identity. Into his own rulership Charlemagne incorporated notions of lordship, freedom and reciprocal duty that would have universal appeal. Demanding an oath of fidelity from 'all',[254] Charlemagne sent *missi* to explain that he was 'well aware that many complain that their law had not been kept for them; and that it is totally the will of the lord king that each man should have his law fully kept'. What *lex sua* meant can be reconstructed from two later statements. A further oath of fidelity in 802, Charlemagne said, meant that each was thereby obliged not to harm 'the *honor* of the realm' but to be faithful 'as a man in right ought to be to his lord'.[255] In a near-contemporary capitulary Charlemagne forbade anyone to abandon his lord having once accepted the symbolic lordly gift of a shilling[256] '*unless*' – and here follow four conditions: 'unless his lord seeks to kill him, or assaults him with a stave, or debauches his wife or daughter, or takes away his allodial property'. Life, personal immunity from degrading physical violence, patriarchal rights in his female dependants, patrimony: these constituted a man's *lex*, and at the same time, by setting limits to what a lord could do, provided legitimate grounds for rejecting lordship. In 843, Charles the Bald elaborated on his grandfather's words: while his *fideles* promised in turn to uphold the king's *honor*, Charles promised to keep for each his due law in each rank and status (*lex competens... in omni dignitate et ordine*), and not to deprive anyone of his *honor* without just cause.[257] Other mid-ninth-century capitularies throw light on the notion of different social ranks: Carolingian brother-kings are 'peers' (*pares*); faithful men have their peers, with whom they must co-operate, if necessary, to restrain the king from acting against the *lex* of any one of them.[258] There is a sense of plural ranks among the

---

253 Compare the blessing-prayer, '*Prospice*', Nelson (1993a), p. 58.

254 *MGH Cap.* I, no. 25 (787/792), c. 4, p. 67: the list, including all men, free and slave (*coloni, servi*) who 'having been given an office hold benefices and official dues (*honorati beneficia et ministeria tenent*) or have been given an office as vassals (*vel in bassallitico honorati sunt*) and are able to have horses and weapons...' concludes: 'omnes iurent'.   255 *MGH Cap.* I, no. 34, p. 101.

256 *MGH Cap.* I, no. 77, c. 16 (King, p. 245); Campbell (1989), p. 36.

257 *MGH Cap.* II, no. 254, c. 3, p. 255; cf. no. 204, *adnuntiatio Karoli*, c. 2, p. 71: the provision that everyone must choose a lord reinforced, rather than reduced, hierarchical authority.

258 *MGH Cap.* II, no. 205 (851), c. 3, p. 72, no. 264 (856), c. 4, p. 284. Compare free peasant *pares* in Aquitaine, Nelson (1986b), p. 49.

aristocracy, perhaps corresponding to those sketched in *The Government of the Palace*: *consiliarii, optimates, minores*.

What Hincmar stressed above all, however, was the collective body, the *generalitas universorum maiorum*, the *universitas*, which, acting at and through assemblies, together with the king, maintained the well-being of the whole realm. Here he was typical of the ninth century's much more articulate expression of ideas of shared participation in public duties and benefits, of generalised commitment. The idea of the state revived. Compare Charlemagne's admonition that 'everyone should personally strive to maintain himself in God's service, because the lord emperor cannot himself provide the necessary care and discipline for each man individually', with Louis the Pious' committing of 'ourself, our sons and our associates (*socii*), in the administration of this realm', to ensure that 'peace and justice be kept in the whole generality (*generalitas*) of our people'.[259] Louis envisaged that this should be 'especially striven for in all assemblies', and declared that while 'by divine authority and by human governmental arrangements (*ordinatio*) the whole of our own office (*ministerium*) rests in our person, it is divided into shares in such a way that each of you in his place and in his *ordo*, has a share in our office – so that I am the adviser of all of you, and all of you must be our helpers'. Louis clearly had counts particularly in mind (he seems to refer to an oath of office taken by each one of them, to be 'the ruler's helper and the people's preserver') but he enjoined *all* to mutual 'love and peace, and to show honour to his representatives (*missi*)'. Louis' programme was summed up as the securing of *communis utilitas*. The conflicts of the early 840s evoked further explicit statements of collective political action. In the Strasbourg Oaths, the aristocracy as a group underwrote the kings' commitments to each other, and used the threat of collective withdrawal of obedience as a sanction to guarantee the kings' fulfilment of their oaths. At Coulaines, and again in the 850s, Charles the Bald and his advisers developed the idea of a *societas*, and of political advice and military support – *consilium et auxilium* – as the shared business of faithful men to maintain the *honor regni*, not just what individuals owed to the king. Inspired by the Theodosian Code, Charles 'with the counsel of his faithful men' laid down that 'all without exception had to come to the defence of the *patria*'; and when the king chose to pay attackers tribute instead, all must contribute.[260] 'All' was meant literally: it included dwellers in *civitates* as well as rustics; traders as well as peasants; Jews as well as Christians.[261] Royal demands weighed on

---

[259] *MGH Cap.* I, no. 33, c. 3, p. 92, trans. p. 234; no. 150 (823/825), c. 2, p. 303; see Guillot (1990).

[260] *MGH Cap.* II, no. 273, c. 27, p. 322; compare no. 271 (861), pp. 301–2: people (*homines*) are to be assured by *missi* that the tax recently collected from them has been 'necesse ... pro regni salvamento'.   [261] *MGH Cap.* II, no. 281, c. 31, p. 361.

villagers as well as on the lordly residents of estates. Even slaves were not excluded from the purview of capitularies. Charles' kingship was at once weaker and stronger than that of his predecessors. Ruler of a kingdom racked by internal conflict and menaced by external attack, Charles could justify imposing heavier burdens on his people. Charlemagne's gloss on the oath of fidelity had been negative in tone: his grandson's stress was on universal obligations that were positive contributions to the common good. In Wessex, Alfred would make similarly insistent and generalised demands. The *princeps* of Brittany, allied with one Viking warlord against others, 'sent messengers to all parts of his *regnum* for them to come with their weapons and bring support'.[262]

In Carolingian texts the concept of *honor* shows the private absorbed, but also ensconced, within the public. *Honor* meant, first, high office. When Louis the Pious deprived two magnates of their *honores* – countships – for incompetent management of a campaign, the pair spent the rest of their careers attempting (ultimately unsuccessfully) to recover what they had lost. Louis the German stripped Duke Ernst of 'all his public *honores*, as a man who was guilty of infidelity'.[263] The derivatives *inhonoratio, dehonorare, exhonorare* likewise referred to deprivation of office. By extension, *honor* came to have the sense of lands attached to office, then to any lands granted by the ruler, so that benefices could be *honores* too.[264] But *honor* retained its link to the notion of royal concession, denoting property received from king as distinct from allods. Its further and fundamental sense (reinforced in early modern states) was identified with rank and status, and linked a man's social standing to recognition by public authority. In a saint's Life produced in West Francia *c.* 800, the parents of a seventh-century saint are said to have 'introduced him to the court and commended him to the king of the Franks to serve in the military household with great *honor* so that by the pathway of this service (*militia*) he could attain the due *honor* of his ancestors'.[265] The aristocrat's *honor* was achieved and deployed through public service to the realm.

In the eighth century, the biblical David offered an attractive general model of consecrated kingship over a chosen people. Perhaps because ecclesiastical theorists laid too much stress on David's humility in face of prophetic chastisement for his failings, Solomon tended to replace him as a royal model in ninth-century Wessex as in Francia. Solomon personified the justice, the wisdom and (as important) the wealth of the good king, his prime function to bring peace.[266] The shift in emphasis coincided with the

---

[262] *Gesta Sanctorum Rotonensium* III, 9, pp. 214–15.
[263] *ARF(2) s.a.* 828, p. 122; *AF(3) s.a.* 861, p. 47.   [264] *AB(3) s.a.* 839, p. 45.
[265] *Vita Ermelandi, MGH SRM* v, pp. 674–710, cited Werner (1985), p. 194.
[266] Anton, (1968), pp. 112, 420–30; Nelson (1993c).

decline in aggressive warfare for Franks and for Anglo-Saxons. Ninth-century writers were well aware that bloodshed would be necessary in the pursuit of peace: indeed they devoted considerable thought to the justifica-tion of violence at the king's command to defend the realm, repress crime, protect the church and the weak. The king acknowledged these realm-wide responsibilities, and justified on these grounds the call for *milites*. As sole legitimate declarer of (public) *bellum*: he must prevent others from waging (private) *werrae*. To the Augustinian notion of just war, Hincmar added his own recommendation that prayers be offered for dead warriors,[267] and later in the ninth century, Frankish churchmen would offer a blessing 'over fighting men' (*super militantes*). Yet in the image of Louis the Pious as *miles Christi*, the Cross-standard had taken the place of the sword.[268] The king had his generals, his *milites*. Under his strategic direction, others could do the fighting. Charles the Bald like a Roman emperor received the weapons and standards of Northmen vanquished by his faithful man Count Robert.[269] Though Charles did not cease to lead armies, he was more prominent, and more successful, in other roles, as assembly-president, judge, man-manager, and manipulator of public opinion.

Charles nevertheless, like other high-status Franks, had been invested with *arma*, surely including a sword, when he came of age.[270] The sword was the prime symbol of a noble's *honor*. A surviving fresco painted on the wall of a church at Mals in the Dolomites shows the noble patron offering his sword to Christ.[271] Armed service was as acceptable to God as to the king. Bretons surrendering to Charlemagne in 799 handed over their swords with their names inscribed on them 'for it was by these weapons that each one of them yielded himself, land and people'.[272] The sword defined and displayed a man's public status. Depriving a man of his sword and belt was a punishment prescribed by councils as part of penance for a range of offences including homicide – that is, misuse of violence: a symbolic obliteration of the noble's status. Here, as in the case of sexual offences, the ideological weight of ecclesiastical sanctions reinforced secular ones.[273] The uses of ritual as social control were well understood by the Carolingians. The

---

[267] *De Regis Persona et Regio Ministerio*, c. 15, PL 125, col. 844.

[268] Sears (1990).   [269] *AB s.a.* 865, p. 127. Compare McCormick (1986).

[270] 838 Nithard I, 6: *arma et corona et pars regni*; compare other references to royal swords (or sword-belts) in *AB(3) s.a.* 844, p. 57, and 877, p. 203: 'spata quae vocatur sancti Petri per quam eum [Louis the Stammerer] de regno revestiret [Richildis, his step-mother]'; for the prayer *Accipe gladium* in royal *ordines* from the late ninth century onwards, see Flori (1983).

[271] Bullough (1965), plate 71. MGH *Cap.* I, no. 75, p. 168, specifies that each horseman (*cabalarius*) must be equipped with a sword (*spata*).

[272] *ARF(2) s.a.* 799, p. 92. For the wider social and symbolic context, see Geary (1987).

[273] Leyser (1984); compare Nelson (1989a).

imposition of the *harmscar*, public humiliation in which a man carried a saddle on his shoulders, was threatened in a number of the capitularies of Louis the Pious and Charles the Bald as the penalty for dereliction of public duties.[274] Bishops played an increasing role in political ritual: after the battle of Fontenoy in 841, bishops were asked by the victors to perform rites of reconciliation, and in 842 bishops declared Lothar, *in absentia*, to lack the 'knowledge for governing the state' and hence to have forfeited his kingship.[275] When Charles the Bald threatened the kingship of his nephew Louis the Younger in 876, Louis had ordeals performed to ascertain the judgement of God.[276] On all these, and other occasions, laymen invoked ecclesiastical intervention in order to legitimise, and shift responsibility for, dangerous political decisions arising from conflicts between Carolingians and so between Franks. Feasts and processions at court, assembly proceedings themselves, were rituals of participation rather than exclusion which kings staged, often with the help of senior churchmen, to enhance their authority within their own realms.[277] The inauguration of Charles the Bald when he acquired Lothar II's kingdom in 869 is the first full king-making rite extant, designed to evoke a sense of common Frankish identity among Charles' old and new subjects. Bishops played a central part: Hincmar of Rheims consecrated Charles with oil allegedly brought from heaven to St Remigius for the baptismal anointing of Clovis, the first king of the Franks whom Hincmar claimed (wrongly) as Charles' ancestor.[278] Ritual was used by rulers to construct fictive kin-relationships that denoted political hegemony and subordination, as when Louis the Pious stood godfather to the Danish king Harald in 826,[279] or Charles the Bald to the son of the Breton prince Salomon, probably in 863,[280] or Alfred of Wessex to the Viking Haesten in 893.[281] With the acquisition of Lothar's kingdom, Charles the Bald 'ordered himself to be called emperor and *augustus* as one who was to possess two kingdoms'.[282] This non-Roman imperial tradition was echoed just a few years later in the Asturias with Alfonso III's interest in acquiring an 'imperial' crown from Tours.[283] It was the Roman empire of Charlemagne and Louis the Pious that finally passed to Charles the Bald when he was consecrated by the pope at St Peter's on Christmas Day 875, in a re-run of Charlemagne's coronation 75 years before.[284] Alfred in turn imitated *his* grandfather when in 886 he marked his acquisition of London – latterly a Mercian city but once the metropolis of Britain – with a coin-issue evoking

[274] De Jong (1992). [275] Nithard IV. I. [276] *AB(3)* s.a. 876, p. 196.

[277] Nelson (1987). [278] *AB(3)* s.a. 869, p. 161.

[279] *ARF(2)* s.a. 826, p. 119; Angenendt (1984), pp. 215–23. [280] Smith (1992), p. 112.

[281] *ASC* s.a. 893. [282] *AF(3)* s.a. 869, p. 61. [283] Linehan (1992), pp. 145, 154.

[284] *AB(3)* s.a. 876, p. 189.

Roman Londinium, 'and all Englishkind bowed to him'.[285] All of these great public rituals, directly involving the aristocracy, witnessed by many people and designed to lodge in the memory, not only enhanced rulers' authority but helped create a collective consciousness of belonging to recently constructed realms. History was invoked to the same end. Charlemagne had the *antiquissima carmina* written down and preserved; historical writing took the place of ancient songs at the court of Louis the Pious; and ninth-century aristocrats who read up their Frankish history in Gregory of Tours and the *Liber Historiae Francorum* also formed an audience for contemporary *Gesta Regum*. Chroniclers in the reign of Alfonso III, probably working to a royal commission, constructed an account of the eighth century to establish the kingdom of the Asturias as the lineal descendant of the Visigothic kingdom, while a parallel strain of prophetic history defined Spain's destiny in terms of Christian *reconquista*.[286] The author(s) of the *Anglo-Saxon Chronicle*, under Alfred's inspiration, made the dynasty of Cerdic the linking theme of a story that culminated in the ninth century, with Egbert the Bretwalda, Æthelwulf the defender of his realm against the heathen, and the trials and triumphs of Alfred's reign.[287] The symbolic representation of the present, and the construction of the past, were ways in which kings attempted to involve contemporaries in shaping the future: as such they were essential elements in royal government.

[285] *ASC s.a.* 886; Keynes and Lapidge (1983), p. 266.
[286] Gómez-Moreno (1932), pp. 592–3, 596; Fernandez-Armesto (1992), p. 130.
[287] Davis (1971); Wormald (1982).

CHAPTER 16

THE ARISTOCRACY

Stuart Airlie

THE barbarian west was dominated throughout the period 700–900 by an hereditary aristocracy, that is, by a ruling elite, membership of which depended on birth. Byzantium, by contrast, was not; only towards the end of the eighth century can we see a truly hereditary aristocracy emerging there.[1] But early medieval western society was not dominated by closed castes exclusively based on birth or service. The ruling aristocracies were 'open', not monolithic, to the extent that royal patronage could promote lowly men; noble birth did not in itself guarantee a glittering career.[2]

The essentials of the secular aristocratic way of life in the west remain fairly constant from 700 to 900 and indeed beyond: pride in ancestry, possession of landed wealth, leadership and participation in warfare and government, not forgetting conspicuous consumption and hunting.[3] But in this chapter we shall be studying the dynamics of the aristocracy, primarily in the Carolingian realms, by examining its relations with royal patrons and the workings of its family structures. Thus some lines of approach may be opened up that have not been fully covered by the otherwise prodigious work of other scholars on this topic, work to which this chapter is nonetheless heavily indebted.

The expansion of Carolingian rule offered great opportunities to the aristocracy, whose leading members were able to enrich themselves and to widen the scope of their activities. Was this aristocracy therefore a Carolingian creation? An older historiographical tradition stressed the importance of Carolingian patronage together with its restriction to a few favoured families from the Carolingians' own 'homeland' in Austrasia.[4] Members of the Austrasian nobility enjoyed a privileged position; thus the

---

[1] Patlagean (1984).
[2] Reuter (1979), pp. 5–6. This, with a substantial bibliography, is an indispensable starting-point for the study of the aristocracy; orientation is also provided in Freed (1986).
[3] Goetz (1983); Airlie (1992).   [4] Poupardin (1900), p. 81.

expansion westwards into Neustria after the battles of Tertry (687) and Vinchy (717) resulted in the gradual filling of offices with Austrasian rather than Neustrian appointees.[5]

Study of those aristocratic families that are visibly active in the Meuse-Moselle region around 700, however, shows that phrases such as the 'rise of the Carolingians' beg some questions. M. Werner's survey of relations between the Carolingians of *c.* 700 and two noble families, that of Irmina of Oeren and that of Adela of Pfalzel, demonstrates that, far from being an all-powerful presence in the landscape showering patronage onto politically passive followers, the early Carolingians were in fact *dependent* on such 'followers', their fellow-aristocrats. Thus Pippin II's marriage to Plectrude some time before 668/70 was a political necessity for him, not for her, as it brought him rich estates at a time when he needed them badly. The power of Austrasian noble families such as that of Plectrude therefore pre-dated the rise of the Carolingians and actually made it possible.[6] Such figures created the new royal dynasty, rather than the reverse.

The Carolingians were therefore not entirely free agents; the aristocracy was too potent a force to be merely an instrument of their will. From the beginning the Carolingians had to work with members of the aristocracy from the whole Frankish world and not simply with an elite group of Austrasians.[7] Regional aristocracies survived. In Alsace, the ducal house of the Etichonids went into eclipse after the Carolingian take-over of the mid-eighth century, but descendants of the family re-emerged under Charlemagne and went on to have glittering careers in Neustria, Italy and Lotharingia.[8] Connections between the Carolingians and the aristocracies of those regions which they incorporated into their empire were intimate: Charlemagne's wife Hildegard was a descendant of Gotefridus, *dux* of Alemannia *c.* 700.[9] The tide of the empire's expansion did not obliterate native aristocracies. As a result, old rivalries between aristocratic families continued to be fought out using royal favour as a weapon. Thus Hildegard's brother and uncle deployed Charlemagne's support in order to win back influence in Alsace which they had lost decades before to the Etichonids.[10]

The creation of the Carolingian empire offered opportunities to regional

---

[5] Hennebicque-Le Jan (1989), pp. 234–5.

[6] M. Werner (1982), pp. 30–1; Gerberding (1987), p. 95.

[7] K.-F. Werner (1965), also in Reuter (1979).

[8] Vollmer (1957); Wilsdorf (1964). On the integration of regional aristocracies into the empire, Bosl (1969), p. 114.

[9] Thegan, *Vita Hludowici*, c. 2, p. 216; Leyser (1968), also in Leyser (1982), at p. 171.

[10] Borgolte (1983), pp. 23–4.

nobilities to act on a European stage. For this elite, however, local origins were less important as a form of identity than membership of a group that governed the empire, a truly imperial aristocracy, the *Reichsaristokratie*. This term, *Reichsaristokratie*, was given wide currency by Tellenbach in 1939 and is used to refer to an elite upper stratum of the nobility, distinguished by its exceptional riches and power and its holding of lands and offices scattered throughout the empire. This office-holding was a product of its closeness to the ruling Carolingian dynasty (*Königsnähe*), a closeness which obviously benefited both partners. Tellenbach listed those members of the aristocracy who formed this group: 111 men belonging to forty-two families.[11] Since this elite was relatively small its genealogical ramifications and the ups and downs of its members' careers could be worked out in detail and thus the political and social history of the Carolingian empire could be more fully understood.

The particular achievement of this research has been its success in 'activating' the seemingly inert data banks of some of the most rebarbative and austere early medieval sources, the *Libri Memoriales*. Essentially these are commemoration books maintained by abbeys in which lists of names of those wishing to be remembered in prayer were entered. These books survive from an area that stretches from Durham in England to Brescia in Italy. Once historians understood how the thousands of names contained in such books had been entered and could then identify group-entries, a rich new source became available to prosopographers who could now trace patterns of kinship and association among the aristocracy to an extent hitherto undreamed of.[12]

The sheer extent of these patterns is important. What emerged was a picture of the aristocratic kin group of the period up until the tenth century as large, extended and drawing its noble ancestry from both the paternal and maternal lines of descent and diffusing it among all members of the kin. In turn, these large kins and family structures became explanatory tools for understanding the politics of the period. If members of these large kin groups were aware of their interrelationship and acted upon this consciousness then the Carolingian empire could be seen as a great network of family relationships, and through the wires of this network kin consciousness transmitted its messages. Thus, painstaking detective work on the commemoration books of the eastern abbeys of Pfäfers and Reichenau enabled Tellenbach to discover hitherto unknown members of the immediate family

---

[11] Tellenbach (1939), pp. 42–55.
[12] Tellenbach (1957b); Schmid (1983). The most 'user-friendly' edition of a *Liber Memorialis* is that of Remiremont, *MGH Lib. Mem.*; helpful discussion in Constable (1972).

of Rudolf, abbot of St Riquier and Jumièges in the western kingdom of
Charles the Bald.[13]

The fact that some members of this aristocracy have dropped from view
and need to be rediscovered in this way points to areas where the concept of
the *Reichsaristokratie* needs refining. It is important not to see it as a closed
caste. It was, rather, the tip of an iceberg. Men of high birth had obscure
relatives and not all offices in royal government were held by men of the very
highest birth. To that extent the Frankish world of the eighth and ninth
centuries was more socially flexible than, say, the kingdom of Germany in
the tenth.[14] Uncovering the *Reichsaristokratie* is therefore a complex business, more complex than merely finding new candidates to add to Tellenbach's 1939 list, as he and his pupils have pointed out.[15] It was royal favour
that enabled a man to rise above his fellows, though social values and
political pressures meant that the king's choice was not entirely free; in no
sense was the aristocracy a royal creation.[16] The concept of the *Reichsaristokratie*, however, is worth preserving as a useful tool as it offers insights into
the structure of the empire and the social history of the aristocracy.

The motor that propelled fortunate members of the aristocracy across
Europe was royal favour and patronage. Thus the grandchildren of Adela of
Pfalzel can be found in the first half of the eighth century working for
Charles Martel in Burgundy and Provence, far from their homeland in the
Meuse-Moselle region. Nor was such movement simply a one-way traffic
from Austrasia; present among Charles Martel's following in Trier in 722 is
one Abbo, a Gallo-Roman magnate from Provence, where he laboured to
establish Frankish hegemony.[17] Such mobility lasted as long as the empire
did; its most egregious example is perhaps Boso, right-hand man of Charles
the Bald from 869 to 877.[18] Bernard of Septimania, who played a leading role
in the high politics of the 830s and 840s, did not confine himself to
Septimania in the Spanish March where he held office. The royal court
exerted a strong gravitational pull: he was married in Aachen in 824; in 829
he became the guardian of the young Charles the Bald but had to flee the
court a year later after rebellion had broken out, his overweening power
being one of the rebels' main targets. He reappeared in Aachen in 832; he
appeared in Burgundy in 833 and seems to have spent the last part of the
decade back in Septimania. It is not surprising that in the text written by his

---

[13] Tellenbach (1957a).

[14] Bullough (1970), pp. 73–84 and Airlie (1990); on tenth-century conditions, Reuter (1991), p.
221.

[15] Schmid (1974), reprinted in Schmid (1983) at pp. 5–9; Tellenbach (1979), p. 246 n. 30.

[16] K.-F. Werner (1965), translated in Reuter (1979).

[17] M. Werner (1982), pp. 302–3; Geary (1985), pp. 33–4.   [18] N. 83 below.

wife Dhuoda for their son he is almost always 'off-stage'. In its essentials, Bernard's career, with its continual shifts of scene and gaining and losing of royal favour, is typical of his class.[19]

But more than royal favour, or its loss, was involved in the making and sustaining of the *Reichsaristokratie*. Patterns of office-holding were underpinned by family structures. Members of this aristocracy may have passed from one region of the empire to another because of royal command, but while the kings provided a framework and opportunities for such movement, it was the family connections of the aristocracy that made it possible.

Hennebicque, for example, has uncovered an aristocratic family group anchored between the Meuse and the Rhine; its members, identifiable through such names as Heriricus, Albericus, Wernharius and Hunfridus can be found, as a group, in the same area in documents stretching across a century, roughly from 760 to 870. This group, composed of various families coalesced into a larger association, was itself linked to some of the most prominent kin groups of the more politically visible members of the *Reichsaristokratie* such as the 'Adalhards' and the 'Unruochs'. Hennebicque has successfully demonstrated that the high-profile members of the *Reichsaristokratie* such as Adalhard 'the seneschal' were able to move from one Carolingian court to another because in each kingdom there was an infrastructure, consisting of members of their kin, with which they could align themselves on arrival. Some time between 844 and 849 Adalhard 'the seneschal' himself left the court of Charles the Bald for that of Lothar I, where he gained offices (*honores*). Not all his contacts were confined to court; we can see him in contact with one Heriricus, presumably a lowly member of his kin group, in 853.[20] This network of patronage and support is a crucial factor in explaining how the *Reichsaristokratie* worked. Great men such as Adalhard moved from one 'support group' to another and acted as channels of royal patronage for the members of the 'support groups'. The movements and activity of the members of the *Reichsaristokratie* were complemented, and made possible, by the existence of the humbler branches of the kin who safeguarded kin interests while the great men moved from *honor* to *honor*. Thus a 'supporting cast' for the prominent members of the 'Widonid' group can be traced through Lorsch charters.[21]

Such structures and the pattern of holding property across the empire appear to have been little disturbed by the empire's division in the Treaty of

---

[19] Dhuoda, *Manuel* at e.g. Praefatio, pp. 84–6 and x.4, pp. 350–2; Störmer (1973), p. 469.

[20] Hennebicque (1981), pp. 294–9, 321–3; cf. the local context in Kuchenbuch (1978), pp. 346–54.

[21] *Codex Laureshamensis* II, nos. 511, 656 and 813; Metz (1965), pp. 4–6, 14. Note also the humbler member of Hugh of Tours' kin-group visible in his entourage in his 820 charter for Weissenburg, *Traditiones Wizenburgenses*, no. 69.

Verdun of 843. Although this meant that members of the aristocracy could now hold office in only one kingdom, they retained property and family interests in other kingdoms. We can gain some idea of how properties were maintained across the boundaries created in 843 by looking at the case of Eberhard of Friuli. Eberhard was a Frankish magnate who had married into the Carolingian family and who held office in the kingdom of Lothar I. Not only did he retain his property in all three post-Verdun kingdoms, he successfully bequeathed it to his children, one of whom, Unruoch, inherited estates in Alemannia and Italy, that is, in the kingdoms of Louis the German and Louis II respectively, and held on to them by remaining on good terms with both rulers.[22]

The fact that the high aristocracy was so mobile owing to royal patronage and the infrastructure of clientage has important consequences for our understanding of family structure. There appears to have been no fixed point, no family seat, around which these aristocrats organised themselves. We have already observed this in the career of Bernard of Septimania. In the *Liber Manualis*, written by his wife Dhuoda in Uzès, the focus is not on Uzès, but on the inheritance of Bernard's brother, Theudericus, in Burgundy. This explains why Dhuoda also focused on the royal court, for it was the king who distributed *honores*.[23]

This lack of a central base in Dhuoda's work stands in stark contrast to aristocratic texts of a later date, such as the twelfth-century *Historia Welforum*, which lay stress on the possession of a fixed residence (*habitatio certa*) as a key element in a noble family's make-up.[24] This absence of conceptual traces of a centre is paralleled by an absence of physical ones. It is difficult to find a fixed point of residence for aristocratic families of the early middle ages. Great aristocrats of this period do not appear to group themselves around a residence such as a castle, as was to happen later. Their properties were too scattered, the theatre of their operations was too wide, for them to be as confined as, relatively speaking, their descendants were.[25] Thus the aristocracy from, say, 1100 on was different in type from its Carolingian predecessor. The appearance of castles functioning as fixed centres of lordship meant that families shrank and organised themselves

[22] *Cartulaire de l'abbaye de Cysoing*, no. 1; cf. Hlawitschka (1960), pp. 60–6 and p. 276.

[23] *Manuel*, III.4, pp. 148–52, VIII.15, pp. 320–2; Wollasch (1957), p. 187 and Störmer (1973), pp. 467–8. Bernard's striving for the Burgundian *honores* was noted by other contemporaries, Nithard, *Histoire* III.2, p. 84.

[24] *Historia Welforum*, c. 1, p. 4; Schmid (1988), p. 13 and Wollasch (1957), pp. 170–2.

[25] Schmid (1957), reprinted in Schmid (1983), here at pp. 213–14; Schmid (1988), pp. 30–1, Borgolte (1988), p. 52 and Althoff (1990), pp. 62–4. One reason for the absence of traces of residence is the lack of integrated historical and archaeological analysis of the type called for by Schmid (1988), pp. 36–7.

around such centres, whence they derived their surnames, a name element quite foreign to the aristocracy of 700 to 900. Broadly speaking, a tighter, more patrilineally organised aristocracy, with a smaller pool of heirs, thus came into being in western Europe.[26]

We must not be tempted, in looking at the 'streamlined' aristocratic family of the high middle ages, to think of the early medieval aristocratic family as vast and amorphous. We have seen that members of the *Reichsaristokratie* did indeed have links with their humbler kin, but these were links of patronage and clientship; figures such as Heririicus were in no sense the equals of figures such as Adalhard 'the seneschal'. What then was the shape of the early medieval aristocratic family? The negative approach to this question will show that the aristocracy did not operate in terms of great clans, that is, homogeneous units composed of members with common interests. The positive approach will demonstrate and examine the essentially dynamic and fluid nature of the aristocratic family and explore the consequences of this for our understanding of the period.

Some of the problems in this area stem from the very success of research into sources such as the *Libri Memoriales* and aristocratic naming patterns. The means by which family groups have been constructed has come under critical scrutiny. First, the name material is technically difficult to handle and philologists can reveal the work of historians to have been imprecise.[27] Naming patterns alone are an insufficient basis for establishing affiliation. It is now generally accepted that coincidence of name between two individuals widely separated in space and time is not in itself sufficient to establish a connection between them.[28]

Not only is it often difficult to establish connections between members of the great aristocratic kin groups; such connections, once established, can themselves possess limited explanatory value. Study of aristocratic behaviour under the pressure of conflicts of loyalty, as in the struggle for power among members of the Carolingian dynasty in the 830s and 840s, shows that families could split. Thus in 834, on the Breton border, we find two brothers, Lambert and Wido, on opposite sides in a clash between partisans of Lothar and Louis the Pious. Their family had a strong tradition of office-holding in this region. One might be tempted to think that the brothers' being on different sides was a means of safeguarding family interests in troubled times were it not for the fact that Wido was killed in a pitched battle against his brother's forces.[29] Such tensions between close relatives are

---

[26] Schmid (1957), reprinted in Schmid (1983); Störmer (1973), pp. 93–7; Althoff (1990), pp. 55–67; for English-language accounts, see Holt (1982) and Arnold (1991), pp. 135–51.

[27] For an example, Gockel (1970), p. 298 n. 739.   [28] M. Werner (1982), pp. 21–5.

[29] Nithard, *Histoire* I.5, p. 20; Hennebicque-Le Jan (1989), pp. 258 and 267.

frequently visible at times of political crisis; the family of the counts of Paris split in the civil wars of the 840s, with one brother, Adalhard 'the seneschal', fighting for Charles the Bald while another, Gerard, fought for Lothar.[30] Attempts by scholars to explain choices of loyalty along lines of family identity alone are bound to fail.

To allocate an individual to a large family group is only a first step towards understanding his or her behaviour. Family membership was only one component of an aristocratic identity made up of bonds of friendship, political allegiance and spiritual alliance.[31] Other priorities could cut across family ties. We have seen this happen in war, but such claims were heard in peace time too. For example, Bishop Megingoz of Würzburg worked actively, some time between 754 and 782, to prevent his niece, whom he saw as unworthy, becoming abbess of the convent of Wenkheim in succession to his sister. His failure shows the power of family claims; his effort shows that such claims were not unchallenged.[32] The charting of kin groups, therefore, does not necessarily shed much light on political activity. To some extent, these kin groups have not been so much discovered as constructed. Names of families such as the Welfs, Widonids, etc. are not contemporary but are labels of modern historians.

What constituted family identity? Debates as to whether the early noble family was agnatic or cognatic in structure obscure the point that family structure was flexible.[33] Thus, if a man gained status through marriage the new wife's kin would provide the name-pool for the descendants of the marriage. This can be seen in the case of the Carolingians themselves who seldom took names from Bishop Arnulf of Metz and his son Ansegisel but frequently took them from the family of Pippin, whose daughter Begga had married Ansegisel.[34] Such thought patterns reveal a perception of the family group as potentially wide, and it is such a perception that is reflected in many of the entries in the *Libri Memoriales*. But such perceptions were not constant and concentration on the *Libri Memoriales* may be positively misleading.[35]

The perception of family structure varied for contemporaries, depending on vantage point. Thegan, for example, opened his Life of Louis the Pious by tracing Charlemagne's ancestry back to Arnulf in a strictly agnatic line, a simplified and striking image of the smooth transmission of power from generation to generation. But he described the ancestry of Hildegard, Louis'

---

[30] Nithard, *Histoire* II.3, p. 44.

[31] This point cannot be overstressed; see Tellenbach (1979), p. 248.   [32] Bosl (1969), p. 65.

[33] Fichtenau (1984), pp. 119–20, and in more lightly annotated English translation, Fichtenau (1991), pp. 85–7.

[34] Goetz (1986), pp. 37–8; cf. Schmid (1957), reprinted in Schmid (1983), pp. 204–9.

[35] Leyser (1968), reprinted in Leyser (1982), p. 170, formulates the essential warning.

mother, on a broader canvas, tracing her membership of the *cognatio* of Duke Gotefridus of Alemannia through the maternal line in order to highlight her maternal ancestry.[36] On occasion, then, the role of women as powerful ancestors could be highlighted but this does not mean that all families looked continuously to female ancestors as the source of their status. The fact that they did so, however, when it was suitable means that we must not seek to discover a single, cast-iron structure for the noble family. Instead we must grasp how flexible family structure was for contemporaries.

Definitions of identity and status were made within families and could be fluid. This emerges clearly from Dhuoda's text in two ways. First, she herself draws a distinction between a broad and a narrow view of family when she commemorates eight dead members of her son William's kin whom she seems to regard as a *genealogia*, before going on to talk of other relatives who form a *stirps*.[37] Second, she selects one of William's relatives as being his most important connection in the family: his paternal uncle Theodericus. Here the biological bonds were supplemented with cultural ones: Theodericus was both William's godfather and his guardian (*nutritor*). These bonds were strengthened through the transmitting of property.[38] Dhuoda does not give William an exhaustive list of his kin group. She does not, for example, refer in her list of the deceased members of William's *genealogia* to his father's *consobrinus* Count Odo of Orléans, though it was precisely Odo's connection to Bernard of Septimania that had earned him the fatal enmity of Lothar.[39] Dhuoda was thus not striving for a complete picture of family membership.

It is in the area of inheritance that we can see claims and definitions at their sharpest. Dhuoda locates William's place in a double line of descent of blood and of property: William should pray for the *parentes* of his father who have bequeathed him their property as his heritage and although she reassures him that this heritage had remained safely in the possession of the family, she does so in terms that betray anxiety.[40] Entitlement to property is therefore a key factor in family identity; Dhuoda is determined to draw lines, to make such identity exclusive. Her terminology here recalls that of an aristocrat from the previous century, Abbo of Provence, who in his will (739)

---

[36] Thegan, *Vita Hludowici*, cc. 1 and 2, p. 216; Tremp (1988), pp. 26–7; Borgolte (1986), pp. 184–5. A similar pattern of thought is visible in Notker, *Gesta Karoli* I, c. 13, p. 17 and II, c. 8, pp. 60–1; commentary in Schmid (1988), p. 16 and Borgolte (1986), pp. 152–3.

[37] Dhuoda, *Manuel* x.5, p. 354; Oexle (1988), p. 104. Compare Nithard's distinction between a broad and narrow family group, *Histoire* IV, c.5, p. 138; comment and further references in Nelson (1985), reprinted in Nelson (1986), here at pp. 231–2.

[38] Dhuoda, *Manuel* VIII.15, pp. 320–2; Wollasch (1957), pp. 187–8.

[39] Dhuoda, *Manuel* x.5, p. 354; for the attack on Odo and on Bernard's brother in 830, Astronomer, *Vita Hludowici*, c. 45, p. 336. [40] Dhuoda, *Manuel* VIII.14, pp. 318–20.

designates as kin '*only* those persons from whom he had inherited property'.[41] We are thus vividly reminded of how inheritance claims can bring one type of kinship definition into sharp, and, it would seem, restricted focus.

Inheritance patterns and practice among the early medieval nobility remain relatively understudied. But there is evidence to suggest that Dhuoda's testimony is representative, that is, that the circle of heirs was a restricted one, or even 'determinedly patrilinear'.[42] The will of Eberhard of Friuli (867) shows him, together with his wife, bequeathing properties to their four sons and three daughters; here, decisions are made by parents alone and the heirs are their children.[43] The family unit on this occasion was small; although we know that Eberhard was a member of a great clan, there is no indication of this in his will. After all, early medieval law-codes stressed that not all members of a family were equally entitled to inherit. A text such as the *Edictum Chilperici* from the late sixth century points to an agnatic pattern: the inheritance (referred to simply as land, *terra*) is to go to sons, or in their absence, daughters. The inheritance rights that counted were those of a privileged circle.[44] This can be seen very clearly in an inheritance dispute over the rights of daughters dating from the late ninth century. It appears that Ingeltrude, the daughter of Count Matfrid of Orléans and thus a member of the Frankish high nobility, had, after an eventful career that involved abandoning her husband Boso, made arrangements for her property that effectively excluded her and Boso's daughters in favour of members of her own kin. But Pope John VIII argued that Ingeltrude's dispositions were invalid because she issued them while under sentence of excommunication from the church and because 'in matters of inheritance children take precedence over all other types of relative'.[45]

The pattern revealed by the above evidence is one of a small circle of heirs; children, including daughters, are to be preferred to more distant kin. This tightly linear structure is visible over several generations in a text such as the *Translatio Sanguinis Domini*. From mid-tenth-century Reichenau, this preserves information about and, importantly, the priorities of, a noble family, the descendants of Hunfrid of Rhaetia who obtained the precious double

---

[41] Geary (1985), p. 116.

[42] Bouchard (1986), p. 644; general discussion in Murray (1983) and Hartung (1988a).

[43] *Cartulaire de l'abbaye de Cysoing*, no. 1.

[44] Murray (1983), pp. 195–7; cf. Hartung (1988b), pp. 54–6.

[45] 'Omnibus gradibus cognatorum in hereditate sumenda preferendi sunt filii...nec cognati eorum, nisi ipse filie, quae sunt legitime, illos alodes habere debent', *MGH Epp.* VII, no. 111, p. 103 and cf. nos. 129 and 130, pp. 114–15. On this case, Hlawitschka (1969), pp. 159–61 and Wemple (1981), p. 87 and p. 249 n. 64; Roman custom may have helped the pope favour Ingeltrude's daughters: Wemple, p. 113.

relic of some of Christ's blood and a fragment of the True Cross after a visit to Jerusalem *c* 800.[46] The text is concerned with the transmission of the sacred relic through Hunfrid's descendants. This transmission is clearly linear as we observe it passing from Hunfrid to his son Adalbertus, and then to his son Odalricus, to his daughter Hemma and then to her son Odalricus. Only one member of the family in each generation enjoys possession of the relic, which is seen as a key element in the family's patrimony. The focus of the text is on only those members of Hunfrid's line who inherited the relic. It is significant that this linear pattern is not disturbed by the fact that one of the eventual heirs was a woman, Hunfrid's great-granddaughter Hemma; she gains the relic through hereditary right, cares for it and transmits it, along with the name of her own father, to her son Odalricus.[47]

A similar pattern emerges from a survey of who controlled the 'family monasteries' that so often acted as a focus for aristocratic wealth. The Saxon noble Count Waltbert and his wife Aldburg founded Wildeshausen in the 860s as an *Eigenkirche* that was always to be controlled by a fittingly pious member of his line.[48] What Waltbert intended by this is quite clear: his own descendants, and no distant relatives, were to control Wildeshausen; his son Wibert was to be *rector*, to be succeeded by his brother's son or, if this was impossible, by the son of his sister. This is what happened. Given the clerical status of the persons involved here, straightforward father–son succession was problematic, but a restricted pool of 'heirs' was envisaged, heirs in direct line of descent from Waltbert. South of Saxony, in Alemannia, one notes another family monastery, at Aadorf, founded by Count Udalrich some time before 866. This was intended as a resting-place for his family, but the people involved were, again, the founder's immediate relatives: his wife, his daughters, his son.[49]

For some purposes, then, the aristocratic family appears to have been a large kin; for others, a much smaller unit. Distant kin could matter less to contemporaries than they do to modern historians, anxious to chart a 'total' picture for their own purposes. Sometimes there was tension between these two concepts of large and small family units. Such tension can be fruitfully explored in two areas: the position of women and the struggle for offices.

Frankish law-codes suggest that women were postponed, not excluded, as heirs; daughters could inherit property if there were no sons.[50] But at the

---

[46] Text in *MGH SS* IV, pp. 444–9; commentary in Borgolte (1984a), pp. 221–9.
[47] *Translatio Sanguinis Domini*, cc. 14–18, p. 448.
[48] Schmid (1964), reprinted in Schmid (1983).
[49] *Urkundenbuch der Abtei Sanct Gallen* II, nos. 655, 691 and 697; Borgolte (1984b), pp. 597–9. It is, however, difficult to generalise about sites of aristocratic burial: Schmid (1957), reprinted in Schmid (1983), here at pp. 227–9.
[50] Wemple (1981), pp. 44–50; Murray (1983), pp. 183–215.

beginning of our period we do find cases of women inheriting property quite straightforwardly; such heirs do not have to be brotherless daughters or childless widows. Thus the Neustrian noblewoman Erminetrude, in a will from *c.*700, left vineyards and slaves to her granddaughter and daughter-in-law, as well as bequeathing substantial properties to her grandson.[51] How typical was this? On the basis of law-codes and formularies, scholars thought that it was only as the eighth century wore on that Frankish daughters came to share inheritance with their brothers. In fact, however, there is charter evidence showing that women were inheriting property alongside their brothers (and disposing of it with them) as early as the late seventh century.[52]

Such evidence reveals that, to some extent, a bilateral system of inheritance existed. This is not to say that sisters inherited equally with brothers, but it is now possible to make a more positive assessment of women's participation in inheritance than hitherto. Social constraints could work in women's favour. Women had legitimate claims which the family group could be compelled to recognise. We have seen this with regard to Ingeltrude's daughters and the niece of the bishop of Würzburg

Women's grip on property may not always have been firm, but they could share fully in the status that high birth conferred. The ancestry of noble women was celebrated, as we have seen in the case of Hildegard. Women could in fact outrank their husbands in terms of ancestry and in such cases children took their names from the maternal side of the family.[53] The aura of nobility surrounded aristocratic women; in eighth-century Bavarian documents women are grouped together with men under such titles as *praeclari homines*.[54] Here the individual woman, or man, is subsumed within the group identity of the noble family. This is not to say that all members of a given noble family were equal, but differentiation of noble status within a family was not exclusively dependent upon gender. The noble family was a complex organism; no one model suffices to describe it.

A key function of women within their family was as a focus, and indeed constructor, of family identity. High-ranking women in the Carolingian world were well educated themselves and passed on their education, which would include family traditions, to their offspring and indeed to a wider audience. Thus Dhuoda's *Liber Manualis*, in listing her son's ancestors and urging him to pray for them, reproduces in miniature the gigantic apparatus

---

[51] Erminetrude's will: *ChLA* xiv, no. 592 (where it is dated to the sixth or seventh century); Wemple (1981), p. 49; Heidrich (1988), pp. 1–2. The dispute over the date of this document does not affect my argument.   [52] M. Werner (1982), pp. 131–2.

[53] Hennebicque (1981), p. 296; Borgolte (1986), pp. 234–5.   [54] Störmer (1973), pp. 208–9.

of the *Libri Memoriales*.[55] Outside the secular household, women as well as men could preside over the commemoration of their own family, as Count Udalrich's daughters did at Aadorf.[56] Richardis, wife of Charles the Fat, used her royal connections to build up Andlau in Alsace, an abbey that acted as a focus for her family's power and a counterweight to the nearby Etichonid foundation of Erstein.[57]

Dhuoda's overwhelming stress on her husband and his family may therefore be misleading, suggesting as it does that aristocratic women sank their own family identities upon marriage. Husbands 'recognised' their wife's family, as can be seen in the bequests of Eccard of Mâcon (d. 876), who died childless, to a wide circle that included female relatives of his wife.[58] Richgard's case shows that the gravitational pull of the royal family itself was not sufficient to obliterate a noble wife's consciousness of her own descent, and ambition for her family.[59] Not surprisingly, when women of the royal family married they too remembered their ancestry and status.[60]

It should now be clear that the social and political history of the aristocracy can only be understood in dynamic terms. Nowhere is this more true than in office-holding. The relationship of the nobility to the royal dynasty, differentiation within the nobility as a social group, competition between and within noble families, can all be seen at their starkest here.

The offices that the aristocracy competed for so fiercely can generally be described as *honores*: the public offices and benefices which gave their holders prestige and political muscle.[61] Those men who gained an office such as a countship were aware that it was a *ministerium* for which one had to show oneself to the king as a worthy candidate, but they also saw themselves as having a claim on such offices because their noble status entitled them to rule.[62] Kings' extensive power of patronage was therefore subject to

55 Dhuoda, *Manuel* VIII, x.5, pp. 306–24 and p. 354; on the education of women, McKitterick (1989), pp. 223–7.

56 Above, n. 49. The *Vita Odiliae*, which dates from the end of the ninth century, highlights, as an essential facet of Odilia's sanctity, her family piety, as seen in her successful prayers for her father to be released from the torments of the after-life, *Vita Odiliae*, cc. 12 and 22, *MGH SRM* VI, pp. 44 and 49; cf. Cardot (1983). 57 Borgolte (1983), pp. 27–8, 34–5.

58 *Recueil des chartes de l'abbaye de Saint-Benoît-sur-Loire*, nos. XXV, XXVI and XXVII; commentary in Schmid (1965), reprinted in Schmid (1983), pp. 566–71.

59 Within a family's 'commemoration policy', women's initiatives could of course be later taken over by men, Martindale (1990).

60 The names of two of Eberhard of Friuli's daughters, Judith and Heilwig, are those of his wife Gisela's mother and maternal grandmother, *Cartulaire de l'abbaye de Cysoing*, no. I; cf. Gisela's perception of her *cognatio*, *ibid.*, no. VI.

61 On definitions of *honor*, Niermeyer (1976), pp. 495–8 and compare Fichtenau (1984), pp. 193–4 and, without the references, (1991), p. 141. 62 Hlawitschka (1986), pp. 182–5; Zotz (1988).

constraints, in the form of the claims of the aristocracy as a group and, more particularly, the claims of certain families to specific offices. This holds true throughout our period. As the grip of the Carolingians on Neustria tightened, so did that of noble families on comital office. The countship of Meaux passed from Helmgaudus to his son Gauzhelmus and to his son Helmgaudus in what looks like uninterrupted succession from 744 to 813, while the countship of Paris was dominated by the descendants of Count Gerard between 753 and 858.[63] The combination of hereditary claims and the royal granting of a *ministerium* is clearly expressed in an 814 charter of the Bavarian Count Orendil in which he refers to his sons as his potential successors, should one of them be worthy of obtaining the office (*ministerium*).[64] (One notes that only one son could succeed.) The famous Capitulary of Quierzy of 877 in which Charles the Bald recognised hereditary claims to counties and benefices is not therefore such a landmark as used to be thought.[65]

This, however, does not mean that kings' powers of patronage were limited to the extent that succession to office was a foregone conclusion. It was precisely the nobility's hunger for office and the importance of office-holding that gave kings their enormous political leverage. The ascent of the low-born Ebbo to the see of Rheims shows something of the scope of royal patronage.[66] The behaviour of Charles the Bald in 868 shows the continuing importance of the royal will in the distributing of *honores* in the second half of the ninth century, and this in a case where hereditary claims were perceived even as they were passed over: 'Those of Robert's *honores* which Charles had granted to his son after his father's death were now taken away and distributed among other men. The sons of Ranulf also had their father's *honores* taken away from them.'[67] In the light of this the resentment felt by Charles the Simple's magnates in 920 at his promotion of his favourite, Hagano, is less noteworthy than the fact that royal power of promotion was still potent.[68]

Both Charles the Bald's success and Charles the Simple's problems stemmed from the fact that the distribution of *honores* was a matter of political skill and negotiation; there were always more claimants than rewards, a timeless political problem. The great political crisis of the ninth century involved struggles between rival kings and their followers over

---

[63] Hennebicque-Le Jan (1989), pp. 236–7.   [64] Störmer (1973), p. 458; Zotz (1988), p. 4.
[65] Nelson (1992), pp. 248–9.   [66] Airlie (1990).
[67] 'Ablatis denique a Rotberti filio his quae post mortem patris de honoribus ipsius ei concesserat et per alios divisis, sed et a filiis Ramnulfi tultis paternis honoribus...', *AB(3) s.a.* 868, pp. 141–2; the translation is from Nelson (1991), pp. 143–4.
[68] Martindale (1977), p. 15; Althoff (1990), p. 165.

honores; this was, for example Hincmar's view of the civil war ended by the Treaty of Verdun in 843: 'the magnates of the realm began to fight among themselves for *honores*, to see which of them might obtain the lion's share'.[69] The Treaty of Verdun itself was concerned to ensure that each king received an adequate share of the empire's resources with which to reward his following. But the splitting up of those resources guaranteed that politics after 843 would be dominated by royal efforts to gain more of them and that members of the *Reichsaristokratie* would come under severe pressures of conflicting loyalties.[70]

The importance of the holding of *honores* cannot be overestimated as a factor in explaining aristocratic political behaviour. Kings deployed the threat of loss of *honores* or the offer of them as routine methods of gaining aristocratic loyalties.[71] Loss of *honores*, which involved loss of royal favour, was not merely a loss of resources, but exposed one to the pent-up hostility of one's rivals: Matfrid of Orléans lost his offices in 828 and in 829 Louis the Pious announced an investigation into Matfrid's past conduct as an official, encouraging complainants to come forward.[72] Matfrid's determination to regain his lost countship of Orléans was matched only by the determination of the new incumbent, Odo, to hold on to it. Thus, when Louis' sons rose against him, Matfrid regained Orléans, only to lose it again to Odo when Louis was reinstated. The next round of fighting saw Matfrid and Odo clash again over possession of the county, with fatal results for Odo, though Louis' restoration in 834 meant exile and definitive loss of Orléans for Matfrid.[73] *Honores* were worth fighting and dying for.

Aristocrats who had 'invested' too heavily in a particular Carolingian as a patron found it hard to switch to a replacement if their patron faltered. Thus, the death of Charlemagne's brother Carloman in 771 resulted in the flight of several of his supporters to the Lombard court; they knew that there would be no place for them under Charlemagne, who had his own office-hungry magnates to reward. Similarly, the followers of Bernard of Italy in 817 rebelled with him against Louis the Pious' plans for the succession which threatened to exclude Bernard.[74] For such men the death or threatened downgrading of their Carolingian patron meant that the flow of favour dried up. There was no real security of tenure. It has been estimated that in Charlemagne's forty-five-year reign there were ten

---

[69] 'coeperunt regni primores...singillatim certare de honoribus, quique illorum, unde majores et plures possent obtinere', *Ad Ludovicum Balbum*, PL 125, col. 985.

[70] Nithard, *Histoire* IV, c. 3, p. 128; Tellenbach (1979), pp. 261–5.

[71] Tellenbach (1979), pp. 261–5. [72] *MGH Cap.* II, no. 188, c. 3, p. 10.

[73] Astronomer, *Vita Hludowici*, c. 44, p. 334 and c. 52, p. 352.

[74] Carloman: Brunner (1979), pp. 41–2; Bernard: Schmid (1976), reprinted in Schmid (1983).

dismissals from secular office and that in Louis' twenty-six years there were twenty-one.[75] Such figures are almost certainly an underestimate, but the pattern is clear. Amidst such upheaval the determination of magnates to hold their office was a constant. This was so whether the *honor* was a county such as Orléans or a lucrative benefice such as Neuilly which the family of Count Donatus of Melun strove for a generation to retain in the face of intense pressures.[76]

What made *honores* so important? This returns us to the subject of family structure. The eighth and ninth centuries were in general a time of partible inheritance, not of primogeniture. This did not mean that all children inherited equally; sons, for example, gained more than daughters. There was also regional variation; for example, fathers west of the Rhine could favour certain sons or indeed one son above others. In general, however, it can be said that the widespread practice of partitioning inheritances threatened the fortunes of a family.[77] Nor was it only the petty nobility that faced such threats. The fact that aristocratic estates were often scattered across a wide area and were more frequently split up than either royal or ecclesiastical estates again meant that a given family's power could fluctuate dangerously from generation to generation.[78] It is not surprising, therefore, that divisions of inheritance could be tense occasions, when frustrated expectations burst into conflict, sometimes resulting in fratricide.[79]

The importance of office-holding is now clear. Only the possession of *honores* provided 'security' by raising a man above the pressure on inheritance of property. This explains why a man like Bernard of Septimania was willing to hand his son over to Charles the Bald in 841, in effect as a hostage, in return for the king's promise to grant him *honores* in Burgundy. The possession of such *honores* was a more stable power base than family estates.[80]

As we have seen, however, *honores* in fact offered little security, given the rivalries within both the aristocracy and the royal house. Insecurity and conflicts are therefore the hallmarks of the social and political history of the Carolingian aristocracy. Its members strove to rise above their rivals and that included their own relatives.[81] The possession of *honores* also meant that there was differentiation of status within families. When the Welfs Hugh and Conrad left Louis the German's court for that of Charles the Bald in the 850s they gained rich *honores* in Burgundy; but their brother Welf (II) remained

---

[75] Krah (1987), pp. 38, 80–2.

[76] Hincmar, *De Villa Noviliaco*, MGH SS xv, pp. 1168–9; Krah (1987), pp. 73–5.

[77] Duby (1953), pp. 54–60; Hartung (1988a), pp. 421–2 and 432–5.   [78] Rösener (1989).

[79] *Gesta Sanctorum Rotonensium* iii, c. 8, ed. C. Brett, p. 206.   [80] Nithard, *Histoire* iii, c. 2, p. 84.

[81] Brunner (1979), pp. 27–35; Hartung (1988a), p. 423.

behind in Alemannia and obscurity.[82] The disparity of fortune in the 'Bosonid' family is even more striking.[83] In both these cases we are not dealing with a gulf between distantly related members of extended kin groups, but with one between brothers. Also visible here is the swift abandonment of the old family stamping-ground if promotion beckoned. The importance of royal favour in enabling a man to rise above his fellows should by now be evident, as should the restricted nature of the circle touched by that favour.

Conflict *within* as well as between families should therefore come as no surprise. We have seen this happen in the civil wars of the 830s and 840s. The great magnates often rose either in isolation from their relatives or at their expense. When Eberhard of Friuli's son Rudolf, who was abbot of both St Bertin and St Vaast, died in 892, Count Baldwin II of Flanders claimed the abbacies on the grounds that he was Rudolf's cousin (*consobrinus*); he paid no heed to closer claimants.[84]

Access to an *honor* such as a countship meant access to the powers of lordship, to income (for example, profits of justice) and to lands. Marriage into the royal family brought political favour, which could be translated into very concrete terms. Judith's marriage to Louis the Pious in 819 brought important fiscal lands in Schussengau into Welf hands.[85] Access to such resources enabled counts to strengthen their hold over their own following by acting as channels through which royal favour could be directed further down the hierarchy. Thus in June 859 Hunfrid, marquis of Gothia, successfully petitioned Charles the Bald at Attigny to grant land in Narbonnais and Ampurias to members of his entourage there.[86] What the great magnates gained for themselves, they had to redistribute. They accumulated in order to spend.

Differentiation of status within family parallels, and helps explain, differentiation within the nobility as a social group. Magnates did not always manage to put down deep roots. Of the two great administrators of eighth-century Carolingian Alemannia, Ruthard and Warin, only the former managed to entrench himself and his descendants there. Warin's son

---

[82] Althoff (1990), p. 50; Borgolte (1986), pp. 290–1.
[83] Boso, a magnate from Lotharingia, travelled west with his brother-in-law Charles the Bald in 869, held offices in Vienne and Lyonnais and built up a network of power stretching from Cambrai to Pavia; contrast his brother Bivinus, who remained in obscurity in Lotharingia and pursued family claims to land around the abbey of Gorze, hitherto a focus of the family's power: Airlie (1985), pp. 194–201, 214–19. Churches, of course, were very often far from being a mere second best as an anchor for aristocratic power, see Hartung (1988a) and Nightingale (1988).
[84] *Annales Vedastini s.a.* 892, p. 71; Airlie (1985), pp. 137–8.
[85] Fleckenstein (1957), p. 90; Rösener (1989), p. 143.   [86] Airlie (1985), pp. 212–13.

Isanbard succeeded him as count in Thurgau but was squeezed out in 779 by hostile nobles.[87] A century later, similar short tenure of office can be observed: Boso of Vienne and Bernard of Gothia held the county of Berry in quick succession in the 870s but they looked upon it merely as a source of troops and money; they had no interest in making it a permanent power base.[88] An important consequence of this pattern is that humbler members of the nobility, broadly defined, may have been able to secure themselves more firmly in localities. Counts came and went in Linzgau and Argengau, for example, but a series of charters from there reveals the continuous presence in witness-lists from 793 to 885 of men called Sigibert; they are probably related to each other and at least one of them was a *vicarius*. Beneath the *Sturm und Drang* of high politics we may have here a 'dynasty' of the petty nobility.[89] In Boso's career we can detect a *vicecomes* and *missus* of his called Erlulfus at a *mallus* in Provence between 871 and 876. In 870, in the entourage of Boso's predecessor Gerard of Vienne there is an Erlulfus, almost certainly the same man. Gerard had been dismissed from office in 870, to be replaced by Boso; Erlulfus, at a less exalted level, had survived.[90] In Italy the families with a future in the post-Carolingian world were those of the second rank who had consolidated their status in confined regions, often by leasing estates from more prominent office-holders such as bishops.[91]

The ultimate evolution of the great magnates, the 'super-magnates' who rose to become kings themselves, remains to be considered. Of course there had always been distinctions among the nobility, but the men who rose to regal or quasi-regal status at the end of the ninth century were distinctive indeed. Boso of Vienne was only one member of that elite group upon whose help Charles the Bald was depending in Italy in 877. This group included Hugh the Abbot, a Welf, Bernard of the Auvergne, the son of Bernard of Septimania, and Bernard, marquis of Gothia, a 'Rorgonid'.[92] High birth and royal favour enabled them to outrank their peers and to monopolise certain offices. When Bernard of Gothia fell from power in 878 his *honores* were secretly carved up among a charmed circle which included Boso and Bernard of the Auvergne.[93] Such men did not threaten royal power; they were strong agents of a strong king. High administrative tasks and military commands were the traditional preserves

---

[87] Borgolte (1984a), pp. 191–2 and Borgolte (1986), pp. 150–6.
[88] Devailly (1973), pp. 83–4.   [89] Borgolte (1988), pp. 44–5.
[90] Airlie (1985), pp. 303–4; compare Theis (1990), pp. 212–16. Important analysis of Robert the Strong's entourage in K.-F. Werner (1959).   [91] Wickham (1981), pp. 141–3, 181–2.
[92] AB(3) s.a. 877, p. 216.   [93] AB(3) s.a. 878, pp. 229–30.

of favoured aristocrats and these men carried out such tasks on a large scale at a time of Viking and Hungarian attacks. In West Francia such men as Boso ran the 'provinces' of Charles the Bald's empire; in East Francia men such as the Liudolfings' ancestor Brun, who was also a royal brother-in-law, held the title of *dux* and died fighting a Viking host in Saxony in 880.[94]

Such men profited from royal service. In no sense can they be described as 'anti-Carolingian'. They would fight to retain their status and this could involve defying an individual king; their resistance prevented Louis the Stammerer from redistributing *honores* as he wanted to on his accession in 877.[95] But it was crises in Carolingian kingship itself that triggered the rise of the great magnates to royal status; that status had not been the target of the dynasty's followers. The death of Louis the Stammerer in 879 saw Boso's bid for a crown, but it was the deposition and death of Charles the Fat, the last legitimate adult male Carolingian, in the winter of 887–8 that heralded the appearance of the new rulers. The great men who had risen in Carolingian service now stepped in to fill the power vacuum. A contemporary identifies them: in Italy, Berengar, the son of Eberhard of Friuli, in Burgundy, Conrad, son of Rudolf, in Provence and Gaul, Louis(!), the son of Boso, and Wido, son of Lambert, in the northwest, Odo, son of Robert the Strong.[96] These men were the privileged members of privileged families. They had benefited from the success, not the failure, of the Carolingians' partnership with the aristocracy; to that extent they were the Carolingians' natural heirs. They do not represent a take-over by the aristocracy.[97]

What does explain 888 is the all-too-successful integration of Carolingians and aristocrats. This is not to downplay the crisis of legitimacy. Regino's contemporary account remains the most acute analysis; the 'kinglets' were indeed distinguished by high ancestry and power, but none had the royal charisma that would enable him to dominate.[98] Nevertheless Carolingian favour had marked these men out and the structure of the Carolingian empire itself was the foundation of the new powers in both East and West Francia. The new dukedoms and kingdoms reflected the old duchies and sub-kingdoms, the administrative regions, of that empire. The new powers were formed in old moulds.[99] The new potentates thus modelled themselves on their Carolingian predecessors. What else could they do? They failed to match their intensity of rule, in both east and west, as the history of the tenth century shows. But they bore a Carolingian stamp. Boso of Vienne's brother, Richard the Justiciar, who dominated Burgundy

---

[94] Boso, n. 83 above; Bruno: *AF(3) s.a.* 880, p. 94.   [95] *AB(3) s.a.* 877, p. 218.

[96] *AF(3) s.a.* 888, p. 116.   [97] Brühl (1990), pp. 373–4.

[98] Regino, *Chronicon s.a.* 888, p. 129.   [99] Brühl (1990), pp. 303–29.

from the 890s to his death in 921, was commemorated in a poem which not only praised his military achievements, important as those were, but also described him as 'the shield of the church', and provider of justice for his people.[100] It is a fine epitaph for a ruling elite.

[100] K.-F. Werner (1986). I am grateful to Rosamond McKitterick for editorial advice and patience and to Janet Nelson for critical encouragement.

CHAPTER 17

SOCIAL AND MILITARY
INSTITUTIONS

Hans-Werner Goetz

INTRODUCTION

SOCIAL history deals mainly with two topics: (1) social order, concerning the structure of a (former) society and the criteria for its subdivision, and (2) social bonds, informing us about the organisation of social groups and the mechanisms which regulate social life. The individual is always part of several, overlapping communities, from household and family, the village community, the community of serfs on estates, the parish congregation, or voluntary associations, to political orders, like tribes, peoples or nations. The integration of individuals into communities and their dependence on social bonds in the early middle ages can hardly be overestimated.

Before venturing to describe the little we know of early medieval society, it is wise to remember the problems of such an undertaking. These result mainly from a deep discrepancy between the evidence of our sources on the one hand and modern fields of interest on the other. Whereas modern historiography lays a distinct emphasis on social developments, writers of the early middle ages had not the slightest interest in social phenomena as we conceive of them. This means that the evidence is widely dispersed and is to be found in completely different contexts, in a distinct phraseology and under diverse aspects. Social structures, which alter slowly, were not perceived by early medieval authors and often were not even perceivable. Those medieval social 'theories' that are known to have existed are inappropriate to satisfy modern needs, whereas the social criteria of modern historians are widely influenced by sociological theories whose application to pre-industrial times still has to be proved valid (which one should not expect to be too successful concerning the middle ages). Moreover, in discussing former societies, we have to distinguish between the social theory or ideal, as expressed in laws and moral treatises, and the real manifestation, which is often neglected by our sources and only known from indirect and almost unintentional remarks. Considering all these problems, we have to distinguish (a) between the former and the modern mode of perception (social history in itself is a modern approach), (b) between former and modern terminology, and (c) between 'norm' and 'reality'. Nevertheless a great many uncertainties and questions remain, which increase, of course, if the society is seen, as it is here, in a European or Occidental context. Social history, more than any other branch of historiography, is therefore compelled to adopt explicative theories which often remain hypothetical. In spite of the great amount of research carried out during the last decades, it is only possible here to present a preliminary concept of early medieval society, open to criticism and improvement. My discussion will be largely restricted to the Frankish empire, which is the best-known area, but reference will be made to other regions wherever possible to make clear that there were vast geographical differences within Europe. It is evident from the preceding remarks that there are no particular sources for the social historian who finds evidence, however dispersed, in all kinds of sources: historiography and hagiography, liturgical, exegetical and dogmatical texts, polyptychs, letters and fiction. Most of the evidence, however, is provided by legal sources, particularly by the *leges* of the early medieval peoples, the Frankish capitularies, the ecclesiastical (canon) law and, of course, by charters and *formulae*. The following examples taken from sources are therefore meant rather as an illustration than as a representative survey. Such a survey would require discussions which are not possible in this context.[1]

THE SOCIAL ORDER

Problems in applying modern categories to social history: the character of early medieval society

The commonest way of dividing a society is by speaking of castes, classes, and 'estates' or 'orders' (*ordines*),[2] but none of these categories applies sufficiently to the early middle ages. Its society did not consist of *castes*, because its social groups were not completely distinct from each other and not primarily of religious origin; social structures were older than the introduction of Christianity, though they might have changed under

---

[1] I am extremely grateful to Rosamond McKitterick and Chris Wickham for helpful suggestions and discussions as well as stylistic emendations.

[2] The German term is *Stand*, for which there is no exact English equivalent. For further discussion see Bosl (1969a).

Christian influence. Nor can we talk of medieval 'classes' (in the sense of German *Klassen*), since medieval theories do not underline their role in the process of economic production and, at least in the early middle ages, there are no signs of a real class consciousness and a common interest of its members. More appropriately, we might describe early medieval society as being divided into social orders (*ordines*) which were, at least theoretically, divided on the grounds of birth and function and – more importantly – by legal distinctions. Moreover, medieval theorists recognised *ordines*. Yet modern historians are reluctant to acknowledge the existence of a society differentiated in such a way before the twelfth century, when we perceive an apparently stricter consciousness of social status which led to the definition of legal and social barriers; in the early middle ages, the nobility still did not form a 'legal estate'. Nevertheless, early medieval society was rather a society of estates than of classes or even castes.

Another possibility of dividing and describing a society and one which is more widespread nowadays is the method of *stratification*, which has the advantage of being applicable to every developed society consisting of vertically organised social strata. The normal custom is to distinguish between upper, middle and lower class(es) which again are subdivided internally. It is no doubt possible to distinguish between upper and lower classes (and perhaps a middle class of free peasants, too) during the early middle ages, but it is by no means easy to separate them distinctly. This is partly due to the lack of corresponding terms in medieval texts, but mainly to a multiplicity of different criteria.[3] Modern standards like profession or income had little or no relevance in the middle ages, when measures like rank (status) or authority were far more important. The significance of these, however, can hardly be estimated today. Social status was dependent on one's legal status, on custom and tradition, on social, political and ecclesiastical functions. It should be noted, however, that medieval thinkers did not make clear distinctions between these three aspects. Secondarily, within the classes, it was possibly also dependent on age and sex, and of course on rights of possession, power and domination, on the degree of rulership and of subjugation and on the rank of one's master (thus the king's serfs had a higher status than the serfs of a nobleman). All these criteria overlapped, making it impossible to create a clear-cut social order.

Under such circumstances, a description of early medieval social order cannot be more than a cautious one. If past periods of research chose to see medieval society as one of enormous stability, this seems true for medieval ideology, but it far from characterises reality. Social mobility was probably

---

[3] These problems are discussed by Mitterauer (1977).

not the pre-eminent feature, but one that should by no means be underestimated. Early medieval society is readily described as being homogeneous
with very little division of labour, which is true in comparison with late
medieval urban society, but this should not obscure the fact that social
distinctions and graduations did actually exist. We should, however, always
remember the fact that these depended on vague criteria of overlapping
systems.

Early medieval 'theories' of social classification

If we look at the early medieval 'social theories' first, we find that
contemporary authors, though they did not spend a lot of time reflecting on
social affairs, had at least a certain concept of social order, which was, of
course, a Christian concept. 'Society' as a whole was a Christian society
manifested in the 'church' (*ecclesia*), a term that must not be misunderstood
as the body of ecclesiastics in an institutional sense; by the 'church', all
Christians were meant. For Boniface, the *ecclesia* formed one body (*corpus*)
consisting of a large number of different 'members', such as authorities
(*officia*) and honours (*dignitates*).[4] This Christian society, according to
contemporary conception, was solid and characterised by its order – and
ordo was the central term of medieval social theory – arranging everything
according to measure, number and weight. This order was part of the divine
system of the world and, moreover, a reflection of the celestial order (which
was seen from an earthly perspective).[5] Medieval 'social theory' was thus
embedded in the vision of the world as a whole. According to the
Augustinian tradition, everybody was expected to have his or her proper
place and function.[6] On the one hand, this included the acknowledgement of
social inequality, of *a vertical division of society*. On the other hand, however, it
meant a certain respect for each function (an important aspect which should
not be neglected) and thus created *a horizontal conception of society* at the same
time; early medieval society had a hierarchical structure, but with regard to
its function (and, of course, to the prospect of salvation) each class was
equal, to be judged by God respectively by the accomplishment of its proper
charge,[7] thus contributing to universal welfare. Each subject, we learn from
a capitulary of Louis the Pious, was admonished to serve the king within his
proper place and order, thus participating in the realm and the king's office.[8]

---

[4] Boniface, Sermo 9, 1, *PL* 89, col. 860.   [5] Compare Dinzelbacher (1979).

[6] Compare Augustine, *De Civitate Dei* 19, 13: 'ordo est parium dispariumque rerum sua cuique
loca tribuens dispositio'.   [7] Compare Tellenbach (1972).

[8] *Admonitio ad omnes regni ordines* (*s.a.* 823/825), *MGH Cap.* I, no. 150, c. 3, p. 303: 'unusquisque
vestrum in suo loco et ordine partem nostri ministerii habere cognoscatur'.

When we look for more concrete attempts at social division, various concepts present themselves.

1. The most common social classification, which was based on the legal order as it is found in the Germanic laws as well as in other sources characterising the legal classes, was the following: (sometimes) the nobility (*nobiles*), (always) the freemen (*liberi, ingenui*), (mostly) the half-free (*liberti, lidi*) and (always) the unfree (*servi*).[9] The fundamental distinction was the one between free and unfree (*liberi* and *servi*), sometimes seen as a division of the whole society: *non est amplius nisi liber et servus*.[10]

2. A later system reflected a growing domination of an upper class (the nobility). This development sometimes, and especially in the Frankish capitularies, was reflected by a distinction between *potentes* and *pauperes*, meaning those who dominated and those who were dominated (*Herrschende und Beherrschte* in the terminology of Karl Bosl[11]). One has to recall, however, that *pauper* is an ambiguous term covering meanings from the conscious – religious – 'poverty' of the monks (*pauperes Christi*) to an economic poverty in our sense.[12] In a social context the term seemed to signify above all impoverished freemen lacking adequate shelter and care, as distinct from the *servi* who were unfree, but sheltered and cared for by their master.[13] The capitularies emphasised the duty of the *potentes* to protect the *pauperes*. This scheme displays the development of a consciousness of a society that was vertically divided, with differences among the free people regarding their power and rights.

A more widespread and more appropriate bipartition of early medieval society was to distinguish between lords and servants, *domini* and *servi*. This seems similar to the afore-mentioned classification, but it was more appropriate to characterise the relation of tenancy and dependence between a lord and his bondsmen (that is, the serfs). Once again, *servus* is an ambiguous term since it covered slaves and legally unfree as well as serfs. In both cases, certain terms, though specific in themselves, were chosen to refer to the mass of the society in a generalising manner, thus revealing a significant feature of social thinking: *pauperes* and *servi* were apparently perceived as the 'normal case' of subordinate people.

A third division of the whole society was made by distinguishing 'warriors' and 'peasants' (*milites* and *rustici*).[14] This did not mean, of course, that all people were either combatants or peasants, but it sheds a light on the normal agrarian character of early medieval society as well as on the fact that

[9] See pp. 457–61 below.   [10] *MGH Cap.* I, no. 58, c. 1, p. 145 (*s.a.* 801/14).
[11] Compare Bosl (1963).   [12] Compare Mollat (1978).   [13] Compare Goetz (1981).
[14] Compare Duby (1973).

the 'peasants' (who formerly *were* the soldiers) began to be excluded from military service from the end of the eighth century.

3. A very different system was to distinguish between ecclesiastics and laymen (*clerici et laici*), for ecclesiastical office in itself set the clergy apart both socially and legally. Theoretical definitions emphasised the different function (obviously on an equal level), as seen for example in a letter written by Pope Zacharias to the mayor of the palace, Pippin, in 747 which attributed the task of defending the country from the enemy to the (upper-class) laity, whereas priests and monks had to pray for the salvation of the others.[15] Sometimes we find a triple system distinguishing between clergy, monks and laymen, but with a growing approximation of monks and clergy concerning their way of life and their concept of themselves, the dual system became the standard scheme of Carolingian society.

4. It was not until the end of our period, once the clergy and monks were seen as one *ordo*, that, according to social theory, the laity began to divide into an upper and a lower 'class', the result being a (much discussed) triple division of the whole society into those who pray (*oratores*), those who fight (*bellatores*) and those who work (*laboratores*).[16] Its first appearance was in King Alfred's Old English version of *De Consolatione Philosophiae* by Boethius,[17] another version was developed in the school of Auxerre,[18] while its most famous manifestation is found in Adalbero of Laon's satirical poem written in the early eleventh century (1025/7) and addressed to King Robert II of France. The origins of this idea, therefore, seem to come from England and northern France. Further groups – such as merchants (*mercatores*) – were rarely included.[19]

5. There were, however, completely different ways of dividing the society according to theological or moral criteria (which we would not classify as being 'social' systems), for example, the distinction between the learned (*doctores*), the 'chaste' (*abstinentes*) and the married (*coniugati*),[20] or between *coniugati*, *continentes* and *virgines*,[21] between men and women, chosen and

---

[15] *Codex Carolini* 3, *MGH Epp.* III, p. 480; 'Principes et seculares homines atque bellatores convenit curam habere et sollicitudinem contra inimicorum astutiam et provintiae defensionem, praesulibus vero sacerdotibus adque Dei servis pertinent salutaribus consiliis et oracionibus vacare, ut, nobis orantibus et illis bellantibus, Deo prestante, provincia salva persistat fiatque vobis in salutem laudem et mercedem perpetuam.'

[16] Compare Oexle (1978); Duby (1978).

[17] Ed. Walter John Sedgefield, *King Alfred's Old English Version of Boethius* 17 (Oxford 1899), p. 40: *gebedmen, fyrdmen, weorcmen* (the king needs the help of all of these groups).

[18] Compare Iogna-Prat (1986).

[19] Compare Pseudo-Bede, *De Quatuor Ordinibus*, PL 94, cols. 556–7.

[20] Compare Jonas of Orléans, *De Institutione Laicorum* 2, 1, PL 106.

[21] Thus (later on) Abbo of Fleury, *Apologeticus*, PL 139, cols. 463/4, from about 994.

damned, rich and poor, young and old.[22] Such descriptions were normally part of a 'mirror of virtues' (*Tugendspiegel*) defining the duties or functions of different groups. They again display the idea of different groups distinguished by their functions, each being important and in a sense equal, though ranked in a hierarchical order consisting principally of ecclesiastical and secular offices (as in Walahfrid Strabo).[23] It is in this (functional) respect that certain 'professions' such as judges or merchants formed part of such systems.

Social reality in the early middle ages: some main features

With a knowledge of medieval social concepts, one can better understand the thought of these former times. These concepts do not lack any reference to reality,[24] but offer an ideal and often simplified reflection of actual social conditions. What they neglect is, primarily, a consideration of social mobility and change on the one hand, and of an interdependence and a superposition of different systems on the other. In reality, there is *not* such a distinct demarcation as reflected in theory. This means that the attempts to classify early medieval society that have been outlined above and are reviewed here once again with respect to their practical impact turn out to be much more complicated when we try to describe the real circumstances.

1. The distinction of different **legal classes** is so widespread and frequently documented throughout the west that it must be judged as one of the most important (perhaps the most important) social phenomenon of this period. In the course of the ninth century, however, legal class lost much of its importance to other factors, though this was only the beginning of a long development. Whereas the legal significance of being free meant, first of all, having full legal capacity in the count's court, it is not easy to value its social implication. The graduated *wergeld* and the attempts to retain one's liberty prove, however, such a portent: in the ninth century, land donations made by peasants in order to preserve their own liberty or that of their wives and children testify the continuing appreciation of being legally free (independent of the fact that these people had long since become dependants). Moreover, the period considered here was one of significant changes.

If we take a brief look at the single legal classes, we at once face the problem of whether or not there was a **nobility**, though this is a question

---

[22] Thus Boniface, Sermo 9, 1, *PL*89, col. 860.
[23] Walahfrid Strabo, *De exordiis et incrementis rerum ecclesiasticarum* 32, *MGH Cap.* II, p. 515.
[24] Compare Oexle (1987).

that concerns Merovingian more than Carolingian times.[25] Although some
tribal laws such as the Salic law do not testify to the existence of a nobility as
a legal class with a distinct *wergeld* – a fact that might be interpreted as the
absence of legal prerogatives, but which has also been understood as
indicating that the nobility was beyond the royal law and authority[26] – there
is absolutely no doubt of the existence of a social, economic and political
upper class which was called 'nobility' by Carolingian sources[27] and was
defined by birth (*maiores natu*). It is difficult to say whether the Frankish
noblemen were descended from an old Frankish nobility (*Uradel*) joined by
the Gallo-Roman senatorial aristocracy or, as were the Anglo-Saxon earls,
from a younger nobility risen in the ranks of the king's service, but it seems
most probable that the Carolingian nobility had several roots. In the ninth
century, members of the leading Frankish and Burgundian families, called
the 'Frankish imperial aristocracy' by German historians, were sent to the
new provinces east of the Rhine and south of the Alps, and again, in the
course of a few generations, they merged with the provincial aristocracy. In
principle, we must distinguish between these political leaders and the
broader social class of noblemen from which they were recruited. Nevertheless, it can be said that the early medieval nobility as a distinct class was more
or less identical with the political and economic leaders (the landowners) as
well as the secular and ecclesiastical office-holders. A few *leges barbarorum*,
such as the Saxon laws written down during the reign of Charlemagne,
defined them as a legal class as well. The *wergeld* of the Anglo-Saxon 'noble'
was six times the amount of a freeman's. Moreover, from the end of the
eighth century, the nobility gradually began to acquire the monopoly of
military service. Thus, on the whole, the nobility was a class above the
others. Though it is difficult to define its limits, in spite of the criterion of
being noble by virtue of birth, we have to assume that it was possible to
become noble on the grounds of one's outstanding reputation. It was also
possible to suffer a decline in social status and cease to be noble.

The ordinary **freemen** (*ingenui*, *liberi*) represented the standard class of the
Germanic laws and the addressees of the state authority. Legal decrees still
fostered the illusion that the freemen were the basic element of the early
medieval state, though the power had long since passed into the hands of the
nobility. The freemen still held their legal rights, including the right of
possession and of being free to move, but their original prerogatives to
attend and share the political and legal decisions of the public assemblies and

---

[25] For details, compare Airlie, chapter 16 above.

[26] Compare Karl Bosl, in *Handbuch der deutschen Wirtschafts- und Sozialgeschichte* (1971) I, p. 141.

[27] Goetz (1983).

to do military service were restricted more and more during the eighth and particularly the ninth century. According to one capitulary, a peasant had to possess twelve *mansi* to be an armoured horseman.[28] In spite of the impression created by the legal sources that there existed a homogeneous and influential class of freemen, the weakening of the social position of this group is one of the main characteristics of our period. The other main feature is the fact that this apparently homogeneous legal class actually was extremely heterogeneous in its social manifestation. There has been a long dispute concerning the character of these freemen. Former historians believed in the existence of one homogeneous Germanic class of 'freemen' (*Gemeinfreie*), a view that was abandoned by the discovery of a noble class. In the late 1940s and 50s, German scholars (such as Dannenbauer, Mayer and Bosl) thought that all freemen were 'the king's freemen', who settled on his land and were obliged to do military service, but were actually dependent tenants (Bosl ambiguously called them the 'free unfree'). Both theories have turned out to be wrong in so far as they presume a uniformity of this class that never existed.[29] The theory of the king's freemen rightly took into account the medieval system of domination, but it judged from the state of the ninth century when 'freedom' was beginning to lose its social relevance. There *were* 'king's freemen' (being nothing else than legally free people on the king's land and in the king's service), but they were different from 'ordinary freemen', perhaps socially elevated by the status of their lord, but complemented by other groups such as those living on church land, for example, or being completely independent. Freemen could be rich or poor, lords or vassals, dependent or independent, peasants, artisans or merchants. What is most important, however, is that we have to distinguish between legal and social status, especially when contrasting *ingenui* and *servi*: the state of being free in the early middle ages implied a legal uniformity, but a vast social diversity. In the eighth and ninth centuries, a freeman (in the legal sense of the word) could well be a tenant, though, of course, not all freemen were dependents. Legally, there was the possibility of liberation of a *servus* to full or restricted freedom by an ecclesiastical or a secular act (men so freed were called *tabularii* and *cartularii* respectively). There were other social climbers (such as *censuales* and *ministeriales*) who acquired a better economic situation and a higher rank as officials of the landlord, though they experienced no improvement in their legal status. In Christian Spain, particularly along the border, the distinction between free and unfree may

[28] *MGH Cap.* I, no. 44, c. 6, p. 123. For a full discussion of the meaning of the word *mansus* see Verhulst, pp. 493–5 below.
[29] Compare Müller-Mertens (1963); Schulze (1974); Schmitt (1977).

have become irrelevant in favour of a class of small tenants who had to protect the border, but were not allowed to move.[30]

The **half-free** (often called *liti* or *laeti*), a term for a multiplicity of different states between free and unfree, had a number of different origins: they might have derived from a subdued population (as in the case of the Saxons), or be fallen freemen, risen *servi* or children from unequal marriages, or, of course, the descendants of half-free parents. The half-free had a restricted legal capacity, but were personally dependent. Again the legal status covered a variety of distinct social functions.

Finally, the **unfree** had no personal legal capacity, but were owned by a lord who could punish or sell them or give them away (to a church, for example). They were distinguished from freemen by different (corporal) penalties and certain restrictions. Contrary to their position in Roman law, the unfree in the early middle ages tended to be treated more and more as people rather than as objects (though this is a question fervently discussed), and they were allowed to have a limited amount of property and were able to marry with the consent of their master. In the case of the unfree there is not the same discrepancy between legal and social status as for freemen because a person who was legally unfree was personally unfree as well. Socially, however, there could be great differences among the unfree, ranging from homeless servants, obliged to do their master a permanent service, to those who had an official function as stewards of a large estate (compare below).

Legal status depended on one's kinship to such a degree that, in extreme cases, one might be tempted to slay a relative who could endanger one's freedom by revealing his lower status.[31] Though the classes were separated legally and some laws, such as those of the Saxons, prohibited any intermarriage,[32] we normally find a toleration of mixed marriages. Despite their strict prohibition in the *Lex Salica* (tit. 98), these in fact seemed fairly widespread among peasants. The superior partner's status did not suffer as a result, as we are informed by the polyptych of St Germain-de-Prés from the early ninth century, according to which nearly 20% of all tenant couples differed in their legal status. Moreover, a great number of lawsuits[33] reveal that, despite the criterion of birth, the legal status of partners was not at all clear in certain cases: the status of a *servus* or a freeman was not unchangeable and often had to be inquired about legally.[34] The main problem in our period is, however, that the distinction of being free or unfree was only part

---

[30] Glick (1979), pp. 146–53.   [31] *MGH Cap.* I, no. 39, c. 5, p. 113 (*s.a.* 803).

[32] Compare Rudolf of Fulda, *Translatio s. Alexandri*, ed. Bruno Krusch, *Nachrichten der Gesellschaft der Wissenschaften zu Göttingen, phil.-hist. Klasse* (1933), p. 423.

[33] Epperlein (1969), p. 108–26.

[34] *MGH Cap.* I, no. 16, c. 8, p. 40 (*s.a.* 758/68); no. 138, c. 6, p. 276–7 (*s.a.* 818/19).

of a complicated social system and that, in the eighth and ninth centuries, it was no longer an indicator of the social *function* of the individual. Thus, to conclude, legal status was no more than *one* aspect of a social classification.

2. The legal system was particularly encroached upon by the new dependency within the manorial system (which is dealt with below): the *servus* could be a slave or a dependent tenant (with very different functions respectively). Regardless of the continuing existence of real slaves, especially in the Mediterranean countries, we may proceed from the assumption that the slavery of antiquity was replaced by the serfdom of the early middle ages. However, it is important to keep in mind that, serfdom being arguably a consequence of the manorial system, the categories of 'slave' or 'serf' are imbedded in different social contexts, that is: a legal and a 'manorial' context, though the sources use *servus* for both groups; there is no contemporary term for being a dependant except that such are occasionally referred to as having landowners as their masters. Most important for the characterisation of social reality was the distinction between masters and servants (reflected by the sources, as described above, p. 455) or between lords and dependants in the manorial system on the one hand and, among the peasants, between free (that is, independent and 'allodial') owners and tenants on the other. Although we have only indirect evidence and independent peasants (mostly in the form of documents that recorded them giving their lands away to churches), we have to proceed from the assumption that there still existed a great number of free peasants. There was also an increasing loss of freedom in favour of serfdom. A lot of freemen became tenants of a noble or ecclesiastical landlord, thus retaining their legal freedom, but actually losing their independence, partly owing to a crime or debt, partly by submitting themselves to a lord, partly by the effect of precarial contracts, partly by force, and at any rate, by the custom of paying taxes and rendering services to their lords. It is impossible to determine the scale on which men bound themselves to a lord by becoming his dependants, but it was sufficient for Carolingian capitularies to remark on the need to protect freemen.[35] In the ninth century, 'freedom' (as a social, not as a legal term) was becoming dependent on the amount and kind of services due to a lord. These were new criteria. They established a new order which in turn affected the legal status.

3. Apart from these systems, there can be no doubt about a growing tendency to separate the **clergy** as a distinct class, exempted (legally and socially) from the normal classification, and elevated by the fact that they were among the educated members of society and had easier access to

---

[35] *MGH Cap.* i, no. 39, c. 1, p. 114; no. 44, c. 16, p. 125; no. 73, cc. 2–3, p. 165; *MGH Conc.* iii, no. 41, c. 14, p. 422.

learning and scholarship. Yet, since the clergy could not be recruited by
birth because of the celibacy observed at least by the higher clergy,
ecclesiastics always remained within the social system, with strong secular
and spiritual connections between laymen and clergy in the early middle
ages. These connections are particularly evident between the bishops and
their (lay) families, a fact which we are able to determine from the collective
entries in memorial books, the existence of *Eigenkirchen und -klöster*
(churches and monasteries within a particular lord's jurisdiction and on his
estates conceived as family churches and monasteries), and the collective
family domination of a bishopric, especially in France where the see was
often regarded as part of the patrimony of a leading family.[36] Apart from
this, we have to keep in mind that there was a social hierarchy within the
clergy; bishops, abbots, and monks too with rare exceptions, came from
noble families, whereas priests may have originated from the free families of
the local society or, in rural seigneurial churches, had often formerly been
serfs who were set free according to the canonical prescription that the priest
should not be legally unfree.

4. The existence of a (more or less separate) clergy is a sign that legal and
social status was already encroached upon by the distinction of **functional
positions**. These did not correspond with the functional estates of the
contemporary social theories mentioned above, but resulted rather from
practical needs revealed in administrative documents. The most significant
characterisation is found within the manorial system by distinguishing
between tenants, that is, peasants holding a farm including their own house
(*servi casati*) and landless workers living in the manor (*servi non casati*) – with
intermediate stages, like the *haistaldi* in Prüm, whom Ludolf Kuchenbuch
defines as serfs with a small area of agricultural land, waiting to be loaned a
mansus.[37] Of these serfs, a small group entrusted with a special task or office,
the *ministri* or *ministeriales*, began to rise to more elevated positions, as
millers, foresters, priests attached to the estate, and, above all, as stewards in
charge of a manor (*villici*). In the ninth century these *villici* continued to be
serfs, peasants mostly (contrary to a widespread opinion that they originally
were *servi non casati*), but held a position from which they could rise into the
local nobility within the next two centuries. The existence of artisans and
merchants – within and outside the manorial system – leads us to a further
social differentiation according to profession; different terms for various
activities and occupations prove that early medieval society was already
characterised by a division of labour, though it remained, of course, a largely
agricultural society. Beyond such classifications, there were enormous social

<hr>

[36] Kaiser (1981).   [37] Kuchenbuch (1988), p. 255–60.

differences between members of the same 'class' or function, even among the tenants: peasants enjoyed a different status dependent on whether they held a 'free' or an 'unfree' *mansus (mansus ingenuilis et servilis)*, each having different duties. These duties were originally likely to correspond to the legal status of the tenant, but had completely lost such a connotation by the ninth century. It depended on the size of the family, the number of servants, the extent of their arable and other agricultural land, the amount of services and payments they owed the lord; the most favourable state was that of the *censuales* who rendered nothing but a money rent, or the *cerocensuales* paying a rent in wax to a church. It is not possible to define fixed groups (or strata) within the early medieval population, but there can be no doubt that there were profound social differences everywhere.

5. Not all people were respected as full members of society. Serfs, though they were dependent on their masters, were integrated in the social system because they had someone by whom they were cared for and sheltered. Others often termed **marginal groups** by social historians were not in such a position. These groups could be of a very different nature, with nothing in common but the fact that they stood outside Christian or Catholic society and therefore were despised in some way or other. This could derive from religious reasons, as in the case of the **Jews**, who seemed to live mainly in the big cities (not yet in closed quarters, but in increasing concentrations in certain urban areas) and who worked as merchants, artisans or physicians, and in southern Europe also as peasants. Though anti-Jewish statements (such as Agobard of Lyons' invectives from 822–8 directed against the influence of the Jews in the king's court) were still being made for religious and political reasons, Jews seemed on the whole to be tolerated; they lived under their own law, fostered their own religion, and had their own authorities, supervised by a *magister Iudeorum* who was appointed by the king. We have evidence of religious discussions and conversions in both directions, though these were despised on both sides. Ecclesiastical decrees were restricted to the prohibition of intermarriage, joint meals, offices giving Jews power over Christians and the possession of Christian servants, and certain Jews were even protected by the royal precepts (in exchange for a tax). The documents preserved refer, however, rather to single cases than to the whole 'race'.[38] Some Jews at least seemed to be wealthy. In these centuries, Jews were restricted in their social possibilities, regarded as foreigners and as a threat to the Christian cult, yet they were granted complete religious liberty and were not yet persecuted. Like the Jews, heretics were also regarded as outsiders for religious reasons, but unlike the

---

[38] *Formulae Imperiales*, nos. 30–1, *MGH Form.*, pp. 309–11.

HANS-WERNER GOETZ

Jews they were not tolerated; heretics did not, however, play an important role in the eighth and ninth centuries.

The **mendicants** were a completely different case of a marginal group; despised because they did not fit into an orderly society, they were at the same time needed as objects of Christian charity. In fact, one has to distinguish between the poor, whose income did not suffice, but who were nevertheless respected and explicitly sheltered by the king's protection, and those beggars who did not work properly and who were disapproved of. Carolingian capitularies tried to prohibit begging (in vain, of course) whereas an anecdote handed down by Notker the Stammerer seems to imply that sometimes, at least, beggars formed a community of their own with a 'beggar king' as their head.[39] At any rate, poverty was so widespread that there was a constant need for welfare which was institutionalised by the monasteries' care for the poor, the ill and the pilgrims (a continuation of the Merovingian *xenodochia*).[40]

A further marginal group is represented by strangers of all kinds: travellers and pilgrims perhaps or even merchants (who left their home only temporarily), and particularly vagrants and vagabonds who had no constant home at all. Minstrels and other 'dishonourable professions', including prostitutes, came very close to this group. In addition there were those who were excluded from society because of contagious diseases, particularly leprosy. And finally there were criminals and outlaws, damned by secular courts and free to be killed by anybody, or those excommunicated by ecclesiastical authorities and therefore prohibited from communicating with anyone. Once again, it is misleading to consider all these different people as being closely connected by classifying them as marginal groups. Each group was formed according to different criteria and was therefore socially distinct. What they had in common was the lack of 'normal' social bonds.

6. It is no doubt also somewhat misleading to deal with **women** as a distinct social group, because women were, of course, primarily part of their respective classes. Their position was first and foremost determined by their social status, and gender was only of secondary importance. Thus what has been said above is mostly true for men *and* women. Yet there were some common features that suggest that it might be wise to insert a small section on the social status of women as a whole. Though there were certain improvements in the course of the early middle ages owing to the influence of the church,[41] the common opinion is (not quite unjustly) that women were

---

[39] Notker, *Gesta Karoli* II. 21, ed. Hans F. Haefele, *MGH SRG* n.s. XII, 2nd edn (1980), p. 91.
[40] Boshof (1976; 1984).   [41] Compare e.g. Ketsch (1982).

completely subordinated, living in a patriarchal society and subjected to the dominion (*munt*) of their male guardian: 'Medieval society was essentially a society of men.'[42] Legal discriminations no doubt affected the social position of women with regard to their right to marry and to get divorced, to inherit or to be in possession: according to the Salic law (tit. 98 of the Carolingian version of 100 titles), a man was allowed to dismiss his wife, but had to respect her dowry. The same law (tit. 93, 6) excluded daughters from the inheritance of certain categories of land (*terra salica*), which was to be retained by the *virilis sexus*.[43] Southern European and southern German laws were less strict in these respects. Moreover, women were excluded from public and ecclesiastical offices. On the other hand, the laws protected them from importunities and injuries to an extent that reveals a great deal of respect; the *wergeld* for women, especially when they were able to bear children, sometimes was, as in the Salic law, three times higher than a man's *wergeld*, and the forfeit for blocking a woman's way when travelling exceeded the male counterpart by the same measure. The fine for cutting a girl's hair was higher than for cutting a boy's hair.[44] The suggestion that there was widespread infanticide of girls[45] is absurd and has widely been rejected.

Moreover, we are beginning to realise more and more that legal norms reflect moral ideals which may deviate completely from social reality. There is, for example, sufficient evidence showing that women (especially noble-women) did have possessions as well as the right to dispose of them. Women had their share in the household management or, in the case of the peasant family, in the domestic economy: the *opera muliebria* (such as textile work) formed a constitutive part of the peasant economy.[46] Finally, women played an important part in family politics and in 'family consciousness', even among peasant families,[47] in religious and cultural life (e.g. as nuns and canonesses[48] as well as founders of monasteries), and some women even gained a decisive political influence.[49] In other words, women participated in the early medieval 'ways of life' (*Lebensformen*) which included possibilities of self-development. It remains true, however, that the wife's position depended on the status of her husband. Marriage, therefore, was a kind of precondition to develop a certain standing and influence, thus resulting in the normal 'career' for women (and men), though there seem to have been a

---

[42] Compare van Houtte (1980), p. 144: 'Die mittelalterliche Gesellschaft war im wesentlichen eine Gesellschaft von Männern.'
[43] Compare also Chilperic's edict (561/84), 3, *MGH Cap.* I, p. 8, granting daughters hereditary rights only if there were no sons. See Ganshof (1962).   [44] See *Lex Salica* 26, 22, 33.
[45] Coleman (1974).   [46] See Herlihy (1990); Kuchenbuch, in Goetz (1991), pp. 139–75.
[47] See Goetz (1987).   [48] Baltrusch-Schneider (1985); Hochstetler (1991).
[49] Goetz (1991); Affeldt (1990).

certain number of unmarried people too. For noblewomen, religious life
was an alternative to marriage, but this should not be interpreted as a flight
from man's domination,[50] since the religious impetus was the same for both
sexes. Recent studies have shown that monasteries formed an integral part
of family politics,[51] which warns us against neglecting the mutual relations
between the 'secular' and 'spiritual life'. The latter was an alternative only
from the religious point of view. While marriage still was seen as a hindrance
to becoming a saint, socially, it enjoyed high esteem. A last point: early
medieval society, especially in the areas of household and marriage, was
based on a complementary collaboration between men and women, husband and wife, the latter being integrated into the economic 'family
enterprise'. At the same time, both sexes were expected to meet specific
needs, according to nature and ability, founded on the conception of a basic
difference between the two sexes. Textile work was considered to be the
typical *opus muliebre* (though, in reality, this was only one of many female
activities). Ideologically, at least, this distinction encouraged different
'spheres of the sexes', though current differentiations, such as inside and
outside, household and public, are ideological simplifications of the actual
sphere of activity. Woman's nature, connected with her frailty and weakness
– it is significant that some female saints developed a 'virility' through their
religion – demanded respect and protection, but could also be a barrier to
certain female activities. It did not, however, completely exclude female
power and influence, especially at the side of her husband.

If we try to characterise early medieval society from a modern point of
view, it was divided into a certain number of classes and strata, but at the
same time we can observe a clear distinction between an upper and a lower
class. The upper class (the nobility) still lacked the legal status and the social
implications it gained in later centuries, but was identical with the great
landowners and the political and ecclesiastical leaders: early medieval
society was a society dominated by and organised round the nobility.
Nevertheless it was an agricultural society, in which the beginnings of a
social and functional differentiation – into peasants, artisans, merchants and
officials – can be discerned.

SOCIAL BONDS

Whereas social order represented the theoretical and structural classification
of medieval society, social life was rather determined by the various
relations between people or classes, by natural or 'artificial' bonds between

---

[50] Thus Wemple (1981), pp. 190–1.   [51] Compare n. 46.

human beings and groups on an equal as well as on a hierarchical level. Following a categorisation devised by Gerd Althoff, we can distinguish between 'natural' bonds, such as those within the family, bonds resulting from lordship, and bonds of association as in membership of a particular group.

Family and kindred[52]

The family was the most natural and primary social institution at all levels of society. Moreover, the 'natural' family (that is household and kindred) served as a model for more sophisticated forms of political and social life: for the early medieval polity which was, in effect, governed by an extended household administration; for the monastery, conceived of as a community of brethren or sisters under the rule of a 'father' (the abbot) or 'mother' (the abbess); for the bishop and his *familia* of cathedral clergy; and also for the community of serfs on particular estates known as the *familia*.

The family in the proper sense of the word was, no doubt, of great importance in the early middle ages, though its influence and character are controversial issues. First of all, the term 'family' can have various meanings which are not congruent, though there are certain overlappings: It can mean (1) the **household** as a spatially limited unit of all those living under one roof and under the authority of one person (the head of the house) and including non-relatives such as servants and guests. In the early middle ages, the house was a relatively independent district of peace and law excluded from the public administration. The family can also represent (2) the **kindred**, members being united by kinship links, perhaps including the relations of the wife (the latter form is sometimes called *Sippe* in German research work). In relation to the household, the kindred may (a) be restricted to the **nuclear family** of husband, wife and children, sometimes extended to include lateral relatives, or (b) cover all relatives as the **extended family**. The crucial questions are: what was the social and political relevance of each of these different forms and what was the size and structure of the household family?

The **kindred** or **clan** as the whole body of relatives (*Sippe*) seems to have played an important part in earlier times when the *leges barbarorum* gave evidence of their legal function during the contraction of marriage, as oath-helpers at court, in distributing or receiving penalties and forfeits, as guardians of the morals of the family members, or as guarantors for

---

[52] See Duby and LeGoff (1977); Flandrin (1979); Schuler (1982); Murray (1983); Herlihy (1985); Gies (1987).

damages. First and foremost, however, it was *the* single institution on whose help and protection the individual could count in times of need. It seems that, in the eighth and ninth centuries, the kindred was still an acknowledged and respected unit in political, legal, social and economic life (though of a gradually diminishing influence), whereas it was no longer a settlement unit, not even in regions with a strong family tradition such as Wales[53] (there were, however, some exceptions, as, for example, in Lombard Italy or in certain parts of Spain where extended families may still have formed the basic land-tenure unit,[54] or in Celtic Scotland where the *cenél* implied kindred and a territorial unit at the same time[55]). It was by no means a typically Germanic institution as German historians used to think. In fact, by this time, the Germanic tribes, as Alexander C. Murray has shown, no longer had a 'clan structure' in a strictly agnatic sense but included bilateral relations as well.[56] The individual, however, was incorporated into his or her family and judged by his or her family origin.

The nuclear family was created by the act of **marriage**,[57] which at the same time was conceived of as a contract to combine two kin groups. It was on these grounds, and also to enlarge their possessions or raise their esteem, that kings and noblemen often contracted a 'political marriage'. In reaction to this, some laws prohibited marriages to women of other *gentes*, or partners of lower classes. In particular, the bride's family had to consent to the marriage, though the fact that the laws opposed a violent abduction of the bride implied that it was not extraordinary either to take a wife without her and her parents' consent or to elope with her. For the church, in spite of the ideal of virginity, marriage was considered a good institution that was in accordance with the will of God as long as it served procreation and helped to discourage fornication.[58] During the Frankish period, the church supported legal and official marriage (the so-called *Muntehe*) as the only kind of matrimony. This included a formal contract between two families and the gift called *dos* given by the husband to his wife as a surety in the event of his premature death. The so-called *Friedelehe*, however, was considered to be a concubinage. In the ninth century, it was no longer permitted to have two wives simultaneously, and the occasions for a divorce, too, became increasingly restricted until close kinship and affinity (including spiritual relationship) remained the only grounds. Thus the church helped the nuclear family to prevail as the norm. The household family was responsible for the education of the children, it had a certain religious function and, in

[53] Davies (1982), pp. 71–81.   [54] Glick (1979), pp. 141–6.
[55] Dickinson (1977), pp. 46–55.   [56] Murray (1983).
[57] Compare Ritzer (1962); Gaudemet (1963); *Il matrimonio* (1977); Mikat (1978); Gaudemet (1980).
[58] Compare Jonas of Orléans, *De Institutione Laicali* 2, 1, *PL* 106, cols. 167–70.

most cases, it formed an economic unit of production. According to canon law, the partners were equated morally and religiously, whereas secular law emphasised a patriarchal structure. The house was normally inherited by the eldest son who 'took home' his bride, whereas the wife played an important part in the family consciousness (for example by naming children after her or after members of her own family) and in the housekeeping (compare above p. 465). Ecclesiastical prescriptions also tried to influence sexual life by creating periods of continence (during menstruation and pregnancy, on fasting and festive days and on Sundays). According to the penitentials, only about ninety days a year (on average) remained on which copulation was allowed.[59]

The **size** of the family is one of the crucial issues of medieval social history. Earlier theories of the extended family as a unit of settlement have now generally been abandoned in favour of a recognition that the nuclear family constituted the household as early as the eighth century.[60] The average number of children in these households was between two and three, though the number of children was considerably higher in some cases and the household could be extended by a grandparent or by sisters and brothers of the parents. According to the information acquired from polyptychs, the average size of the peasant household depended on the extent of arable land (St Germain) and related closely to the number of livestock (Farfa).[61] We have to account not only for a high mortality rate among newborn children, but also for attempts at birth control and perhaps also for the system of 'fostering', i.e. giving the children away to other households from a certain age to be educated, in return for which the children served their host families. Contrary to some theories, children were wanted and were normally loved and cared for;[62] childlessness was regarded as an evil, and saints like Verena in Swabia were implored to help women give birth, especially to a son.[63] As far as people living in extreme poverty are concerned, however, there is evidence of the practice of abandonment of children.[64] The inheritance of landowning families was divided (according to rules differing from region to region); some of the sons founded their own families, whereas others were destined to become monks or clerics, and the daughters moved to the houses of their husbands. Thus, on the one hand, we see small households whose members still remain firmly integrated amongst their kin group. On the other hand, there are enough examples to prove that relatives did not always live in harmony or support each other.

---

[59] Flandrin (1983); Payer (1984); Brundage (1993).
[60] Mitterauer and Sieder (1982), p. 38–65; Guichard (1979).   [61] Ring (1979).
[62] Richard B. Lyman Jr., in de Mause (1974), pp. 75–100; Platelle (1982); Herlihy (1978); Schwarz (1993).   [63] Schmid (1977).   [64] Boswell (1984).

Another major problem concerning the early medieval family is the determination of the exact relationship of members to one another since these bore only one **name**, which was a Christian name and a 'family name' at the same time. In all classes, typical names, or in the case of the bipartite Germanic names at least one part of the child's name, were taken from the names of the parents or other relatives.[65] The name, therefore, is an indicator of a family consciousness. The importance of the female kinship resulted in changes of the names and shape of the family according to the standing of its members,[66] but it adds to the relevance of the wife for the social rank of the family. Family ties become visible in the frequent entries in confraternity books indicating the solicitude of the family for the memory of its dead members, regardless of their sex and status and even including ecclesiastical family members.[67]

The **family consciousness** or sense of family, though not limited to certain classes, found its most characteristic expression where the 'nobility' was concerned. The noble families tried to preserve their possessions, to raise their members to high positions and to guard their social rank by according marriages. The extent to which those ideals were also shared by the women is shown by Dhuoda's famous 'Manual', a book of advice written by a noblewoman (the wife of Count Bernard of Septimania) for her son William at a time when her husband was in exile (841–3).[68] Dhuoda identified herself with her family (and her husband), and she took care of its temporal and heavenly welfare;[69] she admonished her son to guard his religious belief, his proximity to the king and the family tradition. Whereas the early medieval noble family often lacked a permanent residence or at least an ancestral seat, it could produce a new centre in the form of a family convent. This was often founded and led by widows, daughters or younger sons, and here the monks, nuns, canons or canonesses prayed for the salvation of the family members.

In principle, the lower classes led a similar life and also created a family consciousness. Marriage seems to have been the rule even among the *mancipia* of the manors, who first needed the consent of the masters. In Lauterbach in Lower Bavaria, 41% of the servants are known to have been married, though the actual number would have exceeded this percentage.[70] Among the dependent peasantry, the *mansus* (probably equivalent to the hide, which, according to Bede, is the land able to support one family in

---

[65] Goetz (1985; 1987); Mitterauer (1993).

[66] Schmid (1957; 1959); Werner (1965); Leyser (1970); Schmid (1977); Fussen (1991). Bouchard (1986) doubts that the names were taken from other members of the wife's family than the wife herself.   [67] Schmid (1965).   [68] Wollasch (1957).

[69] Dronke (1984), pp. 36–54; Marchand (1984).   [70] Hammer (1983).

early Anglo-Saxon England)[71] was most often inhabited by one (nuclear) family; on the estates of the monastery of St Germain-des-Prés near Paris as well as the monastery of Farfa in northern Italy about 60% of the *mansi* were occupied by one family, whereas 5% were single households; others, however, in St Germain at least, were inhabited by up to five families, each having its own 'hearth' (i.e. house). The names of their members, however, imply a consanguinity,[72] thus revealing that the *mansus* had become hereditary in the ninth century (and probably even earlier), a fact confirmed by the capitularies. In Farfa, 15% of the households accommodated three generations, and 20% included sisters and brothers.

On the whole, the importance of the early medieval family should not be underestimated since it exercised public functions and (despite a great many family quarrels, especially among the nobility) served as a means of close relationship and integration. The fact that family consciousness normally exceeded other bonds is shown indirectly by the exceptional case of the Irish and Anglo-Saxon monks who left their families for reasons of a *peregrinatio* as an element of ascetism. On the other hand, the family still retained its influence over monasteries and other religious institutions. In the course of the eighth and ninth centuries, however, its importance was restricted, partly by public measures but above all by the growth of other social bonds overlapping these natural relations, such as the oaths between lords and their *fideles* creating bonds between members of the upper classes and the bonds of dependency between peasants and their lords.

The warrior retinue and 'feudal institutions'

The warrior retinue (*Gefolgschaft*) is a modern term for the Germanic *comitatus* (*truht* or *trustis* in Old High German), which describes a community of free warriors led by a highly respected person. It was established by a voluntary personal bond between the leader and his followers, who swore an oath of allegiance and fidelity and received subsistence in return. It can be traced back to the early history of the Germanic people (cf. Tacitus' 'Germania'), and continued to be a decisive element in all of the Germanic kingdoms of late antiquity. In fact, it was from such *Gefolgschaften* that the hordes and kingdoms of the Great Migration originated. Conflicts were very likely to arise between sworn fidelity to a leader and family bonds. The king's followers (like the Visigothic *saiones*, the Lombard *gasindii*, the Anglo-Saxon *gesiths* and *ealdormen*, or the Frankish *antrustiones*), some of whom were sent out to control or govern the country as officials, were widely respected,

---

[71] McGovern (1972). For *mansus*, compare above n. 28.   [72] Bessmertny (1984).

and protected by a higher *wergeld* than they would otherwise have had. The historical relevance of the Germanic *Gefolgschaft*,[73] however, has been seriously challenged.[74] Actually, the warrior retinue was not an exclusively Germanic institution but was also found in other European cultures. Beginning as a private bond, it often acquired a public character. It would be wrong, however, to insist that the whole state was based on such communities. During the eighth and ninth centuries, at least, it was not so much the warrior retinue as an institution that was important, but the form and content as well as the personal affinity it transmitted to other institutions, particularly what are often called feudal institutions (*Lehnswesen*). In some regions, such as Scandinavia, however, it survived as a public organisation; the raids of the Vikings, for example, are at least partly to be considered as marauding expeditions of such warrior retinues; the Scandinavian *lið* was a body of warriors in the same sense as the Germanic *comitatus*.[75]

Medieval society as a whole is often misleadingly characterised as a 'feudal society'.[76] In a technical sense, however, 'feudal' (a term corresponding with medieval expressions) denotes the relationship between a lord and his *fideles* or vassals.[77] The origins of this network of dependency, which culminated in the eleventh to thirteenth centuries in what has been described as the 'classic age of feudalism', lay in the Frankish kingdoms. It was based on several precursors and was in fact an amalgamation of various elements, namely the late Roman commendation into the *patrocinium* of a senatorial aristocrat, the (Germanic) warrior retinue with its obligation to faithfulness as described above, and in particular the Celtic vassalage, originally a bond creating servitude, but by and by one that changed into an individual relationship between freemen. These features established a personal element within the links formed by lords with their *vassi* or *fideles* whose special character lay in the increasing association of the oath with the originally independent institution of the benefice (the 'material' element). This was a lease of land under extremely favourable conditions in the form of a donation *per precariam*. A comparable form was the southern French and Catalan *aprisio*, a donation of land that had not yet been cultivated, especially land near the border. From the eighth century onwards, these elements grew together: the *beneficium* became the equipment of a vassal and was meant to secure his maintenance in return for his obligation to give counsel and help

---

[73] See above all Schlesinger (1953); more recently von Olberg (1983); Kienàst (1990); for the Visigoths: Kienast (1984).   [74] Kuhn (1956).   [75] Thus Lund (1981).

[76] For the history of this term which was created in the eighteenth century as a devaluating expression for the *ancien régime*, see Brunner (1959); Guerreau (1980).

[77] Principal works are by Bloch (1949), Boutrouche (1959), and Ganshof (1968b); for later times, Mitteis (1962). See now Reynolds (1994).

(*consilium et auxilium*), consisting mainly of military help (thus *miles* could come to mean 'vassal' too). Established possibly in the times of Charles Martel as a form of payment to his followers, the system spread particularly during the age of Charlemagne. The vassals received a high reputation which made it possible for noblemen to become vassals of a king, another nobleman or an ecclesiastical prelate.

Whereas the form (the act of commendation) and substance of the feudal system are well known (though one cannot always be sure of the beginning of certain rituals) it is more difficult to consider their expansion and success in regions outside the Frankish empire. In Italy, it was no doubt introduced by the Carolingians.[78] It seems, however, that the institution did not reach the British Isles until after the Norman Conquest, or Spain before the eleventh century. Other lands, such as Poland or Hungary, remained untouched by the feudal system, although comparable social bonds existed there. The period considered here saw but the beginnings of 'feudal institutions', which were far from being a phenomenon of the whole west.

In the Frankish empire, however, 'feudal institutions' developed a deep relevance as the dominating social bond between noblemen, and they took on great influence in institutional and military life because the king's officials were bound to him as his vassals and the office itself was gradually considered to be a fief. While under Charlemagne feudal tenures were held for life, they became hereditary as from the ninth century and ultimately merged with private property. Multiple vassalic bonds in the western parts of the realm undermined the efficiency of the system, while the fief was no longer seen as a reward but became a precondition of being a vassal. The fief still secured a social bond among the leading classes, whereas, institutionally, the mass of their followers, dependants and serfs were separated from the king, who could only reach them by way of his vassal.

Landlordship and estate management

The **manorial system** (as a rough translation for the French *seigneurie* or the German *Grundherrschaft*), which was the other predominant economic institution of the time, was of comparable or even greater importance as a social bond and, at the same time, the substantial way of life of a rural community.[79] Like vassalage, it created a social bond, but this time not between freemen and noblemen, but between the leading class of landowners (the lords or masters) on the one hand, and their servants (of all

---

[78] Compare Keller (1979) pp. 303–42.

[79] The economic aspects are dealt with below by Verhulst, chapter 18; for rural society compare Wickham's contribution, chapter 19 below.

ranks), tenants and manorial serfs, on the other (compare above, p. 461).
The basic assumption is that the king, a church or a nobleman was lord over
the people who lived and worked on his land. The term (*seigneurie*,
Grundherrschaft), however, is a modern expression[80] for a certain kind of
social, economic and administrative organisation, particularly the combination of a demesne on the one hand and tenures held by dependent tenants
on the other, both grouped around a *curtis* (manor) as the administrative
centre and, in smaller systems, the residence of the landlord. (This is the so-
called 'classical' or bipartite form of the manorial system.) The tenure was a
kind of rural fief, the material bond between the peasant and his lord, which
always remained the property of the landowner, but was more and more
considered to be hereditary: the capitulary of Pîtres from 864 gives evidence
of a *mansus hereditarius*.[81]

The origins of the manorial system are rather controversial and by no
means homogeneous. In some aspects (such as the *patrocinium* and the
colonate), they go back to late antiquity, a time in which they were not,
however, predominant; moreover, a straight line of unchanged continuity
up to the early middle ages does not seem to exist. The bipartite system is
considered to be a creation of the king's estates in the northern parts of
France during the first half of the seventh century,[82] as it was in this region
that it is documented for the first time. While in Merovingian times the
manorial system existed, but was no more than one form of land organisation, in Carolingian times it no doubt became the decisive rural institution,
manifesting itself in a number of different ways.

Landlordship was sometimes complemented by the possession of a rural
Eigenkirche, jurisdictional rights and the domination of whole villages. The
lord, therefore, was a kind of public authority for his dependants, though his
dominion was far from being a closed or coherent territory, and a village
was often divided among several great landowners. Problems arose when
serfs belonging to different lords married, and laws were consequently made
to regulate the lord's rights held over the offspring.[83]

Recent research, particularly on the ninth-century West Frankish kingdom, has been concerned more with the economic than with the social
aspects of the manorial system.[84] Socially, landlordship and estate management had a number of different roots which become apparent when studying
the lord's rights. These derived partly from his position as head of the
household, partly from a proprietorial control exercised over the unfree

---

[80] Schreiner (1983).   [81] *MGH Cap.* II, no. 275, c. 12, p. 337. Compare also p. 471 above.
[82] Thus Verhulst (1966).   [83] *MGH Cap.* I, no. 58, c. 1/8, pp. 145f.
[84] Bleiber (1981); Verhulst (1985); Rösener (1989); Kuchenbuch (1991); Devroey (1993); Elmshäuser and Hedwig (1993); a critical survey of recent research is given by Morimoto (1988); for
the monastic seigneurial system see Kuchenbuch (1988).

(called *Leibeigenschaft* in German), partly from a patronage-based dominion held over freemen, and probably partly from the use of force to suppress free peasants. All of these groups became dependants and, later on, serfs of the lord, independent of their legal status (compare above, p. 461). United by their subjection to the same lord, they all were joined in a body called the *familia* of the lord who rendered them protection and maintenance. The latter was provided either by living in the manor (*servi non casati*), or by holding land by tenure (*servi casati*) for which the tenant was obliged to pay dues and render the lord his services: the *mansus* was the administrative and economic unit of the duties owed to the lord and the social unit and the living space of one or more peasant families (compare above, pp. 470–1). In the eighth and ninth centuries, in some regions, lords increasingly transformed their demesne into *mansi* or divided these into several parts.

The *familia* can be classified into several groups according to their functions as servants, peasants or officials (*ministeriales*) (compare above, p. 462), and also as artisans and merchants. The peasants (*servi casati*) could be former freemen or *servi* who were provided with a *mansus*. Initially, *servi* and *liberi* (or *coloni*) were charged with different obligations which, however, might be gradually adjusted to each other. In 861, sixty people claimed to be *liberi coloni* who therefore were not obliged to render low-status services.[85] It should be noted that these charges were *not* unalterable. Yet there were vast differences among the tenants (compare above, pp. 462–3).

The ideal balance of the estate management does not, of course, mean that there were no social tensions: we have sufficient evidence of bondmen's attempts to reduce or deny their lord certain services, generally or individually, by legal (in court) or illegal actions, and of attempts to run away from one master generally to take refuge with another.[86] In 828, for example, the *coloni* of a northern French village called *Antoniacum* refused to pay their dues and services because their parents had not paid them either.[87] As far as we can see, these attempts, which almost always referred to customary rights, were made in the belief that their cause was a just one. There is, however, absolutely no indication of general opposition to landlordship and the manorial system as such. A lord could claim his right to a fugitive successfully, but he had to maintain it personally.[88] If he neglected to do so, this might have caused social changes and, contrary to the lords' interest, led to increased mobility on the part of the peasant populations.

While recent research allows us to give an adequate description of this type of estate management as a model, we are not at all clear about its

---

85 *Recueils Charles II le Chauve* II, no. 228, p. 7.
86 For the evidence see Epperlein (1969), pp. 29–41.
87 *Recueils des actes de Pépin I et de Pépin II. Pépin I*, no. 12, pp. 46–7.
88 Cf. *Pactus Legis Salicae* 90, 2, *MGH Leges nat. germ.* IV: 1, p. 252.

expansion and its regional diversities. There are claims that it did not even exist in southern France, where more traditional forms of social and economic life persisted;[89] in most regions of Spain, freemen did not seem to become dependent upon lords until the ninth century,[90] and the manorial system in England, of course, is only faintly documented in pre-Conquest times, though modern historians tend to think that its origin might be earlier.[91] A bipartite system in which a lord could require services on his demesne of peasants whom he had provided with a house and land is to be found as early as in Ine's law (688/726, clause 67), and in Wales a distinction was also made between *servi* and dependent tenants.[92] There is no doubt, therefore, that we find rights of lordship exercised over the unfree and peasant population everywhere, creating social bonds that, in my opinion, can be called a 'manorial' or even 'seigneurial system' (which are modern terms anyway), though its actual manifestation displayed a great variety of social, administrative and economic forms.[93] East of the Rhine, for example, the percentage of the *servi non casati* seems to have been higher than in the western parts of the Frankish kingdoms. Thus while the 'classic' bipartite organisation only spread gradually, different forms of estate management established the basic social bonds in most parts of early medieval rural society.

Community life and local associations

The household and manorial systems were more than mere social bonds in so far as they at the same time represented forms of community life within a certain social context: on the one hand the family, on the other the seigneurial *familia*. The latter, however, formed a community only in a limited sense, as its members were normally dispersed over a wide area. The rural population lived in the village community,[94] which might but need not have been a conglomeration of dependants of the same *familia*. Normally, this community comprised smaller landlords, independent and servile peasants, servants as well as artisans, the village priest and others, and in some cases it could reach a respectable size of several hundred houses. Thus the village community was in itself a graded 'class society' which called for regulations. In the early middle ages, it was not yet established as a rural community in the institutional sense of a local authority, since it belonged to

---

[89] Compare, for example, the works of Magnou-Nortier (1981–4).
[90] Dufourcq and Gautier-Dalché (1976), pp. 24–6.   [91] Loyn (1962), chapter 19, pp. 163–98.
[92] Davies (1982), pp. 67–71.   [93] Verhulst (1983).
[94] For this aspect, see Wickham, chapter 19 below.

one or several lords. Initially, indeed, a terminological difference between rural individual and group settlement did not exist. Yet the village community undermined the bonds of lordship and should be considered as a kind of community of neighbours – *vicini* is the term used in legal sources – whose members shared common interests and were disposed to mutual help; in a famous article of the Salic law called *De migrantibus* (tit. 45), for example, the *vicini* were granted the right to refuse to consent to anyone settling down in their village.

'Urban' communities ˙also began to take shape at this time. These consisted of a more or less dense population of craftsmen and tradesmen rather than of peasants (though it is often difficult to draw strict dividing-lines between towns and villages).[95] In the episcopal sees, of course, administrative officials also formed an important part of the population. All of these people, however, were dominated by kings, bishops and other lords. A completely different and in some ways alternative communal way of life relevant for both sexes, though separated, was the religious variety: a monastic life dictated by strict rules and with a regulated daily routine, which became increasingly dominated by the rule of St Benedict.[96] It cannot be said that entering a convent in the eighth and ninth centuries was a voluntary decision since most monks, nuns, canons and canonesses were destined for a religious life by their parents while they were children.

For the individual, all these communal ways of life were predestined by one's social origin or affiliation. We also have evidence of voluntary local associations based on co-operative bonds. These were constituted by joint banquets (*convivia*) and oaths,[97] and were founded on friendship (*amicitia*) and alliances (which were both of considerable political and social import). Such bonds, which were long neglected by social historians in favour of households and local communities, are known under different names, such as *consortium* or *confratria* and, above all, *coniuratio*, a term that reveals the fact that these bonds both were constituted by an oath and also might have formed a kind of conspiracy. In fact, these *coniurationes* were forbidden by Frankish capitularies. The term, however, seems to be a self-denomination.[98] The early medieval *coniurationes* have been widely discussed and interpreted recently as 'guilds' – according to the Old German term *gildonia*, which was used for the first time in the capitulary of Herstal in 779.[99] These 'guilds' were unions of different kinds – there were, for example, *coniurationes clericorum* as well as *coniurationes servorum*. According to Otto Gerhard

---

[95] For the economic aspects of urban community life, see the contribution of Verhulst, chapter 18 below. [96] This aspect is dealt with below, chapter 23.
[97] Althoff (1990), pp. 85–133. [98] Alcuin, *Ep.* 291, *MGH Epp.* IV, p. 449.
[99] *MGH Cap.* I, no. 20, c. 16, p. 51.

Oexle,[100] however, 'guilds' were first and foremost local communities uniting different legal classes and including clergy and women. It is likely that they also served a religious purpose or at least were held together by religious rituals. They were not unions of certain professions; the medieval guilds of merchants and the corporations of artisans came later (the first reliable evidence of a merchants' guild is from the eleventh century), although in southern Italy the *scholae* of artisans may be considered as followers of the ancient *collegia*.[101] Their function seems to have been a legal one (as guarantors of peace and law); their particular purpose, however, was to provide mutual help to members, as these were bound by an oath to assist each other and, contrary to the natural and seigneurial bonds, considered themselves equal. Sometimes they organised a defensive body to ward off alien intruders (like the Vikings). What it was they opposed and why they were attacked by the authorities can hardly be explained with any certainty. They were not, however, conspiracies of dependants opposed to the lords, since the lords themselves had to be warned by the king not to support them.[102] It is possible that church officials objected to certain doubtlessly religious forms of community life that were strongly suggestive of pagan rituals, but it seems more likely that these 'guilds' were opposed by the authorities because they traversed the official bonds and were regarded as a rival to the parishes as well as to the local authorities. These guilds, therefore, give evidence of the existence of co-operative social bonds.

A last point to be mentioned is the system of **hospitality**, which provided social contacts and liabilities rather than bonds.[103] This was understood in a wide sense in the middle ages and included social welfare and nursing. Though in the southern parts of Europe taverns may still have existed from ancient times in addition to the so-called *xenodochia*, which served as poorhouses, pilgrims' inns and hospitals at the same time (compare above, p. 464), there is no sign of any professional hospitality or public welfare. Both of these services came to be offered by the monasteries. The famous plan of St Gall displays three distinct districts reserved for these charges inside the monastery: a poorhouse, a guesthouse for noble visitors, and a boardinghouse for monks. Welfare and hospitality were considered first and foremost to be a responsibility of the family. It is widely assumed that there was a common obligation to receive strangers and pilgrims as guests, but it is more likely that hospitality was considered a virtue rather than a duty,[104] except for charges of hospitality towards one's own lord. Once a guest was

---

[100] Oexle (1981; 1985); Althoff (1990), pp. 119–33.   [101] Barni and Fasoli (1971), pp. 341–3.
[102] *MGH Cap.* I, no. 148, c. 7, p. 301 (*s.a.* 821).   [103] Peyer (1983; 1987).
[104] See Hellmuth (1984), regarding the Scandinavian hospitality system.

accommodated under one's roof, however, the host was responsible for his protection. Nevertheless, hospitality merely created temporary bonds.

People living in the early middle ages were born in certain social conditions and in social bonds that in some cases could change, but which rather expanded by virtue of additional voluntary associations. Men and women needed these bonds in order to lead a life of security, protection and order. It is exactly this element that was responsible for the fact that early medieval society and the early medieval state were characterised by personal associations. The different bonds overlapped and interfered with each other, causing social conflict and tension, which in turn led to social mobility and change. But they always remained a characteristic feature of the period.

SOCIAL ASPECTS OF MILITARY INSTITUTIONS

Military institutions are a vivid reflection of social order and social change, particularly in these centuries. Conscription into the army is dependent on social and political conditions and social and legal status, but is also able to affect the social hierarchy. The following remarks are concerned with the social aspects of military institutions rather than with the art of warfare. For this reason, they can be dealt with briefly by referring to the preceding passages.

At the beginning of the period considered here, military institutions still maintained something of their traditional appearance. Military service was obligatory for all freemen within the realm. Principally, freemen and soldiers were identical groups (which is reflected by the Lombard term *arimanni* in the sense of 'armymen'); thus, the public assembly was at the same time an assembly of the army. In the Frankish kingdoms, the army was levied every year at varying locations in spring. On a local level, the soldiers were levied and commanded by counts, margraves, dukes and other officials, whereas the army as a whole was led by the king.

In the eighth and ninth centuries fundamental changes are known to have taken place within the armed forces, particularly in the Frankish empire. The frequent campaigns of Charles Martel, Pippin and Charlemagne and, in later years, the civil wars of Louis the Pious' sons and the invasions of the Vikings, Hungarians, Slavs and Saracens required new and stricter structures, and they were an enormous burden for the peasant warriors, particularly since the soldiers had to provide their own food. A great many chapters in various capitularies are concerned with the army and its equipment.[105] It was still the freemen that were conscripted into the army, but conscription was now linked with property ownership. A capitulary from the year 807, for example, obliged all freemen who possessed three or more manses to do military service personally; one year later this measure was raised to four manses. All those who owned less had to serve as soldiers alternately: for every four manses one soldier had to be provided.[106] This did not yet mean an abandonment of the freemen's obligation to do military service, but displays the expenses it incurred. Moreover, a change in the structure and leadership of the army is apparent from the time of Charles Martel, but may have begun even earlier; whereas the early medieval army consisted mainly of footsoldiers, there was a constant increase and finally a prevalence of mounted warriors from the sixth to the ninth centuries (after the introduction of the stirrup in about 600), which meant, of course, because of the need to provide horses and fodder, a further rise in costs and a growing social differentiation. It was particularly the noblemen and their vassals who served on horseback. Gradually, the army changed from a general levy of all freemen to a mounted contingent of vassals commanded by powerful noblemen. This development, which began in the early eighth century, culminated in the tenth century; by that time, military service had become feudal service and a duty of the vassals. By the end of the ninth century the king no longer levied all the freemen, but only his vassals, including his officials and ecclesiastical leaders, particularly bishops and abbots, who were explicitly exempted from the prohibition against ecclesiastics performing military service.[107] This marks the (faint) beginning of knighthood and of a social distinction between noble-born soldiers (*milites*) and peasants (*rustici*).[108] In the ninth century, however, there were still remnants of a universal levy on all freemen, which is evident, for example, in the military tax imposed upon those tenants who were legally free. On the other hand, this tax is proof of a discharge from military service by a rural due owed in money or natural products. This change in military institutions again corresponded to the social order: the decline of the free peasants and the rise of noblemen and vassalage. In later centuries, when peasants were to become disarmed and defenceless, military institutions would continue to fit the social order.

---

[105] Compare *MGH Cap.* I, no. 46, c. 5, p. 131; no. 64, c. 12, p. 153; no. 74, c. 5, p. 167 (and many more).   [106] *MGH Cap.* I, no. 48, c. 2, pp. 134–5; no. 50, c. 1, p. 137.
[107] Prinz (1971).   [108] Nelson (1989).

CHAPTER 18

ECONOMIC ORGANISATION

Adriaan Verhulst

DEMOGRAPHIC DEVELOPMENT

THE population of western Europe appears to have increased from the mid-seventh century onwards. Archaeological investigation of two burial fields near Cologne in Germany allows a comparison between the sixth and seventh centuries, and points to an increase in population in that part of the Rhineland of up to 60% in 100 years. This is not particularly high, since in Alemannia an extraordinary increase of three to six times the population of the sixth century is probably due to external causes such as immigrations. Pollen analyses in various areas of Germany such as the Rhön and Eifel show a clear increase in grain pollen from the seventh century onwards. This points to the extension of arable land, which is also borne out indirectly by some admittedly rare and isolated texts from the seventh century.

The earliest more explicit written records of land clearance concern the surroundings of Fulda in Thuringia during the second half of the eighth century. Particular mention is made of well-delimited virgin lands called *porprisum*, *bifang* or *captura* in which estates and farms were established by reclamation of new land.[1] There were twelve in the eighth century and thirty-six in the first thirty to forty years of the ninth century. These clearances were not primarily the work of the abbey but of laymen who subsequently donated the *bifang* to the abbey for further extension. Elsewhere in Germany, more particularly in southwest Germany and especially in the Odenwald, numerous reclamations in the form of *bifang* or *captura* are mentioned in the records of the abbeys of Lorsch and Fulda in the ninth century. Again they were, in a first phase, the work of laymen who may be characterised as entrepreneurs. Despite these examples mainly being located in Germany, the phenomenon is so widespread in western Europe that it cannot reflect local coincidences.

---

[1] Lohrmann (1990), pp. 110–12.

In some regions of western Europe, however, the presence of large areas of arable land is probably responsible for the absence of written documents on new reclamations. Some of them, moreover, had, as early as the beginning of the ninth century, very high population densities. The area of Paris, the Île de France, is often mentioned as an example in this respect, partly because demographically useful data can be found in the famous polyptych of Abbot Irmino of the abbey of St Germain-des-Prés, which dates from shortly before 829.[2] On the basis of this document, population densities of thirty-nine inhabitants per square kilometre have been calculated for a number of abbey estates in the southern area of Paris, and appear to be indirectly confirmed by high densities of approximately thirty-four inhabitants per square kilometre on some estates of the abbey of St Bertin in the vicinity of St Omer. Concerning the latter, however, Schwarz has proposed a reduction to an average of twenty inhabitants per square kilometre.[3] A similar figure has been advanced for the most densely populated area of Friesland (Westergo) around 900.[4] It is probably the case, however, that apart from these privileged areas (both demographically and as far as documents are concerned), the population density in many areas, even though they had been largely reclaimed, was much lower, and probably from four or five to between nine and twelve per square kilometre. There is general agreement on one thing in this respect: the population density and degree of arable could vary largely from area to area and even from locality to locality, according to the age of occupation, the relative fertility and productivity of the soil, and types of land use. In opposition to the areas of southern Gaul and the Île de France in the north, to the Rhine/Moselle area, to the area between Scheldt and Dender in Belgium and others, there were thinly populated regions such as southwest and western France (Maine) or the northern half of Belgium.

More interesting and more reliable than these largely hypothetical estimates of population densities in certain areas are some recent attempts, exploiting modern demographic methods, to investigate Carolingian polyptychs from St Germain-des-Prés for the Île de France and from St Victor de Marseille for Provence.[5] Fertility coefficients, for example, have been derived from the proportion of adults to children. They make it possible to assume that the population of certain estates in the eighth and ninth centuries doubled in a time span of half to one and a half centuries. A doubling in 100 years, that is a growth of 1% per year, is accepted by several authors and probably occurred from as early as the seventh century.

There is less agreement on the answer to whether this growth, which can

[2] *Pol. Irm.*, ed. Longnon, VIII, xv. Zerner (1979), pp. 17–24.   [3] Schwarz (1985), p. 37.
[4] Slicher van Bath (1965), pp. 100–3.   [5] Toubert (1986), pp. 336–41.

be considered moderate to considerable, was a continuous process or whether it was interrupted by times of crisis. Many authors refer in this respect to the numerous famines which struck the central areas of the Carolingian empire in the northern half of France at the end of the eighth and the beginning of the ninth century. These famines were so severe that they forced Charlemagne to take general and drastic measures in 794 such as setting maximum prices for bread and grain, introducing new units of measurement, weight and currency, establishing help for the needy and requiring the saying of prayers in churches and monasteries.[6] Usually, however, these famines are interpreted as accidents of growth, as expressions of a disproportion between a rapidly growing population and a rigid economic structure, especially on the large estates, where the so-called overpopulation of the *mansus* is in this respect referred to, both in the Île de France and in parts of northern Italy.[7] It is, however, not established that these consecutive famines had cumulative effects as was the case in the fourteenth and fifteenth centuries. There may have been rapid recovery after a famine, which in turn could have been the result of the dynamic qualities of a young population. A sensitivity to crises, more particularly to grain crises, and the rapid and dynamic reactions afterwards, may be responsible for the apparently somewhat chaotic and uneven growth. Such a characteristic of early medieval demographic evolution is probably partly responsible for the fact that these fluctuations cannot be determined or delimited chronologically.

AGRICULTURAL TECHNIQUES

During the eighth century clear indications appear in written sources that in large parts of western Europe, from Switzerland to southwest Germany, northeast France and the south of Belgium, two kinds of grain instead of one were grown in regular rotation side by side during the same harvest year, namely, winter-sown corn and spring-sown corn. Every third year the fields that had produced spring corn the year before were left lying fallow for a year, before being sown, after two ploughing turns in June and October, with winter corn, followed in the subsequent spring by the sowing of spring corn. This regular fallow system superseded in many areas a system with one grain crop and with longer, three-year, periods of fallow, that in its turn had replaced an irregular fallow system, in which the soil was used for growing the same crop for several years in a row before being left fallow for a similar

---

[6] *MGH Cap.* I, no. 28, c. 4. Verhulst (1965), pp. 175–89; Devroey (1987), pp. 68–92.

[7] Toubert (1990), p. 64.

length of time. These fields were allowed to grow wild while adjacent plots were burnt off and brought into cultivation. This irregular primitive system had disappeared almost everywhere in Europe by the eighth century. The new three-year crop rotation system, which had originated in the eighth century or so in various places between the Alps and the North Sea, made the cultivation of two different and complementary grain crops possible: one, spelt, rye and wheat, was meant for human consumption as grain for bread, while the other, mainly barley and oats, was used as animal feed. All these grains had the advantage of being sown and harvested at different times (autumn and spring) thus distributing field work more evenly and lessening the risk of a failed harvest. It was even possible in spring to sow a field with spring corn in those plots where the winter crop appeared to have failed. The proportion of fallow land was, furthermore, reduced from at least a half to a third, which led to a more intensive use of arable soil and a larger volume of production. This important innovation can first be observed with certainty in the eighth century on the demesnes of large ecclesiastical landowners, cultivated directly for the landlords by dependent farmers. The services the tenants were required to perform on the fields of their lord – ploughing, sowing, harvesting – were entered meticulously in polyptychs and other kinds of descriptions of the landowners' rights and goods.[8] These records make it possible to confirm the existence of the three-course rotation system. The texts, however, are unfortunately far less explicit about plots cultivated by farmers for their own benefit. Although dependent farmers most probably knew the three-course rotation system, because their services were organised in accordance with it, it is not certain that they were able to apply it themselves to their own land, even if they wanted to. The system implies that all plots that are cultivated according to it undergo the same kind of tillage at the same time and that once they have been sown they are not indiscriminately accessible to humans or animals. This is most easily achieved when all plots are located within the same field complex and are cultivated by and for the benefit of one owner, who is not obliged to take into account other farmers and neighbours. This was true for the few larger complexes called *culturae*, of which the demesne of a large landowner usually consisted. The plots of individual farmers, however, were usually well clear of the lands of the demesnes but were often intermingled with each other, which meant the three-course system could only be applied if all involved were in agreement. It may be that development of the village community in the eighth and ninth centuries would have been too limited for the community to play a role as regulating authority of

[8] Schroeder-Lembke (1961; 1969); Hildebrandt (1988).

farming practices and achieve such agreement and consensus.[9] This is probably also the reason why a clearly visible topographic division of arable land into three-field complexes can only have been applied (and not even generally at that) on the demesne lands in so far as they consisted of one or more of such complexes. This was not yet the case in all areas in the ninth century. Those scholars who presumed grouping in three units for those demesne lands that consisted of numerous complexes (*culturae*), even if their total number were a multiple of three, therefore, were wrong. The estate of Prüm in Mabompré in the Belgian Ardennes, for example, consisted of fifteen scattered *culturae*.[10] In fact, these were only sown with oats which, since oats were at that time still considered to be a forest crop, points to their recent cultivation after forest clearance. The terms *zelga*, *campus*, *satio*, *aratura*, used in many contemporary texts in connection with the three-course crop rotation systems, should therefore not yet be interpreted as topographic-geographic subdivisions of agricultural land, but merely as a reference to arable lands of the demesne sown with the same crop.

Thus the open field most probably did not yet exist. The field complexes – either demesne lands known as *culturae* or *accara* groups of individual farmers – did not yet form continuous open areas and were still separated by woods, heath or other uncultivated plots and possibly even enclosed by hedgerows or trees. Only within the complexes did the plots probably together constitute a kind of micro open field. Their division into narrow strips must primarily have been the result of later partitions relating to the inheritance of freehold property or partitions and subdivisions of demesne lands, such as by the separating off of *ancingae* (see below).

The origins of these long narrow strips have often been attributed to the introduction of the heavy asymmetrical plough with mould board, an innovation that is again incorrectly placed in the eighth or ninth century. The heavy plough was indeed fitted with a mould board and a coulter knife, mounted on a square wooden frame, unlike the Roman *aratrum* or the prehistoric *ard*, which consisted of a simple digging stick with a symmetrical ploughshare. The front train on two wheels of the heavy plough, however, may already have been present sometimes in the primitive *ard*. The asymmetrical plough had been in use in central Europe as early as the second century or so, and spread from there over the Alps into northern Italy. The light plough remained in use throughout the middle ages there, however, more especially in the valley of the Po. It is nevertheless possible that the distribution of the heavy plough during the eighth and ninth centuries was stimulated by the general economic expansion of the period and the use of

[9] Genicot (1990), pp. 44–5.   [10] Despy (1968), p. 161; Kuchenbuch (1978), p. 101.

iron, especially on large estates, and newly assarted lands. The expansion of
the cultivation of summer grain, barley and oats within a three-course
rotation may also have favoured the use of the heavy plough. It enabled
farmers to keep more oxen, at least four of which were needed to pull a
heavy plough. By the late ninth and tenth centuries leaseholders in the Paris
region began to be classified according to the size of the team, whether of
two or four oxen, they owned. Farms with a small team will have had to co-
operate with each other. Moreover, it is probable that not everyone had a
heavy plough of his own and that it may have been necessary to borrow one
from a large farmer or from the landlord. In fact, farmers were required to
render services to the demesnes, usually with their own oxen, but probably
without their own ploughs.

The raising of cattle was far less common than that of smaller domestic
animals such as pigs or sheep in the early middle ages, even on demesnes.
The prevalence of pigs (on average 40%) in comparison to sheep and
especially to cattle (22%), on both desmesne land and farms held in tenure,
points to mixed farming in which the stock economy was subordinate to an
agricultural economy centred on grain production. This was true for both
northern and southern Europe, which have been contrasted too strictly as a
Germanic animal-fat economy as against a Roman olive and grain producing economy. Yet, there were some regions in northern Europe in the
eighth and ninth centuries where cattle raising was more important than
agriculture. In Frisia the area of land ownership of the abbey of Fulda was
expressed in terms of the animals, cattle, sheep and pigs, that could be put to
pasture on it. In East Anglia, and especially along the coasts of the Low
Countries, huge flocks of sheep were kept. Their enormous wool production largely surpassed the needs of the abbeys that possessed them. A
pastoral specialisation of this kind does not point to an underdeveloped
economy but, on the contrary, presupposes a specialised trade in and
processing of wool, both in the country, mainly in Frisia, and in the
developing towns of, for example, Flanders. In this respect, the church with
its widely scattered landowning, which made it easier to run the risks
associated with specialisation, played an important role.

In spite of the importance of the sylvo-pastoral element in the form of
hunting, fishing or wild fruits in the early medieval economy and food
supply, there is no doubt that grain production made considerable progress
and had become more important than cattle raising or other forms of
agrarian economy. This was even the case in a country such as Italy, where a
proportion of half and half between wild and cultivated land in the triangle
Milano–Como–Varese was considered very high for arable land. It was a
higher proportion than the as yet little-exploited valley of the Po with its

numerous and extensive boglands. The pollen diagrams and the increase in three-course crop rotations, among other less direct indications, prove this. At the same time summer grain (mainly barley), probably prevalent formerly in the two-course rotation system, was sown less and less in the eighth and ninth centuries in favour of winter grain, mainly spelt, rye and, to a lesser extent, wheat. In southwest Germany, northeast France and the southern half of Belgium, there was a very great prevalence of spelt. It accounted for between 50% and 80% of grain production. Elsewhere in Europe spelt declined, mainly in favour of rye, the importance of which increased during the whole of the early middle ages. In northern Italy, where (summer) barley had been the most important crop and where few oats had been cultivated, rye became the principal bread grain in the ninth and tenth centuries. It was twice as important as wheat and millet, constituting a great break with ancient tradition.

Apparently, these developments are unrelated to the yield ratios of the various grain crops, for which only very rare, unreliable and ambiguous figures are available. It is now accepted that the very low yield ratios that were calculated on the basis of the inventory of grain stocks at the royal estates near Lille around 800 (mainly at Annappes), 3, 1.6, 1.3, 1.8, 2.15 for spelt, wheat, rye, barley and oats respectively should be increased slightly in order to express real physical gross yields.[11] Although it is therefore no longer possible to refer to these yield ratios as catastrophic, the expansion in the Carolingian period did not entail an increase in efficiency but rather a production increase due to reclamations and the adoption of the three-course crop rotation system. In itself this important progress in agricultural technique did not lead to an increase in physical efficiency. Agricultural technology remained too underdeveloped for that. More particularly, the fertiliser problem was not solved by extensive dressing with cow manure, nor by the exhortation to marl the land that was proclaimed in 864 by Charles the Bald at Pîtres. Manuring and marling only became possible when stock raising and stabling increased within the framework of a grain economy. In the ninth century only a modest step was taken in that direction. The increase in the production of grain in the eighth century is also apparent from the large number of watermills in this period. A very large proportion of them were grain mills. Though a number of them were originally built by laymen, for example in northeast Spain and western central Italy where several were even collectively owned (and continued to be owned) by village communities, in the central regions of the Frankish empire they were usually in the ownership of a large ecclesiastical landowner

---

[11] *MGH Cap.* I, no. 128, cc. 25, 30, 32, 34. Montanari (1985), pp. 46–9.

as part of the demesne, but operated by the more prosperous tenants at a fairly high rent.[12] The latter fact points to the recent introduction of the mills. In the valleys of the Seine and its tributaries alone, the abbey of St Germain-des-Prés owned eighty-four grain mills (*farinarii*) *c.* 820. In those places where fewer or almost no references to watermills exist, as is the case in northwest France (St Omer) and the southern Low Countries, the grain crop was probably milled mainly by means of hand mills. Finally, it should be pointed out that the residue of grain mills was important as fodder for oxen, pigs, poultry and even horses.

When seen against these clear and numerous signs of expansion of grain production, the famines of the eighth and ninth centuries are difficult to explain. It has been pointed out, possibly rightly, that they were less numerous in the two centuries before than after 1000, a fact which was considered to be related to the increased importance of grain in the diet after that date.[13] It could also be said, however, that when we view these four centuries together, famine was more frequent in the ninth and in the twelfth centuries, that is, in the most expansive centuries at least as far as reclamations are concerned. This might lead to the conclusion that the famines in those centuries should not be interpreted primarily as a result of an underdeveloped agricultural economy, but rather as a consequence of too rapid an increase in population in comparison with the available means in terms of arable land or technology. They should perhaps, therefore, be seen as 'accidents' of expansion.

STRUCTURE AND EXPLOITATION

From about the middle of the eighth century onwards, the structure and exploitation of land ownership in the Frankish empire between Loire and Rhine, between Rhine, Elbe and Alps, and in northern and central Italy underwent profound changes. At different times, and in different ways, depending on the region and many other factors, the so-called bipartite structure was introduced. In its most mature form the bipartite system consisted of an equilibrium between, and a close link in terms of exploitation with, the two parts that together constituted the unit of ownership referred to as a *villa*: one part, that is the demesne (French: *réserve*, German: *Salland*), was cultivated directly for the lord of the domain mainly by the farmers among whom the other part of the estate was divided, the so-called tenements or holdings. The tenants could cultivate the latter for themselves in exchange for services, deliveries of goods and payments to the lord and

---

[12] Lohrmann (1989), pp. 367–404; (1990), pp. 112–13; Toubert (1990), pp. 68–9.

[13] Curschmann (1900), pp. 82–5; Riché (1973), pp. 294–5; Montanari (1979), p. 436.

his demesne. This mostly abstract model, the so-called classical form, occurred almost nowhere in its ideal form. And the model was not static, but constantly in evolution.

The general impression is that the bipartite system probably originated in the central parts of the Frankish realm, more particularly in the regions between Seine, Meuse and Rhine, approximately along an imaginary line between Paris and Aachen. This impression is based on the fact that at the edges of these areas, such as the delta of the Meuse and Rhine rivers or in Maine, as well as in little-exploited and densely wooded parts of the central regions themselves, such as the Ardennes in southeast Belgium or the Argonne Forest in northeast France, the system was still in full development as late as the middle of the ninth century, and often was unable to mature fully. Obviously, this was even more true further afield in, for example, Thuringia. On the other hand the bipartite system had evolved centrally, primarily in the Paris region, by the beginning of the ninth century, to such an extent that it showed signs of 'decline'. On the other hand, the only Mediterranean area in which the classical manorial system developed was in Italy after 774, and in fact it did so fully only in the north, especially in Lombardy. On the basis of this chronological and geographical configuration, and given that the classical manorial system was mainly to be found on royal estates, on church lands that came from royal gifts and on estates of the high nobility, who were often of royal blood as well, it may be that the system owed its existence, or at least its introduction, to the initiative of the Frankish king and his entourage.[14] Conversely, this would explain why it hardly existed in the Carolingian period in the area between the Loire and the Pyrenees, brought within the Carolingian sphere of influence only late in the eighth century.[15]

Royal initiative alone, even if also promoted and applied by the Carolingian church, was obviously insufficient to integrate big farms, that had been cultivated directly by slaves, or small enterprises that had been more or less independent, into single large estates that were to be exploited in a different way from then onwards. In order for this system to be introduced more or less completely and for it to be exploited more or less efficiently still other factors must have been at work. Reclamation of wooded but fertile soils, usually covered with loess, enlarged the amount of arable land in the demesne, often in the form of extensive homogeneous and compact agricultural complexes called *culturae* between the Seine and the Rhine and *territoria* in central Germany. They were the result of the labour not only of serfs who lived on the demesne without their own farms, but also of free and

---

[14] Verhulst (1966); Fumagalli (1980); Poly (1980); Morimoto (1988), pp. 103–4, 109–13.

[15] See Fouracre, chapter 3 above.

semi-free newcomers. In exchange, these people of diverse origins and status were allowed to cultivate a small part of the unexploited part of the demesne for themselves and to keep it as a holding. They were obliged to make payments and provide supplies and they had to render agricultural services to the lord to help out on the enlarged demesne, which in this way could muster added labour. Obviously, all this was only possible on extensive estates and those were largely in the hands of the king, bishoprics, monasteries and the nobility. An additional beneficial factor of the establishment of a classical bipartite exploitation scheme was the concentration of ownership and the location of those possessions in the vicinity of the owners' power centres, that is the royal palaces, the bishops' cities and the abbeys.

This largely abstract and ideal model of the classical manorial structure and the history of its origins and expansion can be made more concrete by means of extant management documents and inventories (*polyptyca, descriptiones, brevia*), which almost without exception date back to the ninth century and usually form part of an ecclesiastical archive.[16] In these, the lord had had the composition of the demesne in terms of land, buildings, personnel and infrastructure, but more particularly the obligations of the tenants with respect to services, deliveries of supplies and payments, recorded. Often this had been done on the orders of the king. In principle the surveys of fiefs (*beneficia*) and possessions held as *precaria*, the income of which was not directly to the benefit of the lord, were also noted down in such documents, but few of these survive. These managerial documents obviously present no picture of evolution unless a similar document of some decades later has been preserved, as in the rare case of Bobbio (with records for 862 and 883).[17]

Indeed, the purpose of these documents was primarily to determine the obligations of the inhabitants of the estate, probably after consultation and in agreement with them, in order to be able to standardise and in this way optimise the structure and exploitation of the estate. Even then, this normalisation took place separately from estate to estate, or in terms of geographical grouping of estates, which means that in spite of a certain common basic structure, which the lord attempted to introduce among

---

[16] The most famous of these documents are the polyptychs of the abbeys of Weissenburg (before 818–19) (Dette 1987), St Germain-des-Prés (before 829) (Guérard 1844; Longnon 1886–95; Devroey 1989), Montiérender (before 845) (Droste 1988), St Bertin (844–59) (Ganshof 1975), St Remi de Reims (after 848) (Devroey 1984), Bobbio (862 and 883) (Castagnetti *et al.* 1979), Lobbes (868–9) (Devroey 1986), St Maur-des-Fossés (869–78) (Hägermann and Hedwig 1990), Prüm (893) (Schwab 1983). Among the rare inventories of royal estates the most famous is the so-called *Brevium exempla* (*MGH Cap.* i, no. 128; Brühl 1971).

[17] Fumagalli (1966); Toubert (1973b), p. 99.

other means through the elaboration of these managerial documents, a great variety can still be observed. This variety is often regionally determined. The lord's control was probably limited, therefore, not only because of geographic differences such as the presence or not of extensive loess plateaux, mountains, infertile soils, woods or bogs, but also as a result of pre-existing economic and social structures, especially as far as the legal status of large parts of the population was concerned (with possible groups of freemen, freed men, half-free *coloni* or slaves). This variety makes it hardly sensible to describe one concrete domain as the ideal example of a classical bipartite estate, even though a domain of the abbey of St Germain-des-Prés from the immediate vicinity of Paris such as Palaiseau is often taken as a model for it.[18] That is why we limit the following description to some general characteristics of the directly exploited part of the estate – the demesne – on the one hand, and those of the holdings on the other hand.

The demesne consisted of various kinds of uncultivated as well as arable land that could extend to several hundred hectares. Examples in this respect from *c.* 825–50 can be found among the estates of St Germain-des-Prés: 396 hectares in Palaiseau. Their demesne consisted on average of three times as much arable land as the estates of Montiérender, which were situated some 150 km to the east and were still in full expansion as classical estates, mainly through deforestation. The Paris estates of St Germain-des-Prés were probably arable land that had been in use long before the advent of the Carolingians. Some large demesnes, however, must have carried out reclamations for arable land during the eighth and ninth centuries. This was probably true for certain estates of royal origins to the east of the Rhine, where the acreage of arable land within the demesne (250 to 300 hectares on the demesne of the bishop of Augsburg at Staffelsee in south Bavaria for example) was five times as extensive as the average acreage of 40 to 50 hectares on less classical domains both in Bavaria and in Saxony. Depending on the geographical conditions, the arable land could be largely concentrated together in extensive *culturae*, in which case they were not very numerous, or they could be distributed over a large number of smaller *culturae* or *territoria* (as in Villance in the Belgian Ardennes), without ever being mixed with the individual fields of the tenants. The latter situation, the so-called *Gemengelage*, was mainly to be found in the border areas of the classical estate (western France, Saxony, Rheinhessen).

From an economic point of view, the proportion between the total area of the demesne and that of the holdings is important. It provides us with an indication of the number of labourers required for the cultivation of the

---

[18] Longnon (1886–95) II, 2, p. 8; Ganshof (1980), pp. 177–8.

demesne. The larger the area of arable land in the demesne the more labour was required. In evenly developed classical estates the proportion was around 1 in 2.5 and 1 in 3, as was the case on the estates of St Germain-des-Prés, Lorsch and the Staffelsee estate between 800 and 820 and on the former *fiscus* Friemersheim on the lower Rhine around 890.

Because of the large extent of arable land in the demesne on some estates the proportion between demesne and tenures could sometimes rise to 1:1, as was the case on some domains of royal provenance belonging to the abbey of Weissenburg.[19] For the exploitation of such relatively large demesnes even the rather onerous services of the tenants were no longer sufficient. It must therefore be assumed that even on these classical estates fairly heavy use was made of resident slaves without holdings. This can even be proved in some cases, as at Staffelsee, where in spite of a basic service of three days a week by slaves who were housed on nineteen *mansi serviles* and who in addition cultivated 17% of the fields of the demesne in plots according to the system of the *riga/ancinga*, there were an additional seventy-two *provendarii* without holdings at the disposal of the demesne. In a more general sense this was also the case on most of the still expanding estates of Montiérender shortly before 845, where on average thirteen slaves can be counted per demesne, especially on the smaller domains that were given in *precaria*.

The data concerning the smaller estate units of the nobility in various regions of Germany, such as Saxony and Bavaria, also indicate that the smaller the manors, the more use of resident slaves was made for the exploitation of the demesnes.[20] The exploitation of the demesne by means of services by tenants therefore seems to have been a system that was mainly developed on large estates, usually owned by the king or donated by him. A typical example of this is the abbey of Fulda. Here only estates with demesnes of more than 150 hectares of arable land were organised according to a bipartite system and largely dependent on the services of tenants for their exploitation.[21]

Certain rights were attached to the holding in exchange for payments to the lord, both in kind and in money, and for services on his demesne. Only in the course of the ninth century did rents and services sometimes come to be based on tenants personally, instead of on their holding, as on the estates of St Bertin abbey in northern France.[22] This does not mean that the person of the tenant, more particularly his legal status of free, freed, half-free or slave, will not have played a role initially in the imposition on his holding of service obligations, especially in their size and nature.

[19] Dette (1987), pp. 54–7.   [20] Rösener (1989b), pp. 158–67.
[21] Weidinger (1989), pp. 251–65.   [22] Ganshof (1975), p. 32.

From the middle of the seventh century, the term *mansus* is used as a technical term for a holding in a bipartite manor in the region of Paris. A *mansus* consisted of a complete farm with farmhouse, farm buildings, fields and sometimes also meadows, or even, in some rare cases, woods. The introduction of this new term, *mansus*, is related to the development of the classical, bipartite manorial system based on services. The Frankish kings played as important a role in the introduction of the use of the term *mansus*, which they also used for fiscal and related matters as a unit of assessment, as they had in the rise of the bipartite manorial system. This is suggested by the spread of the use of the term *mansus*, from the Paris region in all directions, corresponding to the region in which the manorial system developed in its classical form. In most regions *mansus* replaced older terms such as *coloni(c)a*, *casata*, *factus* and *hoba*, though *coloni(c)a* and *factus* continued to exist to the south of the Loire with their simple original meaning of a holding not necessarily being part of a larger domanial unit; *casata* and *hoba* were retained in Germanic-speaking areas, often with the same meaning as *mansus*.

Mansus essentially means a unit of assessment for payments, in kind and money and for services, even though on the other hand – as was the case with the hide in large parts of England outside Kent – *mansus* was also used to express rough estimates of the value of some land or of whole regions. It was also used by the king as a basis for various taxes and military obligations. This is why some modern authors consider it a purely fiscal unit, which they trace back, incorrectly in our view, to the Roman taxation system that persisted here and there in the Merovingian period.[23] The problem is that the *mansus* is no fixed unit, either in terms of area or in terms of the charges and obligations connected with it, though the normal occupancy of a *mansus* is supposed to be by one tenant. In estates where the *mansus* organisation seems to be fairly recent, as is the case of the estate of Poperinge near Ypres, belonging to the abbey of St Bertin about the middle of the ninth century, the areas of the *mansi* are rather large. They constitute groups in which all the *mansi* have an area of either 24, 20, 15 or 13 bonniers. In Palaiseau, a *villa* near Paris of the abbey of St Germain-des-Prés, where the arable land and its organisation within a manor are of much older origin, the size of the *mansi* is much smaller. It is by no means certain that there is a connection with the so-called overpopulation of the *mansus*, in which the latter was inhabited by more than one family. This was the case with half the total number of *mansi* at Palaiseau.

As far as payments in kind and money or labour services are concerned, it is even more difficult to distinguish specific, let alone standard types. What

---

[23] Durliat (1990), pp. 195–203.

does occur is that within one particular estate all *mansi* of a category that may or may not be juridically defined were subject to the same obligations, which meant that these obligations had to be entered only once in the chapter of the polyptych concerned. Such uniformity occurs mainly in the case of *mansi serviles*, as, for example, on the manor of Staffelsee belonging to the bishop of Augsburg.[24] It may be explained by the fact that *mansi serviles* were usually created anew and that it was easier to impose uniform obligations on slaves than on free or half-free *coloni*. The holdings of the latter may indeed have been previously independent farms that had been integrated in an estate only later, in which case an agreement had possibly to be concluded with the free person or *colonus* concerned. This difference in juridical status might also explain the fact that *mansi serviles* or *servi* personally were usually taxed much more heavily in services than *lidi*, *coloni* or *ingenui*. On most bipartite estates in the Frankish regions to the east of the Rhine the lowest burden of field work of the *mansi serviles* was two to three days a week, in addition to other labour services. On top of that, they often had to be available at any moment, whenever they were ordered to do so.

In the regions to the east of the Rhine and in Italy as well as in some areas to the west of the realm such as the Argonne forest around the abbey of Montiérender, the services required of free and half-free tenants were normally limited to some transport services mentioned above, to agricultural services during a few periods of two weeks (*noctes*) in the year and to the cultivation of a fixed plot of the demesne. This limitation was possible because there were many slaves available. In the western part of the realm in the ninth century, on the other hand, the number of slaves had been severely reduced, probably because of the process of settling them on holdings. This process in its turn had obscured the difference in social position between these former slaves and the free and half-free tenants within the same estate. The difference between, for instance, the *mansi ingenuiles* and the *mansi serviles* had thus largely disappeared in these regions. In order to ensure the exploitation of large demesnes free and half-free tenants in the western part of the realm were therefore requested to perform practically the same services as slaves elsewhere. This presupposes a strong hold on the population by the authority of the king and the church, but may, on the other hand, be due to the heavy population pressure discussed above (p.482).

In the payments in kind and money that *mansi* as holdings in an estate were required to perform there was not any consistency, or any correlation between the payments and the size or the status of the *mansus*. Payments in

---

[24] Elmshäuser (1989), p. 365.

money were insignificant before the end of the ninth century and usually served to buy off military service (*hostilitium*) when it concerned *mansi ingenuiles*. Towards the end of the ninth century and thereafter some supplies in kind (e.g. pigs, wood or linen) were increasingly frequently bought off with annual payments in money. Most supplies or payments in kind consisted still of small quantities of chickens and eggs. Supplies of grain or industrial products (made of wood or iron if the geographical area was rich in these raw materials) were only relatively large when no or few services were requested from the *mansi*.

The classical manorial organisation was manifestly a phenomenon that was limited in time and space. Under the influence of various factors such as population increase, divisions of estates owned by the king and nobility by means of enfeoffments, gifts, sales, inheritance and the expansion of trade and money, the relationship based on services between the demesne and holdings classified as *mansi* evolved, as is clear from various polyptychs of a later date or younger parts of them from the abbeys of Lobbes, Prüm, Rheims and St Maur-des-Fossés.[25] It is possible therefore to work out a chronologically and geographically determined typology of those manorial forms and structures which diverge from the classical model, even though they occurred in its range of distribution or at least at the edge of it.

At the beginning of the development there is the type that during the Merovingian period must have been present in almost all parts of western Europe. This type consisted of an estate or agricultural enterprise of from about 40 to 150 hectares of arable land, directly cultivated by slaves, who had no holding and lived on or near the centre of the estate. If a few holdings were administered from within this centre, they were in any case limited in numbers and only obliged to provide supplies and payments, not services. Often these domains were situated in hardly exploited areas, where they often played a pioneering role. In such cases stock breeding, especially of pigs, became very important. Examples of this type can be found among the estates of the abbey of Fulda in central Germany at the beginning of the ninth century, among the possessions of the abbey of Montiérender in the Argonne forest in northeast France, and in Italy among the lands of the abbey of Farfa at the estuary of the Po, as well as in the mountainous regions of Piemonte and the central Apennines.[26]

In these large farms, often simply called *curtes*, some holdings may have been included or their number extended. This could be done by assigning part of the demesne either to freed or unfree slaves as has been observed as

---

[25] See note 16 above.

[26] Fulda: Weidinger (1989), pp. 254–6; Montiérender: Droste (1988), p. 143; Italy: Toubert (1973b), pp. 105–6.

early as the eighth century in some places in Italy, or by assigning not yet
exploited parts of the demesne to new holdings. This is known to have been
carried through in Italy as late as the second half of the ninth century.
Between 862 and 883, the two different stages of the polyptych of Bobbio,
the number of holdings increased from 74 to 123. The complex that was
henceforth often called *villa* rather than *curtis* had in this way evolved into a
bipartite manor. Because slaves were still used on the demesne, the new
holdings were not always made serviceable to the demesne upon their
integration. Many factors are at work in the development of this type of
organisation, among them the legal status of the tenant, the origin of the
holding, the needs of the lord and the balance of power between his
authority and the resistance of his subjects.

The integration or creation of holdings did not always lead to a bipartite
estate, even without services from them. When holdings were scattered over
several villages, for example, next to and among lands of other lords, the
demesne court, exploited with the help of a number of slaves, simply became
a rent-collecting centre, with no additional links to the holdings. Examples
of this type can be found among the possessions of Corvey, Fulda and, at the
end of the ninth century, on certain possessions of the church of Lucca
consisting of holdings (*sortes*) that were granted in *beneficium* as a whole and
only yielded payments in money for the holder of the *beneficium*.[27]

So far, I have referred to such indications of 'decline' as the overpopulation of the *mansus* and its small size on some estates of St Germain-des-Prés
in the vicinity of Paris. Yet the case of the lands of the abbey of Prüm at
Villance in the Belgian Ardennes proves that we have to be careful with the
term 'decline'. The overoccupation of four tenants per *mansus* on twenty-
two of the thirty-five *mansi* cannot easily be interpreted as decline since it
concerns a 'classical' estate that originated in the course of the ninth century
as a result of clearances. In a similar way it has been possible to prove that the
vacant *mansi* (*mansi absi*) that occurred in great numbers on the lands of the
abbey of Montiérender *c.* 850 (around 20% of the total number of *mansi
ingenuiles*) and the numerous *sortes absentes* that represented up to one sixth of
the total number of *sortes* in the mid-ninth and early tenth century in Italy
(near cities this proportion was as high as 50%), were not 'abandoned' *mansi*
or *sortes*, but holdings that had temporarily no official tenant and had been
granted to other landholders. Their presence is evidence of great mobility
within the domanial structures, to which the management of the estate could
react with great flexibility because of the concept of 'vacant' holdings.

In the same way half *mansi* should not always be interpreted as the

---

[27] Corvey: Rösener (1985), pp. 200–3; Fulda: Weidinger (1989), pp. 256–8; Lucca: Toubert (1983),
p. 27.

consequences of a division of a *mansus* and therefore as a sign of decline, but often as *mansi* in development, as was the case on some estates of St Bertin around 850. When, on the other hand, Charles the Bald complained in the Edict of Pîtres (864) that the '*mansa*' became ever smaller because essential elements of it had been alienated, this did concern in his opinion a process of decline, which even threatened the smooth operation of the state institutions.[28] The reduction of the demesne that can be observed mainly on some estates of the abbey of Bobbio from the middle of the ninth century onwards was a conscious policy aimed at multiplying the number of holdings and keeping alive a parallel and more intensive cultivation of a reduced demesne by means of the services created in this way. While here the phenomenon can be interpreted as an attempt at optimising efficiency, its general introduction on the estates of the abbeys of Prüm and Weissenburg at the end of the ninth and during the tenth century should probably indeed be interpreted as a decline of the classical domanial system.

The manorial system was at that time in fact clearly past its peak and it is possibly not without significance that its decline coincided with the reduction of royal authority. As argued above, the original development of the manorial system had clearly been linked to the rise and expansion in all senses of the power of the Carolingian rulers, and may even have been a component of a 'Carolingian agrarian "policy"'. The promotion of the small farm enterprise, the mitigation of slavery and the reduction of the number of slaves, compensated for by the introduction and increase of services, were probably consequences rather than aims of this policy. In our opinion, its fundamental aim was an increase of production through an optimisation of efficiency. This production increase was in manual crafts as well as in agriculture with the aim of increasing deliveries of supplies to the court, the church and probably also to the army.

Let us now consider areas that were brought under Carolingian authority only late in the eighth century. These areas cannot be considered together. A distinction should be made between, on the one hand, Catalonia and Roussillon, about which there are fairly extensive if somewhat late sources, and on the other, Auvergne, Charente, Poitou, the Limousin and Provence. It is no coincidence that there are almost no documents available concerning these southern parts of France, and certainly no polyptychs. The structure and exploitation of large landownership was indeed very different here from that of the classical manorial organisation, of which the polyptychs were the tools of operation *par excellence*. Outside Catalonia and Roussillon: the main characteristics were first the prevalence of the small farm enterprise, usually

---

[28] *MGH Cap.* II, no. 273, c. 30. Zotz (1989), p. 123.

in allodial property, or, as in the Auvergne, as tenements, and secondly the small size and significance of the demesne, cultivated directly for the lord by a few slaves, without services from holdings, for which the demesne was only a rent-collecting centre without any close links.

The numerous small *allodia* between the Loire and the Pyrenees may date from the late Roman period or may have originated through reclamations according to the system of the *aprisio* which had a great success in Catalonia and Roussillon in the ninth and tenth centuries. The holdings, on the other hand, owe their existence partly to the large-scale assignment of land to former slaves, as is apparent at the beginning of the ninth century from the polyptych of St Pierre-le-Vif concerning Mauriac in the Central Massif, in the southwest of Auvergne.[29] Most of the holdings are much older and probably originated as possessions of late Roman *coloni*. Their principal obligation consisted of the payment of a levy in kind that amounted to one tenth of the harvest. It occurs in 672–6 under the name of *agrarium* in the oldest tax list of the abbey of St Martin in Tours and is also mentioned in the seventh-century *Formulae Wisigothorum*. It was later converted to a fixed payment as in Mauriac in the Auvergne and at the beginning of the tenth century was still referred to with the telling name of *tasca*. Additionally,. *colonicae* had to pay for the right to pasture (*pascuarium*, *pasquier*), again consisting of one tenth of the yield of cattle raising, chickens and eggs as oblations (*eulogiae*) and a *tributum* in money as a sign of dependence. A *colonica* had an average size of 16 hectares and could provide for the needs of one canon which appears to make it similar to the *mansus* to the north of the Loire. The term *mansus*, however, only began to be used to the south of the Loire in the ninth century, first and foremost in Auvergne, with a slightly divergent meaning, of which the exploitation of buildings and garden in the immediate vicinity, and orchard, were the most important elements. Rarely or never did there exist an obligation for agricultural services for the *mansus*. Elsewhere the term *mansus* was only found in the meaning of seigneurial *mansus* (chef-manse), exploited directly for the lord, as in Limousin.

In lower Catalonia, as well as in Roussillon, 80% to 90% of the land in the ninth and tenth centuries was taken up by the allodial property of small peasants. Many of these *allodia*, however, were transformed into holdings in the tenth and eleventh centuries after they had been sold to large land-owners. In exchange for part of the yield, they became part of the large estates that were built up by new, large abbeys from the ninth century onwards in the northeast of the county of Barcelona (around Gerona and

---

[29] Bonnassie (1990), p. 28.

Ampurias) and in Roussillon, as a result of the clearances of large forests and garrigues.[30] These most southern regions of the Frankish empire thus developed in their own separate way.

Outside the Frankish empire England and Brittany have to be discussed. Although no actual written record survives on the subject, it may perhaps be surmised that England was a society with many slaves cultivating the demesne without much help from rent-paying tenants, the so-called 'ceorls', half-free persons who can be compared to *coloni* in the Frankish empire. They were probably rarely obliged to render services.[31] Outside Kent, the unit of assessment for the determination of the obligations of the tenants was the hide, which was also used to give a rough indication of the value of a plot of land or even of whole regions. In both aspects the hide may be compared with the *mansus* on the Continent, a word that is often used next to *mansio* and *mansiuncula* to translate the term in Latin charters. Just like the *mansus*, the hide was in principle sufficient to maintain one family, even though up to four households could live on one hide. In Kent the unit of family holding was not the hide but the area of arable land (OE *Sulung*) that could be ploughed in one year by a team of eight oxen, and equivalent to two hides. The obligations that were calculated on these units of assessment are unknown. A charter from Edward the Elder, granted to Winchester in 900, however, reveals that a holding with the size of a hide was taxed fairly heavily in the form of a payment in money and supplies of beer, bread, barley, wood, sheep and lambs.[32] In addition the tenant had to cultivate three acres of the demesne fully and mow half an acre of meadow. He was even obliged to work for the lord whenever he was asked to do so, except for a period of three weeks a year. On top of that he was subjected to various public duties, mainly military. It is impossible to determine whether such a situation, if representative, had been in existence for a long time or whether it was the beginning of a new development.

In the ninth century, land ownership in Brittany consisted exclusively of large or small *allodia*. When large-scale land ownership became important, especially that of abbeys such as Redon, the small *allodia* were incorporated by gifts to the abbey and held from it in *precaria*. The large *allodia* were mostly transformed into fiefs. Here again, as in Catalonia and Roussillon, there appears to have been an abrupt change from a society characterised by small peasant properties to one dominated by large estates.[33]

---

[30] Bonnassie (1975–6), p. 233.   [31] Finberg (1972), p. 447.

[32] *Cart. Saxonicum*, 592, 594. Finberg (1972), pp. 452–3.

[33] Chédeville and Tonnerre (1987), pp. 204–6.

CRAFT AND INDUSTRIAL PRODUCTION

Textiles, tools, weapons and other iron and wooden objects, glass, pottery and salt were manufactured almost exclusively in the countryside in Carolingian Europe. Production only merits the term industrial when it largely exceeds local demand and was suited to or even intended for export.

The deliveries by landholders, within a manorial framework or outside it, of woven pieces of linen cloth (*cam(i)siles*), of wool or flax (*sar(i)ciles*), both materials usually produced for the manufacturing of shirts (*camisiae*), or the supply of the shirts themselves in addition to that of coats and capes made of wool (*pallia, saga*), is very common in the Carolingian period and mentioned frequently in polyptychs and donation charters. The abundantly found loom weights, with the literary evidence, confirm that textile production was a normal side-activity for most tenants in Carolingian Europe.[34] Women were usually active in it, for example the many unfree and free women on different estates of St Bertin in northwestern France. Exceptionally, they only had to supply spindles of spun flax. It remains unknown who actually used these in weaving. It might be supposed that this happened in the workplaces for women (*gynaecea*) that are mentioned from the eighth century onwards in various places in Europe, the Low Countries, Germany, France and Italy as part of the demesne of an estate. Both female slaves without a holding of their own and half-free women with holdings, who were married to *coloni*, had to come and work there as an obligatory service that more or less corresponded to the agricultural seigneurial services of the men on the demesnes. In the *Capitulare de Villis* and the *Brevium Exempla* such workplaces are also mentioned, which might mean that they were installed on royal domains (*fisci*), as was the case for other non-agricultural activities that had a more industrial than artisanal character.[35] Whether this situation was also true for the textile production of the *gynaecea* is a question that cannot be answered positively, even though it is raised by the famous *pallia fresonica*. This was woollen cloth of a high quality that was renowned throughout the whole of the Frankish empire in the ninth century and therefore was probably manufactured, either in Frisia itself or in England and Flanders and carried by Frisian middlemen, on an industrial scale.[36] The production of wool from sheep that were put to pasture by the thousands on the numerous saltmarshes along the Flemish, Zeeland and Frisian coasts was so important along the North Sea coast of the Low Countries from the eighth to the tenth centuries that several abbeys located further away (St

[34] Toubert (1990), pp. 75–80.

[35] *MGH Cap.* I, no. 32, cc. 31, 43, 49; no. 128, c. 7. Toubert (1990), p. 79; Ganshof (1980), pp. 183–6. See p. 501 below.   [36] Lebecq (1983) I, pp. 76–7, 131–4; Schmid (1991), pp. 12–15.

Wandrille, Fulda, Lorsch and others) brought in their wool from flocks of sheep that they owned there themselves or took delivery of large annual supplies of woollen monks' clothes and other woven materials.[37] Whether this large production was still locally processed by craftsmen is a question that is important in view of the high quality of textile produced by these areas in later centuries, albeit mainly within a city context.

Iron-working, like textiles, was associated with agricultural needs, though smiths ranked as specialised artisans within the peasant community. Archaeological excavations have uncovered 'mines' or surface furrows, pits and funnel shafts, dated between the eighth and tenth centuries, from which iron ore was extracted. These were often donated with the surrounding land by smaller private landowners to abbeys such as Fulda, Lorsch and St Gall. In the south German Franconian Alps a settlement of artisans has been discovered in the vicinity of a Carolingian iron mine. Only one written reference to a miner (*fossarius*) is known on the lands of the abbey of Prüm in Houmont in the Belgian Ardennes. Whether the *fossa ferraricia sive plumbaricia*, shallow shafts of iron ore and lead that are mentioned in the *Capitulare de Villis* (c. 62) as elements of the royal estate, were indeed mainly to be found on *fisci* is unclear, even though the only proof for the existence of industrial iron-working concerns possessions of the Carolingian king, and iron objects for the army (*ferramenta*) are also mentioned in the *Capitulare de Villis* (c. 42). In the well-known inventory of the estates of the bishopric of Chur, the income of a complete *ministerium* from the vicinity of Bregenz in the Vorarlberg consisted mainly of supplies of iron products paid as *census regis* to the representative of the king named *schulteiss* in the *ministerium*. Eight furnaces are mentioned. This substantial production clearly exceeded local needs and can therefore be termed 'industrial'. Since *capitularia* from 779 onwards reiterate the prohibition against the export of weapons and military equipment, such as the metal shirt (*brunia*), it is probable that the excess was marketed. Almost all other written documents from such abbeys as Bobbio, St Remi of Rheims, Weissenburg, Lorsch and St Gall in the Carolingian period record deliveries of iron, either as rough ingots (referred to by weight) or as finished products such as ploughshares, horseshoes and weapons, which served as rents from peasants for their holdings.[38] These peasant farmers would appear, therefore, to have been miners on the side.

The abbey of St Germain-des-Prés received 100 *librae de ferro* from each of its 25.5 *mansi serviles* in the *villa* of Boissy-Maugis in the Perche (western France).[39] This may indicate a community of iron smelters that lived somewhat isolated in one of the numerous extensive forests of this region. It

---

[37] Lebecq (1983 1), pp. 126–8, 132–3.   [38] Sprandel (1968), pp. 357–8.
[39] Longnon (1886–95) II, pp. 192–200.

is likely that the rather small and strongly decentralised production of iron was processed locally by smiths. Apart from some isolated literary references to a *faber*, with no hint of his social or professional status on the estate, there is archaeological evidence of the activity of smiths between 600 and 900 from the region of the upper Rhine (Schaffhausen) and the lower Rhine (Krefeld), from a mound in the Wesermarsch, in the Carolingian lost village under the Kootwijkerzand and in other places on the Veluwe (Holland) and especially in the village of Warendorf (Westfalia).[40] Here, not only were large parts of smelting furnaces found, but it was also possible to locate the workplace of a smith, which led to the conclusion that there was always one smith present per group of farms. It has been deduced from this evidence that these blacksmiths were probably integrated in the manorial structures.

As decentralised as textile and iron processing was the manufacture of wooden objects, even though there were several specialised woodworkers at the abbeys themselves (see below). Apart from this group the only information at our disposal on woodworking concerns deliveries of wooden objects such as wooden eating plates, spoons, wooden roof shingles, slats, vats, barrels and even carts that tenants were often obliged to make.[41]

The production of glass and ceramics is almost exclusively identified from archaeological evidence.[42] The quality and quantity of the production, especially as measured against its export in the Carolingian period to faraway regions such as Scandinavia via Dorestad to Hedeby (Haithabu) and Birka, allow us to surmise that the production was on an industrial scale. The only two written references, in each case to a glazier who is specifically named (*vitrearius*) as holder of a *mansus* and half a *mansus* in the vicinity of Douai (northern France) and in Barisis (*département* of Aisne) on possessions of the abbey of St Amand in 864, are difficult to interpret.[43] It seems probable that these glaziers were, with other specialised artisans, normally active in the buildings of St Amand and of its *cella* in Barisis. Despite the numerous examples of Merovingian glasswork that have been dug up, mainly in Scandinavia, the oldest excavated place of glass manufacturing in the countryside, located in the wooded region called Hochwald in Kordel near Trier, dates to the Carolingian period. Hochwald's renowned products have been found in Hedeby and Birka.[44] Another glass-making workshop has been found in the Carolingian palace at Paderborn.[45]

---

[40] Janssen (1983), pp. 342–6.
[41] Kuchenbuch (1978), pp. 136, 150; Ganshof (1980), p. 179; Droste (1988), pp. 112, 115 e.o. (*scindela*), 98, 100 (*faccule*); Hägermann and Hedwig (1990), p. 94.
[42] Janssen (1983), pp. 320–31, 348–84.   [43] Ganshof (1980), p. 184 and p. 188 n. 27.
[44] Janssen (1983), p. 323.
[45] Janssen (1983), p. 392 (on the basis of literature cited p. 300 nn. 119–20).

Much more is known of Carolingian pottery production. One of the main centres of industrial production was located in the village of Badorf, between Cologne and Bonn, a site primarily determined by the presence of the necessary clay and sand and by the proximity of sources of energy such as water and wood.[46] Another important Carolingian pottery centre was situated in Saran, in the forest of Orleans, but, unlike Badorf, outside the neighbouring settlement.[47] The quality of the production in terms of the material, the shape, the decorations and the standardisation, and the sheer quantity apparent from the massive exports, clearly point to the industrial nature of Badorf and Saran. That the quality and quantity of pots produced in the Carolingian period was greater than that of the Merovingian period, and the centres of production were different, points to better organisation, probably within the manorial framework. Reference is made in this respect to the later possessions of the archbishop of Cologne and the chapter of St Pantaleon of Cologne in the vicinity of Badorf. Next to the king, these church institutions are considered possible patrons of the specialised craftsmen, who are believed, rightly or wrongly, to have had no independent status at all.[48]

Ipswich in East Anglia was an important centre for pottery production on an industrial scale during this early period. Ipswich ware was exported to the whole of southern England. There was a separate pottery-making zone of the settlement. By contrast, other activities at Ipswich such as textile, leather and bone-working, which were already more important in Ipswich than agriculture, were spread over the whole settlement.[49] This was also the case in the important proto-town of Hamwic (Southampton) on the Channel coast, where production consisted mainly of textiles and iron. Pottery was largely imported from the Continent.

Documents concerning salt production on the estates of the abbey of Prüm in Lorraine, not far from Metz in Vic-sur-Seille, Moyenvic and Marsal provide some notion of industrial organisation.[50] Other abbeys with an eye to their need for salt, such as those of St Denis, Montiérender and Weissenburg, also had estates in this region. The salt was crystallised in large cooking pots by means of boiling the water from salt-rich sources in the vicinity. In Prüm's case, the sources of salt and the collecting basins and workplaces with pots were all owned by the abbey. The manual workers (*operatores*) were Prüm's tenants working in exchange for holdings where they could also grow crops.[51] They could use the collecting basins and other utensils in exchange for a payment of a tax that was calculated per boiling

---

[46] Janssen (1983), pp. 348–73.   [47] Janssen (1983), pp. 383–4.
[48] Janssen (1983), pp. 390–2.   [49] Clarke and Ambrosiani (1991), pp. 19–22, 34–5.
[50] Kuchenbuch (1978), pp. 293–8.   [51] Kuchenbuch (1978), p. 295.

pot. They were allowed to keep part of their production for sale. Most of it, obviously, went to the abbey, which had it transported by means of transport services of tenants via Metz along the Moselle to the main seat of the abbey in Prüm. The salt that was not used in the abbey itself was sold on the local markets in the vicinity of Prüm.

Elsewhere in Europe there were only references to salt extraction or processing. Many abbeys had rights in salines along the coast, mainly at the estuaries of rivers and streams such as the Loire (St Mesmin in Orléans) and the Seine (St Wandrille), on which they often had toll privileges for the transport of salt. Several of these salt basins with sea water seem to have been exploited by associations of manual workers. The salt production in the lagoons in Venice and at the estuary of the Po (in Comacchio) was so important that it led in the ninth century to a wide network of inter-regional trade upstream along the Po.[52] On the Zeeland islands in the estuary of the Scheldt too, salt was produced by abbeys such as that of Lorsch. In 775/6 it owned seventeen saltpans (*culinas*) to extract salt from sea water or peat.[53] Inland, salt was also produced in salt mines such as the Salzkammergut and in Reichenhall in south Bavaria.[54]

Manual workers with diverse specialities such as leather-working, metalworking as smiths and weaponmakers, woodturners and other woodworkers and fur-makers had to provide for the needs of very large abbey communities. Gifts of swords by the abbeys of Fulda, Lorsch and St Gall might point to the fact that this production sometimes exceeded their own requirements. In St Riquier the settlement consisted of districts or streets (*vici*) where the artisans lived together grouped by speciality.[55] Even though the artisans seem to have been more independent than the numerous unskilled *provendarii* that lived near the abbey as well, they did in fact belong to the unfree or half-free *familia* of the abbey. It is therefore questionable whether they worked for their own benefit.

TRADE AND TOWNS

As a result of the dominant role of manorial organisation in agrarian and industrial production, the exchange of goods and trade were also to a large extent dependent on the large estate and its production. The manorial centres of the king and the church played a centralising and at the same time redistributive role in this respect. The surplus of the agrarian and industrial production of the demesnes and the deliveries in kind of agrarian and craft products by the tenants of the estate were transported by means of various

[52] Violante (1953), pp. 4–6.   [53] Koch (1970), pp. 9–10.   [54] Ganshof (1980), p. 184.
[55] Hariulf, *Chron. Centulense*, ed. F. Lot (1894), VII, p. 307. Schwind (1984), pp. 101–23.

transport services imposed on the tenants (*angariae, scarae, navigia*). They were taken via country road and waterways to regional estate centres or else directly to the *palatia* and abbey seats. This was primarily the case for specialised products such as salt, oil and wine which sometimes had to be transported over long distances, but less so for products such as corn which were only transported to the abbey itself. Whatever was not used or stored for later use in these secondary or main centres was sold at nearby markets or ones further afield where there was a demand for a particular commodity not produced locally. The first and foremost objective of the large landowners was always to ensure their own provisioning with the most diverse products from their own production and supply centres. Only if this was not possible did they try to obtain the goods that were lacking by purchase or exchange.

Markets were organised in ever increasing numbers with royal permission in or near to certain estates in the ninth century, especially under Louis the Pious and Charles the Bald. Examples of such markets can be found on several estates of the abbey of St Denis: in the region of Paris, at Néron, Faverolles (774) and Saclas (814), in southwest Germany at Esslingen (866–8). On the estates of Prüm in the Eifel regional markets were established at Rommersheim (861) and Münstereifel (898).[56] These markets were situated in the countryside, while others were established in the neighbourhood of large abbeys (St Vaast 867, St Amand 872, St Bertin 874). Older markets, dating from before the ninth century, were mostly established in or close to *civitates* of Roman origin such as Nantes, Angers, Langres, Troyes, Sens and Orléans. Often coins were minted there as well. Coining rights were sometimes granted by the king when a new market was organised, as was the case in Rommersheim and Münstereifel.[57] Although tradesmen were present at these local weekly markets it was mostly the producers themselves – peasants and craftsmen, even unfree tenants – who offered their produce directly for sale. Craftsmen who did not have a holding or had one that was too small probably bought corn, chickens or eggs with the money from the sale of their craft products. Peasants bought tools from the craftsmen or obtained them through exchange. From passing traders or from agents of large landowners both groups probably bought rare products that were not produced in the region such as salt, oil and wine.

Other products that circulated in the international trade circuit were such things as wax and honey, horses and even slaves. Examples of foreign merchants are the Russians and Czechs operating a salt trade (*salinarium mercatum*) along the mid-Danube in Bavaria. They are mentioned in the well-

---

[56] Kuchenbuch (1978), pp. 304–5; Ganshof (1980), p. 191 and 197 n. 38; Bleiber (1982), pp. 106–7.
[57] Bleiber (1982), pp. 112–13; see also chapter 20 below.

known inquiry on the toll at Raffelstetten at the end of the ninth century.[58]
Foreign merchants also appeared on a market at Walenstadt in Rhaetia.[59]
The pricing policy for life-ensuring products such as corn was severely
controlled by the authorities in times of famine and gave rise to the far-
reaching measures under Charlemagne in 794 and in 805–6 referred to
earlier.

Because of the continuity of towns from late Roman times to the early
middle ages, Italy, and especially northern Italy, forms an exception to this
picture of local and regional trade in the Carolingian empire. In Italy trade,
even local and regional retail trade, was mainly concentrated in towns. The
markets organised in the ninth century outside the walls of the town by
churches and monasteries and authorised by the king or owned by the
abbeys, such as Bobbio (860), Volterra, Piacenza and Mantua (894), were in
fact annual fairs functioning in international trade.[60]

In towns such as Pavia, Milan, Mantua, Parma, Cremona and Piacenza,
large landowners such as the abbeys of Bobbio, Sta Giulia di Brescia,
Novalesa and others possessed subsidiaries to which they brought surpluses
from their estates, especially corn and oil along the Po and its tributaries, to
sell them there. Places at the estuary of the Po, such as Comacchio, or to the
north of it, like Venice, had a great need for agrarian products because they
produced little more than salt. Initially, since a charter on that matter had
been granted by King Liutprand in 715, this salt was transported upstream
along the Po to its confluence with the Oglio between Cremona and Mantua
by agents of Comacchio privileged as *milites*. Soon though, in the second half
of the ninth century, the Comacchesi were elbowed out of this traffic by
traders from Cremona (852) and by Venetians who in 862 owed payments in
pepper and cinnamon to the office of the abbey of Bobbio in Mantua.[61] These
products had clearly been brought to Italy by international traders. Owing to
the lasting importance of towns in Italy, this international circuit was more
inter-woven here with regional and inter-regional trade than in other parts of
Europe.

During the eighth and ninth centuries international trade from Italy in the
Mediterranean area was largely restricted to the Adriatic Sea because of the
insecurity caused by Arab pirates in the western Mediterranean. Only some
coastal navigation to the ports in Provence was possible during the first half
of the ninth century. It was Venice that gained most from this situation. The
treaty of 812 between Charlemagne and the Emperor Michael of Byzantium
had given Venice great possibilities in the eastern basin of the Mediterra-

---

[58] *MGH Cap.* II, 253. cc. 1, 6, 7. Ganshof (1966), pp. 221–2.
[59] Ganshof (1980), pp. 192, 195 and nn. 42 and 95.
[60] Violante (1953), pp. 5–6; Toubert (1983), p. 42.   [61] Violante (1953), p. 8.

nean where only some southern Italian ports such as Naples, Salerno, Gaeta and Amalfi had kept up trade.[62] On the other hand, the *pactum Lotharii* of 840, which exempted Venice from toll and berthing taxes (*ripaticum*), made it possible for Venice to expand to the central and northern parts of the Frankish empire, while traders from the continental parts of the empire were given concessions in the shipping trade by the Venetians and even participated in the Venetian commercial enterprises with money.[63]

Through Venice and the north Italian cities of the Po valley, which gained from Venetian prosperity, spices, expensive Oriental textiles, furs from the Black Sea region – given by the abbot Ansegisus to his abbey of Fontenelle[64] – and other goods were brought from the Near East across the Alps to the central parts of the Frankish empire. In the opposite direction slaves from the regions east of the Elbe and from the Balkans, reaching Italy via Chur, were sold to Arabs in the south of Italy and Sicily.[65]

Apart from Italy the centre of international trade from and to the Frankish empire during the eighth and ninth centuries lay very clearly in the central and northern parts of the empire and in the adjacent regions of England, Scandinavia and eastern Europe. The cities (*civitates*) of Roman origin, Aix, Narbonne, Arles, Nîmes in southern Gaul, however, decayed in the course of the eighth century and were destroyed or occupied by Muslims for a long time. They lost their commercial importance almost completely in favour of their military role. The revival of trade and urban life in Provence only took place from about 980 onwards.

International trade was concentrated in places along the frontier of the Frankish empire where, in addition, important royal tolls were established: on the Channel and the southern North Sea coast at Rouen and Amiens, but especially at Quentovic, Domburg and Dorestad; on the frontier with Denmark at Hedeby (Haithabu-Schleswig); on the frontier with the Slavs along the Elbe at Bardowiek and Magdeburg; along the Danube at Raffelstetten and Regensburg.[66] Inland, international trade took place along some important traffic arteries such as the Rhine, the Meuse, the Danube and at some annual fairs dating from before the ninth century, such as the fair of St Denis near Paris, which had existed since the seventh century.[67]

The most important of the border places, to wit the *emporia* of Quentovic, Dorestad and Hedeby, share characteristics with a number of trading places outside the Frankish empire with which they traded, such as Hamwic, Lundenwic (the trading place that originated from the end of the seventh century along the street still known in London as the Strand, running

[62] Violante (1953), p. 20.   [63] Violante (1953), pp. 6–7.   [64] Violante (1953), p. 34.
[65] Violante (1953), pp. 31–4.   [66] Johanek (1987), pp. 14–16.
[67] Ganshof (1980), p. 191; Johanek (1987), pp. 19–20.

parallel to the Thames to the west of the Roman *Londinium* which was
largely uninhabited until the end of the ninth century); Birka, an island in
what is now called the Mälar lake, a former bay of the Baltic Sea to the west
of Stockholm; Kaupang, not far from Oslo, and many smaller trading places
in the Baltic area from Denmark to northwestern Russia. The most striking
characteristic of most of these trading places is their ephemerality. Their
short-lived prosperity is linked both to their specialisation and to the
protection afforded Quentovic and Dorestad at least by Carolingian royal
authority.[68] The decline of the *emporia* situated outside the Carolingian
empire is usually explained by the close commercial ties they maintained
with the Carolingian *emporia* whose fate they largely shared, as well as by the
changes and decline of the political authority with which they were often
connected.[69] Trading places of lesser importance, called *portus* and situated
further inland along the Rhine at Duisburg, Cologne, Mainz, along the
Meuse at Maastricht, Huy, Dinant and along the Scheldt at Ghent, Tournai,
Valenciennes, became the true precursors of medieval towns in the west.[70]
Their trade was supported to a large extent by a network of domanial centres
and by their surplus of food and consumable goods.[71] The maritime *emporia*
along the borders of the empire exported and imported mainly luxury
goods, sometimes in large quantities. Through Dorestad and Domburg,
wine from the upper Rhine area was exported to England and Scandinavia,
ceramics from the region of Cologne and Bonn (Badorf), millstones from
the Eifel (Mayen), glass (funnel-shaped and globular cups) from Kordel
close to Trier and metal ornaments. After the conquest of Saxony and the
Danube region, slaves, furs and wax from Saxony and eastern Europe were
imported from the end of the eighth century along the Elbe-Saale-Danube
border, at, for example, Bardowiek (on the lower Elbe) and Magdeburg,
mentioned in the capitulary of Thionville. Slaves were sold to the Arab
regions along the Mediterranean either via Venice or via the Meuse at
Verdun, the Saône–Rhône river and the northeast of Spain.

Who were the carriers of goods such as ceramics, glass, wine and
millstones into the trade circuit? Large landowners such as the king and
certain churches were probably often the producers of luxury goods in
addition to large quantities of food. Kings, abbeys and bishops mostly sold
these products through the mediation of agents in their service who enjoyed
their special protection. Among the commercial agents of the king, the
Jews, who acted mainly in groups, especially in the valley of the Rhône
(Lyons) and Septimania, took a special place.[72] One reason for this is that
they were dominant, as non-Christians, in the slave trade.

[68] Van Es (1990), pp. 178–9.   [69] Clarke and Ambrosiani (1991), pp. 174–5.
[70] Verhulst (1989), pp. 1–35.   [71] Toubert (1990), pp. 81–4.
[72] Johanek (1987), pp. 55–60.

Traders in the service of abbeys were often not free, though that they also traded on their own account appears from the well-known *Praeceptum negotiatorum* of Louis the Pious.[73] In addition to these groups, independent free merchants were active as well, among whom the Frisians were the most active and the best known. They mainly operated along the Rhine, between Dorestad and the Alps. Along the Rhine in some river ports (*portus*) such as Mainz they had separate living quarters.[74] In Duisburg they lived at the same time as agents of the abbey of Prüm, to which they owed large sums of money.[75] Well known is the case of a Frisian trader Ibo who was in the service of the abbey of St Maximin in Trier at the beginning of the ninth century.[76] Possibly as part of this employment he sailed in association with other merchants with no less than six ships overseas, possibly to England, where the Frisians were also very active.

Finally, it can be stated that trade in Carolingian times was indeed more important than earlier scholars, especially Pirenne, would have us believe.[77] Yet this importance should not be overestimated. It was to a large extent a local and inter-regional trade which had its roots in the great estates which were also the bases for agriculture, crafts and industry. The trade in luxury goods was, compared to the trade in food, consumable goods and objects of daily use, of lesser importance. Outside Italy, the places where trade was conducted were not yet cities in the full sense of the word. With some exceptions these centres cannot be considered as the precursors of the later medieval towns. The people who supported trade were acting primarily as agents in the service of the king and large ecclesiastical landowners. In that they nevertheless were professional traders who maintained some independent commercial dealings, they can be regarded as the 'precursors' of the later medieval merchants.

[73] *MGH Form., Form. Imper.* 37. Ganshof (1957), pp. 101–12.
[74] Lebecq (1983), pp. 230, 240–1.   [75] Kuchenbuch (1978), pp. 302–3.
[76] Lebecq (1983), pp. 28–9.   [77] Johanek (1987), pp. 66–8.

CHAPTER 19

RURAL SOCIETY IN CAROLINGIAN
EUROPE

Chris Wickham

W H E N, around 897, Helmstan of Fonthill in Wiltshire stole Æthelred's belt, he found himself in serious trouble. Helmstan was a king's man, probably a thegn, and a medium landowner, that is to say someone with several tenants: a man of local standing, at least in his village, and with royal connections – though these were not as hard to come by near to the centre of the still small kingdom of Wessex as they were in the huge Frankish empire, and Helmstan was not important enough to be recorded elsewhere. But a belt was not a small matter (it may well have been a *cingulum militare*, the symbol of military obligation itself); and proven theft cast doubt on Helmstan's entire capacity to act at law. His enemies immediately began to claim his lands, including land to which he had clear written title, for Helmstan arguably was no longer legally able to defend himself, and anyway, as a thief, was now bereft of the friends and allies without whose supporting oaths no one could win at court. Helmstan had to go to an old patron, the ealdorman Ordlaf, and promise him the land itself in order to get the backing Helmstan needed to keep it; Ordlaf promised him life tenure, if he kept himself out of trouble, and then arranged both the court strategy and the oath-helpers that Helmstan needed. Helmstan, thanks both to Ordlaf's backing and to his own charters, won his case. Helmstan was a bad lot, however, and soon after that was caught stealing cattle; Ordlaf ended up with the land, although not without trouble both from the king's confiscators and from Helmstan's rivals.[1]

The Helmstan case is well known to Anglo-Saxon historians, and is at the centre of debates about the relative importance of documents and of oaths at court. No one disputes, however, that it shows, more clearly than do most texts, that legal success in the early middle ages depended on the building up of political support as much as on being in the right.[2] And this was not

---

[1] Text ed. in Harmer (1914), no. 18; trans. in Whitelock, *EHD*, no. 102. For the belt, see Leyser (1984), p. 553, for a plausible hypothesis; for the date, Wormald (1988), p. 261.

[2] See, in general, Davies and Fouracre (1986).

restricted to court cases, either; local political and social relationships, between a person and his or her kin, friends, neighbours, patrons and enemies, created the practically relevant world in which each person lived. So they have done in all societies; but in our period this presents problems of evidence. We cannot get at these little worlds through law-codes, for laws merely show us the basic ground-rules that each Helmstan was supposed by some king to live by, not how they actually behaved. Nor can we, for the most part, get at them through historical narratives, for these are focused almost exclusively on the king's court and the upper aristocracy. Hagiography can give us local vignettes, though these tend to be isolated, and socially decontextualised by their moral purpose and their topoi. In the Carolingian period, however, from 750 or so onwards, we begin to be able, for the first time in European history, to see rural society more directly, thanks to the steady expansion in the documentation of individual land transactions. Not many land transactions have the detail and human interest of the Helmstan case, unfortunately; they are legal documents, and are generally as arid and formulaic as any modern written contract. (The Helmstan case actually survives in a letter, from Ordlaf to King Edward the Elder; it is not a 'proper' document.) But when large numbers of such charters survive for a single area, or even sometimes a single village, their authors, local landowners, can be seen more clearly and continuously, as they sell land to each other, give to local churches, lease to tenants, or go to court to make claims against opponents. A rural sociology of people dealing with other people can, in some parts of western Europe, be built up, in a way that cannot be done for any earlier period, even the Roman empire.

The Romans had immense quantities of documents, but they are mostly on papyrus, and very few have survived, except in the dry sands of Egypt. Only parchment allowed the possibility of very long-term record-keeping, and it only became common after 700. The eighth century, too, saw a rapid expansion in the number of written transactions after a post-Roman low point, especially as the church, in our period the most important focus for the culture of writing, began to seek and get private gifts of land. As a result, well-documented areas in our period are, essentially, areas in which large numbers of people gave land to a church or monastery whose archives have survived, and are only well documented for as long as people kept giving. They are also, essentially, areas in which late Roman land law survived, for it was on this legal system that the documentary traditions of Europe themselves depended.[3] All the same, within these constraints, we are reasonably well informed about the local societies of certain regions of

---

[3] See Levy (1951), the classic survey of 'vulgar' Roman law; for non-Roman areas see, for varying observations, Charles-Edwards (1976); Davies (1978b), pp. 16–21; Gurevič (1982); Wickham (1989), pp. 484–99.

Europe for at least parts of the eighth and ninth centuries: notably the
Catalan mountains, Languedoc, the Breton march, southeast Wales, southern Burgundy, the middle and upper Rhineland, Hesse, the Alpine foothills
of Alemannia (in modern Switzerland) and Bavaria, the middle Po plain,
northern Tuscany and the central Apennines. Northern France, so rich in
estate records, was as yet relatively poor in private documents; England
would be relatively poor in both for some time yet. There are other gaps,
some of them substantial. But this spread is otherwise reasonably wide, and
allows us to make a start in an understanding of how rural social
relationships actually worked in practice, on the ground. I will take four
areas as brief examples of such local societies, and then discuss what their
similarities and differences might tell us about the vast range of small-scale
realities that made up Europe as a whole. The four are two small Catalan
counties, Urgell and Pallars; the villages north of the Breton monastery of
Redon; Dienheim in the middle Rhine, just upstream from Mainz; and
Cologno Monzese, a settlement just east of Milan: from, respectively, a
marginal frontier area, a more prosperous marchland, a core area for
Frankish political power, and the urbanised heartland of the Lombard-
Carolingian kingdom of Italy.

URGELL AND PALLARS

The impetus of the Arab and Berber conquest of Spain took the invaders
well into Gaul, through the low passes at both ends of the Pyrenees; but
there is little evidence that they occupied the mountains themselves on a
permanent basis, and it is likely that the highest valleys of the central
Pyrenees saw few Arabs at all except the occasional raiding party – the latter
probably more common after the Frankish occupation of the mountains in
the 780s than before. Pallars and Urgell were two of these valleys; narrow
defiles cut into the limestone, and isolated from the plains to the south by
gorges. Pallars was the more remote and barren; Urgell, slightly nearer to
the sea, had better communications with both the Frankish and the Arab
worlds, and a fertile upland basin at its centre. Urgell had and maintained a
bishop, whose diocese covered the whole of the high Catalan Pyrenees
(Felix, bishop *c*. 782–99, was at the centre of the Adoptionism debate). Both
areas had counts, although Pallars was nominally controlled from Toulouse
from the 780s until the appearance of a locally based and effectively
autonomous comital family headed by Ramon I in the 870s. In the same
decade Guifré (Wifred) the Hairy was count of Urgell, and he extended his
control across most of the counties that would later become Catalonia. Both
of these counts were loyal to the Carolingians, but Carolingian loyalism was a

convenient cover for independent-mindedness, especially under the Robertian King Odo in the 890s; by 900, Frankish power was not very immediate in this area. But it never had been, really; like the Asturias, the Catalan Pyrenees can be seen as a long-surviving area of Visigothic provincial culture, isolated by the mountains, with both local aristocratic families and a strong tradition of Visigothic law and institutions.[4]

Three religious institutions kept enough documents to allow us to say something about mountain society in the ninth century: Urgell cathedral, and two monasteries in parallel valleys in Pallars, Gerri and Alaó, both of them established around 810. All three archives include a wealth of land transactions, both sales between private owners and gifts or sales to the church. The scale of these deals is generally very small: a field here, a vineyard there. The geographical range is very small as well: nearly all the charters in the Alaó archive, the richest of the three, are for the high side-valleys inside a 10 km radius of the monastery. Few landowners are recorded as owning in more than a couple of contiguous village territories; the exceptions are often counts, who must have already taken over the royal lands in the area. We cannot draw any conclusions about the wealth of landowners from the size of individual land transactions, for kings can alienate single fields as easily as peasants can. But their localisation is indicative; we are dealing with people who lived inside two or three hours' walk of all their fields. And the fact that people rarely alienated whole estates, or even tenant houses, may be significant, too. Highly fragmented and localised property-owning in a marginal area, owned by substantial numbers of different people, has led historians to conclude that we are here dealing with a society with a wide stratum of landowning peasant cultivators, alongside the larger landowners who certainly existed everywhere, and this is indeed the most likely interpretation of the texts. Most people were free, too; slaves, generally tenants, are rarely referred to in these areas.

Pallars and Urgell are and were ecologically marginal; but they were heavily populated. Lists of all or most of the family-heads of a village, which we have in a few cases such as Baén above Gerri in 920, or the settlements around the nunnery of Sant Joan de les Abadesses slightly to the east of our valleys in 913, show population levels equivalent to those of the nineteenth century. Unsurprisingly, we have references to small-scale land clearance (*aprisio* or *ruptura*); these peasants must have been on the edge of survival, even with the help of the hunter-gatherer economy in the mountains and the woodland around them, and needed all the land they could get. Colonists

---

[4] The key surveys here are Bonnassie (1975); Abadal (1955; 1980); Salrach (1987; 1988), Martí (1993). For Adoptionism, see chapter 28 below, pp. 762–6. Texts for Pallars, with commentary, are in Abadal (1955); for Urgell, in Baraut (1978; 1979).

were probably moving out of the valleys into the relatively less peopled lowlands, nearer to the frontier, as well.[5] It is interesting, however, that we find references above all to grain and even wine in our texts, and very rarely to the silvo-pastoral resources of the mountains. Horses and cows appear, it is true, in particular as currency (along with grain): the area presumably had little access to coin. Sheep, however, are rarely emphasised as yet, even though they would become the classic resource of the Pyrenean pastoral economy. One has the impression of a society relatively little orientated to what we would see as the potential of its environment, and trying instead to imitate the agriculture of the plains.[6] Woods and pastures were, so far, only accessories to a peasant subsistence agriculture, and not objects of exploitation in their own right; this would only come with the seigneurial power and the commercial upturn of the twelfth century. The only exceptions to this subsistence economy were iron- and salt-working, for these two natural products were locally abundant; iron tools were unusually widely available, and even tithes could be in iron.

Society was isolated in Pallars and Urgell, then. But it was not quiescent. For one thing, there was a pullulation of land-sales; a field or vineyard could easily be bought and sold several times in a generation. These sales could certainly result in the accumulation of properties by an individual, as with the acquisitions of Goltered and his wife Gerosolima in the hills just east of La Seu d'Urgell between 860 and 895, or those of Tedila, southwest of Alaó, between 893 and 911; respectively, seven and nine texts, nearly all involving single fields. Goltered was a judge for the bishop, in his cathedral at La Seu, in 872; Tedila was a priest, which in these valleys seems to have involved considerable social prominence; both of them could well have been local notables profiting from the poverty of their neighbours in hard times. So could the monasteries; both Alaó and Gerri built up very large estates, second only to the counts, through sale as well as gift.[7] But most sales seem to have been between equals, and perhaps for social as much as for economic reasons; even a sale to Alaó could have represented a relationship of clientele as much as an economic transaction. Social relationships can also be seen,

---

[5] Texts: Abadal (1955), no. 132; Udina (1951), no. 38, with Appendix IIA; for commentary, Abadal (1955), pp. 22–4*; (1980), pp. 108–12; Feliu (1984); Bonnassie (1975), pp. 86–91. For clearance, Bonnassie (1975), pp. 99–106 and Salrach (1988) are the most sensible surveys, as against, e.g., Abadal (1980), pp. 75–120.

[6] There are parallels to this in Tuscany: Wickham (1988), e.g. pp. 24–6; but contrast Castile, in Wickham (1983), pp. 434–48. For animals as currency in northwest Spain, see for example, Gautier Dalché (1969). For late medieval Catalan mountain pastoralism, see Le Roy Ladurie (1975), pp. 133–98.

[7] Goltered and Gerosolima: Baraut (1979), nos. 19, 22, 24–7, 37–8; Tedila: Abadal (1955), nos. 88–9, 98, 103, 111–12, 114–16, 120; for Gerri's property see e.g. Abadal (1955), no. 108.

quite explicitly, in church foundations. Most private churches in Europe in this period were founded by single families, as a mark of status and even aristocratic identity. In the Pyrenees, however, most visibly in Urgell, and in Cerdanya and the Berguedà to its east and south, churches in the ninth and early tenth century were founded by their villagers. Between 833 and 913, surviving documents record the consecration of twenty-four new churches by the bishop of Urgell; only seven, all of them after 900, were built by a single person. The others were founded either by a whole village, or by a substantial proportion of it.[8] We should not hypothesise from this a set of economically coherent and organic (still less immemorial) mountain village communities; although uncultivated land, of which there was much in the mountains, was controlled collectively, most of these churches were given lands by local inhabitants on a strictly individual basis, and were indeed ceded to the bishop at their consecration. But it seems clear that village collectivities were strong, and mattered enough to their members that they did not, for a long time, break ranks over such an important issue as the building of a local church. The village, and its constituent families, were the first points of reference; wider political structures, however important, probably came second.

This very local, largely peasant-based society may have been helped to survive not only by the mountains but by the frontier. It was a military zone; the valleys had numerous *castra*, fortified settlements as it would seem from our earliest references, between the more normal open villages; the army-service theoretically due from all freemen in the Carolingian period was perhaps in practice more widely required here than elsewhere. It may be relevant that *Hispani* from south of the Pyrenees, fleeing from the Arabs in the first half of the ninth century, were settled by kings on uncultivated land in Languedoc and explicitly held to military service; these certainly included peasants.[9] But it was not an egalitarian society. The *Hispani* in Languedoc had clearly defined clienteles, with leaders (John of Fontjoncouse near Narbonne under Louis the Pious was a *patronus* to his *commendati*); and even the Catalan villagers who founded their own churches had, in nearly every case, a single leader who gave by far the largest gift, and who was sometimes put in charge of the church by the bishop. These village leaders were usually

---

[8] Baraut (1978), nos. 1, 4–26; see comments in Bonnassie and Guichard (1982), pp. 79–83.

[9] *Castrum* as a settlement, i.e. not just a fortification: see Baraut (1979), nos. 39, 40 for Bar by La Seu. For *Hispani*, see *MGH Dip. Kar.* I, nos. 179, 217, III, no. 10; *MGH Cap.* I, nos. 132–3, II, no. 256; Tessier 40, 43, 46, 94, 118, 164; *HGL* nos 40, 84–5, 150 (*HGL* II, 85 is the most substantial text for John of Fontjoncouse). Most of these texts are republished in Abadal (1952) II. The fullest discussion is Dupont (1965); see also, for sharper surveys, Müller-Mertens (1963), pp. 61–5, 77–8, 85–7; Lewis (1965), pp. 69–74, 159–65.

priests, though sometimes called *viri illustres* or *milites*. As the richest local owners with special social characteristics, already including, sometimes, a specific military identity, they would in the tenth century slowly develop into a local aristocratic stratum to match that in the entourages of counts – if, indeed, these two were ever fully distinct. They would then, in the eleventh century, here as elsewhere in France and the Iberian peninsula, establish seigneurial powers over peasantries, often by force.[10] But these changes were still very much in the future in 900. There are some signs of it already: in 913 the villagers around Sant Joan de les Abadesses found themselves tenants of the nunnery against their will, thanks to a comital grant of their lands over their heads; the inhabitants of Baén in 920, perhaps even more remarkably, granted their whole village to the local count in return for his promise to be their *senior et defensor* against others. But most local power was as yet informal, inside a framework of strong public institutions run by the counts. It was the combined strength of public power and of peasant property-owning that meant that the shift to seigneurial relationships in this area would have to be unusually violent.[11]

EAST BRITTANY

The Breton march was another fringe of the Carolingian world, but a much less marginal one. The area I will discuss here, between Rennes and Redon, was and is a fairly prosperous lowland mixed farming area, with grain-fields intercut with pasture (especially for pigs and sheep) and woodland, in a way totally characteristic of much of ninth-century northern Europe, at least in areas (the great majority) which had not yet developed open-field farming. There was some wine, and ample salt not too far away, on the coast. Money was reasonably easily accessible and there were markets too, at least on a small scale. But it was beyond the edge of Frankish society; it was an area of Breton language and customs, and in the ninth century it was ruled by Breton *principes*, even if these were, except for brief periods, nominally subject to Frankish kings. Frankish institutions had some impact, but only as a veneer, as we shall see. Perhaps the only significant contribution the Franks made to our area was some of the grants the kings made to the monastery of Redon.[12]

Redon's charters are our source for the society of its hinterland; they are,

---

[10] Bonnassie (1980); Pastor (1980); Poly and Bournazel (1980).

[11] Texts as in n. 5; in general, Bonnassie (1975).

[12] See, for this section, the works of Wendy Davies, notably (1985; 1986; 1988). For open-field farming, see pp. 483–5 above; for the Breton *principes*, see chapter 6, p. 185 and Smith (1992).

like those for Catalonia, ninth-century, and peak between 830 (Redon itself was founded in 832) and 875. Their wealth in itself marks a moment of change; Redon was to become, particularly after 860, the dominant power in the area, notably in the ten or so villages to its north. But these villages are reasonably clearly illuminated at that moment, at least. The word I translate as 'village' is the latin *plebs*; this is a term with considerable wealth of nuance, but here it meant a local territory, probably centred on a population nucleus (though it would usually have had more than one settlement in it), and in most cases with a church as an important focus. All significant local transactions took place in the framework of the *plebs*: sales, pledges, dispute settlements, with local inhabitants as witnesses, sureties and judges; the village, that is to say, stands out as a social unit even more clearly than it did in Catalonia.

Most of the inhabitants of the average well-documented *plebs*, Ruffiac or Carentoir or Bains, seem to have been landowning peasant cultivators. The arguments, as in Catalonia, are largely indicative, but they are convincing. Few people can be seen to own more than a single holding; conversely, although the set of charters is unusually rich in sociological detail, relatively few can be seen to be tenants. Proprietors were also, even more than in Pallars, almost all restricted to their own *plebs* as landowners, and are rarely much beyond it even as witnesses to documents and in court cases. Perhaps a quarter of the population were unfree, servile tenants of more prosperous local owners or of aristocrats; as Redon increased its holdings, many free owners became its tenants too. At the other end of the scale there were richer peasants, and then the various strata of what we would call the aristocracy, presumably separated from each other by fairly narrow bands of wealth (though there was less fragmentation of land than in Catalonia, and inevitably less flexibility as a result; single peasant holdings were apparently normally single blocs of land, and much less often divided). The aristocracy did not, as a whole, intervene in village society, and much of it operated more on a 'national' level, in the entourage of the Breton *princeps*. There was one important exception, however, the families of 'machtierns'. Machtierns were, in some ill-defined way, the leaders of *plebes*; they presided over public gatherings, and sometimes over courts. They had local political authority, that is to say, and were mostly not very close to the *principes*. But they did not have a clear power to coerce, or even control: *plebes* tended to run themselves, through a wide stratum of local notables who all knew each other, rather than simply being the fields of action of machtierns.

This, in fact, is the real originality of the Breton material. It is most visible in court cases. These have some of the terminology of the Frankish court; they were sometimes called the *placitum* or the *mallus*, just as in Francia, and their leading men were sometimes called *scabini* or *boni viri*. But their presuppositions were quite unlike those of the Carolingian world. There were no legal experts of any kind, and no references to law. Judges were not professional, and a *iudex* in one case could simply appear as a witness in the next. Where judgement was needed, local *seniores* ('elders') could provide it, sometimes from their own personal knowledge. The people who ran courts were not, in fact, any sort of clearly defined elite. Thus, judges were more often substantial owners than others were, but not all of them were more than cultivators; and most other court figures were simply peasants, their only qualifications being that they were free, male, and probably experienced and well-thought-of. They ran a strictly local justice, based on the structures of the community. We have documents that record some classic village negotiations, as a result. When in the 860s Wordoital of Ruffiac made an accusation against the priest Maenweten, the latter began to gather evidence together to be used in court. Seeing this, Wordoital retreated: he did not want to lose Maenweten's friendship, as he would if the case became public, and he offered compromise terms, which involved a pay-off to him of 4 shillings; Maenweten accepted. Such a transaction, however common, would probably never have been recorded elsewhere; here, it seemed close enough to a public dispute to be worth writing down. When people went to court, negotiations could still continue; courts tended to prefer compromises, which would restore social equilibrium without trouble, and often actively worked to achieve them. In part they had to, for this society had no regular means of enforcing judicial decisions publicly; losers were bound only by their obligations to the men who had stood surety for them in court. *Principes* were very distant; machtierns (unlike counts in Francia) had no visible policing functions. Villagers had to do it themselves, through the mixture of petty hatreds and family or neighbourly solidarity that can be found in most peasant societies.[13]

Court cases are, as we have already seen for Helmstan, key guides to how society really works, and in the Redon area they are particularly clear – as well as being unusually coherently analysed in Wendy Davies' work. They show a world which, while easily understandable in terms of modern peasant sociology, is quite alien to that assumed by the fixed procedures, run by counts, of the classic Carolingian *placitum*; even the remote Catalan Pyrenees, thanks to a strong Visigothic institutional tradition, shows more formality and hierarchy in its courts than does Brittany. Again, we have to

---

[13] The clearest parallel to this in medieval Europe is probably eleventh- to thirteenth-century Iceland: see e.g. Byock (1988); Miller (1990). For Wordoital and Maenweten, see *CR* no. 144.

recognise that hierarchies did exist. Apart from machtierns, there were families of rich peasants and quasi-peasants, who had considerable local influence in the Redon area. (Many, as in Catalonia, were dynasties of priests.) And Redon itself was increasing its lands and influence dramatically, often at the expense of the local priests, who were drawn into the monastery; after *c.* 850 it gained direct judicial control over the four nearest *plebes*, as the beginning of a much more structured political power bloc than had existed in the area before. But Redon was at least local; and, outside its four *plebes*, its influence, while great, was not different in type from that of machtierns or even village elders: it was informal, based on negotiation rather than control. The absence of stable hierarchies, and of any formal dependence that might have subjected an extremely localised day-to-day social activity to some political control, seem to have been the major distinguishing features of east Breton village society up to 850 at the earliest. Everyone else, even the Breton *princeps*, impinged on the *plebs* from outside, and intermittently at that.

DIENHEIM

Moving from Brittany to the Rhineland, we see a much sharper contrast. The Rhineland was the main through-route in Frankish Europe. Its pottery and its natural products (such as timber, or quern-stones) could be found in much of the North Sea commerce area; some of its cities, like Mainz and Cologne, were among the few in northern Europe to have maintained relatively substantial populations and some true urban functions, in an economic sense, from the Roman period onwards. The middle Rhine valley was, furthermore, one of the heartlands of the Frankish kingdoms, with major eighth- and ninth-century royal residences such as Worms and Frankfurt, and a dense network of palaces and other royal estates along the river, such as Gernsheim, Trebur and Ingelheim. The alluvial land of the wide valley south of Mainz and Frankfurt is rich, and has long been heavily settled. It is flanked by low hills covered in vineyards, before one reaches the thick woodland of the higher hill-country, the Odenwald or the Taunus; and specialist wine-producing villages already existed in 800. One of these was Dienheim, a village on the Rhine halfway between Mainz and Worms, which is mentioned in over 150 documents from the years between 750 and 840, mostly from the cartularies of the monasteries of Fulda and Lorsch. The Lorsch texts, which are the majority, are heavily abbreviated, and both the sets are more formulaic than many early medieval charter traditions, thus reducing the amount of incidental material we can use. Nonetheless, the

village is far more densely documented than any other rural settlement in
Europe in our period; it thus fits well into our gallery of examples.[14]

The documents we have for Dienheim are almost all gifts to the church;
there are few sales, or private transactions of any kind. They are mostly of
small plots of land, either vineyards (the great bulk) or grain fields, in the
village or its *marca*, the territory immediately around it. A minority of gifts,
some two dozen, are of house-plots, *mansi* or *areae*, usually with their lands,
and often with servile tenants (*mancipia*); the texts indicate that such tenant
plots consisted of scattered fields, as in Catalonia, interspersed with those of
other owners and tenants. A very few gifts were probably somewhat larger,
for they included many *mancipia*, who are, as is often the case in German
documents, named; one, a cession by Adalhart to Fulda in 796 of all his lands
in Dienheim, lists eighteen (or, in another version of the text, forty-seven).
Dienheim had a river-port by the 790s, and presumably exported its wine
down the Rhine to northern Europe.[15] This may have been one of the
reasons why so many people owned land there, although it was certainly not
the only one – there were many other wine villages in the middle Rhineland,
as a glance at the Lorsch documents will show.

Despite the fragmentation of property, one cannot in Dienheim immediately deduce the existence of peasant proprietors, as in our two previous
examples. The number of *mancipia* in the village was high, for a start; it is
clear that much land was cultivated by men and women of servile status. It is
also clear that many of the donors to Fulda and Lorsch were reasonably rich.
One, indeed, was the king, who gave his estate there, and most (although
not quite all) of his land, to Fulda in 782.[16] Others were major middle
Rhenish aristocrats, from many of the numerous great and (often) old
families of the area, such as the 'Rupertiner', or the family network who
controlled the church of St Lambert in Mainz, including close associates of
the Carolingians. Even otherwise unknown donors, in fact, frequently gave
land spread over several villages, often stretching across the whole middle
Rhine region and beyond. And the steadily expanding properties of Lorsch
and Fulda, not to speak of five other less well-documented churches and

---

[14] For Dienheim, see Gockel (1970), pp. 184–203, 222–7; Gensicke (1973); Staab (1975), pp. 262–
78; Freise (1978), pp. 1187–98. The texts are nearly all in *UF*, *CDF* and *CL*, all of which have
good indexes; Gockel (1970) pp. 190ff. lists the others. Gockel and Staab give overviews of the
Rhineland; see further Ewig (1980), with bibliography; Falck (1972) and Staab (1975), pp. 122–32
for Mainz; Hodges (1982) for trade; Déléage (1941), pp. 200–26 and Schwind (1977) for
fragmentation of property in villages.

[15] *UF* nos. 237, 246. *Mancipia* with agricultural duties could be either demesne slaves or – perhaps
more often – tenants; in areas of fragmented landowning they were usually tenants (see, for this
area, Staab (1975), pp. 331–51, esp. p. 346).

[16] *UF* no. 149 (*MGH Dip. Kar.* I, no. 145).

monasteries which came to possess property locally thanks to gifts from the period between 750 and 840, added further to the lands of outside owners in Dienheim. German medievalists, reacting against nineteenth-century nationalist theories of Germanic freedom and village community, have become the most cautious historians in Europe when it comes to looking for early medieval peasant owners, and Dienheim has been used as an example of this caution: it is argued that all the landowners about whom one can say anything at all seem to own a lot of property, spread widely; whether or not they are aristocrats, they certainly cannot be said to be peasants.[17]

This is not the whole story, however. Most of the Dienheim donors are unidentifiable, even in the thousands of Fulda and Lorsch charters; and one might well feel that, in a world of partible inheritance, which certainly helped to create the fragmented tenure of most of the Rhine villages, over-prolific and otherwise unlucky branches even of aristocratic families could well end up pretty poor. And in Dienheim our donors are not actually the only documented figures. In the Fulda charters, which survive in fuller versions than those for Lorsch, we find a coherent group of regular witnesses to Dienheim documents – thirty-six, on Eckhard Freise's figures – only a third of whom are documented as giving land to the church; conversely, most donors rarely if ever witnessed documents at all. These witnesses were largely local, especially those who were not donors; at least, they rarely witnessed in texts outside Dienheim, even for neighbouring villages. Who were these people? They were by definition free and law-worthy; they seem from their witnessing to have constituted the backbone of Dienheim's public activity. They must have been an elite inside the village, but quite possibly only by contrast with its servile inhabitants. Whether they cultivated the soil or not, they made up a village-based society. Something of the flavour of their known actions can be gained by looking at one active member of the group, Batucho (*fl. c.* 790–828), whose name is rare enough for us to be able to presume that most references to it are to the same person. Batucho witnessed twenty-three times in Dienheim and three times in neighbouring villages (two of them just across the Rhine to the east), and also three times in and around Kreuznach, 20 km to the west. Dienheim looked regularly across the Rhine, as also north to Mainz, as the overall distribution of properties in the area makes clear: these were the major directions of its social – and doubtless commercial – contacts. The Kreuznach link is less explicable, though two out of the three charters are

[17] So, especially, Staab (1975), pp. 262–78; critical are Gockel (1976) and, implicitly, Freise (1978), pp. 1187–98, who has worked most systematically on the witness-lists. For the intellectual background, see Staab (1980) and Schulze (1974) among others, and chapter 18 above, pp. 454–7.

for the same man, Ediram, a local aristocrat, and Batucho here, along with other Dienheim witnesses, may simply have been following a patron. He is recorded as a donor only once, giving portions of two tenant houses near Alzey, 15 km to the southwest, to Lorsch in 813. If this is really the same man, he had a certain range as a property-owner, and could perhaps be classed as a medium owner, with enough land for him not to have to cultivate. But other than that he was overwhelmingly a Dienheim figure, and certainly ceded none of his land there to any documented church. This was a common feature of the village witnesses. Even those who did give land in Dienheim might only give a single field; an example is Waldleih (*fl. c.* 790–818, a witness twelve times, always in Dienheim), who gave a vineyard to Lorsch in 817, probably just before he died.[18]

This sort of information is sparse enough, but it does enable us to draw some conclusions with wider implications. It is seldom possible to be sure one is dealing with peasant owners in this period; only a charter of gift or sale of all an owner's possessions, clearly itemised, gives a clear guide to the landed resources of any proprietor, rich or poor, and these are rare. But in Dienheim – one is tempted to say, even in Dienheim – one can isolate a highly localised stratum of freemen with public standing, who constituted village society, and may well have included cultivators. What they did in their village apart from witness is far less clear than in our previous two examples; we have no court cases or collective acts for Dienheim, or for any of its neighbours. But Dienheim had a certain role as a public centre (it is called a *vicus publicus* in some texts), and there may have been, for example, a court there, at least occasionally. With all these aristocrats about, it is unlikely to have been run through the almost organic consensus we saw around Redon; this was an area of formalised hierarchies of dependence, both on aristocratic or royal land and in aristocratic entourages; and, in the arena of the public, if there was ever a part of the Frankish world where the clear-cut responsibilities and procedures of the capitularies actually worked, it would have been in a core royal region like the middle Rhine. But Dienheimers kept their identity nonetheless. Precisely the fact that, in the midst of all this aristocratic gift-giving to Fulda and Lorsch, so many local inhabitants gave little or nothing to those monasteries is at the very least

---

[18] Batucho: *UF* nos. 169, 213, 261, 278; *CDF* nos. 198–9, 201, 212–13, 216–17, 250–1, 264, 281–3, 285, 335, 338, 378, 421, 431, 459, 464, 478, 487 (and perhaps, rather later, 534); *CL* nos. 208, 1107; see also Weirich (1936), n. 26, an isolated Hersfeld text. *CDF* no. 388 lists a slave called Batucho, who is evidently a different person; the references in *CL* nos. 2666, 2701 (*s.a.* 770–3), for higher up the Rhine, seem too early to be for the same man. Waldleih: *UF* nos. 169, 213, 237, 257; *CDF* nos. 198, 212–13, 216–17, 282, 328, 338; Weirich (1936), no. 26; *CL* no. 1701. For Ediram, see Staab (1975), pp. 386–7.

suggestive: they may have wanted to keep a certain distance from the networks of clienteles that criss-crossed the middle Rhine, run as these clienteles were by aristocrats and abbots who were potentially, and would become, threats to the public autonomy and the very existence of small owners. Further than this, however, we cannot speculate.

Milan too was a major political and economic centre, second in the Lombard-Carolingian kingdom of Italy only to neighbouring Pavia, which was the capital; indeed, it was probably larger than Pavia, and is a good candidate for being the second or third largest city in early medieval Latin Europe, after Rome and maybe Naples. Its artisans and merchants often appear in surviving texts, even though these, as usual, only relate to their ownership of land. Its market is documented, as are numerous churches and public buildings; it expanded further in the tenth century, too, as references both to new suburbs and urbanising rural families clearly demonstrate. Its hinterland was fertile, and there is some evidence for crop specialisations, such as, for instance, the olive-groves on Lake Como. It had a large and complex society of judges, clerics, merchants and aristocratic landowners, and since all of these people owned land, usually in widely scattered units, the complexity of its social structure spilled out into the countryside and integrated rural and urban society quite tightly. Milan was entirely typical of documented Italian cities in this; before 900 we can see it in Lucca, Verona and Ravenna; and, after 900, in many more.[19]

Our guide to Milanese society is the charter collection of the suburban monastery of S. Ambrogio, and, as usual, we are restricted to the field of S. Ambrogio's interests. It expanded rather late by the standards of other major churches in Carolingian Italy. Most sets of gifts to churches in Italy, as in Germany, peak around 800, and dry up around 830. But S. Ambrogio only became a monastery in the 780s, thanks to patronage from Charlemagne and the archbishop of Milan (previously, it had been a rather somnolent late Roman basilica), and only began to collect land on a large scale after 835. Perhaps for this reason, it had relatively little in Milan, where it had numerous well-established ecclesiastical rivals for patronage; it mostly obtained properties in the villages outside town. One of these was Cologno Monzese, a village some 10 km to the northeast of Milan, a

---

[19] For Milan and the Milanese, see Violante (1953); Bognetti (1954); Keller (1979), pp. 304–22; Rossetti (1986); Balzaretti (1989). For Milanese urban archaeology, see Lusuardi Siena (1986); Andrews (1986). Parallels in Italy: Bullough (1966); Wickham (1981), pp. 80–92, 101–4; Bullough (1972) for background.

medium-sized grain-growing village, which is quite well documented as a result, and can serve as our model here. The number of documents for ninth-century Cologno number only about twenty, far less than for Dienheim, but they are often very detailed, and we can learn a good deal that is hidden from us in Germany.[20]

S. Ambrogio moved into Cologno by two different routes. One was by buying up land from local owners. The 'Leopegisi', as they are now called, are the best attested of these owners, and are documented between 830 and 882. They were a family with several houses in our earliest texts for them, all in or near Cologno, but with no links to city officials or church or lay elites; one could call them medium owners, for they were not cultivators, and they may indeed have been Cologno's richest family around 850, but they were not aristocrats. In the 860s they, or some of them at least, needed money, for they seem to have pledged increasing amounts of their land to S. Ambrogio, presumably for concealed loans; and it is certain that S. Ambrogio had acquired a high percentage of their property by 880 or so. In 865 one of them, Walpert, resisted, and occupied some of the ceded property, by cutting down woodland and ploughing it, but he could not defeat S. Ambrogio's charters and its political support, and the monastery won the resultant court case. By 876 Walpert was dead, and his children were reduced to poverty; the family survived, but maybe only as cultivators.[21] We only know about the Leopegisi because S. Ambrogio kept their charters, which in itself makes them atypical; other, more prudent, landowning families sold much smaller amounts of property to the monastery, and did not lose their position. Most of those we can say something about were nonetheless local medium owners like the Leopegisi, though others were certainly always peasants. (There is no doubt of the existence in Italy of a substantial stratum of peasant cultivators in and among the scattered lands of medium and large owners; they are explicitly attested in many places.) One of these families moved into the city in the tenth century. Milanesi appear as local owners and witnesses, too, well before 900, and some of them are called *negotiantes*, merchants.[22] It is likely enough that not only S. Ambrogio was buying into Colognese society.

S. Ambrogio's other entrée into Cologno landowning was by the gift of an estate (*curtis*) by a royal follower (*gasindio*), Aribert, maybe around 800, including part of a church, S. Giorgio. This property, the monastery's first

---

[20] Rossetti (1968) is the basic analysis for Cologno; the other Milan surveys cited in n. 19 also discuss it. Texts are in Porro, which I cite for convenience; the recent edition by Natale (1970) is not yet widely available.

[21] Porro nos. 113, 142, 214, 216, 222–3, 226, 228, 234 (= Manaresi no. 67), 239, 260–1, 267, 315; Rossetti (1968), pp. 101–22; Balzaretti (1989), pp. 164–73.

[22] Porro nos. 216, 226, 239, 260, 339, 352; Rossetti (1968), pp. 128–34, 155–6, 172–82.

and largest in the village, caused more problems than did those of the local lay owners, for Archbishop Angilbert I ceded most of it in benefice in 822–3 to his vassal Lupus of Schianno, and the monastery did not get it back for nearly four decades, despite repeated attempts. In the end, the archbishop (by now Angilbert II) relented; in a court case of 859 between S. Ambrogio and Lupus, held in the archiepiscopal palace in the city, Lupus appealed to Angilbert for proof that he held the *curtis* legally from him, and the archbishop refused, stating that his predecessor's benefices were illegal. Lupus had to cede, although not without recompense. A month later, in a private agreement, but one witnessed both by the representatives of the bishop and by some of the lay participants in the case, Lupus got for his Cologno lands a life-time cession by the monastery of lands in Balerna (somewhat closer to Schianno, in fact, which is over 40 km from Cologno, to the northwest).[23] Only after this agreement was S. Ambrogio free to expand in Cologno. Significantly, it was in the years immediately after this that it took over the Leopegisi lands; after 892 it was the largest local owner, and in the 920s it built a castle there as well.

The interest for us here is less, perhaps, the simple fact of the expansion of the lands of the monastery of S. Ambrogio, and more the social context in which it occurred. It should be clear that we are dealing with a sharply hierarchical society here, with landowning peasants (and certainly tenants, both servile and free), but also many strata of landowners, right up to counts and bishops. It was also explicitly a society linked by ties of private dependence. Aristocrats were archiepiscopal vassals; counts, too, could get major churches in benefice from the king. The archbishop, who was S. Ambrogio's patron, seems to have been in practice free to dispose of monastic land, even if this had no basis in law; S. Ambrogio could only win it back in court with his support, and then had to pay off the loser. This was how major monasteries had to operate, even at the heart of the Italian kingdom, and even though the framework of public power was very carefully respected by all. The Leopegisi, who had no powerful friends, did not stand much of a chance once their position became weak. This intercutting of public and private power was a constant reality in Carolingian Europe. On the other hand, it was, in this region, a stable system. The Leopegisi went under, but many of their equals and inferiors survived. Other medium owners were *scabini*, and had some public influence;[24] they could even rise, if they were lucky. In the hinterland of cities, there were too

---

[23] Porro nos. 179, 207 (= Manaresi no. 64), 208 for Lupus; see Rossetti (1968), pp. 65–95; and, in general, Wickham (1986), Padoa Schioppa (1988), Bonacini (1991) for courts. S. Ambrogio did not get S. Giorgio back until 892: Porro no. 352 (cf. 142).

[24] See Fumagalli (1968), pp. 22–31 for profiles of *scabini* in Italy, and Estey (1951) for parallels in Francia.

many rival families and churches for one easily to gain dominance in any given area, and the poor were protected by this power balance. Similarly, they were, at least minimally, protected by the continuing structures of the Carolingian state, which never entirely failed in the Italian plains. In Italy, unlike in (for example) Catalonia or France, the socio-political patterns of the ninth century would not be all that different in the eleventh, and even, in some respects, the twelfth.

These four societies were not in any sense 'typical', even of their immediate surroundings; they just happen to be well documented. Still, there are some clear similarities between them, which are not obscured by the different stresses on particular aspects of their social structures that different sorts of evidence tend to produce. By what criteria should we compare them? We are dealing with four different legal traditions in these societies, Visigothic, Breton, Frankish and Lombard; that we can nonetheless see close analogies between their local practices illustrates very clearly the limits of law as a guide to rural society. Rather, the bases of any comparison between them need to be wider, more sociological, categories. Here, I will discuss four such features that are common to all four of our societies: the patterns of landholding, the nature of the village, patronage and violence.

In each of our societies, land tenure was very fragmented. This is a typical result of partible inheritance, and it is considered normal and even desirable by many peasant societies; there is no need to regard it as unstable or irrational. Land often, as a result, had to be described field by field, and such descriptions were pretty similar throughout Europe. Fields tended to be defined by their neighbours on each side, or by the streams and innumerable public roads or tracks that bordered them. Neighbours, above all, mattered: they were authorities, often the only authorities, as to which land belonged to whom, or – most importantly – where its bounds actually lay.[25] Public rituals of 'bounding' land, with public surveyors and witnesses, were common across Europe (those for the ex-Visigothic provinces seem to have been the most elaborate). Such rituals were as important an element in the construction of local identity as any of the more obvious ceremonies of belonging, such as attendance at church or (for the free) at court. Precisely because land was so divided, its exploitation required the recognition that other owners or holders had rights; one regularly depended on one's neighbours, or some of them, both for support at court, and for loans of

---

[25] See, in general, Dopsch (1962) I, pp. 249–51, 306–9; Déléage (1941), pp. 200–51 (an unjustly neglected classic); Schwind (1977); Conti (1965), pp. 133–43, 212–15 (covering eleventh-century Tuscany, but with endless extension). For the anthropology of fragmented land, see Davis (1973), pp. 107–45 for a Mediterranean case.

produce and labour, in a give and take without which one could hardly expect to survive. The friendless, like Helmstan, could lose their lands entirely; or, if they were poorer, maybe not get through a hard winter. In constructing such support networks, kinship was obviously crucial, but there are consistent signs that it was not the only link early medieval villagers recognised. How one actually determined which of one's neighbours were to be friends and which enemies, however, we rarely know.

Fragmented land was not, it should be recognised, characteristic of the whole of Europe. Already in Brittany we saw less of it, for there inheritance divisions stopped short of dividing tenures unless there were no other way of apportioning land. And to an extent this stress on fragmentation is implicitly due to the bias of our evidence: villages owned by a single proprietor, or two or three, appear in fewer documents, for there were fewer people to alienate land. In Anglo-Saxon England, at least after 800 or so, much of the land seems to have been in the hands of kings, churches and aristocrats, often in large blocs; single estates (which were often single villages) frequently had only one charter, which was handed from owner to owner somewhat like a modern title-deed. Northern France, too, had many areas of fiscal (royal) land, handed *en bloc* to monasteries; the only evidence we have for such estates after the initial gift may be the estate-record of its owner, its 'polyptych', in the run of such records that we have for the ninth century. Even in the Rhineland, although Dienheim was an anthill of tiny properties, neighbouring Guntersblum may have belonged entirely to a single owner, St Ursula's church in Cologne.[26] It is very hard to assess the relative frequency of fragmented land and large concentrated estates, for they intercut so much, and our evidence is so chancy. In Italy, scholars concur that very few villages were single estates, except for fiscal and ex-fiscal properties, the latter usually in the hands of the church; and big fiscal blocs were, in most of the country, restricted to marginal land, especially in the mountains. In Germany, old-settled land like the Rhine and Danube valleys was more likely to be divided between many proprietors than was the hill country of Hesse or the Ardennes; in France we could say the same, though the rich Seine valley, an old Merovingian power base, seems to have had more fiscal land than elsewhere. Overall, nonetheless, it is hard to avoid the conclusion that tenure was a great deal more likely to be fragmented than not. The reasons for regional divergences largely lie in variations in the development of concepts of property itself, and cannot be dealt with here.[27]

[26] For England, Maitland (1897), pp. 272–307 and *passim*; for Guntersblum, Gockel (1970), pp. 57, 226.

[27] Déléage (1941), pp. 200–26 is the widest ranging survey for northern France and Germany; it has been updated only in detail. For concepts of property, see n. 3.

But they are important; rural social relationships are going to be very different if villagers are all or mostly owners, tenants of many lords, or tenants – free or servile – of only one.

Fragmentation led to flexibility. There could be a very wide variety in levels of land owning in any village, from regional and local aristocrats, through village notables with dependent tenants, small owners, cultivators who owned some of their land and rented the rest, and free tenants, down to servile tenants and landless slaves. There were many intermediate grades between these, as well. None of the divisions was entirely clear-cut. Even that between free and unfree, in principle the fundamental division in early medieval society, could be unclear in practice, as the substantial number of court cases in which tenants claim their freedom show – the criteria courts used to determine free or slave status could in practice be very *ad hoc*. This flexibility was one of the most important elements, in fact, that underpinned the informality of Carolingian society. Status groups were almost never clearly bounded. The notorious difficulty involved in defining the aristocracy of early medieval Europe has one of its origins at the local level: we can seldom be certain about the status of the people for whom we have documents, and we can at least conclude from this that exact levels of free status were not sufficiently important to be recorded in written transactions. One should contrast with this the importance of titles like *miles* and *dominus* in documents of around 1100;[28] although such terms can be found in early medieval charters, they are far rarer. There were, it is true, societies like Lombard Italy, where in the eighth century and into the ninth titles like *vir devotus*, *vir honestus* and *vir magnificus* appear quite often in land transactions; they were already less common before the Frankish conquest in 774, however, and may have represented an earlier (and by now vestigial) public division inside the armed Lombard people.[29] The word 'public' is crucial here, in fact: for, normally, the only consistent marks of status we find in documents for lay society are official titles like count or *scabinus*, rather than any broader social categories. Although it would be ingenuous to believe that there was no aristocracy in Carolingian Europe, at least as a *de facto* class of large landowners, with privileged access to public office and the king, it was not a legally defined stratum, and *local* status did not necessarily depend on belonging to it.[30]

In the light of local realities such as these, it is at least less surprising that Carolingian legislation – like the Romano-Germanic law-codes before it – gave so much space to the position of the free; free status (however defined)

---

[28] See e.g. Duby (1973), pp. 416–20. For free and unfree, see chapter 18 above, pp. 460–1.

[29] Tabacco (1969), pp. 234–46.

[30] See e.g. Tabacco (1972); Goetz (1983); and chapter 18 above, pp. 457–66.

was still the normal criterion for participation in public life, theoretically independent of the clienteles of the powerful. And the predominantly agricultural interest of much early medieval law makes sense as well: although not all cultivators were free, many were; and some, at least, owned land too. One does not have to be tied to the romantic image of the free Germanic peasantry, the *Gemeinfreie* of nineteenth-century scholarship, to recognise that at least some early medieval peasants could be landowners, for at least part of their land, nearly everywhere in Europe, and could have access to public rights and burdens as a result – characteristically, army-service, public works such as road- and bridge-building, and attendance at law-courts. However little this meant in practice, it was important in theory, and was consistently upheld by kings.

The normal geographical basis for the social activity of the peasantry was the village. Words and phrases that one could translate as references to villages and their territories appear in all four of our examples, as also in nearly every charter collection in Europe: *vici*, *loci* and *villae*, each with a wide distribution across Europe, or more localised words like *fundus* (or *locus et fundus*) and *casale* in Italy, *marca* in Germany, *plebs* in Brittany. Historians sometimes argue as to how far these words really mean 'village': *villa*, to name only one, has had many meanings across the millennia, and had meant 'estate unit' with some regularity in the Roman world. Some historians have, indeed, gone so far as to doubt whether villages existed at all in the early middle ages, arguing that settlement units were too small, mobile, randomly arranged, and conceptually and socially weak to be designated as such.[31] This is an argument only about words; if a village is a rural settlement in a geographically defined territory, then the words listed above certainly meant 'village' in our documents. They were not all large, though some were (Dienheim must have had a couple of hundred inhabitants at the very least, and Baén in Pallars perhaps a hundred; Palaiseau, one of St Germain's villages outside Paris, had over six hundred). They were sometimes concentrated settlements, and sometimes more dispersed: the micro-regional differences uncovered by archaeological, geographical and documentary research are too complex to be summarised here, but it can at least be said that the bewildering contrasts in settlement layout that can be seen in twentieth-century Europe all had their analogues before 900. There is some sign that in parts of Europe, such as Denmark, Germany and much of

---

[31] Chapelot and Fossier (1985), pp. 71, 129. On the conceptual uncertainty of the word *villa*, which still in *Lex Salica* ranges from 'village' to 'house', see Schmidt-Wiegand (1977), but Heinzelmann (1993) shows that *villa* normally means village in Gregory of Tours.

England, settlement could move around inside given village territories, at least up to the ninth century, and often later. In the tenth and eleventh centuries, by contrast, villages sometimes became more nucleated, whether on the tops of hills and behind fortifications as in the *incastellamento* process of central Italy or southern France, or in the centre of the relatively fixed and organised structure of the open-field system, as in much of northern Europe – the growing concerns of lords with local control had a good deal to do with both.[32] But these developments need not be seen as the 'invention of the village'; even dispersed and shifting settlements can easily have inhabitants with a clear sense of territorial identity and a commitment to social and economic co-operation (and also, for that matter, lords with considerable local involvement). Such identity and co-operation can be seen consistently in our eighth- and ninth-century documentary material, all over Europe, with only a few exceptions.[33]

This said, however, it should also be stressed that village communities were rarely as clearly bounded and structured in the Carolingian period as they would be in the twelfth century. The coherent local collectivities that we saw in the Pyrenees and in Brittany are not so visible elsewhere in Europe. Villages as yet rarely had any type of formalised local institutions that we can see in our sources. Local public administrative units, such as the *centenae* of the Frankish world (whatever these actually were), were too large or vague; in the ecclesiastical sphere, a widespread village-based parish structure was still centuries in the future.[34] Local public figures, such as the *boni homines* that appear frequently in court cases from all over Europe, were notables from given communities, rather than representatives of them. It is beyond doubt true that the exploitation of uncultivated lands, woodland and pasture and marsh, was usually village based, and, where these lands were systematically exploited, this could produce an early coherence for village society, as we can see not only in Catalonia, but in Castile and the Asturias, and in the central Italian Apennines. In northern Europe, at least in strip-farming areas, agriculture already involved collective decisions, for example, over when and what to sow. And villages could have local customs (*consuetudo loci*) that included standard rents payable on different kinds of

---

[32] Settlement mobility: Bernhard (1982) for one example, Vogelgesang, outside Speyer; Hvass (1986) for Vorbasse in Denmark; Steuer (1989), pp. 117–19; Taylor (1983), pp. 117–50 and Hamerow (1991), for mobility and nucleation in England in general. *Incastellamento*: Bourin-Derruau (1987); Toubert (1973), pp. 303–68; Settia (1984); Wickham (1985); Montarrenti (1989). For settlement diversity, Chapelot and Fossier (1985) is probably the best general survey.

[33] The most notable contrast with the world of villages can be found in the ex-Byzantine areas of Italy, which maintained a territorial structure based on fragmented estates that went back to the Roman empire: Castagnetti (1979), pp. 169–204; Toubert (1973), pp. 455–65.

[34] For parishes, Reynolds (1984), pp. 81–90; for *centenae*, Murray (1988).

holding, which could be, at least in theory, safeguarded as landlords changed.[35] Some of these collective arrangements covered not only free villagers but also the unfree, those technically with no rights; even slaves, for example, often owed standard rents, and cultivators of all statuses must have co-operated in strip farming. Others, however, were restricted to the free: every reference to a village in a law-code, for example, described its free society by definition, as with the famous clause in the *Pactus Legis Salicae* that granted a (somewhat restricted) right of veto to *vicini* if a newcomer wanted to settle in their village.[36] Servile *vicini* certainly did not have that right, or any other local legal right, whether to witness publicly or to seek the support of their kin and neighbours at law. The village community would not be fully complete until the unfree had more local rights, and this was a slow development: in Continental Europe it would not be achieved until the eleventh century at the earliest.

European villages in our period thus existed, and had clear identities and even local customs; in some areas they had quite extensive collective functions. But they did not yet in most places constitute well-defined legal communities. They were, as were many other elements of Carolingian rural society, still relatively informally organised. Nonetheless, inside these limits, villages could often operate as effective *de facto* units of horizontal social solidarity, in conjunction with the structures of kinship already outlined in chapter 18; these were the counterweights to the (more often discussed) vertical structures of lordship and patronage in the interplay of mutual obligations in society as a whole.

Personal lordship has been analysed in the previous chapter, but at the local level formal dependence was only one element in the construction of a social world. One could seek patrons and allies in many ways, as one can see in a brief example from one of Einhard's letters. Einhard wrote from Seligenstadt to Hraban Maur in Fulda, perhaps in the 830s, about the plight of one of Hraban's men, Gundhart, who had been called to the army. It appears that Gundhart was in feud, and one of his worst enemies was the count under whom he would have to march; Einhard was interceding with Hraban not to object when Gundhart reneged on his military obligations and paid the subsequent fine. Gundhart clearly had many superiors: his public commander, the count; his personal lord, Hraban, whose vassal he

---

[35] Village collectivities of various kinds: Pastor (1980); García de Cortázar (1988), pp. 10–27; Wickham (1982), pp. 18–28, 69. Locally based rent traditions: Kuchenbuch (1978), pp. 236–44; Kuchenbuch (1983); Goetz (1989) – though see also the cautionary remarks in Goetz (1984) and Verhulst (1983).   [36] *Pactus Legis Salicae* (ed. *MGH Leges nat. germ.* IV: 1), c. 45.

presumably was; but also Einhard, as a much more informal friend and patron (and perhaps a necessary one, in view of Hraban's notorious authoritarianism and narrow-mindedness). He had pressing – not to say threatening – family obligations, too; we are only lacking his neighbours, and maybe the church he was closest to, for the characterisation of his immediate world to be complete.[37] How one dealt with, or chose, one's patrons is unfortunately as hard to analyse, given our sources, as how one dealt with, and chose friends from, one's neighbours, precisely because patronage as a whole was so much less formal than lordship. The only informal social bond that is at all consistently documented in our texts – so visibly, in fact, that it is often scarcely noticed as a social bond at all – is that between lay owners and churches, as expressed in grants of land to them. We do at least have thousands of attestations of this; one can construct, as a result, entire patronage networks for individual churches and monasteries, even if one can usually only speculate about their content and about what for example, led one person with land in Dienheim to give it to Fulda, but his or her neighbour to donate instead to Lorsch, or to no church at all.

Why did people give land to the church, in fact? Sometimes they did it for the pious reasons they generally claimed in their charters, without doubt; or at least as part of the more prosaic gift-exchange that the church had encouraged since the fifth century, of prayers, or even entry into heaven, in return for material cessions. Sometimes they did it as a family preservation strategy, as when a family founded its own private church or monastery, which it would in future control collectively, as the undivided focus for increasingly scattered individual holdings. Sometimes they did it for status: a generous donor or founder gained a name, simply through what in the present century would be called conspicuous consumption, as both powerful and saintly. Sometimes, at the other end of the scale, they did it to relieve debt (as with the Leopegisi in Cologno) or desperation (as with the self-commendations that are prominent in modern literature, although rather more infrequent in our sources). Sometimes, too, they did it to obtain or reward a patron or ally, whom they needed to meet the social pressures of society at large: we would hardly be surprised, for example, if we had the documents for Seligenstadt, to find that Gundhart was reasonably generous to that monastery, whether before or after Einhard's letter. It is interesting, however, that people rarely gave more than small proportions of their lands, except some of the childless; they kept the rest back for their more ordinary

---

[37] Einhard, *Epistolae* (ed. *MGH Epp.* v), no. 42. Gundhart may have been the witness who appears in several Fulda acts in and around Nordheim u.d. Rhön to the southeast of the monastery in 824, *CDF* nos. 423–6, (?) 435; if so, we probably know his friends and neighbours as well. He gave no land to Fulda.

secular obligations. Nor were they generous to individual houses over unbroken periods of time. Both Lorsch and Fulda got the vast majority of their gifts between 760 and 840, roughly the three generations after their foundations; the later ninth century is badly documented in both places. Bavarian patterns are similar, as Störmer has shown; so are they in much of Italy. The consistency of the pattern reflects the fact that the mid-eighth century was a common time for church foundation in much of Europe. By contrast, the later ninth century, despite its importance in three out of our four examples, seems to have been a good time for gifts only for the rather fewer houses founded after 800, and even then not consistently: some late-founded establishments, especially in areas where there were already popular churches, had to buy much of their land. The issue of why churches and monasteries were founded in different periods will be dealt with later; but why people, usually unrelated to the founders, gave them land, and why they stopped, usually between one and three generations after the foundation, no matter when the foundation took place, is relevant here, for it must be linked to the changing structures of local societies.[38] As a generalisation over the whole of Europe, one could propose that donors saw churches as patrons for as long as they were reasonably external to the political affairs of their own communities; when churches, thanks to these same gifts, became too rich and powerful in any given area, gifts dried up. This was a pattern that seems to have been consistent across space, time and social class, alongside the differences in local developments that certainly existed as well.

The final feature common to all these societies that needs to be stressed here is violence. Even in the laconic land transactions that are the bulk of our local evidence one can see that people fought a lot. Feuds are well documented in aristocratic society (in the lowest stratum of which Gund-hart perhaps was); but peasants attacked each other too. The endless lists of penalties for the cutting off of body parts in all the law-codes are the clearest indication of it; we sometimes have more casual examples of it, too, as when Yspalaric sued Leofred in the bishop's court of Urgell in 872 for hitting him with a stick and locking him up in two houses, 'moved by anger', or when in 870 S. Ambrogio fined one of its dependants for killing another on an Alpine estate, Delebio. The fact that these two ended up in court at all may have been still unusual, in fact; although courts tried to regulate inter-personal violence, it was and remained normal to deal with it privately, with

---

[38] Störmer (1973), pp. 374–81; comp., for Italy, Wickham (1988), pp. 54–5; Fumagalli (1979) for an alternative context. For the varying dates of monastic foundations, see chapter 23 below, pp. 623–6.

family support, either through more violence, or through agreement, or both. And even inside the more normal field of interest of our documents, namely claims to land, violent dispossession seems to have been common – indeed, it seems sometimes to have been a strategy in dispute settlement itself, as a way to force the other party into the usually disadvantageous position of plaintiff at court.[39] It is an abiding impression left by all early medieval documentation that people behaved, or could behave, dreadfully to each other, whether or not moved by anger (an anger that anyway seems to have been pretty close to the surface); by the Carolingian period we may possibly have left behind the ultra-violence recorded in Merovingian sources, but brute force remained an entirely normal element in social interaction. Not least, it was a basic element in the way men behaved towards women.

The existence of this violence underlay most of the relationships between rich and poor, too: it was, or could be, class violence. In the Carolingian period, the poor free were on the defensive, as capitularies show in both Francia and Italy, against aggressions by all kinds of powerful people: private lords, churches, and even (or especially) counts, the nominal guardians of the weak. Even in court, the locus of justice and peaceful resolution, the importance of allies and patrons reflects the fact that those without powerful friends tended to lose; judges could be suborned or biased, witnesses could be bribed or cowed. The Leopegisi of Cologno are only one out of many examples of a weak family failing in court to get out of the clutches of a powerful church; and, while it is not surprising that churches won nearly all our surviving court cases (for why else would they have preserved the documents?), it is nonetheless striking that most of the instances we have of losers openly protesting at the injustice of judgements are of peasants: they seem to have been conscious that courts were biased against them – that is, that the public world itself was constructed on the basis of armed force. Out of court, the relationships between the strong and the weak were even less mediated. In Languedoc, for example, counts felt resentful at kings putting *Hispani* on fiscal land; they reacted, quite simply, by dispossessing the newcomers on every occasion they could find (John of Fontjoncouse, even though not a powerless man, had his land contested three times between 812 and 834, and was expelled once). The free peasants neighbouring on the Alpine estates of a monastery in Verona commended themselves to the monastery's protection, in return for rent and labour; they found, in 845, that this could be legally construed as a cession of their own lands, and they narrowly avoided being declared unfree. On estates,

---

[39] Baraut (1979), no. 25; Porro no. 249 (cf. Balzaretti (1989), p. 240); for violence as a court strategy, Davies and Fouracre (1986), pp. 232–5.

consuetudo loci or no, landlords often put up rents if they could get away with it, even for their free tenants, never mind their unfree ones.[40] And, as the powerful increased their local land owning and local power (the accumulations of land by churches in all of our examples are only the best-documented illustration of it), these possibilities for aggression increased. We do not have to be apocalyptic about the collapse of non-aristocratic land owning and political autonomy in the years of Carolingian decline; it did not happen quite yet, anywhere in Europe. But the stability and internal consistency of the social and political patterns in each of our four examples should not mislead us into hypothesising a world of tranquillity and justice. The public institutions of the Carolingian period reached surprisingly far into local society, but they did not lessen, and nor were they probably even supposed to lessen, the violence people used against their equals, and, above all, their inferiors.

Up to a point, these broad analyses fit all our four examples, and some of the similarities between them can indeed be generalised to most of Latin Europe, whether inside the Carolingian frontiers or beyond them. But there were many differences between them, too; and, even when they were similar, we should not necessarily assume that they were always the same in other areas, especially those that did not yet have a documentary tradition.

The extent of such differences across Europe can only be hinted at here, however. The concept of property-owning, for example, as I have already indicated, was not homogeneous across Europe; even in Carolingian Europe, with its strong tradition of property law inherited from Rome, not all public land seems to have been held by tenants according to Roman procedures; and in England, the Celtic lands or Scandinavia, much land holding was for a long time associated with very loose systems of dependence. Indeed, the way one constructed alliances and hierarchies of dependence through the distribution of wealth, whether in land or moveables, varied very greatly, and the social structures of the Carolingian world are here no guide to those in the rest of Europe.[41] Other clear contrasts in the way people constructed social relationships can be seen even inside the relatively homogeneous world of our four examples. The first two, Catalonia and Brittany, with their relatively accentuated local peasant

---

[40] Protests: e.g. Manaresi, nos. 36, 89; Nelson (1986), pp. 56–9. Corruption: see, emblematically, *Epitaphium Arsenii*, ed. Dümmler (1900). John of Fontjoncouse: *MGH Dip. Kar.* I, 217; *Histoire générale de Languedoc* II, 85. Verona: Manaresi, no. 49. Landlords and rents: e.g. Goetz (1984); for one case, the Limonta estate on Lake Como, see Castagnetti (1968); Balzaretti (1989), pp. 219–36. For resistance, see, in general, Epperlein (1969); for Italy, e.g. Wickham (1982), pp. 18–28.

[41] See Wickham (1992) for a development of this argument.

societies, can be opposed to Dienheim and Cologno, where regional aristocracies are much more in evidence. Brittany can, in particular, be opposed to the others in the informality of its procedures for local regulation, which have little to do with either codified law (unlike in Catalonia, and probably Italy) or with formal court rituals, backed up by the coercive powers of counts (as in all our other areas). Cologno, too, shows up features that cannot be seen in our other areas, notably in the articulation of its public hierarchies and its private bonds of dependence. Although this may be simply because of the sort of evidence we have (it is hard to imagine, for example, that there were not quite complex private clienteles in and around Dienheim, for there certainly were elsewhere in the Rhineland), it does at least seem that, at Cologno, these hierarchies linked the strata of free society together to an extent that we cannot assume in our other examples.

This brief analysis of difference can in fact already lead us to some positive conclusions, for the issue of how coherent local hierarchies are is an important one for understanding how societies work in different places. Villagers around Milan were not just surrounded by the rich and powerful, landowners and officials and churchmen, but were frequently associated with them, as tenants and clients and vassals. They were part of a network of mutual obligation that, while not being especially supportive to the weak, at least connected them to the leaders of political society. This private network ran contrary to the public rules of the Lombard-Carolingian state, but in reality made the latter procedures more effective, at least when they did not undermine real power relationships. One cannot conclude from this that public strength naturally went together with private strength; public institutions were regular and coherent in peasant Catalonia, for example. The social stability implied in our Italian evidence, too, should not blind us to the fact that it was precisely private systems of dependence that would lead to the breakup of the Carolingian state structure itself, and this in some parts of Europe was already imminent in 900. But regular public procedures, run by powerful aristocrats, do work quite effectively if these aristocrats have their own clients who will do their bidding, and this pattern is one that has lasted without a break from the Roman world. Conversely, while the informal, locally orientated operation of Breton courts may well have had analogues at village level in any part of Europe in which local custom had more immediacy than codified 'national law', their dominance by peasants, and an apparently community-based law-finding, would have been hard to maintain if aristocrats with armed clienteles had been an influential part of local society, as they were in very many places in the Carolingian world. Peasant justice thus, perhaps, presupposes not only a landowning peasantry, but also an absence of systematic hierarchies that link villagers to lords. When a more organic aristocracy developed in Brittany, village law-finding would be weakened there; in Catalonia, too, such a newly formed aristocracy would after 1000 destroy both peasant autonomies and the public framework within which they existed. If the public framework lasted longer in Italy, it is largely because it was more hierarchical, and thus served aristocratic interest better, to start with.

Land transactions and disputes have their limitations. The richness of modern ethnography, with its complex levels of social intercourse and ritual, is impossible to reconstruct through them. We can tell little about the thoughts or the values of villagers in Carolingian Europe. But something of their relationships can be seen for all that; land was the sole basis for survival, after all, for all but a tiny minority, and what people did with it, and who they dealt with, is a good guide to what they really needed, and who they believed they could trust. There are clear similarities in the basic patterns of their behaviour in our four examples, as we have seen, and these are in the last analysis not entirely surprising: for all our examples were agrarian, peasant-based societies, at a similar level of technological development; and all four were taken from the Carolingian world, with its relatively influential and homogeneous network of public institutions, inherited, ultimately, from the Roman empire. There were considerable differences as well, however, linked to the very various patterns of land tenure and local economic organisation in neighbouring regions – sometimes neighbouring villages – in Europe. We have to grasp both the similarities and the differences before we can arrive at any generalisations as to how its society (its societies) worked.[42]

[42] I am very grateful to Ross Balzaretti, Leslie Brubaker, Wendy Davies, Hans-Werner Goetz, Rosamond McKitterick and Jinty Nelson for comments on this chapter, some of them at extremely short notice.

CHAPTER 20

MONEY AND COINAGE

Mark Blackburn

CHANGES in coinage and monetary circulation in Europe were as radical as the political developments they accompanied during the eighth and ninth centuries.[1] The period saw the virtual extinction of gold coinages and their replacement with silver in almost all areas of Europe. The new silver denomination, the penny, introduced in Francia and England towards the end of the seventh century, subsequently took on a broader, thinner appearance and in this form it became the standard currency unit of medieval Europe, marking the final break with the monetary system of late antiquity. In the Frankish and Anglo-Saxon kingdoms the currency developed a fiscal role in addition to its important commercial function, accompanied by tightening royal control, although by the end of the ninth century in Francia the first signs of feudal usurpation of minting rights can be detected. Elsewhere, the impact of the Muslim conquests of Spain and Sicily were to change their entire monetary systems. In Germany, the use of coin became established in the Rhineland and Bavaria, but to other parts it scarcely penetrated. Further east and north, in eastern and central Europe and in Scandinavia, silver dirhems from the Near East began to arrive in enormous quantities. Yet at just this time there are signs of a possible shortage of silver for currency in western Europe resulting in widespread debasement and perhaps a contraction in the amount of coinage in circulation.

Coinage was used in a variety of ways in the early middle ages according to the sophistication of the economy and the level of society, and it must

---

[1] For a general survey of European coinages other than Byzantine and Arab issues, see Grierson and Blackburn (1986); for Byzantine issues see Grierson (1982); for Muslim Spain, Miles (1950), and the Arab possessions in Sicily, Spahr (1976) and Balog (1979). A general account of the use of money from the standpoint of an economic historian can be found in Spufford (1987, 1988) for western Europe, although the strength of these two works lies in the sections on the later middle ages, and in Hendy (1985) for the Byzantine state.

always have been accompanied by alternative forms of payment, such as barter or credit, although our knowledge of these is slight in a period when there is so little documentary evidence for the workings of the economy and trade. Indeed this dearth of information has enabled scholars to form radically different interpretations based on the same evidence, some minimising and some maximising the degree of monetisation and the role of commerce.[2] Europe in the eighth and ninth centuries can be divided into two broad regions, the coin-producing areas in the west and south where coinage circulated in specie, being normally counted out in transactions, and the areas to the north and east with their bullion economies in which imported coinage and other forms of precious metal were used together by weight. The boundary between the two regions remained remarkably static between the eighth and eleventh centuries, although by the end of the twelfth century most of Europe had some form of regulated currency system. On the extreme fringes, such as Ireland and Scotland before the Viking age, there is little surviving evidence of monetary exchange, but the Irish law tracts, thought to reflect the situation in the early eighth century, provide a rare insight into how payments could be made in goods or weighed metal in a primitive coinless non-market economy.[3]

THE RETREAT OF GOLD

During the first two centuries following the collapse of the western empire, the currencies of the new barbarian kingdoms were based largely on locally produced gold coins. Only in Italy under Ostrogothic and later Byzantine control was a range of silver and bronze coins also issued in substantial quantity. The Franks, Burgundians, Suevi, Visigoths, Lombards and Anglo-Saxons all had essentially mono-metallic currency systems based on the gold solidus and increasingly the tremissis (one-third solidus). However, apparent shortages of gold for currency in western Europe resulted in progressive reductions in fineness, seen first in the late sixth-century coinage of Visigothic Spain and during the early seventh century in that of the Franks. By the third quarter of the seventh century the fineness of the Frankish and Anglo-Saxon coins had fallen to as little as 25% gold or less alloyed with silver, and during the 670s these base gold tremisses were replaced by new coins of virtually pure silver. The old tremisses were quickly driven out of circulation leaving once again a mono-metallic currency in Francia and England.

---

[2] The minimalist view is exemplified by Grierson (1959) and Hendy (1988), while Metcalf, in particular, has championed the commercial approach, e.g. Metcalf (1967; 1984a).

[3] Gerriets (1985).

Elsewhere in Europe, in Italy and briefly in Spain, the use of gold coinages lingered on. The Visigothic tremisses of the late seventh century were heavily debased, but their issue continued until the Arab conquest of Spain in 711–15. The Umayyad governors replaced the Germanic system of coinage with an Arabic one, consisting initially of gold dinars and their fractions similar to those of North Africa but of inferior and very variable fineness.[4] These coins belong to a transitional phase in which pseudo-Byzantine types were still giving way to purely Islamic ones in the western provinces of the caliphate. Between 711/12 and 720/1 (AH 93–102) three successive types of gold coinage were issued in Spain: Arab-Byzantine types with Latin inscriptions, Arab-Byzantine types with bilingual inscriptions, and Arabic types with entirely Kufic inscriptions.[5] These Kufic dinars, of restored (c. 98%) fineness, were struck in small numbers down to 744/5 (AH 127),[6] after which no further gold was issued in Spain for some two hundred years, until the Spanish Umayyads conquered North Africa, gaining access to Sudanese gold. The currency became one based essentially on silver dirhems weighing c. 2.9 g, more than twice as heavy as the Frankish denier, supplemented with some low-value copper coins. Unlike the Visigothic coinage for which more than twenty mints are recorded in its later stages, the Islamic issues from Spain in the eighth and ninth centuries carry only the name of the province al-Andalus (Andalusia, i.e. Spain), and we do not know whether there was just one or several mints producing the coinage, although differences of style and ornamentation suggest that at times there may have been more than one.[7] Córdoba is likely to have been the principal mint, at least after its establishment as the capital of the Islamic province in about 719. The earlier issues could have been struck at Seville, the initial seat of the Umayyad governors.

In Italy, the diverse nature of the Lombard (later Carolingian), Byzantine, Papal and Arab states was reflected in their coinages. Each had a different monetary system and separate currency, yet inevitably their economies were influenced by those of their neighbours. Thus, although the mint at Constantinople throughout the period maintained a gold coinage of the highest purity (c. 96%), the Byzantine mints in Italy followed a course of debasement as the western kingdoms had done.[8] Arabic Sicily, on the other hand, managed to match the high (c. 95% +) standards of the North African and Near Eastern mints throughout the ninth century, but thereafter its gold coinage declined in quality.[9] The history of the various coinages is

---

[4] Balaguer (Prunes) (1976), pp. 95–103; Balaguer (Prunes) (1979), p. 239.
[5] Miles (1950), pp. 113–18; Walker (1956), pp. xxxix–li, lv–lix; Balaguer (Prunes) (1976; 1979).
[6] Bates (1992).   [7] Miles (1950), pp. 33–42.   [8] Oddy (1988).
[9] Balog et al. (1981); al-'Ush (1982), p. 24.

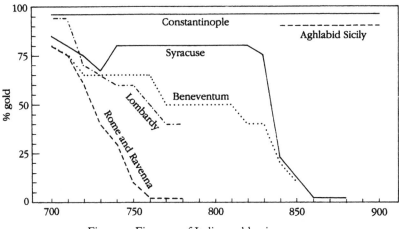

Figure 1 Fineness of Italian gold coinages

complicated to follow, but the pattern of debasement (Fig. 1) shows a common trend.

The Lombard coinages of north Italy and of Tuscany developed in different ways.[10] In the north a regal coinage replaced the earlier pseudo-imperial issues by the end of the seventh century, while in Tuscany municipal issues were produced by the towns of Lucca, Pisa, Chiusi (?) and Pistoia. Aistulf (749–56) brought the Tuscan mints under royal control, but not until the reign of Desiderius (757–74) was a uniform coinage achieved. In contrast to the Merovingian and Visigothic coinages, the gold content of the Lombard tremisses had remained relatively high until the end of the seventh century, rarely dropping below 75% gold.[11] The first regal coins were over 90% fine, but the standard declined to around 50–60% by the mid-seventh century and perhaps 30% by the end of Desiderius' reign. In the late seventh and early eighth centuries it was supplemented by an issue of tiny silver coins weighing less than 0.3 g. After the Frankish conquest of 774, Charlemagne continued striking base gold tremisses of Lombardic design for a few years, replacing them with silver pennies of Frankish type probably in 781. The Lombard duchy of Benevento in southern Italy, which was quite independent of the northern kingdom, struck gold solidi and tremisses of Byzantine design in the names of the dukes (from 774 princes) until the mid-ninth century.[12] After an initial fall in fineness from *c*. 75% gold in the early eighth century, the Beneventan mint maintained a standard of around 50–60% for the next hundred years until the second quarter of the

[10] Arslan (1978), pp. 16–19; Bernareggi (1983); Grierson and Blackburn (1986), pp. 55–66.

[11] Oddy (1972).   [12] Grierson and Blackburn (1986), pp. 66–72.

ninth century when it shared in the precipitous decline of the dominant Syracuse mint.[13]

At the beginning of the eighth century there were five Byzantine mints in western Europe – Ravenna, Rome, Naples, Syracuse, Sardinia – but by the late ninth century they had all ceased to be under imperial control.[14] In northern and central Italy, the Byzantine mints of Ravenna and Rome produced debased gold coinages until the Lombards captured Ravenna in 751 and the pope assumed formal control of the Rome mint in the 770s or early 780s. At both mints debasement had begun in the late seventh century, falling to around 50% gold by 720 and then accelerating into a cataclysmic decline so that by the mid-eighth century the ostensible gold coinage was composed largely of base copper alloy coins that had perhaps been lightly gilded before issue at the mint. The Ravenna mint continued to operate for a few years after the city's capture, striking pale gold solidi and tremisses, and even copper folles in the name of Aistulf but of Byzantine design. At Rome the mint continued to issue a purely token 'gold' coinage for some thirty years, during which time Syracuse in Sicily was producing a very respectable gold coinage in large quantity. Clearly the coins of Rome can have circulated only very locally, and by this date it may be wrong to regard them as imperial in any meaningful sense. Political control of the city was effectively exercised by the papacy, and from the late seventh or early eighth century initials or monograms of the popes appear on the small silver coins from Rome, combined with the bust of the emperor. Several new varieties of this 'papal-imperial' coinage were discovered in a hoard from Rome or its environs in the early 1980s.[15] Popes Gregory III (731–41) and Zacharias (741–51) also struck copper pieces exclusively in their own names, and although their function is disputed – whether coins, tokens or weights[16] – they are another indication that the Rome mint was effectively under papal control, and the reference to the emperor as the traditional minting authority was little more than a formality.[17] Pope Hadrian I (772–95) was the first to strike purely papal coins, possibly following the visit of Charlemagne to Rome in 781 since they are silver denari of Carolingian fabric, even if their designs are Byzantine in taste.

In the south, at Naples, solidi and tremisses of distinctive fabric were

[13] Oddy (1974).

[14] For the Byzantine issues of Italy and Sicily see Grierson (1982), pp. 129–44, 165–71, 185–7; and for the fineness of their gold issues see Oddy (1988).

[15] O'Hara (1985); Morrisson and Barrandon (1988).

[16] Grierson and Blackburn (1986), pp. 644–5.

[17] A parallel could be drawn with the Lombards, who had minted gold coins in the name of the emperor until the late seventh century in Lombardy and Tuscany and until the mid-eighth century in Benevento.

struck from the later seventh until the mid-eighth century with finenesses similar to those from Rome and Ravenna, and an aberrant group of solidi of the first half of the ninth century have been tentatively attributed to the mint by then controlled by the duke of Naples. The dukes went on to strike large copper folles of Byzantine type but in the name of Sergius I (duke 840–61) or of S. Gennaro.[18] The island of Sardinia briefly supported a Byzantine mint striking gold and bronze for some twenty-five years from the early 690s until the reign of Anastasius II (713–16). It appears to have inherited some of the business of the Carthage mint after the city's conquest by the Muslims in 695, but it failed to flourish. It adopted the high gold standard of Carthage, *c.* 95% fine, although latterly there is evidence of a slight decline to *c.* 90%.

The most important Byzantine mint in the west was that of Syracuse, which produced substantial issues of gold and bronze coinage until the middle of the ninth century, when production declined and then ceased altogether on its capture by the Arabs in 878. Initially, in the early eighth century the gold solidi, semisses and tremisses were debased in line with those from the mints of Ravenna and Rome to *c.* 65%, but their fineness was restored under Leo III (717–41) to *c.* 80% at which level it was held until the 820s and the first Arab conquests on the island. It then fell away rapidly, managing only 20% gold in the final issues under Michael III (842–67) and Basil I (867–86). The weights of Sicilian issues were also notably lighter than those from Constantinople, and during the ninth century their flans became smaller and thicker. It is this distinctive fabric, their linear style and the find distribution that serves to justify their attribution to Sicily, since latterly few of the coins carry any identification of their mint.

Arabic coins had been struck in Sicily since the first arrival of the Aghlabids on the island in 827. They appear to have been struck in both gold and silver, although only those in silver specify their origin.[19] Silver dirhems with the name *Siqilliya* (Sicily) were issued in 829/30 (AH 214) by the commander-in-chief, Muḥammad ibn al-Jawārī, presumably struck at his siege-camp outside the city of Enna. These were followed after the capture of Palermo in 831 by a series of half- and later quarter-dirhems with the mint-name *Siqilliya*, *Madīna-Balarm* or *Madīna*, all thought to have been struck at Palermo. They were in turn replaced in the late ninth century by tiny silver coins known as *kharrūbas*, weighing *c.* 0.2 g and valued at one-sixteenth of a dirhem. Although struck without mint-names, their find distribution shows them to be Sicilian rather than North African. The attribution of Aghlabid gold coins to specific mints or regions is more problematic; their distributions are not as clear as those of the silver, since

---

[18] Grierson (1991), pp. 45–6.   [19] Balog (1979); al-'Ush (1982).

gold was used more widely in international trade. However, it is clear that the coins used in Sicily in the ninth century were small quarter-dinars of fine gold, and they may well have been struck on the island.[20] The currency of Sicily under the Fāṭimids and Normans continued to consist mainly of small denominations, which has been seen as evidence of a weak economy. However, it might rather signify a more highly monetised economy in which smaller change was required for regional and local trade,[21] as was also the case in southern Scandinavia where finely cut-up dirhems and hacksilver predominate in the tenth-century hoards.[22]

None of the Arabic settlements of mainland Italy or Malta is known to have struck coinage in this period, but the obscure amirs who ruled over Crete from 827/8 until its reconquest in 961 by Nicephorus Phocas issued their own coinage, mainly in copper with just a little gold and silver, essentially for local use.[23] Of the other Byzantine provinces in or around the eastern Mediterranean, much of the Balkans by the early eighth century was in Slav hands and no coinage was struck there, while Byzantine Greece looked to Constantinople for its currency.

In Constantinople coins of fine gold continued to be struck in quantity, and in Islamic North Africa gold was plentiful in the ninth century as a result of the exploitation of trans-Saharan trade routes bringing gold from the Sudan.[24] The reasons for the loss of gold from the currency of Europe have been much debated.[25] Pirenne argued that it was symptomatic of an economic and cultural decline that western Europe suffered during the eighth century as a result of the Arab conquests around the Mediterranean which inhibited international trade.[26] Grierson, on the other hand, saw it as a consequence of the monetary reforms of ʿAbd al-Mālik in the 790s which valued gold more highly in relation to silver than it was in the west, hence prompting a wholesale export of gold to the east.[27] Neither of these theories, however, will stand as the sole cause of the change in the light of the revised chronologies for the Merovingian gold and silver coinages and the demonstration that there had been progressive debasement in the west since the late sixth or early seventh centuries. Another argument runs that the gold was being converted into ornaments and plate for the church and nobility and used for gilt decoration on books and woodwork, for which there is much evidence in literature.[28] Unfortunately, it is impossible to quantify the amount of ornamental metalwork that existed in any one

---

[20] Spahr (1976), p. 105, no. 5.; Balog *et al.* (1981), pp. 162, 171.   [21] Travaini (1990), p. 12.

[22] Hårdh (1976) I, pp. 128–45.   [23] Miles (1970).   [24] Fomin (1990).

[25] For recent reviews see Suchodolski (1981a); Hendy (1988), pp. 70–7.

[26] Pirenne (1939), pp. 107–17, 173.   [27] Grierson (1960).

[28] Dodwell (1982); Elbern (1988).

period, but surviving artefacts suggest that gold was not as freely available for decorative purposes after the mid-seventh century, since gold jewellery and ornaments then became scarcer and the metal less fine, silver gilt and copper gilt being common substitutes.[29] Undoubtedly some of the gold from the coinage was turned into ornaments or used for decorative purposes, but the progressive debasement and replacement of gold coinages in all regions of Europe over a protracted period of some two centuries is cogent evidence for a real and dramatic reduction in general stocks of the metal available in the west. The decline in the use of gold currency was probably the result of a number of factors, but in essence Europe no longer had access to sufficient supplies of new metal to compensate adequately for the natural wastage that always occurs through wear and loss, through conversion into ornaments, and through exports in trade with the east or by way of political payments.

THE NEW SILVER CURRENCY

The first silver pennies were probably introduced in Neustria in the early 670s. Few Merovingian silver coins bear the names of individuals who can be dated independently, but among the earliest is one of Childeric II of Austrasia (662–75) from the mint of Tours and hence struck after his acquisition of Neustria in 673. Two others bear the name EBROINVS, the great Neustrian mayor of the palace (*c.* 660–73, 675–80/3), who may indeed have been responsible for the monetary reform.[30] If the Franks were the first to replace the base gold with silver coins, the Anglo-Saxons soon followed their example, introducing distinctive silver pennies it would seem also during the 670s. The word 'penny' (German *Pfennig*, Dutch *penning*, etc.) is itself first recorded in the late seventh century when it appears in its Old English form (*pening*) in the laws of King Ine of Wessex and in glosses from the school of Hadrian and Theodore of Canterbury. We do not know the vernacular name used by the Franks for these coins; their Latin sources use the Roman term *denarius* (DINARIOS inscribed on one coin of Lyons), which gave rise to the later French *denier*.

The pennies were struck to the same weight standard (*c.* 1.3 g = *c.* 20 Troy grains) and were of similar module to the tremisses that they replaced in both Francia and England. New designs were adopted at most mints to distinguish the silver coins from the previous base gold types, but the administrative arrangements for their issue seem to have been largely

[29] Hawkes, Merrick and Metcalf (1966); Webster and Backhouse (1991), pp. 47, 220–1.
[30] Grierson and Blackburn (1986), p. 94.

unchanged. Under the Merovingians the coinage has the appearance of a series of more or less private issues, in that the king's name rarely occurs on the gold coins and only once on the silver (that of Childeric II mentioned above), and usually the inscriptions specify only the place of production and the moneyer responsible, or on occasion an ecclesiastical foundation or 'the Palace'. Still, there must have been regulations governing at least the circulation of coins, and it is possible that rather more royal control in fact lay behind the neutral face of the coinage. The dies used to strike the silver coins are in general more poorly engraved and less literate than those for the gold, but this could as well reflect a general relaxation of standards.

The pennies or so-called 'sceattas'[31] produced at Frisian and Anglo-Saxon mints are mostly uninscribed. A few merely reproduce legends from Roman or Merovingian prototypes, but when they bear a meaningful word – often in runic script[32] – it is normally the name of a moneyer or mint, as on the Merovingian deniers. The only series in which an Anglo-Saxon ruler's name and title appears is the Northumbrian coinage under Aldfrith (685–704), Eadberht (736–54) and Archbishop Ecgberht (c. 732–66). For the southern English issues, it has been argued that they are also royal or ecclesiastical coinages and that there was essentially one mint in each of the kingdoms, but the case is not clearly established.[33]

Detailed study of the Anglo-Saxon issues, which have recently been found in large numbers in excavations and as stray finds by metal-detector users, has helped to clarify the chronology and the patterns of minting and circulation.[34] During the last quarter of the seventh century minting appears to have been concentrated at London and in Kent, as it had been in the gold phase, but output increased somewhat. The circulation of these 'Primary sceattas', as they are known, was concentrated in southeast England. The first decade of the eighth century saw an influx of imported silver coins from Frisia, the 'porcupine' and 'Continental runic' types, which circulated in England more widely than the Anglo-Saxon issues had done and quickly came to dominate the currency, constituting for example two-thirds of the 324 coins from the Aston Rowant, Oxfordshire, hoard, deposited c. 710. This influx of foreign currency not only had the effect of extending the area of monetary circulation to most of England apart from the northwest, but it

---

[31] The Anglo-Saxon and Frisian pennies of the period c. 675–750 have since the seventeenth century generally been called 'sceattas', but this is a misnomer based on a wrong interpretation of the early seventh-century laws of Æthelberht of Kent, where the term is used for a weight of gold; Grierson (1961b).

[32] Frisian and Anglo-Saxon coins with runic inscriptions are surveyed in Blackburn (1991).

[33] Metcalf (1977; 1993); Grierson and Blackburn (1986), p. 159.

[34] Metcalf (1994), a major study in a field that has been advancing rapidly.

prompted the establishment or re-establishment of local mints in Northumbria (York), East Anglia (Ipswich?), Wessex (Southampton) and perhaps Essex and Mercia, and facilitated a dramatic growth in the volume of coinage in circulation generally.

In Frisia itself minting and coin circulation seem to have expanded substantially from the late seventh century, presumably prompted by the availability of silver on a scale unknown before, though where this was coming from is not clear. Frisia had no silver mines, and the metal is unlikely to have been from Melle in Aquitaine, subsequently to become the principal silver source within the Frankish kingdoms, since in the late seventh century the Frankish coinage does not appear to have grown in the same way. The silver probably reached Frisia, therefore, from Germany or central Europe. The Frisian coins are of a limited number of types, but, apart from an early issue of Dorestad, they are either uninscribed or crudely copy a runic legend from an English issue. Their mint attributions are therefore uncertain, though Dorestad is likely to have continued as a major mint along with other *wics* having access to the North Sea. One issue, the 'Wodan/Monster' type, has been found extensively in southern Scandinavia and is now thought to have been struck at the Danish town of Ribe, shortly after its establishment in the early eighth century.[35]

Our knowledge of the Merovingian silver coinage is much less clear. The surviving evidence is very uneven, based largely on six French hoards, five of which were deposited during the first two decades of the eighth century,[36] and the sixth being a comparatively small group of mainly local coins. Single-finds from excavations or casual discoveries add to the picture, but they are far less plentiful and less well recorded than the English finds. Moreover, the deniers did not travel abroad to the same extent as the gold tremisses, and foreign finds are comparatively few. The number of minting places in the silver phase cannot be gauged accurately, for although far fewer are named on surviving deniers than the eight hundred or so on the Merovingian tremisses, this must in part be because a smaller proportion of the coins have clear inscriptions and the survival rate in the silver coinage is lower than in the gold. However, they are likely to have numbered a few hundred, and a hundred or so mints were active in the succeeding coinages of Pippin III and Charlemagne. At many of these places very little coinage was produced and they cannot have been regular establishments, but some substantial mints can be identified, at Paris, Poitiers, Marseilles, Lyons, Chalon-sur-Saône and elsewhere. Some of the mints producing the

[35] Metcalf (1984b); Jonsson and Malmer (1986); Metcalf (1986).
[36] For their dating see Grierson and Blackburn (1986), pp. 140–4.

anonymous Frisian coinages would also have been under Merovingian control, as the northern border was pushed progressively northwards, although this does not seem to have had a discernible influence on their coinages.

Although there were many more minting places in the Frankish kingdoms than in England, the find evidence suggests that coinage was used more intensively in England than in France. Moreover, the Merovingian denier no longer enjoyed the prominent role in international trade that the gold tremissis had done; this was now assumed by Frisian and Danish issues, which travelled widely, not only to England, but to western France and up the Rhine. Many of the Rhineland finds come from graves, since the practice of making grave deposits continued well into the eighth century. But the discovery in the early 1980s of at least twenty-two 'porcupine sceattas' of the first half of the eighth century as stray finds from a market site near the river front at Mainz shows that they also played a commercial role in the Rhine valley.[37] Anglo-Saxon coins are also found on the Continent, though in smaller numbers than the Frisian types. In Italy, by contrast, the new Lombard and papal-imperial silver issues were for purely local use, providing small change to supplement the main gold coinages.

Within a few years of assuming the title of king of the Franks, Pippin III (751–68) had implemented a radical reform that changed fundamentally the appearance and outward status of the coinage.[38] Henceforth all Frankish coins would identify the royal authority under which they were issued and usually their mint of origin. The small dumpy fabric typical of the Merovingian period gave way to larger thinner coins, apparently the result of a technical change in the minting process whereby the coins were struck on flans cut from sheet metal rather than on individually cast blanks. This technique had already been used by the neighbouring Visigoths, Lombards and Arabs, and the Visigothic and Lombard coinages also provided precedents for naming the ruler and mint on the coins. The silver denier of the later seventh century had weighed c. 1.3 g, but subsequently it had fallen in some regions of Francia to c. 1.1 g or less.[39] Pippin restored the weight standard to one approaching that of the original deniers, and legislation is preserved in a capitulary of 754/5, which may indeed be the date of the coinage reform, decreeing that there shall be no more than twenty-two

---

[37] Blackburn (1993), pp. 42, 48, citing unpublished work of C. Stoess.
[38] Lafaurie (1974), pp. 35–44.
[39] Lafaurie (1969), pp. 144–8, although the chronology and stepped weight standards are now doubted.

solidi (i.e. 264 deniers) struck from a pound of silver.[40] Pippin also introduced a second denomination, the halfpenny, although it was not widely struck until the ninth century.

Pippin's sons, Carloman (768–71) and Charlemagne (768–814), brought some standardisation to the coin designs, although the reverses could still display considerable variety. Charlemagne also extended minting of the broad denier to his newly acquired Lombard kingdom in Italy, probably in 781 if, as seems likely, the provision in the Capitulary of Mantua relates to this recoinage.[41] As we have seen, it was also at this time that the first purely papal coinage was struck at Rome, taking for its model the Carolingian denier, although the designs were Byzantine in inspiration. In Aquitaine Charlemagne issued a small coinage in the name of his young son Louis, probably to mark his coronation as sub-king in 781. This was an exception to the general rule that sub-kings did not strike their own coinages. The second major monetary reform of the eighth century was instituted by Charlemagne in the early 790s, probably in 793/4,[42] increasing the weight of the coins by some 30% to *c.* 1.7 g and imposing still greater standardisation in the design, the principal motif of which was the royal monogram of *Karolus* used to validate his diplomas. There was also a reduction in the number of mints, this heavier denier being struck at some forty places across the kingdom, compared with perhaps one hundred recorded in the lighter issue, many of them small, apparently unimportant localities with minting rights surviving from the Merovingian period.

The Anglo-Saxon coinage underwent two reforms which more or less paralleled those of Pippin and Charlemagne. By the mid-eighth century a monetary crisis had developed in southern England, as the coinages became severely debased and reduced in weight and production at several mints seems to have ceased.[43] In the 750s, an East Anglian king, Beonna (749–57 or later), improved the silver content of the East Anglian coinage to *c.* 70%,

---

[40] *MGH Cap.* I, p. 32, c. 5. This passage has prompted various estimates of the weight of the early Carolingian pound, but it may be a weight particular to the mint for buying silver, Lyon (1986), pp. 183–4.

[41] 'After the first day of August let no one dare to give or receive the pennies now current; anyone who does so is to pay our fine', *MGH Cap.* I, p. 191, c. 9; trans. after Loyn and Percival (1975), p. 50. The capitulary is not dated and it could be from 774, 781 or 787. Grierson (1954) has argued that 781 is the most probable, but alternative interpretations have been offered by Suchodolski (1981b).

[42] The dating is based mainly on a reference to these 'new coins' bearing 'the monogram of our name' in the Synod of Frankfurt 794 (*MGH Cap.* I, p. 74, c. 5), on the composition of the Ilanz hoard, and on Charlemagne's known movements in the early 890s; Grierson (1965), pp. 507–11. Suchodolski (1981b), however, prefers a date of *c.* 790.   [43] Metcalf (1988), pp. 236–7.

although it subsequently fell again, and placed his name and title on the obverse of the coins, [44] inspired it would seem by Northumbrian coin types. Within a few years Offa of Mercia (757–96) had conquered East Anglia and instituted his own more radical monetary reform, in which the penny was restored to full fineness (c. 96% silver) and weight (c. 1.3 g). The new thinner Carolingian fabric was adopted, and the king's name and title, together with that of the moneyer, but not the mint, was placed on the coins. There had been doubts as to whether Offa or two minor Kentish kings, Heabert and Egbert, were originally responsible for the reform, [45] but recent finds suggest that Offa's first coins were struck in London or East Anglia and that the Kentish kings followed them with an issue from Canterbury. Offa's coinage is one of the most varied and artistic of the English series, yet its internal chronology remains problematic. Towards the end of his reign, c. 792 on the evidence of the archiepiscopal issues, Offa instituted another reform, increasing the weight standard of the penny from c. 1.3 g to c. 1.45 g (not the Frankish standard), and imposing greater uniformity of design through the adoption of a common obverse type with the inscription in three horizontal lines. Three mints were operating south of the Humber, London, [46] Canterbury and East Anglia, all controlled by Offa. This was rather fewer than had struck the 'sceattas' of the early eighth century, yet the circulation area of Offa's coins was similar to that of the 'sceattas'. One significant difference, however, is the scarcity of foreign coins among the finds. In the Anglo-Saxon and Frankish kingdoms from the second half of the eighth century it seems that foreign money had to be exchanged before it could be used, and in practice its circulation would have been difficult once the reforms of the 790s had brought a divergence in the weight standards either side of the Channel.

In Umayyad Spain the first silver dirhems were struck in 721/2 (AH 103), initially in parallel with the gold dinars discussed above. Their inscriptions and design were the same as those introduced by ʿAbd al-Mālik in about 695 (AH 75), carrying the Islamic profession of faith, the date, and the name of the mint or in this case the province al-Andalus, but not that of the ruler. Coins of the Umayyad governors are scarce, but dirhems are known for all years down to 739/40 (AH 122), after which production became erratic owing to political upheavals in the province. Shortly after Spain's secession from the ʿAbbasid caliphate in 756, regular minting was resumed with dirhems of the same anonymous Umayyad type, so that the names of the new independent amirs do not appear on the coinage. There is then a virtually unbroken sequence of dirhems for every year until the late ninth century

---

[44] Archibald (1985).   [45] Blunt (1961).

[46] The case for London being a major mint under Offa is put in Stewart (1986).

when in the face of local rebellions the minting of silver became sporadic and finally ceased in 905/6 (AH 293), not to be restored until ʿAbd al-Raḥmān III's major monetary reform of 928/9 (AH 316). In addition to the silver, at times low-value copper *fulus* were struck. These are mostly undated, but they have been attributed to the period of the Governors and to the late ninth and early tenth centuries when the production of dirhems was reduced or had ceased. Many of the Spanish dirhem hoards contain a substantial proportion of irregularly cut fragments of coins that must have been used by weight as small change, yet it would be wrong to regard Spain as having a wholly bullion economy comparable to that of Scandinavia and eastern Europe, for the hoards never contain foreign coin or silver ingots and ornaments.

COINAGE IN THE NINTH CENTURY

Charlemagne's coronation as emperor by Pope Leo III in Rome at Christmas 800 was not reflected in the Frankish coinage, which continued to accord him the title of *rex Francorum*. Only on Leo III's own coinage of Rome was Charlemagne accorded the title *imperator*, as his name was joined with that of the pope marking the start of a new 'papal/imperial' series, though one that now looked west rather than east. Towards the end of his reign, possibly in 812 when the eastern emperor Michael I recognised Charlemagne's imperial title,[47] a new type was introduced with a laureate bust of classical style and the titles IMP*erator* AUG*ustus* and occasionally D*ominus* N*oster*. The type was continued by Louis the Pious (814–40) during the first five years of his reign, and he additionally struck a small number of splendid gold solidi. The imperial pretensions are clear. Louis then instituted two recoinages in rapid succession, in 818 and 822/3.[48] His second issue, with the mint name written across the field, was struck at some forty-five mints and to an enhanced weight standard of *c.* 1.8 g. This apparently proved unviable, for the third type with a 'Temple' design[49] returned to the former 1.7 g standard, and it remained in circulation for some forty years from 822/3 until Charles the Bald's reform of 864. On the reverse, the mint name was suppressed in favour of the invocation *Christiana religio*, and only recently through stylistic analysis has it proved possible to attribute a significant number of coins to mints, although there remains a substantial proportion that are unidentified.[50]

Despite the division of the empire between Louis the Pious' three sons

---

[47] Grierson (1965), pp. 524–7; Lafaurie (1978); Grierson and Blackburn (1986), p. 209.

[48] Coupland (1990), pp. 24, 28.

[49] Arguably representing a baptistery; Robert, Desnier, and Belaubre (1988).

[50] Coupland (1990).

under the *Ordinatio imperii* of 817, the coinage continued to be minted in
Louis' name at all mints until his death in 840. The exceptions to this were
few and short lived.[51] In Aquitaine Louis issued a small coinage in the name
of Pippin I to mark his coronation as sub-king there in 817, just as
Charlemagne had done for Louis when he was a child. Two groups in the
name of Lothar appear to have been minted during his father's life. One is a
portrait issue which is most plausibly attributed to the years 822/3 when
Lothar went to Italy and was crowned emperor of Italy. The second group,
which copies Louis' *Christiana religio* type, comes from Dorestad and other
unidentified but non-Italian mints, and has been attributed to Lothar's
revolt of 833–4. Overall, the uniformity and strength of control over the
administration of Louis' coinage down to 840 is impressive. The coinage
was plentiful and the hoards suggest a free and rapid circulation of issues
throughout the empire. Such uniformity and freedom of circulation would
not be achieved again in the middle ages over so vast an area. With the
political fragmentation of the empire and loosening control, regional
differences of design and fabric soon developed, and circulation became
more localised. Thus in 849 Lupus of Ferrières, planning to visit Rome,
anticipated problems as he had been told that only 'Italian silver coinage'
(*Italica moneta argento*) was current in that country.[52]

    Even within Charles the Bald's West Frankish kingdom, the heart of the
Carolingian world, the uniformity and quality of the coinage were soon lost.
During the earlier years of the reign several coin types were issued, but the
changes of type were not accompanied by general recoinages as occurred
under Louis, and they do not appear to have been closely co-ordinated, so
that it is difficult to determine the sequence and chronology of the issues.[53]
In broad terms, outside Aquitaine the mints seem to have continued striking
the Temple type though in the name of Charles, and initially with the
anonymous *Christiana religio* reverse inscription but subsequently replacing
this with the name of the mint. Later several mints adopted their own
distinctive designs, a city gate at Chartres and Orléans, the mint-name-in-
field at Meaux, Paris and Sens, and a cross at Rheims. In Aquitaine the
pattern of minting is complicated by the war that was waged between
Charles and Pippin II during most of the 840s and by the fact that the
kingdom acted with a degree of independence. Early in the reign, before the
Treaty of Verdun (August 843), some deniers and oboles were struck by
Pippin II in the name of his ally the Emperor Lothar at Bordeaux. Pippin's
coinage in his own name, however, belongs essentially to the period 845–9,

---

[51] Coupland (1989), pp. 195–9; Coupland (1990), pp. 27, 45–8.
[52] Lupus of Ferrières, *Correspondance*, L. Levillain (ed.), II, pp. 18–21, no. 76.
[53] For a survey of Charles' earlier coinage, 840–64, see Coupland (1991).

interrupting the issues of Charles the Bald. In the early 840s the mints of Bourges, Melle and Toulouse struck a Monogram type for Charles, but in or before 845 at Bourges and Melle this was changed for the mint-signed Temple type in use at other West Frankish mints. Toulouse, however, had fallen to Pippin II in late 842 or 843 and Melle likewise fell in 845, and at these mints Pippin struck coins bearing his own monogram. He also minted coins at Bordeaux, Dax and three new mints, Cahors, Limoges and Poitiers, and perhaps elsewhere since some of the coins have the reverse inscription *Aquitania* but no mint-name. When in 848 Pippin eventually captured Bourges, the capital of Aquitaine, he issued a celebratory portrait coinage, reminiscent of that struck for his father in 817. However, Pippin's success was short lived, and when Charles regained control of the region during 848–9 he produced his own version of the portrait coinage at Bourges, a mint-name-in-field type at Melle, and the former Monogram type at Toulouse. There are also coins of Charles the Bald from Clermont and ones reading *Aquitania* struck at Bordeaux and elsewhere which we cannot date precisely.

The earlier coinage of Charles the Bald not only shows signs of weak administrative control, but it quite soon suffered serious debasement, so that by the 860s the coins contained no more than 50% silver.[54] By 864 Charles was in a position to tackle the poor state of the currency and he undertook a thorough reform of the coinage, introducing a new uniform coinage throughout the kingdom with his monogram surrounded by the legend *Gratia Dei Rex*, and struck in fine (*c.* 96%) silver. By chance, detailed provisions for carrying out this recoinage have been preserved in the Edict of Pîtres of 25 June 864.[55] On 1 July the count in whose district a mint was situated was to send his viscount, two men of property and the moneyer to Senlis where they would receive on loan five pounds of silver with which to begin minting. After Martinmas (11 November) the old coinage would no longer be legal tender. The edict limited production to the Palace and ten named mints, but in practice the type was struck at some seventy West Frankish mints and at a further nineteen mints after the annexation of Lotharingia in 869. This dramatic expansion from the fifteen mints operating during the first twenty-four years of the reign evidently represents a deliberate policy to ensure that coinage was available for trade, and more importantly for the payment of taxes and other renders.[56] The *Gratia Dei*

[54] Metcalf and Northover (1989), pp. 114–15; Coupland (1991), pp. 151–2.

[55] *MGH Cap.* II, pp. 315–16, cc. 10–12, 14.

[56] Grierson (1990) has argued that it was initially intended to facilitate the collection of tribute to pay the Vikings in 866, but this would not explain the extension of minting in Lotharingia after 869; Metcalf (1990), p. 88.

Rex coinage was so successful that the designs and inscriptions were immobilised at some mints until the tenth century and even later. Immobilisation was but one symptom of the loosening of royal control and the emergence of local 'feudal' authority as counts and ecclesiastical authorities were granted or simply assumed the right to control the mints and retain the profits from the coinage. The abbots of Corbie went so far as to place their initial or monogram on the coins, a practice that became widespread in later centuries.[57]

Lothar (840–55) inherited the third share of Louis the Pious' empire known as the Middle Kingdom, a long piece of territory that stretched from Frisia to Provence and south of the Alps to Italy. It was an anomalous political unit that remained intact only during Lothar's lifetime. His coinage was struck mainly at Dorestad[58] and in Italy, where there were four mints, Milan, Pavia, Treviso and Venice, although the status of the latter was unusual since the Venetians regarded themselves as subjects of the Byzantine empire. Indeed towards the end of Louis' reign Venice had struck coins of the Temple type but inscribed + DS CVSERVA ROMA NP ('O God, preserve the emperor of the Romans') and + XPE SALVA VENECIAS ('O Christ, save Venice'), leaving ambiguous which emperor it was saluting. Lothar's Italian coins were of the mint-name-in-field type, but his successors reverted to the *Christiana religio* Temple type struck on flans that grew progressively thinner and much larger than the dies, resulting in some extraordinarily delicate saucer-shaped coins by the end of the ninth century. At Rome the papal coinage of silver denari continued to acknowledge the Carolingian emperor but, after the death of Louis the Pious, the Frankish weight standard of 1.75 g was abandoned in favour of a lower one of *c.* 1.3 g, possibly reverting to an earlier Roman weight system. Further south at Benevento, denari of Carolingian fabric but for the most part of novel design were struck to a standard of *c.* 1.4 g, falling in the second quarter of the ninth century to 1.3 g. A Carolingian ruler is referred to on the Beneventan coinage on just two occasions. Once was when Grimoald III (788–806) was obliged to recognise Charlemagne's overlordship during the first two years of his reign, and the coins carry both their names. The second occasion was during 866–71, when Louis II campaigned against the Arabs in southern Italy and made himself master of Benevento, where he struck denari, some in the joint names of himself and his wife Angilberga.

The eastern portion of the empire, assigned to Louis the German (840–76), comprised all Germany east of the Rhine plus the towns of Mainz, Worms and Speyer on the west bank, and this was expanded in 870 after the

---

[57] Lafaurie (1970), pp. 132–3.   [58] On Lothar's Dorestad coinage see Coupland (1988).

death of Lothar II to incorporate part of Lotharingia with Cologne, Trier, Metz, Strasbourg, Basel, Toul and Liège, the latter two shared with Charles the Bald. Outside the Rhineland and Bavaria, Germany had essentially a non-monetary economy to judge from the pattern of minting and of coin finds. Louis the Pious had struck coinage at Cologne, Mainz, Strasbourg, Regensburg and three unidentified mints, all of them probably situated in Germany, *Alaboteshain, Aldunheim* and *Stottenburg,* but the only coins attributable to Louis the German before 870 are ones from Mainz, and thereafter the coins of Louis and his successors are almost entirely ones struck in their Lotharingian territories to the west of the Rhineland. Arnulf of Carinthia (887–99) struck a substantial coinage at Mainz and a small issue at Regensburg, but it was only under Louis the Child (899–911) that the Rhineland mints of Cologne and Strasbourg were brought back into operation after an interval of sixty years or more. Coin finds from the eighth and ninth centuries present a similar pattern, being moderately plentiful from the middle Rhineland and Bavaria, while further east and north they are very scarce.[59] It was the tenth century, under the new dynasty of Saxon kings, that saw the great expansion of minting and coin circulation in Germany.

In England, after Offa's death in 796, Mercia's supremacy over Kent and East Anglia was challenged, and the moneyers of Canterbury and the East Anglian mint struck their coins in the names of local kings, Eadberht Præn of Kent (796–8) and Eadwald of East Anglia (*c.* 796–800). Within a few years Offa's successor, Cenwulf, had regained control of the two kingdoms and of their mints. In the 820s political control of these kingdoms again changed hands, Kent to a local king Baldred in *c.* 823 and thence to Egbert of Wessex in 825, and East Anglia to a local king Æthelstan in 827. On each occasion the mints continued operating with the same moneyers, and so far as one can judge little interruption in minting. Moneyers, although men of wealth and moderately high status, were evidently not political appointees, and the mints were not institutions of the court. The moneyers would have belonged to the mercantile community, which was also the principal customer of the mint bringing in foreign coin and bullion for conversion into legal currency. The mints were situated at or near the principal ports: London, Canterbury, Rochester (from *c.* 810), Ipswich (?), and Southampton or Winchester (intermittently from the 790s). There were fluctuations in output, notably at London which, after being the second mint in the later

---

[59] Blackburn (1993).

eighth and early ninth centuries, produced virtually no coinage in the 830s and 850s. Presumably Mercia's political decline had dire consequences for London's foreign trade. In the middle of the ninth century there are signs of greater central control being exercised over the mints, as their fiscal and revenue-collecting roles became more important. The coin types were becoming more standardised, initially bringing uniformity to the products of all the moneyers within a mint, and subsequently between mints. The Kentish mints of Canterbury and Rochester adopted a common type from the late 840s, and in the mid 860s Burgred of Mercia (852–74) and Æthelred I of Wessex (865–71) must have agreed a form of monetary alliance whereby the same coin type should be used in both kingdoms. The number of moneyers was increased significantly in Wessex during the 850s and in Mercia in the 860s.

For Northumbria, its physical isolation and political turmoil had allowed the monetary developments of western Europe to pass it by. The kings and the archbishops of York continued to strike small thick pennies of Merovingian or 'sceat' fabric, although since the early ninth century these had become increasingly debased so that by c. 850 they were of pure brass (the so-called 'stycas') and of such low value that they were used and hoarded in vast numbers. Their circulation was essentially limited to the Northumbrian kingdom, although in the middle of the ninth century some seem to have been used as a supplementary currency in Lindsey (north Lincolnshire) and East Anglia. The series came to an end with the Viking conquest of York in 865.

Northumbria was not alone in suffering debasement, for the southern issues were progressively debased from c. 840 so that by the 870s the coins of Wessex and Mercia were barely 25% fine and much reduced in weight.[60] It fell to Alfred of Wessex (871–99) to overhaul the monetary system, which he did with two major coinage reforms and a radical reorganisation of the mints. In about 875, probably before the decisive battle of Edington (878), he ordered a recoinage replacing the base Lunette coins with a Cross-and-Lozenge type in fine (c. 95%) silver and of restored weight of c. 1.4 g. A few years later, c. 880, with another recoinage he raised the weight standard to c. 1.6 g, and introduced the halfpenny for the first time in England. As a more gradual process, starting in the later 870s, he embarked on a programme of creating a series of inland mints, in parallel with his establishment of the network of defensive boroughs. By the end of his reign the number of mints in Wessex and English Mercia had increased from two to at least eight, and the policy was continued by his successors so that by the

[60] Metcalf and Northover (1985).

reign of Athelstan (924–39), after the reconquest of the Danelaw, there were some forty mints operating in England. Like his contemporary Charles the Bald, Alfred could see the commercial and fiscal advantages of having a sound currency and accessible mints.

By the end of the ninth century the geographical pattern of minting in England had changed radically, owing in part to Alfred's reorganisation of the mints, but also to the impact of the Viking settlement of the Danelaw. The Vikings had scarcely any experience of minting in their homelands, but they knew the utility of coinage, having campaigned in Francia and England for several decades and received many payments of tribute. Within a few years of their settlement in the Danelaw they established a series of mints in East Anglia and the east Midlands during the 880s and at York in the 890s. Initially they copied Alfred's coins, although retaining the older *c.* 1.4 g weight standard, but soon they developed their own distinctive coinages, south of the Humber in the name of the martyred East Anglian king Edmund, and at York in the names of the Viking kings.[61] Their mints in the southern Danelaw were established not by English or Scandinavian moneyers, but by men with Continental names, presumably brought for the purpose from Francia.[62] Although in some cases the die-cutting is poor and the inscriptions are illiterate, the Danelaw coinages were produced in fine silver, with fairly well-controlled weights, and on a very substantial scale.

There is here a conundrum for the monetary historian, for while the mint organisations in Francia and England expanded during the second half of the ninth century, the number of stray finds of coins recovered falls off over the ninth century, and single-finds from the last third are notably scarce. This suggests that the volume of coinage in general circulation had shrunk. A similar pattern has been observed in England and on the Continent, [63] which when coupled with the evidence of silver debasement in both countries in the mid-ninth century, suggests that there may have been a shortage of silver for currency purposes in western Europe lasting for a century or so until the discovery of new ores in the Harz mountains.

THE BULLION ECONOMIES OF NORTHERN AND EASTERN EUROPE

At the end of the seventh century in vast areas of Europe north and east of the Rhine and Danube valleys there was no coin production and virtually no coinage to be found, although Roman silver *denarii* of the second and third centuries and gold solidi of the late fourth and fifth centuries had circulated to some extent in previous times. The growth of the 'sceat' currency of

---

[61] Lyon and Stewart (1961); Blackburn (1989).   [62] Smart (1986).
[63] Blackburn (1993).

Frisia and England also led to its limited penetration into southern
Scandinavia, and the establishment of a mint probably at Ribe in Jutland in
the first quarter of the eighth century, flourishing for some twenty to thirty
years. There was a revival in minting towards the end of the eighth century,
not at Ribe but probably at Hedeby, and there followed almost two
centuries of intermittent production of light-weight pennies with designs
derived from Charlemagne's Dorestad coinage.[64] However, this small
coinage had little economic impact, for its circulation by tale was very
restricted, perhaps merely to the *wic* of Hedeby itself, and although the coins
did reach other parts of Scandinavia and beyond it was an insignificant
element of the stock of bullion silver.

The major economic change in the region came with the establishment of
links to the east which brought Islamic silver dirhems into the northern
lands in huge quantities. For more than 150 years, until the 970s, Arabic
dirhems dominated the currency of European Russia, the lands of the
southern Baltic, and Scandinavia. They travelled from the regions south and
east of the Caspian Sea via a number of routes across Russia to the Baltic, but
Russia was not a mere transit area, for dirhems have been found there in
hoards widely dispersed, suggesting they were actively used and stored as
wealth.

The date for the establishment of links between Scandinavia and the east,
which has been taken to mark the dawn of the Viking age, has been
disputed.[65] The hoards suggest that the first dirhems arrived in Scandinavia
c. 800 but, since they had only just appeared in Russia perhaps a decade
earlier, and were immediately able to pass on to Scandinavia, it is quite likely
that trade or other links between Russia and Scandinavia, already existed.[66]
The initial appearance of the dirhems, therefore, may not have the
significance that some scholars have attached to it. During the course of the
ninth and tenth centuries there were ebbs and flows in the import of Islamic
coinage into the northern lands. There was a temporary reduction between
the 820s and 840s, and a more marked decline from the 870s.[67] When the
importation resumed *c*. 900, it was from quite a different region, from the
Sāmānid lands of central Asia rather than the heart of the ʿAbbasid caliphate
in the Near East.

Within Europe the dirhems are found in hoards, sometimes of immense
size, containing a mixture of silver ornaments, ingots and coins, often cut up
and covered in 'peck-marks' indicating they had been tested for their quality
with a sharp blade. Later in the tenth century, as west European pennies
replaced the dirhems as the main source of imported silver into the northern

[64] Malmer (1966).   [65] Linder Welin (1974); Callmer (1976).
[66] Jonsson (1994).   [67] Noonan (1985).

lands, the hoards retained their mixed character. It was not until the eleventh and twelfth centuries that this vast area of northern and eastern Europe would develop its own national coinages and regulated monetary economies.

Looking forward from the year 900, what do we see?[68] The unified currency system of the Carolingians, at its strongest under Louis the Pious, would become still more fragmented as the new kings of France lost effective control over the provinces. Most coinage was struck by and for the profit of the local nobility, lay or ecclesiastical, who proceeded to reduce the weight and fineness of the denier at differing rates, resulting in regionalisation of the currency. The Saxon kings, as has been indicated, greatly expanded the area of minting and coin circulation in Germany, but they achieved this largely by granting minting rights to local magnates and, as in France, regional weight standards began to develop in the late tenth century. In England, by contrast, the trend towards strong central control continued. After the reconquest of the Danelaw in the middle of the tenth century, the new unified kingdom devised perhaps the most sophisticated fiscal currency system medieval Europe would see. With hindsight the seeds of these various developments were there to be found at the end of the ninth century, but it would have required considerable talent to predict exactly how they would grow.[69]

[68] For a survey of coinage and currency in tenth-century Europe see Dumas (1991).

[69] *Acknowledgements.* I am grateful to Helen Brown, Alberto Canto and Lucia Travaini for advice on the Arabic coinages of Spain and Sicily, and to Philip Grierson for his comments on a draft of this chapter.

PART III

CHURCH AND SOCIETY

CHAPTER 21

THE PAPACY IN THE EIGHTH AND NINTH CENTURIES

Thomas F.X. Noble

FROM the election of Sergius I in 687 to the death of John VIII in 882, what counted most was the unspectacular and relentless emergence of the papacy as a local and then, slowly, as a western European institution. The central theme in this chapter, then, will be local history.[1] Papal history must first be understood in its own terms, and those terms are rooted in and around Rome.

THE SOURCES FOR PAPAL HISTORY

The most important source for papal history in the eighth and ninth centuries is the *Liber Pontificalis*,[2] a collection of contemporary or near-contemporary papal biographies written in the Lateran. These Lives vary in length, and also in the quality and detail of the information they provide. As a rule, the accounts tell something of the parentage of the pope and something about his personal characteristics. Then the text might give a long narrative of significant political or diplomatic events, or it might provide brief, catalogue-like statements about routine ecclesiastical business. The biographies, coming as they do from the Lateran, and intended as they must have been both for reference and for the education of young men beginning their careers in the papal administration, have an official quality. This means that they are valuable both for what they tell us and for the slant or interpretation that they give to events.[3] The second critical source is the

---

[1] Among relatively recent papal histories, mention may be made of: Ullmann (1970; 1972); Pacaut (1976); Richards (1979); Zimmermann (1981); Fink (1981); Franzen and Bäumer (1982); Schimmelpfennig (1984); Anton (1984); Fried (1984). The most detailed accounts of individual pontificates are still to be found in Mann (1925). Zimmermann (1981), pp. 7–10 discusses pointedly and concisely the emergence of the polemical tradition of the papacy. The classic treatments in the Protestant tradition of papal history are Caspar (1930; 1933; 1956) and Haller (1951). For the fullest presentation of the Catholic view see Seppelt (1954).

[2] *Le Liber Pontificalis*, ed. Duchesne, 2d edn (1955–7).   [3] Noble (1985); Bertolini (1970).

more than 1200 surviving papal letters from Sergius I to John VIII.[4]
Originally these letters would have been kept in registers in the archive of
the Lateran, but from our period we have only a fragment of the register of
Gregory II (716–31) and a large extract from that of John VIII (872–82).
Thus, for the most part, it is recipients' copies that have chanced to survive.[5]
Vast quantities of letters have been lost. The surviving material treats a wide
array of subjects of concern to the churches of Byzantium and western
Europe. Letters provide a good impression of the kinds of issues that came
to the attention of the popes. If the surviving letters of the eighth and ninth
centuries are compared to the large surviving extract from the register of
Gregory I (590–604: 866 letters) or even to the fragment from Gregory II, it
will be seen that the loss has been especially acute in materials detailing the
mundane business of operating the Roman church province. Papal letters
have generally been neglected as sources of spirituality. Most historians
have used them to document particular papal claims in the realms of
ideology or politics. Recent work on the Register of Gregory I proves that
more than 60% of his letters were rescripts, that is, direct responses to
petitions that were directed to Rome by private individuals or by officers of
the papal administration.[6] Should further research arrive at similar findings
for the letters of later popes, then it will be necessary to stress even more
emphatically that papal letters primarily reveal the quotidian concerns of the
Lateran administration and not the personal interests or ideas of individual
popes.

Few documentary materials are extant from our period, even though
there is plenty of reason to think that various branches of the papal
administration produced and conserved records.[7] The *Liber Diurnus*, a
collection of formulae used in the Lateran chancery, survives only in north
Italian manuscripts.[8] The published version, therefore, is not the actual
formula book of the Roman church, but it does contain many actual
formulae bearing on a wide array of routine administrative matters. The
formulae reveal the range of documents that might have survived, were all
papal registers extant. Another quasi-documentary source for the activities
of the papal administration is the *Ordines Romani*, which contain the rites for
virtually all liturgical celebrations involving the pope or his highest
subordinates. *Ordo Romanus I*, in particular, lays out in great detail all the
arrangements for a major papal Mass.[9] From this text we can see who

---

[4] There is no comprehensive, critical edition. Some texts are in *MGH* volumes, many more in *PL*.
Critical to research is Jaffé (1885).   [5] Noble (1990), pp. 84–93.   [6] Pitz (1990).
[7] Noble (1990), pp. 93–5.   [8] *LD*; Noble (1990), pp. 95–6 and n. 49.
[9] *Ordo Romanus I*, ed. Andrieu, *Les ordines* II, pp. 67–108.

accompanied the pope, how a procession was organised, what activities took place and who filled what roles. It is a superb, but still not fully exploited, source for public ritual in the early middle ages.

Rome did not produce additional historical accounts, but, at the turn of the seventh century, papal Rome began to be a subject of intense interest among historical writers in Francia, England and northern Italy. These records fill a few gaps in the papal sources and sometimes permit us to draw alternative interpretations of key developments. Byzantine writers, who had never paid much attention to the popes, almost totally lost sight of them in the eighth and ninth centuries, although some treatises and letters emanating from anti-iconoclast circles, chiefly monastic ones, illuminate papal activities. Several popes in this period – Zacharias I (741–51), Hadrian I (722–95), Leo III (795–816), Paschal I (817–24), Gregory IV (827–44), Leo IV (847–55), Nicholas I (858–67) – were energetic builders, restorers and embellishers of Roman churches, as the *Liber Pontificalis* informs us, even though little of this art and architecture survives.[10] Beginning with Gregory III and Zacharias, the popes issued coins and, starting with Hadrian I, they issued beautiful gold coins.[11] These contribute to our understanding of papal history in the areas of political symbolism and manifestations of public authority and they shed some light on the economic life of papal Rome.

THE PAPACY IN ITS ROMAN AND ITALIAN SETTING

The great fact of papal history in the early middle ages is the papacy's alienation from Byzantium and alignment with the Franks. Viewed through the pellucid lens of hindsight that fact has acquired an inevitability that robs it of all sense of contingency. For the papacy to have abandoned its familiar moorings in the Roman world cannot have been easy. The church had arisen and spread in the Roman world. Its sense of universality, its catholicity, was partly, but importantly, Roman. It had inherited, but also redefined, the Roman idea of destiny. The church's leaders, the popes, had defined themselves in part in relation to the emperors: 'Two there are, august emperor, by which this world is chiefly ruled, the sacred authority of the priesthood and the royal power' is how Gelasius I (492–6) had put it.[12]

When the break with Byzantium came in the eighth century, it stood

---

[10] *LP*, ed. Duchesne, I, pp. 432–3, 434–5, 499–514; II, pp. 1–3, 7–34, 74–83, 111–34, 152–3, 163–4, 166–7. Geertman (1975).   [11] Grierson and Blackburn (1986), pp. 259–66.

[12] Gelasius I, *Letter to the Emperor Anastasius*, ed. E. Schwartz, pp. 20–1, at p. 20.

against a background of long and complicated relations. The Byzantine version of Rome provided a sense of historical and cultural orientation.[13] The imperial authorities had occasionally afforded some help against the incursions of the Lombards. But there was also the sorry tale of imperial interference in dogma. To the popes, the Council of Chalcedon (451) had settled the critical points of Trinitarian and Christological teaching and its formulations required neither amendment nor correction. The emperors could not be so certain. Some, Justinian for example and perhaps Heraclius, harboured genuine doubts about the strict dyophysitism proclaimed at Chalcedon. But most emperors, and not least Heraclius and his seventh-century successors, had to contend with rich and vital provinces, Syria for instance, that were devoutly monophysite. The popes, except Honorius momentarily, were unprepared to yield to political exigencies and determined to condemn imperial intervention in the realm of dogma. Papal principle, or obstinacy as it was seen in Constantinople, led to the humiliating capture and abuse of Martin I in 649, and to the haughty displays of Constans II on his visit to Rome in 663 – the last imperial visit to Rome until a western emperor was made there in 800. Still, it had been possible to live with these difficulties.

The decades after 692 brought shocks that could not be endured.[14] In that year Justinian II held a council, called the *Quinisext* because it issued disciplinary canons meant to complement the dogmatic decisions of the fifth and sixth ecumenical councils.[15] The canons would have had the effect of making binding in Rome a number of practices that were not in force there, and Sergius I summarily rejected them. Justinian sent an envoy to Rome to seize Sergius but the Romans protected the pope. In 695 Justinian was deprived of his throne but his successor was no more pleased with Sergius than Justinian had been. Again, officials were sent to discipline the pope and again they were forced to withdraw. Justinian recovered his office in 705 and tried to punish the Italians, including the pope and the Romans, whom he held partially accountable for his deposition. Yet again, the Romans thwarted the Byzantines.

Political confusion at Constantinople, coupled with short reigns and Arab attacks, produced a lull in papal–Byzantine relations until the Emperor Leo III ascended the throne, defeated the Arabs and turned his attention to the west. Leo significantly raised the taxes of the imperial provinces in Italy to raise funds for his wars in the east. These taxes would have been burdensome for peasants and landlords alike, but were especially resented because the imperial authorities were providing no help in Italy

[13] For the following see, in greater detail, chapters 13 and 14 above.
[14] Noble (1984), pp. 1–60.   [15] Mansi, XI.912C–1006B.

itself, where the Lombards were menacing the lands from Ravenna to Rome. Gregory II raised staunch opposition to the new taxes and, as under Justinian II and Sergius I, officials who were sent to Rome to force compliance with imperial policy were driven off.

Then came what turned out to be the defining issue: Iconoclasm.[16] In 726 Leo III began agitating against figural representations in Christian art and by 731 he formally banned them. He even dismissed the patriarch of Constantinople and tried to win the pope to his views. Gregory II and Gregory III resolutely refused to engage in a discussion of the image question and solemnly denied that the emperor had any right to involve himself in such matters in the first place. Leo III discovered that, once again, he could coerce neither the pope nor the population of central Italy. Accordingly, the emperor decided to cut his losses by withdrawing Dalmatia, Illyricum and southern Italy along with Sicily from the Roman church province and by denying to the Roman church some valuable revenues. By the middle 730s it appeared that the break between Rome and Constantinople was complete.

Yet the reality was more complex. Relations between Rome and the east had always been difficult. The situation in Constantinople might change, as indeed it seemed to do briefly in 741 when the iconodule usurper Artavasdos came to power.[17] The pope was now the key figure in a widespread movement that was mixed in its allegiances and motivations, and that involved people in Venice, Ravenna, Rome and many rural regions. And the Lombards were potentially more menacing now that they had been shown the impotence of the Byzantine authorities in Italy. Under the popes Gregory III and Zacharias, there were a few attempts to reach an accommodation with Byzantium, but these were doomed because the Byzantines could not provide assistance in Italy and would not abandon Iconoclasm. These popes also carried on an intense diplomacy with the Lombard court, while also appealing to the Bavarians and Franks for assistance. The popes even tried to use the Lombard dukes of Spoleto and Benevento against the kings in Pavia. A Franco-papal alliance was only one somewhat remote possibility among several.

In 751 the Lombard king, Aistulf, captured Ravenna and began making threatening gestures towards Rome. It was in this context that Stephen II appealed again to the Franks.[18] What the pope wanted was protection, not a new master. Stephen had to overcome serious opposition at the court of the new Frankish king Pippin, but he finally did so by 754. Stephen travelled to the Frankish kingdom and engaged in several meetings with Pippin. Pippin

---

[16] Martin (1930), pp. 5–84; Beck (1966), pp. 13–61; Haldon (1977); Stein (1980).

[17] Speck (1981). [18] Noble (1984), pp. 61–98 with further literature and sources.

and the Frankish magnates agreed to help the pope in Italy, and Pippin and Stephen concluded a personal alliance of *amicitia, pax et caritas*. In 755 and again in 756 Pippin campaigned in Italy, defeated Aistulf, and forced the Lombard king to return to the pope the lands which he had seized in central Italy. Under Pippin's protection the papal state that had been emerging since the 730s came fully into being.

In the 760s and early 770s Desiderius, the new Lombard king, struggled to recapture valuable lands which his predecessor had been forced to hand over to Rome.[19] The popes continually appealed to the Franks to fulfil the terms of their alliance. Pressing military problems in the Frankish realm, and a change of rulers when Pippin died in 768, precluded active Frankish intervention in Italy. The pope and the people of central Italy were still vulnerable when in 773 Charlemagne agreed to come to the aid of Hadrian I. Charlemagne defeated the Lombard king, as his father before him had done, but to avoid a continuing nuisance in Italy, Charlemagne deposed Desiderius and made himself king of the Lombards. Charlemagne also renewed the Franco-papal alliance and guaranteed the pope's possessions in Italy. For some years, however, there were sharp disagreements between the papal and Frankish courts about just what lands the popes could legitimately claim. In 781 and again in 787 Charlemagne made major territorial settlements in Italy that left the popes in secure possession of a wide swathe of lands in Italy running from Ravenna to Rome.[20] Some lands which the popes had been claiming since the 730s were not handed over, but in a few areas new lands were actually added to the papal territories. The settlements are known to us in some detail from their confirmation between Louis the Pious, Charlemagne's successor, and Paschal I in 817.[21]

As the papal administration assumed the leadership of the lands and people of central Italy, the former military aristocracy which had been ascendant under the Byzantine regime was partly eclipsed and partly absorbed by the papal government. Stephen II (752–7) and his brother Paul I (757–67) were the first Roman nobles elected to the papal office in the eighth century. Paul's death brought violent factional squabbles at Rome that were not resolved until the eminent Hadrian I was elected in 772. During Hadrian's long pontificate, noblemen were promoted to important offices and there was a large degree of symbiosis between the papal administration and the Roman nobility. One result of this situation was that quarrels that had always existed within the Roman nobility were now domesticated in the Lateran. One such quarrel, whose exact bases are unknowable, broke out during the early years of the pontificate of Leo III.

[19] Noble (1984), pp. 99–137.   [20] Noble (1984), pp. 138–83.
[21] *Pactum Hludowicianum, MGH Cap.* I, ed. A. Boretius, no. 172, pp. 352–5.

He was attacked by a mob led by some relatives of Hadrian I. Leo fled to Charlemagne who, as the pope's ally and protector, first restored him to Rome and then resolved to go to Rome himself and investigate the matter. Inquiries were indeed held in Rome in December of 800, but the Franks were careful to respect the autonomy of the pope. Although charges of papal misconduct had been bruited abroad, Leo was not put on trial. Instead, the pope swore publicly that he was guiltless. On Christmas Day 800 Charlemagne was crowned emperor in St Peter's by Leo. Whatever the contemporary or later significance of that event, it seems that Leo III was merely trying to strengthen the hand of his ally and protector. Charlemagne's imperial dignity did not fundamentally change his position in Rome or the basis of his alliance with the pope.[22]

The last year of Leo's pontificate was disturbed by another uprising in Rome, and his successor, Stephen IV (816–17), rushed to Francia to confer with Louis the Pious. At Rheims Stephen crowned Louis emperor and concluded an agreement which was reaffirmed a year later between Louis and Stephen's successor, Paschal I. This agreement was the *Pactum Ludovicianum*, mentioned already as containing the earliest surviving list of the papal territories in central Italy. The document also spelled out the terms under which the Carolingians would provide their by now customary protection for the papacy. Louis agreed not to intervene in Rome unless asked to do so. In other words, he confirmed the autonomy of the pope and his lands. Paschal, however, soon found himself in the middle of a bloody aristocratic quarrel that took the lives of some prominent Lateran officials. Louis, and his son Lothar who was then active in Italy and who had been crowned co-emperor by the pope in 823, were prevented from taking decisive action but heard enough reports to suggest to them that partisan strife in Rome was reaching a ferocious level. When Paschal died in 824 and was succeeded by Eugenius I, Louis and Lothar issued a new statement of the Franco-papal alliance. The *Constitutio Romana*[23] achieved a clarification of the position of the pope in Rome and secured a clearer framework for the imperial protection of the papacy. From now on, popes were, after their elections but before their consecrations, to swear the traditional oath of alliance and friendship with the Frankish emperor. The Romans were, at the same time, to swear allegiance to the pope. Moreover, an imperial and a papal *missus* would henceforth sit together in judgement in Rome to hear appeals against officials of the papal administration. Throughout the rest of the ninth century the popes tended to observe the terms of the *Constitutio*,

---

[22] For two anthologies containing a wide array of interpretations of these events see Sullivan (1959) and Wolf (1972). See also Noble (1984), pp. 256–75, 278–308.

[23] *Constitutio Romana, MGH Cap.* 1, ed. A. Boretius, no. 161, pp. 322–4.

although occasionally popes were consecrated without first confirming their
bonds with the emperor. John VIII got the imperial *missus* removed from
Rome, largely because by then neither the emperor nor the *missus* exercised
effective power of protection.[24]

Some problems that were but dimly visible in the time of Leo III and
Paschal I became more acute in the middle years of the ninth century. New
problems arose too. In the former category must be placed the social and
political strife in Rome. It seems absolutely clear that the papal administration, although solidly aristocratic, had been riven by faction. What is not
clear is what issues set the factions off against one another. There are hints,
however. One is that, according to a late ninth-century source, at the time of
the disturbances under Paschal I, 'all the greater men of the city were of the
imperial party'.[25] Under Sergius II a gang, including soldiers from south of
Rome, invaded the Lateran and held it for a time. Sergius, like his successor
Leo IV, refused to send notice of his election to the emperor. When Benedict
III was elected in 855 he sent envoys to the emperor but they were
intercepted by men devoted to Arsenius, the bishop of Porto, who was the
head of the imperial party and father of the defeated candidate, Anastasius.
The men who overtook Benedict's envoys were led by another of Rome's
suburbicarian bishops and a *magister militum*. Nicholas I and Hadrian II were
both opposed by the party, called 'imperial', of Arsenius and Anastasius.
Hadrian suffered the indignity of an attack on Rome by Duke Lambert of
Spoleto, and so did John VIII, who was actually driven out of the city in
878. Obviously, there were persons in Rome who were members of the
papal administration and simultaneously allies of military officers outside
the city. These people were usually not in control of the papal office and the
partisan papal sources call them an 'imperial' party.

A second hint may be concealed in several statements in the *Liber
Pontificalis* to the effect that certain popes had great concern for the 'poor'
and strong support from the 'people'.[26] In the social lexicon of the early
middle ages, poverty meant powerlessness more than penury.[27] And
'people' can mean almost any group not immediately identifiable with an
elite. In other words, it may be that as some persons in the papal
administration looked to the imperial officers in Italy and to the local
military magnates, others in the papal government drew support from the
populace of Rome itself. Some confirmation for this point of view may be
found in the attempt by Nicholas I to restore the papal election decree of

---

[24] Bertolini (1956); Noble (1984), pp. 308–22.

[25] *Libellus de imperia potestate in urbe Roma*, ed. Zuchetti, pp. 197–8.

[26] *LP* II, p. 52 (Paschal I), pp. 142–3 (Benedict III), p. 173 (Hadrian II). Each of these popes was
opposed by military, or 'imperial', aristocrats.   [27] Bosl (1964); Duby (1974), pp. 93–4.

769.[28] That decree had restricted participation in papal elections to the cardinal clergy of Rome and had thus excluded the laity. This action was taken early in the history of the papal state when the local aristocracy and the papal administration were first attaining a high degree of identification. Louis, in the *Pactum Ludovicianum*, reopened participation to all Romans but then guaranteed orderly and canonical elections. It seems that Nicholas was trying, once again, to restrict the participation of the lay nobility in the selection of Rome's leader.

A third hint points to family aggrandisement. Hadrian I had come from a powerful landed family some of whose members had been implicated in the strife of the years 767–9. Hadrian promoted members of his own family to high office and some of them attacked Leo III. Stephen IV was the candidate of a faction of the nobility and popes Sergius II and Hadrian II were from the same family as Stephen, although their exact relationships cannot be determined. The point is that any noble family might put some of its members into the Lateran but others would remain participants in the wider society. Doubtless such families saw the Lateran administration as a means of protecting and promoting their interests.

Raising political and economic interests brings up a fourth hint that in some ways ties all the others together. Elite families in seventh- and early eighth-century Italy had possessed significant landholdings and military offices in the Byzantine administration.[29] When the Byzantine government was eclipsed by the papal in the 730s and 740s, some members of those elite families, as we have already noted, began to enter the Lateran. They did not thereby, as individuals or as families, lose their connections to the country-side. The Lateran, indeed, enhanced and complicated those links precisely because it was the largest landholder in Italy. Some papal lands were directly exploited but others were leased. The fate of the secular and of the ecclesiastical nobility was closely interwoven, but the real jurisdictional power was in the hands of the clergy.

By the ninth century, signs point to the growing importance of that power. As the Carolingians and the popes produced peace in central Italy, removed onerous Byzantine taxation and put land back into cultivation, there can be no doubt about rising prosperity in the Italian countryside.[30] It is surely no coincidence that the Carolingian-induced *Pax Italiae*, coinciding as it did with the aristocratisation of the Lateran administration, issued in a stream of massive building projects in and around Rome along with the donation of literally thousands of pounds of gold and silver objects to

---

[28] Roman Council of 862, c. 6: Jaffé, *Regesta Pontificum Romanorum*, p. 345.　　[29] Brown (1984).
[30] But prosperity in general did not necessarily mean prosperity for all: Wickham (1981), pp. 80–114; Tabacco (1989), pp. 4–6, 109–76.

various churches in the city. Control of the Lateran had come to mean control of vast wealth. Wealth was sought for its own sake but also because it generated patronage. The Lateran was owed a great measure of loyalty by the people who benefited from buiding projects and charitable benefactions. It is hardly surprising that factions formed in attempts to control that patronage.

Conditions in Rome were made more difficult in the middle years of the ninth century by a weakening of the Carolingian ability to intervene effectively in Rome and by the appearance of Arab raiders all over Italy, and even in the eternal city. In 830 and again in 833 the sons of Louis the Pious rose up in rebellion against their father. Although peace of a sort was patched up in 835, the Carolingian imperial office, with its obligation to defend Rome, was never restored to its former glory. Louis died in 840; his eldest son Lothar succeeded to the imperial office but his brothers Charles and Louis contested his authority at every turn. Lothar sent his son Louis II to Italy as king but Pope Gregory IV took a very independent line *vis-à-vis* his putative ally. In 844, on Gregory's death, Louis marched to Rome to investigate Pope Sergius' title because he had been elected and consecrated without reference to the emperor or to the king of Italy. Sergius closed the gates of Rome to Louis, a sure sign of the change in papal relations with the Carolingians. Sergius was finally prevailed upon to agree that henceforth papal consecrations would not take place without imperial approval and that imperial *missi* would be present. Sergius refused to swear allegiance to Louis because he wished to avoid any implication that the papal state depended upon the kingdom of Italy. When Lothar died in 855, Louis succeeded him as emperor, but because Lothar had divided his 'Middle Kingdom' into three parts, Louis was effectively confined to Italy. He lacked the power, prestige and material resources to be really effective in Italy or elsewhere in the Frankish world. When the south Italian princes of Capua, Salerno and Beneventum plotted and schemed with and against one another, or when Lambert of Spoleto ravaged Rome, Louis was nearly powerless. Nor could he suppress factional strife in Rome itself. Down to his death in 875 Louis enjoyed generally cordial relations with the popes, but he was not of much use to them, nor they to him. After Louis' death, Italian magnates invited Karlmann, son of Louis the German, to take the imperial office, while John VIII turned to Charles the Bald and, after his death, to Charles the Fat. John even appealed to the Byzantines in his quest to secure protection in Rome. John's pontificate shows us both the pope as the final arbiter of the imperial office and the imperial office shrunk to a shadow of its former majesty.[31]

---

[31] Kreutz (1991), pp. 18–74; see chapters 5, 6, 10 and 13 above.

Pope John VIII, who was brutally murdered in Rome, had needed protection from the Romans, just as a number of his predecessors had done. But he, and the popes going back to Gregory IV, had another pressing threat: the Arabs.[32] Città Vecchia was raided in 813 and Sicily was attacked in 827 by Muslim marauders operating from North Africa and from islands in the western Mediterranean. South Italian princes, who were competing for control of Beneventum, called in Muslims as mercenaries but, as so often happened, the hirelings soon discovered the relative weakness of their paymasters. Down to about 850 Muslims raided the western coast of Italy with virtual impunity, often launching their ventures from a secure base at Bari.

Late in his pontificate Gregory IV built fortifications at Ostia, called Gregoriopolis.[33] These did not prevent the raiders from going right up the Tiber to Rome in 846. Leo IV then undertook massive repairs and fortifications around Rome.[34] He refurbished the old city walls and constructed some fifteen towers. He constructed additional fortifications along the Tiber. Finally, and most famously, he built a massive wall – 40 feet high and 12 feet thick with forty-four towers – around St Peter's and the Vatican palace. Rome's old city walls had not sheltered any of the portions of the city across the Tiber from the city centre. He also rebuilt the old fortress at Portus and garrisoned it with Corsicans who had lost their island to the Muslim. Pope Nicholas I subsequently tried to enlist the south Italian princes in his wars against the Muslims but was unable to secure order in that turbulent region. John VIII directed a successful fleet in the waters near Ostia and gained some measure of security when the Byzantines retook Bari in 876. He also had to endure the danger of a secure Muslim base in Sicily after the seizure of Syracuse in 878.

There are many ironies in this tale of the papacy's position in central Italy. For a long time the papal administration was less important than the Byzantine and did not attract Rome's elite. Then, when the papal administration began to take control of central Italy, the elite entered that administration. The Lateran thus acquired power and prestige as never before, but was also embroiled in the social struggles that had arisen in the wider society. The Carolingians for a time provided protection from both external foes and internal strife, but some at least in Rome began to chafe under Frankish 'protection'. As the precise terms of this were being renegotiated, the Carolingians were diverted from Italian concerns by civil strife and foreign attacks. In the short term, the absence of effective Carolingian power in Rome led to increased violence and factional strife in the city. In the

---

[32] Kreutz (1991), pp. 18–35; see chapter 10 above.   [33] *LP* II, p. 82.
[34] *LP* II, pp. 115, 123; Mann (1925) II, pp. 262–7; Krautheimer (1980), pp. 117–20.

longer term, the power vacuum left Rome at the mercy of the Arabs. The popes always desired freedom and the Franks had wished to accord them wide autonomy. In the end papal freedom collapsed in the political and social strife of the tenth century and papal autonomy became meaningless in view of the weakening of the imperial office.

THE INSTITUTIONS OF THE ROMAN CHURCH

The assumption of territorial rule and the entry of the local Roman nobility into the clergy brought about an increase in the routine business and a refinement of the structures of the Roman church. In late antiquity the bishop had become the focus of Christian instruction and of sacramental celebration in towns. In large cities, such as Rome, the press of affairs had forced bishops to decentralise many of their responsibilities. Beginning in the fourth century, moreover, the imperial administration had begun assigning to the church a variety of formerly public responsibilities such as legal jurisdiction in relatively minor cases and a wide array of charitable services. In eighth- and ninth-century Rome, therefore, the popes found themselves at the head of both a religious and a secular administration that had been growing for centuries.

The key figure was, of course, the pope. Throughout our period the popes can, with only a few exceptions, be characterised as Roman, noble and experienced. Those popes who did not come from Rome itself, Leo III for example, were Italians from families of long residence. The Romanisation of the papacy is the predictable result of the far-reaching identification of the Roman nobility and the papal administration that has already been mentioned. Beginning with Stephen II there is no pope who can, with absolute certainty, be excluded from the nobility. The *Liber Pontificalis* almost always provides details of the previous careers of the men who were elected pope and among these details emphasis is usually laid both on the offices held and on the name of the pope who first promoted the later pope to a major position. It is hard to say exactly how long men served before election. For example, Sergius II, who was elected in 844, entered the *schola cantorum* under Leo III, who died in 816. He had a minimum of twenty-eight years' service, and perhaps many more given that Leo was elected in 795. Leo IV, who became pope in 847, was brought into the Lateran by Gregory IV, who served from 827 to 844. He had at least three and possibly as many as twenty years' experience. All these popes served for a long time before election and they usually held both pastoral and administrative offices.

Except when there was strife, papal elections were carried out in the Lateran palace.[35] From at least the fifth century, the electors were the 'clergy

[35] Noble (1984), pp. 188–205.

and people' of Rome. It is impossible to say precisely what this meant in practice. Across the eighth century, papal elections were routinely tumultuous, all the more so as the popes became both secular and spiritual leaders. The ninth century saw increasingly violent and corrupt elections such that the decree of 769 and the value of Carolingian protection both became dead letters. It was not until the middle of the eleventh century that effective reform was instituted in the papal election process.

The priestly side of the papal office centred on the provision of liturgical and sacramental services throughout the city.[36] By the eighth century, these were accomplished through five major basilicas and twenty-eight title churches.[37] Each title church had several priests, the most senior of whom was the *presbyter prior*. The senior *presbyter* was the archpriest of the church and the head of the ecclesiastical personnel as a whole. The twenty-eight *presbyteri priores* were the 'cardinal priests' of the Roman church. They were called cardinals partly because they were the elite clergy of the church and partly because they were 'incardinated' to serve in the patriarchal basilicas such as St Peter's, St Paul's Outside the Walls, St Mary Major and St Lawrence. Seven priests were posted to each basilica and celebrated the daily eucharistic liturgy there. St John Lateran was the pope's own basilica and Rome's cathedral church. Its daily liturgies were celebrated by one of Rome's seven suburbicarian bishops. Gradually, each basilica also had a monastery attached to it which saw to the perpetual prayer (*laus perennis*) in that building.[38] The popes had a regular routine of 'stational' liturgical celebrations throughout the city.

Further officers of the spiritual administration of the Roman church were the regional deacons.[39] Since perhaps the third century Rome had been divided into seven regions. Each region had been assigned a deacon, with subordinate subdeacons and acolytes, who were essentially ministers for charitable services. Their head was the archdeacon, one of the great officers of the church.

The archpriest and archdeacon were headquartered in the Lateran along with some other high offiers. The *vicedominus* was the *maiordomo* of the papal household. The *nomencolator* was the chief protocol officer. He arranged ceremonies and controlled personal access to the pope. The *vestararius prior* had charge of the moveable wealth of the church, for example liturgical vessels and vestments. He also supervised the upkeep of the title churches and basilicas.

A range of administrative responsibilities was also centred in the Lateran. Each region of the city had been furnished with a notary who kept church

[36] Noble (1990), pp. 98–101.   [37] Kuttner (1945); Fürst (1967).
[38] Ferrari (1957), pp. 365–75.   [39] Noble (1984), pp. 217–18.

records of all kinds.[40] The *primicerius* of the notaries was one of the greatest officers of the Roman church. He not only superintended the notaries in the city but also headed the papal chancery and archives. The library had once been under the jurisdiction of the *primicerius* of the notaries but in the eighth century, if not before, a separate *bibliothecarius* appeared. The regions were also equipped with *defensores* who were, in a sense, the legal staff of the Lateran. Their original purpose, going back to the fifth century, was to handle minor legal cases and to hear appeals against misconduct by imperial or ecclesiastical officials.[41] As the role of the church became more prominent, their responsibilities grew. There were also two financial officers, the *arcarius*, or treasurer, and the *saccellarius*, or paymaster.[42] They may have received fees and offerings from pious Christians everywhere, for example 'Peter's Pence', but probably spent more time handling revenues from the papal patrimonies and dispensing them again to repair churches, to build walls and to defend Rome.

The Roman church also exercised significant jurisdiction and influence in and around Rome in ways that were only marginally connected to the spiritual functions of the church. Central Italy was dotted with estates both large and small, both nucleated and dispersed, that made up the patrimonies of the church.[43] Some of these had been let out on leases but many more were farmed and managed by an army of peasants and minor officials. From the time of Gregory the Great, the popes called their patrimonies the 'endowment for the poor'. That is, the revenues, in cash and in kind, generated by those lands went to feed the populace of Rome. Food distributions were carried out at institutions called *diaconiae* that were concentrated in the old city centre near the former *stationes annonae* where the Roman state had distributed food.[44] The country around Rome also had estates called *domuscultae*.[45] These first appear in the sources in the middle of the eighth century and were still being reorganised under Gregory IV. *Domuscultae* were large farms. They were regarded as inalienable and were exploited directly by the church. The peasants on them could bear arms. Given that they were concentrated right around Rome, that they appeared when the Lombard threat was most acute, that they were ravaged by the opponents of Leo III and that they appear again when the Arab threat raised its head, it seems safe to conclude that they had always formed a type of papal self-defence force around the city. If sources were richer, they might well show the *domuscultae* playing a major role in the factional strife of the ninth century

[40] Noble (1984), pp. 218–22; Noble (1990), pp. 84–92.   [41] Fischer (1939).

[42] Noble (1984), p. 225.

[43] Spearing (1918); Recchia (1978); Castagnetti (1979).

[44] Lestocquoy (1930); Bertolini (1968).   [45] Bertolini (1952); Noble (1984), pp. 246–9.

when military officers from just outside the city seem often to have been implicated.

Apart from some differences in the scale of its operations and the grandeur of its ritual, the Roman church was little different from any other metropolitan or patriarchal church. The challenges of the eighth and ninth centuries produced some unique responses in the shape of the papal administration, but it is also important to see that that administration had been evolving consistently ever since the third century. The papal relationship with the Carolingians had virtually no impact on the development of the pastoral administration of the church, and that aspect of the papacy has survived in traceable form to this day. The Carolingians initially made it possible for the popes to assume temporal rule in central Italy. While it might be true to say that the inability and unwillingness of the Carolingians to provide continuously effective protection in the ninth century hastened the collapse of papal rule, it is no less true that social and political dynamics in and around Rome contributed materially to the failure of the papacy's first attempt at secular rule.

THE PAPACY AND THE CHRISTIAN WORLD

It is easy enough to list all the occasions when a pope dealt with some ecclesiastical matter. It is much harder to provide a secure interpretative framework for discussing such a list. Even if one believed that late antique popes achieved a clearly defined and well-understood jurisdictional primacy in the church, one would be left having to explain how, when, where and why that primacy was invoked and applied. On the other hand, one can suggest that the popes were accorded a good measure of moral and spiritual prestige and precedence, that Rome was often seen as a source of information and of authentic teaching, and that papal power grew as individual incidents turned into precedents and then into traditions. In that case, it becomes possible to watch the papal role in the church grow, not as the inevitable consequence of ancient theory, but as the unpredictable result of precise historical circumstances.

One might begin by looking at the popes as the guardians of the *catholica fides*. Our period saw Iconoclasm and Adoptionism and also a dispute over the procession of the Holy Spirit, to mention only some controversies in which the popes played a fairly significant role. In each case, it is interesting to note that the popes did not cause the problem, did not play the leading role in combating it, and basically took the position that because the *status quo ante* was correct, there was no point in engaging in serious discussion. Iconoclasm is a good case in point. Emperor Leo III and the Bithynian bishops who were his chief supporters did not have a very complex position with respect to images. Essentially, they equated them with idols and convinced themselves that images were offensive to God. Iconodules, chiefly John Damascene, weighed in with elaborate theological defences of images and provoked a slightly more sophisticated attack on images from Constantine V and his circle. This, in turn, let loose a torrent of iconodule writing, some of which shows real depth. Through all of this the popes took a remarkably simple position: emperors had no business intruding themselves into dogmatic questions; general, and more particularly Roman, ecclesiastical traditions admitted the use of images. What the popes did not do was engage the Iconoclasts on the field of debate. When Theodulf, one of Charlemagne's court theologians, sent to Rome an outline of his *Libri Carolini*,[46] a massive treatise against the restoration of images by the second Council of Nicaea in 787, Pope Hadrian I did send back a long reply, and that reply does attempt to refute many of Theodulf's specific points.[47] What is most interesting in Hadrian's reply, however, is his exasperation at Theodulf's departure from the ancient traditions of the church. At any rate that is how Hadrian depicted things. In the pope's view, II Nicaea had put an end to the iconoclast heresy and had restored the ancient custom of the church. Theodulf, to Hadrian's mind, went too far in challenging the appropriateness of images, although less far than the Iconoclasts had done. In the end, though, the papacy adhered to tradition in each case.

The Adoptionist controversy is instructive too.[48] This was a heresy that the Franks encountered and brought to the attention of the pope. Two Spanish bishops, Elipandus of Toledo and Felix of Urgel, had begun teaching, perhaps in the early 780s, that Christ in his humanity was the adoptive son of God. Traditionally Adoptionism has been seen as a very mild form of Arianism: a slight de-emphasis of Christ's divinity so as to preserve the oneness of God. The matter was brought to Charlemagne's attention and he assembled his palace theologians who produced massive treatises condemning Elipandus and Felix. The Franks actually laid hands on Felix, more than once, and forced him to recant. Hadrian approved all that the Franks had done in the name of the unity of the church and the integrity of the faith. It was Rome's view that the Council of Chalcedon (451) had settled the fundamental mysteries surrounding the person of Christ. The Franks were then full of intellectual enthusiasm and keen to prove themselves worthy of the political leadership of the west. Some experts therefore massively refuted the Adoptionists while others shadow-

---

[46] *Libri Carolini*, ed. Bastgen.

[47] Letter of Hadrian I, *MGH, Epp. Sel. Pont. Rom.*, no. 2, *MGH Epp.* v, pp. 5–57.

[48] Cavadini (1993).

boxed with the Byzantines over images. The pope did not involve himself in particulars.

The *filioque* controversy reveals once again the papal adherence to tradition while also pointing to an interesting aspect of Franco-papal relations. The basic issues were these.[49] After the councils of Nicaea and Constantinople set down the precise phraseology of the creed, it slowly emerged that the eastern and western churches differed in their understanding of the Procession of the Holy Spirit. The east believed (and believes) that the Spirit proceeded 'from the Father through the Son'. The west, on the contrary, held that the Spirit proceeded 'from the Father and from the Son'. Some time in the seventh century, probably in Spain, some in the west began to insert *et filio* or *filioque* ('and from the son') into the creed. On a few occasions in the eighth century, the Franks aggressively asserted that the Byzantines were wrong in their interpretation of the Procession of the Holy Spirit. Then in 808 or 809 some Frankish monks in the Holy Land were accused of heresy for chanting *filioque* and they appealed to Pope Leo III to defend themselves against this charge.[50] The principal evidence they cited on their own behalf was that they had heard *filioque* chanted at the Frankish court. Leo simply referred the matter to the Franks who then sent a delegation to Rome to confer with the pope. It turned out that the pope and the Franks agreed on the theological issue: the Holy Spirit did indeed proceed from the Father and from the Son. But the Franks had inserted the word *filioque* into the creed whereas Rome had not done so (and would not until 1014). The Franks and the popes simply agreed to disagree. This point is important in view of the tendency by some historians to believe that Charlemagne simply overwhelmed the pope on theological matters.

A few ninth-century cases bear out the general line of interpretation we have been developing. Iconoclasm reappeared after the Council of St Sophia in 815.[51] Emperor Michael II wrote to Louis the Pious to enlist his aid against the pope.[52] Specifically, he seems to have wanted Louis to compel the pope to stop aiding iconodule monks who were fleeing the empire in some numbers and settling in Rome. Michael may well have known that the Franks were by no means ardent iconodules, but he was certainly mistaken in supposing that a Carolingian emperor could or would bully a pope the way his own ancestors had done, or that Louis would imagine himself to have the role in dogma that Roman emperors had always claimed. Louis collected his key advisers in 825 and they produced a series of lengthy

---

[49] Haugh (1975).
[50] Jaffé, *Regesta*, no. 2519; letter of Jerusalem monks to Leo III, *Epp. Sel. Pont. Rom.*, no. 7, *MGH Epp.* v, pp. 64–6.   [51] Alexander (1953; 1958); Martin (1930), pp. 150–221.
[52] *Michaelis epistola ad Hludowicum imperatorem directa*, *MGH Conc.* II:2, no. 44A, pp. 475–80.

treatises that harshly criticised Hadrian for what they regarded as his excessive zeal in the defence of images.[53] But then Louis gave letters to his envoys to Rome urging them to use every art of flattery and persuasion to get Eugenius I to agree to the Frankish view on images. Louis warned his envoys, however, that 'Roman obstinacy' would probably foil their efforts. In other words, the Franks and the popes, close allies in so many ways, again agreed to disagree. And sometimes the Franks were prepared to handle theological quarrels on their own. The predestinarian speculations of Gottschalk of Orbais[54] and the eucharistic contention between Ratramnus and Paschasius were settled among the Franks themselves with virtually no reference to Rome.[55] There is every reason to believe that the official Frankish view and the papal view were the same. What is interesting here is that the Franks did not feel compelled to refer the cases to Rome, and that the popes did not insist on giving their stamp of approval to the proceedings.

It is, therefore, comparatively easy to say that in dogmatic issues the popes saw themselves as the guardians of the *catholica fides* as it had been defined in the ecumenical councils of antiquity. It is less easy, in the early middle ages, to say how that guardianship would be exercised.

The church in Rome, and everywhere else, was a hierarchical organisa-tion and the pope was at the head of that hierarchy. One area where papal authority was exercised and papal assistance provided was in the develop-ment of the hierarchy where it did not already exist. Gregory I sent a mission to England, of course, and for two centuries his successors worked to shape the English church. The sending of Theodore of Tarsus to England in 668 was an important step, as was the reception in Rome, more than once, of Wilfrid of Ripon. Papal envoys were sent to England in 786[56] and, on the request of King Offa of Mercia, they raised Lichfield to metropolitan status.[57] A few years later Leo III, having been assured that Offa had misrepresented things to Hadrian I, returned Lichfield to simple diocesan rank.[58] This case, incidentally, displays clearly the trouble the popes had in getting timely and adequate information. Popes Gregory II, Gregory III and Zacharias supported Boniface in his efforts to convert the peoples of central Germany and to procure for those regions a proper hierarchy. At first Boniface was archbishop without see, and then he and his successors officiated from Mainz.[59] The dukes of Bavaria first appealed to Rome for the

---

[53] *MGH Conc.* II:2, nos. 44B–E, pp. 480–551.   [54] Vielhaber (1955).

[55] Bakhuizen van den Brink (1954); Bouhot (1976); see below, pp. 767–73; 777–80.

[56] Alcuin, ep. no. 3, ed. Dümmler, *MGH Epp.* IV, pp. 19–29; Wormald (1991), pp. 28–36.

[57] Jaffé, *Regesta*, no. 2456; Godfrey (1962), pp. 263–7.   [58] Jaffé, *Regesta*, no. 2494.

[59] Reuter (1980), pp. 78–9 and McKitterick, above, pp. 72–6.

erection of a hierarchy in their province as early as 716. Not until Salzburg was made an archbishopric on Charlemagne's request in 798 was the Bavarian hierarchy completed.[60] The Bavarian dukes, just like their Carolingian contemporaries, saw the creation of an ecclesiastical hierarchy as a means of enhancing their own prestige and of solidifying their own local control. Surely Offa of Mercia had the same thing in mind; Canterbury and York, England's old archbishoprics, were in the kingdoms of Kent and Northumbria, outside the effective control of the Mercian king. In the ninth century, the dukes of Brittany attempted to detach their province from its customary allegiance to Tours, reorganise the local church, and subject the province to a new archdiocese at Dol.[61] The papacy continually refused to countenance these Breton initiatives. The early medieval popes did not initiate the creation of new hierarchies, but it was widely understood that papal approval was necessary for such tasks to be legitimately accomplished.

The popes also had to deal with existing hierarchies. Such dealings could take many forms. From the seventh century to the ninth, the popes tried to extend their authority to the Venetian region, while at the same time trying to heal the rift between the patriarchs of Aquileia and Grado.[62] As the papacy and central Italy were emancipated from the Byzantines, the popes laid claim to Ravenna. Rarely, however, would the archbishops of Ravenna submit to the bishops of Rome.[63] The papacy got involved with the Frankish episcopate on several occasions. Ebbo of Rheims, for example, had played a decisive role in the deposition of Louis the Pious in 833. Subsequently Ebbo was himself deposed and his successor, the redoubtable Hincmar, challenged the legitimacy of a number of bishops, among whom was Wulfad of Bourges, who had been consecrated by Ebbo. Wulfad appealed to Rome and Pope Leo IV insisted that the whole matter be opened up for papal review.[64] It was not that Leo and Hincmar really disagreed on the fundamental point of Wulfad's suitability. Rather, Leo was trying to establish the point that suffragans could appeal to Rome against their metropolitans and that in such cases the decision of the pope took precedence over and could even overrule that of archbishop. Later Hincmar found himself embroiled with Rome again when he sought to depose Rothad of Soissons and when he disciplined his own nephew, Hincmar of Laon.[65] Once again, the issue was papal versus metropolitan jurisdiction. The popes did not confine their interest to the west. Leo IV objected sharply

---

[60] Jaffé, *Regesta*, nos. 2495, 2496.　　[61] Smith (1992).

[62] Some sense of the issues can be gained from *Codex Carolinus*, no. 54, ed. Gundlach, *MGH Epp.* v, pp. 576–7. Papal relations with northeastern Italy lack a comprehensive study.

[63] Noble (1984), pp. 250–53 and *passim*.　　[64] Jaffé, *Regesta*, nos. 2631–3.

[65] McKeon (1978).

when Patriarch Ignatius of Constantinople deposed Bishop Gregory Asbestas of Syracuse,[66] and Nicholas I objected to the elevation of Photius to the
Constantinopolitan patriarchate, producing in the process a schism that
lasted several years.[67] These cases make quite clear both the papacy's lofty
claims to jurisdiction in the church, and the reality of the weakness of the
pope's actual position. No ninth-century pope had much influence in
Constantinople; if various popes succeeded in wearing down the indefatig-
able Hincmar of Rheims this owned much to momentary circumstances
when Hincmar found himself abandoned by the West Frankish king or his
episcopal colleagues.

The ironies in the papal position are revealed in the divorce case of Lothar
II and his wife Theutberga.[68] Lothar had inherited the northernmost
portion of his father's middle kingdom, that is, Lotharingia (Lorraine).
Lothar's wife was apparently unable to produce an heir but his mistress
Waldrada had done so. Lothar thus wished to divorce his wife and to marry
Waldrada. He even found compliant bishops who were prepared to assist
him in his scheme. Pope Nicholas I, like several of his predecessors, was
staunch in his support of the integrity of marriage. He refused to let Lothar
have a divorce, even though he was politically closely allied to Lothar's
brother, Louis II, in Italy. In the end, though, Lothar would almost
certainly have gained his divorce had not Hincmar of Rheims and Charles
the Bald entered the fray against him. They appear to have been hoping to
incorporate Lotharingia into the West Frankish kingdom and wished to see
Lothar die childless. Nicholas I upheld the sanctity of matrimony and
Lothar II did not get his divorce. But papal authority in marriage cases was
much less important than Frankish politics in the resolution of the case.

Throughout our period popes were involved in missionary endeavours.[69]
After Gregory I's initiative in England, one might have thought that the
early medieval papacy would have been active in extending the faith. In fact,
the popes after Gregory took no more initiative than his predecessors had
done in winning souls. Missionary endeavours tended to be presented to the
popes for their support and approval. Boniface has already been mentioned.
He went to Germany of his own volition and then went to Rome to secure
papal approval for his work. In 822 Louis the Pious resolved to send Ebbo
of Rheims as a missionary to the Danes.[70] The emperor sent Ebbo to Rome
to secure a pallium and papal support. These were forthcoming and when
Ebbo was replaced a few years later by Anskar he too had full papal support.
Benedict III received the great missionaries to the Slavs, Constantine-Cyril

---

[66] Jaffé, *Regesta*, nos. 2629, 2654, 2661.   [67] Dvornik (1948).
[68] McKeon (1978), pp. 39–56.   [69] Sullivan (1955).
[70] Sawyer, Sawyer and Wood (1987), pp. 36–67.

and Methodius, in Rome and he and his successors supported them, not least against the bishops of Bavaria who were profoundly jealous at the successful growth of churches in Bohemia and Moravia.[71] Nicholas I, Hadrian II and John VIII all tried at one time or another to extend papal influence over the Bulgars and the Slovenes.[72] In the latter effort, Rome was largely successful, but the Bulgars were eventually won over to the Orthodox faith. The popes, therefore, were neither ignorant of nor uninterested in the substantial expansion of Christianity in the early middle ages. But they did not plan or direct that expansion, and they did not set down a principle that such expansion was somehow papal prerogative.

In many cases, parties outside papal Rome turned to the popes when there was no reason to expect that they should have done so. The Franks are said to have turned to Rome for chant masters[73] and certainly did so for a Roman sacramentary.[74] The Franks promoted the cult of St Peter and built churches, for example St Denis and Fulda, that depended heavily upon papal-Roman models.[75] It was the Carolingians as much or more than the popes who set the papacy at the very heart of western Christianity.

THE IDEA OF THE EARLY MEDIEVAL PAPACY

The early medieval papacy inherited from late antiquity two important sets of ideas about its place in the world. A number of popes, but especially Leo I (440–61), emphasised the Petrine foundations of papal power. As it was articulated, this idea held that a clear primacy had been assigned by Christ to Peter (Matthew 16. 18–19) and that primacy had been handed down to Peter's successors, the popes. Gelasius I (492–6), in rejecting the emperor's interference in a dogmatic controversy, wrote a famous letter which said that the world was governed by the power of kings and the authority of priests, and that priestly authority, in so far as it was concerned with immortal souls, was superior to kingly power. His use of the words power (*potestas*) and authority (*auctoritas*) is revealing because the former suggested mere force and police power whereas the latter signified legitimacy and dignity. These Leonine and Gelasian themes appeared from time to time in papal writings from the sixth, seventh and eighth centuries but for most of that time the papal position was too precarious to permit even theorising about the nature of the pontifical dignity.

---

71 Vlasto (1970).   72 Sullivan (1966).
73 Jaffé, *Regesta*, no. 2371 (Paul I); Mann (1925) II, pp. 228–30 (Gregory IV), John the Deacon, *Vita Gregorii* II, c. 9, 10, PL 75, cols. 91–2 and Notker *Gesta Karoli*, c. 10, ed. Rau, pp. 334–6. See also Rankin (1993) and her references.   74 *Codex Carolinus*, no. 89, MGH Epp. V, p. 626.
75 Krautheimer (1969); Heitz (1976).

In the ninth century, the popes began to reassert themselves. Gregory IV, for example, explicitly quoted Gelasius in a letter dated 833 to some Frankish bishops.[76] They had written to the pope to inquire about his intentions in the dispute that was then raging between Louis the Pious and his sons. Gregory, on his arrival in Francia, claimed that he had come to restore the peace of the Christian world, while the bishops told him he had no business sitting in judgement upon the emperor. Gregory told the bishops that they were wrong to insist that the imperial power, which was mortal, was greater than the pontifical, which was immortal.

Gregory's claims are interesting, but their context must not be lost sight of. Gregory had been brought to Francia by Lothar to condemn Louis. Lothar then discovered, to his dismay, that the pope aimed to carry out a genuine inquiry into the strife of Francia. From then on, he prevented the pope from playing a real role in the whole affair. The Frankish bishops were in a curious position. Some supported Louis and some Lothar. Virtually all agreed, however, that the pope had no business interfering in the affairs of the Frankish realm or anticipating the decisions of the Frankish clergy. The bishops of the Frankish empire adhered to an ecclesiology that emphasised the unity of the church and the essential equality of all bishops more than the leadership of the pope.[77]

Regino of Prüm once said of Nicholas I that 'he commanded kings and tyrants and surpassed them in authority as if he were the lord of the world'.[78] The St Bertin annalist quotes a Frankish bishop who used almost the same language in saying that 'the lord Nicholas makes himself master of the whole world'.[79] Nicholas was imperious to a fault, but he was not especially original in his thinking. Leo IV once said to Louis II: 'As you know, we received the pontifical summit in order that we might have care and concern for everything that is to be found in the world.'[80] Since the days of Leo I, words like those of Nicholas and Leo had been used in papal documents, but often without practical effect. The pontificate of Nicholas I is an especially good example of the disparity between papal claims and historical realities. Nicholas sought to enforce his authority in Constantinople in a long controversy with the Patriarch Photius. Likewise, he attempted to reduce the patriarch of Ravenna to subjection. His letters confidently asserted great authority but he failed to bend either foe to his will. Nicholas sought without full success to maintain control of missionary endeavours. The work of Cyril and Methodius as well as the mission to Khan Boris of the

---

[76] Gregory IV, *Epp. Sel.*, no. 14, *MGH Epp.* v, pp. 72–81.
[77] Agobard of Lyons, ep. no. 16, *MGH, Epp.* iv, p. 277; Morrison (1969), pp. 213–51, 363–72.
[78] *MGH SS* i, p. 579.   [79] *AB(1) s.a.* 864, p. 107.
[80] Leo IV, ep. no. 10, *MGH Epp.* v, p. 589.

Bulgars involved too many people, places and problems for Nicholas to have been the sole influence upon them. We have seen that Nicholas appeared to have prevailed in the divorce case of Lothar II, but the fact remains that his victory was secondary to the victory of Hincmar of Rheims and Charles the Bald. Nicholas managed to gain a compromise on his terms in the case of Frankish bishops who appealed to him against what they regarded as arbitrary judgements by their metropolitans. Here again, though, the reality is more complex. Somewhere in western Francia an astonishingly clever forger produced a set of allegedly ancient papal and conciliar documents purporting to place the pope at the summit of the ecclesiastical hierarchy and to guarantee to suffragan bishops the right to appeal to the pope against their metropolitans.[81] Nicholas became the first pope to receive these 'Pseudo-Isidorian Decretals' and their ardent papalism certainly squared with his own view of the world. But the forgeries had been produced in a context where many local bishops resented the powers of their superiors and sought a way of escaping their power. As a means to that escape, the forgers created a papacy and a papal authority that had never existed. The Frankish clergy had not, in a fundamental way, come around to Nicholas' views on papal leadership. And just as Agobard and his contemporaries had bitterly resented the involvement of Gregory IV in the troubles of the 830s, so too Hincmar and many of his fellows saw Nicholas as a tiresome meddler. An understanding of the ninth-century papacy, in theory or in practice, must be grounded in an understanding of actual power relationships and of competing ecclesiologies. There is a profound danger in assuming that the papacy of 1870 was always organically present in all the earlier papacies.[82]

In the ninth century a fortuitous set of circumstances made the popes secure enough to raise again the kinds of grand claims that had been expressed in late antiquity. The Carolingians were generally friendly and supportive. Lothar more than once spoke of the pope as the 'head of all churches'[83] and Frankish bishops could use the same language. During the iconoclastic disputes, Greek monks such as Theodore of Studion wrote to Leo III and affirmed the petrine terms of papal power as strongly as any pope had ever done.[84] But when these expressions came from Francia and Byzantium, they were usually flattering introductions to requests to the pope for some grant or concession. When the popes refused, which they often did, letters full of abuse sometimes followed. The point is that papal

---

[81] Fuhrmann (1972), pp. 195–236; (1973), pp. 237–88.   [82] Markus (1970).

[83] Lothar, ep., apud *Epp. Sel. Leonis IV*, no. 46, *MGH Epp.* v, p. 609.

[84] Theodore of Studion, *Epistolae*, Book I, nos. 33, 34, Book II, nos. 12, 13; *PG* 90, cols. 1017B–C, 1021B, 1152C, 1153D.

statements about power and authority were usually considerably grander than actual papal power and authority. The Carolingian period in papal history provided the peace and security necessary for the elaboration of a papal government and for papal rule in central Italy. The Carolingians themselves sought to sanctify society and government and actively cooperated with the popes in the process of achieving their ends. Frankish protection curbed the worst social and political abuses in Rome. It was only in this context that the papacy could feel encouraged to make bold claims about its power. But as soon as the Carolingian protectorate disappeared, the papacy sank into a morass of social upheavel and political corruption. Papal pronouncements had a hollow ring. But the papacy was an institution with tremendous structural continuity and an elephantine memory. The papacy of the eighth and ninth centuries contributed in important ways to the development of the oldest surviving institution in the western world.

CHAPTER 22

THE ORGANISATION, LAW AND LITURGY OF THE WESTERN CHURCH, 700–900

Roger E. Reynolds

IN the history of the western church the eighth and ninth centuries have generally been recognised as pivotal in the development of ecclesiastical organisation, canon law and the liturgy, and it is on these therefore that this chapter will concentrate. This was a period that saw the establishment of a dominant theory of episcopal primacy and of a hierarchy of clerical personnel; some of the purest texts of early Christian conciliar and papal law were collected and disseminated but there was also the concoction and wide distribution of some of the most audacious forgeries of these same two types of law. Both the genuine and the false came to influence the law of the church throughout the middle ages. Synodical legislative activity, which had virtually ceased in the late seventh century, was revived, to be supplemented by a host of episcopal and secular capitularies setting down legal norms intended to revitalise the church. It was in the late Merovingian and Carolingian periods, moreover, that in the liturgical rite of the western church Roman texts were mixed with earlier indigenous material, thereby creating a hybrid Roman rite that would be used in the worship of the western church down to the modern period.

ECCLESIASTICAL ORGANISATION

Territorial structures in the organisation of the western church

The territorial organisation of most of the western church in the eighth and ninth centuries was ultimately based on civil structures inherited from late antiquity. A remarkable number of early medieval canon law manuscripts contain a list of provinces and cities inherited from the early fifth century, now called the *Notitia Galliarum*,[1] suggesting that it was considered to be an

---

[1] *MGH AA* IX, p. 1. An example is BN lat. 12097, s. VI, in which the heading *Series episcoporum* is provided.

ecclesiastical document. In the middle of the ninth century the *Notitia Galliarum* was used, as will be seen in this chapter, for polemical purposes by the compilers of the Pseudo-Isidorian Decretals to assert the primacy of one see over another, and more specifically, one metropolitan over another. The intent was to adduce evidence for certain positions on the basis of antique, even pagan, precedent. Even before the middle of the ninth century, however, the *Notitia Galliarum* was being copied and modified to reflect actual changes in civil and ecclesiastical territorial organisation. Although most of the eighth- and ninth-century redactions of the text to some extent reflect contemporary understanding of the ecclesiastical organisation of the church, one in particular is worth considering in more detail. It appears in the *Collection in Two Books* extant in BN n.a. lat. 452, written in Salzburg *c.* 821–36, perhaps under the direction of Baldo *scolasticus*,[2] and in two other codices: Vat. reg. lat. 407, written in the vicinity of St Gall about the middle of the ninth century, and a miscellaneous codex, St Gall 397, written largely at the court of Louis the German in the ninth century and used by Grimoald, the archchancellor of Louis as his *vademecum*.[3] The first section of the *Collection in Two Books* largely comprises liturgical material, the second more ordinary matters of canon law legislated by the ancient Gallican councils. The redaction of the *Notitia Galliarum* begins, surprisingly, not with Gallican material but with a list of the 'patriarchal' or metropolitical cities in Italy: Rome, Ravenna, Aquileia and Milan. Grado, whose bishop was called patriarch by the people only in 775 and who was a rival to Aquileia, in dispute with Salzburg over the question of jurisdiction in Carinthia, was added to the ancient group of four. Following the five Italian cities, the *Notitia Galliarum* proper begins. It differs in a number of respects from the Carolingian system of ecclesiastical provinces as it has been reconstructed (see Map 19).

The changes made in the Salzburg redaction reflect the new developments, the establishment of new sees and suppression of old ones in the Frankish church, not least Carolingian reorganisation at the beginning of the ninth century. Only a few examples can be given here. Several of the sees founded by missionaries from the seventh to the ninth century and associated with Cologne found in other manuscripts of the *Notitia Galliarum* were omitted, either deliberately or owing to ignorance, such as Utrecht, Osnabrück, Münster and Bremen, or Paderborn, Verdun, Halberstadt and Hildesheim, founded from Mainz. Yet in other respects, the *Collection in Two Books* clearly reflects the reorganisation of the Roman province of *Germania II* in the light of the missionary activity of the eighth century. By 742 sees

[2] Reynolds (1980).   [3] Bischoff (1981).

had been established at Würzburg and Eichstätt, and at Buraburg and Erfurt, although these last two were *oppida* not *civitates*. Further, Augsburg, which had formerly belonged to Rhaetia, and Constance, to which the bishopric of Windisch in the province of *Sequanorum* had been transferred, were brought within the province of Mainz in 746. The first formal ecclesiastical organisation in Bavaria came with Boniface, who created residential sees with the approval of Pope Gregory III in 739. By 798, at the behest of Charlemagne, Bavaria was made an ecclesiastical province headed by Arno of Salzburg. The compiler of the *Collection in Two Books* took special care to uphold the newly gained rights of Salzburg, by, for example, calling the city by its ancient Roman name, thereby attempting to give it antique dignity and including in its province sees that had but an ephemeral existence as bishoprics, namely Eichstätt and Neuburg on the Danube. Only two ninth-century sees in *Sequanorum* are given correctly, Besançon and Basle: the others either never were episcopal sees in the middle ages or their bishops had long been moved to other sees. In separating Vienne into two parts, moreover, the *Collection in Two Books* records one of the earlier compromises in the struggle between Arles and Vienne for metropolitan status.

While versions of the *Notitia Galliarum* such as that in the *Collection in Two Books* present a reasonably accurate structuring of the provinces and cities extant in the Frankish realms, one must depend on other types of documentation for the church in Italy, Spain, England and Ireland. For Italy, there was the ancient list in the *Laterculus Provinciarum* and such documents as the *De Terminatione Provinciarum Italiae* and *De Provinciis Italiae* of the ninth or tenth century, but these only give the barest of information. One must look, rather, to local lists of bishops, signatories to councils, and the letters of popes to appreciate the large numbers of bishops within the areas under the four great sees of Rome, Ravenna, Aquileia/Grado and Milan. From 700 to 900 there is evidence for nearly 185 bishops on the peninsula itself as well as in Sicily, Sardinia and Corsica.

The ecclesiastical organisation of the Iberian peninsula before the invasion of the Muslims in 711 is clear in such documents as the *De Provinciis Spaniae* with its list of episcopal cities from the seventh century and in the lists of the signatories of councils held in Visigothic Spain. Thus under Toledo there were, according to the *De Provinciis Spaniae*, twenty-one episcopal cities: under Seville ten, under Mérida thirteen, under Braga nine and under Visigothic Narbonne nine. By the time of Charlemagne, however, the only Christian parts of Spain were the Spanish March, including only the very northern sections of the old province of Tarragona and Narbonne, and the kingdom of Galicia and Asturias, crossing the old

Map 19 The ecclesiastical provinces of western Europe 700–900 (for list of metropolitan bishoprics and their suffragans, see pp. 592–6).

Archbishoprics

● Bishoprics (some added for orientation)

Many bishoprics were created and some elevated to archbishoprics in the course of the tenth and early eleventh centuries, especially in German and Italy, and Northern Spain.

Some of the provinces indicated outside the Carolingian heartlands are conjectural.

PRAGUE

Prague
(from 973)

ssau

Salzburg

SALZBURG

QUILEIA

Aquileia

OME

Rome

CAPUA

Capua
(from 966)

Dyrrachium

Thessalonica

Preslav

Pliska

Develtos

Constantinople

BLACK SEA

SEA

Metropolitan bishoprics and their suffragans, in so far as these can be determined for the period before 900.

The list includes all those sees for which incumbents are recorded at some stage during the period 700–900, though not necesssarily in continuous succession. The boundaries marked for some dioceses are necessarily only approximate. (Map and list compiled by RMcK)

England
Situation by *c.* 850; there were many changes in the tenth century.

YORK
Hexham, Lindisfarne

CANTERBURY
London, Sherborne, Winchester, Rochester, Selsey, Dunwich, Elmham, Lichfield, Worcester, Leicester, Lindsey, Hereford

Ireland

ARMAGH
Emly, Meath, Clogher, Raphoe, Glendalough, Kildare-Leighlin, Mayo, Ossory, Cork, Lismore, Tuam, Clonfert, Clonmacnois

Wales
Llandaff, Llandeilo Fawr, St David's, Bangor

Scotland
Candida Casa – Whithorn (Galloway)

Frankish kingdoms
RHEIMS
Thérouanne, Cambrai, Arras, Noyon, Laon, Soissons, Beauvais, Senlis, Châlons-sur-Marne

ROUEN
Bayeux, Evreux, Lisieux, Sées, Avranches, Coutances

TOURS
Alet, Rennes, Le Mans, Léon, Quimper, Vannes, Nantes, Angers

TRIER
Maastricht, Cologne, Metz, Verdun, Toul, Strasbourg, Speyer, Worms, Mainz

In 748 the metropolitanate was restored to Mainz (under Boniface) and in 811 it was restored to Cologne, so that the ecclesiastical provinces, with the new bishoprics established in Germany, thereafter were as follows:

TRIER Metz, Toul, Verdun

MAINZ
Worms, Speyer, Strasbourg, Constance, Chur, Paderborn, Augsburg, Eichstätt, Halberstadt, Hildesheim, Würzburg, Verdun. In the tenth century Bamberg, Olmütz and Prague (briefly) were added.

COLOGNE
Liège, Utrecht, Tongres-Maastricht, Münster, Bremen, Minden, Osnabrück

HAMBURG-BREMEN
Became an archdiocese after 831 and included in due course: Mecklenburg, Oldenburg, Ratzeburg, Schleswig

SENS
Paris, Meaux, Troyes, Auxerre, Nevers, Orléans, Chartres

BORDEAUX
Saintes, Angoulême, Périgueux, Agen, Poitiers

EAUZE (later moved to AUCH)
Dax, Labourd, Béarn, Comminges, Oloron, Aire, Bigorre, Conserçens, Lectoure, Baxas. Information from this province is very sparse during this period and many of these sees may have remained vacant.

NARBONNE
Carcassonne, Elne, Agde, Béziers, Maguelonne, Nîmes

ARLES
Uzès, Gap, Vaison, Orange, Trois Châteaux, Digne, Nice, Sisteron, Antibes, Fréjus, Riez, Toulon, Aix, Marseilles, Apt, Glandève, Carpentras, Vence, Alais, Vivier (later in province of Vienne), Die (later in province of Vienne), Embrun

Not all these bishoprics had incumbents between 700 and 900. In 811 Embrun became a metropolitan and the province consisted of EMBRUN, Digne, Vence, Nice, Orange, Cavaillon, Trois Châteaux

Similarly, Aix was the metropolitan by the end of the eighth century and consisted of AIX, Apt, Fréjus, Gap, Sisteron, Antibes

LYONS

Mâcon, Autun, Chalon, Langres, Besançon, Basle, Lausanne, Sion (later in province of Tarentaise)

In 811 Besançon was made a metropolitan and the province consisted of BESANÇON Bellay, Constance (later in province of Mainz), Civitas Helvetiorum (Windisch, Avenches, Lausanne)

VIENNE

Geneva, Tarentaise, Grenoble, Maurienne, Valence, Die, Viviers

Tarentaise was made a metropolitan in 811 and included the dioceses of TARENTAISE, Aoste, Sion

BOURGES

Limoges, Clermont, Javols, Velay, Cahors, Rodez, Albi, Toulouse

SALZBURG

Passau, Freising, Regensburg. In the tenth century Seben (moved to Brixen) and Gurk were also included.

In 988 the archdiocese of Magdeburg was created, including MAGDEBURG, Brandenburg, Havelburg, Meissen, Merseburg, Zeitz-Naumburg

Spain

In northern Spain there seems to be considerable doubt about the existence of metropolitanates and the continued incumbency of many sees. Sees that were occupied at some stage between 700–900 (in the south probably not after 711), and in some cases continuously, are as follows

LUGO (possibly archbishopric from 747)
Malaga, Dumium, Oviedo (created between 802 and 812), Orense (Auria), Palentia, Osma (Auxuma), Pamplona, Toledo,

Salamanca, Seville, Segontia, Tuy (Tude), Urgel, Vich (archbishopric 971–1091), Braga, Coimbra, Lamego, Porto, Viseu, Iria

Italy

In Italy the history of many sees for the most part is not at all clear before the tenth century, nor is any system of ecclesiastical provinces definite, apart from the provinces of Rome, Milan, Ravenna and Aquileia. Even there, the jurisdiction of Rome or Ravenna over dioceses within the Lombard kingdom is uncertain. The following purport to have had incumbents during the period 700–900, if not always continuously, and this list is, therefore, to be understood as conjectural.

ROME

(1) *Suburbicarian or cardinal bishoprics*
Ostia, Velletri, Tres Tabernae, Porto, Cere, Sabina (Sedes Foronovo; Sedes Curium or St Anthemius), Palestrina, Gabii, Frascati, Silva Candida

(2) *Ancient dioceses in the Tusculan regions*
Albano, Labico
(3) *Others directly (in theory) under Rome's ecclesiastical jurisdiction*
Castro et Aquipendente, Alatri, Amelia, Anagni, Ancona, Umana, Ascoli, Assisi, Bagnorea, Benevento (archbishopric from 969), Forlimpopoli, Bomarzo, Cagli, Camerino, Ficocle, Cesena, Città di Castello, Orte, Comacchio, Faenza, Fano, Ferentino, Fermo, Ferrara, Foligno, Forlì, Fossombrone, Gubbio, Iesi, Imola, Montefeltre, Narni, Nepi et Sutri, Nocera, Norcia, Orvieto, Osimo, Perugia, Pesaro, Rieti, Rimini, Segni, Sinigaglia, Spoleto, Sutri, Terni (not after 742), Terracina, Tivoli, Todi, Urbino, Viterbo, Veroli, Lucca, Arezzo, Cortona, Piacenza, Florence, Fiesole, Pistoia, Siena, Chiusi, Grosseto, Massa Maritima (Populonia), Suana, Reggio, Pisa, Volterra

(4) *Corsica*
Aleria

(5) *Sardinia*
Ales, Bosa, Cagliari, Nuovo Galtelli, Iglesias, Ogilastra, Sassari

RAVENNA (archbishopric)
Sarsina, Cesena, Forlimpopoli, Forlì, Faenza, Imola, Bologna,
Modena, Parma, Piacenza, Brisello, Ferrara

AQUILEIA
Grado, Adria, Aemonia, Altino, Asolo, Belluno, Caorle,
Castello, Capodistria, Cenda, Chioggia, Concordia, Equilio,
Padua, Pedena, Pola, Treviso, Cerona, Vicenza

MILAN
Bergamo, Brescia, Como, Cremona, Lodi, Mantua, Pavia

GENOA (archbishopric from 1163)
Tortona, Turin, Acqui, Alba, Aosta, Asti, Ivrea, Luni,
Vercelli, Novara, St John de Maurienne

Bulgaria

This list is not comprehensive, nor are all the bishoprics
known to have particular, named individuals as incumbents.
But these are the sees which, beyond reasonable doubt,
existed, had a bishop (albeit identity unknown) *and* were
subject to the jurisdiction of the archbishop of Bulgaria and
under the khan's rule during the second half of the ninth
century.

No list of Byzantine bishoprics under the jurisdiction of the
patriarch of Constantinople can be attempted here. Lists of
metropolitanates and bishoprics do exist, but as the editor of a
large collection of them, J. Darrouzès, emphasised, they do
not necessarily bear any relation to reality at any particular
moment and they are anyway very difficult to date more
narrowly than a century or two. However, if it is desired to
identify those places featuring in Map 16 of the Balkans in the
ninth century which were sees, the following are relevant:
Thessalonica (metropolitanate); Dyrrachium
(metropolitanate); Develtos (bishopric)

PLISKA; PRESLAV (in succession to Pliska; date of
succession unknown)
Bregalnitsa, Belgrade, Dorostolon (Dristra), Philippopolis,
Morav-Margus, Ochrid

province of Braga and the northeastern reaches of the *Tarraconensis* province. Bishoprics nevertheless continued to exist even in the areas dominated by the Muslims, and from 711 to 900 there is evidence of no less than forty bishops spread over the whole of the Iberian peninsula.

With the Anglo-Saxon invasions there was a breach with the Roman past in Britain. When Pope Gregory I sent missionaries to this area, he seems to have considered Britain to be a lost Roman province and devised a scheme, accordingly, with two ecclesiastical provinces centred on London and York. As matters turned out, it was Canterbury that took the place of London under Augustine, the first 'archbishop'. York, after a false start, was established as a metropolitan, with its first archbishop, Egbert, only in the eighth century. A number of additional dioceses were established by Augustine, but the system was reorganised under Archbishop Theodore (602–90) into a network of some fifteen dioceses, arranged for the most part in relation to the emerging Anglo-Saxon kingdoms, though many sees were physically centred on an old Roman *civitas*.[4] Thus sees were established at York and Lindisfarne (later moved to Durham) in the kingdoms of Deira and Bernicia as well as at Whithorn in Galloway (for ministry to the Picts). The boundaries of the dioceses of Hereford and Worcester preserved until the Reformation the ancient borders of the two ancient kingdoms of the Hwicce and the Magonsaetan. Theodore divided Mercia between the main diocese with its centre usually in Lichfield and the diocese that sprawled from Oxfordshire to Lincoln, which eventually became the see of Lincoln. In Wessex there were the southern sees of Winchester, Salisbury and Exeter. The southern dioceses reflected the early kingdoms of East Anglia (with bishops at Elmham and Dunwich), Essex (with a bishop at London), Sussex, and Kent (with bishops at Canterbury and Rochester as well as at Selsey and Lindsey) (see Map 19).[5]

Nearly as important as these episcopal sees themselves in Anglo-Saxon England were the minsters, a word deriving from the Latin *monasterium*. These minster churches, which in some cases were the seats of bishops, might be served either by monks (or even nuns) or by canons and might have a full complement of monastic or canonical personnel. In any event, they were generally large churches serving an area wider than a village.[6] With the Viking attacks of the late eighth and ninth centuries, many of the great minsters and towns with their churches were burned and plundered.[7] As for other bishops' sees in the time of the Danish raids, there was probably no complete breakdown of pastoral care, but records are sketchy. It appears

[4] Bede, *HE*, ed. Colgrave and Mynors, v. 23, p. 559; Brooke (1982).   [5] Basset (1989).
[6] Blair and Sharpe (1992) and Foot (1992).   [7] Foot (1991).

that some sees may have remained vacant for a while or moved to other safer locations.

The territorial structure of the churches in lands where Celtic Christians lived has always been an enigma in that Roman territorial structures had not existed in these areas. It used to be maintained that when St Patrick came to Ireland he brought with him notions of Roman ecclesiastical structures, founding his archiepiscopal see at Armagh and his other churches throughout the land. Because of the lack of urban centres, however, this Roman structure was submerged in a monastic pattern from the sixth century onwards. Because monasteries were the centres of Christianity both in Ireland and wherever Celtic wanderers settled, it followed that abbots held ecclesiastical jursidictional power in Celtic lands and that the bishop was kept largely within monastic communities for administering the sacraments. More recently, however, it has been established that the Irish church was not organised into regular dioceses under Armagh, though by the eighth century Armagh was being recognised as a type of 'mother' church over a larger *paruchia*, whatever area this may have been. Certainly there was an extensive network of monasteries, often thought of as towns and places of refuge, and said to be modelled on the celestial city of the heavenly Jerusalem. The inhabitants of these monastic 'towns' were not simply monks, but might include many ordained clerics, laymen and even political figures. These monasteries were usually on 'virgin' sites that had not been pagan cult centres but, as Kathleen Hughes has shown, early diocesan churches situated on or close to ancient cult centres such as Armagh, Kildare, Kilcullen, Killashee, Ardbraccan, Seir and Emly.[8] Moreover, there were smaller churches – unfree churches – built by or under the hereditary control of families that might develop into much larger churches and perhaps even be called monasteries.

That there were jurisdictional bishops in the Celtic churches is clear from both Latin and vernacular documents, some of these bishops being called *Romani*, others *Hibernici*, implying perhaps adherence to two different types of jurisdictional systems, Episcopal jurisdiction appears to have entailed ministrations to the laity and also sometimes to the monasteries. Although evidence is still very sketchy, it seems that some bishops lived outside what is conventionally said to be a monastic context while others lived in collegiate or monastic communities made up of monks and secular clergy, not unlike the minsters in Anglo-Saxon England. Perhaps in these communities the abbot, as *princeps* or ruler, would have had control of the lands and revenues and the bishop would have had the responsibility for pastoral care

---

[8] Hughes (1966) and her references to the older literature.

not only in the monastery but also in the local churches that might be attached to the monastery.[9] Ireland, in short, may not have been so very different from other parts of early medieval Europe as was once supposed.

Ecclesiastical structures

Within the diverse geographical areas in western Christendom in the eighth and ninth centuries there were a number of common ecclesiastical structures, although their names and exact configurations, and the duties of the personnel within them (see below) could vary from place to place and time to time. At the highest level was the patriarchate, which by the fifth and sixth centuries was taking on the more technical attachment to the bishops of the five great sees of Rome, Alexandria, Antioch, Jerusalem and Constantinople and by the eighth century was equated with that of primate. Before the eighth century there were a number of other sees that used the title itself, including Lyons, Bourges, Ravenna, Milan and Besançon, though without any claim to be of equal rank with Rome. A number of Carolingian bishops claimed primatial status, but it was only with the Pseudo-Isidorian forgers in the mid-ninth century that the patriarchal primacy took on a meaning that would be repeatedly used later into the middle ages. According to the forgers, the primate was the metropolitan of the first province. The bishop of the metropolitan see of *Belgica Prima*, for example, would be the primate over the metropolitan bishop of *Belgica Secunda*. In such a structure a suffragan bishop in these provinces would have the right of appeal beyond his own metropolitan to the provincial primate when he felt his own metropolitan was partial or the findings of his own comprovincials were suspect.

Countering the idea of primacy put forward in the Pseudo-Isidorian Decretals, Hincmar, archbishop of Rheims, argued that the metropolitan bishops, who were compared to primates, should decide major cases (usually reserved to the pope), the point being that the patriarchate or primacy would be limited to a single province. Basically, Hincmar wanted such a province of a metropolitan primate to include from ten to twelve cities. Hincmar's idea of primacy was, as it turned out, too closely tied to the circumstances of Rheims and hence was not very influential later, while that of the Pseudo-Isidorian forgers was used again in a variety of cases in the eleventh century in 'refounding' primatial sees.

Below the patriarch/primate in the western church were the metropolitans and archibishops, and, under them, the suffragan bishops who

---

[9] Sharpe (1984).

governed their dioceses. In the 740s the title of archbishop was assigned to a number of metropolitan bishops in Francia, namely Boniface of Mainz, Grimo of Rouen, Abel of Rheims and Hartbert of Sens, symbolised by the sending of the pallium, a band of white wool, to each new archbishop by the pope.[10] With Charlemagne and the reorganisation of the church in his realm, the title became more common and was used to designate all bishops who held metropolitical sees. New metropolitical sees were established, such as Salzburg in 798, whose first archbishop was Arno.

In the Roman empire, the diocese had been a territory dependent for its administration on a city or *civitas*. Since early Christian bishops generally lived in a *civitas*, the territory over which they exercised juridical authority was called by its usual civil term, diocese. The churches or groups of the faithful subject to a bishop were known not only as a diocese but also a *parochia*, meaning a neighbourhood or parish. While in the eastern church the term diocese was reserved for territories governed by a patriarch, in the west the terms diocese and parish were used interchangeably to designate the territory subject to the jurisdiction of a bishop. Even in the ninth century, Pope Leo IV could call such a territory a parish, and so flexibile was the word diocese that Archbishop Hincmar of Rheims could even call his province a diocese.[11] According to canon law, dioceses were not to be created in towns not populous enough to support the dignity of episcopal residences. On the other hand, in a number of instances dioceses in the western church might contain several *civitates*. The creation of new dioceses belonged, according to canon law, to provincial synods with the consent of the *primas* and the bishop of the diocese to be divided, but the papacy was also active in the creation of new dioceses, as we have seen in the case of Pope Gregory I in Anglo-Saxon England. This was the pattern followed in the eighth century as well with the creation of new bishoprics in missionary lands by Boniface with the approval of Pope Zacharias.

The term parish gradually came to be applied to smaller basic units of pastoral care. Even within *civitates* there could be urban parishes. As Christianity spread to rural areas, rural parishes also grew up. Bishops began to create these parishes in the *vici* or villages where clergy would be appointed for pastoral care. Smaller churches might have only one priest, perhaps assisted by several lower clerics. Larger rural churches might have several priests under the direction of an archpriest. Some indication of the links between the bishop and his parish priests is provided by the episcopal statutes, such as those of Theodulf of Orléans or Hildegar of Meaux, where

---

[10] Boniface, *Epp.* ed. Tangl, no. 57.

[11] In the Isidorian version of the Council of Antioch (341), c. 9, the word *parochia* was translated as diocese.

the bishop proffered advice on how the clergy should care for their people.[12] Other churches were established by individuals for or on their own estates or *villae*. These *Eigenkirchen* or proprietary churches were the private properties of the owners of land on which the church stood and provided the same range of services as those in the *vici* churches.

Yet such private churches were a cause of tension within the organisation of the church. The 'owners' of the churches felt it their right to control them in any way they pleased but bishops attempted to control the deliverance and quality of religious service provided by clergy appointed by the founders and subsequent 'owners' of the church. Legislation under the Carolingians attempted to balance these positions and to see that the churches which cared for the needs of the local populace were adequately supported. Because the Carolingian rulers themselves were heavily involved in the control of churches in their realm, they could hardly deny the rights of private ownership over churches, and hence owners were assured of their rights to select priests, define terms of office, and even dispose of churches. Legislation also reaffirmed the bishops' rights over the practice of religion in their dioceses. Special attention was given to the support of local churches so that they would have adequate means to provide the spiritual services required of them. Christians were required to pay tithe, and efforts were made to define the minimum size of the grant or benefice given to a parish priest in return for his pastoral service.

THE ORGANISATION OF PERSONNEL IN THE CHURCH

Personnel in the church in Spain

Visigothic Spain had an ecclesiastical organisation highly peculiar to that church. Despite its distinctiveness, however, this organisation of personnel was enormously influential, not only in the churches of the Asturias, the Spanish March, Catalonia and the Narbonne region, where it was combined with Gallican and Frankish usages, but also in many regions beyond the Iberian peninsula: in Ireland and wherever the Irish wandered in Europe, in territories under Frankish domination, and even in Italy.

Sources describing the ecclesiastical personnel in Visigothic churches are manifold and include saints' Lives, the acts of synods, episcopal letters, inscriptions and manuscript illuminations. The principal sources, however, are the rites of ordination of ecclesiastical personnel which are assumed to bear some relation to actual practice. There is also a treatise of the fifth (?)

---

[12] Brommer, *MGH Cap. episc.*, and McKitterick (1977), pp. 45–79.

century attributed to Jerome, and the works of Isidore of Seville, both genuine and spurious.

The ordination texts are found in the *Liber Ordinum*, whose only manuscript (Silos, Bibl. del Monast. 4) was written in Silos in the mid-eleventh century, shortly before the 'Old Spanish' rite it contains was superseded by the Roman rite. The *Liber Ordinum* includes ordination rites for the presentation and tonsuring of young clerics who were placed in the cathedral schools. Whether these were singing schools, like the *scola cantorum* in Rome, is impossible to determine. There are also rites for the sacristan and for the *custos librorum et senior scribarum* whose ordination gave him charge over the books and the scribes who copied them. A rite for the consecration of a bishop is lacking, but it is present in other 'Old Spanish' liturgical books. Episcopal subscriptions, moreover, appear frequently in synodal acts.

The *Ordo de Celebrando Concilii* was diffused widely through the churches of western Europe and provided the basis for conciliar structuring and prayers even down to the Second Vatican Council. In it, there are instructions regarding several ecclesiastical officials who do not have ordination rites in the *Liber Ordinum*, namely the doorkeepers, and the notaries who transcribed the acts of the councils. In fact, in the illustrations of the councils of Toledo and the *Ordo de Celebrando Concilii* in two renowned Mozarabic manuscripts, the *Codex Aemilianensis* and *Codex Vigilanus* (El Escorial d.1.1 and d.1.2), both written in northern Spain in the tenth century but whose illustrations are thought to reflect Visigothic originals, both doorkeepers and notaries are clearly depicted among other ecclesiastical and lay dignitaries attending councils.

While the ordination rites of the *Liber Ordinum* largely emphasise the liturgical duties of most of the grades, other types of document describe in fuller detail both the liturgical and administrative duties of ecclesiastical personnel in the Spanish churches and add further officers among them. Thus the *De Septem Ordinibus Ecclesiae*, for example, adds one, the gravedigger, whose origins go back to antiquity. This text, moreover, appears to have played a major role in the composition of two of the most influential descriptions of ecclesiastical personnel in the middle ages, the authentic works of Isidore of Seville: the *De Ecclesiasticis Officiis* and the *Origines* or *Etymologiae*. Although Isidore described the duties of the grades in terms of the contemporary liturgy of the Visigothic church, these descriptions were adapted to their own regional and local situations by writers throughout western Europe and the texts were copied in their thousands, for many different purposes, during the middle ages. Isidore describes, in addition to the grades of the *Liber Ordinum*, the lector, psalmist and exorcist, the chorbishops (assistant or rural bishops) and the *custos sacrorum* (who had the care of the liturgical vessels).[13]

One of the most important Isidorian texts for its description of the duties of ecclesiastical personnel in Spain is found in a letter said to have been written by Isidore to a fellow bishop, Leudefredus of Córdoba. The Pseudo-Isidorian *Epistula ad Leudefredum* is important for several reasons. In the original Spanish recension (El Escorial d.i.1 and 1623) it describes more independent grades, and describes them more fully, than any other tract: doorkeeper, acolyte, exorcist, psalmist, lector, subdeacon, deacon, priest, bishop, archdeacon, *primicerius, thesaurarius, oeconomus* and *pater monasterii.* The grades and descriptions of functions, the *thesaurarius, oeconomus* and *pater monasterii,* are found in no other tract.

While the ecclesiastical personnel described in the authentic works of Isidore and the *Epistula ad Leudefredum* would be appropriate to a large royal city such as Visigothic Toledo, it is less likely that they would have persisted in the churches of the Iberian peninsula reduced by the Muslim invasions and in the churches of the Asturias and Catalonia of the eighth and ninth centuries. Nonetheless, at least a knowledge of these grades was maintained as late as the eleventh century, even if they were not actively used all the time.[14]

The problem of the organisation of personnel in the Irish church is closely connected with the problem of the structure of the Irish church as a whole outlined above. If the structure of the Irish church was essentially monastic,[15] would monks, who were usually laymen, be among the personnel of the Irish church? Thus, there would have been abbots (usually ordained as priests) as well as all of the other officers in a monastery as part of the ecclesiastical hierarchy. Even according to more recent revisionist notions on the organisational structure of the Irish church – one in which monks and clergy lived side by side – monastic personnel would have to be part of the ecclesiastical organisation of the church. Yet in terms of the sacraments it would have been the ordained clergy who would have served the inhabitants of the monastery. As to ministration to the lay population outside the monasteries, there is precious little documentary evidence, but the early *Penitential of Vinnian*[16] and the *Synodus Episcoporum*[17] speak only of clergy ministering to the lay populace.

Who were these clergy and what were their duties? The Irish annals and Lives of saints often mention clerics, but these are usually in the upper reaches of the clerical grades – bishops, priests and deacons – and little is said

---

[13] Excellent discussion of chorbishops in Levison (1946), pp. 66–8.

[14] Reynolds (1979; 1987).   [15] Sharpe (1984).

[16] *Penitential of Vinnian*, ed. Wasserschleben.   [17] Ed. Bieler (1963).

about their precise functions. On the other hand, there are legal texts, in Latin and Old Irish, that describe both the clerical hierarchy and obligations and are now believed to reflect conditions in Ireland far more accurately than has hitherto been thought.

Chief among the Latin sources has been the *Collectio Canonum Hibernensis*,[18] compiled some time between the beginning of the eighth century and *c.* 763, either in Ireland itself or by Irish compilers elsewhere but reflecting both Continental and Insular conditions.[19] Within the *Hibernensis* the septiformity of the ecclesiastical hierarchy is stressed, as it is in numerous liturgical and theological tracts in Ireland. Probably, however, this emphasis derives from the Irish love of numerology, such as is found in the Irish *Liber de Numeris*,[20] and not from the actual numbers of clerical personnel found functioning in the Irish church. In the *Hibernensis* the first section is devoted to a description of the clerical hierarchy, their origins, obligations and canonical rules under which they live. The structure and order of the grades described is very much like that in the works of Isidore of Seville, something not surprising given the heavy use of Isidore's work in the *Hibernensis*. Described in descending order are the bishop, presbyter, deacon, subdeacon, lector, exorcist and doorkeeper, with several significant modifications of the older sources used. The chorbishop is not described and higher offices of patriarch, archbishop and metropolitan are not mentioned. Despite the claims made in the non-canonistic sources for a primatial or archiepiscopal position for Armagh this episcopal rank is not reflected in the *Hibernensis*. Further, there is no description of the acolyte,[21] the lector has been placed hierarchically above the exorcist,[22] at least in the fuller description of the grades, and the psalmist is considered only as an addendum after all the grades.[23] The full descriptions of the grades in the *Hibernensis* are perhaps not wholly reflective of the situation in Ireland, but two other texts, an Ordinal of Christ,[24] and the *De Distantia Graduum*, probably Irish in origin, reflect actuality in Ireland.[25] In a fashion similar to the details given in the *De Distantia Graduum*, another Irish text lays out the obligations of a bishop. The *Riagail Phátraic*, a document found only in a sixteenth-century manuscript but dating to the eighth century,[26] states that it is the duty of the chief bishop in each *tuath* to ordain clergy, consecrate churches, act as a soul friend to rulers and *erenachs*, and sanctify and bless

[18] Ed. Wasserschleben (1885).   [19] Reynolds (1984).   [20] Reynolds (1972).

[21] Reynolds (1978).

[22] As this was also true of Isidore of Seville's work it is possibly a sign of Isidore's influence.

[23] Mentioned in the Uraicecht Becc, ed. Breatnach (1987) and in the Synod I of St Patrick, ed. Bieler (1963).   [24] Reynolds (1978).

[25] Reynolds (1972). There are also resemblances to the fifth-century Gallican *Statuta Ecclesiae Antiqua*, ed. Munier (1960).   [26] Sharpe (1984).

children after baptism. In a later provision of the tract the bishop is also charged with overseeing clergy and laity, ascertaining that churches' oratories and burial grounds are undefiled, and seeing that the altar is properly furnished and ready for use by the clergy. There are a number of other early Irish law texts, such as the *Bretha Nemed* and *Uraicecht Becc*,[27] that lay down the obligations of the clergy, particularly of the higher clergy. Others give detailed lists of clerical personnel, sometimes those who have not been ordained. Clearly there was much thought given to the practical and symbolic importance of these officers, and the forms in which these thoughts were expressed link them clearly to similar expression on the Continent.

Personnel in the Gallo-Frankish churches

In the churches of western Europe north of the Alps of the eighth and ninth centuries the organisation of ecclesiastical personnel was nearly as complex as it was in the Visigothic territories, but the number of clerics for which there was a specific ceremony of ordination was somewhat more limited. The reason for this may be that the text presenting rubrics for ordinations, the fifth-century Gallican *Statuta Ecclesiae Antiqua*, was so widely diffused both in canon law and liturgical material from the eighth century onwards that it virtually submerged other ordination texts from other areas of Europe.[28]

The *Statuta* itself was compiled *c.* 475 in southern Gaul, probably by Gennadius of Marseilles. The text as a whole has been described as a bishop's ordination manual and contains a credal statement indicating what a cleric should believe, a substantial number of short canons according to which a cleric should conduct his life, and finally a list of rubrics for the liturgical ordination of clerics. These clerical personnel are similar to those found in the ancient Roman *Orationes Solemnes*: bishop, priest, deacon, subdeacon, acolyte, exorcist, lector, doorkeeper, psalmist (to which are added virgins and widows). During the ordination of the several grades of clerics symbolic instruments are received which make their function in the church clear. For example, the subdeacon receives eucharistic vessels from the bishop and archdeacon; the acolyte receives a candle and wax as well as eucharistic vessels; the exorcist receives a booklet of exorcisms for use in pre-baptismal rites; the lector receives a codex of lessons; the doorkeeper receives keys to open and close the doors of the church.

---

[27] Ed. Breatnach (1987).

[28] It played a role, for example, in the structuring of the *Institutio Canonicorum* of 816. *MGH Conc.* II:1.

During the eighth and ninth centuries modifications were also made by the Franks in some of the older, non-Gallo-Frankish texts describing the obligations of the clerics. These presumably represent an attempt to make the texts a more accurate description of everyday practice. In various Frankish recensions of the Irish *De Distantia Graduum*, for example, the doorkeeper no longer carries the codex for the reader; the lector no longer blesses the bread and new fruits; the subdeacon reads the Epistle at Mass; the deacon does not give communion in the form of the Viaticum, but is specifically obliged to read the Gospel at Mass; and when the acolyte is added to the text, he is to light the candles to be carried before the Gospels at Mass.[29]

Many other clerical officers who functioned in the late Merovingian and Carolingian churches appear to have been introduced to take on new functions within the churches of Francia. At the lower end of the hierarchical scale the *Regula Canonicorum* of Chrodegang of Metz outlines liturgical duties for cantors, the *primus scolae, notarii* (who recite the names of the baptisands) and *stationarii*. Other 'minor' ecclesiastical functionaries such as the cellarer and porter are assistants not so much in the liturgy but in economic matters and in the care and fabric of the church. Several of these are mentioned later in the *Institutio Canonicorum* of 816.

Until the eighth century the archdeacon had been responsible for the governance of clerics in a diocese, especially those in the *domus ecclesiae* or under the direct control of the bishop. Further, this officer had charge to some extent of the clergy in rural areas, where he might even institute and control rural archpresbyters. According to the Gallican councils, whose texts were frequently reproduced in manuscripts of the eighth century and beyond, the archdeacon had among his obligations the oversight of instruction of young clerics, denouncing and punishing clerical faults, oversight of vestments and habits, assistance in episcopal ceremonies and councils, representation of a bishop in councils, presentation of clerical ordinands to the bishop and involvement in the tradition of symbols in ordination ceremonies. By the mid-ninth century, the archdeacon's role had been so enhanced that Archbishop Hincmar of Rheims called him *comministrum nostrum* and some scholars have even argued that for all practical purposes the archdeacon was an episcopal vicar, although he was clearly *post episcopum*. In any event, according to Walahfrid Strabo, the archdeacon was the first person in the bishop's *familia*, and as such might make visitations, examine clergy, assist in ordination ceremonies, examine the faith and sacramental practices of priests, and even direct the diocese on the death of

[29] Reynolds (1972; 1978; 1984).

the bishop.[30] In some ninth-century dioceses there might be multiple archdeacons, who oversaw territories called *parrochia*. Because of their power, abuses by archdeacons seem to have been common in the ninth century, and hence in a number of conciliar canons and capitularies, there were attempts to curtail their pretensions and especially their economic power.

The office of the archpriest, like that of the archdeacon, had originated in the western church at least by the fifth century. By the eighth and ninth centuries the archpriest in an urban setting was charged primarily with the oversight of the liturgical practices of other priests in the cathedral and parochial churches in the city. In rural settings, the position of the archpriest was somewhat greater, although his jurisdictional power was less than that of the archdeacon. In the late Merovingian period the archpriest in rural areas seems to have ruled over smaller groups of priests with whom he lived in a paternal, non-coercive way. In the eighth century more and more churches came to be placed in *villae* and over them were priests. There was a tendency for these churches to become autonomous, and hence, as a means of control, deaconries or archpriests developed in the ninth century, over which rural archpriests were set as deans. Among their many duties these archpriests transmitted and assured publication of orders from their superiors to the priests; they made visitations to churches to verify titles of ordination of clerics and the regularity of their inscriptions to churches; and they made inquiries regarding liturgical fabric and vestments. In his *Capitula quibus de rebus magistri et decani singulas ecclesias inquirire*, Hincmar of Rheims laid out a long series of obligations of the deans.

During the eighth and ninth centuries a variety of episcopal officers was active. One of these was the chorbishop or assistant bishop.[31] By the early ninth century there are indications, particularly in the province of Rheims, that abuses involving some chorbishops had arisen, perhaps concerning irregular ordinations and confirmations. Hence ways were sought to diminish their powers despite their justification in canon law. The Pseudo-Isidorian forgers of the mid-ninth century devised spurious evidence that they were to be regarded as simple priests. Nevertheless, the institution was slow to die out. Relations between the suffragan bishops and their metropolitan could be strained. Again, affairs in the province of Rheims afford us a glimpse of this. The Pseudo-Isidorian forgers drew on no less a text than the *Notitia Galliarum* to safeguard the position of the suffragan bishops. Thus, Trier as the first city of the province of *Belgica Prima* would hold primacy over Rheims, which was the first see of the province of *Belgica*

---

[30] Walahfrid Strabo, ed. Knoepfler; and see Corrêa (1994).   [31] Gottlob (1928).

Secunda. The motive behind such political use and distortion of ancient lists was to give the suffragan bishops under Archbishop Hincmar of Rheims the right to appeal in major cases to a primatial see, even the ancient primatial see of Rome. The theoretical structures and positions defined in texts in use in the Frankish church in the eighth and ninth centuries, therefore, were vulnerable to the politics and circumstances of individual bishops. In the career of Bishop Hincmar of Laon, who resisted with every weapon in his ecclesiastical armoury the ultimately successful attempt of his uncle, Archbishop Hincmar of Rheims, to enforce his jurisdiction, we see how theory and practice could clash.[32]

Personnel in the church of Rome

Although Rome's population was far less by the early eighth century than it had been, it was still a large city by early medieval standards, and as such the church needed an administrative personnel larger than most cities. Heir to a complex governmental system of classical Rome, moreover, the church of Rome had adopted an ecclesiastical organisation and hierarchy of lay and clerical officials far surpassing in complexity other sees in the western church, many of whose ancient features were maintained in the eighth and ninth centuries.[33] Three sources are particularly rich: the *Liber Pontificalis*, comprising papal biographies, includes accounts of the positions individuals had filled before becoming pope as well as descriptions of the personnel that surrounded the pope and administered Rome; the *Ordines Romani*[34] describe liturgical ceremonies in Rome and the officials who took part in them; the *Liber Diurnus*,[35] a collection of standard formulae used in papal correspondence, mentions various members of the Roman church. For the purposes of this discussion the personnel may be divided into the ordained clergy on the one hand and, on the other, laymen or possibly ordained officials, though it is often very difficult to establish who was ordained or not in early medieval Rome. Because of this uncertainty, which includes the issues of whether Frankish or Gallican rites were used in Rome and the degree to which texts were adjusted to take account of practical changes made in response to new needs, it is perhaps prudent here to deal first with those ordained according to rites represented in *Ordo Romanus* XXXIV, and then with others represented in such documents as the *Statuta Ecclesiae Antiqua* or the *Gelasian Sacramentary of the Eighth Century*.

Supreme among the Roman bishops was the pope himself, ultimately responsible, in theory at least, for the administration, religious life and

[32] McKeon (1978). [33] Noble (1984; 1990). [34] Ed. Andrieu (1951).
[35] Ed. Sickel (1931–61); Santifaller (1978).

liturgy of the city of Rome. Besides the pope there were other bishops who functioned in the city, although they drew their jurisdictional status from their ordination to the ancient sees encircling the city of Rome: Ostia, Porto, Silva Candida, Albano, Velletri, Palestrina and Gabii. These bishops were seconded from their own sees to the Lateran basilica and accompanied the pope to stational churches, where they took part in the liturgy with him.

Although they shared in a common *sacerdotium* with the bishop of Rome, the priests of Rome enjoyed administrative positions and prestige far below even the deacons. They were generally attached to one of the twenty-five or twenty-eight *tituli* or titular churches, the 'parish' churches within the walls of Rome, where Mass, baptisms and penance took place. Two or three priests, the chief bearing the title *prior presbyter*, were responsible for the religious and liturgical life of their 'titles', where, on occasion, there might be a stational Mass with the pope. They celebrated the liturgies of their own churches especially on Sundays, and because they also assisted in the liturgical rites, in particular baptism and penance, in the seven major patriarchal basilicas, they were on occasion designated as *presbyteri cardinales*. On certain days, especially ferias, they might join with the pope in a stational Mass, after which they would return to their titular churches to celebrate for their own people. As a sign of their unity with the papal liturgy, the sacred *fermentum*, consecrated at the papal Mass, was brought by an acolyte to place in the chalice at the commixture. Beyond Eucharistic celebrations, the titular priests were responsible for baptisms, penance and burials. The titular churches were said to be quasi-dioceses or quasi-parishes, serving the population but not a defined area. Outside the city walls the titular priests of the city were in charge of the martyrial and cemetery shrines. Also outside the city walls were *presbyteri parrochiales* responsible for baptisms and penances in the 'parishes'. The *fermentum* was not sent to them, since it was thought improper to carry it for long distances, and hence the *presbyteri parrochiales* had full power to consecrate the sacrament without the commixture.

Rome had been divided into seven regions at least since the fourth century, and to each of these regions was attached, if only in name, a deacon, who had considerable administrative and liturgical power. Often in the early middle ages, popes were chosen from the ranks of the Roman deacons because of their administrative abilities.[36] As administrative officers, the regional deacons, were often in charge of the patrimony of the Roman church and eleemosynary activity, such as provision of food for the poor, and were involved in papal diplomatic missions. As well as the seven

[36] Reynolds (1979).

regional deacons, there were also simple deacons (called *diaconi forenses*) in the diverse churches who served the priests in liturgical services. As liturgical officers, the deacons were of special importance in that they read the Gospel.

The continued importance of subdeacons in the eighth and ninth centuries is suggested by the fact that a number of popes were elevated from the rank of subdeacon. Each of the seven regions of Rome had a group of subdeacons who assisted the deacons in vesting the pope in the stational liturgies. Other groups of subdeacons such as the *subdiaconi sequentes* and *subdiaconi oblationarii* were assigned distinct liturgical functions, whether as thurifer, as bearer of the wine before consecration, or as reader of the Epistle. Acolytes were also attached to the seven regions in Rome, and it is thought that there were many more of these than of the *subdiaconi sequentes*. The functions of the acolytes were primarily liturgical, but they were no more than the simple acolytes of the later middle ages. By the early tenth century *Ordo Romanus* xxxv had made provision for the ordination of lectors in Rome.[37] Even in the eighth-century *Ordo Romanus*, however, there is a reference to cantors and lectors. For cantors there was no ordination rite in any of the Roman *ordines* nor in the *Statuta Ecclesiae Antiqua* or *Gelasian Sacramentary of the Eighth Century*. Nonetheless, in the *Statuta Ecclesiae Antiqua* there was a rite of ordination for *psalmistae*. It is thus conceivable that this rite was extended to *cantores* who, *Ordo Romanus* i states, were responsible for singing the gradual with its psalmic elements between the Epistle and Gospel. Exorcisms were performed only by those given the power by bishops. The tendency to give this power to the grades from acolyte upwards is clear in the Roman baptismal *Ordo Romanus* xi, which may have been compiled as late as 700. There it is the acolyte who exorcises baptismal candidates.[38]

The *scola cantorum* in Rome had a number of *cantores* who went under a variety of titles; these are found in the extensive directions for chanting in *Ordo Romanus* i. Heading the *scola* was the *primus* or *prior scolae*. It is uncertain if he had administrative or pedagogical duties in the *scola*, but it is generally agreed that liturgically he acted as precentor. As well as three other *scolae*, there were the *paraphonistae* who sang the melody. It has been argued by some musicologists that in the 'Old Roman' chant in use in Rome until it was replaced by the 'Gregorian' chant, it was the *paraphonistae* who sang a lower chant, somewhat in Byzantine style, as the other members of the *scola* sang the upper chant.[39] Also in the *scola* were the *infantes* or children,

---

[37] See the *Liber Pontificalis*, ed. Duchesne.   [38] Ed. Andrieu.   [39] Ed. Andrieu.

presumably either orphans or those who had been sent to the *scola* by their parents as one avenue to clerical advancement.

The administrative and jurisdictional importance of the archdeacon, a *vicarius* of the pope, is stressed in the first section of *Ordo Romanus* I. The term *primicerius* could be applied to an officer often mentioned without qualification in documents of the eighth and ninth centuries. Among other duties, the *primicerius* aided the pope in discussions of councils, acted as master of ceremonies, as *apocrisiarius* or envoy for the pope in distant lands, and as judge; he witnessed donations and was involved in the production of papal letters. The *primicerius* also replaced an archdeacon or priest when they were absent or there was a papal vacancy. It is probable that most of the *primicerii* were clerics, although some, like a certain Gregorius *primicerius* whose son Georgius was excommunicated by John VIII before 876, may have been laymen. Close in dignity to the *primericus* was the *secundicerius*, also mentioned in the *Ordo Romanus* I in close proximity to the pope during stational Masses. Among the administrative duties performed by this individual were accompanying the pope on missions, acting in financial and property matters, witnessing donations or papal *acta*, involvement in the issuance of papal bulls, and assisting the *primicerius* and pope in receiving oaths of new bishops. *Defensores* are frequently mentioned in *Ordo Romanus* I as administrative officers and envoys but of far greater importance were the notaries. There were seven regional notaries in Rome, headed by the *primicerius notariorum*, who was one of the chief senior officials of the Roman church; his office handled most of its daily business. The *primicerius notariorum* had direction of the papal offices in the Lateran, the *scrinium* (hence the alternative term for the notaries of *scriniarii*), where he managed the correspondence and records and was responsible, where necessary, for their production. It was his office that drew up the standard formulae found in the *Liber Diurnus*. The office received notices of the election of new bishops and declarations of orthodoxy; it was responsible for the issuance of papal approbation; permissions were given for the building of new churches and the translations of relics; exchanges of private lands for those belonging to the Roman church were entered; notification of the deaths of popes was given to the exarch, to the emperor and to the archbishop and city council of Ravenna to use their influence in the quick choice of a successor; notices were sent out summoning Italian bishops to the annual Synod of Rome and regrets received for age or illness; appointments were made of rectors and stewards of patrimonies and of wardens of charitable institutions such as orphanages and pilgrim hostels within the city. The office of the *primicerius notariorum* provided mounts for papal notaries and envoys.

There remains a handful of dignitaries with ceremonial or advisory functions, such as the *bauili, stratores lauci, ordinator*, and *vicedominus*, who was the *majordomo* of the pope's palace or *patriarchium* at the Lateran, the *advocatores ecclesiae*, or lay or clerical advocates who represented the church in legal issues, and the archpriest, who was usually the senior priest of a city, whether in terms of years since appointment or in terms of age. On occasion, however, they might be called upon for administrative assistance to the pope, as was the case when Pope Hadrian II sent the archpriest Peter as his envoy to Constantinople.

In addition there were officials who performed essential functions within the papal household and chapel such as the *vestararii*, in charge of the papal *vestiarium* or sacristy at the Lateran palace and of the rich liturgical apparatus belonging to the pope: chalices, patens, sumptuous Gospel Books and vestments. This office in the ninth century tended to be held by well-to-do magnates, who used these treasures as a basis for dynastic ambitions. Beyond their capacity as keepers of papal liturgical wealth, some *vestararii* were placed in charge of the affairs of abbeys, as was Micco, a regional notary and the first mentioned *vestararius*, appointed in charge of Farfa by Pope Hadrian I in 772. Further, there was, from at least the eighth century, the *bibliothecarius* in charge of the papal library, the best known of whom is Anastasius. The officer, who could be a cleric or bishop, who oversaw the papal financial office was the *arcarius*. He received claims upon papal revenue, and disbursed funds, payment of officials and ordinary expenditure for which he depended on the *saccellarius*. In addition, some lay officials appear to have been guards with military functions of some kind, such as the *milites draconarii* and the *superisra* charged with military matters and the military quarters at the Lateran. It will be evident from the diversity of grades that most might be described as the designation of a role in the liturgy rather than necessarily entailing the performance of any other clerical or pastoral function. There were a number of minor servants with small liturgical or administrative roles such as the *oblationarius*, who provided lights, bread and wine for feast-day Masses, the overseer of the *diaconia* responsible for distribution of food to the poor, almoners, *mansionarii* or sacristans and various other attendants.[40] It would appear that only those from the rank of subdeacon upwards actually performed any administrative or clerical task. They indicate an apparently labyrinthine complexity and extraordinarily self-conscious display of ritual dignity on the part of the pope, the roots of which most probably lie in the late Roman imperial past. Designated roles no doubt carried with them hosts of opportunities for

[40] *Liber Pontificalis*, ed. Duchesne.

patronage; bribes and salaries were required. It is essential for an understanding of Roman politics in the eighth and ninth centuries to appreciate the relatively large and complex organisation that dominated the city and acted as a focus of ambitions in every sphere.

THE LAW OF THE WESTERN CHURCH FROM 700–900

At the beginning of the eighth century the creation and collection of ecclesiastical law had reached a nadir. Enactments of councils in Gallican lands had virtually ceased. The brilliant Visigothic legislative activity reflected in the national and local councils of Toledo, Seville and elsewhere in the sixth and seventh centuries had come to an end; the golden age of councils of the African church had ended with the invasions of the Vandals, Byzantines and Muslims. Even in Italy, where canonistic legislation had been dominated by popes and Roman synods since the fourth century, the decline of papally initiated legislation by 700 is striking; in the *Regesta Pontificum Romanorum* the fifty-seven pages of entries of papal decrees of Gregory I up to 604 contrast tellingly with the mere twenty-five pages for the next twenty-two popes down to 700.[41]

Nevertheless the collections of older canon law such as those of conciliar and papal decrees compiled by Dionysius Exiguus in the late fifth and early sixth centuries, the *Collectio Dionysiana*, continued to circulate and were undergoing modifications in the late seventh and early eighth centuries. We cannot assume therefore that there was neither knowledge of nor active interest in the law of the church. The proliferation of highly local and individual collections, indeed, witnesses to the contrary. Pre-700 manuscript evidence for the copying of such *Dionysiana* derivates as the *Collectiones Quesnelliana*,[42] *Vaticana*, *Justelli*[43] and *Wirceburgensis*, however, is virtually non-existent. Even such modified forms of the *Dionysiana* as the *Collectio Dionysiana Bobbiensis* and *Adaucta* exist in manuscripts only after 700, and the systematic *Concordia Canonum Cresconii*,[44] widely circulated from the eighth century and beyond, is found in only one manuscript dated before the eighth century. Likewise, the systematic African *Breviatio Canonum* of Fulgentius Ferrandus[45] is found in only one pre-eighth-century manuscript. Other collections of canons from the Gallican and ecumenical councils and on the Acacian Schism are also extremely rare in manuscripts copied before 700. Most of these collections were very local, but there was one extremely

---

[41] Ed. Jaffé.   [42] *PL* 56, cols. 359–746.   [43] *PL* 56, cols. 747–817.
[44] *PL* 88, cols. 829–942; Verona, Biblioteca capitolare, LXI.
[45] *CCSL* 149; BN lat. 12097.

significant systematically arranged collection, the *Collectio Vetus Gallica*,[46] designed *c.* 600 as an easy-to-use systematic collection of authentic texts. It had among its major concerns the regular assembly of synods, the ordination, deposition and duties of clerics, the rights of the metropolitan, and the administration of the sacraments and ecclesiastical properties. The author appears to have worked in Burgundy, almost certainly in Lyons itself, and was in all likelihood the well-known correspondent of Gregory I, Eutherius of Lyons.

From the beginning of the eighth century to the early 780s manuscript evidence for the dissemination of older collections increases dramatically and for the Frankish lands has been examined systematically by Rosamond McKitterick.[47] Together with these new copies of older collections, modified versions of these as well as new collections were made. From Lyons the *Vetus Gallica*, for example, had travelled northward, where it was augmented in a redaction in the circle of Leudegar of Autun. When Lendegar was exiled to Luxeuil, the *Vetus Gallica* may have gone with him, and then to the centre responsible for the production of the distinctive pre-Carolingian a-b script where the earliest extant manuscript of the collection was written.[48] Three more additions were made, resulting in the *General-redaktion* of the second quarter of the eighth century that was widely spread throughout Europe into the eleventh and twelfth centuries.

Although no extant pre-700 manuscripts of them are known, it is clear that a number of Visigothic collections were in circulation by 700,[49] notably the massive *Collectio Canonum Hispana* containing Oriental, African and Gallican synodical and papal legislation, which by 700 was disseminated in at least three or four redactions.[50]

Beyond these collections of more formal canonical enactments of councils and popes, there had also developed by the late seventh century collections of penitential canons, used especially by confessors in the practice of private penance and diffused widely in the Insular and Continental churches. Again, pre-eighth-century manuscript evidence for these collections is virtually non-existent, but the best known are those attributed to Vinnian, Columbanus and Cummean and the anonymous *Poenitentiale Mediolanense*, now dated to the sixth or seventh century.[51] From the eighth century, however, a host of Insular and Continental penitentials, with several attributed to such notable figures as Gregory, Basil, Egbert, Theodore and Bede, and two significant Irish collections of canons were compiled, the *Liber ex Lege Moysi*[52] and the *Collectio Canonum Hibernensis*. The former, dated *c.* 700,

---

[46] Mordek (1975). This collection was formerly known as the *Collectio Andegavensis* II.
[47] McKitterick (1985).   [48] McKitterick (1992).   [49] Firey and Reynolds (1993).
[50] Ed. Martinez Dies (1966–).   [51] Vogel (1978).   [52] Firey and Reynolds (1993).

contains exclusively moral and legal precepts drawn from the Pentateuch and seems to have enjoyed some popularity in Brittany and the Frankish territories. The latter, far more popular and widely disseminated, was compiled some time between about 700 and *c.* 763, perhaps in Ireland or on the Continent by Irish canonists, and has an intensely complex text history. It not only survives in many manuscripts and abridged versions but miscellaneous canons from it are scattered throughout canonical collections, theological and liturgical florilegia, biblical commentaries and even Irish and Welsh law-codes reaching well into the twelfth century. It is arranged in a systematic fashion under titles on a variety of disciplinary, social and spiritual topics. Each title is followed by a group of canons drawn and often creatively altered from the Old and New Testaments, Greek and Latin patristic writers and various synods. Developments in canon law and penitential literature are part of the reforms initiated by the early Carolingian rulers. Charlemagne in particular aimed to reform the decadence and misrule of the Merovingian church and to counteract its particularism.

Together with greatly increased conciliar activity[53] there was an outpouring of capitularies, both secular and episcopal, recommending a host of specific reforms.[54] In penitential discipline there was a reform of the older types of penitential books, the new books attempting to use largely antique and universally recognised canons. Prominent among these were the Penitentials of Halitgar of Cambrai and Hraban Maur.[55] In early attempts at ecclesiastical reform and unification, collections of canon law played a major role, and it is generally held that Charlemagne ordered a return to antique, universal and genuine ecclesiastical law by suppressing the older collections and introducing what he believed was a 'pure' collection of Roman canon law in the form of the *Collectio Dionysio-Hadriana* procured from Pope Hadrian I. To some extent this is true, but it is now known that the popularity of many of the older collections reached a zenith precisely in the Carolingian era. Hubert Mordek has shown, for example, that most of the manuscripts of the *Vetus Gallica* were copied during this period, one even in the court of Charlemagne.[56] Raymund Kottje has established that in northern Italy the *Concordia Cresconii* was the preferred collection.[57] The *Collectio Hibernensis* manuscripts indicate that it continued to be a popular collection in western and northern France.[58] Further, even the *Collectio Dionysiana* was heavily augmented with subscriptions of conciliar participants after the lists of conciliar canons, creeds, papal decrees, and a series of letters of Pope Gregory II (715–31). Older material lacking in the *Dionysio-Hadriana* that could be of value in ecclesiastical reform was provided in part

---

[53] McKitterick (1977).   [54] Hartmann (1989).   [55] Kottje (1980).
[56] Mordek (1975) and Reynolds (1984).   [57] Kottje (1965).   [58] Reynolds (1883).

by forms of the *Collectio Hispana* brought into the Frankish territories by contacts with the former Visigothic territories and the Christian kingdoms of Spain.[59] This influenced two collections compiled in the Carolingian period, the systematic *Collectio Dacheriana*[60] and the chronological *Collectio Hispana Gallica Augustodunensis*, as well as other systematic collections drawing on the older Frankish material, such as the *Collectio Sangermanensis* based on the *Vetus Gallica*.[61] Another example is the liturgico-canonical *Collectio Duorum Librorum* or Collection in Two Books discussed in relation to the *Notitia Galliarum* above. Its aim seems to have been to supplement the *Dionysio-Hadriana* with didactic liturgical texts and Gallican canons.[62]

The ecclesiastical reforms undertaken by Pippin, Charlemagne and Louis the Pious had been of great benefit to the church. Its hierarchical ordering had been regularised; the lives and education of clerics had been improved; large parts of the empire had been Christianised; and some of the best and most genuine texts of antique canon law had been reinstated. In order to effect these reforms, however, secular rulers had to involve themselves in the control of the church. This they had done directly and indirectly through the appointment of archbishop-metropolitans. But by the second quarter of the ninth century this interference had created a tension among the bishops. There was also another remnant of ecclesiastical government left over from patristic antiquity that created tension among the bishops by undercutting their authority. This was the continued existence of chorbishops, who were at times created irregularly by single bishops and who wandered about without fixed sees.

It was in this climate of both reform and tension that the so-called Pseudo-Isidorian forgeries were composed, the extent of which is still not fully understood.[63] They were the product of a highly organised, skilled and clever atelier working in the archdiocese of Rheims, probably in the employ of Hincmar, bishop of Laon, who was locked in a bitter feud with his uncle, Hincmar, archbishop of Rheims.[64] Four major collections are known to have been issued by the forgers. The *Collectio Hispana Gallica Augustodunensis*[65] was a revised version of the *Collectio Hispana Gallica*, with many of its canons altered and apocryphal sections added to deal with such issues as legal procedures against bishops, matrimony and chorbishops. The *Capitula*

---

[59] Reynolds (1979b).

[60] Ed. d'Achery (1723). Abigail Firey has shown that this bears the clear stamp of Florus the Deacon of Lyons; it contains three books, on penance, matrimony and the ecclesiastical hierarchy.

[61] BN lat. 12444, ed. Nürnberger (1890) and see Reynolds (1984).

[62] See p. 615 above. Another farragious collection, the *Collection of Laon*, was compiled in the vicinity of Cambrai from the *Dionysio-Hadriana*, *Vetus Gallica*, *Collectio Hibernensis*, liturgical, didactic and formulaic texts.   [63] Fuhrmann (1972–4).   [64] McKeon (1978).

[65] Named after a manuscript once in Autun but now Vat. lat. 1341, s.IX ex, written at Corbie.

Angilramni,[66] consisting of some seventy-one capitularies attributed to Angilramnus of Metz (768–91) and purporting to be a gift to or from Pope Hadrian I, is concerned particularly with the rights of clerics *vis-à-vis* seculars, such as the *privilegium fori* and accusations, and drew on both canon and Roman law from the Breviary of Alaric. The *Capitularia Benedicti Levitae*,[67] purports to be a continuation of the ninth-century *Capitularia* by Ansegis and in manuscripts often follows that work as books 5 to 7. The author misleadingly calls himself a deacon from Mainz. The *Capitularia* is an attempt to gain support for the forgers' cause, especially regarding lay incursions and chorbishops, by citing secular sources and showing their agreement with ecclesiastical decrees and the works of the Fathers. Among its many sources are the Frankish capitularies, Roman law, Germanic *leges*, the *Dionysio-Hadriana*, *Vetus Gallica*, *Hibernensis*, penitentials, the Bible and patristic Fathers. The fourth and largest section of the forgers' work, the Pseudo-Isidorian Decretals, is a magnificently forged set of papal decretals reaching back to the primitive age of the church based on at least 10,000 textual fragments woven together. They were especially designed to support the claims to the independence of clergy from lay control, to inhibit judicial actions by laity against the clergy and to diminish the power of the metropolitans by making appeals to Rome available to lower clergy.

The earliest collections to follow the Pseudo-Isidorian Decretals after the mid-ninth century were largely those based directly on it, despite contemporary suspicions of their authenticity.[68] Certainly the most important and widely diffused of these were, first, the *Collectio Canonum* attributed to Remedius of Chur (790–806)[69] but probably produced in southern Germany *c.*870, and second, the *Collectio Anselmo Dedicata*,[70] dedicated to Bishop Anselm II of Milan (882–96) by a cleric who calls himself the smallest sheep in Anselm's flock. The latter's twelve books deal with the Roman church and the higher ecclesiastical dignitaries, bishops, councils, priests and deacons, lower clerics, religious and widows, the laity, virtues, liturgy and sacraments, heretics, Jews and pagans. Each book is divided into three sections corresponding to the category of source exploited: canon and Roman law and papal decrees.

THE LITURGY OF THE WESTERN CHURCH FROM 700–900

Like ecclesiastical law at the beginning of the eighth century, the liturgical practices of the western church were as diverse and 'national' as the

---

[66] Fuhrmann (1972–4). 　　[67] Ibid.
[68] For example, the collection in Berlin Phillipps 1764, the *Pittaciolus* of Hincmar of Laon and a group of collections in single manuscripts, including Troyes Bib. Mun. 1406 and BN lat. 2449.
[69] Ed. John (1976). 　　[70] Firey and Reynolds (1993).

organisational and geographical structures of the church at that time. There were more general rites celebrated by 'national' churches and others of a more regional, local and even urban character. It is textbook wisdom that Carolingian domination of most of Europe from the later eighth to the ninth century brought a unification of liturgical rites and uses and a triumph of the Roman rite. To some extent this is true, but modern scholarship has shown that great diversity of liturgical practices continued throughout the ninth century and beyond.

Of the liturgical rites in use in the western church at the beginning of the eighth century, the most widely used were those within the so-called broader Gallican family, namely the Gallican, Old Spanish, Milanese and Celtic rites, related to most western rites of late antiquity.[71] Many Gallican rite sacramentaries, lectionaries, benedictionals, baptismal *ordines* and passionals were copied in the eighth century and thus witness to a great deal of creative work in the liturgy of the eighth century.[72] In the Gallican Mass there were many peculiarities, such as the three lessons (also a feature of the Milanese and Old Spanish rites), often highly prolix and long.[73]

Because the rite perceived as Roman became the dominant rite in the western church from the period of Charlemagne, its importance when it had been simply one of many local rites in use in Rome, reflected in the renowned *Ordo Romanus* I,[74] is often overestimated. The Roman rite was modified as it was taken from Rome by travellers and pilgrims in *libelli* and manuscripts, and was adapted to local circumstances and local liturgical preferences.

Thus in some of the most famous early 'Roman' sacramentaries still extant, copied outside Rome and north of the Alps, Gallican-rite elements and feasts were quickly introduced. In the Reginensis codex of the Gelasian Sacramentary (Vat. reg. lat. 316), for example, copied at Jouarre in the mid-eighth century in a scriptorium of nuns, Gallican-rite ordination rubrical directions from the *Statuta Ecclesiae Antiqua* were inserted.[75] Gallican-rite influence is even more clear in many manuscripts of the so-called *Gelasian Sacramentary of the Eighth Century*, such as the famous *Gellone Sacramentary* (BN lat. 12048), where feasts of Gallican and Frankish saints have been added. Into the high middle ages there was used in Rome, especially at the Lateran, a chant called by musicologists the Old Roman,[76] evidence of

[71] Vogel (1986).
[72] McKitterick (1992a,b) and p. 687 below. The Mass liturgy of the Gallican rite is found in such sacramentaries as the *Libellus Missae* with so-called Masses of the Mone (Karlsruhe Aug. ccliii), the *Missale Gothicum* (Vat. reg. lat. 317), *Missale Gallicanum Vetus* (Vat. pal. lat. 493), *Missale Francorum* (Vat. reg. lat. 257) and the *Bobbio Missal* (BN lat. 13246).
[73] To be found, for example, in the Lectionary of Luxeuil, BN lat. 9427.
[74] Ed. Andrieu (1977).   [75] McKitterick (1992a).   [76] Rankin (1994).

which is only extant in notated manuscripts from the eleventh century, so much remains highly speculative as far as the early middle ages is concerned. This chant was based on the indigenous one used in the Roman church since patristic times, but from the middle of the seventh century it had been modified by the influx of foreigners into the south of Italy and Rome itself fleeing the troubled lands of the east. Fourteen out of the twenty popes between 644 and 772 were Greek speaking, and the *Liber Pontificalis* reported on the musical competence of three of them: Leo II from Sicily, and Sergius I and Gregory III from Syria. Under the influence of the easterners, the Roman liturgy assumed a number of 'orientalisms', and the chant took on certain modal, cadential and ornamental formulae reminiscent of eastern chant. Because of the links between the Franks and Rome in the mid-eighth century, and the liturgical reforms in which the Carolingian rulers began to take an interest, Chrodegang, bishop of Metz, Pippin III's ecclesiastical adviser, introduced what he understood to be (or claimed as) Roman liturgical practice and chant to Metz. Singers went to Metz to study the Roman chant. As these singers tried to master by heart a new chant repertoire – neumed chant books were common only from the later ninth century and beyond – their indigenous Gallican musical traditions were mixed with the Roman, producing what scholars now think of as Gregorian chant.

Before the time of Charlemagne the Romanisation of rites appears to have been a gradual and voluntary process. But with Charlemagne and his successors there was a programmatic, official attempt to see that it was the rite of the ancient, universal see of Rome that was followed in the lands controlled by them. In many capitularies and canons of councils it is the liturgical *mos Romanorum* or at least what is understood to be or proclaimed as Roman, that is imposed on the churches of the Carolingian realm. To effect this change it was insufficient simply to legislate. Charlemagne therefore also sent a request to Pope Hadrian I asking that a pure Roman Sacramentary with the Lateran liturgy be transmitted to the Carolingian court, there to be used and copied by scribes. Hadrian sent a Mass Book, the so-called *Hadrianum*.[77] In 812 Charlemagne also sent out a questionnaire to clerics in his empire presenting what Charlemagne thought was the Roman rite of Baptism and asking his respondents to inform him as to the extent to which they were adhering to the elements of this rite.[78] There were, moreover, several attempts to suppress non-Roman rites in parts of the empire under Carolingian control, such as the Spanish March where the

[77] Now extant only in Cambrai Bib. Mun. 164; see McKitterick (1977), pp. 115–54; Deshusses (1971). It is possible that the Rule of St Benedict with its instructions as to the monks' performance of the divine office was also used in relation to this need.   [78] Keefe (1981).

language of the Mass in the Old Spanish rite was thought by the Franks to perpetuate the ancient heresy of Adoptionism, and in Lombardy where the Milanese rite was practised.

Roman books and liturgical customs were undoubtedly introduced into parts of the Carolingian realm where indigenous rites had earlier prevailed. In the gloriously illustrated Gospel Books, for example, one finds Roman stational churches noted with the lessons, and in some cities, such as Metz, there were attempts to copy the Roman stational liturgies. In Carolingian Sacramentaries it is the Roman canon of the Mass and Roman calendar that are followed. But great admixtures of indigenous rites nevertheless remained or were inserted into the Roman-rite books themselves. To the *Hadrianum*, for example, was added a plethora of older, indigenous prayers, rubrics and occasional rites. The most substantial Carolingian augmentation of the Gregorian Sacramentary was the Supplement compiled by Benedict of Aniane.[79] The majority of the added texts in the Supplement are from the Gallican rite; the ordination texts from the *Statuta Ecclesiae Antiqua*, prefaces, texts for liturgical feasts dear to Gallican-rite hearts, and the like. But it has not been adequately appreciated that Benedict of Aniane, who, after all, was a Visigoth from Septimania, also added a number of texts from the Old Spanish rite. Other Carolingian innovations were the introduction of a new Hymnal and the rearrangement of the Antiphonary by Amalarius of Metz and Agobard of Lyons. In the Benedictine office, new prayers were inserted by means of the supplemented Gregorian Sacramentary and Carolingian Prayer Books with their Gallican-type prayers.[80]

Baptismal practices were highly local and astonishingly diverse in the Carolingian realm, with many elements of older indigenous liturgical practices. The same can be said of the ordination rites[81] and of the rites for the dying.[82] New aids for the soul in the after life were added in the Frankish rites of death such as votive Masses and informal confraternities of prayers. The latter are recorded in remarkable confraternity books, *Libri Vitae* and *Libri Memoriales*, containing thousands of names of monks, nuns, secular clergy and lay benefactors which reveal enormous networks of communities, bound together by prayer.[83]

The late eighth and ninth centuries saw an outpouring of liturgical commentaries unmatched since patristic times. For many of the major liturgical rituals dozens of tracts were written. For Baptism there were nearly eighty, most of them anonymous, but some belong to such figures as Alcuin, Magnus of Sens, Theodulf of Orléans, Amalarius of Metz, Leidrad of Lyons, Jesse of Amiens, Angilmodus of Soissons, Maxentius of Aquileia,

---

[79] Deshusses (1971).   [80] Black (1987).   [81] Reynolds (1975c).   [82] Paxton (1990).
[83] Hlawitschka, Schmid and Tellenbach (1981); Gerchow (1988).

and perhaps Arno of Salzburg and Hildebald of Cologne.[84] There were expositions of the office by Alcuin, a Pseudo-Alcuin, a Pseudo-Jerome, and many anonymous pieces, and a plethora of anonymous texts on the Mass written in the late eighth and very early ninth centuries with such titles as *Dominus Vobiscum* or *Quotiens contra Se*. In the ninth century some of the major Carolingian thinkers wrote tracts on the Mass: Alcuin, Amalarius, Agobard of Lyons, Florus of Lyons, Hraban Maur and Walahfrid Strabo, to mention only the most significant. Characteristic of all these liturgical expositions was the mixture of Roman, Gallican, Milanese, Old Spanish and even Celtic traditions. In the most elaborate of all Carolingian liturgical commentaries, the *Liber Officialis* of Amalarius, this mixture of older indigenous liturgical texts and explanations of them reached a level not to be matched until the late thirteenth century with the *Rationale* of William Durandus.[85]

By the end of the ninth century liturgical rites in western Europe, whether daily or occasional, were perhaps even more varied and rich than they had been at the beginning of the eighth century. The Roman rite had been introduced almost everywhere both voluntarily and by legislation, but the traditional liturgical preferences of the indigenous non-Roman rites were not suppressed or lost. Rather, they were incorporated into the liturgy of the western church, there to remain into modern times. Similarly, the fundamental contributions made to canon law and the internal and external structures of the church described in this chapter provided the bases for the subsequent development of the western church in its various regions.

---

[84] Keefe (1981; 1984) and forthcoming.   [85] Reynolds (1992).

CHAPTER 23

CAROLINGIAN MONASTICISM: THE POWER OF PRAYER

Mayke de Jong

MONASTERIA

WHEN Folcuin, abbot of Lobbes (d. 990) wrote the *Gesta* of his predecessors, he did so in a nostalgic vein.[1] His *Deeds of the Abbots of Lobbes* sang the praises of the lost glory of Carolingian times. His Lotharingian abbey had been founded on royal soil, it had enjoyed royal protection, and from time to time had been governed by abbots of royal blood.[2] Folcuin himself was very much part of this past, for he could trace his ancestry to Charles Martel.[3] He looked hopefully towards the German emperor: from him, Folcuin expected the restoration of direct royal protection (*tuitio*) and immunity for the abbey in his charge.

The lost world for which Folcuin yearned came into being after 700. It rose and flourished in the Carolingian age; towards the end of the ninth century it went into decline in the West Frankish kingdom as well as in Lotharingia. The old order remained best preserved in the German empire. There, the traditional close interdependence between cloister and royal power still existed; hence, Folcuin hoped that Emperor Otto II might restore Lotharingian abbeys such as Lobbes to their former glory. Carolingian monasteries had been at the very centre of social and political life, while royal service had deeply affected the internal life of these religious communities.

[1] Carolingian monasticism has been the subject of much excellent scholarship in recent years, especially of German origin. The required brevity of references has made it impossible to acknowledge all relevant publications. However, a more extensive selection has been included in the bibliography. While writing this chapter, I have gratefully benefited from the supportive criticism of Esther Cohen, Bram van Hoven van Genderen, Geoffrey Koziol, Albert de Leeuw and, above all, Rosamond McKitterick.
[2] Folcuin, *Gesta Abbatum Lobiensium*, c. 3, p. 57: '*quod videlicet locus regius, regia munificentia constructus, regio, ut dictum est, palatio contiguus*'. About Lobbes, see Dierkens (1985), pp. 91–125.
[3] Folcuin, *Vita Folcuini*, c. 3, p. 427.

This chapter is about the impact of the powerful – kings and aristocrats – on the inner world of the cloister. Monastic life was lived in close contact with the world outside, and responded to its needs. This constant proximity necessitated a repeated redrawing of boundaries and renewal of distance, which is usually called 'monastic reform'. The tension between separation and integration is a recurrent theme in the writings of Carolingian monastic authors, precisely because their communities were so much at the centre of social and political life. As is explained below, the architectural solution to this problem was the *claustrum*, an inner enclosure within the monastery which should keep the outside at bay. The first section of this chapter deals with the demands of society on monks and nuns, and with the political function of *monasteria*; the second one treats the way in which these demands shaped the *vita communis* – the persisent ideal of a communal life within the cloister.

Unavoidably, the emphasis will be on the larger abbeys, for their history is best documented. Still, this bias in favour of large abbeys can be justified, in that they were characteristic of the Carolingian era. Their very size symbolised their wealth and power. Monasteries were prominent in the overwhelmingly rural landscape, harbouring hundreds of people; their economic, social and cultural impact has been compared to that of towns in a later age.[4] Moreover, the prayer of thousands of monks and nuns played a vital part in safeguarding the ruler and his realm. In other words, monasteries were indispensable to those wielding power.

Royal abbeys

Such large abbeys often had modest origins. A network of new monasteries grew in Germany, inspired by the Anglo-Saxon missionary Boniface and his disciples. Apparently Boniface knew the monks in various foundations well enough to supervise even the minutiae of their organisation. Thus, when Abbot Wigbert of Fritzlar had died in 732 he sent personal instructions to the community:

I call upon your affection in fatherly love to maintain the order of your monastic life more strictly now that our father Wigbert is gone. Let the priest Wigbert and the deacon Megingoz expound the rule to you. Let them have charge of canonical hours and of the office of the church. They are to give advice to the others, instruct the children, and preach the word of God to the brethren. Let Hiedde rule the servants, and let Hunfrid assist him, if need be. Sturm will take charge of the kitchen,

---

[4] Wollasch (1978).

Bernhard is to be the labourer and will build our cells as needed. In all matters, wherever necessary, consult Abbot Tatwin and do whatever he may direct.[5]

Fulda had started on as small a footing as Fritzlar. In 744 seven monks accompanied the Bavarian Sturm to start a monastery 'in the middle of the wilderness, and amidst the people to whom we are preaching'.[6] Like other monastic foundations inspired by Boniface, it served as a pastoral centre and missionary station. Soon, Fulda harboured 400 monks, not counting novices and children.[7] Boniface remained Fulda's informal leader and source of inspiration; here he wished to be buried, rather than in his see of Mainz. Sturm, who was Fulda's first abbot, remained in his shadow until Boniface's death in 754.[8] Then, dissension arose between Abbot Sturm and Archbishop Lull of Mainz concerning who was to wield power in Fulda. The conflict between Boniface's two disciples was resolved in a manner typical of the time: King Pippin stepped in, reinstated Sturm and made Fulda into a royal abbey, 'completely free of Lull's dominion'.[9]

Fulda's fate after Boniface's death highlights an important change within contemporary monasticism. Monasteries were gradually withdrawn from the bishop's power, coming to enjoy royal protection and becoming subject to royal *potestas*. This situation was a far cry from the the episcopal control of monasteries affirmed time and again in sixth-century synods.[10] In Merovingian times, the only foundations which had enjoyed relative independence were the royal ones. For the rest, bishops held sway over monastic communities within their diocese. They were responsible for internal discipline, which meant that they supervised monastic customs as well as the appointment of abbots. Moreover, as administrators of ecclesiastical property they had to oversee the economic management of monastic

---

[5] Boniface, *Epistolae*, no. 40, p. 65: 'Paterno amore dilectionem vestram obsecro, ut eo maiore monasterialis normam vitae custodire studeatis, quo pater noster Uuigbertus defunctus est. Uuigbertus presbiter et Megingotus diaconus regulam vestram vobis insinuent et spiritales horas et cursum ecclesiae custodiant et ceteros admoneant et magistri sint infantum et predicent verbum Dei fratribus. Hiedde sit prepositus et servos nostros admoneat; et Hunfridus adiuvet illum, ubicumque opus sit. Styrme in coquina sit. Bernardus operarius sit et edificet domuncula nostra, ubi opus sit. Et de omnibus, ubicumque vobis necesse sit, Tatuuinum abbatem interrogate, et quodcumque vobis insinuet, hoc facite.' About the date of this letter, see Schmid (1978a), pp. 119–27.

[6] Boniface, *Epistolae*, no. 86, p. 193: 'Est preterea locus silvaticus in heremo vastissimae solitudinis in medio nationum praedicationis nostrae, in quo monasterium construentes monachos constituimus sub regula sancti patris Benedicti viventes.'

[7] Liudger, *Vita Gregorii*, c. 5, p. 72.   [8] Schmid (1978a), pp. 129–30.

[9] Eigil, *Vita Sturmi*, c. 20 (version EPB), p. 155: 'et absolutum ab omni dominio Lulli episcopi'. Schmid (1978a), p. 111.

[10] Semmler (1974), pp. 379–85. Council of Orléans (511), c. 17, *Concilia Galliae*, p. 9; Council of Arles (554), c. 2, *Concilia Galliae*, p. 171.

possessions. Although ecclesiastical law prohibited their outright owner-ship of monastic lands, successive bishops did enjoy usufruct and could dispose of oblations. Lay founders of monasteries were only allowed such rights of usufruct during their lifetime; this barred aristocratic families from using their monastic foundations as sources of dynastic power.

Given this situation, the new model provided by Columbanus' influential monastery of Luxeuil (590) was as attractive to lay founders as it was unattractive to bishops. Luxeuil – and monastic foundations inspired by it – remained outside the scope of episcopal *potestas*, with abbot and lay founder being in full control. The first wave of Columbanian monasteries were royal ones, founded by kings and their relatives, but soon, lay aristocrats followed suit. Significantly, such monasteries were mainly located in the outlying areas of dioceses.[11] In the early decades of the seventh century episcopal power was still too strong to be challenged.

Monastic property bolstered the veritable 'episcopal states' which grew in the course of the sixth and seventh centuries. Bishops exercised royal rights such as mint and toll; dioceses such as Trier, Chur, Rouen, Rheims, Sens, Tours and Auxerre became the strongholds of powerful aristocratic families. Any mayor of the palace or king who wanted to rule had to break these states up. One effective way to go about this was to undermine the direct episcopal control over monasteries. This strategy was used consis-tently from 714 onwards, when Charles Martel set about recovering the severe losses of the preceding decades.[12] Whenever the mayor of the palace managed to isolate a wayward bishop, the latter would be banished, while the victor quickly assumed his enemy's rights over the monasteries in his diocese. Pippin II had thus chased bishops out of Rouen and Nantes after his victory at Tertry (687), and Charles Martel did likewise in 717 when the incumbent of Rheims tried to counter him. In most cases the pattern was similar, with growing military might enabling the Pippinids to topple yet another episcopal state, establishing their own *fideles* on confiscated eccle-siastical property.

It is tempting to view this battle between bishops and mayors of the palace over monasteries as a road which led directly to kingship. As often, however, hindsight is misleading. During the early decades of the eighth century, the mayors of the palace did not operate as future kings, but as magnates struggling for power.[13] For all magnates, Pippinid and otherwise,

---

11 Semmler (1974), pp. 388–9.   12 Semmler (1974), esp. pp. 392–5.

13 Conversations with Geoffrey Koziol and Ian Wood have clarified this issue for me. The latter kindly allowed me to read several chapters of his book, Wood (1993), in advance of publication, in which the same point is made, esp. chs. 15 and 16. About the relatively tardy dominance gained by the Pippinids over St Denis, see Semmler (1989b), pp. 89–97.

control of monastic wealth and the sacred was an important asset. Like other lay lords, therefore, Pippin II and his descendants founded their own monasteries (*Eigenklöster*) over which they retained complete control. As they grew more powerful, their patronage became more sought after; hence, lesser lords would strengthen their bond with the rising power by placing their own monastic foundation under the protection (*tuitio*) of the mayor of the palace. It is no coincidence that an early instance of such a *traditio* by a lay founder of a monastery to Pippin II occurred after the latter's victory at Tertry (687).[14] However, a severe set-back for Pippinid power followed soon afterwards; and as late as the 730s, Charles Martel was still fully engaged in dismantling the episcopal states.

When Pippin III became king in 751, all those monasteries which had sustained his family's rise to power became royal monasteries, sharing in its glory. Their importance to the new dynasty's power is evident from the fact that the mayors of the palace generally reserved control of the monasteries for themselves, instead of handing them over to *fideles*. The same course of action was taken by the new king and his successor. In 806 Charlemagne finally succeeded in dismantling Chur, the last of the episcopal states. He established a count within this diocese, but the three most important monasteries became royal ones, instead of becoming part of the comital endowment. This gathering of major monasteries into the fold of royal protection was systematic. Whenever conflict over succession to the abbacy opened the possibility of a solution in the shape of royal *tuitio*, the king made the most of the opportunity, as Pippin III did in Fulda. He would step in as an arbitrator, upholding monastic liberty against the bishop and placing the community under his personal protection. Successive kings firmly held on to their monasteries. When Charlemagne restored extensive property to the bishop of Auxerre, he gave back some small and insignificant *monasteria*; wealthy ones such as St Germain d'Auxerre continued to be royal abbeys.[15] Monastic lands had become indispensable, for they yielded a significant proportion of the royal army.[16]

Once the new dynasty was established and the episcopate sufficiently tamed, co-operation between kings and bishops became yet again imperative. New ground rules had to be established for the governance of monasteries as well. They were laid down in 755 at the synod of Ver: monasteries were to be either episcopal or royal, and Pippin and Charlemagne acted upon this, ruling vigorously.[17] Thus, the efforts of lay aristocrats to use monasteries as building blocks for independent power

---

[14] Semmler (1974), p. 305.

[15] *Gesta Episcoporum Autissiodorensium*, p. 395; Semmler (1974), p. 351.

[16] Prinz (1971); Nelson (1983).   [17] Synod of Ver (755), c. 20, *MGH Cap.* I, p. 36.

were effectively checked for some four generations. Only in the 880s was royal monopoly of monasteries seriously threatened, with lay lords assuming control of monastic resources.

Abbots and bishops, monks and clerics

In the eighth century, episcopal and abbatial roles were still curiously intertwined. Not only did bishops assume the function of abbot, but abbots also became bishops. The subscriptions of the Synod of Attigny (762) distinguished between 'bishops with a diocese' and 'bishops from a monastery', and furthermore spoke of 'abbots who are not bishops' as if those were the exception rather than the rule.[18] Apparently, ecclesiastical leadership comprised these three categories: bishops, abbots and those who combined both roles. In Ireland, where monastic communities dominated the church and diocesan structure was lacking, the so-called monastic bishop was a familiar figure, as he would become in Anglo-Saxon monasteries of the eighth century. Such monastic bishops had no circumscribed diocese; they lived in the cloister and were full members of their community, taking charge of pastoral care and the ordination of the clergy. A monastic bishop did not need to be an abbot; the office could also be filled by plain monks.

The continent also had its share of abbot-bishops in the eighth century, as is clear from the above-mentioned Synod of Attigny. Their existence suited peculiar circumstances, especially in missionary regions where no diocesan organisation existed as yet. In the seventh and eighth centuries Lobbes harboured a number of monastic bishops, much to the confusion of its tenth-century historian Folcuin. How could Lobbes have counted several bishops at the same time, he wondered, some of whom could not even be clearly identified as abbots?[19] Lobbes provides an interesting example of how monastic bishops could become pawns in the Pippinid struggle for power, for this foundation did belong to a proper diocese, Cambrai. Pippin II appointed a missionary bishop named Ursmar (d. 713) to the abbacy of Lobbes, thus undermining the control of the local suffragan, while deftly gaining a foothold on the border between Austrasia and Neustria.[20] Lobbes indeed proved a staunch ally of the mayors of the palace. When Pippin III had become king, however, the toleration of abbot-bishops ceased. He now took control of the bishoprics, imposing a diocesan organisation, Roman style. This left no room for monastic independence. The Synod of Ver (755)

---

[18] Synod of Attigny (762), *MGH Conc.* II:I, p. 73; Dierkens (1985), p. 298, n. 108.
[19] Folcuin, *Gesta Abbatum Lobiensium*, cc. 6–7, pp. 58–9. Dierkens (1985), pp. 105, 297–9, 321–5.
[20] Dierkens (1985), pp. 298–9.

attempted to eradicate all that was disorderly: double monasteries led by an abbess, vagrant monks travelling without permission of their abbots, and dioceses containing more than one bishop.[21] The new ruler intended to control the *monasteria*, through and with the bishops. Significantly, the reign of the abbot-bishops in Lobbes ended in 776.[22]

Bearing this in mind, it is not surprising that the eighth-century notion of *monasterium* should be complicated. Certainly its meaning was not restricted to that of a group of monks or nuns devoted to contemplation, living under an abbot or abbess and subject to a rule of life. The Anglo-Saxon church in particular was familiar with a wide variety of communities called *monasteria*, of which some harboured priests carrying out pastoral duties in the neighbourhood, while others had a more contemplative orientation.[23] Therefore, a clear distinction between contemplative monasticism on the one hand and active secular clergy on the other would be an anachronism. The hallmark of a *monasterium* seems to have been a communal and corporate life, no matter whether this was directed more towards prayer or to pastoral care. Usually, both activities were combined. This also holds true for the Continent. Here, groups of 'secular' clergy leading a communal life were nothing out of the ordinary either. Willibrord's missionary see of Utrecht had such a *monasterium*, in the charge of Abbot Gregory.[24] The second half of the eighth century saw the first tentative efforts to differentiate between monks and clerics. However, this entailed an even further monasticising of cathedral clergy. Bishop Chrodegang of Metz (d. 766) founded Gorze, a community bound to the Rule of Benedict, while at the same time organising his clergy as a *coenobium*, living within the walls of a cloister. For the latter he composed a rule of life, similar to the rules that had long governed monastic life.[25]

The fluid nature of the boundaries between monks and clerics is understandable, given the fact that both groups shared a central task, the *Opus Dei*, and a way of life, the *vita communis*. Many of those who, according to their own lights, belonged to the so-called monastic order (*ordo monasticus*) were in fact part of the cathedral clergy, or of communities founded by bishops to take charge of pastoral care in the less accessible regions of their large dioceses. And even those monasteries that understood themselves to be 'Benedictine' were so in spirit, but not to the letter, and remained open to customs derived from the *ordo canonicus*.[26]

---

[21] Synod of Ver (755), cc. 1, 6 and 10, *MGH Cap.* I, pp. 33–5.   [22] Dierkens (1985), p. 108.
[23] Foot (1992b).   [24] Angenendt (1973), pp. 64–85; Angenendt (1990b).
[25] Paulus Diaconus, *Liber de Episcopis Mettensibus*, p. 268: 'ad instar coenobii infra claustrorum septa conversari fecit, normamque eis insituit, qualiter in ecclesia militare deberet'. Semmler (1980), p. 79; Semmler (1973).   [26] Semmler (1980).

Yet another reason for the increasing similarity between monks and clerics lay in the widespread conviction that only those who lived a *vita communis*, in the sense of living in a state of ritual purity, could be effective mediators between God and mankind.[27] This notion is already evident in the *Concilium Germanicum* of 743, convened by Carloman and dominated by Boniface. The church had to be purified; no clergy living an unchaste life could be tolerated within the *ecclesia*.[28] This called for ascetic priests; thus monks were turned into priests, and conversely, cathedral clergy into ascetic communities.[29] During the second half of the eighth century, all efforts to distinguish clearly between monks and communally living clerics failed.[30] It took the next generation of reform-minded churchmen to create the phenomenon of the 'canon' (*clericus canonicus*) as opposed to the monk *monachus*, who by definition lived under the Rule of Benedict. This new distinction implied that monks were to concentrate on prayer, leaving pastoral care to the canonical clergy.

In practice, however, monks remained very much involved in pastoral care; an increasing number of private churches still ended up in monastic hands, for the aristocrats donating them were convinced that the *cura animarum* was best taken care of by ascetic specialists.[31]

Reform

The councils organised in the 740s by Boniface had already made an effort to bring monks and nuns under one rule, that of Benedict. This endeavour gained momentum at the beginning of the ninth century. The Rule of Benedict had long been held in high esteem in the Frankish kingdoms; from the 630s onwards it had often been combined with Columban's monastic rule.[32] The few extant examples of these mixed rules (*regulae mixtae*) suggest that Benedict's influence was strong, but not to the extent of excluding other traditions.[33] Only very gradually, the Rule of Benedict was to gain

---

[27] Angenendt (1978/9) pp. 36–42; cf. also Angenendt (1983). This notion was contrary to St Augustine's doctrine of *ex opere operato*, according to which priestly ordination validated the sacraments, and not the life-style of the individual priest. Still, the opposite attitude dominated early medieval practice.

[28] *MGH Conc.* II:1, cc. 1–2, 6–7, pp. 3–4; Hartmann (1989), p. 52.

[29] Angenendt (1983), esp. pp. 217–21; Angenendt (1990a), pp. 345–7.

[30] Semmler (1980); Hartmann (1989), p. 55.   [31] Constable (1982), pp. 366–8.

[32] Prinz (1965), pp. 267–88; Dubois (1981), pp. 23–35; Moyse (1982), pp. 3–19. However, the notion that the *Regula Benedicti*, the *Regula Columbani* or their combination were the only alternatives open to monasticism tends to deny the diversity and vitality of monastic life in the Merovingian realm. Cf. Wood (1982).

[33] Waldebert, *Cuiusdam Patris Regula ad Virgines*, PL 88, cols. 1053–70; Donatus, *Regula ad Virgines*, ed. A. de Vogüé (1975).

supremacy within the Carolingian realm. Anglo-Saxon influence aided this development, for English monasticism – although certainly not 'Benedictine' – was conscious of its ties with Rome. In the Anglo-Saxon church, Benedict was regarded as 'the Roman abbot' (*abbas Romensis*) and his Rule as the *regula Romana*.[34] When Carolingian rulers and their ecclesiastical advisers sought to establish religious unity in the realm of the Chosen People of the Franks, they turned to the Roman abbot, and to Monte Cassino. From this 'source and head' (*fons et caput*) of all monastic inspiration Charlemagne was sent an authoritative copy of the Rule, believed to be a copy of the autograph itself.[35]

The thrust of reform which was to make all monks and nuns into Benedictines – though by no means uniformly – was intensified from 800 onwards. This tied in with a more general endeavour to 'correct'. The key notions of the so-called Carolingian renaissance were unification and *correctio*; these were to touch all aspects of Christian life and liturgy.[36] Because the Christian cult was grounded in texts, it was of crucial importance that these be the correct ones, used by the whole of the *populus christianus*. For how could God be honoured by faulty ritual? A strong belief in the efficacy of correctly performed ritual underpinned these strenuous efforts to improve the knowledge of Latin grammar in all those concerned with liturgy. As Charlemagne wrote to Abbot Baugulf of Fulda, those in bishoprics and monasteries who can teach and learn should do so, 'so that those who desire to please God by living rightly should not neglect to please him also by speaking correctly'.[37] Obviously, the Carolingian God liked to be addressed only in correct Latin.

Within the reform-minded clergy, Benedict of Aniane increasingly came to the foreground. This 'second Benedict' was born *c.* 750 as Wittiza, the son of a Gothic count.[38] He converted to monastic life in adulthood, rather an exceptional act for an age in which most people entered religious life in childhood. The fact that he became the mentor of young King Louis the Pious contributed much to his success, drawing him nearer and nearer to the centre of power.

Benedict of Aniane's influence made itself felt in the steadily increasing efforts to bind all monks and nuns to the Rule of Benedict. At the same time, the monastic order became more distinct from the other orders of the realm. Accordingly, the various *ordines* started to meet more often in separate assemblies. In 802 abbots and monks flocked to Aachen to discuss life

[34] Wollasch (1973), pp. 41–6; Wollasch (1982).   [35] McKitterick (1983), pp. 119–20.
[36] Schramm (1964).
[37] *Epistola de litteris colendis, MGH Cap.* I, no. 29, p. 79; 'ut, qui Deo placere appetunt recte vivendo, ei etiam placere non negligant recte loquendo'.   [38] Semmler (1983), pp. 5–9.

according to the Rule, with Benedict taking the lead. In Mainz in 813 three groups (*turmae*) met separately: bishops, abbots and monks, and counts and judges.[39] This gathering was one of five reform councils convened simultaneously by the emperor, to meet in the early summer of 813 in Rheims, Arles, Tours, Mainz and Chalon-sur-Saône. The councils of Tours and Mainz stressed that all monasteries should live in accordance with the Rule, while in Rheims it was even deemed necessary to read the Rule to the abbots, in order to familiarise them with it.[40] The five synods of 813 show that the Rule of Benedict was by no means universally obeyed yet, least of all in the heartland of the realm.[41] Ancient sees like Rheims harboured rich and staunchly defended older monastic traditions. Old and venerable communities like St Denis, St Maur-des-Fossés and Stavelot-Malmédy, moreover, had joined the *ordo canonicorum*, which permitted the possession of personal property. This choice for the canonical life was not necessarily a sign of flagrant lack of discipline, for together with the obligation of stability (*stabilitas loci*), the prohibition of personal property was virtually the only feature distinguishing monastic from canonical life. This much is certain: by 813 the era of the mixed rules was hardly over. And monastic foundations with a long tradition of their own were definitely not yet ready for the next stage of reform, which entailed not only one rule (*una regula*), but also a unified custom (*una consuetudo*).[42]

For this was the twofold goal of the great reforming councils held in Aachen in 816 and 817, orchestrated by Benedict of Aniane. When Louis became emperor in 814, Benedict was soon at his side as religious adviser. The chronicle of Moissac notes for this year: 'In the first year of his reign the Emperor Louis recalled the Abbot Benedict from his monastery in Aniane, because of the fame of his life and saintliness, so that he would establish himself in the vicinity of the palace of Aachen in the forest of Ardennes.' To ensure Benedict's presence, Louis founded the monastery of Inden (Kornelimünster), close to Aachen.[43] Benedict has been branded as an 'imperial abbot' (*Reichsabt*), who tried to root out older monastic traditions in the Carolingian realm, acting strictly and rigidly against communities that had lapsed into canonical life. None of these judgements stands up to close scrutiny.[44] The religious houses reformed by Benedict were loosely joined together, having abbots and abbesses of their own; they may have looked up

---

[39] *MGH Conc.* II:1, c. 14, p. 273.

[40] Council of Tours, c. 26, *MGH Conc.* II:1, p. 290; Council of Mainz, c. 11, *MGH Conc.* II:1, p. 263; Council of Rheims, c. 9, *MGH Conc.* II:1, p. 255.   [41] Semmler (1965; 1983).

[42] Moyse (1982); Semmler (1983).

[43] *Chronicon Moissiacense* (*s.a.* 814), p. 311; further sources compiled by Semmler (ed.), *Legislatio Aquisgranensis*, CCM I, p. 426, n. 10.   [44] Geuenich (1989), pp. 81–2.

to him as their guiding spirit, but they did not treat him as some super-abbot.[45] And the rich monastic tradition of the Frankish empire is still known precisely because Benedict took the trouble to gather it into two major compilations, the *Concordia Regularum* and the *Codex Regularum*. These were to be the manifold source of inspiration from which the 'one custom' was to be drawn. Some contemporaries found Benedict much too lenient towards monastic communities changing over to the canonical life. With his fellow reform abbot, Arnulf of Noirmoutier, Benedict travelled in 817 to St Martin of Tours to pacify the quarrelling monks; the majority of them opted for the canonical life, apparently with their visitors' approval. When in 832 Louis the Pious brought back St Martin into the monastic fold, his charter depicted Benedict and Arnulf as two 'good and pious, but extremely simple fathers', who had allowed themself to be lured into compliance.[46]

The monastic and canonical orders became the object of intense scrutiny and debate at the councils of Aachen in 816 and 817. The emperor himself attended, intervening personally, along with many abbots, monks, bishops and lay magnates.[47] They first issued the *Institutio Canonicorum* and the *Institutio Sanctimonialum* for canons and canonesses respectively. These read as a compilation of patristic texts, with additional decrees of a more practical kind.[48] The council of August 816 also legislated for monks and nuns. The sources for this meeting are very interesting, for they include the official capitulary as well as several unofficial eyewitness reports, all of these testifying to heated debate and much controversy.[49]

What were the main issues of the Aachen councils? Acceptance of the Rule as the one law governing monastic life was not the problem; predictably, it was the uniform interpretation of it that met with most resistance. First, there was the matter which the emperor personally supported: the general and uniform compliance with St Benedict's Office. This trend conflicted with the current Frankish observance of the Roman Office, which was the consequence of King Pippin's liturgical innovations half a century earlier.[50] Next, there was the controversy over the *laus perennis*, the continual singing of the Psalms all year round. This custom is already mentioned in sixth-century sources, and was still widely observed when the 816 decrees forbade it. The *laus perennis* implied the non-stop singing of

---

[45] Semmler (1963; 1983; 1992).

[46] *Monuments historiques*, ed. J. Tardif (1866), no. 124, p. 88: 'Idem veri boni et devoti, sed simplicissimi patres.'   [47] Semmler (1963), esp. pp. 13–21; Semmler (1960).

[48] Edited in *MGH Conc.* II:2, pp. 394–421 and 422–56.

[49] Semmler (1960); edited by J. Semmler, *Legislatio Aquisgranensis, CCM* I, pp. 423–82.

[50] Angenendt (1972), p. 213–15; Semmler (1975), pp. 139–42. Cf. Paulus Diaconus, *Liber de Episcopis Mettensibus* p. 286, about Bishop Chrodegang's introduction of the *Romana cantilena* among the clergy of Metz.

some 450 Psalms within twenty-four hours, with sections of the community taking turns, whereas the custom proposed in Aachen demanded only 138 Psalms, sung by all.[51] Still, monastic prayer in the *consuetudo* of 816 had tripled compared to the original requirements of the Rule of Benedict, and had become a much more communal and intensive preoccupation. The question of cloister schools was also hotly debated; should these receive other children than the child oblates who were bound to monastic life? In 817, the final answer was an emphatic negative.[52] The most contentious issue, however, was the relation between abbot and community. Many abbots by now had become powerful men with an aristocratic life-style, demanding a separate abbot's house where they could receive their distinguished guests in suitable splendour. Henceforth, abbots were to be denied any special privileges; their place was in the refectory and dormitory along with the rest of the community.[53] This stern attitude towards worldly abbots fits in with the overall concern with the distinction between the various orders: monks and canons, the clergy and the laity. The endeavour to separate the inseparable shows in the decrees concerning the schools and the abbots, and also in those regulating estate management. Abbots were to reduce their tours of inspection, and monks were not to be sent out at all.[54]

The Aachen reform had a mixed success, if only because estates needed to be managed, monastic schools remained attractive to all contemplating a career in the church, and abbots still owed royal service. Neither was the *una consuetudo* ever achieved.[55] However, the Rule of Benedict did gain preeminence: though local custom varied widely, the *Regula Benedicti* became the foundation of monastic identity. This was hammered home once more by yet another meeting in Aachen in 818/19, leading to far-reaching changes within individual monasteries. Some became staunchly Benedictine, others opted for the canonical order.[56] In following years, *missi* were sent out to check on compliance with the reforms. Not all bold dreams came true, but the scale and impact of the undertaking can hardly be overestimated. The ultimate purpose was unification of the church within an undivided Christian empire. After all, 817 was also the year of the *Ordinatio Imperii*, issued to safeguard the future cohesion of the realm. The strenuous efforts to distinguish between monastic and canonical life, along with the demand for

---

[51] Hallinger (1979), pp. 134–46.
[52] Council of Aachen (817), c. 5, *Legislatio Aquisgranensis*, p. 474.
[53] *Statuta Murbacensia*, c. 4, *Legislatio Aquisgranensis*, p. 443; Council of Aachen (816), c. 23, *Legislatio Aquisgranensis*, pp. 464–5. Cf. Semmler (1963), pp. 40–9.
[54] *Statuta Murbacensia*, c. 10, *Legislatio Aquisgranensis*, p. 445; Semmler (1963), pp. 55–8.
[55] Kottje (1965), pp. 331–5; Semmler (1980); Donat (1990).
[56] Hlawitschka (1961); Semmler (1980).

unity (*forma unitatis*) served to underpin a larger operation: the building of one Christian empire.[57]

Lay abbots

The names of nine leading abbots who supported the Aachen reforms were entered together in 824 in the confraternity book of Reichenau, under the heading of 'the names of our living friends' (*nomina amicorum viventium*). The list is headed by Hilduin, abbot of St Denis, St Médard of Soissons, St Germain-des-Prés, St Ouen in Rouen, and Salonnes; to cap it all, Hilduin became chaplain of the palace, bearing from 825 the title *archicapellanus*. His accumulation of abbacies was the reward for long service to the emperor. Second in the list came Einhard, Charlemagne's famous biographer.[58] His career was very much the result of the blurring of boundaries between the cloister and the outside world. Educated in Fulda, he remained a layman and became a courtier. As such, he received the abbacy of St Peter in Ghent and several others as benefices. Einhard is one of the earliest lay abbots that can be identified. The institution of the lay abbot has in the past come in for much abuse from historians, who have made them into the symbol of all that was worldly and wicked in the Carolingian church. Recently, however, the balance has been redressed in their favour.[59] Their virtues as benefactors and reformers of their monasteries have been eloquently extolled.

Indeed, Einhard's career supports this contention. He not only was one of the central figures of the 816/17 reforms, but also made material provisions for the prayer of at least twenty-four canons in Ghent.[60] The background to the lay abbot was the growing economic and political importance of monasteries and their abbots. Abbots became mainstays of royal power, courtiers, trusted counsellors and envoys. They also controlled vast economic resources; church property supported a substantial part of the Carolingian army. To gain constant access to rich monastic lands kings needed faithful abbots, so they accorded abbacies to their loyal followers, monks and laymen alike. The number of abbacies gathered by Hilduin and Einhard speaks for itself. Hilduin was a monk, Einhard a layman and Alcuin, who ruled the abbey of St Martin in Tours, was technically a secular cleric, having been brought up in the cathedral *monasterium* of York. Before the Aachen councils, no clear-cut distinction was made between the various *monasteria* or their abbots. The specifically defined *abbas laicus* was a creation of the ninth century. Surprisingly, the Aachen councils were remarkably

---

[57] Ardo, *Vita Benedicti*, c. 36, p. 215: 'Cunctaque monasteria ita ad formam unitatis redacta sunt.'
[58] Geuenich (1989), pp. 89–93.   [59] Felten (1980).   [60] Felten (1980), p. 49.

silent on this topic, although much debate raged on the extent to which a 'regular' abbot should be part of his community. A lay nobleman in charge of a religious house – monastic or canonical – seems to have been tacitly accepted, provided he did not plunder the resources to the extent that a regular life within the cloister became impossible. This was to be prevented by a division between the lands of the abbot (*mensa abbatis*) and those destined for the upkeep of the community (*mensa fratrum*). Einhard shortly after his appointment made this arrangement in St Peter at Ghent. The Council of Paris (829) was equally lenient, limiting itself to some sound advice to the lay abbots on how to carry out their functions. Kings unabatedly continued rewarding their followers with abbacies and thus with monastic wealth, in spite of a capitulary of 818/19 granting the free election of an abbot to all royal monasteries.[61] A study of the career of ten important abbots during the reign of Louis the Pious shows that none of them achieved his position as a result of a free election. Between them they were in charge of over thirty monasteries.[62]

It was only in 844 that lay abbots really came under attack. After the partition of the realm in 843 it was apparently now time for reassessment and reconstruction, and conciliar activity peaked, especially in the realm of Charles the Bald. Usurpation of church lands by the laity was condemned in general, and lay abbots were commanded to restore their abbacies. Nothing came of it, for reasons that the bishops themselves stated: lay abbots were necessary in times of 'pressing public need' (*propter imminentem rei publicae necessitatem*).[63] And the bishops' very vexation with ecclesiastical property in lay hands shows the extent to which kings had come to rely on trusted lay abbots. Rich monastic lands yielded political and military service without depleting the royal fisc.[64] Bishops and abbots, regular and irregular, contributed substantially to the royal army. The ramshackle but functional state of Charles the Bald was 'held together by a thousand special personalised arrangements', among which the lay abbacy proved indispensable.[65] The king himself was lay abbot of St Denis from 867 onwards, using the institution as a political tool.

The history of Lobbes offers an enlightening example of the mixed blessings of lay abbacy. In 864 the brother of Queen Theutberga of Lotharingia, Hubert, invaded the abbey and ousted the abbot. Hubert was killed in the same year, but in the meantime he had managed to divide the estates into a meagre *mensa fratrum* and a lavish *mensa abbatis*: off the latter

[61] *Capitulare Ecclesiasticum* (818/19), c. 5, *MGH Cap.* II, p. 276.   [62] Geuenich (1988), p. 184.
[63] Council of Yütz, c. 5, *MGH Conc.* III, p. 34.   [64] Nelson (1992), pp. 58–62.
[65] Nelson (1992), p. 67.

lived his own followers.[66] Perhaps Folcuin has drawn too bleak a picture of his activities, but the fact of the sudden raid and its consequences are indisputable. The division of property remained in force in the following decades, when Lobbes was ruled by lay abbots of Carolingian blood. Between 864 and 881, Lothar II, Carloman (son of Charles the Bald), Charles the Bald himself, Louis II the Stammerer, Louis the German and Hugo, son of Lothar and Waldrada, all benefited from Lobbes.[67] Folcuin wrote of them without one word of disapproval, probably because all these abbots were blood relations of kings. Therefore, they belonged in this *locus regius*.[68] Hubert, however, lived on in Lobbes as the devil incarnate.

In other words, lay abbots came in all shapes and sizes. On the one hand, there were villains like Hubert who violently raided a monastery, on the other hand there were models of piety such as Einhard, who ensured the regularity of their communities. Probably, the majority of lay abbots occupied some middle ground. In a world of personalised arrangements and wealthy monasteries, they were a fact of life.

VITA COMMUNIS

Claustrum versus saeculum

One of the most controversial sources for Carolingian monasticism is the so-called Plan of St Gall. This beautifully executed ground plan of a large abbey was never used as a practical guide for building in St Gall; this much is clear from archaeological data. It therefore soon earned the qualification of a paradigmatic vision of how a large abbey should be planned. Some maintained that the Plan was the direct architectural outcome of the Aachen reforms of 816/17,[69] others have doubted this close connection.[70] Where did it originate? A good case has been made for Reichenau, although the exact authorship remains uncertain.[71]

The St Gall Plan illustrates the problems that large Carolingian abbeys were facing. All aspects of life are represented here, many resulting from constant interaction with the outside world. These include guest houses, a school, buildings for artisans, animals and servants, a brewery, a bakery and a hospice. The central task of the community had to be carried out amidst all

---

[66] Folcuin, *Gesta Abbatum Lobiensium*, c. 12, pp. 60–1; Dierkens (1985), pp. 109–10.
[67] Dierkens (1985), pp. 129–30.
[68] Folcuin, *Gesta Abbatum Lobiensium*, c. 3, p. 57; see above, n. 2.
[69] Horn and Born (1979); Hecht (1983).
[70] De Vogüé (1984); Sanderson (1985); Zettler (1990).   [71] Zettler (1990).

this hustle and bustle. How was one to safeguard prayer and stability? The architectural solution was the cloister (*claustrum*). In this inner sanctuary only monks were to be admitted; their coming and going was subject to the abbot's approval, as was the highly exceptional admittance of outsiders. According to the Plan of St Gall the *claustrum* encompassed all buildings for exclusive monastic use, such as the dormitory, refectory, kitchen and lavatories. Above all, the three places around which religious life revolved were secluded from intrusion by outsiders: the monastic choir, library and scriptorium. With respect to learning, Carolingian monasticism differed markedly from that in Benedict's time. Benedict attached no particular significance to intellectual activity or the monastic school: according to his prologue, monastic life itself was the 'school of the service of the Lord'. By the ninth century, however, the study and production of texts had assumed paramount importance in the cloister. Not all monks and nuns participated equally in literate culture, but those who did constituted an elite within their communities. There existed no contradiction between intellectual and religious activity. On the contrary, the study of texts meant meditation, in the sense of really 'digesting' their spiritual significance, and work in the scriptorium belonged as much to the *Opus Dei* as did prayer.

This claustral structure was to be built around a central square court adjoining the southern side of the church. Hence, the authors of the Plan created a sacred space within the monastery, where prayer and study could continue unhindered. This was no ninth-century invention, but from this time on the *claustrum* became a characteristic feature of western monastic architecture.[72] Local conditions might call for adaptations of this scheme, but the general principle remained the same; the duties of the inside and the outside world had to be combined as well as separated. Hildemar of Civate, author of an extensive commentary on the Rule of St Benedict (*c.* 845), gave detailed instructions to this effect.[73] Preferably, visiting monks, abbots, bishops and prominent laity were all to have their own guest quarters. If for some reason it proved impossible to have a separate guest house for visiting bishops and prominent laymen, they could lodge in the same building, but in rooms of their own. Under no circumstances, however, should these guest rooms be adjacent to the hospice for visiting abbots, monks and the poor.[74] Vassals should also join their lords in the separate guest house, which was to be as far removed as possible from that intended for the visiting monks. After all, 'the laity may stay up till the middle of the night,

[72] Zettler (1990), pp. 677–80.
[73] For biographical data, see Hafner (1959), pp. 97–8, 107–8; Semmler (1963), p. 33.
[74] Hildemar, *Expositio*, c. 53, pp. 507–8.

talking and feasting, while the monks are not allowed to do this; instead, they have to be silent and pray'.[75]

Communication between the *claustrum* and the outside was a delicate affair at all times. Hildemar envisaged a separate dwelling for the abbot, with its own kitchen. This kitchen also catered to the needs of the guests and could not be reached directly from the *claustrum*. The abbot's kitchen was served by a canon (*clericus canonicus*), while the monks' kitchen was run by a *monachus*. For practical purposes – apparently the larder was inside the cloister – a window was to be built to connect the two kitchens, enabling the monk to hand fish and other food to the canon in charge of cooking. Obviously, Hildemar's monastery harboured a number of canonical clergy, who were probably trained within the monastic confines. Because of their intermediate status, they were employed in the transitional areas between cloister and outside world. Different monks were to receive the various guests in a way that befitted their station in life, 'for it may happen that all come at the same time, counts and bishops and abbots and poor'.[76]

Hildemar's commentary has rightly been called a 'textbook of ninth-century monastic life'.[77] His career shows how much monastic life in northern Italy was part of Carolingian monasticism. He dictated his commentary on the Rule to his pupils in Civate, where he was *magister*. Hildemar had wide experience of actual custom in all its variety, having been raised in Corbie, and having travelled widely in the Carolingian empire. He was obviously much impressed by Reichenau, and it is no coincidence that the earliest manuscripts of his commentary originate from there.[78] One could very well envisage the daily routine that Hildemar depicts within the spatial setting of the Plan of St Gall.[79] Both sources, one textual and the other visual, show how busy monasteries had become since the days of St Benedict. The porter and cellarer now were important functionaries with a special staff to aid them. The continuous presence of outsiders had become a burden, but an inescapable one, for at the same time the guests and the outside world guaranteed the existence of the community. Hildemar's attitude towards the powerful (*potentes*) makes this crystal clear. These easily affronted men were to be handled with care, otherwise the community might lose their generosity, and be harmed by their wrath.[80] A good grasp of status differences was essential for a monk. For example, a poor man would

---

[75] Hildemar, *Expositio*, c. 65, pp. 611–12: 'eo quod laici possunt stare usque mediam noctem et loqui et jocari, et monachi non debent, sed magis silentium habere et orare'.

[76] Hildemar, *Expositio*, c. 58, p. 507: 'quia solet evenire, ut veniant uno tempore et comites et episcopi et abbates et pauperes'.   [77] Semmler (1963), p. 81. See also K. Zelzer (1989).

[78] Hafner (1959), pp. 7–21.   [79] Hafner, (1962), p. 192; Zettler (1990), p. 661.

[80] Hildemar *Expositio*, c. 51, p. 497; de Jong (1992), pp. 37–8.

be honoured by monks washing his feet, but a mighty one could feel ridiculed and take his revenge.[81] Such were the realities of life that Hildemar observed, and they must have been similar in all monasteries dealing with the powerful.

Guarding the *claustrum* was a full-time occupation. Departure and return were surrounded with ritual, and the traveller had to remain silent on what he had seen in the outside world.[82] But Hildemar also deemed claustrality an interior affair. Even when one left the monastic precincts, one remained in the cloister in spirit. A monk ordered to visit the cobbler's workshop, outside the *claustrum*, stayed 'inside' as long as he did not exceed his brief. However, if he disobeyed, he left his internal cloister.[83] The tension between inside and outside, *claustrum* and *saeculum*, is expressed in terms of the dichotomy of mind and body; claustral activities were connected with the *homo interior*, business outside with the *homo exterior*.[84] The abbot served as link between the inside and the outside world. As the Rule dictated, he supervised all comings and goings in the monastery.[85] At the same time, he had to be capable of handling all outside business. Ekkehard's history of Carolingian St Gall illustrates this vividly. In Ekkehard's opinion, 'saintly simplicity' (*sancta simplicitas*) and too great a concern with life inside would not make a good abbot, for the management of the monastic estates called for permanent vigilance.[86] The ideal abbot felt at home within the cloister as well as outside, and could easily adapt his behaviour to different circumstances. He would impose strict monastic discipline, while allowing his community some relaxation – provided that monastic *hilaritas* took place behind the walls of the *claustrum*, and was never witnessed by the laity. In the outside world, however, the abbot was a mighty lord, with a firm grip on his vassals. They were to serve him properly when he dined outside the cloister. In turn, he supervised the education of their sons, from backgammon to falconry, and provided them with armour when they came of age.[87] In other words, a good abbot was a flexible one: a benevolent but strict father to his

---

[81] Hildemar, *Expositio*, c. 53, p. 502.

[82] Hildemar, *Expositio*, c. 67, pp. 612–13.

[83] Hildemar, *Expositio*, c. 67, p. 613.

[84] Hildemar, *Expositio*, c. 4, 184: 'Et hoc notandum est, quia multa sunt, quae dixi, quae quantum ad exteriorem hominem attinent, in claustra non possunt fieri, veluti est mortuum sepelire aut infirmum visitare. Sed tamen omnia in claustra possunt fieri, quantum ad interiorem hominem attinent, id est si voluntas fuerit alicui in corde id agendi. Et ideo si infirmum infra claustram non possunt visitare, quia domus infirmorum non est infra claustram, tamen infra claustrum possum visitare, si voluntas mihi fuerit visitandi. Similiter et in caeteris officiis ita intelligendum est.'

[85] *Regula Benedicti* c. 67, 7: 'Similiter et qui praesumpserit claustra monasterii egredi vel quocumque ire vel quippiam quamvis parvum sine iussione abbatis facere.'

[86] Ekkehard, *Casus*, c. 47, p. 106.   [87] Ekkehard, *Casus*, cc. 134–5, pp. 262–4.

community; a powerful and efficient ruler in the outside world. Only by combining both roles could he secure the continuity of his abbey.

Recruitment

Most monks and nuns were raised within the confines of the cloister. Thus, the opposition between the inner and outer world became part of their psychological make-up as they grew up. This attitude can be observed in the letters of Boniface, who had entered a monastery when he was not yet six years old. He always preserved his distinctly monastic outlook, for he had known no other way of life.

Child oblation became the predominant gateway to monastic life in the course of the ninth century.[88] The Rule of Benedict provides a brief but influential instruction for the *oblatio puerorum*. The child was to be offered 'to God in the monastery' (*Deo in monasterio*) by his parents, within the context of Mass. Thus, the boy was offered at the altar with bread and wine, to remain in the monastery forever. All ties with his worldly possessions had to be severed, though the parents were free to make a gift to the monastery. No mention was made of a personal confirmation of the parental oblation.[89]

The chapter in the Rule of Benedict on child oblation contrasts strangely with the preceding one on the entry of adult novices. Their acceptance is treated with great circumspection. The Rule was read to them thrice over, and only after a probationary period of one year was the novice allowed to take his final vows. This divergent approach within one text has long puzzled historians, who have chosen to disregard child oblation as something relatively unimportant, and typical of the 'dark ages' of medieval monastic history.[90] This is mistaken, for the child oblates who in Benedict's time were a minority became a majority in the Carolingian age. Adult novices now were an exception rather than the rule.

This major change occurred as gradually as the diffusion of the Rule itself. In fact, the *oblatio puerorum* confirms the overall impression that the age of the *regulae mixtae* lasted for a very long time indeed. Sources from the period between 650 and 750, in which the *Regula Benedicti* progressively became an integral part of the mixed rules, give no indication of an oblation ritual performed at the altar. Surely, the idea of offering one's offspring to God

---

[88] De Jong (1986), pp. 181–90; idem (1989). About Fulda, see Schmid (1978b), pp. 582–7; Freise (1989), pp. 1018–27.   [89] *Regula Benedicti*, c. 59.

[90] Dom David Knowles expressed this widespread and understandable uneasiness when he devoted only a few pages to child oblation in his *History of the Monastic Orders in England*, deeming the phenomenon suitable to 'the early centuries or backward countries of medieval times'. Cf. Knowles (1949), pp. 9 and 418–22.

was as familiar as the story of young Samuel which served as the biblical model for child oblation. Yet there is no sign before 750 of formalised oblation ritual. Rather, the entry of young boys into monastic life was described in terms of *commendatio*. Parents informally 'commended' their sons to an individual abbot or bishop, thus ensuring their upbringing within the church, just as other sons were commended to kings and mayors of the palace, to receive their military training at court.[91] In contrast, the Rule of Benedict prescribes a more impersonal and solemn transaction, which barred any possibility of returning to the world. Indeed, ecclesiastical legislation from the mid-eighth century onwards hammered home this unpalatable truth. As Pope Gregory II already wrote to Boniface in 726, 'it is an impious (*nefas*) thing that the restraints of desire should be relaxed for children offered to God by their parents'.[92]

More legislation was to follow, for the practice of child obation became common enough to invite abuse.[93] The Council of Aachen (817) proclaimed that the oblation of a child was to be performed during the Offertory of Mass, in the presence of witnesses, stressing that the boy should confirm the parental vow once he reached the age of understanding.[94] Some monasteries indeed demanded a personal profession from the oblate at the *aetas intelligibilis*, but one should not imagine that the youth then was at liberty to make a choice between the cloister and the world outside. His confirmation of parental vows was treated as a matter of course. Some, however, begged to differ. A famous and nasty confrontation erupted in 829 between Hraban Maur, abbot of Fulda, and his former pupil Gottschalk, son of a Saxon count. Gottschalk fought to be released from Fulda and his vow on the grounds that his oblation had been unlawfully witnessed by Frankish instead of Saxon witnesses; and he accused Hraban of having forced him to comply with profession, tonsure and monastic garb.[95] At first Gottschalk seemed to be winning his case, but Hraban fought back, submitting a 'Book on Child Oblation' to Louis the Pious himself.[96] The struggle over Gottschalk's property, handed over to Fulda at his oblation, was the crux of the affair. In the end, the rebel was allowed to leave his hated abbot, but he was still a monk, while Hraban remained in full control of his inheritance.

---

[91] De Jong (1989), pp. 71–3.   [92] Boniface, *Epistolae*, no. 26, p. 46.

[93] General complaints about grasping abbots who had their eye on the newcomers' possessions must also have pertained to child oblates. Council of Frankfurt (794), c. 16, *MGH Conc.* II:1, p. 168; Council of Chalon (813), *ibid.*, p. 275; *Capitulare Ecclesiasticum* (818–19) c. 8, *MGH Cap.* I, p. 277. Cf. Semmler (1963), pp. 46–7. Specifically about child oblation: *Capitulare Ecclesiasticum* (818–19), c. 20, *MGH Cap.* I, p. 278.

[94] Council of Aachen (817) c. 17, *Legislatio Aquisgranensis*, p. 477.

[95] Freise (1978), pp. 1021–9; Rädle (1980).

[96] Hraban Maur, *Liber de Oblatione Puerorum*, PL 107, cols. 419–40.

Hraban and Gottschalk were to cross swords once more in 848–51, when Gottschalk was cruelly punished for his heterodox views on predestination.[97]

Complaints were voiced that 'all too often' (*frequentissime*) oblates tried to leave monastic life.[98] A certain drop-out rate should be taken into account, and it may indeed have had interesting consequences for the transmission of literate skills from monasteries to the outside world.[99] On the other hand, Gottschalk was an exceptionally strong personality. For many ordinary oblates the monastery where they were raised became 'our nest', the world they knew and trusted.[100] They had left their families as soon as they could walk and talk; what did the world outside mean to them? In his letters, Alcuin praised the 'maternal affection' of the brothers of York who had educated him, expressing his desire to be buried in the place where he had been raised.[101] His hagiographer described him as a young child, being transferred from his mother's carnal breasts to the church's spiritual ones – a revealing metaphor.[102]

Some quantitative data illustrate the predominance of child oblates in the ninth century. In St Rémi at Rheims, when Archbishop Hincmar (845–81) was abbot, all newcomers were registered; their oblation or profession charters were entered in full into a book. The remaining fragments yield thirty-seven child oblates as against only one adult novice.[103] The *Liber Memorialis* of the royal nunnery of San Salvatore/Santa Giulia in Brescia contains a list of forty-one oblates offered between *c.* 837 and 848; this *notitia* was drawn up on the occasion of the oblation of Gisela, the daughter of Lothar I. Comparison with a list of nuns living in San Salvatore around 850 shows only fourteen names that do not figure in the *notitia* of 848. Of these, some may have been former child oblates as well, who had entered San Salvatore before 837 and were still alive in 850.[104] There was thus an overwhelming presence of child oblates at San Salvatore, though admittedly their numbers were swelled thanks to the staggering generosity of one Radaldus, who donated no less than seven daughters to the nunnery.[105]

Such an act raises a persistent question: was child oblation a means of ridding oneself of superfluous children, especially of daughters? Radaldus may have been a case in point, but generally this approach does not

---

[97] Ganz (1990a).   [98] Smaragdus, *Expositio*, c. 59, p. 301.

[99] McKitterick (1989), pp. 216–23.

[100] Ekkehard, *Casus*, c. 5, p. 24 ('intima nostra') and c. 75, p. 156 ('nidus noster'); both expressions refer to the *claustrum*.   [101] Alcuin, *Epistolae*, no. 42, pp. 85–6.

[102] *Vita Alcuini* c. 2, p. 185: 'qui cum matris ablactaretur carnalibus, ecclesiae traditur misticis imbuendis uberibus.'

[103] BN lat. 13090, fols. 72–77b; de Jong (1986), pp. 90–4; Stratmann (1991), pp. 72–8.

[104] Becher (1983), pp. 303–5.   [105] Becher (1983), pp. 304–5, no. 25–31.

correspond with reality as far as it can be observed in sources of this period. Oblation was as important in male as in female communities: the biographies of leading churchmen speak for themselves. Willibrord, Boniface, Alcuin, Hraban Maur, Hincmar: they all started their life in the cloister at an early age. The rich material of Fulda shows that between 826 and 835 this abbey recruited some 100 to 130 very young monks.[106] Narrative sources concerning Fulda yield many *pueri nutriti*, but only two monks who entered the abbey as adults (*conversi*).[107] No wonder that magister Hraban Maur complained that all his time was taken by the caring for 'the little ones' (*parvuli*).[108] The substantial gift to the monastery required of parents, moreover, made the dumping of an unwanted child a rather expensive affair. In Carolingian times, the optional gift of the parents (*eleemosyna*) mentioned by Benedict had become the total inheritance of the child.[109] So it was no mere rhetoric when Hraban denounced Gottschalk and his associates as opponents of monastic life itself.[110] Child oblation was the lifeline of monasteries, providing recruits as well as property. Thus, economic considerations neatly coincided with religious ones.[111]

Thus it is not surprising that the anonymous monk who reported back home on the Aachen Council of 816, spoke of his community as 'we, who have lived this kind of life virtually from our cradle, instructed by our elders'.[112] It would be a mistake, however, to regard all those reared within the monastic confines as child oblates in the strict sense of the word. The anonymous monk mentioned two categories of newcomers in his monastery about which the council had not yet taken a decision: priests and *scholastici*.[113] The latter category must have included child oblates as well as others, for one year later the Aachen reformers came to a decision, banning all except *pueri oblati* from monastic schools.[114] From what our anonymous reporter has to say about the education of the *scholastici*, it is clear that they were trained for a life as an intellectual elite, within the church. They had to speak Latin at all times, and proceeded from basic education – psalms, hymns and the Rule – to Scripture, patristic writing and saints' Lives, whereas lay adults who converted to monastic life could restrict themselves

---

[106] Schmid and Althoff (1980), pp. 211–15; Schmid (1978a), pp. 116–17.

[107] Freise (1978), pp. 1018–19.   [108] Hraban Maur, *Epistolae*, no. 5, p. 389.

[109] Smaragdus, *Expositio*, c. 59, p. 300; Hildemar, *Expositio*, c. 59, p. 550. The latter gave the parents two options: either completely disinheriting the child, or handing over his inheritance (*portio eius*) to the monastery.   [110] Hraban Maur, *Liber de Oblatione Puerorum*, cols. 437–40.

[111] De Jong (1986; 1989).

[112] *Statuta Murbacensia, Legislatio Aquisgranensis*, p. 442: 'Nos vere qui ab ipsis pene cunabilis a maioribus nostris eruditi in eadem dispositione viximus'.

[113] *Statuta Murbacensia*, c. 20, *Legislatio Aquisgranensis*, p. 447.

[114] Council of Aachen (817), c. 5, *Legislatio Aquisgranensis*, p. 474.

to the Lord's Prayer, the Creed, the penitential psalms and, if they were able to, the whole Psalter.[115]

In so far as the *scholastici* were not child oblates, they must have been mostly young clerics. Their presence in the monasteries is manifest in many sources, also in those dating from after the 817 prohibition. It has already become clear that Hildemar considered canonical clergy living within a monastic community as nothing out of the ordinary. He was not alone in this, for a letter from St Gall of 887 mentions Waldo, who had 'applied himself under the strictest discipline and supervision to literary study and the principles of monastic life'; he had done so as a *clericus*, and was sent for further training to the bishop of Augsburg.[116] And the *clericus* Gundram, nephew of Hraban Maur was brought up in Fulda, and from there he went to the court. Only at a later age did Gundram become a priest as well as a monk of Fulda.[117] Obviously, in spite of the prohibition of 817, monasteries remained a preferred training ground, also for the secular clergy. Some went elsewhere, while others opted for monastic life. Given the fact that their education was no different from that of oblates, many might indeed have stayed on as monks. The famous 'external school' of the Plan of St Gall, a bone of contention since the last century, may simply have been intended for the use of all *scholastici*, oblates and clerics alike, plus the occasional lay boy.[118] After all, the Plan's author called it the 'common house of the school' (*domus communis scolae*).

Discipline

Carolingian monks and nuns living under the Rule of Benedict promised obedience first and foremost. Although the additional third part of the profession (*conversio*, or rather *conversatio morum*) became more common in the ninth century, this triple formula did not render older forms obsolete.[119] Given the fact that most vows were made by parents or relatives on behalf of very young children, a profession formula referring to a change from a secular to a monastic way of life would not have made much sense anyway. Obedience to the abbot did, however, and so did stability. Early medieval

---

[115] *Statuta Murbacensia*, c. 2, *Legislatio Aquisgranensis*, p. 442. Cf. the epilogue, p. 449, which mentions Latin as the language for the *scholastici* on a day-to-day basis: 'Usum latinitatis potius quam rusticitatis qui inter eos scolastici sunt sequuntur.'

[116] *Collectio Sangallensis*, no. 24, *MGH Form.* pp. 409–10: 'sub artissima disciplina et custodia litterarum monasterialibusque rudimentis insistens'.

[117] Ermanricus, *Sermo de Vita Sualonis*, c. 10, p. 161; Sandmann (1978), p. 761.

[118] De Jong (1986), pp. 165–75; Hildebrandt (1991), pp. 99–107.

[119] Leclercq (1971); Constable (1987), p. 785.

relations between abbots and their monks have been compared to those between a lord and his followers.[120] Personal loyalty pervaded the concept of obedience. For those who became monks at a later age after a military life, this may indeed have been the case. Hildemar counted on adult novices who generally came from the arms-bearing classes, for he prescribed a profession ritual entailing a deposition of arms onto the altar, after only two months.[121] This profession was binding, but much instruction was yet to follow, most of all in the art of humility.

Humility was the stuff that Benedictine monasticism was made of, for it represented the complete antithesis of aristocratic life outside the cloister. The Rule elaborates the twelve stages of humility, of which obedience forms an integral part. A proper monk had to obey his superiors in all matters, no longer had a will of his own and remained obedient even in the face of unjust demands.[122] As Benedict's chapter on profession has it, he was no longer his own man.[123] This must have been a difficult proposition for adult novices, especially for the aristocrats among them. Therefore, monastic authors doubted whether these adults would ever make good monks, some frankly preferring child oblates. Garrulous Hildemar was the most outspoken in this preference.[124] His elaborate system of *custodia et disciplina* aimed at moulding young boys into perfect monks. Three to four masters were responsible for guarding the children at all times, leaving them no opportunity for sin. They were to be strictly supervised at school, during meals, in the bathroom and in the dormitory. Once a month they were allowed to play, again within sight of their masters. Supervision would surely have been more lax at times, and some as Gottschalk did must have rebelled. With the large majority, however, the strategy of constant *custodia* must have worked.

A long training in monastic discipline was to mould the minds and actions of the monks. According to the Rule, the height of humility is reached,

when the monk is not only humble at heart, but when he also makes this always visible to onlookers through his external behaviour, which means that during the *Opus Dei*, in the Oratory, in the monastery, in the garden, on the road, on the land, or where he sits or walks or stands, he should always keep his head bowed and his eyes directed downwards.[125]

---

[120] Frank (1951), pp. 107–11; Constable (1987), p. 788–9.

[121] Hildemar, *Expositio*, c. 58, pp. 537–8.   [122] *Regula Benedicti*, c. 68.

[123] *Regula Benedicti*, c. 58, 25: 'quippe qui ex illo die nec proprii corporis potestatum se habituro scit'.

[124] De Jong (1983), esp. pp. 122–3.

[125] *Regula Benedicti*, c. 7, 62–3: 'Duodecimus humilitatis gradus est si non solum corde monachus sed etiam ipso corpore humilitatem videntibus se semper indicet, id est in opere Dei, in oratorio, in monasterio, in horto, in via, in agro, vel ubicumque sedens, ambulans vel stans, inclinato sit semper capite, defixis in terram aspectibus.'

Physical behaviour was regarded as a necessary expression of an internal
state and even as its most perfect reflection. Hildemar warned monks who
had to prune vines above their heads to be extra humble while standing on
their toes.[126] It would be a mistake to deem this one more instance of
'ritualistic' early medieval monasticism. In a world in which cloister and
outside world were so intimately connected, an internal *claustrum* which was
implanted from childhood might be the best guarantee for keeping the
boundaries around the community intact.

The small-scale organisation that Benedict had experienced and for which
he wrote, with its moderate balance between prayer and work, had vanished
in the ninth century. The overall picture is that of large monasteries. This
holds true for the whole of the Carolingian empire, including northern Italy.
The convent of Remiremont was a community of a little over eighty nuns in
the first half of the ninth century;[127] St Riquier, however, counted some 300
monks at the same time, and 100 boys who were brought up to be monks.[128]
The size of Fulda was even more astounding: under abbot Hraban Maur in
825/6 a list of over 600 *fratres* of Fulda was entered into the confraternity
book of Reichenau.[129] Specialisation was unavoidable in such a situation,
and Hildemar's commentary bears witness to this. Numerous masters
minded the children, others supervised work on the estates, toiled in the
garden, assisted in the kitchen and at the porter's lodge, received the guests
and cared for the sick. Every department had its specialist, from the
scriptorium to the stables. Inside the *claustrum*, the monks seem to have
carried out the household chores. Outside, however, they served more as
supervisors than as manual workers. Here lay servants, members of the
monastic *familia*, did the hard work.[130]

In ninth-century Fulda, not all monks lived in the central cloister. This
was mainly the habitat of the old and the young, while those in the prime of
life served in the numerous monastic outposts (*cellae*), for purposes of estate
management.[131] The ambitious Abbot Ratger almost brought ruin to his
prosperous community by forcing it to build a large church, 'an immense
and superfluous building', as disapproving monks called it.[132] Laymen were
enlisted for household chores and the supervision of monastic property,
while liturgical services were shortened and the monks of Fulda were
converted into an army of reluctant builders. The community suffered acute

---

[126] Hildemar, *Expositio*, c. 7, p. 286.   [127] Hlawitschka (1978), pp. 38–9.
[128] Angilbert, *Institutio*, praefatio, p. 291.   [129] Schmid (1978b), pp. 588–97.
[130] About the *familia* and their activities: Kuchenbuch (1978), pp. 343–6; Schwind (1984);
Weidinger (1991).   [131] Schmid (1978b), pp. 587–8.
[132] *Supplex Libellus*, c. 12, p. 324: 'Ut aedificia immensa atque superflua et cetera inutilia opera
omittantur.'

distress, aggravated by an epidemic in 806 which claimed many victims among the exhausted monks. In 812 their patience finally ran out, and Ratger's opposition sought the support of the emperor himself. The petition (*Supplex Libellus*) they offered to Charlemagne in 812 demanded that the management of the mill, the garden, the kitchen and agriculture should be restored to the hands of the monks.[133] The *Supplex Libellus* is extremely instructive, for it shows what standards had been in Fulda until Ratger took over. Revealing details, such as the request that the elderly monks should once more be allowed to use staffs and hassocks, suggest that he indeed deserved the name of tyrant.[134] But in spite of the material hardship they had suffered at their tyrant's hands, the monks of Fulda suffered most keenly from forced neglect of their liturgical duties. The bulk of their grievances was concerned with what they felt to be their primary responsibility: prayer.

Communities of prayer

The monks of Fulda demanded a restoration of the liturgical practice customary before Ratger's time. This practice entailed substantial obligations, such as daily prayer for the ruler, his children and the entire Christian people (*populus christianus*); prayer for all living benefactors each Monday; a commemoration of all deceased brothers, twice a day, and for the same a vigil and fifty psalms each month; and an annual vigil and a Psalter for Abbot Sturm and the founders of Fulda on their anniversary. In addition, they requested that priests be given the opportunity to celebrate Mass more often, as they had done previously, and that the major saints' days be yet again honoured with traditional Masses and vigils.[135]

It is clear that liturgical activity had greatly increased, certainly in comparison with the days of Benedict.[136] The *Supplex Libellus* reflects a changed reality, in which priests played a key role. They were indeed numerous in Fulda, as well as in other abbeys. If one includes subdeacons, 70% of the monks during the abbacy of Hraban were of clerical rank – and of those monks who were still in minor orders, many were destined to be ordained when they were old enough.[137] The lay monastic community of late antiquity had become one of monks in holy orders by the ninth century.

---

[133] *Supplex Libellus*, c. 16, p. 325; Semmler (1958).
[134] *Supplex Libellus*, c. 5, p. 323; tyrant: *ibid*, c. 20, p. 327.
[135] *Supplex Libellus*, cc. 1–3, pp. 321–2; Oexle (1978b), pp. 140–50. However, celebration of Mass did not yet play a central role in the commemoration of the dead; cf. Angenendt (1983), p. 206.
[136] Angenendt (1990a), pp. 401–2. See also Nussbaum (1961), pp. 77–90; Haüssling (1973), pp. 298–347.   [137] Schmid (1978b), pp. 592–7; Schmid (1982), p. 133.

And as their numbers rose, so did the number of altars in the churches.[138] The Plan of St Gall mentions nineteen altars in the main church alone.

Various factors contributed to this process. Certainly the increasing missionary and pastoral activity of monks played a part.[139] But the determining influence was the perception of prayer in general and Mass in particular, which was shared by religious and laity alike. It was widely believed that a Mass could be a gift to God: to express gratitude, to beg for assistance or to placate impending wrath. A glance at Carolingian sacramentaries, many of them originating from monasteries, shows immediately that there were Masses for all purposes, from warding off bad weather to safeguarding a traveller. The central ritual of the church had become a gift (*munus*), for which a counter-gift (*remuneratio*) was to be expected.[140]

The proliferation of votive Masses (*missae speciales*) was such that they tended to distract the attention of the faithful from the communal Mass (*missa publica*).[141] This development was inevitable, since the laity had a vested interest in such Masses. Penitential practice had flourished on the Continent since Irish and Anglo-Saxon monks had introduced private penance; having Masses said or Psalters sung had become one way of fulfilling one's penitential obligations. Conversion tables were drawn up to calculate the exact relation between alms and prayer. One *solidus* represented two Masses or one hundred psalms, ten *solidi* could substitute for six Masses or six Psalters, and twenty *solidi* represented twelve Masses or twelve Psalters.[142] Amalarius of Metz neatly summed up the penitential aspect of Mass: 'All these sacrifices have been offered by the priest as well as by the people, so that the Almighty God will not count our sins.'[143]

The load of this increased demand for prayer fell onto the shoulders of monks and canons. Unlike the ordinary village priests, they had the time and liberty to devote themselves to these duties, provided they did not have Ratger of Fulda as an abbot. More importantly, unlike village priests, monks and canons lived in ascetic communities and therefore were reliable mediators between God and mankind. Whoever dared to approach the 'terrible sacraments' in a state of impurity could not perform an effective sacrifice, and also ran the risk of illness and even death; such at least was the moral of miracle stories.[144] On the road to monastic priesthood, child

---

[138] Häussling (1973).   [139] Vogel (1980; 1981); Constable (1982).

[140] Angenendt (1983), esp. pp. 181–3; Angenendt (1990a), pp. 331–4. Amalarius of Metz opposed *munera* to *dona*; while the former would lead to a remuneration, the latter were freely given, without expectation of reward. Amalarius, *Expositio*, c. 27, p. 306.

[141] Angenendt (1983), p. 179.   [142] Angenendt (1984b), pp. 143–50.

[143] Amalarius, *Expositio*, c. 55, p. 322: 'Haec omnia sacrificia ideo sunt offerta, tam a sacerdote tam a populo, ut omnipotens Deus peccata nostra non reputet.'

[144] Notker, *Gesta Karoli*, c. 25; cf. Angenendt (1978/9), pp. 39–40; Angenendt (1990a), pp. 345–6.

oblates had a decided advantage over adult *conversi*, for they became literate early on, which was a prerequisite for priesthood. Moreover, they embodied the ritual purity demanded of true mediators. As Alcuin wrote of Willibrord: 'he was taken to Ripon right after having been weaned, and grew up there seeing and hearing nothing but good and saintly things'.[145]

Not all shared an identical burden of prayer. Customs varied, and of course women could not say Mass. But women did participate in all other duties such as singing of psalms and other prayers pertaining to the Office. In the *Liber Memorialis* of Remiremont the names of founders, abbesses, kings and the dead sisters were recorded for commemoration.[146] Prayer for one's own dead was of primary importance, especially for founders and abbots/abbesses. In Fulda, the cult of the dead seems to have gained a particular momentum; Annals of the Dead were kept there from 779 onwards, to be continued up to the eleventh century.[147] But the commemoration of the living required intensive activity as well. In the second half of the eighth century, so-called confraternities of prayer began developing. At first, these were restricted to abbots and bishops, although their communities were also mobilised to prayer and thus took part. Most famous is the agreement (*conventum*) of the Synod of Attigny in 762. The bishops and abbots present promised to have one hundred Psalters sung and one hundred Masses read for each other in the event of death. In addition, thirty Masses were to be said by participants personally.[148]

Until well into the ninth century, the confraternities of prayer were predominantly an internal affair for religious communities. Rulers excepted, the laity did not participate. Several Carolingian 'memorial books' (*libri memoriales*), also called 'books of life' (*libri vitae*), are still extant. Among those, the Reichenau confraternity book is certainly the most spectacular. When it was first conceived – probably *c*. 824 – no less than fifty monasteries with the names of dead and living brothers and sisters were entered.[149] The organisation behind such large volumes must have been stupendous. The lists of names are a treasure trove for the social historian, even more so from the late ninth century onwards, when the laity increasingly had their names inscribed. A veritable network of prayer spanned the Carolingian empire. Traditionally, the Anglo-Saxon missionaries were held to be the creative force behind liturgical commemoration, but this view does not stand up to

---

[145] Alcuin, *Vita Willibrordi*, c. 3, p. 186.

[146] Schmid and Oexle (1974), pp. 79–80; Jakobi (1986).

[147] Oexle (1978b).

[148] *MGH Conc.* II:1, pp. 72–3; Schmid and Oexle (1974), esp. pp. 85–6.

[149] Edited as *Das Verbrüderungsbuch der Abtei Reichenau: Einleitung, Register, Faksimile*, eds. J. Authenrieth, D. Geuenich and K. Schmid, *MGH Lib. Mem.* I; cf. Schmid (1977), pp. 24–8.

close scrutiny. Rather, the phenomenon was a legacy of late antiquity to which Anglo-Saxons and Franks were both heirs.[150]

It is no coincidence that the first networks of prayer developed in the very area and period which saw the consolidation of Carolingian power.[151] The authority of this dynasty was founded on prayer as well as on military might. Rulers and their families were the first of the laity to have their names recorded in the books of life, and special prayers were devoted to them. Those abbeys that gained the status of 'royal' under the Carolingians owed the king prayer first and foremost. And at times of crisis, kings made the prayer mills turn faster. The Annals of Fulda recorded the disastrous year of 874, when an exceptionally cold winter claimed many human and animal victims. King Louis the German anxiously conferred with his counsellors on 'concord and the state of the realm' (de concordia et statu regni), and devoted himself to prayer during Lent. Then, one night, he had a vision of his dead father, Louis the Pious, who addressed him – in Latin! – from the hereafter to tell him how much he was tormented, and how badly he needed the assistance of prayer to gain eternal life. The shocked king immediately sent out letters to all monasteries of the realm, requesting them to intervene with God for his father's soul.[152] Ultimately, the bad winter was interpreted as a punishment for the failure to pray for the dead emperor.

This spirit of penance and prayer was at the very heart of monastic identity, as Fulda's crisis of 812 amply shows. The Aachen councils of 816/17 aimed at safeguarding and restoring liturgical duties: prayer had to be welded into a unified and forceful endeavour. The claustrum was to protect the inner world of prayer. The ousting of Ratger in 817 and the restoration of the old order were closely connected with the Aachen reforms, which were now fervently embraced in Fulda. The presence of the names of reform-minded abbots in the first layout of Reichenau's confraternity book also shows an intimate link between intensified prayer and reform.[153] This is understandable, for both stemmed from the same root. A feeling of crisis seems to have been the catalyst for the large-scale confraternity of prayer at Reichenau. It was eloquently voiced in the vision of Wetti. This vision was recorded from the monk's mouth shortly before he died on 4 November 824.[154] It expresses deep anxiety in the face of impending death. Have I failed in my duties, and have I done sufficient penance? Wetti wrote to ten brothers in particular, requesting them to commemorate him with one hundred

---

[150] Schmid and Oexle (1974), p. 75; Gerchow (1988), pp. 7–16.
[151] Schmid and Oexle (1974), pp. 94–5.   [152] Annales Fuldenses s.a. 874, p. 94.
[153] Geuenich (1989).
[154] Haito of Reichenau, Visio Wettini; Walahfrid Strabo, Visio Wettini. Cf. Traill (1974); Schmid (1977).

psalms and one hundred Masses.[155] His vision reminded its readers of their task of commemorating the dead, and hammered home that those neglecting this duty would be punished for this in the hereafter.[156]

In short, the need for monastic prayer was clear to monks and rulers alike. This was the pre-eminent function of 'royal abbeys'. They were indispensable to the common prosperity and salvation of the religious communities, but even more of those outside, who had entrusted monks and nuns with the task of intercession. Between 700 and 900, monasteries became veritable powerhouses of prayer. They were part of the Carolingian order, which was built on the ideal of harmony between God and his Chosen People, the Franks.

The strong bond between kings and abbeys started to disintegrate in the last decades of the ninth century, especially in the West Frankish kingdom and in Lotharingia. The history of Lobbes is yet again illuminating. From 864, the monastery was ruled by a number of lay abbots, who were all members of the Carolingian family. Lobbes' status as a royal abbey came to an end in 881/2, when Bishop Franco of Liège received Lobbes as a benefice, probably as a reward for his energetic resistance against Viking attacks. This personal union between episcopacy and abbacy was institutionalised in 889 by Arnulf of Carinthia. Until 957, the bishop of Liège remained the rightful abbot of Lobbes, enjoying the benefits of the *mensa abbatis*.[157] An abbey that had been a mainstay of Carolingian authority was now taken over by the bishops of Liège – and by local aristocrats gaining control over the episcopal office. Folcuin described the abbacy of Bishop Balderic (954–7) as an all-time low in the history of his abbey. Lobbes was attacked by the Magyars, and its immunity was violated by Balderic's uncle, Régnier III, count of Hainault. He went so far as to pursue an enemy into the monastery, finally decapitating him in the *atrium* of the church of Notre-Dame.[158] Together with his spouse and Bishop Balderic, the count celebrated a sacrilegious Christmas within the cloister, desecrating the holiest places of Lobbes' inner sanctuary: he lodged in the sacristy, and used the table where the host was kept as a storage cupboard for shoes and dishes.[159] On top of all this, he replaced the duly chosen *praepositus* of Lobbes by his favourite, Erluin, who was a first abbot

---

[155] Walahfrid, *Visio Wettini*, pp. 332–3, lines 912–30; Traill (1974), p. 206.
[156] Walahfrid, *Visio Wettini*, p. 318, lines 430–4.   [157] Dierkens (1985), pp. 111–13.
[158] Folcuin, *Gesta Abbatum Lobiensium*, c. 26, p. 68.
[159] Folcuin, *Gesta Abbatum Lobiensium*, c. 26, p. 68: 'Nam comes cum coniuge in sacrario ecclesiae mansitabat, et mensa, qua sacratissimum Domini corpus absumebatur, ministerium calciamentorum et paterarum seu scutellarum efficiebatur.'

of Gembloux. From the very beginning, the monks of Lobbes hated their new leader. When he was promoted to abbot and chased a large part of the recalcitrant monks from Lobbes, the latter retaliated. Three of them entered the dormitory at night and lifted Erluin from his bed; once outside the cloister, they blinded him and cut off part of his tongue, before sending him on his way back to Gembloux.[160]

The disappearance of the Carolingian order severely affected monastic life, materially as well as spiritually. Ecclesiastical institutions and their wealth bore the brunt of Viking and Magyar raids. Monastic authors may have exaggerated the general impact of the attacks, but undoubtedly their own communities suffered heavily. On Epiphany of 882, Prüm was set ablaze by Vikings. According to Regino, the defence of the monastery was left to 'ignoble folk' (*ignobile vulgus*) who were armed, but lacked military training; they were slaughtered like animals.[161] Ten years later, the abbot and monks had to flee from Prüm again, barely escaping yet another Viking raid. Understandably, monastic discipline suffered in such turbulent times. Shortly after the onslaught of 892, a crisis over the abbacy broke out. Regino replaced the abbot that had fled, but only managed to hang on to the office for seven years. Two local counts forced him out and gave the abbacy to their brother.[162] External attack easily led to internal disruption, for monastic discipline was dependent on the *claustrum* remaining intact. When a fire destroyed St Gall in 937, lack of discipline was the immediate result; monks wandered freely outside the cloister, and some 'threw off their yoke and fled'.[163] The physical and the mental *claustrum* were closely connected; hence, its violation could have long-term and traumatic effects on monastic communities. This partly explains the so-called 'exaggerated' reaction of monastic authors to Viking and Magyar raids.

In spite of all this turbulence, which deeply affected the *vita communis*, it should be kept in mind that the tenth century witnessed yet another wave of monastic reform. In the German realm, concern for monastic discipline remained very much a royal prerogative. Kings made it their business to go on personal visits of inspection within the *claustrum*; in St Gall, tales were told about Otto I testing discipline in the choir by throwing his staff on the floor, being overjoyed that none of the monks batted an eyelid.[164] Elsewhere, bishops and lay aristocrats instead of kings took the lead. They built on Carolingian traditions, not only because they drew upon the Aachen

---

[160] Dierkens (1985) pp. 117–19; Folcuin, *Gesta Abbatum Lobiensium*, c. 26, pp. 68–9.

[161] Regino, *Chronicon* (882), pp. 260–2.

[162] Regino, *Chronicon* (892), pp. 294–6. Regino's angry tale about this was originally in his *Chronicon*, but is missing in all extant manuscripts. It therefore seems to have been erased from the original.

[163] Ekkehard, *Casus*, c. 68, p. 144.   [164] Ekkehard, *Casus*, c. 146, p. 282.

reforms as a source of inspiration,[165] but also in that they considered monastic reform the hallmark of a proper ruler. Once counts and dukes consolidated their power, they set about reforming monasteries or lending their support to reform.

Even Folcuin's scapegoat Régnier may have aspired to reform Lobbes, thus enhancing his authority. It was he who brought the hated Erluin from Gembloux to Lobbes. The monks wanted no part of this stranger and considered him a tyrant, a point of view which Folcuin shared completely. Yet, the tradition of Gembloux sheds a very different light on Erluin. Here, he was remembered as a dedicated and exemplary reform abbot.[166] Probably Lobbes was put in Erluin's charge by a count who had monastic reform in mind, as befitted a true ruler. But Régnier's precarious hold on power was broken by the Ottonians; in 958, the new duke of Lotharingia – Archbishop Bruno of Cologne – chased him into exile. Given Folcuin's loyalty to everything Ottonian, it is likely that his malicious account of Erluin was coloured by the latter's close association with Régnier. The unfortunate reformer simply had the wrong backer: one who was not royal. Erluin's successor Aletran was from Gembloux as well, but he went down in the history of Lobbes as the abbot who restored monastic life, ensuring independence and wealth for the abbey. He did so with the full support of Archbishop Bruno, the king's brother, which may account for his popularity with the historiographers of Lobbes. Were Erluin's aims so very different from those of Aletran? It seems as if the impatient reformer clashed head-on with a proud royal abbey and its Carolingian past, which was still very much alive in the tenth century.

---

[165] Semmler (1989a), pp. 29–50.
[166] Sigebert, *Gesta abbatum Gemblacensium*, c. 13, p. 530: 'qui etiam martyrium pro Dei amore subire erat paratus'.

CHAPTER 24

RELIGION AND LAY SOCIETY

Julia M.H. Smith

DOMINATED by the establishment of the Carolingian empire and the extension of its political and religious influence beyond the imperial frontiers, the centuries from 700 to 900 witnessed a vigorous effort by ecclesiastical authorities to transform the religious life of the laity. Influenced by ideals originating in monastic and missionary circles, ideologues at the Carolingian court set out to establish a comprehensive code of conduct for the laity and a firm place for them within the Christian church. Reformers concentrated on encouraging education in the basic tenets of Christian doctrine, channelling lay people's spiritual needs into directions approved by the upper echelons of the clerical hierarchy and imposing a Christian moral code formulated for those in secular occupations. In so doing, clergy (often themselves from a monastic background) encountered beliefs, practices and social customs of which they disapproved. From lay people's point of view, the rituals of the Christian church in which they were encouraged – or coerced – to participate were often only one of a number of possible ways of making sense of the world, placating its hostile forces and ensuring social harmony. When men and women did follow preachers' exhortations, they may have seen a significance in their actions that differed from what the clergy hoped to inculcate. The religion of lay society *c.* 700– 900 by no means always conformed to the ideal which the ecclesiastical establishment struggled to impart.

Young and old, male and female, rich and poor, lord and slave, illiterate and learned, the laity constituted the vast majority of Christians. With the exception of kings and queens (for the most part excluded from this discussion), the activities and beliefs of lay men and women have usually left little direct trace. With the single exception of the enchiridion of spiritual advice written for her son in 843 by the Frankish noblewoman Dhuoda, a work as remarkable in its survival as in its composition, no lay person has left us an authorial account of his or her own life and beliefs. Dhuoda apart, we have to reconstruct the religion of the laity from fragmented information in many different sources, whose male authors were usually members of the clerical or monastic elite. None of these texts offers a simply descriptive position. Sometimes the perspective is exemplary, in the form of accounts of good deeds to be emulated or bad conduct to be shunned. More often it is hortatory, such as sermons or handbooks of moral instruction written by clerics for lay recipients. It may even be prescriptive: legislated norms of appropriate conduct and belief, promulgated by kings acting in consultation with their religious advisers, by church councils or by individual bishops. In reading these sources, we run hard up against the predilection of all early medieval writers for drawing both inspiration and the form of words from earlier authors. The dominant patterns of thought might blunt an author's sensitivity to many of the social realities of their day. Carolingian moralists often tell us much more about how the laity ought to behave than about what they were actually doing and thinking. To offer hypotheses about lay religion, we must proceed by assembling fragmentary evidence, and penetrate the rhetoric of reform to reconstruct underlying patterns of human behaviour.

In exploring the religion of the eighth and ninth centuries, we inevitably explore its society too. The vocabulary of the period makes this clear, for *Christianitas* meant the Christian faith, the way of living which it entailed, and the area within which Christianity was professed. When the Bulgars began to convert in the middle years of the ninth century, the comprehensive nature of their new faith became abundantly clear. Confused by the competing efforts of both Greek and Roman missionaries, they wrote to Pope Nicholas I in 866. His precise answers to their 106 questions gave instruction on everything from prayer, sexual ethics and days of fasting to those days on which it was permissible to bathe, whether it was permissible to carry a horse's tail into battle as a standard, and why hunting was banned during Lent.[1] As propounded by Carolingian moralists and missionaries, *Christianitas* embraced all aspects of human existence from bedchamber to battlefield and from church to farmyard. It left no room for secularity; its only antithesis was paganism.

Early medieval confessors were urged to pay heed to 'the qualities of times and persons, of places and ages' whenever they administered penance.[2] This essay will do the same. Distinctions of time – of changing religious practices over the course of these two centuries – have been particularly prominent in discussions of the gradual process of Christianisation which

---

[1] *MGH Epp.* vi, pp. 568–600; Sullivan (1966).

[2] For example, the Council of Worms (868), c. 25, 'Temporum etiam et personarum, locorum quoque et aetatum qualitates inspicere', Mansi xv, p. 873.

followed upon the formal adoption of Christianity by early medieval peoples. Distinctions of place have long been apparent in the contrasts between religious organisation and forms of spirituality which characterise Ireland as opposed to Anglo-Saxon England or Gaul. More recently, historians have placed much emphasis on the regional variations in the liturgy, saints' cults, penitential practices and cultural life of the Frankish lands, even in the heyday of Carolingian court culture. Much less attention has been paid to distinctions of persons and ages. To remedy this deficiency becomes a particular theme of this chapter. In the paragraphs which follow, differentiations of religious experience by gender and by status will be pointed out repeatedly. The religion of the laity was as variegated as lay society itself.

BAPTISM AND COMMUNITY

In surveying the religion of Europe over two centuries of pervasive change, we may well ask what the religion of the urban population of, say, early medieval Milan had in common with that of the new converts in Charlemagne's Saxony. Baptism provides an answer. This rite of Christian initiation identified membership of Christendom; indeed, both the Old English and the Old Welsh words for baptism (OE *fulwiht*, OW *bedydd*) served on occasion as synonyms for *Christianitas*.[3] From the reign of Charlemagne onwards, if not from the conversion in the 680s of the last pagan Anglo-Saxon kingdom, that of the South Saxons, it is safe to say that 'kingship and christening manifestly went together'.[4]

Baptism distinguished Christians from non-Christians, the *fideles* from the *pagani*. Within Christendom, it was shared by everyone without regard for distinction of gender, status or occupation. Nevertheless, individuals' experience of baptism will have varied greatly, for even in Charlemagne's empire, liturgical uniformity was an ideal rather than a reality. By 700, the early Christian rite of initiation for adults had long since been adapted to accommodate a society in which everyone was baptised as an infant, though the missionary activity on the northern and eastern frontiers of Europe led Alcuin (*c.* 730–804) in particular to reflect upon the appropriate rite for new, adult converts.[5] Except at a synod convened on the Danube in 796 to organise missionary work among the Avars, Anglo-Saxon and Frankish legislation concerned itself with the appropriate form of baptism for infants or, in cases of urgent necessity, for the dying. Most is known about the liturgy for infant baptism, and even in this regard, the rituals in use lacked

---

[3] Pryce (1992), p. 42; Foot (1992), p. 191.   [4] Van Engen (1991), p. 23.
[5] *MGH Epp.* IV, nos. 111, 113, pp. 159–62, 163–6.

uniformity, and indeed changed considerably in the two centuries under discussion here. In the Carolingian lands north of the Alps, the spread of the Roman rite from the early eighth century onwards introduced a dominant theme on which local variations were numerous. But in the north Italian dioceses within the province of Milan and in Ireland and Anglo-Saxon England (so far as extremely scanty evidence permits us to say), non-Roman rites remained in use. Within the area of Carolingian liturgical change and experimentation, a further tendency reinforced the various local forms of the ritual which people underwent, namely the tendency to compress into a single ceremony a ritual whose full form was intended to be spread out over the entire period of Lent. Nevertheless, underlying the varying liturgical details was a common fundamental structure: baptism everywhere meant an initiation process comprising instruction, exorcism, immersion in or aspersion with water, usually ending with episcopal confirmation and the celebration of Mass.[6]

What did baptism involve for the family of the young infant? In Wessex, laws issued by Ine in 693 fined parents if their child was not baptised within thirty days of birth; if the child died without baptism, they were fined everything they owned.[7] Carolingian clergy, on the other hand, tried to restore the ancient custom of baptising only at Easter or Pentecost, and restricted the rite to baptismal churches under episcopal control, that is, those churches whose clergy enjoyed the right to collect the chrism from the bishop. The intention was to baptise infants at the first Easter or Pentecost after birth, when they were not yet weaned but were still *parvuli lactantes*.[8] Many parents, Charlemagne included, ignored this. When Hadrian I baptised the king's son Pippin, at the Easter service in Rome in 781, the boy was already aged four or five. Dhuoda implies that her second son, born on 22 March 841, had not yet been baptised by the time she started writing her handbook of spiritual advice for her elder son, commenced on 30 November in the same year.[9] The Franks were not subject to the same harsh penalty for tardiness that Ine had decreed in Wessex.

Taking a baby for baptism could involve many journeys, sometimes over considerable distances, for not every place of worship could be used for the rite. Those parents living within the shadow of the urban cathedral of Milan would have only needed to carry their child a short walk around the block. The 'Troyes Anonymous', an unidentified bishop writing within the province of Sens in 812, reminds us that, within his diocese, the procedure

[6] Fisher (1965); Angenendt (1985); Keefe (forthcoming).
[7] Laws of Ine, c. 2, Whitelock, *EHD* no. 32, p. 399.
[8] Council on the Danube (796), *MGH Conc.* II: 1, pp. 172–6.
[9] Dhuoda, *Liber Manualis* 1.7, XI.2. In 841, Easter fell on 17 April.

for baptism varied between the city and rural areas.[10] By about 900, the Gallo-Roman dioceses of Gaul each had hundreds of baptismal churches, one in almost every village of any size. The pattern did not extend, however, to more remote areas, for at the same date only forty parish churches served the entire region of the Ardennes.[11] In the huge dioceses of early Anglo-Saxon England and of the missionary church in Carolingian Germany, where priests were few and far between and bishops even scarcer, baptism, or any other sacrament, must have been very hard to obtain, and it was certainly impossible for episcopal confirmation to follow directly upon the baptism which a priest had administered. In Northumbria in the early eighth century, Bede (673/4–735) tells us that many remote settlements never saw a bishop to confirm people from one year's end to the next.[12] Getting an infant baptised in these circumstances must have entailed arduously long journeys and careful planning.

The text of the full Roman rite of initiation included seven scrutinies during Lent, spread out between the Wednesday of the third week of Lent and the day before the Easter vigil itself. It culminated in baptism during the Easter vigil, immediately followed by confirmation by the bishop and then Eucharist. A northern Italian Order of Scrutinies dating back to the eighth century expected some thirteen meetings of priest and catechised (and parents) to precede baptism itself.[13] Such demands placed upon families were often too great to be practicable. The repeated visits for the scrutinies of the Roman rite were frequently omitted or reduced to three in places where the distances to be travelled were too great, clergy too few or parents lax. In the diocese of the 'Troyes Anonymous', two scrutinies were performed, one postponed (unusually) until the second Monday after Easter Sunday. When confirmation became established as a separate rite, performed a matter of days or months after baptism, that placed a further burden on parents, and many seem not to have bothered at all.[14] Whether all the stages of baptism were completed on one occasion at a missionary church far from where the parents lived, or whether repeated visits were made to a cathedral by those who lived nearby, initiation of a child into the Christian faith demanded that parents commit time and energy, quite apart from the fees which some clergy improperly extorted.[15]

In the eighth and ninth centuries, having a child baptised may have been a

[10] Keefe (1986), p. 76.   [11] Genicot (1990), pp. 24–5.

[12] Bede, 'Epistola ad Ecgbertum episcopum' in HE, ed. Plummer, 1. 405–23 at p. 410.

[13] Lambot (1928); Fisher (1965), p. 40; Keefe (forthcoming) for demonstration that this ordo was in use by the Carolingian period.   [14] Jonas of Orléans, De Institutione Laicali 1. 7.

[15] First statutes of Gerbald of Liège, c. 12. MGH Cap. episc. 1, p. 19 and further references there cited.

time-consuming business, but its purpose became clear when translated into the metaphor of the secular social hierarchy. At baptism, the catechumen exchanged bondage to Satan for the lordship of Christ. Writing in 819, Hraban Maur (*c.* 780-856) described the exsufflation which formed one stage in this rite of initiation in language redolent of contemporary social relations of commendation, servitude and lordship: 'after he has commended himself into the lordship of the other by his confession of the true faith, and has separated himself from the servitude of his previous owner, the evil power is blown out of him ...'.[16] Hraban has left us with a clear statement of the religous identity of ninth-century society, and the way in which social cohesion was rooted in baptism.

That cohesion rested upon firm assumptions about the relative social positions of male and female. Baptism made this explicit. From the moment of entry into the Christian community, girls were treated differently from boys. As the children came into church for the various stages of the Roman rite, the boys were grouped on the right-hand side, girls on the left. At each stage – scrutiny, exorcism, receiving the creed, at the font – boys preceded girls.[17] Different prayers were said over each sex; Archbishop Hincmar of Rheims (845–82) expected his priests to know them all by heart.[18] The priority accorded to males found an echo in the rules for purification after childbirth which some penitential codes specified: following the Levitical code the new mother had to purge herself by sexual abstinence for up to twice as long after the birth of a girl as she did after the birth of a son.[19] The moment of entry into the Christian community gave ritual confirmation to the distinctions of gender which underlay all early medieval social relationships.

Baptism shaped those social relations in other ways too. Candidates for baptism had always needed a sponsor; by the seventh century, the sponsor's role was to make the profession of faith on behalf of the child.[20] Carolingian legislation forbade parents to sponsor their own children, and thereby encouraged the use of godparents: those who, through sponsoring a child, became its spiritual parents at its second, spiritual birth. Godparents were a child's *fideiussores*: they vouched for the child before God with their own pledge, and might be called to account if they defaulted.[21] Godparenthood had far-reaching implications and obligations. Churchmen tried to persuade

---

[16] 'At postquam se per confessionem verae fidei in alterius commendaverit dominium, et per abrenuntionem a prioris possessoris se alienaverit servitio, exsufflatur ab eo saeva potestas...' *De Clericorum Institutione* I. 27.   [17] *Ordo Romanus XI*, ed. Andrieu (1931–61), II, pp. 417–47.
[18] *Capitula Presbyteris Data* (852), c. 3, *PL* 125, col. 773.
[19] Flandrin (1983) pp. 17, 77 gives details.   [20] Lynch (1986).
[21] Legatine mission to England (786), c. 2, *MGH Epp.* IV, p. 21.

godparents to take a hand in religious instruction, and stipulated that they be able to teach the Apostles' Creed and Lord's Prayer to their godchildren. They were also concerned to prevent marriage, or any sexual relationship, between those who were spiritually kin, whether godfather and god-daughter or biological mother and godfather. In 879, a man named Stephen baptised his own dying son and acted as godfather, receiving the child from the font, as was permissible in an emergency when a priest was not present.[22] Because Stephen was now the spiritual 'co-father' of the child's mother, Bishop Anselm of Limoges ordered the couple to separate. The intervention of Pope John VIII saved the marriage, but the episode makes clear the way in which the clerical ban on sexual relations between spiritual kin had the power to disrupt medieval marriage patterns.

Nevertheless, the institution of godparenthood offered other compensations. Certainly Carolingian kings and magnates exploited it to form bonds of deep personal obligation. In addition to baptising the young Pippin in 781, Hadrian I also stood sponsor to him, thereby creating ties of spiritual kinship between biological father and spiritual father, in this instance Charlemagne and the pope. In 851 and 863, Charles the Bald stood sponsor to the sons of two successive Breton princes, part of a carefully executed move to undercut the Breton propensity to rebel. William, son of Bernard of Septimania and Dhuoda, had as his godfather his paternal uncle Theoderic, and Dhuoda wrote to William that, had Theoderic lived, 'he would have nurtured you and been your loving supporter in all things'.[23] For many laity, baptism may have been as much an opportunity to extend and manipulate their network of kindred as a moment of deep sacramental significance.

Festivals and worship

'If you fully desire to be a Christian', asserted the anonymous author of a treatise for use in instructing pagan converts, 'you can escape the great darkness of ignorance and unbelief. If you can keep the precepts of divine law, you will truly be a Christian.'[24] Baptism formed the point of entry into a rule-bound society. We can best explore the implications of those rules by following the themes underlying this writer's tenfold law of God. The author has combined some of the Ten Commandments with precepts of

---

[22] John VIII, ep. 195, *MGH Epp.* VII, p. 156.

[23] 'Nutritor etenim atque amator tuus fuerat in cunctis, si ei licuisset.' *Liber Manualis* VIII.15.

[24] 'Si ergo perfecte christianus esse desideras, magnas ignorantiae et infidelitatis poteris evadere tenebras. Nam si divinae legis praecepta seruare potueris, recte christianus eris.' *Ratio de Cathechizandis Rudibus* 2, Heer (1911), p. 80. According to its editor, this treatise was compiled c. 800, probably in Bavaria.

Jesus and early Christian exhortations into a statement outlining forms of worship and ritual, relations between the individual and God, and rules of conduct constraining an individual in his or her relations with family and community.[25] This and the following two sections address these issues.

Our catechetical treatise defined forms of worship and ritual through a series of negatives: prohibitions on worshipping idols, on the casting of spells and on divination, on making sacrifices to trees, springs and the like, and on taking offerings to any place other than the Christian church. Throughout eighth- and ninth-century legislation recur constant objections to rites and to ways of influencing events or predicting the future that were deemed un-Christian. Meeting the challenge of imposing Christian rituals and religious practices absorbed much energy. Although particularly acute in missionary areas, the clash of interests occurred everywhere: Boniface (672/5–754) reported stories of people celebrating the new year in 'pagan fashion' with singing, shouting, dancing and feasting right outside St Peter's basilica in Rome.[26]

Churchmen responded by urging lay participation in the festive cycle of the Christian year in ways which gave liturgical structure to the passing seasons and the week's work. They also encouraged visits to healing shrines and gave the clergy opportunities to preach to the assembled congregations. Accounts in saints' Lives offer assurance that laity did attend the major church festivals, often in large numbers. People flocked to saints' shrines on the annual feast days and rushed to attend the ceremonial translation of relics into new shrines. These large, religiously charged gatherings provided an environment in which reputed miracles of healing were particularly liable to occur. Huge crowds assembled whether for local celebrations, such as the festival of Germanus of Auxerre in a church dedicated to him in the diocese of Langres, or for the transfer of prestigious relics to shrines of international importance, such as the arrival of relics of St Denis at Fleury.[27] The laity also participated in the main annual feasts, notably Christmas and Easter. In the Easter Sunday liturgy at St Riquier in the 790s, for example, two priests administered communion to the laity, one to the men and the other to the women at the same time as the monks received the sacrament, and at the end of the service, all processed out of the church together.[28]

The church demanded more than seasonal participation in its liturgical cycle, however. At the heart of the efforts of Carolingian reformers lay an effort to impose a weekly rhythm of work and rest. Frequent legislation

---

[25] *Ratio de Cathechizandis Rudibus* 2, Heer (1911) p. 81 and pp. 18–23 on the sources for this passage.

[26] Boniface, ep. 50, *MGH Epp.* III, pp. 299–302.

[27] Heiric of Auxerre, *Miracula Sancti Germani* I, 5, *PL* 124, cols. 1232–3; Adrevald, *Miracula Sancti Benedicti* I, 28.   [28] Angilbert of St Riquier, *Institutio de Diversitate Officiorum*, 8.

stressed the obligation to keep the Sabbath – and acknowledged how widely it was flouted.[29] Charlemagne supplied a detailed list of all the agricultural tasks which men might not perform, but specifically exempted military service, the transport of foodstuffs and the carrying of the dead to the grave site. He also specified the range of prohibited women's work – weaving and spinning and production of cloth – but made no mention of the preparation of food.[30] Church councils enacted supplementary restrictions, such as a ban on markets and law courts.[31] Days of rest were for all: 'May your serfs and your serving women and your oxen and asses and horses have rest on the Lord's day and on saints' days, in the same way that you do.'[32] Women who worked at their looms on Sundays were particularly liable to find their hands crippled as a divine punishment.[33]

Keeping the Sabbath by no means entailed going to church. Though individual bishops and preachers might urge regular church attendance, neither kings nor councils legislated on the subject. The Anglo-Saxon Council of Clovesho in 747, for example, simply stated that the populace was to be invited to church on Sundays and feast days. No evidence permits any estimates of the frequency with which people attended church, though we do know that when they did attend, they sometimes left part way through the service.[34] Exhortations to attend church had to be tempered by recognition of the practical difficulties involved. As an anonymous ninth-century north-Italian preacher said to his congregation on the subject of church attendance during Lent: 'I urge each of you who lives next to the church and can get there, to hear Mass daily, and each who can should attend Matins every night. But those who live far from the church should make the effort to come to Matins every Sunday, that is, men and women, young and old, except for the sick. However one or two people may remain at home to guard the house.'[35] Church attendance may not have been more than erratic.

---

[29] For detailed references, Hartmann (1989), pp. 433–5 and Brommer (1974), pp. 63–5. Flouting of the Sabbath: Council of Paris (829), c. 50, *MGH Conc.* II:2, p. 643.

[30] Admonitio Generalis, c. 81, *MGH Cap.* I, p. 61.

[31] For example, Council of Arles (816), c. 16. *MGH Conc.* I, p. 252.

[32] 'Diem dominicam uel sollempnitates sanctis, quomodo uos habetis requiem, sic habeant et serui uestri, et ancillae uestrae, et boues et asini et caballi uestri.' Quoted from an anonymous, untitled sermon of the eighth or ninth century: Morin (1905), pp. 515–19 at p. 517.

[33] Heiric, *Miracula Germani* I, 5, *PL* 124, col. 1234; *Vita Arnulfi* 28, *MGH SRM* II, pp. 444–5.

[34] Admonitio Generalis, c. 71, *MGH Cap.* I, p. 159 is typical of the many injunctions against leaving before the end of the service.

[35] *Sermo in Quadragesima*, Mercier (1970), pp. 186–95. 'Moneo etiam ut qui iuxta ecclesiam est, et occurrere potest, quotidie audiat missam; et qui potest omni nocte ad matutinum officium veniat. Qui vero longe ab ecclesia manent, omni dominica studeant ad matutinas venire, id est viri et feminae et iuvenes et senes, praeter infirmos. Unus tantum aut duo remaneat, qui domum custodiant.'

Frequency of communion did receive more attention from legislators. According to Bede, lay people in early eighth-century Northumbria only received the sacrament at Christmas, Epiphany and Easter; most Carolingian bishops settled for similar injunctions to communicate three times a year.[36] Only in ninth-century Italy, it seems, did the laity receive communion with any regularity.[37] A powerful disincentive must have been the universal prohibition on any sexual activity for several days before receiving the Eucharist, though as Bede pointed out, there was no reason why the young and the elderly (who were not sexually active) could not take the Eucharist at least on all Sundays and feast days.[38] In practice, cautions about lay people communicating in a state of impurity suggest that these rules were honoured at least as much in the breach as the observance.[39]

Receiving communion from time to time may have been obligatory, but did not form the primary focus of public religious observance. It is not only the silence of sermons and of the handbooks of spiritual advice for lay people which suggests this. Even for those lay people whose devotional life approached the intensity of a monastic existence, receiving the sacrament appears to have been marginal to their main spiritual concerns. Gerald of Aurillac (*c.* 855–909), the only lay person in this period to be hailed as a saint, is certainly reported to have heard Mass frequently, but is never described receiving communion; in her *Liber Manualis*, Dhuoda never made any mention at all of the sacraments. Both Gerald and Dhuoda commissioned Masses for themselves or others; but for both of them, prayer, recitation of the psalms and observing the monastic offices formed the essence of their religious life.[40]

Gerald, as befitted a man of his wealth and status, had his own private travelling altar, which accompanied him wherever he went.[41] Judging by the descriptions of the altar fittings in two ninth-century wills, the private chapels of the Carolingian aristocracy were sumptuous places indeed, replete with gold crowns, candelabra, silver censers, rich textiles and precious reliquaries.[42] Such people evidently preferred not to slum it in the local parish church, which was liable to be used as a granary or to have a leaky roof. There might be animals wandering in and out, nesting birds

---

[36] Bede, 'Epistola ad Ecgbertum episcopum' in *HE*, ed. Plummer, p. 419; Browe (1921).

[37] Mercier (1970), p. 193.

[38] 'Epistola ad Ecgbertum episcopum', in *HE*, ed. Plummer, p. 419.

[39] For example the first statutes of Theodulf of Orléans, c. 44, *MGH Cap. episc.*, p. 140; Jonas of Orléans, *De Institutione Laicali* II, 18.

[40] Odo of Cluny, *Vita Geraldi* II, 17, IV, 60, 66; Dhuoda, *Liber Manualis* II, 3, XI, 1.

[41] Odo, *Vita Geraldi* III, 32, IV, 67, V, 72.

[42] Will of Heccard, count of Mâcon: Prou and Vidier (1900–7) I, pp. 59–67; will of Eberhard, marquis of Friuli: Coussemaker (1885) I, pp. 1–5.

polluting the sacred space with their excrement, women singing and dancing in the forecourt, people gossiping and story-telling.[43] Prohibitions against the nobility hearing Mass in their private houses surely acted as inducements to social mixing.[44]

Behaviour in churches, or expectations about it, hint at the ways in which social attitudes might find expression within an ecclesiastical context. There are obvious distinctions here of both gender and wealth. For women, access to saints' shrines, to the sacraments and to the altar was sometimes impossible. Two strands run through the penitential and legislative texts which deal with women in church: one, conventionally indebted to Gregory the Great, did not penalise women as impure; the other, under the influence of the penitential ascribed to Theodore of Tarsus, prohibited women from receiving communion during menstruation, imposed a period of purification after childbirth and refused to allow women to approach the altar at any time.[45] Many monasteries prohibited women from entering the cloister and church. Women could approach relics when they were taken outside the enclosure; otherwise they had to resort to other tactics. A blind woman entrusted her candle to a man to take to the shrine of St Leutfred; another woman, who dressed as a man in order to get close to the relics of St Carilef, was struck blind.[46] In both secular and monastic churches, local custom or direction was responsible for regulating access. No overall pattern can be discerned.

Social status also affected the way people participated in ecclesiastical celebrations. For the rich, festivals such as Christmas were opportunities to bedeck themselves in their finest apparel, 'so that on that day they might be seen to be more honourable than other people'.[47] On these occasions, displays of status and of conspicuous wealth had an immediate audience. Hraban Maur complained that on Rogation Days, when his congregation should have been purging themselves with fasting, clad in hair shirts or in mourning, both men and women were wearing all their finery. Having spent

---

[43] First statutes of Theodulf of Orléans, c. 8; statutes of Radulf of Bourges, cc. 2–3; statutes of Ruotger of Trier, c. 2, *MGH Cap. episc.*, pp. 108–9, 235–6, 62–3; Regino, *Libri II de Synodalibus Causis*, Bk I, Inquisitio cc. 1, 72–3, II.v.87–8.

[44] *Duplex Legationis Edictum* (789), c. 25, *MGH Cap.* I, p. 64; Council of Paris (829), c. 47, *MGH Conc.* II:2, p. 641.

[45] Gregory the Great, ep. XI (56a), *MGH Epp.* II, pp. 338–9; Penitential of Theodore, I.xiv, cc. 17–18, in Schmitz (1883), pp. 524–50. Both these texts were highly influential in eighth- and ninth-century Anglo-Saxon and Frankish legislation. Also Regino, *Libri II de Synodalibus Causis* I, 200–2.

[46] *Vita Sancti Leutfredi* 4, *AASS* Jun IV, p. 112; *Miracula Sancti Carilefi* 11, *AASS OSB* I, pp. 653–4.

[47] *Sermo in Adventu Domini*, Mercier (1970), pp. 150–3: 'ut honorabiliores caeteris videantur in illa die'.

the day riding through the fields on their caparisoned horses, they ended it by feasting late into the night with drinking, music and bawdy singing, their guests not the beggars and cripples from outside their gate but their own like-minded neighbours and cronies.[48] All too easily did a day intended for penance and humility become an excuse for affirming the distance that separated feasting *potentes* from suffering *pauperes*. The worship and ritual of the ninth-century church was as much about social rank as it was about Christian religion.

SIN AND SALVATION

Through baptism, the new Christian entered a relationship with the Christian God which would not culminate until the Last Judgement. At its core, the clergy preached, lurked all-pervasive sin. Fear of punishment and the certainty of impending judgement combined put great stress on expiation. Coupled with the belief that, after death, the just passed straight to paradise to await judgement but the impure would be purified by fire, an ideology of sin and atonement permeated the lives of both clergy and laity throughout the early middle ages.

By *c.* 700, belief in purgatory had spread from monastic to lay circles, and had taken hold even in the far north of Christendom, on the northerly fringes of Northumbria. Dryhthelm, a *paterfamilias* who led a religious life within his household, had a glimpse of purgatory and paradise, after which he had himself tonsured and joined a monastery. His vision of the souls of men tossed between raging fire and icy tempest in a valley that lay in front of the mouth of the stinking pit of hell, and of bands of happy people on the fragrant, sunlit plain which lay just outside the kingdom of heaven, captures for us the beliefs and fears which helped shape men's and women's conduct. As Dryhthelm's angelic guide explained to him, the souls being chastened by fire and ice were those people who had delayed confessing and repenting their sins until the very moment of their death. Along with their own penitence, the prayers, alms, fasts and Masses of the living would help these souls finally reach heaven. The white-clad people enjoying the flowery meadow were those who had died performing good works, but who were not so perfect as to enter immediately the kingdom of heaven.[49] For Dryhthelm and his contemporaries, good works, confession and the repentance of sin during this life affected what happened beyond the grave. The Christian religion demanded that quotidian affairs be conducted in accordance with a rigorous ethic of self-restraint and good deeds.

[48] Hraban Maur, *Homiliae* XIX, PL 110, col. 38.
[49] Bede, *HE* v.12, ed. Plummer, I, pp. 303–10.

A system of private confession followed by penance, first developed by Irish monks in the sixth century, became the chief means through which clergy tried to exercise disciplinary control over the behaviour of the laity. Through tariffs of penance, graduated according to the severity of each sin, and repeated each time another sin was confessed, confessors could help the penitent cancel out his or her ill deeds. Regular confession was desirable: Dhuoda urged young William to 'offer your true confession, in privacy, with sighing and with tears' and to devote fully one half of his time to penance and reparation.[50] Confession and penance became an urgent necessity to those on their deathbeds, and all priests were expected to be able to administer it. Bede told the admonitory tale of a Mercian warrior in the opening years of the eighth century who continually refused to do penance, even when very ill. Angels showed him the brief list of his good works; devils the tome of his sins. He died unshriven, condemned to everlasting torment.[51] As Alcuin reminded Count Wido, God never spurned penance, however short its duration, if done with true contrition, but there was no possibility to repent after death.[52]

Within the context of beliefs about an after-life where each individual's fate turned upon his or her good deeds, penance brought together social behaviour and divine judgement in a framework of ecclesiastical discipline and clerical ritual. Accounts of sinners hastening to holy men and priests to confess suggest that ecclesiastical teaching on the need for penance was often taken to heart.[53] The survival of vernacular *ordines* for hearing confession and administering penance points in a similar direction.[54] To work, however, the system relied upon the voluntary co-operation of lay people with their priests. Herein lay the difficulty. One ninth-century bishop admitted the problems he encountered in making penance an effective disciplinary tool. Isaac of Langres (859–80) commented that he had decided to take action 'because of the idleness of those who were uncooperative, and their complaints about pastoral solicitude, and because of the insolence of wicked men who assert that all the things which are said for their own improvement or security are dreamed up and invented and imagined by us'.[55]

Some of those difficulties lay in the strategies people devised to fulfil the

---

[50] *Liber Manualis* III. 11: 'Da illis, ut melius nosti, tuam occulte cum suspirio et lachrymis ueram confessionem.'   [51] *HE* v.13, ed. Plummer, I, pp. 311–13.

[52] *De Virtutibus et Vitiis*, 13.   [53] Vogel (1956).   [54] Steinmeyer (1916), pp. 306–36.

[55] 'Propter quorundam minus acquiescentium desidiam, et querelam contra pastoralem sollicitudinem, atque improborum insolentiam, qui omnia quae ad emendationem vel ad suam cautelam dicuntur, a nobis ficta et excogitata garriunt et inventa, utile duximus, quaedam saluberrimarum capitula sanctionum. . .colligere et in unum corpusculum aggregare.' *PL* 124, col. 1075.

letter, but not the spirit, of a penitential sentence. Penitentials most commonly imposed sentences of fasts of specified duration, which might be many years for the most serious offences. By the middle of the eighth century, the Irish practice of commuting a penance had become widespread: in 747 the Council of Clovesho inveighed against the practice. Commutation enabled a penitent to avoid the inconvenience of fasting by giving alms or donating land to the church. Alternatively, someone else could be hired to perform the fast on the penitent's behalf, or a priest paid to say Masses.[56] In 829, the Council of Paris, apropos of the correct administration of penance, cautioned priests who 'determine the duration and nature of the penance according to the penitent's pleasure, for the sake of a gift or love or fear or favour', and Hincmar likewise commanded his priests not to accept hush-money.[57]

Efforts to minimise the inconvenience of a penitential sentence doubtless sprang from a deep concern about the possible fate of one's soul, coupled with a reluctance to allow clerical stipulations to circumscribe every action. On no aspect of people's conduct did Christian *mores* have a greater effect than on their sexual behaviour. In the many extant eighth- and ninth-century penitential codes, sexual irregularities form the most notable category of offence. In an effort to impose as nearly a monastic morality on lay society as possible, clerical reformers and legislators viewed even conjugal sexuality as deeply polluting and quite incompatible with participation in the worship of the Christian community. Intended for procreation only, intercourse was not permissible at many stages of a woman's physiological cycle – menstruation, pregnancy, breast-feeding – nor at many specified times in the liturgical calendar.

Historians have debated the possible demographic effects of restrictions so stringent that they would allow the well-behaved Christian couple to have intercourse on fewer than fifty days of the year.[58] Equally difficult to establish is any sense of how widely these rules of conduct were observed. Jonas' pastoral experience as bishop of Orléans (818–43) certainly led him to conclude that many people ignored injunctions to refrain from sexual activity before marriage and, since nuptial Masses were reserved for virgins, he observed that they thereby denied themselves the chance of having their marriage blessed in church.[59] Much of the work of explaining the church's teaching must have been left to individual priests and confessors, but when

---

[56] Vogel (1978), pp. 47–52 for further details.
[57] 'Sacerdotes vero qui aut muneris aut amoris aut timoris aut certe favoris causa tempora modumque paenitentiae ad libitum penitentium indicunt.' *MGH Conc.* II:2, p. 633; Hincmar, *Capitula Presbyteris Data* (852) c. 13, *PL* 125, col. 776.   [58] Flandrin (1983), pp. 41–71.
[59] *De Institutione Laicali* II. 2.

flagrant flouting of the code of sexual ethics occurred, harsh punishment might ensue. The bishops who attended the general assembly at Epernay in 846 may at least have connived at the decision 'by the judgement of the Franks' to burn alive a man who indulged in bestiality with a mare during the holy season of Lent.[60]

Alongside hints that the sexual *mores* promulgated by the clergy were disregarded, we need to set evidence that other people attempted to order their lives appropriately. Two rare examples suggest that at least some members of the ninth-century aristocracy had taken these restrictions to heart. In August 822, Northild publicly complained to Louis the Pious about 'dishonourable goings-on' between herself and her husband Agembert, though the bishops to whom the emperor referred the case decided that it lay outside their competence, and should be referred to married lay people to resolve.[61] More telling still is the attitude of Gerald of Aurillac, whose horror of 'carnal obscenity' led him to wash away the stain of 'nocturnal illusions' by bathing and by shedding tears of penance. 'One could demand nothing more, or more excellent', declared his biographer, Odo of Cluny (c. 879–944), 'for nothing is to be compared to virginity.'[62] In matters of sexuality more than any other sphere of human activity, the conduct of an individual became an expression of adherence to the Christian religion.

When Dryhthelm had his vision of purgatory and paradise, the angel reminded him that suffering souls could be helped by the prayers, alms, fasting and Masses of the living. Acceptance of the intercession of others characterised much of the religious practices of the eighth and ninth centuries; so too did the emphasis on almsgiving and fasting as aids to salvation. A Lenten sermon stressed the theme. 'For it is written: "As water extinguishes fire, so alms extinguish sin." And you ought to know that each person ought to give to the poor according to what he possesses; in other words, he who has much, should give much, and he who has very little, should give very little.'[63]

In this respect too, however, practical consequences might differ from clerical intentions. Certainly many churches grew extremely wealthy on the pious donations made to them as alms to assist the donors' souls (about three-quarters of the approximately 800 original charters dating from the eighth and ninth centuries in the St Gall archive record grants made *pro*

---

[60] *AB s.a.* 846, p. 52.

[61] 'Femina quaedam non ignobilis genere, nomine Northildis, de quibusdam inhonestis inter se et virum suum vocabulo Agembertum, ad imperatorem publice proclamavit.' Hincmar, *De Divortio Lotharii Regis et Tetbergae Reginae*, interrogatio v, *PL* 125, col. 655.

[62] *Vita Geraldi* III, 41.   [63] *Sermo in Quadragesima*, Mercier (1970), pp. 186–95.

salute animae[64]), but the poor often appear to have been marginalised by the rich. As Alcuin urged a noble woman and her daughter, 'the feeding of the hungry is the salvation of the rich';[65] however another preacher had to warn his congregation not to retain for their own use the food that they saved by fasting during Lent, but to be sure to distribute it to the poor.[66] Fasting and almsgiving might be performed in a spirit of self-gain: 'for there are some, who seizing the property of others, pretend that they give alms: but by imagining that they show mercy to some, they oppress others'.[67] Emphasis on almsgiving as a religious activity acknowledged and – in practice – reinforced a highly stratified social order.

The essence of early medieval teaching on the relationship of all people to God lay in fear of judgement and damnation in the face of the overwhelming presence of sin. In this climate, a penitential discipline of monastic origin came to pervade norms of lay conduct. Whether almsgiving, intercessory prayer or penance helped one person towards salvation, other people were necessarily involved. The struggle for salvation was fought – or abandoned – in the arena of social relationships.

INDIVIDUAL IDENTITY AND SOCIAL ORDER

The intrusion of clerical rituals into the everyday lives of men and women had become marked by the ninth century. Nothing demonstrates this more clearly than the development of ecclesiastical rites which regulated people's identity and standing within their community, or which made a bid to maintain order and affirm social cohesion. The former category of rituals can only be discussed briefly; the practical effects of rituals to regulate public conduct can, on the other hand, be traced directly through narrative accounts.

First witnessed in the closing years of the ninth century, a prayer to be said *super militantes* marks a preliminary stage in the elaboration of a 'liturgy of knighthood'.[68] Not until the end of the eleventh century did there emerge a full ecclesiastical rite of passage for making a knight, but the Carolingian clergy evinced a decided interest in other status-changing rituals. Invoking a common procedure, the archbishop of Sens, for example, manumitted serfs of the church, pronouncing their freedom 'in front of the corner of the holy

---

[64] Angenendt (1984), p. 141.
[65] *MGH Epp.* IV, pp. 73–4: 'quia refectio egeni salus est divitis'.
[66] *Sermo in Quadragesima*, Mercier (1970), pp. 186–95.
[67] Paulinus of Aquileia, *Liber Exhortationis ad Hericum Comitem* 31. PL 99, col. 227.
[68] Nelson (1989), p. 259 and note 26.

altar, in the sight of the assembled priests and clergy and populace'.[69] Manumission marked a permanent change in an individual's social standing and necessitated careful record in a charter.[70] To preserve for posterity the life changes of humble men and women, some English churches developed the practice of entering the names of those who had been manumitted, and of the witnesses to the ceremony, on the fly-leaves of Gospel Books.[71] Equally significant as a change in social status, marriage too might be accompanied by an ecclesiastical ceremony. It remains unknown how common this may have been, for no literary or documentary evidence survives to set alongside the liturgical texts of nuptial Masses, and the only individuals known to have been married in church are members of the Carolingian dynasty.[72] Through prayer confirming the warrior status of Carolingian aristocrats, and through rites of manumission or of marriage which transformed social identity, ninth-century clergy ensured their own role in delimiting social relationships. In establishing a place within the church for such hitherto secular matters as warfare and marriage, Carolingian churchmen inaugurated profound social transformations, ones whose full impact was not realised for centuries to come.

Carolingian clergy also took an interest in maintaining the solidarity and tranquillity of lay society. In particular, they did so in rituals which formally excluded someone from the Christian community of the church or – conversely – gave expression to reconciliation and social cohesion. Such rites were not new in the ninth century, but rather originated in the practices of the early church. Publicly proclaimed excommunications placed ecclesiastical and spiritual strictures of varying degrees of severity on those offenders who could not be disciplined by other means.[73] Hincmar of Rheims, for example, authorised the excommunication of those who had publicly committed crimes such as homicide, adultery or perjury, and who refused to appear before the bishop for a penitential sentence.[74] As 'putrid limbs, beyond all hope' such people were to be amputated from the body of the church.[75] Rites for the expulsion from the church of those undergoing public penance (and for their subsequent reconciliation) also derived from ancient practices, and became important when the tradition of public penance was revived early in the ninth century.

[69] Regino, *Libri II de Synodalibus Causis* I, 413–18; *Formulae Senonenses Recentiores*, 9, *MGH Form.*, pp. 215–16. [70] Nelson (1990), p. 262. [71] Whitelock, *EHD*, nos. 140–8, pp. 607–10.
[72] Vogel (1976). [73] Regino, *Libri II de Synodalibus Causis* II, 412–17.
[74] *Capitula Superaddita* (857) c. 1, PL 125, col. 793.
[75] 'Et tamquam putrida ac desperata membra ab universalis ecclesiae corpore dissecandi; cuiusmodi iam inter christianos nulla legum, nulla morum, nulla collegii participatio est'. Synod of Pavia (850), c. 12. *MGH Cap.* II, p. 120.

The importance of public penance as a religious means of identifying and punishing malefactors, of distancing them from the community and stripping them of their status may be illustrated by the case of the Lombard Haistulf, who killed his wife amid accusations of adultery in or about 794. Paulinus, patriarch of Aquileia (787–802), gave him the choice between entering a monastery or undergoing a rigorous public penance for the remainder of his life. In addition to stringent dietary restrictions, the obligation to spend his time in fasting, prayer and almsgiving, and in absolute sexual continence, the penitential sentence forbade him to receive the Eucharist, stripped him of the right to carry arms (a right which denoted his free – and doubtless noble – status), forbade him ever to bring a lawsuit and condemned him to stand by himself at the door of the church, commending himself to the prayers of those who passed in and out. For the sake of his soul, Haistulf thus became socially dead, denied the status of a warrior or the right to remarry.[76] By stripping aristocratic males of their right to bear arms, public penance restored social cohesion by disciplining and humiliating fractious and unruly men.

In the course of the ninth century, the demarcation between royal judicial powers and the episcopal prerogative of imposing public penance became increasingly blurred in the Frankish lands. By the reign of Charles the Bald, royal *bannum* and public penance were effectively intertwined.[77] Offenders such as Frotmund, a Lotharingian noble who together with his brothers killed his uncle at a date between 855 and 858, received sentence from king and bishops acting in concert – in his case a penitential journey in sackcloth and chains around the shrines of Christendom and the Holy Land.[78] Ecclesiastical rites had become an instrument of public policing.

Formal oaths sworn on Gospel Books or saints' relics commonly created the social obligations of lordship and vassalage; appropriately, the maintenance of public order also depended upon Christian rituals. This is particularly evident in the procedures for conducting ordeals – the search for divine judgement, the *iudicium Dei*, on matters incapable of human resolution. An ordeal commenced when the presiding priest said Mass, and adjured those about to undergo the ordeal to admit their guilt. If they did not confess, he gave them the sacrament, and then blessed the instruments of the ordeal. Where possible, the ordeal took place within the church; in the case of trial by hot water or hot iron, the priest built a fire in the church forecourt. After having been sprinkled with holy water, and having kissed the Gospel Book and Cross, each person proceeded to the *iudicium*, guided by the priest in the

---

[76] *MGH Epp.* IV, pp. 520–2.
[77] *MGH Cap.*, no. 203, c. 6; no. 259, c. 9; no. 272, c. 3; no. 275, c. 10; no. 287, c. 4; II, pp. 66, 269, 307, 335–6, 373.   [78] *GSR* III, 8.

presence of the assembled crowd. Representing the bishop of Paris in an ordeal of the Cross conducted in the royal chapel in 775, Corellus 'appeared terrified and overcome' and thus the *iudicium Dei* resolved the case.[79]

Both the ordeal (regulated in legislation from the sixth century onwards) and public penance emphasise far more steadily than sermons or prescriptive codes the ways in which early medieval men and women shaped their conduct, and constrained that of others, in accordance with an interpretation of Christian teaching which made sense in a practical rather than a doctrinal sense. Public or private, penance most clearly indicates the way in which 'religion' and 'society' are synonymous.

DEATH AND BURIAL

Although the clergy were concerned to ensure that all people entered into the life of the Christian community through baptism, they were not always so worried about their manner of leaving this world for the next. As reflected in ecclesiastical statutes, a concern with death and burial only developed during the later stages of the Carolingian reform movement. It is nevertheless possible to sketch in outline some of the main shifts in funerary practice of the eighth and ninth centuries, especially in the Frankish lands.

Burial is above all about place. The grave is a place of leave-taking. Living members of a family remember their dead at the graveside. At the grave of a holy man or woman, miracles may occur. The most terrible of the maledictions heaped upon excommunicated thieves, perjurors and despoilers of church property culminated in the imprecation that their bodies be buried in the graves of asses and treated as dung on the face of the earth.[80] To violate a grave was odious impiety.[81] Where, then, were lay people buried in the eighth and ninth centuries?

In the Mediterranean littoral and its hinterland, the desire for burial *ad sanctos* meant that by the end of sixth century, burial took place in or close to suburban shrines. In areas of less persistent Roman influence, burials were by no means always in churchyards until very much later. Since the 1970s, an archaeological pattern has been well established in early medieval Celtic Britain of essentially 'secular' cemeteries which were gradually either abandoned or brought within the sphere of influence and control of the

---

[79] 'Quod ita et in capella nostra recensenda missa Harnaldo presbitero visi fuerunt stetisse et ea hora protegente devina dextera dei deus omnipotens suum iustum iudicium declaravit, ut homo memmorato Herchenrado episcopo nomine Corellus ad ipso dei iudicium ad ipsa crucem trephidus et convictus aparuit.' *MGH Dip. Kar.* I, no. 102, pp. 146–7. The earliest *ordines* for conducting an ordeal are ninth-century: *MGH Form.*, pp. 619–20, 638–40.

[80] Regino, *Libri II de Synodalibus Causis* II, 416.   [81] Jonas, *De Institutione Laicali* III, 15.

church. The earliest such cemeteries, in the post-Roman period, were generally unenclosed, often on the same sites as earlier pagan cemeteries. At some point, a boundary ditch or wall might be added, or a cross-incised pillar or a special grave would form a focus for subsequent burials. A timber chapel, later replaced with a stone building, completed the transformation into parish graveyard. This slow sequence spanned the early middle ages.[82] A comparable sequence is now becoming evident in Anglo-Saxon England and in northern Gaul, although the clergy probably managed to establish their monopoly over burial grounds somewhat earlier.[83] However, this control of death and burial had not yet been fully established by 900: even if most local churches had a graveyard by this date, in no part of Latin Christendom were lay people obliged to carry their dead to them. Burial remained the responsibility of family and kindred.

Wherever people were laid to rest in the eighth and ninth centuries, one thing is clear: burial was expensive. The cost incurred before or after death might take several forms: grave goods, burial fees, gifts to monasteries, guild fees. Fifth-, sixth- and early seventh-century sites in the Germanic regions of Europe reveal the wealth that accompanied the aristocratic dead into their graves. Until the middle of the seventh century, aristocratic burial in richly furnished graves remained a widespread custom, whether in field cemeteries or in churches. But from the mid-century, habits changed, and aristocratic burials in Frankish churches from the 650s onwards show a move towards a monastic austerity. One of the founding saints of the Carolingian dynasty, Geretrud, initiated this trend; the rise to hegemony of the Austrasian aristocracy may have reinforced the new taste. Only in peripheral regions did traditions of burials with grave goods persist: furnished graves have been found in early eighth-century churches in southern Germany, for example, or at early Christian sites of the ninth century in Greater Moravia. In both these cases, there is a clear contrast between the funerary culture of Frankish heartlands and non-Carolingian periphery.[84]

Even though the taste for richly equipped interments faded, burial remained costly, whether in a field cemetery or an ecclesiastical space. In 828, Jonas of Orléans railed against those magnates who neglected their obligations to bury the dead as an act of charity, not bothering to give funerals for the *pauperes* and even charging for them to be buried in the fields.[85] Funerary chapels subordinate to mother churches within the archdiocese of Rheims catered for the *pauperculi* who were unable to carry

---

[82] Thomas (1971), pp. 48–68.

[83] Morris (1983), pp. 49–62; Blair (1988), pp. 35–58; Young (1977; 1986).

[84] Young (1977), pp. 59, 65; Dierkens (1981).   [85] *De Institutione Laicali* III, 15.

their dead further than their own village, presumably those who were so poor that they lacked access to a cart to carry the body.[86] Several monasteries had cemeteries set aside for the burial of the poor, and Charles the Bald took care to ensure that the one run by the monks of St Martin at Tours had its own adequate endowment.[87] Throughout the ninth century, bishops repeatedly forbade their priests to charge for funerals, but to no avail, for the burial fee became a well-established parochial perquisite.[88]

On the other hand, priests were explicitly allowed to accept gifts made freely by the family and followers of the dead person. Such gifts were often made by those for whom transport of the dead over a considerable distance was no problem. For the *potentes* of the ninth century, burial at a church or monastery was normal, and was but one stage in the continuing web of relationships and property transactions that bound landowning families over generations to the shrine of their preferred saintly patron. We may glimpse the Christian death rituals typical of the landowning elite in a late ninth-century charter relating to the deaths of Deurhoiarn and his wife Roiantken, both substantial landowners in eastern Brittany.[89] On 29 June 875, the couple asked the monks of Redon at their dependent church of St Maixent in Plélan to show them where they might be buried. The abbot indicated a space in the monastery's forecourt and husband and wife each gave a gift of land to the monks to secure their spot. Ninth-century legislation had repeatedly addressed the problem of tombs crowding inside churches and hindering worship: burial in the forecourt, in side-chapels (*porticus*) or in an *abhedra* (whose nature is uncertain) was permissible, and efforts were made to restrict the privilege to priests and lay people of worthy and upright life.[90] In practice, this meant those who gave ante-mortem gifts to a church in anticipation of burial there, as Deurhoiarn and Roiantken had done. When Deurhoiarn died six months later, we may guess that a priest was at hand to hear his confession, anoint him and administer the viaticum, as almost all ninth-century episcopal statutes required. His widow and son led the funeral procession from their house to St Maixent, and were met *en route* by the monks, carrying relics. Once in the monastery, Deurhoiarn was buried 'with dignity, in the Christian custom'. By the late ninth century, burial for the laity 'in Christian custom' had come to mean a liturgical rite,

---

[86] Hincmar, *Collectio de Ecclesiis et Capellis*, p. 76.

[87] Tessier (1943–55), I, pp. 298–300, no. 112.

[88] Carolingian synodical and episcopal leglislation on burial is summarised by Regino of Prüm, *Libri II de Synodalibus Causis* I, 123–9.   [89] CR 236.

[90] First statutes of Theodulf, c. 9; second statutes, cc. 10, 11. *MGH Cap. episc.*, pp. 109, 153, and further references given there.

involving at the very least the singing of psalms and antiphons.[91] By the time Deurhoiarn died, the full monastic funerary Mass was beginning to be used for laity, notably in East Frankish regions, and perhaps this Breton funeral took such a form.[92] Certainly Deurhoiarn, and also Roiantken who died very shortly after him, were the subjects of commemorative Masses on the first Sunday after their death, and again on a subsequent Sunday, probably the anniversary. On both these occasions, their son visited the graves and made further donations to the monks, for the sake of his parents' souls.

At the time of Deurhoiarn's death, the monastery of St Maixent had not been in existence for more than a few years. He could not, therefore, have been claiming an hereditary right to a family grave site, as some people tried to do.[93] As landowners, however, Deurhoiarn and Roiantken's relations with the monks of Redon and St Maixent neither began nor ended with their death. In return for the lands and support which their families gave to the monks over many years, they were given the privilege of burial near to the miracle-working relics of St Maxentius. As described briefly in this charter, their burial indicates the way in which, from the late ninth century onwards, the rituals which had been worked out in monastic communities for easing the passage of the soul into the after life were beginning to be extended to the laity.

The commemorative masses said for this Breton couple are a further indication of another significant development in the ways by which the laity of the eighth and ninth centuries coped with death. Jonas of Orléans reminded Count Matfrid of the obligation of all family, kin and friends to help the souls of the deceased with their prayers and almsgiving.[94] As a theology developed which stressed that the soul of the deceased needed the help of the prayers of the living in order to make its way to heaven, so the laity (or at least, those who could afford to) found ways of instituting prayers, Masses and works of charity for the salvation of themselves and those dear to them. The obligation lay heavily on family members themselves. As Dhuoda faced her own impending death in 843, she wrote to her son William that 'your frequent prayer and that of others is necessary to me now. It will be more and more so in time to come, if, as I believe, my moment is upon me.'[95]

---

[91] Statutes of Radulf of Bourges, c. 18, statutes of Ruotger of Trier, c. 20, *MGH Cap. episc.*, pp. 68, 246–7; Council of Trier (927), c. 9, *MGH Conc.* IV:1, p. 82.

[92] Frank (1962); Paxton (1990b) on the use of the *agenda mortuorum* for the laity.

[93] Hincmar, *Capitula Superaddita* (857), c. 2, PL 125, col. 794.

[94] *De Institutione Laicali* III, 15.

[95] *Liber Manualis* x, 4: 'Est michi modo necesse tua uel aliorum frequens oratio: erit postea plus et per amplius, ut credo citius ita esse uenturum.'

In addition to kin, monks and clergy might also be requested to help the souls of lay men and women through their Masses and prayers. Lists of thousands of names in monastic memorial books testify to the overwhelming concern felt by everyone from peasant to king to seek the help of monks' prayers in defeating death. Wills elaborate on the arrangements which might underlie these requests for spiritual patronage. When Count Eccard of Mâcon drew up his will in 876, he stipulated that his remains he buried in the church of St Benedict at Fleury. He also left an endowment to ensure that at both Fleury and Faremoutiers (where his sister was abbess) annual Masses would be said for himself and his family, to mark the anniversary of his death.[96] Arrangements for intercession could be quite complex. 'In the hope, and for the reward, of eternal and future life, and for the salvation of our own souls and those of our children' the Kentish ealdorman Oswulf and his wife Beornthryth made a grant to Christ Church, Canterbury in c. 806. In return for a generous donation of land, they requested annual commemorative prayers and almsgiving from the cathedral community, possibly even including membership in the monastic prayer confraternity during their own lifetime. Archbishop Wulfred declared that the couple should be jointly commemorated on the day of Oswulf's anniversary, with religious offices, almsgiving and a banquet for the community. He also made provision for specified amounts of food from named estates to be given out as alms, for wax to be set aside for candles for Oswulf and Beornthryth's sake, for each priest in the cathedral community to sing two Masses for each of the couple, for the deacons likewise to make two Gospel readings and all the other members of the community to sing two 'fifties' of psalms for each of them.[97]

At a lower social level, commemorative prayer was amongst the functions of the guilds which can be traced in the Frankish countryside of the late ninth century and in England from the tenth century onwards. Members paid their fees or dues in cash or kind – burial and spiritual assistance were never free – and in return provided each other with both practical and prayerful help. In early tenth-century Exeter, for example, when a guild brother died, each member was to pay for six Masses or six Psalters of psalms.[98] Hincmar of Rheims allowed the guilds which flourished within his diocese to bring offerings to Mass, to offer candles at the altar, to assist in each other's funerals, and to undertake almsgiving and other works of charity.[99]

---

[96] Prou and Vidier (1900–7), no. 25, I, pp. 59–67.

[97] Harmer (1914), no. 1, pp. 1—2; English translation pp. 39–40, with the suggestion that Oswulf and Beorthryth were requesting entry to the confraternity at p. 72.

[98] Whitelock, *EHD*, no. 137, p. 605.   [99] *Capitula Presbyteris Data* (852), c. 14, *PL* 125, col. 778.

The concern of guildsmen to provide for each other's spiritual welfare suggests the extent to which religious values of clerical and monastic origin had become widely diffused by *c.*900. By the end of the ninth century, bishops had begun to demand that their parish clergy know by heart the rituals for the last rites and burial as well as for baptism: the extension into the parochial community of clerical management of death marks one of the most significant changes in the religious experiences of the laity in this period.

Nevertheless, not all of the ways in which lay people coped with death met with episcopal approval even by the end of the ninth century. Certainly in the archdioceses of Rheims and Trier, people had their own sense of how to mourn and commemorate a death. A wake, lasting all night, took place in the house where the death had occurred. Food and drink were served. Family and friends gathered to sing, joke and dance. On the third, seventh and thirtieth days after the burial and again at the anniversary, they gathered for commemorative feasts. The drink flowed; people invoked the saints in their cups and paraded masks representing demons in front of the local priest; storytelling, raucous games, singing and dancing again whiled away the night.[100] Such feasts not only bound together the living and the dead members of a single community. As at any early medieval drinking session, funerary feasts could be occasions for settling old scores, or beginning new feuds. Both Halitgar, bishop of Cambrai (817–31), and Hincmar of Rheims warned against the anger and quarrels at feasts for the dead that resulted in fights and sometimes in killings.[101]

Halitgar, Hincmar and other concerned bishops could no more eradicate these practices or stop village priests participating in them than they could bring all the laity into church on Sundays. Nevertheless, their legislation was but a part of a much greater effort to extend to the laity, at all social levels, the solace and help which they believed the church could offer in the face of death. Certainly by the end of the ninth century, lay men and women were laid to rest and their deaths commemorted in ways which owed much more to ecclesiastical, and particularly monastic, influence than had been the case in 700. By 900, most people in Latin Christendom were probably buried in mortuary chapels or graveyards associated with churches, and death was widely understood in terms of impending judgement and the efficacy of intercession. Only in such an environment could the denial of Christian rites to those who had committed suicide, been killed in judicial duels or failed to

---

[100] Regino of Prüm, *Libri II de Synodalibus Causis*, episcopal *inquisitio*, cc. 40, 73 and 1.216, 304, 398, II.5.55; Hincmar of Rheims, *Capitula Presbyteris Data* (852), c. 14, *PL* 125, col. 776.

[101] Hartmann (1979), p. 390, 'De sinodo quarto', c. 6; Hincmar, *Capitula Presbyteris Data* (852), c. 14.

confess before being swung on the gibbet be an effective sanction.[102] By 900, death was becoming as much a clerical as a familial affair.

The religion of the laity in the early middle ages cannot be abstracted from its human environment. Matters of sickness and health, sex and kinship, public order, social hierarchy and gender differentiation all found religious expression. In the course of the eighth and ninth centuries, the clergy of the Christian church took a steadily growing part in shaping the ritual and liturgy which encompassed so many aspects of human existence. In their efforts to steer people towards an after life of salvation, they created a 'liturgical civilisation', which swathed men and women in a mesh of ecclesiastical ritual.[103] By 900, many more aspects of life fell under the scrutiny of the church than had been the case in 700: clerically orchestrated liturgy came to mark all stages of life from the cradle to the grave. The intrusion of clerical norms into every aspect of everyday life which so characterises the Christian middle ages had its origins in these centuries.

[102] Council of Mainz (847), c. 27; Council of Valence (855), c. 12, *MGH Conc.* III, pp. 174–5, 360.
[103] Vauchez (1975), p. 14.

PART IV

CULTURE AND INTELLECTUAL DEVELOPMENTS

CHAPTER 25

EIGHTH-CENTURY FOUNDATIONS

Rosamond McKitterick

IN about 780, Charlemagne sent out an appeal for copies of remarkable or rare books.[1] Its success is documented, first, by the number of extant ninth-century manuscripts which appear to emanate from the court or depend on court exemplars and, second, by the short list of books in Berlin, Diez B. Sant. 66, a late eighth-century grammatical collection. The list includes many unusual texts and has been identified as a catalogue of some at least of the books in the Carolingian court library.[2] That such an appeal for texts could be made, and, apparently, responded to, is an indication that knowledge existed within the Frankish kingdoms by the 780s both of particular texts and of centres likely to contain ancient books of some kind. Levels of interest and the availability of texts are, therefore, interlocking problems in any assessment of the pre-Carolingian period. Although it is certainly relatively thinly documented, the evidence exists nevertheless to suggest distinct centres of intellectual activity and spheres of interest in the eighth century. The eighth century is to be understood not merely as a tail end of the four centuries of change and innovation which divide the world of Augustine and Jerome from that of Alcuin and Charlemagne, but as a time of new developments and fresh beginnings. Substantial foundations began to be laid all over Western Europe, in the Frankish kingdoms, Spain, Italy, Anglo-Saxon England and Ireland, for the remarkable efflorescence of culture in the ninth century discussed in the ensuing chapters of this book.

There was some degree of continuity throughout the period from the fifth to the eighth centuries.[3] Before the eighth century, distinctive intellectual contributions were made by many individuals such as Boethius, Cassiodorus, Gregory of Tours, Caesarius of Arles and Isidore of Seville. Learning became increasingly the prerogative of monastic and cathedral centres. There was a shift in emphasis from secular and classical to Christian

---

[1] Bischoff (1981b), p. 14.   [2] Bischoff (1981c), pp. 149–69.   [3] Riché (1962; 1976).

knowledge and texts.[4] Yet among the difficulties in assessing eighth-century developments are the nature of the evidence and the criteria employed in assessing levels or areas of cultural activity. The latter have to be understood within the framework provided by an educational curriculum in the form in which it survived into the early middle ages, and by the Christian authors and writings which served as its bedrock.[5] It is the extant manuscript evidence above all which enables us to document precise topics of interest, the contributions of individuals and the degree of innovation. Thus this crucial category of evidence augments what is known from texts and authors whose original manuscripts no longer survive.[6] In many cases, apart from the liturgy and canon law, we are admittedly not dealing so much with the creation of new work as with the transmission and augmentation of existing knowledge. We can observe how the technical mastery of literate skills was disseminated, how libraries were formed, and how centres capable of copying books were established. Without this fundamental framework, nothing subsequently would have been possible; it is vital that we do not underestimate its importance. The manuscript evidence can be exploited to shed light on the intellectual and religious vigour of a period. It provides some idea of the number of scribes trained to copy texts, the books copied, the books available and the contacts formed between one centre and another, often in different regions. The forms of the letters themselves can reflect the diverse influences present in a culture.

Let us compare, for instance, Anglo-Saxon intellectual culture with that of Frankish Gaul. Northumbria's culture is dominated by Bede, whose ecclesiastical history, biblical exegesis and treatises on time and metrics were also in great demand on the Continent.[7] The schools of York under Ælberht and Whitby under Hild were much praised by Alcuin and Bede respectively.[8] In the southwest of England the giant is the poet and moralist Aldhelm, author of a fearsome tract on virginity and many admonitory letters. An Englishman famed for his teaching and, as the Latin prose style of his letters strongly indicates, trained in the traditions of Aldhelm, moreover, was Boniface. He clearly had many pupils, both in Wessex and in the monasteries he established on the Continent, and a number of them wrote to him for advice on their Latin style as well as on religious matters. Some idea of what all these scholars had read can be determined from what they wrote; this augments our knowledge of texts available in early Anglo-Saxon England.[9] Learning was also a marked feature of monastic life in the

---

[4] Fontaine (1959); Fontaine and Hillgarth (1992).   [5] Glauche (1970).
[6] Berschin and Lehner (1990).   [7] Ed. Tangl 116, Whitelock (1974).
[8] Alcuin, *Versus de Patribus, Regibus et Sanctis Euboricensis Ecclesiae*, line 1536; Bede *HE* iv. 23.
[9] Laistner (1957); Lapidge and Herren (1979); Szarmach (1986); Biggs, Hill and Szarmach (1990); Ogilvy (1961).

south of England generally, both in the various religious communities of men and women for which we have the occasional poem, letter or passing reference and, most notably, at the school of Canterbury under Theodore and Hadrian. [10] Here, to Bede's information that Theodore and Hadrian 'gave their hearers instruction not only in the books of holy scripture but also in the art of metre, astronomy and *computus*',[11] Aldhelm adds that Roman law was also taught.[12] This was possibly from the Digest of Justinian rather than from the Breviary of Alaric, the collection from which those on the Continent normally derived their knowledge of Roman law. Theodore's qualities as a teacher and scholar emerge from his own *canones*, a creed, and contributions to medical recipes and the liturgy. A more impressive dossier is derived from the evidence of the original English collection of glosses, now extant in Leiden Voss. lat. Q.69, fols. 20r–36r, which Lapidge rightly describes as a 'wonderful treasury of evidence for the books which were known and studied in early England' and associates with the school of Canterbury. Beside church canons and papal decretals, the glosses derive from Eusebius' ecclesiastical history and the works of Gildas, Sulpicius Severus, Isidore, the Rule of Benedict, Athanasius' *Life of Anthony*, Jerome's *De Viris Illustribus*, Eucherius, Orosius' *Historia*, Augustine's Sermons, the grammars of Donatus and Phocas, glosses to many books of the Bible (possibly to be attributed to Theodore himself), and Gregory the Great's *Dialogues* and *Regula Pastoralis*.[13]

There is no scholar of comparable stature to Bede, Aldhelm or Theodore in Frankish Gaul. Nor can we as yet define any one centre of education and learning that can be compared to the account now possible for Canterbury, apart from Corbie, with its library and the activities of its abbots in the late seventh and the eighth centuries.[14] If we compare the intellectual resources as reflected in the extant manuscripts of both Frankish Gaul and Anglo-Saxon England, even taking the knowledge revealed in the writings of Bede, Aldhelm and Theodore into account, however, a rather different picture emerges; the clear limitations of English resources in this period can be recognised.

Both Anglo-Saxon England and Frankish Gaul inherited the Roman script system: the Franks by direct continuity and the English largely indirectly through the British and Irish churches (who preserved the script and book-making practices from the late Roman period) and the Italian missionaries who brought their literate practices and their books with them from the Continent. The manuscript to which the Durham Maccabees fragment belonged, a sixth-century uncial codex from Italy, for example,

[10] Sims-Williams (1991); Lapidge (1986).   [11] *HE* IV.2.
[12] Aldhelm, *Opera*, ed. Ehwald, pp. 476–7.   [13] Lapidge (1986).   [14] Ganz (1981; 1990).

served as an exemplar for the famous Codex Amiatinus, a pandect or complete Bible produced at Wearmouth-Jarrow at the turn of the seventh century. Thus in England we can observe the reception of Irish Christianity, the introduction there of insular minuscule and half-uncial as well as the effects of Roman (or Frankish) books and script brought by missionaries and pilgrims. Just over one hundred English manuscripts dating from before the ninth century are extant; a great proportion of these, produced in association with such centres as Lindisfarne, Jarrow, Wearmouth and Canterbury, are Gospel texts or other biblical books, though there are also important commentaries by such authors as Gregory the Great, Cassiodorus and Jerome, the works of Bede and Aldhelm, and a few of the rarer authors such as Junilius, Phillipus and Paterius.[15] The script types of the south of England and Mercia, which differ significantly from those of Northumbria, confirm the impression offered by the literary evidence, namely, that communications between the north and the rest of England were not good. Generally the provision of books is very basic indeed; the range is small and the Bible predominates. Thus even with scholars of the stature of Bede, Theodore and Aldhelm, the range of their learning was limited according to what was available to them.

The remarkable range of texts and authors in Francia, and the chronological distribution of the Frankish evidence is instructive in contrast to that of England and helps to account for the Carolingian efflorescence of learning and intellectual activity in the later eighth and the ninth centuries. There are about 500 Frankish manuscripts dating from the eighth century or earlier, that is, five times as many as from England: 400 Frankish manuscripts are extant from the eighth century alone; about 300 can be dated between c. 500 and c. 750,[16] with a further 200 datable to the last half of the eighth century. Thus there would appear to be an enormous increase in either production, or survival rate, or both, in the course of the eighth century. Many of the later eighth-century manuscripts from both Francia and Italy, of course, reflect the early years of the Carolingian Renaissance; my remarks here, therefore, primarily concern the evidence from before about 780.

Unlike the overwhelming proportion of Gospel texts in England, there are few Merovingian Gospel texts before the mid-eighth century.[17] On the other hand there are many Sacramentaries (Mass Books) and an enormous range of classical, legal and patristic texts. Lyons, for example, had enjoyed a reputation as a centre for the book trade in antiquity, and the region retained something of this reputation in the sixth, seventh and eighth centuries. It was there that Wilfred of Hexham had spent three years in the 650s imbibing

---

[15] Brown (1975; 1993) and Gneuss (1981).

[16] Discussed in detail, McKitterick (1981 and 1994).   [17] McGurk (1960).

learning, and from Vienne and elsewhere in Burgundy that Benedict Biscop acquired many of the books he subsequently took back with him to Jarrow.[18] Texts copied in Burgundy in the early eighth century include Jerome on the Psalms, Maximus of Turin's Homilies, Julianus Pomerius, the Breviary of Alaric, and the *Vetus Latina* collection of canon law, a vital witness to canon law compilation and formulation of *c.* 600 which was subsequently disseminated from the Autun region at the turn of the seventh century.[19] The writings of many of the Gallo-Roman authors of Gaul, such as Hilary of Poitiers and Eucherius of Lyons, quite apart from those of the principal church fathers such as Origen, Augustine, Ambrose, Gregory the Great and Jerome, are represented. At Luxeuil, whose scriptorium was at the peak of its activity at the end of the seventh century, and at the constellation of convents producing books in the Seine basin in the early eighth century, we can gain a representative impression of the types and range of books being produced. From Luxeuil, for example, there are twenty-eight codices still surviving. Twenty-one of these are written in the distinctive and ornate Luxeuil calligraphic minuscule developed from the elongated Merovingian chancery hand. The centre wrote for export as well as for its own liturgical needs, library and monastic reading.[20] Its influence appears to have been spread as monks from Luxeuil were called on to assist the setting up of religious foundations elsewhere such as Corbie, Jouarre, Chelles, Remiremont, Faremoutiers and the convent of St Mary and St John at Laon.[21] Generally the texts produced at Luxeuil are Christian – biblical commentaries, theological treatises, canon law collections, some grammars and liturgical books, including Augustine on Genesis, Isidore of Seville's *Synonyma*, the *Cura Pastoralis* and Homilies of Gregory the Great, the sermons and letters of Augustine and Jerome, and the famous Luxeuil Lectionary. Similarly, in the Seine basin convents, the nuns copied such heavy-weight patristic works by Augustine and Gregory the Great as the *De Trinitate, De Genesi ad Litteram* and the *Homilia in Ezekielem, Dialogi* and *Moralia in Job*, many Mass Books, Isidore of Seville, Eusebius and Symphosius and Gregory of Tours' *Historiae*. A glance at the late Merovingian library of Corbie confirms the impression of relative comprehensiveness: it adds to the heavy-weight authors familiar from other Merovingian centres not only more works by them but also the *Regula Magistri*, an Epitome of Gregory of Tours, secular law-codes, Jerome-Gennadius' *De Viris Illustribus*, the Rule of Basil, and various works by Tertullian, John Chrysostom, Ephraemus Syrus, Caesarius of Arles, Ambrose, John Cassian, Isidore,

[18] Eddius Stephanus, *Vita Wilfridi*, ed. Colgrave, c. 6 and Bede, *Historia Abbatum*, ed. Plummer, c. 4 and c. 6.   [19] Mordek (1975).   [20] Löwe (1972).   [21] Prinz (1965, 2nd edn 1988).

Cassiodorus and Paterius.[22] Rich resources can also be attributed to Fleury library, for it is there that we can observe not only a substantial base in patristic writings, but also the beginnings of what was to become a major concentration of classical texts in the ninth century.[23] Even with such evidence as this, there is a danger in seeing the contrast with English resources too starkly. First it is essential that the complex network of relations of all kinds, reflected in the manuscript evidence, that criss-crossed the Channel be borne in mind.[24] Secondly, it should be noted that some insular manuscripts, such as that of Theodore of Mopsuestia's *Commentary on the Epistles of St Paul*, Phillipus on Job, Jerome on Isaiah, Boniface's *Aenigmata* and *Carmina* by Paulinus of Nola and many minor works by Isidore of Seville, were in Corbie library by 800.[25] In other words, the accidents of survival may well have distorted our understanding of the range of insular learning in some respects.

Overall, the Frankish evidence tells of continuing book production, in however small a way, throughout the Merovingian period, with many new centres being established in the Loire river valley as well as in the region north of the Loire, especially in the Seine basin and Picardy, in the early eighth century. All these centres produced many key texts for the Christian faith and Christian learning. They were sometimes in the form of intelligent compilations of material for particular purposes put together in the early eighth century, such as the didactic moral *florilegium* compiled by Defensor of Ligugé *c.* 700, or the compendium of strange lore, a precursor of the bestiary, gathered together in the *Liber Monstrorum de Diversis Generibus*.[26] An extraordinary assembly of fantastic knowledge is the mid-eighth-century Cosmography of Aethicus Ister, now generally attributed to the Irishman Virgil, bishop of Salzburg, who had inadvertently annoyed the English missionary Boniface. Among the strange and miscellaneous information Virgil included in his book was an account of the inhabitants of the Antipodes. Strange visions were recounted in the eighth-century *Visio Barontii* as well as in the *Revelationes Methodii*. A further eighth-century text with marvellous stories of the unknown is the *Hodoeporicon* written by Hugeburc, an English nun at Heidenheim in Germany. Contained within the conventional framework of an account of the life of Willibald, she provides a lively account of Willibald's travels to and adventures in the Holy Land and Asia Minor; he is thrown into the dungeon by the Saracens, smuggles out balsam hidden in bamboo poles topped up with petroleum to mask the smell, gazes at the awesome sight of Vesuvius and visits with great

---

[22] Ganz (1981).   [23] Mostert (1989) and McKitterick (1990).   [24] McKitterick (1989b).
[25] Ganz (1990), pp. 129–30.   [26] Brunholzl (1990), pp. 148–50.

devotion many of the Holy Places themselves, including the site of the Council of Nicaea.[27]

While the preoccupations of English book production are similar to those of the Franks, such as the stress on the Bible and biblical exegesis, the Frankish manuscripts also witness to much creative activity in the spheres of liturgy and canon law compilation. Reference has already been made to the remarkable *Vetus Gallica* canon law collection, but there are also the crucial developments in the Frankish Mass Books, apparent in such codices as Vat. reg. lat. 316, a mid-eighth-century copy of a text compiled 628–715, Vat. reg. lat. 317, Vat. reg. lat. 257 and 493. These reveal the active composition of new prayers, the reorganisation and elaboration of many ecclesiastical rituals and a concentration on the provision of a reformed liturgy for the entire Frankish church which were to culminate in the reforms presided over by Pippin III and Chrodegang of Metz and, in their footsteps, Charlemagne and Benedict of Aniane.[28] An important indication of the assessment and definition of a canon of knowledge, moreover, was the drawing up of the text *De Libris Recipiendis et non Recipiendis*, a list of approved and unapproved books, whose earliest extant manuscript is from northern Francia of *c.*700.[29] It can be set beside the possession, by such centres as Corbie, of the Jerome-Gennadius bibliographical guide *De Viris Illustribus*. Already in the late Merovingian period, therefore, is apparent the preoccupation with authority, orthodoxy and correctness that was to become such a prevailing characteristic of Carolingian scholarship. By implication, furthermore, the books produced in the eighth century reveal what enormous traffic there must have been from scriptorium to scriptorium in texts for copying and palimpsesting. Many codices are still in the old Roman scripts, uncial and half-uncial, but minuscule experiments, based on half-uncial cursive and charter hands, can also be observed. We are witnessing in fact the active and creative response of scribes to the need for texts, just as at Wearmouth-Jarrow we see how capitular uncial and then minuscule were developed to facilitate the dissemination of the texts of Bede.[30] It was the primitive minuscule forms of the early eighth century that were to be regularised as Caroline minuscule; we can observe these in many different centres throughout the Frankish, Bavarian and Alemannic regions.[31]

As emphasised in chapter 2(c) above, many of these manuscripts come from centres where individual Englishmen and women were members of

---

[27] Dronke (1984); Bischoff (1931) and above, p. 78.

[28] Moreton (1976); McKitterick (1992); Vogel (1981), Deshusses (1971) and compare Reynolds above, ch. 22.   [29] McKitterick (1989a).   [30] Parkes (1983).

[31] Bischoff (1974; 1980; 1990); McKitterick (1981; 1989b).

the community, but there are important links evident in the manuscripts with centres like Spain and Italy as well. Lyons in particular reveals many contacts with Spain, while such centres as Verona and Bobbio had links with Frankish centres such as Luxeuil.[32] Italian and Spanish book production in the late seventh and the eighth centuries, moreover, was very similar in emphasis to that of the Frankish regions. If we look at the extant manuscripts from such major centres as Bobbio, Nonantola, Ravenna, Verona, Vercelli or Monte Cassino, it is clear that Lombard intellectuals shared the preoccupations of the Franks. In Italy, too, therefore, there is an active and creative interest in canon law, though the collections formed appear to be more idiosyncratic and less widely disseminated than the Frankish *Vetus Gallica*. There is manifest an interest in the texts accompanying the liturgy, such as the Homiliaries put together by Agimundus, probably a priest in Rome, in the first part of the eighth century, and by Alan of Farfa, quite apart from the many copies made of the homilies of Gregory the Great and the volume of Maximus of Turin's Homilies in Bobbio library. As in Francia, so in Italy there are the same Gallo-Roman theologians such as Hilary of Poitiers; the same impressive collections of the theological treatises and biblical commentaries of the main patristic authors, and of sixth-century authors such as Augustine, Orosius, Gregory the Great, Jerome, Ambrose, Isidore of Seville, Maximus of Turin, Ambrosiaster and Cyprian. Yet in Italy there are various additional features. It is noticeable, for example, that there is a greater number of classical works such as Juvencus, Virgil and Juvenal surviving in sixth-century manuscripts in Italian monastic libraries. It should be stressed that the numbers of such early codices are nevertheless extremely small in comparison with those produced in the ninth century. But such small indications of classical survivors help to account for the dedicated copying and preservation of such works in the Carolingian period.[33] Historical writing is notable too in the form of the *Liber Pontificalis*. Two editions of this extraordinarily rich text had been made in the course of the sixth century, with the record kept up to date right through until the end of the ninth century, with many local recensions apparent, as in the 'Lombard' recension in Lucca, Biblioteca Capitolare 490. Such historiographical influence as the *Liber Pontificalis* may have exerted is apparent at least in the *Gesta Episcoporum Mettensium* of Paul the Deacon, as well as later, ninth-century, works, and it may be that information the *Liber Pontificalis* contained was also useful to Paul when he wrote his History of the Lombards in the 780s at Monte Cassino. Certainly an interest in the history of the Lombards in the course of the seventh

---

[32] *CLA* VI, pp. xv–xvii.   [33] See Contreni and Ganz below, chapters 27 and 29.

century is evident from the *Origo Gentis Langobardorum* and the annalistic collection of Secundus. The existence, moreover, of the *De Libris Recipiendis et non Recipiendis,* Jerome-Gennadius' *De Viris Illustribus,* Augustine's *Retractationes* (in which he lists many of his works) and Cassiodorus' *Institutiones* at Vercelli, and at least one other seventh- or eighth-century copy of Jerome-Gennadius' *De Viris Illustribus* suggests a similar interest in expanding library resources to that we have observed in Francia. There are very few new authors but a great many copyists, extractors and compilers with a creativeness in gathering together useful material for the Christian faith and Christian learning, especially in the spheres of liturgy and canon law. Nowhere is this more apparent than in the massive commentary on the Apocalypse (Book of Revelation) by Ambrosius Autpertus of San Vincenzo al Volturno, produced 758–67. He incorporated the interpretations of a great many patristic authors, familiar and rare, in the course of his exposition. As with the evidence from Frankish scriptoria, so in Italy we may observe an impressive demonstration of scribal discipline and co-operation. In the course of the eighth century we witness consolidation of the uncial script and forms or pre-Caroline minuscule in Rome and in many of the north Italian centres, as well as the gradual emergence of new letter forms in central Italy, especially at Monte Cassino.[34]

The Spanish manuscript evidence, from both the Mozarabic communities in Muslim Spain and the northern Christian kingdoms, is much more meagre, but it tells a similar story: liturgical and canonical texts in new arrangements are to the fore, as well as a respectable corpus of the standard patristic works. Yet there was also a move to record the past, evident in the Arabic-Byzantine Chronicle of 741 and the Mozarabic Chronicle of 751.[35] Those manuscripts which can be attributed to Ireland, on the other hand, far more closely resemble the Anglo-Saxon books in their basic emphasis, but the seventh and eighth centuries saw particularly influential developments in the composition of insular grammars for the learning of the Latin language by non-native speakers,[36] and of distinctive exegesis of the Bible.[37]

With all the eighth-century evidence in every region there is a growing intensity of production. The recurrence of such principal bibliographical aids as Jerome-Gennadius demonstrates a consciousness in the acquisition and expansion of knowledge. Teaching was being carried out in the monasteries and cathedral schools, even if only at a limited level at which we can only guess from the results reflected in the manuscripts copied. Certain methods of scholarship were apparent and these remained the guiding

[34] Petrucci (1969; 1971; 1973).
[35] Wolf provides a convenient introduction and translation (1990).
[36] Law (1982); Holtz (1992).   [37] Bischoff (1954).

principles for intellectual endeavour subsequently. The discipline established in particular scriptoria for the production of all these texts, and all the training, communication and discipline they embody, are a crucial element in the assessment of eighth-century culture. Both learning and scribal capacity, after all, were sufficient for Charlemagne to be able to be confident that the work he required was actually feasible.

The manuscript evidence also gives us clear indications of many new centres being established, particularly in those areas in which English men and women set up new monasteries – in Hesse, Franconia and Thuringia, Bavaria and the northern Rhineland – such as Echternach, Würzburg, Fulda or Hersfeld, or in those areas in which native Alemans or Bavarians, inspired in some cases by visiting Frankish or Irish missionaries, established new houses, such as St Gall and Reichenau, Regensburg, Salzburg and Freising.[38] All these from frail beginnings gradually built up their intellectual resources along similar lines to those already customary in the older centres of learning and the religious life. These new foundations were to emerge as major centres of book production and Christian learning in the Carolingian Renaissance.

So far I have stressed on the one hand the importance of the preservation of knowledge, copying of essential texts, compilations of excerpts from a range of authoritative authors and the building up of libraries with mainline as well as more obscure patristic and early medieval writers. The evidence also clearly reveals considerable activity in the spheres of liturgy and canon law, and in texts related to the liturgy such as homilies. There is one further genre of Christian writing to which many individuals, in every part of western Europe, made particularly creative contributions in the eighth century, and this is hagiography. Most literary histories dismiss these works as being of little merit, but they have much to tell us, not only concerning the currents of religious devotion in many different localities, and of the actions of the influential individuals,[39] but also of the way a cult was promoted and how writing was put to the service of religion. The Corbie collection (BN lat. 12598) is a case in point. In Corbie's library soon after it had been completed at a centre somewhere nearby, it included accounts of the lives and virtues of Martin, Remedius, Medard, Vedast, Fuscian and Victor, Landebert, Columba, Juliana, Agatha, Euphemia, Crispin and Crispianus, Justis and Lucian, Caecelia and Agneta. Thus local Frankish saints are commemorated alongside saints and martyrs of early Christianity. Many new saints' Lives were written in the eighth century, from Ireland and England across to Italy, such as the Lives of Emmeram and

---

[38] Duft (1990); Bischoff and Hofmann (1952; 1974; 1985); Netzer (1994).
[39] Fouracre (1990).

Corbinian by Arbeo of Freising, Willibald's Life of Boniface and the anonymous Irishman's Life of Willibrord. In northern Francia, the richest fund for this genre, there are Lives of Bonitus, Lambert of Liège, Hugobert, Arnulf of Metz, Ermino and Ursmar of Lobbes, Rigobert of Rheims, Eucherius and Pardulf. A large proportion of these were 'corrected' by Carolingian scholars in the ninth century and transformed in various ways. These Lives were often of family saints as well as of local saints; they reflect a degree of family and aristocratic self-interest and form part of a carefully nuanced campaign on the part of a particular church or family to enhance its prestige together with that of the monastery whose patron the saint was. Yet the religious devotion they mirror and the contribution the laity made to the development of the cult of a saint are also very real and not to be underestimated. In this respect they link up with the appearance of local annals and rather more substantial historical works such as the so-called Metz Annals, the Continuations made to the Chronicle of Fredegar, or the *Liber Historiae Francorum*, all of which witness to political ideals and ambitions on the part of particular families as well as to a wish to shape posterity's understanding of the past.[40]

Not all intellectual energy in the eighth century was channelled into Christian education and learning, however. This was also a dynamic period in the formulation and revision of secular laws, and we can observe in relation to this the increasing resort to the written record in legal transactions and disputes.[41] To the impressive base provided in the mid-seventh century by Rothari, king of the Lombards, for example, were added many new provisions and judgements by Kings Liutprand and Ratchis, who had particular concern for the rules of inheritance and abuse of power by *iudices*. Lombard law occasionally shows that Roman practice, especially in the laws of property and possession, the notion of the state and its administrative role and the distinction between public and private, made some impact.[42] Among the Franks, a redaction of the sixth-century *Lex Salica* was put together early in the reign of Pippin III. The *Lex Ribuaria*, compiled in Austrasia in the mid-seventh century, of which the Carolingian mayor issued his own recension in the mid-eighth century, provides a crucial context for the subsequent assumptions and procedures of the Carolingian mayors of the palace and Austrasian nobles in the conduct of legal business. They make room in particular for the use of written documents in a number of important instances. Other laws appear to have been formulated either as a result of Frankish initiative or as a form of assertion against the political dominance of the Francs. The *Lex Baiuuariorum*, for example, was

---

[40] Innes and McKitterick (1994). [41] Davies and Fouracre (1986); McKitterick (1989a).
[42] Wickham (1982), pp. 43–6, 69 and Delogu, above, p. 292.

promulgated under Duke Tassilo between 744 and 748 before he was crushed under his uncle's and cousin's expansionist greed. A remarkable prologue to the Bavarian laws called attention to the legislation of the Hebrews, the Greeks, the Egyptians and the Romans, and cited by name the great law-givers of history such as Solon, Lycurgus, Numa Pompilius, Pompey, the 'authors' of the Twelve Tables, the Caesars, Constantine and Theodosius. It provided a definition of 'custom' and 'law' and evoked the law-giving of the ancient Frankish kings. The *pactus legis Alemannorum* was drawn up in the early seventh century, but the *Lex Alemannorum*, compiled about a century later, may be expressive of a brief period of independent power on the part of the dukes before 724.

Like the Edict of Rothari, the *Liber Iudiciorum* of the Visigoths was promulgated in the mid-seventh century. Similarly, subsequent rulers, notably Erwig in 681, and Egica and Witiza, revised and added to it.[43] The effect of the legislation was to make Roman law in the Visigothic kingdom redundant; the *Liber Iudiciorum* has been characterised, rightly or wrongly, as the first territorial law-code of early medieval Europe, which applied to all inhabitants within the kingdom irrespective of racial or cultural affiliations. New laws were formulated, moreover, which sought to contain a possible abuse of power on the part of the king, defined a distinction between personal property and property pertaining to the office of king, and explicitly subjected the ruler to the law. This body of laws remained that consulted by judges in the Christian kingdoms of northern Spain after the Arab conquest in 711. Roman law, however, as the number of manuscripts of the Breviary of Alaric available in the eighth century attest, was still widely in use in early medieval Europe. The Breviary, a Digest of the Theodosian Code compiled in southern Gaul at the beginning of the sixth century, continued to provide a source for Roman legislation and Roman jurisprudential ideas throughout the ninth century as well.[44] In many of the early 'Germanic' codes there are indications of a knowledge and application of Roman principles on many topics. There is also evidence of an attempt to accommodate, if not Christianity itself, then certainly the needs of the Christian church, into the framework of the laws. This is particularly evident in the laws of the earliest English kings, such as those of Æthelberht, Hlothere, Eadric and Wihtred, kings of Kent in the course of the seventh century, of Ine of Wessex (688–94) and no doubt Offa of Mercia, allusion to whose laws is made by Alfred of Wessex. Yet the English laws differed in that, unlike their continental counterparts, they were, although consciously

---

[43] Collins (1983), p. 123; King (1980).   [44] Gaudemet (1955); Nelson (1989).

emulating Roman example, written in a Germanic vernacular.[45] In Ireland too, problems of secular law and thinking about legal questions concerning power, rights, status, the enforcement of law, property, authority and the distinction between public and private are all embodied in a series of vernacular Irish tracts compiled in the seventh and eighth centuries and apparently comprising statements of customary practice.[46]

Thus a great deal of thinking about status and power in the course of the seventh and eighth centuries was embodied in these legal compilations. They witness, furthermore, not only to the application of ideas to the practical spheres of government and ordered society, but also to the maintenance of legal training to some degree, even if those versed in the law or acting as judges did so as part of a package of other administrative, martial or ecclesiastical obligations. The wider context of such legal provision, as the prologue to the eighth-century redaction of the *Lex Salica* and the *Lex Baiuuariorum* make clear, and as Wormald has stressed,[47] was a wish on the part of the Germanic kings both to emulate the literary and legal aspects of the Roman and Judaeo-Christian culture to which they were heirs, and to reinforce the links that bound a ruler or dynasty to his people. But we also witness the coincidence of an appreciation in many different parts of western Europe of the practical significance of the written word in relation to the exigencies of enforcing justice.[48] The ideological, symbolic and practical functions of the law are all intertwined and interdependent. Those concerned with government were, as Nelson has shown,[49] able to build on the work of the eighth-century rulers, lawyers and legal advisers.

The many endeavours in different branches of learning and technical skills that have been surveyed in this chapter mirror the formation of particular mental attitudes that were to have a profound influence in the subsequent centuries. A particular image and conception of the church and Christianity was formed through the liturgical and canon law collections, as well as by means of biblical study, knowledge of the writings of the great church fathers and of the histories and accounts of the institutions of the early Christian church. Efforts were being made in many different ways to understand God's purpose for his people. From the overwhelmingly biblical and patristic orientation of early medieval intellectual endeavour we gain a crucial indication of the formative influences and characteristics of early medieval religion and the institutional and intellectual frameworks

---

[45] Kelly (1990).
[46] Still an excellent introduction is Hughes (1972), 43–64. See Ó Corráin, p. 50 above.
[47] Wormald (1977).   [48] McKitterick (1989a) and Sellert (1992) with further references.
[49] Nelson, ch. 15 above.

established to support it. In the eighth century in particular, the tools were honed, methods refined, links joined and essential principles established for the exuberant manifestations of learning, thought and art in the later eighth and ninth centuries that are characterised as the 'Carolingian Renaissance'.[50]

[50] McKitterick (1994).

CHAPTER 26

LANGUAGE AND
COMMUNICATION
IN CAROLINGIAN EUROPE

Michel Banniard

LINGUISTIC FRONTIERS

THE period from the eighth to the tenth centuries is highly original from the cultural, literary and linguistic points of view. Thanks to the high reputation of the Carolingian Renaissance,[1] it has been the subject of much research, but whatever the discipline – linguistics, culture, history, literature[2] – many questions remain unanswered. To summarise in a few words the complex problems posed to and by current research, we need to ask the following questions. Which language(s) corresponded to which culture(s) and to which audience(s) did each language communicate?[3]

Three crucial and significant thresholds were successively established during the period from, say, the reign of Dagobert to that of Charles the Bald. Over time, in the Latin-speaking regions, the popular spoken language underwent a metamorphosis by the end of which imperial Latin had given way to early Romance dialects. In the western world, four distinct main groups emerged, some old, some new: the Latin areas (Italy, Gaul, Spain, etc.), the Germanic areas (Old High German, Old English, etc.), the Greek areas (southern Italy, the Peloponnese, Palestine, etc.), and the Arabic areas (Arabia, Syria, Egypt, Spain, etc.). Lastly, within the variable fabric of society, a number of 'splits' separated the learned culture of speakers endowed with autonomous access to the written tradition from the popular culture of speakers possessing only collective oral knowledge. How are we to establish a clear chronology for these cumulative 'broken lines'? The most rational approach is to conduct a systematic study on the basis of

---

[1] On the controversial question of the appropriate terminology, I have followed Lehmann (1941), pp. 109–38.

[2] Recent works on these questions include Fleckenstein (1953); Borst (1958); Braunfels (1965); McKitterick (1977; 1989); Fontaine (1981); Guerreau-Jalabert (1982); Banniard (1992).

[3] Battisti (1960); Lentner (1963); van Uytfanghe (1975; 1977); Wright (1982); Richter (1982; 1983); Banniard (1992), chapter 6.

contemporary evidence, using, by extrapolation, methods honed in the context of historical anthropology and here focused on the application of modern socio-linguistic advances to the Carolingian period.[4]

Naturally, the *testimonia* assembled are ambiguous. Possible readings of the famous Canon 17 of the Council of Tours held in 813[5] are today so numerous, and so divergent, that this document, which the researcher might at first think of as constituting a clear-cut reference point in historical research, seems to have been transformed into a thicket of enigmas. So, let us pose our questions as directly as possible. Following the chronological splits mentioned above, we will concentrate on the region where, in the fifth century, Latin was the mother tongue of the whole community of speakers. Three questions need to be asked. First, up until what diachronic limit could late spoken Latin,[6] at the elementary level of the *sermo humilis*, be employed for the religious instruction of illiterate people? Second, what role did late Latin, in its learned forms (history, and, above all, poetry) play in the culture of the social elite, that is, the lay aristocracy? Lastly, what diachronic linguistic models can accommodate the answers to the first two questions? To establish the current state of our knowledge, it will be helpful first to put down a few socio-linguistic markers, then note breaks and continuities, before trying to compile an account, a good deal more complex than might at first have been imagined, of the changing linguistic and cultural structures which have existed during these centuries.

EUROPEAN LANDMARKS

The term 'Europe', by convention, is applied to the group of western countries where Latin and Christian civilisation spread, that is, from its start, in the Roman, and in the later Carolingian empire, to which it is thereupon convenient to add the British Isles and Spain. Within this area, which varies in size over time, we can follow the fortunes of medieval Latin, from its roots in late antiquity to its branches, some of them, popular and Romance, growing in the ancient Latin-speaking lands, and some of them aristocratic and learned, as they were following the *dilatatio christianitatis*.

This brief backwards glance is essential to emphasise the vitality of the language of Rome, even after the 'fall' of its empire. The relatively recent reassessment not only of our knowledge but of our perception of the late

---

[4] For a fuller explanation of these ideas see Banniard (1992), chapter 1, pp. 32–8. There is an interesting preliminary discussion in van Uytfanghe (1976).

[5] *MGH Conc.* II:1, p. 288 and compare Banniard (1992), p. 408.

[6] For this specifically linguistic problem see E. Löfstedt (1933) II, chapter 12, esp. pp. 355–64; Norberg (1943); Reichenkron (1965); B. Löfstedt (1982).

empire has of course echoed through those auxiliary domains of history, the history of culture and the history of languages. The period which begins in the third century has now to be seen not as an accidental and decadent appendix to glorious antiquity, but as an original and creative extension to the old classical civilisation.[7] The consequences for literary and linguistic history are considerable, at a number of levels. First, late Latin literature, pagan and Christian, has achieved the cultural status which is its due; no one now regards Sidonius Apollinaris as a *momie peinturlurée*.[8] Next, *ipso facto*, we now see the imperial elites as displaying not so much an artificial taste for a past long gone as a dynamic loyalty to aesthetic values which had undergone a revival in a new way. The rise of Christianity provoked a revolution in men's minds and literary models: the power of the Christian mission imposed new linguistic compromises; alongside the recognised literature, based on the elevated language to which succeeding centuries would give the significant name of *sermo sc(h)olasticus*, there emerged a new eloquence intended for the faithful masses, the *plebs christiana*. Initially regarded as having no place in either education or grammar by the intellectual elite, already repelled by a Latinity as crude as that of the first Latin translations of the Bible, the new language slowly won itself an honourless but unavoidable function, before receiving from Augustine its baptismal name, the *sermo humilis*, the 'earth-bound language'.[9]

Three conclusions follow from these considerations: first, that the period of cultural and linguistic change which began in the fourth and fifth centuries concerned, at all levels of culture and communication, a vivid Latinity; second, that the social spread of late Latin, a living, spoken language, was extensive, for the linguistic and archaeological indicators combine to confirm the extent of Romanisation; third, that Latin was deep rooted among the populations of the empire. However peculiar the accents of spoken Latin might be, diachronically and synchronically, conceiving a vulgar Latin as radically different from ordinary Latin is simply a lure. These are conclusions based both upon the internal facts of linguistic evolution and, above all, on the external facts provided by socio-linguistic research. It was therefore from the basis of a Latinity which was not a dying language but a living one that these transitional periods began.[10]

Such a reassessment of the basic facts is a prerequisite to understanding the direct *testimonia* of the early middle ages. Then we can attempt to provide a more comprehensive interpretation of the functions achieved by the

---

[7] A revision due largely to Marrou (1958; 1977); also to Brown (1971; 1978).

[8] Lot (1931), p. 128.

[9] See Norden (1898), II, pp. 529–654; Auerbach (1965), chapter 8; Meershoek (1966).

[10] For a brief summary of recent works see Banniard (1992), chapter 1, pp. 17–48.

698 MICHEL BANNIARD

learned literary production from the eighth to tenth centuries. During the period which extends from about 450 to 850, we do know, from objective evidence, that Latin ceased to be a spoken language as it was growing into different Romance languages.[11] We need here to note three points: first, it was not because the diachronic link between Latin-speaking generations proceeded without interruption that there was no abrupt linguistic caesura (in other words, one language died and others were born); second, this diachronic metamorphosis of the spoken living tongue did not preclude communication between speakers of different generations; third, we must gather from these two points that the linguistic situation needs to be studied as one that was changing over time, and that we should take care to avoid looking at the fifth century as if it were, so to speak, identical with the eighth. We must strive, on the contrary, after the distinguishing of the various diachronic strata in the evolution of late Latin.[12]

For thirty years, we have been struggling to move beyond both the out-dated teaching of the Romance philologists who argued that the popular spoken language had become Romance by the fifth century at least, and the position of the Latin philologists who, while pushing the date forwards to around 600, have left this matter in a state of flux, for the period 600–800. Taking as our principal focus of interest Francia, that is, the country which is richest in *testimonia*, and is most precocious in the appearance of the first glimpses of texts in a written vernacular (*scripta vulgaris*), it now seems advisable to propose a protracted chronology, based on the criterion of 'vertical communication'.[13] Let us refer to the example of the sermons written in *sermo humilis*, or the saints' Lives worded in *sermo rusticus* (the 'language of general communication'); all the textual evidence, collected from contemporary authors, shows that the mass of illiterate hearers understood this Latin without difficulty when it was read aloud to them.[14] Moreover, internal analysis suggests that the structure of the spoken language (its diasystem) remained Latin, *lato sensu*, up to 650. Accordingly, I propose the following phases for Francia:[15]

1. 450–650: late Latin remains a living language, since it is not only understood but spoken;
2. 650–750: the popular spoken language fairly rapidly loses much of its Latin diasystem, at the level of 'active competence' (or performance);

[11] For a detailed report compare Banniard (1992), chapter 8, pp. 369–422 and chapter 9, pp. 485–533.
[12] For a more detailed discussion see Banniard (1992), chapter 1, p. 2 and chapter 9, p. 486.
[13] On this criterion see Banniard (1992), chapter 1, pp. 38–40.
[14] See Banniard (1992), chapter 5, pp. 254–63. [15] Banniard (1992), chapter 9, pp. 519–33.

illiterate people cease to be Latin native speakers in less than one hundred years;

3. 750–850: a rapid loss by the mass of the illiterate, of 'passive competence' (or performance); they prove unable or unwilling to retain more than a ragged contact with the grammatical structures of late spoken Latin;

4. 850–1000: surge of the same phenomenon as in (2) and (3) among the lay aristocracy.[16]

With appropriate modifications, this chronology applies to the other Romance countries. In the current state of research, one can only put forward the hypothesis that Spain and, above all, Italy, experienced a quite similar, but rather later, development.[17] From the socio-linguistic point of view, the transition from different kinds of spoken Latin to the Romance languages, and the corresponding wreck of general Latin communication, led, from the 750s onwards, to the establishment of a situation of diglossia (where different languages in the same society fulfil different social functions).

BREAKS AND CONTINUITIES

At the beginning of the eighth century, therefore, we enter a specific phase in the linguistic and cultural history of the west. On the one hand, we see signs of a linguistic crisis, soon to be followed by a sudden awareness of its existence, which itself culminated in a mental revolution. On the other, initiated by the will of a Carolingian monarchy intent on promoting an intellectual revival, there was a rise of a vital, learned and once more multi-faceted Latinity. This gives us such an impression of continuity with antiquity that it has been suspected of being merely an illusion. At this point, it is helpful to introduce a distinction between changes in society as a whole and continuities within particular groups. The former are obvious but their scale remains debatable; the latter, equally noticeable, give rise to even more complex questions.

The question of breaks with old customs is introduced by the obligation imposed on bishops or priests at the reform council of Tours in 813 to *transferre* their sermons into a language the people could understand: this verb, *transferre*, is decisive evidence of a major break in practice; yet it remains to some degree enigmatic. It is today generally accepted that the reformation of Latin, begun under Pippin III and pursued even more

---

[16] For a somewhat converging view, see Wright (1982) chapters 4 and 5. Compare Banniard (1992), chapter 9, pp. 492 and 534.   [17] Banniard (1992), Annexe 3, pp. 544–51.

actively under Charlemagne, gave rise to a linguistic crisis. The *sermo rusticus*, that is, the Latin intended for the illiterate, which had hitherto been accepted by both literate speakers (sometimes reluctantly) and illiterate hearers (now and then with some toil) as a common means of vertical communication, gradually lost its status as universal linguistic mediator between the educated and the uneducated.

When asked to raise the level of the style they used, some of the professional 'mediators' became aware that the reform of oral communication bred a host of difficulties in transmitting the Christian message. At the same time, the specialists in the standard normative language had a keen sense of the lamentable state of the language in everyday use: Latin had never been so badly spoken. Two tendencies came face to face within the Carolingian court: one party proposed to compel the masses to raise themselves to a higher linguistic level; the more realistic decided to adopt this level of language, however much they disliked it.

This is how it came to be laid down in the province of Tours that preachers should 'openly endeavour to translate sermons into the Latin of the illiterate' (*transferre in romanam linguam rusticam*) in order that 'all might the more easily understand'.[18] Against this evidence, attempts have been made to diminish the width of the gulf created by this injunction, arguing that *transferre* could mean simply 'pronounce' (a phonetic adaptation)[19] or, an even subtler hypothesis, 'transcribe' (that is, adapt into Romance *scripta*).[20] But the most obvious meaning is also the one justified by all contextual studies: that it was a question of 'translating' from one language to another. The change under way since the fifth century had now been completed in the spoken popular language and noticed by many of the *eruditi*.[21]

At the same time, the linguistic proximity of the 'grammatical' language and of the non-standard language was emphasised, since *lingua romana* meant 'Latin' and *rustica* meant 'illiterate'. It was still the same popular spoken language that had always been so unamenable to the art of the grammarian

---

[18] Banniard (1992), chapter 8, pp. 405–13. This is the only possible translation. Indeed, if *romana lingua* means 'Latin' and *rusticus* means 'illiterate', then *romana lingua rustica* can only mean 'Latin spoken by illiterate people'. In other words, 'bad spoken Latin' versus 'good spoken Latin'. Continuity and discontinuity are both implied by these words. The gap between the two levels of old and new language is not indicated by *romana lingua rustica*, but by *transferre*. This is my point of departure with Roger Wright's interpretation, for Wright does not think this is a matter of translation *stricto sensu*.   [19] This thesis is brilliantly argued in Wright (1982).

[20] This is the interesting interpretation of Cerquiglini (1991).

[21] It was noticed everywhere in Francia, for canon 17 of Tours was but a peculiar and local settlement of a general prescription emanating from Aachen (Banniard (1992), pp. 407–9).

(from Varro to Priscian, intellectuals had been aware of this distinction, which proves essentially obvious and trivial); and now it had become alienated from its own ancient structure, as a result of a somewhat strange process of auto-allophonismus.[22] It was the paradox of a bi-dialectalism which emerged in this way into the consciousness of literate Carolingians.[23] In the literal sense, they were witnesses to what was, from their point of view, a linguistic catastrophe: they watched impotently as the vernacular was irrevocably separated from the traditional ensemble of different kinds and levels of Latin. Hitherto, there had existed, and could officially be authorised, only *traditio* (explanation); translation had now been sanctioned.[24]

The precision of the *testimonia* is such that we should have confidence in their authors, and accept that late Latin disappeared as one living language of the whole community during the course of the eighth century. Nevertheless, the popular spoken language retained a relationship, discrepant and loose but real, with the traditional language. In other words, although a diachronic linguistic frontier emerged, there yet remained some tiny and troublesome contact points. This last observation makes it possible, it seems to me, to resolve the difficult problem raised by the existence of a learned Latin culture within the lay aristocracy.[25] Can we apply such terms to the Frankish *potentes*? This highly controversial question is neatly exemplified in the question of Charlemagne's relations with the Latin language, culture and literature. In spite (or because?) of the formal testimony not only of Einhard but of Alcuin, it has recently been argued that Charlemagne did not even speak Latin.[26] Taking such interpretations further, it has been claimed that, with very few exceptions, the Frankish aristocracy was remote from a Latinity which was exclusively for the use of the clergy. This very clergy therefore appears to have utterly deluded modern scholars so that they think laymen were, so to speak, locked up in their own Romance language and, in a sense, deaf and dumb to Latin words.[27]

There is ample evidence, however, of an output in the learned language which was aimed at an audience of lay aristocrats. First, there is Carolingian

[22] Auto-allophonismus is a linguistic concept that is indispensable to the argument. It is intended to show in a clear-cut way that late spoken Latin (fifth-century) changed into a new spoken tongue by the eighth century: that is to say, it went through an internal structural metamorphosis.

[23] See Koll (1957–8); B. Muller (1983).

[24] For a fuller discussion see Banniard (1992), chapter 7, pp. 402–5.

[25] See the classic studies of Laistner (1957); Riché (1972; 1979); Simonetti (1986). See also the works of Rosamond McKitterick.   [26] In particular, this is argued in Richter (1982).

[27] This is indeed a commonplace if one takes the theories of the romanist philologists into account and thinks of the work of Le Goff (1977) and Riché (1972).

legislation, then the politically 'committed' works of Einhard, Thegan, Nithard and Hincmar of Rheims, whose audience raises difficult questions.[28] More surprising still is the flowering of poetry; Theodulf's poem describing his mission to the Narbonnaise is hardly likely to have been addressed only to a few devotees of the hexameter; there must surely have been a real audience for the famous poem about the battle of Fontenoy.[29] Would it not be more logical to attribute its existence to a vital need for a literature indispensable to a Frankish aristocracy, which was sorely tried physically and psychologically? Lastly, sufficient attention has perhaps not been paid to the socio-linguistic implications of the appearance of such a text as the *Liber Manualis* of Dhuoda.[30] This formidable woman seems not to have enjoyed an exceptional intellectual education; only, unlike many other persons of her social level, she had a vocation to write. However, she does appear to have been familiar with learned Latin, in which she immersed herself without apparent difficulty. Further, in spite of some stylistic unorthodoxies, only to be expected from a largely autodidact authoress, she expressed her views firmly in quite respectable language. Nor is there any reason to suppose that her son William, destined for an active public career, had any difficulty in understanding the *vademecum* addressed to him by his mother. So, his ability to understand a Latinity which was, after all, of a quite educated level was not the exclusive preserve of the professional expert in Latin grammar.[31] By reading it for himself, or by listening to a reader, William could enjoy his mother's private lessons.

So, everything points to a reassessment of the socio-linguistic history of the Carolingian period. Indeed, the *testimonia* which we have briefly described, and which are independent of each other, combine to link themselves into a convincing body of evidence. The way in which both the discontinuities in general social practice and the continuities within particular social groups are revealed gives them reciprocal authentication. If the language spoken by the illiterate was, in practice, still close to that spoken by the literate, to the extent that the possibility of vertical communication, however disturbed, was nevertheless not utterly broken, we must conclude that this same spontaneous spoken language provided an adequate base for ready access to literary forms, that is, to the successive levels of the grammatical language. From access only to the lowly style (*sermo humilis*) for the majority of the *potentes*, perhaps, to access to scholarly elaborations

---

[28] See Brunhölzl (1976).

[29] For Carolingian poetry, see Godman (1985 and 1987).

[30] Edited by Riché and Mondésert (1975).

[31] On this theme, see, in addition to the works already cited, Godman and Collins (1990); Iogna-Prat (1991).

(*sermo politus, carmina*) for the elite among them,[32] the aristocratic laity was yet eager and receptive to old Latin works.

LINGUISTIC LATTICES AND CULTURAL NEBULAE

It is possible to explain the contradictions between the different cultural and linguistic interpretations of the Carolingian centuries, but to do so we have to accept that the analytical tools hitherto employed were inadequate, since they reduced phenomena of great complexity to oversimplified and geometric schemata. The contribution of parallel sciences such as dialectology, socio-linguistics and anthropology[33] will make it possible, or so one hopes, to overcome these difficulties, though at the cost of a considerable lengthening of the logical processes employed.

Let us recall a few of the conceptual oppositions which may make more refined analyses possible: written/oral; scholarly/popular; aristocratic/collective; traditional/innovative; grammaticality/ungrammaticality; dominant/dominated; pleasant/repellent; vertical communication/horizontal communication; Christian/non-Christian; biblical/non-biblical; etc. This tool-box employed for synchronic analyses by linguists and/or ethnologists, has produced minute descriptions of modern societies, studied *in vivo*, that is, as it happens. By extrapolation into societies of the past, it is reasonable o assume that the manifold phenomena which induced the transformations of the sixth to ninth centuries were of at least equal intricacy.[34] This leads us to paint a many-sided picture of the linguistic and cultural *nature* of the years 700–900.

To see the everyday socio-linguistic situation as a binary opposition between the language of the church and that of the people gives a wholly inadequate picture of reality. The linguistic situation involves facts so complex that I propose to use Goebl's concept of a 'linguistic lattice' to describe it. In particular, we find the following.

First, two categories of competence can be identified. Every native speaker is endowed with both an active competence (performance), that is, the ability to express himself in his mother tongue, and a passive competence, that is, the capacity to understand other speakers whose linguistic characteristics do not correspond exactly to his own. The second level of

---

[32] This idea, recently revived by McKitterick (1989), first appeared in Schuchardt (1886), pp. 64, 75, 101–3. It is also present in H.F. Muller (1921; 1929; 1945); it reappeared in Zumthor (1963), then in van Uytfanghe (1977) and Wright (1982). Lastly it is central to some of the discussion in the collection of essays published by Wright (1991).

[33] Labov (1976; 1977); Cortelazzo (1976); Le Goff (1977); Goebl (1983).

[34] For a methodological discussion, see Banniard (1980).

competence comprises a range of very variable abilities, which are stored in the memory of the speaker. These include not only the ability to understand surviving linguistic forms inherited from an earlier stage of the language, but also to grasp linguistic structures which are just emerging, or, so to speak, crystallising, at the very origin of a later new stage of his language, and accents varying for geographical and/or social reasons, etc.

Second, there are many levels of spoken language whose use varies according to the speaker's education or culture and according to the context within which he is speaking (or listening). By way of an example, we will use the convergent/divergent opposition to show that, according to his frame of mind, a speaker of low cultural level will try to imitate the linguistic level of a speaker of higher cultural level, or, on the contrary, will reject it completely.[35]

Third, there are many kinds of relationships between the spoken and the written word, which suggest the existence of different levels of literacy and illiteracy, the transition from one to the other condition not being achieved by a discontinuous leap.[36] Thus, a modest country priest may read the Gospel with difficulty, an accountant in an abbey confine himself to figures, while a more enterprising well-off peasant may be able to make out a few lines of a charter, and so on. Of course, given our knowledge of civilisation, we can postulate that, the higher the level of literacy, the rarer it was.

Lastly, as all language is a matter of human interrelations, communication, in a society which was far from uniform, and was increasingly fragmented both socially and geographically, often depended on linguistic compromise. Illiterate speakers can (in a spontaneous and unconscious manner) hold in their memory the passive linguistic competences essential to participate in, for instance, the festivals of the patron saint of their church; the reverse kind of collaboration is found, when, for example, a preacher attempts to adapt his pronunciation to local peculiarities, in order to get his message over,[37] he might have been equally well understood had he

---

[35] See Banniard (1992), chapter 1, pp. 38–44 and chapter 7, pp. 397–401, and an even more detailed system in Swiggers (1987).   [36] See Richter (1979); Stock (1983); Goody (1986).

[37] This does not mean, in any case, that in 813 it was a single matter of phonetic adaptation. I think it was really a translation, in the full sense of the word. Of course, a part of this translation was a matter of pronunciation. On the other hand, it is not the same thing to accept some of the characteristics peculiar to vulgar local pronunciation, as a kind of *pacamentum*, and to speak or to read with *all* the vulgar phonetic patterns. Last but not least, I do believe that a linguistic change took place between, say, 650 and 750, and that this was not a mere matter of phonetics; morphology and syntax were also involved. Nor was the gap which opened between the usual spoken and skilled written language after the Carolingian reforms a mere matter of phonetics. See Banniard (1992), chapter 8, pp. 398–404 and chapter 9, passim. *Contra*, see Wright (1982).

preserved a *more* scholarly diction, but by this means he won his way into the hearts of his audience.[38]

These specifically linguistic considerations lead on to a similar kind of statement on the matter of culture in general, the best image for which seems to me to be the 'nebula'. Within this ensemble, we find sub-groups of the following type:

1. Places of obligatory mediation, that is, of preaching and evangelisation; places for the proclamation and exercise of royal (capitularies) or private justice (wills) respectively, and places for issuing orders to the army.

2. Places where mediation was available if required, such as the Carolingian court, with its scholars, counsellors and *nutriti*; episcopal palaces; abbeys; the households of the *potentes*; hermitages.

3. Clerics with a very high level of education (abbots, or counsellors at court such as Alcuin, Theodulf, Lupus of Ferrières, Hincmar, Smaragdus and others). For these persons there was' a deepened distinction between Latin (the learned language) and Romance (the vernacular).

4. Clerics with a middling or lower level of education, in particular copyists, notaries, chancery scribes and accountants. For them, the distinction between Latin and Romance was far from always clear. One suspects that there was frequent flux and interchange between their acquired *latinitas minor* and native *romanitas maior*.

5. Similar distinctions can be upheld for the laity.[39] In the case of lay people educated to a high level such as Guido, Dhuoda, William or Nithard we need to employ the concept of passive competence. That they had access to even the very formal works of the court poets is, in my view, certain. Their situation also makes them the natural mediators between *latinitas*, even *maior* (the Latin spoken by those who did not speak Romance) and the *romanitas maior* of those who did not know Latin.

6. The category of lay persons educated at a lower level. The case of Charlemagne's famous referendary, Maginarius, would appear to have been typical. His literacy, as shown in his letter to the sovereign, was of a middling level.[40] It is in the nature of things that these last mix their acquired *latinitas minor* and their natural *romanitas maior*. Secured by their passive competence, and heartened by the attraction of the court models, they grew into a considerable potential audience for literary works in Latin.

7. There is, in addition, the category of illiterate laity, the largest, naturally, almost cut off from acquired *latinitas minor* but also far from being totally

---

[38] Banniard (1989), chapter 6, pp. 202–8.   [39] See the recent discussion of Chelini (1991).
[40] See the apposite analysis of his relationship with Latin in Pei (1932), pp. 9–10, 390.

fluent in a general *romanitas maior*.[41] This was the world of over-dialectalisation within Romance, of a locally autonomous folklore, fragmented and evolving.

8. The last factor, not to be forgotten, is that of the 'time shift': the socio-linguistic structure was not the same from the seventh to the tenth centuries, but distinct structures succeeded each other.[42]

I have come to be certain that the linguistic processes, cultural exchanges and channels of communication in our period require an analytical representation of considerable complexity. Unfortunately, we need to admit that the socio-linguistic reality of that time extends beyond the framework of the logical categories so far employed by modern scholars; on the other hand, it is pleasant to be able to conclude that the Carolingian world, even the lay world, was by no means remote from the literary renaissance of the ninth century.

ORDER FROM CHAOS

During the early Carolingian period (650–750), by means of overlapping and entangling processes, a linguistic revolution was effected, in the course of which the common spoken language ceased to be organised according to an essentially Latin structure and was instead restructured into a diasystem which was essentially Romance (at an early stage, of course). A Latin-speaking society was succeeded by a Romance-speaking society. During the following century, cultural conflicts resulted in the decay of the passive competence of the mass of uneducated speakers.[43] The coexistence of different Latinities was superseded by a situation of diglossia: the Latin of the illiterate won a status within general communication, a status which in part sanctioned its linguistic identity. While the literate unwillingly acknowledged this status, they showed quite clearly their own scorn for this wild spoken language as dissociated from the norms of *grammatica*.

---

[41] These words *romanitas maior* designate, in my opinion, a level of language due to appear later on, in the ninth and tenth century, through unitary written forms such as those used in the Strasbourg oaths or even in the so-called Eulalia Sequence. We catch it again in the eleventh century, when the court poetry of the troubadours is born: their language, though not a Latin one, is nevertheless literate, unitarian and, so to speak, 'grammatical' as well.

[42] Banniard (1992), chapter 9, pp. 505–10 and 519–28.

[43] Neither the linguistic characteristics nor the socio-linguistic implications of the reform of singing have been sufficiently analysed. See Huglo (1988), pp. 56–7, 81–4 and Elich (1988) I pp. 86–93, 227–30.

Nevertheless, the distinction between Latin and Romance was not so sharp as one might think. Channels remained open which made it possible, even for lay speakers who were so inclined, to participate in the *latinitas maior*. This linguistic proximity can be illustrated by referring yet again to the famous glosses of Reichenau.[44] After much effort, to some extent justified, philologists have succeeded in establishing that these glosses contained Romance words. This is undeniable inasmuch as we know that the words referred to can properly be regarded as having the status of belonging to Romance. But the distinction between Latin and Romance is highly debatable at the level of the actual consciousness of the compilers of the glosses: first there is a circularity in the glosses, since a word now classifiable as Romance is sometimes glossed by a classical word,[45] secondly, however relaxed, the spelling respected the Latin forms; lastly, even in the glosses described as Romance, the inflectional morphemes follow the standard forms. We can only conclude that, between 750 and 850 at least, Latin unity, even if broken, had not yet involved a great drifting apart of its constituent linguistic continents.[46]

The later transition from diglossia to clear bilingualism will only be gradual.[47] It was not enough, in practice, for the literate to have acknowledged the conceptual autonomy of the spontaneous spoken language. It had also to be sanctioned by a written form whose conception was difficult and whose necessity was far from obvious, since, for the literate, Latin spelling was perfectly satisfactory. In fact, the written forms and conventions of Romance did not really become widely used until the emergence of a desire to create a Romance literature, that is to say, until the emergence of a new aristocratic laity.[48]

The end of the Merovingian centuries and the whole of the Carolingian period in the linguistic and cultural history of Europe can be described in a way which, however complex its elements, reveals a creative development, much less confused than appeared at first sight; the ills and the disorders which the language of the Merovingian charters appears, time and time

---

[44] References taken from Klein (1968), with a lot of probing samples!

[45] For detailed analysis see Banniard (forthcoming).

[46] There is an interesting example of a description of this diachronic linguistic frontier on the basis of a morphosyntactic category by Beckman (1963). See also an analogous and very enlightening inquiry by Green (1991).

[47] For a definition of these concepts and a discussion of their reality and chronology see Banniard (1992), chapter 9, pp. 515–19.

[48] Delbouille (1972) I, pp. 3–56, 560–84, 604–22 and Banniard (1989), p. 219–25 and (1990) p. 220–9.

again, to display are the indirect sign of an intense linguistic activity, from which would emerge the new and unforeseen perfection of the Romance dialects, fruit of a process by which final order was born of apparent chaos.

CHAPTER 27

THE CAROLINGIAN RENAISSANCE: EDUCATION AND LITERARY CULTURE

John J. Contreni

THE IMPETUS FOR LEARNING

WRITING towards the end of the ninth century, Notker Balbulus, teacher, scribe and librarian at the monastery of St Gall, recorded what he and doubtless many others thought about the origins of the Carolingian revival of learning. Two Irishmen, he claimed in his *Gesta Karoli Magni*, came to the Continent hawking wisdom and were eventually brought to the attention of Charlemagne who 'was always an admirer and great collector of wisdom'. Soon after, Notker reported, the Anglo-Saxon Alcuin heard of the king's love of wisdom and took to sea to meet him.[1] Although the simplicity of Notker's explanation of the wellspring of the Carolingian renaissance is attractive, it reduces a complex phenomenon to virtual parody. Irishmen, Anglo-Saxons, Visigoths and Italians were instrumental in defining the renaissance, but the programme had its roots in the eighth century with missionaries like Boniface and with political leaders such as Charlemagne's father, Pippin III. What Charlemagne and his coterie of scholars, principally Alcuin but others as well, contributed to the revival of learning was a sense of mission, constancy, example, reinforcement and support.

The mission, defined in the *Admonitio Generalis*, in the *Epistola de Litteris Colendis* and in other programmatic documents, was simple enough but had profound implications.[2] What the leaders of Carolingian society wanted to do was to prepare the clergy, 'the soldiers of the Church', to lead 'the people of God to the pasture of eternal life'. The evidence of poorly written letters that had come to the court signalled that the clergy needed schooling, for ignorance of language went hand in hand with a more serious lack of

---

[1] *Gesta Karoli* I, 1–2 (*MGH SS* II, p. 731); Ganz (1989), pp. 175–6; Rankin (1991).

[2] *Admonitio Generalis*, *MGH Cap.* I, pp. 52–62, especially pp. 59, line 42 to 60, line 7 (trans. King (1987), pp. 209–20); *Epistola de Litteris Colendis*, *MGH Cap.* I, p. 79, especially lines 37–42 (trans. Loyn and Percival (1975), pp. 63–4); Scheibe (1958), pp. 221–9; Wallach (1968), pp. 198–226.

wisdom. The key passage in the *Epistola de Litteris Colendis* called for a fundamental change in the relationship between the clergy and the people of Carolingian Europe. It was no longer sufficient that the people be impressed by the *sight* of the clergy, they had also to be instructed by the *words* monks read and sang.[3] Carolingian leaders in their efforts to broadcast sacred wisdom to society had before them the example of King Josias (II Kings 22: 11) who by correction and admonition called the Israelites back to God, but they also needed the help of a reformed, wise clergy: 'For although it is better to do what is right than to know it, yet knowledge comes before action.'[4]

A programme of such ambitious scope might well have remained only a set of ideals had it not been pursued with the kind of determination that Charlemagne directed towards the Saxons. It is worth noting, too, that his longevity meant that he was able to give continued impetus to the programme. His sons and grandsons in their legislation and the clergy in episcopal councils and statutes throughout the ninth century continued to emphasise the importance of book learning and study.[5] Although Charlemagne's own intellectual achievements seem modest, they should not be underestimated. His biographers credit him with an incisive, questioning mind. When Einhard recorded that his patron was talkative to the point of verbosity (*dicaculus*), he was describing a confident political leader and military commander who was not intimidated by the superior learning of scholars, bishops and abbots.[6] The example Charlemagne set at his court enlivened the prescriptions of the documents. Courts were political, military and administrative centres, often on the move, and constantly receiving and sending delegations and embassies. Amid the hubbub and contributing to it were scholars, poets and artists. Proximity to the centres of power gave new eminence to intellectual life and to intellectuals. Charlemagne's successors, especially Louis the Pious and Charles the Bald, continued to attract scholars to their courts and consulted them on a wide range of topics from calendar

---

[3] *MGH Cap.* I, p. 79, lines 38–42: 'Optamus enim vos, sicut decet ecclesiae milites, et interius devotos et exterius doctos castosque bene vivendo et scholasticos bene loquendo, ut, quicunque vos propter nomen Domini et sanctae conversationis nobilitatem ad vivendum expetierit, sicut de aspectu vestro aedificatur visus, ita quoque de sapientia vestra, quam in legendo seu cantando perceperit, instructus omnipotenti Domino gratias agendo gaudens redeat.'

[4] *Ibid.*, lines 16–17: 'Quamvis enim melius sit bene facere quam nosse, prius tamen est nosse quam facere.'

[5] Riché (1989), pp. 69–79; McKitterick (1977), pp. 1–79; Hildebrandt (1992), pp. 49–71; McKitterick (1992a).

[6] *Vita Karoli* 25 (ed. Halphen (1947), p. 74): 'Adeo quidem facundus erat ut etiam dicaculus appareret'; Ring (1978), pp. 263–71.

reform to predestination.[7] Royal patronage inspired an outpouring of panegyric poetry, biblical commentaries, histories, translations of the Greek Fathers into Latin, and even the financing of three schools.[8] Ecclesiastical authorities such as Claudius, bishop of Turin, Theodulf, bishop of Orléans, Hraban Maur, abbot of Fulda and archbishop of Mainz, Lupus, abbot of Ferrières, and Hincmar, archbishop of Rheims, among others, were also formidable scholars who made their cathedrals and monasteries intellectual and educational centres.

Seen from the top down in this fashion, the Carolingian renaissance appears as a well-organised programme which, given the authority behind it, could not help but achieve its goals. Observers from the time of Notker Balbulus and Heiric of Auxerre, who celebrated the intellectual brilliance of Charles the Bald's court, to the present day have been impressed by the Carolingian achievement.[9] Monastic, cathedral and court scriptoria toiled industriously to provide Carolingian Europe with the texts needed for serious study, worship and government – perhaps as many as 50,000 in the ninth century alone by one estimate.[10] Books counted as treasure and formed an important part of the venerable gift-giving tradition among the Franks. When Emperor Lothar made peace with his brother, Charles, in 849, he entered into a spiritual association with one of the foremost monasteries of his brother's realm, St Martin at Tours, and sealed his commitment to the community by underwriting the copying and decoration of a sumptuous Gospel Book, the Lothar Gospels.[11] Librarians and teachers carefully built up the collections of their local libraries and constantly sought copies of books they did not possess. The libraries supported schools, many of which in the ninth century offered sustained instruction for two or three generations of masters.[12] Carolingian scholars were as productive as their colleagues in the scriptoria. They revised the biblical text several times, produced compilations of patristic works, wrote their own commentaries on the Bible and classical texts, and glossed treatises on the arts for their students. They wrote histories and poetry and exchanged innumerable letters among themselves.

These accomplishments give substance to the notion of a renaissance in

[7] See the relevant articles and references in *Karl der Grosse* II; Godman and Collins, *Charlemagne's Heir* (1990); Gibson and Nelson, *Charles the Bald*, (1990); also Bullough (1973).

[8] Brunhölzl (1975), pp. 241–494, 545–75, and below, note 62.

[9] Heiric of Auxerre, *Vita Sancti Germani Episcopi Autissiodorensis*, MGH Poet. III, p. 429, lines 13–26.   [10] McKitterick (1989), p. 163.

[11] McKitterick (1989), pp. 148–64; Bullough (1991a), p. 39.

[12] Bischoff (1981), pp. 213–33; McKitterick (1989), pp. 165–210.

the modern sense of the word, a rebirth of learning, even if what the Carolingians really wanted to achieve was reform and correction of their society. But neither *renovatio*, their word, nor our term conveys adequately the shape of the world of learning in the ninth century. Despite the important impetus given to learning by central authority in the Carolingian realms, the reality of literary culture and education was less schematic and more decentralised than official mandates suggest. Much of the variety inherent in Carolingian learning can be attributed to differences in resources, talents and interests across the cultural landscape. More fundamentally, neither the Christian heritage nor the antique tradition that Carolingian scholars grappled to understand and to blend were monolithic. Each bore its own internal dissonances and seemed even to contradict each other, thereby making the goal of a unitary culture illusory. The results of concentrated intellectual energy in areas as fundamental to Carolingian society as the theology of baptism and law were surprisingly pluralistic.[13]

The prismatic effects of the Carolingian programme were further refracted by the stances thoughtful writers took about the shape of their society. Enthusiastic court, cathedral and monastic scholars responded to the challenges of the Carolingian reform programme, but they were no mere puppets. While some 'Christianised' the arts, others worried about the revival of pagan models.[14] In the heady days of the great king and emperor, Charlemagne, court scholars used their talents to legitimise and praise authority; a later generation of intellectuals would criticise and instruct errant political leaders.[15] And in what is perhaps the surest sign of the vitality of learning in the Carolingian realms, scholars engaged in polemic on critical political and theological issues and even proved themselves adept at forgery.

The injunction to instruct God's people through proper use of language in reading and in song thus brought forth a luxuriant and in some ways an unintended harvest, a harvest that was sown first in the schools of Carolingian Europe.

SCHOOLS AND LEARNING

The schools of the Carolingian realms were at once the training ground for the educated elite and the arena in which the new Christian culture was hammered out. By the ninth century these schools had begun to feel the twin effects of royal mandates such as the *Epistola de Litteris Colendis*, (which was

---

[13] Leonardi (1981a), pp. 459–506; Keefe (1986), pp. 48–93; Reynolds (1983), pp. 99–135; Contreni (1992a), chapter 3; Contreni (1992b), chapter 4.

[14] Giacone (1975), pp. 823–32; Nees (1991).   [15] Godman (1987); Anton (1968).

intended for all monasteries and bishoprics) and of the contact the Franks had established in the eighth century with cultural centres peripheral to their *regnum*. The learning, curriculum, and books of Anglo-Saxon, Irish, Lombard, Roman and Visigothic schools and even of the Byzantine world began to circulate in Francia thanks to the expansion of Carolingian power and authority and to the pull of patronage.

The Carolingian court provided the setting for one kind of school, the palace school. All the Carolingian monarchs, but especially Charlemagne, Louis the Pious, Lothar I, Lothar II and Charles the Bald drew scholars to their courts. These masters acted as advisers on all sorts of matters for their patrons, wrote poetry for them, and dedicated their books to them. They also had a hand in teaching royal and aristocratic children such as the young Charles the Bald who was tutored by Walahfrid Strabo. The court school, as far as it can be detected, was a loosely organised institution. Its members were transient, and after its heyday in the 780s and 790s its leading members dispersed to the monasteries and cathedrals of the realms where they established more formal educational institutions.[16]

The legislation of the closing decades of the eighth century clearly assigned to monasteries and cathedrals responsibility for educating the clergy who would lead God's people. Neither the *Admonitio Generalis* nor the *Epistola de Litteris Colendis* distinguished between the different functions of monasteries and cathedrals, no doubt because in missionary and frontier regions monks had long functioned as secular clergy. One of the provisions of Bishop Theodulf of Orléans' *capitula* for his parish priests suggests how blurred the lines were between clerical and monastic education. Priests in Theodulf's diocese who wished to send any of their relatives to school had the bishop's permission to send them to the cathedral school *or* to any one of the monastic schools under the bishop's jurisdiction.[17] There is no hint here that those who chose to learn their letters in a monastic school intended to become monks. Theodulf was not an innovator nor was his invitation for students to use the resources of local monasteries unique. When Louis the Pious and Benedict of Aniane set out to reform monastic life, the presence of so many non-monks within the monastic precincts and within the routine of monastic life was, from the perspective of the reformers, alarming. In 816, the Council of Aachen established guidelines to reform cathedral canons along monastic lines and to isolate young men training to become canons

---

[16] Bullough (1991b), pp. 123–60; McKitterick (1983), p. 161; Godman (1985), pp. 6–8.

[17] *Erstes Kapitular*, c. 19 (*MGH Cap. episc.* I, pp. 115–16): 'Si quis ex presbyteris voluerit nepotem suum aut aliquem consanguineum, ad scholam mittere, in ecclesia sanctae Crucis aut in monasterio sancti Aniani aut Sancti Benedicti aut Sancti Lifardi aut in ceteris de his coenobiis, quae nobis ad regendum concessa sunt, ei licentiam id faciendi concedimus.'

from those training to become parish priests.[18] The next year, 817, a second reforming council at Aachen even more emphatically barred everyone except oblates from monastic schools.[19] To Hildemar of Corbie the distinction was fundamental: monastic schools offered training in monastic discipline, ecclesiastical schools taught the liberal arts.[20]

These new directives flew in the face of tradition. The 'external school' depicted on the Plan of St Gall may have represented an attempt to observe the letter of the 817 council but not its spirit by locating the school for non-monks literally on the perimeter of the monastic complex.[21] The remarkable literacy of some Carolingian aristocrats (Angilbert, Einhard, Nithard and Dhuoda are the best examples) no doubt owed something to tutelage by monks and nuns. But it was not only that the education of the privileged was threatened by the movement for monastic purity. By restricting access to what presumably were the best and most stable schools in the Carolingian world, the reform programme itself was jeopardised. Who would train the rural clergy? Louis the Pious threw this responsibility onto the bishops, but these hard-pressed leaders were unable to shoulder the financial burden of maintaining schools. Bishops meeting at the great reform synod of Paris in 829 chided their colleagues for their lacklustre support of schools and tried to energise support for schools by requiring bishops to bring their students to provincial councils so that episcopal support for schooling would be 'obvious to all'.[22] Adequate assistance for parish schools was even more problematic. Bishop Theodulf tried to get his priests to offer instruction without pay in schools he was trying to set up, but parish priests living on

---

[18] *Concilium Aquisgranense*, c. 135 (*MGH Conc.* II, p. 413): 'Ut erga pueros, qui nutriuntur vel erudiuntur in congregatione canonica, instantissima sit adhibenda custodia.'

[19] *Synodi Secundae Aquisgranensis Decreta Authentica (817)*, c. 5 (ed. Hallinger (1963), I, p. 474): 'Ut scola in monasterio non habeatur nisi eorum qui oblati sunt.'

[20] Hildemar of Corbie, *Expositio Regulae*, prologue: 'In hoc enim loco scholam nominat monasticam disciplinam; nam sunt et aliae scholae; est enim schola ecclesiastica disciplina, schola est liberalium artium' (ed. Mittermüller (1880), p. 65).

[21] Hildebrandt (1992), pp. 91–3; for the problematical external school at St Riquier, *ibid.*, pp. 79–85.

[22] *Capitula ab Episcopis Attiniaci Data* (822), c. 3 (*MGH Cap.* I, p. 357): 'Scolas autem . . . omnino studiosissime emendare cupimus, qualiter omnis homo sive maioris sive minoris aetatis, qui ad hoc nutritur ut in aliquo gradu ab ecclesia promoveatur, locum denomit natum et magistrum congruum habeat. Parentes tamen vel domini singulorum de victu vel substantia corporali unde subsistant providere studeant, qualiter solacium habeant, ut propter rerum inopiam doctrinae studio non recedant'; *Admonitio ad Omnes Regni Ordines* (825), c. 6 (*MGH Cap.* I, p. 304); *Concilium Parisiense a. 829*, c. 30 (*MGH Conc.* II, p. 632): 'Sed super hac eiusdem principis ammonitione, immo iussione a nonnullis rectoribus tepide et desidiose hactenus actum est. . . . [E]t quando ad provintiale episcoporum concilium ventum fuerit, unusquisque rectorum . . . scolasticos suos eidem concilio adesse faciat, ut suum sollers studium circa divinum cultum omnibus manifestum fiat.'

slender means like the hermits who taught children could not bypass the extra income.[23] A generation later Bishop Herard of Tours (855–66) and Bishop Walter of Orléans (?869–91) could only urge their priests to maintain schools 'if possible'.[24] When at the end of the ninth century Fulco became archbishop of Rheims (833–900) to succeed Hincmar, one of the great Carolingian churchmen, he found both the school for canons and the school for rural clergy in disarray and could restore them only by calling in outside help in the form of two monastic teachers, Remigius of Auxerre and Hucbald of St Amand.[25]

Fulco knew that parish priests bore primary responsibility for the religious education of the Christian people. They had to make sure that godparents knew both the Lord's Prayer and the Creed before they could sponsor a child in baptism and that they could teach these basic Christian formulae to their godchildren.[26] The few parish inventories surviving from the ninth century suggest that rural priests stocked modest libraries and, therefore, could read and presumably teach reading and writing to children.[27] It is most unfortunate that so little is known of these elementary schools for through them some measure of literacy, enough to assure minimal participation in the liturgy, reached the broadest level of Carolingian society – the children of free parents as well as the children of peasants if the *Admonitio Generalis* was obeyed.[28] Angilbert assumed that the men, women and children of the seven communities near St Riquier would participate actively, singing and following banners which probably bore legends, in intricate processions during the liturgy for Rogations; Paschasius Radbertus envisaged peasants lamenting the death of Adalhard of Corbie in their own tongues and also joining in with clergy in an antiphonal

---

[23] *Erstes Kapitular* 20 (*MGH Cap. episc.* I, p. 116): 'Presbyteri per villas et vicos scolas habeant. Et si quilibet fidelium suos parvulos ad discendas litteras eis commendare vult, eos suscipere et docere non renuant, sed cum summa caritate eos doceant ... Cum ergo eos docent, nihil ab eis pretii pro hac re exigant nec aliquid ab eis accipiant excepto, quod eis parentes caritatis studio sua voluntate obtulerint'; Grimlaic, *Regula Solitariorum*, c. 52 (*PL* 103, col. 644); McKitterick (1989), pp. 219–20.

[24] *Capitula Herardi*, c. 17 (*PL* 121, col. 765c): 'Ut scholas presbyteri pro posse habeant et libros emendatos'; *Capitula a Walterio reverendo pontifice compresbiteris promulgata in sinodo apud Bullensem fundum* II, 6 (*MGH Cap. episc.*, p. 189): 'Ut unusquisque presbiter suum habeat clericum, quem religiose educare procuret et, si possibilitas illi est, scolam in ecclesia sua habere non negligat sollerterque caveat, ut, quos ad erudiendum suscipit, caste sinceriterque nutriat.'

[25] Flodoard, *Historia Remensis Ecclesiae*, c. 9 (*MGH SS* 13, p. 574).

[26] Lynch (1986), pp. 305–32.

[27] Hammer (1980), pp. 5–17.

[28] *Admonitio Generalis*, 72 (*MGH Cap.* I, pp. 59–60): 'Sacerdotis ... ut eorum bona coversatione multi protrahantur ad servitium Dei, et non solum servilis conditionis infantes, sed etiam ingenuorum filios adgregent sibique socient'.

lament expressed in Latin.[29] Some lay men and women no doubt learned enough formal Latin as boys and girls in these schools to be able to participate later in life in disputes with monks about documents and to participate in the Carolingian literate community.[30] Some students received enough schooling to master the priests' service books, to learn the duties of the priesthood through imitation, to demonstrate competence to the bishop and thereby become country priests themselves.[31] With such rudimentary training, no wonder bishops worried about the qualifications of their priests. Many in the diocese of Rome were reputed to be uneducated and illiterate; Hincmar of Rheims wondered if the priests who taught in schools in his diocese could read; Bishop Sigemund of Meaux was not certain that his priests measured up to new intellectual expectations.[32]

Which of the children who received the rudiments of an education at the parish level went on to monastic and episcopal schools for further religious instruction and a more rigorous education? Those who had connections, like the relatives of the priests in the diocese of Orléans or Hincmar of Rheims' nephew, the younger Hincmar, had the best opportunity. But an ecclesiastical career and with it higher education must also have been available to the children of the poor, otherwise Notker's classic account of Charlemagne examining the talented low-born and lazy noble pupils of Clement Scottus would not have had its intended effect.[33] Notker's sympathies clearly lay with the *pauperes* and perhaps he was one of them. Walahfrid Strabo came from humble circumstances and Archbishop Ebbo of Rheims (816–35) was the son of serfs.[34]

The dearth of known women writers during the Carolingian period does not necessarily mean that only boys went on for further schooling and that opportunities for creative intellectual activity were non-existent for

---

[29] Angilbert, *Institutio de Diversitate Officiorum*, c. 9 (ed. Hallinger (1963), pp. 296–9); Paschasius Radbertus, *Egloga Duarum Sanctimonialium*, lines 5–20 (*MGH Poet.* III, pp. 45–6).

[30] Nelson (1986a), pp. 56–7; McKitterick (1989), pp. 77–134.

[31] Vykoukal (1913); Amiet (1964), pp. 12–82.

[32] *Capitula Admonitionis ab Eugenio II proposita*, 6 (*MGH Conc.* II, p. 557): 'Cauendum quippe est, ut non ineruditi ad ministerium Christi vel inlitterati, ut dedecet, accedant'; *Capitula quibus de rebus magistri et decani per singulas ecclesias inquirere, et episcopo renuntiare debeant*, c. 11 (*PL* 125, col. 779): 'Si habeant clericum qui possit tenere scholam, aut legere epistolam, aut canere valeat, prout necessarium sibi videtur'; Flodoard, *Historia Remensis Ecclesiae* III, 3, 23 (*MGH SS* XIII, p. 534): 'Item interrogationem eius, quid ipse scientiae requireret a presbiteris suae parrochiae' (synopsis of a letter from Hincmar of Rheims to Sigemund).

[33] *Gesta Karoli*, c. 3 (*MGH SS* II, pp. 731–2).

[34] Walahfrid Strabo, *Gotesscalcho monachi, qui et Fulgentius*, line 23 (*MGH Poet.* II, p. 363): 'Atqui in pauperie, passa est quam nostra iuventus'; Thegan, *Vita Hludowici*, 44 (*MGH SS* II, p. 599): 'Elegerunt ... qui dicebatur Ebo, Remensis episcopus, qui erat ex originalium servorum stirpe.'

Carolingian women.[35] When Hincmar of Rheims recommended that *puellulae* not be taught in the same place as boys, he bore tacit witness to a Carolingian tradition of female education.[36] The patristic giants whom Carolingian scholars so much admired inhabited an intellectual world which included educated women. The example of Jerome and his Roman female companions loomed especially large in the minds of ninth-century men and women. Benedict of Aniane in the *De Institutione Sanctimonialium* used Jerome's letter to Laeta which outlined the young Pacatula's education to describe the education girls should receive in monasteries.[37] When Paschasius Radbertus wrote a treatise on the Assumption of Mary for the nuns at Soissons, he cast his work in the form of a letter from Jerome to Paula and Eustochium.[38] Gisela and Rotrud, respectively sister and daughter of Charlemagne, found the example of Jerome useful when they cajoled busy Alcuin into writing a commentary on the Gospel of John for them. They reminded Alcuin that Jerome had never spurned the pleas of women and had in fact dedicated many of his works on the prophets to them. Blessed Jerome, they pointedly added, continued to correspond with Roman women after he had moved to Bethlehem despite the dangerous distance across the Tyrrhenian Sea. In comparison, the little Loire and the short distance between Tours and Paris offered no obstacles to their request.[39] But, it was not imitation of past traditions that drove education for girls and women. Everyone in the Carolingian world was supposed to know the Lord's Prayer and the Symbol.[40] Women in religious houses, like their male counterparts, as religious 'professionals' had to know more, how to pray, to chant and to read, in order to participate fully in their faith.

A capitulary intended to establish empire-wide policy in 802 barred all men from female monasteries except for priests who, accompanied by a witness, could visit the sick; they could also say Mass for the nuns, but were

---

[35] Wemple (1981), pp. 187–8.

[36] *Collectio de Ecclesiis et Capellis*, MGH *Fontes* xiv, c. 100: 'Ut divinum officium non dimittant et scolarios suos modeste distringant, caste nutriant et sic litteris imbuant, ut mala conversatione non destruant, et puellas (*al. cod.* puellulas) ad discendum cum scolariis suis in scola sua nequaquam recipiant.'

[37] *Institutio Sanctimonialium Aquisgranensis* (*Concilium Aquisgranense a. 816*), c. 22 (*MGH Conc.* 1, pp. 452–4): 'Ut erga puellas in monasteriis erudiendas magna adhibeatur diligentia'; Morrison (1983), pp. 50–2.   [38] *De Assumptione Sanctae Mariae Virginis*, CCCM 56c, pp. 109–62.

[39] MGH *Epp.* iv, p. 325: 'Minore vadosum Ligeri flumen quam Tyrreni maris latitudo periculo navigatur. Et multo facilius cartarum portitor tuarum de Turonis Parisiacam civitatem, quam illius de Bethleem Romam, pervenire poterit.'

[40] *Admonitio Synodalis*, 61 (ed. Amiet (1964), p. 58): 'Videte ut omnibus parrochiariis vestris simbolum et orationem dominicam insinuetis.'

to leave immediately afterwards.[41] Thus, young girls in monastic communities must have been taught by women. The *Vita Liutbergae* mentions that its heroine taught chant to young girls, but such direct evidence is rare.[42] A number of sources, however, do shed indirect light on schooling for women. Gisela and Rotrud wrote to Alcuin after they had already tried to understand St John's Gospel by tackling Augustine's commentary. Paschasius Radbertus, who had been raised as an orphan by the nuns at Soissons and received his early education from them, wrote, in addition to the treatise on the Assumption, two other works at the request of the Soissons community.[43] These kinds of requests testify to a high level of intellectual inquiry and to study programmes in female monasteries. Women also functioned as teachers outside monastic walls. Wiborada, a female hermit, taught Oudalricus, a young monk from St Gall.[44] In the communities around St Riquier, women (*geniciariae*) helped prepare children for participation in liturgical processions.[45] Hincmar of Rheims must have anticipated that girls would be taught by women when he prohibited them from attending the priest's school along with boys.

The most visible female teacher of the Carolingian period is also its only known female author. Dhuoda's case is made even more remarkable by her lay status. She wrote her *Liber Manualis* in the early 840s to instruct her son, William, in a way of life that blended Christian principles with the aristocratic virtues of family loyalty and respect for paternal authority. That she expected her sixteen-year-old son to read her book and went on to urge him to read many of the books of the learned masters to learn more about God suggests that William was himself well educated and that Dhuoda may have been his first teacher.[46] The roster of lay women who participated in literary culture extends beyond Dhuoda. Judith, the second wife of Louis

[41] *Capitulare Missorum Generale*, c. 18 (*MGH Cap.* I, p. 95): 'Et ut in claustra vel monasterium earum vir nullus intret, nisi presbiter propter visitationem infirmarum cum testimonio intret, vel ad missam tantum, et statim exeat.' *Capitularia ecclesiastica ad Salz data a. 803–804*, c. 5 (*MGH Cap.* I, p. 119): 'Ut nullus in monasterio puellarum vel ancillarum Dei intrate praesumat.'

[42] *Vita Sanctae Liutbirgae*, 35 (*MGH SS* IV, p. 164): 'Cui ad divini operis implementum, quibus illa iugiter summo inhaerebat studio, puellas eleganti forma transmiserat, quas illa et in psalmodiis et in artificiosis operibus educaverat, et edoctas libertate concessa seu ad propinquos, sive vellent, ire permisit.'

[43] *Expositio in Psalmum XLIV*, PL 120, cols. 993–1060; *De Partu Virginis*, CCCM 56c, pp. 47–89.

[44] Hartmann, *Vita Sanctae Wiboradae*, c. 39 (*MGH SS* IV, p. 456): 'Quidam iuvenis monachus in venerandi patris nostri Galli congregatione, Oudalricus nomine, sub scolari disciplina degebat.'

[45] Angilbert, *Institutio de diversitate officiorum*, c. 9 (ed. Hallinger (1963), p. 298): 'Nam pueri forinseci et puellae sine litteris auxilium habeant de scolariis et geniciariis, ut in his, que ceperant, et sciunt psallentes existere possint.'

[46] *Liber Manualis* I, 7, lines 2–7 (ed. Riché (1975), p. 114): 'Admoneo te etiam ... ut inter mundanas huius saeculi curas, plurima volumina librorum tibi adquiri non pigeas.'

the Pious, impressed contemporaries with her intellect. Her grand-daughters, the three daughters of Eberhard of Friuli, inherited along with their brothers part of their father's extensive library; one of the women received a copy of the Lombard laws![47] The unnamed mother of Sado gave her son a copy of Aelius Donatus' *Ars Maior*, a book which she may have used herself.[48] It is not surprising that these women and others of high social and political status were educated. Evidence of various sorts, however, has begun to fill in a picture of even wider participation by women in the world of Carolingian learning.

Women active as scribes supplied the needs of their own communities as well as those of other houses. The list of female writing centres, Chelles, Jouarre, Remiremont, Säckingen, Poitiers, Herford, Soissons, Essen, Brescia, continues to grow. Nuns at Vreden and Neuenheerse copied out reliquary tags and probably also books. The important 'Corbie a-b' script which survives in thirty-nine manuscripts and fragments has been attributed to the skill of female scribes.[49] Copying, like embroidery and working with cloth, could at one level be viewed as manual labour which in the monastic routine along with reading and prayer was both pleasing to God and a useful antidote to idleness.[50] But books were meant to be read and to be pondered and occasionally to beget new books. Women read intelligently, as the examples of Gisela and Rotrud, Dhuoda and the nuns of Soissons demonstrate. But with the exception of Dhuoda, did they contribute to Carolingian literary culture? From the time of Peter of Pisa in the last quarter of the eighth century to the time of Remigius of Auxerre (died 908), approximately sixty male authors are known by name. These authors did not write everything that has survived from the period and many works remain unattributed. Of these, histories such as the *Liber Historiae Francorum*, the *Annales Mettenses Priores*, the *Annales Quedlinburgenses*, as well as *Vitae* of founders of female monastic houses may well have been written by women.[51] And just as recent palaeographical research suggests that it is no longer possible to assume that unattributed manuscripts were copied in male scriptoria, so too the large collection of excerpts, glosses, and pedagogical and devotional extracts that survive cannot be attributed solely to the activity of male compilers and readers.

While much remains to be learned about the participation of women in

---

[47] Riché (1963), pp. 87–104; McKitterick (1989), pp. 245–50. [48] McKitterick (1976), p. 228.
[49] Bischoff (1966a), pp. 16–34; McKitterick (1991), pp. 69–95; Bishop (1990), pp. 521–36; McKitterick (1992b).
[50] *Institutio Sanctimonialium Aquisgranensis (Concilium Aquisgranense a. 816)*, c. 14 (*MGH Conc.* II, p. 448): 'Provideant etiam, ut otio vacare non possint, sed potius aut orationi aut lectioni aut manuum operationi insistant.' [51] McKitterick (1991), pp. 95–111; Nelson (1990c).

Carolingian literary culture, it is clear that since women could never become priests they could not write the guidebooks, the scriptural commentaries, the theological treatises, the sermon collections intended to form and arm the 'soldiers of the Church'.[52]

For most young boys, the path to that vocation began approximately at age seven in the monasteries and two or three years later in the cathedral schools. School was but one part of their daily routine. Children engaged in appropriate forms of work, assisted in prayer services, and, in general, were acclimatised to the ecclesiastical regime. Ninth-century monasteries and cathedral cloisters were generally solicitous of their young charges. They constituted the next generation of clergy raised up from a tender age within a religious atmosphere and therefore uncontaminated by the evils of the world.[53] Precise information on the number of students at any one time is difficult to come by. If the lists of monks and *scholastici* from Fulda's dependencies are representative, students could account for between 26 and 49 percent of the adult population.[54] In small monasteries and cathedrals, young pupils studied with a *magister* or *grammaticus* who did everything, even tripling as the director of the scriptorium and as the librarian. Larger, better endowed schools with more pupils might have several masters who would teach a speciality: chant, copying, grammar, explication of Scripture. The relationship between students and masters was an intensely spiritual and personal as well as academic one. Alcuin remembered fondly all his former pupils, called them by pet names, and lamented that his students came and went, but that the 'old man' remained.[55] Heiric of Auxerre published part of the lectures of both his teachers, Lupus of Ferrières and Haimo of Auxerre, and prefaced them with a poem in praise of his masters.[56] Ercanbert of Fulda wrote down the lectures of his master, Rudolf, because he was concerned that the master's instruction would fade from memory if not committed to writing.[57]

Masters frequently corresponded with each other. They wrote to maintain personal contact, to query experts about particularly thorny intellectual matters, to borrow books, and to request that books be written.[58] These contacts proved useful when masters wanted to send their best students, ones they might be grooming as successors, to other centres for further study. Heiric of Auxerre spent several years at Soissons before returning to

---

[52] *Epistola de Litteris Colendis*, c. 38 (*MGH Cap.* I, p. 79); 'Optamus enim uos, sicut decet ecclesiae milites.'   [53] De Jong (1983), pp. 99–128; Quinn (1989).

[54] Hildebrandt (1992), pp. 119–29, 147–50; K. Schmid (1978) I, pp. 221–3.

[55] *MGH Epp.* IV, p. 359: 'O quam felix dies fuit, quando in laribus nostris pariter lusimus litterali tessera. Sed nunc omnia mutata sunt. Remansit senior, alios generans filios, priores dispersos gemens.'   [56] Quadri (1966), pp. 77–161.   [57] *MGH Epp.* V, pp. 358–9.

[58] Contreni (1992c).

Auxerre. Lupus of Ferrières sent monks from his abbey to Prüm in order to learn German. Hraban Maur studied at Tours. Hucbald of St Amand and Remigius of Auxerre were recruited to Rheims by Archbishop Fulco. Some teachers also became authors when bishops, abbots, kings and learned lay men and women needed a concise historical commentary on a Gospel or a *vita* of a local saint. Their learning, experience and contacts made masters prime candidates for higher ecclesiastical appointments. Alcuin, Hraban Maur, Lupus of Ferrières and Paschasius Radbertus all began their careers as school teachers.

Approximately seventy schools were sufficiently active in the ninth century to leave some record of their activity.[59] On a map these centres form a rough triangle with the broad base extending from Hamburg in the north to Tours in the southwest and with the apex in Italy, roughly near Monte Cassino (see Map 20). Most of the schools in this area were concentrated in four regions: north of the Loire, in northern Italy in the former Lombard kingdom, in the parts of Germany that had seen the most intense missionary activity in the eighth century, and in the Spanish March and Septimania. Among major regions, only Aquitaine stands virtually devoid of known schools although some forty saints' Lives were composed in Carolingian Aquitaine and the historian Ermoldus Nigellus and the author of the *Waltharius* poem – if they are not the same person – came from that region.[60] The influence of the Carolingian courts along with epistolary and personal exchanges combined to establish loose networks among the schools. At the diocesan level, bishops such as Theodulf of Orléans and Hincmar of Rheims could exert some measure of control and organisation over the schools in their jurisdictions. Lothar I authorised an ambitious scheme in 825 which would have funnelled masters and students from throughout northern Italy into nine centres (Pavia, Ivrea, Turin, Cremona, Florence, Firmo, Verona, Vicenzo and Cividale) for further schooling. He even offered to provide for the schools to encourage participation.[61] Four years later the bishops gathered at the Council of Paris tried to enlist the support of Lothar's father, Louis the Pious, to establish three schools under royal patronage.[62] But both these efforts appear to have been stillborn. Dungal, the Irish master placed in charge of the school at Pavia, retired to Bobbio within two years. Lothar's

---

[59] Riché (1989), pp. 97–101.   [60] Poulin (1975); Werner (1990), pp. 101–23.

[61] *Capitulare Olonnense Ecclesiasticum Primum*, c. 6 (*MGH Cap.* I, p. 327): 'Propter oportunitatem tamen omnium apta loca distincte ad hoc exercitium providimus, ut difficultas locorum longe positorum ac paupertas nulli foret excusatio'; Bullough (1964), pp. 120–1.

[62] *Concilium Parisiense a. 829*, cc. 3, 12 (79) (*MGH Conc.* II, p. 675): 'Similiter etiam obnixe ac suppliciter vestrae celsitudini suggerimus, ut morem paternum sequentes saltim in tribus congruentissimis imperii vestri locis scole publice ex vestra auctoritate fiant, ut labor patris vestri et vester per incuriam, quod absit, labefactando non depereat.'

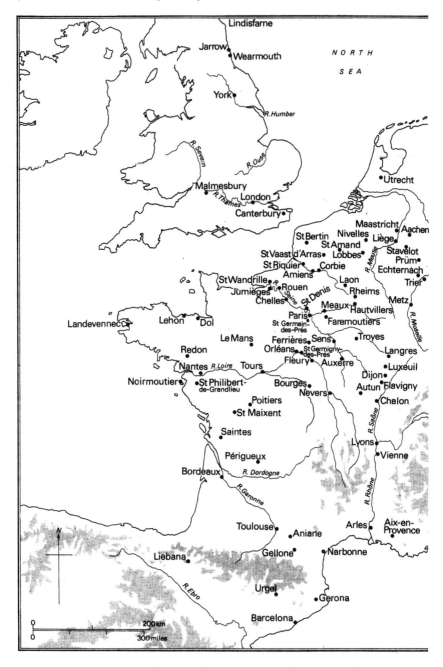

Map 20 Carolingian schools, scriptoria and literary centres

presence in Italy in the 820s was limited. In 830, the year after the Council of Paris, Louis' reign was convulsed by rebellion, the aftermath of which, and not schools, preoccupied both him and Lothar during the 830s. What this meant was that Carolingian achievements in education and literary culture were going to be based for the most part on local initiatives.

Only a few of the Carolingian schools have been studied systematically. While the published sources have been analysed with great care, the complete picture of Carolingian education will only begin to emerge when the manuscripts used in the schools are studied in detail. Enough is known about the major centres, St Amand, Corbie, St Denis, Auxerre, Laon, Lyons, Lorsch, St Gall, Fulda, Tegernsee, Reichenau, Verona, Milan and Pavia among others, to permit a few generalisations. As this list indicates, antiquity and past glory offered no guarantee of high achievement as a Carolingian school. Relatively newly established centres such as ninth-century Fulda achieved equivalent status to older centres such as Milan and Pavia and even surpassed Rome. The sixty-two bishops from the province of Rome called together by Pope Eugenius in 826 listened as Deacon Theodore recited a sad tale of abandoned churches in villages, parishes and cities and had to be reminded not to appoint uneducated or illiterate priests lest the blind lead the blind. When the bishops drafted a plan of action, they patterned it on Carolingian reform legislation, including a call for the establishment of schools to teach the liberal arts and holy dogma.[63] That the same recommendation had to be repeated in 853 suggests the difficult nature of educational reform and may explain why Rome never became a leading intellectual centre in the ninth century.[64]

An active and influential school depended for its vitality on the resources necessary to copy books or to obtain them from other centres. Hameln, a tiny dependency of Fulda with its twelve monks and eleven students, must have had minimal library resources in contrast to St Gall and Lorsch, whose ninth-century library catalogues list 264 and more than 450 codices respectively, or Corbie, from whose library almost 250 manuscripts and manuscript fragments survive.[65] Books were at the heart of Carolingian education. Cathedrals and monasteries that were endowed by their patrons

---

[63] *Capitula Admonitionis ab Eugenio II Proposita*, c. 6 (*MGH Conc.* II, pp. 556–7): 'Primis omnium de ecclesiis Dei, quae per singula loca in parroechiis, per vicos vel civitates in ruinis neglectae reiacent ... Cavendum quippe est, ut non ineruditi ad ministerium Christi uel inlitterati, ut dedecet, accedant ...'; *Concilium Romanum a. 826*, c. 34 (*ibid.*, p. 581): 'De scolis reparandis pro studio litterarum'; Noble (1976).

[64] *Concilium Romanum a. 853*, c. 34 (*MGH Conc.* III, pp. 327–8); Leonardi (1981b).

[65] McKitterick (1989), pp. 169–96; Bischoff (1974), p. 15; Ganz (1990a), pp. 124–58.

and masters with books and had the institutional stability to protect their collections possessed one essential ingredient for achieving the goals of the Carolingian reform movement. The other ingredient was the gifted and dedicated master. What gave a school stability and prominence was its success in establishing a tradition of teaching. Few centres could match the record of Auxerre, whose known masters, Murethach, Haimo, Heiric and Remigius, span the course of the ninth century. Corbie comes close with Hadoard, Paschasius Radbertus and Ratramnus. St Gall had its three Notkers and later four Ekkehards. Martin Scottus taught at Laon for nearly twenty-five years until his death in 875 and was followed by Manno, Bernard and Adelelm.[66]

Sustained material and human resources combined to support the Carolingian educational programme. Despite inevitable differences in interests and talents among individual masters and despite sometimes vast differences in local resources, masters and students in Carolingian Europe concentrated their energies on what had become a common body of knowledge – always expanding, sometimes problematical and contradictory, always subject to misinterpretation and dispute – that furnished the essential intellectual grounding for thought and letters in the ninth century and, indeed, beyond to the twelfth and thirteenth centuries.

THE CURRICULUM

When the *Epistola de Litteris Colendis* called Carolingian monks and priests to the *litterarum studia*, the study of letters, it meant to reform the way they spoke Latin. It was the 'uncouth speech' (*sermones inculti*), the 'verbal mistakes' (*errores verborum*), the 'unskilled language' (*lingua inerudita*) that had to be corrected so that the men of God by their 'holy conversation' (*sancta conversatio*) in reading and in singing (*in legendo seu cantando*) could instruct the faithful.[67] In urging clergy to speak Latin like the Fathers, scholars such as Alcuin, who as an Anglo-Saxon learned Latin as a foreign language, set the reform on a fateful course. To the degree that they succeeded, proponents of the new language ran the risk of distancing the clergy from the Carolingian people. In 813, three separate church councils at Mainz, Rheims and Tours urged bishops to preach in the language of their parishioners, either German (*Thiotiscam*) or the rustic Latin (*rustica Romana lingua*) the *Epistola de Litteris Colendis* aimed to correct, so that their homilies might be more easily

---

[66] Iogna-Prat *et al.* (1991); Ganz (1990a); de Rijk (1963); Contreni (1978).
[67] *MGH Cap.* I, p. 79; Wright (1982).

understood; in 847 another council at Mainz repeated the canon.[68] Parish priests no doubt already used the languages of their flocks. The requirements of pastoral care took precedence over scholarship.

For the sixty or so authors of the Carolingian world and their disciples as well as several generations of unknown masters and their disciples proper use of language, however, was paramount. To mispronounce a word in the liturgy or to use the wrong case ending, as Gunzo of Novara learned, was to reveal oneself as uneducated. Lupus of Ferrières, who had a keen interest in word use and pronunciation, thought that emphasis on proper language had gone too far: his contemporaries, he wrote, were more concerned to weed out the errors in their language than the errors in their lives.[69] Hypercorrectness in some quarters was only one result of the reforms and not the most typical. The modest requirements of the reform set in motion an ambitious programme of higher learning throughout Carolingian Europe. The germ of the programme was already embedded in the *Epistola de Litteris Colendis* ('figures of speech, tropes and the like') and more precisely in the *Admonitio Generalis* ('the reading of Psalms, Tironian notes, chant, reckoning and grammar').[70] These elements of the reform programme went beyond the correct pronunciation of words to focus attention on the proper meaning and use of words. When Carolingian teachers sought direction on how to achieve these goals in practice, they had available Augustine's *De Doctrina Christiana*, Cassiodorus' *Institutiones Divinarum et Humanarum Lectionum* and Isidore of Seville's *Etymologiae*, as well as Martianus Capella's allegory of the arts, the *De Nuptiis Philologiae et Mercurii*. These works all helped to shape the Carolingian curriculum. They each provided a systematic introduction to knowledge and learning and in the cases of Augustine,

---

[68] *Concilium Moguntinense a. 813*, c. 25 (*MGH Conc.* II, p. 268): 'De officio praedicationis: si forte episcopus non fuerit in domo sua aut infirmus est aut alia aliqua causa exigente non valuerit, numquam tamen desit diebus dominicis aut festivitatis qui verbum Dei praedicet iuxta quod intellegere vulgus possit'; *Concilium Remense a. 813*, c. 15 (*MGH Conc.* II, p. 255): 'Ut episcopi sermones et omelias sanctorum patrum, prout omnes intellegere possent, secundum proprietatem linguae praedicare studeant'; *Concilium Turonense a. 813*, c. 17 (*MGH Conc.* II, p. 288): 'Visum est unanimitati nostrae, ut quilibet episcopus habeant omelias continentes necessarias ammonitiones ... Et ut easdem omelias quisque aperte transferre studeat in rusticam Romanam linguam aut Thiotiscam, quo facilius cuncti possint intellegere quae dicuntur'; *Concilium Moguntinum a. 847*, c. 2 (*MGH Cap.* II, p. 176): reiterates canon 17 from Tours (813); McKitterick (1977), pp. 184–209; Wright (1982), pp. 118–22; Banniard, p. 696 above.

[69] Gunzo of Novara, *Epistola ad Augienses* (ed. Manitius (1958)); Lupus of Ferrières, *Ep.* no. 35, 2 (ed. Marshall (1984), p. 48): 'Sic linguae vitia reformidamus et purgare contendimus, vitae vero delicta parui pendimus et augemus'; Contreni (1992c), pp. 95–6.

[70] *Epistola de Litteris Colendis*, *MGH Cap.* I, p. 79: 'Cum autem in sacris paginis schemata, tropi et caetera ...'; *Admonitio Generalis*, c. 72 (*MGH Cap.* I, p. 60): 'Et ut scolae legentium puerorum fiant. Psalmos, notas, cantus, compotum, grammaticam.'

Cassiodorus and Isidore of Seville explicitly tied secular learning to divine learning. The antique liberal arts programme found fertile ground in Carolingian schools. The liberal arts, singly or as a group, were favourite subjects of Carolingian poets who helped to canonise the arts programme as the basic framework for studies in schools. Their verse accompanied artistic renderings of the arts so that students learned through images and words.[71] Individuals as different as Wetti, the visionary monk (d. 824), and Wicbald, bishop of Auxerre (879–887), were praised for their command of the liberal arts.[72] Teachers created anthologies of texts on the arts to support their instruction.[73]

Despite the pervasiveness of the arts in the schools and in academic discourse, it would be misleading to compress the reality of Carolingian learning to the liberal arts programme. First of all, on a theoretical level many rival schemata of the arts competed with each other. The question of the priority, order and relationship of the arts to each other remained a vexing issue to masters throughout the Carolingian period and beyond.[74] Alcuin helped to 'Christianise' the arts by demonstrating how grammar could serve as the handmaiden of theology. His description of the temple of Christian Wisdom supported by the seven 'columns' of the arts put into graphic form the relationship between secular and divine learning.[75] So did the notion of John Scottus approximately fifty years later when he taught that the arts come together as the tributaries of a stream to be united in the contemplation of Christ.[76] Such confident assertions were not without their critics and throughout the ninth century nagging questions about the appropriateness of the arts to Christian education persisted. John Scottus' use of the art of dialectic to understand the issue of predestination was roundly criticised by Bishop Prudentius of Troyes (*c*. 846–61).[77] Agobard of Lyons was concerned that specialised study in music produced cantors who were very narrowly educated, deficient in their spiritual formation and

---

[71] 'Hibernicus exul', *De Artibus Liberalibus*, MGH Poet. I, pp. 408–10; Theodulf of Orléans, *De Septem Liberalibus Artibus in quadam pictura depictis*, ibid. I, pp. 544–7; also ibid. I, pp. 347, 542, 607–15, 616–17, 625–8, 629–30; II, pp. 359, 667–8; IV: 249–60, 339–43; Ganz (1990a), pp. 159–60.

[72] Walahfrid Strabo, *Visio Wettini* 176–7, MGH Poet. II, p. 309: 'Nam Wettinus erat celebri rumore magister / Artibus instructus septem de more priorum'; *Gesta Episcoporum Autissiodorensium*, MGH SS XIII, p. 399: 'Hic vir a primo etatis tyrocinio spiritualibus inbuitur disciplinis, liberalium artium studiis adprime instructus...'

[73] BN lat. 13955 (Ganz (1990a), pp. 152–3, 159–60); Laon, Bib. Mun. 468 (Contreni (1984)).

[74] Contreni (1992d).

[75] *De Grammatica*, PL 101, col. 853; Brunhölzl (1965); Leonardi (1981a).

[76] *Expositiones in Ierarchiam Caelestem* I, lines 540–55 (*CCCM* 31, p. 16); Giacone (1975).

[77] *De Praedestinatione contra Iohannem Scottum*, c. 1 (PL 115, cols. 1013–14).

puffed up by their pride.[78] One anonymous master regretted the time he had spent in his youth studying the arts.[79] Another felt compelled to rehearse once again the patristic arguments for incorporating secular learning in a Christian curriculum.[80] Ermenric of Ellwangen at the end of the ninth century recorded a dream in which the fundamental crisis of a Christian scholar who loved the classics – an issue that had disturbed the sleep of Jerome 500 years earlier – haunted him in the form of the ghost of Virgil.[81] Theodulf of Orléans, whose poem *De libris quos legere solebam et qualiter fabulae poetarum a philosophis mystice pertractentur* provides one of the best guides to the pagan and Christian 'school-authors' who formed the bases of the curriculum, was himself deeply troubled by the prospect of the revival of Roman pagan trappings in a Christian empire.[82] Hincmar of Rheims seventy-five years later shared Theodulf's antipathy towards Rome.[83] The Carolingian revival of learning did not put to rest these kinds of perennial questions that plague societies which try to establish themselves on religious foundations. Nevertheless, in the context of the ninth-century Frankish kingdoms, the imperative to Christianise the people and to appropriate the divine wisdom of the sacred text drove secular and religious culture together. Even Theodulf saw that, though much in the works of pagan authors was worthless, yet there were also many truths hidden under their false covers.[84]

Hraban Maur's *De Institutione Clericorum* illustrates well how secular and divine wisdom complemented each other in the Carolingian classroom.[85] This handbook for the training of clergy obviously depicts an ideal programme. Young men studying for the priesthood were expected to know the liberal arts – grammar, rhetoric, dialectic, mathematics, arithmetic, geometry, music, astronomy and what Hraban called the 'philosophical books'. At the same time, they received moral and spiritual training and prepared themselves to preach to their flocks. This is the programme of Augustine, judiciously supplemented by Cassiodorus, Isidore of Seville and Gregory the Great's *Pastoral Care*. But before students could embark on their studies, they had first to master the elements of learning and religious life – reading, writing, computus and chant. Training in these basic skills

---

[78] *De Antiphonario*, c. 18 (*CCCM* 52, p. 350).

[79] *Sollers artis eram prima florente iuventa* (ed. Leonardi (1961), p. 150).

[80] BN lat. 5600, fols. 130v–131r, 'incipit: Interrogatio: Cur autem grammaticam ab homine pagano edita vir christianorum legere praesumat?' (ed. Contreni (1992e), note 37).

[81] *MGH Epp.* V, pp. 561–2; also *Vita Alcuini* II (*MGH SS* xv: 1, p. 185).

[82] *MGH Poet.* I, pp. 543–4; Glauche (1970), pp. 11–12; Nees (1991), pp. 65–7, 77–143.

[83] Wallace-Hadrill (1981), pp. 49–50; Nees (1991), pp. 210–11, 235–57.

[84] *De libris quos legere solebam*, cc. 19–20 (*MGH Poet.* I, p. 543): 'In quorum dictis quamquam sint frivola multa / Plurima sub falso tegmine vera latent'.   [85] (Ed. Knoepfler (1900)).

was complementary. Children learned to recognise individual letters by copying them out. Most of this early instruction took place on wax tablets and pieces of slate, but sometimes early efforts to enter the world of Latin literacy left their marks on parchment.[86] Inscriptions in buildings provided more public opportunities for students to learn how to read.[87] For some, reading was a lifelong challenge. Hildemar, a monk of Corbie, described in his commentary on Benedict's *Rule* how the abbot would question monks about their Lenten reading. If he learned that the monastery's librarian had assigned a monk a reading that was too difficult, the abbot would give him a second, more appropriate book.[88] Hildemar's commentary is a model of a text written in simple, direct Latin, accessible to the young monks who received their first introduction to the *Rule* while still learning Latin. Even when they were ready to tackle more advanced reading, they needed their teachers to rearrange the word order of Virgil, Priscian and other classical authors with syntactical glosses to make the texts easier to understand.[89]

Elementary instruction in reading and speaking Latin was not limited to classroom exercises. Daily participation in the liturgy and communal readings reinforced the lessons of the *schola*. The Psalter was the first major text students mastered. Singing and recitation of the Psalms embedded the sounds of Latin in their minds while at the same time initiating students to the kind of moral formation Hraban Maur described in his *De Institutione Clericorum*. The Psalter remained a lifelong companion of Carolingian scholars. When testing new quills out on the fly-leaves of the manuscripts they were copying, scribes often used as a pen-trial the phrase *Beatus vir* from the first Psalm. The Psalms came to mind almost automatically when Carolingian authors wrote. Lupus of Ferrières drew inspiration from Augustine seventeen times and from Priscian and Virgil thirteen times each in his letters, but it was the Psalms that came more frequently to mind in forty-four cases.[90] Even in a relatively esoteric work such as the *Exposition on the Celestial Hierarchy*, John Scottus recalled Psalm verses fifteen times, second only to his penchant for the Gospel of John which he quoted twenty-one times.[91]

As Carolingian students mastered the rudiments of reading, copying and chant, they also began to study the first art, grammar, which included the

---

[86] Bischoff (1966b), pp. 74–87; Ganz (1987), pp. 34–5.   [87] Mitchell (1990), pp. 186–225.

[88] Hildemar, *Expositio Regulae*, c. 48 (ed. Mittermüller (1880), p. 487): 'Si autem cognoverit abbas, illi non esse aptum, tunc dicet illi: Non est iste liber tibi aptus, sed talis aptus est tibi; et non dabit illi, quem quaesivit, sed quem cognovit illi esse aptum'; Ganz (1990a), pp. 70–1.

[89] Draak (1957), pp. 216–82; (1967), pp. 100–44; Robinson (1973), pp. 443–75; Wieland (1983), pp. 98–107.   [90] Lupus of Ferrières, *Epp.* (ed. Marshall (1984), pp. 133–42).

[91] *Expositiones in Ierarchiam Coelestem*, *CCCM* 31, pp. 222–4.

rules of grammar as well as the study of texts. Grammar was the pre-eminent art of the Carolingian period. Grammatical studies prepared students not only to read, write and speak correctly, it also taught them how to think and provided them with a methodological tool for plumbing the mysteries of divine wisdom. The pervasiveness of grammar in Carolingian culture can be observed in the routine injunction of Archbishop Herard of Tours that priests not say Mass alone because the words 'Lift up your hearts' would be meaningless, and in the wholesale appropriation of grammatical methodology into scriptural exegesis and theological debate.[92]

Carolingian masters and students drew on a wide range of grammatical resources when they embarked on the systematic study of language. In addition to the works of the Latin grammarians, depending on local networks and influences, they might also consult Anglo-Saxon and Irish grammatical treatises.[93] Carolingian commentaries such as those of Alcuin or Sedulius Scottus provided a third resource. The manuals could be complementary. Donatus' *Ars maior* and *Ars minor*, for example, might be supplemented by Sedulius Scottus' commentaries on those texts or by the *Ars Laureshamensis*. The Carolingian commentaries testify to the challenge masters faced when they taught grammar. The Lorsch commentary required forty lines to explain the six words which began Donatus' commentary on the *Ars maior*: 'Incipit ars Donati grammatici urbis Romae.' The master responsible for this introduction to Donatus explained that the word *incipit* derived from *coepi* ('I begin'), not from *cepi* ('I took'). The teacher then followed this clarification with a question: How can it be said that the arts 'begin' since they are inanimate? The answer was that the term was being used metaphorically to apply to the inanimate.[94] Clearly what was apparent to Jerome who studied with Donatus in the fourth century was not so obvious to Carolingian students in the ninth century. Carolingian students had to work at grammar day and night.[95]

The study of Latin vocabulary went hand in hand with the study of the mechanics of the Latin language, as the Lorsch master's lesson about the difference between *coepi* and *cepi* suggests. Masters expanded the storehouse of their students' vocabulary in several ways. First, they glossed authoritative texts such as the Bible and the works of the school authors with simple

---

[92] *Capitula Herardi*, c. 28 (*PL* 121, col. 766): 'Ne presbyter solus missam canat: non enim potest dicere Dominus vobiscum, Sursum corda, et caetera'; Jolivet (1958); Ferrari (1972), p. 33 ('Dungal fu più filologo che filosofo'); Colish (1984), pp. 757–95.

[93] Holtz (1981), pp. 315–26; Law (1982), pp. 98–105.

[94] *Ars Laureshamensis*, lines 13–21 (*CCCM* 40A, p. 3).

[95] *Ad quendam inpubem*, lines 11–14 (*MGH Poet.* III, p. 355): 'Unum te moneo: semper certare studeto. / Quo valeas fisus ludere litterulis / Cum sociis, tecum qui discunt nocte dieque / Artem grammaticam; sicque valeto bene.'

lexical equivalents of new or unusual words: 'A gloss is the definition of a single word, as "sharp" means "intelligent".'[96] They also compiled glossaries, alphabetised wordlists culled from numerous sources and constantly augmented. The *Liber Glossarum*, the most important Carolingian glossary of all, with its more than 500,000 entries, constituted a veritable encylopaedia of Latin language and lore.[97]

Carolingian students inhabited several linguistic worlds. They never left their first languages behind, be they rustic Latin or German, when they embarked on the formal studies that aimed to prepare them to speak and write like the church Fathers. Hraban Maur quoting Augustine in the *De Institutione Clericorum* thought it prudent to remind his German-speaking students that when Augustine wrote 'our language' he meant Latin.[98] Learning Latin did not mean that students turned their backs on their first languages. They continued to need to communicate in those languages and actively studied the vernaculars. Lupus of Ferrières sent some of his monks to Prüm precisely to learn German which he thought would be a useful acquisition.[99] As future priests learned Latin biblical, theological and ecclesiastical concepts they also had to learn how to express them in the vernacular to the people. Bilingual Latin–vernacular glossaries helped them to explain their new learning in their first languages and doubtless proved useful to missionaries and teachers as a springboard into the world of Christianity and Latin learning.[100]

Study of Latin authors, especially the patristic authorities, sometimes led to the study of Greek which, during the third quarter of the ninth century, constituted one of the special achievements of the Carolingian renaissance. Continental knowledge of Greek was once thought to be an import from Ireland and limited to Irish masters such as John Scottus. But the widespread evidence of wordlists and Greek terms in poetry and exegesis suggests that some Carolingian students were taught this second of the three sacred languages, enough at least to understand a Greek term encountered in Jerome.[101]

Instruction in Hebrew in Carolingian schools, despite the evidence of trilingual Latin–Greek–Hebrew glossaries and of consultations with contemporary Jews on particular linguistic matters, appears to have been non-

---

[96] *Ars Laureshamensis*, lines 73–4 (*CCCM* 40A, p. 5): 'Glosa est unius verbi interpretatio, ut catus id est doctus.'

[97] Goetz (1888–1923); Lindsay (1926–31); Ganz (1990a), pp. 53–4; Ganz (1993).

[98] *De Institutione Clericorum* III, 9 (ed. Knoepfler (1900), p. 204): 'Si autem ipsius linguae nostrae, *id est latinae*, aliqua verba locutionesque ignoramus . . .'; Blumenkranz (1977a), p. 100.

[99] *Servati Lupi Epistolae*, Epp. 70, 2, and 91, 5 (ed. Marshall (1984), pp. 73–4, 89).

[100] Steinmeyer and Sievers (1879–1922); Bischoff (1966e), pp. 90–1; McKitterick (1977), pp. 184–205.   [101] Herren (1988); Berschin (1988).

existent.[102] This indifference to Hebrew in a society impregnated with Old Testament models such as Josias and David and connected to a living tradition of Hebrew language in its indigenous Jewish communities is difficult to explain. Despite the hostility of Agobard of Lyons' anti-Jewish tracts, Carolingian Jews interacted freely with Christians and at a rather high level.[103] Agobard fulminated especially at their presence in the court of Louis the Pious, the site of the most spectacular episode in ninth-century Christian–Jewish relations. Deacon Bodo, an Alemannian by birth, established a reputation at court as a scholar versed in secular and sacred learning. His contacts with Jews led him in 839 to convert to Judaism, change his name to Eleazar, and marry a Jewish woman. Along with his nephew who also converted, Bodo went to Spain where it was reported that he actively encouraged Christians to convert to Judaism or to Islam. Bodo-Eleazar defended his new faith against Paul Alvar, a Cordoban Jew who had converted to Christianity. The *Annales Bertiniani* report that these events greatly troubled Louis the Pious, but they seem not to have affected relations between Jewish and Christian scholars. Hraban Maur, Paschasius Radbertus, Amalarius of Metz and others continued to consult Jews, but never apparently studied Hebrew themselves.[104] Christian scholars may have thought that everything worth learning from the Hebrew tradition had already been made available to them in the Old Testament and in the works of the church Fathers, notably Jerome, whereas the Greek works of a Pseudo-Dionysius or Maximus Confessor offered exciting new insights.

Glossaries and grammatical studies went hand-in-hand with the study of texts. Carolingian masters faced an enormous challenge when they introduced their students to the study of the Bible and the school-authors. The example of the royal nuns, Gisela and Rotrud, is worth recalling. They asked Alcuin to explain the Gospel of John to them because Augustine's commentary was too difficult.[105] If these educated women whose intelligence permeates their letters found Augustine difficult, understanding the

---

[102] Thiel (1973); Herren (1989a); Riché (1989), pp. 96–98.

[103] Agobard of Lyons, *De Baptismo Mancipiorum Iudaeorum*, CCCM 52, pp. 113–17; *Contra Praeceptum Impium de Baptismo Iudaicorum Mancipiorum*, ibid., pp. 183–8; *De Insolentia Iudaeorum*, ibid., pp. 189–95; *De Iudaicis Superstitionibus et Erroribus, ibid.*, pp. 197–221; Blumenkranz (1960); Bachrach (1977).

[104] *AB(1) s.a.* 839, 847, (pp. 27–8, 53–4); Paul Alvar, *Epp.*, 14–20 (ed. Gil (1973) I, pp. 227–70); Cabaniss (1953); Blumenkranz (1977b); Blumenkranz (1963), pp. 144–217.

[105] *MGH Epp.* IV, p. 324: 'Habemus siquidem clarissimi doctoris Augustini homeliatico sermone explanationes in eundem evangelistam, sed quibusdam in locis multo obscuriores maiorique circumlocutione decoratas, quam nostrae parvitatis ingeniolo intrare valeat. Sufficit vero nostrae devotioni de rivulis dulcissimae aquae potare, non profundissimis gurgitum fluminibus nostras immittere carinas'.

Fathers must have been a considerable challenge for most students. Christian of Stavelot's students complained to him that Jerome's explanation of Matthew was beyond them even after studying his commentary twice.[106]

Carolingian masters responded to the pedagogical challenge of accommodating the wisdom and language of the Fathers to new readers by writing their own commentaries on the sacred and secular texts. The new commentaries aimed for a simple, straightforward style, eliminated philological discussions, and preferred the literal, historical interpretation to the mystical. Carolingian commentators also increased the utility of their commentaries by synthesising the work of several authors in their own.[107] Irish masters and texts played a key role in the development of a new Carolingian-style commentary when they brought to the Continent and helped to propagate in Carolingian schools a new, 'technical' approach to the explication of texts. The special demands of teaching Latin in a Celtic culture forced Irish masters to go beyond the grammar of Donatus and to draw on a wide variety of late antique grammatical works – many of which had been supplanted on the Continent by the very success of Donatus. The work of the Irish grammarians began to make its mark in the eighth century when Anglo-Saxon and Irish missionaries came to the Continent. Both Alcuin and Peter of Pisa were familiar with the Irish grammatical tradition. In the ninth century, some time around 840, a new Irish commentary based on Donatus' *Ars maior* and complemented by commentaries on Donatus and on Priscian's grammar began to change the shape of grammatical studies in Carolingian Europe. Murethach of Auxerre and Metz and Sedulius Scottus taught their own versions of the new commentary. Two other versions survive from the teaching of anonymous masters. These commentaries adopted what might be termed an exegetical approach to their text. The master in explicating Donatus' text supplemented it with examples of specific grammatical doctrines taken from other grammarians and thus implicitly compared and contrasted authorities. Grammatical instruction became a dialectical commentary on a text. In the process of paraphrasing and commenting on the text and developing the 'sense' of an author's grammatical doctrines, ninth-century Irish teachers and their students refined a study technique that inevitably spilled over into other areas. The technique consisted of constant, almost formulaic questioning (*Querendum est*; *Quaestio*) justification of doctrines, comparison where relevant with practices *apud modernos*, and the consultation of additional authorities.[108]

The brand of textual scholarship promoted by the Irish had its greatest

[106] *MGH Epp.* vi, p. 177.   [107] Contreni (1992f), pp. 84–93.
[108] Holtz (1972), pp. 45–73; Holtz (1977a), pp. 69–78.

impact on the study of the sacred text itself. Carolingian scholars from the time of Alcuin at the end of the eighth century to the time of Remigius of Auxerre at the beginning of the tenth century wrote more than 150 biblical commentaries.[109] Some commentaries undoubtedly did not survive – Rudolf of Fulda's teaching would have been lost had not his student, Ercanbert, transcribed his comments[110] – but the ones that have are representative. Carolingian commentators clearly had students – both young and adult – in mind. They avoided the allegorical approach for the historical and literal and aimed at brevity and clarity in their expositions. Originality was not one of their goals. Over and over they stressed in the prefaces to their works how dependent they were on the patristic giants who preceded them. But when they excerpted, combined and rephrased their exegetical predecessors, Carolingian masters did in fact produce new works that helped to make the ninth century the first great age of patristic scholarship.

The interplay between Irish and Continental biblical scholars was complex. Carolingian schools from the eighth century on assimilated an Irish biblical tradition that was perfectly suited to the needs of students like Gisela and Rotrud, and those of Christian of Stavelot. The Irish approach to the Bible favoured literal and historical interpretation, compilation, the dialogue format, and what seemed to some like an excessive fondness for lists and pedantic detail and a fascination for first-time occurrences. Theodulf thought Irish scholars were like jacks-of-all-trades who mastered none.[111] But the widespread acceptance of Hiberno-Latin exegesis is amply demonstrated by many surviving Continental examples and, especially, by the massive compilation known as the Reference Bible, an exegetical compendium that ranged over the entire Bible.[112] By the middle of the ninth century, Carolingian masters had begun to apply the methodology they learned from the grammarians to the Bible to develop their own more 'scientific' approach to the sacred text. Haimo of Auxerre, a pupil of Murethach, was instrumental in formulating Carolingian scholastic exegesis.[113] Other Carolingian masters such as Christian of Stavelot also helped to popularise the grammatical approach to biblical pedagogy. Christian's commentary on Matthew opens with a paean to the liberal arts and a discussion of the *tempus, locus* and *persona* of the Gospel. [114]

---

[109] McNally (1959), pp. 89–117.   [110] *MGH Epp.* v, p. 358.

[111] *Ad Carolum Regem*, lines 233–4 (*MGH Poet.* i, p. 489): 'Multa scis et nulla sapis, plura, inscie, nosti, / Quid dicam inde magis? non sapis atque sapis'; Bischoff (1967a).

[112] Bischoff (1966c), pp. 205–73.   [113] Holtz (1977b), pp. xxi–xxxv; Bertola (1961a and b).

[114] *Expositio in Matthaeum Evangelistam* i (*PL* 106, col. 1264): 'In omnium principiis librorum tria quaerenda sunt, tempus, locus, persona. Similiter de isto evangelio haec tria tenenda sunt.'

Any Carolingian student would have recognised Christian's themes from study of the Carolingian commentaries on secular authors. In addition to the commentaries on the grammarians, the ninth century produced glosses and commentaries (partial and whole) on Virgil, Boethius, Sedulius and Martianus Capella among others. The commentaries usually begin with an *accessus*, or introduction, organised around the seven *periochae*: an account of the author's life; an explanation of the work's title; a description of the nature of the text; the author's intention in writing the work; the number of books contained in the work; the order of the books; and a summary of the work.[115] The commentary then proceeded to explicate the text. Comments ranged from the lexical to the mythological and historical to the philosophical and theological. The commentaries tended to have lives of their own and seem to have continually developed from year to year as the master taught. A written version of a commentary might enshrine a set of notes in a tradition that was free to grow prompted by the demands of the classroom, the use of new texts or the incorporation of comments by other masters. The complicated textual history of the ninth-century Martianus Capella commentaries and of John Scottus' *Periphyseon* testify to creativity and continual revision on the part of Carolingian masters.[116]

Grammar and the explication of secular and religious literature were fundamental to Carolingian schools and literary culture. Grammar was but one constituent of wisdom. Mastery of the first art opened the way to vigorous study of the other arts. When Carolingian masters taught about learning, wisdom and the relation of the arts to each other, they abandoned the schema of the traditional seven liberal arts canonised in Martianus Capella and in Isidore of Seville's *Etymologiae*, preferring instead that of Isidore's *Differentiae* in which wisdom is subdivided among physics, ethics and logic. Physics includes the quadrivial arts, arithmetic, geometry, music and astronomy as well as astrology, the mechanical arts and medicine. Ethics embraces the four principal virtues of prudence, justice, fortitude and temperance. Logic, the study of words, consists of rhetoric and dialectic to which grammar 'adheres'.[117] The relationship among grammar, rhetoric and dialectic was indeed one of adhesion since they all focused on the proper comprehension and use of words. As Carolingian students studied grammar and secular and divine literature, they also began to learn how to manipulate language through rhetorical and dialectical studies.

Hraban Maur in the *De Institutione Clericorum* began his discussion of rhetoric with Cassiodorus' classical definition of rhetoric's usefulness in 'civil questions', but quickly moved to Augustine and the *De Doctrina*

---

[115] Huygens (1954).   [116] Schrimpf (1973); Jeauneau (1989); Zier (1989); Smith (1989).
[117] *Differentiae* II.39 (*PL* 83, pp. 93–5); Bischoff (1966d); Contreni (1992d), p. 7.

Christiana to appropriate rhetoric for Christian uses, especially for the
'preacher of the divine law'.[118] What Augustine had in mind was classical
rhetoric, the art of persuasion, an art which Carolingian preachers eschewed
when composing their sermons. As Sulpicius Severus, Paulinus of Nola and
others saw centuries earlier, the medieval preacher's audience was made up
of sinners, not scholars – a point Hraban seems to have taken when he
recommended that preachers adapt their words to their audiences and cited
Gregory the Great's *Pastoral Care* at length on how to do that.[119] Carolingian homiletic tradition fostered homilies which inspired monastic meditation and sermons accessible to the people in their own language – neither
of which would have been well served by classical and patristic rhetorical
canons. The purpose of rhetorical studies in the Carolingian schools was, in
the words of the *Epistola de Litteris Colendis*, to enable *readers* to comprehend
the figures of speech, tropes and metaphors found in the sacred writings.
Bede blazed the path Carolingian rhetorical studies would take when he
illustrated the figures of speech in his *De Schematibus et Tropis* with examples
from the Bible. Thus, for epizeuxis, Bede offered 'Awake, awake, stand up,
O Jerusalem' ('Elevare, elevare, consurge Hierusalem') from Isaiah 51,
17.[120]

   Study of the figures of speech and especially of the writings of late antique
Christian authors enabled masters who wrote and scholars – an Alcuin, a
Theodulf of Orléans, a Lupus of Ferrières – to embellish their prose not only
with rhetorical figures, but also with rhyme and parallelism. For most
students, however, rhetorical studies amounted to the mastery of appropriate prose styles. The letters of Lupus of Ferrières offered models that they
might emulate in their own correspondence. The master who used Lupus'
letters in his teaching peppered the margins of the unique copy of the letters
with observations such as 'an excellent plea' (*optima supplicatio*), 'excellent
encouragements' (*optimae adhortationes*), 'Note a humble and prudent
request' (*Nota humilem et prudentem implorationem*).[121] Collections of model
letters also prepared students to write all kinds of letters.[122] Carolingian
students learned how to write letters of condolence, how to describe a king,
how to compose a debate between winter and spring, and how to write
letters and poems of praise and flattery. The results of this training in the use
of stock phrases and exempla crop up everywhere in Carolingian literature.

---

[118] *De Institutione Clericorum* III, 19, lines 28–36 (ed. Knoepfler (1900), pp. 225–7, 245–60).
[119] Riché (1978), p. 90; *De Institutione Clericorum* III, 37 ('De discretione dogmatum iuxta qualitatem auditorum') (ed. Knoepfler (1900), pp. 260–72).
[120] *De Schematibus et Tropis* I, 8 (*CCSL* 123A, p. 147).
[121] BN lat. 2858; Lupus of Ferrières, *Epp.* (ed. Marshall (1984), pp. 24, 44, 54).
[122] *MGH Form.*

When Einhard needed to describe Charlemagne's physical characteristics, he naturally drew from Suetonius' portraits of Roman emperors. Biblical commentators when defending their use of a variety of sources compared their works to the pipes of an organ which when sounded individually are discordant, but when played together emit a pleasing sound. Paschasius Radbertus justified the compilatory method of his commentary on Matthew by repeating Cicero's story from the *De Inventione* of the painter Xeuxis who painted parts of the five prettiest girls he could find to create an adequate portrait of Helen of Troy. He used the same story but to a different end in his *Vita Adalhardi*.[123]

The most original development in Carolingian rhetorical studies linked rhetoric with rulership. Alcuin's *Disputatio de Rhetorica et Virtutibus*, dedicated to Charlemagne, was only the first of many hortatory treatises Carolingian authors wrote to guide their leaders. Smaragdus of St Mihiel's *Via Regia* for Louis the Pious, Jonas of Orléans' *De Institutione Regia* for Louis' son, Pippin, Hincmar of Rheims' *De Regis Persona et Regio Ministerio* for Charles the Bald, and Sedulius Scottus' *De Rectoribus Christianis* for Lothar firmly established a Carolingian tradition of political moral suasion that grounded contemporary politics in rhetoric. These authors and others such as Cathwulf and Lupus of Ferrières exemplified Isidore of Seville's definition of rhetoric as 'skill in speaking well on civil matters and a flow of eloquence intended to persuade men to do what is just and good.'[124]

The revival of rhetorical studies in the schools and of rhetoric in scholarly and intellectual discourse in the ninth century was accompanied by intense study of dialectic and the application of dialectic to the problems intellectuals debated in the Carolingian realms. It is no longer possible to imagine a long period of dormancy in dialectical studies between the time of Augustine and Boethius on the one hand, and the eleventh century on the other.[125] Nor is it possible to understand the fundamental nature of dialectical studies in the ninth century only by saluting John Scottus' use of dialectical reasoning in his works or by belittling Fridugisus of Tours' treatises on the reality of 'shadow' and 'nothing'. In the ninth century a broad range of masters and their students considered seriously the problems of essence and universals and applied Aristotle's categories and syllogistic reasoning to theological speculation.

The recovery in the curriculum of works such as Aristotle's *Categories* and

---

[123] *Expositio in Matheo libri XII*, prologue (*CCCM* 56, p. 6); *Vita Sancti Adalhardi* 20 (PL 120, cols. 1518–19).

[124] *Etymologiae* II, 1, 1 (ed. Lindsay (1911)): 'Rhetorica est bene dicendi scientia in civilibus quaestionibus, eloquentia copia ad persuadendum iusta et bona'; Anton (1968).

[125] D'Onofrio (1986).

Boethius' *Opuscula Sacra* as well as Augustine's *De Trinitate* gave Carolingian
dialectical studies their impetus. Once again, Alcuin led the way with his *De
Dialectica* which presents the elements of basic dialectical reasoning in the
form of a dialogue between Alcuin and Charlemagne. Alcuin's role in
making dialectic accessible to Carolingian students extended far beyond the
composition of this one text. He taught his students to apply dialectical
reasoning to contemporary theological issues such as the Adoptionist
controversy. Alcuin's teaching survives in a series of texts known in the
manuscripts as the *Dicta Albini*. The *dicta*, defined in the *De Dialectica* as 'the
same as dialectic because dialectic investigates statements (*dicta*)',[126]
consider such topics as the Trinity, the existence of God, the existence of
God before time and the creation of man in God's image.[127] One of the texts,
set in the form of a dialogue, gives a sense of the nature of dialectical inquiry
as well as the level of sophistication of the instruction. The *interrogatio* opens
with a request: 'You, who want to know if God is, tell me what you think
God to be, if he is.' 'He is the good', comes the *responsio*, 'of which there is
none better, and the power of which there is none more powerful.'
Seventeen exchanges later the interrogator succeeds in convincing the
responder that God must exist not on the strength of any authority, but on
the internal logic of the argument.[128]

   This dialectical approach to theology was also broadcast by Candidus,
Alcuin's pupil, from whose teaching a similar set of *dicta* survives. Extracts
from the *dicta* appear in the *Libri Carolini* and in Benedict of Aniane's
Munimenta Fidei. It is in this context of growing interest in the technique of
dialectical inquiry that Fridugisus' *De Nihilo et Tenebris* must be seen.[129]
Fridugisus was concerned to discuss the reality of negative qualities, a
question that was assuming greater urgency as thinkers attributed negative
predicates to God. Fridugisus also broached the question of the pre-
existence of the soul before union with the body and was rebutted by
Agobard of Lyons who marshalled patristic and biblical citations against
him.[130] Agobard was not alone in questioning the results of the new
methodology. Theodulf of Orléans, Benedict of Aniane and Prudentius of
Troyes also reacted against what they thought was excessive reliance on
syllogistic reasoning – a defect they tended to ascribe to Irish masters. But
dialectic proved so useful in exploring perennial problems of Christian
theology that ninth-century debates on the Eucharist, the world soul and
predestination all depended on it. Indeed, in combating John Scottus,

---

[126] *De Dialectica*, c. 1 (*PL* 101, col. 953): 'Dicta est dialectica, quia in ea de dictis disputatur.'
[127] Marenbon (1981), pp. 144–70.   [128] *Ibid.*, pp. 154–7.   [129] *MGH Epp.* IV, pp. 552–5.
[130] *Ibid.* V, pp. 210–21; Marenbon (1981), pp. 64–6.

Prudentius of Troyes proved himself no neophyte in dialectical debate.[131] Although few Carolingian students could engage in this kind of theological speculation at the level of a Ratramnus of Corbie, John Scottus or Prudentius of Troyes, the evidence is abundant that dialectical studies formed an important part of their training in the arts. The evidence consists of extensive Carolingian glosses to key school texts, the *De Nuptiis* of Martianus Capella, the *Opuscula Sacra* of Boethius, and, especially, the *Categoriae Decem*.

Dialectical studies complemented the study of grammar and rhetoric since all three aimed to understand words: written words, spoken words, words used in texts, in prayer, in argument and in speculation. The other arts which formed the school curriculum concerned number. Carolingian students studied the mathematical arts for obvious practical reasons. The *Admonitio Generalis* required that young students learn to master the computus, the early medieval method of reckoning time and determining dates. They would also have to know how to manipulate numbers when it came to collecting the tithe and dividing it into fourths, when calculating the harvests from fields or the rents due from farmers. The vast building programme promoted in the Carolingian realms stimulated the study of ratio, architecture and geometry as evinced by the careful proportions of surviving buildings and by the meticulous draftsmanship of the Plan of St Gall. The increasingly theoretical nature of ninth-century chant likewise required keen understanding of harmony and measure.[132]

Number also had a deeper significance for Carolingians thinkers. It reflected the inherent order of the divinely created universe. The rationality and system of number often appealed to religious peoples who, like the Mesopotamians or Pythagoreans, seek to understand the world through numerical relations. For Christians of the ninth century, the key text could be found in the Book of Wisdom (11:16–21) which describes the apocalyptic fury God might have unleashed on the Egyptians for their worship of 'mindless reptiles and contemptible beasts'. But the God of Israel was a lenient, patient God who 'ordered all things by measure, number, weight'. The study of measure, number and weight became, with the study of the word, a means to approach the Creator.[133] It is not only that numbers have an allegorical significance – the seven days of Genesis, the dimensions of Noah's Ark. Jerome in his comment on Ezekiel 45, 12 ('The shekel shall be twenty gerahs; five shekels shall be five shekels, and ten shekels shall be ten

---

[131] *De Praedestinatione contra Iohannem Scottum*, PL 115, cols. 1009–1366; Ganz (1990b), p. 293.

[132] Ullman (1964); Ilmer (1984); Borst (1988), pp. 19–27; Crocker (1975), pp. 341–9; Stevens (1979a), pp. 165–75; Horn and Born (1979) I, pp. 53–63.

[133] Wallace-Hadrill (1983), pp. 215–16; Jeauneau (1990), pp. 126–41.

shekels, and your mina shall be fifty shekels') saw that scriptural concern for correctness of weights and measures extended beyond the needs of commerce and daily life. Numerical correctness is a metaphor for correctness of speech, action and thought. Jerome's point did not escape Hraban Maur in his ninth-century commentary on Ezekiel.[134] Time was equally fundamental. Creation was measured in days in Genesis and the heavenly bodies were established by the Creator as 'signs' to mark the seasons, the days and the years (Genesis 1, 14). And since the Creator entered time through the Incarnation and changed the course of sacred history through His Passion and Resurrection, the proper observance of these moments in time through the liturgy and the celebration of feast days became charged with sacral significance. Determination of appropriate dates was more than a matter of convenience.

The movements and characteristics of the heavenly bodies fascinated Carolingian observers. Alcuin had to respond to Charlemagne's questions on the subject. Dungal too was called on by the emperor to explain the eclipse of the sun in 810. Lupus of Ferrières and 'the Astronomer', the anonymous author of a *Vita Hludowici Imperatoris*, were both intelligent observers of astronomical phenomena.[135] In the schools, instruction in the technically rigorous computus, specifically called for in the *Admonitio Generalis*, included arithmetic as well as knowledge of the courses of celestial bodies. The fundamental texts masters used included Victorius of Aquitaine's *Liber Calculi*, Boethius' *De Arithmetica*, the works of Euclid, Pliny and Bede as well as numerous computistical manuals and tables and ingenious mnemonic verses which helped students to learn and remember complicated relationships.[136] One teaching text suggests that Carolingian students were the first in the west to learn the rules for adding positive and negative numbers.[137]

The abundance and variety of arithmetical and scientific texts in Carolingian libraries and classrooms sometimes caused confusion and led to debate. In 809 a meeting of computists (*compotistae*) was held at Aachen to try to clarify the most vexing problems. The assembled experts were asked

---

[134] Jerome, *Commentariorum in Hiezechielem libri XIV* 14, 45 (*CCSL* 75, pp. 679–81); Hraban Maur, *Commentariorum in Ezechielem libri viginti* 18, 45 (*PL* 110, cols. 1026–7).

[135] Alcuin, *Ep.* 145 (*MGH, Epp.* IV, pp. 231–2); Dungal, *Ep.* 1 (*MGH Epp.* IV, pp. 570–8); Lupus of Ferrières, *Ep.* 20, 13 (ed. Marshall (1984), p. 28); *Vita Hludowici Imperatoris, MGH SS* II, pp. 604–48.

[136] *MGH Poet.* II, pp. 422–3, 604–18, 644–5; IV, pp. 670–702, 937–43, 1119–22; Pacificus of Verona, *Manuale di computo con ritmo mnemotecnico* (ed. Meersseman and Adda (1966)); Jones (1943), pp. 3–122; Walsh and Ó Cróinín (1988), pp. 3–47; Stevens (1979b), pp. 27–63; Stevens (1993); Eastwood (1993); Dekkers and Gaar (1961), pp. 502–18; Beaujouan (1972), pp. 639–67.

[137] Folkerts (1972).

twenty-three questions, some of which they could answer satisfactorily and others which they could not: 'xv. With regard to the lunar cycle, why does it not begin with the paschal terms? Then, what is the use of it? Regarding the utility of that cycle they had something to say; but regarding its inauguration, nothing.'[138] The conference of computists was the first step in an attempt to standardise Carolingian computus. The second was the compilation and publication of two massive collections known as the 'Three-Book Computus' and the 'Seven-Book Computus' which integrated arithmetic, computus and astronomy with bits of theology and history to produce a Carolingian *summa* on computus.[139] Dicuil, an Irishman in the court of Louis the Pious, added his *Liber de Astronomia et Computo* to the growing body of Carolingian computistical literature.[140] The most important computistical works used in Carolingian classrooms were Bede's treatises, *De Natura Rerum, De Temporibus Liber* and *De Temporum Ratione*. Dozens of ninth-century manuscripts of the Bedan computistical corpus survive attesting to its widespread use in the schools. More significantly, Bede's texts were commented on and glossed a number of times by Helperic, by Hraban Maur, by Martin Scottus and by other, anonymous masters who simplified Bede for their students. They even worked through examples using the current year or used familiar geographical references to elucidate complex computistical formulae and concepts.[141]

Clear pedagogical concerns are also evident in what may have been the most significant development in computistical instruction in the ninth century. Some time early in the century, a Carolingian master gathered together a series of excerpts bearing on astronomy from the second book of Pliny's *Naturalis Historia*. The selections discuss the positions and courses of the seven planets, the intervals between their circular orbits, their apsides and, finally, their travels through the bands of the zodiac. The excerpts appear in thirty-eight manuscripts dating from the ninth to the twelfth centuries and attest to the widespread interest in these sections of the *Naturalis Historia*. The Plinian texts also were available to Carolingian teachers in both the 'Three-Book Computus' and the 'Seven-Book Computus'. The Plinian excerpts attracted the attention of teachers because they

---

[138] *Capitula de quibus convocati compotistae interrogati fuerint, MGH Epp.* IV. 4, pp. 565–6; Jones (1963), p. 27. [139] Borst (1993); Stevens (1993), p. 375; Bischoff (1981), pp. 228–9.

[140] Esposito (1990).

[141] See Stevens (1985), pp. 39–42 and the introductions to Jones (1975–80), *Bedae Venerabilis Opera: Opera didascalica, CCSL* 123A, B, C. *De Temporum Ratione*, c. 27, line 18 (*CCSL* 123B, p. 363) is glossed: '[PORRECTARUM] Longarum quarum sit una hic in Francia et altera in Burgundia'; also, at c. 47, line 40 (*CCSL* 123B, p. 429): '[PARTIAMUR] Verbi gratia, habemus nunc ab incarnatione domini annos DCCCLXXIII; adde unum annum decennovenalis cicli et fiunt DCCCLXXIIII, partire per XVIIII et invenies quotus annus sit circuli decennovenalis.'

furnished much greater and more precise detail about planetary motion than
did the standard accounts of Isidore of Seville and Bede. Pliny also provided
a theoretical framework to account for the variety and complexity of the
behaviour of planets that was lacking in the medieval treatises. When
Carolingian masters taught the Plinian system to their students, they
achieved a pedagogical innovation by supplementing the text with
diagrams. These ninth-century diagrams were conceptually more sophisticated than the *rota* associated with Isidore of Seville's text which essentially
served as graphic equivalents of Isidore's words. The ninth-century Plinian
diagrams represent Carolingian reworkings of the Plinian doctrine so that
students could appreciate in a simplified, visual format the intricacies of
Plinian astronomy. The diagrams which evolved through the course of the
ninth century to include circular, tabular and grid formats encouraged
students to think by means of verbal and pictorial representations about
computistical and astronomical phenomena.

Intense study of Martianus Capella in Carolingian schools reinforced the
impact the Plinian texts made on Carolingian teaching. In Book VIII of the
De Nuptiis, Martianus described circumsolar orbits for Venus and Mercury.
He adopted Pliny's concept of the force of solar rays as the cause of the
regular variations in planetary paths and then applied the same mechanism
to account for the restriction of Mercury and Venus to the neighbourhood
of the sun. The Capellan text was ambivalently understood in the early
middle ages to suggest both concentric and intersecting orbits for the two
planets around the sun. Further study of the text and of earlier authorities
produced various circumsolar paths for Mercury and Venus that were
assigned to Pliny and to Bede. Many Carolingian masters came to consider
the combined planetary doctrine of Pliny and Martianus Capella as reigning
authority in their diagrams and glosses on other astronomical texts.[142]

The study of music in the Carolingian world mirrors the study of
computus. There was a practical need, the requirements of the Christian
liturgy, as well as intellectual imperative, the study of music, its harmonies,
its measure, as one of the arts.

Students received their introduction to music when they began to learn
the Psalms by chanting them. The study of chant was controversial in
Carolingian Europe. As early as the 750s, Chrodegang of Metz urged Pippin
III to encourage the spread of Roman chant in his realm. Chrodegang had
been to Rome and had established a *schola cantorum* at Metz modelled on the
one there.[143] Pippin supported Chrodegang's efforts and so did his son,

[142] Eastwood (1982), pp. 145–55; (1986a), pp. 183–208; (1986b); (1987), pp. 141–72; Mostert and
Mostert (1990), pp. 248–61; Eastwood (1993).
[143] Paul the Deacon, *Gesta Episcoporum Mettensium*, MGH SS II, p. 68; Vogel (1979), pp. 13–34.

Charlemagne. When Charlemagne visited Rome he was reported to have compared Roman chant to the clear waters of a well and the chant of his own kingdom to the muddy waters of a creek and resolved to go back to the supposed source of authentic Christian music, back to Pope Gregory the Great. An antiphonary and responsorial were sent north from Rome to help with the effort. Archbishop Arn of Salzburg reflected this Romanising enthusiasm when he ordered his bishops to establish schools of chant according to the Roman tradition.[144] Archbishop Leidrad of Lyons reported to Charlemagne that he did everything commanded of him, including the establishment of a *schola cantorum* led by a monk from Metz skilled in Roman chant.[145] According to the *Libri Carolini*, Roman chant followed in the wake of Carolingian conquest.[146]

Political initiatives in cultural matters can be tricky, however, and Carolingian efforts to standardise chant according to the Roman model were no exception. The reality of the musical scene at the beginning of the ninth century was more complex than Charlemagne or his advisers imagined. For one thing, Carolingian reformers were way out ahead of Rome which, except with the churches of suburbicarian Italy, was quite liberal when it came to chant and liturgical practices.[147] For another, Roman chant of *c.* 800 had continued to evolve from that of the seventh and eighth centuries which had been exported north earlier. Cantors from Metz who went down to Rome thinking themselves experts were surprised to find that they were out of tune with their Roman colleagues. What was thought to be authentic, fixed and immutable had actually changed considerably. Notker Balbulus, who had a special interest in chant, attributed the chaotic musical situation of Charlemagne's day to sabotage by the twelve Roman monks Pope Stephen had sent to Francia. 'Envious of the glory of the Franks', the Roman cantors deliberately taught incorrect chant and different systems of chant in the twelve centres to which they were assigned.[148] But variety and change are hardly to be wondered at in a tradition where everything depended on oral transmission from master to student from generation to generation.[149] Carolingian masters tried to curb diversity by continually correcting books and a New Hymnal was established during the reign of Louis the Pious.[150] But the long-sought-after uniformity remained elusive.

---

[144] *Concilium Rispacense a. 798* VIII (*MGH Conc.* II, p. 199): 'Episcopus autem unusquisque in civitate sua scolam constituat et sapientem doctorem, qui secundum traditionem Romanorum possit instruere et lectionibus vacare et inde debitum discere, ut per canonicas horas cursus in aecclesia debeat canere.'   [145] *MGH Epp.* IV, p. 370.

[146] *Libri Carolini* I, 6 (*MGH Conc.* II (suppl.), p. 21); Levy (1987); Hughes (1987); Treitler and Levy (1988); Bullough (1991c), pp. 7–8.   [147] Vogel (1967), p. 217.

[148] *Gesta Karoli Magni Imperatoris* I, 10 (*MGH SS* II. 735).

[149] Treitler (1974; 1981); Levy (1990).   [150] Bullough (1991d), pp. 241–71.

When Helisachar, the archchaplain in the court of Louis the Pious, brought out a new, supposedly definitive antiphonary, he admitted in his preface that the work was going to be controversial.[151] In the end what came to be known as 'Gregorian' chant was actually a hybrid of Carolingian and Old Roman texts and melodies.

As Carolingian masters worked to fix texts, they also tried to regularise the melody of chants for their pupils. The system they used to accomplish this was a series of raised marks, visual cues, that indicated the range of a melody from high to low, but these notes, called neumes, did not indicate pitch or intervals. Although neumic notation was fairly primitive in the ninth century, it was a significant pedagogical breakthrough because it provided an enduring graphic representation of melody.[152] Major centres of musical instruction developed characteristic forms of notation known today as Messine for those of Metz, St Gall notation for those associated with that monastery, Aquitainian, Breton and other regional varieties. In an effort to improve on neumic notation by clearly indicating pitch, some masters created a system of Greek-letter and then Latin-letter notation.[153] Monks apparently from Jumièges developed a clever mnemonic device for remembering the very long melodies of the Kyrie and Alleluia. One Jumièges monk fleeing the Vikings came to St Gall with his antiphonary which incorporated the innovation and showed it to young Notker Balbulus. Notker, who was searching for just such an aid, shared the new technique with his teachers, Iso and Marcellus, who pressed it into service for their students.[154] It was in the Carolingian monastic and cathedral schools where masters were hard taxed to help their students learn an expanding and increasingly more complicated musical repertoire that these pedagogical devices, the neumes, the tropes and the sequences, were invented. Like the opening words of the first Psalm, medieval students copied verses from hymns and tropes into the margins of manuscripts, even non-musical manuscripts, and signed them with neumic notes by way, apparently, of practice as the melodies ran through their heads.

The same belief that animated compustitical and astronomical studies, that basic religious truths could be detected in measure, number and order, inspired the theoretical study of music as an art. Music considered as a mathematical discipline with cosmological implications had a long pedigree stretching from the Greeks, through Augustine, Boethius, Cassiodorus and

[151] *MGH Epp.* v, pp. 307–9; Huglo (1979), pp. 87–120.
[152] Corbin (1977); Treitler (1982); Bénédictines de Solesmes (1889–).
[153] Crocker (1979), pp. 79–104.
[154] *Liber Ymnorum*, preface (ed. von den Steinen (1948) II, pp. 8–10); Crocker (1975), pp. 341–51; Crocker (1977); Rankin (1993).

Isidore of Seville into the Carolingian period. Music was the art practised by angels; its harmonies regulated the movements of the heavenly bodies; and it was the most perfect art because its powers encouraged warriors and soothed the beasts of land, sea and air.[155] In contrast to the *cantor* who taught his charges how to sing, the *musicus* introduced his students to a world of ratios, rhythm and mathematical proportions heavily laced with Pythagorean philosophical speculation. In the words of Boethius, scholars such as himself were the architects of music, while the cantors were the mere bricklayers. Aurelian of Réôme in the middle of the ninth century altered the image only slightly in his *Musica Disciplina* when he compared singing to reading and the study of music to the study of grammar – the one was like manual labour, the other like reasoning.[156] The air of superiority implicit in these comparisons derived from the encounter of Carolingian masters with Greek musical theory. Boethius was the chief conduit to the Carolingian world of Greek musical doctrine. His *De Institutione Musica* along with the more accessible ninth book (*De Musica* or *De Harmonia*) of Martianus Capella's *De Nuptiis* fuelled interest in musical speculation. The treatise of Aurelian of Réôme, the anonymous *Alia Musica*, Hucbald of St Amand's *De Harmonica Institutione*, the *Musica Enchiriadis*, and the *Scolica Enchiriadis* all bear witness to the assimilation of ancient musical theory in the Carolingian classroom.[157] The commentaries on Martianus Capella's *De Musica* played an especially significant role. Capella helped Carolingian masters to understand Greek musical theory and technical musical terms. When masters such as John Scottus and Remigius of Auxerre glossed the *De Nuptiis* for their students and later readers, they placed musical study within the framework of the study of the liberal arts: it was one of the ways to approach divine truth. Liturgical music and music studied as one of the arts thus pointed in many directions – to the divine, to the cosmos and to the microcosm, to human self-knowledge and awareness.[158]

The arts of words and of numbers were not the only ones jostling for attention in the Carolingian curriculum. On a theoretical level, the 'mechanical' or 'minor' arts such as ploughing, fulling and stonecutting were acknowledged, but only surveying seems to have been studied formally, especially at centres with extensive landed holdings such as Fulda and

---

[155] Aurelian of Réôme, *MGH Epp.* VI, p. 130 (= *Musica Disciplina* 20, 29–31 (ed. Gushee (1975), p. 132). [156] *Musica Disciplina* 7, 1 (ed. Gushee (1975), p. 77).

[157] *Alia Musica* (ed. Chailley (1965)); Hucbald of St Amand, *De Harmonica Institutione* (ed. Gerbert (1784), pp. 104–21) and Weakland (1956), pp. 66–84; *Musica Enchiriadis* (ed. Schmid (1981), pp. 3–59); *Scolica Enchiriadis* (ed. Schmid (1981), pp. 115–56).

[158] Duchez (1980), pp. 165–87; Duchez (1989), pp. 553–92; Pérès (1991), pp. 435–42; Morrison (1992).

Corbie.[159] One would like to know more about training in the technical arts since, judging from the buildings built and by the draftsmanship of the Plan of St Gall, achievement was high. Einhard the 'engineer-architect' and craftsman is as interesting as the biographer although it is the wordsmith who is better known.[160] Nothing remains of the works that earned Donadeus of St Riquier a reputation as a leading geometrician who used his skill in the mechanical arts to create all kinds of beautiful things.[161]

Several texts, however, do break the general silence of the sources on the practical arts. While no treatise explains the art of writing in Carolingian schools and scriptoria, it is clear that training in copying was essentially imitative and repetitive. The writing master either wrote out a short text which was then copied by beginners in practice sessions or the master actually began to copy a few lines of a manuscript from an exemplar, leaving the remainder to the work of younger hands.[162] Surviving manuscripts and occasional comments from scribes, masters and book owners bear abundant witness that the art of the scribe received scrupulous attention. Carolingian scribes were responsible for two innovations which profoundly affected literary culture. They perfected and broadcast throughout Europe Carolingian minuscule script. At the same time they became adept in the use of Tironian notes – specifically recommended in the *Admonitio Generalis* – and extended their use from administrative documents through the entire range of Carolingian literary culture and into the classroom.[163] The educational and religious programme that formed the core of the Carolingian reform agenda depended on the production of manuscripts, manuscripts that were accurately copied from authentic exemplars. The process of book production, from the preparation of parchment, to ruling and lay-out, preparation of ink and of writing instruments, consignment of quires to copyists, supervision of copying and correction, and finally to binding, demanded organisational skill to accumulate the necessary material and human resources and technical skill to produce the desired results.[164] While they pursued the goal of accurately copied and readable manuscripts, Carolingian masters were mindful of the deeper significance of their work. Some scribes, more impressed by the physical labour involved, compared the quill as it

[159] *De Proprietate Philosophiae et de VII Liberalibus Artibus*, cc. 8–9 (ed. Contreni (1992d), p. 18); *MGH Epp.* VI, p. 184, lines 23–26; Riché (1989), pp. 221–45, 276–80; Folkerts (1978; 1993); Ilmer (1984), pp. 49–58; Ullman (1964).   [160] Stevens (1979b), p. 36; Bullough (1991a), p. 65.

[161] Mico of St Riquier, *Epytafium*, c. 36, ll. 2–5 (*MGH Poet.* III, p. 311): 'Donadeus monachus nec non geometricus unus / Optimus ex multis, mechanica doctus in arte; / Auctor enim diversarum pulcherrimus ipse / Artium.'

[162] Clm 6233 (Bischoff, *Schreibschulen* I, p. 136); MS Laon, BM 468 (ed. Contreni (1984)).

[163] Ganz (1983), pp. 58–75; Bischoff (1990), pp. 112–18; Ganz (1990c).

[164] McKitterick (1989), pp. 135–64.

made its way across the page to the farmer's plough moving through the field, while other scribes, who worked on sacred texts, Bibles and liturgical books, saw their work as charged with religious meaning. They were the agents of God who transferred his words to his people and provided those people with the words by which he might be worshipped.[165]

Medicine was another practical art studied in the schools. Doubtless, throughout the Carolingian world medical practitioners, clergy as well as lay men and women conversant with folk medicine tended the sick. In the ninth century a learned tradition of medicine developed which was supported by medicine's inclusion among the liberal arts and also by Carolingian legislation.[166] Evidence for the study of medicine in the schools shows up, for example, on the fly-leaves of the unique ninth-century manuscript of Einhard's letters (BN lat. 11379) or in the equally rare copy of Lupus of Ferrières' correspondence (BN lat. 2858). Hundreds of medical recipes, dietary recommendations and medical explanations are scattered throughout other manuscripts along with numerous citations and lengthy extracts from Hippocrates, Galen, Oribasius, Dioscorides, Soranus, Alexander of Tralles, Theodorus Priscianus, Pliny, Quintus Serenus, Cassius Felix and Marcellus Empiricus.[167] In the ninth century it was not unusual for ecclesiastics and scholars of the mettle of Walahfrid Strabo, Lupus of Ferrières, Abbot Dido of St Pierre-le-Vif or Bishop Pardulus of Laon to be knowledgeable about medical matters and, in the case of Hincmar of Rheims, to integrate concepts of disease and health into systems of thought.[168]

LITERARY CULTURE

When Carolingians wrote about schooling they invariably described its goal in spiritual terms. It was not only that the study of the arts would provide some technical assistance in comprehending the sacred texts, but also that the arts themselves had value as conduits to the knowledge of God.[169] The study of the arts generated its own abundant literature in the form of manuals, commentaries and glosses. Some writers in the Carolingian world scaled the heights of wisdom and produced works that made the ninth century the first great age of European philosophical and theological speculation.[170] But philosophy and theology were not the only beneficiaries of the Carolingian reform programme. The process of governing increas-

[165] Ganz (1987), pp. 23–44.
[166] Hibernicus Exul, *De Artibus Liberalibus*, c. 8 (*MGH, Poet.* I, p. 411); MacKinney (1937), pp. 84–96; Baader (1972), pp. 669–718.   [167] Beccaria (1956); Wickersheimer (1966).
[168] Contreni (1990), pp. 267–82; Morrison (1981), pp. 583–712.
[169] Leonardi (1981a), pp. 473–5.   [170] See chapter 28.

ingly buttressed traditional sources of power with its own literary forms.[171] The Carolingian age also saw significant new developments in the study of law, the writing of history and the uses of poetry.

The centrality of law to Carolingian concepts of social structure and order, the presence of legal texts of all sorts in the cupboards of monastic, cathedral and lay libraries and the involvement of important lay and ecclesiastical officials in adjudication demonstrate that the study of law was part and parcel of the learned culture of the ninth century.[172] Law, like the study of medicine and training in writing, served eminently practical needs. But law also was fundamental to Christian notions of right order and the proper maintenance of society. Isidore of Seville began the fifth book of his *Etymologiae*, 'De legibus et temporibus', by listing Moses as the first law-giver (*auctor legum*).[173] When Charlemagne issued the *Admonitio Generalis*, he referred for precedent to Josias, the Hebrew king who, when the lives of his people did not conform to 'the words of the book of the law' (II Kings 11), admonished and corrected his subjects in order to restore his kingdom to the worship of the one true God. Alcuin taught Charlemagne that rhetoric had as its proper focus *quaestiones civiles*.[174] The last great Carolingian king, Charles the Bald, was portrayed as a law-giver in a Psalter illustration. The inscription entered above his head in the illustration compares the Frankish king both to Josias and to the Roman emperor, Theodosius the Great.[175] The juxtaposition in this portrait of Frankish, Roman and Hebrew law-givers neatly captures one of the dynamic elements of legal studies in the ninth century – the multiplicity of legal codes. When Charlemagne issued the *Admonitio Generalis*, in 789, he incorporated in it a summary of canons from the collection known as the *Dionysio-Hadriana*, a compilation put together in the sixth century by Dionysius Exiguus and supplemented in the eighth century by Pope Hadrian I (772–95). The pope presented a copy of the collection to Charlemagne in 774. Whether Charlemagne intended the *Dionysio-Hadriana* to serve as his equivalent of Josias' 'book of the law' cannot be said. He still remained keenly interested in Frankish law and was troubled at the end of his life by the separate codes of law that governed the Franks.[176] The expansion of the Carolingian realm at the end of the eighth century brought Carolingians into contact with the laws of other peoples, the Lombards and Alemans, notably. The Carolingian legal *armamentarium* also contained texts from the Roman tradition. Some of that tradition was

---

[171] Nelson (1990a), pp. 258–96.   [172] McKitterick (1989), pp. 23–75; Riché (1965), pp. 12–19.
[173] *Etymologiae* 5, 1 (ed. Lindsay (1911)).
[174] *Disputatio de Rhetorica et de Virtutibus Sapientissimi Regis Karli et Albini Magistri* 1, 13 (ed. Howell (1965), p. 66).   [175] BN lat. 1152, fo. 3v; Hubert (1968), p. 147 (fig. 135).
[176] Einhard, *Vita Karoli* III, c. 29 (ed. Halphen (1947), pp. 80–2).

embedded in the laws of barbarian peoples who had settled in Romanised lands; the *Lex Romana Burgundionum* and the *Lex Romana Visigothorum* are notable examples. The principal source for the study of Roman law in the ninth century was the Theodosian Code, most of the surviving manuscripts of which date from the reigns of Louis the Pious and Charles the Bald.

Carolingian society also produced its own law in the form of numerous royal capitularies, episcopal statutes and synodal canons. Land conveyances, manumissions, wills and a host of other legal and quasi-legal documents attest to the penetration of law into all levels of Carolingian society. The rich fund of evidence generated by attempts to resolve disputes in the Carolingian world reveals a keen interest in procedure, the use of documents and judicial inquiry even in the midst of customary law and oral traditions.[177] Clerics who functioned in this environment as parish priests responsible for the souls of their congregations, as managers of church land, as bishops and as abbots, as notaries and as confidants to kings and counts had to know how to interpret and apply complex and often inconsistent legal codes. Rustic lay men and women such as those from the *villa* of Mitry, who came to the court of Charles the Bald in 861 to argue their status as free *coloni* against the abbey of St Denis which claimed they were unfree *servi*, were also active participants in the world of Carolingian law.[178] So, too, were lay aristocrats such as Count Eccard of Mâcon and Count Eberhard of Friuli whose libraries contained law-books.[179]

The evidence for the *learning* of the law in contrast to the abundant evidence for its practice is sparse. A diploma of 751 from Pippin III mentions *legis doctores*[180]; 'masters of the law' participated in a mid-ninth-century dispute involving Fleury.[181] But were these teachers or simply experienced practitioners? The evidence of manuscripts and of texts suggests that law was indeed studied in the schools, at least in those schools that had the legal resources and special interest in the subject. Isidore of Seville's *De Legibus* from the *Etymologiae*, useful for its handy précis of legal terminology, was copied into manuscripts of legal texts. The texts themselves were glossed, epitomised and made the subjects of *interpretationes*. Bishops throughout the Carolingian realms compiled digests of capitularies and canons for the use of their priests, implying thereby that parish clergy possessed the basic skills to read, understand and apply ecclesiastical law, although Bishop Sigemund of Meaux had doubts on this score.[182] The

---

177 *Gerichtsurkunden der Fränkischen Zeit* (1891, 1893); Nelson (1986a), pp. 45–64; Davies (1986), pp. 65–84; Wickham (1986), pp. 105–24. 178 Nelson (1986a), pp. 51–3.

179 Riché (1963), pp. 87–104. 180 Riché (1989), p. 259. 181 Nelson (1986a), p. 63.

182 *MGH Cap. episc.* and *ibid.* preface, pp. viii–ix; Flodoard, *Historia Remensis Ecclesiae* 3, 23 (*MGH SS* XIII, p. 534); Stratmann (1991), pp. 59–60.

modest church libraries of the Bavarian priests, Egino and Baldric, contained among their titles books of 'canons' which the priests undoubtedly used in the performance of their pastoral duties.[183]

The clearest evidence for a learned tradition of legal studies once again comes from those who wrote the most – the great ecclesiastics and scholars of the Carolingian world. Alcuin and Theodulf of Orléans were locked in a bitter struggle over the law of sanctuary that required Charlemagne's intervention.[184] It was a palace chaplain and abbot, Ansegisus of St Wandrille, who compiled the first systematic and widely copied collection of Carolingian capitularies.[185] Archbishop Magnus of Sens (801–18) presented Charlemagne with a compilation of *notae iuris*, a specialised collection of legal abbreviations, for the use of the royal chancery.[186] The bishops of Lyons put together an exceptional collection of law-books, some of which undoubtedly served as sources for the collection compiled *ex lege et canone* by Florus (d. *c.* 860), the prolific deacon of that city.[187] Archbishop Hincmar of Rheims possessed formidable knowledge of Roman and church law and presented the younger Hincmar with a canon law collection as well as a copy of the decretals of Gelasius on the day of his ordination to the bishopric of Laon.[188] Lupus of Ferrières copied one of Eberhard of Friuli's law-books and was probably the legal expert the abbey of St Denis called in to defend its claims against Fleury.[189]

Legal disputes over matters of property and jurisdiction generated the most original creations of Carolingian legal culture: forgeries. The Le Mans forgeries aimed to establish the claims of the bishopric of Le Mans over property in the diocese by creating a history of the diocese which placed the monasteries and many estates of the diocese under the control of the bishop. In addition to a series of poems about Bishop Aldric of Le Mans (832–57) and a series of spurious saints' Lives, the collection includes a history of the bishops of Le Mans and a biography of Aldric. The history and the biography contain eighty-six royal, episcopal and private charters, many of which were forged in favour of the claims of Le Mans.[190] The origin of the Pseudo-Isidorian forgeries cannot yet be localised with the same precision as the Le Mans collection, but manuscript and historical evidence places the brain-trust that produced this complex collection somewhere in the

---

[183] Hammer (1980), pp. 14, 16.   [184] Wallach (1968), pp. 97–140.

[185] *Ansegisi Abbatis Capitularium Collectio*, MGH Cap. I, pp. 382–450; McKitterick (1983), pp. 126, 331–2.   [186] Ed. Keil (1857–80), IV, pp. 285–300.

[187] McKitterick (1977), pp. 29–30.

[188] Hincmar of Rheims, *Opusculum LV Capitulorum*, PL 126, cols. 292, 421; *Epistola ad Hincmarum Laudunensem*, PL 126, col. 544; Devisse (1962); Nelson (1986b).

[189] *MGH Poet.* IV, p. 1059; Nelson (1986a), p. 63.   [190] Goffart (1966).

archdiocese of Rheims between the years 847 and 852. Pseudo-Isidore consists of a series of conciliar canons attributed to Spain, two sets of capitularies attributed to Bishop Angilram of Metz and to a Deacon Benedict of Mainz, and a collection of papal decretals assigned to an Isidorus Mercator. A composite of spurious and genuine documents, the Pseudo-Isidorian collection, despite its complexity, is remarkably unified. Its more than 10,000 citations are massed to defend the episcopal church against interference by archbishops, church councils and laymen.[191] The sophistication and success of Pseudo-Isidore and other ninth-century collections of forged legislation were owed to the close study of Roman and church law that enabled the forgers to make their new documents both consistent and credible.

The forgeries attempted to manipulate history. In a society where tradition, religious, dynastic and familial, counted for everything and where the present was not so sharply delineated from the past, the writing of history inevitably constituted an important element of Carolingian literary culture. But history writing was not an ivory-tower enterprise. History was used to justify the present and its writing was a partisan activity that reflected all the tensions inherent in a complex, multi-layered culture. When Carolingian writers turned their minds to history for their own personal reasons, as Nithard and Hincmar seem to have done, or for the edification of their contemporaries and posterity as Einhard and Notker in their lives of Charlemagne did, each wrote in support of his particular agenda.[192] Agnellus of Ravenna's history of the deeds of the bishops of his town boosted the church of Ravenna against that of Rome and also gave Agnellus the opportunity to celebrate his family.[193] In the famous opening chapter of Einhard's life of Charlemagne, the last Merovingian is ridiculed as he no doubt was when Einhard was a young man in Charlemagne's court. But Hilduin of St Denis was more interested in the continuities between early Frankish history and his day when he wrote on his house's patron, reputedly Dionysius the Areopagite, and when he produced a laudatory life of the Merovingian Dagobert.[194]

History-writing took many forms in the eighth and ninth centuries.[195] The most rudimentary consisted of glosses entered more or less annually in the margins of Easter tables, a practice that may have been brought to the

[191] Hinschius (ed.) (1863); Williams (1971); Fuhrmann (1972–4) I, pp. 195–224, III, pp. 625–33, 651–72.   [192] Wallace-Hadrill (1981); Nelson (1990b); Nelson (1986c).

[193] Fasoli (1970); Brown (1986).

[194] *Vita Karoli* I (ed. Halphen (1947), pp. 8–10); *Vita Sancti Dionysii, AASS*, Oct. IV (1856), pp. 696–987; *Gesta Dagoberti, MGH SRM* II, pp. 401–25; Gauert (1984); Wallace-Hadrill (1981), pp. 43–8.

[195] Levison and Löwe (1953–73); Ganshof (1970); Innes and McKitterick (1994).

Continent by Anglo-Saxon missionaries. These entries consisted essentially of memoranda of all sorts on unusual meteorological phenomena, the death dates of political and ecclesiastical dignitaries, local events such as miracles, Carolingian warfare, and raids by Northmen, 'Huns' (Magyars) or Saracens, and occasionally biographical information about the annalist.[196] Annals such as the *Royal Frankish Annals* or the *Annals of St Bertin*, unfettered by the space constraints of margins, provided longer, more detailed accounts of the year's events. The manuscript tradition of most annals is limited and it is difficult to argue that they represent an official record or served as propaganda. But that does not mean that Carolingian annals are bland, objective records of the year's events. Rather, annals are highly idiosyncratic and reflect the points of view of those who kept them up.[197]

Chronicles such as that of Freculph of Lisieux or Ado of Vienne attempted to capture the broad sweep of history from Creation to the present, but most history-writing in the eighth and ninth centuries was considerably more local and specific. Although the *Liber Historiae Francorum* of the early eighth century provided a promising start, the closest that Carolingian literary culture came to producing historical work in the mould of Bede or Gregory of Tours ironically was with Paul the Deacon's *Historia Langobardorum*.[198] The Carolingian continuators of Fredegar's chronicle, Count Childebrand and his son, Count Nibelung, were interested primarily in family history and when writers thought about the Franks in panoramic terms their attention was attracted to the past of the ancient Trojans and the Israelites.[199]

Local history and biography provided greater inspiration to historically minded writers in the Carolingian realms. The *gesta* of bishops and abbots emerged as an especially important historical genre. The model was Rome's *Liber Episcopalis* which was also known in the ninth century as the *Acta Pontificum* and the *Gesta Pontificum* before it assumed its better-known title, *Liber Pontificalis*, some time before the twelfth century.[200] The history of the Roman bishops circulated widely and rapidly – sometimes even before the notice concerning the reigning pope could be completed.[201] Writers who emulated the *Liber Pontificalis* at Metz, Ravenna, Le Mans, St Wandrille, St Gall, Auxerre, Rheims and St Bertin implicitly and sometimes spuriously

---

[196] Freise (1984).   [197] Nelson (1990b).

[198] Gerberding (1987); Sestan (1970); Bullough (1991e).

[199] *Fredegarii Chronicorum Liber Quartus cum Continuationibus* 34 (ed. Wallace-Hadrill (1960), pp. 102–3); McKitterick (1989), pp. 236–41; *Historia Daretis Frigii de Origine Francorum, MGH SRM* II, pp. 194–200.   [200] Bertolini (1970), pp. 408–9; Noble (1985), pp. 349–50.

[201] Bertolini (1970), pp. 445–6.

claimed ancient and triumphant heritages for their houses.[202] The *gesta* should also be read as collective biographies, proud records of the achievements of the men who led episcopal and monastic communities. All Carolingian writers realised that successful human agency required divine assistance, but despite themselves these writers filled the pages of their manuscripts with impressive records of human, individual achievement. These records took two forms, *Vitae* of the long dead such as Remigius, Dionysius, Dagobert, Germanus of Auxerre and a host of Merovingian saints whose lives were reworked by Carolingian hagiographers, and *Vitae* (more commonly, *Gesta*) of more contemporary heroes such as Boniface, Charlemagne, Alcuin, Louis the Pious, Benedict of Aniane, Wala and Adalhard. Nithard in his *Histories*, an eyewitness account of the eventful years 840–2, and Abbo of St Germain-des-Prés in his *Bella Parisiacae Urbis*, a versified account of the Danes' harrowing siege of Paris in 885–6 and its aftermath, were inspired by the momentous events of their own day.[203] To read all these works simply as sources from which the raw facts of Carolingian history might occasionally be gleaned is to miss their meaning. Schooling in the secular and divine arts taught Carolingian writers how to use words reflectively to tell their stories and to signify something of their society. In the purposeful words of a Notker Balbulus history offered a storehouse of anecdotes by which a young prince might be instructed while for Nithard, Hincmar and Paschasius Radbertus the tensions and disappointments of the very recent past prompted deeply personal, sophisticated commentary.[204]

Poetry offered Carolingian writers an especially powerful and expressive means to teach, plead, thank, praise, condemn, memorialise, poke fun, pray, celebrate and lament. The moral and didactic themes of Carolingian religious culture, biblical lessons, the emblematic lives of saints, the glories of monastic life, the virtues and vices, all found in verse a convenient vehicle. Carolingian poetry, some 3200 pages of which survive in the major modern collection, was an ubiquitous feature of Carolingian literary culture

---

[202] Paul the Deacon, *Gesta Episcoporum Mettensium, MGH SS* II, pp. 260–70; Agnellus of Ravenna, *Liber Pontificalis Ecclesiae Ravennatis, MGH SRL*, pp. 265–391; *Actus Pontificium Cenomannis in Urbe Degentium* (ed. Busson and Ledru (1901)); *Gesta Sanctorum Patrum Fontanellensis Coenobii* (ed. Lohier and Laporte (1936)); Ratpert and Ekkehard IV, *Casus Sancti Galli, MGH SS* II, pp. 59–147; Rainogala and Alagus, *Gesta Episcoporum Autissiodorensium, MGH SS* XIII, pp. 393–400; Flodoard, *Historia Remensis Ecclesiae, MGH SS* XIII, pp. 409–599; Folcuin, *Gesta Abbatum Sancti Bertini Sithiensium, MGH SS* XIII, pp. 607–35.

[203] *Nithard: histoire des fils de Louis le Pieux* (ed. Lauer (1964)); *Abbon: le siège de Paris par les Normands: poème du IXe siècle* (ed. Waquet (1964)); Nelson (1986c).

[204] Ganz (1989); Wallace-Hadrill (1981); Nelson (1986c; 1990b); Ganz (1990a), pp. 103–20.

and one of its most impressive achievements.[205] The roster of Carolingian poets is the same as the roster of leading Carolingian ecclesiastics, teachers and prose-writers: Paul the Deacon, Paulinus of Aquileia, Alcuin, Angilbert of St Riquier, Theodulf of Orléans, Hraban Maur, Walahfrid Strabo, Florus of Lyons, Paschasius Radbertus, Sedulius Scottus, John Scottus, Hincmar of Rheims, Heiric of Auxerre, Gottschalk of Orbais, Dhuoda, Lupus of Ferrières, Hucbald of St Amand, Pacificus of Verona, Notker Balbulus and a host of others, some known by name, but many known only by their verse. Their ability to oscillate comfortably between verse and prose bespeaks a literary versatility that can only partially be explained by earlier, especially Merovingian, precedent.[206] Widespread poetical skill and a ready willingness to use that skill in a variety of circumstances was also a function of schooling. Students learned to read by reading the Psalms, the songs of David, trained their ears while learning chant, and were introduced to metre when they tackled Virgil and other Latin poets. Further grammatical and rhetorical training sharpened their skills. Poetry was everywhere around them – in the Bible, in their schoolbooks, and in the *vulgaria carmina* which celebrated the Carolingian family and other heroes right through the ninth century.[207] In their turn, Carolingian poets placed their verse everywhere. Leaving aside for a moment learned compositions that took form on parchment and circulated or were read to limited circles of friends and patrons, readers could encounter verse on tombstones and tables, on vases and vestments, on altars and on altar vessels, on fans and on clocks. Readers of Alcuin's verse posted in a latrine could contemplate his lesson on gluttony.[208] Verse explained pictorial programmes on the walls of churches and decorated the entrances to libraries, infirmaries, scriptoria and even the apple house at St Riquier.[209] Verse enlivened festive and ritual drinking and eating in monastic communities.[210]

Verse was equally versatile on more formal occasions. Paul the Deacon used poetry to plead with Charlemagne for the freedom of his brother and the restoration of his family's Lombard holdings.[211] Alcuin, Ermoldus Nigellus, Abbo of St Germain-des-Prés and the 'Saxon Poet' put history

---

[205] *MGH Poet.*; von den Steinen (1948); Schaller (1962); Düchting (1968); Dronke (1977); Lapidge (1977); Norberg (1979); Godman (1981; 1982; 1985, pp. 1–80; 1987; 1990); Dutton (1986); Meyers (1986); Brooke (1990); Nees (1991), pp. 21–109.   [206] Godman (1987), pp. 1–37.

[207] *Poetae Saxonis Annalium de Gestis Caroli Magni Imperatoris* 5, 117 (*MGH Poet.* IV, p. 58).

[208] *In latrinio*, *MGH Poet.* I, p. 321.

[209] *Versus in domo pomorum*: 'Hic redolere solent autumni pendula mala / Tempore, sed rigida diffugiunt hiemis' (*MGH Poet.* III, p. 323).

[210] *MGH Poet.* III, p. 690 (VII, i–ii); IV, pp. 350–3 (*Carmina Potatoria*); Bischoff (1967b).

[211] *MGH Poet.* I, pp. 47–8 (x).

into verse.[212] Verse dedications accompanied gifts of Bibles and Psalters and especially copies of an author's own works such as Ansegisus' capitulary collection, John Scottus' translations and Heiric of Auxerre's *Collectanea*.[213] Poetry celebrated victories – Charlemagne over the Saxons, Pippin over the Avars, Charles the Bald over Louis the German – as well as the fame of towns, monasteries and churches.[214] Verse served also to memorialise the dead and while many of the laments for abbots, bishops, aristocratic patrons and members of religious communities tended towards the formulaic, poets on occasion could convey genuine pathos as when Angelbert, a frontline participant in the battle of Fontenoy (841) and perhaps a layman, wrote a short, moving lament for those who fell in a battle that deserved neither praise nor poetry.[215] Theodulf of Orléans, Dhuoda and Gottschalk of Orbais found verse useful to give voice to the pain of exile, loss or persecution and demonstrated with other writers a highly personal and individual strain in Carolingian poetry.[216]

Verse was a natural ally of teachers throughout the Carolingian period in many different centres. Mnemonic and rhythmic verse helped students memorise complex material. Poetry provided the appropriate means to remember one's own masters and to humour and scold one's pupils. The poet's art dedicated books to friends and patrons and appealed to readers to remember the scribe who copied the book. Teachers used verse to describe the arts and their properties. They wrote of their students, prodding them on to study and remembering them when they died young.[217] And it is the

---

212 Alcuin, *Versus de Patribus Regibus et Sanctis Euboricensis Ecclesiae* (ed. Godman (1982)); Ermoldus Nigellus, *In Honorem Hludowici Christianissimi Caesaris Augusti* (ed. Faral (1964)); *Poetae Saxonis Annalium de Gestis Caroli Magni Imperatoris*, MGH Poet. IV, pp. 7–71; Abbo, *Bella Parisiacae Urbis* (ed. Waquet (1964)).

213 *MGH Poet.* I, pp. 283–6; III, pp. 243–64; Ansegisus, *MGH Poet.* II, p. 672 (= *MGH Cap.* I, p. 394); John Scottus, *Carmina 7–8* (*MGH Poet.* III, pp. 547–50); Heiric of Auxerre, *Collectanea*, preface (ed. Quadri (1966), p. 77).

214 *De Conversione Saxonum Carmen*, MGH Poet. I, pp. 380–1, long attributed to Angilbert of St Riquier, but now to Paulinus of Aquileia, see Schaller (1989); *De Pippini Regis Victoria Avarica*, *MGH Poet.* I, pp. 116–17; John Scottus, '*Hellinas Troasque*', *MGH Poet.* III, pp. 527–31; *Laudes Mediolanensis Civitatis*, MGH Poet. I, pp. 24–6; *Laudes Veronensis Civitatis*, MGH Poet. I, pp. 118–22; Hraban Maur, *Denotatio Dedicationis Ecclesiae Sancti Salvatoris Constructae in Monasterio Fuldae*, *MGH Poet.* II, pp. 205–8; John Scottus, '*Aulae sidereae*', *MGH Poet.* II, pp. 550–2; Riculf, *De Conditore Ecclesiae Sancti Albani*, MGH Poet. I, p. 431.

215 *Versus de Bella Quae Fuit Acta Fontaneto* 11: 'Laude pugna non est digna, nec canatur melode' (*MGH Poet.* II, pp. 138–9); Godman (1985), pp. 48–50.

216 Theodulf, *Ad Modoinum Episcopum Scribens ei de Exilio*, MGH Poet. I, pp. 563–5, 569–73; Dhuoda, *Liber Manualis*, '*Epigrama operis subsequentis*' (ed. Riché (1975), pp. 72–8); Gottschalk, '*Ut quid iubes?*', *MGH Poet.* III, pp. 731–2; *idem*, '*O mi custos*', *MGH Poet.* VI, pp. 89–97; Godman (1985), pp. 37–42, 69–71.

217 *MGH Poet.* I, pp. 403, 558; II, 39–87, 403–4; III, pp. 351, 355, 363–4, 427–8; IV, pp. 78–9, 657–8.

soaring, exuberant court poetry of Angilbert, Alcuin and Theodulf rather than the more modest terms of the *Admonitio Generalis* or the *Epistola de Litteris Colendis* that limns the modern view of the Carolingian renaissance.[218] But it is the very private poem of a seasoned scholar that captures the tension and ambivalence inherent in Carolingian education and learning. 'In the first flower of my youth', the late ninth-century teacher wrote on the fly-leaf of a Virgil manuscript, 'I was clever in the arts by which the one, the highest God is worshipped. It delighted me then to collect piles of books.' The master was especially taken with Martianus Capella, but recognised that the gods of Capella were false gods and Mercury led only to them.[219] Wisdom built on book-learning could never be an end in itself. Learning was important because it furnished part of the equipment of 'the soldiers of the church' which along with inward devotion would enable the clergy to penetrate the mysteries of Scripture and lead God's people to paradise.[220]

The accomplishments of the Carolingian reform programme outlived the dynasty that gave initial impetus and support to the reforms. At the most fundamental level, Caroline minuscule continued to be used as an effective means of communicating thought and language and was even adopted in Anglo-Saxon England during the tenth century. The institutional underpinnings of learning, schools and scriptoria, continued to function with a greater degree of stability and continuity than the politically troubled tenth century would suggest. The example Carolingian leaders provided in their courts and legislation and which Notker Balbulus enshrined in his emblematic account of Charlemagne's life was not lost on later politicians who believed that learning was important for the spiritual health of the individual and also for Christian society. The Ottonians, the Capetians and the descendants of Alfred the Great all valued and supported Christian learning and reform. The Carolingian book forged links between the ninth century and the world of learning in the tenth, eleventh and twelfth centuries. Between the covers of Carolingian manuscripts, the Carolingian

---

[218] Godman (1985), pp. 9–33; Garrison (1994).

[219] 'Sollers artis eram prima florente iuventa, / Qua colitur summus, unus et ipse Deus; / Hoc mihi tunc placuit multis conquirere libris, / Nunc nimium fallor, me mala causa tenet. / Ille Capella strio, translato nomine Felix, / Nos fallit vetulos; nam vetus ipse fuit. / Hymeneum cecinit carmen Kartaginis arvis, / Femineo vultu numina falsa docet: / Aetherios superasse polos talaribus altis / Mercurium finxit duceret inde deam' (ed. Leonardi (1961), p. 150).

[220] Theodulf of Orléans, *Erstes Kapitular* 2: 'Oportet vos assiduitatem habere legendi et instantiam orandi, quia vita viri iusti lectione instruitur, oratione ornatur... Haec sunt enim arma, lectio videlicet et oratio, quibus diabolus expugnatur. Haec sunt instrumenta, quibus aeterna beatitudo acquiritur. His armis vitia comprimuntur, his alimentis virtutes nutriuntur', *MGH Cap. episc.* i, p. 105.

curriculum and literary culture with all its variety and with all its internal dissonances lived on to help form new generations of learners – Berengar, Abelard, Anselm of Laon, Lanfranc, Anselm of Canterbury, Peter Lombard – pioneers of a new order.[221]

All of this was far from the minds of Carolingian masters and students who were very much interested in their present, not in the recovery of past learning nor in its preservation for some vague future. Their enduring accomplishment, one that would frame intellectual life for centuries to come, was to provide a meaningful rationale for rigorous and sophisticated study and research. In responding to the call for reform, they purposefully drew from historical sources of learning to fashion their own luxuriant programme of studies and literary culture based on the mastery of secular letters and pointing in the direction of divine wisdom. As it worked its way through the schools of the ninth century, this process transformed both secular and sacred learning. The study of the Scriptures and of theology was pursued with all the new information and methodologies gained from specialised study of the arts. At the same time, the arts became sacralised, no longer mere secular learning, but paths to a higher wisdom. 'Therefore we urge you, not only not to neglect the study of literature, but with a resolve that is humble and pleasing to God eagerly to learn it, so that you can more easily and correctly penetrate the mysteries of the divine scriptures.'[222]

---

[221] *Settimane* 37; Berschin (1991); Riché (1989), pp. 125–31, 334–44; Bullough (1991f–g); Rosenthal (1969); Fichtenau (1984), pp. 376–96; Hoffmann (1986); Bishop (1971).

[222] *Epistola de Litteris Colendis*, lines 30–3, *MGH Cap.* I, p. 79: 'Quamobrem hortamur vos litterarum studia non solum non negligere, verum etiam humillima et Deo placita intentione ad hoc certatim discere, ut facilius et rectius divinarum scripturarum mysteria valeatis penetrare.'

CHAPTER 28

THEOLOGY AND THE
ORGANISATION OF THOUGHT

David Ganz

THE Carolingian age saw a vast expansion of Christian territory, and a systematic attempt to establish a Christian civilisation throughout that territory. 'The doctrine of the evangelists shines through the whole world; we hold it in unanimity and faithfully preach it',[1] Alcuin wrote to Felix during the Adoptionist controversy, and he told Charlemagne, 'Your holy will and the power ordained by God everywhere defends the catholic and apostolic faith and works strongly to expand the Christian empire and you are zealous to defend, to teach and to propagate the truth of the apostolic faith.'[2]

The faith was defended through affirming the authority of bishops and archbishops: the clergy were trained to understand the Creed, celebrate the Mass and baptism and use penitentials, and their flocks were instructed by means of explanations of the Trinity, the Lord's Prayer, the Ten Commandments and the Creed, and through the reading of homilies.[3]

This expansion involved explanations of the Christian faith to recent converts from Germanic paganism, who had to learn what comprised 'the cup of life and salvation'[4] which they were offered. At the same time clergy familiar with Carolingian education tried to formulate accounts of the nature of the redemptive power of the church and the meaning of its doctrine and worship, raising the threat of heresy and challenging the Carolingian episcopate to pronounce formulae of orthodoxy. In contrast to later Merovingian synods, Carolingian synods and the assemblies of nobles and clergy were often concerned with statements of Christian faith and the correct interpretation of religious principles. Their decrees might be

---

[1] Alcuin to Felix, *PL* 101, col. 120.
[2] Alcuin to Charlemagne in the dedication to the Seven Books against Felix, *PL* 101, col. 127.
[3] McKitterick (1977); Keefe (1983); Chelini (1991), pp. 75–101.
[4] Pope Boniface to Edwyn. Bede *HE* II. x.

incorporated into the annals which recorded the notable events of any year.[5] One reason was that the writers of those annals, and of the verses, panegyrics, letters, treatises on administration and advice to rulers which are our chief sources for Carolingian history were monks and bishops trained in Christian doctrine who attended the assemblies where it was defined. To understand the ideology which motivated these men it is crucial to explore the ways in which they affirmed their faith, and the nature of the disputes which divided them. The relations between God and his subjects were the chief concern of Carolingian thinkers: to understand their thought we cannot ignore its preoccupations. Theological debates explored in what way and how many of mankind were saved.

Any account of Carolingian discussions of theological problems must ascertain the categories which Carolingian authors would have assumed and acknowledged appropriate to such discussions, and must provide classifications which extract Carolingian theological debates from realms of obscurity. Narrative surveys of the development of dogma in the ninth century can be found in general histories,[6] but treatments of Carolingian theology are restricted to surveys or to sections in the biographies of Alcuin,[7] Theodulf,[8] Agobard,[9] Hincmar[10] and John Scottus.[11] This chapter will explore how Carolingian writers on theology defined their topics, and with what methodologies they hoped to resolve uncertainties in a domain allowing little speculation and less doubt. Instead of presenting a chronological account, it focuses on attitudes to the Trinity, to the process of salvation and the damnation of the wicked, to the ways in which the Eucharist, and the worship of images and relics, might assist in human salvation, and on the mysteries of the soul. In conclusion it explores differences between eastern and western ecclesiology.

The concept of theology as 'an organised and learned understanding of the doctrine of revelation'[12] was not a Carolingian one. John the Scot

---

[5] The Royal Frankish annals record the history of Felix and the Council of Frankfurt in 794. The Annals of St Bertin, Fulda and Xanten all describe Gottschalk's condemnation at Mainz in 848. The Annals of St Bertin describe the condemnation at Quierzy in 849 and the Synod of Quierzy in 853 and the synods of Langres and Savonierres in 859. Ado of Vienne includes an account of the condemnation of Felix and the pseudosynod of Nicaea II in his Chronicon, *PL* 123, col. 128.

[6] Von Harnack (1898); Pelikan (1978). There is an excellent discussion of theology in Amann (1947).

[7] The dissertations of Frobenius Forster and J.B. Enhueber on Adoptionism printed in *Beati Flacci Albini Opera, PL* 101, cols. 299–438; Gaskoin (1904); Kleinclausz (1948); Bullough (1991). [8] Dahlhaus-Berg (1975). [9] Boshof (1969). [10] Devisse (1975).

[11] Cappuyns (1933); Schrimpf (1982a and b).

[12] M.D. Chenu, *La théologie au douzième siècle* (Paris, 1966), p. 376.

borrowed the term from Pseudo-Dionysius, affirming that: 'Theology is the first or highest part of wisdom, concerned wholly or for the most part with speculations about the divine nature',[13] and in a celebrated passage of Book III of his *Periphyseon* he treated theology as a part of the fourfold division of wisdom: practical, natural, theological and rational.[14] Few of his contemporaries accepted such a category of thought. The term 'theology' was used by Boethius in chapter 2 of his *De Trinitate*, and by Cassiodorus in the *Historia Tripartita* 2, 11. But for most Carolingian writers, the understanding of the divine nature was a part of faith or doctrine. The discipline of theology was no part of their intellectual equipment: it was recovered from the writings of the church Fathers and the acts of the ecumenical church councils.

The term *doctrina* is used in the Gospels (Mark 1, 27: 'What new doctrine is this?' and John 7, 16: 'My doctrine is not mine, but his that sent me,') and by Augustine.[15] The great regional reform councils of 813 promulgated a creed, 'the doctrine which we have received from the holy fathers'.[16] The creed was to be taught to the people, according to councils of 794, 802 and 822.[17] Before consecration bishops and priests were examined on their faith.[18] *Doctrina* was closely related to faith. Alcuin writes of 'the walls of the faith of the church and the doctrine of the apostles'.[19] Agobard of Lyons affirmed that the clarification of doctrine was the precondition for the strengthening of faith.[20] At baptism and at the consecration of priests an explicit profession of faith was required.[21] It might involve the 'Athanasian' Creed (the *Quicumque vult*), sung at St Riquier on Rogation Days, quoted to clergy by Theodulf and Haito of Basel, and which Hincmar required his clergy to learn. It might be the creed of Constantinople, used in the baptismal liturgy of the Gelasian Sacramentary, and recommended as the best counter to Adoptionism by Paulinus of Aquileia.[22] The Athanasian Creed affirms that 'those who do not hold this faith pure and undefiled, without doubt shall perish eternally' and Carolingian commentaries interpret this as a requirement that priests should teach it.[23]

Alcuin affirmed the integrity of the faith, seen as a consensus of the

---

[13] *Periphyseon* 2.30 (ed. I.P. Sheldon-Williams, Dublin (1981), p. 166).

[14] *Ibid.* 3. 29 (ed. I.P. Sheldon-Williams, Dublin (1981) pp. 222–3, depending on III, 3, p. 48). Compare the account of John the Evangelist as theologian, *Hom. in John*, c. 14, ed. E. Jeauneau, pp. 270–2.   [15] *De Civitate Dei* XIII, 16; XVIII, 51.

[16] *MGH Conc.* II:I, pp. 249–50, compare pp. 255, 259.   [17] *MGH Conc.* II:I, pp. 245, 271.

[18] *MGH Conc.* II:I, p. 471.   [19] *MGH Epp.* IV, p. 61.   [20] *MGH Epp.* VI, p. 166.

[21] Hartmann (1979), pp. 383, 387.

[22] Walahfrid records that the creed of Constantinople was widely used in the Mass following the Gospel reading, both in France and Germany after the deposition of Felix of Urgel in 798: *MGH Cap.* II, p. 500.   [23] Burn (1896), p. 20.

Fathers, affirmed by ecumenical councils and Catholic synods.[24] But in the dispute with Felix he stressed that the mystery of the Incarnation and the Redemption should be venerated in faith rather than discussed by reason, for where reason fails there faith is necessary.[25] Faith always incorporated an area beyond the reach of human reason, and reason was checked when it attempted to explore mysteries beyond its grasp. Hincmar compared those treating doctrine to a man standing before a bright fire with his eyes closed, knowing that the fire is there, yet unable to see it clearly.[26] The majesty of the mystery of the Christian faith cannot be explored beyond the capacity of man's weakness, so that orthodox repetition of patristic thought can become the testimony to a sense of the weakness of fallen man. In contrast diversity of belief was heresy. Claudius of Turin defined heresy as 'everyone choosing for himself a discipline which he thinks best'.[27] Behind dogma lay experience, as Benedict of Aniane wrote in his *Munimenta Fidei*: 'An acutely sensed experience alone makes one a friend of God: it is through this wisdom that one becomes a friend of God and obeys Him. In this manner faith will remain pure and it will grow until faith's content is revealed.'[28]

The most widely used synthesis of doctrine was Augustine's *Enchiridion* on Faith, Hope and Charity, a long exposition of the Apostles' Creed, and at least twenty-five Carolingian copies survive. Notker Balbulus recommended it as securing victory over present and future heresy; to Alcuin it offered the means to define the Incarnation.[29] It was quoted by Hincmar, Lupus, Prudentius, Florus and John the Scot in the debate on Predestination.[30] A Carolingian copy now in Harvard has notes besides passages on Predestination.[31] Victorinus' *Commonitorium* and the writings of Fulgentius of Ruspe offered other syntheses, but they supplemented the orthodoxies of the *Dionysio-Hadriana* and the other collections of church councils. This emphasis on conciliar thought was to develop after 787 when the Byzantine church challenged the concept of an ecumenical council. As Ratramus noted when defining the Eucharist, Paul had affirmed the importance of uniformity in what we know and what we say.[32] This was the Carolingian ideal.

A crucial feature of Carolingian religion was the dichotomy between the thought of Frankish prelates, secure in a national tradition of church councils and continuities, and the concerns of converts whom the expansion

---

[24] Compare Hincmar, *De Una et Non Trina Deitate*, PL 125, col. 561.
[25] PL 101, col. 134; compare *Adversus Elipandum*, PL 101, cols. 298–300.
[26] PL 125, col. 533.   [27] PL 105, 901.   [28] Leclercq (1948), p. 63.
[29] PL 101, cols. 183, 268.   [30] Gorman (1985), pp. 194–5.
[31] Gorman (1985). For a manuscript of the *Enchiridion* from Trier with passages from Alcuin's circle added to it, compare Marenbon (1981), pp. 58–60, 168–72.
[32] Ratramnus, *De Corpore*, c. xii, p. 45.

of Frankish territories had made Christian. The faith had to be expounded to speculative thinkers condemned for heresy, and to uncomprehending unbelievers compelled into a fearsome fold. Unity of faith was seen as imperative, but we should perhaps acknowledge the degrees of diversity and the extent to which issues of dogma had replaced the meditative spirituality of the Merovingian age.

Most Carolingian theology is rebarbative, because it offers an accumulation, a plurality of human texts as the only adequate exegesis of the divine text. When Hincmar quotes Ambrose on faith thirty times, seven passages of Boethius' *De Trinitate* twenty-two times, Augustine on the Trinity twenty-nine times, Alcuin on the Trinity twenty one times, and the same passage from Pseudo-Athanasius on the Trinity twenty-six times it is hard to admire his methodology.[33] But the validity of any revival of studies is the usefulness of what is revived. Wisdom required the cumulative experience of a plurality of exegetical discourses, and that shared experience was a process of intellectual growth.

ADOPTIONISM[34]

The issues raised in the Adoptionist debate were to recur throughout the Carolingian age. The debate centred on the nature of Christ's true humanity, the ways in which He had become man to redeem mankind. The Council of Toledo in 675 had condemned the teaching that the Son was adopted into the Trinity, but the term 'adopted son' was retained in the Mozarabic liturgy. Bishops Felix of Urgel, in the region reconquered by Charlemagne, and Elipand of Toledo, renewed this teaching in opposition to the doctrines of one Migetius, who was accused of teaching Christians in Muslim Spain that there were three corporeal persons in the Trinity, the persona of the father being David and that of the Holy Spirit St Paul. This was a vision of God's appearance in history through union with corporeal beings. Migetius also claimed that the power of God is in Rome alone, perhaps to defend the church against Islamic and Jewish influences,[35] but if Elipand's report is correct he was clearly unorthodox.

Elipand and Felix were concerned to establish the identity of Christ with the logos, and so spoke of His assumption and adoption of humanity, using terminology which was found in Spanish Christianity and, in respect to

---

[33] Devisse (1975), pp. 181–2.

[34] This section owes much to Cavadini (1993).

[35] He prohibited eating with pagans (*PL* 96, cols. 865–6), claimed to be a prophet, and identified Rome with the New Jerusalem, *ibid.*, col. 866. Cavadini argues for a more orthodox interpretation.

Christ's humanity, in the teachings of Augustine.[36] Elipand seems to have used 'adoption' to describe how the incarnate Word was born, but never spoke of it as an active process. This emphasis on the distinction between humanity and divinity in Christ provoked papal accusations of a revival of the Nestorian heresey, though Felix and Elipand called Jesus, in so far as He was divine, God's son by nature from eternity, not by grace.[37] For Felix, the adoption of Christ was an assurance that the elect, servants of God like Christ Himself, would also become godlike, brothers of Christ in the fullest sense.[38] His concern for Christ's real humanity was the source of his bias.[39]

Elipand's attack on Migetius was challenged by Beatus, abbot of Liebana, and Bishop Etherius of Osma. Already threatened by the isolation of life in Muslim Spain, Elipand saw this as a challenge to the primacy of Toledo.[40] Pope Hadrian, appealed to by Beatus, condemned Migetius, but objected to Elipand's use of the term 'adoptive son'. Felix wrote a treatise to support Elipand, but in 792, summoned to a council of bishops at Regensburg, he recanted, and he repeated his recantation at Rome. In 794 Charlemagne held an assembly at Frankfurt where bishops from Francia, Italy and Germany condemned Adoptionism, and Charlemagne sent their decision to Elipand. Felix continued to define his view of how Christ became man and to influence the Christians of Septimania, though most of our knowledge of his teaching derives from his opponents. In late 797 or early 798 Alcuin sent the octogenarian Elipand a brief treatise (letter 23): by March 798 he had written a *libellus* against the heresy of Felix consisting chiefly of patristic testimonies, most notably from Augustine on John, with its discussion of the divine and human natures of the incarnate Christ.[41] Pope Leo III condemned Felix at Rome in October of 798, and in 799 at the Council of Aachen Felix recanted after a debate with Alcuin, and was deposed and sent to Lyons, where he died in *c.* 818.

The threat of Adoptionism was its novelty, its separatism and its vision of Christ as a subject in His humanity. 'To deny that in his humanity as well as in his divinity Christ was begotten of God would make it more difficult to sustain the view that godlikeness lies within man's potential.'[42] It gained converts among the clergy, including monks and bishops.[43] Alcuin insisted

---

[36] For the Augustinian background see von Harnack (1890), pp. 278–86. Even Alcuin speaks of an assumption of humanity: *PL* 101, cols. 172, 213. For the connotations of *adoptio* compare Heil (1965), pp. 118–25.

[37] Elipand's *Confessio, PL* 96, col. 916. Cavadini, in his chapter on Elipand, argues convincingly that he was not a Nestorian.   [38] *PL* 101, col. 173.

[39] Von Harnack (1890), pp. 279–81.

[40] The regional tensions are well conveyed by Heil (1965).   [41] Ed. Blumenshine (1980).

[42] Bullough (1991), p. 187.

[43] Alcuin, *MGH Epp.* IV, p. 346. Alcuin estimated that there were 20,000 converts.

that Christ's death on the Cross was not by necessity but by compassionate choice.[44] He challenged Felix to find support in the Gospels, Epistles, Prophets, the Fathers, the creeds and the synods for the novelties he was expounding.[45] Felix was compared to Nestorius, and accused of following Pelagius:[46] the tradition of the church's condemnation of heresies defined the narrow path of orthodoxy. The debate also involved defining who were the members of Christ's body, which Felix asserted could not share in His divinity.[47] What was the nature of Christ's humanity, which He shared with mankind?[48]

Felix argued: 'If in His flesh our Redeemer is not the adoptive son of the Father but is the true and proper Son, how can you avoid saying that this flesh of His was not created and made from the mass of the human race, but was begotten from the essence of the Father.'[49] Christ, said the Adoptionists, cannot be both the proper son of David and the son of God.[50] Felix had referred to Christ in His humanity as *nuncupativum Deum*, God in name only, which Alcuin saw as equating Christ's natures with two persons, God and not God.[51] Alcuin stressed how Felix and his followers were isolated from the universal Catholic church, and challenged him to find one race or city or church which agreed with his teaching.[52] The heresy was both new and parochial. Felix had destroyed the Catholic peace and unity of apostolic faith of the church.

Alcuin offered the analogy of mortal man with an immortal soul for the human and divine natures in Christ.[53] Felix affirmed that Christ had two fathers, God and David, and so could not be a true son of God. But this is to deny God's explicit testimony and Christ's own statements.[54] Alcuin saw the Adoptionists as confusing the grace of assumption with the grace of adoption.[55] Alcuin, like Augustine, saw participation in divinity as an exaltation of Christ's humanity but felt that Felix regarded the Incarnation as a diminution of His divinity.[56] To speak of our adoption among the saints is to honour us, but to speak of Christ's adoption is to debase Him.[57]

For Felix, mankind is adopted as the children of God and must have an adopted head, and Christ's baptism is His adoption, but Christ needed no such regeneration, for He was without sin.[58] The assumption of humanity in Christ was equated with adoption by Alcuin, but while every adoption was

---

[44] *PL* 101, cols. 140–1, compare cols. 235–40.   [45] *PL* 101, col. 129.
[46] *PL* 101, cols. 136, 164, 186, 189, 223, 289–90.   [47] *PL* 101, cols. 149–50.
[48] *PL* 101, col. 247.   [49] *PL* 101, col. 155.   [50] *PL* 101, col. 137.
[51] *PL* 101, cols. 129, 136–7 and especially 173–5.   [52] *PL* 101, cols. 131–2.
[53] *PL* 101, cols. 134–5, 163, 166.   [54] *PL* 101, cols. 138–9.
[55] Ed. Blumenshine (1980), pp. 95–6.   [56] *PL* 101, cols. 149–50.   [57] *PL* 101, col. 154.
[58] *PL* 101, cols. 157–9.

an assumption, not every assumption was an adoption.[59] Felix affirmed that only a servant could be born of Mary, who was a maidservant.[60] Once God had decided to adopt a man, the Son of Man had to be His servant and fulfil His will. Only belief in Christ's adoption, as a man, offers the certainty of our own adoption. The reference to Christ as servant horrified Hadrian and the Frankish bishops, for it properly indicates man's bondage to sin. Alcuin objected that God can create whatsoever He chooses, and what could be born of God save God?[61] Though the Son was good, as a man He was not good from Himself.[62] Felix argued that Christ's ignorance of where Lazarus was buried was a further sign of His adoption: the proper Son of God should be omniscient.[63]

Paulinus of Aquileia, in his attack on Adoptionism, saw it as a challenge to Christ's humanity, and so he confessed the unity of God and man. Christ was not *homo purus* but *homo verus*.[64] The Crucifixion was not a humbling of God; the unity of God's will was what made the redemption possible.[65] As in the debate on Predestination, the issue of how mankind was saved was central.

In 800 Alcuin wrote four books against the teachings of Elipand, archbishop of Toledo, who continued to support Felix's doctrine after Felix's recantation.[66] At the same time Alcuin was working on a commentary on the Gospel of John, which he saw as particularly concerned with the divinity of Christ and His equality with the Father.[67] Elipand accused Alcuin of corrupting Charlemagne, but Alcuin said that Charles could not be corrupted, for Felix and his sect had been condemned at Regensburg and by Pope Hadrian. Elipand denied human freedom by making Christ the liberator a captive.[68] He had misused passages from Augustine and Ambrose.[69] An anthology of patristic texts showed that no council had ever taught Adoptionism, and even the Spanish church, as Isidore and Julian of Toledo made clear, taught the unity of Christ's person, had rejected it. Like a chalice of gold and silver Christ is both God and man, His two natures are one.[70]

After Felix's death, Agobard of Lyons found a set of questions and answers which suggested that he had not recanted. Agobard, challenged by Felix's supporters in Lyons, sent a refutation to Louis the Pious.[71] Although he had not read Alcuin or Paulinus he returned to the charge of Nestorianism and false interpretation of Scripture, quoting passages from Latin

---

[59] *PL* 101, col. 167.　　[60] *PL* 101, cols. 164, 202.　　[61] *PL* 101, col. 143.
[62] *PL* 101, col. 198.　　[63] *PL* 101, col. 196, compare Paulinus *PL* 99, cols. 444–5.
[64] *PL* 99, col. 379.　　[65] *PL* 99, cols. 378–80.　　[66] *PL* 101, cols. 243–304.
[67] *PL* 100, cols. 743–1008; compare Bullough (1991), pp. 100–2.　　[68] *PL* 101, col. 259.
[69] *PL* 101, cols. 261–2, 268–70.　　[70] *PL* 101, cols. 295–6.
[71] *PL* 104, cols. 29–70. Agobard, *Opera*, pp. 71–111.

translations of Nestorius. Agobard provides evidence of what Felix taught, claiming that he said that God was not crucified, but the man whom He assumed, just as a ram was sacrificed in place of Isaac.[72] God gave birth to a Son by nature, not by will or necessity, for in God there is no necessity. Agobard accused Felix of subjecting God to time and mocked the categories Felix had used for describing Christ's nativity.[73] The work ends with a dossier of quotations from Cyril, Augustine, Vigilius of Thapse and Hilary, confirming the importance of church councils in establishing Catholic orthodoxy. Most important in this treatise is Agobard's clear evidence that Adoptionism was a doctrine which attracted followers.

THE DEBATE ON THE TRINITY

The western church had affirmed the doctrine that the Holy Spirit came from the Father and Son and not from the Father alone (the *filioque*),[74] at Gentilly in 767 and at Aachen in 809, with support from treatises by Smaragdus and Theodulf of Orléans.[75]

In the mid-ninth century the proper definition of the Trinity again became an issue when Hincmar objected that certain innovators affirmed that the expression *trina et una deitas* was as catholic in doctrine as *trinus et unus deus*.[76] Among them were Ratramn of Corbie, who had prepared a dossier of texts from Hilary and Augustine for Bishop Hildegar of Meaux. When Gottschalk learned of this discussion he wrote a schedula affirming the correctness of *trina deitas*. Following on the Adoptionist controversy and the question of the *filioque*, Gottschalk's references to *trina deitas* were suspect to Hraban Maur and Hincmar.[77] Hincmar forbade the clergy of his diocese to use the refrain 'Te trina deitas unaque poscimus' found in a hymn for the common of several martyrs and used by Gottschalk to support his views, and Bishop Rudolph of Bourges followed him, though other bishops allied with Gottschalk.[78] Hincmar affirmed that Gottschalk's heresy was spread among his people.[79] Gottschalk's defence of his stance included an attack on Hincmar as a swollen and turgid skin charged with heresy.[80] In his view all of God's attributes, including His deity, are one in essence and

---

[72] *PL* 104, col. 38. Agobard, *Opera*, p. 77.

[73] *PL* 104, cols. 41, 48–9; Agobard, *Opera*, pp. 80, 95–7; Lambot, pp. 295–6.

[74] Hincmar's request to Odo of Beauvais, *MGH Epp.* VIII, pp. 225–6. For the response of the East Frankish bishops compare Hartmann (1977).

[75] *PL* 105, cols. 239–76; *MGH Conc.* II:1, p. 236.

[76] Hincmar, *De Una et Non Trina Deitate*, *PL* 125, cols. 473–5.

[77] *MGH Epp.* V, p. 500, Hraban to Hincmar.

[78] Hincmar, *De Una et Non Trina Deitate*, *PL* 125, cols. 473–4, 504.   [79] *PL* 125, col. 503.

[80] Lambot, p. 96.

threefold in persons. Only by means of this division of deity could God have suffered on the Cross, for it was only the deity of the Son who suffered. So each person of the Trinity has his own proper deity, for person is a special substance. Gottschalk appealed to the grammarians, deriving *persona* from *per se una*,[81] and to expressions found in Prosper, Prudentius and the Council of Constantinople of 680.[82] But the dispute on Adoptionism had affirmed that deity was indivisible. Hincmar procured from Hraban Maur a copy of Alcuin's *De Trinitate* which was to provide twenty-one quotations used to refute Gottschalk.

In 856–7, after his second treatise on Predestination, Hincmar wrote his *De Una et Non Trina Deitate*,[83] and was to use some of its formulae at the 860 Council of Tusey which resolved the Predestination debate. Gottschalk was condemned as a known heretic inspired by the devil, who should remain silent. Hincmar's concern was to defend the unity of the deity, a part of God's indivisible substance.[84] Three persons did not entail a threefold deity, that would be Arianism.[85] The archbishop defended his position by quotations from church councils, grammarians, the Scriptures and the Fathers, especially Pseudo-Athanasius, Ambrose, Augustine and Boethius. Hincmar accused Ratramn of defending the usage of *trina deitas* in a volume prepared for Bishop Hildegar of Meaux, and of supporting his views with a forged quotation from Augustine.[86]

The debate involved a clarification of different interpretations of grammar: the term *trina* introduced plurality into what, above all other things, is unity.[87] Hincmar also used number theory: *tres* shows plurality by a repetition of unities, as does its derivative *trina*. In contrast, *ter* expresses only unity with a collective signification.[88] Hincmar's fear is that divine essence is being divided, just as Alcuin had feared the Adoptionists had done. The terminology of distinction was also to cause Gottschalk problems when he came to talk of two kinds of Predestination.[89]

THE DEBATE ON PREDESTINATION

The debate on Predestination is the clearest evidence of those tensions in Carolingian culture which underlay the frequent expressions of unity and harmony. In councils and sermons Carolingian society affirmed that God

---

[81] *PL* 125, col. 586.   [82] *PL* 125, col. 477.
[83] *PL* 125, cols. 473–618. The work opens with Gottschalk's schedula. According to Flodoard 3, 15, Hincmar also wrote a work on the Trinity addressed to Charles the Bald. On the debate, compare Davis (1971), pp. 455–68 and Jolivet (1958).   [84] *PL* 125, col. 526.
[85] *PL* 125, cols. 490, 533.   [86] *PL* 125, col. 515.   [87] *PL* 125, cols. 565–6.
[88] *PL* 125, cols. 566–8.   [89] Lambot, p. 67, cf. John Scottus, *De Praedestinatione*, c.1.

punished sin. In 829 the disasters of the empire were 'what our iniquity
deserves', and a three-day fast and general examination of conscience was
the remedy.[90] In 843 there was 'such sense of discord that we clearly lack
divine grace'.[91] The 857 Synod of Quierzy gave a full definition of sin, and
the Annals of St Bertin record the Anglo-Saxon vision of a priest who saw
God with books written in black letters and letters of blood. The Annals tell
how in 845 God, offended by sins, sent the Viking invaders, and in 865
'divine judgement' allowed them to burn Fleury and Orléans. Sin and its
punishment was a necessary category of social order, but when the implicit
values and laws of society were made explicit, then theological debate
became a redefinition of that society.

The monk Gottschalk was the son of a Saxon noble who had been an
oblate at Fulda, and who had studied with Hraban Maur and at Reichenau
with Abbot Wetti.[92] At Fulda he was the friend of Walahfrid Strabo and
Lupus of Ferrières. In 829, after the Council of Mainz had heard his appeal,
he left Fulda and visited Corbie and Rheims, where he debated in the royal
presence with a person who asserted that one might speak of the blood of the
Holy Spirit, a reminder of how frequent and public theological debate must
have been.[93]

After teaching in the monastery of Orbais, Gottschalk was ordained a
priest and took pupils on a pilgrimage to Rome. In 845/6 he was at the court
of Eberhard of Friuli and teaching a doctrine of Predestination which
aroused the hostility of Hraban Maur, his former abbot.[94] From Friuli
Gottschalk entered the land of the Bulgars, perhaps in connection with
Eberhard's missionary activities, and was present at a battle between the
Slav King Trpimir and the Byzantine *patricius*.[95] On his return to the diocese
of Mainz, Gottschalk was required to present his teachings on Predestination to Hraban at the synod of Mainz and was condemned and flogged and
sent to Hincmar, his metropolitan. In the spring of 849 he was again
condemned at the Synod of Quierzy, declared to have been uncanonically
ordained, and forced to burn the dossier of biblical and patristic quotations
he had prepared in his own defence. But he sent a work on Predestination to
his friend the monk Gislemar of Corbie, wrote an attack on Hraban and sent
a treatise to Hincmar.

Gottschalk attempted to establish the church's teaching on Predestination as clearly as possible.[96] His God inspired fear, and Predestination was

[90] *MGH Cap.* II, p. 27.   [91] *MGH Conc.* II:1, p. 384.
[92] For Fulda cf. E. Friese (1978), pp. 1021–9. Wetti of Reichenau is called *magistro meo*: Lambot, p.
170. In Alemannia Gottschalk read the City of God, *ibid.* p. 163.
[93] Lambot, pp. 298–300.   [94] *MGH Epp.* v, pp. 481–7.   [95] Lambot, pp. 169, 325.
[96] Vielhaber (1956); Nineham (1989).

the proof of His love, and of our love for the vision of God. Human nature was fallen and powerless, grace was omnipotent.[97] Gottschalk took comfort in the certainty that God had predestined some to eternal life, but because he was concerned with the inner life his teaching was seen as a threat to the system of sacraments and works. Hraban claims that people were affirming that Gottschalk's teaching meant that they did not need to practise Christian worship.

But Gottschalk was concerned with how human language can approach God. If God had not predestined future things by eternal disposition, nothing would ever be created by Him. Nothing else is sufficient for a reasonable and intellectual creature save God.[98] If God had willed universal salvation then He would also have said so, but He did not save the wicked, and so He did not die for the wicked.[99] Gottschalk's writings record his doubt, his fear of his own damnation, his inability to weep. In eloquent and original verse confessions he debated with God. For Gottschalk, the immutable identity of divine nature was the central fact of human history.[100]

Hincmar wrote a treatise for the priests and monks of his diocese, warning them against Gottschalk's teachings: double Predestination, that Christ was not crucified for all men, and that faith and works will not save those who have been baptised if they are not predestined to salvation.[101] The archbishop says that his clerics will know Gottschalk by name, and warns them that he has been excommunicated. He provides a dossier of texts to refute him, and urges them to ask teachers to explain to them the etymologies of *praescientia* and *praedestinatio*, which Gottschalk has confused. Christ will convert sinners to justice, and so bring men to join the angels. Sinners deny this redemption and blame God for their own neglect of their lives. But God only condemns those who abandon Him. God's justice is linked to His grace. At the same time Hincmar sought advice from Lupus of Ferrières, Prudentius of Troyes, Amalarius of Lyons and Hraban. Prudentius and Lupus both supported Gottschalk's position, and Hincmar sent Prudentius' treatise to Hraban, who replied urging that Gottschalk be silenced. Charles the Bald asked for explanations of Predestination from Lupus and Ratramn of Corbie.

Lupus affirmed that despite the truth of Predestination man need not despair. The doctrine is defended with quotations from Augustine, Gregory, Fulgentius and Isidore. God did not make man knowing that he could easily avoid sin. Man cannot know whom God saves.[102] No Christian should think himself one of the damned and believe that he cannot be turned from

---

[97] Lambot, pp. 52–5, 185.   [98] Lambot, pp. 185–7.   [99] Lambot, pp. 156–7.
[100] Lambot, pp. 56–7.   [101] Ed. Gundlach (1889).   [102] *PL* 119, col. 636.

evil and saved by God.[103] David and Peter who repented and the penitent thief should serve as examples to sinners.[104] God preferred to convert the wicked than to allow no sins.

Ratramn assembled dossiers of patristic texts in defence of double Predestination. The prophets affirmed the justice of Predestination, and God allowed mankind time to repent before He sent the flood. He distinguished between how God is the author of good projects, but merely the ordainer of evil ones.[105] We cannot know why one man is greater than another, one wretched, another happy, one weak, another strong, but we do not need human arguments to justify God's acts. Evil acts result from the desires of rational men, not from God. Only by grace can men attain salvation, for grace removes the blindness of man's heart and gives the fullness of virtue.[106] Because God's foreknowledge does not compel anyone to sin, the ordering of the world, its misfortunes and the Last Judgement, are a part of divine justice. To deny God's predestination is to deny His judgement of the world.[107] The work closes with a long commentary on Isidore's definition of Predestination.

Pardulus of Laon appealed to John Scottus, who dedicated his treatise on Predestination to Charles the Bald. Like Gottschalk, John was concerned with God's vision of Predestination, not with the teaching mission of the church. He differs from other contributors to the debate in the logical method of procedure, and his radical account of evil and its punishment. John started from an account of philosophy, and a discussion of how it might be possible to talk about God. To distinguish between His Predestination and His prescience, as in a doctrine of double Predestination, is wrong. God is absolutely one; any indication of division is a metaphor. Predestination implies time, but since God exists in eternity He cannot have *fore*knowledge. Gottschalk's teaching is a refutation of divine authority and annuls the rules of reason. For John, Gottschalk denies that grace aids man to do justice. God's justice depends on freedom, so that man keeps God's commandments, and to do this he needs free will, for God must command what lies within man's power.[108] But while Adam could have kept the commandments by free will alone, fallen man needs grace to use his free will rightly.

John resolved the question of Predestination to punishment in a highly original way. God cannot punish His creation, sinners are punished by their own wickedness.[109] Evil is an absence of good, a deficiency and not a

---

[103] *PL* 119, cols. 645–6.   [104] *PL* 119, col. 640.   [105] *PL* 121, col. 15.

[106] *PL* 121, col. 63.   [107] *PL* 121, col. 76.

[108] *De Praedestinatione*, c. 5, p. 40. There are helpful accounts of John's position in Marenbon (1990) and Schrimpf (1982a and b).   [109] *De Praedestinatione*, c. 17, p. 110.

substance. Otherwise God must have created evil, yet He is perfectly good. So God cannot predestine man to an evil life, because this is a deficiency, not a thing, and so without any cause.[110] Predestination, like law, enables God to define the limits of man's action. Evil consists of an inability to exist within the bounds of the law, but the wicked cannot escape from the law. The law never compels man to sin, but it ensures that sinners are punished.[111]

John's arguments were refuted by Prudentius, and Gottschalk reproached Prudentius for his stance.[112] Prudentius blamed John for his reliance on the liberal arts and logic, though he used the ten categories to refute John.[113] He questioned John's restrictive definition of free will without grace. Using the example of Peter's denial of Christ, where Christ's look brought Peter to contrition, and of Christ's look converting Matthew, Prudentius saw grace as creating the will to good; it is a conversion. John seemed to deny God's power to change the world. The punishment of rulers results from God's Predestination.[114] Prudentius strove to explain how God worked immutably in time to redeem or to punish men.

Florus of Lyons also attacked John and his many admirers.[115] Gottschalk was wrong to assert that some men are inevitably predestined to evil.[116] John's teaching is opposed to the truth of faith, the authority of Scripture, the sincerity of patristic dogma and all divine and human reason.[117] Florus strove to defend God's justice, which all the church accepts and praises. Just as the sun shines on just and unjust alike, so there is one Predestination with two effects. Florus also attacked Hincmar and Hraban in his *De Tribus Epistolis*, affirming that the five errors which Hincmar had condemned in Gottschalk's teaching were in agreement with Augustine. Establishing seven rules of faith he affirmed that Predestination is eternal and unchanging, and that nothing in creation is not predestined and foreknown. God's predestination involves no compulsion to sin. The elect cannot perish and the condemned, who include pagans, Jews and heretics, cannot be saved.[118] Gottschalk was wrong on free will, but his writings should have been discussed and not burned.[119]

In 853 at Quierzy, Charles the Bald and a hastily convened group of clerics drew up four *capitula* stating orthodox doctrine on Predestination.[120] By free will man fell, losing free will, which was recovered through Christ. With grace it is used for good, without grace, for evil. God wills all to be saved, but those who are not saved perish for their merits. Christ suffered for all,

---

[110] *De Praedestinatione*, c. 10, pp. 62–5.   [111] *De Praedestinatione*, c. 18, p. 114.
[112] Raedle (1988), pp. 315–25.   [113] *PL* 115, col. 1037.   [114] *PL* 115, col. 1045.
[115] *PL* 119, col. 103.   [116] *PL* 119, col. 128.   [117] *PL* 119, col. 150.
[118] *PL* 121, cols. 989–92.   [119] *PL* 121, col. 1030.
[120] Quierzy, *MGH Conc.* III, pp. 198–9.

but did not redeem all by His passion. The *capitula* were opposed by Florus of Lyons and in January 855 were condemned because of their silence on grace by fourteen Lotharingian bishops at the Council of Valence.[121] In May 856 Prudentius of Troyes required Aeneas to accept a set of *capitula* opposing those of Quierzy before he could be appointed bishop of Paris. Hincmar wrote a treatise attacking Gottschalk, Prudentius and Ratramn, unfortunately lost.[122] In June 859 the Lotharingian bishops met at Langres and issued a set of decrees on Predestination which implicitly retracted the condemnation of Quierzy while attacking John Scottus, and at the Frankish Synod of Savonières in June 859 six *capitula* on Predestination were issued.[123]

Charles asked Hincmar to respond to the Langres *capitula* and he wrote his third treatise in defence of Quierzy. Long and disordered, it emphasises Gottschalk's condemnation, listing the bishops who were present in 849. Each chapter of Quierzy is defended at length. He attacks Valence and Prudentius' capitula for Aeneas' election, and quotes passages of Florus to refute them. Hincmar defended himself against the charge that he saw God as the author of sin.[124] Predestination is a socially dangerous doctrine, for it undermines human responsibility.[125] To secure its condemnation Hincmar resorted to the standard practice of showing that it had already been condemned, and gave a long and unreliable account of Predestinarians who had been forced to recant in the sixth century. Baptism was the election of those to be saved, offering them the means of salvation, the Eucharist the salvation of the elect.[126] Grace is offered to fallen man, enabling him to choose good, but man must choose grace.[127] Penance can redeem the sinner.[128] Christ wished to save all of mankind, but his death only benefits those who believe in Him.[129] The *De Praedestinatione* defended the church against those who sought to make its sacraments void.[130] But the work is also a defence of Hincmar's ecclesiastical policy, for the seventh *capitulum* at Valence had suggested that ignorant men had been appointed to bishoprics and urged rulers to proceed to canonical election and an examination of royal clerics before they are appointed.[131]

In October 860 at Tusey a synod met under the authority of Charles and Lothar II to resolve the sins of the people which had caused evil Christians and the cruel race of the Northmen to burn and ravage many places consecrated to God. The idea of Predestination to damnation was rejected.

---

[121] Valence, *MGH Conc.* III, pp. 347–65; c. 4 against John the Scot.
[122] Devisse (1975), pp. 215–19. McKeon (1974), p. 91 suggests that this treatise was never issued.
[123] McKeon (1974), pp. 75–110.   [124] *PL* 125, col. 215.   [125] *PL* 125, col. 97.
[126] *PL* 125, cols. 301, 304.   [127] *PL* 125, col. 111.   [128] *PL* 125, cols. 240–1.
[129] *PL* 125, col. 213.   [130] *PL* 125, col. 365.   [131] *PL* 125, cols. 383–92.

Christ had sought to redeem all by His sacraments, and to assemble them into one flock led by His saints. By endowing church lands men became the heirs of God and co-heirs of Christ.[132] Predestination had become a nuisance to bishops concerned with penance and with the security of church property. In June 863 Nicholas I sought a meeting at Metz between Gottschalk, Hincmar and two papal legates, but Hincmar defied the summons. In 866 a monk named Guntbert brought a copy of Gottschalk's writings to Rome and begged Nicholas to intervene, but the pope's death in November 867 ended the possibility of papal involvement. It is assumed that Gottschalk died before 870.

ICONOCLASM AND THE TOOLS OF SALVATION

Beside debates on the nature of Christian dogma, Carolingian clerics defined the means of salvation, exploring how images of Christ and His saints, relics of the saints and the mystery of the Eucharist could assist believers on their earthly pilgrimage to the heavenly kingdom. The debate on the role of images enabled rulers, clergy and people to deploy their new learning so as to explain their ecclesiology. The Byzantine church had condemned the worship of images of the saints as idolatrous but in 787 a council assembled at Nicaea restored their worship with incense.[133] The council gave an account of the place of images in Christian history and a refutation of the definition of 754.[134] When the acts of this council reached Rome their doctrine of image worship provoked a reaction in the churches of the west. In 792 Angilbert, the abbot of St Riquier, took the Frankish *Capitulare adversus Synodum* (now lost) to Rome to be examined by the pope.[135] He took Felix of Urgel for the same purpose, and certain passages in the *Libri Carolini* reflect a response to the Adoptionist, as well as to the Nicaean challenge.[136] The harmony between Charlemagne and Hadrian which had made the response to Adoptionism so effective was not matched when it came to images, in part because the Latin translation of the acts of Nicaea II was so inaccurate that Charlemagne accused the Greeks of saying what Hadrian knew they had not said.

In 793 the ideas formulated in the *Capitulare* were fully expounded in the *Libri Carolini*, the most substantial piece of theological writing of the early Carolingian period, composed between 790 and 793 by Theodulf and

---

[132] *PL* 126, col. 126.

[133] Mansi, *Concilia* XII, cols. 984–6, with Hadrian's response at 1056–72.

[134] Dumiège (1978). There is an English translation of the sixth session in Sahas (1986).

[135] The Capitulare are mentioned by the 825 Council. For their contents, and Hadrian's response, see *MGH Epp.* v. 7, Freeman (1985), pp. 81–5.   [136] Freeman (1985), pp. 87–90.

discussed at the Frankish court: 'So that the enemy advancing from the east may be struck helpless and harmless, by the judgement of the holy Fathers in the western lands given us by God's grace.'[137] While Theodulf composed the bulk of the text, as the use of Bible quotations remembered from the Mozarabic liturgy and the Visigothic orthography make clear, some passages may derive from work by Alcuin or his pupils, and the margins of the earliest manuscript record Charlemagne's own appreciation of Catholic or reasonable teaching.[138] Charlemagne's preface stresses his obligation to defend the church 'against the novelties of foolish synods and emperors who blasphemously claim to rule with God'.

The *Libri* explain how the eastern church had misunderstood the doctrine of images, believing that images were owed the same worship reserved to the Trinity. This teaching is derived from biblical passages which Nicaea had offered in defence of images but which were interpreted literally rather than typologically. Only the church can decide what constitutes an ortho-dox reading of Scripture, and only the Roman church has never vacillated in faith, based on a divine primacy. The new patriarch, Tarasius, was extraordinarily elected and has misled his church. The work explains what images are and what place they hold in the church. Images are made by men and not by God, and cannot in themselves be pious. They are not necessary to recall Christ or any other memory.[139] The Apostles did not sanction adoration of images, nor are images made by men to be linked to the Ark of the Covenant, made at God's command, or to the Eucharist. It is wrong to burn incense or candles before images. Adoration belongs to God and His saints alone. After a Frankish profession of faith and an attack on statements made by individual bishops at Nicaea and the empress who had the audacity to preside at a council, the work closes with a condemnation of Byzantine errors on images and Byzantine divergence from the universal teachings of the church and communion with Rome. Writing is to be preferred to images as a means of teaching, for images are mere reminders of what they represent. The Franks have never broken with Rome, and strive to bring new peoples into the Roman fold.[140] Charlemagne and his advisers regarded the decisions of Nicaea as a deliberate attack on their own doctrines.[141]

Pope Hadrian's support of the Greek position may have been the death blow to the influence of the *Libri Carolini*. There is little evidence that the work circulated, though Hincmar had a copy made.[142] At Frankfurt in 794 the Frankish episcopate discussed Adoptionism and Iconoclasm at a general

---

[137] *Libri Carolini Praefatio*, p. 5.
[138] Freeman (1971) with the comments of Bullough (1991), pp. 184–7.
[139] *Libri Carolini* II. 21, p. 80.   [140] *Libri Carolini* I. 6, p. 20–22.
[141] *Libri Carolini* II. 12, p. 72; III. 11, p. 124; III. 18, p. 141.   [142] Freeman (1965; 1985; 1988).

council dealing with a great volume of business. Hadrian offered Charlemagne the chance to distance himself from the *Libri*, in keeping with the stance taken by the bishops at Frankfurt.[143]

In 824 the Emperor Michael II wrote to Louis the Pious condemning the worship of images, which had been condemned by a Byzantine synod in 815. Louis consulted Pope Eugenius, who approved a Frankish synod. The synod, which was a hastily convened gathering of a few key bishops,[144] condemned Pope Hadrian's support of Nicaea II, 'contrary to divine authority and the teachings of the fathers'.[145] This was presented as a middle way – 'We neither destroy with some, nor worship with others' – urging that those who wanted images abstain from worship, but that those who do not wish for images do not reject those who have images or the images which they have. Images instruct the illiterate and arouse memory and imitation of the saints portrayed.[146] The *Libellus Synodalis* of 825 affirmed that worship of the Cross was more important than the worship of images, for it has far greater powers.[147] The synodal proceedings were approved by Louis the Pious, who advised his messengers to Rome to find out if Eugenius was sending legates to Byzantium, and if so, to ask if Frankish legates might accompany them. Ann Freeman has suggested that the 825 synod echoes the 'irreconcilable conflict, on a matter of doctrine, between the papacy and what may perhaps already be called a national church'.[148]

The teachings of Claudius, bishop of Turin, a pupil of Felix of Urgel and an exegete who had been the protégé of Louis the Pious, renewed interest in the status of images. Sent to Turin he tried to correct the local worship of images and also removed crosses and attacked relics. Claudius sent an *Apologeticum* to Abbot Theodemir of Psalmody which must be reconstructed from the works of his opponents, in which he explains his views.[149] His opposition to images seems to have been a puritanical objection to veneration of objects rather than spiritual development. It may derive from his close reading of St Paul's Epistles.[150] Claudius wished to defend the church against images, for he regarded image worshippers as still worshipping idols.[151] He also attacked the cult of relics and the practice of pilgrimage. Christians should seek the same faith, justice and truth which the saints held instead of trusting in their power to aid us.

He was opposed by the Irish scholar Dungal, a distinguished astronomer

143 Ep. Hadriani, no. 2, *MGH Epp.* IV, pp. 55–7.
144 Boshof (1969), p. 141 gives a list of participants.   145 *MGH Conc.* II:2, p. 481–2.
146 *MGH Conc.* II:2, pp. 483–7.   147 *MGH Conc.* II:2, pp. 478–532.
148 Freeman (1985), p. 104.   149 Excerpts are in *MGH Epp.* IV, pp. 610–13.
150 Compare *PL* 104, cols. 900, 926. For doctrinal links between opposition to images and relics and Adoptionism cf. von Harnack (1890), p. 282.   151 *PL* 106, col. 325.

who had read Lucretius and taught at Pavia. Dungal feared the growth of a party who supported Claudius and rejected images of the Passion as idolatry, the Cross as a mockery of Christ's death, and the veneration of the saints and pilgrimages to Rome as ineffectual.[152] His *Responsa* were written around 827. He knew of the interrogation in the palace in 825 and its support of the Gregorian view of the place of images in the church, and he made use of passages quoted by the council.[153] Dungal showed how often patristic authors referred to the use of images of the saints, and how Jerome had reminded Vigilantius of the legitimate veneration of images and saints. Constantine had brought relics to Constantinople (just as Charlemagne and Louis had done for their empire) and Fortunatus had praised the Cross. Dungal used Priscian and Augustine to clarify the meanings of worship.[154] The Cross may lead us to the celestial homeland, it was prefigured in the Old Testament, and it was the sign of membership of the Christian community where charity extended wide as the arms of the Cross.[155]

Using Augustine's distinction between things to be used and to be enjoyed, Dungal explained how we are to love things as signs of God. His main concern was with relics, and he used the poems of Paulinus of Nola and Prudentius to show their merits. The intercession of the saints benefits the living and the dead.[156] The most severe charge was that Claudius was seeking to ally with Jews and Muslims.[157] Claudius had apparently refused to attend a council, but he was condemned for his contempt of the Cross.[158]

At about the same time Agobard of Lyons wrote on images, providing an elaborate definition of what worship entailed and quoting Augustine to show that even pagans worshipped without images.[159] Those who claim to worship saints through their images are liars.[160] In places Agobard quotes from Claudius,[161] though he accepts that the saints may intervene for those who pray to them, and he respects those who worship the Cross, though not those who depict Christ upon it.[162]

Jonas of Orléans wrote his *De Cultu Imaginum* for Charles the Bald.[163] Louis the Pious had sent him excerpts from Claudius' *Apologia* which he and his courtiers had examined and rejected. Though Jonas had learned that Claudius had died, he claimed that his doctrine was not erased. For Jonas, Felix was reborn in Claudius his disciple. He had transgressed the boundaries of the Fathers.[164]

[152] *PL* 105, col. 465.   [153] Ferrari (1972), pp. 16–32.   [154] *PL* 105, col. 486.
[155] *PL* 105, cols. 486–94.   [156] *PL* 105, col. 526.   [157] *PL* 105, col. 528.
[158] *PL* 105, cols. 529–30.   [159] *PL* 104, cols. 218–20; Agobard, *Opera*, pp. 172–3.
[160] *PL* 104, cols. 216, 224; Agobard, *Opera*, pp. 169–70, 179.   [161] Boshof (1969), pp. 155–6.
[162] *PL* 104, cols. 216–17; Agobard, *Opera*, pp. 168–70.   [163] *PL* 106, cols. 303–87.
[164] *PL* 106, col. 311.

Rumour of Claudius' heresy had come from Italy to Gaul and Spain, and seduced many, though Claudius denied that he taught a sect.[165] To worship images, Jonas stated, is not to worship idols as Claudius had affirmed. Images of saints and histories were not for worship but to give beauty to the churches.[166] Jonas used Augustine's definition of the degrees of worship to distinguish between the adoration due to God from that which mortals show to mortals.

Jonas defended the cult of relics, for the bones of saints repel demons. If they were like animals, stones or wood, as Claudius stated, how do they perform miracles? The Cross was feared by demons and was the only support for the faithful crossing the sea of this world.[167] Claudius said that if we wish to worship the Cross as an emblem of the Passion then we should adore virgins, manger, swaddling clothes, ships, asses, lambs, lions, rocks and thorns, and Jonas made a detailed mockery of these views.

Book II of Jonas' treatise is in praise of the Cross. Not only is it a spiritual figure in memory, but when it is gazed at it prefigures the victory of the Lord's Passion.[168] In Book III he defends the cult of relics and affirms the intercession of the saints and the benefits of pilgrimage. By seeing relics we are more likely to feel remorse; the saints' bodies are the habitations of God.[169]

DEFINING THE EUCHARIST

Carolingian sacramentaries and exegetes had emphasised the symbolism of the Mass, in which the faithful shared in the Holy Spirit, and were united in the body of Christ, the community of the faithful. There were several brief expositions of the Mass, and in his treatise on the instruction of the clergy Hraban Maur devoted a chapter to a systematic exposition of what the Mass meant.[170] Amalarius of Metz, an eager student of the liturgy, sought the spiritual meaning behind each detail of the Eucharistic ceremony and of the other services of the church in a series of allegorical explanations.[171] Louis the Pious made Amalarius bishop of Lyons in 835, and when he urged his congregation to read his *Liber Officialis* this provoked hostile reactions from Agobard and Florus. Dom Wilmart published critical marginalia in a manuscript of the *Liber Officialis* which describe the work as *vanitas, confusa*

---

[165] *PL* 106, col. 314.   [166] *PL* 106, col. 318.   [167] *PL* 106, col. 333.

[168] *PL* 106, col. 342.   [169] *PL* 106, col. 378–9.

[170] *De Institutione Clericorum* I, cc. 32–3, ed. A. Knoepfler (1900), pp. 69–77. On the elementary treatises, A. Wilmart in *DACL* v, pp. 1014–27.

[171] On the dispute between Amalarius and Florus see Kolping (1951), pp. 424–64. For Amalarius' views see the edition by Hanssens, *Studi e Testi* 138–40 (1948–50).

rabies, insania and so forth, and attributed them to Florus of Lyons.[172] Florus
rejected the process of allegorisation, in which the chalice was called Christ's
sepulchre, the priest Joseph of Arimathea, the archdeacon Nicodemus, the
deacons apostles, and the subdeacons the women at the tomb,[173] asserting
that allegory was not designed to commemorate, but to foreshadow and
could not depend on the human authority of Amalarius.[174] Agobard also
objected to a liturgy with inventions and human lies in his *Liber de
Correctione Antiphonarii*, a collection of quotations which he refuted.[175] He
was especially concerned with Amalarius' comments about Christ's human
nature. Christ did not submit to the Father when He was crucified; that
happened when He took on the form of a slave.[176] Florus' condemnation
was echoed in 838 at the Synod of Quierzy, and Amalarius was charged with
separating the person of Christ. At the same time Carolingian monasteries
were celebrating frequent Masses at their separate altars, and all monks were
supposed to attend these Masses and to take communion frequently. Masses
were also said for the souls of the dead.[177] The close connection between the
Eucharist as Christ's body, and the church, also Christ's body, is one of the
keys to Carolingian interpretations of the sacrifice of the Mass.[178]

   The monks of Corvey, the Saxon daughter-house of the abbey of Corbie,
asked their abbot for an explanation of the nature of the eucharistic
elements. Paschasius Radbertus answered them between 831 and 833 and his
treatise was later revised and presented to Charles the Bald, probably in 843.
For Radbert the words Christ spoke at the Last Supper must be understood
as literally true, for God is truth and His will governs all things.[179] Thus
Christ's flesh and blood are actually present in the consecrated elements at
the Mass, though they are imperceptible. If the Eucharist were not Christ's
body and blood, then it would not provide the certainty of salvation for
those who consume it.[180] For sinners the Eucharist serves as a judgement
confirming their exclusion from the church. But confession and penance can
heal the sinner and restore him to the church.[181] Only a real presence can
transfer to Christians the benefits of Christ's sacrifice on the Cross and
remove the stains of sin which blemish the souls of baptised Christians: they
share in Christ's body.[182] This body has three meanings: the church, the
body born of Mary which is identical to the Eucharist, and the Scriptures.[183]
(A remarkable analogy to this doctrine is found in an entry in the Annals of

---

[172] Wilmart (1924), pp. 320—9.   [173] Florus, *Opusc.* I. 4, *PL* 119, col. 74.
[174] *Opusc.* I. 6, *PL* 119, col. 76.   [175] *PL* 104, cols. 329–40.
[176] Agobard, *PL* 104, cols. 343–6.   [177] Browe (1921); Haussling (1973).
[178] Cristiani (1968; 1987); Picasso (1987).   [179] Radbert, *De Corpore*, p. 104.
[180] *Ibid.*, pp. 23, 53, 96, 101–2.   [181] *Ibid.*, pp. 49–50.   [182] *Ibid.*, pp. 23, 53, 96.
[183] *Ibid.*, pp. 37–40; compare Picasso (1987).

St Bertin for 873, which tells how Satan, disguised as an angel, enticed the future Charles the Fat into a church and gave him the Eucharist, and 'passing into his mouth Satan entered him'.) Those who partake of the Eucharist are joined with Christ in one body, the body of Christ which is the church, because that body is now within the believer and has become a part of his physical being.[184] Consecration of the elements is a miracle, confuting the natural order. The Mass is thus a daily sacrifice, replicating Christ's sacrifice.[185] For, since there is daily sin, there has to be a daily sacrifice. Christ's humanity is the figure of His divinity, just as letters are the figures of the spoken words they transcribe. In the later editions of the treatise Radbert augmented the number of miracle stories which served to establish the real presence of the Eucharist, derived from Gregory's dialogues and Paul the Deacon's Life of Gregory.[186]

After Radbert's treatise had been presented to Charles the Bald he asked Ratramn, a monk of Corbie, to explain 'whether the Eucharist contains something hidden which reveals itself only to the eyes of the faith, or whether without the veil of any mystery bodily sight beholds outwardly what the sight of the mind gazes at inwardly; and whether it is that body which was born of Mary, suffered, died and was buried, and which, rising again and ascending into heaven, sits at the right hand of the Father'.[187]

Ratramn distinguished two errors in the discussion of the Eucharist, the belief that Christ's body and blood are sensibly present in the Eucharist, and their identification with the historical flesh and blood of the Incarnation. He began his treatise by defining figure and truth 'to prevent ourselves being stopped by the ambiguity of language'[188] in an effort to attack the doctrine of a real presence. For the Eucharist to be a mystery, it must be a figure. In the second part he attacked the notion of a historical presence, explaining the difference between Christ's real and His spiritual body. For Ratramn figure and truth are incompatible, the true physical body of Christ must have solely attributes of Christ's physical body and blood and all of those attributes should be present. The body of Christ will be revealed to the saved at the end of time, when there will be no need of the Eucharist, for the saved will contemplate the truth itself.[189] In the present Christ's body can only be experienced imperfectly. In the true body there is no figure or signifier. The consecrated elements contain the divine power, the spiritual body and blood, which is not visible or tangible, in contrast to the bread and wine which believers see, touch and taste.[190] The bread and wine are corruptible,

---

[184] Radbert, *De Corpore*, pp. 112–13, 116.   [185] *Ibid.*, pp. 23, 52–3.
[186] A second edition was presented to Charles the Bald in 843–4. For added miracles, pp. 60–5.
[187] Ratramnus, *De Corpore*, c. 5, p. 44.   [188] *Ibid.*, c. 6, p. 44.
[189] *Ibid.*, c. 97, p. 68, compare c. 100.   [190] *Ibid.*, c. 9, pp. 44–5.

but Christ cannot be corruptible. 'Nothing, therefore is here to be experienced corporally but spiritually.'[191] This does not mean that the consecrated elements cannot be recognised as the truth of Christ's body and blood. But only the faithful can recognise such a truth, which signifies the reality of Christ's separately existing historical body and blood of which it is the pledge. Ratramn insists that he does not deny the presence of Christ's body and blood in the Eucharist, but he distinguishes between the Eucharistic body, which is temporal, and the historical body, which is eternal.[192]

Gottschalk quotes from Radbert's treatise, but affirms that we cannot eat the body born of Mary, which has risen and is in heaven, but we can eat the body of Christ consecrated by the priest.[193] Hincmar condemned those who saw the sacraments of the altar as a remembrance of the true body and blood of Christ[194] and the monk Adrevald of Fleury assembled a florilegium on the Eucharist directed against John Scottus.[195] Fredugard, a pupil of Radbert, questioned him about his use of Augustine and Ambrose and in his response of c.856 Radbert assembled an anthology of patristic quotations in support of his position, affirming that many were in doubt about the problem.[196] He explained the Last Supper, quoting from Book 12 of his great commentary on Matthew, and warned Fredugard that errors in the understanding of the Eucharist depended on a false concept of Christ. He defended himself against Ratramn's use of Ambrose, and opposed Amalarius' doctrine of a *corpus triforme*, the holy and immaculate body born of Mary, the earthly body and the body in the sepulchre.[197] For Radbert the Mass was a sacrifice, enabling the faithful to make contact with Christ as God and man. For Ratramn the sacrifice was made once and for all, at the crucifixion and the Eucharist was a spiritual reality.[198]

THE DEBATE ON THE SOUL

The writings of Ambrose, Augustine, Claudianus Mamertus and Cassiodorus transmitted a long-standing debate on the nature of the soul, its relation to other souls and the world soul, and the time of its initial connection with the body. Alcuin and Hraban Maur composed treatises on the soul and both Ratramn and Hincmar attempted to discuss whether the

---

[191] *Ibid.*, cc. 59–60, p. 58.
[192] On Ratramnus, compare Fahey (1951). On the eucharistic controversy, Geiselmann (1926), de Lubac (1949) and the articles by Cristiani (1968), pp. 167–233 and Chazelle (1992).
[193] Lambot, p. 325.   [194] *De Praedestinatione*, PL 125, col. 296.
[195] PL 124, cols. 947–54.   [196] Ed. Paulus, *CCCM* xvi, pp. 145–73.   [197] *Ibid.*, p. 173.
[198] Ratramnus, p. 44.

soul might be localised and whether it had limits.[199] Hincmar was responding to questions posed by Charles the Bald and his responses may be linked to questions explained by Gottschalk in a set of answers sent to a young monk.[200] Both Hincmar and Ratramn used passages from Augustine, Ambrose and Cassiodorus. Ratramn's first treatise explored the relationship of the soul to space, and defended its incorporeal nature on the basis of patristic authority.[201] At the same time, Hraban Maur was composing a treatise on the soul, closely following the treatise by Cassiodorus.

In 863 Ratramn composed a treatise against the teachings of a monk of St Germer de Fly who affirmed the existence of a universal soul following the teachings of an Irishman named Macarius.[202] Augustine had distinguished three possibilities concerning the soul, including the existence of a world soul which was both one and many, divided among mankind. For Augustine this was absurd; for Macarius apparently it was credible. Ratramn sent a short refutation to the monk, who defended his position, and he then composed a fuller version, the sole text in the debate to survive. The monk had affirmed that if nouns refer to individual things then, if applied to anything more general, they are meaningless. Ratramn argued that the universal soul is only an abstraction, since universals are merely mental concepts taken from particular things.[203] For Ratramn the only true substances are individuals. The individual things are substances but genera and species are more truly called subsistentia; formed in human thought, they do not constitute concrete things.[204] Ratramn explored Augustine's three questions on the soul, and his account of the relationship between genera and species, relying on Boethian logic and the *De Decem Categoriae*. He refuted the use of a passage from Boethius' *Contra Eutychen* on Christiology, exploring the meaning of nature, to explore the world soul.

THE PHOTIAN SCHISM[205]

In 859 Photius was elected archbishop of Constantinople in place of Ignatius, and the Emperor Michael III urged the pope to send legates to Constantinople to discuss the question of images. Nicholas, surprised at the news of the deposition of Ignatius, asked for an inquiry which could also

---

[199] Mathon (1964), pp. 226–358 treats the writings of Alcuin, Hraban, Hincmar, Ratramn and Gottschalk. On Ratramn, compare Colish (1984), esp. pp. 788–95; Delahaye (1951). For the date, compare Bouhot (1976), pp. 8–11.   [200] Lambot, pp. 283–94.

[201] Ed. A. Wilmart, *RB* 43 (1930): 210–23.

[202] *Liber de Anima ad Odonem*, ed. C. Lambot, Namur (1952).

[203] *Liber de Anima*, pp. 27–8.

[204] *Liber de Anima*, pp. 71, 74.   [205] Haugh (1975); Dvornik (1948).

treat the question of images. For Nicholas the question of the Roman primacy was at stake, not least because Byzantine and Roman missionaries were competing to convert the Bulgars. He emphasised the blasphemy of the Byzantine government towards the papal office, and he went so far as to instruct Michael not to call himself an emperor of the Romans 'when you don't even understand the Latin language and for that reason call it barbarous'.[206] In 863 Nicholas summoned a synod, concerned with Illyria and deposing Photius. Meanwhile the Byzantines had baptised Khan Boris, and the emperor had condemned the pope for his support of Ignatius. Nicholas challenged Michael, and Khan Boris appealed to Nicholas and Louis the German for a patriarch for Bulgaria. A Byzantine synod in 864 condemned the heresies of the Frankish church, including priestly celibacy, fasting in Lent and the use of the *filioque* formula. Greek missionaries in Bulgaria attacked further Latin practices, including priestly shaving and the practice of offering a lamb at the Easter Mass.[207] An embassy from Nicholas was forced to acknowledge Photius as patriarch of Constantinople. In 867 Nicholas wrote to East and West Frankish metropolitans asking for help against Photius, who had presided at the council which had deposed Nicholas and excommunicated all his followers. Photius was in contact with the Emperor Louis II and the archbishop of Cologne, both hostile to the pope.[208] Nicholas appealed to Hincmar for a united protest of all the west against those who contradicted the doctrine and practice of the church.[209]

Hincmar defended the western church and the doctrine of the *filioque*. The replies of Aeneas of Paris and Ratramn of Corbie to Hincmar's request for a defence of the western church are preserved.[210] Aeneas saw the authority of Constantinople as dependent on the primacy of Rome. He acknowledged the need to fight enemies of the church and their poisons.[211] In the reign of Louis the Pious, Greece, which strove to be called mother of philosophers and words, tried to distinguish true and false superstitions. East and west contained just and reprobate mixed, but by free will humanity moved from right to left. So it is no surprise that disputes had grown in Constantinople, and the history of church councils show that heretics chiefly arose there. Aeneas discussed the *filioque* and clerical celibacy, unction of priests and bishops, fasting, beards and the supposed migration of the church to Constantinople. Rome's position was one of command; in Pseudo-Isidore Aeneas found evidence that it was the pope who had convoked the first

[206] *MGH Epp.* VI, pp. 454–9.   [207] Dvornik (1948), pp. 117–19.

[208] Dvornik (1948), pp. 120–1.   [209] *MGH Epp.* VI, pp. 169–71, 601–5.

[210] Hincmar's request to Odo of Beauvais, *MGH Epp.* VIII, pp. 225–6. For the response of the East Frankish bishops compare Hartmann (1977).   [211] *PL* 121, cols. 685–762.

Council of Nicaea.[212] Rome was the final arbiter of disputes; it judged but might not be judged. It taught, and learned from none.[213] The status of Constantinople as an imperial city was irrelevant to the status of the Byzantine church: the translations of the empire and the creation of a New Rome were rejected. Instead, the Donation of Constantine showed that Rome had primacy over all other churches.[214] Aeneas then offered a battery of quotations, chiefly from western authors, which supported his stance.

Ratramn's *Contra Grecorum Opposita* is a more subtle work.[215] He was concerned to defend the Roman church which Michael and Basil had attacked, and affirmed that bishops, not emperors, should debate. Emperors may discuss earthly laws but it is for bishops to consider divine dogmas. His first three books are on the *filioque*, the procession of the spirit. He treats the absurdity of Greek accusations about Latin use of chrism and the bringing of a lamb to Easter Mass. Book II objects to the ways laymen are making rules for the church.[216]

The Greeks want to be the summit of all kingdoms and to change ecclesiastical laws.[217] For Ratramn only the pope can hold universal councils. Chalcedon and the Emperor Leo show Rome's supervisory role. The Greek emperors had no ecclesiastical function and therefore they should learn and not teach.[218] The Constantinople Synod of 869, after the death of Nicholas and Michael III, praised Nicholas and condemned Photius, who dared to judge a pope. In 873 Photius and Basil were reconciled.

THE NATURE OF DEBATE

Carolingian theological debates were public; they took place at assemblies of bishops in the presence of rulers, and so the dogmas which they defined were the expression of a collective and a national faith. This is clearest in the debates against the Byzantine church about icons and the procession of the Holy Spirit, and in the stance of Nicholas I and his Frankish supporters against Photius. In the mission to the Bulgars eastern and western Christianity were in active competition. At St Gall Latin creeds were translated into Greek, and Carolingian scholars explored the Greek Scriptures.[219] But such dialogue was very limited, and the hostile response to John the Scot's mastery of the thought of Pseudo-Dionysius, Maximus the Confessor and Gregory of Nyssa confirmed the sense of divergence which the Iconoclast controversy had revealed.[220] In part religious differences

[212] *PL* 121, cols. 748–9.   [213] Kennedy (1983), pp. 105–16.   [214] *PL* 121, col. 758.
[215] *PL* 121, cols. 225–316.   [216] *PL* 121, col. 243.   [217] *PL* 121, col. 335.
[218] *PL* 121, col. 331.   [219] Kaczynski (1988).   [220] Jeauneau (1983).

expressed a political divergence, just as the Adoptionist debate had centred on the independence of the archbishop of Toledo, and decisions about Predestination had exploited tensions between the Frankish kingdoms of Charles the Bald and Lothar.[221]

Carolingian theology cannot be studied in isolation from this political background: the ruler was of necessity a theologian. Old Testament rulers and the Christian emperors were the models for sovereigns who spoke with God and guided their people. Alcuin reminded Elipand that Charlemagne was 'Catholic in faith, a king in power, a priest in preaching, a philosopher in liberal studies'. With his two swords he defended the church from heretics and from pagans. Similar language was used to Louis the Pious and to Charles the Bald.[222]

The methods of debate are the clearest evidence we have for the categories of Carolingian thought, and the ways in which it remains remote from us. Often argument proceeds from the assembling of quotations from patristic sources, which may extend to Bede. The quotations are not so much a monolithic block as a process of continual new beginnings, imposing a proper contemplation of the testimony of Scripture as it has been interpreted consistently by the church. This helps to explain why disputants rarely try to reconstruct their opponents' positions; instead they raid their works for quotations which, removed from their context, can be condemned as heresy.

The arguments which Carolingian thinkers formulated in order to refute one another might centre on the correct interpretation and use of texts, as we have seen in the debates on Predestination and the soul. Gottschalk, Hincmar, Ratramn and John quoted the *Hypomnesticon* as an authentic work of Augustine, but Prudentius and Florus both showed why it could not be authentic, both because it was not quoted by Possidius or in Augustine's *Retractationes*, and because it ignored or contradicted Augustine's teachings on punishment.[223]

The *Libri Carolini* make use of logical writings by Boethius and Apuleius to apply logic to the question of whether what is held dear is adored, and frequently quote the account of the ten logical categories, attributed to Augustine.[224] Charlemagne praised their use of syllogisms.[225] Alcuin raised questions of method by his use of dialectic as well as patristic authority to refute Felix, and in his letter to Gisela he deployed dialectic interrogations to

[221] Ganz (1990).
[222] Nelson (1977) with references to the oath to preserve the honour of God administered by Hincmar to Charles the Bald in 869. Schieffer (1989).
[223] *PL* 115, cols. 1199–2000 (Prudentius); *PL* 121, cols. 1044–5 (Florus).
[224] *Libri Carolini* II, 31, p. 102; IV, 23, p. 220.   [225] Freeman (1971), p. 60.

destroy the error of Adoptionist teaching.[226] Claudius of Turin applied grammar to the terminology of image worship, and was attacked by the schoolmaster Dungal.[227] In addition Gottschalk affirmed that the syllogism was a tool which he had received from God to refute his opponents.[228] Florus attacked the false syllogisms by which John the Scot equated Predestination and foreknowledge. Ratramn attempted to proceed from clear definitions in his works on Predestination, the Eucharist and the soul.

Few of the texts of theological debates circulated widely but several of the manuscripts are heavily annotated by Carolingian readers.[229] Notes in patristic manuscripts from Carolingian libraries show that the debates reached a wider audience, for readers have marked passages which treat of Predestination or the Eucharist or the virginity of Mary. In some cases it is possible to see how patristic dossiers were assembled, and autograph notes by Alcuin, Ratramn, Florus and Hincmar have been identified. Two Irish copies of the Greek text of the Gospels and Epistles have notes identifying passages which can be used to oppose him, and an Irish manuscript of Servius' commentary on Virgil also has notes referring to Gottschalk, Ratramn and John the Scot. So the debates reached a learned audience beyond the participants. Beyond the monastery both Felix and Gottschalk had a wider circle of supporters, showing that theological ideas affected their society. Carolingian theological discussion was a recognition that the practices of the Christian church needed a fuller definition. Baptism and the Eucharist, the workings of penance and the intervention of saints and images and relics were all to be challenged from within the church. The rapid increase in the circulation and study of patristic writings provided a set of authorities to explain practice and dogma, and to preserve the vision of orthodoxy. But the debates with Rome over the *filioque* and over images revealed the local features of this orthodoxy. The Christian world became articulate by recreating theological tradition. For many it was a painful process, but the issues at stake were nothing less than the relations between society and its vision of redemption.

---

[226] *MGH Epp.* iv, pp. 337–40.   [227] *PL* 104, cols. 879–80; *PL* 105, col. 479.
[228] Lambot, pp. 156–7, 173–4, 206–7, 418–19.   [229] Ganz (1990).

CHAPTER 29

BOOK PRODUCTION IN THE CAROLINGIAN EMPIRE AND THE SPREAD OF CAROLINE MINUSCULE

David Ganz

If we were to inspect a beautiful writing somewhere, it would not suffice for us to praise the hand of the writer, because he formed the letters even, equal and elegant, if we did not also read the information he conveyed to us by those letters.
(Augustine in *Iohannis Evangelium Tractatus*, ed. R. Willems (*CCSL* 36), Turnhout (1954), XXIV, 2)

THE reigns of Charlemagne and Louis the Pious saw a remarkable expansion in the copying of manuscripts throughout the Carolingian empire and a steady increase in uniformity about the choice of scripts in which texts were copied. Some 500 manuscripts survive from Merovingian Gaul copied before *c.* 750: some 7000 manuscripts survive copied in the Carolingian empire between *c.* 750 and 900.[1] Without this expansion, patristic, classical and vernacular writings would not have been studied in the ninth century or read in our own. Because many of the kinds of books and the literary standards of the Roman empire, with its booksellers, law-schools and letter-writers, were replaced, most of our reconstruction of that earlier literary culture relies on extrapolation from stray references in hagiographical and other sources and scanty manuscript survivals. But since every Carolingian manuscript of an earlier text was a copy, to ignore the implications of the discarded exemplars is to misread this evidence. What is clear is that these exemplars were disparate. Only after the ninth century could readers in the lands of the Carolingian empire find a recognisable and accessibly uniform Latin word in the manuscripts which they used. The diversity of scripts which had characterised Europe in 700 was restricted by Carolingian policies. The choice of scripts, and the extent and nature of book production in Spain, Britain and southern Italy, serve as a reminder of what might have

---

[1] Bischoff (1990), p. 208.

happened without the resources of Carolingian faith and Carolingian power.[2] In those, diversity of letterforms, a wealth of cursive features, elaborate calligraphic virtuosity and very poor levels of orthography and Latinity go hand in hand with libraries which seldom owned as many as fifty volumes.

Our evidence for the manuscripts which could be used by Carolingian readers is twofold: manuscripts which have survived in whole or in part, and the few Carolingian catalogues of libraries.[3] The earliest book catalogue from Würzburg, a cathedral founded in the 730s, can be dated to *c.* 800.[4] It lists thirty-six volumes, of which twenty still survive, copied at different times and places. They include a sixth-century bilingual manuscript of Acts in Greek and Latin, copied in southern Italy and used by Bede (*CLA* 251), a sixth-century Italian copy of Jerome on Ecclesiastes which had belonged to an Anglo-Saxon nunnery (*CLA* 1430) and a manuscript of Augustine on the Trinity copied in the nunnery of Jouarre into which the catalogue was copied (*CLA* 252). Gregory's *Dialogues* came from Lorsch, the *Regula Pastoralis* was copied at Mainz (*CLA* 1400), Juvencus from Fulda. (Four titles on the list are noted as loans to Fulda and one to Holzkirchen.) So to assemble thirty-six books, even with a scriptorium working at the cathedral, manuscripts had to come from several places. Similarly Alcuin in 796 sought books from England for Tours. These books may be compared with the thirty-two books listed in the earliest Fulda catalogue.[5] It is probable that Würzburg in 800 owned more books, including Irish copies of the Pauline Epistles and a grammar, copies in Insular script of Gregory on Ezekiel, Augustine on the Psalms (*CLA* 1419) and Isidore's *Synonyma*.) Some 140 manuscripts and fragments from before the mid-ninth century survive from Würzburg, and most of them had been copied there. St Gall owned 395 works in 835, Reichenau's catalogue listed some 400 volumes, Murbach some 300.[6] The catalogue of Cologne cathedral library, dated to 833, lists 108 items.[7] Where catalogues are missing, we depend on the evidence of surviving manuscripts for an estimate of the scale of book production. Some 350 Carolingian manuscripts survive from Tours, some 300 from Rheims (where there were several scriptoria, but also a disastrous fire in 1774), about 300 from Corbie, more than 100 from Freising, Salzburg and Lyons.[8] There are only twenty-five manuscripts and fragments surviving from the great

---

[2] Cf. Morrish (1988) and Bischoff (1990), pp. 96–100.
[3] For manuscripts, *CLA* and the works of Bischoff; for catalogues Lehmann (1917–) and Becker (1885); McKitterick (1989).   [4] Bischoff and Hoffmann (1952), pp. 142–8.
[5] Lehmann (1925), pp. 48–52; (1926), pp. 52–3.   Lehmann (1918).
[7] Dekker (1895).   [8] Bischoff (1990), p. 208.

Merovingian scriptorium of Luxeuil, and fewer pre-Carolingian manuscripts survive which were copied at St Gall, Fleury or Corbie.

This rapid expansion in library holdings throughout the empire between 790 and 840 depended on the widespread development of scriptoria which could supply the needs of libraries throughout the Carolingian realms. Bernhard Bischoff surveyed the centres of book production in the realm of Charlemagne, some of which produced over fifty surviving volumes. We know of writing centres at the palace, which influenced the scripts used at Metz, Lorsch and Weissenburg.[9] Mainz, Ecthernach, Werden, Fulda, Hersfeld and Würzburg used the Insular scripts of Anglo-Saxon missionaries. Manuscripts copied under Charlemagne survive from Cologne and Trier. St Germain and St Denis were quick to develop excellent Caroline minuscule scripts, and volumes survive copied at both houses in the 790s. In Picardy books were copied at Amiens for the bishop, at Beauvais, Corbie and at St Riquier, most of whose extensive library has perished, and St Wandrille, where the abbey chronicle lists works copied for successive abbots. To the north the abbeys of St Amand, St Vaast and St Bertin, which obtained hunting rights to secure hides to bind its books, remained influential throughout the Carolingian age. The cathedral of Laon developed a distinctive minuscule script in the second half of the eighth century, which was replaced by Caroline minuscule. Rheims had a scriptorium by *c.* 800. Along the Loire the great scriptorium of Tours, where Insular scribes had worked, soon developed a majestic Caroline minuscule, and the many volumes copied there for export made that script influential as a standard throughout the empire. Further upstream, the cathedral of Orléans and the scriptorium of Micy copied for Archbishop Theodulf, and the abbey of Fleury supplemented its many late antique volumes, in fragments today, with a wide variety of scripts, some influenced by Irish and Breton practices. A handful of manuscripts copied in the reign of Charlemagne can be localised in Brittany.[10]

In southern France the great library of Lyons, rich in superb late antique volumes, copied books for Archbishop Leidrad, who wrote to tell Charlemagne how he had augmented his library. Luxeuil revived its output, as did Autun. One or two volumes reveal the scriptoria at Bourges, St Claude in the Jura and Strasbourg. Several volumes copied in the reign of Charlemagne survive from the rich library at Murbach. To the southeast the great abbeys of St Gall and Reichenau on Lake Constance have preserved their substantial catalogues and holdings. Chur in eastern Switzerland had a distinctive local script with looped t. In Bavaria a Gospel Book survives

---

[9] Bischoff (1989).   [10] Smith (1992), pp. 162–77.

from Augsburg with illustrations derived from a late antique model, while the monasteries of Stafelsee, Freising, Tegernsee, St Emmeram at Regensburg, Salzburg and Mondsee followed Insular scribal practices, though Salzburg was soon influenced by the scripts of St Denis and St Amand.[11]

In northern Italy, conquered by Charlemagne in 774, the ancient centres of Verona, Ravenna and Vercelli preserved some continuity of writing around a cathedral. Books may also be localised at Cividale, Novara, Ivrea, Aosta and the monasteries of Nonantola and Bobbio. Lucca was one of several Italian centres where books were copied in uncial scripts. Important uncial manuscripts were also copied in Rome and Perugia. In southern Italy Monte Cassino and Naples preserved independent traditions of Beneventan script.[12] Series of charters from Chiusi, Lucca, Milan, Pavia, Piacenza, Pisa, Pistoia and Salerno preserve the cursive scripts used for recording property transactions, often the first scripts that Italian writers learned.[13] The evidence of private documents from north of the Alps is almost entirely from the archives of St Gall, but a few Frankish documents reveal how much has been lost. The royal chancery also copied large numbers of charters, confirmations and judgements.[14] In addition to localising manuscripts from these named centres, Bischoff has grouped other manuscripts copied in Charlemagne's reign on the grounds of their script, though those scripts cannot be localised to a centre. There were at least 650 monasteries north of the Alps. So the development of script under the Carolingians, like that of language or learning, depended on the diversity of energies of a vast periphery.

Production of books throughout the empire on such a scale required an increase in the number of scribes, and the formalisation of their training. Learning to write was often a new and unfamiliar skill, and scribes in their colophons compared it with other forms of toil, stressing the merits of their labour. 'The art of scribes is the hardest of arts. It is a difficult toil, it is hard to bend the neck and to plough the pages for three hours' (*Anthologia Latina* II, xxvii). 'Three fingers write, but the whole body toils. Just as it is sweet for the sailor to reach harbour, so sweet is it for the writer to put the final letter on the page.'[15]

Carolingian scriptoria developed a uniform script, Caroline minuscule, which could be used to copy texts in Greek, Latin, Old Irish, Old Saxon, and what we regard as the different dialects of German and Romance. This script was well proportioned, was fairly easy to learn to write competently and

---

[11] Bischoff (1980).   [12] Bischoff (1981a).   [13] *ChLA* xxx–xxxix.

[14] *ChLA* xiv–xix.

[15] *MGH Poet.* I, p. 284; IV, p. 1062. Similar terms are found in the Gundohinus Gospels datable to 754.

imposed clarity on the texts before a reader. This clarity is twofold: the letters are part of a uniform alphabet with no cursive letterforms and they seldom alter their shape, and a line of writing may use word separation, punctuation and other visual clues to convey information about how the text may be read.[16] The script was so influential that some Irish scholars on the Continent adopted it in place of their own Irish scripts, and it came to replace Insular scripts in the Insular foundations at Würzburg, Fulda, Mainz and in Bavaria. In the tenth and eleventh centuries it was introduced into Spain and England, Hungary and Iceland.

To learn this new script was a difficult process, for the technique of using a quill requires precision and some training in reading and forming the strokes of letters. Letters and syllables were often taught in a crude basic script, which survives in signatures to charters and in pentrials, before the scribe learned formal bookscripts by imitating the writing of a master.[17] On entry into a monastery monks needed to be able to sign their names and the abbey of St Gall preserves the volume in which this was done, the best evidence for the range of skills and alphabets in use in one community.[18] The monks copied a promise of obedience and stability to God and his saints, starting with a simple cross. After the first seven pages, copied by one scribe, several other scribes with cruder letterforms each write their own profession or a group of professions and the range of ligatures and letterforms can vary greatly. Some of the monks seem to have had little formal training in writing and use an ill-cut pen to write their names.

When learning to write the beginner first learned simple penstrokes, then letters and syllables, then mnenomic verses which used the complete alphabet, and all of these often survive in the pentrials of scribes testing a pen or a fresh batch of ink.[19] The separate strokes of a letter might be given names.[20] Often manuscripts preserve passages which the master wrote to start a page or a quire as a model for a less skilled scribe. A volume from Tegernsee (*CLA* 1252) has eleven passages by the master scribe Dominicus, which set the standard for a group of unskilled scribes who have difficulty forming letters and use few ligatures.[21] Such models are found in manuscripts from Lorsch (Oxford Bodleian Library, Laud Misc. 130, fol. 3r, Laud Misc. 132, and Laud Misc. 141) and at Salzburg, in Salzburg St Peter Stiftsbibl. a vii 33 and Clm 5508, where the main scribe, trained in France, is followed by several pupils who write much shorter stints (*CLA* 1247).[22] In Leiden, Bibliotheek der Rijksuniversiteit Voss. Lat. Q 108, a Weissenburg copy of Jerome-Gennadius, a scribe who is learning writes short passages

---

[16] Knight (1989).   [17] Petrucci (1986).   [18] Krieg (1931).

[19] For plates of pentrials, compare Ganz (1990), plate 13; Bischoff (1981), plate xviii.

[20] Leiden BPL 135.   [21] Clm 6233; Bischoff (1981b), plate 10.   [22] Bischoff (1980).

on fols. 44r–v, 52–53v, and 60–60v. The master scribes, like Dominicus at Tegernsee, Adalandus at Weissenburg[23] or Adalbaldus at Tours, and many others whose names are lost, developed their local styles of Caroline minuscule, which make it possible to localise manuscripts copied at different centres. At St Gall distinctive fr and fu ligatures were used, at Rheims the steep a, triangular ascenders at Mainz, distinctive ra and oru ligatures at St Amand, the half-uncial g at Tours. Elsewhere characteristic punctuation marks or abbreviations identify a scriptorium.

The hallmark of a scriptorium is a shared scribal discipline: most scribes are trained to write alike, using the same sequence of penstrokes to form letters and abbreviations, and the parchment on which they write is ruled and assembled according to a house style. The verse *tituli* for the scriptorium written by Alcuin and prayers for the scriptorium in the Gregorian Sacramentary see the scribal discipline as a part of monastic discipline. 'May those who copy the pronouncements of the holy law and the hallowed sayings of the saintly Fathers sit here. Here let them take care not to insert their vain words, lest their hands make mistakes through such foolishness. Let them resolutely strive to produce emended texts and may their pens fly along the correct path.'[24] The scriptorium was a place where a group of scribes shared standards of correct writing. The scribes at St Riquier were urged to keep the law of blessed Benedict night and day as they 'ploughed the sacred books'.[25] Apart from a three-line composition by Isidore of Seville these *tituli* are the earliest examples of verses composed for the scriptorium. The blessing for the scriptorium urged the scribes to grasp the sense of the Scripture which they copied. To do this involved a shared discipline of book production and common attitude to written language.

We know very little about the layout of a Carolingian scriptorium. Hildemar said that 'the tools of scribe are pen, reed, penknife, razor, pumice, parchment and other things like these, with which a book is made'.[26] The Carolingian plan of a monastery preserved at St Gall shows a scriptorium with a central table and seven writing desks beside six windows. More than seven monks may well have been writing in the scriptorium at the same time, for we know that scribes used portable desks.[27] Bruckner estimated the number of scribes at St Gall as twenty-one from 750 to 770, eighty under Abbot Waldo, and around 100 under Abbot Gozberet, when some seventy volumes were copied.[28] There were around 100 scribes active at Corbie between 770 and 830. Occasionally colophons reveal how long it took to copy a manuscript. In 793 at St Gall the twenty-three folios of the *Lex*

---

[23] Palazzo and Parisse (1991), pp. 28–9; Butzmann (1964).   [24] Alcuin, *MGH Poet.* I, p. 320.
[25] *MGH Poet.* III, p. 296.   [26] Hildemar, p. 139.   [27] Ganz and Rodgers (forthcoming).
[28] Bruckner (1938), pp. 19–22.

Alemannorum were copied in two days (*CLA* 950). In 823, Augustine's commentary on the Epistle of John, Clm 14437, 109 leaves of twenty lines was copied by two Regensburg scribes in seven days. The 182 leaves of thirty-two lines of Valenciennes 59 were copied in 806 from 1 July to 4 August. A manuscript of canons of 218 leaves, Clm 5508 (*CLA* 1247), was copied over 146 days at Salzburg, at a rate of $2\frac{2}{3}$ pages per day. A manuscript of saints' Lives of 291 leaves (Brussels 8216–18) was copied by a Regensburg scribe in 819 during the campaign against the Avars from 2 June to 12 September.[29] While the quality of the script might deteriorate, it seems reasonable to assume that a skilled scribe could copy up to seven pages of twenty-five lines in a day.

The supply of parchment for such a project might vary from the excellent uniform white leaves of Tours Bibles copied from 830 to 860 to the crude skins with holes in them and hair still attached found in several eighth-century manuscripts. At Corbie the sheep on the abbey's estates were tithed and the tithed sheep were kept in ten flocks at the abbey, controlled by a master. There was also a lay parchmentmaker, as at Bobbio.[30] A two-month-old lamb skin measures 300 x 600 mm, large enough to make a bifolium. While most Carolingian manuscripts were copied on sheepskin the earliest books copied at Lorsch were copied on calf, as were many Insular volumes. Goat was used at Chelles and Echternach and in early books from Corbie and St Gall. The earliest St Gall charters were copied on sheep, but goat and calf were used from 760 and the parchment was probably surplus scraps from the stock prepared for the copying of books.[31] Parchment was prepared by soaking the skin in lime for three days to remove the fat, scraping it and then letting the skin dry under tension.[32] A St Gall colophon suggests that some scribes prepared their own parchment for writing (*MGH Poet.* IV, p. 314). At Corbie in the mid-ninth century the flesh side of the parchment was uppermost at the outside of the quire into which the pages were assembled; elsewhere the hair side was uppermost. Ruling of the lines for writing might be done so that the impression was always on the hair side, with a ridge on the flesh side, or both hair and flesh sides might be grooved and ridged.[33] These different practices serve to identify different centres. The need for a steady supply of parchment was reflected in substantial expansion of pastoral farming on monastic estates, and improved systems of monastic rent. In his commentary on the Rule of St Benedict written *c.* 840 Hildemar describes a book of thirty sheets of parchment which was to be sold for 60 *denarii*.[34] The survey detailing the estates of the abbey of Prüm

---

[29] *New Palaeographical Society*, ed. E.M. Thompson, London (1903) I, Plate 31.
[30] *CCM* I, pp. 367 (Corbie), 422 (Bobbio). [31] Eisenlohr (1991), pp. 62–95.
[32] Ruck (1991). [33] Rand (1929), pp. 12–18. [34] Hafner (1959), pp. 139–40.

values a young pig at 4 *denarii* and a sheep with its fleece at 15 *denarii*.[35] So a small Carolingian manuscript might be the equivalent in price of fifteen pigs or four mature sheep, or of 120 days of work on the Rheims estates, though to produce it needed thirty sheepskins.

Not only did parchment vary; not all scribes who wrote on it were equal. In 789 Charlemagne decreed that liturgical manuscripts, Gospel Books, Psalters and missals be copied by those of mature age, and written carefully.[36] In 805 Charlemagne ordered that 'scribes not write badly', and Louis the Pious wanted the decrees of his reform council of 816 'copied clearly and openly, lest they be corrupted by the error of the scribe or abridged by anyone'.[37] Scribal norms were also social norms: 'correcting errors, removing what is superfluous, affirming the right' were what Charlemagne urged on his clergy in 789.

Hildemar states that if the books readers use have errors or are not properly punctuated, then the lector reading during the office need not be punished for mistakes in reading. A brother was to stand beside the lector to correct him.[38] Abbot Maurdramn of Corbie, in the colophon in a volume of his Bible, the earliest datable example of Caroline minuscule, said that he commissioned the book for the love of God and for the convenience of readers (Amiens BM 11, *CLA* 707).[39] That convenience depended on clarity of script and layout, the quality of the text, and ideas of how written language could guide the reader.

Scribal colophons often ask pardon for the errors of the scribe.[40] The head of the scriptorium often corrected texts himself and the inscription *requisitum est*, meaning collated with the original, is found at the ends of the quires of several Tours Bibles and other Tours manuscripts, along with evidence that the text has been corrected.[41] At Salzburg the monk Baldo corrected biblical commentaries, added texts to manuscripts of letters by Augustine, Jerome and Alcuin, and supplied glosses to Boethius and Alcuin's treatises on the Trinity. In addition he wrote the Salzburg Annals, an account of how Charlemagne conquered and ruled Bavaria.[42] At Corbie the librarian Hadoard corrected the texts of Cicero's philosophical writings before a Corbie copy was made, and also corrected Augustine's *City of God*. At Ferrières Lupus edited classical authors, noting variant readings and revising word division.[43] Elsewhere correctors are often anonymous, but sometimes proved excellent textual critics like Lupus.

Copying texts might involve the transformation of the exemplar being

[35] Schwab (1983); Kuchenbuch (1978), pp. 146–8.   [36] *Admonitio generalis, MGH Cap.* I, c. 2, p. 60.
[37] *MGH Cap.* I, pp. 121, 339.   [38] Hildemar, pp. 469–71.   [39] Ganz (1990), p. 44.
[40] Karlsruhe Aug. Perg. 82; St Gall 20.   [41] *CLA* VI, 762; Rand (1929).
[42] Bischoff (1980), pp. 78–81 and 90–134.   [43] Bischoff (1981), pp. 63–7.

copied. In Carolingian copies word division was often emphasised, in contrast to Merovingian scripts where ligatures might link letters from different words, or late antique manuscripts where the lack of word division caused errors in transcription. The library of the University of Leiden owns two manuscripts of the Natural History of Pliny the Elder. Voss. lat. F. 61 (*CLA* 1580) of 130 folios contains books XXI–XXXII, a portion of a volume copied at a centre in northeastern France close to the court, and Lipsius 7 of 377 folios contains a complete text copied by scribes trained at Murbach and Luxeuil. Fols. 214–377 of the Lipsius manuscript copy the whole of the Vossianus manuscript (the first half of the text is now in Paris). The Vossianus was corrected before it was copied, and then corrected again in the ninth century. By placing these volumes side by side we can see how scribes copied an exemplar. To copy a difficult text quickly it was split into quires which were assigned for copying, and both the finished copy and the exemplar were extensively corrected. The Lipsius copy of the nineteen quires of Vossianus is the work of at least ten scribes, who copy one or more quires, or finish the quires begun by other scribes. In order to avoid mistakes, they copy slavishly, column by column. Fols. 232–4 are exact copies of fol. 19v – 21v. Fols. 81–8 corresponded to fols. 292–9. Fol. 103 is exactly copied on Fol. 314r. At times the scribe alters the size of script he is using, compressing at the ends of quires lest they run over and cause problems for the scribe who is copying the next quire, who was probably working at the same time. Word division, in a difficult technical text with unfamiliar vocabulary, presented problems to all scribes. Confusion of letters produces *fontem* for *pontem*, *aquartheopompus* for *aquas theopompus*, *hannibale* and *ham nabalem*.

In order to tackle the problems involved in copying at this level, scribes had to master Latin grammar. The major Carolingian scriptoria were quick to copy collections of grammatical texts and of treatises on spelling, which not only served as reference works for teaching correct Latinity, but also provided the standards for the analysis of language which were a part of the clarity of Caroline minuscule.[44] Bede's and Alcuin's works on orthography each survive in a dozen Carolingian copies from Auxerre, Corbie, Freising, Fulda, Luxeuil, Lyons, Monte Cassino, St Gall and Salzburg.[45]

The Life of Benedict of Aniane, who reformed Benedictine monasticism throughout the Carolingian empire, tells how he trained cantors, taught lectors, had grammarians and those skilled in the science of the scriptures, and how he assembled a multitude of books (Adrevald, *Vita Benedicti*, c. 18[46]). The Aachen reform council of 816 required that monks should learn

---

[44] Holtz (1981), pp. 354–405.   [45] Dionisotti (1982).   [46] *MGH SS* xv, pp. 208–9.

the Psalter and hymns by heart, and then read the Rule and the *liber comitis*, and then the Bible and those who expounded it. After they had mastered these they could proceed to the art of literature and to spiritual flowers.[47] Hildemar recommends that pupils read the expositions of those doctors in whose books no error is found, that is, Augustine and Gregory or Ambrose and other Catholic Fathers.[48] Writing and teaching went hand in hand. The Carolingian schools needed libraries where texts on the liberal arts or on exegesis or anthologies of grammatical texts were systematically assembled.[49] Charlemagne also assembled books in his palace library, and Louis the Pious and Charles the Bald continued this practice.[50] Lectors, grammarians and books taught the skills which scribes needed.

Early medieval grammar defines the relationship between the voice and the letter, and definitions of grammar reveal Carolingian attitudes to written language. Letters had a shape (*figura*), a name and the sound to which the letter referred (*potestas*). Another grammar in Leiden, BPL 135, notes that some add *anima, virtus* and *cor* (spirit, strength and heart) to this list. A grammar copied at Charlemagne's court asked: What are letters, in meaning or power or shape?[51]

The four functions of grammar are reading, pronunciation, correction and judgement. Reading is correct pronunciation according to the requirements of meaning and accent. The four parts of reading are accent, *discretio*, pronunciation and modulation. Accent is the correct pronunciation of each syllable, short or long. *Discretio* is the clear rendering of confused meanings. Pronunciation is a proper and appropriate rendering of the people to whom the words refer, the sobriety of an old man, the bravery of a youth or the tenderness of a woman. Modulation is an artificial inflection to make speech more pleasant. Narration is the description of everything, or the explanation of obscure meanings. Emendation is the correction of the errors of poets or historians. Judgement is the approval of what is well said.

This text derives from the late antique grammars of Victorinus and Audax and is transmitted by the Northumbrian Anonymous *ad Cuimanum* (*CLA* 1452), a text annotated at Murbach in the Carolingian age and quoted by Hildemar in his commentary on the Rule of St Benedict.[52]

In a poem which prefaces his edition of the Bible, Alcuin said, 'Whosoever as a reader in church reads in the sacred body of this book the high words of God, distinguishing the meanings, the truth, the cola and commata with his voice, let him pronounce as the accent sounds.'[53] And to enable the reader to distinguish and convey the meanings of the text, the scribes had to clarify those meanings by their methods of laying out and punctuating the

[47] *Statuta Murbacensia, CCM*, p. 442.   [48] Hildemar, p. 281.   [49] Bischoff (1981b).
[50] Bischoff (1981), pp. 149–69, 171–86.   [51] Berlin, Diez B Sant 66, p. 121.
[52] Hildemar, pp. 428–9.   [53] *MGH Poet.* I, p. 292.

text. Carolingian scribes wrote texts to be read aloud. In the poems of the calligraphers at Charlemagne's court words flow, shine, echo and resound.

Carolingian writers were aware of the complexities involved in creating an extensive written culture. Anglo-Saxon bookriddles were widely copied on the Continent, and explore the mysteries of letters, which are described as 'offering sweet cups to thirsty lips and serving dainty dishes on snowwhite tables'. 'The tears of the pen fill the arid furrows'. We quickly and silently give our ready words' (Aldhelm Riddle 30). The quill 'travels a narrow path over white-glowing fields, leaving black footprints along the shining way, covering the bright fields with my blackened windings' (Riddle 59). Aldhelm also wrote of the bookchest filled with divine words, but denied the gift of understanding (Riddle 89).[54]

A Lorsch riddle describes how and why words appeared on the page: 'As the white virgin sows her black tears she leaves black traces in the white fields leading to the shining halls of starry heaven.'[55] It is no accident that these riddles were used to teach verse composition, involving grammar and pronunciation.

This awareness of the novelty and mystery of written language was explored in reflections on language and memory. A Carolingian grammar copied at the court of Charlemagne asks: 'For what purpose were letters invented? For the renewing of memory so that all you wish may be said, because of the variety of language memory grew weak and letters were invented.'[56] An early medieval commentary on the Creed explains 'that the Creed is better remembered if it is not written down for what is safely written down is not reviewed every day, but what you daily fear you may forget is reviewed every day'.[57] This constant reviewing and ruminating of texts was replaced by copying books in which a passage might be located and referred to. Carolingian texts have marginal indexes listing topics or rare vocabulary. Following Bede, Carolingian exegetes identified the sources which they quoted by placing the authors' names in the margin. (Lazy scribes often left them out.[58]) This was a new way of reading, in which the text became an authority, rather than a partner in dialogue or a spur to a spiritual progress or prayer.

The act of writing could also serve as a form of meditation on the text being copied and this underlines much Carolingian thought about the scribe. Cassiodorus saw each word as a blow against the devil (*Inst.* 1, xxx). Hraban Maur wrote a poem to abbot Eigil of Fulda about how in copying the law of God, 'the fingers joy in writing, the eyes in seeing and the mind

---

[54] Tatwine, Riddles 4, 6, *CCSL* 133, pp. 171, 173; Aldhelm, *ibid.* pp. 413, 455, 509.
[55] *MGH Poet.* 1, pp. 22–3. [56] Berlin, Diez B Sant 66, pp. 345–6 (*CLA* 1044).
[57] Casparri (1964), pp. 221–2. [58] Laistner (1933).

turns over the mystical words of God in meaning' (*MGH Poet.* ii, p. 186). A treatise on letters gives a symbolic meaning to the number of strokes which make up the letter, so that A represents the Trinity, B the Old and New Testaments, C the ever open church, and so forth.[59]

For the Spanish theologian Beatus the letter of Scripture was identified with the Body of Christ: 'What is read by the tongue, what is understood in syllables, what sounds in the ears and is heard by men, all this is a body, all this is a book. The letter is the body of Christ, in reading and hearing it is eaten. No book is without letters and no letter without understanding.'[60] Isidore in his *Libri Sententiarum* iii, xiv 8–9 praised silent reading: 'The understanding is more fully instructed when the voice of the reader is silent.'

As well as a new sense of a corporate endeavour in the scriptorium and discussion of the attitudes to written language which readers and scribes shared, the Carolingian achievement involved the widespread use of a standard minuscule script which replaced the variety of scripts in use across western Europe in the eighth century. By 750 a few writing centres had developed distinctive scripts, some of which were stylised calligraphic achievements, but most writing was in undistinguished scripts, crude uncials or minuscules rich in ligatures which made the shape of any letter vary greatly. Spelling is confused 'e' and 'i', 'o' and 'u' and 'b' and 'v' seem interchangeable and 'ci' replaces 'ti'.[61] There were seldom fixed canons of script, in part because few centres attained the level of organisation or continuity such developments entailed. Outside these few centres scripts were simplified, and letters were written separated, with infrequent liga-tures. Such simplifications prepared the path for diverse minuscule scripts, found at Tours by *c.* 730, in the early charters of St Gall, in Bavaria from *c.* 770. But in these centres minuscule is often combined in the same volume with cursive, half-uncial and uncial scripts; there is no sense of a normative script shared by all the scribes. Rand identified twenty-three different minuscule hands in the 226 folios of a Tours manuscript copied around 730 (*CLA* 530) and eight uncial, three half-uncial and at least ten minuscule hands in the 138 folios of a slightly later Tours manuscript (*CLA* 682).[62]

The success of such minuscule scripts depended on scribal discipline, but did not require the calligraphic skills needed to master the distinctive scripts used at Luxeuil, Laon, Chelles or Corbie, or the verve of Insular minuscule. Caroline minuscule had a roundness and a clarity and discipline which secured its triumph throughout the Carolingian empire, from the Pyrenees to Salzburg. Written with a slanted pen, and with few strokes used to form

---

[59] Hagen (1870), pp. 302–7, a text also in BN lat. 13025 and Leiden BPL 135.
[60] Beatus, *Adversus Elipandum*, i. 66, *CCCM* 59, p. 50.
[61] For examples Ganz (1987), pp. 28–9, 37–8.   [62] Bischoff (1990), pp. 100–9.

each letter, it was easier to learn than other contemporary scripts. Because it
required limited calligraphic skills, it was possible to create a large skilled
labour force to produce many books quickly, akin to the slaves who had
copied most books in the early Roman empire. In Byzantium at the end of
the eighth century a minuscule script was also developed to meet the need to
communicate and disseminate ideas, as the instrument of a new culture.[63]

Carolingian scribes used enlarged letters to indicate the start of a new
section, and punctuation marks to guide the reader in different kinds of
graded pause and in recognising questions. In some scriptoria word division
at line ends followed the teaching of classical grammarians. Consistent and
accurate formation of letters ensured a certainty of deciphering, and made it
easier to read a text. The ideal of invariable forms for the same letter was
developed by Insular scribes, who also developed a set of punctuation marks
graded so that a more important pause had a greater number of marks. The
abbreviations for *tus* and *tur* were separated. The question mark was
invented in the reign of Charlemagne. Beyond these graphic aids, legibility
was enhanced by a degree of word separation, and clearer spacing between
lines to emphasise ascending and descending strokes. Words were seldom
separate but were grouped by the reader into conceptual units, such as
sermodomini (for *sermo domini*, the word of the Lord) or *intelligibileest* for
intelligibile est in a Rheims copy of Hilary on the Trinity made from an uncial
exemplar in which there was no word separation. Close packing of
individual letters made words more readable.[64]

In addition to letterforms and punctuation, a hierarchy of different scripts
enabled the reader to identify titles of works or sections, or the opening, the
contents or the end of the text. In the complete Bibles copied at Tours, this
hierarchy was lavishly deployed. It drew on a command of classical scripts,
capitals, rustic capitals, uncials and half-uncials, a willing acceptance and
mastery of the legacy of scripts transmitted by late antique manuscripts at
the same time as scribes abandoned the strivings towards cursive minuscules
and the crude versions of uncial and half-uncial which had characterised pre-
Carolingian scripts in Gaul and Italy.

The discovery of late antique manuscripts transformed standards of book
production.[65] A letter of Lupus of Ferrières asked Einhard for the uncial
scripts constructed according to ancient models by the royal scribe Bertcaudus,[66] and excellent capitals and uncials are found on title pages, prefaces and
the openings of the Gospels, probably influenced by the lettering of Roman
inscriptions. (Examples are the Metz Gospels, BN lat. 9388 with elegant
tapering strokes in N, M, V and very open spacing, lucidity and serenity, or

---

[63] Lemerle (1986), pp. 135—6.   [64] Parkes (1992).   [65] Autenrieth (1988).
[66] *MGH Epp.* VI, no. 5, p. 17.

the capitals in Donatus on Virgil, Vat. reg. lat. 1484.) In the Bible of Tours incipits occupy several lines in pen-written square capitals, followed by uncials for the opening lines of the book of the Bible. Explicits are always in rustic capitals with a steep pen angle. Chapters begin on a new line, with an initial in the margin. Prologues are copied entirely in half-uncial. Red ink is used for the capitals in the text, for the incipit or explicit, and for initials at the start of a book.[67] The revival of half-uncial to set off the opening lines of a text was also practised at St Amand and St Germain. But if these systems of scripts are compared with the Insular scripts used in Anglo-Saxon centres on the Continent like Echternach, Mainz, Werden, Fulda and Hersfeld, and influential at Lorsch, Salzburg, Freising and Regensburg, the degree of individual virtuosity attained by the scribe is much less. The grace of Caroline minuscule depended on a discipline of learned conventions about the shapes of letters and the layout of the page: Insular scribes could see such rules as a starting-point for their own creative talent.

To see the result of these changes it is worth looking at the copying of a single text at a single scriptorium. The great Bibles of Tours were copied from 800, and were among the earliest single- or two-volume complete Bibles. It is remarkable that the same scriptorium was able to copy two complete Bibles every year for more than half a century. Alcuin's prefatory poems make it clear how these Bibles were to be used. 'It should be in ' e church for the readers ... I pray you take care of the reading, so that you resound the heavenly words of God with the right meaning and the great reward of Christ will remain for you' (Alcuin, *Carmen* 66[68]). So Tours Bibles are community books, read aloud for the praise of Christ. To copy a Tours Bible required some 215–25 skins, measuring 760 x 525 mm. This format was a marked improvement on the 460–515 leaves used for the Wearmouth-Jarrow pandects, and though the size of the sheet was larger, the total number of leaves was less than in the multivolume Carolingian Bibles of Corbie, St Gall, Freising or Würzburg. This single- or two-volume Bible was a new format, adopted by many Carolingian centres; it had been used at Metz and at Reichenau before 800, and by Theodulf of Orléans, who had at least eight copies of his small three-column 61-line Bible (*CLA* 576, 768).[69] While the Tours pandects did not replace other copies or texts of the Vulgate, there is evidence of Tours texts being collated to improve the biblical text across the Carolingian empire. Forty-six Bibles and eighteen Gospel Books have survived from before 853, only three Bibles and seven Gospel Books from *c.* 854–900. This shows the effect of Viking attacks in

---

[67] Knight (1989); Autenrieth (1988), pp. 17–25. [68] *MGH Poet.* I, p. 285.
[69] Dahlhaus-Berg (1975), pp. 39–91.

853, 872 and 902, when St Martin's was burned. The Tours scriptorium was copying to supply the needs of a community of libraries.[70]

The number of scribes in Tours Bibles has not yet been studied. Bruckner distinguished twenty-four in Moutier Grandval often writing very similar script, Rand found sixteen in BN lat. 11514, twelve in the surviving portion of BN lat. 68, twelve in Harley 2805, eight in BN lat. 3, and six in Zurich. But other Bibles in Berne and Paris seem to have only one or two scribes. The labour force varied as more scribes were trained, and as speed of production became important.

As the copying advanced, the scribes of Tours refined their script, and by the 830s ligatures between 'r' and following letters are rare, and open 'a' is no longer used. At the ends of quires scribes often had to compress the text they were copying to fit the text into a predetermined format, because other scribes had already begun the following section in a fresh quire. The Gospels and Pauline Epistles frequently begin a new page or quire. The ruling of these quires is remarkably standard in its measurements. Such standardisation meant that scribes knew how much parchment would be needed for each section of text, and so the task of copying a complete Bible could be easily divided among scribes.[71]

Tours Bibles were seen as royal Bibles and as normative Bibles, and Tours Bibles and Gospel Books were presented to emperors and to their relatives. Charles the Bald and Lothar each owned Bibles later presented to Metz and Prüm. Charlemagne's grandson Rorigo, Lothar's brother-in-law Liutfrid and at least two royal archchancellors owned Bibles. It is hard to believe that they were not produced for specific foundations, or for individual prelates. Like lesser books they could easily fit into a network of patronage and gift-giving beyond their literary merit. The great Carolingian Bibles are not only lavishly decorated and illustrated, they contain poems in which the book, the true wisdom of eternal life, and the ruler for whom each is copied, are celebrated. The scribe is to rejoice as he lays down his pen like the sailor safe home, snatched from the savage waves (*MGH Poet.* I, p. 284, compare I, p. 293; III, p. 254).

Tours also produced at least fifteen copies of a collection of texts concerning St Martin, the patron of Tours, which were exported to Corbie, Metz, St Amand and Regensburg. St Amand produced sacramentaries for Le Mans, Chelles, Tournai, St Denis, Rheims, St Germain and Sens.[72] Here one centre controlled production. For other widely circulated texts created in the Carolingian age, such as the homiliaries of Paul the Deacon, the

---

[70] Fischer (1985); Ganz (1994) and McKitterick (1994).

[71] This section draws on the study of Tours Bibles in Paris, London, Munich, Wolfenbüttel, Trier, Chapel Hill and Yale.   [72] McKitterick (1990).

Dionysio-Hadriana (a collection of church councils and papal decrees presented by Pope Hadrian to Charlemagne), copies of the *Lex Salica* and of Ansegisus' collection of Frankish capitularies, and computistical texts, copying depended on finding an exemplar.[73]

Bede's *De Temporum Ratione*, composed in 725, established the western calendar of the church. It survives in two Insular copies sent from Wearmouth-Jarrow to German monasteries (*CLA* 1233, 1822), three Continental copies made before *c.* 795 (*CLA* 1398, 1413), eleven copies or excerpts made between· 795 and 820, thirty-six chapters and excerpts made between *c.* 820 and 850, and twenty-nine copies and excerpts made before 900. This rapid dissemination shows how a standard text could be created. Many copies are glossed, some in German or Old Irish (*CLA* 1511). But the surviving manuscripts cannot represent the full diffusion of the text, for in many cases we have multiple copies from the same major library. Cologne, Lorsch, St Gall, Auxerre and Trier each owned two copies by 830, Fulda, Corbie and Reichenau all had three copies.[74] Major scriptoria could supply the needs of their monastic schools, and pupils could get textbooks when they needed to use computus either at school or if they became bishops.

Merovingian Gaul and Anglo-Saxon England seem to have been satisfied with a few large monastic and cathedral libraries, as at Lyons or Wearmouth-Jarrow, and many others which may not even have owned all of the books of the Bible – libraries where meditation was more important than erudition. The expansion of Carolingian libraries owed much to Charlemagne's educational vision and to Louis the Pious' reform of monastic life. Charlemagne wanted homiliaries and sacramentaries for the churches of the empire. Scribes were also needed to record legislation, property transactions and taxation. Certain texts were copied to meet the needs of those redefining religious orthodoxy. Because texts were not copied by chance, it is worth exploring the reasons why they were copied.

The increase in book production in the Carolingian period ensures the preservation of certain texts which seem not to have been used in the seventh and eighth centuries. The Carolingians secured their classical and patristic heritage. There are no Merovingian manuscripts of Virgil. Carolingian copies are the earliest witnesses for the philosophical and rhetorical works of Cicero, the works of Caesar, the poems of Lucretius, Horace, Martial and Statius and the illustrated manuscripts of Terence and of the astronomical poem *Aratea*.[75] These works were not copied in the seventh century. Carolingian copies are the earliest witnesses for the late antique writings of Boethius and Martianus Capella, which were soon studied in

---

[73] Bühler (1986); McKitterick (1990).   [74] Stevens (1985).   [75] Bischoff *et al.* (1989).

manuscripts with wide margins ruled for glosses. In place of the syllabic shorthand used in France and Italy, the late antique dictionary of some 15,000 shorthand words, the *Commentarium Notarum Tironianum*, was copied at Rheims, Corbie, St Amand (*CLA* 1132), Tours, St Germain, Auxerre and other Frankish centres. Shorthand made it possible to record Charlemagne's views on the *Libri Carolini*, to write extensive commentaries on classical and patristic texts and to draft letters and charters.[76]

There was some revival of the study of Greek, especially at St Gall, where portions of the Carolingian liturgy were translated into Greek, and bilingual manuscripts of the Psalter, the Gospels and the Pauline Epistles were copied, together with the only Greek–Latin grammar of late antiquity. Elsewhere scholars attempted to compose verses in Greek, and to assemble glossaries and paradigms of Greek declensions, using late antique materials created for Greeks studying Latin. They also copied bilingual conversation exercises, chiefly fables and descriptions of elementary school, but including an epitome of Homer. Greek alphabets might be used by clever scribes: only at St Gall, Auxerre and Laon did people try to learn it, and only John Scottus was able to translate Greek texts well.[77]

Carolingian expansion aided similar developments in the copying of patristic texts. Both Bede and Hraban Maur had composed their commentaries in part because of the scarcity of elaborate commentaries such as Ambrose on Luke or Jerome on the Prophets. Hraban's commentaries were not widely copied in Francia because their sources were available as a result of the expansion of monastic libraries. In the East Frankish kingdom they circulated more: Hraban was the friend of more abbots and bishops, and their libraries, further from the court, often had not had access to exemplars which circulated in the west. His *De Clericorum Institutione* survives in copies from Fulda, Regensburg (one copy was sent to St Gall), Salzburg, Trier, Reichenau and the region of Tours.[78] In contrast, major works of patristic theology often required more parchment to be copied, and their circulation depended on the discovery of an exemplar and the desire of a Carolingian reader to use it. Hilary's treatise on the Trinity was copied at Rheims from a sixth-century exemplar kept at St Denis when Hincmar needed to refute Gottschalk, and at Reichenau Gottschalk found a copy made from a Verona exemplar. Jerome's *Questions on Genesis* survive in two mid-eighth-century Corbie copies and sixteen ninth-century copies. There are no early copies of his commentary on Ezekiel, but in the ninth century it was at Corbie, Fleury, Cologne, Regensburg, Lyons, St Gall and Rheims. Carolingian copies of the commentary on Daniel survive from Verona, Trier, Corbie, Freising, St

---

[76] Ganz (1991).   [77] Herren (1988).   [78] Kottje (1975).

Gall and Regensburg, but no earlier witnesses are known. Ambrose's Commentary on Luke was available in a sixth-century copy at Bobbio which was copied at St Gall in the ninth century, at Corbie in the 760s, at Boulogne, Freising and Lorsch. Even Augustine on the Psalms, which was too long to be copied without substantial resources, seems to have first crossed the Alps in the eighth century. Insular scribes made copies preserved at Würzburg, and there were Merovingian copies at Luxeuil and Lyons, but it was the Carolingian copies from Corbie and Chelles (copied for Cologne), Rheims, Laon, Fulda, Reichenau, Weissenburg, Lorsch, Regensburg and St Amand (for Salzburg) which ensured that the work circulated.[79] Augustine's *Confessions* survive in two sixth-century Italian manuscripts and fourteen ninth-century witnesses, from Auxerre, Tours, Weissenburg, Lyons and the Loire, and other centres.[80] The *De Doctrina Christiana* survives in a North African volume dating from before 426 and in a fragment from Bobbio (*CLA* 1613, 343 and 356) and in fifteen Carolingian manuscripts. A copy at Charlemagne's court was the exemplar for copies from Cologne, Lyons, St Riquier and the court of Louis the Pious; Würzburg and Lorsch copied a further exemplar.[81] But such texts did not reach wide audiences outside these major centres: Carolingian book production never supplied the 'general reader' except as a reader of the liturgy.

New kinds of text were also created: Otfrid in the monastery of Weissenburg in Alsace copied psalters and books of the Bible which had an extensive marginal gloss.[82] The Irish had done this to explain words: Carolingian glossed biblical texts expounded the spiritual meaning, just as glossed texts of Virgil and Christian poets had done. The development of anthologies of grammatical texts, of the Christian epic poets, of collections of the works of church Fathers, rather than epitomes and digests, and of glossed texts of Scriptures and glossed manuscripts of pagan and Christian poets all represent not merely an expansion but a transformation of the Merovingian library. In many cases they reflect the presence of teachers: glosses to Bede's computistical works, to Prudentius, Martianus Capella or Boethius circulated from master to master, sometimes independently of the texts which they explained. As learning became more systematic the fixed text could be adorned with the various accessories of glosses and commentary as master and pupils decided. This made manuscripts harder to copy, for the layout was more complex, and the needs of one teacher were trivial for another.

---

[79] The details above combine the information in the most recent editions with current work on the manuscripts of these texts.   [80] Gorman (1983).   [81] Gorman (1985).
[82] Palazzo and Parisse (1991), pp. 23, 31, 43; Butzmann (1964).

We may contrast the growth of the library at Corbie, a Merovingian royal monastery which has preserved many of its early manuscripts, with the new foundation of Lorsch. At Corbie, the minuscule script which developed under Abbot Maurdramnus (c. 771–80) and his successor Adalhard (781–826) was regular, with few variant letterforms. In a large format it could be majestic, enhanced by title pages with large display capitals in red, green, blue and violet, often in alternating lines of colour. The script was used for a major increase in the library's holdings, in part the result of the friendships which Adalhard made at court. He knew Alcuin, Paul the Deacon and Angilbert of St Riquier, and he was Charlemagne's cousin, entrusted with the government of Italy, where he became a friend of Pope Leo III. The library copied commentaries on almost every book of the Bible, including the multivolume commentary by Augustine on the Psalms, as well as Gospel and Epistle lectionaries, works of Alcuin, and the *Dionysio-Hadriana*. In addition, works of theology by Augustine, Hilary and Ambrose, Cassiodorus' commentary on the Psalms, Gregory's *Regula Pastoralis*, Cassian's *Collationes* and works on grammar and computus were copied – a total of over sixty volumes. By the end of Louis the Pious' reign the library had doubled these holdings, with over 120 volumes.[83] The Corbie theologians Paschasius Radbertus and Ratramn were using these books to define the Eucharist and the soul, to expound the Gospel of Matthew, and to praise dead abbots in fitting prose.

Lorsch's earliest manuscripts are copied in a script close to the round minuscule used by calligraphers at Charlemagne's court but with Anglo-Saxon display scripts and initials. Abbot Richbod of Lorsch was a friend of Alcuin, educated at court, and probably chose his models there. The texts he wanted include Hegesippus, Jerome (letters and treatises and the Commentary on Matthew), Augustine's *De Consensu Evangelistarum*, *De Genesi ad Litteram* (copied from a Luxeuil exemplar), Iohannis' *Evangelium Tractatus*, Julius Pomerius' *De Vita Contemplativa*, and Cassian and medical texts. For history Lorsch owned Josephus, Eusebius-Rufinus, Orosius, Gregory of Tours and Bede's *Historia Ecclesiastica*. To learn Latin, two anthologies of Insular and late antique grammarians were completed by Bede and Aldhelm on metre. Richbod's successor Adalung (804–37) was abbot of Lorsch and of St Vaast. During his abbacy the earlier script was modified as scribes trained elsewhere co-operated in copying, variant letterforms were eliminated, and uncial became the standard display script. Major works of theology were now copied: Hilary on the Trinity, Augustine's *De Civitate Dei* and Gregory's *Moralia*, together with Isidore's *Etymologiae* and Pris-

---

[83] Ganz (1990).

cian's grammar. Commentaries include Bede on Ezra and on Proverbs, Hesychius on Leviticus, Jerome on Ecclesiastes and the Pauline Epistles, Arnobius on the Psalter, and a complete large-format two-volume Bible. Lorsch also copied some ten manuscripts in a script used at St Vaast.[84] This diversity was not matched by the kind of study found at Corbie; not every library inspired active scholarship.

Before his death in 819 Archbishop Hildebald of Cologne had obtained copies of works of Augustine, *De Doctrina Christiana* and the *Ennarationes in Psalmos*, Isidore's *Chronicon* and Bede's *De Temporum Ratione* with other computistical texts, Bede's *De Natura Rerum* and *De Temporibus*, Jerome on Ezekiel and the Minor Prophets, the letters of Gregory the Great, a homiliary, John Chrysostom on Hebrews and the *Dionysio-Hadriana*. The volumes carry inscriptions on their title pages recording that they were copied for him and many are still in the cathedral library. Many were not copied at Cologne itself; expansion required the products of scriptoria working on copies for export, such as those of the nuns at Chelles and the scribes of the archaic ab script.[85] The works copied were not easily available; to procure them required organisation. Carolingian scribes and libraries might not always be able to procure the texts they needed, but with effective organisation they could secure important texts. Similar donation inscriptions to those for Hildebald are found in twenty-two Rheims manuscripts presented by Hincmar (843–82), which include a two-volume two-column 47-line Bible, and works of Augustine, Ambrose, Jerome, Gregory's *Moralia* in three volumes, Bede, Alcuin and Hilary. Hincmar had these works copied in order to fuel his campaigns against Gottschalk and his nephew Hincmar of Laon.[86] The cathedral of Laon also procured most of its library from outside, though many of the books had been collected by the teachers at the cathedral school.[87]

The scriptorium of the cathedral at Auxerre was slower to provide for the needs of the clergy there, and its expansion came in the second half of the ninth century, when many classical texts were copied, including works by Caesar, Lucan, Martianus Capella, Sallust, Petronius, Macrobius, Solinus, Servius and Virgil. The earliest books copied at Auxerre were less ambitious: Fredegar's Chronicle, Jerome on the Minor Prophets and against Rufinus, Gregory's *Homilies on the Gospel* and the *Regula Pastoralis*, Eusebius' *Ecclesiastical History*, Isidore's *Etymologiae*, the *Liber Pontificalis*, Jerome and Gennadius' *De Viris Illustribus*, the sermons of Effrem the Syrian and treatises of Cyprian.

These examples show how Carolingian libraries grew chiefly through the

---

[84] Bischoff (1989).   [85] Dekker (1895).
[86] Devisse (1975), pp. 917–64; 1055–88; 1469–1514.   [87] Contreni (1978).

copying of manuscripts in the scriptorium of the abbey or cathedral to which the library belonged. But some volumes were procured from outside, or left as gifts to the library, and some libraries depended on such acquisitions, such as the cathedral school at Laon. Quite a number of books, then, entered a library after having been written elsewhere. But it is equally true that many books written inside a scriptorium left it. Salzburg owned volumes copied at Freising, a copy of Gennadius from Würzburg, volumes from northern Italy and northern France, Orosius copied at Reichenau. Lorsch owned some late antique volumes, and volumes from Luxeuil, the Rhineland, Worms, Mainz, Weissenburg, St Gall, the palace scriptorium, St Amand, Rheims and the Loire. Corbie had works of theology, canon law and monastic rules from Italy, Insular volumes of Aldheim and Lathcen, a set of volumes of Gregory's *Moralia* copied at Tours, Hraban Maur's *De Laudibus Sanctae Crucis* from Fulda and saints' Lives copied at the centres where they were venerated. Corbie could apparently find copies of most of the texts the monks wanted. But growth was not always steady or systematic. While one or two centres might search for the works of Bede, or the books listed by Cassiodorus, most libraries got what they could as circumstances allowed.

As well as cathedral, monastic and royal libraries, individuals also owned books, which they either copied, bought or inherited. Between 822 and 833, in a list which identifies the books of twenty-three priests, one deacon and eight others, St Gall acquired eighteen Psalters from six priests and four other donors, and twenty-one missals from nineteen priests, one deacon and two others. Noctrim had two Psalters copied for him, Eto bought two psalters, Wito wrote half of a Psalter which Ruadhelm finished and donated.[88] The Rheims *polyptique* records books in the churches of six Rheims estates. Most had a missal, a Psalter, a lectionary and an antiphonary. Three had penitentials, two had computistical materials. Bavarian inventories list the same texts, and also collections of homilies. This was a world in which each parish church had a bookshelf, and bishops listed the texts which it should hold. If such collections existed in the parishes of seventh-century Gaul no trace survives; it seems unlikely that such texts were readily available or that clerics had formal training in how to copy them. By the ninth century books were ubiquitous; even laymen owned them.

The private libraries of scholars, teachers and clerics might amount to some thirty volumes with several texts in each volume. The teacher Martin of Laon owned twenty-one manuscripts, some from St Amand, Corbie, northern France and north Italy,[89] Eccard, count of Mâcon owned twenty-

---

[88] Lehmann (1917), pp. 255–6.   [89] Contreni (1978).

eight and Gerward, the palace librarian of Louis the Pious, owned twenty-seven. Such evidence only provides a hint of the extent of lay literacy or private ownership, but it suggests that book ownership was not confined to religious houses. When Charlemagne died his books were sold, not least because people wanted to buy them.

But writing in the Carolingian age was not confined to books. Writing one's name served as a form of authentication, or a record of a ceremony. Written names might be marks of ownership, and could also have a magical function. Inscriptions on swords and jewellery were not always in Latin, or in Latin characters, and such writing, on the fringes of Christian book-making, was the earliest encounter with letters most converts would have. Runes were used to inscribe brooches, axes and caskets from Frankish sixth- and seventh-century graves from Burgundy to Saxony and Munich, and were used on caskets, coins, gravestones and monuments in Anglo-Saxon England.[90] A pilgrim wrote runic graffiti on an Italian fresco of St Luke at S. Angelo.[91] Runic alphabets were used for signatures in manuscripts, and were incorporated into collections of different alphabets in several Carolingian manuscripts. Walahfrid Strabo copied Hebrew, Greek and runic alphabets with the names of the letters.[92] So writing was never exclusively Latin or Christian, and Latinity's potential for restrictiveness was an advantage for many who used it. While Latin was privileged, accounts of letters derived from Isidore set the Latin alphabet beside Greek and Hebrew letters, so that the question of whether k and x were Latin letters was discussed by Isidore, Bede and others.

Latin characters were used to copy Germanic texts, from glosses, charms and baptismal and credal formulae to the Christian literature composed in the vernacular. Here Anglo-Saxon runes were used for w and th. The chief centres for copying Old High German texts were monasteries at Fulda, St Gall, Reichenau, Regensburg, Weissenburg, Mainz and Murbach. A few vernacular texts survive in more than one copy: the Old High German translation of Isidore was copied at Mondsee and in Alsace; there are two Carolingian copies of Otfrid's *Liber Evangeliorum* made at Weissenburg; the Old Saxon biblical epic the *Heliand* was copied at Corvey and two other north German centres.[93] As in England, the vernacular was chosen as a means of instruction, and there are vernacular glosses to the law-codes. At the same time, Irish scholars crossing Europe took manuscripts with extensive Old Irish glosses. These include the poem in which a monk describes how he hunts words and his white cat hunts mice.[94]

The Carolingian world used writing extensively. Merchants carried

[90] Duwel (1983).   [91] Derolez and Schwab (1983).   [92] Bischoff (1967).
[93] Bischoff (1981c).   [94] Flower (1947), pp. 24–5; *Thesaurus PalaeoHibernicus* II, p. 293.

letters of protection, freed serfs needed a charter of manumission, bailiffs
rendered written accounts (*MGH Cap.* I, p. 172). Huntsmen and other royal
officials might have written instructions. Written surveys of lands were
common; counts and powerful magnates often had their own notary (*De
Exordiis*, c. 32). But there were also non-practical writings – written
winileodas or love songs forbidden in *MGH Cap.* I, p. 23, charms and
phylacteries, spells, the letters from Heaven condemned by Charlemagne in
789, cures for baldness or for the bite of mad dogs. Hildemar implies that the
doctor will have a book, and medical manuscripts survive. If the doctor was
unhelpful, texts of the Gospels and Psalter could be used for divination or to
cure the sick.[95]

In this world of writings the question of what was read by a reader
confronting a text becomes crucial. Many people only heard texts read
aloud, and because we cannot tell if texts were read or heard we cannot
assume that the owner of a written text was able to read it himself. But what
was heard was often remembered verbatim. For this reason I have avoided
using 'literacy' in Carolingian contexts: ears were more effective than eyes.
While some readers read silently, most may have read aloud, using
expression to convey what they were reading and who was speaking.
Sometimes passages from Virgil or Horace have musical notation, implying
that these texts were sung. As standards of Latinity improved, Latin became
the language of a more restricted group: those who had been taught
grammar. Some writers distinguished between the language of the Franks
or Germans, the *lingua barbara* and the Latin language. When people learned
Latin letters, they moved beyond the *lingua rustica*.[96] Though they might
choose a simple style to instruct a large audience, in contemplative reading
complexity was often seen as the mark of profundity. But to master the
complexity of a text, it was important to articulate that text with the visual
aids the trained scribe could deploy. While the scribes and witnesses of
charters might keep the basic alphabets they learned in order to form letters,
the scribes of books sought to discipline letters, words and sentences to
enhance understanding. In the Carolingian age, they found what they
sought, and the type in which this book had been printed, preserving the
letterforms of Caroline minuscule instead of Anglo-Saxon, Gothic or
Roman capitals, is the measure of their achievement. Without the Carolingians neither Latin script nor Latin texts would have secured the
continuities this volume affirms.

---

[95] Poulin (1979).   [96] Wright (1991), pp. 101–74, and Banniard, above, p. 696.

CHAPTER 30

ART AND ARCHITECTURE

Lawrence Nees

INTRODUCTION

T H E eighth and ninth centuries were a formative period for medieval art. By the end of the ninth century fundamental attitudes to art had been established in the Latin, Greek and Islamic worlds, and the essential architectural forms that would characterise their religious structures for centuries to come had been defined. Moreover, the role of pictorial arts in religious practice had been actively contested, debated, and eventually largely established. Western Christendom adopted a position between the aniconism of Islam and the intense veneration of sacred icons in Byzantium, emphasising the role of art to embellish holy places and objects and to communicate Christian ideas and Christian history.

The historical significance of medieval art and the conscious intentions of medieval artists have long been defined primarily in referential rather than contextual terms, emphasising copying rather than creation as the fundamental character of early medieval art. Certainly many links between the art of the early middle ages and that of early Christian antiquity have been discovered and explicated in terms of both form and content, style and iconography.[1] Indeed the understanding of an artistic creation such as the Douce ivory book cover (Plate 1) requires the identification of the pictorial models upon which some of its images closely rely.[2] Even when early sources were clearly followed and evoked, however, their meaning was often altered in original ways,[3] in this example so as to bear upon contemporary Carolingian political and theological controversies. Engagement with the present far outweighed interest in the past, and recent studies have sought to understand how early medieval western art contributed to

---

[1] Krautheimer (1942).

[2] Goldschmidt (1914), no. 5. See discussion in Hubert, Porcher and Volbach (1970), p. 229, emphasising the derivative quality and stylistic 'misunderstandings'.

[3] Kessler (1990a); Nees (1992a).

the central mission defined in contemporary documents, leading the Christian community towards salvation.[4]

Rome plays a large role in the art of the early middle ages, but not as the Rome of Augustus or even of Constantine so much as of St Peter. The eighth and ninth centuries witnessed the emergence of the papal temporal state, of the notion of the papacy as a supreme ecclesiastical and even secular power, of attempts to emulate Roman liturgy and canon law, and of artistic references to Rome. The Godescalc Gospel Lectionary from AD 781–3, for example, contained an image of the fountain of life which recalled the occasion in whose honour the book was made, the baptism of Charlemagne's sons by the pope in the Lateran Baptistery at Rome. As had been the case in the series of paintings and books brought to Northumbria by Benedict Biscop at the end of the seventh century,[5] the Roman material evoked by this image was venerable but not ancient, for it was either still in contemporary use or apparently was regarded as such. In this light even the conscious evocation of the great early Christian basilicas of Rome in early Carolingian architecture can be seen not as a retrospective 'renaissance' but as linkage with the living tradition of papal Rome.[6]

The problematic tendency to see the early medieval west in the Hegelian sense of a recipient rather than a creative culture[7] also underlies the historiographical tradition of asserting dependence upon borrowings from the earlier and contemporary cultures of the eastern Mediterranean,[8] which accepts the mechanism of external reference while altering the source of influence. A significant body of scholarship has sought to document with specific examples the conception of oriental influence,[9] but all such examples have been contested.[10] The fundamental evidence adduced is primarily based upon supposed stylistic and to a lesser extent iconographic similarities with eastern Mediterranean art commonly later in date, relying upon the imaginative historical reconstruction of an eastern Mediterranean art of the

[4] See the *Admonitio Generalis* of 789, in *MGH Cap.* i, no. 22, also trans. in King (1987), p. 209. See also discussion of this document and related questions by Contreni, pp. 709–73 above.

[5] Neuman de Vegvar (1987), pp. 112–67.

[6] The essential guide for what the Carolingian court actually sought and acquired from Rome, at least in regard to books, is Bullough (1977).   [7] Hegel (1899), pp. 341–2.

[8] The theory of 'oriental influence' can be traced back at least to the beginning of the twentieth century, in Josef Strzygowski's sensational and controversial theory that the essential elements of medieval art were derived not from debased classical forms but from a living Near Eastern tradition which determined the anti-classicism of the Germanic north; see Strzygowski (1901), a later formulation in Strzygowski (1923).

[9] See Hodges and Whitehouse (1983), and for important early studies, Åberg (1943–6); Ebersolt (1928); Demus (1970), pp. 45–50; Kitzinger (1977), pp. 113–22. For a bibliography on the topic see Nees (1985a), pp. 122–37.

[10] Raftery (1965); Schapiro and Seminar (1973); Nees (1978).

early period now largely absent because of the destruction wrought by Byzantine Iconoclasm in the eighth and early ninth century. Only in recent years have attempts been made to explain some similarities between prior western and subsequent eastern material by positing autonomous western creativity that played a significant role in influencing the east,[11] and in broader terms by a recognition that already in the late antique period the west neither was, nor saw itself as, an inferior cultural backwater eager for any and all eastern fashions in art or thought.[12] Most recently historians and art historians have attempted to define in a more subtle way the connections between related phenomena in both east and west.[13]

No single approach to early medieval art holds sway in contemporary scholarship,[14] and it would be both idiosyncratic and perverse to deny that the source- and style-criticism that previously dominated the field remain widely practised and fruitful approaches. Of growing importance is contextual criticism, seeking to understand the work of art in relation to specific contemporary concerns of many differing natures, for example those having to do with the liturgy.[15] In the Latin west, service books such as lectionaries and sacramentaries became, for the first time during this period, major recipients of luxurious artistic treatment (Plates 15, 16), and the subject matter of the decoration is often directly liturgical.[16] Indeed the altar came to be the focus of luxurious objects in many different media, including ivory fans, diptychs and combs, enamel and metalwork chalices, patens, reliquaries, and covers of the liturgical books. On the other hand, increasing attention has been paid to what have sometimes been termed 'popular' attitudes towards early medieval art, for example the production of images with distinctly magical and protective qualities, and of images used in connection with pilgrimages and other popular religious practices, in both the east and the west.[17] Even illuminated manuscripts partook of this trend, in a number of instances being associated with burials or carrying images of a distinctly apotropaic character.[18]

PATRONAGE

In late antiquity, the traditional concentration of patronage in urban centres changed, as throughout the Roman world country villas became primary

---

[11] Buckton (1988); Osborne (1990).   [12] Brown (1976).   [13] McCormick (1986).
[14] For a descriptive overview see Kessler (1990b).
[15] Galavaris (1970), with literature, to which may be added the important remarks with reference to Byzantine architecture in Krautheimer (1975), pp. 312–15. For the west a leading exponent of liturgical connections with respect to architecture is Heitz (1980).
[16] Reynolds (1983).   [17] Vikan (1982). See also Brown (1981).
[18] Nees (1987), pp. 189–212; Caviness (1989); Wharton (1990).

aristocratic residences, with elaborate floor mosaics and wall-paintings, and collections of objects in precious metals, especially silver. The eighth and ninth centuries were in many respects the culmination of this development, when artistic patronage and activity did continue in such surviving cities as Rome, Trier and Cologne, but came increasingly to be concentrated in royal courts and especially in monasteries, both of which were generally located away from cities.[19]

Court patronage was scarcely new to this period, but its focus and character had shifted with the decline of the cities. Public works such as large baths and markets ceased to be produced at all, and even such urban churches as continued to be built or rebuilt were carried out by bishops and local clergy from their own resources. Court patronage shifted primarily to luxury arts in textiles and precious metals, often decorating objects intimately connected with imperial and royal symbolism such as crowns.[20] The elaborate devices surrounding the imperial throne in the palace at Constantinople, with twittering mechanical birds and other spectacular automata, were first described and probably created in this period,[21] and a number of elaborate thrones survive such as the probably ninth-century bronze 'Throne of Dagobert',[22] and the carved ivory throne of the Carolingian Charles the Bald, now in the Vatican where it has long been venerated as the *Cathedra Petri* or throne of St Peter (frontispiece).[23]

Imperial and aristocratic villas had been decorated with scenes of hunting and combat throughout the Roman world and beyond in late antiquity, and the Great Palace of the Byzantine emperors, which may have been executed and was certainly visible during the eighth and ninth centuries, showed a magnificent hunt.[24] Pictish monuments of the eighth or ninth centuries such as the large stone from Hilton of Cadboll show the currency of related iconography in the west in the period, even if its precise relationship to religious or historical ideology, rather than to contemporary aristocratic life, has not been clearly defined (Plate 2).[25] The royal hunt was a prominent feature of western aristocratic life at this period, as throughout the middle ages and beyond, and was an important theme in contemporary poetry.[26] It is not surprising to find hunting scenes entering sacred contexts, as for example stag hunts in the illustrations of the ninth-century Utrecht Psalter, and combats with animals decorating canon tables of a number of ninth-century Carolingian manuscripts. The metaphoric conception of the ruler as

[19] See Verhulst, chapter 18, above.
[20] Schramm and Mütherich (1981), no. 39.   [21] Mango (1972), pp. 160–5.
[22] Roth (1986), pl. 68; Schramm and Mütherich (1981), no. 57.   [23] Nees (1991).
[24] Nordhagen (1963), arguing for a date *c.* 700.
[25] I. Henderson (1989); Ritchie (1989), p. 9; I. Henderson (1986), p. 91 and fig. 5.7b.
[26] Godman (1990).

triumphator over malevolent beasts or human enemies is indeed a favourite image of early Carolingian art related to the court, with the ruler appearing as the Christian soldier (Plate 3).[27] In a more distant sense the very frequent image of Christ trampling upon beasts was evidently a special favourite of the court art of Charlemagne (Plate 1).[28]

The focus of court art was the palace. In Byzantium the great city of Constantinople remained the essential imperial seat and also fortress, but elsewhere rural palace-villas became characteristic. Early Islam is characterised by a long series of such structures, notably the Umayyad palaces at Mshatta, Qasr al-Hayr and Khirbat al-Mafjar, all characterised by at least symbolic if not necessarily effective fortification, private religious centre, imposing vaulted reception chambers, elaborate mosaic and painted decoration, and luxurious baths and other living areas.[29] The complex as a whole is strikingly comparable to the best preserved of western palace complexes of the period, Charlemagne's Aachen, which was also a non-urban seat with baths, large formal reception room and imposing vaulted octagonal chapel (Plate 4).[30]

Aachen was by no means a unique type of complex in the west at this period, even if its specific form and scale were unusual. Its construction was preceded and influenced by smaller court centres such as Lombard Cividale in northern Italy, Bavarian Regensburg, and earlier Frankish villas at Worms and elsewhere.[31] Aachen asserts the royal capital as a symbolic centre, at least in the later years of Charlemagne and early years of Louis the Pious, although the Frankish court long remained itinerant among many different villas, some of which were themselves impressive artistic centres. The villa at Ingelheim was used by Charlemagne from the 780s, and by the 820s under Louis the Pious was provided with extensive cycles of wall-paintings in its chapel and its separate royal hall.[32] In the middle of the ninth century Charles the Bald, inspired by Aachen, built a palace and chapel for himself at Compiègne.[33]

Luxurious objects in precious metals and gems had always been associated with court patronage. Whereas those works had in antiquity often been for private use, their eighth- and ninth-century equivalents were essentially public political statements.[34] The use of gold jewellery to mark aristocratic and royal status had long been true of Celtic and Germanic

---

[27] Sears (1990); also Goldschmidt (1914), no. 10.   [28] Goldschmidt (1914), nos. 1, 5, 13.
[29] O. Grabar (1973), pp. 139–87; Ettinghausen (1972).
[30] Schramm and Mütherich (1981), nos. 1–6. For the chapel at Aachen, see also Bandmann (1965); Kreusch (1965); Hugot (1965).   [31] Ewig (1963).
[32] Lammers (1972). For an English translation of the description of the decoration see Godman (1985), pp. 250–7.   [33] Vieillard-Troiekouroff (1971).
[34] Riché (1972).

practice in the west, as seen for example in the great Sutton Hoo ship-burial of the seventh century, and the elaborate grave goods in Frankish and other Continental royal and aristocratic cemeteries from the fifth to the seventh century. In the British Isles and the Scandinavian north the eighth and ninth centuries represent the pinnacle of this tradition in the technical brilliance, complexity and scale of personal jewellery such as the magnificent Hunter-ston and Tara brooches of eighth-century Britain and Ireland (Plate 5) or a silver-gilt brooch in the Borre style from Rinkaby.[35] Nothing so elaborate survives on the Continent, although some enamelled and gold jewels are impressive, while the richest decoration was reserved for elaborate reliquar-ies, some of which were apparently for private courtly use.[36] Carved rock crystals constitute a distinctive class of Carolingian luxury production, the great majority decorated with crucifixions and closely associated with the altar and liturgical objects, but the largest of the group, telling the story of Susanna and the Elders in a series of lively narrative scenes, was made for, or at the behest of, a Frankish king and certainly reflects royal political concerns (Plate 6).[37]

If court patronage may be said to be an intensification and narrowing of earlier practice, monastic patronage may be said to be a dramatically new and broadening phenomenon. The later seventh century saw a notable shift throughout the Christian world. From this period monasteries in the British Isles and those founded or stimulated by Insular pilgrims and clerics across the western European Continent were clearly functioning as major collec-tions of imported works of arts, as architectural centres, often with impressive stone carvings, such as the Ruthwell cross of the eighth century (Plate 7),[38] and as active scriptoria producing increasingly elaborate sacred manuscripts for their own use and, in many cases, for export. The religious foundations on the Continent were in the eighth century provided with increasing royal support and given a central role in royal administration. St Denis was not only the site of Pippin's coronation; it was also his place of burial. Abbot Fulrad of St Denis was the royal chaplain, and Pippin's last testament ordered the rebuilding of the church on an exceptionally large scale for its new consecration in the presence of Charlemagne in 775.[39] Major foundations, often with enormous new church buildings, were constructed in the East Frankish territories at Lorsch, Fulda and other centres.[40] The major monastic reform council held under Louis the Pious' direct imperial patronage in 816–17 probably resulted, if only indirectly, in new building

---

[35] Stevenson (1974); Youngs (1989), no. 69; Graham-Campbell and Kidd (1980), fig. 91.
[36] Schramm and Mütherich (1981), nos. 17 and 24.
[37] Schramm and Mütherich (1981), no. 31; Kornbluth (1992).
[38] Schapiro (1944); Meyvaert (1982).   [39] Crosby (1987), pp. 51–83; Jacobsen (1983b).
[40] Krautheimer (1942).

projects and conceptions, of which the fullest surviving evidence is the Plan of St Gall of *c.* 820 (Plate 8).[41] The design and construction of such a large and complex monastic institution, whose central enclosed courtyard, the cloister, sought to preserve the isolation of the monks from the large surrounding lay community, is both a characteristic and highly original element of the art of the ninth century and a precondition for much of the artistic production of that and later periods, such as architectural sculpture and mural painting.

Luxuriously decorated books, some with figural illustrations, were produced in the Roman world from at least the fourth and increasingly from the fifth century with both secular and Christian content,[42] but few would argue that book illumination held a central place in early Christian art, as it clearly did in the art of the eighth and ninth centuries, to be discussed in detail below.[43] Production of books was essential in the west at this time, for use in pastoral and missionary work. Increasingly important links between the monasteries and royal patrons also encouraged the production of luxurious books within monastic scriptoria for the personal use of royalty and for royal gift-giving, and the growing educational enterprise increasingly concentrated in the monasteries resulted in the production of large numbers of books, some of which were decorated with ornaments and figures. Production and illumination of religious texts were also pious labours undertaken by monks in hope of furthering their own salvation, as numerous inscriptions and images attest. The introductory miniature in a late eighth-century psalter with commentary from Weissenburg in Alsace (Vat. pal. lat. 67) shows Erembertus, possibly the scribe or painter as well as donor, as a humble servant supplicating his saintly patron Martin of Tours for the latter's indulgence (Plate 9).[44] Lists of names of the monks in monasteries linked by prayer confraternities were on some occasions richly illustrated with ornament and figures (Plate 10), as in the splendid *Liber Viventium* from the monastery of Pfäfers (St Gall, Stiftsarchiv, cod. Fab. 1).[45]

THE PERSONALITY OF IMAGES

Works of art of the eighth and ninth centuries were frequently personal in subject matter and reference. The icon won its central place in Byzantine art

---

[41] Horn and Born (1979) I, pp. xx–25, arguing for a direct copying of a plan drawn up at the conference and preserved at court. For different views see Nees (1986) and Jacobsen (1992).

[42] Weitzmann (1971), pp. 96–125, and for an overview Weitzmann (1977).

[43] Scant evidence connects book art with monasteries in the late antique period, the few surviving de luxe manuscripts seeming, whether having Christian or secular content, more probably associated with either urban or aristocratic patronage.

[44] Eggenberger (1982).   [45] Euw (1989).

and spiritual life, where 'the experience it offers – in a sense, demands – is intensely personal and immediate'.[46] Icon is a term conventionally used by historians to refer to a special class of images which are at once sanctified through ritual procedures of various kinds, and sanctified as channels for the transmission of prayer from earth to heaven and for the transmission of the holy from heaven to earth.[47] Icons could be and were made of any material, whether paint, mosaic, stone sculpture, metal or ivory, and could portray any sacred subject, such as an event from the Gospel narrative like the Crucifixion, or an image of Christ or the Virgin.[48] A most common and characteristic form is the image of the saint or holy man whose protection was sought by all levels of society from the emperor to the common folk.

The production of iconic and other forms of highly personal images was not limited to Byzantium. Byzantine icons found their way to Rome, where some icons of this early period are still preserved at Sta Maria Antiqua, Sta Maria Nova, Sta Maria in Trastevere and elsewhere,[49] and thence spread elsewhere in the west, even as far as Northumbria, where local artists could take up and develop the type translated into stone or wood carvings.[50] Portraits, not usually regarded as icons, were in fact characteristic of much of the figural artistic production of the period, including not only the common portraits of Evangelists in Gospel manuscripts (Plate 32) but of other authors such as David. Portraits of patrons and even self-portraits of scribes are another feature of works of this period, at least in the west. The Carolingian King Charles the Bald was portrayed kneeling before the Cross, in his private Prayer Book (Plate 11),[51] or receiving the gift of a great Bible from his monks (Plate 12);[52] the monk Erembertus (Plate 9) stands humbly before his saintly patron. Artists of the period sometimes appear to have closely identified with the images they created. Thus the scribe Thomas of the Gospel Book in the cathedral treasury of Trier, cod. 61 (Plate 13), not only signs his name beside his own most original creation, a tetramorphic image, but writes Thomas as an identifying inscription beside only that single apostle in a cycle including portraits of all twelve apostles.[53]

The image of the holy man or of his miraculous deeds was in north-western Europe accompanied by the association of important works of art with him as either maker or user. Thus both the so-called Cathach of St Columba and the Book of Durrow, respectively a small Psalter and small Gospel Book of the seventh century, were from a very early date associated

[46] Vikan (1988), p. 24.   [47] Beck (1975), with literature.
[48] For the most important group of icons from this period see Weitzmann (1976).
[49] Bertelli (1961); Kitzinger (1955); Belting (1990).
[50] Nees (1983b); Neuman de Vegvar (1987), pp. 203–37.
[51] Deshman (1980).   [52] In general on ruler portraits see Bullough (1975).
[53] Alexander (1978), no. 26; Netzer (1989, 1994).

with St Columba (or Columcille) of Iona, while later the Book of Kells came to be seen as one of his chief relics.[54] Patterns of patronage and gift-giving reinforced the personal character of art, and luxury illuminated manuscripts from the Carolingian courts lend support to the view that artistic production occurred to a very large degree on an *ad hoc* basis, at the behest of individual donors.[55]

ICONOCLASM AND THE IMAGE QUESTION

The expanded role given to images during the seventh and early eighth centuries led in the Byzantine world to the sharp reaction known as Iconoclasm, and ironically gave new force and definition to religious images. In 787, the Seventh Ecumenical Council reversed the acts of the iconoclastic synod of Constantinople of 754, which had condemned all production and use of sacred images. The Acts of Nicaea II declared that the manufacture and use of holy images were not only permissible but indeed necessary for Christian worship. Icons in general, and the icons of Christ in particular, upon which the entire debate essentially depended, were seen as a necessary acknowledgement of the reality of the Incarnation of Christ, and a channel through which, along with the sacred relics, Scripture and holy liturgy, the Christian believer came into direct contact with God.[56]

Iconoclasm returned in Byzantium with a new emperor in 815, but between that time and the ultimately definitive restoration of holy images in 843 no new council was held, and the second period of Iconoclasm was apparently a far less violent confrontation of rival views of Christian art. Nevertheless, the iconoclastic controversy played a major role in Byzantine culture and necessarily dominated Byzantine art for the greater part of the eighth and ninth centuries.[57] Associated with it, if by no means necessarily either its cause or its effect, was the absence of all figural imagery from Islamic religious art from the early eighth century, when the first great Islamic monuments of the Dome of the Rock in Jerusalem and the Great Mosque of Damascus were built and decorated.[58]

The medieval west also responded to Byzantine Iconoclasm, although in a manner which is much more difficult to describe, especially in relation to

---

[54] George Henderson (1987), pp. 179–98. For crosses in Ireland connected with holy men see Stalley (1990), with bibliography; for metalwork see especially the seventh-century Frankish objects associated with St Eloi (or Eligius) of Noyon, discussed in Vierck (1974).

[55] Wirth (1989), pp. 142–3 for a list of manuscripts and donations.

[56] The material upon which this abrupt summary depends may be found in A. Grabar (1957), with references and documents. See also Cormack (1985), and for a stimulating overview Brown (1973).

[57] For a range of essays on different aspects of the issue see Bryer and Herrin (1977).

[58] O. Grabar (1973), pp. 75–103 and 131–6.

the nature and development of western art. The iconoclastic position itself was rejected by the papacy and the rest of the western church, but apart from Rome itself and such works as the Theodotus Chapel at Sta Maria Antiqua (Plate 30),[59] there is only scanty and isolated evidence of reaction to the dramatic changes taking place in the east.[60] The official restoration of images through the Council of Nicaea in 787 led to a sharp response at the court of Charlemagne, where the very lengthy treatise known as the *Libri Carolini* was written probably during the years 792–3.[61] What influence did the *Libri Carolini* have upon the course of Carolingian or, more broadly, of western art? What does this treatise tell us about the west's conception of and attitude towards art?

The *Libri Carolini* vociferously rejects the Nicene contention that images of Christ or the saints could be termed sacred things that can establish contact with divinity, and hence were appropriately venerated by the faithful. Images were to be sharply distinguished from the truly sacred things such as relics, and eucharistic sacrifice and the liturgical vessels essential for its performance, the Cross and Scripture.[62] Images could function in two ways, by decorating and enhancing beauty, and by activating a memory, functioning as what might be termed a sign. The *Libri Carolini* often speaks of beauty; from his poetry and from works of art made for him, it is clear that Theodulf of Orléans, the work's primary author, himself had a very lively sense of visual aesthetics and a strong taste for beautiful ornamental decoration.[63] The adoption of decoration, which might well be purely ornamental and non-figural, as a central feature of works of art is indeed a central characteristic of art during the eighth and ninth centuries not only in the west but also in Islam and the Byzantine world. The second function of images propounded in the *Libri Carolini* is connected to the famous earlier pronouncements by Pope Gregory the Great that images could serve for the illiterate as did books for the literate, allowing the biblical stories to be recalled and ultimately helping to bring the observer to prayer.[64] This statement is explicitly quoted in the *Libri Carolini*, but in such a way as not to emphasise the propaedeutic role of images suggested by Gregory. On the other hand, the *Libri Carolini* clearly agrees with Gregory's statement that images with religious subjects should

[59] Belting (1987).
[60] For one possible reaction in Francia see Nees (1987).
[61] Freeman (1985). The work is edited by Hubert Bastgen in *MGH*, but a new edition by Freeman is shortly to appear in the same series, and it is hoped that a translation will follow.
[62] Chazelle (1986).   [63] Nees (1991), pp. 21–46.
[64] Davis-Weyer (1971), pp. 47–9. The interpretation and meaning of this text has recently been the subject of a series of studies, including Kessler (1985), Duggan (1989), and especially Chazelle (1990).

not be either avoided or destroyed, but rather corrected and subordinated to words, which alone can clearly inform.[65]

It seems at first remarkable that the *Libri Carolini* says so very little about actual works of art. When specific images are mentioned, these are frequently vague 'straw men' designed to fit the author's argument rather than descriptions or analyses that can be related to contemporary Byzantine or Carolingian art. Indeed the peculiar disengagement between words and specific images was commonplace in the Carolingian period.[66] Even in cases like the Dagulf Psalter, where unusual prefatory texts inside the book explain the unusual iconography of the ivory covers, the juxtaposition must be made by the medieval and modern reader, not being explicit in the text, the dedication only specifying that the covers are made of ivory.[67] Theodulf has in fact long been famous for his apparently almost archaeologically accurate descriptions of several works of art such as an ancient silver vase and a painting of a tree with images of the liberal arts, but the former seems most likely to be an imaginary vessel rather than a real one.[68] Generally one should be careful not to accept Carolingian literary descriptions as simply accurate renderings of images into words, for the descriptions follow their own conventions.

Only one Carolingian work of art can be confidently related to the *Libri Carolini* in a direct way, the apse mosaic in Theodulf's own oratory at Germigny-des-Prés, depicting the Ark of the Covenant in Solomon's Temple, with two sets of cherubim stretching their wings over it (Plate 14).[69] Far from setting a new trend, the mosaic of Germigny remains isolated as a direct outcome of the arguments of the *Libri Carolini*, although some other attempts to trace a direct impact of the *Libri Carolini* upon Carolingian art have been made.[70] The *Libri Carolini* text in fact never criticises the making of images of Christ or the saints, only the allegedly idolatrous misuse of such images approved by the Nicene synod, and the absence of figural decoration in the several illuminated manuscripts associated with Theodulf need not imply total aniconism on his part either by virtue of personal conviction or alleged Visigothic heritage.[71] Nevertheless, although direct influence of the *Libri Carolini* upon the course of Carolingian and western art cannot be asserted,[72] the debate clearly joined with many other artistic and cultural factors to separate further the traditions and

---

[65] Chazelle (1986), pp. 180–2. [66] Ganz (1992).
[67] See Goldschmidt (1914), nos. 3–4; Holter (1980), pp. 58–66. [68] Nees (1991), pp. 21–46.
[69] Bloch (1965).
[70] Schnitzler (1964), and Schrade (1965), followed more recently and rejected by Wirth (1989), pp. 111–66.
[71] Vieillard-Troiekouroff (1975). [72] Mütherich (1979).

arts of the Greek east and Latin west at a moment when the already growing separation might have been reduced. At the same time, the Gregorian view that images could serve a useful role in teaching certainly is consistent with the growing tendency during the ninth century to create works of art with increasingly complex didactic messages.

ICONOGRAPHY

Eighth- and ninth-century artists introduced new treatments of established image types, developed image cycles for newly composed or newly illustrated texts, created new types of portraits of authors and donors, and produced many unique images intended for special settings or functions. Although drawing upon earlier traditions, artists also altered or adapted those images to express new meanings or serve new functions of contemporary significance, as demonstrated by the few examples chosen from among a great many possibilities to be mentioned here.[73] This is not to say that artists of the period were unwilling to invent what seem to be entirely novel images without essential pictorial forerunners, such as the tetramorphic figure included in the early eighth-century Trier Gospels,[74] or the apse mosaic from Germigny (Plate 14). Rich meanings and functions penetrated apparently purely ornamental compositions, so that in this period one can meaningfully discuss non-figural iconography.[75]

The importance of new liturgical imagery has already been mentioned, citing illustrations in ivory of the new Roman liturgy introduced in ninth-century Francia.[76] Sacramentaries became an important class of illuminated manuscript, apparently for the first time, during this period. Already in the mid-eighth century sacramentaries have large cross frontispieces, and elaborate initial pages.[77] From the end of the eighth or the early ninth century, the Gellone Sacramentary (BN lat. 12048) uses a wide range of ornaments and figures in the margins and as initial letters. The opening initial I of the title for the first text is made up of a standing iconic image of the Virgin in elaborate courtly costume, wielding a cross in one hand and a censer in the other (Plate 15).[78] A new emphasis upon the Virgin's role in the Incarnation and in the liturgical life of the church is also evident in such stylistically unrelated works as the fresco cycle from Castelseprio in northern Italy.[79]

The mid-ninth-century Sacramentary of Bishop Drogo of Metz (BN lat. 9428) also uses letters as the basis for figural illumination, but does so in a

---

[73] Nees (1992b).   [74] Alexander (1978), no. 26, fig. 110.   [75] Elbern (1971).

[76] Reynolds (1983); Calkins (1983), pp. 161–93.

[77] Hubert, Porcher and Volbach (1969), pp. 164–81, with illustrations.

[78] Teyssèdre (1959).   [79] Leveto (1990).

variety of ways. Some letters simply provide a frame for a scene, but others are opened up so as to provide within the letter itself space for appropriate figures, as the Old Testament prefigurations of the eucharistic sacrifice who are shown within the letter T opening the Canon of the Mass (Plate 16).[80] The sacramentary from Marmoutiers made in Tours in the mid-ninth century has not only a portrait of the 'author', Gregory the Great, and a page showing the donation of the book to Abbot Raganaldus by his monks but also a large miniature showing the different grades of the ecclesiastical hierarchy from lector up to bishop.[81]

Other new texts were illustrated during this period, of which the most famous is probably the commentary by Beatus of Liebana on the Apocalypse, written in northern Spain during the later ninth century. Certainly meant from its inception to receive some illustrations, the earliest surviving illustrated Beatus dates from the tenth century (Plate 17).[82] The interest in the Apocalypse as a subject for large-scale illustration is a feature of art certainly in Francia and perhaps also in Britain. The municipal libraries of Trier, Cambrai and Valenciennes all preserve late eighth- or ninth-century richly illustrated copies of the Apocalypse.[83] Classical texts such as the plays of Terence and the astronomical books known as Aratea were copied, the illustrations in some cases following those in the late Roman manuscripts that were the source for the text.[84] Such manuscripts had not been produced since late antiquity and reflect the important role of ancient secular learning in Carolingian education. Other texts used in the schools, such as Boethius, *De Arithmetica*, occasionally received elaborate frontispiece miniatures,[85] as did some legal collections, even manuscripts which on the basis of style do not closely connect with courtly classicism (Plate 18).[86]

Iconographic patterns also included new treatments of established types. For example, a common arrangement found in a number of early illustrated Psalters is used in the Corbie Psalter of the early ninth century for the combat of David and Goliath, but the artist adds the blessing hand of God at the centre of the scene in order to make more explicit the salvific power. The little demonic creature above the head of the Philistine giant characterises the satanic enemy (Plate 19).[87] An especially important example of new forms and interpretations of traditional iconography is the image of the Crucifixion. Crucifixion images were in fact rare in early Christian art, and,

---

[80] Mütherich and Gaehde (1976), pls. 29 and 28 respectively.   [81] Koehler (1930), pl. 61a.

[82] Dodwell (1971), pp. 96–105, and Williams (1977), pp. 24–8.

[83] Hubert, Porcher and Volbach (1970), figs. 167–9; Braunfels (1968), figs. on pp. 301–7. See also in general Landes (1988).   [84] Mütherich (1990), pp. 597–601.

[85] Hubert, Porcher and Volbach (1970), figs. 117–18.

[86] BN lat. 4404, fols. 1v–2, for which see Porcher (1965), and especially now Nelson (1989).

[87] Hubert, Porcher and Volbach (1969), fig. 206, and for a larger selection of illustrations and discussion Braunfels (1968), pp. 156–8, pl. xxii a–d and figs. 68–83.

viewed from the standpoint of later Christian art, continued to be surprisingly infrequent up to the early ninth century. At the same time early Crucifixions tended to focus on the triumphal interpretations of the scene, depicting a living Christ, often in an overtly apocalyptic context. Towards the end of the seventh century the monk Anastasius Sinaites in his *Hodegon*, ironically wishing to demonstrate that the Logos never died, called for a diagram depicting the human Christ dead on the Cross.[88] This new iconography appears in Byzantine icons of the eighth and ninth centuries showing Christ with eyes closed, and from approximately the second quarter of the ninth century appears in western images. The new iconography, evidently appealing to new doctrinal and devotional concerns, formed the most frequent subject of late Carolingian ivories and crystals, and appeared often in manuscripts, of which one of the most interesting is the image before the kneeling King Charles the Bald in his private prayer book (Plate 11). Here linked with an inscription referring to the wounds of Christ, and with the liturgy for Good Friday, the image is paired with the humbly petitioning posture of the ruler to make a powerful statement about the ruler's connection with the suffering human Christ.[89]

The portrait of Charles the Bald is only one of a series remarkably varied in form and contents.[90] The presentation image of the Bible from Tours (Plate 12) shows him enthroned with his soldiers and courtiers in a composition derived from late Roman images of imperial majesty, but here adapted to suit a particular occasion and a very un-Roman crowd of monks. The extraordinary double-page image of Charles the Bald in a Gospel Book made *c.* 870 has him seated under a great canopy looking across the page at the image of the apocalyptic Lamb adored by twenty-four crown-bearing elders,[91] creating an unprecedented combination of celestial majesty and almost visionary personal contemplation. Other ruler portraits include Charles' father Louis the Pious from Hraban Maur's *In Praise of the Holy Cross* (Plate 3), in which the Carolingian interest in acrostic poems creating internal images is raised to a new level. The image of Louis as a Christian soldier, derived from images in contemporary psalters and in such allegorical works as Prudentius' *Psychomachia*, is actually composed of another series of verses spelled out by the letters upon his shield and staff and those making up his body. The text itself becomes an image, as original and rich in content as it is peculiar and, linked to Hraban's important essay on the cult of the Cross, was repeatedly copied not only in the ninth century but in later medieval centuries.[92]

[88] Kartsonis (1986), pp. 40–57.   [89] Deshman (1980).

[90] Schramm and Mütherich (1981), nos. 51, 52 and 58; Schramm (1983).

[91] Fuhrmann and Mütherich (1986), no. 2 and pls. 3–4.

[92] Sears (1990).

ARCHITECTURE

Across much of Italy, northern Spain and to a lesser extent Francia, buildings of the late Roman world remained in use for private and public purposes into, and in some cases throughout, the eighth and ninth centuries. The great churches of early Christian Rome are the outstanding example of architectural continuity and are important for understanding the new constructions of the period here under review, but late Roman churches also remained in use in Milan and Ravenna, in Paris and Toulouse, in Trier and Cologne among many other sites.[93] In a poem of *c.* 799 Theodulf of Orléans describes visiting Narbonne in southern Francia and finding the Roman forum and hall for justice still in use.[94] Continuity of use from the past is important, and should not be forgotten in turning to a consideration of the new building of the period. Yet across northern and eastern Francia, Scandinavia and much of the British Isles surviving Roman masonry buildings were rare or non-existent, and a very different tradition of timber architecture was practised. Because wood is far less permanent than stone, knowledge of this tradition is scanty, consisting largely of excavations of post-holes, later buildings believed to be based upon the same tradition, and indirect evidence in the form of pictorial representations. The so-called stave churches of Norway, although surviving only from a later date, convey something of the imposing beauty and grandeur that wooden churches could attain,[95] and literary sources tell of the rich decoration of wooden churches in Ireland. Most of the knowable timber buildings, however, are domestic in nature, living halls of nobles and farmers, and barns.[96] The Plan of St Gall (Plate 8) offers rich insight into a wide range of barns, sheds and workshops, and a rare, and therefore doubly precious, insight into everyday secular life in the period.[97] It is also possible to argue that the tradition of timber building played a role in the development of a new medieval aesthetic and structural system,[98] but nevertheless architecture of the eighth and ninth centuries can be known primarily from stone ecclesiastical buildings.

The study of western European church architecture of the eighth and ninth centuries has been dominated for the past half-century by Richard Krautheimer's great article treating 'the Carolingian revival of early Christian architecture'.[99] Focusing upon the use of a large, continuous transept in the court-supported monastery church at Fulda, as enlarged by Abbot Ratger from 802 to 819, which he saw as a direct and deliberate

[93] Krautheimer (1965).   [94] Nees (1991), pp. 51 and 59.
[95] Anker (1970), pp. 201–419.
[96] Sage (1965); Graham-Campbell and Kidd (1980), pp. 75–80.
[97] Horn and Born (1979) II, pp. 1–314.   [98] Horn (1958).   [99] Krautheimer (1942).

evocation of the Vatican Basilica of St Peter in Rome, Krautheimer compellingly linked this new plan-type with a broad cultural programme in which Charlemagne and his court sought to attach themselves through art and other means to the early Christian Roman empire, especially at the time of Constantine. He connected other important architectural works with the same historical moment and programme, suggesting that the Torhalle or Gatehouse from Lorsch specifically evoked the Arch of Constantine in Rome, and that the Palace Chapel at Aachen could be linked with Constantine's Lateran Palace in Rome.

Subsequent research on the chronology, morphology and terminology of several buildings has cast doubt upon or invalidated a number of Krautheimer's specific claims and arguments, as he himself acknowledged in important postscripts attached to reprintings of his article.[100] For example, St Peter's now seems not to have provided a precedent for the continuous transept of Fulda, the other apostolic basilica of St Paul's being in fact the only major Roman precedent. St Denis, dedicated in 775, seems to be more important than ever as the earliest post-antique example of this transepted basilica type. Church buildings from the time of Louis the Pious appear not to have continued the transepted basilica type but rather favoured a triple-apsed plan of the sort used by Benedict of Aniane's newly founded abbey at Cornelimünster. Only after c. 830 with Einhard's church at Seligenstadt and the basilicas at Corvey and St Gall does the transepted or T-basilica re-emerge.[101] Yet Krautheimer's conception remains a vivid account of a decisive moment in European architecture. Beginning with St Denis, Carolingian and other western monastery and cathedral churches are executed on a newly enlarged scale, and follow the basic pattern of the aisled basilica with an enhanced focus upon the chief altar, often located at the crossing of nave and transept.

Burial within the church, as with Pippin's burial at St Denis, is a leading motif of major architecture, most often focusing upon a holy relic. The cult of relics was intensified in the Carolingian period, and an earlier ecclesiastical canon requiring that all altars should contain relics was promulgated for the entire Frankish realm in 801.[102] One architectural development associated with the growing relic cult rather than with possible reminiscences of an early Christian past is the development of large crypts giving access to the holy tombs, such as the crypts added during the later eighth century to both the eastern and western ends of St Maurice-d'Agaune, now in Switzerland.[103] The church of the St Gall plan (Plate 8), also double-ended, has a major crypt for the relics of the patron saint, as is the case in Seligenstadt in

---

[100] See Krautheimer (1942), postscripts (1969) and (1987).   [101] Jacobsen (1983a; 1990).
[102] See Geary (1990), pp. 36–43 with references.
[103] Oswald et al. (1966), pp. 298–9. On the double-ended churches see Mann (1961).

Germany, Nivelles in Belgium, Wilfrid's churches of Hexham and Ripon, and a number of churches in Rome and central Italy such as Sta Prassede and Farfa.[104]

An essentially new feature of architecture of the eighth and ninth centuries is the double-ended church already mentioned, and possibly related to it, the development of monumental, frequently towered, façades, the so-called Westworks.[105] Charlemagne's palace chapel at Aachen was provided with a tall structure, distinct from the octagon to which it was attached, whose second-floor gallery provided an elevated position from which the ruler could observe the liturgical services and also appear to those assembled in the atrium before the building.[106] Best preserved is Corvey in Saxony, built 873–85, with tall towers flanking the central block on the exterior and a large tribune on the upper storey overlooking the nave (Plate 20).[107] These new buildings either focus upon the chief relic or patron of the church, or provide a setting for the ruler or patrón, or both at once, and testify again to the concentration upon powerful individuals as a central characteristic of the art of this time. This is probably the proper context in which to understand the 'triumphal arch' added in the ninth century to the royal abbey at Lorsch, which marked the way to the royal necropolis.[108]

The city of Rome was the major Italian centre of architectural production during the eighth and ninth centuries, especially in the first half of the latter, which saw the construction of such major new works as Sta Prassede, built by Pope Paschal I, 817–24. This church stems from a major effort to provide adequate space for the collection of relics of the martyrs, and like Fulda and other Carolingian churches was a spacious church featuring a continuous transept (Plate 21), in this case also richly decorated with mosaics and *opus sectile* pavements.[109] Outside the city itself, the great imperial abbey at Farfa employed many of the same features of annular crypt and continuous transept used both in Rome and in great Carolingian churches as a means for the accommodation of the relic cult. The adoption at Farfa of a western apse, however, relates exclusively to transalpine churches.[110] Evidently architectural ideas moved in both directions.

English ecclesiastical architecture produced large masonry churches from the late seventh century. Some of the early churches had distinctive aisle-less forms, sometimes with chambers called *porticus* flanking

---

[104] See Taylor and Taylor (1965), pp. 297–312 and 516–18 respectively; McClendon (1987), pp. 57–62. [105] See Möbius (1968), pp. 9–22 and 131–48 for discussion and bibliography.

[106] Kreusch (1965); Heitz (1987), pp. 139–44.

[107] Hubert, Porcher and Volbach (1970), pp. 63–4 and figs. 51–4; Conant (1978), pp. 63–4 and figs. 22–3. [108] Jacobsen (1985).

[109] Krautheimer, Corbett and Frankl (1967), pp. 235–62; Krautheimer (1980), pp. 109–42. See, on the pavements, McClendon (1980). [110] McClendon (1987), pp. 54–75.

the nave, as at Canterbury, and sometimes with a monocellular nave leading to a smaller rectangular sanctuary, as in the well-preserved late seventh- or possibly early eighth-century church at Escomb not far from Durham.[111] Such early types continued in use, as at Brixworth (Northamptonshire), dated to the early ninth century.[112] Elsewhere, morphologically distinct churches were produced, as in the basilica with true aisles rather than *porticus* chambers erected at Hexham in the later seventh century by Wilfrid.

To a surprising degree Ireland remained architecturally distinct. Monastic sites ranged from small hermitages of sometimes awesome asceticism, as at Skellig Michael off the western coast,[113] to such large complexes as Clonmacnoise and Armagh. Still relatively little known archaeologically, the larger sites appear generally to have followed the earlier tradition of building within circular enclosures marked by banks or walls. Best known are the sites of Nendrum and Armagh in the north, which had a series of enclosure rings about the major churches and domestic structures at the centre. Multiple churches were a common feature, probably reflecting differences in function rather than deriving from the multi-church monasteries known in England and on the Continent at this period.[114] Only in the eighth century is the first Irish church built of stone mentioned, and it is clearly then unusual, for until the eleventh century most church buildings in Ireland were made in wood. The small dry-stone oratories from western Ireland that may perhaps be dated to this period are in their small scale and rude construction characteristic of hermitages, and must not be taken to represent the achievements of Irish architects in the large and rich centres of the northern and eastern parts of the country. There wooden churches known from literary and historical sources were from the seventh century large and ornate, with decoration in painting and sculpture. The church of St Brigit at Kildare was divided into three main spaces, with a sanctuary containing the altar and tombs of the patron saint as well as of an archbishop, and with separate halls for male and female worshippers.[115]

Spanish architecture followed diverse patterns distinct from those elsewhere in early medieval western Europe. Spanish building traditions, moreover, offer an especially enlightening commentary upon the engagement of architectural design with broader political and social issues of the period. Surviving buildings datable to the Visigothic period include aisled basilicas such as Quintanilla de la Viñas and San Juan de Baños, while others such as San Pedro de la Nave and Santa Comba de Bande have a distinctive

---

[111] Fernie (1983), pp. 54–6.   [112] Fernie (1983), pp. 65–9.
[113] Horn, Marshall and Rourke (1990).   [114] Edwards (1990), pp. 104–21.
[115] Edwards (1990), pp. 121–4, with the text of Cogitosus' description. For that text see also Davis-Weyer (1971), pp. 71–2.

cross-shaped plan difficult to parallel in other earlier or contemporary tradition. Both basilican and central-plan churches sharply segregate the spaces, especially the liturgical chancel area from the nave, dramatic brightly lit spaces alternating with penumbrally dark. The frequent use of horseshoe-shaped arches along the nave arcades and at the entrance to chancel and sanctuary, a feature that was formerly thought to reflect Islamic influence although it demonstrably pre-dates the arrival of Muslims in Spain, contributes to the closing and partitioning of spaces, as seen for example at Quintanilla de las Viñas (Plate 22). Strict separation of clergy and laity was especially featured in early Spanish legislation, and the development of distinctively Spanish liturgical prayers and practices were part and parcel of the same local phenomenon.[116]

International architectural styles are reflected in Spanish monuments of the late eighth and early ninth centuries. The Great Mosque of Córdoba was built *c*. 786 by Abd al-Raḥmān I, founder of the Umayyad state in Spain, closely following in its hypostyle plan the pattern established in earlier Umayyad mosques in Damascus and Jerusalem, while its startling construction of doubled arcades with contrasting voussoirs probably also recalls early Umayyad architecture.[117] At the turn of the ninth century the Asturian kingdom produced at San Julian de los Prados a very large open basilica with spacious continuous transept, a radical departure from the previous Spanish Christian tradition recently interpreted as a deliberate attempt to evoke the great Carolingian churches discussed previously.[118] A different Mozarabic style developed among the Christians living under or fleeing Muslim rule. At San Miguel de Escalada at the beginning of the tenth century, the consistent use of horseshoe arches and arcade across the nave so as to separate it from the chancel (Plate 23) harks back to churches of the Visigothic period, which were arguably evoked with special intensity as a response to persecution of the Christians under Muslim rule during the later ninth century.[119]

SCULPTURE, IVORY CARVING, METALWORK AND TEXTILES

Stone sculpture was a major form of artistic expression throughout western Europe between the seventh and tenth centuries,[120] taking the form of architectural sculpture as in such important Visigothic churches as Quintanilla de las Viñas (Plate 22) and S. Pedro de la Nave, church furnishings such

---

[116] Dodds (1990), pp. 16–26.
[117] Dodds (1990), pp. 94–5; O. Grabar (1973), pp. 130–1.   [118] Dodds (1990), pp. 27–37.
[119] Dodds (1990), pp. 47–70.
[120] See among the important catalogues Fossard, Vieillard-Troiekouroff and Chatel (1978); Cramp (1984); for the Italian series Nees (1985a), pp. 219–26.

as the grand baldacchinos and altars of eighth-century Lombard northern Italy, especially in the reign of Cividale,[121] and free-standing monumental sculpture in northern regions. Large dressed limestone memorial stelai were produced in large numbers in Scandinavia, especially on the island of Gotland, from sub-Roman times. By the eighth century truly monumental stones standing over 4 m high were produced, as for example the Lärbro monument (Plate 24). This and related stones were carved, or perhaps more properly incised, in very low relief, and were probably originally coloured (the black backgrounds that today allow the designs to be seen are modern). Interpretation of the imagery is difficult; whether the depictions of travel, warfare and ritual relate primarily to a mythological or contemporary context remains controversial.[122] Also difficult to assess is the chronological, functional and possible historical relationship to stone carvings elsewhere, notably the Pictish stones of Scotland (Plate 2) and the high crosses of Scotland (Plate 7), northern England and especially Ireland.

Monumental in scale, ranging from under 3 to over 7 m in height, the best known and most elaborate stone crosses of Ireland date only from the early tenth century, but others such as the north cross from the now desolate site at Ahenny (Co. Tipperary) (Plate 25) date from the ninth century at the latest, and probably from as early as the mid-eighth. The Ahenny cross is a monolith set into a separate base, and with a ring that structurally helps support the heavy arms of the cross while conveying a Christian symbolic message derived from earlier Christian iconography. The prominent rounded bosses accord with the complex interlacing ornamental designs on both faces of the cross to suggest the influence of early metal-covered wooden crosses. Although shallow and flat in such early examples as Ahenny, the carving is in true relief, with the patterns and figures standing out against a background chiselled away, and hence quite distinct in workmanship from the Scandinavian or earlier Pictish carvings, which incise the patterns into the stone. From the ninth century Irish crosses are generally dominated by panels of Christian figural iconography carved in high and rounded relief. The function and interpretation of the Irish high crosses is difficult to assess. They seldom if ever had a funereal function, but are strongly linked to monasteries. They certainly identified themselves as sacred Christian presences, often associated with the borders of the monastic enclosure and perhaps endowed with some apotropaic significance,[123] and probably served as the focus of prayers and processions.[124] As is true of their material and style, function probably varied from site to site and may also

[121] See Hubert, Porcher and Volbach (1969) for what remains the most convenient assemblage of monuments.   [122] Anker (1970), pp. 184–92, pl. 90.
[123] Nees (1983a).   [124] See discussion in Edwards (1990), pp. 163–4; Stalley (1990).

have altered over time. The tradition of stone sculpture throughout northern Britain and Ireland may have been stimulated initially by Roman art and early Christian imagery, but developed within the complex and shifting context of a distinctive north Insular cultural milieu also apparent in metalwork and manuscript illumination.[125]

The Pictish stones of northern and eastern Scotland began with a so-called Class I series, incised designs of stereotyped patterns known as Pictish symbols, placed on undressed or roughly shaped stones, that stem from the pre-Christian period. If correctly interpreted as memorial stones in association with graves,[126] they are more analogous to the Gotlandic stones than to high crosses in Ireland. The Class II series continues to use some Pictish symbols, but now worked in high relief on carefully shaped and generally two-sided slabs, and includes elaborate figural iconography, as on the Hilton of Cadboll stone (Plate 2) with its large symbol in the upper square panel and hunting scene in the lower. The abstractly rendered vine border with birds on this stone ultimately reflects the Mediterranean tradition, probably in this case as transmitted through Northumbrian works such as the Ruthwell cross (Plate 7), which employs similar patterns on its side faces. The Pictish Class II stones frequently carry large crosses on at least one side, crosses sometimes as at Aberlemno with rings and interlace ornament evoking the Irish series, but distinct from those monuments in being always relief slabs rather than free-standing crosses fully in the round.[127]

The Ruthwell cross itself (Plate 7), erected and preserved in what is now southwesternmost Scotland but closely linked stylistically and linguistically with the Northumbrian Anglo-Saxon kingdom, is but the best known representative of an imposing mass of stone sculpture and architecture produced in the northern Anglo-Saxon kingdoms, whose complete cataloguing opens many ways for further research.[128] Its elaborate and difficult iconographic programme, which continues to be the focus of controversy and debate, both reflects the monastic spirituality of the Insular monks and responds to the cult of iconic images then so important an issue throughout the Mediterranean world and its hinterlands.[129]

Sculpture on the Continent seems at first sharply different from that seen in Scandinavia and the British Isles, far more likely to be architectural in context and function, flat relief in technique, and less likely to be figural. Stone sculpture appears to have been consistently associated with high

---

[125] Edwards (1990), pp. 161–71; essays in Higgitt (1986).   [126] Thomas (1984).

[127] For a convenient and richly illustrated introduction to the Pictish stones see Ritchie (1989).

[128] Cramp (1984). For a convenient study of the monument in context, with earlier literature, see Neuman de Vegvar (1987), pp. 203–37. For the proceedings of an important recent conference devoted to the Ruthwell cross see Cassidy (1992).

[129] See Ó Carragáin (1986); and Haney (1985).

aristocratic and royal patronage, in Spain (Plate 22) as elsewhere.[130] In the
Lombard duchy of Spoleto, an altar slab of the mid-eighth century from S.
Pietro in Ferentillo bears a long inscription naming Duke Ilderic Dagileopa,
and showing the duke as a praying figure standing beside another man
identified by inscription as the sculptor Ursus.[131] The altar, inscribed with
the names of Dukes Pemmo and Ratchis (duke and then king 744–9) from
San Martino in Cividale, depicts the majestic Christ enthroned and surrounded by angels on the front, and the Adoration of the Magi on one of the
sides, images of authority perhaps of special interest to the patron.
Iconographically linked to works from the Christian northwest and southeast,[132] the workmanship is in a very flat relief, with very awkwardly
proportioned figures. It is then startling to look at the eighth-century
sculpture from the 'Tempietto' of Sta Maria in Valle also in Cividale, which
has a row of naturalistic standing female saints above the door (Plate 26).
The difference between the Ratchis altar and the 'Tempietto' figures may be
related not only to the latter's later date,[133] but also to the different material
employed, stucco rather than stone.[134]

Unfortunately stucco is far more perishable than stone, and its general
disappearance no doubt distorts our picture of large-scale sculpture,
especially in the Frankish kingdom, where it seems to have been very
popular. The virtually complete disappearance of wood-carving from the
entire region save the Scandinavian north, where magnificent architectural
carving in wood survives, especially in the stave-churches of Norway, to
give a hint of the lost achievements in this medium,[135] is no doubt an even
greater and more distorting loss. Chance survivals from early Mediterranean
sites, such as the carved doors and ceiling beams from the sixth-century
church of Justinian at Mount Sinai,[136] support the literary and archaeological
evidence for the importance of wood carving.[137]

Perhaps a preference for carving in wood and moulding in stucco helps to
explain the small amount and modest quality of figural stone carving in the
Frankish heartlands.[138] Architectural sculpture such as capitals continued to

---

[130] Hubert, Porcher and Volbach (1969), pp. 84–7; Thilo (1970).

[131] Hubert, Porcher and Volbach (1969), fig. 278.

[132] For the use of this relief in a major argument for the importance of 'oriental influence' see
      Francovich (1961).

[133] Many dates have been proposed, but this position was argued in great detail in the exhaustive
      study by L'Orange and Torp (1977).   [134] See in general *Stucchi* (1962).

[135] Anker (1970), pp. 201–452.

[136] Forsyth and Weitzmann (1965), pp. 8–10 and pls. XLIII–LVII and LXVI–LXXIX.

[137] See Dodwell (1982), index s. v. 'wood.'

[138] For an overview see Hamann-MacLean (1974). Arguments for a dating into the Carolingian
      period of some important sculptural monuments such as the tomb of Willibrord (Beutler,
      [1978]), though provocative, have not been persuasive.

Plate 1 Oxford, Bodleian Library, cod. Douce 176, ivory cover (photo: Bodleian Library)

Plate 2 Pictish symbol stone, from Hilton of Cadboll (photo: Royal Commission on the Ancient and Historical Monuments of Scotland, Edinburgh)

Plate 3 Vatican, Bibliotecca Apostolica Vaticana, cod. Reg. lat. 124, fol. 4v, Hraban Maur, *De Laudibus S. Crucis*, Emperor Louis the Pious (photo: Biblioteca Apostolica Vaticana)

Plate 4 Aachen, Palace of Charlemagne, model by Leo Hugot (photo: Lawrence Nees)

Plate 5 Hunterston brooch, National Museum of Antiquities of Scotland, Edinburgh (photo: National Museums of Scotland, Edinburgh)

Plate 6 Susanna crystal, British Museum, London (photo: British Museum)

Plate 7 Ruthwell cross, oblique view (photo: Royal Commission on the Ancient and Historical Monuments of Scotland, Edinburgh)

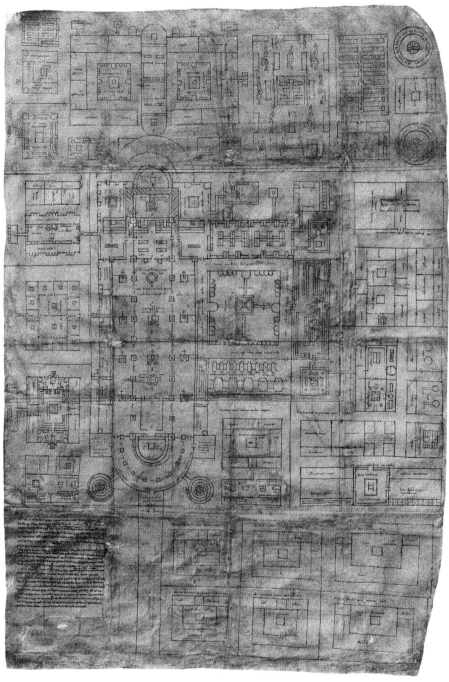

Plate 8 St Gall, Stiftsbibliothek, cod. 1092, Plan of St Gall (photo: Stiftsarchiv St Gallen)

Plate 9 Vatican, Biblioteca Apostolica Vaticana, cod. Pal. lat. 67, fol. 5r, dedication page, Erembertus before St Martin (photo: Biblioteca Apostolica Vaticana)

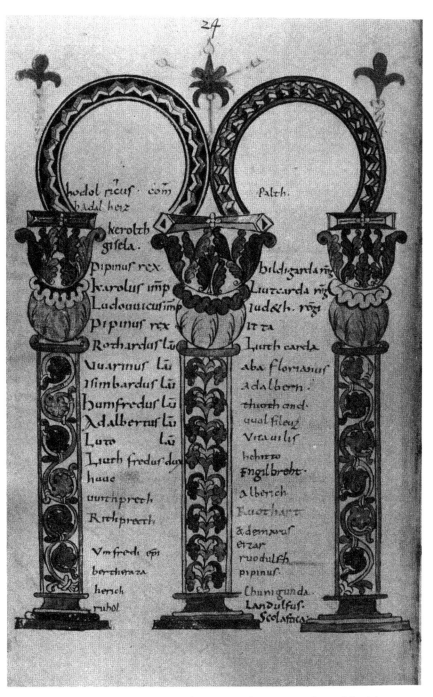

Plate 10 St Gall, Stiftsarchiv, cod. Fab. 1, p. 24, *Liber Viventium* from Pfäfers (photo: Stiftsarchiv St Gallen)

Plate 11 Munich, Schatzkammer der Residenz Prayerbook of Charles the Bald, fols. 38v–39r, Crucifixion and Charles the Bald (photo: Bayerische Verwaltung der staatliche Schlösser Garten und Seen)

Plate 12 Paris, Bibliothèque Nationale, cod. lat. 1, fol. 423r, Vivarian Bible, Presentation of book to Charles the Bald (photo: Bibliothèque Nationale)

Plate 13 Trier, Domschatz, cod. 61, fol. 1v, Christ and Evangelist symbols (photo: Ann Münchow)

Plate 14 Germigny-des-Prés, Oratory of Theodulf, apse mosaic with Ark of the Covenant, (photo: J. Feuille / CNMHS /SPADEM)

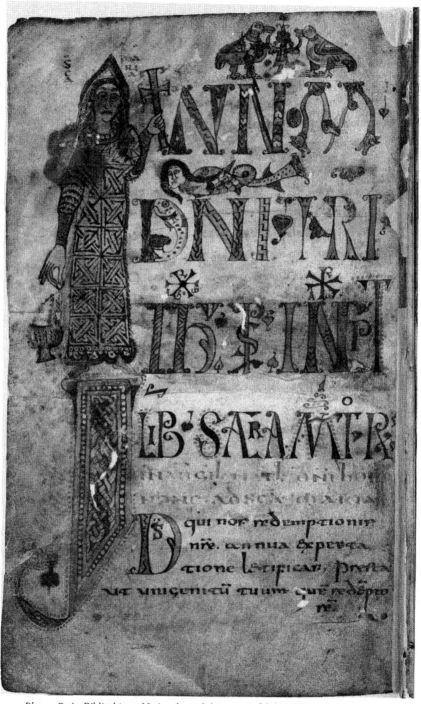

Plate 15 Paris, Bibliothèque Nationale, cod. lat. 12048, fol. lv, Gellone Sacramentary, Virgin Mary (photo: Bibliothèque Nationale)

Plate 16 Paris, Bibliothèque Nationale, cod. lat. 9428, fol. 15v, Drago Sacramentary, Te Igitur (photo: Bibliothèque Nationale)

Plate 17 Paris, New York, Pierpoint Morgan Library, cod. M. 644, fols. 152v–153r, Morgan Beatus, Woman clothed in the Sun, and Dragon (photo: The Pierpoint Morgan Library, New York)

Plate 18 Paris, Bibliothèque Nationale, cod. lat. 4404, fols. IV –2r, Legal collection, Emperor Theodosius with Roman lawyers (photo: Bibliothèque Nationale)

ce eum mchox dif &
orgáno ·
laudate eum mcfm
balif. benefónanrbs;
laudate eum mcim
balif iubilauonif om
nif fpr laudæ dñm ·

SED HE ALXX
ni quid Jnter
PRETIBUS e
di aus EST ·

hnc PSALMUS
PRO PRIE SCRIP
dis DAUID ex
exJRAUUME
dim:

illuf era
inter fratruf
meof ·&adu
lefcencior in
domo patrif mei
pafcebám ouef
patrif mei
anuf meae
fecerunr organú

Plate 19 Amiens, Bibliothèque Municipale, cod. 18, fol. 123v, Corbie Psalter, David and Goliath (photo: Bibliothèque Municipale)

Plate 20 Corvey, interior of western end (photo: Westfälisches Amt für Denkmalpflege)

Plate 21 Rome, Sta Prassede, interior towards aspe (photo: ICCD, Roma, neg. E-112365)

Plate 22 Quintanilla de las Viñas, interior with entrance to chancel (photo: J. D. Dodds / C. A. Gifford)

Plate 23 San Miguel de Escalada, interior (photo: J. D. Dodds/C. A. Gifford)

Plate 24 Lärbro, sculptured stele (Bunge Museum; photo: Lawrence Nees)

Plate 25 Ahenny, North Cross (photo: Catherine Herbert)

Plate 26 Cividale, Sta Maria in Valle ('Tempietto'), entrance wall with stuccoes and wall-paintings (photo: ICCD, Roma, neg. E-115903)

Plate 27 Ivory with Ascension of Virgin and scenes of St Gall, by Tuotilo (St Gall, Stiftsbibliothek, cod. 53; photo: Stiftsbibliothek St Gallen)

Plate 28 Drawing of lost Arch of Einhard (Paris, Bibliothèque Nationale, cod. fr. 10440, fol. 45r; photo: Bibliothèque Nationale)

Plate 29 Milan, S. Ambrogio, altar of Wulvinus, back, detail: images of donor Angilbertus and artist Wolvinus (photo: Lawrence Nees)

Plate 30 Rome, Sta Maria Antiqua, Chapel of Theodotus, (photo: ICCD, Roma, neg. E-51242)

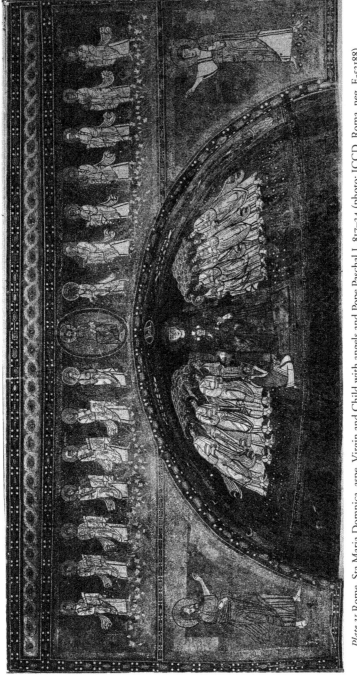

Plate 31 Rome, Sta Maria Domnica, aspe, Virgin and Child with angels and Pope Paschal I, 817–24 (photo: ICCD, Roma, neg. E-52188)

Plate 32 Paris, Bibliothèque Nationale, cod. n. a. lat. 1203, fols. 2v–3r, Godescalc Evangelistary, Evangelist John and Christ (photo: Bibliothèque Nationale)

Plate 33 Vatican, Biblioteca Apostolica Vaticana, cod. Barb. lat. 570, fol. 11v, Barberini (Wigbald) Gospels, Evangelist Matthew (photo: Biblioteca Apostolica Vaticana)

Plate 34 Essen Munsterschatz Gospels, pp. 55–6, Cross with Evangelist symbols, and initial page (photo: Lawrence Nees)

Plate 36 Paris, Bibliothèque Nationale, cod. lat. 12168, fol. 1r, Augustine, *Quaestiones in Heptateuchon*, from Laon (photo: Bibliothèque Nationale)

Plate 35 Paris, Bibliothèque Nationale, cod. lat. 9332, fol. 140r, Medical compendium, Alexander medicus and salvific cross (photo: Bibliothèque Nationale)

be produced in such Carolingian building campaigns as St Denis from the eighth and Lorsch from the ninth century,[139] continuing most probably an unbroken tradition going back through the Merovingian to the late Roman period.[140] Fine slabs used as altar enclosures from such sites as Metz and Schänis (near St Gall) testify to the currency of both ribbon interlace and classicising vegetal ornament into the ninth century.[141] A very fine slab with peacock from the Carolingian royal site of Ingelheim, datable to 773–4, has been used to show the connections of Carolingian sculpture especially with the Italian sculpture of the eighth century,[142] with which it shares fine carving in very flat relief, a tradition distinct from that of free-standing sculptural monuments with fully rounded relief seen in Insular sculpture of this period. However, in general it seems that monumental decoration was, in the Carolingian context, largely limited to painting, while figural sculpture was restricted to small-scale work in ivory and in metal.

Ivory carving was a major art form in the Carolingian period, with nearly two hundred surviving examples.[143] The important Byzantine production does not begin until the tenth century, and then apparently suddenly, at a very high level of craftsmanship and patronage, in a manner analogous to the Carolingian phenomenon.[144] Especially in the light of the fact that new ivory was virtually unobtainable, and many if not most Carolingian ivories were made by re-carving ancient panels,[145] Carolingian ivory producti n clearly represents a highly self-conscious art, largely sponsored by Charlemagne himself and his successors. It is very probably no coincidence that the earliest securely datable Carolingian ivories (*c.* 795) are the panels that originally formed the covers of the Dagulf Psalter, according to the dedicatory poems written inside, intended as a special gift from Charlemagne to Pope Hadrian.[146] Closely associated with these ivories is the Oxford panel with Christ trampling the beasts (Plate 1), which is, I believe, the original cover of a Gospel lectionary written in the first years of the ninth century for Charlemagne's sister Gisela in her nunnery at Chelles.

The Carolingian ivories include groups of carvings that have been connected with the important sees of Rheims and especially Metz, as well as smaller groups stemming from such centres as Trier.[147] Although some

---

[139] See respectively Vieillard-Troiekouroff (1976), and Jacobsen (1985).

[140] In general see James (1977).

[141] Hubert, Porcher and Volbach (1970), pp. 31–32 and fig. 27. See Doberer (1965).

[142] Paeseler (1966).   [143] Goldschmidt (1914); Volbach (1976).

[144] Goldschmidt and Weitzmann (1930–4); Cutler (1994).

[145] Weitzmann (1973), pp. 25–9; in general, Cutler (1985, 1994).

[146] Goldschmidt (1914), nos. 3 and 4; Gaborit-Chopin (1978), p. 45. For the dating see Nees (1985b). For an undated but probably earlier related ivory see Neuman de Vegvar (1990); Webster and Backhouse (1991), no. 141, who still press a claim for English production, provide a colour plate of this important work.   [147] For the latter see Sanderson (1974).

pyxides, combs, reliquary chests and one magnificent liturgical fan were produced in ivory for the luxurious enhancement of the altar,[148] and we have written testimony for the existence of ivory doors at St Denis,[149] the greatest number of ivories were panels that served as book covers. The ivory covers of the Dagulf Psalter stand at the beginning of this class, which also includes a series of ivories decorating the Psalter and the Prayer Book of Charles the Bald that are of superlative richness and technical brilliance, with many lively figures engaged in fervent interaction expressing the narrative action. The links between these ivories and the illustrations in manuscripts such as the Utrecht Psalter are many and sometimes specific, leading Goldschmidt to suppose that the same workshop or workshops produced ivories and illumination. The illustration of liturgical rites as well as scenes from the life of Christ on the covers of the Drogo Sacramentary from mid-ninth-century Metz demonstrate with special clarity both *ad hoc* creation and close linkage to the text.[150] At least in the case of the monk Tuotilo, who at the very end of the ninth or early tenth century carved the ivory covers of a luxurious Gospels in and for his monastery of St Gall, it appears that the monk was not only a very accomplished ivory carver but also a painter and a master musician. His ivories reveal an ability to copy closely earlier Carolingian ornamental ivory panels with inhabited rinceaux available to him at St Gall, while also drawing upon figural sources of disparate kinds for his images of Christ in Majesty, the Assumption of the Virgin, and his patron saint's encounter with a bear (Plate 27).[151]

The craft of ivory carving was connected not only with manuscript illumination but also with metalworking. A number of Carolingian ivories retain evidence of metal inserts and fittings, including extensive use of gold inlay and coloured paste ornaments on the largest complex of Carolingian ivories, the so-called *Cathedra Petri* (Throne of St Peter), in fact the throne of Charles the Bald (frontispiece).[152] This work was probably originally made for Charles the Bald's coronation at Metz in 869, and was decorated with relief ivories showing combat scenes, drawing upon ancient traditions of ruler iconography previously discussed, to which were subsequently added the twelve labours of Hercules.[153]

Bravura carving upon hard and recalcitrant surfaces produced during the Carolingian period a unique series of rock crystals. Several of the smaller examples served as seals, that of Archbishop Radbod of Trier being a

---

[148] See Goldschmidt (1914); for the Flabellum from Tournus, the liturgical fan, see also the excellent illustrations in Gaborit-Chopin (1978), pp. 58–61, pls. 49–52 and no. 51.

[149] Bischoff (1981).

[150] Reynolds (1983); the ivories are also illustrated in Hubert, Porcher and Volbach (1970), figs. 214 and 215.   [151] Duft and Schnyder (1984), pp. 58–75.

[152] Weitzmann (1973); Nees (1991).   [153] Nees (1991), with earlier literature.

characteristic example, and indicative of original inspiration from ancient glyptics preserved to the Carolingian period and still in use, as well as of production in the lower Rhineland. The majority of the crystals have the Crucifixion as their central subject, and were certainly employed in liturgical contexts, such as reliquaries.[154] The largest of the group (Plate 6) is a unique work made for a special occasion. Identified by inscription as having been made at the order of a 'rex Lottarius', possibly Lothar II (d. 869), it tells in eight episodes the apocryphal story of Susanna and the Elders, using the lively figures and emphatic story-telling gestures associated with the style of the Utrecht Psalter to make the story vivid and emotionally involving, and to point a moral lesson for the ruler.[155] Perhaps no other work shows so clearly the manner in which, starting perhaps from an ancient inspiration, early medieval artists developed original and effectively didactic images.

Sculpture in ivory and rock crystal was closely associated with Carolingian Francia during this period, and especially with the Frankish king, but the other major medium for what may be thought of in the context of sculptural art, various kinds of metalworking, was widely employed across western Europe. Widespread archaeological and historical evidence indicates continuity from pre-Christian into Christian art in terms of style, technique, and even centres of production and organisation of work,[156] but continuity went hand in hand with originality on many stylistic and technical levels. It has recently been argued, for example, that cloisonné enamel work was not a technique borrowed from Byzantium, as had long been thought, but very probably an indigenous western invention.[157] Certainly the abundant surviving evidence shows the metalworkers' delight in new ornamental patterns, in combining different techniques such as filigree, repoussé, enamel, set jewels and ivories to achieve effects of vivid colour and pattern. Aesthetic preference is manifestly for brilliance and variety. Metalsmiths, and especially goldsmiths, had in the pre-Christian societies of northern Europe commonly enjoyed high social status. Some may have been itinerant, although the evidence of workshops active over long periods of time rather more strongly argues for marketing over an extensive area, working for different wealthy patrons. High-calibre metalwork travelled easily, and aristocratic new styles spread rapidly, as seen in the eighth-century Hunterston brooch (Plate 5).[158]

By the eighth century the primary focus of luxurious metalwork was the altar. Only from Derrynaflan in Ireland does a complete altar service survive

[154] The only study of the entire group is the unpublished doctoral dissertation by Kornbluth (1986).
[155] See Kornbluth (1992).   [156] Craddock (1989); Roth (1986), pp. 40–79.
[157] Buckton (1988).
[158] Stevenson (1974); Youngs (1989), no. 69, the latter arguing for production by a Celtic smith drawing on Germanic techniques and styles.

from this period, including chalice, paten and stand, and strainer, the objects produced at differing times during the ninth century.[159] Many other liturgical objects were decorated with metalwork, often combined with jewels, enamel work, ivory and other materials. Reliquaries are among the most numerous surviving works, but there were also many large altar and processional crosses, book covers, ewers, ciboria, censers, croziers and elaborate portable altars. Some works appear to have been unique creations demanded by special patrons and circumstances. The grand reliquary given by Charlemagne to St Denis is now known only from drawings and a few fragments, the drawing showing an unparalleled three-storeyed arcaded superstructure rising high above the chest.[160] One of the most original works of the period is the silver base for an altar cross ordered by Einhard in the early ninth century (Plate 28), taking the form of a triumphal arch of Roman type, but thoroughly Christianised through an elaborate pro-gramme including large figures of military saints on the lowest level, the four Evangelists on the middle level along with the Annunciation and Baptism, and at the top Christ enthroned, surrounded by His Apostles.[161] The work clearly relates to the cult of the Cross, a central theological and devotional theme of Carolingian culture about which Einhard himself composed an important treatise, and thereby bespeaks the intimate connec-tion between works of art, their individual patron's interests, and contem-porary issues of broad cultural import.

Only one metalwork-decorated altar survives from this period, although literary evidence tells us that such magnificent works were found in a number of great churches. The fortunate survival, made by Wulvinus at the order of Archbishop Angilbert II (824–59) for the church of S. Ambrogio in Milan, brings together many characteristic elements of early medieval metalwork.[162] The altar consists primarily of gilt repoussé panels, each framed by elaborate enamelled borders. Wulvinus appears on the back of the altar (Plate 29) in a large medallion, offering his work to the local saint, here the great St Ambrose. The aristocratic Frankish episcopal donor appears in an adjacent matching medallion; both donor and artist are rendered on the same scale, and both receive crowns from Ambrose. This self-portrait is perhaps the clearest, if extreme, example of artistic self-consciousness, even self-promotion, of the entire period.[163] The artist is described by name as the maker, and is identified as a *magister*, presumably meaning a secular master

---

[159] Youngs (1989), pp. 130–3; Ryan (1990).

[160] Elbern (1965), p. 140 and fig. 22.   [161] Hauck (1974); Belting (1973).

[162] The clearest concise summary, with helpful iconographic drawings and bibliography, is *Karl der Grosse* (1965), no. 559. See more recently Haseloff (1990), no. 51, with colour reproductions of front and back and of many details.

[163] For colour reproductions of these panels see Hubert, Porcher and Volbach (1970), figs. 220 and 222.

and not a cleric. His name is Germanic, and most scholars have seen him as someone trained north of the Alps, perhaps at Tours or in Charlemagne's court at Aachen, but called to Milan for this grand commission, upon which he may have worked with other artists. The back of the altar is decorated not only with the images of the donor and artist, each beneath a protective archangel, but also with twelve scenes from the life of the patron saint. Each narrow side panel features a large cross adored by deacons and surrounded by saints. On the front is Christ enthroned in Majesty at the centre of another cross, flanked by twelve scenes of His life, scenes including the Crucifixion and Resurrection but especially emphasising miracles.

Monumental bronze casting was also practised during the period, the outstanding example being the enormous bronze doors made for Charlemagne's palace chapel at Aachen, and the bronze railings which run around the second floor of the building's central space. It seems that the workshop producing such varied and spectacular works, which draw upon the abstract and optically complex patterns seen in other metalwork and also in manuscript painting, must have been located in Aachen itself.[164] At least one life-size image of Christ on the Cross was made in metal in the ninth century; the silver original is now known only in the form of a sixteenth-century leather replica, but is described as a papal gift to the Vatican basilica during the ninth century.[165]

The tremendous losses of metalwork pale into insignificance beside the loss of textile work of the period, which has almost entirely vanished. Textiles are not only necessities of life but occasions for artistic display in most cultures, and literary sources confirm the importance of textile work in the early medieval west.[166] Much of that fine textile work seems to have been done by women, both aristocratic women in secular life, for whom weaving and sewing had been since Penelope a primary occupation, and nuns in the monastic life. By nature fragile, cloth has usually survived only in scraps, such as the bits of imported silks used to wrap relics, and even collected in liturgical books. Little has survived burial in the damp conditions of northern and western Europe, an important exception being the fragments from the ninth-century ship-burial at Oseberg in Norway, in which Queen Asa was interred.[167] The fabrics found there included woollen tapestry borders ranging from six to nine inches in breadth, depicting long processions of horses, wagons, men and women, and providing a precious glimpse of the kind of works that must stand behind such famous later textiles as the Bayeux Tapestry. The most significant discovery of recent years is the large collections of textiles from the church at Maaseik in

---

[164] Braunfels (1965).
[165] Elbern (1965), p. 123. The copy is reproduced in Lasko (1972), pl. 18.
[166] Dodwell (1982), pp. 129–69.   [167] Anker (1970), pp. 192–3.

Belgium.[168] Including woven silks and flat embroideries with much laid-work, the earliest examples of what was in the middle ages known as an English technique, *opus anglicanum*,[169] here including gold-wrapped threads, the cloths show such patterns as arcades with inset interlace and floral patterns, and strips of medallions containing birds. Pearls were sewn to the cloth along the arches of one fabric, a detail which is only one of many which closely link the textiles to other arts of the period, and especially to manuscript illumination. The Maaseik fabrics provide direct evidence for the plausible supposition that textiles indeed served as important carriers of artistic ideas.

PAINTING AND BOOK ILLUMINATION

Painting on panels was a significant artistic medium in the period, although few examples survive. In the eastern Mediterranean both portrait and narrative icons were produced in painted form, and eastern images reached the west and influenced painting there, such as the Crucifixion painted on the wall of Sta Maria Antiqua in the Theodotus Chapel (Plate 30). Rome itself produced painted icons on panels, including small portraits of Peter and Paul from the late eighth century now in the Vatican Museum, and the monumental image of the Virgin enthroned between saints presented to Sta Maria in Trastevere by Pope John VII (705–7), who kneels before the throne to receive a blessing.[170] Literary evidence indicates the production of panels with narrative scenes.[171]

Painting on walls generally played a more didactic role than did panels. A notable example of the range and richness of mural decoration of the period is provided by the three major campaigns carried out in Rome during the pontificate of Paschal I (817–24). Sta Maria Domnica received a new apse with a figure of the pope kneeling before a huge enthroned Virgin and Child flanked by clouds of angels, a composition adapted from the earlier Virgin icon of John VII in Sta Maria in Trastevere, but given a more intimate and literally touching character through the new motif of the pope taking the Virgin's foot in his hands (Plate 31).[172] Paschal's other two mosaic programmes seem at first highly conventional in comparison to Sta Maria Domnica, for the apses of both Sta Cecilia in Trastevere and Sta Prassede

---

[168] Budny and Tweddle (1984); Webster and Backhouse (1991), no. 143.

[169] The next earliest examples are a stole and two maniples from the early tenth century, gifts from Queen Ælfflaed to the bishop of Winchester preserved in the tomb of St Cuthbert at Durham; see Battiscombe (1956), pp. 375–432.

[170] See Bertelli (1961); Belting (1990), pp. 131–163, these examples fig. 73 and pl. II.

[171] Davis-Weyer (1971), p. 74; Meyvaert (1979).

[172] Oakeshott (1967), pp. 203–4, figs. 114–20 and colour pl. xx.

(Plate 21) closely follow the precedent of the sixth-century apse of SS. Cosma e Damiano, and they have accordingly been cited as primary evidence of the retrospective character of this art, a feature linking it with the spirit of the Carolingian Renaissance.[173] Sta Prassede, however, was built for a novel reason, namely to house in its crypt over two thousand relics removed from the catacombs. Moreover, the triumphal arch opening from the nave to the transept has an unparalleled composition apparently showing large groups of saints led by angels to the bejewelled heavenly city, in which Christ, the Virgin and the apostles await them.[174]

The mosaic medium is extremely costly, and only a few other surviving examples were produced during this period either in or outside Rome. Of the latter, two stand out: the dome of Charlemagne's palace chapel at Aachen, and the apse of Theodulf's oratory at Germigny. Because the mosaic at Aachen was totally remade in the nineteenth century, little can be said about its style, or about the origin of the workshop that produced it, so most discussion has centred upon its iconography.[175] The basic reference is to the Apocalypse, with the Elders gathered about the throne of God in adoration, representing the chosen people of God, with whom the Franks identified. The emphasis upon the divine throne is linked to the royal Frankish throne in this highly idiosyncratic palace church.[176] It is surprising that such a small foundation as Theodulf's oratory at Germigny should have received any mosaic decoration whatsoever (Plate 14). The choice of the same conspicuously luxurious medium just deployed in Aachen and in Rome[177] links Germigny to those programmes and renders even more forceful the sharp break in its iconography. No earlier apse decoration has as its subject the Ark of the Covenant set within the Temple of Solomon. Evidently the subject appears here illustrating Theodulf's argument in the *Libri Carolini* that the Ark is the only image that can be said to be worthy of veneration, because explicitly authorised by God.[178]

Iconoclasm made Byzantium largely inactive in monumental painting until near the end of the period,[179] so that western Christendom developed

---

[173] See for example Dodwell (1971), pp. 10–14, figs. 1–3, who emphasizes the 'absorption in the past' in those mosaics even while noting that some portions display originality and seem 'quite new'.

[174] Oakeshott (1967), pp. 204–7 and fig. 121. For colour details of the apse mosaic see Grabar and Nordenfalk (1957), pp. 40–3. The church is the subject of the Bryn Mawr College Master's thesis by Judith Freda, from which I have learned much, and which I will hope soon be published.

[175] Schnitzler (1964), rejected by Schrade (1965).

[176] Schnitzler (1964) and Schrade (1966); for a discussion of the controversy concerning the iconography of the Aachen dome in the appropriate royal context see Bullough (1975), pp. 241–6.

[177] Belting (1978). Texts describing the mosaics are available in English translation in Davis-Weyer (1971), pp. 88–92.   [178] Chazelle (1986).   [179] Mathews (1988).

this medium more or less in isolation. Almost nothing survives of mural painting outside Italy and the Frankish territories during this period.[180] Painters working within an Italo-Byzantine tradition continued to be active in Rome, as witnesses the Theodotus Chapel (Plate 30) from the mid-eighth century, only one example of a series of paintings in the church of Sta Maria Antiqua starting in the late sixth century and continuing until the end of the eighth.[181] Whether the tradition is truly continuous in terms of masters and workshops remains a very difficult problem even in regard to Italy, as there is some evidence suggesting an important impact of Frankish art upon the peninsula during the ninth century.[182] Painting styles were clearly diverse, with such late eighth- or early ninth-century wall-paintings as those at Brescia and Castelseprio sharing enough similarities to suggest a direct link with each other, while participating in a lively narrative style.[183]

From the Frankish territories to the north few wall-paintings survive, although literary sources suggest that they were common, including the decoration with many narrative scenes of both the church and the royal hall in the palace at Ingelheim.[184] The Lorsch Gatehouse has architectural paintings in its upper room, and two later ninth-century crypts have extensive mural paintings. At St Germain at Auxerre architectural and decorative paintings accompany lively and expressively painted narrative scenes from the life and passion of St Stephen, including his martydom.[185] Most important of surviving Carolingian mural decorations is the Johanneskirche at Müstair. Here all four walls of a very large hall church dating from the early ninth century were covered with paintings, now in heavily restored condition. The east wall has three niches whose lower sections illustrate saints' lives, and which rise to large apses whose subjects include Christ in Majesty and a huge cross. On the western entry wall above the doorway is an enormous Last Judgement, the earliest preserved example of what becomes a standard feature in later churches,[186] while the lateral walls each have five rows of eight rectangular narrative panels with biblical scenes.[187]

If it is difficult to assess monumental painting because so little survives, at least outside the city of Rome, almost the reverse is true in regard to book

---

[180] Backhouse, Turner and Webster (1984), no. 25. On Spanish works see Grabar and Nordenfalk (1957), pp. 2–68; Dodds (1990), pp. 37–46.

[181] Belting (1987), and in general Belting (1990). For an important earlier campaign see Nordhagen (1968).   [182] Belting (1967).   [183] Leveto (1990), with earlier bibliography.

[184] The texts related to Ingelheim are conveniently edited in Faral (1964), pp. 157–65). Many others are gathered in von Schlosser (1892).

[185] Hubert, Porcher and Volbach (1970), figs. 4–8. For the Trier paintings see Sanderson (1974), esp. 170–2 and figs. 21–5. For colour reproductions of the procession see Grabar and Nordenfalk (1957), pp. 74–5.   [186] Brenk (1966).

[187] Hubert, Porcher and Volbach (1970), figs. 20–3. Cwi (1983), with convenient list of iconographic subjects and drawings showing their placement on the walls.

illustration, of which so much survives, often in wonderful condition, ironically from almost everywhere except Rome.[188] Books are enormously complex physical objects, constructed from parchment that must be manufactured, ordered into gatherings, folded, trimmed and ruled for writing.[189] Books are, of course, first and foremost carriers of texts, texts whose arrangements and contents are essential evidence relating to the images, particularly as far as the relationship between the textual content and the illustration is concerned.[190] Thousands of books, many elaborately decorated with ornament and figural miniatures, were produced in literally dozens of major scriptoria. The most famous books are closely or loosely connected with the royal Carolingian courts and the principal monasteries associated with the kings; the importance of courtly and monastic patronage is seen nowhere so clearly as in the area of book-painting. However, the stupendous quality and well-established renown of the courtly manuscripts, of which the Godescalc Evangelistary (Plate 32) made for Charlemagne *c*. 781–3 is one of the most significant, should not cause us to forget that the great majority even of richly illuminated manuscripts were made not for royal but for ecclesiastical, most often monastic, patrons and purposes. Indeed the most extraordinary feature of book-painting in this period, its emergence as a pre-eminent artistic medium, begins not at the Carolingian court at all but in the monasteries of the Merovingian and especially of the Irish and Anglo-Saxon world from the later seventh century and throughout the eighth.

From at least the second half of the seventh century, books in Francia, Ireland and in the newly Christianised areas of England began to be produced in which the ornamental designs of high-prestige native secular arts, especially metalwork, transform the appearance and status of books. Especially the books of Holy Scripture, above all others the Psalter and Gospels, became venerated objects, on some occasions carried into battle as palladia, associated with tombs and apotropaic magical practices, preserved as relics.[191] By the late seventh century, with the writing and painting of the Book of Durrow at an unknown monastery variously identified as Iona or a site in Ireland or northern England, the fundamentally new idea of a completely decorated book is established, along with the essential cycle of illustrations that would long characterise medieval Gospel Books.[192] The book opens with an image of the Cross, followed by prefatory texts and

[188] Osborne (1990).

[189] Shailor (1991); Bischoff (1989); McKitterick (1989a), pp. 135–64; Ganz, p. 792 above.

[190] Fundamental for this approach remains Weitzmann (1947). See more recently Calkins (1983).

[191] G. Henderson (1987), especially pp. 179–99.

[192] For the manuscript see Alexander (1978), no. 6; G. Henderson (1987), pp. 19–56; and Calkins (1983), pp. 33–63 and pls. 9–25 for the most easily grasped descriptive account of all the decorative elements of the book.

decorated so-called canon tables, tables of concordance originally compiled by Eusebius in the fourth century and preserved in most elaborately decorated Gospel manuscripts thereafter.[193] Each of the four Gospels is preceded by a full-page miniature of the Evangelist, here represented by the Evangelist's symbolic creature alone but more commonly in later manuscripts by the Evangelist and symbol together, as in the portraits of the Godescalc Evangelistary (Plate 32). The Gospel text itself begins with a large initial letter or letters treated as works of art, with ornamental elongation of stem ends, and complex interlace and other patterns filling the letters themselves. Finally, each of the Gospel texts is preceded, and the volume opened and closed, by full pages of ornament, many featuring the cross motif, which have long been inaccurately but conveniently known as carpet pages. On these pages the stunning decorative quality and sheer aesthetic bravura is most purely expressed, and the links with Celtic and Germanic metalworking traditions are most obvious, while ornament is also used to carry sophisticated ideological messages and even protective functions.[194]

The Lindisfarne Gospels[195] and the Book of Kells are only the most famous among the Insular books that during the eighth century continue and develop the decorative ideas and structure announced in the Book of Durrow, adding a far greater range of colours and patterns, and human figures that derive in some instances from contact with Mediterranean traditions. To the established cycle of canon tables, initial pages and Evangelist portraits presented by the Books of Durrow and Lindisfarne, the Book of Kells, variously dated between the second quarter of the eighth century and the early ninth century, introduces episodes from the Gospel narrative, including the Temptation and Arrest of Christ, and a powerfully iconic image of the Virgin and Child enthroned.[196] Great Gospel Books such as these received the most elaborate decoration, but some other text types borrow from their vocabulary. For example, the Book of Cerne, probably produced in central England for Bishop Æthelwald of Lichfield (818–30), draws upon some Gospel texts but is essentially a collection of prayers.

Grotesque ornamental heads constitute only one of several features linking the Book of Cerne with a probably earlier Gospel Book signed by a scribe Wigbald now in the Vatican, cod. Barb. lat. 570, a large and magnificently decorated book from southern England or possibly from an

[193] The fundamental study remains Nordenfalk (1938).   [194] Elbern (1971).

[195] G. Henderson (1987), pp. 99–122; for discussion along with colour reproductions of the major decoration Backhouse (1981).

[196] Alexander (1978), no. 21; G. Henderson (1987), pp. 130–78; for convenient colour reproductions of the major decoration see Henry (1977).

Insular centre across the Channel. However, in its Evangelist portraits the Barberini Gospels follow an altogether different path, eliminating the Evangelist's symbol altogether, and showing a massive figure actually writing the holy words, with penknife in one hand and pen dipping into an inkwell with the other (Plate 33). The Evangelist is set into a landscape whose paradisiac connotations are conveyed by the rich vines at either side, and indeed the conception brings us very close to the kind of work which would have been one of the sources upon which Charlemagne's *famulus* Godescalc drew in making his great Evangelistary in the early 780s (Plate 32). Even some small details of ornament link the manuscripts, showing one manner in which the earliest artist of Charlemagne's court drew upon the Insular heritage in specific details as well as in the more important respect of treating even the pages of text in his book as luxurious images, set against coloured backgrounds and surrounded by elaborate ornamental frames.

It is arguable that the type of decorative structure and, even more important, the attitude towards the decoration of the holy book was transmitted by Insular missionaries to the Continent well before the end of the eighth century.[197] By the second quarter of the eighth century the Trier Domschatz cod. 61 Gospel Book was produced at Echternach (founded 690). In its prefatory miniature of the four symbols of the Evangelists grouped about a cross (Plate 13) it closely reflects the traditions of the Book of Durrow. Already in this case the Insular or Insular-trained scribe Thomas, responsible for this miniature, was working with a Continental, Frankish collaborator, and later books from Echternach such as a mid-eighth-century Psalter in Stuttgart and manuscripts such as a late eighth-century or early ninth-century Gospels from the Essen Treasury (Plate 34) or a little-known collection of monastic homilies now in Cracow show the growing interaction between the different traditions.[198] The style of drawing and iconographic features of the Essen miniature are varied, but the style of interlacing terminals of the cross and the extensive use of red dotting is an Insular feature, as is in one sense the huge initial I on the facing page.

Yet that initial page of the Essen Gospels has its smaller letters formed from the bodies of birds and fish, a characteristic not of Insular art but of the Continent. Since late antiquity, some letters had been enriched with animal and vegetal ornament, and by as early as the sixth century the beasts sometimes took over the letters entirely.[199] This tradition was richly developed in Continental scriptoria of the seventh and eighth and indeed

---

[197] See McKitterick, chapter 25 above, p. 683.

[198] Alexander (1978), no. 28; Webster and Backhouse (1991), no. 128, with colour plates; David (1937).

[199] Fundamental is Nordenfalk (1970), and more accessible are Pächt (1986), pp. 45–82 and Netzer (1994).

well into the ninth century, when, as has recently been shown, this western tradition, transmitted through Latin and Greek scriptoria in Rome, becomes a starting point for middle Byzantine types of ornamental script.[200] Indeed there are other relationships between eastern and western illumination in the period, including the prevalence of large ornamental pages featuring the cross, which occur before, after and even during Iconoclasm.[201] Crosses had featured and would continue to feature prominently in both eastern and western manuscripts from an early period, and the cross is always an essential and potent Christian sign,[202] but there is evidence for its special association with military and spiritual victory during the eighth and ninth centuries.[203]

Cross pages are common in book illumination in the west during the seventh and eighth centuries, occurring frequently in such Frankish examples as an eighth-century compendium of medical texts in Paris, BN lat. 9332 (Plate 35), in which a cross with inscription invoking the Cross along with the blood of Christ as an instrument of salvation is paired with the portrait of the medical author Alexander. Such illumination, drawing upon a Mediterranean ornamental koine of guilloche, knot and acanthus patterns along with bird and fish patterns, was reorganised into a recognisable tradition from the late seventh century, with the major centres of production at foundations such as Luxeuil in Burgundy and Corbie in Picardy.[204] Many of these centres developed distinctive styles of script as well as ornament. Laon produced in the middle of the eighth century a series of books, including not only liturgical books but very elaborately ornamented library volumes such as a manuscript of Augustine's *Quaestiones in Heptateuchon* in whose initial page (Plate 36) Frankish beasts and leaves are combined with Insular interlace and dots, the two traditions seeming almost to go to war with each other in the strange beast eating pen flourishes at the lower left corner. The same page shows three lines of a distinctively Laon conception, in which the letters are solid black but played against complex coloured background, reversing the normal relationship between figure and ground in a manner not enhancing legibility but reflecting scribal play and interest in variety for its own sake.[205]

Manuscripts continued to be decorated in the established Frankish traditions of 'Insular' and 'Merovingian' styles into the ninth century in many centres, examples of which have previously been mentioned (Plates 13, 34, 35 and 36), including works of great aesthetic and creative

---

[200] Osborne (1990).
[201] Nordenfalk (1970), pp. 189–90 and fig. 54. For the liturgical formula see Galavaris (1970), pp. 65–76.   [202] Nees (1980–1).   [203] Bischoff (1963).   [204] McKitterick (1981).
[205] Hubert, Porcher and Volbach (1969), fig. 190; on Laon see *ibid.*, pp. 192–3.

achievement. Royal manuscripts were also produced in this venerable tradition to the end of the century, such as the magnificent Second Bible of Charles the Bald, written probably at St Amand and presented to the king in the 870s. The associated manuscripts are sometimes called Franco-Saxon because of their obvious dependence upon the Insular tradition, but in fact works in this style had been produced for decades in the Frankish territories, at Echternach and in related scriptoria of northern Francia,[206] and this royal manuscript is neither retardataire nor a return to 'barbarian' traditions under the impact of Viking invasions or anything of the sort. Indeed its extensive use of gold leaf relates it to the Carolingian court workshops of the ninth century, and the beautifully clear word *principio* at the bottom of the page is written with some of the most elegant Roman lapidary-style capitals of the period. The book is of a different tradition, but of no lesser quality, than the better-known because more apparently classicising First Bible of Charles the Bald, whose presentation scene (Plate 12) relies upon ultimately Roman iconographic and stylistic formulae.

Production of luxurious illuminated books for, and possibly at, the Frankish court is first attested by the Godescalc Evangelistary of 781–83 (Plate 32). Although some scholars believe that a 'court school' produced a continuous series of books for the three decades from the Godescalc book to Charlemagne's death in 814, books of which ten or so survive, including the extraordinary luxurious Gospel Books from Soissons, Trier and Lorsch among others,[207] production was probably sporadic, guided by specific circumstances, and concentrated in the last decade of the eighth century following the establishment of Aachen as a court centre in 794.[208] A second group of manuscripts, exhibiting what some have termed a 'Hellenistic' manner with active and loosely painted figures set into spacious landscapes, may have been associated with the court of Charlemagne or of Louis the Pious, and in some aspects related to the episcopal scriptoria of Rheims.[209] It is indeed difficult, and has long been a matter of controversy whether books written for or presented as gifts by Frankish kings after Charlemagne, such as Louis the Pious[210] or Lothar I,[211] were written at the court itself or, as it were, subcontracted through monasteries, as certainly happened in some cases.[212] Most problematic is Charles the Bald; clearly a large group of magnificent books was written for him, including his Prayer Book (Plate 11)

---

[206] Nordenfalk (1931); Euw (1990).
[207] Mütherich (1965), conveniently summarized in Mütherich and Gaehde (1976).
[208] See Nees (1986; 1985b).   [209] Braunfels (1968), pp. 137–50; Euw (1990), no. 8, pp. 62–5.
[210] Mütherich (1990).   [211] Koehler and Mütherich (1971).
[212] See Contreni, p. 711 above.

and the great *Codex Aureus* from St Emmeram,[213] but no one has yet established where the scribes and artists were working, or how they were organised.[214]

There is no doubt that the great books associated with the Frankish kings exerted a powerful influence on some monastic scriptoria. Tours and Rheims both produced illuminated books for royal patrons in the luxurious styles associated with the court, whether or not the books were intended for court-related functions or royal gifts. Tours was especially prolific, producing many elaborately decorated Gospel Books and even full Bibles annually during the period of its greatest flourishing in the second quarter of the ninth century.[215] Rheims probably had not a single scriptorium but several associated scriptoria, produced books in the time of Ebbo and also of Hincmar,[216] and also developed a series of manuscripts illustrated with pen drawings of great expressive vivacity, including the Utrecht Psalter, a style that had enormous impact not only upon contemporary but upon later illuminated manuscripts, and also appealed to workers in ivory and metal.[217] Fulda produced Gospel Books closely related to those from Charlemagne's court, while at the same time producing luxurious copies of the work of its own abbot, Hraban Maur's *De Laudibus Sanctae Crucis*, all of which included the image of Emperor Louis the Pious, to whom the work was dedicated (Plate 3), along with other acrostic figure-poems, mostly devoted to and illustrating the cult of the Cross. Fulda possibly initiated the series of extensively, if less richly, illustrated copies of Hraban's widely read encyclopaedic work, *De Universo*.[218] Other scriptoria followed or developed their own traditions of decoration. St Gall, for example, produced at the end of the ninth century such different and highly original works as the Golden Psalter, St Gall Stiftsbibliothek cod. 22. That book's programme of miniatures draws upon a wide variety of sources, some reminiscent of earlier 'court' products. Yet the Golden Psalter and other Carolingian books must be understood not just as results of their sources but of the particular functions they were intended to serve at the time of their making.[219] The rich complexity of these works brought a wide range of aesthetic and intellectual challenges and rewards to their early medieval audiences, and can still do so today.

[213] Calkins (1983), pp. 119–45.
[214] Koehler and Mütherich (1971).
[215] Koehler (1930–3); Kessler (1977); Calkins (1983), pp. 93–118.
[216] Rome, Abbazia di S. Paolo fuori le mura; see Mütherich and Gaehde (1976), no. XIX, pls. 42–5.
[217] Braunfels (1968), pp. 158–79, figs. 84–115.
[218] Mütherich (1980). On the illustrations of *De Universo* see Le Berrurier (1978).
[219] Eggenberger (1987).

CONCLUSION

Rosamond McKitterick

IN all the chapters in this volume, far more has been documented than mere change and adjustment. It is not for nothing that recent studies have invoked phrases such as the 'formation of Europe' in relation to the early middle ages and in particular to the two centuries between 700 and 900, the period examined in such detail in this book. Since the planning got under way in the late 1950s for the splendid Council of Europe exhibition on Charlemagne, mounted at Aachen in 1965, the Carolingian ruler has been the symbol, rightly or wrongly, of European unity and the common cultural heritage of Europe. The Carolingian period and the role of Frankish political expansion and cultural imperialism have taken their place in the historiography of most European countries as an essential phase in those countries' development. As is clear from the relevant chapters above, some areas, such as Ireland, Scotland, Wales, Bulgaria or Scandinavia, were outside the direct sphere of influence of the Franks, yet cannot be said to be totally unaffected by events within the Frankish world. Peripheral regions, at the *fines imperii*, were affected in one way or another. Not one region of the area we now think of as Europe was so self-contained as to remain entirely untouched by events in the Carolingian heartlands, even among those for whom the benefits of Carolingian rule may not have been either welcome or obvious. To this extent, therefore, the Frankish dominance of the historical evidence is not entirely unaccountable. It is arguable, however, that it was not so much the political successes and failures of the Franks, or those of their allies and supporters or opponents and enemies, which impinged most on the regions encompassed in this book and for which they and this period as a whole need to be remembered. Rather it is their political ideologies, methods of ruling, social organisation, economic innovations, religious zeal and intellectual and cultural traditions that have left their lasting legacy.

The principles embodied in Frankish kingship and royal administrative methods had rested on a relatively influential and homogeneous network of

845

public institutions, inherited, ultimately, from the Roman empire. In many other respects, indeed, the Roman roots of early medieval public life are readily discernible, not least in the resort to the written word for records and in legal transactions. The unified currency system of the Carolingians, in which the Carolingian *denarius* was used throughout western Europe, became increasingly fragmented as the kings lost direct control over the various provinces. On a smaller scale and especially in England, however, the trend towards strong central control of the currency was maintained. Trade on a local and inter-regional level, based on the agricultural, craft and industrial products of the great estates, and patterns of estate management with the manorial system as the peak of a developing economy, were the beginnings of the organisation that underpinned the later development of towns and merchants. Although a society dominated by and organised round the nobility, it was an agricultural society with the beginnings of social and functional differentiation, coherent local hierarchies, a considerable degree of social mobility, flexibility and informality, and characterised by personal associations of great, if overlapping, variety which formed an elaborate network of mutual obligation. As Wickham commented, 'brute force remained an entirely normal element of social interaction', but there was also a strong sense of coherence and identity within settlements and a considerable degree of social and economic co-operation among the inhabitants. Within the public life of the areas ruled by the Franks, office holding, the provision of justice, the accretion of wealth and land and participation in government led to the successful integration of the aristocracy within the administrative structures of the kingdoms as well as laying the foundations for new political constellations of power, in the old moulds, in both the eastern and the western kingdoms. The Frankish exercise of power, like that of other rulers of the peripheral regions in the early middle ages, was one that depended above all on loyalty. This entailed the agreement to carry out orders without which government would have been inconceivable, and the bonds of mutual obligation and dependence existing between different individuals and groups. Such loyalty had its ritual expression in attendance at the assemblies convened by the king in which both lay and ecclesiastical magnates joined. At every level of society, moreover, women can be observed in influential roles within the royal household, the family, on the great estates, within communities and in the church. It is for this reason that, rather than allotting women a separate section, they were integrated into most of the chapters in this book. They manifestly did not experience a decline in their position in the Carolingian period as is sometimes supposed.

The reality underlying the order imposed or implied by so many of our sources, and their often symbolic representation of the present, most notably in 'court' historiography, was anything but tidy. Throughout our period, despite the efforts to maintain strong centralised government, there was tension between central and local powers as well as between centre and peripheries. The manifestation and exertion of power in the secular world that the chapters above have documented is also to be observed in the control, power and influence exerted by the church over, and over the church by, secular magnates and rulers. The identification of the ideals of rulership with those of a Christian ruler are of paramount importance. Further, the impact of the powerful on both the secular and inner worlds of the church and its monasteries led to tensions not always happily resolved and which were to re-emerge frequently in the years that followed.

Yet the church also exerted a power of prayer. This too was fully acknowledged and exploited by the laity, for they invested in this power to an extraordinary degree. We thus see not just ecclesiastical intrusion into secular life but also the reception of religious norms in every aspect of quotidian lay life. Political power was linked with spiritual and religious power: reform and expansion went hand in hand. Political leaders encouraged the reform of a church which was directed at the moral welfare of all their subjects, and thereby widened the brief for the state's intervention in the life of its subjects.

In canon law and liturgy, as well as in the internal and external structures of the church, the developments and adjustments of the eighth and ninth centuries provided the bases for the subsequent development of the western church in its various regions. We observe the appropriation of the arts to a Christian education. Learning furnished part of the equipment of a soldier of Christ; it was linked with the spiritual health of society, and thus its material prosperity. Rulers learnt to take an active interest in events to make their own distinctive contributions for the promotion of learning and education. The Carolingians, their contemporaries and their successors all valued and supported Christian learning and ecclesiastical reform. Contreni and Ganz have stressed, moreover, how Carolingian books and texts bridged the centuries between late antiquity and the scholarly world of the tenth and eleventh centuries, and how, without the Carolingians, neither Latin script nor Latin texts would have secured the continuities that this volume affirms. The enduring achievement of ninth-century scholars was to provide a meaningful rationale for rigorous and sophisticated study and research, with the arts sacralised as paths to higher learning.

Carolingian learning, in all its variety and internal dissonances, was nevertheless at the heart of the intellectual and cultural legacy of the Carolingians to Europe as a whole. By the end of the ninth century, moreover, fundamental attitudes towards art had been established in the Latin, Greek and Islamic worlds. In book-painting, sculpture, the decorative arts and architecture, forms closely related to and expressive of their religion as well as buildings characterising their religious institutions were defined. The role of the pictorial arts in religious practice in particular was established. It became accepted that art could embellish a holy place or object. In all the promotion of art, architecture and learning the ruler, and the personal patronage of other like-minded individuals, played a crucial role.

It was Latin and Christian civilisation above all which provided the common links between Ireland and Anglo-Saxon England, Francia, northern Spain and Lombardy, Carinthia, Rome, Bulgaria and Scandinavia and elsewhere. Individuals moved throughout this world. Many, as we have seen with the Irish and English missionaries in Germany, the Irish, English, Lombard, Spanish, Greek and Italian scholars at the Frankish court, the Franks who established themselves in Italy and the Greeks who settled in the Exarchate of Ravenna, were able to uproot themselves. They made a life for themselves elsewhere in a way that questions the appropriateness of national boundaries in our assessment of the coherence of the early medieval world.

There is no doubt that the foundation for the wealth and variety of European civilisation was laid in these centuries, and naturally enough, in the centuries before 700, as the preceding volume to this one makes clear. Of what artificially created period of history can this not be said? Nevertheless, it remains the case that the years between 700 and 900, despite the varying fortunes of political conquest and territorial aggrandisement, were years of remarkably accelerated cultural and political formation, when ideologies and institutions were determined, social structures coalesced, and religious, intellectual and cultural traditions were established. The remaining volumes in this series will demonstrate the degree to which they endured in the succeeding centuries in medieval Europe.

APPENDIX:
GENEALOGICAL TABLES

In the tables, rulers are indicated in italics.

Table 1 ANGLO-SAXON RULERS, *c*.700–*c*.900

For reference: E.B. Fryde, D.E. Greenway, S. Poole and I. Roy (eds.) *Handbook of British Chronology*, 3rd edn, London 1986. Ancestors of eighth- and ninth-century kings are included where relevant.

1 NORTHUMBRIA (Bernicia + Deira)
Rulers of either Bernicia or Deira only are not indicated

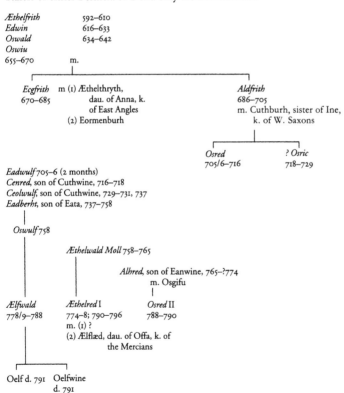

Æthelfrith   592–610
Edwin   616–633
Oswald   634–642
Oswiu
655–670   m.

Ecgfrith   m (1) Æthelthryth,   *Aldfrith*
670–685   dau. of Anna, k.   686–705
                   of East Angles   m. Cuthburh, sister of Ine,
                   (2) Eormenburh   k. of W. Saxons

                                Osred   *? Osric*
                                705/6–716   718–729

Eadwulf 705–6 (2 months)
Cenred, son of Cuthwine, 716–718
Ceolwulf, son of Cuthwine, 729–731, 737
Eadberht, son of Eata, 737–758

Oswulf 758

                Æthelwald Moll 758–765

                        Alhred, son of Eanwine, 765–?774
                                m. Osgifu

Ælfwald   *Æthelred* I   *Osred* II
778/9–788   774–8; 790–796   788–790
               m. (1) ?
               (2) Ælflæd, dau. of Offa, k. of
                       the Mercians

Oelf d. 791   Oelfwine
              d. 791

Osbald 796 for 27 days

Eardwulf 796–806; ? restored ?806
        through intervention of Charlemagne and Pope Leo III

| *Ælfwald* 806/8–808/10

Eanred 808/10–840/1
|
Æthelred II 840/1/844–?848

Rædwulf 844

Osberht 848/9/50–862/3, 867

Ælle 862/3 or 867

II   BERNICIA after 867

Ecgberht I 867–872; d. 873

Ricsige 873–876

Ecgberht II 876–?878

Eadwulf ?878–913

| *Aldred*   Uhtred
913–? after 927

III   SCANDINAVIAN KINGDOM OF YORK after 867

Halfdan I d. 873

Guthfrith I 883– 895

Sigfrid 895

Knútr ? c. 895

Æthelwald c. 899/900–?903

Halfdan II ?902–910

IV SOUTH SAXONS

Ælle ?477– after 491
Æthelwalh before 674–680/5
Berhthun ⎱
Andhun ⎰
Nothelm [Nunna] ?*c.* 692–*c.* 710
Watt ?692
Æthelstan c. 714
Æthelberht c. 744–733 x 754
Osmund 762/4 ?772
?Oswald, dux c. 772
Osloc, dux c. 772
Ealdwulf, rex, dux ?772 x 787–791
Ælhwald, rex c. 765

V EAST ANGLES

Aldwulf 663/4–713
|
Ælfwald 713–749
Hun, Beonna and Alberht 749
Æthelberht ?–794
Eadwald c. 796–800
?Æthelstan c. 825
?Æthelweard c. 850
Edmund 855–869
Guthrum 878–889/90

East Anglia conquered by King Edward of Wessex, 917

VI HWICCE

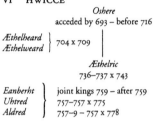

Oshere
acceded by 693 – before 716

Æthelheard ⎱ 704 x 709
Æthelweard ⎰

Æthelric
736–737 x 743

Eanberht ⎱ joint kings 759 – after 759
Uhtred ⎭ 757–757 x 775
Aldred ⎰ 757–9 – 757 x 778

Æthelmund ealdorman 793 x 796–802

VII EAST SAXONS

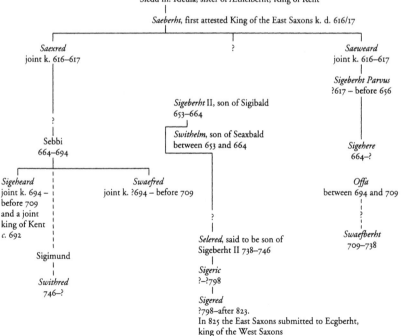

Sledd m. Ricula, sister of Æthelberht, King of Kent

Saeberht, first attested King of the East Saxons k. d. 616/17

Saexred
joint k. 616–617

?

Saeweard
joint k. 616–617

Sigeberht Parvus
?617 – before 656

Sigeberht II, son of Sigibald
653–664

?

Sebbi
664–694

Swithelm, son of Seaxbald
between 653 and 664

Sigehere
664–?

Sigeheard
joint k. 694 –
before 709
and a joint
king of Kent
c. 692

Swaefred
joint k. ?694 – before 709

Offa
between 694 and 709

Sigimund

?

Selered, said to be son of
Sigeberht II 738–746

?

Swaefberht
709–738

Swithred
746–?

Sigeric
?–?798

Sigered
?798–after 823.
In 825 the East Saxons submitted to Ecgberht,
king of the West Saxons

VIII   KENT

In the ninth century Kent, Sussex and Essex normally formed an apanage for the heir to the West Saxon throne

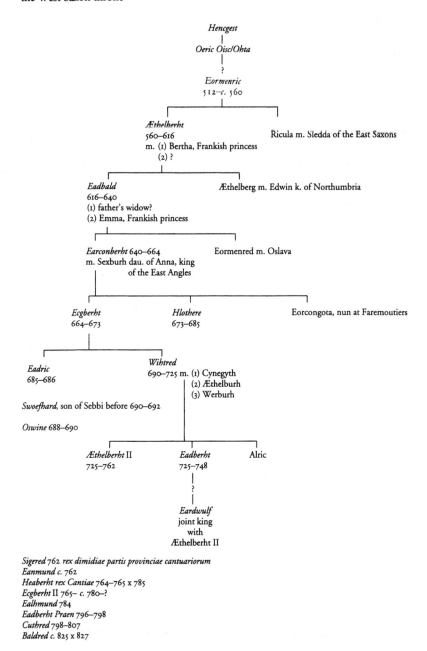

Sigered 762 *rex dimidiae partis provinciae cantuariorum*
Eanmund c. 762
Heaberht rex Cantiae 764–765 x 785
Ecgberht II 765– c. 780–?
Ealhmund 784
Eadberht Praen 796–798
Cuthred 798–807
Baldred c. 825 x 827

IX   MERCIA

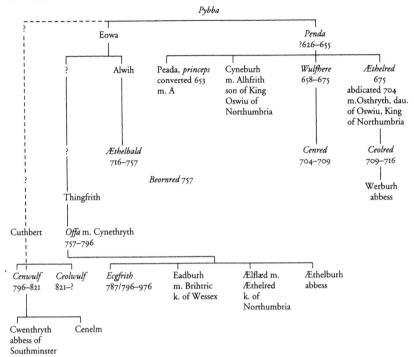

Beornwulf 823–825

Ludeca 825

Wiglaf 827–840 m. Cynethryth

Berhtwulf 840–?852

Burgred ?852 m. Æthelswith, dau. of
                    Æthelwulf, King of
                    W. Saxons, buried at
                    Pavia *en route* to Rome

Ceolwulf II puppet king, 873/4–?
Æthelred II ?ealdorman
?879–911   m. *Æthelflæd*, dau. of Alfred, King of Wessex
                    Queen 911–918

            Ælfwynn, Queen 918–?

Thereafter Mercia was ruled directly by the Kings of Wessex

Genealogical table of the kings of Wessex.

Cerdic 519–534
Creoda
Cynric 534–560

Ceawlin 560–591
Cuthwine/Cutha 560–591
Ceolwulf
Cuthwulf

Cutha
Ceol 591–597
Ceolwulf 597–611

Cynegils* 611–642
Cenwealh 642–645
m. (1) sister of Penda king of Mercians
(2) *Seaxburh* Queen 672–674

Centwine 676–685
m. sister-in-law of Ecgfrith k. of Northumbria

Bugge, correspondent of Boniface

daughter
m. Oswald. k. of Northumbria

Cenberht
Coelwald
Cenred

Cædwalla 685–688
Ascwine 674–6

Ine 688–726
m. Æthelburh

Ingild
son/dau.
g'son/g'dau.
Ealhmund

Æthelheard 'of Cerdic's stock' 726–740
Cuthred 740–756
Sigeberht 756–?757
Cynewulf 757–786
Brihtric 786–802
m. Eadburh, dau. of Offa of Mercia

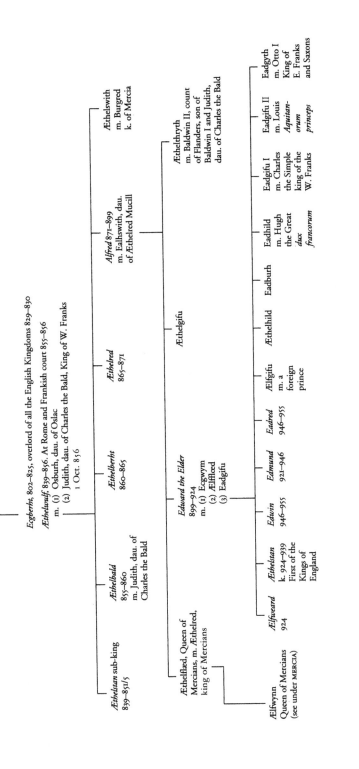

Egberht, 802–825, overlord of all the English Kingdoms 829–830

Æthelwulf 839–856. At Rome and Frankish court 855–856
m. (1) Osburh, dau. of Oslac
(2) Judith, dau. of Charles the Bald, King of W. Franks
1 Oct. 856

Æthelstan sub-king 839–851/5

Æthelbald 855–860 m. Judith, dau. of Charles the Bald

Æthelberht 860–865

Æthelred 865–871

Alfred 871–899 m. Ealhswith, dau. of Æthelred Mucill

Æthelswith m. Burgred k. of Mercia

Æthelflæd, Queen of Mercians, m. Æthelred, king of Mercians

Edward the Elder 899–924 m. (1) Ecgwyn (2) Ælfflæd (3) Eadgifu

Æthelgifu

Æthelthryth m. Baldwin II, count of Flanders, son of Baldwin I and Judith, dau. of Charles the Bald

Ælfwynn Queen of Mercians (see under MERCIA)

Ælfweard 924

Æthelstan k. 924–939 First of the Kings of England

Edwin 946–955

Edmund 921–946

Eadred 946–955

Ælfgifu m. a foreign prince

Æthelhild

Eadburh

Eadhild m. Hugh the Great dux francorum

Eadgifu I m. Charles the Simple king of the W. Franks

Eadgifu II m. Louis Aquitanorum princeps

Eadgyth m. Otto I King of E. Franks and Saxons

* Cynegils was either the son of Cuthwine/Cutha son of Ceawlin or the son of Ceol son of Cutha, Cynric's son.

Table 2 THE LAST MEROVINGIANS

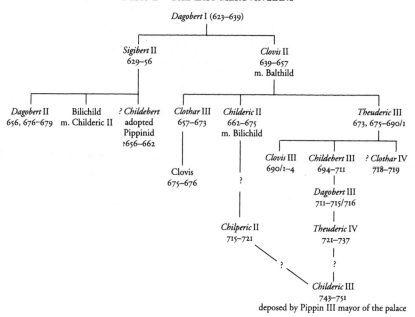

Table 3 THE ARNULFINGS

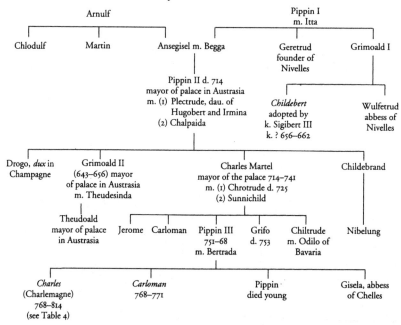

Table 4 PIPPIN III AND CHARLEMAGNE

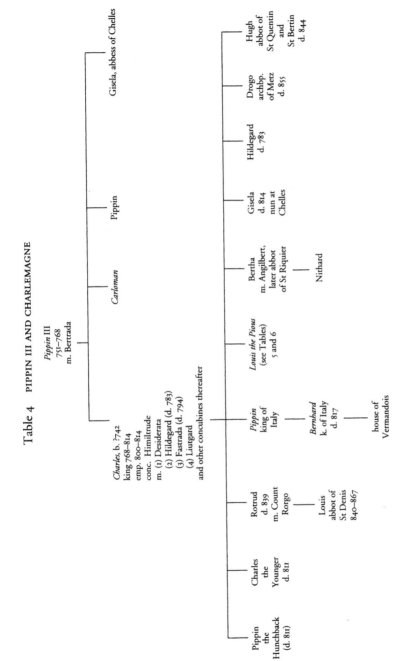

Table 5   THE SONS OF LOUIS THE PIOUS (1): THE DESCENDANTS OF GISELA AND CHARLES THE BALD,

CHILDREN OF LOUIS THE PIOUS AND JUDITH

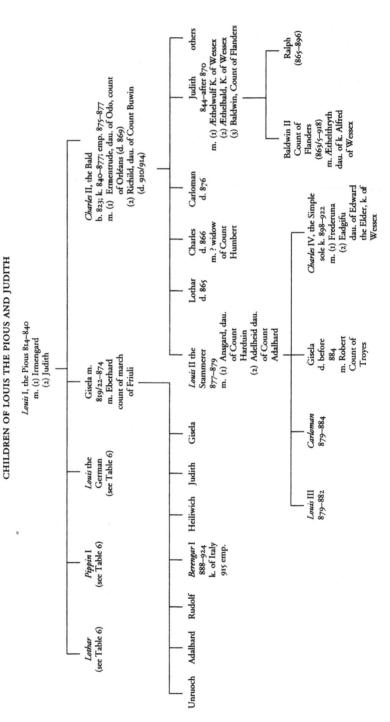

Table 6   THE SONS OF LOUIS THE PIOUS (2): THE DESCENDANTS OF LOTHAR, PIPPIN I AND LOTHAR, CHILDREN OF LOUIS AND IRMENGARD

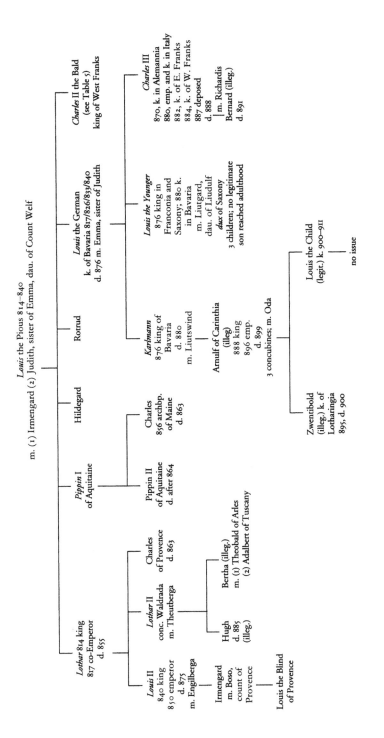

Table 7 SCANDINAVIAN RULERS

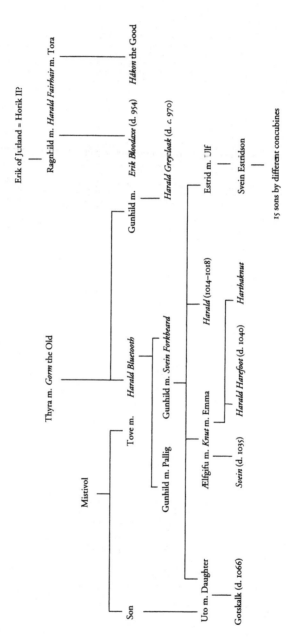

Table 8   RULERS IN THE BALKANS, *c.* 700 – *c.* 900

Many of the dates and some of the names are debatable. This list is therefore provisional.

I   BULGARS

Teletz *c.* 760–763
Sabinos 763
Umar *c.* 765
Paganos *c.* 765–(?) *c.* 770
Telerig *c.* 770–776
Kardam 776–*c.* 802
Krum *c.* 802–814
Omurtag 815–831
Malamir 831–836
Presian 836–852
Boris I 852–889, 893
Vladimir 889–893
Symeon 893–927

II   CROATS
No certainty before the middle of the ninth century

Trpimir I, *c.* 845–864
Zdeslav, 864, 876–879
Domagoj, 864–876
?, son of Domagoj, 876
Branimir, 879–92
Mutimir, 892–910

III   SERBS

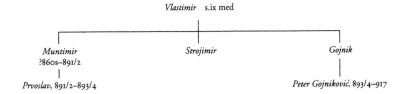

Vlastimir   s.ix med

Muntimir
?860s–891/2

Strojimir

Gojnik

Prvoslav, 891/2–893/4

Peter Gojniković, 893/4–917

Table 9   RULERS OF SPAIN, *c.* 700 – *c.* 900

I   VISIGOTHS

Erwig k. 680–687
Egica k. 687–70; son-in-law of Erwig and Kinsma of Wamba; k. (672–680)
Witiza k. 701–708/9

?*Achila*, son of Witiza; k. 709–10
Roderick, duke of Baetilia, k. 710–713, last Visigothic King of Spain
Agila II 710/711–713
Ardo 713–720

II   ARAB GOVERNORS and AMIRS OF CÓRDOBA

Mūsā ibn Nuṣayr	711–713/14
'Abd al- 'Aziz ibn Mūsā	713/14–715/16
Ayub ibn Ḥabīb al Lakhmi	6 months, 716–early 717
Al-Horr ibn 'Abd al-Raḥmān	
ibn 'Uthman al-Thakifi	Jul/Aug 717–April/May 718
Al-Samh ibn Malik al-Khaulani	April/May 718–May 721
'Abd al-Raḥmān ibn 'Abd-Allāh	
al-Ghafeki	May–Aug 721
Anbasah ibn Sohaym al-Kalbi	Aug 721–Dec 725/Jan 726
Odhrah ibn 'Abd-Allah	
al-Fihri	Jan–Aug (?) 726
Yahya ibn Sallamah al-Kalbi	late 726–Nov/Dec 727
'Uthman ibn Abi Nasah	
al-Khathami	Dec 727–June/July 728
Hodjefah ibn al-Ahwan al-	
Kaysi	June/July 728–April 729
Al-Haythan ibn Ubeyd	
al-Kelabi	April 729–March 731
Muḥammed ibn 'Abd-Allāh	
al-Ashjai	March–May 731
'Abd al-Raḥmān ibn 'Abd-Allāh	
al-Ghafeki	(again) May 731–Oct 732
'Abd al-Mālik ibn Kattan	
al-Fihrī	Oct 732–Oct/Nov 734
Ukbah ibn al-Hejaji	
al-Saluli	Oct/Nov 734–739
'Abd al-Mālik ibn Kattan	(in revolt) 739–Sept/Oct 741
Balj ibn Bashir	Sept/Oct 741–Sept 742
Tha'labah ibn Sallamah	
al-Amali	Sept 742–May 743
Abu al-Khattar Husam ibn	
Dhirar al-Khalbi	May 743–April 745
Thuabah ibn Yezid	April 745–746/7

III   UMAYYAD AMIRS OF CÓRDOBA

'Abd al-Raḥmān I	756–788
Hishām I	788–796
Al-Hakem I	796–822
'Abd al-Raḥmān II	822–852
Mohammed I	852–886
Al-Mundhir	886–888
'Abd-Allāh	888–912
'Abd al-Raḥmān III	912–929

Table 10   RULERS OF THE CHRISTIAN KINGDOMS OF NORTHERN SPAIN *c.* 700 – *c.* 900

I   KINGS OF THE ASTURIAS

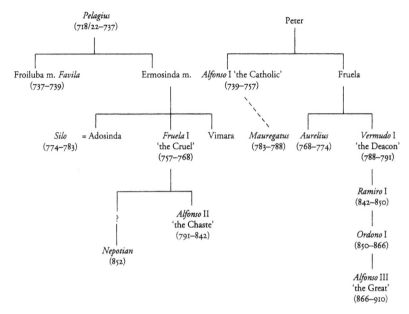

II   KINGS OF LEON

Garcia 910–914
Ordono II 914–924
Fruela II 924–925

III   KINGS OF PAMPLONA

Enneco (Iñigo) Arista early ninth century–852(?)
García Iníguez 850s/860s
García Jiménez (?)
Fortun Garcés c. 882–905

IV   COUNTS OF BARCELONA

Bera, 801–820
Bernard 'of Septimania', by 827–829, 835–844
Berenguer, *c.* 830–835
Sunifred I, 844–848
William, son of Bernard, by seizure, 848–849/50
Aleran, 848–852
Odalric, 852–*c.* 858
Humfrid, *c.* 858–864
Bernard 'of Gothia', 865–878
Wifred I, 878–897/8
Wifred II Borrell, 897/8–911/12
Sufier, 911/12–954

Table II   RULERS IN ITALY, *c.* 700 − *c.* 900

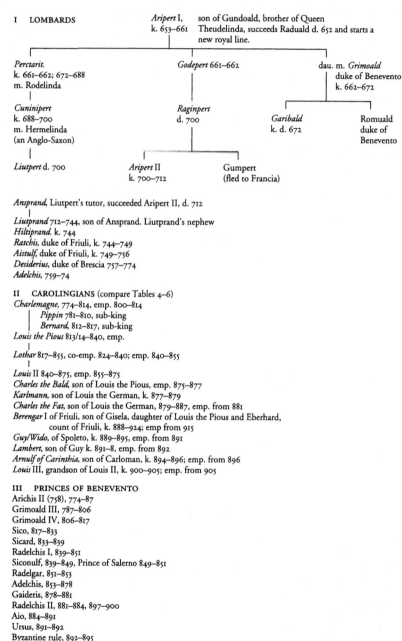

I   LOMBARDS

Aripert I, k. 653–661   son of Gundoald, brother of Queen Theudelinda, succeeds Raduald d. 652 and starts a new royal line.

Perctarit. k. 661–662; 672–688 m. Rodelinda

Godepert 661–662

dau. m. *Grimoald* duke of Benevento k. 662–672

Cuninipert k. 688–700 m. Hermelinda (an Anglo-Saxon)

Raginpert d. 700

Garibald k. d. 672

Romuald duke of Benevento

Liutpert d. 700

Aripert II k. 700–712

Gumpert (fled to Francia)

Ansprand, Liutpert's tutor, succeeded Aripert II, d. 712

Liutprand 712–744, son of Ansprand. Liutprand's nephew
Hiltiprand. k. 744
Ratchis, duke of Friuli, k. 744–749
Aistulf, duke of Friuli, k. 749–756
Desiderius, duke of Brescia 757–774
Adelchis, 759–74

II   CAROLINGIANS (compare Tables 4–6)
Charlemagne, 774–814, emp. 800–814
    Pippin 781–810, sub-king
    Bernard, 812–817, sub-king
Louis the Pious 813/14–840, emp.

Lothar 817–855, co-emp. 824–840; emp. 840–855

Louis II 840–875, emp. 855–875
Charles the Bald, son of Louis the Pious, emp. 875–877
Karlmann, son of Louis the German, k. 877–879
Charles the Fat, son of Louis the German, 879–887, emp. from 881
Berengar I of Friuli, son of Gisela, daughter of Louis the Pious and Eberhard,
     count of Friuli, k. 888–924; emp from 915
Guy/Wido, of Spoleto, k. 889–895, emp. from 891
Lambert, son of Guy k. 891–8, emp. from 892
Arnulf of Carinthia, son of Carloman, k. 894–896; emp. from 896
Louis III, grandson of Louis II, k. 900–905; emp. from 905

III   PRINCES OF BENEVENTO
Arichis II (758), 774–87
Grimoald III, 787–806
Grimoald IV, 806–817
Sico, 817–833
Sicard, 833–839
Radelchis I, 839–851
Siconulf, 839–849, Prince of Salerno 849–851
Radelgar, 851–853
Adelchis, 853–878
Gaideris, 878–881
Radelchis II, 881–884, 897–900
Aio, 884–891
Ursus, 891–892
Byzantine rule, 892–895
Guy IV of Spoleto, 895–897
Atenulf, 900–910
Landulf I, 910–943

Table 12   BYZANTINE RULERS, *c.* 700 – *c.* 900

I   HERACLIANS

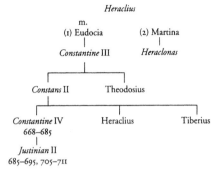

Heraclius

m.

(1) Eudocia   (2) Martina

Constantine III   *Heraclonas*

Constans II   Theodosius

Constantine IV   Heraclius   Tiberius
668–685

Justinian II
685–695, 705–711

Leontius, 695–698
Tiberius II, 698–705
Philippicus, 711–713
Anastasius II, 713–715
Theodosius III, 715–717

II   SYRIANS

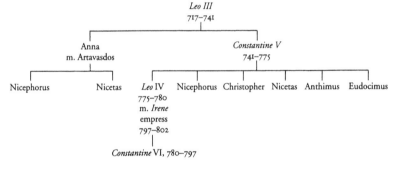

Leo III
717–741

Anna
m. Artavasdos

Constantine V
741–775

Nicephorus   Nicetas   *Leo* IV   Nicephorus Christopher Nicetas Anthimus Eudocimus
775–780
m. *Irene*
empress
797–802

Constantine VI, 780–797

Nicephorus I, 802–811
Staurakios, 811
Michael I, 811–813
Leo V, 813–820

III   AMORIANS

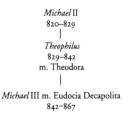

Michael II
820–829

Theophilus
829–842
m. Theodora

Michael III m. Eudocia Decapolita
842–867

Table 12   BYZANTINE RULERS, *c.* 700 – *c.* 900 (cont.)

IV   MACEDONIANS

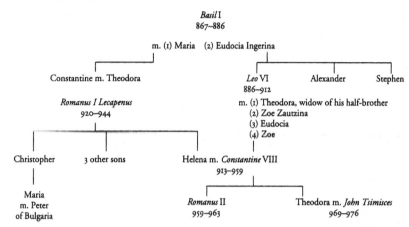

PRIMARY SOURCES

The list represents those primary sources referred to in the text of all the chapters in this book or cited in the notes, arranged in alphabetical order of author. Anonymous works and collections of documents have been listed in alphabetical order of title. In the case of the saints' *Vitae* the word *sanctus* has been removed from the title in order to preserve the alphabetical sequence of names. Collections of sources are to be found under the editor's name.

Abbo of St Germain-des-Prés, *De Bello Parisiaco*, ed. W. Waquet, *Abbon: le siège de Paris par les normands*, Paris (1964)

Abbreviatio Rufini, ed. C.H. Turner, *Ecclesiae Occidentalis Monumenta Iuris Antiquissima, Canonum et Conciliorum Graecorum Interpretationes Latinae*, Oxford (1939)

Actus Pontificium Cenomannis in Urbe Degentium, ed. G. Busson and A. Ledru (Archives historiques du Maine 2), Le Mans (1901)

Adam of Bremen, *Gesta Hammaburgensis Ecclesiae Pontificum*, ed. W. Trillmich and R. Buchner (*AQ* 11), Darmstadt (1961)

    English trans. F.J. Tschan, *History of the Archbishops of Hamburg-Bremen by Adam of Bremen*, New York (1959)

Adler, A. (ed.) *Suidae Lexikon* 5 vols., Leipzig (1928–38) reprinted Stuttgart (1971)

Admonitio ad Omnes Regni Ordines (825), ed. A. Boretius, *MGH Cap.* I, Hanover (1883), pp. 303–7

Admonitio Generalis, ed. A. Boretius, *MGH Cap.* I, Hanover (1883), pp. 52–62

Admonitio Synodalis, ed. R. Aimet, 'Une *Admonitio Synodalis* de l'époque carolingienne: étude critique et édition', *Mediaeval Studies* 26 (1964), pp. 12–82

Adomnán, *De Locis Sanctis*, ed. D. Meehan (*SLH* 3), Dublin (1958)

Adrevald of Fleury, *Miracula Sancti Benedicti*, PL 124, cols. 909–48

    ed. G. Waitz, *MGH SS* xv:1, Hanover (1887), pp. 474–97

    ed. E. de Certain, *Les miracles de Saint Benoît écrits par Adrevald, Aimon, André, Raoul Tortaire et Hugues de Sainte Marie, moines de Fleury*, Paris (1858), pp. 15–83

Aethicus Ister, ed. H. Wutke, *Die Kosmographie des Istries Aithikos im lateinischen Auszuge des Hieronymus*, Leipzig (1853)

Agobard of Lyons, *Contra Praeceptum Impium de Baptismo Iudaeorum Mancipiorum*, ed. L. van Acker (*CCCM* 52), Turnhout (1981), pp. 183–8

Agobard of Lyons, *De Antiphonario*, ed. L. van Acker (*CCCM* 52), Turnhout (1981), pp. 335–51

Agobard of Lyons, *De Baptismo Mancipiorum Iudaeorum*, ed. L. van Acker (*CCCM* 52), Turnhout (1981), pp. 113–17

Agobard of Lyons, *De Insolentia Iudaeorum*, ed. L. van Acker (*CCCM* 52), Turnhout (1981), pp. 189–95

Agobard of Lyons, *De Iudaicis Superstitionibus et Erroribus*, ed. L. van Acker (*CCCM* 52), Turnhout (1981), pp. 197–221

Agobard of Lyons, *Opera*, ed. L. van Acker (*CCCM* 52), Turnhout (1981)

Aistulf, *Leges*, ed. F. Beyerle, *Leges Langobardorum, 643–866*, Witzenhausen (1962), pp. 194–204

al-Akhbar al-Maimu'ah, ed. E. Lafuente y Alcantara, Madrid (1867)

Al-Makkarī, ed. P. de Gayangos, *The History of Mohammedann Dynasties in Spain*, 2 vols., London (1840–3)

Al-'Udhri, Ahmad b., *'Umar, Nusus 'an al-Andalus*, ed. A.A. al-Ahwani, Madrid (1965)

Alagus, see under Rainogala

Alan of Farfa, see R. Grégoire, *Les homéliaires du moyen âge: inventaire et analyse des manuscrits*, Rome (1966)

Alcuin, *Carmina*, ed. E. Dümmler, *MGH Poet.* I, Berlin (1881), pp. 160–351

Alcuin, *De Dialectica*, *PL* 101, cols. 949–76

Alcuin, *De Virtutibus et de Vitiis*, *PL* 101, cols. 613–38

Alcuin, *Disputatio de Rhetorica et de Virtutibus Sapientissimi Regis Karli et Albini Magistri. The Rhetoric of Alcuin and Charlemagne*, ed. with English trans. W.S. Howell, New York (1965)

Alcuin, *Epistulae*, ed. E. Dümmler, *MGH Epp.* IV, Berlin (1895)
  English trans. (selection) S. Allott, *Alcuin of York: His Life and Letters*, York (1974)

Alcuin, *Libellus contra Haeresim Felicis*, ed. G.B. Blumenshine (*Studi e Testi* 285), Vatican (1980)

Alcuin, *Versus de Patribus, Regibus et Sanctis Euboricensis Ecclesiae*, ed. and trans. P. Godman, *The Bishops, Kings and Saints of York*, Oxford (1982)

Alcuin, *Vita Sancti Willibrordi*, ed. W. Levison, *MGH SRM* VII, Hanover (1920), pp. 81–141
  English trans. C.H. Talbot, *The Anglo-Saxon Missionaries in Germany*, London (1954), pp. 3–22

Aldhelm, *Opera Omnia*, ed. P. Ehwald, *MGH AA* 15, Berlin (1919)

Alfred, *Gregory's Pastoral Care*, modern English trans. in S. Keynes and M. Lapidge, *Alfred the Great*, Harmondsworth (1983), pp. 124–30

Alia Musica (Traité de musique du IXe siècle), ed. J. Chailley (Publications de l'Institut de Musicologie de l'Université de Paris 6) Paris (1965)

Die althochdeutsche Glossen, ed. E. Steinmeyer and E. Sievers, 5 vols., Berlin (1879–1922)

Amalarius of Metz, *Expositio Missae 'Dominus Vobiscum'*, ed. J.M. Hanssen, *Amalarii Episcopi Opera Liturgica Omnia* II (Studi e Testi 139), Vatican (1948)

Ambrosius Autpert, *Opera*, ed. R. Weber (*CCCM* 27, 27A, 27B), Turnhout (1975–9)

Anastasius Bibliothecarius, *Epistulae sive Praefationes*, ed. E. Casper, *MGH Epp.* VII, Berlin (1928), pp. 395–442

Andrea Dandolo, *Chronica per Extensum Descripta*, ed. E. Pastorello, Bologna (1938–58)

Andrew of Bergamo, *Historia*, ed. G. Waitz, *MGH SRL*, Hanover (1878)

Angelbert, *Versus de Bella quae fuit Acta Fontaneto*, ed. E. Dümmler, *MGH Poet.* II, Berlin (1884), pp. 138–9

Agnellus of Ravenna, *Liber Pontificalis Ecclesiae Ravennatis*, ed. O. Holder-Egger, *MGH SRL*, Hanover (1878), pp. 265–391

Angilbert of Saint-Riquier, *Institutio de Diversitate Officiorum*, ed. K. Hallinger, M. Wegener and H. Frank (*CCM* 1), Siegburg (1963), pp. 283–303

Anglo-Saxon Chronicle, ed. B. Thorpe, Rolls Series, London (1861), English trans. G.N. Garmonsway, London (1953)

Annales Bertiniani, ed. G. Waitz, *MGH SRG* 5, Hanover (1883)
    ed. F. Grat, J. Vielliard and C. Clémencet, *Annales de Saint-Bertin*, Paris (1964)
    English trans. J. Nelson, *The Annals of Saint-Bertin*, Manchester (1991)

Annales Fuldenses, ed. F. Kurze, *MGH SRG* 7, Hanover (1891)
    ed. with German trans. R. Rau, *QK* 3 (= *AQ* 7), Darmstadt (1960), pp. 19–117
    English trans. T. Reuter, *The Annals of Fulda*, Manchester (1992)

Annales Lauresbamenses, ed. G. Pertz, *MGH SS* 1, Berlin (1826), pp. 22–30

Annales Mettenses Priores, ed. B. von Simson, *MGH SRG* 10, Hanover (1905)

Annales Mosellani, ed. I.M. Lappenberg, *MGH SS* XVI, Hanover (1859), pp. 494–9

Annales Regni Francorum, ed. F. Kurze, *MGH SRG* 6, Hanover (1895)
    English trans B. Scholz, *Carolingian Chronicles*, Ann Arbor (1970)

Annales Sancti Amandi, Tiliani, Laubacenses, Petaviani, ed. G. Pertz, *MGH SS* 1, Berlin (1826), pp. 6–10

Annales Vedastini, ed. B. von Simson, *MGH SRG* 12, Hanover (1909)

Annales Xantenses, ed. B. von Simson, *MGH SRG* 12, Hanover (1909)

Annals of Inisfallen, ed. S. MacAirt, Dublin (1951)

Annals of the Kingdom of Ireland by the Four Masters, ed. J. O'Donovan, 7 vols., Dublin (1851)

Annals of Ulster 1, ed. S. MacAirt and G. MacNiocaill, Dublin (1983)

Ansegisus of Saint-Wandrille, *Capitularium Collectio*, ed. A. Boretius, *MGH Cap.* 1, Hanover (1883), pp. 382–450

Arbeo of Freising, *Vita Corbiniani*, ed. F. Brunhölzl, H. Glaser and S. Benker, *Vita Corbiniani, Bischof Arbeo von Freising und die Lebensgeschichte des hl. Korbinian*, Munich (1983)

Arbeo of Freising, *Vita Haimhrammi Episcopi*, ed. B. Krusch, *MGH SRG* 13, Hanover (1920)
    ed. B. Bischoff, *Arbeo, Vita et Passio Haimhrammi Martyris: Leben und Leiden des hl. Korbinian*, Munich (1953)

Ardo, *Vita Benedicti Abbatis Anianensis*, ed. G. Waitz, *MGH SS* XV:1, Hanover (1887), pp. 200–20

Arnulf, *Diplomata*, ed. P. Kehr, *Arnolfi Diplomata, MGH Dip. Germ.* 3, Hanover and Leipzig (1940)

Ars Lauresbamensis: Expositio in Donatum Maiorem, ed. B. Löfstedt (*CCCM* 42A), Turnhout (1977)

Asser, *Life of King Alfred*, ed. W. Stevenson, rep. by D. Whitelock, Oxford (1959)
    English trans. S. Keynes and M. Lapidge *Alfred the Great*, Harmondsworth (1983), pp. 67–110

Astronomer, *Vita Hludovici Pii Imperatoris*, ed. G. Pertz, *MGH SS* II, Berlin (1829), pp. 604–48

ed. and trans. R. Rau, *QK* 1 (= *AQ* 5), Darmstadt (1955)

English trans. A. Cabaniss, *Son of Charlemagne*, Syracuse, NY (1961)

Aurelian of Réômé, *Musica Disciplina*, ed. L. Gushee (Corpus Scriptorum de Musica 21) (1975)

Beatus, *Adversus Elipandum*, ed. B. Löfstedt (*CCCM* LIX), Turnhout (1984)

Bede, *De Schematibus et Tropis*, ed. C.B. Kendall (*CCSL* 123A), Turnhout (1975), pp. 142–71

Bede, *De Temporibus*, ed. T. Mommsen and C.W. Jones (*CCSL* 123C), Turnhout (1980), pp. 585–611

Bede, *De Temporum Ratione*, ed. C.W. Jones (*CCSL* 123D), Turnhout (1977), pp. 463–544

Bede, *Historia Abbatum*, ed. C. Plummer, *Venerabilis Bedae Opera Historica*, Oxford (1896)

Bede, *Historia Ecclesiastica Gentis Anglorum*, ed. and trans. B. Colgrave and R.A.B. Mynors, *Bede's Ecclesiastical History of the English People*, Oxford (1969)

Bede, *Opera de Temporibus*, ed. C.W. Jones, Cambridge, MA (1943)

Bede, *Vita Sancti Cuthberti*, ed. and trans. B. Colgrave, *Two Lives of Saint Cuthbert*, Cambridge (1940)

Bell, H.I., *The Aphrodito Papyri* (Greek Papyri in the British Museum 4) London (1910)

Benedict of Aniane, *Institutio Sanctimonialium Aquisgranensis (Concilium Aquisgranense a. 816)*, ed. A. Werminghoff, *MGH Conc.* II: 1, Hanover (1906), pp. 312–456

Berengar, *Diplomata*, ed. L. Schiaparelli, *I diplomati de Berengario*, Rome (1903)

Bieler, L. (ed.), *The Irish Penitentials*, Dublin (1963)

Bieler, L., *The Patrician Text in the Book of Armargh* (*SLH* 10), Dublin (1979)

Binchy, D.A., *Corpus Iuris Hibernici*, 6 vols., Dublin (1978)

Binchy, D.A., *Crith Gablach*, Dublin (1941)

Bobbio Polyptych of 862, ed. A. Castagnetti *et al.* (*FSI* 104) (1979), pp. 121–44

Böhmer, J.K., *Regesta Imperii* I: *Die Regesten des Kaiserreichs unter den Karolingern 751–918* (Innsbruck, 1908; rep. Hildesheim, 1966), rev. edn of Bd 3: *Die Regesten des Regum Italiae des Kaiserreiches und der Burgundischen Regna*, Teil 1: *Die Karolinger im Regnum Italiae (840–887)*, ed. H. Zielinski, Vienna (1991)

Boniface, *Epistulae*, ed. M. Tangl, *Die Briefe des heiligen Bonifatius and Lullus*, MGH *Epp. Sel.* 1, Hanover (1916)

ed. and trans. (selection) R. Rau, *Briefe des Bonifatius, Willibalds Leben des Bonifatius nebst einigen zeitgenössischen Dokumenten*, *AQ* IVb, Darmstadt (1968)

English trans. E. Emerton, *The Letters of Saint Boniface*, New York (1940)

English trans. (selection) C.H. Talbot, *The Anglo-Saxon Missionaries in Germany*, London (1954)

Bovo of Corvey, *Commentary on Book III, m.ix of Boethius, De Consolatione Philosophiae* in R.B.C. Hugyens, 'Mittelalterliche Kommentare zum *O qui perpetua*', *Sacris Erudiri* 6 (1954), pp. 373–428

Breatnach, L., 'The first third of Bretha Nemed toísech', *Ériu* 40 (1989), pp. 1–40

Breve Commemoratorii de illis causis dei vel monasteriis, ed. T. Tobler and M. Molinier (*Itinera Hierosolymitana* 1), Geneva (1880), pp. 301–5

Breviarium Ecclesiae Ravennatis (Codice Bavaro) secoli VII–X, ed. G. Rabotti (*FSI* 92), Rome (1985)

Brevium Exempla ad describendas res ecclesiasticas et fiscales, ed. A. Boretius, *MGH Cap.* 1, Hanover (1883), no. 128

Brühl, C. and Violante, C. (eds), *Die 'Honorantie civitatis Papie': Transkription, Edition, Kommentar*, Cologne (1983)

Candidus Wizo, *Philosophical and Theological Passages*, ed. J. Marenbon, *From the Circle of Alcuin to the School of Auxerre: Logic, Theology and Philosophy in the Early Middle Ages*, Cambridge (1981), pp. 152–70

Capitula ab Episcopis Attiniaci Data (822), ed. A. Boretius, *MGH Cap.* 1, Hanover (1883), pp. 357–8

Capitula ad Quibus Convocati Compositae Interrogati Fuerint, ed. E. Dümmler, *MGH Epp.* IV, Hanover (1895), pp. 565–6

  ed. C.W. Jones, 'An early medieval licencing examination', *History of Education Quarterly* 3 (1969), pp. 19–29

Capitula Angilramni, ed. P. Hinschius, *Decretales Pseudo-Isidorianae et Capitula Angilramni*, Leipzig (1863)

Capitula Episcoporum, ed. P. Brommer, *MGH Cap. episc.* 1, Hanover (1984)

Capitulare de Villis. Cod. Guelf. 254 Helmst. der Herzog August Bibliothek Wolfenbüttel, ed. C. Brühl, *Dokumente zur deutsche Geschichte in Faksimilis* 1, Mittelalter 1, Stuttgart (1971)

Capitulare Missorum Generale, ed. A. Boretius, *MGH Cap.* 1, Hanover (1883), pp. 91–9

Capitulare Olonnense Ecclesiasticum Primum, ed. A. Boretius, *MGH Cap.* 1, Hanover (1883), pp. 326–7

Capitularia Benedictae Levitae, ed. G. Pertz, *MGH Leges* II:2, Berlin (1837)

Capitularia Ecclesiastica ad Salz data a. 803–804, ed. A. Boretius, *MGH Cap.* 1, Hanover (1883), pp. 119–20

Capitularia Regum Francorum, ed. A. Boretius and V. Krause, *MGH Leges* sectio III, 2 vols., Hanover (1883–97)

  English trans. (selection) P.D. King, *Charlemagne: Translated Sources*, Kendal (1987)

  English trans. (selection) H. Loyn and J. Percival, *The Reign of Charlemagne: Documents on Carolingian Government and Administration*, London (1975)

Cartulaire de l'abbaye de Cysoing et de ses dépendances, ed. I. de Coussemaker, Lille (1883)

Cartularium Saxonicum, ed. W. de G. Birch, London (1885–93)

Castagnetti, A., Luzzati, M., Pasquali G. and Vasina, A., *Inventari altomedievali di terre, coloni e redditi* (*FSI* 104), Rome (1979)

Cessi, R. (ed.), *Documenti relativi alla storia di Venezia anteriori al Mille* 1, Padua (1940)

Charles III (the Fat), *Diplomata*, ed. P. Kehr, *MGH Dip. Germ.* 2, Hanover and Leipzig (1936–7)

The Charters of St Augustine's, Canterbury, ed. S. Kelly, Oxford (1994)

Christian of Stavelot, *Expositio in Matthaeum Evangelistam*, *PL* 106, cols. 1259–504

Chronica di Monemvasia, ed. I. Dujčev, Palermo (1976)

Chronicle of 754, ed. E. López, *Cronica mozarabe de 754: edición crítica y traducción*, Zaragoza (1980)

Chronicle of Alphonso III, ed. J. Gil Fernández, J.L. Moralejo and J. Ruíz de la Peña,

Crónicas Asturianas, Oviedo (1985)

Chronicon Altinate, ed. R. Cessi, *Origo civitatum Italiae seu Venetiarum (FSI)*, Rome (1933)

Chronicon Aquitanicum, ed. G. Pertz, *MGH SS* II, Berlin (1829)

Chronicon Centulense see under Hariulf

Chronicon Fontanellense, ed. J. Laporte, *Mélanges de la société de l'histoire de Normandie*, Paris and Rouen (1951), pp. 63–91

Chronicon Moissacensis, ed. G. Pertz, *MGH SS* II, Berlin (1829), pp. 282–313

Chronicon Monasterii Beneventani Sanctae Sophiae, ed. F. Ughelli, 2nd rev. edn by N. Coleti (Italia Sacra 10), Venice (1722)

Chronicon Vulturnense, ed. V. Federici, 3 vols., Rome (1925–38)

Clement of Ochrid (Kliment Okhridsi), *S'brani s'chineiia*, ed. B.S. Angelov *et al.*, Sofia (1971–7)

Codex Carolinus, ed. W. Gundlach, *MGH Epp.* III, Berlin (1892)

English trans. (selection) in P.D. King, *Charlemagne: Translated Sources*, Kendal (1987)

Codex Laureshamensis, ed. K. Glöckner, 3 vols., Darmstadt (1929–36)

Codice Diplomatico Longobardo I and II, ed. L. Schiaparelli, Rome (1929–33); III and IV, ed. C.R. Brühl, Rome (1973–81); V, ed. H. Zielinski, Rome (1986)

Collectio Canonum Hibernensis, ed. F.W.H. Wasserschleben, *Die irische Kanonensammlung*, 2nd edn, Leipzig (1885)

Collectio Canonum Remedio Curiensi Episcopo Perperam Ascripta, ed. H. John, *Monumenta Iuris Canonici*, ser. B: Corpus Collectionum 2, Vatican (1976)

Collectio Concilii Secundi Arelatensis, ed. C. Munier, *Concilia Gallia A. 314–A. 506* (*CCSL* 148), Turnhout (1963), pp. 111–30

Collectio Dacheriana, ed. L. d'Achery and L.F.J. Le Barre, *Spicilegium sive collectio veterum aliquot scriptorum qui in Galliae bibliothecis delituerant* I (Paris, 1723)

Collectio Dionysio-Hadriana, ed. J. Hartzheim (Concilia Germania 1), Cologne (1759)

Collectio Herovalliana, PL 56, cols. 11–354

Collectio Hispana et Collectio Hispana Systematica, ed. G. Martínez Díez (*La Colección canonica hispana*), Madrid (1966)

Collectio Justelli, PL 56, cols. 747–817

Collectio Novariensis, ed. G. Martínez Díez, 'La Colección del ms. de Novara', *Annuario de Historia del Derecho Español* 33 (1963), pp. 391–538

Collectio Quesnelliana, PL 56, cols. 359–746

Collectio Sangermanensis, ed. A.J. Nürnberger, 'Über eine ungedruckte Kanonessammlung aus dem 8. Jahrhundert', *Bericht der Wissenschaftlichen Gesellschaft Philomathie in Neisse vom Oktober 1888 zum Oktober 1890*, Neisse (1890), pp. 125–97

Collectio Veronensis, ed. E. Schwartz, *Publizistische Sammlungen zum Acacianischen Schisma* (Abhandlungen der bayerischen Akademie der Wissenschaften phil.-hist. Abteilung, Neue Folge 10), Munich (1934)

Collectio Vetus Gallica, ed. H. Mordek, *Kirchenrecht und Reform im Frankenreich*, Berlin (1975)

Concilios Visigóthicos e Hispano-Romanos, ed. J. Vives (España Christiana, Textos 1) (Madrid, 1963)

Concilium Moguntinense a. 813, ed. A. Werminghoff, *MGH Conc.* II:1, Hanover (1906), pp. 259–73

Concilium Moguntinum a. 847, ed. A. Boretius and V. Krause, *MGH Cap.* II, Hanover (1987), pp. 173–84

Concilium Parisiense a. 829, ed. A. Werminghoff, *MGH Conc.* II:2, Hanover (1908), pp. 606–80

Concilium Remense a. 813, ed. A. Werminghoff, *MGH Conc.* II:1, Hanover (1906), pp. 254–8

Concilium Rispacense a. 798, ed. A. Werminghoff, *MGH Conc.* II:1, Hanover (1906), pp. 196–9

Concilium Romanum a. 826, ed. A. Werminghoff, *MGH Conc.* II:2, Hanover (1908), pp. 552–83

Concilium Romanum a. 853, ed. W. Hartmann, *MGH Conc.* III, Hanover (1984), pp. 317–39

Concilium Turonense a. 813, ed. A. Werminghoff, *MGH Conc.* II:1, Hanover (1906), pp. 286–933

Concordia Canonum Cresconii, PL 88, cols. 829–942

Concilia Galliae A. 314 – A. 695, ed. C. Munier and C. de Clercq (*CCSL* 148 and 148A), Turnhout (1963)

Constantine Porphyrogenitus, *De Administrando Imperio*, ed. G. Moravcsik and R.J.H. Jenkins (Dumbarton Oaks Texts 1), Washington DC (1967)

Constantine VII, *De Ceremoniis Aulae Byzantinae*, ed. J.J. Reiske, Bonn (1829)

Constantine VII, *De Thematibus*, ed. A. Pertusi (Studi e Testi 160), Vatican (1952)

Constitutio Romana, ed. A. Boretius, *MGH Cap.* I, Hanover (1883), pp. 322–4

Conversio Bagoariorum et Carantanorum, ed. H. Wolfram, Vienna (1979)

Corpus Consuetudinum Monasticarum I: *Initia Consuetudinis Benedictinae. Consuetudines Saeculi Octavi et Noni*, ed. K. Hallinger, Sieburg (1983)

Corpus Glossariorum Latinorum, ed. G. Goetz, 7 vols., Leipzig and Berlin (1888–1923)

La Cronaca Veneziana del diacono Giovanni (Chronicum Venetum), ed. G. Monticolo, *Cronache Veneziane Antichissime (FSI 9)*, Rome (1890), pp. 57–172

Danmarks Runeindskrifter, ed. L. Jacobsen and E. Moltke, Copenhagen (1941–2)

Dares Phrygius, *Historia de Origine Francorum*, ed. B. Krusch, *MGH SRM* II, Hanover (1888), pp. 194–200

Davies, W. (ed.), *The Llandaff Charters*, Aberystwyth (1979)

Davis-Weyer, C. (ed.), *Early Medieval Art 300–1100* (Sources and Documents in the History of Art Series), Englewood Cliffs (1971)

Decretales Pseudo-Isidorianae et Capitula Angilramni, ed. P. Hinschius, Leipzig (1863)

Defensor of Ligugé, *Liber Scintillarum*, ed. H. Rochais (*SC* 77 and 86), Paris (1961–2)

Deusdedit, *Collectio Canonum*, ed. V. Wolf von Glanvell, *Die Kanonessammlung des Kardinals Deusdedit*, Paderborn (1905)

Devroey, J.P. (ed.), *Le polyptique et les listes de biens de l'abbaye Saint-Pierre de Lobbes (IXe–XIe siècles): édition critique*, Brussels (1986)

Devroey, J.P. (ed.), *Le polyptique et les listes de cens de l'abbaye de Saint-Remi de Reims (IXe–XIe siècles)* (Travaux de l'Académie Nationale de Reims 163), Rheims (1984)

Dhuoda, *Liber Manualis*, ed. and French trans. P. Riché (*SC* 225 bis), Paris (1975) English trans. C. Neel, *Handbook for William: A Carolingian Woman's Counsel for her Son*, Lincoln, NB (1992)

Dicta Albini/Dicta Candidi, ed. J. Marenbon, *From the Circle of Alcuin to the School of Auxerre: Logic, Theology and Philosophy in the Early Middle Ages*, Cambridge

(1981), pp. 151–70

Dicta Pirminii, ed. G. Jecker, Münster (1927)
 reprint with German trans. U. Engelmann, *Der heilige Pirmin und sein Pastoralbüch-lein*, Sigmaringen (1976)

Dicuil, *Liber de Astronomia*, ed. M. Esposito, 'An unpublished astronomical treatise by the Irish monk Dicuil', *Proceedings of the Royal Irish Academy* 26 c (1907), pp. 378–46

Dicuil, *Liber de Mensura Orbis Terrae*, ed. J.J. Tierney (*SLH* 6), Dublin (1967)

Droste, C.D. (ed.), *Das Polypticon von Montierender: kritische Edition und Analyse*, Trier (1988)

Eddius Stephanus, *Vita Sancti Wilfridi*, ed. W. Levison, *MGH SRM* vi, Hanover (1913), pp. 193–263
 ed. and trans. B. Colgrave, *The Life of Bishop Wilfrid by Eddius Stephanus*, Cambridge (1927)

Eigil, *Vita Sturmi Abbatis Fuldensis*, ed. P. Engelbrecht, *Die Vita Sturmi des Eigils von Fulda: Literarkritische-historische Untersuchung und Edition*, Marburg (1968)
 English trans. C.H. Talbot, *The Anglo-Saxon Missionaries in Germany*, London (1954), pp. 181–202

Einhard, *Translatio Sanctorum Marcellini et Petri*, ed. G. Waitz, *MGH SS* xv:1, Hanover (1887), pp. 238–64

Einhard, *Vita Karoli*, ed. G. Waitz, *MGH SRG* 25, Hanover (1911)
 ed. with French trans. L. Halphen, *Eginhard: vie de Charlemagene*, 3rd edn, Paris (1947)
 English trans. L. Thorpe, *Two Lives of Charlemagne*, Harmondsworth (1969)

Ekkehard IV, *Casus sancti Galli*, ed. H.F. Haefele, *AQ* 10, Darmstadt (1980)

Encomium Emmae Reginae, ed. A. Campbell (Camden Third Series 72), London (1949)

Epistula ad Leudefredum, ed. R.E. Reynolds, 'The "Isidorian" *Epistula ad Leudefre-dum*: an early medieval epitome of the clerical duties', *Mediaeval Studies* 41 (1979), pp. 252–330

Epistulae Selectae Pontificum Romanorum Carolo Magno et Hludowico Pio Regnantibus Scriptae, ed. K. Hampe, *MGH Epp.* v, Hanover (1898), pp. 1–84

Erchempert, *Historia Langobardorum Beneventanorum*, ed. G. Waitz, *MGH SRL*, Hanover (1878)

Ermanricus of Ellwangen, *Sermo de Vita Sualonis*, ed. O. Holder-Egger, *MGH SS* xv:1, Hanover (1887), pp. 153–63

Ermentarius, *De Translationibus et Miraculis Sancti Filiberti Libri II*, ed. R. Poupardin, *Monuments de l'histoire des abbayes de Saint-Philibert*, Paris (1905)

Ermold the Black (Ermoldus Nigellus), *In Honorem Hludovici Pii Christianissimi Caesaris Augusti*, ed. and trans. E. Faral, *Ermold le Noir: poème sur Louis le Pieux*, 2nd edn, Paris (1964)
 English trans. (selection) P. Godman, *Poetry of the Carolingian Renaissance*, London (1985)

Eugenius III, *Capitula Admonitionis*, ed. A. Werminghoff, *MGH Conc.* I:2, Hanover (1908), pp. 553–8

Fantuzzi, M. (ed.), *Monumenti Ravennati de' secoli di mezzo*, 6 vols., Venice (1801–4)

Felix, *Vita Sancti Guthlaci*, ed. and trans. B. Colgrave, *Felix' Life of Saint Guthlac*, Cambridge (1956)

Ferrandus the deacon of Carthage, *Breviatio Canonum, a. 523–546*, ed. C. Munier, *Concilia Africae A. 315–A. 525 (CCSL* 149), Turnhout (1974), pp. 284–306

Flodoard of Rheims, *Historia Remensis Ecclesiae*, ed. J. Heller and G. Waitz, *MGH SS* XIII, Hanover (1881), pp. 405–599

Florus of Lyons, *Opera*, *PL* 119, cols. 11–424

Folcuin, *Gesta Abbatum Lobiensium*, ed. G. Pertz, *MGH SS* IV, Berlin (1841), pp. 54–74

Folcuin, *Gesta Abbatum Sancti Bertini Sithiensium*, ed. J. Heller and G. Waitz, *MGH SS* XIII, Hanover (1881), pp. 600–35

Formulae Merovingici et Karolini Aevi, ed. K. Zeumer, *MGH Form.*, Hanover (1886)

Fredegar, *Chronicarum quae Dicuntur Fredegari Scholastici libri IV cum continuationes*, ed. B. Krusch, *MGH SRM* II, Hanover (1888), pp. 1–193
ed. and trans. J.M. Wallace-Hadrill, *The Fourth Book of the Chronicle of Fredegar and its Continuations*, Oxford (1960)

Freising Charters, ed. T. Bitterauf, *Die Traditionen des Hochstifts Freising*, Munich (1905)

Fridigisus, *De Nihilo Tenebris*, ed. E. Dümmler, *MGH Epp.* IV, Berlin (1895), pp. 552–5

Ganshof, F.L. (ed.), *Le polyptique de l'abbaye de Saint-Bertin (844–859): édition critique et commentaire* (Mémoires de l'Académie des Inscription et Belles-Lettres 45), Paris (1975)

Gasnault, P. (ed.), *Documents comptables de Saint-Martin de Tours à l'époque mérovingienne, Collection de documents inédits sur l'histoire de France*, Paris (1975)

Gelasius I, *Letter to the Emperor Anastasius*, ed. E. Schwartz, *Publizistische Sammlungen zum Acacianischen Schisma (Abhandlungen der bayerischen Akademie der Wissenschaften*, phil.-hist. Abteilung, Neue Folge 10), Munich (1934), pp. 20–1

Genesius, *Regum Libri IV*, ed. A. Lesmüller-Werner and I. Thurn (*CFHB* 14), Berlin (1978)

Gerichtsurkunden der fränkischen Zeit, ed. R. Hübner, *Zeitschrift der Savigny-Stiftung für Rechtsgeschichte*, Germanistische Abteilung 12 (1891) and 14 (1893); rep. Aalen (1971)

Die Gesetze der Angelsachsen, ed. F. Liebermann, 3 vols., Halle (1903–16)

Gesta Hodoeporicon, ed. O. Holder-Egger, *MGH SS* XV:1, Hanover (1887)
English trans. C.H. Talbot, *The Anglo-Saxon Missionaries in Germany*, London (1954), pp. 153–77

Gesta Pontificum Autissiodorensium, see under Rainogala and Alagus

Gesta Sanctorum Patrum Fontanellensis Coenobii, ed. F. Lohier and J. Laporte (*Mélanges de la société de l'histoire de Normandie*), Paris and Rouen (1936)

Gisela and Rotrud of Chelles, *Epistula*, ed. E. Dümmler, *MGH Epp.* IV, Berlin (1895), pp. 323–5

Glossaria Latina, ed. W.M. Lindsay, J.F. Mountford and J. Whatmough, 5 vols., Paris (1926–31)

Glosses to Boethius, *Opuscula Sacra* (sometimes attributed to Remigius of Auxerre) ed. E.K. Rand, *Johannes Scotus*, Munich (1906)

Glosses to *Categoriae Decem*, ed. J. Marenbon, *From the Circle of Alcuin to the School of Auxerre: Logic, Theology and Philosophy in the Early Middle Ages*, Cambridge (1981), pp. 185–206

Godescalc of Orbais, see under Gottschalk

Gottschalk of Orbais, *De Praedestinatione*, ed. C. Lambert in Gottschalk of Orbais, *Œuvres théologiques*

Gottschalk of Orbais, *O Mi Custes*, ed. K. Strecker, *MGH Poet*. VI, Berlin (1951), pp. 89–97

Gottschalk of Orbais, *Œuvres théologiques et grammaticales de Godescalc d'Orbais*, ed. C. Lambot (Spicilegium Sacrum Lovaniense 20), Leuven (1945)

Gottschalk of Orbais, *Ut Quid Iubes?*, ed. L. Traube, *MGH Poet*. III, Berlin (1896), pp. 731–2

Grimalaic, *Regula Solitariorum*, PL 103, cols. 573–664

Guérard, B. (ed.), *Polyptique de l'abbé Irminon ou dénombrement des manses, des serfs et des revenus de l'abbaye de Saint-Germain-des-Prés sous le règne de Charlemagne, publié avec des prolégomènes*, Paris (1844)

Gunzo of Novara, *Epistula ad Augienses*, ed. M. Manitius, *MGH, Die deutschen Geschichtsquellen des Mittelalters, 500–1500: Quellen zur Geistesgeschichte des Mittelalters* II, Weimar (1958)

Guy and Lambert of Spoleto, *Diplomata*, ed. L. Schiaparelli, *I diplomati di Guido e Lamberto*, Rome (1910)

Haddan, A.W. and Stubbs, W. (eds.), *Councils and Ecclesiastical Documents Relating to Great Britain and Ireland*, 3 vols., Oxford (1869–78)

Hägermann, D. and Hedwig, A. (eds.), *Das Polyptichon und die Notitia de Aries von Saint-Maur-des-Fossés: Analyse und Edition* (Beihefte der Francia 23), Sigmaringen (1990)

Haito of Reichenau, *Visio Wettini*, ed. E. Dümmler, *MGH Poet*. II, Berlin (1884), pp. 267–75

Hariulf, *Chronicon Centulense*, ed. F. Lot, Paris (1894)

Harmer, F.E. (ed.), *Select English Historical Documents of the Ninth and Tenth Centuries*, Cambridge (1914)

Hartmann, *Vita Sanctae Wiboradae*, ed. G. Pertz, *MGH SS* IV, Berlin (1841), pp. 452–7

Hartmann, W. (ed.), 'Neue Texte zur bischöflichen Reformgesetzgebung aus den Jahre 829/31: vier Diözesansynoden Halitgar von Cambrai', *DA* 35 (1979), pp. 368–94

Heer, J.M., *Ein karolingischer Missions-Kathechismus: Ratio de Catecizandis Rudibus* (Biblische und Patristische Forschungen 1), Freiburg-im-Breisgau (1911)

Heiric of Auxerre, *Miracula Sancti Germani*, PL 124, cols. 1207–70

Heiric of Auxerre, *Vita Sancti Germani Episcopi*, ed. L. Traube, *MGH Poet*. III, Berlin (1896), pp. 428–517

Heist, W.W., *Vitae Sanctorum Hiberniae* (Subsidia Hagiographica 28), Brussels (1865)

Herard of Tours, *Capitula*, PL 121, cols. 761–74

Herrmann, E. (ed.), *Slawisch-Germanische Beziehungen im süddeutschen Raum von der Spätantike bis zum Ungarnsturm: Ein Quellenbuch mit Erläuterung*, Munich (1965)

'Hibernicus Exul', *De Artibus Liberalibus*, ed. E. Dümmler, *MGH Poet*. I, Berlin (1881), pp. 408–10

Hildemar of Corbie and Civate, *Expositio Regulae Sancti Benedicti*, ed. R. Mittermüller, *Vita et Regula SS. P. Benedicti, Una cum Expositione Regulae a Hildemaro Tradita*, Regensburg, New York and Cincinnati (1880)

Hilduin of Saint-Denis, *Gesta Dagoberti*, ed. B. Krusch, *MGH SRM* II, Hanover (1888), pp. 396–425

Hilduin of Saint-Denis, *Vita Sancti Dyonisii*, *AASS* Oct. IV, pp. 696–987

Hincmar of Rheims, *Ad Hludovicum Balbum*, *PL* 125, cols. 938–90

Hincmar of Rheims, *Ad Reclusos et Simplices*, ed. W. Gundlach, 'Zwei Schriften des Erzbischofs Hinkmar von Reims 2' (Zeitschrift für Kirchengeschichte 19) (1889), 258–309

Hincmar of Rheims, *Capitula quibus de rebus magistri et decani per singulas ecclesias inquirere, et episcopo renuntiare debent*, *PL* 125, cols. 777–92

Hincmar of Rheims, *Capitula Synodica*, *PL* 125, cols. 773–804

Hincmar of Rheims, *Collectio de Ecclesiis et Capellis*, ed. M. Stratmann, *MGH Fontes* 3, Hanover (1990)

Hincmar of Rheims, *De Divortio Lotharii Regis et Tetbergae Reginae*, *PL* 125, cols. 619–772

Hincmar of Rheims, *De Ordine Palatii*, ed. T. Gross and R. Schieffer, *MGH Fontes* 145, Hanover (1990)

Hincmar of Rheims, *De Regis Persona et Regio Ministerio*, *PL* 125, cols. 833–56

Hincmar of Rheims, *De Villa Novilliaco*, ed. O. Holder-Egger, *MGH SS* xv:2, Hanover (1888), pp. 1167–9

Hincmar of Rheims, *Epistulae*, ed. E. Perels, *MGH Epp.* viii:1, Berlin (1939)

Hincmar of Rheims, *Opusculum LV capitulorum*, *PL* 126, cols. 282–494

Historia Welforum, ed. E. König (Schwäbische Chroniken der Stauferzeit 1), 2nd edn, Sigmaringen (1976)

Hraban Maur, *Commentariorum in Ezechielem libri viginti*, *PL* 110, cols. 493–1084

Hraban Maur, *De Clericorum Institutione*, *PL* 107, cols. 293–420
  ed. A. Knoepfler, *Veröffentlichungen aus dem Kirchenhistorichen Seminar München* 5, Munich (1900)

Hraban Maur, *Denotatio Dedicationis Ecclesiae Sancti Salvatoris Constructae in Monastico Fuldae*, ed. E. Dümmler, *MGH Poet.* II, Berlin (1884), pp. 205–8

Hraban Maur, *Epistula* (to Bishop Noting), *PL* 106, cols. 23–50

Hraban Maur, *Epistulae*, ed. E. Dümmler, *MGH Epp.* v, Berlin (1899), pp. 381–515

Hraban Maur, *Homiliae*, *PL* 110, cols. 9–134

Hraban Maur, *Liber de Computo*, ed. W.M. Stevens (*CCCM* 44), Turnhout (1977)

Hraban Maur, *Liber de Oblatione Puerorum*, *PL* 107, cols. 419–40

Hucbald of Saint-Amand, *De Harmonica Institutione*, ed. M. Gerbert (Scriptores Ecclesiastici de Musica Sacra 1), San-Blasian (1784), pp. 104–21

Hugeburc of Heidenheim, *Hodoeporicon*, ed. O. Holder-Egger, *MGH SS* xv:1, Hanover (1887), pp. 86–117
  English trans. C.H. Talbot, *The Anglo-Saxon Missionaries in Germany*, London (1954), pp. 152–77

Ibn al-Athīr, *al-Kamīl fī'l-ta'rīkh*, ed. C.J. Tornberg, Leiden (1867–74)

Ibn al-Athīr, *Annales du Magreb et de l'Espagne*, trans. E. Fagnan, Algiers (1901)

Ibn al-Qūṭiyyah, *Ta'rīkh iftitaḥ al-Andalus*, ed. J. Ribera, Madrid (1926)

Ibn Idhārī, *al-Bayān al-mughrib fi akhbār al-Maghrib*, ed. G.S. Colin and E. Lévi-Provençal, Leiden (1948–51)

Ibn Rusteh, *Les autors précieux*, trans. G. Weit, Cairo (1955)

Institutio Canonicorum Aquisgranensis, ed. A. Werminghoff, *MGH Conc.* II:1, Hanover

(1906), pp. 308–421

Isaac of Langres, *Canones*, PL 124, cols. 1075–110

Isidore of Seville, *De Ecclesiasticis Officiis*, ed. C.M. Lawson (*CCSL* 113), Turnhout (1989)

Isidore of Seville, *Etymologiarum sive originum libri XX*, ed. W.M. Lindsay, Oxford (1911)

Islendingabók, ed. A. Holtsmark, *Archiv for Nordisk Filologi* A 5 (1951)

Itinerarium Bernardi, ed. T. Tobler and M. Molinier, *Itinera Hierosolymitana* I, Geneva (1880), pp. 309–20

Jerome, *Commentariorum in Hezechielem libri XIV*, ed. F. Glorie (*CCSL* 75 and 75A), Turnhout (1964)

Johannes Scottus Eriugena, see under John Scottus

Johannis de Fordun, *Chronica Gentis Scotorum*, ed. W.F. Skene, Edinburgh (1971)

John VIII, *Epistulae*, ed. E. Caspar, *MGH Epp*. VII, Hanover (1928), pp. 1–272

John VIII, *Fragmenta Registri*, ed. E. Caspar, *MGH Epp*. VII, Hanover (1928), pp. 273–312

John the Deacon, *Cronaca*, ed. G. Monticolo, *Cronache Veneziane antichissime* (*FSI* 9), Rome (1890)

John the Deacon, *Vita Gregorii II*, PL 75, cols. 91–2

John Scottus (Johannes Scottus Eriugena), *Commentarium in Martianum Capellam*, ed. C. Lutz (Cambridge, MA, 1939). A different version of Book I is edited by E. Jeauneau in *Quatres thèmes érigéniens*, Montreal and Paris (1978)

John Scottus, *De Praedestinatione*, ed. G. Madec (*CCCM* 50), Turnhout (1978)

John Scottus, *Expositiones in Ierarchiam Ecclesiam*, ed. J. Barbet (*CCCM* 31), Turnhout (1975)

John Scottus, *Homily on the Prologue to St John's Gospel*, ed. with French trans. E. Jeauneau, Paris (1969)

  English trans. J. O'Meara, *Eriugena*, Oxford (1988), pp. 158–76

John Scottus, *Periphyseon*, I–III, ed. with English trans. I.P. Sheldon-Williams, Dublin (1968–81); IV, ed. with English trans. E. Jeauneau, Dublin (forthcoming); V, ed. H. Floss, PL 122

John Skylitzes, *Synopsis Historiarum*, ed. I. Thurn, Berlin and New York (1973)

Jonas of Orléans, *De Institutione Laicali*, PL 106, cols. 121–278

Jonas of Orléans, *De Institutione Regia*, ed. J. Reviron, *Les idées politico-religieuses d'un évêque du IXe siècle: Jonas d'Orléans et son 'De Institutione Regia'*, Paris (1930), pp. 119–94

Karlmann, *Diplomata*, see under Louis the German

Keynes, S. and Lapidge, M. (eds.), *Alfred the Great: Asser's 'Life of King Alfred' and other Contemporary Sources*, Harmondsworth (1983)

King, P.D., *Charlemagne: Translated Sources*, Kendal (1987)

Koch, A.C.F. *Oorkondenboek van Holland en Zeeland tot 1299* I: *Eind van 7e eeuw tot 1222*, The Hague (1970)

Lambert of Spoleto, *Diplomata*, see under Guy

Lambot, C. (ed.), *North Italian Service Books of the Eleventh Century*, London (1928)

Laudes Mediolanensis Civitatis, ed. E. Dümmler, *MGH Poet*. I, Berlin (1881), pp. 24–6

Laudes Veronensis Civitatis, ed. E. Dümmler, *MGH Poet*. I, Berlin (1881), pp. 118–22

Leges Langobardorum, 643–866, ed. F. Beyerle, Weimar (1947; rep. Witzenhausen, 1962)

  English trans. K.F. Drew, *The Lombard Laws*, Philadelphia (1973)

Legislatio Aquisgranensis, ed. J. Semmler (*CCM* 1), Siegburg (1963), pp. 434–582

Leo III, *Epistulae X*, ed. K. Hampe, *MGH Epp.* v, Hanover (1899), pp. 87–104

Leo IV, *Taktika*, ed. R. Vári, in *A magyar honfoglalás kutföi*, ed. P. Pauler and S. Szilágyi, Budapest (1900)

Lex Salica, ed. K.A. Eckhardt, *MGH Leg. Nat. Germ.* iv:1–2, Hanover (1962–9)
   English trans. K.F. Drew, *The Laws of the Franks*, Philadelphia (1991)
   English trans. T. Rivers, *The Salic and Ripuarian Laws*, New York (1991)

Libellus de Imperia Potestate in Urbe Roma, ed. G. Zuchetti (*FSI* 55), Rome (1920)

Liber Diurnus Romanorum Pontificum ex Unico Codice Vaticano, ed. T. Sickel, Vienna (1889)

Liber Historiae Francorum, ed. B. Krusch, *MGH SRM* ii, Hanover (1888)
   English trans. R. Gerberding, *The Rise of the Carolingians and the 'Liber Historiae Francorum'*, Oxford (1987)

Liber Memorialis von Remiremont, ed. E. Hlawitschka, K. Schmid and G. Tellenbach, *MGH Lib. Mem.* i, Dublin and Zurich (1970)

Liber Monstrorum de Diversis Generibus, ed. F. Porsia, Bari (1976)

Liber Ordinum, ed. M. Férontin, *Le Liber Ordinum en usage dans l'église wisigothique et mozarabe d'Espagne du cinquième au onzième siècle*, Paris (1904)

Liber Pontificalis, ed. L. Duchesne, Paris (1955)
   English trans. R. Davis, *The Book of Pontiffs (Liber Pontificalis to 715)*, Liverpool (1990); *The Lives of the Eighth Century Popes (Liber Pontificalis)*, Liverpool (1992)

Liber Possessionum Wizenburgensis, ed. C. Dette (Quellen und Abhandlungen zur mittelalterlichen Kirchengeschichte 59), Mainz (1987)

Libri Carolini, see under Theodulf of Orléans

Liudger, *Vita Gregorii Abbatis Trajectensis*, ed. O. Holder-Egger, *MGH SS* xv:1, Hanover (1887), pp. 66–79

Liutprand, *Constitutio de Censu Portorum*, ed. L.M. Hartmann, *Zur Wirtschaftsgeschichte Italiens im frühen Mittelalter*, Gotha (1904), pp. 123–4

Longnon, A. (ed.), *Polyptique de l'abbaye de Saint-Germain-des-Prés rédigé au temps de l'abbé Irminon*, Paris (1886–95)

Loyn, H.R. and Percival, J., *The Reign of Charlemagne: Documents on Carolingian Government and Administration*, London (1975)

Lothar I and Lothar II, *Diplomata*, ed. T. Schieffer, *Lotharii I et Lotharii II Diplomata*, *MGH Dip. Kar.* iii, Hanover and Leipzig (1966)

Louis I (the Pious), *Diplomata*, ed. P. Johanek, *Ludowici Pii Diplomata*, *MGH Dip. Kar.* ii, Hanover and Leipzig (forthcoming)

Louis II, *Epistula ad Basilium*, ed. W. Hanze, *MGH Epp.* vii, Hanover (1928), pp. 386–94

Louis the German, *Diplomata*, ed. P. Kehr, *Ludowici Germanici, Karlomani, Ludowici Iunioris Diplomata*, ed. P. Kehr, *MGH Dip. Germ.* i, Hanover and Leipzig (1932–4)

Louis the Younger, *Diplomata*, see under Louis the German

Lull, *Epistulae*, ed. M. Tangl, *Die Briefe des heiligen Bonifatius and Lullus*, *MGH Epp. Sel.* i, Hanover (1916)
   English trans. (selection), Whitelock, *EHD* i

Lupus of Ferrières, *Epistulae*, ed. P.K. Marshall, Leipzig (1984)
   ed. and trans. L. Levillain, *Loup de Ferrières, Correspondance*, 2 vols., Paris (1927–35)
   English trans. G.W. Regenos, *The Letters of Lupus of Ferrières*, The Hague (1966)

Magnus of Sens, *Notae Iuris*, ed. T. Mommsen, in *Grammatici Latini* IV, ed. H. Keil, Leipzig (1864), pp. 285–300

Manaresi, C. (ed., *I placiti del 'Regnum Italiae'*, 3 vols. in 5, Rome (1955–60)

Mercier, P. (ed.) with French trans.), *XIV Homélies du IXe siècle d'un auteur inconnu de l'Italie du nord* (*SC* 161), Paris (1970)

Meyer, K. (ed.), *Bruchstücke der älteren Lyrik Irlands*, Berlin (1919)

Meyer, K. (ed.), *Über die älteste irische Dichtung*, Berlin (1913)

Meyer-Marthaler, E. and Perret, F. (ed.), *Bündner Urkundenbuch*, Chur (1955)

Michael II and Theophilus, *Epistula ad Hulodowicum I*, ed. A. Werminghoff, *MGH Conc.* II:2, Hanover (1908), pp. 475–80

Mico of Saint-Riquier, *Epytafium (xxxvi)*, ed. L. Traube, *MGH Poet.* III, Berlin (1896), p. 311

Milev, A. (ed.), *Gr'tskite Zhitiia na Kliment Okhridski*, Sofia (1966)

Miracula Anastasii, ed. H. Usener, *Acta M. Anastasii Persae*, Bonn (1894), pp. 14–20

Miracula Sancti Bertini, ed. G. Waitz, *MGH SS* XV:1, Berlin (1887), pp. 509–16

Miracula Sancti Carileffi, *AASS OSB* I, pp. 651–4

Miracula Sancti Demetrii, *AASS* Oct. IV, pp. 222–6

Morin, G., 'Textes inédits relatifs au symbole et à la vie chrétienne', *RB* 22 (1905), pp. 505–25

Murethach, *In Donati Artem Maiorem*, ed. L. Holtz (*CCCM* 40), Turnhout (1977)

Murphy, G. (ed.), *Early Irish Lyrics*, Oxford (1956)

Musica Enchiriadis, ed. H. Schmid, *Musica et scolia enchiriadis una cum aliquibus tractatulis adiunctis*, Munich (1981)

Nicholas I, *Epistulae*, ed. E. Perels, *MGH Epp.* VI, Hanover (1925), 267–90

Nicholas I, *Responsa ad Consulta Bulgarorum*, ed. E. Dümmler, *MGH Epp.* VI, Berlin (1925), pp. 568–600

Nithard, *Historiarum Libri*, ed. E. Müller, *MGH SRG* 44, Hanover (1907)
  ed. and trans. P. Lauer, *Histoire des fils de Louis le Pieux* (Les classique de l'histoire de France au moyen âge 7), Paris (1926)
  English trans. B. Scholz, *Carolingian Chronicles*, Ann Arbor (1970)

Notitia Galliarum, ed. T. Mommsen, *MGH AA* IX:1, Berlin (1892), pp. 552–612

Notker Balbulus, *Gesta Karoli Magni Imperatoris*, ed. G. Pertz, *MGH SS* II, Berlin (1829), pp. 726–63
  ed. H.F. Haefele, *MGH SRG* n.s. XII, Berlin (1959)
  ed. and German trans. R. Rau, *QK* 3 (= *AQ* 7), Darmstadt (1960), pp. 322–426
  English trans. L. Thorpe, *Two Lives of Charlemagne*, Harmondsworth (1969)

Notker Balbulus, *Liber Ymnorum*, ed. W. von den Steinen, *Notker der Dichter und seine geistige Welt*, 2 vols., Berne (1948)

O'Brien, M.A., *Corpus Genealogium Hiberniae* I, Dublin (1962)

Odo of Cluny, *Vita Geraldi*, *AASS* Oct. VI, pp. 300–31; English trans. G. Sitwell, *St Odo of Cluny*, London and New York (1958)

The Old English Orosius, ed. J. Bately (Early English Text Society ss 6), Oxford (1980)

The Ordinals of Christ from their Origins to the Twelfth Century, ed. R. Reynolds (*Beiträge zur Geschichte und Quellenkunde des Mittelalters* 7), Berlin and New York (1978)

Ordines Romani, ed. M. Andrieu, *Les Ordines Romani du haut moyen âge*, 5 vols. (Spicilegium Sacrum Lovaniense 11, 20, 23, 24, 28), Leuven (1931–61)

Pacificius of Verona, *Manuale di computo con ritmo mnemotecnico dell'arcidiacono Pacifico di*

Verona (+ 844), ed. G. Meerseman and E. Adda (Italia Sacra 6), Padua (1966)

Pactum Hludowicianum, ed. A. Boretius, *MGH Cap.* I, Hanover (1883), pp. 352–5

Paenitentiale Viniani, ed. L. Bieler, *The Irish Penitentials*, Dublin (1963); ed. F.W.H. Wasserschleben, *Die Bussordnungen der abendländischen Kirche*, Halle (1851)

Parochiale Suevum, ed. P. Geyer and O. Cuntz, *Itineraria et Alia Geographia (CCSL 175)*, Turnhout (1965), pp. 412–20

Paschasius Radbert, *De Assumptione Sanctae Mariae Virginis*, ed. A. Ripberger *(CCCM 56c)*, Turnhout (1985), pp. 97–162

Paschasius Radbert, *De Corpore et Sanguine Domini*, ed. B. Paulus *(CCCM 16)*, Turnhout (1969)

Paschasius Radbert, *De Paratu Virginis*, ed. E.A. Matter *(CCCM 56c)*, Turnhout (1985), pp. 5–96

Paschasius Radbert, *Ecloga Duarum Sanctimonialium*, ed. L. Traube, *MGH Poet.* III, Berlin (1896), pp. 45–51

Paschasius Radbert, *Expositio in Matheo Libri XII*, ed. B. Paulus *(CCCM 56, 56A and 56B)*, Turnhout (1984)

Paschasius Radbert, *Expositio in Psalmum XLIV*, PL 120, cols. 993–1060

Paschasius Radbert, *Vita Sancti Adalhardi*, PL 120, cols. 1507–56

Passio Anastasiae, ed. F. Halkin, *Légendes grecques de 'martyres romaines'* (Subsidia Hagiographica 55), Brussels (1973), pp. 86–132

Paul Alvar, *Epistulae*, ed. I. Gil, *Corpus Scriptorum Mozarabicorum* I, Madrid (1973), pp. 227–70

Paul the Deacon, *Historia Langobardorum*, ed. G. Waitz, *MGH SRL*, Hanover (1878); English trans. W.D. Foulke, *Paul the Deacon's History of the Lombards*, Philadelphia (1907)

Paul the Deacon, *Liber de Episcopis Mettensibus*, ed. G. Pertz, *MGH SS* II, Berlin (1829), pp. 260–70

Paulinus of Aquileia, *De Conversione Saxonum Carmen*, ed. E. Dümmler, *MGH Poet.* I, Berlin (1881), pp. 380–1

Paulinus of Aquileia, *Liber Exhortationis ad Hericum Comitem*, PL 99, cols. 197–282

Pellat, C. (ed.), 'Gahiziana I', *Arabica* 1 (1954), pp. 153–65

Phillimore, E., 'The *Annales Cambriae* and Old-Welsh genealogies', *Y Cymmrodor* 9 (1888), pp. 141–83

Photius, *Epistulae et Amphilochia*, ed. B. Laourdas and L.G. Westernik, 3 vols., Leipzig (1983–5)
    English trans. D.S. White and J.R. Berrigan, *The Patriarch and the Prince: Photius' Letters to Khan Boris*, Brookline, MA (1982)

I placiti del Regnum Italiae, ed. C. Manaresi *(FSI 17)*, Rome (1955)

Polemius (Laterculus Silvius), ed. T. Mommsen, *MGH AA* IX:1, Berlin (1892), pp. 511–51

Poupardin, R., *Recueil des actes des rois de Provence (855–928)*, Paris (1920)

Propositiones ad Acuendos Iuvenes, ed. M. Folkerts, *Die älteste mathematische Aufgabensammlung in lateinischer Sprache: Die Alkuin zugeschriebenen 'Propositiones ad Acuendos Iuvenes' Überlieferung, Inhalt, kritische Edition* (Österreichische Akademie der Wissenschaften, mathematisch-naturwissenschaftliche Klasse Denkschriften, 116 Band, 6 Abhandlung), Vienna (1978)

De Proprietate Philosophiae et de VII Liberalibus Artibus, ed. J.J. Contreni, 'John

Scottus, Martin Hiberniensis, the liberal arts and teaching', in J.J. Contreni, *Carolingian Learning, Masters and Manuscripts*, Aldershot (1992), ch. 6

Provinciale Visigothicum, ed. P. Geyer and O. Cuntz, *Itineraria et Alia Geographia* (*CCSL* 175), Turnhout (1965), pp. 422–48

De Provinciis Italiae, ed. P. Geyer and O. Cuntz, *Itineraria et Alia Geographia* (*CCSL* 175), Turnhout (1965), pp. 366–8

Prudentius of Troyes, *De Praedestinatione contra Iohannem Scottum*, PL 112, cols. 1099–366

Pseudo-Gregory II, *Epistula ad Leonem III*, ed. J. Gouillard, 'Aux origines de l'iconoclasme: le témoignage de Grégoire II?', *TM* 3 (1968), pp. 243–307

Pseudo-Jerome, *De septem ordinibus ecclesiae*, ed. A.W.E. Kalff, Würzburg (1935)

Pseudo-Methodius, ed. E. Sackur, *Sibyllinische Texte und Forschungen*, Halle (1898), pp. 59–96

Rački, F. (ed.), *Documenta Historiae Chroaticae Periodum Antiquam Illustrantia*, Zagreb (1877)

Radner, J.N. (ed.), *Fragmentary Annals of Ireland*, Dublin (1978)

Rainogala and Alagus, *Gesta Pontificum Autissiodorensium*, ed. L. Duru, *Bibliothèque Historique de l'Yonne*, Auxerre (1850), I, pp. 309–57

ed. G. Waitz, *MGH SS* XIII, Hanover (1881), pp. 394–400 and XXVI, Hanover (1882), pp. 584–6

Ratpert and Ekkehard IV, *Casus Sancti Galli*, ed. G. Pertz, *MGH SS* II, Berlin (1829), pp. 57–147

Ratramnus of Corbie, *Liber de Anima*, ed. D.C. Lambot, Namur and Lille (1952)

Rau, R. (ed.), *Quellen zur Karolingischen Reichsgeschichte*, 3 vols., Darmstadt (1972, 1974, 1975)

Recueil des chartes de l'abbaye de Saint-Benoît-sur-Loire, ed. M. Prou and A. Vidier, 2 vols., Paris (1900–12)

Il regesto di Farfa compilato da Gregorio da Catino, ed. I. Giorgi and U. Balzani, 5 vols., Rome (1879–83)

Regino of Prüm, *Chronicon*, ed. F. Kurze, *MGH SRG* 50, Hanover (1890)
ed. with German trans. R. Rau, *QK* 3 (= *AQ* 7), Darmstadt (1960), pp. 180–318

Regino of Prüm, *Libri II de Synodalibus Causis et Disciplinis Ecclesiasticis*, ed. F.W.H. Wasserschleben, Leipzig (1840)

Regula Benedicti, ed. and trans. A. de Vogüé and J. Neufville (*SC* 181–6), Paris (1971–2)

Reichenau confraternity book, ed. J. Autherieth, D. Geuenich and K. Schmid, *Das Verbrüderungsbuch der Abtei Reichenau*, *MGH Lib. Mem.* I, Hanover (1979)

Remigius of Auxerre, *Commentarium in Martianum Capellam*, ed. C. Lutz, Leiden (1962–5)

Remigius of Auxerre, extracts from commentary on Boethius' *De Consolatione Philosophiae*, ed. E.T. Silk, *Saeculi Noni Auctoris in Boetii Consolationem Philosophiae Commentarius*, Appendix, Rome (1935)

Riculf, *De Conditore Ecclesiae Sancti Albani*, ed. E. Dümmler, *MGH Poet.* I, Berlin (1881), p. 431

Rimbert, *Vita Anskarii*, ed. G. Waitz, *MGH SRG* 55, Hanover (1884)
English trans. C.H. Robinson, *Anskar, the Apostle of the North*, London (1921)

Rudolf of Fulda, *Vita Sanctae Liobae*, ed. G. Waitz, *MGH SS* XV:1, Berlin (1887), pp. 127–31

English trans. C.H. Talbot, *The Anglo-Saxon Missionaries in Germany*, London (1954), pp. 205–26

St Gall, charters, ed. H. Wartmann, *Urkundenbuch Abtei Sankt Gallen*, 5 vols., Zurich and St Gall (1863–1921)

Sawyer, P.H., *Anglo-Saxon Charters: An Annotated List and Bibliography*, London (1968); revised edn S. Kelly (London, forthcoming)

Schmitz, H.J. (ed.), *Die Bußbücher und die Bußdisciplin der Kirche*, Mainz (1883)

Schwab, I. (ed.), *Das Prümer Urbar* (Rheinische Urbare 5), Düsseldorf (1983)

Scolia Enchiriadis, ed. H. Schmid, *Musica et Scolia Enchiriadis Una cum Aliquibus Tractatulis Adiunctis*, Munich (1981)

Sedulius Scottus, *Liber de Rectoribus Christianis*, ed. Hellmann (Quellen und Untersuchungen zur lateinischen Philologie 1–1), Munich (1906), pp. 1–91

English trans. E. Doyle, *On Christian Rulers and the Poems: Sedulius Scottus*, New York (1983)

Sickel, T., *Das Privilegium Otto Is für die römische Kirche*, Innsbruck (1883)

Sigebert of Gembloux, *Gesta Abbatum Gemblacensium*, ed. G. Pertz, *MGH SS* VIII, Berlin (1846), pp. 523–42

Skene, W.F. (ed.), *Chronicles of the Picts, Chronicles of the Scots*, Edinburgh (1867)

Smaragdus of Saint-Mihiel, *Expositio in Regulam Sancti Benedicti*, ed. J. Spannagel and P. Engelbert (*CCM* 1), Siegburg (1963), pp. 321–7

Smaragdus of Saint-Mihiel, *Via Regia*, *PL* 102, cols. 931–70

Snorre Sturluson, *Heimskringla*, ed. B. Adalbjarnarson, Reykjavik (1941–51)

English trans. L.M. Hollander, *Heimskringla: History of the Kings of Norway* (1964)

Statuta Ecclesiae Antiqua, ed. C. Munier, Paris (1960)

Steinmeyer, E. von (ed.), *Die kleineren althochdeutschen Sprachdenkmäler*, Berlin (1916)

The Stowe Missal, ed. G. Warren, London (1906–15)

Synaxarium Ecclesiae Constantinopolitanae, ed. H. Delehaye, *AASS* Nov.

Suidae Lexicon, see above under Adler

Synod I of Saint Patrick, ed. Bieler, *The Irish Penitentials*

Synodi Secundae Aquisgranensis Decreta Authentica (817), ed. J. Semmler (*CCM* 1), Siegburg (1963), pp. 473–81

Tatwine, *Ars Tatuine*, ed. M. de Marco (*CCSL 133*), Turnhout (1968)

Tellenbach, G. (ed.), *Römischer und Christliche Reichsgedanke in der Liturgie des frühen Mittelalters* (Sitzungsberichte der Heidelberger Akademie der Wissenschaften, phil.-hist. Klasse 1) (1934–5)

De Terminatione Provinciarum Italiae, ed. P. Geyer and O. Cuntz, *Itineraria et Alia Geographia* (*CCSL* 175), Turnhout (1965), pp. 348–63

Tessier, G. (ed.), *Recueil des actes de Charles II le Chauve*, 3 vols., Paris (1943–55)

Thegan, *Gesta Hludovici Imperatoris*, ed. G. Pertz, *MGH SS* II, Berlin (1829), pp. 585–604

ed. and trans. R. Rau, *QK* 1 (= *AQ* 5), Darmstadt (1955), pp. 213–53

Theodore of Stoudios, *Epistulae*, *PG* 90

Theodulf of Orléans, *Ad Modoinum Episcopum Scribens ei de Exilio*, ed. E. Dümmler, *MGH Poet.* 1, Berlin (1881), pp. 563–5, 569–73

Theodulf of Orléans, *De Libris Quos Legere Solebam*, ed. E. Dümmler, *MGH Poet.* 1, Berlin (1881), pp. 543–4

Theodulf of Orléans, *De Septem Liberalibus Artibus in Quadam Pictura Depictis*, ed. E. Dümmler, *MGH Poet.* 1, Berlin (1881), pp. 544–7

Theodulf of Orléans, *Erstes Kapitular*, ed. P. Brommer, *MGH Cap. Epis.* i:1, Hanover (1984), pp. 73–142

Theodulf of Orléans, *Libri Carolini*, ed. H. Bastgen, *MGH Conc.* ii, Supp., Hanover (1924)

Theophanes, *Chronographia*, ed. C. de Boor, i, Leipzig (1883)
   English trans. H. Turtledove, *The Chronicle of Theophanes*, Philadelphia (1982)

Theophanes Continuatus, *Chronographia*, ed. I. Bekker, Bonn (1838)

Theophilact of Ochrid, *Martyrium Sanctorum Quindecim Illustrium Martyrum*, PG 126, cols. 151–250

Tjäder, J.-O. (ed.), *Die nichtliterarischen lateinischen Papyri Italiens*, 3 vols., Lund and Stockholm (1954–82)

Traditiones Wizeburgenses: Die Urkunden des Klosters Weissenburg 661–864, ed. A. Doll, Darmstadt (1979)

Translatio Sancti Germani Parisiensis, AB (2) (1883), pp. 69–98

Translatione Sanguinis Domini, ed. G. Waitz, *MGH SS* iv, Berlin (1841), pp. 444–9

Uraicecht na Ríar: The Poetic Grades of Early Irish Law, ed. L. Breatnach (Early Irish Law Series 2), Dublin (1987)

Venantius Fortunatus, *Opera Poetica*, ed. F. Leo, *MGH AA* iv:1, Hanover (1881)

Verhulst, A., 'Das Besitzverzeichnis der Genter Sankt-Bavo-Abtei von ca. 800 (Clm 6333)', *FrSt* 5 (1971), pp. 193–234

Vita Alcuini Abbatis Turonensis, ed. W. Arndt, *MGH SS* xv:1, Hanover (1887), pp. 182–97

Vita Amandi, ed. B. Krusch, *MGH SRM* v, Hanover (1910), pp. 428–49

Vita Blasii Amoriensis, *AASS* Nov. 4, pp. 657–69

Vita Eliae Iunioris, ed. G. Rossi Taibbi, *Vita di Sant-Elia il Giovane*, Palermo (1962)

Vita Eliae Speliotis, *AASS* Sep. 3, pp. 848–87

Vita Eligii, ed. B. Krusch, *MGH SRM* iv, Hanover (1902), pp. 634–761

Vita Ermelandi, ed. B. Krusch, *MGH SS* ii, Berlin (1829), pp. 585–604

Vita Eucherii Episcopi Aurelianensis, ed. W. Levison, *MGH SRM* vii, Hanover (1920), pp. 46–53

Vita Faronis Episcopi Meldensis, ed. B. Krusch, *MGH SRM* v, Hanover (1910), pp. 171–203

Vita Folcuini Episcopi Morinensis, ed. O. Holder-Egger, *MGH SS* xv:1, Hanover (1887), pp. 424–30

Vita Geretrudis, ed. B. Krusch, *MGH SRM* ii, Hanover (1888), pp. 447–74

Vita Lebuini, ed. A. Hofmeister, *MGH SS* xxx:2, Hanover (1934), pp. 789–95
   English trans. C. H. Talbot, *The Anglo-Saxon Missionaries in Germany* (London, 1954)

Vita Leutfredi, *AASS* Jun. iv, pp. 105–12

Vita Liobae, see under Rudolf

Vita Liutbirgae, ed. G. Pertz, *MGH SS* iv, Berlin (1841), pp. 158–64

Vita Martini I, ed. P. Peeters, 'Une vie grecque de S. Martin Ier', *AB* 51 (1933), pp. 225–62

Vita Nicetae Patricii, ed. D. Papachryssanthou, 'Un confesseur du second icono-clasme. La vie du patrice Nicétas (+836)', *TM* 51 (1968), pp. 325–7

Vita Odiliae Abbatissae Hohenburgensis, ed. W. Levison, *MGH SRM* vi, Hanover (1913)

Vita Pardulfi Abbatis Waractensis, ed. W. Levison, *MGH SRM* VII, Hanover (1920), pp. 24–40

Vita Sturmi, see under Eigil

Vita Wulframni, ed. B. Krusch, *MGH SRN* V, Hanover (1910), pp. 657–73

Walahfrid Strabo, *De Exordiis et Incrementis Quarundam in Observationis Ecclesiasticis Rerum*, ed. A. Knoepfler, Munich (1890)
  English trans. A. Harting-Corrêa, Leiden (1995)

Walahfrid Strabo, *Gotescalcho Monachi, qui et Fulgentius*, ed. E. Dümmler, *MGH Poet.* II, Berlin (1884), pp. 363–4

Walahfrid Strabo, *Visio Wettini*, ed. E. Dümmler, *MGH Poet.* II, Berlin (1884), pp. 301–33; English trans. D. Traill, *Walafrid Strabo's Visio Wettini: Text, Translation and Commentary* (Lateinische Sprache und Literatur des Mittelalters 2), Frankfurt am Main (1974)

Walter of Orléans, *Capitula a Walterio reverendo pontifice compresbiteris promulgata in sinodo apud bullensem fundum II*, ed. P. Brommer, *MGH Cap. Epis.* I:1, Hanover (1984), pp. 185–93

Wasserschleben, F.W.H. (ed.), *Die Bußordnungen der abendländische Kirche*, Halle (1851; rep. Graz, 1968)

Whitelock, D. (ed.), *English Historical Documents*, I: *c*. 500–1042, 2nd edn, London (1979)

Widukind of Corvey, *Rerum Gestarum Saxonicarum libri III*, ed. A. Bauer and R. Rau (*AQ* VIII), Darmstadt (1969)

Willibald, *Vita Sancti Bonifatii*, ed. W. Levison, *MGH SRG* 57, Hanover (1905)
  ed. with German trans. R. Rau, *Briefe des Bonifatius, Willibalds Leben des Bonifatius nebst einigen zeitgenössischen Dokumenten* (*AQ* IVb), Darmstadt (1968)
  English trans. C.H. Talbot, *The Anglo-Saxon Missionaries in Germany*, London (1954), pp. 25–62

BIBLIOGRAPHY OF SECONDARY
WORKS ARRANGED BY CHAPTER

I INTRODUCTION: SOURCES AND INTERPRETATION

For the primary sources exploited by authors for each chapter, see the composite Bibliography on pp. 867–85. For guides to the sources generally the following are the most helpful:

Buchner, R. (1953), *Die Rechtsquellen*, Weimar
Genicot, L. (1972–), *Typologie des sources du moyen âge occidentale*, Turnhout
McKitterick, R. (1994b), *Carolingian Culture: Emulation and Innovation*, Cambridge
Molinier, A. (1901), *Les sources de l'histoire de France*, Paris
Monod, G. (1898), *Etudes critiques sur les sources de l'histoire carolingienne*, Paris
van Caenegem, R.C. (1978), *Guide to the Sources of Medieval History*, Amsterdam, Oxford and New York
Wattenbach, W., Levison, W. and Lowe, H. (1953–) *Deutschlands Geschichtsquellen im Mittelalter*, Weimar

Reading on matters discussed in the Introduction and cited in the notes

These books and articles represent a selection only. Readers are advised to follow up the references provided by the authors of these articles and books for further studies on the subjects comprised; on law, Schott (1979) and Sellert (1992b) are particularly useful.

Amory, P. (1993), 'The meaning and purpose of ethnic terminology in the Burgundian laws', *EME* 2: 1–28
Balzaretti, R. (1994), 'The monastery of Sant'Ambrogio and dispute settlement in early medieval Milan', *EME* 3: 1–18
Banniard, M. (1991), 'Rhabanus Maurus and the vernacular languages', in Wright (1991), pp. 164–74
Banniard, M. (1992), *Viva voce: communication écrite et communication orale du IVe siècle en occident latin*, Paris
Brown, P. (1981), *The Cult of the Saints*, Chicago
Bühler, A. (1990), 'Wort und Schrift im karolingischen Recht', *Archiv für Kulturgeschichte* 72: 275–96
Bullough, D.A. (1991), *Carolingian Renewal: Sources and Heritage*, Manchester

Bullough, D.A. and Harting-Correâ, A. (1989), 'Texts, chant and the chapel of Louis the Pious', in P. Godman and R. Collins, *Charlemagne's Heir: New Perspectives on the Reign of Louis the Pious*, Oxford, pp. 489–508, reprinted in Bullough (1991), pp. 241–71

Carruthers, M. (1990), *The Book of Memory: A Study of Memory in Medieval Culture*, Cambridge

Classen, P. (1977), *Recht und Schrift im Mittelalter*, VuF 23, Sigmaringen

Coleman, J. (1992), *Ancient and Medieval Memories: Studies in the Reconstruction of the Past*, Cambridge

Collins, R. (1990), 'Literacy and the laity in early medieval Spain', in McKitterick (1990), pp. 109–33

Davies, W. and Fouracre, P. (1986), *The Settlement of Disputes in Early Medieval Europe*, Cambridge

Deshusses, J. (1977), 'Chronologie des grandes sacramentaires de Saint-Amand', *RB* 87: 230–7

Dilcher, G., Lück, H., Schulze, R., Waddle, E., Weitzel, J. and Wolter, U. (1992), *Gewohnheitsrecht und Rechtsgewohnheiten im Mittelalter* (Schriften zur Europäischen Rechts-und Verfassungsgeschichte 6), Berlin

Dronke, P. and U. (1977), *Barbara et Antiquissima Carmina*, Barcelona

Fouracre, P. (1990), 'Merovingian history and Merovingian hagiography', *Past and Present* 127: 3–38

Fuhrmann, H. (1986), *Fälschungen im Mittelalter* (*MGH* Schriften 33), 6 vols., Hanover

Ganz, D. (1990), *Corbie in the Carolingian Renaissance*, Sigmaringen

Geary, P. (1978; 2nd edn 1990), *Furta Sacra: Thefts of Relics in the Central Middle Ages*, Princeton

Goffart, W. (1978), *The Le Mans Forgeries*, Princeton

Goffart, W. (1988), *The Narrators of Barbarian History (A.D. 550–800): Jordanes, Gregory of Tours, Bede, and Paul the Deacon*, Princeton

Hagiographies, cultures et société, IVe–XIIe siècles, Paris (1981)

Head, T. (1990), *Hagiography and the Cult of Saints: The Diocese of Orléans, 800–1200*, Cambridge

Heene, K. (1991), '*Audire, legere, vulgo*: an attempt to define public use and comprehensibility of Carolingian hagiography', in Wright (1991), pp. 130–45

Heinzelmann, M. (ed.) (1992), *Manuscrits hagiographiques et travail des hagiographes*, Sigmaringen

Heinzelmann, M. and Paulin, J.-C. (1986), *Les vies anciennes de Geneviève de Paris: études critiques*, Paris

Herbert, M. (1988), *Iona, Kells and Derry: The History and Hagiography of the Monastic 'Familia' of Columba*, Oxford

Hodges, R. (ed.) (1993), *San Vincenzo al Volturno* I (Archaeological Monographs of the British School at Rome 7) Rome

Hodges, R. and Mitchell, J. (1985), *San Vincenzo al Volturno: The Archaeology, Art and Territory of an Early Medieval Monastery* (BAR International Series 252), Oxford

Innes, M. and McKitterick, R. (1994), 'The writing of history', in McKitterick (1994b), pp. 193–220

Kobler, G. (1971), *Das Recht im frühen Mittelalter*, Cologne and Vienna

Kottje, R. (1986), 'Die Lex Baiuvariorum – das Recht der Beiern', in Mordek (1986), pp. 9–24

Kottje, R. (1987), 'Zum Geltungsbereich der *Lex Alemannorum*', in H. Beumann and W. Schröder (eds.), *Die transalpinen Verbindungen der Bayern, Alemannen und Franken bis zum 10. Jahrhundert*, (Nationes, Historische und philologische Untersuchungen zur Entstehung der Europäischen Nationen im Mittelalter), Sigmaringen, pp. 359–77

Levy, K. (1984), 'Toledo, Rome and the legacy of Gaul', *Early Music History* 4: 49–99

Levy, K. (1987), 'On the origin of neumes', *Early Music History* 7: 59–90

Levy, K. (1990), 'On Gregorian orality', *Journal of the American Musicological Society* 43: 185–227

McKitterick, R. (1977), *The Frankish Church and the Carolingian Reforms, 789–895*, London

McKitterick, R. (1980), 'Charles the Bald (823–877) and his library: the patronage of learning', *ERH* 95: 28–47

McKitterick, R. (1983), *The Frankish Kingdoms under the Carolingians, 751–987*, London

McKitterick, R. (1989), *The Carolingians and the Written Word*, Cambridge

McKitterick, R. (1991), 'Frauen und Schriftlichkeit im Frühmittelalter', in H.-W. Goetz (ed.), *Weibliche Lebensgestaltung im frühen Mittelalter*, Cologne and Vienna, pp. 65–118; revised English version in McKitterick (1994a)

McKitterick, R. (1993), 'Zur Herstellung von Kapitularien: Die Arbeit des *leges* Skriptoriums', *MIÖG* 101: 3–16

McKitterick, R. (1994a), *Books, Scribes and Learning in the Frankish Kingdoms, Sixth to Ninth Centuries*, Aldershot

McKitterick, R. (ed.) (1990), *The Uses of Literacy in Early Medieval Europe*, Cambridge

McKitterick, R. (ed.) (1994b), *Carolingian Culture: Emulation and Innovation*, Cambridge

Martin, H.J. and Vezin, J. (1990), *Mise en page et mise en texte du livre manuscrit*, Paris

Mordek, H. (ed.) (1986), *Überlieferung und Geltung normativer Texte des frühen und hohen Mittelalters* (Quellen und Forschungen zum Recht im Mittelalter 4), Sigmaringen

Morrison, K.F. (1990), *History as a Visual Art in the Twelfth-Century Renaissance*, Princeton

Morse, R. (1991), *Truth and Convention in the Middle Ages: Rhetoric, Representation, and Reality*, Cambridge

Nehlsen, H. (1977), 'Zur Aktualität und Effektivität germanischer Rechtsaufzeichnungen', in Classen (1977), pp. 449–502

Nelson, J.L. (1983), 'Legislation and consensus in the reign of Charles the Bald', in P. Wormald (ed.), *Ideal and Reality in Frankish and Anglo-Saxon Society*, Oxford, pp. 202–27

Nelson, J.L. (1985), 'Public *Histories* and private history in the work of Nithard', *Speculum* 60: 251–93; reprinted in Nelson (1986a), pp. 195–238

Nelson, J.L. (1986a), *Politics and Ritual in Early Medieval Europe*, London

Nelson, J.L. (1986b), 'Dispute settlement in Carolingian West Francia', in Davies and Fouracre (1986), pp. 45–64

Nelson, J.L. (1990a), 'The Annals of St Bertin', in J.L. Nelson and M.T. Gibson (eds.), *Charles the Bald: Court and Kingdom*, 2nd edn, London

Nelson, J.L. (1990b), 'Literacy in Carolingian government', in McKitterick (1990), pp. 258–96

O'Brien O'Keefe, K. (1990), *Visible Song: Transitional Literacy in Old English Verse*, Cambridge

Oexle, O.-G. and Schmid, K. (1974), 'Voraussetzungen und Wirkung des Gebetsbundes von Attigny', *Francia* 2: 71–122

Parkes, M.B. (1993), *Pause and Effect: Punctuation in the West*, London

Paxton, F.S. (1990), *Christianizing Death: The Creation of a Ritual Process in Early Medieval Europe*, Ithaca

Randsborg, K. (1991), *The First Millennium AD in Europe and the Mediterranean: An Archaeological Essay*, Cambridge

Rankin, S. (1993), 'Carolingian music', in McKitterick (1993b), pp. 274–316

Rollason, D. (1989), *Saints and Relics in Anglo-Saxon England*, Oxford

Rollason, D. and Stancliffe, C. (eds.) (1989), *St Cuthbert, His Cult and Community to AD 1200*, Woodbridge

Schott, C. (1979), 'Der Stand der Leges Forschung', *FrSt* 13: 29–55

Sellert, W. (1992a), 'Aufzeichnung des Rechts und Gesetzes', in Sellert (1992b), pp. 67–102

Sellert, W. (ed.) (1992b), *Das Gesetz in Spätantike und frühem Mittelalter* (Abhandlungen der Akademie der Wissenschaften in Göttingen, phil.-hist. Klasse, Dritte Folge 196), Göttingen

Sharpe, R. (1991), *Medieval Irish Saints' Lives: An Introduction to the 'Vitae Sanctorum Hiberniae'*, Oxford

Smith, J.M.H. (1990), 'Oral and written: saints, miracles and relics in Brittany, c. 850–1250', *Speculum* 65: 309–43

Smith, J.M.H. (1992), 'Early medieval hagiography in the late twentieth century', *EME* 1: 69–76

Treitler, L. (1974), 'Homer and Gregory: the transmission of epic poetry and plainchant', *The Musical Quarterly* 60: 333–72

Treitler, L. (1981), 'Oral, written and literate process in the transmission of medieval music', *Speculum* 56: 471–91

Treitler, L. (1982), 'The early history of music writing in the west', *Journal of the American Musicological Society* 35: 237–78

Treitler, L. (1984), 'Reading and singing: on the genesis of Occidental musicwriting', *Early Music History* 4: 135–208

Treitler, L. (1988), 'Communication', *Journal of the American Musicological Society* 41: 566–75

Wolf, K. (1988), *Christian Martyrs in Muslim Spain*, Cambridge

Wormald, P. (1977), '*Lex scripta et verbum regis*: legislation and Germanic kingship from Euric to Cnut', in P. Sawyer and I.N. Wood (eds.), *Early Medieval Kingship*, Leeds, pp. 105–38

Wright, R. (1982), *Late Latin and Early Romance in Spain and Carolingian France*, Liverpool

Wright, R. (1993), 'Complex monolingualism in early Romance', in William J. Ashby (ed.), *Linguistic Perspectives on the Romance Languages: Selected Papers from the XXI Linguistic Symposium on Romance Languages*, Benjamins, pp. 377–88

Wright, R. (ed.) (1991), *Latin and the Romance Languages in the Early Middle Ages*, London

2(a) ENGLAND, 700–900

Bassett, S. (ed.) (1989), *The Origins of Anglo-Saxon Kingdoms*, Leicester

Brooks, N. (1984), *The Early History of the Church of Canterbury: Christ Church from 597 to 1066*, Leicester

Brooks, N. (1989), 'The formation of the Mercian kingdom', in Bassett (1989), pp. 159–70 and 275–7

Bullough, D. (1993), 'What has Ingeld to do with Lindisfarne?' *ASE* 22: 93–126

Campbell, J. (1986), *Essays in Anglo-Saxon History*, London

Campbell, J. (ed.) (1982), *The Anglo-Saxons*, Oxford; reprinted Harmondsworth, 1991

Davies, W. and Vierck, H. (1974), 'The contexts of Tribal Hidage: social aggregates and settlement patterns', *FrSt* 8: 223–93

Dumville, D. (1989a), 'Essex, Middle Anglia and the expansion of Mercia in the south-east Midlands', in Bassett (1989), pp. 123–40 and 270

Dumville, D. (1989b), 'The Tribal Hidage: an introduction to its texts and their history', in Bassett (1989), pp. 225–30 and 286–7

Everitt, A. (1986), *Continuity and Colonization: The Evolution of Kentish Settlement*, Leicester

Goffart, W. (1988), *The Narrators of Barbarian History (A.D. 550–800): Jordanes, Gregory of Tours, Bede, and Paul the Deacon*, Princeton

Grierson, P. and Blackburn, M. (1986), *Medieval European Coinage*, I: *The Early Middle Ages (5th–10th Centuries)*, Cambridge

Hart, C. (1971), 'The Tribal Hidage', *TRHS* 5th series, 21: 133–57

Hodges, R. (1989), *The Anglo-Saxon Achievement: Archaeology and the Beginnings of English Society*, London

Keynes, S. (1990), 'Changing faces: Offa, King of Mercia', *History Today* 40 (November): 14–19

Keynes, S. (1992), 'Rædwald the Bretwalda', in C.B. Kendall and P.S. Wells (eds.), *Voyage to the Other World: The Legacy of Sutton Hoo* (Medieval Studies at Minnesota 4), Minneapolis, pp. 103–23

Keynes, S. (1993), 'The control of Kent in the ninth century', *EME* 2: 111–32

Keynes, S. (1995), 'King Alfred and the Mercians', in M.A.S. Blackburn and D.N. Dumville (eds.), *Kings, Currency, and Alliances: The History and Coinage of Southern England, A.D. 840–900*, Woodbridge

Loyn, H.R. (1984), *The Governance of Anglo-Saxon England 500–1087*, London

Russell, J.C. (1947), 'The Tribal Hidage', *Traditio* 5: 192–209

Sawyer, P.H. (1978), *From Roman Britain to Norman England*, London

Stenton, F.M. (1971), *Anglo-Saxon England*, 3rd edn, Oxford

Wallace-Hadrill, J.M. (1988), *Bede's 'Ecclesiastical History of the English People': A Historical Commentary*, Oxford

Webster, L. and Backhouse, J. (eds.) (1991), *The Making of England: Anglo-Saxon Art and Culture AD 600–900*, London

Wormald, P. (1983), 'Bede, the *Bretwaldas*, and the origins of the *Gens Anglorum*', in P. Wormald *et al.* (eds.), *Ideal and Reality in Frankish and Anglo-Saxon Society*, Oxford, pp. 99–129

2(b) IRELAND, SCOTLAND, AND WALES, *c.*700 TO THE EARLY ELEVENTH CENTURY

Ahlqvist, A. (1982), *The Early Irish Linguist* (Commentationes Humanarum Litterarum 73), Helsinki

Anderson, M.O. (1973), *Kings and Kingship in Early Scotland*, Edinburgh

Anderson, M.O. (1982), 'Dalriada and the creation of the kingdom of the Scots', in D. Whitelock, R. McKitterick and D. Dumville (eds.), *Ireland in Early Medieval Europe*, Cambridge, pp. 106–32

Baldwin, J.R. and Whyte, I.D. (1985), *The Scandinavians in Cumbria*, Edinburgh

Bannerman, J. (1974), *Studies in the History of Dalriada*, Edinburgh

Baumgarten, R. (1985), 'The kinship metaphors in *Bechbretha* and *Coibnes uisci thairidne*', *Peritia* 4: 307–27

Binchy, D.A. (1936), *Studies in Early Irish Law*, Dublin

Binchy, D.A. (1954), 'Secular institutions', in Myles Dillon (ed.), *Early Irish Society*, Dublin, pp. 52–65

Binchy, D.A. (1970), *Celtic and Anglo-Saxon Kingship*, Oxford

Binchy, D.A. (1976), 'Irish history and Irish law: II', *Studia Hibernica* 16: 37–45

Boyle, A. (1967), 'Matrilineal succession in the Pictish monarchy', *Scottish Historical Revue* 56: 1–10

Breatnach, L. (1984), 'Canon law and secular law in early Ireland: the significance of *Bretha Nemed*', *Peritia* 3: 439–59

Breatnach, L. (1986a), '*Airdri* as an old compound', *Ériu* 37: 192–3

Breatnach, L. (1986b), 'The ecclesiastical element in the Old-Irish legal tract Cáin Fhuithirbe', *Peritia* 5: 36–52

Breatnach, R.A. (1953), 'The lady and the king: a theme of Irish literature', *Studies* (Dublin) 42: 321–36

Breen, A. (1992), 'The liturgical materials in MS Oxford, Bodleian Library, Auct. F.4/32', *Archiv für Liturgiewissenschaft* 34: 121–153

Bugge, A. (1900), 'Contributions to the history of the Norsemen in Ireland III: Norse settlements round the Bristol Channel', *Videnskabsselskabets Skrifter*, Phil.-hist. Klasse, pp. 3–11

Byrne, F.J. (1970), *The Rise of the Uí Néill and the High-Kingship of Ireland*, Dublin

Byrne, F.J. (1971), 'Tribes and tribalism in early Ireland', *Ériu* 21: 128–66

Byrne, F.J. (1973), *Irish Kings and High-Kings*, London

Byrne, F.J. (1987), 'The trembling sod: Ireland in 1169', in A. Cosgrove (ed.), *A New History of Ireland*, Oxford, II, pp. 1–42

Carney, J. (1955), *Studies in Irish History and Literature*, Dublin

Carney, J. (1966), *Irish Literature*, London

Carney, J. (1967), *Medieval Irish Lyrics*, Dublin

Chadwick, H.M. (1949), *Early Scotland*, Cambridge

Charles-Edwards, T.M. (1971), 'Some Celtic kinship terms', *BBCS* 24: 105–22

Charles-Edwards, T.M. (1972), 'Kinship, status and the origin of the hide', *Past and Present* 56: 3–33

Charles-Edwards, T.M. (1978), 'The authenticity of the *Gododdin*: an historian's view', in R. Bromwich and R.B. Jones (eds.), *Astudiaethau ar yr Hengerdd*, Cardiff, pp. 44–71

Charles-Edwards, T.M. (1980), 'The Corpus Iuris Hibernici', *Studia Hibernica* 20: 141–62

Charles-Edwards, T.M. (1986), '*Críth Gablach* and the law of status', *Peritia* 5: 53–73

Crawford, B.E. (1987), *Scandinavian Scotland*, Leicester

Crawford, I.A. (1981), 'War or peace – Viking colonisation in the Northern and Western Isles of Scotland', in H. Bekker-Nielsen *et al.* (eds.), *Proceedings of the Eighth Viking Congress*, Odense, pp. 259–69

Davies, R.R. (1990), *Domination and Conquest: The Experience of Ireland, Scotland and Wales 1100–1300*, Cambridge

Davies, W. (1982), *Wales in the Early Middle Ages*, Leicester

Davies, W. (1990), *Patterns of Power in Early Wales*, Oxford

Dillon, M. (1947), 'The archaism of Irish tradition', *Proceedings of the British Academy* 33: 245–64

Doherty, C. (1982), 'Some aspects of hagiography as a source for Irish economic history', *Peritia* 1: 300–28

Doherty, C. (1985), 'The monastic town in early medieval Ireland', in H.B. Clarke and A. Simms (eds.), *The Comparative History of Urban Origins in Non-Roman Europe* (BAR International Series 255), Oxford, pp. 45–75

Dowden, J. (1896), 'An examination of original documents on the question of the form of the Celtic tonsure', *Proceedings of the Society of Antiquaries of Scotland* 30: 325–37

Dumville, D.N. (1975–6), '"Nennius" and the *Historia Brittonum*', *Studia Celtica* 10–11: 78–95

Dumville, D.N. (1977), 'Palaeographical considerations in the dating of early Welsh verse', *BBCS* 27: 246–51

Dumville, D.N. (1982), 'The "six" sons of Rhodri Mawr: a problem in Asser's *Life of King Alfred*', *CMCS* 4: 5–18

Dumville, D.N. (1988), 'Early Welsh poetry: problems of historicity', in B.F. Roberts (ed.), *Early Welsh Poetry: Studies in the Book of Aneirin*, Aberystwyth, pp. 1–16

Duncan, A.A.M. (1975), *Scotland: The Making of the Kingdom* (Edinburgh History of Scotland 1), Edinburgh

Fellows-Jensen, G. (1984), 'Viking settlement in the Northern and Western Isles – the place-name evidence as seen from Denmark and the Danelaw', in A. Fenton and H. Pálsson (eds.), *The Northern and Western Isles in the Viking World*, Edinburgh, pp. 148–68

Fellows-Jensen, G. (1985), 'Scandinavian settlement in Cumbria and Dumfries-shire: the place-name evidence', in J.R. Baldwin and I.D. Whyte (eds.), *The Scandinavians in Cumbria*, Edinburgh, pp. 65–82

Fournier, P. (1899), 'De l'influence de la collection irlandaise sur la formation des collections canoniques', *Nouvelle Revue Historique de Droit Français et Etranger* 23: 27–78

Henry, F. (1965–70), *Irish Art*, 3 vols., London

Henry, F. (1974), *The Book of Kells with a Study of the Manuscript*, London

Henry, F. and Marsh-Micheli, G. (1985), *Studies in Early Christian and Medieval Irish Art*, London

Herbert, M. (1988), *Iona, Kells and Derry: The History and Hagiography of the Monastic 'Familia' of Columba*, Oxford

Holtz, L. (1981), 'Irish grammarians and the continent in the seventh century', in H.B. Clarke and M. Brennan (eds.), *Columbanus and Merovingian Monasticism*, Oxford, pp. 135–52

Hughes, K. (1966), *The Church in Early Irish Society*, London

Hughes, K. (1974), *The Welsh Latin Chronicles: Annales Cambriae and Related Texts*, London

Jackson, K.H. (1955), 'The Pictish language', in F.T. Wainwright (ed.), *The Problem of the Picts*, Edinburgh, pp. 129–66

Jackson, K.H. (1956), 'The poem *A eolcha Alban uile*', *Celtica* 3: 149–67

Jackson, K.H. (1957), 'The Duan Albanach', *Scottish Historical Review*, 36: 125–37

Kelleher, J.V. (1967), 'The rise of Dál Cais', in E. Rynne (ed.), *North Munster Studies*, Limerick, pp. 230–41

Kelly, F. (1988), *A Guide to Early Irish Law*, Dublin

Kelly, J.F. (1988–90), 'A catalogue of early medieval Hiberno-Latin biblical commentaries', *Traditio* 44: 537–71; 45: 393–434

Kirby, D.P. (1976), '. . . *per uniuersas Pictorum prouincias*', in G. Bonner (ed.), *Famulus Christi*, London, pp. 296–334

Lapidge, M. (1986), 'Latin learning in Dark Age Wales', in E. Evans *et al.* (eds.), *Proceedings of the Seventh International Congress of Celtic Studies*, Oxford, pp. 91–107

Lapidge M. and Dumville, D.N. (1984), *Gildas: New Approaches*, Woodbridge

Loyn, H.R. (1976), *The Vikings in Wales*, London

Lucas, A.T. (1967), 'The plundering and burning of churches in Ireland, 7th to 16th century', in E. Rynne (ed.), *North Munster Studies*, Limerick, pp. 172–229

Mac Cana, P. (1955–8), 'Aspects of the theme of king and goddess in Irish literature', *EC* 7: 76–104; 8: 59–65

McCone, K. (1990), *Pagan Past and Christian Present*, Maynooth

Miller, M. (1979a), 'The disputed historical horizon of the Pictish king-lists', *Scottish Historical Review* 58: 1–34

Miller, M. (1979b), 'The last century of Pictish succession', *Scottish Studies* 23: 39–67

Miller, M. (1982), 'Matriliny by treaty: the Pictish foundation legend', in D. Whitelock, R. McKitterick and D. Dumville (eds.), *Ireland in Early Medieval Europe*, Cambridge, pp. 133–61

Mordek, H. (1975), *Kirchenrecht und Reform im Frankenreich*, Berlin

Murphy, G. (1961), *Early Irish Metrics*, Dublin

Ní Dhonnchadha, M. (1982), 'The guarantor list of *Cáin Adomnáin*, 697', *Peritia* 1: 178–215

Nicolaisen, W.F.H. (1979–90), 'Early Scandinavian naming in the Western and Northern Isles', *Northern Studies* 3: 105–21

Ó Corráin, D. (1972a), *Ireland before the Normans*, Dublin

Ó Corráin, D. (1972b), 'Irish regnal succession: a reappraisal', *Studia Hibernica* 11: 7–39

Ó Corráin, D. (1973), 'Dál Cais – church and dynasty', *Ériu* 24: 52–63

Ó Corráin, D. (1978), 'Nationality and kingship in pre-Norman Ireland', in T.W. Moody (ed.), *Nationality and the Pursuit of National Independence* (Historical Studies 11), Belfast, pp. 1–35

Ó Corráin, D. (1979), 'Women in early Irish society', in M. MacCurtain and D. Ó Corráin (eds.), *Women in Irish Society*, Dublin and Westport, CT, pp. 1–13

Ó Corráin, D. (1981), 'The early Irish churches: some aspects of organisation', in D.

Ó Corráin (ed.), *Irish Antiquity: Essays and Studies Presented to M.J. O'Kelly*, Cork, pp. 327–41

Ó Corráin, D. (1985a), 'Irish origin legends and genealogy: recurrent aetiologies', in T. Nyberg *et al.* (eds.), *History and Heroic Tale*, Odense, pp. 51–96

Ó Corráin, D. (1985b), 'Marriage in early Ireland', in A. Cosgrove (ed.), *Marriage in Ireland*, Dublin, pp. 5–24

Ó Corráin, D. (1986a) 'Law and society – principles of classification', in K.H. Schmidt (ed.), *Geschichte und Kultur der Kelten*, Heidelberg, pp. 234–40

Ó Corráin, D. (1986b), 'Brian Boru and the battle of Clontarf', in L. de Paor (ed.), *Milestones in Irish History*, Cork, pp. 31–40

Ó Corráin, D. (1986c), 'Historical need and literary narrative', in E. Evans *et al.* (eds.), *Proceedings of the Seventh International Congress of Celtic Studies*, Oxford, pp. 141–58

Ó Corráin, D. (1987), 'Irish vernacular law and the Old Testament', in P. Ní Chatháin and M. Richter (eds.), *Ireland and Christendom*, Stuttgart, pp. 296–307

Ó Corráin, D. (1989), 'Early Irish hermit poetry?', in D. Ó Corráin, L. Breatnach and K. McCone (eds.), *Sages, Saints and Storytellers: Celtic Studies in Honour of Professor J. Carney*, Maynooth, pp. 251–67

Ó Corráin, D., Breatnach, L. and Breen, A. (1984), 'The laws of the Irish', *Peritia* 3: 390–1

Ó Fiaich, T. (1969), 'The church of Armagh under lay control', *Seanchas Ardmhacha* 5: 75–127

O'Grady, S. (1889), 'The last kings of Ireland', *EHR* 4: 286–303

O'Keeffe, J.G. (1904), 'The rule of Patrick', *Ériu* 2: 216–24

O'Rahilly, T.F. (1946), *Early Irish History and Mythology*, Dublin

Picard, J.-M. (1984), 'Bede, Adomnán and the writing of history', *Peritia* 3: 50–70

Picard, J.-M. (1985), 'Structural patterns in early Hiberno-Latin hagiography', *Peritia* 4: 67–82

Ryan, J. (1967), 'Brian Boruma, king of Ireland', in E. Rynne (ed.), *North Munster Studies*, Limerick, pp. 355–74

Ryan, M. (1987), *Irish and Insular Art, AD 500–1200*, Dublin

Scowcroft, R.M. (1987–8), '*Leabhar Gabhála*', *Ériu* 38: 81–142: 39: 1–66

Seller, W.D.H. (1985), 'Warlords, holy men and matrilineal succession', *Innes Review* 36: 35–41

Sharpe, R. (1984), 'Some problems concerning the organization of the church in medieval Ireland', *Peritia* 3: 230–70

Sharpe, R. (1991), *Medieval Irish Saints' Lives*, Oxford

Smyth, A.P. (1975–9), *Scandinavian York and Dublin*, 2 vols., Dublin

Smyth, A.P. (1984), *Warlords and Holy Men: Scotland AD 80–1000*, London

Swan, L. (1983), 'Enclosed ecclesiastical sites and their relevance to settlement patterns in the first millennium AD', in T. Reeves-Smyth and F. Hammond (eds.), *Landscape Archaeology in Ireland* (BAR British Series 116), Oxford, pp. 269–94

Thurneysen, R. (1891), 'Mittelirische Verslehren', in W. Stokes and E. Windisch, *Irische Texte*, series 3, Leipzig, 1, pp. 1–182

Thurneysen, R. (1915), 'Zum Lebor Gabála', *Zeitschrift für celtische Philologie* 10: 384–95

Thurneysen, R. (1921), *Die irische Helden- und Königsage*, Halle an der Saale

Thurneysen, R. (1923), 'Aus dem irischen Recht I: das Unfrei-Lehen', *Zeitschrift für celtische Philologie* 14: 335–94

Thurneysen, R. (1925), 'Aus dem irischen Recht II: das Frei-Lehen', *Zeitschrift für celtische Philologie* 15: 239–60

Thurneysen, R. (1926), 'Aus dem irischen Recht IV', *Zeitschrift für celtische Philologie* 16: 205–13

Thurneysen, R. (1973), 'Celtic law', in D. Jenkins (ed.), *Celtic Law Papers*, Brussels, pp. 51–70

Wainwright, F.T. (1948), 'Ingimund's Invasion', *EHR* 63: 145–69

Walsh M. and Ó Cróinín, D. (1988), *Cummians's Letter De Controversia Paschali and the De Ratione Conputandi*, Toronto

Wormald, P. (1986), 'Celtic and Anglo-Saxon kingship: some further thoughts', in P.E. Szarmach (ed.), *Sources of Anglo-Saxon Culture*, Kalamazoo, MI, pp. 151–83

2(c) ENGLAND AND THE CONTINENT

Angenendt, A. (1972), *Monachi Peregrini: Studien zu Pirmin und den monastischen Vorstellungen des frühen Mittelalters* (Münstersche Mittelalter-Schriften 6), Munich

Angenendt, A. (1973), 'Willibrord im Dienste der Karolinger', *Annalen des historischen Vereins für den Niederrhein* 175: 63–113

Angenendt, A. (1974), 'Pirmin und Bonifatius. Ihr Verhältnis zu Mönchtum, Bischofsamt und Adel', in Borst (1974), pp. 251–304

Atsma, H. (ed.) (1989), *La Neustrie: les pays au nord de la Loire de 650 à 850*, 2 vols., Sigmaringen

Bange, P. and Weiler, A. (eds.) (1990), *Willibrord zijn wereld en zijn werk* (Middeleeuwse Studies 6), Nijmegen

Barton, P. (1975), *Frühzeit des Christentums in Österreich und Südostmitteleuropa bis 788*, Vienna

Bischoff, B. (1966), 'Wer ist die Nonne von Heidenheim?', *Studien und Mitteilungen zur Geschichte des Benediktinerordens* 49: 387–8

Bischoff, B. and Hofmann, J. (1952), *Libri Sancti Kyliani: Die Würzburger Schreibschule und die Dombibliothek im VIII. und IX. Jahrhundert*, Würzburg

Bonner, D., Rollason, D. and Stancliffe, C. (1989), *St Cuthbert, His Cult and his Community to AD 1200*, Woodbridge

Borst, A. (1974), *Mönchtum, Episkopat und Adel zur Gründungszeit des Klosters Reichenau* (Vorträge und Forschungen 20), Sigmaringen

Braunfels, W. (1965), *Karl der Grosse: Lebenswerk und Nachleben*, 5 vols., Düsseldorf

Brooks, N. (1984) *The Early History of the Church of Canterbury from 597–1066* (Studies in the History of Early Britain), Leicester

Brown T.J. (1974), 'The distribution and significance of membrane prepared in the insular manner', in *La paléographie hébraïque médiévale* (Colloques Internationaux du CNRS 547), Paris, pp. 127–35; reprinted in T.J. Brown, *A Palaeographer's View: Selected Writings of Julian Brown*, ed. J. Bately, M. Brown and J. Roberts, London (1993), pp. 125–40

Brown, T.J. (1975), 'An historical introduction to the use of classical Latin authors in the British Isles from the fifth to the eleventh century', *Settimane* 22: 237–94, reprinted in T.J. Brown, *A Palaeographer's View: Selected Writings of Julian Brown*, ed. J. Bately, M. Brown and J. Roberts, London (1993), pp. 141–78

Bruckner, A. (1967), *Chartae Latinae Antiquiores* iv, Lausanne

Brunhölzl, F. (1990), *Histoire de la littérature latine au moyen âge. De Cassiodore à la fin de la renaissance carolingienne* i: *L'époque mérovingienne*, Leuven (revised French edn of original 1975 German text)

Budney, M. and Tweddle, D. (1984), 'The Maaseik embroideries', *ASE* 13: 65–96

Bullough, D. (1972), 'The educational tradition in England from Alfred to Ælfric: teaching *utriusque linguae*' in *La Scuola nell'Occidente Latino dell'alto medioevo*, *Settimane* 19: 453–94; reprinted in revised version in Bullough (1991), pp. 297–334

Bullough, D. (1991), *Carolingian Renewal: Sources and Heritage*, Manchester

Büttner, H. (1965), 'Mission und Kirchenorganisation des Frankenreiches bis zum Tode Karls des Grossen', in *Karl der Grosse* i, pp. 454–87

Callmer, J. (1984), *Sceatta Problems in the Light of the Åhus Fiads*, Kungliga humanistiska vetenskabssamfundet i Lund (Scripta minora 1983–4: 2), Lund

Cam, H. (1912), *Local Government in Francia and England: A Comparison of the Local Administration and Jurisdiction of the Carolingian Empire with that of the West Saxon Kingdom*, London

Costambeys, M. (1994), 'An aristocratic community on the northern Frankish frontier, 670–726', *EME* 3: 39–62

Crawford, S.J. (1933), *Anglo-Saxon Influence on Western Christendom 600–800*, Oxford

Cubitt, C. (1995), *Anglo-Saxon Church Councils, AD 650–850* (Studies in the History of Early Britain), Leicester

Dahlhaus-Berg, E. (1981), *Nova Antiquitas et Antiqua Novitas: Typologische Exegese und isidorianisches Geschichtsbild bei Theodulf von Orléans* (Kölner Historische Abhandlungen 23), Cologne and Vienna

Dawson, D. (1932), *The Making of Europe 400–1000*, London

Derolez, R. (1974), 'Cross-Channel language ties', *Anglo-Saxon England* 3: 1–15

Dierkens, A. (1989), 'Prolégomènes à une historie des relations culturelles entre les îles britanniques et le continent pendant le haut moyen âge. La diffusion du monachisme dit colombanien ou iro-franc dans quelques monastères de la région parisienne au VIIe siècle et la politique religieuse de la reine Bathilde', in *La Neustrie*, pp. 370–94

Dronke, P. (1984), *Women Writers of the Middle Ages: A Critical Study of Texts from Perpetua (†203) to Marguerite Porete (†1310)*, Cambridge

Ellmers, D. (1990), 'The Frisian monopoly of coastal transport in the 6th–8th centuries AD', in McGrail (1990), pp. 91–2

Evison, V.I. (1965), *The Fifth-Century Invasions South of the Thames*, London

Ewig, E. (1954), '*Milo et eiusmodi similes*', in Boniface (1954): 412–40

Ewig, E. (1962), 'Die älteste Mainzer Patrozinien und die Frühgeschichte des Bistums Mainz', in V. Elbern (ed.), *Das erste Jahrtausend*, Düsseldorf

Ewig, E. (1967), 'Chrodegang et la reforme de l'église franque', in *Saint Chrodegang* (1967)

Foot, S.R.I. (forthcoming), *Anglo-Saxon Minsters AD 597–900*, Cambridge

Frantzen, A.J. (1983), *The Literature of Penance in Anglo-Saxon England*, Brunswick, NJ

Gatch, M.McC. (1977), *Preaching and Theology in Anglo-Saxon England: Aelfric and Wulfstan*, Toronto and Buffalo

Gauthier, N. (1980), *L'évangelisation des pays de la Moselle dans l'haut moyen âge*, Paris

Gerchow, J. (1988), *Die Gedenküberlieferung der Angelsachsen*, Berlin

Gneuss, H. (1981), 'A preliminary list of manuscripts written or owned in England up to 1100', *ASE* 9: 1–60

Grierson, P. (1941), 'The relations between England and Flanders before the Norman conquest', *TRHS* 4th series, 23 (1941): 71–112

Grierson, P. and Blackburn, M. (1986), *Medieval European Coinage, with a Catalogue of the Coins in the Fitzwilliam Museum, Cambridge*, I: *The Early Middle Ages (5th–10th centuries)*, Cambridge

Hauck, A. (1914), *Kirchengeschichte Deutschlands* (5 vols.), Leipzig

Haywood, J. (1991), *Dark-Age Naval Power: A Reassessment of Frankish and Anglo-Saxon Seafaring Activity*, London

Heidrich, I. (1965/6), 'Titulatur und Urkunden der arnulfingischen Hausmeier', *Archiv für Diplomatik* 11/12: 71–279

Heinzelmann, M. (1976), 'L'aristocracie et les évêchés entre Loire et Rhin, jusqu'à la fin du viie siècle', *RHEF* 62: 75–90

Hodges, R. (1989), *The Anglo-Saxon Achievement: Archaeology and the Beginnings of English Society*, London

Hodges, R. and Hobley, B. (1988), *The Rebirth of Towns in the West*, AD 700–1050 (CBA Research Report 68), London

Jelelma, D. (1955), 'Frisian trade in the Dark Ages', *Speculum* 30: 155–36

Johanek, P. (1985), 'Der "Aussenhandel" des Frankenreichs der Merowingerzeit nach Norden und Osten im Spiegel der Schriftquellen', in K. Düwel, H. Jankuhn, H. Siems and D. Timpe (eds.), *Untersuchungen zu Handel und Verkehr der vor-und frühgeschichtlichen Zeit in Mittel- und Nordeuropa*, III: *Der Handel des frühen Mittelalters* (Abhandlungen der Akademie der Wissenschaften in Göttingen, phil.-hist. Klasse, Dritte Folge 150), Göttingen: 214–54

Johnston, D.E. (ed.) (1977), *The Saxon Shore* (CBA Research Report 18), London

Kelly, S. (1992), 'Trading privileges from eighth-century England', *EME* 1: 3–28

Keynes, S. and Lapidge, M. (1983), *Alfred the Great: Asser's 'Life of King Alfred' and Other Contemporary Sources*, Harmondsworth

Kiesel, G. and Schroeder, J. (1989), *Willibrord, Apostel der Niederlande. Gründer der Abtei Echternach. Gedenkgabe zum 1250. Todestag des angelsächsischen Missionars*, Echternach

Le Gentilhomme, P. (1938), 'La circulation des sceattas dans la Gaule mérovingienne, *Revue Numismatique* 2: 23–49; English trans. *British Numismatic Journal* 23 (1943–4): 195–210

Lebecq, S. (1983), *Marchands et navigateurs frisons du haut moyen âge*, 2 vols., Lille

Leeds, E.T. (1913 and 1970), *The Archaeology of the Anglo-Saxon Settlements*, Oxford

Leighton, A.C. (1972), *Transport and Communication in Early Medieval Europe*, Newton Abbot

Levison, W. (1946), *England and the Continent in the Eighth Century*, Oxford

Levison, W. (1940) 'St Willibrord and his place in history', *The Durham University Journal* 32: 23–41, reprinted in W. Levison, *Aus rheinischer und fränkischer Frühzeit*, Düsseldorf (1948), pp. 314–29

Lewis, A.R. (1958), *The Northern Seas*, Princeton

Lohaus, A. (1974), *Die Merowinger und England* (Münchener Beiträge zur Mediävistik und Renaissance-Forschung 19), Munich

Lowe, E.A. (1972), 'An eighth-century list of books in a Bodleian manuscript from

Würzburg and its probable relation to the Laudian Acts', in *Palaeographical Papers*, ed. L. Bieler, 2 vols., Oxford, 1, pp. 239–50

Löwe, H. (1951), *Ein literarische Widersacher des Bonifatius: Virgil von Salzburg und die Kosmographie des Aethicus Ister* (Abhandlungen der Akademie der Wissenschaften und der Literatur in Mainz. Geistes- und sozialwissenschaftliche Klasse, Jahrgang 1951), Wiesbaden

Löwe, H. (1955), 'Bonifatius und die bayerische fränkische Spannung. Ein Beitrag zur Geschichte der Beziehungen zwischen dem Papsttum und den Karolingern', *Jahrbuch für fränkische Landesforschung* 15: 85–128

McGrail, S. (ed.) (1990), *Maritime Celts, Frisians and Saxons* (CBA Research Report 71), London

McKitterick, R. (1977), *The Frankish Church and the Carolingian Reforms 789–895* (Royal Historical Society Studies in History), London

McKitterick, R. (1983), *The Frankish Kingdoms under the Carolingians, 751–987*, London

McKitterick, R. (1985), 'Knowledge of canon law in the Frankish kingdoms before 789: the manuscript evidence', *JTS* 36: 87–117; reprinted in McKitterick (1994)

McKitterick, R. (1989a), 'The diffusion of insular culture in Neustria between 650 and 850: the implications of the manuscript evidence', in *La Neustrie* II, pp. 395–432; reprinted in McKitterick (1994a)

McKitterick, R. (1989b), 'The Anglo-Saxon missionaries in Germany: reflections on the manuscript evidence', *Transactions of the Cambridge Bibliographical Society* 9: 291–329; reprinted in McKitterick (1994a)

McKitterick, R. (1991), *Anglo-Saxon Missionaries in Germany: Personal Connections and Local Influences*, Eighth Brixworth Lecture (Vaughan Paper 36), Leicester

McKitterick, R. (1992), 'Nuns' scriptoria in England and Francia in the early middle ages', *Francia* 19(1): 1–35; reprinted in McKitterick (1994a)

McKitterick, R. (1994a), *Books, Scribes and Learning in the Frankish kingdoms, Sixth to Ninth Centuries*, Aldershot

Morin, G. (1896), 'L'homéliaire de Burchard de Würzburg', *RB* 13: 97–111

Myers, J.N.L. (1986), *The English Settlements*, Oxford

Netzer, N. (1989), 'Willibrord's scriptorium at Echternach and its relationship to Ireland and Lindisfarne', in Bonner, Rollason and Stancliffe (1989), pp. 203–12

Netzer, N. (1994), *Cultural Interplay in the Eighth Century: The Trier Gospels and the Making of a Scriptorium at Echternach* (Cambridge Studies in Palaeography and Codicology 3), Cambridge

Noble, T.F.X. (1984), *The Republic of St Peter: The Birth of the Papal State 680–825*, Philadelphia

Ó Cróinín, D. (1984), 'Rath Melsigi, Willibrord and the earliest Echternach manuscripts', *Peritia* 3: 17–42

Ó Cróinín, D. (1989), 'Is the Augsburg Gospel codex a Northumbrian manuscript?', in Bonner, Rollason and Stancliffe (1989), pp. 189–202

Oexle, G. and Schmid, K. (1974), 'Voraussetzungen und Wirkung des Gebetsbundes von Attigny', *Francia* 2: 71–122

Ortenberg, V. (1990), 'Archbishop Sigeric's journey to Rome in 990', *ASE* 19: 197–246

Parkes, M. (1976), 'The handwriting of St Boniface: a reassessment of the problems', *Beiträge zur Geschichte der deutschen Sprache und Literatur* 98: 161–79

Parkes, M. (1983), *The Scriptorium of Wearmouth-Jarrow*, Jarrow Lecture 1982, Newcastle

Parkes, M. (1991), *Scribes, Scripts and Readers: Studies in the Communication, Presentation and Dissemination of Medieval Texts*, London

Parsons, D. (1983), 'Sites and monuments of the Anglo-Saxon mission in central Germany', *Archaeological Journal* 140: 280–321

Parsons, D. (1988), 'St Boniface – Clofesho – Brixworth', in *Baukunst des Mittelalters in Europa: Hans Kubach zum 75. Geburtstag*, Stuttgart, pp. 371–84

Prinz, F. (1965), *Frühes Mönchtum im Frankenreich*, Stuttgart

Prinz, F. (1988), *Frühes Mönchtum im Frankenreich*, 2nd edn, Darmstadt

Rankin, S. (1985), 'The liturgical background of the Old English Advent lyrics: a reappraisal', in H. Gneuss and M. Lapidge (eds.), *Learning and Literature in Anglo-Saxon Literature: Studies Presented to Peter Clemoes on the occasion of his 65th Birthday*, Cambridge, pp. 317–40

Rankin, S. (1994), 'Carolingian Music', in R. McKitterick (ed.), *Carolingian Culture: Emulation and Innovation*, Cambridge, pp. 274–316

Reindel, K. (1964), 'Bistumsorganisation im Alpen-Donauraum in der Spätantike und im Frühmittelalter', *MIÖG* 72: 277–310

Reuter T. (1980a), 'Saint Boniface and Europe', in Reuter (1980b)

Reuter, T. (1985), 'Plunder and tribute in the Carolingian Empire', *TRHS* 5th series, 35: 75–94

Reuter, T. (ed.) (1980b), *The Greatest Englishman*, Exeter

Sabbe, E. (1950), 'Les relations économiques entre Angleterre et le Continent au haut moyen âge', *MA* 56: 169–93

Saint Chrodegang (1967), Metz

Sankt Bonifatius. (1954) *Sankt Bonifatius. Gedenkgabe zum zwölfhundertsten Todestag*, Fulda

St Kilian (1989), *Würzburger Diözesanblätter*

St Kilian. 1300 Jahre Martyrium der Frankenaposatel, Würzburgere Diözesan-Geschichtsblätter 51

Schieffer, T. (1954), *Winfrid-Bonifatius und die kirchliche Grundlegung Europas*, Freiburg

Schüling, H. (1961–3), 'Die Handbibliothek des Bonifatius', *Archiv für Geschichte des Bibliothekswesen* 4: 285–347

Sims-Williams, P. (1975), 'Continental influence at Bath monastery in the seventh century', *ASE* 4: 1–10

Sims-Williams, P. (1976), 'Cuthswith, seventh-century abbess of Inkberrow, near Worcester, and the Würzburg manuscript of Jerome on Ecclesiastes', *ASE* 5: 1–21

Sims-Williams, P. (1979), 'An unpublished seventh- or eighth-century Anglo-Latin letter in Boulogne-sur-Mer MS 74(82)', *Medium Aevum* 48: 1–22

Spilling, H. (1978), 'Angelsächsisches Schrift in Fulda', in A. Brall (ed.), *Von der Klosterbibliothek zur Landesbibliothek: Beiträge zum zweihundertjährigen Bestehen der hessischen Landesbibliothek Fulda*, Stuttgart, pp. 47–98

Talbot, C.H. (1954), *The Anglo-Saxon Missionaries in Germany*, London

van der Essen, L. (1907), *Etude critique et littéraire sur les Vitae des saints mérovingiens de l'ancienne Belgique*, Brussels

Verbist, G.H. (1938), *Saint Willibrord: apôtre des Pays-Bas et fondateur d'Echternach*, Leuven

Wallace-Hadrill, J.M. (1965), 'Charlemagne and England', in *Karl der Grosse* I, pp. 683–98

Wallace-Hadrill, J.M. (1975), *Early Medieval History*, Oxford

Wallace-Hadrill, J.M. (1983), *The Frankish Church*, Oxford

Wampach, C. (1929–30), *Geschichte der Grundherrschaft Echternach im Frühmittelalter*, Luxembourg

Werner, K.-F. (1976), 'Le rôle de l'aristocracie dans la christianisation du nord-est de la Gaule', *RHEF* 62: 45–73

Werner, M. (1982), *Adelsfamilien im Umkreis der frühen Karolinger. Die Verwandtschaft Irminas von Oeren und Adela von Pfalzel* (VuF, Sonderband 28), Sigmaringen

Whitelock, D. (1960), *After Bede*, Jarrow Lecture 1960, Newcastle, 1961

Wolfram, H. (1972), 'Der heilige Rupert und die antikarolingische Adelsopposition', *MIÖG* 80: 4–34

Wolfram, H. (1979), *Conversio Bagoariorum et Carantanorum*, Vienna

Wolfram, H. (1987), *Die Geburt Mitteleuropas*, Vienna

Wood, I.N. (1981), 'A prelude to Columbanus: the monastic achievement in the Burgundian territories', in H. Clarke and M. Brennan (eds.), *Columbanus and Merovingian Monasticism* (BAR International Series 113), Oxford, pp. 3–32

Wood, I.N. (1983), *The Merovingian North Sea* (Occasional Papers on Medieval Topics 1), Alingsås

Zwink, E. (1983), *Frühes Mönchtum in Salzburg*, Salzburg

3 FRANKISH GAUL TO 814

Boussard, J. (1968), *The Civilisation of Charlemagne*, London

Braunfels, W. (1965 and 1968), *Karl der Grosse: Lebenswerk und Nachleben*, 5 vols, Düsseldorf

Brown, E.A.R. (1974), 'The tyranny of a construct: feudalism and historians of medieval Europe', *AHR* 79: 1063–88

Brunner, H. (1894), *Der Reiterdienst und die Anfänge des Lehnwesens* (Forschungen zur Geschichte des deutschen und französischen Rechtes), Stuttgart

Classen, P. (1972), 'Karl der Grosse und die Thronfolge im Frankenreich', *Festschrift für Hermann Heimpel zum 70. Geburtstag* III, Göttingen, pp. 109–34

Duchesne, L. (1907–15) *Fastes épiscopaux de l'ancienne Gaule*, 3 vols, Paris

Ewig, E. (1953), 'Milo et eiusmodi similes', in *Sankt Bonifatius: Gedenkengabe zum zwölfhundertsten Todestag*, Fulda, pp. 412–40; reprinted in E. Ewig, *Spätantikes und Fränkisches Gallien* II (Beihefte der Francia 3, pt 2), Zurich and Munich (1979), pp. 189–219

Folz, R. (1974), *The Coronation of Charlemagne: 25 December 800*, London

Fouracre, P. (1984), 'Observations on the outgrowth of Pippinid influence in the *regnum francorum* after the battle of Tertry (687–715)', *Medieval Prosopography* 5: 1–31

Geary, P. (1985), *Aristocracy in Provence: The Rhône Basin at the Dawn of the Carolingian Age*, Stuttgart

Gerberding, R. (1987), *The Rise of the Carolingians and the Liber Historiae Francorum*, Oxford

Godman, P. and Collins, R. (eds.) (1990), *Charlemagne's Heir: New Perspectives on the Reign of Louis the Pious (814–840)*, Oxford

Hilton, R. and Sawyer, P. (1963), 'Technical determinism: the stirrup and the plough', *Past and Present* 24: 46–53

Hübner, R. (1891), 'Gerichtsurkunden der fränkischen Zeit', *ZRG GA* 12: 1–118

Jarnut, J. *et al.* (eds.) (1994), *Karl Martell in seiner Zeit* (Beihefte der Francia 37), Sigmaringen

Kottje, R. and Mordek, H. (eds.) (1986), *Überlieferung und Geltung normativer Texte des frühen und hohen Mittelalters* (Quellen und Forschungen zum Recht im Mittelalter), Sigmaringen

McKitterick, R. (1977), *The Frankish Church and the Carolingian Reforms, 789–895*, London

McKitterick, R. (1983), *The Frankish Kingdoms under the Carolingians, 751–987*, London

McKitterick, R. (1989), *The Carolingians and the Written Word*, Cambridge

McKitterick, R. (ed.) (1990), *The Uses of Literacy in Early Medieval Europe*, Cambridge

Mordek, H. (1986), 'Karolingische Kapitularien', in Kottje and Mordek (1986), pp. 25–50

Nelson, J. (1990), 'Literacy in Carolingian government', in McKitterick (1990), pp. 258–96

Noble, T. (1984), *The Republic of St Peter: The Birth of the Papal State, 680–825*, Philadelphia

Nonn, U. (1970), 'Das Bild Karl Martells in den lateinsichen Quellen vornehmlich des 8. und 9. Jahrhunderts', *FrSt* 4: 70–137

Reuter, T. (1985), 'Plunder and tribute in the Carolingian empire', *TRHS* 35: 79–94

Reuter, T. (1990), 'The end of Carolingian military expansion', in Godman and Collins (1990), pp. 391–405

Reuter, T. (1991), *Germany in the Early Middle Ages 800–1056*, London

Reuter, T. (ed. and trans.) (1978), *The Medieval Nobility*, Amsterdam, New York and Oxford

Semmler, J. (1977), 'Zur pippinidisch-karolingischen Suksessionskrise 714–723', *DA* 33: 1–36

Werner, K.-F. (1965), 'Bedeutende Adelsfamilien im Reich Karls des Grossen', in *Karl der Grosse* 1, pp. 83–142

Werner, M. (1980), *Der Lütticher Raum in frühkarolingishcher Zeit* (Veröffentlichungen des Max-Planck-Instituts für Geschichte 62), Göttingen

4 THE FRANKISH KINGDOMS, 814–898: THE WEST

Airlie, S. (1985), 'The political behaviour of secular magnates in Francia, 829–879', Oxford University D.Phil. thesis

Airlie, S. (1990), 'Bonds of power and bonds of association in the court circle of Louis the Pious', in Godman and Collins (1990), pp. 191–204

Angenendt, A. (1984), *Kaiserherrschaft und Königstaufe* (Arbeiten zur Frühmittelalterforschung 15), Berlin and New York

Bautier, R.-H. (1978), Introduction to *Recueil des Actes de Louis II le Bègue, Louis III et Carloman II rois de France, 877–884*, Paris

Borgolte, M. (1986), *Die Grafen Alemanniens in merowingischer und karolingischer Zeit*, Sigmaringen

Boshof, E. (1990), 'Einheitsidee und Teilungsprinzip in der Regierungszeit Ludwigs des Frommen', in Godman and Collins (1990) pp. 161–90

Braunfels, W. (ed.) (1965 and 1968), *Karl der Grosse: Lebenswerk und Nachleben*, 5 vols., Düsseldorf

Brown, G. (1989), 'Politics and patronage at the Abbey of St-Denis (814–98): the rise of a royal patron saint', Oxford University D. Phil. thesis

Brühl, C.R. (1968), *Fodrum, Gistum, Servitium Regis*, Cologne

Brunner, K. (1979), *Oppositionelle Gruppen im Karolingerreich*, Vienna

Cabaniss, A. (1961), *Son of Charlemagne: A Contemporary Life of Louis the Pious*, Syracuse, NY

Calmette, J. (1901), *La diplomatie carolingienne*, Paris

Classen, P. (1963), 'Die Verträge von Verdun und Coulaines, 843, als politische Grundlagen des westfränkischen Reiches', *HZ* 196: 1–35

Classen, P. (1972), 'Karl der Grosse und der Thronfolge im Frankenreich', in *Festschrift für H. Heimpel*, 3 vols., Göttingen, III, pp. 109–34

Collins, R. (1990a), 'Charles the Bald and Wifred the Hairy', in Gibson and Nelson (1990), pp. 169–88

Collins, R. (1990b), 'Pippin I and the Kingdom of Aquitaine', in Godman and Collins (1990), pp. 363–89

Coupland, S. (1987), 'Charles the Bald and the defence of the West Frankish kingdom against the Viking invasions, 840–877', Cambridge University Ph.D. thesis

Coupland, S. (1988), 'Dorestad in the ninth century: the numismatic evidence', *Jaarboek voor Munt-en Penningkunde* 75: 5–26

Coupland, S. (1990), 'Money and coinage under Louis the Pious', *Francia* 17: 23–54

Dahlhaus-Berg, E. (1975), *Nova Antiquitas et Antiqua Novitas*, Cologne

De Jong, M. (1992), 'Power and humility in Carolingian society: the public penance of Louis the Pious', in *EME* 1, pp. 29–52

Depreux, P. (1992), 'Nithard et la *res publica:* un regard critique sur le règne de Louis le Pieux', *Médiévales* 22–3: 149–61

Devisse, J. (1975, 1976), *Hincmar, archevêque de Reims, 845–882*, 3 vols., Geneva

Dhondt, J. (1948), *Etudes sur la naissance des principautés territoriales en France (IXe–Xe siècles)*, Bruges

Dunbabin, J. (1985), *France in the Making 843–1180*, Oxford

Fouracre, P. (1985), 'The context of the OHG *Ludwigslied*', *Medium Ævum* 54: 87–103

Fried, J. (1990), 'Ludwig der Fromme, das Papsttum und die fränkische Kirche', in Godman and Collins (1990), pp. 231–73

Gibson, M.T. and Nelson, J.L. (1990), *Charles the Bald: Court and Kingdom*, 2nd revised edn, Aldershot

Gillmor, C. (1988), 'War on the rivers: Viking numbers and mobility on the Seine and Loire, 841–886', *Viator* 19: 79–109

Gillmor, C. (1989), 'The logistics of fortified bridge building on the Seine under Charles the Bald', *Anglo-Norman Studies* 11: 87–106

Godman, P. (1985), *Poetry of the Carolingian Renaissance*, London

Godman, P. (1987), *Poets and Emperors*, Oxford

Godman, P. and Collins, R. (eds.) (1990), *Charlemagne's Heir: New Perspectives on the Reign of Louis the Pious*, Oxford

Goody, J. (1966), *Succession to High Office*, Cambridge

Grierson, P. (1990), 'The *Gratia Dei Rex* coinage of Charles the Bald', in Gibson and Nelson (1990), pp. 52–64

Guillot, O. (1990), 'Une *ordinatio* méconnue, le Capitulaire de 823–825', in Godman and Collins (1990), pp. 455–86

Hauck, K. (1990), 'Der Missionsauftrag Christi und das Kaisertum Ludwigs des Frommen', in Godman and Collins (1990), pp. 275–96

Hlawitschka, E. (1968), *Lothringen und das Reich an der Schwelle der deutschen Geschichte*, Stuttgart

Houben, H. (1970), '*Visio cuiusdam pauperculae mulieris*: Überlieferung und Herkunft eines frühmittelalterlichen Visionstextes', *Zeitschrift für die Geschichte des Oberrheins* 124: 31–42

Hyam, J. (1990), 'Ermentrude and Richildis', in Gibson and Nelson (1990), pp. 154–68

James, E. (1982), *The Origins of France*, London

Kaiser, R. (1981), *Bischofsherrschaft zwischen Königtum und Fürstenmacht: Studien zur bischöflichen Stadtherrschaft im westfränkisch französischen Reich im früheren und hohen Mittelalter*, Bonn

Kessler, H. (1992), 'A lay abbot as patron: Count Vivian and the first Bible of Charles the Bald', *Settimane* 39: 647–76

Kienast, W. (1990), *Die fränkische Vasallität von den Hausmaiern bis zu Ludwig dem Kind und Karl dem Einfältigen*, ed. P. Herde, Frankfurt

King, P.D. (1987), *Charlemagne: Translated Sources*, Kendal

Leyser, K. (1994), 'Nithard and his Kings', in T. Reuter (ed.), *Communication and Power in Medieval Europe*, 1: *The Carolingian and Ottonian Centuries*, London, pp. 19–26

Lohrmann, D. (1976), 'Trois palais royaux de la vallée de l'Oise d'après les travaux des érudits mauristes: Compiègne, Choisy-au-Bac et Quierzy', *Francia* 4: 121–40

McKeon, P. (1974), 'Archbishop Ebbo of Rheims', *Church History* 43: 437–47

McKeon, P. (1978), '817: une année désastreuse', *Le Moyen Âge* 84: 5–12

McKitterick, R. (1977), *The Frankish Church and the Carolingian Reforms, 789–895*, London

McKitterick, R. (1983), *The Frankish Kingdoms under the Carolingians, 751–987*, London

McKitterick, R. (1989), *The Carolingians and the Written Word*, Cambridge

Martindale, J. (1977), 'The French aristocracy in the early Middle Ages: a reappraisal', *Past and Present* 75: 5–45

Martindale, J. (1985), 'The kingdom of Aquitaine and the dissolution of the Carolingian fisc', *Francia* 11: 131–91

Martindale, J. (1990), 'Charles the Bald and the government of the kingdom of

Aquitaine', in Gibson and Nelson (1990), pp. 115–38

Martindale, J. (1996), *Aquitaine from the Eighth to the Eleventh Centuries*, Cambridge

Metcalf, D.M. (1990), 'A sketch of the currency in the time of Charles the Bald', in Gibson and Nelson (1990), pp. 65–97

Nelson, J.L. (1986), *Politics and Ritual in Early Medieval Europe*, London

Nelson, J.L. (1988), 'A tale of two princes: politics, text and ideology in a Carolingian annal', *Studies in Medieval and Renaissance History* 10: 105–41

Nelson, J.L. (1990), 'The last years of Louis the Pious', in Godman and Collins (1990), pp. 147–60

Nelson, J.L. (1992a), *Charles the Bald*, London

Nelson, J.L. (1992b), 'The intellectual in politics: context, content and authorship in the Capitulary of Coulaines', in L. Smith and B. Ward (eds.), *Intellectual Life in the Middle Ages: Essays presented to Margaret Gibson* London, pp. 1–14

Nelson, J.L. (1993), 'The Franks, the Martyrology of Usuard, and the Martyrs of Cordoba', *Studies in Church History* 30: 67–80

Nelson, J.L. (1995), 'The search for peace in a time of war: the Carolingian *Bruderkrieg*, 840–843', in VuF 42, ed. J. Fried,. Sigmaringen, forthcoming

Noble, T.F.X. (1974), 'The revolt of King Bernard of Italy in 817: its causes and consequences', *Studi Medievali* 3rd series, 15: 315–26

Reuter, T. (1985), 'Plunder and tribute in the Carolingian Empire', *TRHS* 35: 75–94

Reuter, T. (1990), 'The end of Carolingian military expansion', in Godman and Collins (1990), pp. 391–405

Sassier, Y. (1991), 'Les Carolingiens et Auxerre', in D. Iogna-Prat, C. Jeudy and G. Lobrichon (eds.), *L'école carolingienne d'Auxerre de Murethach à Remi*, Paris, pp. 21–36

Schneider, G. (1973), *Erzbischof Fulco von Reims (883–900) und das Frankenreich*, Munich

Schneidmüller, B. (1978), 'Die "Einfaltigkeit" Karls III von Westfrankreich als frühmittelalterliche Herrschertugend. Überlegungen zu den cognomen *simplex*', *Schweizerische Zeitschrift für Geschichte* 28: 62–6

Schneidmüller, B. (1979), *Karolingische Tradition und frühes französisches Königtum: Untersuchungen zur Herrschaftslegitimation der westfränkisch-französischen Monarchie im 10. Jahrhundert*, Frankfurt

Schieffer, R. (1990), 'Väter und Söhne im Karolingerhause', *Beiträge zur Geschichte des Regnum Francorum* (Beihefte der Francia 22), pp. 149–64

Scholz, B. (1970), *Carolingian Chronicles*, Ann Arbor

Schramm, P.E. (1960), *Der König von Frankreich: Das Wesen der Monarchie vom 9. zum 16. Jahrhundert*, 2 vols., 2nd edn, Darmstadt

Schramm, P.E. (1968), *Kaiser, Könige und Päpste*, 4 vols., Stuttgart

Siems, H. (1992), *Handel und Wucher im Spiegel frühmittelalterlicher Rechtsquellen*, MGH Schriften 35, Hanover

Smith, J.M.H. (1992), *Province and Empire: Brittany and the Carolingians*, Cambridge

Stafford, P. (1983), *Queens, Concubines and Dowagers: The King's Wife in the Early Middle Ages*, Athens, GA

Tessier, G. (1942–55), *Recueil des Actes de Charles II le Chauve*, 3 vols., Paris

Vollmer, F. (1957), 'Die Etichonen', in G. Tellenbach (ed.), *Studien und Vorarbeiten zur Geschichte des grossfränkischen Adels*, Freibach, pp. 137–84

Wallace-Hadrill, J.M. (1975), *The Vikings in Francia*, The Stenton Lecture for 1974, Reading; reprinted in Wallace-Hadrill (1976)

Wallace-Hadrill, J.M. (1976), *Early Medieval History*, Oxford

Ward, E. (1990a), 'Caesar's wife: the career of the Empress Judith, 819–29', in Godman and Collins (1990), pp. 205–27

Ward, E. (1990b), 'Agobard of Lyons and Paschasius Radbertus as critics of the Empress Judith', *Studies in Church History* 27: 5–25

Weinrich, L. (1963), *Wala: Graf, Monch und Rebell*, Hamburg

Wemple, S.F. (1981), *Women in Frankish Society*, Philadelphia

Werner, K.-F. (1958), 'Untersuchungen zur Frühzeit des französischen Fürstentums (9.–10. Jht.) IV', *Welt als Geschichte* 19: 146–93

Werner, K.-F. (1965a), 'Bedeutende Adelsfamilien im Reiche Karls des Grossen', in *Karl der Grosse* I, pp. 83–142

Werner, K.-F. (1965b), 'Das hochmittelalterliche Imperium im politischen Bewüsstsein Frankreichs (10.–12. Jhdts)', *HZ* 200: 1–60

Werner, K.-F. (1967), 'Die Nachkommen Karls des Grossen', in *Karl der Grosse* IV, pp. 403–79

Werner, K.-F. (1978), 'Important noble families in the kingdom of Charlemagne', in T. Reuter (ed.), *The Medieval Nobility*, Amsterdam and New York, pp. 137–202

Werner, K.-F. (1979), 'Gauzlin von Saint-Denis und die westfränkische Reichsteilung von Amiens (880)', *DA* 35: 395–462

Werner, K.-F. (1990), '*Hludovicus Augustus*: gouverner l'empire chrétien – idées et réalités', in Godman and Collins (1990), pp. 3–124

Wood, I.N. (1987), 'Christians and pagans in ninth-century Scandinavia', in B. Sawyer, P. Sawyer and I. Wood (eds.), *The Christianization of Scandinavia*, Alingsås, pp. 36–67

Yeandle, D.N. (1989), 'The *Ludwigslied*: king, church and context', in J. Flood and D.N. Yeandle (eds.), '*mit regulu bituungan*': *Neue Arbeiten zur althochdeutschen Poesie und Sprache*, Goppingen

5   THE FRANKISH KINGDOMS, 817–911: THE EAST AND MIDDLE
KINGDOMS

Anton, H.H. (1987), *Trier im frühen Mittelalter*, Paderborn, Munich, Vienna and Zurich

Beumann, H. (1977), 'Die Einheit des ostfränkischen Reichs und der Kaisergedanke bei der Königserhebung Ludwigs des Kindes', *AfD* 23: 142–63

Beumann, H. (1981), 'Unitas ecclesiae – unitas imperii – unitas regni. Von der imperialen Reichseinheitsidee zur Einheit der regna', *Settimane* 27: 531–71

Borgolte, M. (1984), 'Karl III. und Neuendingen', *Zeitschrift für die Geschichte des Oberrheins* 127: 21–56

Bosl, K. (1969), *Franken um 800: Strukturanalyse einer fränkischen Königsprovinz*, 2nd edn, Munich

Brühl, C. (1990), *Deutschland-Frankreich: Die Geburt zweier Völker*, Cologne and Vienna

Brunner, K. (1979), *Oppositionelle Gruppen im Karolingerreich*, Vienna

Classen, P. (1983), *Ausgewählte Aufsätze*, ed. J. Fleckenstein (VuF 28), Sigmaringen

Dümmler, E. (1887–8), *Geschichte des ostfränkischen Reiches*, 3 vols., 2nd edn, Leipzig

Fichtenau, H. (1957), *The Carolingian Empire*, Oxford

Fleckenstein, J. (1959), *Die Hofkapelle der deutschen Könige*, I: *Grundlegung: Die karolingische Hofkapelle*, Stuttgart

Fleckenstein, J. (1978), *Early Medieval Germany*, trans. B.S. Smith, Amsterdam

Fried, J. (1982), 'Der karolingische Herrschaftsverband im 9. Jh. zwischen "Kirche" und "Königshaus"', *HZ* 235: 1–43

Fried, J. (1991), *Die Formierung Europas 840–1046* (Oldenbourg Grundriss der Geschichte 6), Munich

Fried, J. (1994), *Der Weg in die Geschichte: Die Ursprünge Deutschlands* (Propyläen Geschichte Deutschlands 1), Berlin

Gockel, M. (1970), *Karolingische Königshöfe am Mittelrhein*, Göttingen

Godman, P. and Collins, R. (eds.) (1990), *Charlemagne's Heir: New Perspectives on the Reign of Louis the Pious (814–840)*, Oxford

Goetz, H.-W. (1987), 'Regnum: Zum politischen Denken der Karolingerzeit', *ZRG* 104: 110–89

Hannig, J. (1982), *Consensus Fidelium*, Stuttgart

Hartmann, W. (1989), *Die Synoden der Karolingerzeit im Frankenreich und in Italien*, Paderborn, Munich, Vienna and Zurich

Hlawitschka, E. (1986), *Vom Frankenreich zur Formierung der europäischen Staaten- und Völkergemeinschaft 840–1046: Ein Studienbuch zur Zeit der späten Karolinger, der Ottonen und der frühen Salier in der Geschichte Mitteleuropas*, Darmstadt

Jäschke, K.-U. (1975), *Burgenbau und Landesverteidigung um 900* (VuF Sonderband 16), Sigmaringen

Keller, H. (1966), 'Zum Sturz Karls III', *DA* 22 333–84

Löwe, H. (1954, 2nd edn 1990), *Wattenbach-Levison, Deutschlands Geschichtsquellen im Mittelalter: Vorzeit und Karolinger*, III Heft: *Die Karolinger vom Tode Karls des Grossen bis zum Vertrag von Verdun; VI Heft: Die Karolinger vom Vertrag von Verdun bis zum Herrschaftsantritt der Herrscher aus dem Sächsischen Hause. Das Ostfrankenreich*, Weimar

McKitterick, R. (1977), *The Frankish Church and the Carolingian Reforms, 789–895*, London

McKitterick, R. (1983), *The Frankish Kingdoms under the Carolingians, 751–987*, London

Mitterauer, M. (1963), *Karolingische Markgrafen im Südosten*, Vienna

Mühlbacher, E. (1896), *Deutsche Geschichte unter den Karolingern*, Stuttgart

Penndorf, U. (1974), *Das Problem der 'Reichseinheitsidee' nach der Teilung von Verdun (843)*, Munich

Prinz, F. (1985), *Grundlagen und Anfänge: Deutschland bis 1056* (Neue Deutsche Geschichte 1), Munich

Reindel, K. (1953), *Die bayerischen Luitpoldinger 893–989*, Munich

Reuter, T. (1985), 'Plunder and tribute in the Carolingian Empire', *TRHS* 5th series, 35: 75–94

Reuter, T. (1991), *Germany in the Early Middle Ages c. 800–1056*, London and New York

Schieffer, R. (1990), 'Väter und Söhne im Karolingerhaus', in R. Schieffer (ed.),

Beiträge zur Geschichte des Regnum Francorum: Referate beim Wissenschaftlichen Colloquium zum 75. Geburtstag von E. Ewig (Beihefte der Francia 22), Sigmaringen

Schieffer, R. (1992), *Die Karolinger*, Stuttgart, Berlin and Cologne

Schieffer, T. (1986), 'Adnotationes zur Germania Pontificia und zur Echtheitskritik überhaupt. Erster Teil', *AfD* 32: 503–45

Schieffer, T. and Seegrun, W. (1981), *Regesta Pontificum Romanorum*. Germania Pontificia 6, Provincia Hammaburgo-Bremensis, Göttingen

Schlesinger, W. (1963), *Beiträge zur deutschen Verfassungsgeschichte des Mittelalters*, II: *Germanen, Franken, Deutsche*, Göttingen

Schlesinger, W. (1987), *Ausgewählte Aufsätze von Walter Schlesinger 1965–1979*, ed. H. Patze and F. Schwind (VuF 34), Sigmaringen

Schmid, K. (1983), *Gebetsgedenken und adeliges Selbstverständnis im Mittelalter: Ausgewählte Beiträge*, Sigmaringen

Schneider, R. (1964), *Brüdergemeine und Schwurfreundschaft: Der Auflösungsprozess des Karolingerreiches im Spiegel der caritas-Terminologie in den Verträgen der karolingischen Teilkönige des 9. Jahrhunderts* (Historische Studien 388), Lübeck and Hamburg

Schulze, H.K. (1987), *Vom Reich der Franken zum Land der Deutschen*, Berlin

Schwarzmeier, H. (1972), *Lucca und das Reich bis zur Ende des 11. Jahrhunderts. Studien zur Sozialstruktur einer Herzogsstadt in der Toskana* (Bibliothek des Deutsches Historisches Instituts in Rom 41), Tübingen

Simson, B. (1874), *Jahrbücher des Fränkischen Reichs unter Ludwig dem Frommen*, 2 vols., Leipzig

Tellenbach, G. (1979), Die geistigen und politischen Grundlagen der karolingischen Thronfolge', *FrSt* 13: 184–302

Tellenbach, G. (1988), *Ausgewählte Aufsätze und Abhandlungen* II and III, Stuttgart

Tremp, E. (1988), *Studien zu den Gesta Hludowici imperatoris des Trierer Chorbischofs Thegan* (MGH Schriften 32), Hanover

Tremp, E. (1991), *Die Überlieferung der Vita Hludowici imperatoris des Astronomus* (MGH Studien und Texte 1), Hanover

Werner, K.F. (1965), 'Bedeutende Adelsfamilien im Reich Karls des Grossen', in *Karl der Grosse* I, pp. 83–142

Zielinski, H. (1990), 'Ein unbeachteter Italienzug Kaiser Lothars I. im Jahre 847, *QFIAB* 70: 1–22

Zotz, T. (ed.) (1983ff.), *Die deutschen Königspfalzen: Repertorium der Pfalzen, Königshöfe und übrigen Aufenthaltsorte der Könige im deutschen Reich des Mittelalters*, Göttingen

6 FINES IMPERII: THE MARCHES

General

Angenendt, A. (1984), *Kaiserherrschaft und Königstaufe: Kaiser, Könige und Päpste als geistliche Patrone in der abendländischen Missionsgeschichte* (Arbeiten zur Frühmittelalterforschung 15), Berlin

Borst, A. (1965), 'Das Karlsbild in der Geschichtswissenschaft vom Humanismus bis heute', in *Karl der Grosse* IV, pp. 364–402

Dhondt, J. (1948a), *Etudes sur la naissance des principautés territoriales en France, IXe au Xe siècle*, Bruges

Dhondt, J. (1948b), 'Le titre du marquis à l'époque carolingienne', *Archivum Latinitatis Medii Aevi* 19: 407–17

Dopsch, A. (1962), *Die Wirtschaftsentwicklung der Karolingerzeit vornehmlich in Deutschland*, 2 vols., 3rd edn, Cologne

Eadie, J. (1977), 'Peripheral vision in Roman history', in J. d'Arms and J. Eadie (eds.), *Ancient and Modern Essays in Honor of Gerald F. Else*, Ann Arbor, pp. 215–34

Gibson, M.T. and Nelson, J.L. (eds.) (1990), *Charles the Bald: Court and Kingdom*, 2nd rev. edn, Aldershot

Godman, P. and Collins, R. (eds.) (1990), *Charlemagne's Heir: New Perspectives on the Reign of Louis the Pious*, Oxford

Graus, F., Bosl, K., Seibt, F., Postan M.M. and Gieysztor, A. (1970), *Eastern and Western Europe in the Middle Ages*, London

Grierson, P. and Blackburn, M. (1986), *Medieval European Coinage, 1: The Early Middle Ages*, Cambridge

James, E. (1988), *The Franks*, Oxford

Klebel, E. (1938), 'Herzogtümer und Marken bis 900', *DA* 2: 1–53

Klebel, E. (1963), 'Die Ostgrenze des karolingischen Reiches', in H. Kämpf (ed.), *Die Entstehung des deutschen Reiches* (Wege der Forschung 1), Darmstadt, pp. 1–41

Lipp, M. (1892), *Das fränkische Grenzsystem unter Karl dem Grossen*, Breslau

Manteuffel, T. and Gieysztor, A. (eds.), (1968), *L'Europe aux IXe–XIe siècles: aux origines des états nationaux*, Warsaw

Mikoletsky, H.L. (1952), 'Karl Martell und Grifo', in *Festschrift für E.E. Stengel*, Münster, pp. 130–56

Nelson, J.L. (1991), 'La famille de Charlemagne', *Byz* 61: 194–212

Nelson, J.L. (1992), *Charles the Bald*, London and New York

Nitz, H.-J. (1988), 'Settlement structures and settlement systems of the Frankish central state in Carolingian and Ottonian times', in D. Hooke (ed.), *Anglo-Saxon Settlements*, Oxford, pp. 249–73

Noble, T.F.X. (1990), 'Louis the Pious and the frontiers of the Frankish realm', in Godman and Collins (1990), pp. 333–47

Reuter, T. (1985), 'Plunder and tribute in the Carolingian empire', *TRHS* 5th series, 35: 75–94

Reuter, T. (1990), 'The end of Carolingian military expansion', in Godman and Collins (1990), pp. 391–405

Reuter, T. (1991), *Germany in the Early Middle Ages, 800–1056*, London and New York

Werner, K.-F. (1973), 'Les principautés périphériques dans le monde franc du VIIIe siècle', *Settimane* 20: 483–515

Werner, K.-F. (1980), '*Missus – marcio – comes*. Entre l'administration centrale et l'administration locale de l'empire carolingien', in W. Paravicini and K.-F. Werner (eds.), *Histoire comparée de l'administration (IVe–XVIIIe siècles)* (Beihefte der Francia 9), Munich, pp. 191–239

Wood, I.N. (1983), *The Merovingian North Sea*, Alingsås

Brittany

Brunterc'h, J.-P., (1989), 'Le duché du Maine et la marche de Bretagne', in *La Neustrie* 1, pp. 29–127

Chédeville, A. and Guillotel, H. (1984), *La Bretagne des saints et des rois, Ve–Xe siècles*, Rennes

Davies, W. (1990), 'On the distribution of political power in Brittany in the mid-ninth century' in Gibson and Nelson (1990), pp. 98–114

Kerhervé, J. (1980), 'Aux origines d'un sentiment national. Les chroniqueurs bretons de la fin du moyen âge', *Bulletin de la Société Archéologique du Finistère* 108: 165–206

Levillain, L. (1951), 'La marche de Bretagne, ses marquis et ses comtes', *Annales de Bretagne* 58: 89–117

Smith, J.M.H. (1982), 'The "archbishopric" of Dol and the ecclesiastical politics of ninth-century Brittany', *Studies in Church History* 18: 59–70

Smith, J.M.H. (1986), 'Culte impérial et politique frontalière dans la vallée de la Vilaine: le témoignage des diplômes carolingiens dans le cartulaire de Redon', in M. Simon (ed.), *Landévennec et le monachisme breton dans le haut moyen âge*, Landévennec, pp. 129–39

Smith, J.M.H. (1992), *Province and Empire; Brittany and the Carolingians*, Cambridge

Septimania and Hispania

Auzias, L. (1937), *L'Aquitaine carolingienne* (Bibliothèque Méridionale, 2nd series, 28), Toulouse

Bachrach, B.S. (1974), 'Military organization in Aquitaine under the early Carolingians', *Speculum* 49: 1–33

Bonnassie, P. (1975–6), *La Catalogne du milieu du Xe à la fin du XIe siècle: croissance et mutations d'une société*, 2 vols., Toulouse

Collins, R. (1983), *Early Medieval Spain: Unity in Diversity, 400–1000*, London

Collins, R. (1986), *The Basques*, Oxford

Collins, R. (1989), *The Arab Conquest of Spain, 710–797*, Oxford

Collins, R. (1990a), 'Charles the Bald and Wifred the Hairy', in Gibson and Nelson (1990), pp. 169–88

Collins, R. (1990b), 'Pippin I and the kingdom of Aquitaine', in Godman and Collins (1990), pp. 363–89

D'Abadal i de Vinyals, R. (1958), *Els Primers Comtes Catalans*, Barcelona

D'Abadal i de Vinyals, R. (1964), 'La Institució Comtal Carolingia en la pre-Catalunya del segle IX', *Anuario de Estudios Medievales* 1: 29–75

D'Abadal i de Vinyals, R. (1969–70), *Dels Visigots als Catalans*, 2 vols., Barcelona

Dupont, A. (1955), 'Considérations sur la colonisation et la vie rurale dans le Roussillon et le marche d'Espagne au IXe siècle', *Annales du Midi* 67: 223–45

Engels, O. (1970), *Schutzgedanke und Landesherrschaft im östlichen Pyrenäenraum (9.–13. Jahrhundert)* (Spanische Forschung der Görresgesellschaft, 2nd series, 14), Munich

Fontaine, J. (1983), 'Mozarabie hispanique et monde carolingien: les échanges culturels entre la France et l'Espagne du VIIe au Xe siècle', *Anuario de Estudios Medievales* 13: 17–46

Freedman, P. (1988), 'Cowardice, heroism and the legendary origins of Catalonia', *Past and Present* 121: 3–28

Freedman, P. (1991), *The Origins of Peasant Servitude in Medieval Catalonia*, Cambridge

James, E. (1980), 'Septimania and its frontier: an archaeological approach', in E.

James (ed.), *Visigothic Spain: New Approaches*, Oxford, pp. 223–41

Lévi-Provençal, E. (1950), *Histoire de l'Espagne musulmane*, 2nd edn, 2 vols., Paris

Lewis, A.R. (1965), *The Development of Southern French and Catalan Society*, Austin, TX

Nelson, J.L. (1993), 'The Franks, the martyrology of Usuard and the martyrs of Cordoba', *Studies in Church History* 30: 67–80

Rouche, M. (1979), *L'Aquitaine des Wisigothes aux Arabes*, Paris

Ruiz Domenec, J.E. (1975), 'Las Estructuras Familiares Catalanas en la alta Edad Media', *Cuadernos de Arqueología e Historia de la Ciudad* 16: 69–123

Wolff, P. (1965), 'L'Aquitaine et ses marges', in *Karl der Grosse* I, pp. 269–306

Zimmermann, M. (1982), 'Origines et formation d'un état catalan (801–1137)', in J. Nadal Farreras and P. Wolff (eds.), *Histoire de la Catalogne*, Toulouse, pp. 237–71

Zimmermann, M. (1983), 'Aux origines de la Catalogne: géographie politique et affirmation nationale', *MA* 89: 5–40

Bohemia – Moravia – Pannonia

Boba, I. (1971), *Moravia's History Reconsidered: A Reinterpretation of the Medieval Sources*, The Hague

Bosl, K. (1966), *Das Grossmährische Reich in der politischen Welt des 9. Jahrhunderts* (Sitzungsberichte der bayerischen Akademie der Wissenschaften, phil.-hist. Klasse 1966, Heft 7), Munich

Bosl, K. (1967), 'Probleme der Missionierung des böhmisch-märischen Herrschaftsraumes', in F. Graus and H. Ludat (eds.), *Siedlung und Verfassung Böhmens in der Frühzeit*, Wiesbaden, pp. 104–32

Bowlus, C.R. (1987), 'Imre Boba's reconsiderations of Moravia's early history and Arnulf of Carinthia's *Ostpolitik* (887–892)', *Speculum* 62: 552–74

Dittrich, R.R. (1960), 'The beginning of Christianisation in Great Moravia', *Slavonic and East European Review* 39: 164–73

Dopsch, H. (ed.) (1986), *Salzburg und die Slawenmission: zum 1100. Todestag des Hl. Methodius*, Salzburg

Dvornik, F. (1949), *The Making of Central and Eastern Europe*, London

Dvornik, F. (1956), *The Slavs: Their Early History and Civilization*, Boston

Graus, F. (1980), *Die Nationenbildung der Westslawen im Mittelalter* (Nationes 3), Sigmaringen

Herrmann, J. (1985), 'Herausbildung und Dynamik der germanisch-slawischen Siedlungsgrenze im Mitteleuropa', in H. Wolfram and A. Schwarcz (eds.), *Die Bayern und ihre Nachbarn* (Österreichische Akademie der Wissenschaften, phil.-hist. Klasse, Denkschriften 179) Vienna, pp. 269–80

Kuhar, A.L. (1959), *The Conversion of the Slovenes and the German-Slav Ethnic Boundary in the Eastern Alps*, New York

Kuhar, A.L. (1962), 'The growth of monasteries in the Slovene region', in his *Slovene Medieval History: Selected Studies*, New York, pp. 89–113

Löwe, H. (1982), 'Cyrill und Methodius zwischen Byzanz und Rom', *Settimane* 30: 631–86

Mitterauer, M. (1963), *Karolingische Markgrafen im Südosten: Fränkische Reichsaristokratie und bayerische Stammesadel im Österreichischen Raum*, Graz

Mitterauer, M. (1964), 'Wirtschaft und Verfassung in der Zollordnung von

Raffelstetten', *Mitteilungen des Oberösterreichischen Landesarchivs* 8: 344–73
Pohl, W. (1988), *Die Awaren: Ein Steppenvolk im Mitteleuropa, 567–822*, Munich
Poulik, J. (1982), 'Grossmähren zwischen Karolingischen Westen und Byzanz', *Settimane* 30: 157–68
Reindel, K. (1965), 'Bayern im Karolingerreich', in *Karl der Grosse* I, pp. 220–46
Richter, K. (1967), 'Die böhmischen Länder im Früh- und Hochmittelalter', in K. Bosl (ed.), *Handbuch der Geschichte der böhmischen Länder* I, Stuttgart, pp. 165–347
Störmer, W. (1987), 'Zur Frage der Function des kirchlichen Fernbesitzes im Gebiet der Ostalpen vom 8. bis zum 10. Jahrhundert', in H. Beumann and W. Schröder (eds.), *Die transalpinen Verbindungen der Bayern, Alemannen und Franken bis zum 10. Jahrhundert* (Nationes 6), Sigmaringen, pp. 379–403
Vlasto, A.P. (1970), *The Entry of the Slavs into Christendom*, Cambridge
Wolfram, H. (1987), *Die Geburt Mitteleuropas: Geschichte Österreichs vor seiner Entstehung*, Vienna
Zibermayr, I. (1956), *Noricum, Baiern und Österreich*, 2nd edn, Horn

Venice – Friuli – Istria – Dalmatia

Cessi, R. (1940), 'L'occupazione Longobarda e Franca dell'Istria nei secoli VIII e IX', *Atti dell'Istituto Veneto di Scienze, Lettere ed Arte* 100: 289–313
Krahwinkler, H. (1991), *Friaul im Frühmittelalter: Geschichte einer Region vom Ende des fünften bis zur Mitte des zehnten Jahrhunderts* (Veröffentlichungen des Instituts für Österreichische Geschichtsforschung 30), Vienna
Kretschmayr, H. (1905–20), *Geschichte von Venedig*, 3 vols., Gotha
Norwich, J.J. (1982), *A History of Venice*, London
Obolensky, D. (1988), 'The Balkans in the ninth century: barrier or bridge?', *Byzantinische Forschung* 13: 47–66
Ross, J.B. (1945), 'Two neglected paladins of Charlemagne: Erich of Friuli and Berold of Bavaria', *Speculum* 20: 212–35
Sasel, J. (1988), 'L'organizzazione del confine orientale d'Italia nell'alto medioevo', in *Aquileia e le Venezie nell' Alto Medioevo* (Antichità Altoadriatiche 32), Udine, pp. 107–14

Central–southern Italy

Belting, H. (1962), 'Studien zum beneventanischen Hof', *DOP* 16: 141–93
Bertolini, O. (1965), 'Carolo Magno e Benevento', in *Karl der Grosse* I, pp. 609–71
Cilento, N. (1966), *Le Origini della Signoria Capuana nella Langobardia Minore* (Studi Storici 69–70), Rome
Classen, P. (1981), 'Italien zwischen Byzanz und dem Frankenreich', *Settimane* 27: 919–97
Drew, K.F. (1964), 'The Carolingian military frontier in Italy', *Traditio* 20: 437–47
Hlawitschka, E. (1960), *Franken, Alemannen, Bayern und Burgunder in Oberitalien (774–962): Zum Verständnis der fränkischen Königsherrschaft in Italien* (Forschungen zur oberrheinischen Landesgeschichte 8), Freiburg-im-Breisgau
Hofmeister, A. (1907), 'Markgrafen und Markgrafschaften im italienischen Königreich in der Zeit vom Karl dem Grossen bis auf Otto den Grossen (774–962)',

MIÖG (Ergänzungsband 7), pp. 215–428

Kreutz, B.M. (1991), *Before the Normans: Southern Italy in the Ninth and Tenth Centuries*, Philadelphia

Martin, J.-M. (1980), 'Eléments préféodaux dans les principautés de Bénévent et de Capoue (fin du VIIIe siècle – début du XIe siècle): modalités de privatisation du pouvoir', in *Structures féodales et féodalisme dans l'occident méditerranéan (Xe–XIIe siècles)* (Collection de l'Ecole Française de Rome 44), Rome, pp. 553–86

Noble, T.F.X. (1984), *The Republic of St Peter: The Birth of the Papal State, 680–825*, Philadelphia

Toubert, P. (1973), *Les Structures du Latium médiévale: le Latium méridional et le Sabine du IXe siècle à la fin du XIIIe siècle* (Bibliothèque des Ecoles Françaises d'Athènes et de Rome 221), 2 vols., Rome

von Falkenhausen, V. (1983), 'I Longobardi Meridionali' in *Il Mezzogiorno dai Bizantini a Federico II (Storia d'Italia* III, gen. ed. G. Galasso), Turin, pp. 251–364

Wickham, C.J. (1981), *Early Medieval Italy*, London

Frisians – Danes – Elbe Slavs

Bleiber, W. (1965), 'Fränkisch-karolingisch Klöster als Grundherren in Friesland', *Jahrbuch für Wirtschaftsgeschichte* III, pp. 127–75

Blok, D.P. (1979), *De Franken in Nederland*, 3rd edn, Haarlem

Dralle, L. (1981), *Slaven an Havel und Spree: Studien zur Geschichte des hevellisch-wilzischen Fürstentums (6. bis 10. Jahrhundert)* (Giessener Abhandlungen zur Agrar- und Wirschaftsforschung des Europäischen Ostens 108), Berlin

Ernst, R. (1974), *Die Nordwestslawen und das fränkische Reich* (Giessener Abhandlungen zur Agrar- und Wirschaftsforschung des Europäischen Ostens 74), Berlin

Ernst, R. (1977), 'Karolingische Nordostpolitik zur Zeit Ludwigs des Frommen', in C. Goerke, E. Oberländer and D. Wojtecki (eds.), *Östliches Europa: Spiegel der Geschichte. Festschrift für M. Hellmann* (Quellen und Studien zur Geschichte des östlichen Europa 9), Wiesbaden, pp. 81–107

Friedmann, B. (1986), *Untersuchungen zur Geschichte des abodritischen Fürstentums bis zum ende des 10. Jahrhunderts* (Giessener Abhandlungen zur Agrar- und Wirtschaftsforschung des Europäischen Ostens 137), Berlin

Halbertsma, H. (1965–6), 'The Frisian kingdom', *Berichten van die Rijksdienst voor het Oudheidkundig Bodemonderzoek* 15–16: 69–108

Jankuhn, H. (1965), 'Karl der Grosse und der Norden', in *Karl der Grosse* I, pp. 699–707

Kötzschke, R. (1920), 'Die deutsche Marken im Sorbenland', in *Festgabe G. Seeliger*, Leipzig, pp. 79–114

Lebecq, S. (1978), 'Francs contre Frisons (VIe–VIIIe siècles)', in *La Guerre et la paix au moyen âge: Actes du 101e congrès national des sociétés savantes, Lille 1976*, Paris, pp. 53–71

Lebecq, S. (1983), *Marchands et navigateurs frisons du haut moyen âge*, 2 vols., Lille

Lebecq, S. (1986), 'Les Frisons entre paganisme et christianisme', in *Christianisation et déchristianisation: Actes de la 9e rencontre d'histoire religieuse de Fontevraud*, Angers, pp. 19–45

Lund, N. (1989), 'Allies of God or man? The Viking expansion in a European perspective', *Viator* 20: 45–59

Roesdahl, E. (1982), *Viking Age Denmark*, London

TeBrake, W. (1978), 'Ecology and economy in early medieval Frisia', *Viator* 9: 1–29

Wood, I.N. (1987), 'Christians and pagans in ninth-century Scandinavia', in B. Sawyer, P. Sawyer and I.N. Wood (eds.), *The Christianization of Scandinavia*, Alingsås, pp. 36–67

Wood, I.N. (forthcoming), 'Identifying the pagans in conversion history'

7 THE VIKINGS IN FRANCIA AND ANGLO-SAXON ENGLAND TO 911

Blok, D.P. (1978), 'De Wikingen in Friesland', *Naamkunde* 10: 25–47

Brooks, N.P. (1979), 'England in the ninth century: the crucible of defeat', *TRHS* 5th series, 29: 1–20

Coupland, S. (1991a), 'The fortified bridges of Charles the Bald', *Journal of Medieval History* 17: 1–12

Coupland, S. (1991b), 'The rod of God's wrath or the people of God's wrath? The Carolingians' theology of the Viking invasions', *Journal of Ecclesiastical History* 42(4): 535–54

D'Haenens, A. (1970), *Les invasions normandes, une catastrophe?*, Paris

Keynes, S.D. and Lapidge, M. (eds.) (1983), *Alfred the Great*, Harmondsworth

Loyn, H.R. (1977), *The Vikings in Britain*, London

Sawyer, P.H. (1971), *The Age of the Vikings*, 2nd edn, London

Vogel, W. (1906) *Die Normannen und das fränkische Reich bis zur Gründung der Normandie (799–911)*, Heidelberg

Wallace-Hadrill, J.M. (1975), *The Vikings in Francia*, Reading

Zettel, H. (1977) *Das Bild der Normannen und der Normanneneinfälle in westfränkischen, ostfränkischen und angelsächsischen Quellen des 8. bis 11. Jahrhunderts*, Munich

8 SCANDINAVIA, *c.* 700–1066

Andersson, T.M. (1987), 'The Viking policy of Ethelred the Unready', *Scandinavian Studies* 59: 284–95

Bagge, S. (1992), 'Helgen, helt og statsbygger – Olav Tryggvason i norsk historieskrivning gjennom 700 år', in S. Suphellen (ed.), *Kongsmenn og krossmenn: Festskrift til Grethe Authén Blom*, Oslo

Constandse-Westermann, T.S. (1972), 'Genetical affinities between populations in western Europe and Scandinavia', in J.S. Weiner and J. Huizinga (eds.), *The Assessment of Population Affinities in Man*, Oxford, pp. 137–81

Graham-Campbell, J. (1981), *The Viking Age*, London

Gräslund, B. (1986), 'Knut den store och sveariket. Slaget vid Helgeå i ny belysning', *Scandia* 52: 211–38

Helle, K. (1991), 'Tiden fram til 1536', in R. Danielsen *et al.* (eds.), *Grunntrekk i norsk historie fra vikingtid til våre dager*, Oslo, pp. 13–106

Keynes, S. (1986), 'The additions in Old English', in N. Barker (ed.), *The York Gospels*, London, pp. 81–99

Krag, C. (1989), 'Norge som odel i Harald Hårfagres ætt. Et møte med en gjenganger', *Historisk Tidsskrift* (N) 1989: 288–302

Krag, C. (1991), *Ynglingatal og Ynglingasaga: En studie i historiske kilder* (Studia Humaniora 2), Oslo

Liebermann, F. (1903–16), *Die Gesetze der Angelsachsen*, 3 vols., Halle

Löfving, C. (1991), 'Who ruled the region east of Skagerrak in the eleventh century?', in R. Samson (ed.), *Social Approaches to Viking Studies*, Glasgow, pp. 146–56

Lund, N. (1980), 'Svenskevældet i Hedeby', *Aarbøger for Nordisk Oldkyndighed og Historie* 1980: 114–25

Lund, N. (1989), 'Allies of God or man? The Viking expansion in a European perspective', *Viator, Medieval and Renaissance Studies* 20: 45–59

Lund, N. (1991a) 'Denemearc, tanmarkar but and tanmaurk ala', in *People and Places in Northern Europe 500–1600: Essays in Honour of Peter Hayes Sawyer*, Woodbridge, pp. 161–70

Lund, N. (1991b), 'The Danish perspective', in D.G. Scragg (ed.), *The Battle of Maldon AD 991*, Oxford, pp. 114–42

Moltke, E. (1985), 'Det svenske Hedebyrige og Danmarks samling', *Aarbøger for Nordisk Oldkyndighed og Historie* 1985: 16–28

Musset, L. (1959), 'Pour l'étude des relation entre les colonies scandinaves d'Angleterre et de Normandie', in *Mélanges de linguistique et de philologie Fernand Mossé in Memoriam*, Paris, pp. 330–9

Porsmose, E. (1988), 'Middelalder o. 1000–1536', in C. Bjørn *et al.* (eds.), *Det danske landbrugs historie* 1, Copenhagen, pp. 205–417

Randsborg, K. (1980), *The Viking Age in Denmark*, London

Randsborg, K. (1990), *The First Millennium AD in Europe and the Mediterranean: An Archaeological Essay*, Cambridge

Roesdahl, E. (1982), *Viking-Age Denmark*, London

Sawyer, P. (1982), *Kings and Vikings: Scandinavia and Europe AD 700–1100*, London

Sawyer, P. (1987) 'Ethelred II, Olaf Tryggvason, and the conversion of Norway', *Scandinavian Studies* 59: 299–307

Sawyer, P. (1988a), *The Making of Sweden*, Alingsås; Swedish edn, *När Sverige blev Sverige*, Alingsås (1991)

Sawyer, P. (1988b), '"Landamæri I": the supposed eleventh-century boundary treaty between Denmark and Sweden', in A. Andersen *et al.* (eds.), *Festskrift til Olaf Olsen på 60-årsdagen den 7. juni 1988*, Copenhagen, pp. 165–70

Sawyer, P. (1989), 'Knut, Sweden and Sigtuna', in S. Tesch (ed.), *Avstamp – för en ny Sigtunaforskning*, Sigtuna, pp. 88–93

Sawyer, P. (1991), 'Swein Forkbeard and the historians', in I. Wood and G.A. Loud (eds.), *Church and Chronicle in the Middle Ages*, London, pp. 27–40

Wood, I. (1983), *The Merovingian North Sea* (Occasional Papers on Medieval Topics 1), Alingsås

Wood, I. (1987), 'Christians and pagans in ninth-century Scandinavia', in B. Sawyer *et al.* (eds.), *The Christianization of Scandinavia* (Report of a Symposium held at Kungälv, Sweden, 4–9 August 1985), Alingsås, pp. 36–67

9 SLAVS AND BULGARS

Extensive bibliographies of earlier secondary literature may be found in Obolensky (1966); Vlasto (1970); Obolensky (1971). See also, for more recent literature concerning the Avars: Pohl (1989); for the geography and general history of the Balkans: Hösch (1988); and for Sts Constantine-Cyril and Methodius: Mozhaeva (1980); Dujčev, Kirmagova and Paunova (1983).

Ahrweiler, H. (1966), *Byzance et la mer*, Paris

Ahrweiler, H. (1971), *Etudes sur les structures administratives et sociales de Byzance*, London

Ahrweiler, H. (1975), *L'idéologie politique de Byzance*, Paris

Aleksandrov, E. (1991), 'Introniziraneto na kniaz Simeon – 893g.', *Pal.* 15(3): 10–17

Aleksova, B. (1982), 'The episcopal basilica at Stobi (excavations and researches 1970–1981)', *JÖB* 32(4): 481–90

Anastos, M.V. (1954), 'Political theory in the lives of the Slavic saints Constantine and Methodius', *Harvard Slavic Studies* 2: 11–38

Anastos, M.V. (1957) 'The transfer of Illyricum, Calabria and Sicily to the jurisdiction of the patriarchate of Constantinople in 732–33', *Studi Bizantini e Neoellenici* 9: 14–31

Andreev, M. and Milkova, F. (1979), *Istoriia na b'lgarskata feodalna d'rzhava i pravo*, Sofia

Angelov, B.S. (1966), 'Niakolko nabliudeniia v'rkhu knizhovnoto delo na Kliment Okhridski', in B.S. Angelov *et al.* (eds.), *Kliment Okhridski: Sbornik ot statii po sluchai 1050 godini ot sm' rtta mu*, Sofia, pp. 79–105

Angelov, B.S. (1977), *Iz istoriiata na starob'lgarskata i v' zrozhdenskata literatura*, Sofia

Angelov, B.S. (1980), 'Poslanie patriarkha Fotiia bolgarskomu kniaziu Borisu', *Byzbulg* 6: 45–50

Angelov, D. (1978), *Les Balkans au moyen âge: la Bulgarie des Bogomils aux Turcs*, London

Angelov, D. (1979), *Obshtestvo i obshtestvena mis'l v srednovekovna B'lgariia (IX–XIV v.)*, Sofia

Angelov, D. (1980), *Die Entstehung des bulgarischen Volkes*, Berlin

Angelov, D. (1986), 'Das byzantisches Reich und der mittelalterliche bulgarische Staat', *Byzbulg* 8: 9–16

Angelov, D. (1988), 'Methods und seiner Schüler Wirken in Bulgarien', *SM*, pp. 23–31

Angelov, D. (1991) 'Kultur und Sprache in der bulgarischen Geschichte im Mittelalter', *Pal.* 15(3): 3–9

Angelov, D., Kashev, S. and Cholpanov, B. (1983), *B'lgarska voenna istoriia ot antichnostta do vtorata chetv'rt na Xv.*, Sofia

Antoljak, S. (1985), *Srednevekovna Makedonija*, Skopje

Arranz, M. (1988), 'La liturgie de l'Euchologe slave du Sinai', *CAS*, pp. 15–74

Arranz, M. (1989), 'La liturgie slave du IX siècle d'après l'Euchologe slave du Sinai', *MBS* II, pp. 316–40

Aubin, H. (1959), *Die Ostgrenze des alten deutschen Reiches*, Darmstadt

Avenarius, A. (1974), *Die Awaren in Europa*, Bratislava

Avenarius, A. (1985a), 'Die Ideologie der Byzantiner und ihre Widerspiegelung in der Vita Constantini', *BSl* 46: 25–32

Avenarius, A. (1985b), 'Die Konsolidierung des Awarenkhaganates und Byzanz im 7. Jahrhundert', *Byzantina* 13: 1019–32

Avenarius, A. (1988), 'Struktur und Organisation der europäischen Steppenvölker', *Settimane* 35(1): 125–50

Bakalov, G. (1985), *Srednovekovniiat b'lgarski vladetel (titulatura i insignii)*, Sofia

Balint, C. (1989), *Die Archäologie der Steppe: Steppenvölker zwischen Volga und Donau vom 6. bis zum 10. Jahrhundert*, ed. F. Daim, Vienna, Cologne and Graz

Baumann, W. (1988), 'Die Gestalt Methods in der Preisrede Kliment Ochridskis', *SM*, pp. 393–402

Beck, H. G. (1967), 'Christliche Mission und politische Propaganda im byzantinischen Reich', *Settimane* 14: 649–74

Beranová, M. (1988), *Slované*, Prague

Beševliev, V. (1960), 'Tri prinosa k'm b'lgarskata srednovekovna istoriia', in A.K. Burmov *et al.* (eds.), *Izsledvaniia v chest na Marin S. Drinov*, Sofia, pp. 283–300

Beševliev, V. (1962), 'Ein byzantinischer Brauch bei den Protobulgaren', *Acta Antiqua Academiae Scientiarum Hungaricae* 10: 17–21

Beševliev, V. (1963), *Die protobulgarischen Inschriften* (BBA 23), Berlin

Beševliev, V. (1964), *Spätgriechische und spätlateinische Inschriften aus Bulgarien* (BBA 30), Berlin

Beševliev, V. (1971), 'Die Kaiseridee bei den Protobulgaren', *Byzantina* 3: 83–91

Beševliev, V. (1972), 'Eine neue protobulgarische Gedenkinschrift', *BZ* 65: 394–9

Beševliev, V. (1978), *Bulgarisch-Byzantinische Aufsätze*, London

Beševliev, V. (1979), *P'rvo-B'lgarski nadpisi*, Sofia

Beševliev, V. (1981a), *Die protobulgarische Periode der bulgarischen Geschichte*, Amsterdam

Beševliev, V. (1981b), 'Sprachliches aus byzantinischen Bleisiegeln', *JÖB* 30: 63–74

Beševliev, V. (1981c), *P'rvob'lgarite: Bit i kultura*, Sofia

Beševliev, V. (1981, 1984–5), 'Spuren des ehemaligen Doppelkönigtums bei den Protobulgaren', *Byzantine Studies/Etudes Byzantines* 8, 11–12: 13–24

Beševliev, V. (1987), 'Das byzantinische in den protobulgarischen Inschriften', *Byzantiaka* 7: 55–63

Beševliev, V. (1990), 'Eine unbekannte Klausel eines Friedensvertrages zwischen Bulgarien und Byzanz', *JÖB* 40: 167–9

Beshevliev, V., see Beševliev, V.

Birnbaum, H. (1981, 1984–5), 'On the eastern and western components of the earliest Slavic liturgy: the evidence of the Euchologium Sinaiticum and related texts', *Byzantine Studies/Etudes Byzantines* 8, 11–12: 25–44

Boba, I. (1971), *Moravia's History Reconsidered: A Reinterpretation of Medieval Sources*, The Hague

Bon, A. (1951), *Le Peloponnèse byzantin jusqu'en 1204*, Paris

Bona, I. (1988), 'Die Geschichte der Awaren im Lichte der archäologischen Quellen', *Settimane* 35(2): 437–63

Bösl, K. (1966), 'Das Grossmährische Reich in der politischen Welt des 9. Jahrhunderts' (Sitzungsberichte der Bayerischen Akademie der Wissenschaften, phil.-hist. Klasse – nr. 7)

Boyle, L.E. (1988), 'The site of the tomb of St Cyril in the lower basilica of San Clemente, Rome', *CAS*, pp. 75–82

Bozhilov, I. (1983), *Tsar Simeon veliki (893–927): zlatiat vek na Srednovekovna B'lgariia*, Sofia

Bozhilov, I. (1991), '"Oros ton Boulgaron"', *Starob'lgarska Literatura* 25–26: 102–9

Bozhkov, A. (1972), *Miniatiuri ot Madriskiia r'kopis na Ioan Skilitsa*, Sofia

Bratianu, G.I. (1940), 'Le commerce bulgare dans l'empire byzantin et le monopole de l'empereur Léon VI à Thessalonique', *Sbornik v pamet na P. Nikov (Izvestiia na B'lgarskoto Istorichesko Druzhestvo)*, 16–18, pp. 30–6

Brezeanu, S. (1981), 'Grecs et Thraco-Romains au Bas-Danube sous le règne du Tsar Boris-Michel', *RESEE* 19: 643–51

Brezeanu, S. (1982), 'Les roumains et "le silence des sources" dans "le millénaire obscur"', *Revue Roumaine d'Histoire* 21: 387–403

Browning, R. (1975), *Byzantium and Bulgaria: A Comparative Study across the Early Medieval Frontier*, London

Bryer, A. and Herrin, J. (eds.) (1977), *Iconoclasm*, Birmingham

Bujnoch, J. (1972), *Zwischen Rom und Byzanz: Leben und Wirken der Slavenapostel Kyrillos und Methodios nach den Pannonischen Legenden und der Klemensvita* (Slavische Geschichtsschreiber 1), Graz, Vienna and Cologne

Bury, J.B. (1912), *A History of the Eastern Roman Empire from the Fall of Irene to the Accession of Basil I (AD 802–867)*, London

Cankova-Petkova, G. (1968), 'Sur l'établissement des tribus slaves du groupe bulgare au sud du Bas Danube', *Etudes Historiques à l'Occasion du VI Congrès International des Etudes Slaves, Prague* IV, Sofia, pp. 143–66

Cankova-Petkova, G. (1973), 'Contribution au sujet de la conversion des Bulgares au christianisme', *Byzbulg* 4: 21–39

Cankova-Petkova, G. (1976), 'Deux contributions à l'histoire des rapports bulgaro-byzantins au IX siècle', *BSl* 37: 36–45

Cankova-Petkova, G. (1978), 'Über die Bildung des bulgarischen Staates', in V. Vavřínek (ed.), *Beiträge zur byzantinischen Geschichte im 9.–11. Jahrhundert*, Prague, pp. 463–82

Carile, A. (1983), 'La presenza bizantina nell'Alto Adriatico fra VII e IX secolo', *Abruzzo. Rivista dell'Istituto di Studi Abruzzesi* 31: 3–37

Carile, A. (1988), 'I nomadi nelle fonti bizantine', *Settimane* 35(1): 55–87

Carter, F.W. (1972), *Dubrovnik (Ragusa): A Classical City State*, London and New York

Carter, F.W. (ed.) (1977), *The Historical Geography of the Balkans*, London

Cessi, R. (1953), *La Repubblica di Venezia e il problema Adriatico*, Naples

Cessi, R. (1981), *Storia della Repubblica di Venezia*, Florence

Charanis, P. (1950), 'The Chronicle of Monemvasia and the question of the Slavonic settlements in Greece', *DOP* 5: 141–66, reprinted in Charanis (1972)

Charanis, P. (1953), 'On the Slavic settlement in the Peloponnesus', *BZ* 46: 91–103, reprinted in Charanis (1972)

Charanis, P. (1961), 'The transfer of population as a policy in the Byzantine Empire', *Comparative Studies in Society and History* 3(2): 140–54, reprinted in Charanis (1972)

Charanis, P. (1972), *Studies on the Demography of the Byzantine Empire*, London

Cheetham, N. (1981), *Mediaeval Greece*, New Haven and London

Christophilopoulou, A. (1986–92), *Byzantine History, 610–867*, 2 vols., Amsterdam

Christou, P. (1971), 'The missionary task of the Byzantine emperor', *Byzantina* 3: 277–86

Christou, P.C. (1992), 'Who sent Cyril and Methodius into Central Europe: the emperor or the patriarch?', *LSCM*, pp. 109–15

Chrysos, E. (1969), 'Zur Enstehung der Institution der autokephalen Erzbistümer', *BZ* 62: 263–86

Chrysos, E. (1987), 'Die Nordgrenze des byzantinischen Reiches im 6. bis 8. Jahrhundert', in B. Hansel (ed.), *Die Völker Südosteuropas im 6. bis 8. Jahrhundert. Symposion, Tutzing 1985* (Südosteuropa-Jahrbuch 17), Munich, pp. 27–40

Chrysos, E. (1992), 'Byzantine diplomacy, AD 300–800: means and ends', in J. Shepard and S. Franklin (eds.), *Byzantine Diplomacy*, Aldershot, pp. 25–39

Colov, R. (1981), 'Le droit romain en Bulgarie médiévale: diffusion, pénétration, confusion ou interaction?', in *Roma, Costantinopoli, Mosca*, Naples, pp. 399–405

Conte, F. (1986), *Les Slaves: aux origines des civilisations d'Europe centrale et orientale (VI–XIII siècles)*, Paris

Cronţ, G. (1975), 'La loi agraire byzantine dans les pays du sud-est européen', *Actes du XIV Congrès International des Etudes Byzantines* II, Bucharest, pp. 543–53

Cyrillo-Methodianische Fragen, Slavische Philologie und Altertumskunde (1968), *Acta Congressus Historiae Slavicae Salisburgensis in memoriam SS. Cyrilli et Methodii anno 1963 celebrati* (Annales Instituti Slavici 1.4), Wiesbaden

Darrouzès, J. (1975), 'Listes episcopales du concile de Nicée (787)', *REB* 33: 5–76

Darrouzès, J. (1981), *Notitiae Episcopatuum Ecclesiae Constantinopolitanae* (Géographie ecclésiastique de l'empire byzantin 1), Paris

Davidson, M. (1981), 'Sources of art in post-Conversion Bulgaria: the evidence of the Preslav tiles', *PP* III, pp. 71–5

Deér, J. (1965), 'Karl der Grosse und der Untergang des Awarenreiches', in H. Beumann (ed.), *Karl der Grosse, Werk und Nachleben* I, pp. 719–91, reprinted in Deér (1977), pp. 285–371

Deér, J. (1977), *Byzanz und das abendländische Herrschertum* (Vorträge und Forschungen 21), Sigmaringen

Dekan, J. (1980), *Velká Morava: Doba a umění*, Prague

Dewey, H.W. and Kleimola, A.M. (trans.) (1977), *Zakon sudnyj Ljudem (Court Law for the People)* (Michigan Slavic Materials 14), Ann Arbor

Diaconu, P. (1985), 'Extension du premier état bulgare au nord du Danube (VIII–X siècles). La culture matérielle', *EB* 21(1): 107–13

Dimitrov, D.I. (1985), 'La culture matérielle sur la rive septentrionale gauche du Bas-Danube aux VI–X siècles', *EB* 21(1): 114–32

Dimitrov, D.I. (1987), 'Ob osnovnykh protobolgarskikh gruppakh v stepiakh Vostochnoi Evropy v VI–VII vv.', *BHR* 15(1): 58–70

Ditten, H. (1978a), 'Zur Bedeutung der Einwanderung der Slawen', in F. Winkelmann *et al.* (eds.), *Byzanz im 7. Jahrhundert: Untersuchungen zur Herausbildung des Feudalismus* (BBA 48), Berlin, pp. 73–160

Ditten, H. (1978b), 'Bemerkungen zu den ersten Ansatzen zur Staatsbildung bei Kroaten und Serben im 7. Jahrhundert', in V. Vavřínek (ed.), *Beiträge zur byzantinischen Geschichte im 9.–11. Jahrhundert*, Prague, pp. 441–62

Ditten, H. (1981), 'Die Veränderungen auf dem Balkan in der Zeit vom 6. bis zum

10. Jh. im Spiegel der veränderterten Bedeutung der Provinzen der thrakischen Diözese', *Byzbulg* 7: 157–79

Ditten, H. (1983a), 'Zum Verhältnis zwischen Protobulgaren und Slawen vom Ende des 7. bis zum Anfang des 9. Jahrhunderts', in H. Köpstein (ed.), *Besonderheiten der byzantinischen Feudalentwicklung* (BBA 50), Berlin, pp. 85–95

Ditten, H. (1983b), 'Prominente Slawen und Bulgaren im byzantinischen Diensten (Ende des 7. bis Anfang des 10. Jahrhunderts', in H. Köpstein and F. Winkelmann (eds.), *Studien zum 8. und 9. Jahrhundert im Byzanz* (BBA 51), Berlin, pp. 95–119

Ditten, H. (1984), 'Herrschte 837 u.Z. Krieg oder Frieden zwischen Byzanz und Bulgarien?', *EB* 20(4): 62–79

Dittrich, Z.R. (1962), *Christianity in Great-Moravia* (Bijdragen van het Instituut voor Middeleeuwse Geschiedenis der Rijksuniversiteit te Utrecht 33), Groningen

Djingov, G. (1975), 'Sur l'origine de la verrerie en Bulgarie au moyen âge', in *Verre médiéval aux Balkans (V–XV s.), recueil des travaux. Conférence internationale Belgrade, 24–26 avril 1974* (Académie Serbe des Sciences et des Arts, Institut des Etudes Balkaniques. Editions speciales 3), Belgrade, pp. 109–14

Djingov, G. (1979), 'Traditsii i vliianiia v starob'lgarskoto st'klarstvo ot IX—X vek', *B'lgariia v sveta ot drevnostta do nashi dni* 1, Sofia, pp. 239–43

Djingov, G. (1980), 'Za ost'kliavaneto na srednovekovnite sgradi', in G. Gjuzelev (ed.), *B'lgarsko-srednovekovie: B'lgarsko-s'vetski sbornik v chest na 70-godishninata na prof. Ivan Dujčev*, Sofia, pp. 193–6

Djurova, A. (1988/9), 'L'intégration du monde slave dans le cadre de la communauté orthodoxe (IX–XII siècles): notes préliminaires', *Harvard Ukrainian Studies* 12/13: 643–71

Dölger, F. (1939), 'Der Bulgarenherrscher als geistlicher Sohn des byzantinischen Kaisers', *Izvestiia na B'lgarskoto Istorichesko Druzhestvo* 16–17 (= *Sbornik v pamet na prof. Pet'r Nikov*), Sofia, pp. 219–32, reprinted in Dölger (1976), pp. 183–96

Dölger, F. (1976), *Byzanz und die europäische Staatenwelt*, Darmstadt

Döpmann, H.-D. (1967), 'Die jurisdiktionelle Stellung des ersten Erzbischofs von Bulgarien', *Wissenschaftliche Zeitschrift der Humboldt-Universität zu Berlin: Gesellschafts- und Sprachwissenschaftliche Reihe*, 16(5): 803–4

Döpmann, H.-D. (1981), 'Zum Streit zwischen Rom und Byzanz um die Christianisierung Bulgariens', *Pal.* 5: 62–73

Döpmann, H.-D. (1989), 'Die Bedeutung Bulgariens für das Verhalten Roms gegenüber Erzbischof Method', *MBS* 1, pp. 98–103

Döpmann, H.-D. (1990), 'Die Annahme des Christentums bei den Slawen-Völkern Südosteuropas', *EB* 26(1): 46–53

Dostál, A. (1959), *Clozianus codex palaeoslovenicus glagoliticus: Tridentinus et Oenipontanus*, Prague

Dostál, A. (1965), 'The origins of the Slavonic liturgy', *DOP* 19: 67–87

Dostalova, R. (1966), 'Megale Morabia', *BSl* 27: 344–9

Dragojlović, D. (1989), 'Tsrkvene prilike u Dalmatsiji ot razarania Salone do obnove Splitske nadbiskupije', *Balcanica*, Belgrade, 20: 211–26

Ducellier, A. (1968), 'L'Arbanon et les Albanais au XI siècle', *TM* 3: 353–68

Ducellier, A. (ed.) (1986), *Byzance et le monde orthodoxe*, Paris

Duicev, I., see Dujčev, I.

Duichev, I., see Dujčev, I.

Dujčev, I. (1943–4), *Iz starata b'lgarska knizhnina*, 2 vols., Sofia

Dujčev, I. (1949), 'Die *Responsa Nicolai I. Papae ad consulta Bulgarorum* als Quelle für die bulgarische Geschichte', *Festschrift des Haus-, Hof- und Staatsarchivs* I, Vienna, pp. 349–62, reprinted in *MBS* I, pp. 125–48

Dujčev, I. (1951a), 'Au lendemain de la conversion du peuple bulgare. L'épître de Photius', *Mélanges de Science Religieuse* 8: 211–26, reprinted in *MBS* I, pp. 107–23

Dujčev, I. (1951b), 'Zur literarischen Tätigkeit Konstantins des Philosophen', *BZ* 44: 105–10, reprinted in *MBS* II, pp. 69–76

Dujčev, I. (1959a), 'Les sept tribus slaves de la Mésie', *Slavia Antiqua* 6: 100–8, reprinted in *MBS* I, pp. 55–65

Dujčev, I. (1959b), 'Odna iz osobennostei rannevizantiiskikh mirnykh dogovorov', *Vizantiiskii Vremennik* 15: 64–70

Dujčev, I. (1961), 'Une ambassade byzantine auprès des Serbes au IX siècle', *ZRVI* 7: 53–60, reprinted in *MBS* I, pp. 221–30

Dujčev, I. (1964), 'Dragvista-Dragovitia', *REB* 22: 215–21, reprinted in *MBS* II, pp. 137–45

Dujčev, I. (1965), 'La chronique byzantine de l'an 811', *TM* 1: 205–54, reprinted in *MBS* II, pp. 425–89

Dujčev, I. (1967), review of Beševliev (1963) in *BZ* 60: 129–36, reprinted in *MBS* III, pp. 43–56

Dujčev, I. (1968), 'La Bulgaria medioevale fra Bisanzio e Roma', *Felix Ravenna* 46: 67–97, reprinted in *MBS* III, pp. 523–50

Dujčev, I. (1970a), *Slavia Orthodoxa: Collected Studies in the History of the Slavic Middle Ages*, London

Dujčev, I. (1970b), 'The embassy of Constantine the Philosopher to the Arabs', in R. Auty, L.R. Lewitter and A.P. Vlasto (eds.), *Gorski Vijenac: A Garland of Essays offered to Prof. Elisabeth Mary Hill*, Cambridge, pp. 100–4

Dujčev, I. (1972), *B'lgarsko srednovekovie*, Sofia

Dujčev, I. (1981), *Prouchvaniia v'rkhu b'lgarskata istoriia i kultura*, Sofia

Dujčev, I. (1983), 'L'occidente e l'oriente nella civiltà bulgara del medioevo', *Atti dell' 8 Congresso internazionale di studi sull'alto medioevo*, Spoleto, pp. 17–40

Dujčev, I. (ed.) (1976), *Chronica di Monemvasia*, Palermo

Dujčev, I. (1985) (ed.), *Kirill and Methodios: Founders of Slavonic Writing*, trans. S. Nikolov (East European Monographs 172), Boulder, CO

Dujčev, I., Kirmagova, A. and Paunova, A. (eds.) (1983), *Kirilometodievska Bibliografiia 1950–80*, Sofia

Dvornik, F. (1926a), *Les Slaves, Byzance et Rome au IX siècle*, Paris

Dvornik, F. (1930), 'La lutte entre Byzance et Rome à propos de l'Illyricum au IX siècle', in *Mélanges Charles Diehl* I, Paris, pp. 61–80

Dvornik, F. (1933), *Les légendes de Constantin et de Méthode vues de Byzance*, Prague

Dvornik, F. (1948), *The Photian Schism: History and Legend*, Cambridge, reprinted 1970

Dvornik, F. (1956), *The Slavs: Their Early History and Civilization*, Boston

Dvornik, F. (1962), *The Slavs in European History and Civilization*, New Brunswick, NJ

Dvornik, F. (1964), 'Byzantium, Rome, the Franks and the Christianization of the

Southern Slavs', in M. Hellmann *et al.* (eds.), *Cyrillo-Methodiana: Zur Frühgeschichte des Christentums bei den Slaven 863–1963* (Slavistische Forschungen 6) Cologne and Graz, pp. 85–125

Dvornik, F. (1967), 'The embassies of Constantine-Cyril and Photius to the Arabs', *To Honor Roman Jakobson: Essays on the Occasion of his Seventieth Birthday* 1, The Hague and Paris, pp. 569–76

Dvornik, F. (1970), *Byzantine Missions among the Slavs: Saints Constantine-Cyril and Methodius*, New Brunswick, NJ

Dvornik, F. (1971), 'Constantine-Cyril's religious discussions with the Arabs', *Studia Palaeoslovenica*, Prague, pp. 77–8

Dvornik, F. (ed.) (1926b), *La vie de saint Grégoire le Décapolite et les Slaves macédoniens au IX siècle*, Paris

Dzhingov, G., see Djingov, G.

Erdelyi, I. (1988), 'Über die gegossenen Gürtelgarnituren der spätawarenzeit östlich von Karpaten', *Settimane* 35(1): 351–67

Ferluga, J. (1976), *Byzantium on the Balkans*, Amsterdam

Ferluga, J. (1978), *L'amministrazione bizantina in Dalmazia*, Venice

Ferluga, J. (1982), 'Archon. Ein Beitrag zur Untersuchung der südslavischen Herrschertitel im 9. und 10. Jahrhundert im Lichte der byzantinischen Quellen', in N. Kamp and J. Wollasch (eds.), *Tradition als Historische Kraft: Interdisziplinäre Forschungen zur Geschichte des früheren Mittelalters*, Berlin and New York, pp. 254–66

Ferluga, J. (1983), 'Gli Slavi del Sud ed altri gruppi etnici di fronte a Bisanzio', *Settimane* 30(1): 303–43

Ferluga, J. (1984), 'Untersuchungen zur byzantinischen Ansiedlungspolitik in dem Balkan von der Mitte des 7. bis zur Mitte des 9. Jahrhunderts', *ZRVI* 23: 49–61

Ferluga, J. (1985), 'Byzanz auf dem Balkan im frühen Mittelalter', *Südost-Forschungen* 44: 1–16

Ferluga, J. (1987a), 'Überlegungen zur Geschichte der byzantinischen Provinz Istrien', *Jahrbücher für Geschichte Osteuropas* 35: 164–73

Ferluga, J. (1987b), 'Der byzantinische Handel nach dem Norden im 9. und 10. Jahrhundert', in K. Düwel *et al.* (eds.), *Untersuchungen zu Handel und Verkehr der vor- und frühgeschichtlichen Zeit in Mittel- und Nordeuropa. IV: Der Handel der Karolinger- und Wikingerzeit* (Abhandlungen der Akademie der Wissenschaften in Göttingen, phil.-historische Klasse, Dritte Folge, 156), Göttingen, pp. 616–42

Ferluga, J. (1992), *Untersuchungen zur byzantinischen Provinzialverwaltung. VI–XIII Jahrhundert. Gesammelte Aufsätze*, Amsterdam

Fine, J.V.A. (1983), *The Early Medieval Balkans: A Critical Survey from the Late Sixth to the Late Twelfth Century*, Ann Arbor

Florja, B.N. (1981), *Skazaniia o nachale slavianskoi pis'mennosti*, Moscow

Florja, B.N. (1988), 'Priniatie khristianstva v Velikoi Moravii, Chekhii i Pol'she', in G.G. Litavrin (ed.), *Priniatie khristianstva narodami Tsentral'noi i Iugo-Vostochnoi Evropy i kreshchenie Rusi*, Moscow, pp. 122–58

Florja, B.N. and Litavrin, G.G. (1988), 'Christianization of the nations of central and south-east Europe and the conversion of old Rus'', *BSl* 49: 185–99

Galchev, I. (1989), 'Zdravnoto delo na sv. Kliment i sv. Naum', *MBS* 11, pp. 89–92

Gautier, P. (1964), 'Clément d'Ohrid, évêque de Dragvista', *REB* 22: 199–214

Georgiev, E. (1962), *Raztsvet't na b'lgarskata literatura v IX–Xv.*, Sofia

Georgiev, E. (1982), 'Vozniknovenie preslavskoi literaturnoi shkoly', *Pal.* 6(1): 16–28

Georgiev, G.I. *et al.* (1975), 'Archaeological investigations in Bulgaria in the last few decades', *BHR* 3(1): 78–91

Georgiev, P. (1982), 'Za pervonachalnoto sedalishche na b'lgarskata arkhiepiskopiia', *SBC*, pp. 67–78

Gesemann, W. (1988), 'Die altslavische Religion im Lichte der Brüdermission', *SM*, pp. 117–22

Gimbutas, M. (1971), *The Slavs*, London

Gjuzelev, V. (1966), 'Bulgarisch-fränkische Beziehungen in der ersten Hälfte des IX. Jahrhunderts', *Byzbulg* 2: 15–39

Gjuzelev, V. (1969), *Kniaz Boris P'rvi – B'lgariia prez vtorata polovina na IX vek*, Sofia

Gjuzelev, V. (1977), 'Das Papsttum und Bulgarien im Mittelalter (9.–14. Jahrhundert)', *BHR* 5: 34–58

Gjuzelev, V. (1978), 'Allgemeine Charakteristik und Etappen der Errichtung der militarischen und administrativen Verwaltung des ersten Bulgarischen Staates (VII. bis XI. Jh.)', *EB* 14: 71–7

Gjuzelev, V. (1986a), 'Die spätantike und frühmittelalterliche Stadt auf bulgarischem Territorium (6. bis 10. Jahrhundert)', in R. Pillinger (ed.), *Spätantike und frühbyzantinische Kultur Bulgariens zwischen Orient und Okzident* (Schriften der Balkankommission, Antiquarische Abteilung 16), Vienna, pp. 21–4

Gjuzelev, V. (1986b), 'La Bulgarie médiévale et l'Europe occidentale (IX–XIs.)', *Byzbulg* 8: 89–101

Gjuzelev, V. (1988), *Medieval Bulgaria. Byzantine Empire. Black Sea–Venice–Genoa* (Centre culturel du monde byzantin 1), Villach.

Gjuzelev, V. (1991), 'Die bulgarisch-albanische ethnische Grenze während des Mittelalters (6.–15. Jh.)', *EB* 27(3): 78–91

Gojda, M. (1991), *The Ancient Slavs: Settlement and Society. The Rhind Lectures 1989–90*, Edinburgh

Gomolka-Fuchs, G. (1987), 'O kontinuitete mezhdu rannevizantiiskimi i slavianskimi masterskimi VI–VIIvv. na nizhnem Dunae', *TKAS* III, 1(b), pp. 94–100

Gorina, L. (1991), '"Immenik bolgarskikh khanov" v sostave ellinskogo letopistsa pervoi redaktsii', *BHR* 19 (3): 93–6

Goshev, I. (1961), *Starob'lgarski glagolicheski i kirilski nadpisi ot IX i X v.*, Sofia

Goshev, I. (1966), 'Zur Frage der Krönungszeremonien und die zeremonielle Gewandung der byzantinischen und der bulgarischen Herrscher im Mittelalter', *Byzbulg* 2: 145–68

Graebner, M. (1975), 'The Slavs in Byzantine population transfers of the seventh and eighth centuries', *EB* 11(1): 40–52

Graebner, M. (1978), 'The Slavs in Byzantine Empire – absorption, semi-autonomy and the limits of Byzantinization', *Byzbulg* 5: 41–55

Graus, F. (1966), 'L'empire de Grande Moravie, sa situation dans l'Europe de l'époque et sa structure intérieure', in F. Graus *et al.* (eds.), *Das Grossmährische Reich (Tagung der wissenschaftlichen Konferenz des Archäologischen Instituts der Tchechoslowakischen Akademie der Wissenschaften Brno-Nitra 1–4.10.1963)*, Prague, pp. 133–219

Graus, F. (1983), 'Böhmen im 9. bis 11. Jahrhundert (von der "Stammesgesell-schaft" zum mittelalterlichen "Staat")', *Settimane* 30(1): 169–96

Grégoire, H. (1934), 'Les sources épigraphiques de l'histoire bulgare', *Byz* 9: 745–86

Grégoire, H. (1939), 'Une inscription datée au nom du roi Boris-Michael de Bulgarie', *Byz* 14: 227–34

Grierson, P. (1973), *Catalogue of the Byzantine Coins in the Dumbarton Oaks Collection: Leo III to Nicephorus III, 717–1081*, 2 vols., Washington, DC

Grivec, F. (1960), *Konstantin und Method: Lehrer der Slaven*, Wiesbaden

Grivec, F. and Tomšić, F. (1960), *Constantinus et Methodius Thessalonicenses: Fontes* (Radovi Staroslovenskog Instituta 4), Zagreb

Grumel, V. (1936), *Les regestes des actes du patriarchat de Constantinople*, I, fasc. 2: *Les regestes de 715 à 1043*, Chalcedon and Istanbul

Guldescu, S. (1964), *History of Medieval Croatia*, The Hague

Györffy, G. (1988), 'Nomades et semi-nomades: la naissance de l'état hongrois', *Settimane* 35(2): 621–35

Gyuzelev, V., see Gjuzelev, V.

Hahn, J. (1958), *Kyrillomethodianische Bibliographie 1939–1955*, The Hague

Hannick, C. (1978), 'Die Byzantinischen Missionen', in K. Schäferdiek (ed.), *Kirchengeschichte als Missionsgeschichte*, II: *Die Kirche des früheren Mittelalters*, Munich, pp. 279–359

Hannick, C. (1988a), 'Das musikalische Leben in der Frühzeit Bulgariens auf Grund literarischer Quellen des frühslavischen Schrifttums', *BSl* 49: 23–37

Hannick, C. (1988b), 'Das "Slovo na prenesenie mostem sv. Klimenta" als liturgiegeschichtliche Quelle', *CAS*, pp. 227–36

Hannick, C. (1989), 'Das Hirmologion in der Übersetzung des Methodios', *MBS* I, pp. 109–17

Hannick, C. (ed.) (1987), *Sprachen und Nationen im Balkanraum: Die historischen Bedingungen der Entstehung der heutigen Nationalsprachen* (Slawistiche Forschungen 56), Cologne and Vienna

Hauptova, Z. (1978), 'Der altkirchenslawische Vers und seine byzantinischen Vorbilder', in V. Vavřínek (ed.), *Beiträge zur byzantinischen Geschichte im 9.–11. Jahrhundert*, Prague, pp. 335–60

Havlík, L. (1965), 'The relationship between the Great Moravian Empire and the papal court in the years 880–885 AD', *BSl* 26: 100–22

Havlík, L.E. (1989), 'Bulgaria and Moravia between Byzantium, the Franks and Rome', *Pal.* 13(1): 5–20

Havlikova, L. (1991), 'Slavic ships in 5th–12th centuries–Byzantine historiography', *BSl* 52: 89–104

Heiser, L. (1979), *Die Responsa ad consulta Bulgarorum des Papstes Nikolaus I. (858–867)* (Trierer theologische Studien 36), Trier

Hellmann, M. (1976), *Die politisch-kirchliche Grundlegung der Osthälfte Europas* (Handbuch der europäischen Geschichte 1), Stuttgart

Hendy, M.F. (1985), *Studies in the Byzantine Monetary Economy, c. 300–1450*, Cambridge

Henning, J. (1987), *Südosteuropa zwischen Antike und Mittelalter: Archäologische Beiträge zur Landwirtschaft des 1. Jahrtausends u.Z.*, Berlin

Hensel, W. (1965), *Die Slaven im frühen Mittelalter*, Berlin

Hensel, W. and Rauhutowa, J. (1981), 'Archaeological research at Debreŝte (Macedonia), 1974–1978', *Archaeologia Polona* 20: 191–225

Herrin, J. (1973), 'Aspects of the process of Hellenization in the early middle ages', *The Annual of the British School at Athens* 68: 113–26

Herrmann, J. (ed.) (1986), *Die Welt der Slawen*, Leipzig, Jena and Berlin

Hoddinott, R.F. (1975), *Bulgaria in Antiquity: An Archaeological Introduction*, London

Horalek, K. (1959), 'La traduction vieux-slave de l'Evangile: sa version originale et son développement ultérieur', *BSl* 20: 267–84

Hösch, E. (1988), *Geschichte der Balkanländer von der Frühzeit bis zur Gegenwart*, Munich

Iliev, I. (1987), 'Notizen zur literarischen Tätigkeit von Kliment Ochridski (†916)', *Mitteilungen des bulgarischen Forschungsinstitutes in Österreich* 9(1): 67–77

Illyes, E. (1988), *Ethnic Continuity in the Carpatho-Danubian Area* (East European Monographs 249), Boulder, CO

Iordanov, I., see Jordanov, I.

Iurukova, I. See Jurukova, J.

Ivanov, J. (1970a), *B'lgarski starini iz Makedoniia*, Sofia

Ivanov, J. (1970b), *Bogomilski knigi i legendi*, Sofia

Ivanov, S. (1992), 'Slavic jesters and the Byzantine hippodrome', *DOP* 46: 129–32

Ivanova, O.V. (1988), 'Rasprostranenie khristianstva u Slavian v Vizantii (vii–xvv.)', in G.G. Litavrin (ed.), *Priniatie khristianstva narodami Tsentral'noi i Iugo-Vostochnoi Evropy i kreshchenie Rusi*, Moscow, pp. 9–29

Ivanova, O.V. and Litavrin, G.G. (1985), 'Slaviane i Vizantiia', in G.G. Litavrin (ed.), *Ranne-feodal'nye gosudarstva na Balkanakh vi–xiivv.*, Moscow, pp. 34–98

Jakobson, R. (1954), 'Minor native sources for the early history of the Slavic church', *Harvard Slavic Studies* 2: 39–73

Jakobson, R. (1963), 'The Slavic response to Byzantine poetry', *Actes du XII Congrès international d'études byzantines* i, Belgrade, pp. 249–67

Jenkins, R.J.H. (ed.) (1962), *De Adminstrando Imperio* ii: *Commentary*, London

Jireček, C.J. (1877), *Die Heerstrasse von Belgrad nach Konstantinopel*, Prague, reprinted Amsterdam, 1967

Jireček, C.J. (1879), *Die Handelsstrassen und Bergwerke von Serbien und Bosnien während des Mittelalters*, Prague

Jireček, C.J. (1911–18), *Geschichte der Serben*, 2 vols., Gotha, reprinted Amsterdam, 1967

Jordanov, I. (1984), 'Molybdobulles de Boris-Mihail (865–889) et de Siméon (893–913)', *EB* 20(4): 89–93

Jordanov, I. and Aladzhov, D. (1991), 'Nepublikuvani olovni vizantiiski pechati ot Khaskovsko (i)', *Arkheologiia* 1: 44–55

Jurukova, J. (1981), 'Molivdovuli na kniaz Boris I (852–889)', *Numizmatika* 15(2): 3–9

Jurukova, J. (1984), 'La titulature des souverains du premier royaume bulgare d'après les monuments de la sphragistique', in *Sbornik v pamet na Prof. Stancho Vaklinov*, Sofia, pp. 224–30

Jurukova, J. (1985), 'Novi nabliudeniia v'rkhu niakoi redki pametnitsi na sred'novekovnata b'lgarska sfragistika', *Numizmatika* 19(3): 15–24

Kantor, M. (1990), *The Origins of Christianity in Bohemia: Sources and Commentary*, Evanston, IL

Kantor, M. and White, R.S. (trans.) (1976), *The Vita of Constantine and the Vita of Methodius* (Michigan Slavic Materials 13), Ann Arbor

Karayannopoulos, J. (1986), *L'inscription protobulgare de Direkler* (Comité national grec des études du sud-est européen), Athens

Karayannopoulos, J. (1989), *Les Slaves en Macédoine: la prétendue interruption des communications entre Constantinople et Thessalonique du 7e au 9e siècle* (Comité national grec des études du sud-est européen), Athens

Khalikov, A.K., Kazakov, E.P. and Khuzin, F.S. (eds.) (1989), *Rannie bolgary v vostochnoi Evrope*, Kazan

Kiourtzian, G. (1991), 'Note prosopographique sur une inscription du rempart de Thessalonique (861/862)', *REB* 49: 247–53

Kislinger, E. (1981), 'Der junge Basileios I. und die Bulgaren', *JÖB* 30: 137–50

Kiss, A. (1986), 'Die Goldfunde des Karpatenbeckens vom 5.–10. Jahrhundert (Angaben zu den Vergleichsmöglichkeiten der schriftlichen und archäologischen Quellen)', *Acta Archaeologica Academiae Scientiarum Hungaricae* 38: 105–45

Klaić, N. (1984–5), 'Zu Verteidigungssystemen in den mittelalterlichen Kroatischen Ländern', *Balcanoslavica*, Prilep, 11–12: 1–10

Klaić, N. (1985), *Povijest Hrvata u ranom srednjem vijeku*, Zagreb

Klanica, Z. (1988), 'Einige archäologischen Quellen zur Entwicklungsfrage der gesellschaftlichen Organisation Grossmährens', *TKAS* IV, pp. 98–105

Koder, J. (1978), 'Zur Frage der slavischen Siedlungsgebiete im Mittelalterlichen Griechenland', *BZ* 71: 315–31

Koder, J. (1983), 'Zu den Archontes der Slaven in *De Administranao Imperio* 29, 106–115', *Wiener Slavistisches Jahrbuch* 29: 128–31

Koder, J. (1984), *Der Lebensraum der Byzantiner: Historisch-geographischer Abriss ihres mittelalterlichen Staates im östlichen Mittelmeerraum* (Byzantinische Geschichtsschreiber 1), Graz, Vienna and Cologne

Koder, J. and Hild, F. (1976), *Hellas und Thessalia*, TIB 1 (*DÖAW* 125), Vienna

Kodov, K. (1969), *Opis na slavianskite r'kopisi v bibliotekata na B'lgarskata Akademiia na Naukite*, Sofia

Koicheva, E. (1986), 'Zagora, Miziia i etnonim't "Mizi" v'v vizantiiskite pismeni pametnitsi ot kraia na VII do XII vek', *Pal* 10(2): 56–67

Koledarov, P.S. (1973), 'More about the Name "Zagor'e"', *BHR* 1(4): 92–107

Koledarov, P.S. (1979–89), *Politicheska geografiia na srednovekovnata b'lgarska d'rzhava*, 2 vols., Sofia

Koledarov, P. (1980), 'Za b'lgaro-vizantiiskata granitsa v Trakiia po 30-godishniia mir ot 814–815gg.', in V. Gjuzelev (ed.), *B'lgarsko – Srednovekovie. B'lgarsko – s'vetski sbornik v chest na 70 – godishninata na prof. Ivan Dujčev*, Sofia, pp. 55–61.

Konstantakopoulou, A. (1985), 'L'éparque de Thessalonique: les origines d'une institution administrative (VIII–IX siècles)', *Communications grecques presentées au V Congrès international des études du sud-est européen*, Athens, pp. 157–62

Kuev, K.M. (1967), *Chernorizets Khrab'r*, Sofia

Kulturno bogatstvo Prilepa od V–XIX veka (1976), Belgrade

Kuzev, A. (1988), 'Bemerkungen über einige Bistümer in Bulgarien während der ersten Jahrzehnte nach 870', *SM*, pp. 187–92

Kuzev, A. and Gjuzelev, V. (1981), *B'lgarski srednovekovni gradove i kreposti*, I: *Gradove i kreposti po dunav i cherno more*, Varna

Laszlo, G. (1971), *Steppenvölker und Germanen*, Berlin

Laurent, V. (1963–81), *Le corpus des sceaux de l'empire byzantin*, II: *L'administration centrale* v, 1–3: *L'église* (1963, 1965, 1972)

Lemerle, P. (1945), *Philippes et la Macédoine orientale à l'époque chrétienne et byzantine*, Paris

Lemerle, P. (1954), 'Invasions et migrations dans les Balkans depuis la fin de l'époque romaine jusqu'au VIII siècle', *Revue Historique* 211: 265–308, reprinted in Lemerle (1980)

Lemerle, P. (1963), 'La chronique improprement dite de Monémvasie: le contexte historique et légendaire', *REB* 21: 5–49, reprinted in Lemerle (1980)

Lemerle, P. (1965), 'Thomas le Slave', *TM* 1: 255–97, reprinted in Lemerle (1980)

Lemerle, P. (1979–81), *Les plus anciens recueils des Miracles de saint Démétrius et la pénétration des Slaves dans les Balkans*, 2 vols., Paris

Lemerle, P. (1980), *Essais sur le monde byzantin*, London

Lettenbauer, W. (1952), 'Eine lateinische Kanonessamlung in Mähren im 9. Jahrhundert', *Orientalia Christiana Periodica* 18: 246–69

Lishev, S.N. (1970), *B'lgarskiiat srednovekoven grad*, Sofia

Litavrin, G.G. (1985), 'Formirovanie i razvitie bolgarskogo rannefeodal'nogo gosudarstva (konets VII–nachalo XI v.)', in G.G. Litavrin (ed.), *Rannefeodal'nye gosudarstva na Balkanakh VI–XIIvv.*, Moscow, pp. 132–88

Litavrin, G.G. (1988), 'Vvedenie khristianstva v Bolgarii (IX–nachalo X v.)', in G.G. Litavrin (ed.), *Priniatie khristianstva narodami Tsentral'noi i Iugo-Vostochnoi Evropy i kreshchenie Rusi*, Moscow, pp. 30–67

Litavrin, G.G. (ed.) (1987), *Etnosotsial'naia i politicheskaia struktura rannefeodal'nykh slavianskikh gosudarstv i narodnostei*, Moscow

Losert, H. (1991), 'Zur Deutung der Brandgräber in einigen Merowingerzeitlichen Friedhöfen Mittel- und Unterfrankens', *Die Welt der Slaven* 36: 365–92

Löwe, H. (1983), 'Cyrill und Methodius zwischen Byzanz und Rom', *Settimane* 30(2): 631–86

Löwe, H. (1990), 'Consensus-consessus. Ein Nachtrag zum Streit um Methodius', *DA* 46: 507–15

McCormick, M. (1990), *Eternal Victory: Triumphal Rulership in Late Antiquity, Byzantium and the Early Medieval West*, Cambridge

Maksimović, L. (1979), 'O vremenu pokhoda bulgarskog kneza Borisa na Srbiju', *Zbornik Filozofskog Fakulteta*, Belgrade, 14(1): 69–76

Maksimović, L. (1992), 'The Christianization of the Serbs and the Croats', *LSCM*, pp. 167–84

Malingoudis, P. (1978), 'Über drei Titel byzantinischen Ursprungs im mittelalterlichen Bulgarien', *EB* 14(3): 78–83

Malingoudis, P. (1979), *Die mittelalterlichen kyrillischen Inschriften der Hämus-Halbinsel*, I: *Die bulgarischen Inschriften* (Hēllēnik Hetaireia Slabikōn Meletōn 3), Thessalonica

Malingoudis, P. (1981), *Studien zu den slawischen Ortsnamen Griechenlands*, Wiesbaden

Malingoudis, P. (1983), 'Toponymy and history. Observations concerning the Slavonic toponymy of the Peloponnese', *Byzantine Studies/Etudes Byzantines* 7: 99–111

Malingoudis, P. (1987), 'Frühe slawische Elemente im Namensgut Griechensland', in B. Hansel (ed.), *Die Völker Südosteuropas im 6. bis 8. Jahrhundert* (Südosteuropa Jahrbuch 17), Munich, pp. 53–68

Malingoudis, P. (1988), *Slaboi stén mesaioniké Ellada* (*The Slavs in Medieval Greece*), Thessalonica

Mango, C. (1977), 'Historical introduction', in A. Bryer and J. Herrin (eds.), *Iconoclasm*, Birmingham, pp. 1–6

Mango, C. (1980), *Byzantium: The Empire of New Rome*, London

Mango, C. (1983), 'The two Lives of St Ioannikios and the Bulgarians', in *Okeanos: Essays presented to Ihor Ševčenko on his Sixtieth Birthday, Harvard Ukrainian Studies* 7: 393–404

Mango, C. (1985), 'On re-reading the Life of St Gregory the Decapolite', *Byzantina* 13(1): 633–46

Mango, C. (1986), *Byzantine Architecture*, London

Mares, V. (1975), 'Die Anfänge des slavischen Schrifttums und die byzantinisch-griechische Literatur', *Cyrillomethodianum* 3: 1–12

Mathiesen, R. (1981, 1984–5), 'An important early Slavic text of the Apostles' Creed', *Byzantine Studies/Etudes Byzantines* 8, 11–12: 257–64

Mathiesen, R. (1991), 'New Old Church Slavonic manuscripts on Mount Sinai', *Harvard Ukrainian Studies* 15: 192–9

Mavrodinov, N. (1959), *Starob'lgarskoto izkustvo*, Sofia

Metcalf, D.M. (1979), *Coinage in South-Eastern Europe 820–1396* (Royal Numismatic Society, Special Publications 11), London

See Miiatev, K. Mijatev K.

Mijatev, K. (1963), 'L'architecture de la basse antiquité et du haut moyen âge dans les Balkans', *Actes du XII Congrès international des études byzantines* 1, Belgrade, pp. 387–407

Mijatev, K. (1965), *Arkhitektura v srednovekovna B'lgariia*, Sofia

Milkova, F. (1988), 'Le droit byzantin et la première loi écrite bulgaro-slave', *EB* 2: 81–6

Moravcsik, G. (1933), 'Die Namenliste der bulgarischen Gesandten am Konzil von J.869/870', *Izvestiia na B'lgarskoto Istorichesko Druzhestvo* 13: 8–23

Moravcsik, G. (1958), *Byzantinoturcica* (BBA 10–11), 2 vols., Berlin

Mozhaeva, I.E. (1980), *Bibliografiia po Kirillo-mefodievskoi problematike 1945–1970gg.*, Moscow

Mutafchiev, P. (1943–4), *Istoriia na b'lgarskiia narod*, 2 vols., Sofia

Mutafchiev, P. (1973), *Izbrani proizvedeniia*, ed. D. Angelov, 2 vols., Sofia

Naumov, E.P. (1988), 'Obshchestvenno-politicheskie sdvigi v serbskikh i khorvatskikh zemliakh i khristianskaia missiia na Balkanakh', in G.G. Litavrin (ed.), *Priniatie khristianstva narodami Tsentral'noi i Iugo-Vostochnoi Evropy i kreshchenie Rusi*, Moscow, pp. 68–103

Nesbitt, J. and Oikonomides, N. (1991), *Catalogue of Byzantine Seals at Dumbarton Oaks and in the Fogg Museum of Art*, 1: *Italy, North of the Balkans, North of the Black Sea*, Washington, DC

Nichoritis, K. (1989), 'Aton i s'khraniavaneto na Kirilo-Metodievskite traditsii', *MBS* 11, pp. 226–31

Nichoritis, K. (1990), *Atonskata knizhovna traditsiia v rasprostraneneto na Kirilo-Metodievskite izvori* (Kirillo-Metodievski Studii 7), Sofia

Niederle, L. (1923–6), *Manuel de l'antiquité slave*, 2 vols., Paris

Nikhoritis, K., see Nichoritis, K.

Novak, V. (1953–4), 'The Slavonic-Latin symbiosis in Dalmatia during the middle ages', *The Slavonic and East European Review* 32: 1–28

Nystazopoulou-Pelekidou, M. (1985), 'Egemoniké idea kai byzantines epidraseis sté Boulgaria ōs ton egchristianismo (681–864). E martyria tōn prōtoboulgarikōn epigraphōn', *Byzantina* 13(2): 1355–70

Nystazopoulou-Pelekidou. M. (1991), 'Sceaux byzantins improprement appelés protobulgares', *Byzantiaka* 11: 13–22

Obolensky, D. (1948), *The Bogomils: A Study in Balkan Neo-Manicheeism*, Cambridge, reprinted 1972

Obolensky, D. (1966), 'The empire and its northern neighbours, 565–1018', *Cambridge Medieval History* IV.1, Cambridge, pp. 473–518, reprinted in Obolensky (1971b)

Obolensky, D. (1971a), *The Byzantine Commonwealth*, London

Obolensky, D. (1971b), *Byzantium and the Slavs*, London

Obolensky, D. (1986), 'Theophylaktos of Ochrid and the authorship of the Life of St Clement', *Byzantion: Aphieroma ston Andrea N. Straton* II, Athens, pp. 601–17

Obolensky, D. (1988a), 'The Balkans in the ninth century: barrier or bridge?', in J.D. Howard-Johnston (ed.), *Byzantium and the West c. 850–c. 1200* (Byzantinische Forschungen 12), Amsterdam, pp. 47–66

Obolensky, D. (1988b), *Six Byzantine Portraits*, Oxford

Oikonomides, N. (1972), *Les listes de préséance byzantines des IX et X siècles*, Paris

Oikonomides, N. (1981, 1984–5), 'Mesembria in the ninth century: epigraphical evidence', *Byzantine Studies/Etudes Byzantines* 8, 11–12: 269–73, reprinted in Oikonomides (1992)

Oikonomides, N. (1988), 'Tribute or trade? The Byzantine-Bulgarian Treaty of 716', *Studia Slavico-Byzantina et Mediaevalia Europensia: In Memoriam Ivan Dujčev*, Sofia, I: 29–31.

Oikonomides, N. (1992), *Byzantium from the Ninth Century to the Fourth Crusade: Studies, Texts, Monuments*, London

Ostrogorsky, G. (1965), 'The Byzantine background of the Moravian mission', *DOP* 19: 3–18, reprinted in Ostrogorsky (1974)

Ostrogorsky, G. (1974), *Byzanz und die Welt der Slawen*, Darmstadt

Ovcharov, D. (1979), 'Emergence et développement de la ville de Preslav. IX–X siècles (quelques problèmes et aspects)', *BHR* 7 (2): 51–61

Ovcharov, D. (1982a), *B'lgarski srednovekovni risunki-grafiti*, Sofia

Ovcharov, D. (1982b), *Vizantiiski i B'lgarski kreposti v–x vek*, Sofia

Oxford Dictionary of Byzantium (1991), 3 vols., ed. A.P. Kazhdan *et al.*, New York and Oxford

Papachryssanthou, D. (1974), 'La vie de saint Euthyme le jeune et la métropole de Thessalonique à la fin du IX et au début du X siècle', *REB* 32: 225–45

Papastathis, C.K. (1978), *To nomothetikon ergon tés kyrillomethodianés ierapostolés en Megalé Morabiā* (Ellenike Etaireia Slabikōn Meletōn 2), Thessalonica

Papastathis, C.K. (1992), 'The origin of the penances in Methodios' Anonymous Homily', in *LSCM*, pp. 71–4

Parczewski, M. (1991), 'Origins of early Slav culture in Poland', *Antiquity* 65: 676–83

Peri, V. (1983), 'Gli "iura antiqua" sulla patria dei Bulgari: un "topos" canonico per un risveglio missionario', *Atti dell' 8 Congresso internazionale di studi sull'alto medioevo*, Spoleto, pp. 225–68

Petkanova, D. (1988), 'Zur Frage der Autorenschaft der Vita Methodii', *SM*, pp. 485–90

Petrov, P. (1966), 'La politique étrangère de la Bulgarie au milieu du IX siècle et la conversion des Bulgares', *Byzbulg* 2: 41–52

Petrov, P. (1981), *Obrazuvane na b'lgarskata d'rzhava*, Sofia

Picchio, R. (1988), 'Quelques remarques sur l'interpretation du Proglas', *Revue des Etudes Slaves* 70: 313–24

Piffl-Percevic, T. and Stirneman, A. (eds.) (1987), *Der heilige Method, Salzburg und die Slawenmission* (Pro Oriente 11), Innsbruck and Vienna

Pillinger, R. (ed.) (1986), *Spätantike und frühbyzantinische Kultur Bulgariens zwischen Orient und Okzident* (Schriften der Balkankommission. Antiquarische Abteilung 16), Vienna

Pletneva, S.A. (ed.) (1981), *Stepi Evrazii v epokhu srednevekov'ia*, Moscow

Pljakov, Z. (1988), 'La région de la moyenne Struma durant le moyen âge bulgare', *Pal.* 12(1): 101–14

Pljakov, Z. (1989), 'La région de la moyenne Struma aux VII–IX siècles', *Pal.* 13(2): 100–15

Podskalsky, G. (1990), 'Die Organisation der bulgarischen Kirche nach der Taufe des Fürsten Boris-Michael', *EB* 26(1): 54–8

Pohl, W. (1988), 'Ergebnisse und Probleme der Awarenforschung', *Mitteilungen des Instituts für Österreichische Geschichtsforschung* 96: 247–74

Pohl, W. (1989), *Die Awaren: Ein Steppenvolk in Mitteleuropa 567–822 n.Chr.*, Munich

Pohl, W. (1990), 'Verlaufsformen der Ethnogenese – Awaren und Bulgaren', in H. Wolfram and W. Pohl (eds.), *Typen der Ethnogenese unter besonderer Berücksichtigung der Bayern* 1 (*DÖAW* 201), Vienna, pp. 113–24

Popescu, E. (1989), 'Considérations sur les études et l'activité didactique de Constantin-Saint Cyrille', *MBS* 1, pp. 130–7

Popkonstantinov, K. (1985), 'Die Verbreitung des altbulgarischen Schrifttums auf Grund von Inschriften', *Die Slawischen Sprachen* 8: 167–200

Popkonstantinov, K. (1988), 'Traditionen von Kyrill und Methodius im altbulgarischen Literatur- und Ausbildungszentrum des 9. und 10. Jahrhunderts beim Dorf Ravna, Bezirk Varna', *SM*, pp. 491–504

Poulík, J. (1959), 'The latest archaeological discoveries from the period of the Great Moravian Empire', *Historica*, Prague, 1: 7–70

Poulík, J. (1975), *Mikulčice, sídlo a pevnost knížat velkomoravských*, Prague

Poulík, J. (1983), 'Grossmähren zwischen Karolingischen Westen und Byzanz', *Settimane* 30(1): 157–68

Poulík, J. and Chropovsky, B. (1985), *Velká Morava a pocatky československé statnosti*, Prague and Bratislava

Poulter, A.G. (ed.) (1983), *Ancient Bulgaria: Papers presented to the International Symposium on the Ancient History and Archaeology of Bulgaria* 1–11 (University of Nottingham, Department of Classical and Archaeological Studies, Archaeology Section, Monograph Series 1), Nottingham

Primov, B. (1978), 'Bulgaria in the eighth Century. A general outline', *Byzbulg* 5: 7–40

Pritsak, O. (1981), *Studies in Medieval Eurasian History*, London

Pritsak, O. (1983), 'The Slavs and the Avars', *Settimane* 30(1): 353–432

Pritsak, O. (1986), 'The initial formula *Kanasybege* in the Proto-Bulgarian inscriptions', in M. Colucci, G. dell'Agata and H. Goldblatt (eds.), *Studia Slavica Mediaevalia et Humanistica Riccardo Picchio Dicata* II, Rome, pp. 595–601

Pritsak, O. (1988), 'The distinctive features of the *pax nomadica*', Settimane 35: 749–80

Problemi na prab'lgarskata istoriia i kultura (1989), Sofia

Procházka, V. (1967), 'Le zakon' sudnyj'ljud'm' et la Grande Moravie', *BSl* 28: 359–75

Procházka, V. (1968), 'Le zakon' sudnyj' ljud'm' et la Grande Moravie', *BSl* 29: 112–50

Radojičić, G.S. (1952), 'La date de la conversion des Serbes', *Byz* 22: 253–6

Rashev, R. (1982), 'P'rvoto b'lgarsko tsarstvo i moreto', *SBC*, pp. 47–56

Reuter, T. (1991), *Germany in the Early Middle Ages c. 800–1056*, London

Richter, M. (1985), 'Die politische Orientierung Mährens zur Zeit von Konstantin und Methodius', in H. Wolfram and A. Schwarcz (eds.), *Die Bayern und ihre Nachbarn* I, *DÖAW* 179: 281–92

Risos, A. (1990), 'The Vlachs of Larissa in the 10th century', *BSl* 51: 202–7

Ronin, V.R. (1985), 'The Franks on the Balkans in the early ninth century', *EB* 21(1): 39–57

Runciman, S. (1930), *A History of the First Bulgarian Empire*, London

Runciman, S. (1983), 'The Bulgarian princes' list', in Poulter 1983, pp. 232–41

Rybakov, B. (1981), *Iazychestvo drevnikh slavian*, Moscow

Ryszkiewicz, A. *et al.* (1981), *Le bois dans l'architecture et la sculpture slaves*, Paris

Sabev, T. (1988), 'L'œuvre des saints frères Cyrille et Méthode et de leurs disciples dans l'historiographie bulgare au IX–X siècles', *SM*, pp. 255–67

Sakazov, I. (1929), *Bulgarische Wirtschaftsgeschichte*, Berlin and Leipzig

Sansterre, J.-M. (1982), 'Les missionaires latins, grecs et orientaux en Bulgarie dans la seconde moitié du IX siècle', *Byz* 52: 375–88

Schaeken, J. (1987), *Die Kiever Blätter* (Studies in Slavic and General Linguistics 9), Amsterdam

Schramm, G. (1981), *Eroberer und Eingesessene: Geographische Lehnnamen als Zeugen der Geschichte Südosteuropas im ersten Jahrtausend n. Chr.*, Stuttgart

Schreiner, P. (1989), 'Die Byzantinisierung der bulgarischen Kultur', in R. Lauer and P. Schreiner (eds.), *Kulturelle Traditionen in Bulgarien* (Abhandlungen der Akademie der Wissenschaften in Göttingen, phil.-hist. Klasse, Dritte folge 177), pp. 47–60

Schubert, G. (1988), 'Methods Werk in Pannonien und die Magyaren nach der Landnahme', *SM*, pp. 293–305

Schulz, H.-J. (1989), 'Das Missionswerk der heiligen Kyrill und Method: Dienst an Ortskirche und Ökumene', *MBS* I, pp. 71–7

Schütz, J. (1982), 'Methods Grab in der Kathedrale von Morava', *Pal* 6(2): 28–33

Schütz, J. (1985a), 'Konstantins Philosophie und seine Bestellungsurkunde als Philosoph', *Wiener Slavistisches Jahrbuch* 31: 89–98

Schütz, J. (1985b), *Die Lehrer der Slawen, Kyrill und Method: Die Lebensbeschreibungen zweier Missionäre*, Sankt Ottilien

Ševčenko, I. (1964), 'Three paradoxes of the Cyrillo-Methodian mission', *Slavic Review* 23: 220–36

Ševčenko, I. (1967), 'The Greek source of the inscription on Solomon's chalice in the *Vita Constantini*', in *To Honor Roman Jakobson: Essays on the Occasion of his Seventieth Birthday* III, The Hague and Paris, pp. 1806–17, reprinted in Ševčenko (1991), pp. 285–98

Ševčenko, I. (1971), 'On the social background of Cyril and Methodius', *Studia Palaeoslovenica*, Prague, pp. 341–51, reprinted in Ševčenko, (1991), pp. 479–92

Ševčenko, I. (1982), 'Report on the Glagolitic fragments (of the *Euchologium Sinaiticum*?) discovered on Sinai in 1975 and some thoughts on the models for the make-up of the earliest Glagolitic manuscripts', *Harvard Ukrainian Studies* 6: 119–51, reprinted in Ševčenko, (1991), pp. 617–50

Ševčenko, I. (1988/9), 'Religious missions seen from Byzantium', *Harvard Ukrainian Studies* 12/13: 7–27

Ševčenko, I. (1991), *Byzantium and the Slavs in Letters and Culture* (Renovatio 1), Cambridge, MA and Naples

Shepard, J. (1992), 'Byzantine diplomacy AD 800–1204. Means and ends', in J. Shepard and S. Franklin (eds.), *Byzantine Diplomacy*, Aldershot, pp. 41–71

Shepard, J. (forthcoming), 'Bulgaria. The other Balkan Empire', *New Cambridge Medieval History* III

Simeonov, B. (1982), 'Die protobulgarische Inschrift aus Preslav', *Pal* 6(2): 69–77

Simeonova, L. (1988), 'Vizantiiskata kontseptsiia za izkustvoto da se opravliava spored fotievoto poslanie do kniaz Boris I', *Problemi na Kulturata* 4: 91–104

Šišić, F. von (1917), *Geschichte der Kroaten*, Zagreb

Smedovski, T. [Smiadovski] (1978), 'The Latin missions in Bulgaria', *Pal* 2(1): 39–55; 2(2): 39–51

Smiadovski, S. (1991), 'Pokhvalnoto slovo za Irinei (?) ot Kliment Okhridski', *Pal* 15(2): 46–53

Snegarov, I. (1924), *Istoriia na Okhridskata arkhiepiskopiia*, 2 vols., Sofia

Snegarov, I. (1948–9), 'P'rvata b'lgarska patriarshiia: 1', *Godishnik na Sofiiskiia Universitet, Bogoslovski Fakultet* 26: 3–31

Snegarov, I. (1950–1), 'P'rvata b'lgarska patriarshiia (proizkhod, patriarshi i sedalishche): 2', *Godishnik na Dukhovnata Akademiia 'Sv. Kliment Okhridski'*, Sofia, 1(27): 3–26

Snegarov, I. (1954–5), 'Starob'lgarskiiat razkaz "chudo na sv. Georgi s b'lgarina" kato istoricheski izvor', *Godishnik na Dukhovnata Akademiia 'Sv. Kliment Okhridski'*, Sofia, 4(30): 217–41

Snegarov, I. (1962), 'Les sources sur la vie et l'activité de Clément d'Ochrida', *Byzbulg* 1: 79–119

Snegarov, I. (1966), 'Po v'prosa za eparkhiiata na Kliment Okhridski', in B.S. Angelov *et al.* (eds.), *Kliment Okhridsi: Sbornik ot statii po sluchai 1050 godini ot sm'rtta mu*, Sofia, pp. 291–305

Soulis, G.C. (1965), 'The legacy of Cyril and Methodius to the southern Slavs', *DOP* 19: 19–45

Soustal, P. (1983), *Nikopolis und Kephallenia*, TIB 3 (*DÖAW* 150), Vienna

Soustal, P. (1986), 'Bemerkungen zur byzantinisch-bulgarischen Grenze im 9. Jahrhundert', *Mitteilungen des Bulgarischen Forschungsinstitutes in Österreich* 8: 149–56

Soustal, P. (1991), *Thrakien (Thrake, Rodope und Haimimontos)*, TIB 6 (*DÖAW* 221), Vienna

Staňa, Č. (1985), 'Mährische Burgwälle im 9. Jahrhundert', in H. Friesinger and F.

Daim (eds.), *Die Bayern und ihre Nachbarn* II (*DÖAW* 180), pp. 157–200

Stančev, S. (1964), 'L'architecture militaire et civile de Pliska et de Preslav à la lumière de nouvelles données', *Actes du Congrès international d'études byzantines (Ochride 10–16 Septembre 1961)* III, Belgrade, pp. 345–52

Stančeva, M. (1978), 'Sofia au moyen âge à la lumière de nouvelles études archéologiques', *Byzbulg* 5: 211–28

Stanchev, K. and Popov, G. (1988), *Kliment Okhridski: Zhivot i tvorchestvo*, Sofia

Stichel, R. (1988), 'Die "Hohe Rede". Zum Verständnis eines Begriffs in der Predigt auf die Auffindung der Gebeine des hl. Clemens', *SM*, pp. 557–61

Stojanova-Serafimova, D. (1989), 'La culture bulgare du haut moyen âge dans la région de la Rila et du Pirin et sur les versants ouest des Rhodopes', *EB* 24(4): 85–100

Stökl, G. (1980), 'Kyrill und Method – Slawenlehrer oder Slawenapostel, Wirklichkeit und Legende', *Kirche im Osten* 23: 13–31

Sullivan, R.E. (1966), 'Khan Boris and the conversion of Bulgaria: a case study of the impact of Christianity on a barbarian society', *Studies in Mediaeval and Renaissance History* 3: 53–139

Swoboda, W. (1966), 'L'origine de l'organisation de l'église en Bulgarie et ses rapports avec le patriarchat de Constantinople', *Byzbulg* 2: 67–81

Swoboda, W. (1972), 'Bulgaria a patriarchat konstantynopolitanski w latach 870–1018', in *Z Polskich Studiow Slawistycznych, Seria 4: Historia*, Warsaw, pp. 47–65

Synellis, K. (1989), 'Die Entwicklung der Bedeutung des Terminus "pakton" im Rahmen der Entwicklung der "Internationalen" Beziehungen von Byzanz vom 4. bis zum 10. Jahrhundert', in E. Chrysos (ed.), *Studien zur Geschichte der römischen Spätantike: Festgabe für Professor Johannes Straub*, Athens, pp. 234–50

Szekely, G. (1988), 'Die Permanenz der Römer in Pannonien: ein Problem', *Settimane* 35(1): 101–21

Tachiaos, A.-E.N. (1972–3), 'L'origine de Cyrille et de Méthode: vérité et légende dans les sources slaves', *Cyrillomethodianum* 2: 122–40

Tachiaos, A.-E.N. (1988), 'The cult of Saint Methodius in the Byzantino-Slavonic World', *CAS*, pp. 131–42

Tachiaos, A.-E.N. (1989), *Cyril and Methodius of Thessalonica: The Acculturation of the Slavs*, Thessalonica

Tafel, T.L.F. (1839), *De Thessalonica eiusque agro dissertatio geographica*, Berlin; reprinted London, 1972

Tapkova-Zaimova, V. (1963), 'Les voies romaines dans les régions bulgares à l'époque médiévale', *Acta Antiqua Philippopolitana. Studia Historica et Philologica*, Sofia, pp. 165–72, reprinted in Tapkova-Zaimova (1979)

Tapkova-Zaimova, V. (1969), 'L'idée byzantine de l'unité du monde et l'état bulgare', *Actes du I Congrès des études balkaniques et du sud-est européen* III, Sofia, pp. 291–8, reprinted in Tapkova-Zaimova (1979)

Tapkova-Zaimova, V. (1971), 'L'idée impériale à Byzance et la tradition étatique bulgare', *Byzantina* 3: 289–95, reprinted in Tapkova-Zaimova (1979)

Tapkova-Zaimova, V. (1972), 'La ville de Salonique et son hinterland slave (jusqu'au xe siècle), *Actes du II Congrès international des études du sud-est européen* II, Athens, pp. 355–62, reprinted in Tapkova-Zaimova (1979)

Tapkova-Zaimova, V. (1976), *Dolni dunav-granichna zona na vizantiiskiia zapad*, Sofia

Tapkova-Zaimova, V. (1978), 'Les institutions et le régime administratif des pays balkaniques au moyen âge (I): problèmes – mise au point', *EB* 14(3): 35–43

Tapkova-Zaimova, V. (1979), *Byzance et les Balkans à partir du VI siècle*, London

Tapkova-Zaimova, V. (1984), '"Grecs" et "Romains" dans la littérature bulgare' *EB* 20(I): 51–7

Tarnanidis, I.C. (1988), *The Slavonic Manuscripts Discovered in 1975 at St Catherine's Monastery on Mount Sinai*, Thessalonica

Tarnanidis, I.C. (1992), 'Latin opposition to the missionary work of Cyril and Methodius', *LSCM*, pp. 49–62

Teodor, D.G. (1980), *The East Carpathian Area of Romania in the V–XI Centuries* AD (BAR International Series 81), Oxford

Thomson, F.J. (1985), 'Early Slavonic translations – an Italo-Greek connection?', *Slavica Gandensia* 12: 221–34

Thümmel, H.G. (1985), 'Die Disputation über die Bilder in der *Vita* des Konstantin', *BSl* 46: 19–24

Tikhomirov, M.N. (ed.) (1961), *Zakon Sudniy Liudem kratkoi redaktsii*, Moscow

Todorova, E. (1984), 'River trade in the Balkans during the middle ages', *EB* 20(4): 38–50

Totev, T. (1987), 'Les monastères de Pliska et de Preslav aux IX–X siècles', *BSl* 48: 185–200

Totev, T. (1988), 'Epigrafski svidetelstva za starob'lgarskata pismenost', *Pal* 12(2): 83–92

Totev, T. and Georgiev, P. (1980), 'Novi danni za oblika na niakoi manastiri v Pliska i Preslav', in V. Gjuzelev (ed.), *B'lgarsko-srednovekovie: B'lgarsko-s'vetski sbornik v chest na 70-godishninata na Prof. Ivan Dujčev*, Sofia, pp. 130–6

T'pkova-Zaimova, V., see Tapkova-Zaimova, V.

Treadgold, W.T. (1984), 'The Bulgars' treaty with the Byzantines in 816', *Rivista di Studi Bizantini e Slavi* 4: 213–20

Trendafilov, C. (1985), 'Die altkirchenslawische *Vita Constantini* und die Traditionen der altslawischen Exegese', *BSl* 46: 33–9

Tůma, O. (1985), 'Great Moravia's trade contacts with the eastern Mediterranean and the mediating role of Venice', *BSl* 46: 67–77

Turner, D. (1990a), 'The politics of despair: the plague of 746–747 and iconoclasm in the Byzantine Empire', *The Annual of the British School at Athens* 85: 419–34

Turner, D. (1990b), 'The origins and accession of Leo V (813–820)', *JÖB* 40: 171–203

Vaillant, A. (1947), 'Une homélie de Méthode', *Revue des Etudes Slaves* 23: 34–47

Vaillant, A. (1948), 'La préface de l'Evangéliaire vieux-slave', *Revue des Etudes Slaves* 24: 5–20

Vaillant, A. (1956), 'Une poésie vieux-slave: la préface de l'évangile', *Revue des Etudes Slaves* 33: 7–25

Vaillant, A. (1968), *Textes vieux-slaves*, 2 vols., Paris

Vaklinov, S. (1972), 'Pliska prez 1971g.', *Vekove*, Sofia, 3: 3–10

Váňa, A. (1983), *The World of the Ancient Slavs*, London

Vartolomeev, O. (1983), 'I responsi di Papa Nicolo I alle questioni sollevate dai

Bulgari. Una fonte importante per la storia del diritto internazionale privato nel nono secolo', *Atti dell' 8 Congresso internazionale di studi sull'alto medioevo*, Spoleto, pp. 349–57

Vašica, J. (1951), 'Origine cyrillo-méthodienne du plus ancien code slave dit "Zakon sudnyj ljudem"', *BSl* 12: 154–74

Vašica, J. (1959), '*Collectio 87 (93) Capitulorum* dans les nomocanons slaves', *BSl* 20: 1–8

Vašica, J. (1965), *Die Korsuner Legende von der Überführung der Reliquien des heiligen Clemens* (Slavische Propyläen 8), Munich

Vašica, J. (1966), *Literární památky epochy velkomoravské 863–885*, Prague

Vasmer, M. (1941), *Die Slaven in Griechenland* (Abhandlungen der Preussischen Akademie der Wissenschaften, phil.-hist. Klasse 12), Berlin

Vavřínek, V. (1963a), 'Die Christlanisierung und Kirchenorganisation Grossmährens', *Historica*, Prague, 7: 5–56

Vavřínek, V. (1963b), 'Předcyrilometodějské misie na Velké Moravě. (K výkladu V. kapitoly staroslověnského života Metodějova)', *Slavia* 32: 465–80

Vavřínek, V. (1963c), *Staroslověnske životy Konstantina a Metoděje*, Prague

Vavřínek, V. (1964), 'Study of the church architecture from the period of the Great Moravian Empire', *BSl* 25: 288–301

Vavřínek, V. (1978), 'The introduction of the Slavonic liturgy and the Byzantine missionary policy', in V. Vavřínek (ed.), *Beiträge zur byzantinischen Geschichte im 9.–11. Jahrhundert*, Prague, pp. 255–81

Vavřínek, V. (1986), 'Die historische Bedeutung der byzantinischen Mission in Grossmähren', in J. Poulík, B. Chropovsky *et al.* (eds.), *Grossmähren und die Anfänge der tschechoslowakischen Staatlichkeit*, Prague, pp. 245–79

Vavřínek, V. and Zástěrová, B. (1982), 'Byzantium's role in the formation of Great Moravian culture', *BSl* 43: 161–88

Večerka, R. (1988), 'Anmerkungen zu den Kiever glagolitischen Blättern', *BSl* 49: 46–58

Velkov, V. (1969), 'Inscriptions de Mesembria (1956–63), *N*, pp. 179–224

Velkov, V. (1988), *Geschichte und Kultur Thrakiens und Mösiens. Gesammelte Aufsätze*, Amsterdam

Velkov, V. *et al.* (eds.) (1956), *Madarskiiat konnik – prouchvaniia v'rkhu nadpisite i relefa*, Sofia

Venedikov, I. (1962), 'La population byzantine en Bulgarie au début du IX siècle', *Byzbulg* 1: 261–77

Venedikov, I. (1966), 'Kliment Okhridski i Dobeta', in B.S. Angelov *et al.* (eds.), *Kliment Okhridski: Sbornik ot statii po sluchai 1050 godini ot sm'rtta mu*, Sofia, pp. 307–19

Venedikov, I. (1969a), 'La datation des remparts romano-byzantins de Nessèbre', *N*, pp. 125–54

Venedikov, I. (1969b), 'Histoire des remparts romano-byzantins', *N*, pp. 155–63

Venedikov, I. (1979), *Voennoto i administrativnoto ustroistvo na B'lgariia prez IX i X vek*, Sofia

Vilfan, S. (1983), 'Evoluzione statale degli sloveni e croati', *Settimane* 30(1): 103–40

Vlasto, A.P. (1970), *The Entry of the Slavs into Christendom: An Introduction to the Medieval History of the Slavs*, Cambridge

Vryonis, S. (1961), 'St Ioannicius the Great (754–846) and the "Slavs" of Bithynia', *Byz* 31: 245–8

V'zharova, Z.N. (1965), *Slavianski i slavianob'lgarski selishta v b'lgarskite zemi ot kraia na VI–XI vek*, Sofia

V'zharova, Z.N. (1976), *Slaviani i Prab'lgari po danni na nekropolite ot VI–XIv. na teritoriiata na B'lgariia*, Sofia

V'zharova, Z.N. (1981), 'Slaviani i nomadi na teritoriiata na dneshnite b'lgarski zemi ot kraia na vi–xi v.', *PP* iii, pp. 16–65

Waldmüller, L. (1976), *Die ersten Begegnungen der Slawen mit dem Christentum und den christlichen Völkern vom 6. bis 8. Jahrhundert. Die Slawen zwischen Byzanz und Abendland* (Enzyklopädie der Byzantinistik. Grundriss der byzantinischen Philologie, Geschichte und Kunst in Einzeldarstellungen 51), Amsterdam

Wasilewski, T. (1972), *Bizancjum i Słowianie w IX wieku. Studia z dziejów stostunków politycznych i kulturalnych* (Rozprawy Uniwersytetu Warszawskiego 57), Warsaw

Wasiliwski, T. (1985), 'Borys I – Książe czy król Bułgarii?', *Balcanica Posnaniensia* 2: 33–42

Weithmann, M.W. (1978), *Die slavische Bevölkerung auf der griechischen Halbinsel: Ein Beitrag zur historischen Ethnographie Südosteuropas* (Beiträge zur Kenntnis Südosteuropas and des Nahen Orients 31), Munich

Werner, J. (1986), *Der Schatzfund von Vrap in Albanien: Studien zur Archäologie der Awaren* ii (*DÖAW* 184), Vienna

White, D.S. (1987), 'The Hellenistic tradition as an influence on ninth-century Byzantium: Patriarch Photios' letter to Boris-Michael, the Archon of Bulgaria', *The Patristic and Byzantine Review* 6: 121–9

White, D.S. and Berrigan, J.R. (1982), *The Patriarch and the Prince* (trans. of Photius' Letter to Khan Boris), Brookline, MA

Wiita, J.E. (1977), 'The Ethnika in Byzantine Military Treatises' (unpublished Ph.D. thesis), Minnesota

Winnifrith, T. (1987), *The Vlachs: The History of a Balkan People*, London

Wolfram, H. (1979) (ed.), *Conversio Bagoariorum et Carantanorum*, Vienna, Cologne and Graz

Wolfram, H. (1987), *Die Geburt Mitteleuropas: Geschichte Österreichs vor seiner Entstehung 378–907*, Vienna

Zacos, G. and Nesbitt, J.W. (1984), *Byzantine Lead Seals* ii, Berne

Zacos, G. and Veglery, A. (1972), *Byzantine Lead Seals* i.1–3, Basel

Zagiba, F. (1964), 'Die Missionierung der Slaven aus "Welschland" (Patriarchat Aquileja) im 8. und 9. Jahrhundert', in M. Hellmann *et al.* (eds.), *Cyrillo-Methodiana: Zur Frühgeschichte des Christentums bei den Slaven 863–1963* (Slavistische Forschungen 6), Cologne and Graz, pp. 274–311

Zagiba, F. (1967), 'Das Slavische als Missionssprache. Die sog. 'lingua-quarta'-Praxis der bayerischen Mission', *Die Welt der Slaven* 12: 1–18

Zagiba, F. (1971a), *Das Geistesleben der Slaven im Frühen Mittelalter: Die Anfänge des slavischen Schrifttums auf dem Gebiete des östlichen Mitteleuropa vom 8. bis 10. Jahrhundert* (Annales Instituti Slavici 7), Vienna, Cologne and Graz

Zagiba, F. (1971b), 'Das Slavische als Missionssprache (lingua quarta) und das Altkirchenslavische als lingua liturgica im 9.–10. Jahrhundert', *Studia Palaeoslovenica*, Prague, pp. 401–14

Zagiba, F. (1976a), *Musikgeschichte Mitteleuropas von den Anfängen bis zum Ende des 10. Jahrhunderts* (Forschungen zur älteren Musikgeschichte 1), Vienna

Zagiba, F. (ed.) (1976b), *Methodiana: Beiträge zur Zeit und Persönlichkeit sowie zum Schicksal und Werk des hl. Method* (Annales Instituti Slavici 9), Vienna, Cologne and Graz

Zástěrová, B. (1978), 'Über zwei grossmährische Rechtsdenkmäler byzantinischen Ursprungs', in V. Vavřínek (ed.) *Beiträge zur byzantinischen Geschichte im 9.–11. Jahrhundert*, Prague, pp. 361–85

Zástěrová, B. (1983), 'Un témoignage inaperçu, relatif à la diffusion de l'idéologie politique byzantine dans le milieu slave, au 9e siècle', *Okeanos: Essays Presented to Ihor Ševčenko on his Sixtieth Birthday* (Harvard Ukrainian Studies 7), pp. 691–701

Zástěrová, B. (1985), 'A propos de la signification des éléments de l'idéologie politique de Byzance dans les Vies en vieux-slave de Constantin et de Méthode', *Byzantina* 13(1): 155–69

Zettler, A. (1988), 'Methodius in Reichenau. Bemerkungen zur Deutung und zum Quellenwert der Einträge im Verbrüderungsbuch', *SM*, pp. 367–79

Zlatarsky, V.N. (1918–40) *Istoriia na B'lgarskata d'rzhava prez srednite vekove*, 3 vols., Sofia

10 THE MUSLIMS IN EUROPE

The eastern Mediterranean

Ahrweiler, H. (1966), *Byzance et la mer*, Paris

Eickhoff, E. (1966), *Seekrieg und Seepolitik zwischen Islam und Abendland (690–1040)*, Berlin

Fahmy, A. (1966), *Muslim Naval Organization in the Eastern Mediterranean*, Cairo

Hassan, A. (1933), *Les Tulunides*, Paris

Hawting, G.R., (1956), *The First Dynasty of Islam*, London

Kennedy, H.N. (1981), *The Early ʿAbbasid Caliphate*, London

Kennedy, H.N. (1986), *The Prophet and the Age of the Caliphates*, London

Pryor, J.H. (1988), *Geography, Technology and War: Studies in the Maritime History of the Mediterranean, 649–1571*, Cambridge

The Muslims in southern Italy and Sicily

Ahmad, A. (1975), *A History of Islamic Sicily*, Edinburgh

Amari, M. (1880–1), *Biblioteca Arabo-Sicula*, 2 vols., Turin and Rome

Amari, M. (1933–9), *Storia dei Musulmani di Sicilia*, ed. C.A. Nallino, Catania

Guichard, P. (1991), *L'Espagne et la Sicile musulmanes aux XI et XII siècles*, Lyons

Lagumina, B. (1892), *La Cronaca Siculo-Saracena di Cambridge*, Palermo

Lavagnini, B. (1959–60), 'Siracusa occupata degli Arabi e l'epistola di Teodosio Monaco', *Byzantion* 29–30: 267–79

Talbi, M. (1966), *L'Emirat aghlabide 184–296/800–909*, Paris

The Muslims in the Iberian peninsula

Bulliet, R.W. (1978), *Conversion to Islam in the Medieval Period*, Cambridge, MA
Collins, R. (1989), *The Arab Conquest of Spain, 710–797*, Oxford
Creswell, K.A.C. (1940), *Early Muslim Architecture* II, Oxford
Lévi-Provençal, E. (1932), *Inscriptions arabes de l'Espagne*, Leiden and Paris
Lévi-Provençal, E. (1950), *Histoire de L'Espagne musulmane* I, Paris
Guichard, P. (1977), *Structures sociales 'orientales' et 'occidentales' dans l'Espagne musulmane*, Paris and The Hague
Guichard, P. (1983), 'Les débuts de la piraterie andalouse en méditerranée occidentale (798–813)', *Revue de l'Occident Musulmane et de la Méditerranée* 35: 55–76
Manzano Moreno, E. (1991), *La Frontera de al-Andalus en Epoca de los Omeyas*, Madrid
Taha, A.D. (1989), *The Muslim Conquest and Settlement of North Africa and Spain*, London
Wolf, K.B. (1988), *Christian Martyrs in Muslim Spain*, Cambridge

11 SPAIN: THE NORTHERN KINGDOMS AND THE BASQUES, 711–910

Baliñas, C. (1989), *Defensores e traditores: un modelo de relación entre poder monárquico e oligarquía na Galicia altomedieval*, Santiago
Barreiro Somoza, J. (1987), *El señorío de la iglesia de Santiago de Compostela*, La Coruña
Cañada Juste, A. (1980), 'Los Banu Qasi (714–924)', *Príncipe de Viana* 41: 5–95
Casariego, J.E. (1969), 'Una revolución asturiana en el siglo IX: el interregno del conde Nepociano', *Boletín del Instituto de Estudios Asturianos* 68: 3–29
Collins, R. (1983a), *Early Medieval Spain: Unity in Diversity, 400–1000*, London
Collins, R. (1983b), 'Poetry in ninth-century Spain', *Papers of the Liverpool Latin Seminar* 4: 181–95
Collins, R. (1986), *The Basques*, Oxford
Collins, R. (1989a), 'Doubts and certainties on the churches of early medieval Spain', in D. Lomax and D. Mackenzie (eds.), *God and Man in Medieval Spain*, Warminster, pp. 1–18
Collins, R. (1989b), *The Arab Conquest of Spain, 710–797*, Oxford
Collins, R. (1990), 'Pippin I and the kingdom of Aquitaine', in P. Godman and R. Collins (eds.), *Charlemagne's Heir: New Perspectives on the Reign of Louis the Pious (814–840)*, Oxford, pp. 363–89
Fletcher, R. (1984), *St James's Catapult*, Oxford
Floriano A. (1949/51), *Diplomática española del periodo astur*, 2 vols., Oviedo
Gil Fernández, J., Moralejo, J.L. and Ruiz de la Peña, J.I. (1985), *Crónicas asturianas*, Oviedo
Lacarra, J.M. (1945), 'Textos navarros del Códice de Rada', *Estudios de Edad Media de la Corona de Argón* 1: 193–275
Lévi-Provençal, E. (1953) 'Du nouveau sur le royaume de Pampelune au IXe siècle', *Bulletin Hispanique* 55: 5–22
Merea, P. (1949), 'Portugal no seculo IX', in anon. (ed.), *Estudios sobre la monarquía asturiana*, Oviedo, pp. 345–54
Orlandis, J. (1962), *El poder real y la sucesión al trono en la monarquía visigoda* (Estudios visigóticos 3), Rome

Pérez de Urbel, J. (1954), 'Lo viejo y lo nuevo sobre el origen del reino de Pamplona', *Al-Andalus* 19: 1–42

Porres Martín-Cleto, J. (1985), *Historia de Tulaytula (711–1085)*, Toledo

Sánchez-Albornoz, C. (1957), 'Problemas de la historia navarra del siglo IX', *Cuadernos de Historia de España* 25/6: 5–82

Sánchez-Albornoz, C. (1961), 'Otra vez los Jimenos de Navarra', *Cuadernos de Historia de España* 33/4: 314–26

Sánchez-Albornoz, C. (1966), *Población y repoblación del valle del Duero*, Buenos Aires

Sánchez-Albornoz, C. (1967), *Investigaciones sobre historiografía hispana medieval*, Buenos Aires

Sánchez-Albornoz, C. (1969), 'El tercer rey de España', *Cuadernos de Historia de España* 49/50: 5–49

Sánchez-Albornoz, C. (1971), '¿Un regente en Pamplona durante el cautiverio de Fortún Garcés?', in *Homenaje a José Esteban Uranga*, Pamplona, pp. 175–82

Sánchez-Albornoz, C. (1972–5), *El Reino de Asturias*, 3 vols., Oviedo

Ubieto Arteta, A. (1960), 'La dinastía Jimena', *Saitabi* 10: 65–79

Vigil, C.M. (1887), *Asturias monumental, epigráfica y diplomática*, 2 vols., Oviedo

12　LOMBARD AND CAROLINGIAN ITALY

I History of Italy, general

Capitani, C. (1986), *Storia dell'Italia medievale, 410–1216*, Rome and Bari

Hartmann, L.M. (1900–11), *Geschichte Italiens im Mittelalter* II–III, Leipzig and Gotha (still a basic text)

Tabacco, G. (1979), *Egemonie sociali e strutture del potere nel medioevo italiano*, Turin

Wickham, C. (1981), *Early Medieval Italy: Central Power and Local Society, 400–1000*, London

II, 1 The Lombards, general

Bertolini, O. (1968), *Scritti scelti di storia medievale*, 2 vols., Livorno (a collection of studies written between 1920 and 1964)

Bognetti, G.P. (1966–8), *L'età longobarda*, 4 vols. (a collection of studies written between 1938 and 1962), Milan

Cammarosano, P. and Gasparri, S. (eds.) (1990), *Langobardia*, Udine

Delogu, P. (1980), 'Il regno longobardo', in P. Delogu, A. Guillou and G. Ortalli, *Longobardi e Bizantini* (= G. Galasso (ed.), *Storia d'Italia* I), Turin

Jarnut, J. (1982), *Geschichte der Langobarden* (Urban Taschenbücher 339), Stuttgart, Berlin, Cologne and Mainz

Menghin, W. (1985), *Die Langobarden: Archaeologie und Geschichte*, Stuttgart

II, 2 The Lombard state

Bognetti, G.P. (1940), 'Il gastaldato longobardo e i giudicati di Adaloaldo, Arioaldo e Pertarito nella lite fra Parma e Piacenza', in *L'età longobarda* I, pp. 221–74

Brühl, C.R. (1972), 'Zentral- und Finanzverwaltung im Franken- und im Langobardenreich', *Settimane* 20, I: 61–85

Fröhlich, H. (1980), *Studien zur langobardischen Thronfolge von den Anfängen bis zur Eroberung des italienischen Reiches durch Karl den Grossen (774)*, 2 vols., Tübingen

Gasparri, S. (1978), *I duchi longobardi* (Studi Storici 109), Rome

Gasparri, S. (1986), 'Strutture militari e legami di dipendenza in età longobarda e carolingia', *Rivista Storica Italiana* 98: 664–726

Gasparri, S. (1987), 'Pavia longobarda', in *Storia di Pavia* III, Pavia, pp. 19–65

Gasparri, S. (1990), 'Il regno longobardo in Italia. Strutture e funzionamento di uno stato altomedievale', in Cammarosano and Gasparri (1990), pp. 237–305

Harrison, D. (1993), *The Early State and the Towns: Forms of Integration in Lombard Italy, AD. 568–774*, Lund

Mor, C.G. (1958), 'Lo stato longobardo del VII secolo', *Settimane* 5: 271–307

Saracco Previdi, E. (1973), 'Lo sculdhais nel territorio longobardo di Rieti', *SM*, 14: 627–76

Tabacco, G. (1969), 'Dai possessori dell'età carolingia agli esercitali dell'età longobarda', *SM*, 10(1): 221–68

II, 3 Lombard duchies

Conti, P.M. (1973), 'La Tuscia e i suoi ordinamenti territoriali nell'alto medioevo', in *Lucca e la Tuscia nell'alto medioevo (Atti del 5° Congresso internazionale di studi sull'alto medioevo)*, Spoleto, pp. 61–116

Conti, P.M. (1982), *Il ducato di Spoleto e la storia istituzionale dei Longobardi* (Quaderni di 'Spoletium' 2), Spoleto

Gasparri, S. (1983), 'Il ducato di Spoleto. Istituzioni, poteri, gruppi dominanti', in *Il ducato di Spoleto (Atti del 9° Congresso internazionale di studi sull'alto medioevo)*, Spoleto, pp. 77–122

Gasparri, S. (1988), 'Il ducato e il principato di Benevento', in G. Galasso and R. Romeo (eds.), *Storia del Mezzogiorno* II, part I, Naples, pp. 85–146

Hirsch, F. (1890), *Il ducato di Benevento fino alla caduta del regno longobardo* (trans. from German), Rome

Krahwinkler, H. (1992), *Friaul im Frühmittelalter: Geschichte einer Region von Ende des Fünften bis zum Ende des Zehnten Jahrhunderts* (Veröffentlichungen des Instituts für Österreichischen Geschichtsforschung 30), Vienna, Cologne and Weimar

Schneider, F. (1914), *Die Reichsverwaltung in Toskana (568–1268)* I, Rome

Wickham, C. (1980), 'Economic and social institutions in northern Tuscany in the 8th century', in A. Spicciani (ed.), *Istituzioni ecclesiastiche della Toscana medievale*, Galatina, pp. 7–34

II, 4 Ecclesiastical structures and life

Schmid, K. (1967), 'Anselm von Nonantola. Olim dux militum, nunc dux monachorum', *QFIAB* 47: 1–122

Schmid, K. (1991), *Vita Walfredi und Kloster Monteverdi: Toskanisches Mönchtum zwischen langobardischer und fränkischer Herrschaft*, Tübingen

Violante, C. (1982), 'Le strutture organizzative della cura d'anime nelle campagne dell'Italia centro-settentrionale (secoli v–x)', in *Cristianizzazione ed organizzazione ecclesiastica delle campagne nell'alto medioevo: espansione e resistenze, Settimane* 28: 963–1157

II, 5 Political history in the eighth century

Arnaldi, G. (1987), 'Le origini del patrimonio di San Pietro', in G. Arnaldi, P. Toubert, D. Waley, J.C. Maire Vigueur and R. Manselli, *Comuni e signorie nell'Italia nord-orientale e centrale: Lazio, Umbria e Marche, Lucca* (= G. Galasso (ed.), *Storia d'Italia* VII, part 2), Turin, pp. 3–151

Delogu, P. (1991), 'Desiderio', in *DBI* XXXIX, pp. 373–82

Schmid, K. (1972), 'Zur Ablösung der Langobardenherrschaft durch die Franken', *QFIAB* 52: 1–36

III, 1 Carolingians: political history

Arnaldi, G. (1967), 'Berengario I', *DBI* IX, pp. 5–30

Arnaldi, G. (1971), 'La tradizione degli atti dell'assemblea pavese del febbraio 876', in *La critica del testo. Atti del 2° Congresso internazionale della società italiana di storia del diritto* I, Florence, pp. 51–68

Delogu, P. (1968a), 'Strutture politiche e ideologia nel regno di Lodovico II', *Bullettino dell'Istituto Storico Italiano* 80, pp. 137–89

Delogu, P. (1968b), 'Vescovi, conti e sovrani nella crisi del regno italico', *Annali della Scuola Speciale per Archivisti e Bibliotecari* 8: 3–72

Fischer, J. (1965), *Königtum, Adel und Kirche im Königreich Italien (774–875)*, Bonn

Fumagalli, V. (1978), *Il regno italico*, in G. Galasso (ed.), *Storia d'Italia* II, Turin

Hees, H. (1973), *Studien zur Geschichte Kaiser Ludwigs II*, Regensburg

Hlawitschka, E. (1960), *Franken, Alemannen, Bayern und Burgunden in Oberitalien (774–962)* (Forschungen zur Oberrheinischen Landesgeschichte 8), Freiburg im Breisgau

Hlawitschka, E. (1983a), 'Die Widonen im Dukat von Spoleto', *QFIAB* 63: 20–92

Hlawitschka, E. (1983b), 'Die politischen Intentionen der Widonen im Dukat von Spoleto', in *Il ducato di Spoleto (Atti del 9° Congresso internazionale di studi sull'alto medioevo)* I, Spoleto, pp. 123–47

Houben, H. (1987), 'Il principato di Salerno e la politica meridionale dell'Impero d'Occidente', *Rassegna Storica Salernitana* n.s. 4: 59–83

Jarnut, J. (1990), 'Ludwig der Fromme, Lothar und das Regnum Italiae', in Godman and Collins, *Charlemagne's Heir*, pp. 349–62

Manacorda, F. (1968), *Ricerche sugli inizi della dominazione dei Carolingi in Italia* (Studi Storici 71–2), Rome

Ruggiero, B. (1968), 'Il ducato di Spoleto e i tentativi di penetrazione dei Franchi nell'Italia meridionale', *Archivio Storico per le Provincie Napoletane* 84/5: 77–116

Zielinski, H. (1990), 'Ein unbeachteter Italienzug Kaiser Lothars I. im Jahre 847', *QFIAB* 70: 1–22

Zimmerman, H. (1974), 'Imperatores Italiae', in H. Beumann (ed.), *Historische Forschungen für Walter Schlesinger*, Cologne and Vienna, pp. 379–99

III, 2 Institutions of the state

Brunterc'h, J.P. (1983), 'Les circonscriptions du duché de Spolète du VIIIe au XIIe siècle', in *Il ducato di Spoleto (Atti del 9° Congresso internazionale di studi sull'alto medioevo)* 1, Spoleto, pp. 207–30

Castagnetti, A. (1970), 'Distretti fiscali autonomi o sottocircoscrizioni della contea cittadina? La Gardesana veronese in epoca carolingia', *Rivista Storica Italiana* 82: 736–43

Formazione e strutture dei ceti dominanti nel medio evo: marchesi, conti e visconti nel regno Italico (1988) (Nuovi Studi Storici 1), Rome

Fumagalli, V. (1968), 'Un territorio piacentino nel secolo IX: "fines castellana"', *QFIAB* 48: 1–35

Fumagalli, V. (1969), 'Città e distretti minori nell'Italia carolingia. Un esempio', *Rivista Storica Italiana* 81: 107–17

Fumagalli, V. (1981), 'Le modificazioni politico-istituzionali in Italia sotto la dominazione carolingia', *Settimane* 27, 1: 293–318

Gasparri, S. (1990), 'Il regno e la legge. Longobardi, Romani e Franchi nello sviluppo dell'ordinamento pubblico (secoli VI–X)', *La Cultura* 28: 243–66

Krahwinkler, H. (1992), *Friaul im Fruehmittelalter* (see section II, 3)

Keller, H. (1967), 'Zur Struktur der Königsherrschaft im karolingischen und nachkarolingischen Italien. Der "consiliarius regis" in den italienischen Königs-diplomen des 9. und 10. Jahrhunderts', *QFIAB* 47: 123–223

Keller, H. (1969), 'Der Gerichtsort in oberitalienischen und toskanischen Städten. Untersuchungen zur Stellung der Stadt im Herrschaftssystem des Regnum Italicum vom 9. bis 11. Jahrhundert', *QFIAB* 49: 1–72

Keller, H. (1973), 'La marca di Tuscia fino all'anno Mille', in *Lucca e la Tuscia nell'alto Medioevo (Atti del 5° Congresso internazionale di studi sull'alto medioevo)*, Spoleto, pp. 117–42

Saracco Previdi, E. (1973), 'Lo sculdhais nel territorio longobardo di Rieti', *SM* 14(2): 627–76

Sergi, G. (1971), 'Una grande circoscrizione del regno italico: la marca arduinica di Torino', *SM* 12(2): 637–712

Sergi, G. (1985), 'Le città come luoghi di continuità di nozioni pubbliche del potere. Le aree delle marche di Ivrea e di Torino', in *Piemonte medievale: forme del potere e della società*, Turin, pp. 5–27

Sergi, G. (1988), 'Guerra e popolamento nel *regnum Italiae*', in *Castrum 3. Guerre, fortification et habitat dans le monde méditerranéen au moyen âge*, Madrid and Rome, pp. 257–62

Settia, A.A. (1984), *Castelli e villaggi nell'Italia padana. Popolamento, potere e sicurezza fra IX e XIII secolo*, Naples

Tabacco, G. (1968), 'Il regno italico nei secoli IX–XI', *Settimane* 15: 763–90

Taurino, E. (1970), 'L'organizzazione territoriale della contea di Fermo nei secoli VIII–X', *SM* 11(2): 659–710

Taurino, E. (1975), 'Osservazioni sui "missi domini regis" e sui "comites sacri palacii" nel ducato di Spoleto in età carolingia', *Studia Picena* 42: 76–95

Werner, K.-F. (1980), 'Missus, marchio, comes. Entre l'administration centrale et l'administration locale de l'empire carolingien', in W. Paravicini and K.-F.

Werner (eds.), *Histoire comparée de l'administration (IVe–XVIIIe siècles) (Francia,* Beihefte 9), Munich, pp. 191–239

III, 3 Ecclesiastical organisation

Ambrosioni, A.M. (1986), 'Gli arcivescovi nella vita di Milano', in *Atti del 10° Congresso internazionale di studi sull'alto medioevo, Milano 1983,* Spoleto, pp. 85–118

Belletzkie, R.F. (1980), 'Pope Nicholas I and John of Ravenna: the struggle for ecclesiastical rights in the ninth century', *Church History* 49: 262–72

Bertolini, O. (1968), 'I vescovi del "Regnum Langobardorum" nell'età carolingia', in *Scritti scelti di storia medievale,* 2 vols., Livorno, I, pp. 70–92

Castagnetti, A. (1976), *La pieve rurale nell'Italia padana: territorio, organizzazione patrimoniale e vicende della pieve veronese di San Pietro di Tillida dall'alto medioevo al secolo XIII,* Rome

Hartmann, W. (1986), 'Il vescovo come giudice. La giurisdizione ecclesiastica su crimini di laici nell'alto medioevo (secoli VI–XI)', *Rivista di Storia della Chiesa in Italia* 40: 320–41

Hartmann, W. (1989), *Die Synoden der Karolingerzeit im Frankenreich und in Italien* (Konziliengeschichte, Reihe A: Darstellungen), Paderborn, Munich, Vienna and Zurich

Herbers, K. (1991), *Der Konflikt Papst Nikolaus' I mit Erzbischof Johannes von Ravenna (861)* (Diplomatische und Chronologische Studien aus der Arbeit an den *Regesta Imperii:* Beihefte zu J.F. Boehmer, *Regesta Imperii* 8), Cologne and Vienna, pp. 51–66

Picard, J.C. (1988), *Le souvenir des évêques: sépultures, listes épiscopales et culte des évêques en Italie du nord des origines au Xe siècle* (Bibliothèque des Écoles Françaises d'Athènes et de Rome 268), Rome

Tabacco, G. (1986), 'Il volto ecclesiastico del potere nell'età carolingia', in G. Chittolini and G. Miccoli (eds.), *Storia d'Italia. Annali 9. La chiesa e il potere politico dal Medioevo all'età contemporanea,* Turin, pp. 7–41

Violante, C. (1982), 'Le strutture organizzative della cura d'anime nelle campagne dell'Italia centro-settentrionale (secoli V–X)', (see section II, 4)

III, 4 Society in the ninth century

Andreolli, B. and Montanari, M. (1983), *L'azienda curtense in Italia: proprietà della terra e lavoro contadino nei secoli VIII–XI,* Bologna

Bordone, R. (1974), 'Un'attiva minoranza etnica nell'alto medioevo: gli Alamanni del comitato di Asti', *QFIAB* 54: 1–55

Bordone, R. (1980), *Città e territorio nell'alto medioevo: la società astigiana dal dominio dei Franchi all'affermazione comunale,* Turin

Cracco, G. (ed.) (1988), *Storia di Vicenza, II: L'età medievale,* Vicenza

Fumagalli, V. (1976), *Terra e società nell'Italia padana. I secoli IX e X,* Turin

Fumagalli, V. (1978), *Coloni e signori nell'Italia settentrionale: secoli VI–XI,* Bologna

Keller, H. (1979), *Adelsherrschaft und Städtische Gesellschaft in Oberitalien. 9. bis 12. Jahrhundert* (Bibliothek des Deutschen Historischen Instituts in Rom 52), Tübingen

Leicht, P.S. (1954), 'Il feudo in Italia nell'età carolingia', *Settimane* 1: 71–108
Montanari, M. (1988), *Contadini e città fra 'Longobardia' e 'Romania'*, Florence
Rossetti, G. (1973), 'Società e istituzioni nei secoli IX e X: Pisa, Volterra, Populonia', in *Atti del 5° Congresso internazionale di studi sull'alto medioevo, Lucca 1971*, Spoleto, pp. 209–337
Rossetti, G. (1986), 'I ceti proprietari e professionali: status sociale, funzioni e prestigio a Milano nei secoli VIII–X. 1: L'età longobarda', in *Milano e i Milanesi prima del Mille. VIII–X secolo (Atti del 10° Congresso internazionale di studi sull'alto medioevo)* I, Spoleto, pp. 165–207
Sergi, G. (1986), 'I rapporti vassallitico-beneficiari', in *Milano e i Milanesi prima del Mille. VIII–X secolo (Atti del 10° Congresso internazionale di studi sull'alto medioevo)* 1, Spoleto, pp. 137–63
Tabacco, G. (1966), *I liberi del re nell'Italia carolingia e postcarolingia* (Biblioteca degli studi medievali 2), Spoleto
Tabacco, G. (1973), 'Arezzo, Siena e Chiusi nell'alto medioevo', in *Atti del 5° Congresso internazionale di studi sull'alto medioevo, Lucca 1971*, Spoleto, pp. 163–89
Varanini, G.M. (1990), 'Aspetti della società urbana nei secoli IX–X', in A. Castagnetti and G.M. Varanini (eds.), *Il Veneto nel Medioevo: Dalla 'Venetia' alla Marca Veronese*, 2 vols., Verona, pp. 199–236
Vasina, A. (ed.) (1983), Ricerche e studi sul Breviarium ecclesiae Ravennatis (Codice Bavaro): secoli VII–X (Studi Storici 148–9), Rome
Wickham, C. (1986), 'Land disputes and their social framework in Lombard-Carolingian Italy, 700–900', in W. Davies and P. Fouracre (eds.), *The Settlement of Disputes in Early Medieval Europe*, Cambridge, pp. 105–24

III, 5 Town and regional histories

Bergamo e il suo territorio nei documenti altomedievali: atti del Convegno (Contributi allo studio del territorio bergamasco 8) (1989), Bergamo
Carile, A. (ed.) (1992), *Storia di Ravenna, II: Dall'età bizantina all'età ottoniana* (2 vols.), Ravenna
Castagnetti, A. and Varanini, G.M. (eds.) (1989), *Il Veneto nel medioevo: dalla 'Venetia' alla Marca Veronese*, 2 vols., Verona
Cracco, G. (ed.) (1988), *Storia di Vicenza, II: L'età medievale*, Vicenza
Galasso, G. and Romeo, R. (eds.) (1988–90), *Storia del Mezzogiorno* II and III, Naples
Jarnut, J. (1979), *Bergamo 568–1098: Verfassung- Sozial- und Wirtschaftsgeschichte einer langobardischen Stadt im Mittelalter*, Wiesbaden
Schumann, R. (1973), *Authority and the Commune: Parma 833–1133* (Deputazione di Storia Patria per le Provincie Parmensi, Fonti e studi series 2, 8), Parma
Schwarzmeier, H.M. (1972), *Lucca und das Reich bis zur Ende des 11. Jahrhunderts. Studien zur Sozialstruktur einer Herzogsstadt in der Toskana* (Bibliothek des Deutsches Historisches Instituts in Rom 41), Tübingen
Storia di Brescia, della Fondazione Treccani degli Alfieri (1963), I, Brescia
Storia di Milano, della Fondazione Treccani degli Alfieri (1954), II, Milano
Storia di Pavia, II: L'alto medioevo (1987), Pavia
Vasina, A. (ed.) (1983), *Storia di Cesena, II: Il medioevo* I, Rimini
Verona e il suo territorio (1964), 2 vols., Verona

Wickham, C. (1988), *The Mountains and the City: The Tuscan Appennines in the Early Middle Ages*, Oxford

13 BYZANTINE ITALY, *c.* 680–*c.* 876

Alexander, P.J. (1973), 'Les débuts des conquêtes arabes en Sicile et la tradition apocalyptique byzantino-slave', *Bullettino del Centro di Studi Filologici e Linguistici Siciliani* 12: 9–14, reprinted in P.J. Alexander (ed.), *Religious and Political Thought in the Byzantine Empire*. London, (1978), XIV

Anastos, M.V. (1957), 'The transfer of Illyricum, Calabria and Sicily to the jurisdiction of the Patriarchiate of Constantinople in 732–733', *Rivista di Studi Bizantini e Neoellenici* 9: 14–31

Anastos, M.V. (1969), 'Leo III's edict against images in 726–727 and Italo-Byzantine relations between 727 and 730', *Byzantinische Forschungen* 3: 5–41

Arnaldi, G. (1987), 'Le origini del patrimonio di S. Pietro', in *Storia d'Italia*, VII, I, Turin

Bavant, B. (1979), 'Le Duché byzantin de Rome. Origine, durée et extension géographique', *Mélanges de l'Ecole Française de Rome: Moyen Age et Temps Moderne* 91: 41–88

Belletzkie, R.J. (1980), 'Pope Nicholas I and John of Ravenna: the struggle for ecclesiastical rights in the ninth century', *Church History* 49: 262–72

Bertolini, O. (1941), *Roma di fronte a Bisanzio e ai Longobardi*, Bologna

Bertolini, O. (1950), 'Sergio, arcivescovo di Ravenna (744–769) e i papi del suo tempo', *Studi Romagnoli* 1: 43–88

Bertolini, O. (1968a), *Scritti scelti di storia medievale*, 2 vols., Livorno

Bertolini, O. (1968b), 'Quale fu il vero obiettivo assegnato in Italia da Leone III Isaurico all'armata di Manes, stratego dei Cibyrrioti?' *Byzantinische Forschungen* 2: 15–49

Bertolini, O. (1972), *Roma e i Longobardi*, Rome

Bertolini, P. (1974), 'La chiesa di Napoli durante la crisi iconoclasta. Appunti sul codice Vaticano Latino 5007', in O. Banti (ed.), *Studi sul medioevo cristiano offerti a Raffaello Morgen* I, Rome, pp. 101–27

Brown, T.S. (1979), 'The church of Ravenna and the imperial administration in the seventh century', *EHR* 94: 1–28

Brown, T.S. (1984), *Gentlemen and Officers: Imperial Administration and Aristocratic Power in Byzantine Italy, 554–800 AD*, London

Brown, T.S. (1986), '*Romanitas* and Campanilismo', in C. Holdsworth and T. Wiseman (eds.), *The Inheritance of History*, Exeter, pp. 109–10

Brown, T.S. (1988a), 'The interplay between Roman and Byzantine traditions and local sentiment in the Exarchate of Ravenna', *Settimane* 34:127–60

Brown, T.S. (1988b), 'The background of Byzantine relations with Italy', *Byzantinische Forschungen* 13: 27–45

Brown, T.S. (1990), 'Louis the Pious and the papacy; a Ravenna perspective', in P. Godman and R. Collins (eds.), *Charlemagne's Heir: New Perspectives on the Reign of Louis the Pious (814–840)*, Oxford, pp. 297–307

Brown, T.S. (1992), 'Otranto in medieval history', in D. Michaelides and D. Wilkinson (eds.), *Excavations at Otranto* I, Galatina, pp. 27–39

Brown, T.S. and Christie, N. (1989), 'Was there a Byzantine model of settlement in Italy?', *Mélanges de l'Ecole Française de Rome: Moyen Age et Temps Modernes* 101: 377–99

Bulgarella, F. (1983), 'Bisanzio in Sicilia', in *Il Mezzogiorno dai Bizantini a Federico II*, Storia d'Italia III, Turin

Carile, A. (1991, 1992), *Storia di Ravenna* II: *dall'età bizantina all'età ottoniana*, 2 vols., Venice

Carile, A. and Fedalto, G. (1978), *Le origini di venezia*, Bologna

Cessi, R. (1951), *Le origini del ducato veneziano*, Naples

Christie, N. (ed.) (1991), *Three South Etrurian Churches: Santa Cornelia, Santa Rufina and San Liberato*, London

Classen, P. (1951), '*Romanum gubernans imperium*. Zur Vorgeschichte der Kaisertitulatur Karl des Grossen', *DA* 9: 103–21

Classen, P. (1981), 'Italien zwischen Byzanz und dem Frankenreich', *Settimane* 27: 919–67

Curradi, C. (1977), 'I conti Guidi nel secolo x', *Studi Romagnoli* 28: 17–64

Delogu, P., Guillou, A. and Ortalli, G. (1980), *Longobardi e Bizantini, Storia d'Italia* I, Turin

Dölger, F. (1924), *Regesten der Kaiserurkunden des oströmischen Reiches* I, Berlin

Falkenhausen, V. von (1978), *La dominazione bizantina in Italia*, Bari

Falkenhausen, V. von (1980), 'I Longobardi meridionali', in *Il Mezzogiorno dai Bizantini a Federico II, Storia d'Italia* III, Turin, pp. 251–370

Fasoli, G. (1979), 'Il dominio territoriale degli arcivescovi di Ravenna fra l'VIII e l'XI secolo', in C.G. Mor and H. Schmiedinger (eds.), *I poteri temporali dei vescovi in Italia e Germania nel medioevo*, Bologna, pp. 87–140

Ferluga, J. (1988), 'L'Italia bizantina dalla caduta dell' Esarcato di Ravenna alla metà del secolo IX', *Settimane* 34: 169–93

Ferluga, J. (1991), 'L'Esarcato', in Carile (1991), pp. 351–77

Gouillard, J. (1961), 'Deux figures mal connues du second iconoclasme', *Byz* 31: 386–401

Guillou, A. (1969), *Régionalisme et indépendance dans l'empire byzantin au VIIe siècle: l'exemple de l'Exarchat et de la Pentapole d'Italie*, Rome

Guillou, A. (1977), 'La Sicile byzantine. Etat de recherche', *Byzantinische Forschungen* 5: 95–145

Jaffé, P. and Ewald, P. (eds.) (1885), *Registrum Pontificum Romanorum ab condita ecclesia ad annum . . . MCXCVIIII* I, Leipzig

Johns, J. (1995) *Early Medieval Sicily*, London

Kreutz, B. (1992), *Before the Normans: Southern Italy in the Ninth and Tenth Centuries*, College Park, PA

Llewellyn, P. (1971), *Rome in the Dark Ages*, London

Llewellyn, P. (1986), 'The popes and the constitution in the eighth century', *EHR* 101: 42–67

Luzzati Laganà, F. (1980), 'Il Ducato di Napoli', in *Il Mezzogiorno dai Bizantini a Federico II, Storia d'Italia* III, Turin, pp. 327–39

Marazzi, F. (1991), 'Il conflitto fra Leone III Isaurico e il papato fra il 725 e il 733, e il "definitivo" inizio del medioevo a Roma: un'ipotesi in discussione', *Papers of the British School at Rome* 59: 231–57

Mazzarino, S. (1940), 'Su un'iscrizione trionfale di Turris Libisonis', *Epigraphica* 2: 292–313

Merores, M. (1911), *Gaeta im frühen Mittelalter*, Gotha

Noble, T.F.X. (1984), *The Republic of Saint Peter*, Philadelphia

Nordhagen, P.J. (1988), 'Italo-Byzantine wall painting of the early middle ages: an 80-year-old enigma in scholarship', *Settimane* 34: 593–619

Noyé, G. (1988), 'Quelques observations sur l'évolution de l'habitat en Calabre du ve au xie siècle', *Rivista di Studi Bizantini e Neoellenici* n.s., 25: 57–130

Oikonomidès, N. (1964), 'Une liste arabe des stratèges byzantines du vii siècle et les origines du Thème de Sicile', *Rivista di Studi Bizantini e Neoellenici* n.s., 1: 121–30

Oikonomidès, N. (1972), *Les listes de préséance byzantines des IXe et Xe siècles*, Paris

Ruggini, L. (1980), 'La Sicilia tra Roma e Bisanzio', in *Storia della Sicilia* iii, Naples, pp. 1–96

Sansterre, J.M. (1983), *Les moines grecs et orientaux à Rome aux époques byzantine et carolingienne (milieu du VIe s. fin du IX s.)*, Brussels

Schwarz, U. (1978), *Amalfi im frühen Mittelalter. (9.–11. Jahrhundert)*, Tübingen

Skinner, P. (1992), 'Noble families in the Duchy of Gaeta in the tenth century', *Papers of the British School at Rome* 47: 353–77

Toubert, P. (1973), *Les structures du Latium médiéval*, 2 vols., Rome

Zuretti, C.O. (1910), 'L'espugnazione di Siracusa nell'880', in *Centenario della nascità di Michele Amari*, Palermo, pp. 165–73

14 BYZANTIUM AND THE WEST

Aerts, W.J. (1972), 'The Monza Vocabulary', in W.F. Bakker, A.F. van Gemert and W.J. Aerts (eds.), *Studia byzantina et neohellenica neerlandica*, Leiden, pp. 36–73

Ahrweiler, H. (1966), *Byzance et la mer: la marine de guerre, la politique et les institutions maritimes de Byzance aux VIIe–XVe siècles*, Paris

Ahrweiler, H. (1971), 'Les relations entre les Byzantins et les Russes au ixe siècle', *Bulletin d'Information et de Coordination de l'Association Internationale des Etudes Byzantines* 5: 44–70; reprinted in H. Ahrweiler, *Byzance: les pays et les territoires*, London (1976), no. vii

Ahrweiler, H. (1975), *L'idéologie politique de l'empire byzantin*, Paris

Allen, P. (1979), 'The "Justinianic" plague', *Byz* 49: 5–20

Amari, M. (1933), *Storia dei Musulmani di Sicilia*, ed. C.A. Nallino, i, Catania

Bertolini, O. (1968), *Scritti scelti di storia medioevale*, Livorno

Biraben, J.-N. and Le Goff, J. (1969), 'La peste dans le haut moyen âge', *Annales ESC* 24: 1484–1510

Bischoff, B. (1977), 'Irische Schreiber im Karolingerreich', in *Jean Scot Erigène et l'histoire de la philosophie*, Paris, pp. 47–58

Bischoff, B. (1984), *Anecdota novissima*, Stuttgart

Borgolte, M. (1976), *Der Gesandtenaustausch der Karolinger mit den Abbasiden und mit den Patriarchen von Jerusalem* (Münchener Beiträge zur Mediävistik und Renaissance-Forschung 25), Munich

Bouhot, J.P. (1976), *Ratramne de Corbie: histoire littéraire et controverses doctrinales*, Paris

Brown, T.S. (1988a), 'The background of Byzantine relations with Italy in the ninth century', *Byzantinische Forschungen* 13: 27–45

Brown, T.S. (1988b), 'The interplay between Roman and Byzantine traditions and local sentiment in the Exarchate of Ravenna', *Settimane* 34: 127–60

Brühl, C. (1977), 'Purpururkunden', in *Festschrift H. Beumann*, ed. K.U. Jäschke and R. Wenskus, Sigmaringen, pp. 3–21

Buckton, D. (1988), 'Byzantine enamel and the West', *Byzantinische Forschungen* 13: 235–44

Bullough, D. (1955), 'The counties of the *Regnum Italiae* in the Carolingian period (774–888)', *Papers of the British School at Rome* 23: 148–68

Cavallo, G. (1988), 'Le tipologie della cultura nel riflesso delle testimonianze scritte', *Settimane* 34: 467–516

Chiesa, P. (1989), 'Traduzioni e traduttori dal greco nel IX secolo: sviluppi di una tecnica', in *Giovanni Scoto nel suo tempo: l'organizzazione del sapere in età carolingia*, Spoleto, pp. 172–200

Christie, N.J. (1989), 'The archaeology of Byzantine Italy: a synthesis of recent research', *Journal of Mediterranean Archaeology* 2: 249–93

Classen, P. (1983), *Ausgewählte Aufsätze*, ed. J. Fleckenstein *et al.*, Sigmaringen

Classen, P. (1985), *Karl der Grosse, das Papsttum und Byzanz: Die Begründung des karolingischen Kaisertums*, 3rd edn, ed. H. Fuhrmann and K. Märtl, Sigmaringen

Claude, D. (1985), *Der Handel im westlichen Mittelmeer während des Frühmittelalters* (Abhandlungen der Akademie der Wissenschaften in Göttingen, phil.-hist. Klasse, Dritte Folge 144), Göttingen

Corsi, P. (1979), 'La *Vita* di san Nicola e un codice della versione di Giovanni diacono', *Nicolaus* 7: 359–80

Corsi, P. (1983), *La spedizione italiana di Costante II*, Bologna

Dagron, G. (1987), '"Ceux d'en face." Les peuples étrangers dans les traités militaires byzantins', *TM* 10: 207–32

Deér, J. (1972), 'Die Vorrechte des Kaisers in Rom', in G. Wolf (ed.), *Zum Kaisertum Karls des Grossen*, Darmstadt, pp. 30–115

Detorakès, Th. E. (1987), 'Βυζάντιο καὶ Εὐεώπη: ἁγιολογικὲς σχέσεις', in Βυζάντιο καὶ Εὐεώπη. Α'διεθνὴς βυζαντινολογικὴ συνάντηση, Athens, pp. 85–99

Devisse, J. (1976), *Hincmar, archevêque de Reims, 845–882*, Geneva.

Dionisotti, A.C. (1988), 'Greek grammars and dictionaries in Carolingian Europe', in M.W. Herren and S.A. Brown (eds.), *Sacred Nectar of the Greeks: The Study of Greek in the West in the Early Middle Ages*, London, pp. 143–68

Dolbeau, F. (1982), 'La Vie latine de saint Euthyme: une traduction inédite de Jean, diacre napolitain', *Mélanges de l'Ecole Française de Rome. Moyen Age-Temps Modernes* 93: 315–35

Dölger, F. (1924), *Regesten der Kaiserurkunden des oströmischen Reiches von 565–1453* I, Berlin and Munich

Dölger, F. (1953), *Byzanz und die europäische Staatenwelt*, Ettal

Dols, M.W. (1974), 'Plague in early Islamic history', *Journal of the American Oriental Society* 94: 371–83

Dümmler, E. (1887–8), *Geschichte des Ostfränkischen Reiches*, 2nd edn, Leipzig

Dvornik, F. (1948), *The Photian Schism: History and Legend*, Cambridge

Falkenhausen, V. von (1967), *Untersuchungen über die byzantinische Herrschaft in Süditalien vom 9. bis ins 11. Jahrhundert*, Wiesbaden

Falkenhausen, V. von (1968), 'Taranto in epoca bizantina', *SM* 3rd series, 9: 133–66

Falkenhausen, V. von (1968/9), 'A medieval Neapolitan document', *Princeton University Library Chronicle* 30: 171–82

Falkenhausen, V. von (1978–9 [= 1985]), 'Chiesa greca e chiesa latina in Sicilia prima della conquista araba', *Archivio Storico Siracusano* n.s. 5: 137–55

Falkenhausen, V. von (1988), 'San Pietro nella religiosità bizantina', *Settimane* 34, ii: 627–58

Freeman, A. (1985), 'Carolingian orthodoxy and the fate of the *Libri Carolini*', *Viator* 16: 65–108

Gay, J. [= G.] (1917), *L'Italia meridionale e l'impero bizantino dall'avvento di Basilio I alla resa di Bari ai Normanni (867–1071)*, Florence

Grierson, P. (1981), 'The Carolingian empire in the eyes of Byzantium', *Settimane* 27: 885–916

Haendler, G. (1958), *Epochen karolingischer Theologie: Eine Untersuchung über die karolingischen Gutachten zum byzantinischen Bilderstreit*, Berlin

Haldon, J.F. (1990), *Byzantium in the Seventh Century*, Cambridge

Hartmann, L.M. (1904), *Zur Wirtschaftsgeschichte Italiens im frühen Mittelalter*, Gotha

Hartmann, W. (1989), *Die Synoden der Karolingerzeit im Frankenreich und in Italien*, Paderborn

Harvey, A. (1989), *Economic Expansion in the Byzantine Empire, 900–1200*, Cambridge

Hendy, M. (1985), *Studies in the Byzantine Monetary Economy c. 300–1450*, Cambridge

Hergenröther, J. (1867–9), *Photius, Patriarch von Constantinopel: Sein Leben, seine Schriften und das griechische Schisma*, Regensburg

Hiestand, R. (1964), *Byzanz und das Regnum Italicum im 10. Jahrhundert*, Zurich

Irigoin, J. (1969), 'L'Italie méridionale et la tradition des textes antiques', *JÖB* 18: 37–55

Jacob, A. (1972), 'Une lettre de Charles le Chauve au clergé de Ravenne?', *Revue d'Histoire Ecclésiastique* 67: 409–22

Kaczynski, B.M. (1988), *Greek in the Carolingian Age: The St Gall Manuscripts*, Cambridge, MA

Kahane, H. and Kahane, R. (1970–6), '[Abendland und Byzanz:] Sprache', *Reallexikon der Byzantinistik* 1: 345–640, Amsterdam

Kazhdan, A.P. (1974), *Sotsial'nyj sostav gospodstvuyuschego klassa Vizantii xi–xii vv.*, Moscow

Kempf, F., Beck, H.G., *et al.* (1969), 'The church in the age of feudalism', in H. Jedin and J. Dolan (eds.), *Handbook of Church History*, 3rd edn, trans. A. Biggs, New York

Kunze, K. (1969), *Studien zur Legende der heiligen Maria Aegyptiaca im deutschen Sprachgebiet* (Philologische Studien und Quellen, 49), Berlin

Laurent, V. (1978), 'Ein byzantinisches Bleisiegel aus Haithabu', *Berichte über die Ausgrabungen in Haithabu* 12: 36–9

Lewis, B. (1977), 'Sources for the economic history of the Middle East', in *Wirtschaftsgeschichte des Vorderen Orients in islamischer Zeit* i, Leiden, pp. 1–17

Lilie, R.J. (1976), *Die byzantinische Reaktion auf die Ausbreitung der Araber: Studien zur*

Strukturwandlung des byzantinischen Staates im 7. und 8. Jhd. (Miscellanea Byzantina Monacensia 22), Munich

Lilie, R. J. (1984), 'Die zweihundertjährige Reform. Zu den Anfängen der Themenorganisation im 7. und 8. Jahrhundert', *BSl* 45: 27–39 and 190–291

Llewellyn, P. (1981), 'The names of the Roman clergy, 401–1046', *Rivista di Storia della Chiesa in Italia* 35: 355–70

Loenertz, R. (1950), 'Le panégyrique de S. Denys l'Aréopagite par S. Michel le Syncelle', *An. Boll.* 68: 94–107

Loenertz, R. (1951), 'La légende parisienne de S. Denys l'Aréopagite. Sa genèse et son premier témoin', *An. Boll.* 69: 217–37

Loenertz, R. (1974), *'Constitutum Constantini.* Destination, destinataires, auteur, date', *Aevum* 48: 199–45

Lounghis, T.C. (1980), *Les ambassades byzantines en Occident depuis la fondation des états barbares jusqu'aux Croisades (407–1096),* Athens

Luzzati Laganà, F. (1982), 'Le firme greche nei documenti del Ducato di Napoli', *SM,* third series, 23: 729–52

McCormick, M. (1987), 'Byzantium's role in the formation of early medieval civilization: approaches and problems', *Illinois Classical Studies* 12: 207–20

McCormick, M. (1990), *Eternal Victory: Triumphal Rulership in Late Antiquity, Byzantium, and the early medieval West,* 2nd edn, Cambridge

McCormick, M. (1994a), 'Diplomacy and the Carolingian encounter with Byzantium down to the accession of Charles the Bald', in B. McGinn and W. Otten (eds.), *Eriugena: East and West. Papers of the Eighth International Colloquium of the Society for the Promotion of Eriugenian Studies,* Notre Dame

McCormick, M. (1994b), 'Textes, images et iconoclasme dans le cadre des relations entre Byzance et l'Occident carolingien', in *Settimane* 41: 95–158

Mango, C. (1973), 'La culture grecque et l'Occident au VIIIe siècle', *Settimane* 20: 683–721

Mango, C. (1975), 'The availability of books in the Byzantine empire', in *Byzantine Books and Bookmen,* Washington, DC, pp. 29–45

Mango, C. (1980), *Byzantium: The Empire of New Rome,* New York

Mango, C. (1981), 'Daily life in Byzantium', *JÖB* 31(1): 338–53

Mango, C. (1985), *Le développement urbain de Constantinople (IVe–VIIe siècles),* Paris

Mango, C. and Ševčenko, I. (1972), 'Three inscriptions of the reign of Anastasius I and Constantine V', *BZ* 65: 379–93

Margetić L. (1988), 'Quelques aspects du plaid de Rižana', *REB* 46: 125–34

Meersseman, G.G. (1963), *Kritische glossen op de griekse Theophilus-legende (7e eeuw) en haar latijnse vertaling (9e eeuw)* (Mededelingen van de koninklijke Vlaamse academie voor wetenschappen, letteren en schone kunsten van België, Klasse der letteren 25, no. 4), Brussels

Mordek, H. (1988), 'Rom, Byzanz und die Franken im 8. Jahrhundert', *Person und Gemeinschaft im Mittelalter: Karl Schmid zum fünfundsechzigsten Geburtstag,* Sigmaringen, pp. 123–56

Müller-Wiener, W. (1977), *Bildlexikon zur Topographie Istanbuls,* Tübingen

Mütherich, F. (1987), 'Das Verzeichnis eines griechischen Bilderzyklus in dem St-Galler Codex 48', *DOP* 41: 415–23

Nesbitt, J. and Oikonomidès, N. (1991), *Catalogue of Byzantine Seals at Dumbarton Oaks and in the Fogg Museum of Art* 1, Washington, DC

Obolensky, D. (1963), 'The principles and methods of Byzantine diplomacy', in *Actes du XIIe Congrès international des études byzantines* 1, Belgrade, pp. 45–61

Obolensky, D. (1988), 'The Balkans in the ninth century: barrier or bridge?', *Byzantinische Forschungen* 13: 47–66

Panella, C. (1989), 'Gli scambi nel mediterraneo occidentale dal IV al VII secolo dal punto di vista di alcune merci', in *Hommes et richesses dans l'empire byzantin: IVe–VIIe siècle*, Paris, pp. 129–41

Pellat, C. (1954), 'Ğāḥiẓiana, 1', *Arabica* 1: 153–65

Peri, V. (1971), 'Leone III e il "filioque". Echi del caso nell'agiografia greca', *Rivista di Storia della Chiesa in Italia* 25: 3–58

Philippart, G. (1974), 'Jean évêque d'Arezzo (IXe s.), auteur du "De assumptione" de Reichenau', *An. Boll.* 92: 345–6

Pomey, P., Long, L., *et al.* (1987–8), 'Recherches sous-marines', *Gallia Informations* 1: 1–78

Prinz, O. (1985), 'Eine frühe abendländische Aktualisierung der lateinischen Übersetzung des Pseudo-Methodios', *DA* 41: 1–23

Pryor, J.H. (1988), *Geography, Technology and War: Studies in the Maritime History of the Mediterranean, 649–1571*, Cambridge

Riedinger, R. (1989), *Der Codex Vindobonensis 418: seine Vorlage und seine Schreiber* (Instrumenta Patristica 17), Steenbrugge

Sansterre, J.M. (1982), *Les moines grecs et orientaux à Rome aux époques byzantine et carolingienne*, (Académie royale de Belgique, Mémoires de la classe des lettres, Collection in 8°, 2nd series, vol. 66, fasc. 1–2) Brussels

Sansterre, J.M. (1984), 'Où le diptyque consulaire de Clementinus fut-il employé à une fin liturgique?', *Byz* 54: 641–7

Sansterre, J.M. (1988), 'Le monachisme byzantin à Rome', *Settimane* 34, II: 701–50

Schieffer, T. (1935), *Die päpstlichen Legaten in Frankreich vom Vertrage von Meersen (870) bis zum Schisma von 1130* (Historische Studien 263), Berlin

Schreiner, P. (1988), 'Der byzantinische Bilderstreit: kritische Analyse der zeitgenössischen Meinungen und das Urteil der Nachwelt bis heute', *Settimane* 34, II: 319–407

Solier, Y. *et al.* (1981), 'Les épaves de Gruissan', *Archaeonautica* 3: 7–264

Speck, P. (1981), *Artabasdos, der rechtgläubiger Vorkämpfer der göttlichen Lehren* (Poikila Byzantina 2), Bonn

Stiernon, D. (1967), *Constantinople IV* (Histoire des conciles œcuméniques 5), Paris

Strunk, O. (1964), 'The Latin Antiphons for the Octave of the Epiphany', in F. Barišić (ed.), *Mélanges Ostrogorsky*, Belgrade, II, pp. 417–26

Venedikov, I. (1962), 'La population byzantine en Bulgarie au début du IXe siècle', *Byzbulg* 1: 261–77

Wendling, W. (1985), 'Die Erhebung Ludwigs d. Fr. zum Mitkaiser im Jahre 813 und ihre Bedeutung für die Verfassungsgeschichte des Frankenreiches', *FrSt* 19: 210–38

Winkelmann, F. (1987), *Quellenstudien zur herrschenden Klasse von Byzanz im 8. und 9. Jahrhundert* (Berliner byzantinistische Arbeiten 54), Berlin

Zettler, A. (1983), 'Cyrill u. Method im Reichenauer Verbrüderungsbuch', *FrSt* 17: 280–98

15 KINGSHIP AND ROYAL GOVERNMENT

Airlie, S. (1990), 'Bonds of power and bonds of association in the court circle of Louis the Pious', in Godman and Collins (1990), pp. 191–204
Althoff, G. (1990), *Verwandte, Freunde und Getreue*, Darmstadt
Anderson, P. (1974), *Passages from Antiquity to Feudalism*, London
Angenendt, A. (1984), *Kaiserherrschaft und Konigstaufe* (Arbeiten zur Frühmittelalter-forschung 15), Berlin and New York
Anton, H.H. (1968), *Fürstenspiegel und Herrscherethos in der Karolingerzeit*, Bonn
Bachrach, B. (1986), 'Some observations on the military administration of the Norman Conquest', *Anglo-Norman Studies* 8: 11–15
Barnwell, P. (1992), *Emperor, Prefects and Kings: The Roman West 395–565*, London
Bitterauf, T. (1905), *Die Traditionen des Hochstifts Freising*, Munich
Blackburn, M. (1993), 'King Alfred's vision for the coinage', in M. Blackburn and D.N. Dumville (eds.), *Kings, Currency, and Alliances: The History and Coinage of Southern England, AD 840–900*, Woodbridge
Borgolte, M. (1983), 'Die Geschichte der Grafengewalt im Elsass von Dagobert I bis Otto dem Grossen', *Zeitschrift fur die Geschichte des Oberrheins* 131: 3–54
Borgolte, M. (1986), *Die Grafen Alemanniens in merowingischer und karolingischer Zeit*, Sigmaringen
Bouchard, C. (1981), 'The origins of the French nobility: a reassessment', *AHR* 86: 501–52
Bouchard, C. (1986), 'Family structure and family consciousness among the aristocracy in the ninth to eleventh centuries', *Francia* 14: 639–58
Bouchard, C. (1988), 'Patterns of women's names in royal lineages, ninth–eleventh centuries', *Medieval Prosopography* 9(1): 1–32
Bowlus, C.R. (1987), 'Imre Boba's reconsideration of Moravia's early history and Arnulf of Carinthia's *Ostpolitik*', *Speculum* 67: 552–74
Brooks, N. (1984), *The Early History of the Church of Canterbury*, Leicester
Brühl, C.R. (1968), *Fodrum, Gistum, Servitium Regis*, Cologne
Brühl, C.R. (1975), *Palatium und Civitas: Studien zur Profantopographie spätantike Civitates vom 3. bis zum 13. Jht.* I: *Gallien*, Cologne and Vienna
Bullough, D. (1962), '"*Baiuli*" in the Carolingian *regnum Langobardorum* and the career of Abbot Waldo (†813)', *EHR* 77: 625–37
Bullough, D. (1965), *The Age of Charlemagne*, London
Bullough, D. (1975), '*Imagines regum* and their significance in the early medieval West', in G. Robertson and G. Henderson (eds.), *Studies in Memory of D. Talbot Rice*, Edinburgh, pp. 223–76
Bullough, D. (1985), '*Albuinus deliciosus Karoli regis:* Alcuin of York and the shaping of the early Carolingian court', in L. Fenske, W. Rösener and T. Zotz (eds.), *Institutionen, Kultur und Gesellschaft im Mittelalter: Festschrift für J. Fleckenstein*, Sigmaringen, pp. 73–92
Campbell, J. (1989), 'The sale of land and the economics of power in early England: problems and possibilities', *Haskins Society Journal* 1: 23–37
Collins, R. (1983), *Early Medieval Spain*, London
Coupland, S. (1990), 'Money and coinage under Louis the Pious', *Francia* 17: 23–54
Coupland, S. (1991), 'The early coinage of Charles the Bald', *Numismatic Chronicle*: 121–58

Davies, W. (1982), *Wales in the Early Middle Ages*, Studies in the Early History of Britain, Leicester

Davies, W. (1988), *Small Worlds*, London

Davies, W. (1990), 'Charles the Bald and Brittany', in Gibson and Nelson (1990), pp. 98–114

Davies, W. (1993), 'Celtic kingships in the early Middle Ages', in A. Duggan (ed.), *Kings and Kingship in Medieval Europe*, London

Davis, R.H.C. (1971), 'Alfred the Great: propaganda and truth', *History* 56: 169–82

De Jong, M. (1992), 'Power and humility in Carolingian society: the public penance of Louis the Pious', *EME* 1: 29–52

Delogu, P. (1980), 'Il regno longobardo', in P. Delogu, A. Guillou and G. Ortalli (eds.), *Longobardi e bizantini*, Turin

Depreux, P. (1992), 'Nithard et la *res publica*: un regard critique sur le règne de Louis le Pieux', *Médiévales* 22–3: 149–61

Deshman, R. (1980), 'The exalted servant: the ruler-theology of the prayer-book of Charles the Bald', *Viator* 11: 385–417

Devroey, J.-P. (1992), *Etudes sur le grand domaine carolingien*, London

Dhondt, J. (1948), *Etudes sur la naissance des principautés territoriales en France (IXe–Xe siècles)*, Bruges

Dumville, D. (1977), 'Kingship, genealogies and regnal lists', in P. Sawyer and I.N. Wood (eds.), *Early Medieval Kingship*, Leeds, pp. 72–104

Dunbabin, J. (1985), *France in the Making 843–1180*, Oxford

Durliat, J. (1984), 'Le polyptyque d'Irminon et l'impôt pour l'armée', *BEC* 141: 183–208

Durliat, J. (1990), *Les finances publiques de Dioclétien aux Carolingiens (284–889)*, Sigmaringen

Ehlers, J. (1976), 'Karolingische Tradition und frühes Nationalbewusstsein in Frankreich', *Francia* 4: 213–35

Enright, M.J. (1985), *Iona, Tara and Soissons: The Origin of the Royal Anointing Ritual*, Berlin

Ewig, E. (1956), 'Zum christlichen Königsgedanken im Frühmittelalter', in T. Mayer (ed.), *Das Königtum* (VuF 3), Constance, pp. 7–73

Ewig, E. (1965), 'Descriptio Franciae', in *Karl der Grosse* I, pp. 143–77

Faussner, H.C. (1988), *Die Staatsrechtliche Genesis Bayerns und Österreichs*, Sigmaringen

Fernandez-Armesto, F. (1992), 'The survival of a notion of *Reconquista* in late tenth- and eleventh-century León', in T. Reuter (ed.), *Warriors and Churchmen in the High Middle Ages*, London, pp. 123–44

Fleckenstein, J. (1959, 1966), *Die Hofkapelle der deutschen Könige*, 2 vols., Stuttgart

Flori, J. (1983), *L'idéologie du glaive: préhistoire de la chevalerie*, Geneva

Floriano, A.C. (1949, 1951), *Diplomática Española del Periodo Astur*, 2 vols., Oviedo

Fried, J. (1991), *Die Formierung Europas, 840–1046*, Munich

Ganshof, F.L. (1927), 'La "tractoria". Contribution à l'étude des origines du droit de gîte', *Tijdschrift voor Rechtsgeschiedenis* 8: 69–91

Ganshof, F.L. (1971), *The Carolingians and the Frankish Monarchy*, London

Geary, P. (1985), *Aristocracy in Provence*, Berlin

Geary, P. (1987), 'Germanic tradition and royal ideology in the ninth century: the "visio Karoli Magni"', *FrSt* 21: 274–94

Gerberding, R. (1987), *The Liber Historiae Francorum and the Rise of the Carolingians*, Oxford

Gibson M.T. and Nelson J.L. (eds.) (1990), *Charles the Bald: Court and Kingdom*, 2nd rev. edn, Aldershot

Godman, P. (1987), *Poets and Emperors*, Oxford

Godman, P. and Collins, R. (1990), *Charlemagne's Heir: New Perspectives on the Reign of Louis the Pious (814–840)*, Oxford

Goffart, W. (1986), *The Narrators of Barbarian History*, Princeton

Goffart, W. (1990), 'Charters earlier than 800 from French Collections', *Speculum* 65: 906–32

Gómez-Moreno, M. (1932), 'Las primeras crónicas de la Reconquista: el ciclo de Alfonso III', *Boletín de la Real Academia de la Historia* 100: 562–99

Goody, J. (1966), 'Introduction', in J. Goody (ed.), *Succession to High Office*, Cambridge

Guillot, O. (1990), 'Une *ordinatio* méconnue: le Capitulaire de 823–825', in Godman and Collins (1990), pp. 455–86

Hammer, C.J. (1989), '*Lex scripta* in early medieval Bavaria: use and abuse of the *Lex Baiuvariorum*', in E.B. King and S.J. Ridyard (eds.), *Law in Medieval Life and Thought*, Sewanee, pp. 185–95

Hannig, J. (1983), '*Pauperiores vassi de infra palatio?* Zur Entstehung der karolingischen Königsbotenorganisation', *MIÖG* 91: 309–74

Harmer, F. (1952; reprinted 1989), *Anglo-Saxon Writs*, Manchester

Hendy, M.F. (1988), 'From public to private: the western barbarian coinages as a mirror of the distintegration of late Roman state structures', *Viator* 19: 29–78

Hennebicque, R. (1981), 'Structures familiales et politiques au IXe siècle: un groupe familial de l'aristocratie franque', *Revue Historique* 265: 289–333

Hlawitschka, E. (1965), 'Die Vorfahren Karls des Grossen', in *Karl der Grosse* I, pp. 51–82

Hlawitschka, E. (1989), *Stirps Regia: Forschungen zu Königtum und Führungsschichten im früheren Mittelalter*, Frankfurt

Hodges, R. (1990), *Dark Age Economics*, 2nd edn, London

Hodges, R. and Hobley, B. (1988), *The Rebirth of Towns in the West AD 700–1050*, London

Hodges, R. and Whitehouse, D. (1983), *Mohammed, Charlemagne and the Origins of Europe*, London

Hodgson, A. (1993), 'Women in the Frankish church', unpublished University of London Ph.D. dissertation

Houben, H. (1970), '*Visio cuiusdam pauperculae mulieris:* Überlieferung und Herkunft eines frühmittelalterlichen Visionstextes', *Zeitschrift für die Geschichte des Oberrheins* 124: 31–42

Hughes, K. (1966), *The Church in Early Irish Society*, London

Jarnut, J. (1977), 'Studien über Herzog Odilo (736–748)', *MIÖG* 85: 273–84

Jarnut, J. (1984), 'Chlodwig und Clothar. Anmerkungen zu den Namen zweier Söhne Karls des Grossen', *Francia* 12: 645–51

Jarnut J. (1985), 'Die frühmittelalterliche Jagd unter rechts- und sozialgeschichtlichen Aspekten', *Settimane* 31, II: 765–808

Johanek, P. (1987), 'Der fränkische Handel der Karolingerzeit im Spiegel der

Schriftquellen', in K. Düwel (ed.), *Untersuchungen zu Handel und Verkehr der vor- und frühgeschichtlichen Zeit in Mittel- und Nordeuropa* (Abhandlungen der Akademie der Wissenschaften in Göttingen, phil.-hist. Klasse 156, part IV), pp. 7–68

Kaiser, R. (1981), *Bischofsherrschaft zwischen Königtum und Fürstenmacht: Studien zur bischöflichen Stadtherrschaft im westfränkisch-französischen Reich im früheren und hohen Mittelalter*, Bonn

Kantorowicz, E.H. (1946), *Laudes Regiae: A Study in Liturgical Acclamations and Medieval Ruler Worship*, Berkeley, CA

Kelly, S. (1992), 'Trading privileges from eighth-century England', *EME* 1: 3–28

Kessler, H. (1992), 'A lay abbot as patron: Count Vivian and the First Bible of Charles the Bald', *Settimane* 39: 647–75

Keynes, S. (1992), 'The Fonthill Letter', in M. Korhammer (ed.), with K. Reichl and H. Sauer, *Words, Texts and Manuscripts: Studies in Anglo-Saxon Culture presented to Helmut Gneuss*, Cambridge, pp. 53–97

Keynes, S. and Lapidge, M. (1983), *Alfred the Great: Asser's Life of Alfred and Other Contemporary Sources*, Harmondsworth

Kienast, W. (1968), *Studien über die französischen Volksstämme des Frühmittelalters*, Stuttgart

Kienast, W. (1990), *Die Fränkische Vasallität: Von den Hausmeiern bis zu Ludwig den Kind und Karl dem Einfältigen*, ed. P. Herde, Frankfurt

Kirby, D. (1991), *The Earliest English Kings*, London

Konecny, S. (1976), *Die Frauen des karolingischen Königshauses*, Vienna

Lammers, W. (1979), *Vestigia Medievalia: ausgewählte Aufsätze zur mittelalterlichen Historiographie, Landes- und Kirchengeschichte*, Wiesbaden

Leyser, K.J. (1982), *Medieval Germany and its Neighbours 900–1250*, London

Leyser, K.J. (1984), 'Early medieval canon law and the beginnings of knighthood', in L. Fenske, W. Rösener and T. Zotz (eds.), *Institutionem, Kultur und Gesellschaft im Mittelalter: Festschrift für J. Fleckenstein*, Sigmaringen, pp. 549–66

Linehan, P. (1992), *History and the Historians of Medieval Spain*, Cambridge

Lohrmann, D. (1976), 'Trois palais royaux de la vallée de l'Oise d'après les travaux des érudits mauristes: Compiègne, Choisy-au-Bac et Quierzy', *Francia* 4: 121–40

Loyn, H. (1977), *The Vikings in Britain*, London

Loyn, H. and Percival, J. (1975), *The Reign of Charlemagne*, London

Lynch, J. (1986), *Godparents and Kinship in Early Medieval Europe*, Princeton

McCormick, M. (1984), 'The liturgy of war in the early Middle Ages: crises, litanies and the Carolingian monarchy', *Viator* 15: 1–23

McCormick, M. (1986), *Eternal Victory: Triumphal Rulership in Late Antiquity, Byzantium and the Early Medieval West*, Cambridge

McKitterick, R. (1977), *The Frankish Church and the Carolingian Reforms*, London

McKitterick, R. (1980), 'Charles the Bald and his library: the patronage of learning', *EHR* 95: 28–47

McKitterick, R. (1983), *The Frankish Kingdoms under the Carolingians*, London

McKitterick, R. (1989), *The Carolingians and the Written Word*, Cambridge

Maddicott, J. (1992), 'Debate: trade, industry and the wealth of King Alfred. Reply', *Past and Present* 135: 164–88

Magnou-Nortier, E. (1976), *Foi et fidélité: recherches sur l'évolution des liens personnels chez les Francs du VIIe au IXe siècle*, Toulouse

Martindale, J. (1985), 'The kingdom of Aquitaine and the dissolution of the Carolingian fisc', *Francia* 11: 131–91

Martindale, J. (1990), 'Charles the Bald and the government of the kingdom of Aquitaine', in Gibson and Nelson (1990), pp. 115–38

Metcalf, D.M. (1967), 'The prosperity of north-western Europe in the eighth and ninth centuries', *EHR* 2nd series, 20: 344–57

Metcalf, D.M. (1990), 'A sketch of the currency in the time of Charles the Bald', in Gibson and Nelson (1990), pp. 65–97

Metcalf, D.M. and Northover, J.P. (1989), 'Coinage alloys from the time of Offa and Charlemagne to *c.* 864', *Numismatic Chronicle* 159: 101–20

Metz, W. (1960), *Das karolingische Reichsgut: Eine verfassungs- und verwaltungsgeschichtliche Untersuchung*, Berlin

Mordek, H. (1986a), 'Unbekannte Texte zur karolingischen Gesetzgebung. Ludwig der Fromme, Einhard und die *Capitula adhuc conferenda*', *DA* 42: 446–70

Mordek, H. (1986b), 'Karolingische Kapitularien', in H. Mordek (ed.), *Überlieferung und Geltung normativer Texte des frühen und hohen Mittelalters*, Sigmaringen, pp. 25–50

Nelson, J.L. (1986a), *Politics and Ritual in Early Medieval Europe*, London

Nelson, J.L. (1986b), 'Dispute settlement in Carolingian West Francia', in W. Davies and P. Fouracre (eds.), *The Settlement of Disputes in Early Medieval Europe*, Cambridge, pp. 45–64

Nelson, J.L. (1987), 'Carolingian royal ritual', in D. Cannadine and S. Price (eds.), *Rituals of Royalty: Power and Ceremonial in Traditional Societies*, Cambridge, pp. 137–80

Nelson, J.L. (1988a), 'Kingship and empire', in J.H. Burns (ed.), *The Cambridge History of Medieval Political Thought*, Cambridge, pp. 211–51, and reprinted in revised form in R. McKitterick (ed.), *Carolingian Culture: Emulation and Innovation*, Cambridge (1993), pp. 52–87

Nelson, J.L. (1988b), 'A tale of two princes: politics, text and ideology in a Carolingian annal', *Studies in Medieval and Renaissance History* 10: 105–41

Nelson, J.L. (1989a), 'Ninth-century knighthood: the evidence of Nithard', in C. Harper-Bill, C. Holdsworth and J.L. Nelson (eds.), *Studies in Medieval History presented to R. Allen Brown*, Woodbridge, pp. 255–66

Nelson, J.L. (1989b), 'Translating images of authority: the Christian Roman emperors in the Carolingian world', in M.M. Mackenzie and C. Roueché (eds.), *Images of Authority: Papers presented to Joyce Reynolds on the Occasion of her 70th birthday*, Cambridge, pp. 194–205

Nelson, J.L. (1990a), 'The last years of Louis the Pious', in Godman and Collins (1990), pp. 147–60

Nelson, J.L. (1990b), 'Literacy in Carolingian government', in R. McKitterick (ed.), *The Uses of Literacy in Early Medieval Europe*, Cambridge, pp. 258–96

Nelson, J.L. (1991a), *Ninth-Century Histories: The Annals of St-Bertin*, Manchester

Nelson, J.L. (1991b), '"Not bishops' bailiffs but lords of the earth"', in D. Wood (ed.), *The Church and Sovereignty: Essays in Honour of Michael Wilks*, Oxford

Nelson, J.L. (1991c), 'La famille de Charlemagne', *Byzantion. Revue Internationale des Etudes Byzantines* 61: 194–212

Nelson, J.L. (1992a), *Charles the Bald*, London

Nelson, J.L. (1992b), 'The intellectual in politics: context, content and authorship in the Capitulary of Coulaines', in L. Smith and B. Ward (eds.), *Intellectual Life in the Middle Ages: Essays Presented to Margaret Gibson*, London, pp. 1–14

Nelson, J.L. (1993a), 'Women at the court of Charlemagne: a case of monstrous regiment?', in J.C. Parsons (ed.), *Medieval Queenship*, New York, pp. 43–62

Nelson, J.L. (1993b), 'The Franks, the Martyrology of Usuard and the martyrs of Córdoba', *Studies in Church History* 30: 67–80

Nelson, J.L. (1993c), 'The political ideas of Alfred of Wessex', in A. Duggan (ed.), *Kings and Kingship*, London

Nelson, J.L. (1995), 'The search for peace in a time of war: the Carolingian *Bruderkrieg*, 840–843', in *VuF* 42, ed. J. Fried, Sigmaringen, forthcoming

Nightingale, J. (1988), 'Monasteries and their patrons in the dioceses of Trier, Metz and Toul, 850–1000', Oxford University D.Phil. thesis

Nonn, U. (1970), 'Das Bild Karls Martells in der lateinischen Quellen vornehmlich des 8. und 9. Jhdts', *FrSt* 4: 106–14

Odegaard, C. (1945), *Vassi and Fideles in the Carolingian Empire*, Cambridge, MA

Pirenne, H. (1939), *Mohammed and Charlemagne*, English trans. by B. Miall, London

Prinz, F. (1971), *Klerus und Krieg im frühen Mittelalter*, Stuttgart

Randsborg, K. (1980), *The Viking Age in Denmark*, London

Reuter, T. (1982), 'The "imperial church system" of the Ottonian and Salian rulers: a reconsideration', *Journal of Ecclesiastical History* 32: 347–74

Reuter, T. (1985), 'Plunder and tribute in the Carolingian Empire', *TRHS* 35: 75–94

Reuter, T. (1990), 'The end of Carolingian military expansion', in Godman and Collins (1990), pp. 391–405

Reuter, T. (1991), *Germany in the Early Middle Ages*, London

Reuter, T. (1992), *Ninth-Century Histories: The Annals of Fulda*, Manchester

Reynolds, S. (1984), *Kingdoms and Communities in Western Europe, 900–1300*, Oxford

Reynolds, S. (1994), *Fiefs and Vassals*, Oxford

Ritzer, K. (1962), *Formen, Riten und religiöses Brauchtum der Eheschliessung in den christlichen Kirchen des ersten Jahrtausends*, Münster

Rouche, M. (1984), 'Les repas de fête à l'époque carolingienne', in D. Menjot (ed.), *Manger et boire au moyen âge, Actes du Colloque de Nice (15–17 octobre 1982)* 1: *Aliments et société*, Nice, pp. 265–96

Sanchez-Albornoz, C. (1972), *Orígenes de la Nacion Española: El Reino de Asturias* I–III, Oviedo

Sawyer, P.H. (1971), *The Age of the Vikings*, 2nd edn, London

Sawyer, P. (1977), 'Kings and merchants', in P. Sawyer and I.N. Wood (eds.), *Early Medieval Kingship*, Leeds, pp. 139–58

Sawyer, P.H. (1982), *Kings and Vikings*, London

Schieffer, R. (1990), 'Väter und Söhne im Karolingerhause', in *Beiträge zur Geschichte des Regnum Francorum* (Beihefte der Francia 22), Paris, pp. 149–64

Schlesinger, W. (1965), 'Die Auflösung des Karlsreiches', in *Karl der Grosse* 1, pp. 792–858

Schlunk, H. (1947), 'Arte Asturiano', *Ars Hispaniae* 11, Madrid

Schneider, G. (1973), *Erzbischof Fulco von Reims (883–900) und das Frankenreich*, Munich

Schneidmüller, B. (1979), *Karolingische Tradition und frühes französisches Königtum:*

Untersuchungen zur Herrschaftslegitimation der westfränkisch-französischen Monarchie im 10. Jahrhundert, Frankfurt

Schramm, P.E. (1954–6), *Herrschaftszeichen und Staatssymbolik* (MGH Schriften 13), 3 vols., Stuttgart

Schramm, P.E. (1960), *Der König von Frankreich: Das Wesen der Monarchie vom 9. zum 16. Jahrhundert*, 2 vols., 2nd edn, Darmstadt

Schramm, P.E. (1968), *Kaiser, Könige und Päpste*, 4 vols., Stuttgart

Schramm, P.E. and Mütherich, F. (1962), *Denkmale der deutschen Könige und Kaiser*, Munich

Sears, E. (1990), 'Louis the Pious as *Miles Christi*: the dedicatory image in Hrabanus Maurus's *De laudibus sanctae crucis*', in Godman and Collins (1990), pp. 605–28

Siems, H. (1992), *Handel und Wucher im Spiegel frühmittelalterlicher Rechtsquellen* (MGH Schriften 35), Hanover

Smith, J.M.H. (1992), *Province and Empire: Brittany and the Carolingians*, Cambridge

Smyth, A.P. (1977), *Scandinavian Kings in the British Isles 850–880*, Oxford

Spufford, P. (1988), *Money and its Use in Medieval Europe*, Cambridge

Stafford, P. (1981), 'The king's wife in Wessex', *Past and Present* 91: 5–27

Stafford, P. (1983), *Queens, Concubines and Dowagers: The King's Wife in the Early Middle Ages*, Athens, GA

Stafford, P. (1990), 'Charles the Bald, Judith and England', in Gibson and Nelson (1990), pp. 139–53

Stoclet, A. (1986), 'Gisèle, Kisyla, Chelles, Benediktbeuren et Kochel. Scriptoria, bibliothèques et politique à l'époque carolingienne. Une mise au point', *RB* 96: 250–70

Tessier, G. (1955), Introduction to *Receuil des Actes de Charles II le Chauve* III, Paris

Verhulst, A. (1989), 'The origins of towns in the Low Countries and the Pirenne thesis', *Past and Present* 122: 3–35

Wallace-Hadrill, J.M. (1971), *Early Germanic Kingship in England and on the Continent*, Oxford

Wallace-Hadrill, J.M. (1975), *The Vikings in Francia*, The Stenton Lecture for 1974, Reading, reprinted in Wallace-Hadrill (1976), pp. 217–36

Wallace-Hadrill, J.M. (1976), *Early Medieval History*, Oxford

Wallace-Hadrill, J.M. (1983), *The Frankish Church*, Oxford

Ward, E. (1990a), 'Caesar's wife: the career of the Empress Judith, 819–29', in Godman and Collins (1990), pp. 205–27

Ward, E. (1990b), 'Agobard of Lyons and Paschasius Radbertus as critics of the Empress Judith', *Studies in Church History* 27: 15–25

Wemple, S.F. (1981), *Women in Frankish Society*, Philadelphia

Werner, K.-F. (1959), 'Untersuchungen zur Frühzeit des französischen Fürstentums (9.–10. Jht.), IV', *Die Welt als Geschichte* 19: 146–93

Werner, K.-F. (1965), 'Bedeutende Adelsfamilien im Reiche Karls des Grossen', in *Karl der Grosse* I, pp. 83–142

Werner, K.-F. (1967), 'Die Nachkommen Karls des Grossen', in *Karl der Grosse* IV, pp. 403–79

Werner, K.-F. (1978), 'Important noble families in the kingdom of Charlemagne', in T. Reuter (ed.), *The Medieval Nobility*, pp. 137–202

Werner, K.-F. (1980), '*Missus-mancio-comes* entre l'administration centrale et l'administration locale de l'empire carolingien', in W. Paravicini and K.-F. Werner (eds.), *Histoire comparée de l'administration (IVe–XVIIIe siècle)* (Beihefte der Francia 9), Munich, pp. 191–239

Werner, K.-F. (1985), 'Du nouveau sur un vieux thème. Les origines de la "noblesse" et de la "chevalerie"', *Académie des Inscriptions et Belles-Lettres*, Comptes-rendus 1985, Paris, pp. 186–200

Werner, K.-F. (1990), '*Hludovicus Augustus*: gouverner l'empire chrétien – idées et réalités', in Godman and Collins (1990), pp. 3–124

Wickham, C. (1981), *Early Medieval Italy*, London

Wickham, C. (1991), 'Syntactic structures: social theory for historians', *Past and Present* 132: 188–203

Wolfram, H. (1973), 'Lateinische Herrschertitel im neunten und zehnten Jhdt.', in H. Wolfram (ed.), *Intitulatio II. Lateinische Herrscher- und Fürstentitel im neunten und zehnten Jhdt.*, Vienna, Cologne and Graz, pp. 19–178

Wollasch, J. (1984), 'Kaiser und Könige als Brüder der Mönche. Zum Herrscherbild im liturgischen Handschriften des 9. bis 11. Jhdts', *DA* 40: 1–20

Wood, I.N. (1987), 'Christians and pagans in' ninth-century Scandinavia', in B. Sawyer, P. Sawyer and I. Wood (eds.), *The Christianization of Scandinavia*, Alingsås, pp. 36–67

Wood, I.N. (1993a), *Merovingian Gaul*, London

Wood, I.N. (1993b), *The Merovingian Kingdoms 450–751*, London

Wood, I.N. and Harries, J. (eds.), (1993), *The Theodosian Code*, Woodbridge.

Wormald, P. (1977), '*Lex scripta et verbum regis*: legislation and Germanic kingship from Euric to Cnut', in P. Sawyer and I.N. Woods (eds.) *Early Medieval Kingship*, Leeds, pp. 105–38

Wormald, P. (1982), 'The ninth century', in J. Campbell (ed.), *The Anglo-Saxons*, London, pp. 132–59

Wormald, P. (1986), 'Celtic and Anglo-Saxon kingship: some further thoughts', in P. Szarmach (ed.), *Sources of Anglo-Saxon Culture*, Binghampton, NY, pp. 151–83

Yeandle, D.N. (1989), 'The *Ludwigslied*: king, church and context', in J. Flood and D.N. Yeandle (eds.), *mit regulu bituungan: Neue Arbeiten zur althochdeutschen Poesie und Sprache*, Goppingen, pp. 18–79

Zotz, T. (1990), 'Grundlagen und Zentren der Königsherrschaft im deutschen Sudwesten in karolingischer und ottonischer Zeit', in H.-U. Nuber, K. Schmid, H. Steuer and T. Zotz (eds.), *Archäologie und Geschichte des ersten Jahrtausends in Sudwestdeutschlands*, Sigmaringen, pp. 275–93

16 THE ARISTOCRACY

Airlie, S. (1985), 'The political behaviour of the secular magnates in Francia, 829–879', Oxford University D.Phil. thesis

Airlie, S. (1990), 'Bonds of power and bonds of association in the court circle of Louis the Pious', in Godman and Collins (1990), Oxford, pp. 191–204

Airlie, S. (1992), 'The anxiety of sanctity: St Gerald of Aurillac and his maker', *Journal of Ecclesiastical History* 43: 372–95

Althoff, G. (1990), *Verwandte, Freunde und Getreue*, Darmstadt

Arnold, B. (1991), *Princes and Territories in Medieval Germany*, Cambridge

Borgolte, M. (1983), 'Die Geschichte der Grafengewalt im Elsass von Dagobert I. bis Otto dem Grossen', *Zeitschrift für die Geschichte des Oberrheins* 131: 3–54

Borgolte, M. (1984a), *Geschichte der Grafschaften Alemanniens in fränkischer Zeit*, Sigmaringen

Borgolte, M. (1984b), 'Gedenkstiftungen in St Galler Urkunden', in K. Schmid and J. Wollasch (eds.), *Memoria: Der geschichtliche Zeugniswert des liturgischen Gedenkens im Mittelalter*, Munich, pp. 578–602

Borgolte, M. (1986), *Die Grafen Alemanniens in merowingischer und karolingischer Zeit*, Sigmaringen

Borgolte, M. (1988), 'Buchhorn und die Welfen', *Zeitschrift für Württembergische Landesgeschichte* 47: 39–69

Bosl, K. (1969), *Franken um 800* (2nd edn), Munich

Bouchard, C. (1986), 'Family structure and family consciousness among the aristocracy in the ninth to eleventh centuries', *Francia* 14: 639–58

Brühl, C. (1990), *Deutschland-Frankreich: Die Geburt zweier Völker*, Cologne and Vienna

Brunner, K. (1979), *Oppositionelle Gruppen im Karolingzeit*, Vienna

Bullough, D. (1970), Europae pater: Charlemagne and his achievements in the light of recent scholarship', *EHR* 85: 59–105

Cardot, F. (1983), 'Le pouvoir aristocratique et le sacré au haut moyen-âge. Sainte Odile et les Etichonides dans la *Vita Odiliae*', *MA* 89: 173–93

Constable, G. (1972), 'The *Liber Memorialis* of Remiremont', *Speculum* 48: 260–77

Devailly, G. (1973), *Le Berry du Xe siècle au milieu du XIIIe*, Paris

Duby, G. (1953), *La société aux XIe et XIIe siècles dans la région mâconnaise*, Paris

Fichtenau, H. (1984), *Lebensordnungen des 10. Jahrhunderts* (Monographien zur Geschichte des Mittelalters 30), Stuttgart

Fichtenau, H. (1991), *Living in the Tenth Century*, translation of Fichtenau (1984) by P. Geary, Chicago

Fleckenstein, J. (1957), 'Über die Herkunft der Welfen und ihre Anfänge in Süddeutschland', in G. Tellenbach (1957a), pp. 71–136

Freed, J. (1986), 'Reflections on the medieval German nobility', *AHR* 91: 553–75

Geary, P. (1985), *Aristocracy in Provence: The Rhône Basin at the Dawn of the Carolingian Age*, Stuttgart and Philadelphia

Gerberding, R. (1987), *The Rise of the Carolingians and the 'Liber Historiae Francorum'*, Oxford

Gockel, M. (1970), *Karolingische Königshöfe am Mittelrhein* (Veröffentlichungen des Max-Plancks-Instituts für Geschichte 31), Göttingen

Goetz, H.-W. (1983), 'Nobilis. Der Adel im Selbstverständnis der Karolingerzeit', *Vierteljahrsschrift für Sozial- und Wirtschaftsgeschichte* 70: 153–91

Goetz, H.-W. (1986), *Leben im Mittelalter vom 7. bis 13. Jahrhundert*, Munich

Hartung, W. (1988a), 'Adel, Erbrecht, Schenkung. Die strukturellen Ursachen der frühmittelalterlichen Besitzübertragungen an die Kirche', in F. Seibt (ed.), *Gesellschaftsgeschichte: Festschrift für Karl Bosl zum 80. Geburtstag*, Munich, pp. 417–38

Hartung, W. (1988b), 'Tradition und Namengebung im frühen Mittelalter', in I. Eberl (ed.), *Früh- und hochmittelalterlicher Adel in Schwaben und Bayern* (Regio 1), Sigmaringendorf, pp. 23–79

Heidrich, I. (1988), 'Von Plektrud zu Hildegard. Beobachtungen zum Besitzrecht adliger Frauen im Frankenreich des 7. und 8. Jahrhunderts und zur politischen Rolle der Frauen der frühen Karolinger', *RhVjb* 52: 1–15

Hennebicque, R. (1981), 'Structures familiales et politiques au ixe siècle: un groupe familiale de l'aristocratie franque', *Revue Historique* 265: 289–333

Hennebicque-Le Jan, R. (1989), 'Prosopographica neustrica: les agents du roi en Neustrie de 639 à 840', in H. Atsma (ed.) *La Neustrie* 1, Sigmaringen, pp. 231–69

Hlawitschka, E. (1960), *Franken, Alemannen, Bayern und Burgunder in Oberitalien, 774–962*, Freiburg

Hlawitschka, E. (1969), *Die Anfänge des Hauses Habsburg-Lothringen: Genealogische Untersuchungen zur Geschichte Lothringens und des Reiches im 9., 10. und 11. Jahrhundert*, Saarbrücken

Hlawitschka, E. (1986), *Vom Frankenreich zur Formierung der europäischen Staaten- und Völkergemeinschaft 840–1046*, Darmstadt

Holt, J.C. (1982), 'Feudal society and the family in early medieval England: 1. The revolution of 1066', *TRHS* 5th series, 32: 193–212

Krah, A. (1987), *Absetzungsverfahren als Spiegelbild von Königsmacht*, Aalen

Kuchenbuch, L. (1978), *Bäuerliche Gesellschaft und Klosterherrschaft im 9. Jahrhundert*, Wiesbaden

Leyser, K. (1968), 'The German aristocracy from the ninth to the early twelfth century: a historical and cultural sketch', *Past and Present* 41: 25–53, reprinted in Leyser (1982), pp. 161–89

Leyser, K. (1982), *Medieval Germany and its Neighbours 900–1250*, London

McKitterick, R. (1989), *The Carolingians and the Written Word*, Cambridge

Martindale, J. (1977), 'The French aristocracy in the early middle ages: a reappraisal', *Past and Present* 75: 5–45

Martindale, J. (1990), 'The nun Immena and the foundation of the abbey of Beaulieu: a woman's prospects in the Carolingian church', in W.J. Shields and D. Wood (eds.), *Women in the Church* (Studies in Church History 27), Oxford, pp. 27–42

Metz, W. (1965), 'Miszellen zur Geschichte der Widonen und Salier, vornehmlich in Deutschland', *HJb* 85: 1–27

Murray, A.C. (1983), *Germanic Kinship Structure*, Toronto

Nelson, J.L. (1985), 'Public *Histories* and private history in the work of Nithard', *Speculum* 60: 251–93, reprinted in Nelson (1986), pp. 195–237

Nelson, J.L. (1986), *Politics and Ritual in Early Medieval Europe*, London

Nelson, J.L. (1992), *Charles the Bald*, London

Niermeyer, J.F. (1976), *Mediae Latinitatis Lexicon Minus*, Leiden

Nightingale, J. (1988), 'Monasteries and their patrons in the dioceses of Trier, Metz and Toul', Oxford University D.Phil. thesis

Oexle, O.G. (1988), 'Haus und Ökonomie im früheren Mittelalter', in G. Althoff, D. Geuenich, O.G. Oexle and J. Wollasch (eds.), *Person und Gemeinschaft im Mittelalter: Karl Schmid zum fünfundsechzigsten Geburtstag*, Sigmaringen, pp. 101–22

Patlagean, E. (1984), 'Les débuts d'une aristocratie byzantine et le témoignage de l'historiographie: système des noms et liens de parenté aux ixe–xe siècles', in M. Angold (ed.), *The Byzantine Aristocracy: IX to XIII Centuries* (BAR International Series 221), Oxford, pp. 23–43

Poupardin, R. (1900), 'Les grandes familles comtales à l'époque carolingienne', *Revue Historique* 72: 72–95

Reuter, T. (1991), *Germany in the Early Middle Ages c. 800–1056*, London

Reuter, T. (ed.) (1979), *The Medieval Nobility*, Amsterdam, New York and Oxford

Rösener, W. (1989), 'Strukturformen der adligen Grundherrschaft in der Karolingerzeit', in W. Rösener (ed.), *Strukturen der Grundherrschaft im frühen Mittelalter* (Veröffentlichungen des Max-Planck-Instituts für Geschichte 92), Göttingen, pp. 126–80

Schmid, K. (1957), 'Zur Problematik von Familie, Sippe und Geschlecht, Haus und Dynastie beim Mittelalterlichen Adel', *Zeitschrift für die Geschichte des Oberrheins* 105: 1–62, reprinted in Schmid (1983), pp. 183–244

Schmid, K. (1959), 'Uber die Struktur des Adels im früheren Mittelalter', *Jahrbuch für fränkische Landesforschung* 19: 1–23, reprinted in Schmid (1983), pp. 245–67; trans. in Reuter (1979), pp. 37–59

Schmid, K. (1964), 'Die Nachfahren Widukinds', *DA* 20: 1–47, reprinted in Schmid (1983), pp. 59–105

Schmid, K. (1965), 'Religiöses und sippengebundenes Gemeinschaftsbewusstsein im frühmittelalterliche Gedenkbucheinträgen', *DA* 21: 18–81, reprinted in Schmid (1983), pp. 532–97

Schmid, K. (1974), 'Programmatisches zur Erforschung der mittelalterlichen Personengruppen', *FrSt* 8: 116–30

Schmid, K. (1976), 'Zur historischen Bestimmung des ältesten eintrags im St Gallen Verbrüderungsbuch', *Alemannica, Landeskundliche Beiträge: Festschrift für Bruno Boesch zum 65. Geburtstag. Alemannisches Jahrbuch 1973/1975*, Baden, pp. 500–32, reprinted in Schmid (1983), pp. 481–513

Schmid, K. (1983), *Gebetgedenken und adliges Selbstverständnis im Mittelalter*, Sigmaringen

Schmid, K. (1988), 'Adelssitze und Adelsgeschlechter rund um dem Bodensee', *Zeitschrift für Württembergische Landesgeschichte* 47: 9–37

Störmer, W. (1973), *Früher Adel: Studien zur politischen Führungsschicht im Fränkisch-Deutschen Reich vom 8. bis 11. Jahrhundert* (Monographien zur Geschichte des Mittelalters 6), Stuttgart

Tellenbach, G. (1939), *Königtum und Stämme in der Werdezeit des Deutschen Reiches*, Weimar

Tellenbach, G. (1957a), 'Uber die ältesten Welfen im West- und Ostfrankenreich', in Tellenbach (1957b), pp. 335–40

Tellenbach, G. (1979), 'Die geistigen und politischen Grundlagen der karolingischen Thronfolge', *FrSt* 13: 184–302

Tellenbach, G. (ed.) (1957b), *Studien und Vorarbeiten zur Geschichte des Grossfränkischen und Frühdeutschen Adels*, Freiburg im Breisgau

Theis, L. (1990), *L'héritage des Charles: de la mort de Charlemagne aux environs de l'an mil* (Nouvelle histoire de la France médiévale 2), Paris

Tremp, E. (1988), *Studien zu den Gesta Hludowici imperatoris des Trierer Chorbischofs Thegan* (MGH Schriften 32), Hanover

Vollmer, F. (1957), 'Die Etichonen', in Tellenbach (1957b), pp. 137–84

Wemple, S. (1981), *Women in Frankish Society: Marriage and the Cloister 500–900*, Philadelphia

Werner, K.-F. (1959), 'Untersuchungen zur Frühzeit des französischen Fürstentums (9.–10. Jahrhundert) IV', *Die Welt als Geschichte* 19: 146–93

Werner, K.-F. (1965), 'Bedeutende Adelsfamilien im Reich Karls des Grossen', in *Karl der Grosse* I, pp. 83–142; reprinted in Werner (1984) and translated in Reuter (1979), pp. 137–202

Werner, K.-F. (1984), *Vom Frankenreich zur Entfaltung Deutschlands und Frankreichs*, Sigmaringen

Werner, K.-F. (1986), 'Un poème contemporain consacré à la mémoire de Richard le Justicier', *Annales de Bourgogne* 58: 75–7

Werner, M. (1982), *Adelsfamilien im Umkreis der frühen Karolinger: Die Verwandtschaft Irminas von Oeren und Adelas von Pfalzel* (VuF, Sonderband 28), Sigmaringen

Wickham, C. (1981), *Early Medieval Italy*, London

Wilsdorf, C. (1964), 'Les Etichonids aux temps carolingiens et ottoniens', *Bulletin Philologique et Historique du Comité des Travaux Historiques et Scientifiques* 89: 1–33

Wollasch, J. (1957), 'Eine adlige Familie des frühen Mittelalters. Ihr Selbstverständnis und ihre Wirklichkeit', *Archiv für Kulturgeschichte* 39: 150–88

Zotz, T. (1988), 'Grafschaftsverfassung und Personengeschichte. Zu einem neuen Werk über das karolingerzeitliche Alemannien', *Zeitschrift für die Geschichte des Oberrheins* 36: 1–16

17 SOCIAL AND MILITARY INSTITUTIONS

General works

Althoff, G. (1990), *Verwandte, Freunde und Getreue: Zum politischen Stellenwert der Gruppenbindungen im früheren Mittelalter*, Darmstadt

Barni, G.L. and Fasoli, G. (1971), *L'Italia nell'alto medioevo* (Società e costume 3) Turin

Boba, I. (1967), *Nomads, Northmen and Slavs: Eastern Europe in the Ninth Century* (Slavo-Orientalia 2), Wiesbaden

Bosl, K. (1964), *Frühformen der Gesellschaft im mittelalterlichen Europa: Ausgewählte Beiträge zu einer Strukturanalyse der mittelalterlichen Welt*, Munich and Vienna

Bosl, K. (1969a), *Franken um 800: Strukturanalyse einer fränkischen Königsprovinz*, Munich

Bosl, K. (ed.) (1967), *Handbuch der Geschichte der böhmischen Länder* I, Stuttgart

Boussard, J. (1968), *Charlemagne et son temps* (L'univers des connaissances 32), Paris

Campbell, J. (ed.) (1982), *The Anglo-Saxons*, Oxford

Collins, R. (1983), *Early Medieval Spain: Unity in Diversity, 400–1000*, London

Davies, W. (1982), *Wales in the Early Middle Ages*, Leicester

Dickinson, W.C. (1977), *Scotland from the Earliest Times to 1603*, Oxford

Dodgshon, R.A. (1981), *Land and Society in Early Scotland*, Oxford

Dollinger, P. (1982), *Der bayerische Bauernstand vom 9. bis zum 13. Jahrhundert*, Munich

Duby, G. (1973), *Guerriers et paysans, VIIe – XIIe siècle: premier essor de l'économie européenne*, London

Dufourcq, Ch.-E. and Gautier-Dalché, J. (1976), *Histoire économique et sociale de l'Espagne chrétienne au moyen âge*, Paris

Faviaux, J. (1986), *De l'empire romain à la féodalité: droit et institutions* I, Paris

Felio Montfort, G. (1972), 'El condado de Barcelona en los siglos ix y x. Organisación territorial y económico-social', *Cuadernos de Historia Económica de Cataluña* 7: 9–32

Fichtenau, H. (1949), *Das karolingische Imperium: Soziale und geistige Problematik eines Grossreiches*, Zurich; English trans., *The Carolingian Empire*, Oxford (1968)

Finberg, H.P.R. (ed.) (1972), *The Agrarian History of England and Wales* i, Cambridge and New York

Fossier, R. (1970), *Histoire sociale de l'Occident médiéval*, Paris

Fossier, R. (1982), *Le moyen âge* i, Paris

Fossier, R. (1991), *La société médiévale*, Paris

Freed, J.B. (1992), 'Medieval German social history. Generalizations and particularism', *Central European History* 25: 1–26

Ganshof, F.-L. (1968a), *Frankish Institutions under Charlemagne*, Providence, Rhode Island

Glick, T.F. (1979), *Islamic and Christian Spain in the Early Middle Ages: Comparative Perspectives on Social and Cultural Formation*, Princeton

Henning, F.-W. (1991), *Handbuch der Wirtschafts- und Sozialgeschichte Deutschlands* i: *Deutsche Wirtschafts- und Sozialgeschichte im Mittelalter und in der frühen Neuzeit*, Paderborn, Munich, Vienna and Zurich

Herlihy, D. (1978a), *The Social History of Italy and Western Europe, 700–1500*, London

Jarnut, J. (1979), *Bergamo 568–1098: Verfassungs-, Sozial- und Wirtschaftsgeschichte einer lombardischen Stadt im Mittelalter* (Vierteljahrschrift für Sozial- und Wirtschaftsgeschichte, Beiheft 67), Wiesbaden

Kaiser, R. (1981), *Bischofsherrschaft zwischen Königtum und Fürstenmacht: Studien zur bischöflichen Stadtherrschaft im westfränkisch-französischen Reich im frühen und hohen Mittelalter* (Pariser Historische Studien 17), Bonn

Keller, H. (1979), *Adelsherrschaft und städtische Gesellschaft in Oberitalien, 9.–12. Jahrhundert* (Bibliothek des Deutschen Historischen Instituts in Rom 52) Tübingen

Lewis, A. R. (1965), *The Development of Southern French and Catalan Society, 718–1050*, Austin

Loyn, H.R. (1962), *Anglo-Saxon England and the Norman Conquest*, London

Lund, N. (1981), 'Viking Age society in Denmark – evidence and theory', in N. Skyum-Nielsen and N. Lund (eds.), *Danish Medieval History: New Currents*, Copenhagen, pp. 22–35

Sánchez-Albornoz, C. (1980), *La España cristiana de los siglos VIII al XI* i (Historia de España 7), Madrid

Skyum-Nielsen, N. and Lund, N. (eds.) (1981), *Danish Medieval History: New Currents*, Copenhagen

Staab, F. (1975), *Untersuchungen zur Gesellschaft am Mittelrhein in der Karolingerzeit* (Geschichtliche Landeskunde 11), Wiesbaden

Stafford, P. (1985), *The East Midlands in the Early Middle Ages* (Studies in the Early History of Britain), Leicester

Van Houtte, J. (ed.) (1980), *Handbuch der europäischen Wirtschafts- und Sozialgeschichte* ii, Stuttgart

Wickham, C. (1981), *Early Medieval Italy: Central Power and Local Society, 400–1000*, London and Basingstoke

Wickham, C. (1994) *Land and Power: Studies in Italian and European Social History, 400–1200*, Rome

Zettel, H. (1976), *Das Bild der Normannen und der Normanneneinfälle in westfränkischen, ostfränkischen und angelsächsischen Quellen des 8.–11. Jahrhunderts*, Munich

The social order

Social theory

Bosl, K. (1963), 'Potens und Pauper. Begriffsgeschichtliche Studien zur gesellschaftlichen Differenzierung im frühen Mittelalter und zum "Pauperismus" des Hochmittelalters', in A. Bergengruen and L. Deike (eds.), *Alteuropa und die moderne Gesellschaft: Festschrift Otto Brunner*, Göttingen, pp. 60–87

Bosl, K. (1969b), 'Kasten, Stände, Klassen im mittelalterlichen Deutschland. Zur Problematik soziologischer Begriffe und ihrer Anwendung auf die mittelalterliche Gesellschaft', *Zeitschrift für bayerische Landesgeschichte* 32: 477–94

Dinzelbacher, P. (1979), 'Reflexionen irdischer Sozialstrukturen in mittelalterlichen Jenseitsschilderungen', *Archiv für Kulturgeschichte* 61: 16–34

Duby, G. (1978), *Les trois ordres ou l'imaginaire du féodalisme*, Paris

Goetz, H.-W. (1981), '"Unterschichten" im Gesellschaftsbild karolingischer Geschichtsschreiber und Hagiographen', in H. Mommsen and W. Schulze (eds.), *Vom Elend der Handarbeit: Probleme historischer Unterschichtenforschung*, Stuttgart, pp. 108–30

Iogna-Prat, D. (1986), 'Le "baptême" du schéma des trois ordres fonctionnels. L'apport de l'école d'Auxerre dans la seconde moitié du ixe siècle', *Annales ESC* 41: 101–26

Mitterauer, M. (1977), 'Probleme der Stratifikation in mittelalterlichen Gesellschaftssystemen', in J. Kocka (ed.), *Theorien in der Praxis des Historikers*, Göttingen, pp. 13–43

Oexle, O.G. (1978), 'Die funktionale Dreiteilung der "Gesellschaft" bei Adalbero von Laon. Deutungsschemata der sozialen Wirklichkeit im früheren Mittelalter', *FrSt* 12: 1–54

Oexle, O.G. (1987), 'Deutungsschemata der sozialen Wirklichkeit im frühen und hohen Mittelalter. Ein Beitrag zur Geschichte des Wissens', in F. Graus (ed.), *Mentalitäten im Mittelalter: Methodische und inhaltliche Probleme* (Vorträge und Forschungen 35), Sigmaringen, pp. 65–117

Tellenbach, G. (1972), 'Irdischer Stand und Heilserwartung im Denken des Mittelalters', in *Festschrift Hermann Heimpel* II (Veröffentlichungen des Max-Planck-Instituts für Geschichte 361, 2), Göttingen, pp. 1–16

Wunder, H. (1978), 'Probleme der Stratifikation in mittelalterlichen Gesellschaftssystemen. Ein Diskussionsbeitrag zu Thesen von M. Mitterauer', *Geschichte und Gesellschaft* 4: 542–50

Social classes

Bonassie, P. (1991), *From Slavery to Feudalism in South-Western Europe*, Paris

Goetz, H.-W. (1983), '"Nobilis". Der Adel im Selbstverständnis der Karolingerzeit', *Vierteljahrschrift für Sozial- und Wirtschaftsgeschichte* 70: 153–91

Hennebicque, R. (1981), 'Structures familiales et politiques au ixe siècle: en groupe familiale du l'aristocratie franque, *Revue Historique* 265: 289–333

Hoffmann, H. (1986), 'Kirche und Sklaverei im frühen Mittelalter', *DA* 42: 1–24

Loyn, H.R. (1955), 'Gesiths and thegns in Anglo-Saxon England from the seventh to the tenth century', *EHR* 70: 529–49

Müller-Mertens, E. (1963), *Karl der Grosse, Ludwig der Fromme und die Freien: Wer waren die liberi homines der karolingischen Kapitularien?*, Berlin

Runciman, W.G. (1984), 'Accelerating social mobility. The case of Anglo-Saxon England', *Past and Present* 104: 3–30

Schmitt, J. (1977), *Untersuchungen zu den Liberi Homines der Karolingerzeit* (Europäische Hochschulschriften 3, 83), Frankfurt and Berne

Schulze, H.K. (1974), 'Rodungsfreiheit und Königsfreiheit. Zu Genesis und Kritik neuerer verfassungsgeschichtlicher Theorien', *Historische Zeitschrift* 219: 529–50

Schulze, H.K. (1985), *Grundstrukturen der Verfassung im Mittelalter*, 2 vols., Stuttgart

Verlinden, C. (1979), 'Ist mittelalterliche Sklaverei ein bedeutsamer demographischer Faktor gewesen?', *Vierteljahrschrift für Sozial-und Wirtschaftsgeschichte* 66: 153–73

Werner, K.F. (1965), 'Bedeutende Adelsfamilien im Reich Karls des Grossen', *Karl der Grosse* I, pp. 83–142

Minorities

Ben-Sasson, H.H. (ed.) (1979), *Geschichte des jüdischen Volkes* II, Munich

Blumenkranz, B. (1960), *Juifs et Chrétiens dans le monde occidental 430–1096* (Ecole pratiques des hautes études. Etudes juives 2), Paris

Boshof, E. (1976), 'Untersuchungen zur Armenfürsorge im fränkischen Reich des 9. Jahrhunderts', *Archiv für Kulturgeschichte* 58: 265–339

Boshof, E. (1984), 'Armenfürsorge im Frühmittelalter: xenodochium, matricula, hospitale pauperum', *Vierteljahrschrift für Sozial- und Wirtschaftsgeschichte* 71: 153–74

Mollat, M. (1978), *Les pauvres au moyen âge: étude sociale*, Paris

Women

Affeldt, W. (ed.) (1990), *Frauen in Spätantike und Frühmittelalter: Lebensbedingungen – Lebensnormen – Lebensformen*, Sigmaringen

Baltrusch-Schneider, D.B. (1985), 'Anglo-Saxon Women in the Religious Life: A Study of the Status and Position of Women in an Early Mediaeval Society', Ph.D. dissertation, University of Cambridge

Bugge, J. (1975), *Virginitas: An Essay in the History of a Medieval Ideal* (International Archives of the History of Ideas, Series Minor 17), La Haye

Dronke, P. (1984), *Women Writers of the Middle Ages: A Critical Study of Texts from Perpetua (†203) to Marguerite Porete (†1310)*, Cambridge

Ganshof, F.-L. (1962), 'Le statut de la femme dans la monarchie franque', in *La femme* II (Receuil Jean Bodin 12), Brussels, pp. 5–58

Goetz, H.-W. (ed.) (1991), *Weibliche Lebensgestaltung im frühen Mittelalter*, Cologne and Vienna

Herlihy, D. (1990), *Opera muliebria: Women and Work in Medieval Europe*, New York and Hamburg

Hochstetler, D.D. (1991), *A Conflict of Traditions: Consecration for Women in the Early Middle Ages*, Madison

Jesch, J. (1991), *Women in the Viking Age*, Woodbridge

Ketsch, P. (1982), 'Aspekte der rechtlichen und politisch-gesellschaftlichen Situation von Frauen im frühen Mittelalter (500–1150)', in A. Kuhn and J. Rüsen (eds.), *Frauen in der Geschichte* II, Düsseldorf, pp. 11–71

Marchand, J. (1984), 'The Frankish mother: Dhuoda', in K.M. Wilson (ed.), *Medieval Women Writers*, Manchester, pp. 1–29

Mostert, M., Demyttenaere, A., van Hartingsveldt, E.O. and Künzel, R.E. (eds.) (1990), *Vrouw, familie en macht: bronnen over vrouwen in de Middeleeuwen*, Hilversum

Rosenthal, J. (ed.) (1990), *Medieval Women and the Sources*, Cambridge and New York

Rouche, M. and Heuclin, J. (eds.) (1990), *La femme au moyen âge*, Paris

Wemple, S.F. (1981), *Women in Frankish Society: Marriage and the Cloister 500 to 900*, Philadelphia

Social bonds

Family and kindred

Bessmertny, J. (1984), 'Les structures de la famille paysanne dans les villages de la Francia au IXe siècle. Analyse anthroponymique du polyptyque de l'abbaye de Saint-Germain-des-Prés, *MA* 90: 165–93

Boswell, J.E. (1984), '*Expositio* and *oblatio*: the abandonment of children and the ancient and medieval family', *AHR* 89: 10–33

Bouchard, C.B. (1986), 'Family structure and family consciousness among the aristocracy in the ninth to eleventh centuries', *Francia* 14: 639–58

Brundage, J.A. (1993), *Sex, Law and Marriage in the Middle Ages*, Aldershot

Coleman, E.R. (1971), 'Medieval marriage characteristics: a neglected factor in the history of medieval serfdom', *The Journal of Interdisciplinary History* 2: 205–19

Coleman, E.R. (1974), 'L'infanticide dans le haut moyen âge', *Annales ESC* 29: 315–35

Duby, G. and Le Goff, J. (eds.) (1977), *Famille et parenté dans l'occident médiéval* (Collection de l'Ecole française de Rome 30), Paris

Flandrin, J.-L. (1979), *Families in Former Times: Kinship, Household and Sexuality*, Cambridge (French edn 1976)

Flandrin, J. (1983), *Un temps pour embrasser: aux origines de la morale sexuelle occidentale, VIe–XIe siècle*, Paris

Fossier, R. (1980), 'Les structures de la famille en occident au moyen âge', *Congrès international des sciences historiques*, Rapport 2, Bucharest, pp. 115–32

Gaudemet, J. (1963), *Les communautés familiales*, Paris

Gaudemet, J. (1980), *Sociétés et mariage*, Strasbourg

Gies, F. and J. (1987), *Marriage and the Family in the Middle Ages*, New York

Goetz, H.-W. (1985), 'Zur Namengebung in der alamannischen Grundbesitzerschicht der Karolingerzeit', *Zeitschrift für die Geschichte des Oberrheins* 133: 1–41

Goetz, H.-W. (1987), 'Zur Namengebung bäuerlicher Schichten im Frühmittelalter. Untersuchungen und Berechnungen an hand des Polyptychons von Saint-Germain-des-Prés', *Francia* 15: 852–77

Goody, J. (1983), *The Development of the Family and Marriage in Europe*, Cambridge

Guerreau-Jalabert, A. (1981), 'Sur les structures de parenté dans l'Europe médiévale', *Annales ESC* 36: 1028–49

Guichard, P. (1979), 'De l'antiquité au moyen âge: famille large et famille étroite', in *Cahiers d'Histoire* 23: 45–60

Hammer, C.I., Jr (1983), 'Family and *familia* in early-medieval Bavaria', in R. Wall (ed.), *Family Forms in Historic Europe*, Cambridge, pp. 217–48

Herlihy, D. (1974), 'The generation of medieval history', *Viator* 5: 347–64

Herlihy, D. (1978b), 'Medieval children', in *Essays in Medieval Civilization* (The Walter Prescott Webb Memorial Lectures), Austin and London, pp. 109–41

Herlihy, D. (1985), *Medieval Households* (Studies in Cultural History), Cambridge MA and London

Leyser, Karl (1970), 'Maternal kin in early medieval Germany: a reply', *Past and Present* 49: 126–34

Il matrimonio nella società altomedievale (1977), 2 vols. (*Settimane* 24), Spoleto

de Mause, L. (1974), *The History of Childhood*, New York

Mikat, P. (1978), *Dotierte Ehe – rechte Ehe: Zur Entwicklung des Eheschliessungsrechts in fränkischer Zeit*, Opladen

Mitterauer, M. (1993), *Ahnen und Heilige: Namengebung in der europäischen Geschichte*, Munich

Mitterauer, M. and Sieder, R. (1982), *The European Family: Patriarchy to Partnership from the Middle Ages to the Present*, Chicago (German edn 1977)

Murray, A.C. (1983), *Germanic Kinship Structure: Studies in Law and Society in Antiquity and the Early Middle Ages* (Studies and Texts 65), Toronto

Parisse, M. (ed.) (1993), *Veuves et veuvages dans le haut moyen âge en occident*, Paris

Payer, P.J. (1984), *Sex and the Penitentials: The Development of a Sexual Code 550–1150*, Toronto, Buffalo and London

Platelle, H. (1982), 'L'enfant et la vie familiale au moyen âge', *Mélanges de Science Religieuse* 39: 67–85

Ring, R.R. (1979), 'Early medieval peasant households in central Italy', *Journal of Family History* 4: 2–25

Ritzer, K. (1962), *Formen, Riten und religiöses Brauchtum der Eheschliessung in den christlichen Kirchen des ersten Jahrtausends* (Liturgiewissenschaftliche Quellen und Forschungen 38), Münster

Schmid, K. (1957), 'Zur Problematik von Familie, Sippe und Geschlecht, Haus und Dynastie beim mittelalterlichen Adel', *Zeitschrift für die Geschichte des Oberrheins* 105: 1–62

Schmid, K. (1959), 'Über die Struktur des Adels im frühen Mittelalter', *Jahrbuch für fränkische Landesforschung* 19: 1–23

Schmid, K. (1965), 'Religiöses und sippengebundenes Gemeinschaftsbewusstsein in frühmittelalterlichen Gedenkbucheinträgen', *DA* 21: 18–81

Schmid, K. (1977), 'Heirat, Familienfolge, Geschlechterbewusstsein', in *Settimane* 24, I: 103–37

Schuler, T. (1982), 'Familien im Mittelalter', in H. Reif (ed.), *Die Familie in der Geschichte*, Göttingen, pp. 28–60

Schwarz, H.W. (1993), *Der Schutz des Kindes im Recht des frühen Mittelalters: Eine Untersuchung über Totung, Missbrauch, Körperverletzung, Gefährdung anhand der Rechtsquellen des 5.–9. Jahrhunderts* (Bonner Historische Forschungen 56), Sieburg

Stafford, P. (1978), 'Sons and mothers: family politics in the early middle ages', in D. Baker (ed.), *Medieval Women*, Oxford, pp. 79–100

Theis, L. (1976), 'Saints sans famille? Quelques remarques sur la famille dans le monde franc à travers les sources hagiographiques', *Revue Historique* 255: 3–20

Weinberger, S. (1973), 'Peasant households in Provence, ca. 800–1100', *Speculum* 48: 247–57

Wollasch, J. (1957), 'Eine adlige Familie des frühen Mittelalters. Ihr Selbstverständnis und ihre Wirklichkeit', *Archiv für Kulturgeschichte* 39: 150–88

Zerner-Chardavoine, M. (1981), 'Enfants et jeunes au ixe siècle. La démographie du polyptyque de Marseille 813–814', *Provence Historique* 31: 355–80

Followership and feudal institutions

Bloch, M. (1949), *La société féodale*, 2 vols., Paris

Boutruche, R. (1959), *Seigneurie et féodalité: le premier âge des liens d'homme à homme* 1, Paris

Brunner, O. (1959), *Feudalismus: Ein Beitrag zur Begriffsgeschichte*, Wiesbaden

Ganshof, F.-L. (1968b), *Qu'est-ce que la féodalité?* Brussels

Guerreau, A. (1980), *Le féodalisme, un horizon théorique*, Paris

Kienast, W. (1984), 'Gefolgswesen und Patrocinium im spanischen Westgotenreich', *HZ*, 239: 23–75

Kienast, W. (1990), *Die frankische Vasallität: von den Hausmeiern bis zu Ludwig dem Kind und Karl dem Einfältigen*, Frankfurt

Kuhn, H. (1956), 'Die Grenzen der germanischen Gefolgschaft', *ZRG GA* 73: 1–83

Mitteis, H. (1962), *Der Staat des hohen Mittelalters: Grundlinien einer vergleichenden Verfassungsgeschichte des Lehnszeitalters*, Weimar

Olberg, G. von (1983), *Freie, Nachbarn und Gefolgsleute: volkssprachige Bezeichnungen aus dem sozialen Bereich in den frühmittelalterlichen Leges* (Europäische Hochschulschriften 1,627), Frankfurt

Reynolds, S. (1994), *Fiefs and Vassals: The Medieval Evidence Reinterpreted*, Oxford

Schlesinger, W. (1953), 'Herrschaft und Gefolgschaft in der germanischdeutschen Verfassungsgeschichte', *HZ* 176: 225–75 (reprinted in H. Kämpf (ed.), *Herrschaft und Staat im Mittelalter*, Darmstadt (1956), pp. 135–90)

The seigneurial system

Bleiber, W. (1981), *Naturalwirtschaft und Ware-Geld-Beziehungen zwischen Somme und Loire während des 7. Jahrhunderts* (Forschungen zur mittelalterlichen Geschichte 27), Berlin

Coleman, E.R. (1977), 'People and property: the structure of a medieval seigneury', *Journal of European Economic History* 6: 675–702

Devroey, J.-P. (1993), *Etudes sur la grande domaine carolingienne*, Aldershot

Elmshäuser, K. and Hedwig, A. (1993) *Studien zum Polyptychon von Saint-Germain des Prés*, Cologne

Epperlein, S. (1969), *Herrschaft und Volk im karolingischen Imperium: Studien über soziale Konflikte und dogmatisch-politische Kontroversen im fränkischen Reich* (Forschungen zur mittelalterlichen Geschichte 14), Berlin

Kuchenbuch, L. (1978), *Bäuerliche Gesellschaft und Klosterherrschaft im 9. Jahrhundert: Studien zur Sozialstruktur der familia der Abtei Prüm* (*VSWG* 66 Beiheft), Wiesbaden

Kuchenbuch, L. (1988), 'Die Klostergrundherrschaft im Frühmittelalter. Eine Zwischenbilanz', in F. Prinz (ed.), *Herrschaft und Kirche: Beiträge zur Entstehung und Wirkungsweise episkopaler und monastischer Organisationsformen* (Monographien zur Geschichte des Mittelalters 33), Stuttgart, pp. 297–343

Kuchenbuch, L. (1991), *Grundherrschaft im früheren Mittelalter*, Idstein

McGovern, J.F. (1972), 'The hide and related land-tenure concepts in Anglo-Saxon England, AD 700–1100', *Traditio* 23: 101–18

Magnou-Nortier, E. (1981–4), 'La terre, la rente et le pouvoir dans les pays de Languedoc pendant le haut moyen âge', *Francia* 9: 79–115; 10: 21–66; 12: 53–118

Morimoto, Y. (1988), 'Etat et perspectives des recherches sur les polyptyques carolingiens', *Annales de l'Est* 40: 99–149

Rivers, T.J. (1978), 'Pre-Carolingian seigneurial obligations in Lex Alamannorum, XXI–XXII, 1 and their relationship to the St Gall charters (754–770 AD), *Medieval Studies* 40: 374–86

Rösener, W. (ed.) (1989), *Strukturen der Grundherrschaft im frühen Mittelalter* (Veröffentlichungen des Max-Planck-Instituts 92), Göttingen

Rösener, W. (1992), *Grundherrschaft im Wandel: Untersuchungen zur Entwicklung geistlicher Grundherrschaften im südwestdeutschen Raum vom 9. bis 14. Jahrhundert* (Veröffentlichungen des Max-Planck-Instituts für Geschichte 102), Göttingen

Schreiner, K. (1983), '"Grundherrschaft". Entstehung und Bedeutungswandel eines geschichtswissenschaftlichen Ordnungs- und Erklärungsbegriffs', in H. Patze (ed.), *Die Grundherrschaft im späten Mittelalter* (VuF 27), Sigmaringen, pp. 11–74

Verhulst, A. (1966), 'La genèse du régime domanial classique en France au haut moyen âge', *Settimane* 13: 135–60

Verhulst, A. (1983), 'La diversité du régime domanial entre Loire at Rhin à l'époque carolingienne', in *Villa – curtis – grangia. Landwirtschaft zwischen Loire und Rhein von der Römerzeit zum Hochmittelalter* (Beihefte der Francia 11), Munich, pp. 133–48

Verhulst, A. (1988), 'Étude comparative du régime domanial classique à l'est et à l'ouest du Rhin à l'époque carolingienne', *Flaran* 10: 87–101

Verhulst, A. (ed.) (1985), *Le grand domaine aux époques mérovingienne et carolingienne*, Ghent

Local associations

Boshof, E. (1976), 'Untersuchungen zur Armenfürsorge im fränkischen Reich des 9. Jahrhunderts', *Archiv für Kulturgeschichte* 58: 265–339

Boshof, E. (1984), 'Armenfürsorge im Frühmittelalter xenodochium, matricula, hospitale pauperum', *VSWG* 71: 153–74

Davies, W. (1988), *Small Worlds: The Village Community in Early Medieval Brittany*, London

Hellmuth, L. (1984), *Gastfreundschaft und Gastrecht bei den Germanen* (Sitzungsberichte der Österreichischen Akademie der Wissenschaften 440), Vienna

Jankuhn, H., Schützeichel, R. and Schwind, F. (eds.) (1977), *Das Dorf der Eisenzeit und des frühen Mittelalters: Siedlungsform, wirtschaftliche Funktion, soziale Struktur* (Abhandlungen der Akademie der Wissenschaften Göttingen 3,101), Göttingen

Oexle, O.G. (1979), 'Die mittelalterlichen Gilden: Ihre Selbstdeutung und ihr Beitrag zur Formierung sozialer Strukturen', in A. Zimmermann (ed.), *Soziale Ordnungen im Selbstverständnis des Mittelalters* (Miscellanea Mediaevalia 12(1) 1, Berlin and New York, pp. 203–26

Oexle, O.G. (1981), 'Gilden als soziale Gruppen in der Karolingerzeit', in H. Jankuhn *et al.* (eds.), *Das Handwerk, in vor- und frühgeschichtlicher Zeit* I (Abhandlungen der Akademie der Wissenschaften Göttingen 3,122), Göttingen, pp. 284–354

Oexle, O.G. (1985), 'Coniuratio und Gilde im frühen Mittelalter', in B. Schwineköper (ed.), *Gilden und Zünfte: Kaufmännische und gewerbliche Genossenschaften im frühen und hohen Mittelalter* (VuF 29), Sigmaringen, pp. 151–213

Peyer, H.C. (ed.) (1983), *Gastfreundschaft, Taverne und Gasthaus im Mittelalter* (Schriften des Historischen Kollegs. Kolloquien 3), Munich and Vienna

Peyer, H.C. (1987), *Von der Gastfreundschaft zum Gasthaus: Studien zur Gastlichkeit im Mittelalter* (MGH Schriften 31), Hanover

Schwarz, G.M. (1985), 'Village populations according to the polyptyque of the abbey of St Bertin', *Journal of Medieval History* 11: 31–41

Siems, H. (1989), 'Die Organisation der Kaufleute in der Merowingerzeit nach den Leges', *Untersuchungen zu Handel und Verkehr der vor- und frühgeschichtlichen Zeit in Mittel und Nordeuropa*, Göttingen

Military institutions

Beeler, J. (1973), *Warfare in Feudal Europe, 730–1200*, Ithaca and London

Contamine, P. (1980), *La guerre au moyen âge*, Paris

Fleckenstein, J. (1981), 'Adel und Kriegertum und ihre Wandlung im Karolingerreich', *Settimane*, 27, 1: 67–94

Ganshof, F.L. (1968), 'Charlemagne's army', in *Frankish Institutions under Charlemagne*, Providence

Hawkes, S.C. (ed.), (1990), *Weapons and Warfare in Anglo-Saxon England*, Oxford

Nelson, Janet L. (1989), 'Ninth-century knighthood: the evidence of Nithard', in C. Harper-Bill, C. Holdsworth and J.L. Nelson (eds.), *Studies in Medieval History presented to R. Allen Brown*, Woodbridge, pp. 255–66

Oman, C.W.C. (1953), *The Art of War in the Middle Ages, A.D. 378–1515*, rev. and ed. by John H. Beeler, Ithaca

Ordinamenti militari in Occidente nell'alto medioevo (1968), 2 vols. (Settimane 15), Spoleto

Prinz, F. (1971), *Klerus und Krieg im früheren Mittelalter: Untersuchungen zur Rolle der Kirche beim Aufbau der Königsherrschaft* (Monographien zur Geschichte des Mittelalters 2), Stuttgart

Verbruggen, J.F. (1965), 'L'armée et la stratégie de Charlemagne', in *Karl der Gross,* I, pp. 420–36

Verbruggen, J.F. (1977), *The Art of Warfare in Western Europe during the Middle Ages: From the 8th century to 1340* (Europe in the Middle Ages, Selected Studies 1), Amsterdam

18 ECONOMIC ORGANISATION

General and regional

Bonnassie, P. (1975–6), *La Catalogne du milieu du Xe à la fin du XIe siècle: croissance et mutations d'une société,* Toulouse

Bonnassie, P. (1990), 'La croissance agricole du haut moyen âge dans la Gaule du Midi et le nord-est de la péninsule ibérique', in *La croissance agricole du haut moyen âge* (Flaran 10), Auch, pp. 13–35

Bonnassie, P. (1991), *From Slavery to Feudalism in South-Western Europe,* trans. J. Birrell, Cambridge

Chédeville, A. and Tonnerre, N.-Y. (1987), *La Bretagne féodale XIe–XIIIe siècle,* Rennes

Doehaerd, R. (1971), *Le haut moyen âge occidental: économies et sociétés* (Nouvelle Clio 14), Paris

Duby, G. (1962–8), *Rural Economy and Country Life in the Medieval West,* trans. C. Postan, Los Angeles

Duby, G. (1973–8), *The Early Growth of the European Economy: Warriors and Peasants from the Seventh to the Twelfth Century,* trans. H.B. Clarke, Ithaca

Fossier, R. (1968), *La terre et les hommes en Picardie jusqu'à la fin du XIIIe siècle,* Paris and Leuven

Fossier, R. (1981), 'Les tendances de l'économie carolingienne: stagnation ou croissance ?', *Settimane* 27: 261–90

Fournier, G. (1962), *Le peuplement rural en Basse Auvergne durant le haut moyen âge,* Paris

Ganshof, F.L. (1980), 'Das Fränkische Reich', in H. Kellenbenz (ed.), *Handbuch der europäischen Wirtschafts- und Sozialgeschichte* II, Stuttgart, pp. 151–205

Genicot, L. (1990), *Rural Communities in the Medieval West,* Baltimore and London

Rouche, M. (1981), 'Géographie rurale du royaume de Charles le Chauve', in M.T. Gibson and J.L. Nelson (eds.), *Charles the Bald: Court and Kingdom,* Oxford, pp. 192–211

Schwind, F. (1977), 'Beobachtungen zur inneren Struktur des Dorfes in Karolingischer Zeit', in H. Jankuhn and R. Schützeichel (eds.), *Das Dorf der Eisenzeit und des frühen Mittelalters* (Abhandlungen der Akademie der Wissenschaften in Göttingen, phil.-hist. Klasse, Dritte Folge 101), Göttingen, pp. 444–93

Staab, F. (1975), *Untersuchungen zur Gesellschaft am Mittelrhein in der Karolingerzeit,* Wiesbaden

Toubert, P. (1973a), *Les structures du Latium médiéval: le Latium méridional et la Sabine du IXe siècle à la fin du XIIe s.* (Bibl. Ecoles françaises d'Athènes et de Rome 221), Rome

Toubert, P. (1990), 'La part du grand domaine dans le décollage économique de l'Occident (viiie–xe siècles)', in *La croissance agricole du haut moyen âge* (Flaran 10), Auch, pp. 53–86

Demography (including alimentation, clearances)

Devroey, J.-P. (1981), 'Les méthodes d'analyse démographique des polyptyques du haut moyen âge', *Acta Historica Bruxellensia* 4: 71–88

Devroey, J.-P. (1987), 'Units of measurement in the early medieval economy: the example of Carolingian food rations', *Journal of French History* 1: 68–92

Lohrmann, D. (1990), 'La croissance agricole en Allemagne au haut moyen âge', in *La croissance agricole du haut moyen âge* (Flaran 10), Auch, pp. 103–15

Perrin, Ch.-E. (1963), 'Note sur la population de Villeneuve-Saint-Georges au ixe siècle', *MA* 69: 75–86

Riché, P. (1966), 'Problèmes de démographie historique du haut moyen age (ve–viiie siècles)', *Annales de Démographie Historique*: 37–55

Schwarz, G.M. (1985), 'Village populations according to the polyptyque of the abbey of St Bertin', *Journal of Medieval History* 11: 31–41

Slicher van Bath, B.H. (1965), 'The economic and social conditions in the Frisian districts from 900 to 1500', *AAG Bijdragen* 13: 97–133

Toubert, P. (1986), 'Le moment carolingien', in A. Burguière *et al.* (eds.), *Histoire de la famille*, Paris, pp. 333–59

Verhulst, A. (1965), 'Karolingische Agrarpolitik: das *Capitulare de Villis* und die Hungersnöte von 792/93 und 805/06', *Zeitschrift für Agrargeschichte und Agrarsoziologie* 13: 175–89

Zerner, M. (1979), 'La population de Villeneuve-Saint-Georges et Nogent-sur-Marne au ixe siècle d'après le polyptyque de Saint-Germain-des-Prés', *Annales de la Faculté des Lettres et Sciences Humaines de Nice* 37: 17–24

Zerner-Chardavoine, M. (1981), 'Enfants et jeunes au ixe siècle. La démographie du polyptyque de Marseille 813–814', *Provence Historique* 31: 355–77

Technique (including landscape, settlement)

Curschmann, F. (1900), *Hungersnöte im Mittelalter: Ein Beitrag zur deutschen Wirtschaftsgeschichte des 8. bis 13. Jahrhunderts*, Leipzig

Duby, G. (1966), 'Le problème des techniques agricoles', *Settimane* 13: 167–83

Hildebrandt, H. (1988), 'Systems of agriculture in Central Europe up to the tenth and eleventh centuries', in D. Hooke (ed.), *Anglo-Saxon Settlements*, Oxford, pp. 275–90

Lohrmann, D. (1989), 'Le moulin à eau dans le cadre de l'économie rurale de la Neustrie (viie–ixe siècles)', in *La Neustrie*, pp. 367–404

Montanari, M. (1979), *L'alimentazione contadina nell'alto medioevo*, Naples

Montanari, M. (1985), 'Tecniche e rapporti di produzione: le rese cerealicole dal ix al xv secolo', in B. Andreolli, V. Fumagalli and M. Montanari (eds.), *Le campagne italiane prima e dopo il mille*, Bologna, pp. 45–68

Pounds, N.J.G. (1967), 'Northwest Europe in the ninth century: its geography in the light of the polyptychs', *Annals of the Association of American Geographers*: 439–61

Riché, P. (1973), *La vie quotidienne dans l'empire carolingien*, Paris

Schröder-Lembke, G. (1961), 'Zur Flurform der Karolingerzeit', *Zeitschrift für Agrargeschichte und Agrarsoziologie* 9: 143–52

Schröder-Lembke, G. (1969), 'Zum Zelgenproblem', *Zeitschrift für Agrargeschichte und Agrarsoziologie* 17: 44–51

Slicher van Bath, B.H. (1966), 'Le climat et les récoltes au haut moyen âge', *Settimane* 13: 399–425

Verhulst, A. (1990a), 'The "agricultural revolution" of the middle ages reconsidered', in *Essays in Honor of Bryce Lyon*, Kalamazoo, pp. 17–28

White, L. Jr. (1962), *Medieval Technology and Social Change*, Oxford

Wickham, C. (1985), 'Pastoralism and underdevelopment in the early middle ages', *Settimane* 31: 401–51

Manorial organization

General and regional

Andreolli B., Fumagalli, V. and Montanari, M. (eds.) (1985), *Le campagne italiane prima e dopo il mille*, Bologna

Andreolli, B. and Montanari, B. (1985), *L'azienda curtense in Italia. Proprietà della terra e lavoro contadino nei secoli VIII–XI*, Bologna

Devroey, J.-P. (1985), 'Réflexions sur l'économie des premiers temps carolingiens (768–877): grands domaines et action politique entre Seine et Rhin', *Francia* 13: 475–88

Fumagalli, V. (1980), 'Introduzione del feudalismo e sviluppo dell'economia curtense nell'Italia settentrionale', in *Structures féodales et féodalisme dans l'Occident méditerranéen (Xe–XIIIe siècle)* (Collection de l'Ecole Française de Rome 44), Rome, pp. 313–25

Ganshof, F.L. (1949), 'Manorial organisation in the Low Countries in the seventh, eighth and ninth centuries', *TRHS* 31: 29–59

Kuchenbuch, L. (1983), 'Probleme der Rentenentwicklung in den klösterlichen Grundherrschaften des frühen Mittelalters', in W. Lourdaux and D. Verhelst (eds.), *Benedictine Culture, 750–1050*, Leuven, pp. 132–72

Musset, L. (1982), 'Signification et destinée des domaines excentriques pour les abbayes de la moitié septentrionale de la Gaule jusqu'au xie siècle', in *Sous la règle de saint Benoît: structures monastiques et sociétés en France du moyen âge à l'époque moderne*, Geneva and Paris, pp. 167–84

Poly, J.P. (1980), 'Régime domanial et rapports de production "féodalistes" dans le Midi de la France (viiie–xe siècles)', in *Structures féodales et féodalisme dans l'Occident méditerranéen (Xe–XIIIe siècles)* (Collection de l'Ecole Française de Rome 44), Rome, pp. 57–84

Rösener, W. (ed.) (1989a), *Strukturen der Grundherrschaft im frühen Mittelalter* (Veröffentlichungen des Max-Planck-Instituts für Geschichte 92), Göttingen

Toubert, P. (1973b), 'L'Italie rurale aux viiie–ixe siècles. Essai de typologie domaniale', *Settimane* 20: 95–132

Verhulst, A. (1966), 'La genèse du régime domanial classique en France au haut moyen âge', *Settimane* 13: 135–60

Verhulst, A. (1983), 'La diversité du régime domanial entre Loire et Rhin à l'époque carolingienne', in W. Janssen and D. Lohrmann (eds.), *Villa – curtis – grangia: economie rurale entre Loire et Rhin de l'époque gallo-romaine au XIIe–XIIIe siècle*, Munich, pp. 133–48

Verhulst, A. (1990b), 'Etude comparative du régime domanial classique à l'est et à l'ouest du Rhin à l'époque carolingienne', in *La croissance agricole du haut moyen âge* (Flaran 10), Auch, pp. 87–101

Verhulst, A. (ed.) (1985), *Le grand domaine aux époques mérovingienne et carolingienne* (Centre belge d'histoire rurale 81), Ghent

Sources

Birch, W. de G. (ed.) (1885–93), *Cartularium Saxonicum*, London

Boretius, A. (1883), 'Brevium exempla ad describendas res ecclesiasticas et fiscales', *MGH Cap.* I, no. 128

Brühl, C. (1971), *Capitulare de Villis. Cod. Guelf. 254 Helmst. der Herzog August Bibliothek Wolfenbüttel* (Dokumente zur deutschen Geschichte in Faksimiles I, Mittelalter I), Stuttgart

Castagnetti, A., Luzzati, M., Pasquali, G. and Vasina, A. (1979), *Inventari altomedievali di terre, coloni e redditi* (Fonti per la Storia d'Italia 104), Rome

Dette, C. (1987), *Liber possessionum Wizenburgensis* (Quellen und Abhandlungen zur mittelrheinischen Kirchengeschichte 59), Mainz

Devroey, J.-P. (1984), *Le polyptyque et les listes de cens de l'abbaye de Saint-Remi de Reims (IXe–XIe siècles)* (Travaux de l'Académie Nationale de Reims 163), Rheims

Devroey, J.-P. (1986), *Le polyptyque et les listes de biens de l'abbaye Saint-Pierre de Lobbes (IXe–XIe siècles): édition critique* (Commission Royale d'Histoire in-8°), Brussels

Devroey, J.-P. (1989), 'Problèmes de critique autour du polyptyque de l'abbaye de Saint-Germain-des-Prés', in *La Neustrie*, Sigmaringen, pp. 441–65

Droste, C.-D. (1988), *Das Polyptichon von Montiérender: Kritische Edition und Analyse* (Trierer Historische Forschungen), Trier

Ganshof, F.L. (1975), *Le polyptyque de l'abbaye de Saint-Bertin (844–859): édition critique et commentaire* (Mémoires de l'Académie des Inscriptions et Belles-Lettres 45), Paris

Gasnault, P. (1975), *Documents comptables de Saint-Martin de Tours à l'époque mérovingienne* (Collection de documents inédits sur l'histoire de France), Paris

Guérard, B. (1844), *Polyptyque de l'abbé Irminon ou dénombrement des manses, des serfs et des revenus de l'abbaye de Saint-Germain-des-Prés sous le règne de Charlemagne, publié avec des Prolégomènes*, Paris

Hägermann, D. and Hedwig, A. (1990), *Das Polyptychon und die Notitia de Areis von Saint-Maur-des-Fossés: Analyse und Edition* (Beihefte der Francia 23), Sigmaringen

Koch, A.C.F. (1970), *Oorkondenboek van Holland en Zeeland tot 1299*, I: *Eind van de 7e eeuw tot 1222*, The Hague

Longnon, A. (1886–95), *Polyptyque de l'abbaye de Saint-Germain-des-Prés rédigé au temps de l'abbé Irminon*, Paris

Lot, F. (1894), *Chronicon Centulense* (Collection de textes pour servir à l'étude et à l'enseignement de l'histoire), Paris

Meyer-Marthaler, E. and Perret, F. (1955), *Bündner Urkundenbuch*, Chur

Morimoto, Y. (1988), 'Etat et perspectives des recherches sur les polyptyques carolingiens', *Annales de l'Est* 40: 99–149

Schwab, I. (1983), *Das Prümer Urbar* (Rheinische Urbare 5), Düsseldorf

Verhulst, A. (1971), 'Das Besitzverzeichnis der Genter Sankt-Bavo-Abtei von ca. 800 (Clm 6333)', *FrSt* 5: 193–234

Zeumer, K. (1886), *Formulae merovingici et karolini aevi* (*MGH Form.*) Hanover

Monographs

Elmshäuser, K. (1989), 'Untersuchungen zum Staffelseer Urbar', in W. Rösener (ed.), *Strukturen der Grundherrschaft*, Göttingen, pp. 335–69

Goetz, H.-W. (1989), 'Beobachtungen zur Grundherrschafts-entwicklung der Abtei St Gallen vom 8. zum 10. Jahrhundert', in W. Rösener (ed.), *Strukturen der Grundherrschaft*, Göttingen, pp. 197–246

Kuchenbuch, L. (1978), *Bäuerliche Gesellschaft und Klosterherrschaft im 9. Jahrhundert: Studien zur Sozialstruktur der familia der Abtei Prüm*, Wiesbaden

Rösener, W. (1985), 'Zur Struktur und Entwicklung der Grundherrschaft in Sachsen in karolingischer und ottonischer Zeit', in A. Verhulst (ed.), *Le grand domaine aux époques mérovingienne et carolingienne* (Centre belge d'histoire rurale 81), Ghent

Rösener, W. (1989b), 'Strukturformen der adeligen Grundherrschaft in der Karolingerzeit', in W. Rösener (ed.), *Strukturen der Grundherrschaft im frühen Mittelalter*, Göttingen, pp. 126–80

Staab, F. (1989), 'Aspekte der Grundherrschaftsentwicklung von Lorsch, vornehmlich auf Grund der Urbare des Codex Laureshamensis', in W. Rösener (ed.), *Strukturen der Grundherrschaft*, Göttingen, pp. 285–334

Weidinger, U. (1989), 'Untersuchungen zur Grundherrschaft des Klosters Fulda in der Karolingerzeit', in W. Rösener (ed.), *Strukturen der Grundherrschaft*, Göttingen, pp. 247–65

Weidinger, U. (1991), *Untersuchungen zur Wirtschaftsstruktur des Klosters Fulda in des Karolingerzeit* (Monographien zur Geschichte des Mittelalters 36), Stuttgart

Mansus

Devroey, J.P. (1976), 'Mansi absi: indices de crise ou de croissance de l'économie rurale du haut moyen âge ?', *MA* 82: 421–51

Herlihy, D. (1960–1), 'The Carolingian mansus', *EHR* 13: 79–89

Perrin, Ch.-E. (1945), 'Observations sur le manse dans la région parisienne au début du ixe siècle', *Annales d'Histoire Sociale* 8: 39–52

Perrin, Ch.-E. (1960), 'Le manse dans le polyptyque de Prüm à la fin du ixe siècle', in *Etudes historiques à la mémoire de N. Didier*, Paris, pp. 245–58

Schlesinger, W. (1974), 'Vorstudien zu einer Untersuchung über die Hufe', in H. Patze and F. Schwind (eds.), *Ausgewählte Aufsätze von W. Schlesinger* (VuF 34), Sigmaringen, pp. 485–542

Schlesinger, W. (1976), 'Hufe und Mansus im Liber Donationum des Klosters Weissenburg, Beiträge zur Wirtschafts- und Sozialgeschichte des Mittelalters', in H. Patze and F. Schwind (eds.), *Ausgewählte Aufsätze von W. Schlesinger 1965–1979*

(VuF 34), Sigmaringen, pp. 543–86

Schlesinger, W. (1987), 'Die Hufe im Frankenreich', in H. Patze and F. Schwind (eds.), *Ausgewählte Aufsätze von W. Schlesinger 1965–1979* (VuF 34), Sigmaringen, pp. 587–614

Special problems (demesne, services, etc.)

Durliat, J. (1990), *Les finances publiques de Dioclétien aux Carolingiens (284–889)* (Beihefte der Francia 21), Sigmaringen

Fumagalli, V. (1966), 'Crisi del dominico e aumento del masserizio nei beni "infra valle" del monastero di S. Colombano di Bobbio dall' 862 all' 883', *Rivista di Storia dell'Agricoltura* 6: 352–9

Fumagalli, V. (ed.) (1987), *Le prestazioni d'opera nelle campagne italiane del medioevo* (Bibliotheca de storia agraria medievale 3), Bologna

Royal domains

Metz, W. (1971), *Zur Erforschung des karolingischen Reichsgutes* (Erträge der Forschung 4), Darmstadt

Zotz, T. (1989), 'Beobachtungen zur königlichen Grundherrschaft entlang und östlich des Rheins vornehmlich im 9. Jahrhundert', in W. Rösener (ed.), *Strukturen der Grundherrschaft*, Göttingen, pp. 74–125

Economic aspects

Devroey, J.-P. (1979), 'Les services de transport à l'abbaye de Prüm au ixe siècle', *Revue du Nord* 61: 543–69

Devroey, J.-P. (1984), 'Un monastère dans l'économie d'échanges: les services de transport à l'abbaye Saint-Germain-des-Prés au ixe siècle', *Annales ESC* 39: 570–89

Toubert, P. (1983), 'Il sistema curtense: la produzione e lo scambio interno in Italia nei secoli viii, ix e x', in *Storia d'Italia. Annali 6: Economia naturale, economia monetaria*, Turin, pp. 3–63

Craft and industry

Finberg, H.P.R. (1972), 'Anglo-Saxon England to 1042', in H.P.R. Finberg (ed.), *The Agrarian History of England and Wales*, I, ii, AD 43–1042, Cambridge, pp. 385–525

Jankuhn, H., Janssen, W. *et al.* (eds.) (1981–3), *Das Handwerk in vor- und frühgeschichtlicher Zeit* (Abhandlungen der Akademie der Wissenschaften in Göttingen, phil.-hist. Klasse, Dritte Folge 122–3), 2 vols., Göttingen

Janssen, W. (1983), 'Gewerbliche Produktion des Mittelalters als Wirtschaftsfaktor im ländlichen Raum', in H. Jankuhn *et al.* (eds.), *Das Handwerk in vor- und frühgeschichtlicher Zeit* II (Abhandlungen der Akademie der Wissenschaften in Göttingen, phil.-hist. Klasse, Dritte folge 123), Göttingen, pp. 317–96

Schwind, F. (1984), 'Zu karolingerzeitlichen Klöstern als Wirtschaftsorganismen und Stätten handwerklicher Tätigkeit', in L. Fenske *et al.* (eds.), *Festschrift J. Fleckenstein*, Sigmaringen, pp. 101–23

Sprandel, R. (1968), *Das Eisengewerbe im Mittelalter*, Stuttgart

Towns and trade

Bleiber, W. (1982), 'Grundherrschaft und Markt zwischen Loire und Rhein während des 9. Jahrhunderts', *Jahrbuch für Wirtschaftsgeschichte* 23: 105–35

Brisbane, M. (1988), 'Hamwic (Saxon Southampton): an 8th century port and production centre', in R. Hodges and B. Hobley (eds.), *The Rebirth of Towns in the West AD 700–1050* (CBA Report 68), London, pp. 101–8

Clarke, H. and Ambrosiani, B. (1991), *Towns in the Viking Age*, Leicester and London

Clarke, H.B. and Simms, A. (eds.) (1985), *The Comparative History of Urban Origins in Non-Roman Europe* (BAR International Series 225), Oxford

Despy, G. (1968), 'Villes et campagnes aux ixe et xe siècles: l'exemple du pays mosan', *Revue du Nord* 50: 145–68

Duby, G. (1959), 'Les villes du sud-est de la Gaule du viiie au xie siècle', *Settimane* 6: 231–58

Düwel, K., Jankuhn, H., Siems, H. and Timpe, D. (eds.) (1987), *Untersuchungen zu Handel und Verkehr der vor- und frühgeschichtlichen Zeit in Mittel- und Nordeuropa*, iv: *Der Handel der Karolinger- und Wikingerzeit* (Abhandlungen der Akademie der Wissenschaften in Göttingen, phil.-hist. Klasse, Dritte Folge, 156), Göttingen

Ennen, E. (1953), *Frühgeschichte der europäischen Stadt*, Bonn

Ganshof, F.L. (1957), 'Note sur le "praeceptum negotiatorum" de Louis le Pieux', in *Studi in onore di Armando Sapori* i, Milan, pp. 101–12

Ganshof, F.L. (1966), 'Note sur l'Inquisitio de theloneis Raffelstettensis', *MA* 72: 197–224

La genèse et les premiers siècles des villes médiévales dans les Pays-Bas méridionaux: un problème archéologique et historique. Actes du 14e Colloque international (6.–8. sept. 1988) du Crédit Communal (1990) (Crédit Communal de Belgique, Collection histoire, in-8°, 83), Brussels

Hodges, R.C. (1982), *Dark Age Economics: The Origins of Towns and Trade AD 600–1000*, London

Hodges, R. and Hobley, B. (eds.) (1988), *The Rebirth of Towns in the West AD 700–1050* (CBA Research Report 68), London

Jankuhn, H., Schietzel, K. and Reichstein H. (eds.) (1984), *Archäologische und naturwissenschaftliche Untersuchungen an ländlichen und frühstädtischen Siedlungen im deutschen Küstengebiet vom 5. Jh. v. Chr. bis zum 11. Jh. n. Chr.*, Bonn

Jankuhn, H., Schlesinger, W. and Steuer, H. (1973–4), *Vor- und Frühformen der europäischen Stadt im Mittelalter* (Abhandlungen der Akademie der Wissenschaften in Göttingen, phil.-hist. Klasse, Dritte Folge 83–4), Göttingen

Johanek, P. (1987), 'Der fränkische Handel der Karolingerzeit im Spiegel der Schriftquellen', in K. Düwel *et al.* (eds.), *Untersuchungen zu Handel und Verkehr der vor- und frühgeschichtlichen Zeit im Mittel- und Nordeuropa*, iv: *Der Handel der*

Karolinger- und Wikingerzeit (Abhandlungen der Akademie der Wissenschaften in Göttingen, phil.-hist. Klasse, Dritte Folge 156), Göttingen, pp. 7–68

Lebecq, S. (1983), *Marchands et navigateurs frisons du haut moyen âge*, Lille

Lewis, A.R. (1958), *The Northern Seas: Shipping and Commerce in Northern Europe, AD 300–1100*, Princeton

Schmid, P. (1991), 'Mittelalterliche Besiedlung, Deich- und Landesausbau im niedersächsischen Marschgebiet', in H.G. Böhme (ed.), *Siedlungen und Landesausbau zur Salierzeit*, I: *In den nördlichen Landschaften des Reiches*, Sigmaringen, pp. 9–36

Steuer, H. (1987), 'Der Handel der Wikingerzeit zwischen Nord und Westeuropa aufgrund archäologischer Zeugnisse', in K. Düwel *et al* (eds.), *Untersuchungen zu Handel und Verkehr*, IV: Göttingen, pp. 113–97

Steuer H. (1990), 'Die Handelsstätten des frühen Mittelalters im Nord- und Ostseeraum', in *La genèse et les premiers siècles des villes médiévales dans les Pays-Bas méridionaux*, Brussels, pp. 75–116

Studien zu den Anfängen des europäischen Städtewesens (1958) (VuF 4), Lindau and Konstanz

Van Es, W. (1990), 'Dorestad centred', in J.C. Besteman, J.M. Bos and H.A. Heidinga (eds.), *Medieval Archaeology in the Netherlands*, Assen and Maastricht, pp. 151–82

Verhulst, A. (1989), 'The origins of towns in the Low Countries and the Pirenne thesis', *Past and Present* 122: 1–35

Violante, C. (1953), *La società milanese nell'età precomunale*, Bari

19   RURAL SOCIETY IN CAROLINGIAN EUROPE

Abadal, R. d' (1952), *Catalunya carolíngia 2: Els diplomes carolingis a Catalunya* II, Barcelona

Abadal, R. d' (1955), *Catalunya carolíngia 3: Els comtats de Pallars i Ribagorça*, Barcelona

Abadal, R. d' (1969), *Dels Visigots als Catalans* I, Barcelona

Abadal, R. d' (1980), *Els primers comtes catalans*, Barcelona

Andrews, D. (1986), 'Milano altomedievale sotto Piazza del Duomo. Gli scavi del 1982 e 1983', *Atti del 10° Congresso internazionale di studi sull'alto medioevo*, Spoleto, pp. 355–64

Baliñas Pérez, C. (1992), '*Do mito á realidade: a definición social e territorial de Galicia na Alta Idade Media (séculos VIII e IX)*', Santiago de Compostela

Balzaretti, R. (1989), 'The lands of Saint Ambrose', Ph.D. dissertation, University of London

Baraut, C. (1978), 'Les actes de consacracions d'esglésies del bisbat d'Urgell (segles IX–XII)', *Urgellia* I: 11–182

Baraut, C. (1979), 'Els documents, dels segles IX i X, conservats a l'Arxiu capitular de la Seu d'Urgell', *Urgellia* 2: 7–145

Barbero, A. and Vigil, M. (1978), *La formación del feudalismo en la península Ibérica*, Barcelona

Bartmuss, H.-J. (1965), 'Die Genesis der Feudalgesellschaft in Deutschland', *Zeitschrift für Geschichtswissenschaft* 13: 1001–10

Beckmann, G.A. (1963), 'Aus den letzten Jahrzehnten des Vulgärlateins in Frankreich', *Zeitschrift für romanische Philologie* 79: 305–24

Bernhard, H. (1982), 'Die frühmittelalterliche Siedlung Speyer "Vogelgesang"', *Offa* 39: 217–33

Bognetti, G.P. (1954), 'Pensiero e vita a Milano e nel Milanese durante l'età carolingia', in *Storia di Milano* 2, Milan, pp. 719–803

Bonacini, P. (1991), 'Giustizia pubblica e società nell'Italia carolingia', *Quaderni Medievali* 31–2: 6–35

Bonnassie, P. (1975), *La Catalogne du milieu du Xe à la fin du XIe siècle*, Toulouse

Bonnassie, P. (1980), 'Du Rhône à la Galice: genèse et modalités du régime féodal', in *Structures féodales et féodalisme dans l'Occident méditerranéen (Xe–XIIIe siècles)*, Rome, pp. 17–55

Bonnassie, P. and Guichard, P. (1982), 'Les communautés rurales en Catalogne et dans le pays valencien (ixe–milieu xive siècle)', *Flaran* 4: 79–115

Bosl, K. (1969), *Franken um 800*, Munich

Bourin-Derruau, M. (1987), *Villages médiévaux en Bas-Languedoc: genèse d'une sociabilité, Xe–XIVe siècle* 1, Paris

Brooks, N.P. (1984), *The Early History of the Church of Canterbury*, Leicester

Bullough, D.A. (1966), 'Urban change in medieval Italy: the example of Pavia', *Papers of the British School at Rome* 34: 82–131

Bullough, D.A. (1972), 'Social and economic structure and topography in the early medieval city', *Settimane* 21: 351–99

Byock, J. (1988), *Medieval Iceland: Society, Sagas and Power*, Berkeley, CA

Campbell, J. (1989), 'The sale of land and the economics of power in early England', *Haskins Society Journal* 1: 23–37

Castagnetti, A. (1968), 'Dominico e massaricio a Limonta nei secoli ix e x', *Rivista di Storia dell'Agricoltura* 8: 3–20

Castagnetti, A. (1969), 'La distribuzione geografica dei possessi di un grande proprietario veronese del secolo ix: Engelberto del fu Grimoaldo di Erbè', *Rivista di Storia dell'Agricoltura* 9: 15–26

Castagnetti, A. (1979), *L'organizzazione del territorio rurale nel medioevo*, Turin

Chapelot, J. and Fossier, R. (1985), *The Village and the House in the Middle Ages*, London

Charles-Edwards, T.M. (1976), 'The distinction between land and moveable wealth in Anglo-Saxon England', in P.H. Sawyer (ed.), *Medieval Settlement*, London, pp. 180–7

Collins, R.J.H. (1981), 'Charles the Bald and Wifred the Hairy', in M. Gibson and J. Nelson (eds.), *Charles the Bald: Court and Kingdom*, Oxford, pp. 169–89

Collins, R.J.H. (1985), '"Sicut lex Gothorum continet": law and charters in ninth- and tenth-century León and Catalonia', *EHR* 396: 489–512

Conti, E. (1965), *La formazione della struttura agraria moderna nel contado fiorentino* 1, Rome

Croissance (1988), *La croissance agricole du haut moyen âge*, Flaran 10

Dannheimer, H. (1968), (ed.), *Epolding-Mühlthal: Siedlung, Friedhöfe und Kirche des frühen Mittelalters*, Munich

Davies, W. (1978a), *An Early Welsh Microcosm: Studies in the Llandaff Charters*, London

Davies, W. (1978b), 'Land and power in early medieval Wales', *Past and Present* 81: 3–23

Davies, W. (1985), 'Disputes, their conduct and their settlement in the village communities of eastern Brittany in the ninth century', *History and Anthropology* 1: 289–312

Davies, W. (1986), 'People and places in dispute in ninth-century Brittany', in Davies and Fouracre (1986), pp. 65–84

Davies, W. (1988), *Small Worlds: The Village Community in Early Medieval Brittany*, London

Davies, W. and Fouracre, P. (eds.) (1986), *The Settlement of Disputes in Early Medieval Europe*, Cambridge

Davis, J. (1973), *Land and Family in Pisticci*, London

Déléage, A. (1941), *La vie économique et sociale de la Bourgogne dans le haut moyen âge*, Mâcon

Despy, G. (1968), 'Villes et campagnes aux ixe et xe siècles: l'exemple du pays mosan', *Révue du Nord* 50: 143–68

Dollinger, P. (1949), *L'évolution des classes rurales en Bavière depuis la fin de l'époque carolingienne jusqu'au milieu du XIIIe siècle*, Paris

Dopsch, A. (1962), *Die Wirtschaftsentwicklung der Karolingerzeit vornehmlich in Deutschland*, 3rd edn, 2 vols., Cologne

Dubled, H. (1959), 'La notion de propriété en Alsace du viiie au xe siècle', *MA* 65: 429–52

Dubled. H. (1961), 'Étude sur la condition des personnes en Alsace du viiie au xe siècle', *BEC* 119: 21–49

Duby, G. (1971), *La société aux XIe et XIIe siècles dans la région mâconnaise*, Paris

Duby, G. (1973), *Hommes et structures du moyen âge*, Paris

Dümmler, E. (ed.) (1900), 'Paschasius Radbertus, *Epitaphium Arsenii*', Abhandlungen der Preussische Akademie, phil.-hist. Klasse 2, 18–98

Dupont, A. (1965), 'L'aprision et le régime aprisionnaire dans le Midi de la France', *MA* 71: 171–213, 375–99

Epperlein, S. (1969), *Herrschaft und Volk im karolingischen Imperium*, Berlin

Esch, A. (1985), 'Überlieferungs-Chance und Überlieferungs-Zufall als methodisches Problem des Historikers', *HZ* 240: 529–70

Estey, F.N. (1951), 'The *scabini* and the local courts', *Speculum* 26: 119—29

Everitt, A. (1986), *Continuity and Colonisation: The Evolution of Kentish Settlement*, Leicester

Ewig, E. (1980), *Rheinische Geschichte: Frühes Mittelalter*, Düsseldorf

Falck, L. (1972), *Mainz im frühen und hohen Mittelalter* (Geschichte der Stadt Mainz 2, ed. A.P. Brück and L. Falck), Düsseldorf

Feliu, G. (1984), 'Sant Joan de les Abadesses i el repoblament del Vallès', in *Miscel.lània Fort i Cogul*, Montserrat, pp. 129–35

Fossier, R. (1968), *La terre et les hommes en Picardie jusqu'à la fin du XIIIe siècle*, Paris

Fournier, G. (1962), *Le peuplement rural en Basse Auvergne durant le haut moyen âge*, Paris

Freise, E. (1978), 'Studien zum Einzugsbereich der Klostergemeinschaft von Fulda', in K. Schmid (ed.), *Die Klostergemeinschaft von Fulda im früheren Mittelalter* II, 3, Munich, pp. 1003–269

Fumagalli, V. (1968), 'Un territorio piacentino nel secolo ix: "fines Castellana"', *Quellen und Forschungen* 48: 1–35

Fumagalli, V. (1976), *Terra e società nell'Italia padana: i secoli IX e X*, Turin

Fumagalli, V. (1979), 'Le modificazioni politico-istituzionali in Italia sotto la dominazione carolingia', *Settimane* 27: 293–317

García de Cortázar, J.A. (1988), *La sociedad rural en la España medieval*, Madrid
García de Cortázar, J.A. and Díez Herrera, C. (1982), *La formación de la sociedad hispano-cristiana del Cantábrico al Ebro en los siglos VIII a XI*, Santander
Gautier Dalché, J. (1969), 'L'histoire monétaire de l'Espagne septentrionale et centrale du ixe au xiie siècles', *Anuario de Estudios Medievales* 6: 43–95
Geary, P.J. (1985), *Aristocracy in Provence*, Stuttgart and Philadelphia
Gensicke, H. (1973), 'Worms-, Speyer-, und Nahegau', in F. Knöpp (ed.), *Die Reichsabtei Lorsch* I, Darmstadt, pp. 437–506
Gockel, M. (1970), *Karolingische Königshöfe am Mittelrhein*, Göttingen
Gockel, M. (1976), review of Staab (1975), *Nassauische Annalen* 87: 309–15
Goetz, H.-W. (1983), '"Nobilis". Der Adel im Selbstverständnis der Karolingerzeit', *Vierteljahrschrift für Sozial- und Wirtschaftsgeschichte* 60: 153–91
Goetz, H.-W. (1984), 'Herrschaft und Recht in der frühmittelalterlichen Grundherrschaft', *HJb* 104: 392–410
Goetz, H.-W. (1987), 'Herrschaft und Raum in der frühmittelalterlichen Gesellschaft', *Annalen des historischen Vereins für den Niederrhein* 190: 7–33
Goetz, H.-W. (1989), 'Bäuerliche Arbeit und regionále Gewohnheit im Pariser Raum im frühen 9. Jahrhundert. Beobachtungen zur Grundherrschaft von Saint-Germain-des-Prés', in H. Atsma (ed.), *La Neustrie* I, Sigmaringen, pp. 505–22
Gurevič, A. Ja. (1982), *Le origini del feudalesimo*, Bari
Hamerow, H.F. (1991), 'Settlement mobility and the "Middle Saxon Shift": rural settlements and settlement patterns in Anglo-Saxon England', *ASE* 20: 1–17
Hammer, C.I. (1983), 'Family and *familia* in early-medieval Bavaria', in R. Wall (ed.), *Family forms in Historic Europe*, Cambridge, pp. 217–48
Harmer, F.E. (1914), *Select English Historical Documents of the Ninth and Tenth Centuries*, Cambridge
Heinzelmann, M. (1993), '*Villa* d'après les œuvres de Grégoire de Tours', in E. Magnou-Nortier (ed.), *Aux Sources de la gestion publique* I, Lille, pp. 45–70
Hodges, R. (1982), *Dark Age Economics*, London
Hübner, R. (1891), 'Gerichtsurkunden der fränkischen Zeit', *ZRG, GA* 12: Appendix, 1–118
Hvass, S. (1986), 'Vorbasse', *Berichte der römisch-germanischen Kommission* 67: 529–31.
Isla Frez, A. (1992), *La sociedad gallega en la alta edad media*, Madrid
Junyent, E. (1980), *Diplomatari de la catedral de Vic, segles IX–X*, Vic
Karras, R.M. (1988), *Slavery and Society in Medieval Scandinavia*, New Haven, CT
Keller, H. (1979), *Adelsherrschaft und städtische Gesellschaft in Oberitalien 9. bis 12. Jahrhundert*, Tübingen
Kuchenbuch, L. (1978), *Bäuerliche Gesellschaft und Klosterherrschaft im 9. Jht*, Wiesbaden
Kuchenbuch, L. (1983), 'Probleme der Rentenentwicklung in den klösterlichen Grundherrschaften des frühen Mittelalters', in W. Lourdaux and D. Verhelst (eds.), *Benedictine Culture 750–1050*, Leuven, pp. 132–72
Lauranson-Rosaz, C. (1987), *L'Auvergne et ses marges (Velay, Gévaudan) du VIIIe au XIe siècle*, Le Puy
Le Roy Ladurie, E. (1975), *Montaillou, village occitan de 1294 à 1324*, Paris
Levy, E. (1951), *West Roman Vulgar Law: The Law of Property*, Philadelphia
Lewis, A.R. (1965), *The Development of Southern French and Catalan Society 718–1050*, Austin, TX

Leyser, K. (1984), 'Early medieval canon law and the beginnings of knighthood', in L. Fenske, W. Rösener and T. Zotz (eds.), *Institutionen, Kultur und Gesellschaft im Mittelalter: Festschrift für J. Fleckenstein*, Sigmaringen, pp. 549–66

Loring, M.I. (1988), *Cantabria en la alta edad media: organización eclesiastica y relaciones sociales*, Madrid

Lusuardi Siena, S. (1986), 'Milano: la città nei suoi edifici. Alcuni problemi', in *Atti del 10° Congresso internazionale di studi sull'alto medioevo*, Spoleto, pp. 209–40

Lütge, F. (1937), *Die Agrarverfassung des frühen Mittelalters im mitteldeutschen Raum vornehmlich in der Karolingerzeit*, Jena

Magnou-Nortier, E. (1974), *La société laïque et l'église dans la province ecclésiastique de Narbonne (zone cispyrénéenne) de la fin du VIIIe à la fin du XIe siècle*, Toulouse

Maitland, F.W. (1897), *Domesday Book and Beyond*, Cambridge

Martí, R. (1987), 'Els inicis de l'organització feudal de la producció al bisbat de Girona', Doctoral thesis, Universitat Autònoma de Barcelona

Martí, R. (1993), 'La Cerdanya, dels "territoria" al comtat', in *III Curs d'arqueologia d'Andorra*, Andorra

Miller, W.I. (1990), *Bloodtaking and Peacemaking*, Chicago

Mínguez, J.M. (1985), 'Ruptura social y implantación del feudalismo en el noroeste peninsular (siglos VIII–X)', *Studia Historica* 3: 7–32

Montarrenti (1989), articles under the title 'Lo scavo archeologico di Montarrenti e i problemi dell'incastellamento medievale', *Archeologia Medievale* 16: 9–288

Müller-Mertens, E. (1963), *Karl der Grosse, Ludwig der Fromme, und die Freien*, Berlin

Murray, A.C. (1988), 'From Roman to Frankish Gaul', *Traditio* 44: 59–100

Natale, A.R. (1970), *Il museo diplomatico dell'Archivio di Stato di Milano*, Milan

Nehlsen-von Stryk, K. (1981), *Die boni homines des frühen Mittelalters*, Berlin

Nelson, J.L. (1986), 'Dispute settlement in Carolingian West Francia', in Davies and Fouracre (1986), pp. 45–64

Njeussychin, A.I. (1961), *Die Entstehung der abhängigen Bauernschaft als Klasse der frühfeudalen Gesellschaft in Westeuropa vom 6. bis 8. Jahrhundert*, Berlin

Padoa Schioppa, A. (1988), 'Aspetti della giustizia milanese nell'età carolingia', *Archivio Storico Lombardo* 114: 9–25

Pastor, R. (1980), *Resistencias y luchas campesinas en la época del crecimiento y consolidación de la formación feudal Castilla y León, siglos X–XIII*, Madrid

Poly, J.-P. and Bournazel, E. (1980), *La mutation féodale: Xe–XIIe siècles*, Paris

Reynolds, S. (1984), *Kingdoms and Communities in Western Europe, 900–1300*, Oxford

Rösener, W. (ed.) (1989), *Strukturen der Grundherrschaft im frühen Mittelalter*, Göttingen

Rossetti, G. (1968), *Società e istituzioni nel contado lombardo durante il medioevo: Cologno Monzese* 1, Milan

Rossetti, G. (1986), 'I ceti proprietari e professionali: status sociale, funzioni e prestigio a Milano nei secoli VIII–X', 1, in *Atti del 10° Congresso internazionale di studi sull'alto medioevo*, Spoleto, pp. 165–207

Salrach, J.M. (1978), *El procés de formació nacional de Catalunya (segles VIII–IX)*, Barcelona

Salrach, J.M. (1987), *El procés de feudalització (segles III–XII)*, Barcelona

Salrach, J.M. (1988), 'Défrichement et croissance agricole dans la Septimanie et le nord-est de la péninsule ibérique', *Flaran* 10: 133–51

Salrach, J.M. (1991), 'Entre l'estat antic i el feudal', in *Symposium international sobre els orígens de Catalunya* I, Barcelona, pp. 191–252

Sánchez-Albornoz, C. (1965), 'Pequeños propietarios libres en el Reino asturleonés. Su realidad historica', *Settimane* 13: 183–222

Schmidt-Wiegand, R. (1977), 'Das Dorf nach den Stammesrechten des Kontinents', in H. Jankuhn, R. Schützeichel and F. Schwind (eds.), *Das Dorf der Eisenzeit und des frühen Mittelalters*, Göttingen, pp. 408–43

Schmitt, J. (1977), *Untersuchungen zu den Liberi Homines der Karolingerzeit*, Frankfurt and Bern.

Schulze, H.K. (1974), 'Rodungsfreiheit und Königsfreiheit', *HZ* 219: 529–50

Schulze, H.K. (1978), 'Reichsaristokratie, Stammesadel und Fränkische Freiheit', *HZ* 227: 353–73

Schwind, F. (1977), 'Beobachtungen zur inneren Struktur des Dorfes in karolingischer Zeit', in H. Jankuhn, R. Schützeichel and F. Schwind (eds.), *Das Dorf der Eisenzeit und des frühen Mittelalters*, Göttingen, pp. 444–93

Settia, A.A. (1984), *Castelli e villaggi nell'Italia padana*, Naples

Smith, J.M.H. (1992), *Province and Empire: Brittany and the Carolingians*, Cambridge

Staab, F. (1975), *Untersuchungen zur Gesellschaft am Mittelrhein in der Karolingerzeit*, Wiesbaden

Staab, F. (1980), 'A reconsideration of the ancestry of modern political liberty: the problem of the so-called "king's freemen" (Königsfreie)', *Viator* 11: 51–69

Steuer, H. (1989), 'Archaeology and history: proposals on the social structure of the Merovingian kingdom', in K. Randsborg (ed.), *The Birth of Europe*, Rome, pp. 100–22

Störmer, W. (1973), *Früher Adel*, Stuttgart

Tabacco, G. (1969), 'Dai possessori dell'età carolingia agli esercitali dell'età longobarda', *SM* 10: 221–68

Tabacco, G. (1972), 'La connessione fra potere e possesso nel regno franco e nel regno longobardo', *Settimane* 20: 133–68

Taylor, C. (1983), *Village and Farmstead: A History of Rural Settlement in England*, London

Toubert, P. (1973), *Les structures du Latium médiéval*, Rome

Udina, F. (1951), *El Archivo Condal de Barcelona en los siglos IX–X*, Barcelona

Verhulst, A. (1983), 'La diversité du régime domanial entre Loire et Rhin à l'époque carolingienne', in W. Janssen and D. Lohrmann (eds.), *Villa – Curtis – Grangia*, Munich, pp. 133–48

Verhulst, A. (ed.) (1985), *Le grand domaine aux époques mérovingienne et carolingienne*, Ghent

Violante, C. (1953), *La società milanese nell'età precomunale*, Bari

Vollrath, H. (1982), 'Herrschaft und Genossenschaft im Kontext frühmittelalterlicher Rechtsbeziehungen', *HJb* 102: 33–71

Weirich, H. (ed.) (1936), *Urkundenbuch der Reichsabtei Hersfeld* I, Marburg

Wickham, C.J. (1981), *Early Medieval Italy*, London

Wickham, C.J. (1982), *Studi sulla società degli Appennini nell'alto medioevo*, Bologna

Wickham, C.J. (1983), 'Pastoralism and underdevelopment in the early middle ages', *Settimane* 31: 401–55

Wickham, C.J. (1985), *Il problema dell'incastellamento nell'Italia centrale*, Florence

Wickham, C.J. (1986), 'Land disputes and their social framework in Lombard-Carolingian Italy, 700–900', in Davies and Fouracre (1986), pp. 105–24

Wickham, C.J. (1988), *The Mountains and the City*, Oxford

Wickham, C.J. (1989), 'European forests in the early middle ages: landscape and land clearance', *Settimane* 37: 479–548

Wickham, C.J. (1992), 'Problems of comparing rural societies in early medieval western Europe', *TRHS* 6th series, 2: 221–46

Wormald, C.P. (1988), 'A handlist of Anglo-Saxon lawsuits', *ASE* 17: 247–81

Zimmerman, M. (1973), 'L'usage du droit wisigothique en Catalogne du ixe au xiie siècle', *Mélanges de la Casa de Velazquez* 9: 233–81

20 MONEY AND COINAGE

Archibald, M.M. (1985), 'The coinage of Beonna in the light of the Middle Harling hoard', *British Numismatic Journal* 55: 10–54

Arslan, E.A. (1978), *Le monete di Ostrogoti, Longobardi e Vandali: Catalogo delle Civiche Raccolte Numismatiche di Milano*, Milan

Balaguer (Prunes), A.M. (1976), *Las emisiones transicionales árabe-musulmanas de Hispania*, Barcelona

Balaguer (Prunes), A.M. (1979), 'Early Islamic transitional gold issues in North Africa and Spain', *American Numismatic Society Museum Notes* 24: 225–41

Balog, P. (1979), 'The silver coinage of Arabic Sicily', *Atti della Seconda settimana di studi italo-arabi*, Spoleto, pp. 1–21

Balog, P., Mancini, C., Petrillo Serafin, P. and Travaini, L. (1981), 'Nuovi contributi sul contenuto aureo e la tipologia del tarì', *Istituto Italiano di Numismatica Annali* 27–8: 155–84

Bates, M. (1992), 'The coinage of Spain under the Umayyad caliphs of the east, 711–750', in J.I. Sáenz-Diez (ed.), *Jarique* III, Madrid, pp. 271–89

Bernareggi, E. (1983), *Moneta Langobardorum*, Milan

Blackburn, M.A.S. (1989), 'The earliest Anglo-Viking çoinage of the southern Danelaw (late 9th century)', in I. Carradice *et al.* (eds.), *Proceedings of the 10th International Congress of Numismatics, London 1986*, London, pp. 341–8

Blackburn, M.A.S. (1991), 'A survey of Anglo-Saxon and Frisian coins with runic inscriptions', in A. Bammesberger (ed.), *Old English runes and their Continental background* (Anglistische Forschungen 217), Heidelberg, pp. 137–89

Blackburn, M.A.S. (1993), 'Coin circulation in Germany during the early middle ages: the evidence of single-finds', in B. Kluge (ed.), *Fernhandel und Geldwirtschaft*, Sigmaringen, pp. 37–54

Blunt, C.E. (1961), 'The coinage of Offa', in R.H.M. Dolley (ed.), *Anglo-Saxon Coins*, London, pp. 39–62

Callmer, J. (1976), 'Oriental coins and the beginning of the Viking period', *Fornvännen* 71: 175–85

Coupland, S. (1988), 'Dorestad in the ninth century: the numismatic evidence', *Jaarboek voor Munt-en Penningkunde* 75: 5–26

Coupland, S. (1989), 'The coinages of Pippin I and II of Aquitaine', *Revue*

Numismatique 6th series, 31: 194–222

Coupland, S. (1990), 'Money and coinage under Louis the Pious', *Francia* 17(1): 23–54

Coupland, S. (1991), 'The early coinage of Charles the Bald, 840–864', *Numismatic Chronicle* 151: 121–58

Dodwell, C.R. (1982), *Anglo-Saxon Art: A New Perspective*, Manchester

Dumas, F. (1991), 'La monnaie au xe siècle', *Settimane* 38: 565–614

Elbern, V.H. (1988), *Die Goldschmiedekunst im frühen Mittelalter*, Darmstadt

Fomin, A. (1990), 'Silver of the Maghrib and gold from Ghana at the end of the VIII–IXth centuries AD', in K. Jonsson and B. Malmer (eds.), *Sigtuna Papers: Proceedings of the Sigtuna Symposium on Viking-Age Coinage 1–4 June 1989* (Commentationes de Nummis Saeculorum IX–XI, n.s. 6), Stockholm, pp. 69–75

Gerriets, M. (1985), 'Money in early Christian Ireland according to the Irish laws', *Comparative Studies in Society and History* 27: 323–39

Grierson, P. (1954), 'Cronologia delle riforme monetarie di Carlo Magno', *Rivista Italiana di Numismatica* 56: 65–79; reprinted in Grierson (1979), no. XVII

Grierson, P. (1959), 'Commerce in the dark ages: a critique of the evidence', *TRHS* 5th series, 9: 123–40; reprinted in Grierson (1979), no. II

Grierson, P. (1960), 'The monetary reforms of 'Abd al-Malik: their metrological basis and their financial repercussions', *Journal of the Economic and Social History of the Orient* 3: 241–64; reprinted in Grierson (1979), no. XV

Grierson, P. (1961a), 'Monete bizantine in Italia dal VII all'XI secolo', in *Moneta e scambi nell'alto medioevo*, Spoleto, pp. 35–55

Grierson, P. (1961b), 'La fonction sociale de la monnaie en Angleterre aux VIIe–VIIIe siècles', in *Moneta e scambi nell'alto medioevo*, Spoleto, pp. 341–85; reprinted in Grierson (1979), no. XI

Grierson, P. (1965), 'Money and coinage under Charlemagne', in W. Braunfels (ed.), *Karl der Grosse*, I, pp. 501–36; reprinted in Grierson (1979), no. XVIII

Grierson, P. (1979), *Dark Age Numismatics*, London [collected papers]

Grierson, P. (1982), *Byzantine Coins*, London

Grierson, P. (1990), 'The "Gratia Dei Rex" coinage of Charles the Bald', in M.T. Gibson and J.L. Nelson (eds.), *Charles the Bald: Court and Kingdom*, 2nd edn, Aldershot, pp. 52–64

Grierson, P. (1991), *Coins of Medieval Europe*, London

Grierson, P. and Blackburn, M. (1986), *Medieval European Coinage* I: *The Early Middle Ages (5th to 10th centuries)*, Cambridge

Hårdh, B. (1976), *Wikingerzeitliche Depotfunde aus Südschweden*, 2 vols., Lund

Hawkes, S.C., Merrick, J.M. and Metcalf, D.M. (196), 'X-ray fluorescent analysis of some dark age coins and jewellery', *Archaeometry* 9: 98–138

Hendy, M.F. (1985), *Studies in the Byzantine Monetary Economy, c. 300–1450*, Cambridge

Hendy, M.F. (1988), 'From public to private: the western barbarian coinages as a mirror of the disintegration of late Roman state structures', *Viator* 19: 29–78

Jonsson, K. (1994), 'A Gotlandic hoard from the early Viking age', in T. Hackens (ed.), *Festskrift till Birgit Arrhenius* (PACT 38), Strasbourg, pp. 451–8

Jonsson, K. and Malmer, B. (1986), 'Sceattas och den äldsta nordiska myntningen',

Nordisk Numismatisk Unions Medlemsblad 1986: 66–71

Lafaurie, J. (1969), 'Monnaies d'argent mérovingiennes des VIIe et VIIIe siècles: les trésors de Saint-Pierre-les-Etieux (Cher), Plassac (Gironde) et Nohanent (Puy-de-Dôme)', *Revue Numismatique* 6th series, 11: 98–219

Lafaurie, J. (1970), 'Des Carolingiens aux Capétiens', *Cahiers de Civilisation Médiévale* 13: 117–37

Lafaurie, J. (1974), 'Des Mérovingiens aux Carolingiens. Les monnaies de Pépin le Bref', *Francia* 2: 26–48

Lafaurie, J. (1978), 'Les monnaies impériales de Charlemagne', *Comptes Rendus de l'Académie des Inscriptions et Belles-Lettres* 1978: 154–76

Linder Welin, U.S. (1974), 'The first arrival of oriental coins in Scandinavia and the inception of the Viking age in Sweden', *Fornvännen* 69: 22–9

Loyn, H.R. and Percival, J. (1975), *The Reign of Charlemagne*, London

Lyon, C.S.S. (1986), 'Some problems in interpreting Anglo-Saxon coinage', *ASE* 5: 173–224

Lyon, C.S.S. and Stewart, B.H.I.H. (1961), 'The Northumbrian Viking coins in the Cuerdale hoard', in R.H.M. Dolley (ed.), *Anglo-Saxon Coins*, London, pp. 96–121

Malmer, B. (1966), *Nordiska Mynt före år 1000* (Acta Archaeologica Lundensia, 8th series, 4), Lund

Metcalf, D.M. (1967), 'The prosperity of western Europe in the eighth and ninth centuries', *Economic History Review* 2nd series, 20: 344–57

Metcalf, D.M. (1977), 'Monetary affairs in the time of Æthelbald', in A. Dornier (ed.), *Mercian Studies*, Leicester, pp. 87–106

Metcalf, D.M. (1984a), 'Monetary circulation in southern England in the first half of the eighth century', in D. Hill and D.M. Metcalf (eds.), *Sceattas in England and on the Continent* (BAR British Series 128), Oxford, pp. 27–69

Metcalf, D.M. (1984b), 'A note on sceattas as a measure of international trade, and on the earliest Danish coinage', in D. Hill and D.M. Metcalf (eds.), *Sceattas in England and on the Continent* (BAR British Series 128), Oxford, pp. 159–64

Metcalf, D.M. (1986), 'Nyt om sceattas af typen Wodan/Monster', *Nordisk Numismatisk Unions Medlemsblad* 1986: 110–20

Metcalf, D.M. (1988), 'Monetary expansion and recession: interpreting the distribution-patterns of seventh- and eighth-century coins', in J. Casey and R. Reece (eds.), *Coins and the Archaeologist*, 2nd edn, London, pp. 230–53

Metcalf, D.M. (1990), 'A sketch of the currency in the time of Charles the Bald', in M.T. Gibson and J.L. Nelson (eds.), *Charles the Bald: Court and Kingdom*, 2nd edn, Aldershot, pp. 65–97

Metcalf, D.M. (1993–4), *Thrymsas and Sceattas in the Ashmolean Museum, Oxford*, 3 vols., Oxford and London

Metcalf, D.M. and Northover, J.P. (1985), 'Debasement of the coinage in southern England in the age of Alfred', *Numismatic Chronicle* 145: 150–76

Metcalf, D.M. and Northover, J.P. (1989), 'Coinage alloys from the time of Offa and Charlemagne to *c.* 864', *Numismatic Chronicle* 149: 101–20

Miles, G.C. (1950), *The coinage of the Umayyads of Spain*, 2 vols., New York

Miles, G.C. (1970), *The Coinage of the Arab Amirs of Crete*, New York

Morrisson, C. and Barrandon, J.-N. (1988), 'La trouvaille de monnaies d'argent byzantines de Rome (vɪɪe–vɪɪɪe siècles): analyses et chronologie', *Revue Numismatique* 6th series, 30: 149–65

Noonan, T.S. (1985), 'The first major silver crisis in Russia and the Baltic, *c.* 875–*c.* 900', *Hikuin* 11: 41–50

Oddy, W.A. (1972), 'Analysis of Lombardic tremisses by the specific gravity method', *Numismatic Chronicle* 7th series, 12: 193–215

Oddy, W.A. (1974), 'Analysis of the gold coinage of Beneventum', *Numismatic Chronicle* 7th series, 14: 78–109

Oddy, W.A. (1988), 'The debasement of the provincial Byzantine gold coinage from the seventh to ninth centuries', in W. Hahn and W.E. Metcalf (eds.), *Studies in Early Byzantine Gold Coinage* (American Numismatic Society's Numismatic Studies 17), New York, pp. 135–42

O'Hara, M.D. (1985), 'A find of Byzantine silver from the mint of Rome for the period AD 641–752', *Revue Suisse de Numismatique* 64: 105–39

Pagan, H.E. (1986), 'Coinage in southern England, 796–874', in M.A.S. Blackburn (ed.), *Anglo-Saxon Monetary History*, Leicester, pp. 45–65

Pirenne, H. (1939), *Mohamed and Charlemagne*, London

Robert, E., Desnier, J.-L. and Belaubre, J. (1988), 'La fontaine de vie et la propogation de la véritable religion chrétienne', *Revue Belge de Numismatique* 134: 89–106

Smart, V. (1986), 'Scandinavians, Celts, and Germans in Anglo-Saxon England: the evidence of moneyers' names', in M.A.S. Blackburn (ed.), *Anglo-Saxon Monetary History*, Leicester pp. 171–84

Spahr, R. (1976), *Le Monete Siciliane dai Bizantini a Carlo I d'Angiò (582–1282)*, Zurich and Graz

Spufford, P. (1987), 'Coinage and currency', in M.M.E. Postan and E. Miller (eds.), *The Cambridge Economic History of Europe* ɪɪ: *Trade and Industry in the Middle Ages*, Cambridge, pp. 788–873

Spufford, P. (1988), *Money and its Use in Medieval Europe*, Cambridge

Stewart, I. (1986), 'The London mint and the coinage of Offa', in M.A.S. Blackburn (ed.), *Anglo-Saxon Monetary History*, Leicester, pp. 27–43

Suchodolski, S. (1981a), 'Vom Gold zum Silber', in T. Fischer and P. Ilisch (eds.), *Lagon: Festschrift für Peter Berghaus zum 60. Geburtstag am 20. November 1979*, Münster, pp. 97–104.

Suchodolski, S. (1981b), 'La date de la grande réforme monétaire de Charlemagne', *Quaderni Ticinesi di Numismatica e Antichità Classiche* 10: 399–409

Travaini, L. (1990), 'I tarì di Salerno e di Amalfi', *Rassegna del Centro di Cultura e Storia Amalfitana* 10: 9–71

al-'Ush, M. Abū-al-F. (1982) *Monnaies aglabides étudiées en relation avec l'histoire des Aglabides*, Damascus

Walker, J. (1956), *A Catalogue of the Arab-Byzantine and Post-Reform Umaiyad Coins* (Catalogue of the Muhammadan Coins in the British Museum ɪɪ), London

Webster, L. and Backhouse, J. (eds.) (1991), *The Making of England: Anglo-Saxon Art and Culture AD 600–900*, London

21 THE PAPACY IN THE EIGHTH AND NINTH CENTURIES

Alexander, P. (1953), 'The iconoclastic council of St Sophia (815) and its definition (*horos*)', *DOP* 7: 35–66

Alexander, P. (1958), *The Patriarch Nicephorus of Constantinople*, Oxford

Anton, H. (1984), 'Von der byzantinischen Vorherrschaft zum Bund mit den Franken', in M. Greschat (ed.), *Das Papsttum* I: *Von den Anfängen bis zu den Päpsten in Avignon* (Gestalten der Kirchengeschichte 11), Stuttgart, pp. 100–14

Bakhuizen van den Brink, J. (1954), *Ratramnus De corpore et sanguine Domini: Text établi d'après les manuscrits et notice bibliographique* (Verhandelingen der koninklijke nederlandse Akademie van Wettenschappen, afd. Letterkunde, Niewe Reeks, Deel 61, no. 1), Amsterdam

Beck, H. (1966), 'Die griechische Kirche im Zeitalter des Ikonoklasmus', in H. Jedin (ed.), *Handbuch der Kirchengeschichte* III, pt 1, Freiburg, pp. 13–61

Bertolini, O. (1952), 'La ricomparsa della sede episcopale di "Tres Tabernae" nella seconda metà del secolo VIII e l'institutione delle "domuscultae"', *Archivio della Società Romana di Storia Patria* 75: 103–9

Bertolini, O. (1956) 'Osservazione sulla "Constitutio Romana" e sul "Sacramentum cleri et populi" dell'824', in *Studi medievali in onore di Antonio de Stefano*, Palermo, pp. 43–78

Bertolini, O. (1968), 'Per la storia delle diaconie romane nell'alto medioevo sino alla fine del secolo VIII', in his *Scritti scelti di storia medioevale*, ed. O. Banti, Livorno, I, pp. 309–460

Bertolini, O. (1970), 'Il "Liber Pontificalis"', *Settimane* 17: 387–455

Bosl, K. (1964), 'Potens und pauper: begriffsgeschichtliche Studien zur gesellschaftlichen Differenzierung im frühen Mittelalter und zum "Pauperismus" des Hochmittelalter', in his *Frühformen der Gesellschaft im mittelalterlichen Europa*, Munich, pp. 106–34

Bouhot, J.-P. (1976), *Ratramne de Corbie: histoire littéraire et controverses doctrinales* (Études augustiniennes), Paris

Brown, T. (1984), *Gentlemen and Officers: Imperial Administration and Aristocratic Power in Byzantine Italy, AD 554–800*, Rome

Caspar, E. (1930, 1933), *Geschichte des Papsttums von den Anfängen bis zur Höhe der Weltherrschaft* I and II, Tübingen

Caspar, E. (1956), *Das Papsttum unter fränkischer Herrschaft*, Darmstadt

Castagnetti, A. (1979), *L'organizzazione del territorio rurale nel medioevo: circonscrizione ecclesiastiche e civile nella 'Langobardia' e nella 'Romania'*, Turin

Cavadini, J. (1993), *The Last Christology of the West: Adoptionism in Spain and Gaul, 785–820*, Philadelphia

Conte, P. (1971), *Chiesa e primato nelle lettere dei papi del secolo VII*, Milan

Duby, G. (1974), *The Early Growth of the European Economy: Warriors and Peasants from the Seventh to the Twelfth Century*, Ithaca

Dvornik, F. (1948), *The Photian Schism*, Cambridge

Ferrari, G. (1957), *Early Roman Monasteries: Notes for the History of the Monasteries and Convents at Rome from the V through the IX Century* (Studi di antichità cristiana 23), Vatican City

Fink, K. (1981), *Papsttum und Kirche im abendländischen Mittelalter*, Munich

Fischer, B. (1939), 'Die Entwicklung des Instituts der Defensoren in der römischen Kirche', *Ephemerides Liturgicae* 48: 443–54

Franzen, A. and Bäumer, R. (1982), *Papstgeschichte: Das Petrusamt in seiner Idee und seiner geschichtlichen Verwirklichung in der Kirche*, 3d edn, Freiburg im Breisgau

Freeman, A. (1985), 'Carolingian orthodoxy and the fate of the Libri Carolini', *Viator* 16: 65–108

Fried, J. (1984), 'Die Päpste im Karolingerreich', in M. Greschat (ed.), *Das Papsttum* I: *Von den Anfängen bis zu den Päpsten in Avignon* (Gestalten der Kirchengeschichte 11), Stuttgart, pp. 115–28

Fuhrmann, H. (1972–4), *Einfluss und Verbreitung der pseudoisidorischen Fälschungen von ihrem Auftauchen bis in die neuere Zeit* (MGH Schriften 24, 1, 2, 3), Stuttgart

Fürst, K. (1967), *Cardinalis: Prolegomena zu einer Rechtsgeschichte des römischen Kardinalskollegiums*, Munich

Geertman, H. (1975), *More veterum: Il* Liber pontificalis *e gli edifici ecclesiastici di Roma nella tarda antichità e nell'alto medioevo* (Archaeologica Traiectina 10), Groningen

Godfrey, C. (1962), *The Church in Anglo-Saxon England*, Cambridge

Grierson, P. and Blackburn, M. (1986), *Medieval European Coinage* I: *The Early Middle Ages (5th–10th Centuries)*, Cambridge

Haldon, J. (1977), 'Some remarks on the background of the iconoclastic controversy', *BSl* 38: 161–84

Haller, J. (1951), *Das Papsttum: Idee und Wirklichkeit* I and II, Basel

Haugh, R. (1975), *Photius and the Carolingians: The Trinitarian Controversy*, Belmont, MA

Heitz, C. (1976), 'More romano: problèmes d'architecture et liturgie carolingiennes', *Roma e l'età carolingia*, Rome, pp. 27–37

Jaffé, P. (1885), *Regesta Pontificum Romanorum*, 2d edn, I, Leipzig

Krautheimer, R. (1969), 'The Carolingian revival of early Christian architecture', in his *Studies in Early Christian, Medieval and Renaissance Art*, New York, pp. 203–56

Krautheimer, R. (1980), *Rome: Profile of a City, 312–1308*, Princeton, NJ

Kreutz, B. (1991), *Before the Normans: Southern Italy in the Ninth and Tenth Centuries*, Philadelphia

Kuttner, S. (1945), 'Cardinalis: the history of a canonical concept', *Traditio* 3: 129–214

Lestocquoy, J. (1930), 'Administration de Rome et diaconies du VIIe au IXe siècle', *Rivista di Archeologia Cristiana* 7: 261–98

Maccarrone, M. (1991), *Romana ecclesia-cathedra Petri* (Italia Sacra 47), Rome

McKeon, P. (1978), *Hincmar of Laon and Carolingian Politics*, Urbana

Mann, H. (1925), *The Lives of the Popes in the Early Middle Ages*, 2d edn, vols. I–III, London

Markus, R. (1970), 'Papal primacy: the early middle ages', *The Month* 229: 352–61

Martin, E. (1930), *A History of the Iconoclastic Controversy*, London

Meyendorff, J. (1991), *Imperial Unity and Christian Divisions: The Church 450–680*, Crestwood, NY

Morrison, K. (1969), *Tradition and Authority in the Western Church, 300–1140*, Princeton, NJ

Noble, T. (1984), *The Republic of St Peter: The Birth of the Papal State, 680–825*, Philadelphia

Noble, T. (1985), 'A new look at the *Liber Pontificalis*', *Archivum Historiae Pontificiae* 23: 347–58

Noble, T. (1987), 'John Damascene and the history of the iconoclastic controversy', in T. Noble and J. Contreni (eds.), *Religion, Culture and Society in the Early Middle Ages: Studies in Honor of Richard E. Sullivan* (Studies in Medieval Culture 23), Kalamazoo, pp. 95–116

Noble, T. (1990), 'Literacy and the papal government in late antiquity and the early middle ages', in R. McKitterick (ed.), *The Uses of Literacy in Early Mediaeval Europe*, Cambridge, pp. 82–108

Pacaut, M. (1976), *Histoire de la papauté de l'origine au concile de Trente*, Paris

Pitz, E. (1990), *Papstreskripte im frühen Mittelalter: Diplomatische und rechtsgeschichtliche Studien zum Brief-Corpus Gregors des Grossen* (Beiträge zur Geschichte und Quellenkunde des Mittelalters 14), Sigmaringen

Recchia, V. (1978), *Gregorio magno e la società agricola* (Verba Seniorum, n.s. 8), Rome

Reuter, T. (1980), 'St Boniface and Europe', in T. Reuter (ed.), *The Greatest Englishman: Essays on St Boniface and the Church at Crediton*, Exeter, pp. 69–94

Richards, J. (1979), *The Popes and the Papacy in the Early Middle Ages, 476–752*, London

Sawyer, B., Sawyer, P. and Wood, I. (eds.) (1987), *The Christianization of Scandinavia*, Alingsås

Schimmelpfennig, B. (1984), *Das Papsttum: Grundzüge seiner Geschichte von der Antike bis zur Renaissance*, Darmstadt

Seppelt, F. (1954), *Geschichte der Päpste von den Anfängen bis zur Mitte des zwangigsten Jahrhunderts*, 2nd edn, 2 vols., Munich

Smith, J. (1992), *Province and Empire: Brittany and the Carolingians* (Cambridge Studies in Medieval Life and Thought, Fourth Series, 18), Cambridge

Spearing, E. (1918), *The Patrimony of the Roman Church in the Time of Gregory the Great*, Cambridge

Speck, P. (1981), *Artabasdos, der rechtgläubige Vorkämpfer der göttlichen Lehre: Untersuchungen zur Revolte des Artabasdos und ihrer Darstellung in der byzantinischen Historiographie* (Poikila Byzantina 2), Berlin

Stein, D. (1980), *Der Beginn des byzantinischen Bilderstreites und seine Entwicklung bis in die 40er Jahre des 8. Jahrhunderts* (Miscellanea Byzantina Monachensia 25), Munich

Sullivan, R. (1955), 'The papacy and missionary activity in the early middle ages', *Mediaeval Studies* 17: 46–106

Sullivan, R. (1966), 'Khan Boris and the conversion of Bulgaria: a case study in the impact of Christianity on a barbarian society', *Studies in Medieval and Renaissance History* 3: 53–139

Sullivan, R. (ed.) (1959), *The Coronation of Charlemagne: What Did It Signify?*, Boston

Tabacco, G. (1989), *The Struggle for Power in Medieval Italy*, trans. R. Jensen, Cambridge

Ullmann, W. (1970), *The Growth of Papal Government in the Middle Ages*, 3d edn, London

Ullmann, W. (1972), *A Short History of the Papacy in the Middle Ages*, London

Vielhaber, K. (1955), *Gottschalk der Sachse* (Bonner historische Forschungen 5), Bonn

Vlasto, A. (1970), *The Entry of the Slavs into Christendom: An Introduction to the Medieval History of the Slavs*, Cambridge

Wickham, C. (1981), *Early Medieval Italy: Central Power and Local Society 400–1000*, London

Wolf, G. (ed.) (1972), *Zum Kaisertum Karls des Grossen* (Wege der Forschung 38), Darmstadt

Wormald, P. (1991), 'In search of Offa's "Law Code"', in I. Wood *et al.* (eds.), *People and Places in Northern Europe 500–900*, Woodbridge, pp. 25–45

Zimmermann, H. (1981), *Das Papsttum im Mittelalter: Eine Papstgeschichte im Spiegel der Historiographie*, Stuttgart

22 THE ORGANISATION, LAW AND LITURGY OF THE WESTERN CHURCH, 700–900

Amann, E. and Dumas, A. (1948), *L'église au pouvoir des laïques (888–1057)* (Histoire de l'église 7), Paris

Angenendt, A. (1982), 'Die Liturgie und die Organisation des kirchlichen Lebens auf dem Lande', *Settimane* 28: 169–234

Angenendt, A. (1990), *Das Frühmittelalter. Die abendländische Christenheit von 400 bis 900*, Stuttgart

Arnaldi, G. (1964), 'Papato, arcivescovi e vescovi nell'età post-carolingia', in *Vescovi e diocesi in Italia nel medioevo (sec. ix–xiii)*, Rome, pp. 27–53

Autenrieth, J., Geuenich, D. and Schmid, K. (1979), *Das Verbrüderungsbuch der Abtei Reichenau* (MGH Libri Memoriales et Necrologia, nova series 1)

Barion, H. (1931), *Das fränkisch-deutsche Synodalrechts des Frühmittelalters*, Bonn

Basset, S. (1989), *The Origins of Anglo-Saxon Kingdoms*, Leicester

Bethune, B. (1987), 'The text of the Christian rite of marriage in medieval Spain', unpublished Ph.D. dissertation, University of Toronto

Bischoff, B. (1981), 'Bücher am Hofe Ludwigs des Deutschen und die Privat Bibliothek des Kanzlers Grimalt', in B. Bischoff, *Mittelalterliche Studien* III, Stuttgart, pp. 187–212

Black, J. (1987), 'The daily cursus, the week and the Psalter in the divine office and in Carolingian devotion', unpublished Ph.D. dissertation, University of Toronto

Blair, J. and Sharpe, R. (1992), *Pastoral Care before the Parish*, Leicester

Blumenthal, U.-R. (ed.) (1984), *Carolingian Essays*, Washington, DC

Brooke, C.N.L. (1982), 'Rural ecclesiastical institutions in England: the search for their origins, *Settimane* 28: 685–711

Brooks, N. (1984), *The Early History of the Church of Canterbury. Christ Church from 597–1066*, Leicester

Constable, G. (1964), *Monastic Tithes from their Origins to the Twelfth Century* (Cambridge Studies in Medieval Life and Thought), Cambridge

Constable, G. (1982), 'Monasteries, rural churches and the *cura animarum* in the early middle ages' *Settimane* 28: 349–444

Cramer, P. (1993), *Baptism and Change in the Early Middle Ages c. 200–c. 1150* (Cambridge Studies in Medieval Life and Thought)

Cristianizzazione ed organizzazione ecclesiastica delle campagne nell' alto medioevo: espan-

sione e resistenze (1982), *Settimane* 28

Cubitt, C. (1995), *Anglo-Saxon Church Councils c. 650–c. 850*, Leicester

Deansley, M. (1962), *The Pre-Conquest Church in England*, London

Declercq, C. (1936, 1958), *Le législation religieuse franque* I: *De Clovis à Charlemagne (507–814)*; II: *De Louis le Pieux à la fin du IXe siècle (814–900)*, Leuven and Antwerp

Deshusses, J. (1971), *Le sacramentaire gregorien*, Fribourg

Duchesne, L. (1907–15), *Fastes épiscopaux de l'ancienne Gaule*, 3 vols., Paris

Ewig, E. (1979), *Spätantikes und fränkisches Gallien*, Zurich

Firey, A. and Reynolds, R. (1993), *Early Collections of Canon Law and their Manuscripts: A Vademecum*, Toronto

Foot, S.R.I. (1991), 'Violence against Christians? The Vikings and the church in ninth-century England', *Medieval History* 1: 1–16

Foot, S.R.I. (1992), 'Anglo-Saxon minsters: a review of terminology', in Blair and Sharpe (1992)

Fournier, P. (1983), *Mélanges de droit canonique*, ed. T. Kölzer, 2 vols., Aalen

Fournier, P. and Le Bras, G. (1931–2), *Histoire des collections canoniques en occident depuis les fausses décrétales jusqu'au décret de Gratien*, 2 vols., Paris

Frantzen, G. (1973), *Les collections canoniques* (Typologie des sources du moyen âge occidental 10), Turnhout

Fuhrmann, H. (1953–55), 'Studien zur Geschichte mittelalterlicher Patriachate', *ZRG KA* 39: 112–76; 40: 1084; 41: 95–183

Fuhrmann, H. (1972–4), *Einfluss und Verbreitung der pseudo-isidorischen Fälschungen von ihrem Auftauchen bis in die neuere Zeit* (MGH Schriften 24, 1–3), Stuttgart

Gams, P.B. (1973), *Series Episcoporum*, Regensburg

García y García, A. (1967), *Historia del derecho canonico* I: *El primer milenio*, Salamanca

Gottlob, T. (1928), *Der abendländischen Chorepiskopat*, Bonn

Hägele, G. (1984), *Das Paenitentiale Vallicellianum I: Ein oberitalienischer Zweig der frühmittelalterlichen kontinentalen Bussbücher* (Quellen und Forschungen zum Recht im Mittelalter 3), Sigmaringen

Hartmann, W. (1989), *Die Synoden der Karolingerzeit im Frankenreich und in Italien*, Paderborn

Hughes, K. (1966), *The Church in Early Irish Society*, London

Imbart de la Tour, P. (1900), *Les paroisses rurales du 4e au 11e siècle*, Paris

Kaiser, R. (1981), *Bischofsherrschaft zwischen Königtum und Fürstenmacht*, Bonn

Keefe, S.A. (1981), 'Baptismal instruction in the Carolingian period: the manuscript evidence', unpublished Ph.D. dissertation, Toronto

Keefe, S.A. (1984), 'Carolingian baptismal exposition; a handlist of tracts and manuscripts', in Blumenthal (1984): 169–237

Keefe, S.A. (forthcoming), *Water and the Word: Baptism and the Education of the Clergy in the Carolingian Empire: A Study of Texts and Manuscripts*

Kempf, F. (ed.) (1969), trans. A. Biggs, *The Church in an Age of Feudalism* (Handbook of Church History 3), London and New York

Kerff, F. (1982), *Der Quadripartitus: ein Handbuch der karolingischen Kirchenreform* (Quellen und Forschungen zum Recht im Mittelalter 1), Sigmaringen

Körntgen, L. (1993), *Studien zu den Quellen der frühmittelalterlichen Bussbücher* (Quellen und Forschungen zum Recht im Mittelalter 7), Sigmaringen

Kottje, R. (1965), 'Einheit und Vielfalt des kirchlichen Lebens in der Karolingerzeit', *Zeitschrift für Kirchengeschichte* 76: 323–42

Kottje, R. (1980), *Die Bussbücher Halitgars von Cambrai und des Hrabanus Maurus: ihre Überlieferung und ihre Quellen* (Beiträge zur Geschichte und Quellenkunde des Mittelalters 8), Berlin and New York

Kuttner, S. (1945), 'Cardinalis: the history of a canonical concept', *Traditio* 3: 129–214

Lanzoni, F. (1923), *Le origini delle diocesi antiche d'Italia* (Studi e Testi 35), Rome

Lemarignier, J.-F. (166), 'Quelques remarques sur l'organisation écclésiastique de la Gaule du VIIe à la fin du IXe siècle principalement au nord de la Loire', in *Settimane* 13: 451–86

Lesne, E. (1905), *La hierarchie épiscopale: provinces, métropolitains, primats en Gaule et en Germanie depuis la réforme de Saint-Boniface jusqu'à la mort d'Hincmar*, Paris

Lesne, E. (1910–43), *Histoire de la propriété écclésiastique en France*, 6 vols., Lille

Lesne, E. (1910), *L'origine des menses dans le temporel des églises et des monastères de France au IXe siècle*, Paris

Levison, W. (1946), *England and the Continent in the Eighth Century*, Oxford

Lot, F. and Fawtier, R. (1962), *Histoire des institutions françaises au moyen âge* III: *Institutions écclésiastiques*, Paris

Lynch, J. (1986), *Godparents and Kinship in Early Medieval Europe*, Princeton

Maassen, F. (1870), *Geschichte der Quellen und der Literatur des kanonischen Rechts im Abendlande*, Graz

McKeon, P. (1978), *Hincmar of Laon and Carolingian Politics*, Urbana, IL

McKitterick, R. (1977), *The Frankish Church and the Carolingian Reforms, 789–895*, London

McKitterick, R. (1985) 'Knowledge of canon law in the Frankish kingdoms before 789: the manuscript evidence', *JTS* 35: 87–117

McKitterick, R. (1992a), 'Nuns' scriptoria in Francia and England in the eighth century', *Francia* 19, 1: 1–35

McKitterick, R. (1992b) 'Royal patronage of culture in the Frankish kingdoms under the Carolingians: motives and consequences', *Settimane* 39: 93–129

McKitterick, R. (ed.) (1990), *The Uses of Literacy in Early Mediaeval Europe*, Cambridge

McKitterick, R. (ed.) (1994) *Carolingian Culture: Emulation and Innovation*, Cambridge

Mayeur, J.M., Pietri, C. and L., Vauchez, A. and Venard, M. (eds.) (1993), *Histoire du christianisme* IV: *Evêques, moines et empereurs (610–1054)*, Paris

Mordek, H. (1975), *Kirchenrecht und Reform im Frankenreich: die Collectio Vetus Gallica, die älteste systematische Kanonensammlung des fränkischen Gallien: Studien und Edition* (Beiträge zur Geschichte und Quellenkunde des Mittelalters 1), Berlin and New York

Mordek, H. and Reynolds, R. (1991), 'Bischof Leodegar und das Konzil von Autun', in *Aus Archiven und Bibliotheken: Studien zum Recht und zur Kirchengeschichte des Mittelalters: Festschrift für Raymund Kottje zum 65. Geburtstag*, ed. H. Mordek (Freiburger Beiträge zur mittelalterlichen Geschichte 3), Bern, pp. 71–92

La Neustrie: les pays au nord de la Loire de Dagobert à Charles le Chauve (VIIe–IXe siècles) (Exhibition catalogue), ed. P. Perin and L.C. Feffer, Rouen

Noble, T.F.X. (1984), *The Republic of St Peter: The Birth of the Papal State, 680–825*, Philadelphia, PA

Noble, T.F.X. (1990), 'Literacy and the papal government in late antiquity and the early middle ages', in McKitterick (1990), pp. 82–108

Orlandi, G. (1982), 'Dati e problemi sull'organizzazione della chiese irlandese tra v e ix secolo', *Settimane* 28: 713–57

Palazzo, E. (1993), *Le moyen âge des origines au XIIIe siècle* (Histoire des livres liturgiques), Paris

Paxton, F.S. (1990), *Christianizing Death: The Creation of a Ritual Process in Early Medieval Europe*, Ithaca

Pöschl, A. (1908), *Bischofsgut und Mensa Epsicopalis*, Bonn

Rankin, S. (1994), "Carolingian music', in McKitterick (1993), pp. 274–316

Reynolds, R.E. (1970), 'The pseudo-Hieronymian *De septem ordinibus ecclesiae*: notes on its origins, abridgements and use in early medieval canonical collections', *RB* 80: 238–52

Reynolds, R.E. (1972), 'The *De officiis vii graduum*: its origins and early medieval development', *Mediaeval Studies* 34: 113–51

Reynolds, R.E. (1975a), 'Excerpta from the *Collectio hibernensis* in three Vatican manuscripts', *Bulletin of Medieval Canon Law*, n.s. 5: 1–9

Reynolds, R.E. (1975b), 'Isidore's texts on the clerical grades in an early medieval Roman manuscript', *Classical Folia* 29: 95–101

Reynolds, R.E. (1975c), 'A ninth-century treatise on the origins, office and ordination of the bishop', *RB* 85: 321–32

Reynolds, R.E. (1978), *The Ordinals of Christ from their Origins to the Twelfth Century* (Beiträge zur Geschichte und Quellenkunde des Mittelalters 7), Berlin and New York

Reynolds, R.E. (1979a), 'An early medieval tract on the diaconate', *Harvard Theological Review* 72: 97–100

Reynolds, R.E. (1979b), 'The "Isidorian" *Epistula ad Leudefredum*: an early medieval epitome of the clerical duties', *Mediaeval Studies* 41: 252–330

Reynolds, R.E. (1980), 'Canon law collections in early ninth-century Salzburg', in *Proceedings of the Fifth International Congress of Medieval Canon Law: Salamanca 21–25 September 1976*, ed. S. Kuttner and K. Pennington (Monumenta Iuris Canonici, ser. c, subsidia 6), Vatican, pp. 15–34

Reynolds, R.E. (1983a), 'Patristic "presbyterianism" in the early medieval theology of sacred orders', *Mediaeval Studies* 45: 311–42

Reynolds, R.E. (1983b), 'Image and text: a Carolingian illustration of modifications in the early Roman eucharistic *ordines*', *Viator* 14: 59–82

Reynolds, R.E. (1983c), 'Image and text: the liturgy of clerical ordination in early medieval art', *Gesta* 22: 27–38

Reynolds, R.E. (1984) 'Unity and diversity in Carolingian canon law collections: the case of the *Collectio hibernensis* and its derivatives', in Blumenthal (1984), pp. 99–135

Reynolds, R.E. (1987), 'Rites and signs of conciliar decisions in the early middle ages', *Settimane* 33: 207–49

Santifaller, L. (1976), *Liber Diurnus: Studien und Forschungen von Leo Santifaller* (Päpste und Papsttum 10), Stuttgart

Schmidt, H. (1929), 'Trier und Rheims in ihrer verfassungsrechtlichen Entwicklung bis zum Primatialstreit des 9. Jahrhunderts, *ZRG KA* 18: 1–111

Semmler, J. (1982), 'Mission und Pfarrorganisation in den Rheinischen, Mosel-und-Massländischen Bistümern (5.–10. Jahrhundert), *Settimane* 28: 813–88

Sharpe, R. (1984), 'Some problems concerning the organization of the church in early medieval Ireland', *Peritia* 3: 230–70

Sieber, H.J. (1984), *Die Konzilsidee des lateinischen Mittelalters (847–1378)*, Paderborn

Stickler, A.M. (1950), *Historia iuris canonici latini: institutiones academicae* 1: *Historia fontium*, Turin

Stratmann, M. (1991), *Hinkmar von Reims als Verwalter von Bistum und Kirchenprovinz* (Quellen und Forschungen zum Recht im Mittelalter 6), Sigmaringen

van Hove, A. (1945), *Commentarium lovaniense in codicem iuris canonici* 1: *Prolegomena ad codicem iuris canonici*, 2nd edn, Malines

Vogel, C. (1978), *Les 'Libri paenitentiales'* (Typologie des sources du moyen âge occidental 27), Turnhout

Vogel, C. (1986), *Medieval Liturgy: An Introduction to the Sources*, revised and trans. by W.G. Storey and N.K. Rasmussen, Washington, DC

Vollrath, H. (1985), *Die Synoden Englands bis 1066*, Paderborn

Wallace-Hadrill, J.M. (1983), *The Frankish Church* (Oxford History of the Christian Church) Oxford

23 CAROLINGIAN MONASTICISM: THE POWER OF PRAYER

Angenendt, A. (1972), *Monachi Peregrini: Studien zur Pirmin und den monastischen Vorstellungen des frühen Mittelalters* (MMS 6), Munich

Angenendt, A. (1973), 'Willibrord im Dienste der Karolinger', *Annalen des historischen Vereins für den Niederrhein* 63–113

Angenendt, A. (1978/9), 'Religiosität und Theologie. Ein spannungsreiches Verhältnis im Mittelalter', *Archiv für Liturgiewissenschaft* 17: 153–221

Angenendt, A. (1983), '*Missa specialis*. Zugleich ein Beitrag zur Entstehung der Privatmessen', *FrSt* 17: 153–221

Angenendt, A. (1984a), *Kaiserherrschaft und Königstaufe: Kaiser, Könige und Päpste als geistliche Patrone in der abendländischen Missionsgeschichte* (Arbeiten zur Frühmittelalterforschung 15), Berlin/New York

Angenendt, A. (1984b), 'Theologie und Liturgie der mittelalterlichen Totenmemoria', in K. Schmid and J. Wollasch (eds.), *Memoria: Der geschichtliche Zeugniswert des liturgischen Gedenkens im Mittelalter* (MMS 48), Munich, pp. 79–199

Angenendt, A. (1990a), *Das Frühmittelalter: Die abendländische Christenheit von 400 bis 900*, Stuttgart, Berlin and Cologne

Angenendt, A. (1990b), 'Willibald zwischen Mönchtum und Bischofsamt', in H. Dickerhof, Ernst Reiter and Stefan Weinfurter (eds.), *Der heilige Willibald – Klosterbischof oder Bistumsgründer?*, Regensburg, pp. 146–69

Angenendt, A. (1993), '"Mit reinen Händen". Das Motiv der kultischen Reinheit in der abendländischen Askese', in G. Jenal and S. Haarländer (eds.), *Herrschaft, Kirche, Kultur: Beiträge zur Geschichte des Mittelalters. Festschrift für Friedrich Prinz zu seinem 65. Geburtstag.* (Monographien zur Geschichte des Mittelalters 37), Stuttgart

Angerer, J.F. (1977), 'Zur Problematik der Begriffe Regula – Consuetudo – Observanz – Orden', *StMBO* 88: 312–23

Angerer, J.F. (1989), 'Consuetudo und Reform', in R. Kottje and H. Maurer (eds.), *Monastische Reformen im 9. und 10. Jahrhundert*, Sigmaringen, pp. 107–16

Becher, H. (1983), 'Das Königliche Frauenkloster San Salvatore/Santa Giulia in Brescia im Spiegel seiner Memorialüberlieferung', *FrSt* 17: 299–392

Bischoff, B. (1981), 'Die Bibliothek im Dienst der Schule', in B. Bischoff, *MS* 11, pp. 213–33

Bock, C. (1952), 'Tonsure monastique et tonsure cléricale', *Revue de Droit Canonique* 2: 373–406

Boswell, J.E. (1984), '*Expositio* and *oblatio*. The abandonment of children in the ancient and medieval family', *AHR* 89: 10–33

Constable, G. (1964), *Monastic Tithes from their Origins to the Twelfth Century* (Cambridge Studies in Medieval Life and Thought 10), London

Constable, G. (1982), 'Monasteries, rural churches and the *cura animarum* in the early middle ages', *Settimane* 28, 1: 349–89

Constable, G. (1987), 'The ceremonies and symbols of entering religious life and taking the monastic habit, from the fourth to the twelfth century', *Settimane* 33, 11: 771–834

de Jong, M. (1983), 'Growing up in a Carolingian monastery: Magister Hildemar and his oblates', *JMH* 9: 99–128

de Jong, M. (1986), *Kind en klooster in de vroege middeleeuwen*, Amsterdam

de Jong, M. (1989), 'In Samuel's image: child oblation and the Rule of St Benedict in the early Middle Ages (600–900)', *Regulae Benedicti Studia* 16: 69–79

de Jong, M. (1992), 'Power and humility in Carolingian society: the public penance of Louis the Pious', *EME* 1: 29–52

Dierkens, A. (1985), *Abbayes et chapitres entre Sambre et Meuse (VIIe–XIe siècles: contribution à l'histoire religieuse des campagnes du haut moyen âge* (Beihefte der Francia 14), Sigmaringen

Donat, L. (1990), 'Les coutumes monastiques autour de l'an mil', in D. Iogna-Prat and J.-Ch. Picard (eds.), *Religion et culture autour de l'an mil: royaume capétien et Lotharingie (Actes du colloque Hughes Capet, 987–1987)*, Paris, pp. 17–24

Dubois, J. (1981), 'Sainte Bathilde (vers 625–680), reine de France (641–655), fondatrice de l'abbaye de Chelles', *Paris et Ile-de-France, Mémoires* 32: 13–20

Ewig, E. (1982), 'Der Gebetsdienst der Kirchen in den Urkunden der späteren Karolinger', in H. Maurer and H. Patze (eds.), *Festschrift für Bernt Schwineköper: zu seinem siebzigsten Geburtstag*, Sigmaringen, pp. 45–86

Felten, F.J. (1980), *Äbte und Laienäbte im Frankenreich: Studie zum Verhältnis von Staat und Kirche im früheren Mittelalter* (Monographien zur Geschichte des Mittelalters 20), Stuttgart

Felten, F.J. (1988), 'Herrschaft des Abtes', in J. Prinz (ed.), *Herrschaft und Kirche: Beiträge zur Entstehung und Wirkungsweise episkopaler und monastischer Organisationsformen* (Monographien zur Geschichte des Mittelalters 33), Stuttgart, pp. 147–296

Fleckenstein, J. (1953), *Die Bildungsreform Karls des Grossen als Verwirklichung der norma rectitudinis*, Freiburg

Foot, S. (1992a), '"By water in the spirit": the administration of baptism in early Anglo-Saxon England', in J. Blair and R. Sharpe (eds.), *Pastoral Care before the Parish*, Leicester, pp. 171–9

Foot, S. (1992b), 'Anglo-Saxon minsters: a review of terminology', in J. Blair and R.

Sharpe (eds.), *Pastoral Care before the Parish*, Leicester, pp. 212–50

Frank, K.S. (1951), 'Untersuchungen zur Geschichte der benediktinischen Professliturgie im frühen Mittelalter', *StMBO* 63: 93–139

Freise, E. (1978), 'Studien zum Einzugsbereich der Klostergemeinschaft Fulda', in K. Schmid (ed.), *Die Klostergemeinschaft von Fulda im früheren Mittelalter* II, 3 (MMS 8), Munich, pp. 1003–1269

Freise, E. (1984), 'Kalendarische und annalistische Grundformen der Memoria', in K. Schmid and J. Wollasch (eds.), *Memoria: Der geschichtliche Zeugniswert des liturgischen Gedenkens im Mittelalter* (MMS 48), Munich, pp. 441–577

Ganz, D. (1990a), 'The debate on predestination', in M.T. Gibson and J.L. Nelson (eds.), *Charles the Bald: Court and Kingdom*, rev. edn, Aldershot, pp. 281–302

Ganz, D. (1990b), *Corbie in the Carolingian Renaissance* (Beihefte der Francia 20), Sigmaringen

Gerchow, J. (1988), *Die Gedenküberlieferung der Angelsachsen: Mit einem Katalog der Libri vitae und Necrologien* (Arbeiten zur Frühmittelalterforschung 20), Berlin and New York

Geuenich, D. (1988), 'Zur Stellung und Wahl des Abtes in der Karolingerzeit', in G. Althoff, D. Geuenich, O.G. Oexle and J. Wollasch (eds.), *Person und Gemeinschaft im Mittelalter, Karl Schmid zum 65. Geburtstag*, Sigmaringen, pp. 171–86

Geuenich, D. (1989), 'Gebetsgedenken und Anianische Reform: Beobachtungen zu den Verbrüderungsbeziehungen der Äbte im Reich Ludwigs des Frommen', in R. Kottje and H. Maurer (eds.), *Monastische Reformen im 9. and 10. Jahrhundert*, Sigmaringen, pp. 49–106

Grégoire, R. (1967/8), 'Le communion des moines-prêtres à la messe d'après le coutumiers monastiques médiévaux', *Sacris Eruditi* 18: 524–49

Hafner, W. (1959), *Der Basiliuskommentar zur Regula S. Benedicti: Ein Beitrag zur Autorenfrage Karolingischer Regelkommentare* (Beiträge zur Geschichte des alten Mönchtums und des Benediktinerordens 23), Münster

Hafner, W. (1962), 'Der Sankt Galler Klosterplan im Lichte von Hildemars Regelkommentar', in J. Duft (ed.), *Studien zum Sankt Galler Klosterplan* (Mitteilungen zur vaterländischen Geschichte 42), St Gall, pp. 177–92

Hallinger, K. (1977), 'Regula Benedicti c. 64 und die Wahlgewohnheiten des 6. bis 12. Jahrhunderts', in H. Bannest and J. Divjak (eds.), *Latinität und Alte Kirche: Festschrift für Rudolf Hanslik zum 70. Geburtstag* (Wiener Studien, Beiheft 8), Vienna, Cologne and Graz, pp. 119–27

Hallinger, K. (1979), 'Überlieferung und Steigerung im Mönchtum des achten bis zwölften Jahrhunderts', in *Analecta Liturgica* I (Studia Anselmiana 68), Rome, pp. 125–87

Hallinger, K. (1980), 'Consuetudo. Begriff, Formen, Forschungsgeschichte, Inhalt', in *Untersuchungen zu Kloster und Stift* (Veröffentlichungen des Max-Planck-Instituts für Geschichte 68; Studien zur Germania Sacra 14), Göttingen, pp. 140–66

Hartmann, W. (1982), 'Der rechtliche Zustand der Kirchen auf dem Lande: die Eigenkirche in der fränkischen Gesetzgebung des 7.–9. Jahrhunderts', *Settimane* 28, 1: 397–441

Hartmann, W. (1989), *Die Synoden der Karolingerzeit im Frankreich und in Italien*, Paderborn, Munich, Vienna and Zurich

Häussling, A.A. (1973), *Mönchskonvent und Eucharistiefeier: Eine Studie über die Messe in der abendländischen Klosterliturgie des frühen Mittelalters und zur Geschichte der Messhäufigkeit* (Liturgiegeschichtliche Quellen und Forschungen 8), Münster

Hecht, K. (1983), *Der Sankt Galler Klosterplan*, Sigmaringen

Hildebrandt, M.M. (1992), *The External School in Carolingian Society*, Leiden

Hlawitschka, E. (1961), 'Zur Klosterverlegung und zur Annahme der Benedikts-regel in Remiremont', *Zeitschrift für die Geschichte des Oberrheins* 109, NF 70: 259–69

Hlawitschka, E. (1978), 'Beobachtungen und Überlegungen zur Konventsstärke im Nonnenkloster Remiremont während des 7.–9. Jahrhunderts', in G. Melville (ed.), *Secundum regulam vivere: Festschrift N. Backmund*, Windberg, pp. 33–9

Horn, W. and Born, E. (1979), *The Plan of St Gall: A Study of the Architecture and Economy of, and Life in a Paradigmatic Carolingian Monastery*, 3 vols., Los Angeles and London

Jakobi, F.J. (1986), 'Diptychen als frühe Form der Gedenkaufzeichnungen. Zum "Herrscherdiptychon" im Liber Memorialis von Remiremont (Taf. XII–XIII)', *FrSt* 20: 186–212

Kaiser, R. (1988), 'Königtum und Bischofsherrschaft im frühmittelalterlichen Neustrien', in F. Prinz (ed.), *Herrschaft und Kirche: Beiträge zur Entstehung und wirkungsweise episkopaler und monastischer Organisationsformen* (Monographien zur Geschichte des Mittelalters 33), Stuttgart, pp. 83–108

Kottje, R. (1965), 'Einheit und Vielfalt des kirchlichen Lebens in der Karolinger-zeit', *Zeitschrift für Kirchengeschichte* 76: 323–42

Kottje R. (1989), 'Monastische Reform oder Reformen?', in *Monastische Reformen im 9. und 10. Jahrhundert* (VuF 38), Sigmaringen, pp. 9–13

Kottje, R. and Maurer, H. (eds.), *Monastische Reformen im 9. und 10. Jahrhundert* (VuF 38), Sigmaringen 1989

Kuchenbuch, L. (1978), *Bäuerliche Gesellschaft und Klosterherrschaft im 9. Jahrhundert* (*VSWG*, Beiheft 66), Wiesbaden

Kuchenbuch, L. (1988), 'Die Klostergrundherrschaft im Mittelalter. Eine Zwischenbilanz', in F. Prinz (ed.), *Herrschaft und Kirche: Beiträge zur Entstehung und wirkungsweise episkopaler und monastischer Organisationsformen* (Monographien zur Geschichte des Mittelalters 33), Stuttgart, pp. 297–343

Leclercq, J. (1971), 'Profession according to the Rule of St Benedict', in M. Basil Pennington (ed.), *Rule and Life: An Interdisciplinary Symposium* (Cistercian Studies Series 12), Kalamazoo, pp. 117–49

Leclercq, J. (1979), 'New recruitment – new psychology', in J. Leclercq, *Monks and Love in Twelfth Century France: Psycho-Historical Essays*, Oxford, pp. 8–26

McKitterick, R. (1977), *The Frankish Church and the Carolingian Reforms (789–895)*, London

McKitterick, R. (1983), *The Frankish Kingdoms under the Carolingians, 751–987*, London

McKitterick, R. (1989), *The Carolingians and the Written Word*, Cambridge

Metz, W. (1978), *Das Servitium regis: zur Erforschung der wirtschaftlichen Grundlagen des hochmittelalterlichen deutschen Königtums* (Erträge der Forschung 89), Darmstadt

Moyse, G. (1982), 'Monachisme et réglementation monastique en Gaule avant Benoît d'Aniane', in *Sous la règle de St Benoît: structures monastiques et sociétés en France du moyen âge à l'époque moderne* (Hautes études médiévales et modernes V, 47), Geneva and Paris, pp. 3–19

Nelson, J.L. (1983), 'The Church's military service in the ninth century: a contemporary comparative view?', *Studies in Church History* 20: 15–30; (reprinted in J. Nelson (1986), *Politics and Ritual in Early Medieval Europe*, London and Ronceverte, pp. 117–32

Nelson, J.L. (1992), *Charles the Bald*, London

Nussbaum, O. (1961), *Kloster, Priestermönch und Privatmesse: Ihr Verhältnis im Westen von den Anfänge bis zum hohen Mittelalter*, (Theophaneia, Beiträge zur Religions- und Kirchengeschichte des Altertums 14), Bonn

Oexle, O.G. (1978a), *Forschungen zu monastischen und geistlichen Gemeinschaften im westfränkischen Bereich* (MMS 31), Munich

Oexle, O.G. (1978b), 'Memorialüberlieferung und Gebetsgedächtnis in Fulda von 8. bis zum 11. Jahrhundert', in K. Schmid (ed.), *Die Klostergemeinschaft von Fulda im früheren Mittelalter* (MMS 8), Munich, pp. 136–77

Oexle O.G. (1983), 'Die Gegenwart der Toten', in H. Braet and W. Verbeke (eds.), *Death in the Middle Ages* (Mediaevalia Lovaniensia I, 9), Leuven, pp. 365–405

Padberg, L. von (1980), *Heilige und Familie: Studien zur Bedeutung familiengebundener Aspekte in den Viten des Verwandten und Schülerkreises um Willibrord, Bonifatius und Liudger*, Münster

Prinz, F. (1965), *Frühes Mönchtum im Frankenreich: Kultur und Gesellschaft in Gallien, den Rheinländen und Bayern am Beispiel der monastischen Entwicklung (4. bis 8. Jahrhundert)*, Munich, 2nd edn, Darmstadt (1988)

Prinz, F. (1971), *Klerus und Krieg im früheren Mittelalter: Untersuchungen zur Rolle der Kirche beim Aufbau der Königsherrschaft* (Monographien zur Geschichte des Mittelalters 2), Stuttgart

Prinz, F. (ed.), (1988), *Herrschaft und Kirche: Beiträge zur Entstehung und Wirkungsweise episkopaler und monastischer Organisationsformen* (Monographien zur Geschichte des Mittelalters 33), Stuttgart

Rädle, F. (1980), 'Gottschalk der Sachse', in *Die Deutsche Literatur des Mittelalters: Verfasserlexikon* III, pp. 189–99

Sanderson, W. (1985), 'The plan of St Gall reconsidered', *Speculum* 60: 615–32

Sandmann, M. (1978), 'Wirkungsbereiche Fuldischer Mönche', in K. Schmid (ed.), *Die Klostergemeinschaft von Fulda im früheren mittelalter* II (MMS 8), Munich, pp. 692–791

Schieffer, R. (1976), *Die Entstehung von Domkapiteln in Deutschland* (Bonner historische Forschungen 43), Bonn

Schmid, K. (1977), 'Bemerkungen zur Anlage des Reichenauer Verbrüderungs- buches. Zugleich ein Beitrag zum Verständnis der "Visio Wettini"', in K. Elm, E. Gönner and E. Hillenbrand (eds.), *Landesgeschichte und Geistesgeschichte: Fest- schrift für Otto Herding zum 65. Geburtstag*, Stuttgart, pp. 24–41

Schmid, K. (1978a), 'Die Frage nach den Anfängen der Mönchsgemeinschaft in Fulda', in Schmid (ed.), *Die Klostergemeinschaft von Fulda im früheren Mittelalter* I (MMS 8), Munich, pp. 108–35

Schmid, K. (1978b), 'Mönchslisten und Klosterkonvent von Fulda zur Zeit der Karolingen', in K. Schmid (ed.), *Die Klostergemeinschaft von Fulda im früheren Mittelalter* II, 2 (MMS 8), Munich pp. 571–635

Schmid K. (1979), 'Das liturgische Gebetsgedenken in seiner historischen Relevanz am Beispiel der Verbrüderungsbewegung des früheren Mittelalters', *Freiburger*

Diözesan-Archiv 99: 20–44; reprinted in K. Schmid (1985), *Gebetsgedenken und adliges Selbstverständnis im Mittelalter: Ausgewählte Beiträge. Festgabe zu seinem 60. Geburtstag*, Sigmaringen (1983), pp. 620–44

Schmid K. (1980), 'Bemerkungen zum Konstanzer Klerus der Karolingerzeit. Mit einem Hinweis auf religiöse Bruderschaften in seinem Umkreis', *Freiburger Diözesan-Archiv* 100, Dritte Folge 32: 26–58

Schmid, K. (1982), 'Hrabanus Maurus und seine Mönche im Spiegel der Memorialüberlieferung', in R. Kottje and H. Zimmermann (eds.), *Hrabanus Maurus, Lehrer, Abt und Bischof*, Wiesbaden, pp. 102–17

Schmid K. (1984), 'Bruderschaften mit den Mönchen aus der Sicht des Kaiserbesuchs im Galluskloster vom Jahre 883', in H. Maurer (ed.), *Churrätisches und St Gallisches Mittelalter: Festschrift für Otto P. Clavadetscher zu seinem 65. Geburtstag*, Sigmaringen, pp. 173–94

Schmid K. (1986), 'Bemerkungen zu Synodalverbrüderungen der Karolingerzeit', in K. Hauck, K. Kroeschel and S. Sonderegger (eds.), *Sprache und Recht. Beiträge zur Kulturgeschichte des Mittelalters: Festschrift für Ruth Schmidt-Wiegand zum 60. Geburtstag*, pp. 693–710

Schmid K. (1989), 'Mönchtum und Verbrüderung', in R. Kottje and H. Maurer (eds.), *Monastische Reformen im 9. und 10. Jahrhundert* (VuF 38), Sigmaringen, pp. 117–46

Schmid, K. (1991), 'Von den "fratres conscripti" in Ekkehards St Galler Klostergeschichten', *FrSt* 25: 109–22

Schmid, K. and Althoff, G. (1980), 'Rückblick auf die Fuldaer Klostergemeinschaft. Zugleich ein Ausblick', *FrSt* 14: 188–218

Schmid, K. and Oexle, O.G. (1974), 'Voraussetzungen und Wirkung des Gebetsbundes von Attigny', *Francia* 2: 71–122

Schmid, K. and Wollasch, J. (1967), 'Die Gemeinschaft von Lebenden und Verstorbenen in Zeugnissen des Mittelalters', *FrSt* 1: 365–405

Schwind, F. (1984), 'Zu karolingerzeitlichen Klöstern als Wirtschaftsorganismen und Stätten handwerklicher Tätigkeit', in L. Fenske, W. Rösener and Th. Zotz (eds.), *Institutionen, Kultur und Gesellschaft im Mittelalter: Festschrift für J. Fleckenstein zu seinem 65. Geburtstag*, Sigmaringen, pp. 101–23

Semmler, J. (1958), 'Studien zum *Supplex Libellus* und zur anianischen Reform in Fulda', *Zeitschrift für Kirchengeschichte* 69: 268–98

Semmler, J. (1960), 'Zur Überlieferung der monastischen Gesetzgebung Ludwigs des Frommen', *DA* 16: 309–88

Semmler, J. (1963), 'Die Beschlüsse des Aachener Konzils im Jahre 816', *Zeitschrift für Kirchengeschichte* 74: 15–82

Semmler, J. (1965), 'Karl der Grosse und das fränkische Mönchtum', in *Karl der Grosse* II, pp. 255–89

Semmler, J. (1973), 'Chrodegang, Bischof von Metz 747–766', in F. Knöpp (ed.), *Die Reichsabtei Lorsch: Festschrift zum Gedenken an ihre Stiftung, 764*, Darmstadt, pp. 229–45

Semmler, J. (1974), '*Episcopi potestas* und karolingische Klosterpolitik', in A. Borst (ed.), *Mönchtum, Episkopat und Adel zur Gründungszeit des Klosters Reichenau* (VuF 20), Sigmaringen, pp. 305–95

Semmler J. (1975), 'Pippin III. und die fränkischen Klöster', *Francia* 3: 88–146

Semmler, J. (1977), 'Zur pippinidisch-karolingische Suksessionskrise, 714–723', *DA* 33: 1–36

Semmler, J. (1980), 'Mönche und Kanoniker im Frankenreich Pippins III und Karls des Grossen', in *Untersuchungen zu Kloster und Stift* (Veröffentlichungen des Max-Planck-Instituts für Geschichte 68), Göttingen, pp. 78–111

Semmler, J. (1982), 'Iussit…princeps renovare…praecepta. Zur verfassungsrechtlichen Einordnung der Hochstifte und Abteien in die Karolingische Reichskirche' in J.F. Angerer and J. Lenzweger (eds.), *Consuetudines monasticae: Eine Festgabe für Kassius Hallinger aus Anlass seines 70. Geburtstages* (Studia Anselmiana 85), Rome, pp. 97–124

Semmler, J. (1983), 'Benedictus II: una regula – una consuetudo', in W. Lourdaux and D. Verhelst (eds.), *Benedictine Culture, 750–1050* (Mediaevalia Lovaniensia 1/11), Leuven, pp. 1–49

Semmler, J. (1989a), 'Das Erbe der karolingischen Klosterreform im 10. Jahrhundert', in R. Kottje and H. Maurer (eds.), *Monastische Reformen im 9. und 10. Jahrhundert* (VuF 38), Sigmaringen, pp. 27–77

Semmler, J. (1989b), 'Saint-Denis: von der bischöflichen Coemeterialbasilika zur königlichen Benediktinerabtei', in *La Neustrie* II, pp. 75–123

Semmler, J. (1990), 'Renovatio regni Francorum. Die Herrschaft Ludwigs des Frommen im Frankenreich, 814–829/30', in P. Godman and R. Collins (eds.) *Charlemagne's Heir* (Oxford), pp. 125–46

Semmler, J. (1992), 'Benediktinische Reform und kaiserliches Privileg. Zur Frage des institutionellen Zusammenschlusses der Klöster um Benedikt von Aniane', in G. Melville (ed.), *Institutionen und Geschichte: Theoretische Aspekte und mittelalterliche Befunde*, Cologne, Weimar and Vienna, pp. 259–93

Sprandel, R. (1958), *Das Kloster St Gallen in der Verfassung des karolingischen Reiches* (Forschungen zur oberrheinischen Landesgeschichte 7), Freiburg i.B.

Stratmann, M. (1991), *Hinkmar von Reims als Verwalter von Bistum und Kirchenprovinz* (Quellen und Forschungen zum Recht im Mittelalter 6), Sigmaringen

Traill, D.A. (1974), *Walafrid Strabo's Visio Wettini: Text, Translation and Commentary* (Lateinische Sprache und Literatur des Mittelalters 2), Frankfurt am Main

Vogel, C. (1980), 'Une mutation cultuelle inexpliquée: le passage de l'Eucharistie communautaire à la messe privée', *Revue des Sciences Religieuses* 54: 231–50

Vogel, C. (1981), 'La multiplication des messes solitaires au moyen âge. Essai de statistique', *Revue des Sciences Religieuses* 55: 206–13

De Vogüé, A. (1975), 'La Règle de Donat pour L'Abesse Gauthstrude. Texte critique et synopse des sources, *Benedictina* 25: 219–313

De Vogüé, A. (1984), 'Le Plan de Saint-Gall, copie d'un document officiel', *RB* 94: 295–314

Weidinger, U. (1991), *Untersuchungen zur Wirtschaftsstruktur des Klosters Fulda in der Karolingerzeit* (Monographien zur Geschichte des Mittelalters 36), Stuttgart

Wollasch, J. (1973) *Mönchtum des Mittelalters zwischen Kirche und Welt* (MMS 7), Munich

Wollasch, J. (1978), 'Klösterlichen Gemeinschaften als Träger sozialen Lebens vor der Zeit der Städte', in *Prosopographie als Sozialgeschichte? Methoden personengeschichtlicher Erforschung des Mittelalters. Sektionsbeiträge zum 32. deutschen Historikertag*, Munich, pp. 39–43

Wollasch, J. (1982), 'Benedictus abbas Romensis. Das römische Element in der frühen benediktinischen Tradition', in N. Kamp and J. Wollasch (eds.), *Tradition als historische Kraft: Interdisziplinäre Forschungen zur Geschichte des früheren Mittelalters*, Berlin and New York, pp. 119–37

Wollasch, J. (1984), 'Das Mönchsgelübde als Opfer', *FrSt* 18: 529–45

Wood, I.N. (1982), 'The *vita Columbani* and Merovingian hagiography', *Peritia* 1: 63–80

Wood, I.N. (1993), *The Merovingian Kingdoms (450–751)*, London

Zelzer, K. (1989), 'Von Benedikt zu Hildemar. Zu Textgestalt und Textgeschichte der Regula Benedicti auf iheren Weg zu Alleingeltung', *FrSt* 23: 112–30

Zelzer, K. (1981), 'Zur Überlieferung der Regula Benedicti im französischen Raum', in F. Paschke (ed.), *Überlieferungsgeschichtliche Untersuchungen* (Texte und Untersuchungen zur Geschichte altchristlicher Literatur 125), Berlin, pp. 638–44

Zettler, A. (1990), 'Der St Galler Klosterplan. Überlegungen zu seiner Herkunft und seiner Entstehung', in P. Godman and R. Collins (eds.), *Charlemagne's Heir* Oxford, pp. 659–63

24 RELIGION AND LAY SOCIETY

Introductory and general

Angenendt, A. (1982), 'Die Liturgie und die Organisation des kirchlichen Lebens auf dem Lande', *Settimane* 28, 1: 169–226

Angenendt, A. (1984), *Kaiserherrschaft und Königstaufe: Kaiser, Könige und Päpste als geistliche Patrone in der abendländischen Missionsgeschichte*, Berlin

Angenendt, A. (1990), *Das Frühmittelalter: Die abendländische Christenheit von 400 bis 900*, Stuttgart

Brommer, P. (1974), 'Die bischöfliche Gesetzgebung Theodulfs von Orléans', *ZRG KA* 60: 1–120

Chélini, J. (1991), *L'Aube du moyen âge: naissance de la chrétienté occidentale*, Paris

Delaruelle, E. (1954), 'Jonas d'Orléans et le moralisme carolingien', *Bulletin de Littérature Ecclésiastique* 55: 129–43, 221–8

Devailly, G. (1973), 'La pastorale en Gaule au ixe siècle', *RHEF* 59: 23–54

Hartmann, W. (1989), *Die Synoden der Karolingerzeit im Frankenreich und in Italien*, Paderborn

Kottje, R. (1965), 'Einheit und Vielfalt des kirchlichen Lebens in der Karolingerzeit', *Zeitschrift für Kirchengeschichte* 76: 323–42

McKitterick, R. (1977), *The Frankish Church and the Carolingian Reforms, 798–895*, London

Riché, P. (1981), *Instruction et vie religieuse dans le haut moyen âge*, London

Sullivan, R.E. (1966), 'Khan Boris and the conversion of Bulgaria: a case study in the impact of Christianity on a barbarian society', *Studies in Medieval and Renaissance History* 3: 55–139

Vauchez, A. (1975), *La Spiritualité du haut moyen âge occidental, VIII–XIIe siècles*, Paris

Wallach, L. (1955), 'Alcuin on virtues and vices: a manual for a Carolingian soldier', *Harvard Theological Review* 48: 175–95

Baptism and community

Angenendt, A. (1985), 'Der Taufritus im frühen Mittelalter', *Settimane* 33, 1: 275–321

Fisher, J.D.C. (1965), *Baptism in the Medieval West: A Study in the Disintegration of the Primitive Rite of Initiation* (Alcuin Club Collections 47), London

Flandrin, J.-L. (1983), *Un Temps pour embrasser: aux origines de la morale sexuelle occidentale (VIe–XIe siècle)*, Paris

Foot, S.R.I. (1992), '"By water in the spirit": the administration of baptism in early Anglo-Saxon England', in J. Blair and R. Sharpe (eds.), *Pastoral Care before the Parish*, London, pp. 171–92

Genicot, L. (1990), *Rural Communities in the Medieval West*, Baltimore

Gy, P.-M. (1976), 'Evangélisation et sacrements au moyen âge', in C. Kannengiesser and Y. Marchasson (eds.), *Humanisme et foi chrétienne: mélanges scientifiques du centenaire de l'Institut Catholique de Paris*, Paris, pp. 565–72

Gy, P.-M. (1990), 'Du baptême pascal des petits enfants au baptême *quamprimum*', in M. Sot (ed.), *Haut moyen âge: éducation, culture et société. Etudes offertes à Pierre Riché*, Paris, pp. 353–65

Keefe, S.A. (1983), 'Carolingian baptismal expositions: a handlist of tracts and manuscripts', in U.-R. Blumenthal (ed.), *Carolingian Essays*, Washington, DC, pp. 169–237

Keefe, S.A. (1986), 'An unknown response from the archiepiscopal province of Sens to Charlemagne's circulatory inquiry on baptism', *RB* 96: 48–93

Keefe, S.A. (forthcoming), *Water and the Word: Baptism and the Education of the Clergy in the Carolingian Empire: A Study of Texts and Manuscripts*

Kelly, H.A. (1985), *The Devil at Baptism: Ritual, Theology and Drama*, Ithaca

Lynch, J.H. (1986), *Godparents and Kinship in Early Medieval Europe*, Princeton

Morris, R. (1991), 'Baptismal places, 600–800', in I. Wood and N. Lund (eds.), *People and Places in Northern Europe: Studies in Honour of P.H. Sawyer*, Woodbridge, pp. 15–24

Pryce, H. (1992), 'Pastoral care in early medieval Wales', in J. Blair and R. Sharpe (eds.), *Pastoral Care before the Parish*, London, pp. 41–62

Rubellin, M. (1982), 'Entrée dans la vie, entrée dans la chrétienté, entrée dans la société: autour du baptême à l'époque carolingienne', in *Les entrées dans la vie: initiations et apprentissages. XIIe Congrès de la société des historiens médiévistes de l'enseignement supérieur publique, 1981*, Nancy, pp. 31–51

Van Engen, J. (1991), 'Faith as a concept of order in medieval Christendom', in T. Kselman (ed.), *Belief in History: Innovative Approaches to European and American Religion*, Notre Dame, pp. 19–67

Festivals and worship

Amos, T.L. (1989), 'Preaching and the sermon in the Carolingian world', in T.L. Amos, E.A. Green and B.L. Kienzle (eds.), *'De Ore Domini': Preacher and Word in the Middle Ages*, (Studies in Medieval Culture 27), Kalamazoo, pp. 41–60

Browe, P. (1921), 'Die Kommunion in der gallikanischen Kirche der Merowinger- und Karolingerzeit', *Theologische Quartalschrift* 120: 22–54, 133–56

Chélini, J. (1956), 'La pratique dominicale des laïcs dans l'église franc sous le règne de Pépin', *RHEF* 42: 161–74

Dierkens, A. (1984), 'Superstitions, christianisme et paganisme à la fin de l'époque mérovingienne. A propos de l'*Indiculus superstitionum et paganiarum*', in H. Hasquin (ed.), *Magie, sorcellerie et parapsychologie*, Brussels, pp. 9–26

Flint, V.I.J. (1991), *The Rise of Magic in Early Medieval Europe*, Princeton

Goetz, H.-W. (1991), 'Die kirchliche Festtag im frühmittelalterlichen Alltag', in D. Altenburg, J. Jarnut, H.-H. Steinhoff (eds.), *Feste und Feiern im Mittelalter*, Sigmaringen, pp. 53–62

Head, T. (1990), *Hagiography and the Cult of Saints: The Diocese of Orléans, 800–1200*, Cambridge

Heinzelmann, M. (1979), *Translationsberichte und andere Quellen des Reliquienkultes* (Typologie des sources du moyen âge occidental 33), Turnhout

Jungmann, J.A. (1952), *Missarum sollemnia*, 3rd edn, 2 vols., Vienna

Kieckhefer, R. (1990), *Magic in the Middle Ages*, Cambridge

Rollason, D.W. (1989), *Saints and Relics in Anglo-Saxon England*, Oxford

Schneider, H. (1985), '*Aqua benedicta* – das mit Salz gemischte Weihewasser', *Settimane* 33, 1: 327–64

Sin and salvation

Angenendt, A. (1984), 'Theologie und Liturgie der mittelalterlichen Toten-Memoria', in K. Schmidt and J. Wollasch (eds.), *Memoria: Der geschichtliche Zeugniswert des liturgischen Gedenkens im Mittelalter* (MMS 48), Munich, pp. 79–199

Browe, P. (1932), *Beiträge zur Sexualethik des Mittelalters*, Breslau

Brundage, J.A. (1987), *Law, Sex and Society in Christian Europe*, Chicago

Frantzen, A.J. (1983), *The Literature of Penance in Anglo-Saxon England*, New Brunswick, NJ

Kottje, R. (1985), 'Busspraxis und Bussritus', *Settimane* 33, 1: 370–95

Rubellin, M. (1983), 'Vision de la société chrétienne à travers la confession et la pénitence au ixe siècle', in *Pratiques de la confession, des pères du désert à Vatican II: quinze études d'histoire* (Groupe de la Bussière), Paris, pp. 53–70

Southern, R.W. (1982), 'Between heaven and hell', *Times Literary Supplement*, 18 June 1982, pp. 651–2

Vogel, C. (1956), 'La discipline pénitentielle en Gaule des origines au ixe siècle: le dossier hagiographique', *Revue des Sciences Religieuses* 30: 1–26, 157–86

Vogel, C. (1958–9), 'Composition légale et commutation dans le système de la pénitence tarifiée', *Revue de Droit Canonique* 8: 289–318; 9: 1–38, 341–59

Vogel, C. (1978), with supplement by A.J. Frantzen, *Les 'Libri paenitentiales'* (Typologie des sources du moyen âge occidental 27), Turnhout

Individual identity and social order

Browe, P. (1932–3), *De ordaliis*, 2 vols., Rome

Folz, R. (1984), 'La pénitence publique au ixe siècle d'après les canons de l'évêque Isaac de Langres', in *Actes du 109e Congrès national des sociétés savantes (Dijon, 1984), section d'histoire médiévale et de philologie*, Paris, pp. 331–43

Kerff, F. (1989), '*Libri paenitentiales* und kirchliche Strafgerichtsbarkeit bis zum

Decretum Gratiani: ein Diskussionsvorschlag', *ZRG KA* 106: 23–57

Leyser, K.J. (1984), 'Early medieval canon law and the beginnings of knighthood', in L. Fenske, W. Rösener and T. Zotz (eds.), *Institutionen, Kultur und Gesellschaft: Festschrift für J. Fleckenstein*, Sigmaringen, pp. 549–66

Nelson, J.L. (1989), 'Ninth-century knighthood: the evidence of Nithard', in C. Harper-Bill, C.J. Holdsworth and J.L. Nelson (eds.), *Studies in Medieval History presented to R. Allen Brown*, Woodbridge, pp. 255–66

Nelson, J.L. (1990), 'Literacy in Carolingian government', in R. McKitterick (ed.), *The Uses of Literacy in Early Medieval Europe*, Cambridge, pp. 258–96

Reynolds, R.E. (1985), 'Rites of separation and reconciliation in the early middle ages', *Settimane* 33, I: 405–33

Rouche, M. (1985), 'Des mariages païens au mariage chrétien, sacre et sacrement', *Settimane* 33, II: 835–73

Toubert, P. (1976), 'La théorie de mariage chez les moralistes carolingiens', *Settimane* 24: 233–82

Vogel, C. (1964), 'Le pélérinage pénitentiel', *Revue des Sciences Religieuses* 38: 113–53

Vogel, C. (1976), 'Les rites de la célébration du mariage: leur signification dans la formation du lien durant le haut moyen âge', *Settimane* 24: 397–465

Death and burial

Blair, J. (1988), 'Minster churches in the landscape', in D. Hooke (ed.), *Anglo-Saxon Settlements*, Oxford, pp. 35–58

Bullough, D.A. (1983), 'Burial, community and belief in the early medieval west', in P. Wormald, D. Bullough and R. Collins (eds.), *Ideal and Reality in Frankish and Anglo-Saxon Society*, Oxford, pp. 177–201

Bullough, D.A. (1991), *Friends, Neighbours and Fellow-Drinkers: Aspects of Community and Conflict in the Early Medieval West*, Cambridge

Dierkens, A. (1981), 'Cimetières mérovingiens et histoire du haut moyen âge: chronologie – société – religion', in *Histoire et méthode* (Acta Historica Bruxellensia 4), Brussels, pp. 15–70

Frank, H. (1962), 'Der älteste erhaltene *ordo defunctorum* der römischen Liturgie und sein Fortleben in Totenagenden des frühen Mittelalters', *Archiv für Liturgiewissenschaft* 7: 360–415

Kyll, N. (1972), *Tod, Grab, Begräbnisplatz, Totenfeier: Zur Geschichte ihres Brauchtums im Trierer Lande und im Luxemburg unter besonderer Berücksichtigung des Visitationshandbuches des Regino von Prüm* (Rheinisches Archiv 81), Bonn

Morris, R. (1983), *The Church in British Archaeology* (Council for British Archaeology Research Report 47), London

Oexle, O.G. (1976), 'Memoria und Memorialüberlieferung im früheren Mittelalter', *FrSt* 10: 70–95

Oexle, O.G. (1983), 'Die Gegenwart der Toten', in H. Braet and W. Verbreke (eds.), *Death in the Middle Ages*, Leuven, pp. 19–77

Oexle, O.G. (1984), 'Mahl und Spende im mittelalterlichen Totenkult', *FrSt* 18: 401–20

Paxton, F.S. (1990a), *Christianizing Death: The Creation of a Ritual Process in Early Medieval Europe*, Ithaca

Paxton, F.S. (1990b), '*Bonus liber*: a late Carolingian clerical manual from Lorsch

(Bibliotheca Vaticana MS Pal. Lat. 485', in L. Mayali and S.A.J. Tibbetts (eds.), *The Two Laws: Studies in Medieval Legal History Dedicated to Stephan Kuttner*, (Studies in Medieval and Early Modern Canon Law 1), Washington, DC, pp. 1–30

Sicard, D. (1968), 'The funeral Mass', in J. Wagner (ed.), *Reforming the Rites of Death*, New York, pp. 45–52

Thomas, C. (1971), *The Early Christian Archaeology of North Britain*, London

Young, B.K. (1977), 'Paganisme, christianisation et rites funéraires mérovingiens', *Archéologie Médiévale* 7: 5–81

Young, B.K. (1986), 'Exemple aristocratique et mode funéraire dans la Gaule mérovingienne', *Annales ESC* 41: 379–407

25 EIGHTH-CENTURY FOUNDATIONS

General guides

Buchner, R. (1954), *Die Rechtsquellen*, Weimar

Genicot, L. (1972–), *Typologie des sources du moyen âge occidental*, Turnhout

Lowe, E.A. (1935–71), *Codices Latini Antiquiores*, Oxford

Manitius, M. (1911), *Geschichte der lateinischen Literatur des Mittelalters* 1, Munich

Wattenbach, W. and Levison, W. (1952), *Deutschlands Geschichtsquellen im Mittelalter*, Weimar

See also the annual bibliographies in *Medioevo latino. Bollettino bibliographico della cultura europea dal secolo VI al XIII*, Spoleto (1980–)

Works mentioned in the text

Atsma, H. (ed.) (1989), *La Neustrie: les pays au nord de la Loire de 650 à 850* (Beihefte der Francia 16, I and 16, II, Sigmaringen

Berschin, W. (1988), *Greek Letters and the Latin Middle Ages*, Washington

Berschin, W. and Lehner, A. (1990), *Lateinische Kultur im VIII. Jahrhundert*, St Ottilien

Biggs, F.M., Hill, T.D. and Szarmach, P.E. (1990), *Sources of Anglo-Saxon Literary Culture: A Trial Version*, Binghampton, NY

Bischoff, B. (1931), 'Wer ist der Nonne von Heidenheim?' *StMBO* 49: 387–9

Bischoff, B. (1954 and 1966) 'Wendepunkte in der Geschichte der lateinischen Exegese im Frühmittelalter', *Sacris Erudiri* 6: 191–281, reprinted in Bischoff, *MS* I, pp. 205–73; English trans., 'Turning points in the history of Latin exegesis in the early middle ages', in M. McNamara (ed.), *Biblical Studies: The Medieval Irish Contribution* (Proceedings of the Irish Biblical Association 1), Dublin, 1976, pp. 73–160

Bischoff, B. (1965, 1966, 1981a), *Mittelalterliche Studien. Ausgewählte Aufsätze zur Schriftkunde und Literaturgeschichte* I, II, III, Stuttgart

Bischoff, B. (1974), *Die südostdeutschen Schreibschulen und Bibliotheken in der Karolingerzeit* I: *Die Bayerischen Diözesen*, 3rd edn, Wiesbaden

Bischoff, B. (1980), *Die südostdeutschen Schreibschulen und Bibliotheken in der Karolingerzeit* II: *Die vorwiegend Österreichischen Diözesen*, Wiesbaden

Bischoff, B. (1981a), see Bischoff (1965) above

Bischoff, B. (1981b), 'Panorama der Handschriftenüberlieferung aus der Zeit Karls des Grossen', in Bischoff (1981a), pp. 5–38; English trans. in Bischoff (1994)

Bischoff, B. (1981c), 'Die Hofbibliothek Karls des Grossen', in Bischoff (1981a), pp. 149–69; English trans. in Bischoff (1994)

Bischoff, B. (1990), *Latin Palaeography: Antiquity and the Middle Ages*, trans. D. Ó Cróinín and D. Ganz, Cambridge

Bischoff, B. (1994), *Manuscripts and Libraries in the Age of Charlemagne*, Cambridge

Bischoff, B. and Hofmann, J. (1952), *Libri Sancti Kyliani: Die Würzburger Schreibschule und die Dombibliothek im VIII. und IX. Jahrhundert*, Würzburg

Brown, M.P. (1989), 'The Lindisfarne scriptorium from the late seventh to the early ninth century', in G. Bonner, D. Rollason and C. Stancliffe, *St Cuthbert: His Cult and his Community*, Woodbridge, pp. 151–64

Brown, T.J. (1971), 'An historical introduction to the use of classical Latin authors in the British Isles from the fifth to the eleventh century', *Settimane* 22: 237–93

Brown, T.J. (1993), *A Palaeographer's View: The Selected Writings of Julian Brown*, ed. J. Bately, M.P. Brown and J. Roberts, London

Brunhölzl, F. (1990), *Histoire de la littérature latine du moyen âge I/I: L'époque mérovingienne* (Louvain-la-Neuve), a translated and revised edition of the 1975 German version

Collins, R. (1983), *Early Medieval Spain: Unity and Diversity*, London

Davies, W. and Fouracre, P. (1986), *The Settlement of Disputes in Early Medieval Europe*, Cambridge

Deshusses, J. (1971), *Le sacramentaire grégorien*, Fribourg-en-Suisse

Diaz y Diaz, M.C. (1958, 1959), *Index Scriptorum Latinorum Medii Aevi Hispanorum*, Salamanca

Dronke, P. (1984), *Women Writers of the Middle Ages*, Cambridge

Duft, J. (1990), *Die Abtei St Gallen: Beiträge zur Erforschung ihrer Manuskripte*, Sigmaringen

Fontaine, F. and Hillgarth, J. (eds.) (1992), *The Seventh Century*, London

Fontaine, J. (1959), *Isidore de Seville et la culture classique dans l'Espagne wisigothique*, Paris

Fouracre, P. (1990), 'Merovingian history and Merovingian hagiography', *Past and Present* 127: 3–38

Ganz, D. (1981), 'The Merovingian library of Corbie', in H. Clarke and M. Brennan (eds.), *Columbanus and Merovingian Monasticism* (BAR International Series 113), Oxford, pp. 173–207

Ganz, D. (1990), *Corbie and the Carolingian Renaissance*, Sigmaringen

Gaudemet, J. (1955), 'Survivances romaines dans le droit de la monarchie franque du ve au xe siècles', *Revue d'Histoire du Droit*, 23: 149–206

Gerberding, R. (1987), *The Liber Historiae Francorum and the Rise of the Carolingians*, Oxford

Glauche, G. (1970), *Schullektüre im Mittelalter* (Münchener Beiträge zur Mediävistik und Renaissance Forschung), Munich

Gneuss, H. (1981), 'A preliminary list of manuscripts written or owned in England up to 1100', *ASE* 9: 1–60

Gottschaller, E. (1973), *Hugeburc von Heidenheim: Philologische Untersuchungen zu den*

Heiligenbiographien einer Nonne des achten Jahrhunderts (Münchener Beiträge zur Mediävistik und Renaissance Forschung 12), Munich

Heinzelmann, M. (1992), *Manuscrits hagiographiques et travail des hagiographes*, Sigmaringen

Holtz, L. (1992), 'L'enseignement des maîtres irlandais dans l'Europe continentale du Ixe siècle', in J.-M. Picard (ed.), *Ireland and Northern France, AD 600–850*, Dublin, pp. 143–56

Hughes, K. (1972), *An Introduction to the Sources for Early Christian Ireland*, London

Innes, M. and McKitterick, R. (1994), 'The writing of history', in McKitterick (1994b), pp. 193–220

Kelly, S. (1990), 'Anglo-Saxon lay society and the written word', in McKitterick (1990), pp. 36–62

King, P.D. (1980), 'King Chindaswind and the first territorial law code of the Visigothic kingdom', in E. James (ed.), *Visigothic Spain: New Approaches*, Oxford, 131–58

Laistner, M. (1931, reprinted 1957), *Thought and Letters in Western Europe, 500–900*, Ithaca

Laistner, M. (1957), *The Intellectual Heritage of the Early Middle Ages*, Ithaca

Lapidge, M. (1986), 'The school of Theodore and Hadrian', *ASE* 15: 45–72

Lapidge, M. and Herren, M. (1979), *Aldhelm: The Prose Works*, Ipswich and Cambridge

Lapidge, M. and Rosier, J. (1985), *Aldhelm: The Poetic Works*, Cambridge

Lapidge, M. and Sharpe, R. (1985), *A Bibliography of Celtic-Latin Literature 400–1200*, Dublin

Law, V. (1982), *The Insular Grammarians*, Woodbridge

Levison, W. (1946), *England and the Continent in the Eighth Century*, Oxford

Liebermann, F. (1903–16), *Die Gesetze der Angelsachsen*, Leipzig

Lowe, E.A. (1972), 'The script of Luxeuil: a title vindicated', in E.A. Lowe, *Palaeographical Papers*, ed. L. Bieler, 2 vols., Oxford, II, pp. 389–98, reprinted from original 1953 article in *RB* 63: 132–42

Löwe, H. (1952), 'Ein literarische Widersacher des Bonifatius. Virgil von Salzburg und die Kosmographie des Aethicus Ister', *Abhandlungen. der Akademie der Wissenschaften Mainz. Geistes und sozialwissenschaftliche Klasse. Jahrgang. 1951*, Wiesbaden

Löwe, H. (ed.) (1982), *Die Iren und Europa im früheren Mittelalter*, Stuttgart

McCormick, M. (1975), *Les annales du haut moyen âge* (Typologie des sources du moyen âge occidental 14), Turnhout

McGurk, P. (1961), *Latin Gospel Books from AD 400 to AD 800*, Paris, Brussels and Amsterdam

McKitterick, R. (1981), 'The scriptoria of Merovingian Gaul: a survey of the evidence', in H. Clarke and M. Brennan (eds.), *Columbanus and Merovingian Monasticism* (BAR International Series 113), Oxford, pp. 173–207

McKitterick, R. (1989a), *The Carolingians and the Written Word*, Cambridge

McKitterick, R. (1989b), 'The diffusion of insular culture in Neustria between 650 and 850: the implications of the manuscript evidence', in *La Neustrie*, pp. 395–435, reprinted in McKitterick (1994a)

McKitterick, R. (1990b), 'Frankish uncial in the eighth century: a new context for the work of the Echternach scriptorium', in P. Bange and A. Weiler (eds.), *Willibrord, zijn wereld en zijn werk*, Nijmegen, pp. 350–64

McKitterick, R. (1992), 'Nuns' scriptoria in England and Francia in the eighth century', *Francia* 19, 1: 1–35, reprinted in McKitterick (1994a)

McKitterick, R. (1994a) *Books, Scribes and Learning in the Frankish Kingdoms, Sixth to Ninth Centuries*, Aldershot

McKitterick, R. (ed.) (1990a), *The Uses of Literacy in Early Medieval Europe*, Cambridge

McKitterick, R. (ed.) (1994b), *Carolingian Culture: Emulation and Innovation*, Cambridge

Marrou, H.I. (1956), *A History of Education in Antiquity*, trans. G. Lamb, New York

Mordek, H. (1975), *Kirchenrecht und Reform im Frankenreich*, Berlin

Moreton, B. (1976), *The Eighth-Century Gelasian Sacramentary*, Oxford

Mostert, M. (1989), *The Library of Fleury: A Provisional List of Manuscripts*, Hilversum

Nelson, J.L. (1989), 'Translating images of authority: the Christian Roman emperors in the Carolingian world', in C. Roueché and M.M. MacKenzie (eds.), *Images of Authority: Studies Presented to Joyce Reynolds on the Occasion of her Seventieth Birthday* (Cambridge Philological Society, Supplementary volume 16), Cambridge, pp. 194–205

Netzer, N. (1994), *Cultural Interplay in the Eighth Century: The Trier Gospels and the Making of a Scriptorium at Echternach Scriptorium* (Cambridge Studies in Palaeography and Codicology 3), Cambridge

Ó Cróinín, D. (1989), 'The date, provenance and earliest use of the works of Virgilius Maro Grammaticus', in G. Berndt, F. Rädle and G. Silagi (eds.), *Traditio und Werkung*, Munich

Ogilvy, J. (1967), *Books Known to the English, 597–1066*, New York

Ogilvy, J. (1984 for 1981), 'Addenda et corrigenda', *Mediaevalia* 7: 281–325

Parkes, M.B. (1983), *The Scriptorium of Wearmouth-Jarrow* (Jarrow Lecture 1982), Newcastle; reprinted in M.B. Parkes, *Scribes, Scripts and Readers: Studies in the Communication, Presentation and Dissemination of Medieval Texts*, London (1991)

Petrucci, A. (1969 and 1973), 'Scrittura e libro nell'Italia alto medievale', *SM* 10: 157–213; 14: 961–84; 984–1002

Petrucci, A. (1971), 'L'onciale romana. Origini, sviluppo e diffusione di una stillizzazione grafica altomedievali (se. VI–IX), *SM* 12: 75–134

Picard, J.M. (ed.) (1991), *Ireland and Northern France AD 600–850*, Dublin

Prinz, F. (1965, 2nd edn 1988), *Frühes Mönchtum im Frankenreich*, Darmstadt

Prinz, O. (1981), 'Untersuchung zur Überlieferung und zur othographie der Kosmographie des Aethicus', *DA* 37: 474–510

Riché, P. (1962, 1976), *Education and Culture in the Barbarian West, Sixth through Eighth Centuries*, English trans. from 1962 edition with updated bibliography by John J. Contreni, Columbia, South Carolina

Saint Chrodegang (Metz, 1967)

Schieffer, T. (1954), *Winfrid Bonifatius und die christliche Grundlegung Europas*, Freiburg

Sellert, W. (1992), *Das Gesetz in Spätantike und frühem Mittelalter* (Abhandlungen der Akademie der Wissenschaften in Göttingen, phil.-hist. Klasse, Dritte Folge 196), Göttingen

Sims-Williams, P. (1990), *Religion and Literature in Western England, 600–800* (Cambridge Studies in Anglo-Saxon England 3), Cambridge

Szarmach, P.E. (1986), *Sources of Anglo-Saxon Culture*, Kalamazoo

van Uytfanghe, M. (1987), *Stylisation biblique et condition humaine dans l'hagiographie mérovingienne, 600–750*, Brussels

Vogel, C. (1981), *Introduction aux sources de l'histoire du culte chrétien au moyen âge*, Spoleto, and revised, updated version in English by W. Storey and N. Rasmussen, *Medieval Liturgy: An Introduction to the Sources*, Washington, DC (1986)

de Vogüé, A. (1986), *Les règles monastiques anciennes 400–700* (Typologie des sources du moyen âge occidental 46), Turnhout

Whitelock, D. (1974), *After Bede* (Jarrow Lecture 1973), Newcastle

Wickham, C. (1982), *Early Medieval Italy*, London

Wood, I.N. (1993), *The Merovingian Kingdoms (450–751)*, London

Wood, I.N. and Harries, J. (eds.) (1993), *The Theodosian Code*, London

Wormald, P. (1977), '*Lex scripta et verbum regis*: legislation and Germanic kingship from Euric to Cnut', in P. Sawyer and I.N. Wood (eds.), *Early Medieval Kingship*, Leeds, pp. 105–38

26 LANGUAGE AND COMMUNICATION IN CAROLINGIAN EUROPE

Auerbach, E. (1965), *Literary Language and its Public in Late Latin Antiquity and in the Middle Ages*, London

Banniard, M. (1980), 'Géographie linguistique et linguistique diachronique', *Via Domitia: Annales de l'Université de Toulouse II*, 24: 9–43

Banniard, M. (1989), *Genèse culturelle de l'Europe (Ve–VIIIe siècle)*, Paris

Banniard, M. (1990), 'Genèse linguistique de la France', in R. Delort and D. Iogna-Prat (eds.), *La France de l'an mil*, Paris, pp. 214–29

Banniard, M. (1992) *Viva voce: communication orale et communication écrite en occident latin (IVe–IXe siècle)*, Paris

Banniard, M. (1994), 'Seuils et frontières langagiers en Gaule au VIIIᵉ siècle', in J. Jarnut *et al.* (eds.), *Karl Martell in seiner Zeit* (Beihefte der Francia 37), Sigmaringen, pp. 171–92

Battisti, C. (1960), 'Secoli illitterati. Appunti sull crisi del latino prima della riforma carolingia', *SM* 3(1): 362–96

Beckmann, G. (1963), *Die Nachfolgekonstruktionen des instrumentalen Ablativs im Spätlatein und im Französischen* (Zeitschrift für romanische Philologie, Beihefte 106), Tübingen

Borst, A. (1957–8), *Der Turmbau von Babel: Geschichte der Meinungen über Ursprung und Vielfalt der Sprachen und Völker*, 2 vols., Stuttgart

Braunfels, W. (ed.) (1965), *Karl der Grosse: Lebenswerk und Nachleben* II: *Das geistige Leben*, ed. B. Bischoff, Düsseldorf

Brown, P.R.L. (1967), *Augustine of Hippo*, London (French edn, Paris, 1971)

Brown, P.R.L. (1971 and 1978), *The Making of Late Antiquity*, London; 1978 impression, Berkeley, CA

Brunhölzl, F. (1976), *Geschichte der lateinischen Literatur des Mittelalters* I: *Von Cassiodor bis zum Ausklang der karolingischen Erneuerung*, Munich

Cerquiglini, B. (1991), *Naissance du français*, Paris

Chelini, J. (1991), *L'Aube du moyen âge: la vie religieuse des laïcs dans l'Europe carolingienne (750–900)*, Paris

Cortelazzo, M. (1976), *Avviamento critico allo studio della dialectologie italiana: problemi e metodi*, Pisa

Delbouille, M. (1972), 'Tradition latine et naissance des littératures romanes', and 'La formation des langues littéraires et les premiers textes', in *Grundriss der romanischen Literaturen des Mittelalters*, Heidelberg, pp. 3–56; 560–84; 604–22

Duby, G. (1988), *1. La société chevaleresque; 2. Seigneurs et paysans. Hommes et structures du moyen âge*, Paris

Elich, T.W. (1988), 'Le contexte oral de la liturgie mediévale et le rôle du texte écrit', unpublished dissertation of the Institut Catholique de Paris et de l'Université de Paris IV, 3 vols.

Fleckenstein, J. (1953), *Die Bildungsreform Karls des Grossen als Verwirklichung der norma rectitudinis*, Bigge

Fontaine, J. (1981), 'De la pluralité à l'unité dans le 'latin carolingien'?' *Settimane* 27: 765–818

Godman, P. (1985), *Poetry of the Carolingian Renaissance*, London

Godman, P. (1987), *Poets and Emperors: Frankish Politics and Carolingian Poetry*, Oxford

Godman, P. and Collins, R. (eds.) (1990), *Charlemagne's Heir: New Perspectives on the Reign of Louis the Pions (814–840)*, Oxford

Goebl, H. (1983), 'Parquet polygonal et treillis triangulaire: les deux versions de la dialectométrie interpontuelle, *Revue de Linguistique Romane* 187/8: 353–412

Goody, J. (1986), *The Logic of Writing and the Organisation of Society*, Cambridge

Green, J.N. (1991), 'The collapse and replacement of verbal inflection in Late Latin/ Early Romance: how would one know?', in Wright (1991)

Guerreau-Jalabert, A. (1982), 'La "Renaissance carolingienne": modèles culturels, usages linguistiques et structures sociales', *BEC* 139: 5–35

Huglo, M. (1988), *Les livres de chant liturgique* (Typologie des sources du moyen âge occidental), Turnhout

Iogna-Prat, D. Jeudy, C. and Lobrichon, G. (eds.) (1991), *L'école carolingienne d'Auxerre, de Murethach à Remi*, Paris

Klein, H. (1968), *Die Reichenauer Glossen* I: *Einleitung, Text, vollständige Index und Konkordanzen*, Munich

Koll, H. (1957–8), 'Lingua latina, lingua romanica und die Bezeichnungen für die romanischen Vulgärsprachen', *Estudis Romànic* 3: 95–164

Labov, W. (1976), *Sociolinguistique*, Paris

Labov, W. (1977), *Le parler ordinaire*, 2 vols., Paris

Laistner, M.L.W. (1957), *Thought and Letters in Western Europe, 500–900*, Ithaca

Le Goff, J. (1977), *Pour un autre moyen-âge*, Paris

Lehmann, P. (1941), 'Das problem der karolingischen Renaissance', in P. Lehmann, *Erforschung des Mittelalters* I, Leipzig

Lentner, L. (1963), *Volkssprache und Sakralsprache: Geschichte einer Lebensfrage bis zum Ende des Konzils von Trient*, Vienna

Löfstedt, B. (1982), 'Rückschau und Aufblick auf die vulgärlateinischen Fors-chung', *Aufstieg und Niedergang der Römanishen Welt* ser. s 29: 453–79

Löfstedt, E. (1933), *Syntactica: Studien und Beiträge zur historischen Syntax des Lateins,* Oslo

Löfstedt, E. (1959), *Late Latin,* Oslo

Lot, F. (1931), 'A quelle date a-t-on cessé de parler latin en Gaule?', *Archivum Latinitatis Medii Aevi (Bulletin du Cange)* 6: 97–159

Lüdtke, H. (1964), 'Die Entstehung romanischer Schriftsprachen', *Vox Romanica* 23: 3–21

McKitterick, R. (1977), *The Frankish Church and the Carolingian Reforms, 789–895* (Royal Historical Society Studies in History), London

McKitterick, R. (1989), *The Carolingians and the Written Word,* Cambridge

Marrou, H.I. (1958), *Saint Augustin et la fin de la culture antique,* Paris

Marrou, H.I. (1977), *Décadence romaine ou antiquité tardive?,* Paris

Meershoek, G. (1966), *Le Latin biblique d'après Saint Jérôme: aspects linguistiques de la rencontre entre la Bible et le monde classique,* Nijmegen

Muller, B. (1983), 'Zum Fortleben von Latinu und seinen Verwandten in der Romania', *Zeitschrift für Römanische Philologie* 79: 38–73

Muller, H.F. (1921), 'When did Latin cease to be a spoken language in France?', *The Romanic Review* 12: 318–34

Muller, H.F. (1929), *A Chronology of Vulgar Latin,* Halle

Muller, H.F. (1945), *L'époque mérovingienne: essai de synthèse de philologie et d'histoire,* New York

Norberg, D. (1943), *Syntaktische Forschungen auf dem Gebiete des Spätlateins und des frühen Mittellateins,* Uppsala

Norden, E. (1898), *Die antike Kunstprosa vom VI Jahrhundert vor Chr. bis in die Zeit der Rennaissance,* 2 vols., Leipzig

Pei, M. (1932), *The Language of the Eighth-Century Texts in Northern France: A Study of the Original Documents in the Collection of Tardif and Other Sources,* New York

Reichenkron, G. (1965), *Historische Latein–Altrömanische Grammatik, 1: Das sogenannte Vulgärlatein und das Wessen der Romanisierung,* Wiesbaden

Riché, P. (1972), *Education et culture en occident barbare, VIe–VIIIe siècle,* 3rd edn, Paris (1st edn 1962)

Riché, P. (1979), *Ecoles et enseignement dans le haut moyen âge,* Paris

Richter, M. (1979), *Sprache und Gesellschaft im Mittelalter: Untersuchungen zur mündlichen Kommunication in England von der Mitte des elften bis zum Beginn des 14.Jhts,* Stuttgart

Richter, M. (1982), 'Die Sprachenpolitik Karls des Grossen', *Sprachwissenschaft* 7: 412–37

Richter, M. (1983), 'A quelle époque a-t-on cessé de parler latin? A propos d'une question mal posée', *Annales ESC* 38: 439–48

Sabatini, F. (1968), 'Dalla' scripta latina rustica 'alle'scripta romanze', *SM* 3rd series, 9: 320–58

Schurchardt, H. (1866), *Der Vokalismus des Vulgärlateins,* Leipzig

Simonetti, M. (1986), *La produzione letteraria latina fra romani e barbari (sec. V–VIII),* Rome

Stock, B. (1983), *The Implications of Literacy: Written Language and Models of Interpretation in the Eleventh and Twelfth Centuries,* Princeton

Swiggers, P. (1987) 'Compte-rendu du livre de C. Hagège, *L'homme de paroles,* Paris

1985', *Bulletin de la Société de Linguistique* (Paris) 82(2): 20–37

van Uytfanghe, M. (1975), 'De zogehenten Karolingische Renaissance: een breekpunt in de evolutie van de Latijnse taal?', *Handelingen* 29: 267–86

van Uytfanghe, M. (1976), 'Le latin des hagiographes mérovingiens et la protohistoire du français', *Romanica Gandensia* 16: 5–89

van Uytfanghe, M. (1977), 'Latin mérovingien, latin carolingien et rustica romana lingua: continuité ou discontinuité?', in *D'une déposition à une couronnement, 476–800* (Revue de l'Université de Bruxelles), Brussels, pp. 65–88

Wright, R. (1982), *Late Latin and Early Romance in Spain and Carolingian France*, Liverpool

Wright, R. (ed.) (1991), *Latin and the Romance Languages in the Early Middle Ages*, London and New York

Zumthor, P. (1963), *Langue et technique poétique à l'époque romane (XIe–XIIIe siècle)*, Paris

27 THE CAROLINGIAN RENAISSANCE: EDUCATION AND LITERARY CULTURE

Amiet, R. (ed.) (1964), 'Une *Admonitio synodalis* de l'époque carolingienne: étude critique et édition', *Mediaeval Studies* 26: 12–82

Anton, H.H. (1968), *Fürstenspiegel und Herrscherethos in der Karolingerzeit* (Bonner Historische Forschungen 32), Bonn

Baader, G. (1972), 'Die Anfänge der medizinischen Ausbildung im Abendland bis 1100', *Settimane* 19: 669–718

Bachrach, B.S. (1977), *Early Medieval Jewish Policy in Western Europe*, Minneapolis

Beaujouan, G. (1972), 'L'enseignement du *Quadrivium*', *Settimane* 19: 639–67

Beccaria, A. (1956), *I codici di medicina del periodo presalernitano (secoli IX, X, e XI)*, Rome

Bénédictines de Solesmes (1889–), *Paléographie musicale: les principaux manuscrits de chant grégorien, ambrosien, mozarabe, gallican, publiés en fac-similés photographiques*, Solesmes and Bern

Berschin, W. (1988), *Greek Letters and the Latin Middle Ages: From Jerome to Nicholas of Cusa*, trans. J.C. Frakes, Washington, DC

Berschin, W. (ed.) (1991), *Lateinische Kultur im X. Jahrhundert* (Mittellateinisches Jahrbuch Band 24/25), Stuttgart

Bertola, E. (1961a), 'Il commentario paolino di Haimo di Halberstadt o di Auxerre e gli inizi del metodo scolastico', *Pier Lombardo* 5: 29–54

Bertola, E. (1961b), 'I precedenti storici del metodo del *Sic et Non* di Abelardo', *Rivista di Filosofia Neoscolastica* 53: 255–80

Bertolini, O. (1970), 'Il *Liber Pontificalis*', *Settimane* 17: 387–455

Bischoff, B. (1966a), 'Die Kölner Nonnenhandschriften und das Skriptorium von Chelles', in B. Bischoff, *MS* I, pp. 16–34

Bischoff, B. (1966b), 'Elementarunterricht und Probationes Pennae in der ersten Hälfte des Mittelalters', in B. Bischoff, *MS* I, pp. 74–87

Bischoff, B. (1966c), 'Wendepunkte in der Geschichte der lateinischen Exegese im Frühmittelalter', in B. Bischoff, *MS* I, pp. 205–73

Bischoff, B. (1966d), 'Eine verschollene Einteilung der Wissenschaften', in B. Bischoff, *MS* I, pp. 273–88

Bischoff, B. (1966e), 'Über Einritzungen in Handschriften des frühen Mittelalters', in B. Bischoff, *MS* I, pp. 88–92

Bischoff, B. (1967a), 'Theodulf und der Ire Cadac-Andreas', in B. Bischoff, *MS* II, pp. 19–25

Bischoff, B. (1967b), 'Caritas-Lieder', in B. Bischoff, *MS* II, pp. 56–77

Bischoff, B. (1974), *Lorsch im Spiegel seiner Handschriften* (Münchener Beiträge zur Mediävistik und Renaissance-Forschung, Beiheft), Munich

Bischoff, B. (1981), 'Die Bibliothek im Dienste der Schule', in B. Bischoff, *MS* III, pp. 213–33

Bischoff, B. (1990), *Latin Palaeography: Antiquity and the Middle Ages*, trans. D. Ó Cróinín and D. Ganz, Cambridge

Bishop, T.A.M. (1971), *English Caroline Minuscule*, Oxford

Bishop, T.A.M. (1990), 'The scribes of the Corbie a–b', in Godman and Collins (1990), pp. 521–36

Blumenkranz, B. (1960), *Juifs et Chrétiens dans le monde occidental, 430–1096* (Etudes juives 2), Paris and The Hague

Blumenkranz, B. (1963), *Les auteurs chrétiens latins du moyen âge sur les juifs et le judaïsme* (Etudes juives 4), Paris and The Hague

Blumenkranz, B. (1977a), 'Raban Maur et Saint Augustin, compilation ou adaptation? A propos du latin biblique', in B. Blumenkranz, *Juifs et Chrétiens, patristique et moyen âge* (Variorum Reprint, CS 70), chapter 2, London

Blumenkranz, B. (1977b), 'Du nouveau sur Bodo-Eléazar?', in B. Blumenkranz, *Juifs et Chrétiens, patristique et moyen âge* (Variorum Reprint, CS 70), chapter 11, London

Borst, A. (1988), 'Computus: Zeit und Zahl im Mittelalter', *DA* 44: 1–82

Borst, A. (1993), 'Alkuin und die Enzyklopädie von 809', in P.L. Butzer and D. Lohrmann (eds.), *Science in Western and Eastern Civilizations in Carolingian Times*, Basel, pp. 53–75

Brooke, M. (1990), 'The prose and verse hagiography of Walahfrid Strabo', in Godman and Collins (1990), pp. 551–64

Brown, T.S. (1986), '*Romanitas* and *campanilismo*: Agnellus of Ravenna's view of the past', in C. Holdsworth and T.P. Wiseman (eds.), *The Inheritance of Historiography: 300–900* (Exeter Studies in History 12), Exeter, pp. 107–14

Brunhölzl, F. (1965), 'Der Bildungsauftrag der Hofschule', in *Karl der Grosse* II, pp. 28–41

Brunhölzl, F. (1975), *Geschichte der lateinischen Literatur des Mittelalters. Erster Band: Von Cassiodor bis zum Ausklang der karolingischen Erneuerung*, Munich

Bullough, D. (1964), 'Le scuole cattedrali e la cultura dell'Italia settentrionale prima dei Comuni', *Italia Sacra* 5: 111–43

Bullough, D. (1973), *The Age of Charlemagne*, 2nd edn, London

Bullough, D. (1991a), '*Imagines regum* and their significance in the early medieval west', in D. Bullough, *Carolingian Renewal: Sources and Heritage*, Manchester and New York, pp. 39–96

Bullough, D. (1991b), '*Aula renovata*: the Carolingian court before the Aachen palace', in D. Bullough, *Carolingian Renewal: Sources and Heritage*, Manchester and New York, pp. 123–60

Bullough, D. (1991c). 'Roman books and Carolingian *renovatio*', in D. Bullough, *Carolingian Renewal: Sources and Heritage*, Manchester and New York, pp. 1–36

Bullough, D. (1991d), and A. Harting-Corrêa, 'Texts, chant and the chapel of Louis the Pious', in D. Bullough, *Carolingian Renewal: Sources and Heritage*, Manchester and New York, pp. 241–71

Bullough, D. (1991e), 'Ethnic history and the Carolingians: an alternative reading of Paul the Deacon's *Historia Langobardorum*', in D. Bullough, *Carolingian Renewal: Sources and Heritage*, Manchester and New York, pp. 97–122

Bullough, D. (1991f), 'The Continental background of the tenth-century English reform', in D. Bullough, *Carolingian Renewal: Sources and Heritage*, Manchester and New York, pp. 272–96

Bullough, D. (1991g), 'The educational tradition in England from Alfred to Ælfric: teaching *utriusque linguae*', in D. Bullough, *Carolingian Renewal: Sources and Heritage*, Manchester and New York, pp. 297–34

Cabaniss, A. (1953), 'Bodo-Eleazar: a famous Jewish convert', *Jewish Quarterly Review* n.s. 43: 313–28

Colish, M. (1984), 'Carolingian debates over *nihil* and *tenebrae*: a study in theological method', *Speculum* 59: 757–95

Contreni, J.J. (1978), *The Cathedral School of Laon from 850 to 930: Its Manuscripts and Masters* (Münchener Beiträge zur Mediävistik und Renaissance-Forschung 29), Munich

Contreni, J.J. (1984), *Codex Laudunensis 468: A Ninth-Century Guide to Virgil, Sedulius, and the Liberal Arts* (Armarium Codicum Insignium 3), Turnhout

Contreni, J.J. (1990), 'Masters and medicine in northern France during the reign of Charles the Bald', in Gibson and Nelson (1990), pp. 267–82

Contreni, J.J. (1992a), 'The Carolingian renaissance', in J.J. Contreni, *Carolingian Learning, Masters and Manuscripts*, Aldershot, chapter 3

Contreni, J.J. (1992b), 'Inharmonious harmony: education in the Carolingian world', in J.J. Contreni, *Carolingian Learning, Masters and Manuscripts*, Aldershot, chapter 4

Contreni, J.J. (1992c), 'The Carolingian School: letters from the classroom', in J.J. Contreni, *Carolingian Learning, Masters and Manuscripts*, Aldershot, chapter 11

Contreni, J.J. (1992d), 'John Scottus, Martin Hiberniensis, the liberal arts, and teaching', in J.J. Contreni, *Carolingian Learning, Masters and Manuscripts*, Aldershot, chapter 6

Contreni, J.J. (1992e), 'Learning in the early middle ages', in J.J. Contreni, *Carolingian Learning, Masters and Manuscripts*, Aldershot, chapter 1

Contreni, J.J. (1992f), 'Carolingian biblical studies', in J.J. Contreni, *Carolingian Learning, Masters and Manuscripts*, Aldershot, chapter 5

Corbin, S. (1977), *Die Neumen* (Palaeographie der Musik 1–3), Cologne

Crocker, R.L. (1975), 'The early Frankish sequence: a new musical form', *Viator* 6: 341–51

Crocker, R.L. (1977), *The Early Medieval Sequence*, Berkeley and Los Angeles

Crocker, R.L. (1979), 'Alphabet notations for early medieval music', in M.H. King and W.M. Stevens (eds.), *Saints, Scholars, and Heroes: Studies in Mediaeval Culture in Honour of Charles W. Jones*, 2 vols., Collegeville, MN, II: 79–104

Davies, W. (1986), 'People and places in dispute in ninth-century Brittany', in W. Davies and P. Fouracre (eds.), *The Settlement of Disputes in Early Medieval Europe*, Cambridge, pp. 65–84

De Rijk, L.M. (1963), 'On the curriculum of the arts of the Trivium at St Gall from c. 850–c. 1000', *Vivarium* 1: 35–86

Dekkers, E. and Gaar, A. (1961), *Clavis Patrum Latinorum* (Sacris Erudiri 3), Steenbruge

Devisse, J. (1962), *Hincmar et la loi* (Publications de la Section d'histoire 5), Dakar

Draak, M. (1957), 'Construe marks in Hiberno-Latin manuscripts', *Mededelingen der koninklijke nederlandse Akademie van Wetenschappen, Afd. Letterkunde*, n.s. 20–10: 216–82

Draak, M. (1967), 'The higher teaching of Latin grammar in Ireland during the ninth century', *Mededelingen der koninklijke nederlandse Akademie van Wetenschappen, Afd. Letterkunde*, n.s. 30–4: 100–44

Dronke, P. (1977), '*Theologia veluti quaedam poetria*: quelques observations sur la fonction des images poétiques chez Jean Scot', in *Jean Scot Érigène et l'histoire de la philosophie* (Colloques internationaux du Centre national de la recherche scientifique 561), Paris, pp. 243–52

Duchez, M.-E. (1980), 'Jean Scot Érigène premier lecteur du *De institutione musica* de Boèce?', in W. Beierwaltes (ed.), *Eriugena: Studien zu seinen Quellen* (Abhandlungen der Heidelberger Akademie der Wissenschaften, Phil.-hist. Klasse, Dritte Folge, Abhandlung), Heidelberg, pp. 165–87

Duchez, M.-E. (1989), 'Le savoir théorico-musical carolingien dans les commentaires de Martianus Capella: la tradition érigénienne', in *Giovanni Scoto nel suo tempo: l'organizzazione del sapere in età carolingia* (Atti dei Convegni dell'Accademia Tudertina e del Centro di studi sulla spiritualità medievale, n.s. 1), Spoleto, pp. 553–92

Düchting, R. (1968), *Sedulius Scottus: Seine Dichtungen*, Munich

Dutton, P.E. (1986), 'Eriugena, the royal poet', in G.-H. Allard (ed.), *Jean Scot écrivain*, Montreal and Paris, pp. 51–80

Eastwood, B.S. (1982), '"The Chaster Path of Venus" (*Orbis Veneris Castior*) in the astronomy of Martianus Capella', *Archives Internationales d'Histoire des Sciences* 109: 145–58

Eastwood, B.S. (1986a), 'Medieval science illustrated', *History of Science* 24: 183–208

Eastwood, B.S. (1986b), 'Plinian astronomy in the middle ages and Renaissance', in R. French and F. Greenaway (eds.), *Science in the Early Roman Empire: Pliny the Elder, His Sources and Influence*, London and Sydney, pp. 197–251

Eastwood, B.S. (1987), 'Plinian astronomical diagrams in the early middle ages', in E. Grant and J.E. Murdoch (eds.), *Mathematics and Its Applications to Science and Natural Philosophy in the Middle Ages: Essays in Honor of Marshall Clagett*, Cambridge, pp. 141–72

Eastwood, B.S. (1993), 'The astronomies of Pliny, Martianus Capella, and Isidore of Seville in the Carolingian world', in P.L. Butzer and D. Lohrmann (eds.), *Science in Western and Eastern Civilization in Carolingian Times*, Basel, pp. 161–80

Esposito, M. (1990), 'An unpublished astronomical treatise by the Irish monk

Dicuil', in M. Lapidge (ed.), *Mario Esposito: Irish Books and Learning in Mediaeval Europe* (Collected Studies 313), Aldershot, chapter 7

Faral, E. (ed.) (1964), *Ermold le Noir: poème sur Louis le Pieux et épîtres au roi Pépin*, 2nd edn, Paris

Fasoli, G. (1970), 'Rileggendo il "Liber pontificalis" di Agnello Ravennate', *Settimane* 17: 457–95

Ferrari, M. (1972), 'In Papia conveniant ad Dungalum', *Italia Medioevale et Umanistica* 15: 1–52

Fichtenau, H. (1984), *Lebensordnungen des 10. Jahrhunderts: Studien über Denkart und Existenz im einstigen Karolingerreich* (Monographien zur Geschichte des Mittelalters 30, 1–2), Stuttgart

Folkerts, M. (1972), 'Pseudo-Beda: De arithmeticis propositionibus. Eine mathematische Schrift aus der Karolingerzeit', *Sudhoffs Archiv* 56: 22–43

Folkerts, M. (1978), *Die älteste mathematische Aufgabensammlung in lateinischer Sprache: Die Alkuin zugeschriebenen 'Propositiones ad acuendos iuuenes': Überlieferung, Inhalt, kritische Edition* (Österreichischen Akademie der Wissenschaften, Mathematisch-naturwissenschaftliche Klasse, Denkschriften, 116. Band, 6. Abhandlung), Vienna

Folkerts, M. (1993), 'Die Alkuin zugeschriebenen *Propositiones ad acuendos iuuenes*', in P.L. Butzer and D. Lohrmann (eds.), *Science in Western and Eastern Civilization in Carolingian Times*, Basel, pp. 273–82

Freise, E. (1984), 'Kalendarische und annalistische grundformen der Memoria', in K. Schmid and J. Wollasch (eds.), *Memoria: Der geschichtliche Zeugniswert des liturgischen Gedenkens im Mittelalter* (MMS 48), Munich, pp. 441–577

Fuhrmann, H. (1972–4), *Einfluss und Verbreitung der pseudoisidorischen Fälschungen von ihrem Auftauchen bis in die neuere Zeit*, 3 vols. (MGH Schriften 24), Stuttgart

Ganshof, F.L. (1970), 'L'historiographie dans la monarchie franque sous les Mérovingiens et les Carolingiens', *Settimane* 17: 631–85

Ganz, D. (1983), 'Bureaucratic shorthand and Merovingian learning', in P. Wormald, D. Bullough and R. Collins (eds.), *Ideal and Reality in Frankish and Anglo-Saxon Society: Studies Presented to J.M. Wallace-Hadrill*, Oxford, pp. 58–75

Ganz, D. (1987), 'The preconditions for Caroline minuscule', *Viator* 18: 23–44

Ganz, D. (1989), 'Humour as history in Notker's *Gesta Karoli magni*', in Edward B. King, J.T. Schaefer and W.B. Wadley (eds.), *Monks, Nuns, and Friars in Mediaeval Society*, Sewanee

Ganz, D. (1990a), *Corbie in the Carolingian Renaissance* (Beihefte der Francia 20), Sigmaringen

Ganz, D. (1990b), 'The Debate on Predestination', in Gibson and Nelson (1990), pp. 283–302

Ganz, D. (1990c), 'On the history of Tironian Notes', in P. Ganz (ed.), *Tironische Noten* (Wolfenbütteler Mittelalter-Studien 1), Wiesbaden, pp. 35–51

Ganz, D. (1993), 'The *Liber glossarum*: a Carolingian encyclopedia', in P.L. Butzer and D. Lohrmann (eds.), *Science in Western and Eastern Civilization in Carolingian Times*, Basel, pp. 127–38

Gauert, A. (1984), 'Noch einmal Einhard und die letzten Merowinger', in L. Fenske, W. Rösener and T. Zotz (eds.), *Institutionen, Kultur und Gesellschaft im Mittelalter: Festschrift für Josef Fleckenstein zu seinem 65. Geburtstag*, Sigmaringen, pp. 59–72

Gerberding, R.A. (1987), *The Rise of the Carolingians and the 'Liber Historiae Francorum'*, Oxford

Gerbert, M. (ed.) (1784), *Scriptores ecclesiastici de musica sacra* I, San-Blasian

Giacone, R. (1975), 'Giustificazione degli *Studia liberalia* dalla sacralizzazione alcuiniana all'immanentismo di Giovanni Scoto Eriugena', in G.P. Clivio and R. Massano (eds.), *Studi in onore di Renzo Gandolfo nel suo settantacinquesimo compleanno*, Turin, pp. 823–32

Gibson, M.T. and Nelson, J.L. (eds.) (1981, 1990), *Charles the Bald: Court and Kingdom*, Oxford; rev. edn, Aldershot

Gil, I. (ed.) (1973), *Corpus Scriptorum Muzarabicorum*, 2 vols., Madrid

Glauche, G. (1970), *Schullektüre im Mittelalter: Entstehung und Wandlungen des Lektürekanons bis 1200 nach den Quellen dargestellt* (Münchener Beiträge zur Mediävistik und Renaissance-Forschung 5), Munich

Godman, P. (1981), 'Latin poetry under Charles the Bald and Carolingian poetry', in M. Gibson and J. Nelson (eds.), *Charles the Bald: Court and Kingdom* (British Archaeological Reports International Series 101), Oxford, pp. 293–309

Godman, P. (1985), *Poetry of the Carolingian Renaissance*, Norman, OK

Godman, P. (1987), *Poets and Emperors: Frankish Politics and Carolingian Poetry*, Oxford

Godman, P. (1990), 'The poetic hunt from Saint Martin to Charlemagne's heir', in P. Godman and Collins (eds.) *Charlemagne's Heir: New Perspectives on the Reign of Louis the Pious (814–840)*, Oxford, pp. 565–89

Godman, P. (ed.) (1982), *Alcuin: The Bishops, Kings, and Saints of York*, Oxford

Goetz, G. (ed.) (1888–1923), *Corpus Glossariorum Latinorum*, 7 vols., Leipzig and Berlin

Goffart, W. (1966), *The Le Mans Forgeries: A Chapter from the History of Church Property in the Ninth Century* (Harvard Historical Studies 76), Cambridge, MA

Gushee, L. (ed.) (1975), *Aureliani Reomensis Musica Disciplina* (Corpus Scriptorum de Musica 21), n.p.

Hallinger, K. (ed.) (1983), *Corpus Consuetudinum Monasticarum* I: *Initia Consuetudinis Benedictinae. Consuetudines Saeculi Octavi et Noni*, Siegburg

Halphen, L. (ed.) (1947), *Éginhard: vie de Charlemagne*, 3rd edn (Les classiques de l'histoire de France au moyen âge), Paris

Hammer, C.I., Jr (1980), 'Country churches, clerical inventories and the Carolingian renaissance in Bavaria', *Church History* 49: 5–17

Herren, M.W. (ed.) (1988), *The Study of Greek in the West in the Early Middle Ages* (King's College London Medieval Studies 2), London

Herren, M.W. (1989a), 'Gli ebrei nella cultura letteraria al tempo di Carlo il Calvo', in *Giovanni Scoto nel suo tempo: l'organizzazione del sapere in età carolingia* (Atti dei Convegni dell'Accademia Tudertina e del Centro di studi sulla spiritualità medievale, n.s. 1), Spoleto, pp. 537–52

Herren, M.W. (1989b), 'St Gall 48: a copy of Eriugena's glossed Greek Gospels', in G. Bernt, F. Rädle and G. Silagi (eds.), *Tradition und Wertung: Festschrift für Franz Brunhölzl zum 65. Geburtstag*, Sigmaringen, pp. 97–105

Hildebrandt, M.M. (1992), *The External School in Carolingian Society* (Education and Society in the Middle Ages and Renaissance 1), Leiden

Hinschius, P. (ed.) (1863), *Decretales Pseudo-Isidorianae et Capitula Angilramni*, Leipzig (reprinted Aalen 1963)

Hoffmann, H. (1986), *Buchkunst und Königtum im ottonischen und frühsalischen Reich* (MGH Schriften 30, 1–2), Stuttgart

Holtz, L. (1972), 'Sur trois commentaires irlandais de l'Art Majeur de Donat au ixème siècle', *Revue d'Histoire des Textes* 2: 45–73

Holtz, L. (1977a), 'Grammairiens irlandais au temps de Jean Scot: quelques aspects de leur pédagogie', in *Jean Scot Erigène et l'histoire de la philosophie* (Colloques internationaux du Centre national de la recherche scientifique 561), Paris

Holtz, L. (1977b), Introduction to *Murethach (Muridac) In Donati artem maiorem*, *CCCM* 40: i–lxxxvi

Holtz, L. (1981), *Donat et la tradition de l'enseignement grammatical: étude sur l'Ars Donati et sa diffusion (IVe–IXe siècle) et édition critique*, Paris

Horn, W. and Born, E. (1979), *The Plan of Saint Gall: A Study of the Architecture and Economy of, and Life in a Paradigmatic Carolingian Monastery*, 3 vols. (California Studies in the History of Art 19), Berkeley

Howell, W.S. (ed.) (1965), *The Rhetoric of Alcuin and Charlemagne: A Translation, with an Introduction, the Latin Text, and Notes*, New York

Hubert, J., Porcher, J. and Volbach, W.F. (1968), *L'empire carolingien*, Paris

Hughes, D.G. (1987), 'Evidence for the traditional view of the transmission of Gregorian chant', *Journal of the American Musicological Society* 40: 377–404

Huglo, M. (1979), 'Les remaniements de l'Antiphonaire grégorien du ixe siècle: Helisachar, Agobard, Amalaire', in *Culto cristiano [e] politica imperiale carolingia* (Convegni del Centro di studi sulla spiritualità medievale, Università degli studi di Perugia 18), Todi, pp. 87–120

Huygens, R.B.C. (1954), *Accessus ad auctores* (Collection Latomus 15), Berchem and Brussels

Ilmer, D. (1984), 'Arithmetik in der gelehrten Arbeitsweise des frühen Mittelalters: Eine Studie zum Grundsatz *Nisi enim nomen scieris, cognitio rerum perit*', in L. Fenske, W. Rösener and T. Zotz (eds.), *Institutionen, Kultur und Gesellschaft im Mittelalter: Festschrift für Josef Fleckenstein zu seinem 65. Geburtstag*, Sigmaringen, pp. 35–58

Iogna-Prat, D., Jeudy, C. and Lobrichon, G. (eds.), (1991), *L'école carolingienne d'Auxerre, de Murethach à Remi, 830–908*, Paris

Jeauneau, E. (1989), 'L'édition du livre iv du Periphyseon', in *Giovanni Scoto nel suo tempo: l'organizzazione del sapere in età carolingia* (Atti dei Convegni dell'Accademia Tudertina e del Centro di studi sulla spiritualità medievale, n.s. 1), Spoleto, pp. 469–86

Jeauneau, E. (1990), 'Jean Scot et la métaphysique des nombres' in W. Beierwaltes (ed.), *Begriff und Metapher: Sprachform des Denken bei Eriugena* (Abhandlungen der Heidelberger Akademie der Wissenschaften, Phil.-hist. Klasse, 3. Abhandlung), Heidelberg, pp. 126–41

Jolivet, J. (1958), *Godescalc d'Orbais et la Trinité: la méthode de la théologie à l'époque carolingienne* (Etudes de philosophie médiévale 47), Paris

Jones, C.W. (1963), 'An early medieval licensing examination', *History of Education Quarterly* 3: 19–29

Jones, C.W. (ed.) (1943), *Bedae Opera de temporibus* (The Mediaeval Academy of America Publication 41), Cambridge, MA

Jones, C.W. (ed.) (1975–80), *Bedae Venerabilis Opera: Opera didascalica*, CCSL 123A, B, C, Turnhout

de Jong, M. (1983), 'Growing up in a Carolingian monastery: Magister Hildemar and his oblates', *Journal of Medieval History* 9: 99–128

Keefe, S.A. (1986), 'An unknown response from the archiepiscopal Province of Sens to Charlemagne's circulatory inquiry on baptism', *RB* 102: 48–93

Keil, H. (ed.) (1857–80), *Grammatici Latini*, 8 vols., Leipzig

King, P.D. (1987), *Charlemagne: Translated Sources*, Kendal

Knoepfler, A. (ed.) (1900), *Rabani Mauri: De Institutione Clericorum libri tres* (Veröffentlichungen aus dem Kirchenhistorischen Seminar München 5), Munich

Lapidge, M. (1977), 'L'influence stylistique de la poésie de Jean Scot', in *Jean Scot Érigène et l'histoire de la philosophie* (Colloques internationaux du Centre national de la recherche scientifique 561), Paris, pp. 441–51

Lauer, P. (ed.) (1964), *Nithard: histoire des fils de Louis le Pieux* (Les classiques de l'histoire de France au moyen âge 7), Paris

Law, V. (1982), *The Insular Latin Grammarians* (Studies in Celtic History 3), Woodbridge

Leonardi, C. (1961), 'Nuove voci poetiche tra secolo IX e XI', *SM* 2: 139–68

Leonardi, C. (1981a), 'Alcuino e la scuola palatina: le ambizioni di una cultura unitaria', *Settimane* 27, I: 459–506

Leonardi, C. (1981b), 'L'agiografia romana nel secolo IX', in *Hagiographie, cultures, et sociétés, IVe–XIIe siècles* (Centre de recherches sur l'antiquité tardive et le haut moyen âge, Université de Paris X), Paris, pp. 471–89

Levison, W. and Löwe, H. (1953–73), *Wattenbach-Levison: Deutschlands Geschichtsquellen im Mittelalter (Vorzeit und Karolinger)*, Hefte 2–5, Weimar

Levy, K. (1987), 'Charlemagne's archetype of Gregorian chant', *Journal of the American Musicological Society* 40: 1–30

Levy, K. (1990), 'On Gregorian orality', *Journal of the American Musicological Society* 43: 186–227

Lindsay, W.M. (ed.) (1911), *Isidori Hispalensis episcopi Etymologiarum sive Originum libri xx*, 2 vols., Oxford

Lindsay, W.M. (1926–31), Mountford J.F. and Whatmough, J. (eds.), *Glossaria Latina iussu Academiae Britannicae edita*, 5 vols., Paris

Loyn, H.R. and Percival, J. (1975), *The Reign of Charlemagne: Documents on Carolingian Government and Administration*, London

Lynch, J.H. (1986), *Godparents and Kinship in Early Medieval Europe*, Princeton

MacKinney, L.C. (1937), *Early Medieval Medicine with Special Reference to France and Chartres*, Baltimore

McKitterick, R. (1976), 'A ninth-century schoolbook from the Loire valley: Phillipps MS 16308', *Scriptorium* 30: 225–31

McKitterick, R. (1977), *The Frankish Church and the Carolingian Reforms, 789–895*, London

McKitterick, R. (1983), *The Frankish Kingdoms under the Carolingians, 751–987*, London and New York

McKitterick, R. (1989), *The Carolingians and the Written Word*, Cambridge

McKitterick, R. (1991), 'Frauen und Schriftlichkeit im Frühmittelalter', in H.W. Goetz (ed.), *Weibliche Lebensgestaltung im frühen Mittelalter*, Cologne, pp. 65–118

McKitterick, R. (1992a), 'Royal patronage of culture in the Frankish kingdoms under the Carolingians: motives and consequences', *Settimane* 39: 93–129

McKitterick, R. (1992b), 'Nuns' scriptoria in England and Francia in the eighth century', *Francia* 19: 1–35

McKitterick, R. (1994), *Books, Scribes and Learning in the Frankish Kingdoms, Sixth to Ninth Centuries*, Aldershot

McNally, R.E. (1959), *The Bible in the Early Middle Ages* (Woodstock Papers: Occasional Essays for Theology 4), Westminster, MD

Marenbon, J. (1981), *From the Circle of Alcuin to the School of Auxerre: Logic, Theology and Philosophy in the Early Middle Ages* (Cambridge Studies in Medieval Life and Thought, 3rd series, 15), Cambridge

Marshall, P.K. (ed.) (1984), *Servati Lupi Epistulae* (Bibliothecae Scriptorum Graecorum et Romanorum Teubneriana), Leipzig

Meersseman, G.G. and Adda, E. (1966), *Manuale di computo con ritmo mnemotecnico dell'arcidiacono Pacifico di Verona († 844)* (Italia Sacra 6), Padua

Meyers, J. (1986), *L'art de l'emprunt dans la poésie de Sedulius Scottus* (Bibliothèque de la Faculté de Philosophie et Lettres de l'Université de Liège 245), Paris

Mitchell, J. (1990), 'Literacy displayed: the use of inscriptions at the monastery of San Vincenzo al Volturno in the early ninth century', in R. McKitterick (ed.), *The Uses of Literacy in Early Mediaeval Europe*, Cambridge, pp. 186–225

Mittermüller, R. (ed.) (1880), *Expositio Regulae ab Hildemaro tradita et nunc primum typis mandata* in *Vita et Regula SS. P. Benedicti una cum Expositione Regulae*, Regensburg

Morrison, K.F. (1981), '"*Unum ex multis*": Hincmar of Rheims' medical and aesthetic rationales for unification', *Settimane* 27: 583–712

Morrison, K.F. (1983), 'Incentives for studying the liberal arts', in D.L. Wagner (ed.), *The Seven Liberal Arts in the Middle Ages*, Bloomington, IN, pp. 32–57

Morrison, K.F. (1992), '"Know thyself": music in the Carolingian renaissance', *Settimane* 39: 369–479

Mostert, R. and Mostert, M. (1990), 'Using astronomy as an aid to dating manuscripts: the example of the Leiden Aratea Planetarium', *Quaerendo* 20: 248–61

Nees, L. (1991), *A Tainted Mantle: Hercules and the Classical Tradition at the Carolingian Court*, Philadelphia

Nelson, J.L. (1986a), 'Dispute settlement in Carolingian West Francia', in W. Davies and P. Fouracre (eds.), *The Settlement of Disputes in Early Medieval Europe*, Cambridge, pp. 45–64

Nelson, J.L. (1986b), 'Kingship, law and liturgy in the political thought of Hincmar of Rheims', in J.L. Nelson, *Politics and Ritual in Early Medieval Europe*, London and Ronceverte, pp. 133–71

Nelson, J.L. (1986c), 'Public *Histories* and private history in the work of Nithard', in J.L. Nelson, *Politics and Ritual in Early Medieval Europe*, London and Ronceverte, pp. 195–237

Nelson, J.L. (1990a), 'Literacy in Carolingian government', in R. McKitterick (ed.), *The Uses of Literacy in Early Mediaeval Europe*, Cambridge, pp. 258–96

Nelson, J.L. (1990b), 'The "Annals of St Bertin"', in Gibson and Nelson (1990), pp. 23–40

Nelson, J.L. (1990c), 'Perceptions du pouvoir chez les historiennes du haut moyen âge', in M. Rouche and J. Heuclin (eds.), *La femme au moyen-âge*, Maubeuge, pp. 75–85

Noble, T.F.X. (1976), 'The place in papal history of the Roman synod of 826', *Church History* 45: 1–16

Noble, T.F.X. (1985), 'A new look at the *Liber Pontificalis*', *Archivum Historiae Pontificiae* 23: 347–58

Norberg, D. (1979), *L'œuvre poétique de Paulin d'Aquilée*, Stockholm

d'Onofrio, G. (1986), *Fons scientiae: la dialettica nell'Occidente tardo-antico* (Nuovo Medioevo 31), Naples

Pérès, M. (1991), 'Remi et la musique', in D. Iogna-Prat, G. Lobrichon and C. Jeudy (eds.), *L'école carolingienne d'Auxerre de Murethach à Remi, 830–908*, Paris, pp. 435–42

Poulin, J.-C. (1975), *L'idéal de sainteté dans l'Aquitaine carolingienne d'après les sources hagiographiques (750–950)*, Laval

Quadri, R. (ed.) (1966), *I Collectanea di Eirico di Auxerre* (Spicilegium Friburgense 11), Fribourg

Quinn, P.A. (1989), *Better than the Sons of Kings: Boys and Monks in the Early Middle Ages* (Studies in History and Culture 2), New York and Berne

Rankin, S. (1991), '*Ego itaque Notker scripsi*', *RB* 101: 268–98

Rankin, S. (1994), 'Carolingian music', in R. McKitterick (ed.), *Carolingian Culture: Emulation and Innovation*, Cambridge, pp. 274–316

Reynolds, R.E. (1983), 'Unity and diversity in Carolingian canon law collections: the case of the *Collectio Hibernensis* and its derivatives', in U.-R. Blumenthal (ed.), *Carolingian Essays*, Washington, DC, pp. 99–135

Riché, P. (1963), 'Les bibliothèques de trois aristocrates laïcs carolingiens', *Le Moyen Age* 69: 87–104

Riché, P. (1965), 'Enseignement du droit en Gaule du VIe au XIe siècle', *Ius Romanum Medii Aevi* I, 5 b *bb*, Milan, pp. 3–21

Riché, P. (1978), *Education and Culture in the Barbarian West from the Sixth through the Eighth Century*, J.J. Contreni (trans.), Columbia, SC

Riché, P. (1989), *Ecoles et enseignement dans le haut moyen âge: fin du Ve siècle – milieu du XIe siècle*, Paris

Riché, P. (ed.) (1975), *Dhuoda: Manuel pour mon fils* (Sources chrétiennes 225), Paris

Ring, R. (1978), 'Renouatio Karoli Latinitatis', *Res Publica Litterarum: Studies in the Classical Tradition* 1: 263–71

Robinson, F.C. (1973), 'Syntactical glosses in Latin manuscripts of Anglo-Saxon provenance', *Speculum* 48: 443–75

Rosenthal, J.T. (1969), 'The education of the early Capetians', *Traditio* 25: 366–76

Schaller, D. (1962), 'Philologische Untersuchungen zu den Gedichten Theodulfs von Orléans', *DA* 18: 13–91

Schaller, D. (1989), 'Der Dichter des *Carmen de conversione Saxonum*', in G. Bernt, F. Rädle and G. Silagi (eds.), *Tradition und Wertung: Festschrift für Franz Brunhölzl zum 65. Geburtstag*, Sigmaringen, pp. 27–54

Scheibe, F.C. (1958), 'Alcuin und die Admonitio Generalis', *DA* 14: 221–9

Schmid, H. (ed.) (1981), *Musica et scolica enchiriadis una cum aliquibus tractatulis adiunctis*, Veröffentlichungen der Musikhistorischen Kommission, Munich
Schmid, K. (ed.) (1978), *Die Klostergemeinschaft von Fulda im früheren Mittelalter*, 3 vols., Munich
Schrimpf, G. (1973), 'Zur Frage der Authentizität unserer Texte vom Johannes Scottus' *Annotationes in Martianum*', in J.J. O'Meara and L. Bieler (eds.), *The Mind of Eriugena: Papers of a Colloquium, Dublin, 14–18 July 1970*, Dublin, pp. 125–39
Sestan, E. (1970), 'La Storiografia dell'Italia longobarda: Paolo Diacono', *Settimane* 17: 357–86
Smith, L. (1989), 'The manuscript tradition of Periphyseon Book 4', in *Giovanni Scoto nel suo tempo: l'organizzazione del sapere in età carolingia* (Atti dei Convegni dell'Accademia Tudertina e del Centro di studi sulla spiritualità medievale, n.s. 1), Spoleto, pp. 499–512
Steinen, W. von den (ed.) (1948), *Notker der Dichter und seine geistige Welt*, 2 vols., Berne
Steinmeyer, E. and Sievers, E. (1879–1922), *Die althochdeutsche Glossen*, 5 vols., Berlin
Stevens, W.M. (1979a), Introduction to *Rabani Mogontiacensis episcopi De computo*, *CCCM* 44: 163–97
Stevens, W.M. (1979b), 'Compotistica et Astronomica in the Fulda school', in M.H. King and W.M. Stevens (eds.), *Saints, Scholars and Heroes: Studies in Honour of Charles W. Jones*, 2 vols., Collegeville, MN, II: 27–63
Stevens, W.M. (1985), *Bede's Scientific Achievement* (Jarrow Lecture 1985), Newcastle upon Tyne
Stevens, W.M. (1993), 'Computus-Handschriften Walahfrid Strabos', in P... Butzer and D. Lohrmann (eds.), *Science in Western and Eastern Civilization in Carolingian Times*, Basel, pp. 363–82
Stratmann, M. (1991), *Hinkmar von Reims als Verwalter von Bistum und Kirchenprovinz* (Quellen und Forschungen zum Recht im Mittelalter 6), Sigmaringen
Thiel, M. (1973), *Grundlagen und Gestalt der Hebräischkenntnisse des frühen Mittelalters* (Biblioteca di Studi Medievali 4), Spoleto
Treitler, L. (1974), 'Homer and Gregory: the transmission of epic poetry and plainchant', *The Musical Quarterly* 60: 333–72
Treitler, L. (1981), 'Oral, written, and literate process in the transmission of medieval music', *Speculum* 56: 471–91
Treitler, L. (1982), 'The early history of music writing in the west', *Journal of the American Musicological Society* 35: 237–79
Treitler, L. and Levy, K. (1988), 'Communications', *Journal of the American Musicological Society* 41: 566–78
Ullman, B.L. (1964), 'Geometry in the mediaeval Quadrivium', in *Studi di bibliografia e di storia in onore di Tammaro De Marinis*, 4 vols., Verona, IV, pp. 263–85
Vogel, C. (1967), 'La réforme liturgique sous Charlemagne', in *Karl der Grosse* II, pp. 217–32
Vogel, C. (1979), 'Les motifs de la romanisation du culte sous Pépin le Bref (751–768) et Charlemagne (774–814)', in *Culto cristiano [e] politica imperiale carolingia* (Convegni del Centro di studi sulla spiritualità medievale, Università degli studi di Perugia 18), Todi, pp. 13–41
Vykoukal, E. (1913), 'Les examens du clergé paroissial à l'époque carolingienne'.

Revue d'Histoire Ecclésiastique 14: 81–96

Wallace-Hadrill, J.M. (1981), 'History in the mind of Archbishop Hincmar', in R.H.C. Davis and J.M. Wallace-Hadrill (eds.), *The Writing of History in the Middle Ages: Essays Presented to Richard William Southern*, Oxford, pp. 43–70

Wallace-Hadrill, J.M. (1983), *The Frankish Church* (Oxford History of the Christian Church), Oxford

Wallace-Hadrill, J.M. (ed.) (1960), *Fredegarii chronicorum liber quartus cum continuationibus. The Fourth Book of the Chronicle of Fredegar with its Continuations*, London

Wallach, L. (1968), *Alcuin and Charlemagne: Studies in Carolingian History and Literature*, revised and amended reprint, New York

Walsh, M. and Ó Cróinín, D. (eds.) (1988), *Cummian's Letter 'De controversia paschali' and the 'De ratione conputandi'* (Studies and Texts 86), Toronto

Waquet, H. (ed.) (1964), *Abbon: siège de Paris par les Normands: poème du IXe siècle*, Paris

Weakland, R. (1956), 'Hucbald as musician and theorist', *The Musical Quarterly* 42: 66–84

Wemple, S.F. (1981), *Women in Frankish Society: Marriage and Cloister*, Philadelphia

Werner, K.F. (1990), '*Hludovicus Augustus*: gouverner l'empire chrétien – idées et réalités', in P. Godman and R. Collins (eds.) *Charlemagne's Heir*, Oxford, pp. 3–123

Wickersheimer, E. (1966), *Les manuscrits latins de médecine du haut moyen-âge dans les bibliothèques de France*, Paris

Wickham, C. (1986), 'Land disputes and their social framework in Lombard-Carolingian Italy, 700–900', in W. Davies and P. Fouracre (eds.), *The Settlement of Disputes in Early Medieval Europe*, Cambridge, pp. 105–24

Wieland, G.R. (1983), *The Latin Glosses on Arator and Prudentius in Cambridge University Library MS Gg.5.35* (Studies and Texts 61), Toronto

Williams, S. (1971), *Codices Pseudo-Isidoriani: A Palaeographico-Historical Study* (Monumenta Iuris Canonici, series c: subsidia 3), New York

Wright, R. (1982), *Late Latin and Early Romance in Spain and Carolingian France* (ARCA Classical and Medieval Texts, Papers and Monographs 8), Liverpool

Zier, M.A. (1989), 'The shape of the critical edition of Periphyseon IV', in *Giovanni Scoto nel suo tempo: l'organizzazione del sapere in età carolingia* (Atti dei Convegni dell'Accademia Tudertina e del Centro di studi sulla spiritualità medievale, n.s. 1), Spoleto, pp. 487–98

28 THEOLOGY AND THE ORGANISATION OF THOUGHT

Amann, E. (1947), *L'époque carolingienne*, vol. vi of *Histoire de l'église depuis les origines jusqu'à nos jours*, ed. A. Fliche and V. Martin, Paris

Boshof, E. (1969), *Erzbischof Agobard von Lyon: Leben und Werk*, Cologne

Bouhot, J.P. (1976), *Ratramne de Corbie*, Paris

Browe, P. (1921), 'Die Kommunion in der gallikanischen Kirche der Merowinger und karolingerzeit', *Theologisches Quartalschrift* 102: 22–53, 133–56

Bullough, D.A. (1991), *Carolingian Renewal: Sources and Heritage*, Manchester

Burn, A.E. (1896), *The Athanasian Creed*, Cambridge

Cappuyns, M. (1933), *Jean Scot Erigène: sa vie, son œuvre, sa pensée*, Leuven

Cavadini, J. (1993), *The Last Christology of the West: Adoptionism in Spain and Gaul, 785–820*, Philadelpha

Chazelle, C. (1992a), 'The concepts of character and Christ's Glorified Body in the Carolingian Eucharistic controversy', *Traditio* 47: 1–36

Chazelle, C. (1992b), 'Images, scripture, the church and the Libri Carolini' *Proceedings of the PMR Conference for 1992* (forthcoming)

Chelini, J. (1991), *L'aube du moyen âge: naissance de la chrétienté occidentale*, Paris

Colish, M. (1984), 'Carolinigan debates over *Nihil* and *Tenebrae*', *Speculum* 59: 757–95

Cristiani, M. (1968), 'La controversia eucaristica nella cultura del secolo IX', *Studi Medievali* 3rd series, 9: 167–233

Cristiani, M. (1976), 'La notion de loi dans le 'De praedestinatione' de Jean Scot', *Studi Medievali* 3rd series, 17: 81–114

Cristiani, M. (1987), 'Tempo rituale e tempo storico. Communione Cristiana e sacrificio. Scelte antropologiche della cultura altomedievale', in *Segni e Riti nella chiesa altomedievale occidentale*, pp. 439–500

Dahlhaus-Berg, E. (1975), *Nova Antiquitas et Antiqua Novitas: typologische Exegese und isidorianisches Geschichtsbild bei Theodulf von Orleans*, Cologne

Davis, L.D. (1971), 'Hincmar of Rheims as a theologian of the Trinity', *Traditio* 27: 455–68

Delahaye, P. (1951), *Une controverse sur l'âme universelle au IXe siècle* (Analecta Medievalia Namurcensia 1), Namur

Devisse, J. (1975), *Hincmar Archevêque de Reims 845–882*, Geneva

Dumiège, G. (1978), *Nicée II*, Paris

Dvornik, F. (1948), *The Photian Schism*, Cambridge

Fahey, J.F. (1951), *The Eucharistic teaching of Ratramnus of Corbie*, Mundelein

Ferrari, (1972), 'In Papia conveniant ad Dungalum', *Italia Medioevale et Umanistica* 15: 1–52

Freeman, A. (1965), 'Further studies in the Libri Carolini', *Speculum* 40: 203–89

Freeman, A. (1971), 'Further studies in the Libri Carolini III; the marginal notes in Vatican lat. 7027', *Speculum* 46: 597–612

Freeman, A. (1985), 'Carolingian orthodoxy and the fate of the Libri Carolini', *Viator* 16: 65–108

Freeman, A. (1988), 'Additions and corrections to the Libri Carolini; links with Alcuin and the Adoptionist controversy', in S. Krämer and M. Bernhard (eds.) *Scire Litteras*, Munich, pp. 159–69

Ganz, D. (1990), *Corbie in the Carolingian Renaissance*, Sigmaringen

Gaskoin, C. (1904), *Alcuin: His Life and Work*, London

Geiselmann, J.R. (1926), *Die Eucharistielehre der Vorsscholastik*, Paderborn

Gorman, M. (1985), 'Harvard's oldest Latin manuscript', *Scriptorium* 39: 185–96

Gundlach, W. (1889), 'Zwei Schriften des Erzbischofs Hincmar von Reims', *Zeitschift für Kirchengeschichte* 10: 258–309

von Harnack, A. (1898), *History of Dogma* v, London

Hartmann, W. (1977), *Das Konzil von Worms 868: Überlieferung und Bedeutung*, Göttingen

Hartmann, W. (1979), 'Neue Texte zur bischöflichen Reformgesetzgebung aus den Jahren 829/31', *DA* 35: 368–94

Haugh, R. (1975), *Photius and the Carolingians*, Belmont

Haussling, A. (1973), *Mönchskonvent und Eucharistiefeier: Eine Studie über die Messe in der abendländischen Klosterliturgie des frühen Mittelalters und zur Geschichte der Messhäufigkeit*, Münster

Heil, W. (1965), 'Der Adoptianismus, Alcuin, und Spanien', in *Das geistige Leben*, ed. B. Bischoff, *Karl der Grosse* II, pp. 95–155

Jeauneau, E. (1983), 'Pseudo-Dionysius, Maximus the Confessor and Gregory of Nyssa in the works of John Scottus Eriugena', in U.-R. Blumenthal (ed.), *Carolingian Essays*, Washington, pp. 137–49

Jolivet, J. (1958), *Godescalc d'Orbais et la Trinité: la méthode de la théologie à l'époque carolingienne*, Paris

Kaczynski, B.M. (1988), *Greek in the Carolingian Age: The St Gall Manuscripts*, Cambridge

Keefe, S.A. (1983), 'Carolingian baptismal expositions: a handlist of tracts and manuscripts', in U.-R. Blumenthal (ed.), *Carolingian Essays*, Washington, pp. 169–237

Kennedy, K. (1983), 'The permanence of an idea: three ninth century Frankish ecclesiastics and the authority of the Roman see', in H. Mordek (ed.), *Aus Kirche und Reich: Festschrift für F. Kempf*, Sigmaringen, pp. 105–16

Kleinclausz, A. (1948), *Alcuin* (Annales de l'Université de Lyon 3 series, Lettres Fasc. 15), Paris

Kolping, A. (1951), 'Amalar von Metz und Florus von Lyon', *Zeitschrift für katholische Theologie* 73: 424–64

Leclercq, J. (1948), 'Les munimenta fidei de S. Benoît d'Aniane', *Analecta Monastica* 1: 1–74

de Lubac, H. (1949), *Corpus Mysticum: l'eucharistie et l'église au moyen âge*, Paris

McKeon, P.R. (1974), 'The Carolingian councils of Savonières (859) and Tusey (860) and their background', *RB* 84: 75–110

McKitterick, R. (1977), *The Frankish Church and the Carolingian Reforms, 789–895*, London

Marenbon, J. (1981), *From the Circle of Alcuin to the School of Auxerre*, Cambridge

Marenbon J. (1990), 'John Scottus and Carolingian theology', in M.T. Gibson and J. Nelson (eds.), *Charles the Bald: Court and Kingdom*, 2nd edn, Aldershot

Mathon, G. (1964), *L'anthropologie chrétienne en occident de saint Augustin à Jean Scot Erigène*. Thèse Lille, Faculté de Théologie

Nelson, J. (1977), 'Kingship, law and liturgy in the political thought of Hincmar of Rheims', *EHR* 92: 241–79

Nineham, D.E. (1989), 'Gottschalk of Orbais: reactionary or precursor of the Reformation?', *JEH* 40: 1–18

Pelikan, J. (1978), *The Christian Tradition* III: *The Growth of Medieval Theology (600–1300)*, Chicago

Picasso, G. (1987), 'Riti eucarisitici nella società altomedievale. Sul significato storico del trattato eucaristico di Pascasio Radberto', *Settimane* 33: 505–26

Raedle, F. (1988), 'Gottschalk's Gedicht an seinen letzten Freund', in S. Krämer and M. Bernhard (eds.), *Scire Litteras. Forschungen zum mittelalterlichen Geistesleben* (Bayerische Akademie der Wissenschaften, phil.-hist. Klasse N.F. 99), Munich, pp. 315–25

Rivera Recio, J.F. (1980), *El Adopcionismo en Espana (S. VIII)*, Toledo

Sahas, D.J. (1986), *Icon and Logos*, Toronto

Schieffer, R. (1989), 'Regno e Chiesa sotto Carlo il Calvo', in *Giovanni Scoto nel suo tempo*, Spoleto, pp. 1—24

Schrimpf, G. (1982a), *Das Werk des Johannes Scottus Eriugena im Rahmen des Wissenschaftsverstandnisses seiner Zeit*, Münster

Schrimpf, G. (1982b) 'Der Beitrag des Johannes Scottus Eriugena zum Praedestinationsstreit', in H. Lowe (ed.), *Die Iren und Europa im frühen Mittelalter*, Stuttgart, pp. 819–65

Vielhaber, K. (1956), *Gottschalk der Sachse*, Bonn

Wilmart, A. (1924), 'Un lecteur ennemi d'Amalaire', *RB* 34: 320–29

29 BOOK PRODUCTION IN THE CAROLINGIAN EMPIRE AND THE SPREAD OF CAROLINE MINUSCULE

Autenrieth, J. (1988), *'Litterae Virgilianae' Vom Fortleben einer Römischer Schrift*, Munich

Becker, G. (1865), *Catalogi Bibliothecarum antiqui*, Bonn

Bischoff, B. (1973), *Sammelhandschrift Diez B. Sant 66: Grammatici Latini et catalogus librorum*, Graz

Bischoff, B. (1974, 1980), *Die südostdeutschen Schreibschulen und Bibliotheken*, I: *Die bayrischen Diözesen*, II: *Die vorwiegend österreichischen Diözesen*, Wiesbaden

Bischoff, B. (1981a), 'Panorama der Handschriftenüberlieferung aus der Zeit Karls des Grossen', in B. Bischoff, *MS* III, pp. 5–38

Bischoff, B. (1981b), 'Die Bibliothek im Dienste der Schule', in B. Bischoff, *MS* III, pp. 213–33

Bischoff, B. (1981c), *Kailligraphie in Bayern*, Wiesbaden

Bischoff, B. (1989), *Die Abtei Lorsch im Spiegel seiner Handschriften*, Lorsch

Bischoff, B. (1990), *Latin Palaeography: Antiquity and the Middle Ages*, Cambridge

Bischoff, B., Eastwood, B., Klein, T.A.-P., Mütherich, F. and Obbema, P.F.J. (1989), *Aratea: Kommentar zum Aratus des Germanicus MS Voss. lat. Q. 79, Bibliotheek der Rijksuniversiteit Leiden*, Lucerne

Bischoff, B. and Hoffmann, J. (1952), *Libri Sancti Kyliani: Die Würzburger Schreibschule und die Dombibliothek im VIII und IX Jahrhundert*, Würzburg

Bruckner, A. (1938), *Scriptoria Medii Aevi Helvetica* III, Geneva

Buhler, A. (1986), 'Capitularia relecta: Studien zur Entstehung und Überlieferung der Kapitularien Karls des Grossen und Ludwigs des Frommen', *Archiv für Diplomatik* 32: 305–501

Butzmann, H. (1964), *Die Weissenburger Handschriften*, Frankfurt

Casparri, C. (1964), *Alte und Neue Quellen zur Geschichte des Taufsymbols und der Glaubensregel*, Brussels

Contreni, J.J. (1978), *The Cathedral School of Laon from 850–930: its Manuscripts and Masters*, Munich

Dahlhaus-Berg, E. (1975), *Nova antiquitas et antiqua novitas: Typologische Exegese und isidorianisches Geschichtsbild bei Theodulf von Orleans*, Vienna

Dekker, A. (1895), 'Die Hildebold'sche Manuskripten sammlung des Kölner Domes', in *Festschrift der drei und vierzigsten versammlung deutscher Philologen und*

Schülmänner dargeboten von den höheren Lehranstalter Kölns, Bonn, pp. 215–51

Derolez, R. (1954), *Runica manuscripta: The English Tradition* (Rijksuniversiteit te Gent. Werken uitgegeven door te Faculteit van des Wijsbegeerte en Letteren 118), Bruges

Derolez, R. and Schwab, U. (1983), 'The runic inscriptions of San Angelo', *Academia Analecta* 45: 95–130

Devisse, J. (1975), *Hincmar Archevêque de Reims (845–882)*, Geneva

Dionisotti, A.C. (1982), 'On Bede, grammars and Greek', *RB* 91: 111–43

Duwel, K. (1983), *Runenkunde*, Stuttgart

Eisenlohr, E. (1991), 'Die Pergamente der St Galler Urkunden (8–10 Jahrhundert)', in P. Ruck (ed.), *Pergament*, Sigmaringen, pp. 63–95

Fischer, B. (1985), 'Die Alkuin Bibeln', in Bonifatius Fischer, *Lateinische Bibelhandschriften im frühen Mittelalter*, Freiburg, pp. 203–403

Flower, R. (1947), *The Irish Tradition*, Oxford

Gameson, R. (ed.), (1994), *The Early Medieval Bible, its Production, Decoration and Use* (Cambridge Studies in Palaeography and Codicology 2), Cambridge

Ganz, D. (1987), 'The preconditions for Caroline minuscule', *Viator* 18: 23–43

Ganz, D. (1990), *Corbie in the Carolingian Renaissance*, Sigmaringen

Ganz, D. (1991), 'On the history of Tironian Notes', in P.F. Ganz (ed.), in *Tironischen Noten*, Wolfenbüttel

Ganz, D. and R.G. Rogers, (forthcoming) *Depictions of Scribes in the Middle Ages*

Gorman, M. (1983), 'The early manuscript tradition of Saint Augustine's Confessiones', *JTS* n.s. 34: 114–45

Gorman, M. (1985), 'The diffusion of the manuscripts of Saint Augustine's "De Doctrina Christiana" in the Early Middle Ages', *RB* 95: 11–24

Hafner, W. (1959), *Der Basiliuskommentar zur Regula S. Benedicti: Ein Beitrag zur Autorenfrage karolingischer Regelkommentare* (Beiträge zur Geschichte des alten Mönchtums und des Benediktinerordens 23), Münster

Hagen, H. (1870), *Anecdota Helvetica*, Leipzig

Herren, M. (1988), *The Sacred Nectar of the Greeks: The Study of Greek in the West in the Early Middle Ages*, London

Holtz, L. (1981), *Donat et la tradition de l'enseignement grammaticale*, Paris

Irvine, M. (1986), 'Bede the grammarian and the scope of grammatical studies in eighth-century Northumbria', *ASE* 15: 15–44

Knight, S. (1989), 'Scripts of the Grandval Bible', *The Scribe* 45: 6–12

Kottje, R. (1975), 'Hrabanus Maurus – "Praeceptor Germaniae"?', *DA* 31: 534–55

Krieg, P.M. (1931), *Das Professbuch der Abtei St Gallen: St Gallen Stiftsarchiv Cod. Class 1 Cist. c. 3 b. 56*, Augsburg

Kuchenbuch, L. (1978), *Bauerliche Gesellschaft und Klosterherrschaft im 9. Jahrhundert*, Wiesbaden

Laistner, M.W. (1933), 'Source-marks in Bede manuscripts', *JTS* 34: 350–4

Lehmann, P. (1917–), *Mittelalterliche Bibliothekskataloge Deutschlands und der Schweiz*, Berlin

Lehmann, P. (1925–6), *Fuldaer Studien*, Munich

Lemerle, P. (1986), *Byzantine Humanism*, Canberra

McKitterick, R. (1989), *The Carolingians and the Written Word*, Cambridge

McKitterick, R. (1990), 'Carolingian book production: some problems', *The Library* 6th series, 12: 1–33

Morrish, J. (1988), 'Dated and datable manuscripts copied in England during the ninth century: a preliminary list', *Medieval Studies* 50: 512–38

Palazzo, E. and Parisse, M. (1991), *La bibliothèque monastique: le scriptorium oubliée de Wissembourg*, Strasbourg

Parkes, M.B. (1992), *Pause and Effect: An Introduction to the History of Punctuation in the West*, Aldershot

Petrucci, A. (1986), 'Alfabetismo e educazione grafica degli scribi altomedievali sec. VII–X', in P. Ganz (ed.), *The Role of the Book in Medieval Culture*, Turnhout, pp. 109–31

Poulin, J. (1979), 'Entre magie et religion. Recherches sur les utilisations marginales de l'écrit dans la culture populaire du haut moyen âge', in P. Boglioni (ed.), *La culture populaire au haut moyen âge*, Montreal

Rand, E.K. (1929), *A Survey of the Manuscripts of Tours*, Cambridge

Rand, E.K. (1934), *The Earliest Book of Tours*, Cambridge

Rissel, M. (1974), *Rezeption antiker und patristischer Wissensehaft bei Hrabanus Maurus*, Bonn

Ruck, P. (1991), *Pergament Geschichte: Struktur, Restaurierung, Herstellung*, Sigmaringen

Ryder, M.L. (1985), *Sheep and Man*, Duckworth

Schwab, I. (1983), *Das Prümer Urbar* (Rheinische Urbar 5), Düsseldorf

Smith, J. (1992), *Province and Empire: Brittany and the Carolingians*, Cambridge

Spilling, H. (1978), 'Angelsächsische Schrift in Fulda', in A. Brall (ed.), *Von der Klosterbibliothek zur Landesbibliothek: Beiträge zum 200 jährigen Bestehen der Hessischen Landesbibliothek Fulda*, Stuttgart, pp. 47–98

Spilling, H. (1982), 'Das Fuldaer Skriptorium zur Zeit des Hrabanus', in R. Kottje and H. Zimmermann (eds.), *Hrabanus Maurus Lehrer, Abt und Bischoff* (Akademie der Wissenschaften Mainz Einzelveroffentlichung 4), Wiesbaden, pp. 165–91

Stevens, W.M. (1972), 'Fulda scribes at work', *Bibliothek und Wissenschaft* 8: 287–317

Stevens, W.M. (1985), *Bede's Scientific Achievement*, Newcastle

Wright, R. (ed.) (1991), *Latin and the Romance Languages in the Early Middle Ages*, London

30 ART AND ARCHITECTURE

Åberg, N. (1943–6), *The Occident and the Orient in the Art of the Seventh Century*, 3 vols., Stockholm

Alexander, J.J.G. (1978), *Insular Manuscripts 6th to the 9th Century* (A Survey of Manuscripts Illuminated in the British Isles), London

Anker, P. (1970), *The Art of Scandinavia* 1, London

Backhouse, J. (1981), *The Lindisfarne Gospels*, Oxford

Backhouse, J., Turner, D.H. and Webster, L. (1984), *The Golden Age of Anglo-Saxon Art 966–1066*, London

Bandmann, G. (1965), 'Die vorbilder der Aachener Pfalzkapelle', in Braunfels and Schnitzler (1965), pp. 424–62

Barral i Altet, X. (ed.) (1986–90), *Artistes, artisans et production artistique au moyen âge*, 3 vols., Paris

Battiscombe, C.F. (ed.) (1956), *The Relics of Saint Cuthbert*, Oxford

Beck, H.-G. (1975), 'Von der Fragwürdigkeit der Ikone,' *Sitzungsberichte der Bayerischen Akademie der Wissenschaften*, phil.-hist. Klasse. 7

Belting, H. (1967), 'Probleme der Kunstgeschichte Italiens im Frühmittelalter', *Frühmittelalterliche Studien* 1: 94–143

Belting, H. (1973), 'Der Einhardsbogen,' *Zeitschrift für Kunstgeschichte* 36: 93–121

Belting, H. (1978), 'Die beiden Palastaulen Leos III. im Lateran und die Entstehung einer päpstlichen Programmkunst', *FrSt* 12: 55–83

Belting, H. (1987), 'Eine Privatkapelle im frühmittelalterlichen Rom', *Dumbarton Oaks Papers* 41: 55–69

Belting, H. (1990), *Bild und Kult: Eine Geschichte des Bildes vor dem Zeitalter der Kunst*, Munich

Bertelli, C. (1961), *La Madonna di Santa Maria in Trastevere: storia – iconografia – stile di un dipinto romano dell'ottavo secolo*, Rome

Beutler, C. (1978), *Die Entstehung des Altaraufsätzes: Studien zum Grab Willibrords in Echternach*, Munich

Biddle, M. (1975), 'Winchester: the development of an early capital', in H. Jankuhn, W. Schlesinger and H. Steuer (eds.), *Vor- und Frühformen der europäischen Stadt im Mittelalter* 1, pp. 229–61

Bischoff, B. (1963), 'Kreuz und Buch im Frühmittelalter und in den ersten Jahrhunderten der spanischen Reconquista', in *Bibliotheca docet. Festgabe für Carl Wehmer*, Amsterdam, pp. 19–34;- reprinted in B. Bischoff, *MS* II, pp. 284–303

Bischoff, B. (1981), 'Eine Beschreibung der Basilika von Saint-Denis aus dem Jahre 799', *Kunstchronik* 34: 97–103

Bischoff, B. (1989), *Latin Palaeography, Antiquity and the Middle Ages*, trans. D. Ó Cróinín and D. Ganz, Cambridge

Bloch, P. (1965), 'Das Apsismosaik von Germigny-des-Prés. Karl und der alte Bund', in Braunfels and Schnitzler (1965), pp. 234–61

Braunfels, W. (1965), 'Karls des Grossen Bronzewerkstatt', in Braunfels and Schnitzler (1965), pp. 168–202

Braunfels, W. (1968), *Die Welt der Karolinger und ihre Kunst*, Munich

Braunfels, W. (1981), 'Karolingischer Klassizismus als politisches Programm und Karolingischer Humanismus als Lebenshaltung', *Settimane* 2: 821–49

Braunfels, W. and Schnitzler, H. (eds.) (1965), *Karolingische Kunst (Karl der Grosse III)*, Düsseldorf

Brenk, B. (1966), *Tradition und Neuerung in der christlichen Kunst des ersten Jahrtausends: Studien zur Geschichte des Weltgerichtsbildes* (Wiener byzantinische Studien 3), Graz

Brown, P. (1976), 'Eastern and western Christendom in late antiquity: a parting of the ways', in D. Baker (ed.), *The Orthodox Churches and the West* (Studies in Church History 13), Oxford, pp. 1–24

Brown, P. (1981), *The Cult of the Saints: Its Rise and Function in Latin Christianity*, Chicago

Brubaker, L. (1985), 'Politics, patronage, and art in ninth-century Byzantium: the *Homilies* of Gregory of Nazianzus in Paris (BN gr. 510)', *DOP* 39: 1–13

Bryer, A. and Herrin, J. (eds.) (1977), *Iconoclasm: Papers Given at the Ninth Spring*

Symposium of Byzantine Studies, University of Birmingham, March 1975, Birmingham

Buckton, D. (1988), 'Byzantine enamel and the west', *Byzantinische Forschungen* 13: 235–44

Budny, M. and Tweddle, D. (1984), 'The Maaseik embroideries', *ASE* 13: 65–96

Bullough, D. (1975), '"Imagines regum" and their significance in the early medieval west', in G. Robertson and G. Henderson (eds.), *Studies in Memory of David Talbot Rice*, Edinburgh, pp. 223–76

Bullough, D. (1977), 'Roman books and Carolingian *renovatio*', in D. Baker (ed.), *Renaissance and Renewal in Christian History* (Studies in Church History 14), Oxford

Calkins, R. (1983), *Illuminated Books of the Middle Ages*, Ithaca

Cassidy, B. (ed.), (1992), *The Ruthwell Cross*, Princeton, NJ

Caviness, M.H. (1989), 'Broadening the definitions of "art": the reception of medieval works in the context of Post-Impressionist movements', in P.J. Gallacher and H. Damico (eds.), *Hermeneutics and Medieval Culture*, Binghamton, pp. 259–82

Chazelle, C. (1986), 'Matter, spirit, and image in the *Libri Carolini*', *Recherches Augustiniennes* 21: 163–84

Chazelle, C. (1990), 'Pictures, books, and the illiterate: Pope Gregory I's letters to Serenus of Marseilles', *Word and Image* 6: 138–53

Conant, K.J. (1959; revised edn 1978), *Carolingian and Romanesque Architecture 800–1200*, Harmondsworth

Cormack, R. (1985), *Writing in Gold*, London

Craddock, P. (1989), 'Metalworking techniques', in Youngs (1989), pp. 170–213

Cramp, R. (1984), *County Durham and Northumberland* (Corpus of Anglo-Saxon Stone Sculpture), Oxford

Crosby, S.M. (1987), *The Royal Abbey of Saint-Denis from its Beginnings to the Death of Suger, 475–1151*, New Haven

Cutler, A. (1985), *The Craft of Ivory*, Washington

Cwi, J.S. (1983), 'A study in Carolingian political theology: the David Cycle at St John, Müstair', in Schmid (1983) I, pp. 117–25

David, P. (1937), 'Un recueil de conférences monastiques irlandaises du VIIIe siècle. Notes sur le manuscrit 43 de la Bibliothèque du Chapitre de Cracovie', *RB* 49: 62–89

Davis-Weyer, C. (1971), *Early Medieval Art, 300–1100* (Sources and Documents in the History of Art Series), Englewood Cliffs, NJ

De Hamel, C. (1986), *A History of Illuminated Manuscripts*, London

Demus, O. (1970), *Byzantine Art and the West*, New York

Deshman, R. (1974), 'Anglo-Saxon art after Alfred', *Art Bulletin* 56: 176–200

Deshman, R. (1980), 'The exalted servant: the ruler theology of the Prayerbook of Charles the Bald', *Viator* 11: 385–417

Doberer, E. (1965), 'Die ornamentale Steinskulptur an der karolingischen Kirchen-ausstattung', in Braunfels and Schnitzler (1965), pp. 203–33

Dodd, E.C. (1969), 'The image of the word', *Berytus* 18: 35–80

Dodds, J. (1990), *Architecture and Ideology in Early Medieval Spain*, University Park, PA and London

Dodwell, C.R. (1971), *Painting in Europe: 800–1200*, Harmondsworth

Dodwell, C.R. (1982), *Anglo-Saxon Art: A New Perspective*, Ithaca

Duft, J. and Meyer, P. (1954), *The Irish Miniatures in the Abbey Library of St Gall*, Olten and Lausanne

Duft, J. and Schnyder, R. (1984), *Die Elfenbein-Einbände der Stiftsbibliothek St Gallen*, Beuron

Duggan, L. (1989), 'Was art really the "book of the illiterate"?' *Word and Image* 5: 227–51

Ebersolt, J. (1928, 2nd edn 1954), *Orient et occident: recherches sur les influences byzantines et orientales en France avant et pendant les croisades*, Paris and Brussels

Edwards, N. (1990), *The Archaeology of Early Medieval Ireland*, Philadelphia

Eggenberger, C. (1982), 'Eine frühkarolingische Dedicatio in der Lindisfarne-Tradition', in H. Engelhart and G. Kempter (eds.), *Diversarum Artium Studia: Festschrift für Heinz Roosen-Runge*, Wiesbaden, pp. 19–32

Eggenberger, C. (1987), *Psalterium Aureum Sancti Galli: Mittelalterliche Psalterillustration im Kloster St Gallen*, Sigmaringen

Elbern, V.H. (1965), 'Liturgische Gerät in edlen Materialien zur Zeit Karls des Grossen', in Braunfels and Schnitzler (1965), pp. 115–67

Elbern, V.H. (1971), 'Zierseiten in Handschriften des frühen Mittelalters als Zeichen sakraler Abgrenzung', in A. Zimmermann (ed.), *Der Begriff der Repraesentatio im Mittelalter: Stellvertretung, Symbol, Zeichen, Bild* (Miscellanea Mediaevalia 8), Berlin, pp. 340–56

Ettinghausen, R. (1972), *From Byzantium to Sassanian Iran and the Islamic World: Three Modes of Artistic Influence*, Leiden

Euw, A. von (1989), *Liber viventium Fabariensis: Das karolingische Memorialbuch von Pfäfers in seiner liturgie- und kunstgeschichtlichen Bedeutung*, Berne and Stuttgart

Euw, A. von (1990), *Evangéliaires carolingiens enluminés*, The Hague and Brussels

Ewig, E. (1963), 'Résidence et capitale pendant le haut moyen âge', *Revue Historique* 230: 25–72

Faral, E. (1964), *Ermold le Noir: poème sur Louis le Pieux et épîtres au roi Pépin*, Paris

Fernie, E.C. (1983), *The Architecture of the Anglo-Saxons*, London

Fontaine, J. (1973–7), *L'art pré-roman hispanique*, La-Pierre-qui-Vire, 2 vols.

Forsyth, G.H. and Weitzmann, K. (1965), *The Church and Fortress of Justinian*, Ann Arbor

Fossard, D., Vieillard-Troiekouroff, M. and Chatel, E. (1978), *Recueil général des monuments sculptés en France pendant le haut moyen âge*, I: *Paris et son département*, Paris

Francovich, G. de (1961), 'Osservazioni sull'altare di Rathchis a Cividale e sui rapporti fra Occidente ed Oriente nei secoli VII e VIII d. C.', in *Scritti di storia dell'arte in onore di Mario Salmi* I, Rome, pp. 173–236

Freeman, A. (1985), 'Carolingian orthodoxy and the fate of the *Libri Carolini*', *Viator* 16: 65–108

Fuhrmann, H. and Mütherich, F. (1986), *Das Evangeliar Heinrichs des Löwen und das mittelalterliche Herrscherbild*, Munich

Gaborit-Chopin, D. (1978), *Elfenbeinkunst im Mittelalter*, Berlin

Galavaris, G. (1970), *Bread and the Liturgy*, Madison

Ganz, D. (1987), 'The preconditions for Caroline minuscule', *Viator* 18: 23–44

Ganz, D. (1992), '"*Pando quod ignoro*." In search of Carolingian artistic experience', in L. Smith and B. Ward (eds.), *Intellectual Life in the Middle Ages: Essays presented to Margaret Gibson*, London, pp. 25–32

Geary, P.J. (revised edn 1990), *Furta Sacra: Theft of Relics in the Central Middle Ages*, Princeton

Godman, P. (1985), *Poetry of the Carolingian Renaissance*, Norman, OK

Godman, P. (1990), 'The poetic hunt. From Saint Martin to Charlemagne's heir', in Godman and Collins (1990), pp. 565–89

Godman, P. and Collins, R. (eds.) (1990), *Charlemagne's Heir: New Perspectives on the Reign of Louis the Pious (814–840)*, Oxford

Goldschmidt, A. (1914, reprint 1969), *Die Elfenbeinskulpturen aus der Zeit der karolingischen und sächsischen Kaiser* I, Berlin

Goldschmidt, A. and Weitzmann, K. (1930–4), *Byzantinische Elfenbeinskulpturen*, 2 vols., Berlin

Grabar, A. (1957), *L'iconoclasme byzantin: dossier archéologique*, Paris

Grabar, A. and Grabar, O. (1965), 'L'essor des arts inspirés par les cours princières à la fin du premier millénaire: princes musulmans et princes chrétiens', reprinted in A. Grabar (1968), *L'art de la fin de l'antiquité et du moyen âge* I, Paris, pp. 121–44

Grabar, A. and Nordenfalk, C. (1957), *Early Medieval Painting*, Geneva

Grabar, O. (1973, revised edn 1987), *The Formation of Islamic Art*, New Haven and London

Grabar, O. and Ettinghausen, R. (1987), *Islamic Art and Architecture 650–1250*, Harmondsworth

Graham-Campbell, J. (1980), *The Viking World*, New Haven and New York

Graham-Campbell, J. and Kidd, D. (1980), *The Vikings*, London

Hamann-MacLean, R. (1974), 'Das Problem der karolingischen Grossplastik', in Milojcic (1974) III, pp. 21–37

Haney, K.E. (1985), 'The Christ and the beasts panel on the Ruthwell cross', *ASE* 14: 215–31

Haseloff, G. (1990), *Email im frühen Mittelalter* (Marburger Studien zur Vor- und Frühgeschichte), Marburg

Hauck, K. (ed.) (1974), *Das Einhardkreuz*, Göttingen

Hegel, G.W.F. (1956; reprint of 1899 edn), *The Philosophy of History*, trans. J. Sibree, New York

Heitz, C. (1980), *L'architecture religieuse carolingienne: les formes et leurs fonctions*, Paris

Heitz, C. (1987), *La France pré-romane: archéologie et architecture religieuse du haut moyen âge, IVe siècle–an mille*, Paris

Henderson, G. (1972), *Early Medieval*, Harmondsworth

Henderson, G. (1987), *From Durrow to Kells: The Insular Gospel-Books 650–800*, London

Henderson, I. (1986), 'The "David Cycle" in Pictish art', in Higgitt (1986), pp. 87–123

Henderson, I. (1989), *The Art and Function of Rosemarkie's Pictish Monuments*, Inverness

Henry, F. (1977), *The Book of Kells*, New York

Higgitt, J. (1990), 'The stone-cutter and the scriptorium', in *Epigraphik 1988: Fachtagung für mittelalterliche und neuzeitliche Epigraphik, Mainz 10.–14. Mai 1988*, Vienna, pp. 149–62

Higgitt, J. (ed.) (1986), *Early Medieval Sculpture in Britain and Ireland* (BAR British Series 152), Oxford

Hodges, R. and Whitehouse, D. (1983), *Mohammed, Charlemagne and the Origins of Europe: Archaeology and the Pirenne Thesis*, Ithaca

Holter, K. (1980), *Der goldene Psalter 'Dagulf-Psalter': Vollständige Faksimile-Ausgabe im Originalformat von Codex 1861 der österreichischen Nationalbibliothek*, Vienna

Horn, W. (1958), 'On the origins of the mediaeval bay system', *Journal of the Society of Architectural Historians* 17: 2–23

Horn, W. and Born, E. (1979), *The Plan of St Gall: A Study of the Architecture and Economy of, and Life in a Paradigmatic Carolingian Monastery*, Berkeley, CA, 3 vols.

Horn, W., Marshall, J.W. and Rourke, G.D. (1990), *The Forgotten Hermitage of Skellig Michael*, Berkeley and Los Angeles

Hubert, J., Porcher, J. and Volbach, W.F. (1969), *Europe in the Dark Ages*, London

Hubert, J., Porcher, J. and Volbach, W.F. (1970), *Carolingian Art*, London

Hugot, L. (1965), 'Die Pfalz Karls des Grossen in Aachen', in Braunfels and Schnitzler (1965), pp. 534–72

Jacobsen, W. (1983a), 'Benedikt von Aniane und die Architektur unter Ludwig dem Frommen zwischen 814 und 830', in Schmid (1983), pp. 15–22

Jacobsen, W. (1983b), 'Saint-Denis in neuen Licht: Konsequenzen der neuentdeckten Baubeschreibung aus dem Jahre 799', *Kunstchronik* 36: 301–8

Jacobsen, W. (1985), 'Die Lorscher Torhalle. Zum Problem ihrer Datierung und Deutung', *Jahrbuch des Zentralinstituts für Kunstgeschichte* 1: 9–75

Jacobsen, W. (1990), 'Allgemeine Tendenzen im Kirchenbau unter Ludwig dem Frommen', in Godman and Collins (1990), pp. 641–54

Jacobsen, W. (1992), *Der Klosterplan von St Gallen und die Karolingische Architektur*, Berlin

James, E. (1977), *The Merovingian Archaeology of South-West Gaul* (BAR Supplementary Series 25), Oxford

Karl der Grosse. Werk und Wirkung (1965), Aachen

Kartsonis, A.D. (1986), *Anastasis: The Making of an Image*, Princeton

Kessler, H.L. (1977), *The Illustrated Bibles from Tours*, Princeton

Kessler, H.L. (1985), 'Pictorial narrative and church mission in sixth-century Gaul', *Studies in the History of Art* 16: 75–91

Kessler, H.L. (1990a), 'An apostle in armor and the mission of Carolingian art', *Arte Medievale* 2nd series, 4: 17–39

Kessler, H.L. (1990b), 'On the state of medieval art history', *The Art Bulletin* 70: 166–87

Kitzinger, E. (1940; revised edn 1983), *Early Medieval Art, with Illustrations from the British Museum and British Library Collections*, London and Bloomington, IL

Kitzinger, E. (1955), 'On some icons of the seventh century', in K. Weitzmann *et al.* (eds.), *Mediaeval Studies in Honor of Albert Mathias Friend, Jr.*, Princeton, NJ, pp. 233–55

Kitzinger, E. (1977), *Byzantine Art in the Making: Main Lines of Stylistic Development in Mediterranean Art 3rd–7th Century*, Cambridge, MA

Koehler, W. (1930–3), *Die Schule von Tours* (Die karolingischen Miniaturen 1), Berlin

Koehler, W. (1972), *Buchmalerei des frühen Mittelalters*, ed. F. Mütherich, and E. Kitzinger, Munich

Koehler, W. and Mütherich, F. (1971), *Die Hofschule Kaiser Lothars: Einzelhandschriften aus Lotharingien* (Die karolingische Miniaturen 4), Berlin

Koehler, W. and Mütherich, F. (1982), *Die Hofschule Karls des Kahlen* (Die karolingischen Miniaturen 5), Berlin

Kornbluth, G. (1986), 'Carolingian treasure: engraved gems of the ninth and tenth centuries', Ph.D. dissertation, University of North Carolina

Kornbluth, G. (1992), 'The Susanna crystal of Lothar II: chastity, the church and royal justice', *Gesta* 31: 25–39

Krautheimer, R. (1942), 'The Carolingian revival of early Christian architecture', *The Art Bulletin* 24: 1–38; reprinted in R. Krautheimer (1969), *Studies in Early Christian, Medieval, and Renaissance Art*, New York, pp. 203–54, with important 'Postscript', pp. 254–6, and in his (1988), *Ausgewählte Aufsätze zur Europäischen Kunstgeschichte*, Cologne, with important 'Postskript 1987', pp. 272–6

Krautheimer, R. (1965; revised edn 1975), *Early Christian and Byzantine Architecture*, Harmondsworth

Krautheimer, R. (1980), *Rome: Profile of a City, 312–1308*, Princeton

Krautheimer, R., Corbett, S. and Frankl, W. (1967), *Corpus Basilicarum Christianarum Romae* III, Vatican City

Kreusch, F. (1965), 'Kirche, Atrium and Portikus der Aachener Pfalz', in Braunfels and Schnitzler (1965), pp. 463–533

Lammers, W. (1972), 'Ein karolingisches Bildprogramm in der Aula Regia von Ingelheim', in *Festschrift für Hermann Heimpel*, Göttingen

Landes, R. (1988), 'Lest the millennium be fulfilled: apocalyptic expectations and the pattern of western chronography 100–800 CE', in W. Verbeke, D. Verhelst and A. Welkenhuysen (ea), *The Use and Abuse of Eschatology in the Middle Ages*, Leuven, pp. 137–211

Lasko, P. (1972), *Ars Sacra 800–1200*, Harmondsworth

Le Berrurier, D. (1978), *The Pictorial Sources of Mythological and Scientific Illustrations in Hrabanus Maurus' De rerum naturis*, New York

Leveto, P. (1990), 'The Marian theme of the frescoes in S. Maria at Castelseprio', *Art Bulletin* 72: 393–413

L'Orange, H.P. and Torp, H. (1977), *Il tempietto langobardo di Cividale*, 4 vols., Rome

McClendon, C. (1980), 'The revival of *opus sectile* pavements in Rome and the vicinity in the Carolingian period', *Papers of the British School at Rome* 48: 157–65

McClendon, C. (1987), *The Imperial Abbey of Farfa: Architectural Currents of the Early Middle Ages*, New Haven and London

McCormick, M. (1986), *Eternal Victory: Triumphal Rulership in Late Antiquity, Byzantium and the Early Medieval West*, Cambridge

McKitterick, R. (1981), 'The scriptoria of Merovingian Gaul: a survey of the evidence', in H.B. Clarke and M. Brennan (eds.), *Columbanus and Merovingian Monasticism* (BAR International Series 113), Oxford, pp. 173–207

McKitterick, R. (1989a), *The Carolingians and the Written Word*, Cambridge

McKitterick, R. (1989b), 'The diffusion of Insular culture in Neustria between 650 and 850: the implications of the manuscript evidence', in *La Neustrie* II, pp. 395–432

Mango, C. (1972), *The Art of the Byzantine Empire 312–1453* (Sources and Documents in the History of Art Series), Englewood Cliffs, NJ

Mann, A. (1961), 'Doppelchor und Stiftermemorie: Zum kunst-und kultur-geschichtlichen Problem der Westchöre', *Westfälische Zeitschrift* 91: 149–62

Mathews, T. (1988), 'The sequel to Nicaea II in Byzantine church decoration', *Perkins Journal*, July: 11–21

Meyvaert, P. (1979), 'Bede and the church paintings at Wearmouth-Jarrow', *ASE* 8: 63–77

Meyvaert, P. (1982), 'An apocalypse panel on the Ruthwell cross', in F. Tirro (ed.), *Medieval and Renaissance Studies*, Durham, pp. 3–32

Micheli, G.L. (1939), *L'enluminure du haut moyen âge et les influences irlandaises*, Brussels

Milojcic, V. (ed.) (1970–4), *Kolloquium über spätantike und frühmittelalterliche Skulptur*, Mainz

Möbius, F. (1968), *Westwerkstudien*, Jena

Mütherich, F. (1965), 'Die Buchmalerei am Hofe Karls des Grossen', in Braunfels and Schnitzler (1965), pp. 9–53

Mütherich, F. (1979), 'I *Libri Carolini* e la miniatura carolingia', in *Culto Cristiano e Politica Imperiale Carolingia* (Atti del XVIII Convegno di studi, Todi, 9–12 ottobre 1977), Todi, pp. 283–301

Mütherich, F. (1980), 'Die Fuldaer Buchmalerei in der Zeit des Hrabanus Maurus', in W. Böhne (ed.), *Hrabanus Maurus und seine Schule*, Fulda, pp. 94–125

Mütherich, F. (1990), 'Book illumination at the court of Louis the Pious', in Godman and Collins (1990), pp. 595–604

Mütherich, F. and Gaehde, J.E. (1976), *Carolingian Painting*, New York

Nees, L. (1978), 'A fifth-century book cover and the origin of the four Evangelist symbols page in the Book of Durrow', *Gesta* 17: 3–8

Nees, L. (1980–1), 'Two illuminated Syriac manuscripts in the Harvard College Library', *Cahiers Archéologiques* 29: 123–42

Nees, L. (1983a), 'The iconographic program of decorated chancel barriers in the pre-Iconoclastic period', *Zeitschrift für Kunstgeschichte* 46: 15–26

Nees, L. (1983b), 'The colophon drawing in the Book of Mulling: a supposed Irish monastery plan and the tradition of terminal illustration in early medieval manuscripts', *Cambridge Medieval Celtic Studies* 5: 67–91

Nees, L. (1985a), *From Justinian to Charlemagne, European Art, 565–787: An Annotated Bibliography*, Boston

Nees, L. (1985b), review of Kurt Holter, *Der goldene Psalter 'Dagulf-Psalter'*, *Art Bulletin* 67: 681–90

Nees, L. (1986), 'The plan of St Gall and the theory of the program of early medieval art', *Gesta* 25: 1–8

Nees, L. (1987), *The Gundohinus Gospels* (Medieval Academy Books 95), Cambridge, MA

Nees, L. (1991), *A Tainted Mantle: Hercules and the Classical Tradition at the Carolingian Court*, Philadelphia

Nees, L. (1992a), 'The originality of early medieval artists', in C. Chazelle (ed.), *Literacy, Politics and Artistic Innovation in the Early Medieval West*, Lanham, MD, pp. 77–109

Nees, L. (1995), 'Carolingian art and politics', in R. Sullivan (ed.), *The Gentle Voice of Teachers: Aspects of Carolingian Learning*, Columbus, OH

Nelson, J.L. (1989), 'Translating images of authority: the Christian Roman emperors in the Carolingian world', in M.M. MacKenzie and C. Roueché (eds.), *Images of Authority: Papers Presented to Joyce Reynolds on the Occasion of her 70th Birthday*, Cambridge, pp. 191–205

Netzer, N. (1989), 'Willibrord's scriptorium at Echternach and its relationship to Ireland and Lindisfarne', in G. Bonner, D. Rollason and C. Stancliffe (eds.), *St Cuthbert, His Cult and His Community to AD 1200*, Woodbridge, pp. 203–12

Netzer, N. (1994), *Cultural Interplay in the Eighth Century: The Trier Gospels and the Making of a Scriptorium at Echternach* (Cambridge Studies in Palaeography and Codicology 3), Cambridge

Neuman de Vegvar, C. (1987), *The Northumbrian Renaissance*, Selinsgrove

Neuman de Vegvar, C. (1990), 'The origin of the Genoels-Elderen ivories', *Gesta* 29: 8–30

Nordenfalk, C. (1931), 'Ein karolingisches Sakramentar aus Echternach und seine Vorläufer', *Acta Archaeologica* 2: 207–45

Nordenfalk, C. (1938), *Die spätantiken Kanontafeln*, Göteborg

Nordenfalk, C. (1970), *Die spätantiken Zierbuchstaben*, Stockholm

Nordenfalk, C. (1977), *Celtic and Anglo-Saxon Painting*, New York

Nordhagen, P.J. (1963), 'The mosaics of the Great Palace of the Byzantine emperors', *BZ* 56: 53–68

Nordhagen, P.J. (1968), *The Frescoes of John VII (AD 705–707) in S. Maria Antiqua in Rome*, Rome

Oakeshott, W. (1967), *The Mosaics of Rome from the Third to the Fourteenth Centuries*, London

Ó Carragáin, E. (1986), 'Christ over the beasts and the Agnus Dei: two multivalent panels on the Ruthwell and Bewcastle crosses', in P.E. Szarmach (ed.), *Sources of Anglo-Saxon Culture*, Kalamazoo, pp. 377–403

O Cróinín, D. (1982), 'Pride and prejudice', *Peritia* 1: 352–62

O Cróinín, D. (1989), 'Is the Augsburg Gospel Codex a Northumbrian manuscript?', in G. Bonner, D. Rollason and C. Stancliffe (eds.), *St Cuthbert, His Cult and His Community to AD 1200*, Woodbridge, pp. 189–201

Osborne, J. (1990), 'The use of painted initials by Greek and Latin scriptoria in Carolingian Rome', *Gesta* 29: 76–85

Oswald, F., Schaefer, L. and Sennhauser, H.R. (1966–71), *Vorromanische Kirchenbauten: Katalog der Denkmäler bis zum Ausgang der Ottonen*, Munich

Pächt, O. (1986), *Book Illumination in the Middle Ages*, trans. K. Davenport, London

Paeseler, W. (1966), 'Das Ingelheimer Relief mit den Flügelpferden', in *Mainz und der Mittelrhein in der europäischen Kunstgeschichte: Festschrift für W.F. Volbach*, Wiesbaden, pp. 45–140

Palol Sallelas, P. de (1962), *Early Medieval Art in Spain*, London

Palol Sallelas, P. de (n.d. [1968]), *Hispanic Art of the Visigothic Period*, New York

Raftery, J. (1965), 'Ex Oriente ... [sic]', *Journal of the Royal Society of Antiquaries of Ireland* 95: 193–204

Reynolds, R. (1983), 'Image and text: a Carolingian illustration of modifications in the early Roman eucharistic ordines', *Viator* 14: 49–75

Riché, P. (1972), 'Trésors et collections d'aristocrates laïques carolingiens', *Cahiers Archéologiques* 22: 39–46

Ritchie, A. (1989), *Picts*, Edinburgh

Roma e l'età carolingia, Atti delle giornate di studio 3–8 maggio 1976 (1976), Rome

Roth, H. (1986), *Kunst und Handwerk im frühen Mittelalter: Archäologische Zeugnisse von Childerich I. bis zu Karl dem Grossen*, Stuttgart

Ryan, M. (1990), 'The formal relationships of Insular early medieval eucharistic chalices', *Proceedings of the Royal Irish Academy* Section C, vol. 90, no. 10: 281–356

Sage, W. (1965), 'Frühmittelalterliche Holzbau', in Braunfels and Schnitzler (1965), pp. 573–90

Sanderson, W. (1974), 'A group of ivories and some related works from late Carolingian Trier', *Art Bulletin* 56: 159–75

Schapiro, M. (1944), 'The religious meaning of the Ruthwell Cross', *Art Bulletin* 26: 232–45

Schapiro, M. and Seminar (1973), 'The miniatures of the Florence Diatessaron (Laurentian MS Or. 81): their place in late medieval art and supposed connection with early Christian and Insular art', *Art Bulletin* 55: 494–533

Schlosser, J. von (1892; reprinted 1974), *Schriftquellen zur Geschichte der karolingischen Kunst*, Vienna

Schlunk, H. and Hauschild, T. (1978), *Die Denkmäler der frühchristlichen und westgotischen Zeit*, Mainz

Schmid, A.A. (ed.) (1983), *Riforma religiosa e arti nell'epoca carolingia* (Atti del XXIV Congresso internationale di storia dell'arte 1), Bologna

Schnitzler, H. (1964), 'Das Kuppelmosaik der Aachener Pfalzkapelle', *Aachener Kunstblätter* 29: 17–44

Schrade, H. (1966), 'Zum Kuppelmosaik der Pfalzkapelle und zum Theoderich Denkmal in Aachen', *Aachener Kunstblätter* 30: 25–37

Schramm, P.E. (1983), *Die deutschen Kaiser und Könige in Bildern ihrer Zeit 751–1190*, revised edn F. Mütherich, Munich

Schramm, P.E. and Mütherich, F. (1981), *Denkmale der deutschen Könige und Kaiser* I, Munich

Sears, E. (1990), 'Louis the Pious as *Miles Christi*. The dedicatory image in Hrabanus Maurus's *De laudibus sanctae crucis*', in Godman and Collins (1990), pp. 605–28

Shailor, B.A. (1991), *The Medieval Book*, Toronto

Stalley, R. (1990), 'European art and the Irish high crosses', *Proceedings of the Royal Irish Academy* Section C, vol. 90, no. 6: 135–58

Stevenson, R.B.K. (1074), 'The Hunterston Brooch and its significance', *Medieval Archaeology* 18: 16–42

Strzygowski, J. (1901), *Orient oder Rom: Beiträge zur Geschichte der spätantiken und frühchristlichen Kunst*, Leipzig

Strzygowski, J. (1923), *Origin of Christian Church Art*, Oxford

Stucchi e mosaici altomedioevali (1962), Atti dell'ottavo Congresso di studi sull'arte dell'alto medioevo, Milan

Taylor, H.M. and Taylor, J. (1965), *Anglo-Saxon Architecture*, Cambridge

Teyssèdre, B. (1959), *Le Sacramentaire de Gellone et la figure humaine dans les manuscrits francs du VIIIe siècle, de l'enluminure à l'illustration*, Toulouse

Thilo, U. (1970), 'Skulptur in Spanien (6.–8. Jahrhundert)', in Milojcic (1970), pp. 25–34

Thomas, C. (1984), 'The Pictish Class I symbol stones', in J.G.P. Friell and W.G. Watson (eds.), *Pictish Studies: Settlement, Burial and Art in Dark Age Northern Britain* (BAR British Series 125), Oxford, pp. 169–87

Vieillard-Troiekouroff, M. (1971), 'La chapelle du palais de Charles le Chauve à Compiègne,' *Cahiers Archéologiques* 21: 89–108

Vieillard-Troiekouroff, M. (1975), 'Les Bibles de Théodulfe et leur décor aniconi-que', in R. Louis (ed.), *Etudes ligériennes d'histoire et d'archéologie médiévales*, Auxerre, pp. 345–60

Vieillard-Troiekouroff, M. (1976), 'Les chapiteaux de marbre du haut moyen âge à Saint-Denis', *Gesta* 15: 105–12

Vierck, H. (1974), 'Werke des Eligius', in G. Kossack and G. Ulbert (eds.), *Studien zur vor- und frühgeschichtlichen Archäologie: Festschrift für Joachim Werner zum 65. Geburtstag*, Munich, II, pp. 309–80

Vikan, G. (1982), *Byzantine Pilgrimage Art*, Washington, DC

Vikan, G. (1988), *Holy Image, Holy Space: Icons and Frescoes from Greece*, Athens

Volbach, W.F. (1976), *Elfenbeinarbeiten der Spätantike und des frühen Mittelalters*, 3rd edn, Mainz

Webster, L. and Backhouse, J. (eds.) (1991), *The Making of England: Anglo-Saxon Art and Culture AD 600–900*, London

Weitzmann, K. (1947; reprinted with addenda 1970), *Illustrations in Roll and Codex: A Study of the Origin and Method of Text Illustration*, Princeton

Weitzmann, K. (1971), 'Book illustration of the fourth century: tradition and innovation', in his *Studies in Classical and Byzantine Manuscript Illumination*, Chicago, pp. 96–125

Weitzmann, K. (1973), 'The Heracles plaques of St Peter's Cathedra', *Art Bulletin* 55: 1–37

Weitzmann, K. (1976), *The Icons*, I: *From the Sixth to the Tenth Century* (The Monastery of Saint Catherine at Mount Sinai), Princeton

Weitzmann, K. (1977), *Late Antique and Early Christian Book Illumination*, New York

Weitzmann, K. (1986), 'The contribution of the Princeton University Department of Art and Archaeology to the study of Byzantine art', in S. Curcic and A. St Clair (eds.), *Byzantium at Princeton*, Princeton, pp. 11–30

Werner, M. (1984), *Insular Art: An Annotated Bibliography*, Boston

Wharton, A.J. (1990), 'Rereading *Martyrium*: the Modernist and Postmodernist texts', *Gesta* 29: 3–7

Williams, J. (1977), *Early Spanish Manuscript Illumination*, New York

Williams, J. (1980), 'The Beatus commentaries and Spanish Bible illustration', in *Actas del Simposio para el setudio de los codices del 'Comentario al Apocalipsis' de Beato de Liébana, Madrid*, I, pp. 203–27

Wilson, D.M. and Klindt-Jensen, O. (1966), *Viking Art*, London and Ithaca

Wirth, J. (1989), *L'image médiévale: naissance et développements (VIe–XVe siècle)*, Paris

Wood, I. (1989), 'General review: Celts, Saxons, and Scandinavians in the North of England', *Northern History* 25: 302–9

Wright, D.H. (1964), 'The Codex Millenarius and its model', *Münchener Jahrbuch der bildenden Kunst*, 3rd series, 15: 37–54

Youngs, S. (ed.) (1989), *'The Work of Angels': Masterpieces of Celtic Metalwork, 6th–9th centuries AD*, London

Zimmermann, E.H. (1916), *Vorkarolingische Miniaturen*, Berlin

INDEX OF MANUSCRIPTS

GENERAL INDEX

Aachen
  and architecture 824, 825
  and bronze casting 835
  councils 79, 631–6, 641, 643, 650, 652–3,
    713–14, 763, 766, 794–5
  court school 9
  and East Franks 150
  and mosaics 837
  palace complex 3, 105, 111, 145, 386, 393,
    410, 419, 813, Plate 4
abbacies
  and bishops 627–8
  lay 136, 140–1, 149, 394, 414, 634–6, 651
  lifestyle 633, 639–40
Al-ʿAbbās al-Faḍl b. Yaʿqūb 252
ʿAbbasids 249, 250–1, 259–60, 261, 264, 550
  and Charlemagne 102
abbeys
  royal 623–7
  see also monasticism
Abbi, conversion 183
Abbo of Provence 90, 92–3, 211, 434
Abbo of St Germain-des-Prés 753, 754
ʿAbd al-ʿAzīz 257
ʿAbd Allāh of Córdoba 270–1, 284
ʿAbd Allāh b. Ibrāhīm 250–1
ʿAbd Allāh b. Yaʿqūb 254
ʿAbd Allāh, brother of Sulaymān 262–3
ʿAbd al-Mālik 544, 550
ʿAbd al-Raḥmān I of Córdoba 259–62, 276,
    285, 827
ʿAbd al-Raḥmān II of Córdoba 263–8, 269,
    281, 286
ʿAbd al-Raḥmān III of Córdoba 271, 551
ʿAbd al-Raḥmān III, amir 255, 256
ʿAbd al-Raḥmān al-Ghāfiqī 258
ʿAbd al-Raḥmān b. Marwān al-Jillīqī 269
Abelard, Peter 757
Abingdon abbey, charter 32
Abodrites see Obodrites

Abū'l-Shammākh Muḥammed b. Ibrāhīm 266
Acacian Schism 613
Acca, bishop of Hexham 67
acolytes 505, 603, 606, 610
Ad Sebastianum 275
Adalandus, master scribe 791
Adalbaldus, master scribe 791
Adalbero of Augsburg 166
Adalbero of Laon 456
Adalbert of Babenberg 166
Adalbert of Egmond 67
Adalbert, count of Metz 144
Adalbert of Tuscany 165, 316–17
Adaldag, archbishop of Hamburg-Bremen 219
Adalhard 154–5
  and Charles the Bald 120, 134, 404
Adalhard, abbot of Corbie 804
  and Louis I 112, 115, 118, 134
  and monastic schools 715–16
Adalhard, abbot of St Amand 8
Adalhard 'the seneschal' 435, 437, 438
Adalung, abbot of Lorsch 804
Adam of Bremen 211–12, 213, 215, 218, 219
Adaucta 613
Adela of Pfalzel 432, 434
Adelaide, wife of Louis the Stammerer 136,
    138
Adelchis of Benevento 312–13, 329, 366–7
Adelelm of Laon 725
Adelphius, *Vita* 12
administration see government
Admonitio Generalis 709, 713, 715, 726, 739,
    740, 746, 748, 756
Ado of Vienne, Chronicle 752, 759 n.5
Adomnán 45, 54, 55
Adoptionism 762–6, 767
  and Alcuin 738, 758, 785
  and Charlemagne 104, 578
  and papacy 577, 578–9
  and Spain 512, 620, 762–3, 773

Benedict, Rule 82, 187–8, 477, 619 n.77,
628–33, 637–41, 643–7, 729, 792
Benedict of Aniane
and ecclesiastical architecture 824
and education of women 717
Life 794
and liturgy 620, 687
and reform of monasticism 630–1, 713
and theology 738, 761
Benedict Biscop 685, 810
Benedict of Mainz, deacon 751
beneficium 472, 490, 496, 525
Benevento, duchy 175, 184, 186–7, 393, 573
and Byzantine empire 253, 361, 366–7, 372
and coinage 541–2, 554
division 311–13
and Lombardy 291–3, 296–8, 300, 305, 311,
320, 342–4
and Louis II 175, 184, 186, 369, 554
and Muslims 253–4
and papacy 324, 325, 329–30, 567
Beonna, king of East Anglia 549–50
Beornred, king of Mercia 30
Beornwulf, king of Mercia 38–9
Beowulf, and oral tradition 9
Berbers
and conquest of Spain 256, 258, 261, 262,
263–5, 269
rebellions 250–1, 258–9, 266–7, 276
Berengar, count of Le Mans 415
Berengar, nephew of Duke Ernst 154
Berengar of Friuli 160–1, 165, 315–18, 449
Berengar of Tours 757
Berhtwulf, king of Mercia 38
Berlin, Stiftung Preussicher Kulturbesitz,
Diez B. Sant 66 681
Bernard of the Auvergne 448
Bernard, count of Barcelona 116, 117–18,
132
Bernard of Laon 725
Bernard, marquis of Gothia 448
Bernard of Septimania 132, 143, 181, 434–5,
436, 439, 446, 448, 470, 660
Bernard, son of Charles the Fat 159–61
Bernard, son of Charles Martel 403
Bernard, son of Pippin I of Aquitaine 111,
112–15, 304, 402, 403, 445
Bernicia, bishoprics 597
Bersinikia, battle 235
Berta, daughter of Louis the German 148
Bertha, daughter of Charlemagne 115
Bertha, wife of Æthelbert, king of Kent 64
Berthold of Micy, *Vita* 13
Bertrada, wife of Pippin III 77, 111, 301, 400,
424
Bertcaudus, royal scribe 798
Bewcastle cross 55

Bible
commentaries 733–5, 737, 802, 821
copying 799–800, 805
in education 732–3
Greek 375
Reference 734
bibliothecarius 576, 612, *see also* Anastasius
Bibliothecarius
Birka, as trading emporium 502, 508
Birr monastery 48
Bischoff, Bernhard 788, 789
bishops/bishoprics
in Byzantine empire 354–6
and chorbishops 603, 604, 607–8, 616–17
early role 574
and ecclesiastical organisation 599–601, 844
in England 83, 592, 597–8
and episcopal primacy 587, 599
Frankish 73, 76–7, 90–1, 95, 99, 389, 405,
584–5; East 148–9, 161–2, 374; and
education 714, 716; as social order 462; and
solatium 414; territorial organisation
588–97; West 118, 132
and government 414, 428–9
in Ireland 598–9, 604–5
lay 90
in Lombard state 294, 307–10, 314–15
in Rome 603, 609
in Wales 60, 592
Black Hewald 67
Blathmac of Iona 56
Bobbio Missal 618 n.72
Bobbio monastery
book production 688, 789
land ownership 490, 496–7, 506
Bodo, deacon 732
Boethius
eighth-century knowledge of 681, 735,
737–9, 740, 744–5
ninth-century knowledge of 82, 456, 801,
803, 821
and theology 760, 762, 767, 781, 784
Bohemia
and Arnulf 162
and church 583
and Louis the German 151, 184
bonds, social
community life 476–9
family and kin 467–71
landlordship and estate management 473–6
and warrior retinue 479–80
Boniface of Mainz
Aenigmata 686
and Æthelbald 29, 36
as archbishop 73, 580–1, 600
and Carolingian renaissance 709

and liturgy 9
and Lothar II 582, 585
and Louis the German 13, 124, 125–7, 135, 138, 147, 149, 154–5, 182–3
and Middle Kingdom 126, 150
and Neustria 118, 124, 129, 131, 134–5, 181
portrayal 816, 822–3, Plates 11, 12
regnum 118–19, 130–6, 137, 140, 426
and scholarship 710, 711, 713, 795
and the state 426–7
and Strasbourg Oaths (842) 11–12, 120, 126, 145–6
strength 134, 174
and succession 117, 118–21, 136–8, 142–5, 403, 415, 429, 572
and theology 769–72, 776, 778–9, 781, 784
and Tours Bibles 800, Plate 12
and trade 505
see also Aquitaine; Brittany; coinage; Compiègne; Italy; papacy; Vikings
Charles III, the Fat 138, 140, 148, 153, 415, 449
and Alemannia 154, 158, 159
and the church 149, 390, 572
and Italy 157, 158, 314–15, 316, 372
and Lotharingia 156, 167
and Moravia 182
and partition of empire 158–61, 167
and Vikings 158–9, 201
and West Franks 158
Charles of Aquitaine 124–5, 130, 132
Charles Martel
and aristocracy 434
and Austrasia 70, 87–8, 89–90
and Boniface 75
and the church 73–5, 91–2, 95, 109, 326, 365, 388–9, 392, 625–6
and Frisia 89, 99, 174
and military service 479–80
and rise of Carolingians 68, 85, 87–94, 99
and Saxons 73, 88–9, 93, 94
sons 94–6, 180, 182, 403
Charles of Provence 149
Charles the Simple (or 'Straightforward')
and aristocracy 444
and East Franks 167
and England 79
and succession 138, 139, 140–1, 160, 164
and Vikings 201
Charles, son of Pippin III *see* Charlemagne
Charles-Constantine, count of Vienne 373
charters
Asturian 274, 400, 410
Breton 516–17
Castilian 411
English 29–30, 31, 32, 33, 38, 40, 65, 499
Frankish 69, 70, 94, 101, 409

Rhineland 519–23
as sources 17, 20–1, 510–11
Welsh 60
Chartres, battle 201
Chelles
book production 787, 792, 797, 803, 805
convent 8, 719, 831
Chelsea, Synod 79
Childebert III, and rise of Carolingians 86
Childeric II, Merovingian king 545, 546
Childeric III, Merovingian king 94, 97
Chilperic I, and Frisia 67
Chilperic II, and Pippinids 87–8
Chiltrude, sister of Pippin III 96, 400
Chnuba, king of Denmark 215
chorbishop 603, 604, 607–8, 616–17
Christian of Stavelot 733, 734–5
Christianity
in Bulgaria 153, 239–47, 371, 655
and Byzantine empire 320–1, 350, 355
in Celtic areas 43
conversion of pagan rulers *see* baptism
in England 41, 71, 684
and Frisia 66–73, 76, 178 n.30
and frontiers 178
and historiography 10
Latin 384, 418
and learning 756–7
and literacy 4
Orthodox 239–45, 583
and role of Carolingians 758
in Scandinavia 209–10, 217–19, 220–1, 224, 227
and society 452–3, 454, 655–72
see also bishops; church; clergy; iconoclasm; laity; monasticism; papacy
Chrodegang, bishop of Metz
and liturgy 606, 619, 687, 742
and papacy 76–7
Rule 82, 628
Chronicle of Albelda 274, 279, 282–3
Chronicle of Alfonso III 274, 275, 282
Chronicle of Theophanes 97, 325, 331
Chur
book production 788
and Charlemagne 626
and Louis I 117
church, Byzantine 354–6, 361–3, 761, 773–4, 782–4
church, western
baptismal 657–8
in Bulgaria 153
ecclesiastical structures 599–601
in England 20, 26, 64, 71, 77–9, 82–4, 391, 580, 597–8, 670
Frankish 71, 72–84, 90, 96–7, 133, 140–1; and aristocracy 167–8, 513; and frontier

CPSIA information can be obtained
at www.ICGtesting.com
Printed in the USA
BVOW07s0940050218
507186BV00061B/278/P